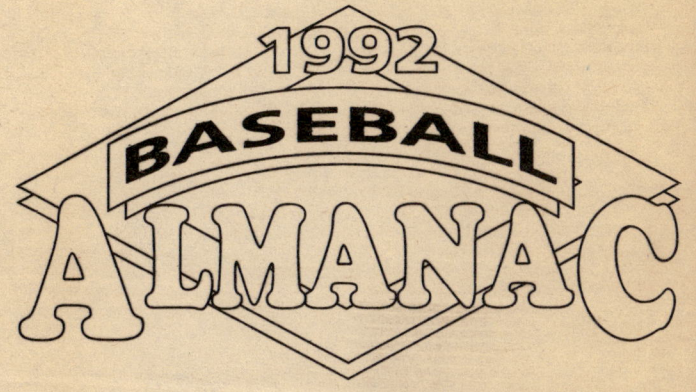

Contributing Writers
Dan Schlossberg
Mike Tully
Michael Bradley
Pete Palmer
Tom Owens

Credits:
Cover Photo: TV Sports Mailbag

All rights reserved under International and Pan American copyright conventions. Copyright © 1992 Publications International, Ltd. This publication may not be reproduced or quoted in whole or in part by mimeograph or any other printed or electronic means, or for presentation on radio, television, videotape, or film without written permission from Louis Weber, C.E.O. of Publications International, Ltd., 7373 N. Cicero Ave., Lincolnwood, Illinois 60646. Permission is never granted for commercial purposes. Printed in U.S.A.

Dan Schlossberg is a free-lance sports writer whose work has appeared in *Grand Slam Baseball Magazine, Petersen's Pro Baseball Yearbook,* and *Street & Smith's Baseball Yearbook.* He is the author of 12 books, including *The Major League Baseball Way to Pitch* and *1991 Baseball's Hottest Players.*

Mike Tully is a former national baseball writer for UPI. He has written six books, including *Leagues and Barons* and *1990-91 Baseball's Hottest Rookies.* His free-lance work has appeared in *The National* sports daily, *Sports Illustrated,* and *The New York Times.*

Michael Bradley is a free-lance writer whose work has appeared in *The Sporting News*, the *Philadelphia Inquirer,* and a variety of national sports publications. He is the coauthor of *1991-1992 Basketball Almanac.*

Pete Palmer edited *Total Baseball* and *The Hidden Game of Baseball* with John Thorn. He was the statistician for *1991 Baseball Almanac* and *1991-1992 Basketball Almanac.* Palmer, a renowned sports statistician, is a member of the Society for American Baseball Research (SABR).

Tom Owens is the author of *Greatest Baseball Players of All Time, Collecting Sports Autographs,* and the *1991 Official Baseball Card Price Guide.* He is a former editor of *Sports Collectors Digest.*

David Nemec is a baseball historian and novelist. He is the author of *Great Baseball Feats, Facts & Firsts,* and a coauthor of the *Ultimate Baseball Book* and *20th Century Baseball Chronicle.* He has written numerous baseball history, quiz, and memorabilia books as well as franchise histories for major league team yearbooks.

Special thanks to Jay Virshbo and Howe SportsData for minor league statistics.

CONTENTS

CURRENT PLAYERS AND ROOKIE PROSPECTS 9

PLAYER PROFILES 10
- Jim Abbott 10
- Paul Abbott 10
- Jim Acker 11
- Juan Agosto 11
- Rick Aguilera 12
- Mike Aldrete 12
- Gerald Alexander 13
- Roberto Alomar 13
- Sandy Alomar 14
- Larry Andersen 14
- Allan Anderson 15
- Brady Anderson 15
- Eric Anthony 16
- Kevin Appier 16
- Luis Aquino 17
- Jack Armstrong 17
- Paul Assenmacher 18
- Don August 18
- Steve Avery 19
- Wally Backman 19
- Carlos Baerga 20
- Jeff Bagwell 20
- Scott Bailes 21
- Harold Baines 21
- Jeff Ballard 22
- Scott Bankhead 22
- Bret Barberie 23
- Jesse Barfield 23
- Brian Barnes 24
- Kevin Bass 24
- Steve Bedrosian 25
- Tim Belcher 25
- Stan Belinda 26
- Derek Bell 26
- George Bell 27
- Jay Bell 27
- Albert Belle 28
- Rafael Belliard 28
- Andy Benes 29
- Todd Benzinger 29
- Juan Berenguer 30
- Dave Bergman 30
- Damon Berryhill 31
- Dante Bichette 31
- Mike Bielecki 32

- Craig Biggio 32
- Bud Black 33
- Jeff Blauser 33
- Mike Boddicker 34
- Joe Boever 34
- Wade Boggs 35
- Tom Bolton 35
- Barry Bonds 36
- Bobby Bonilla 36
- Pat Borders 37
- Chris Bosio 37
- Shawn Boskie 38
- Daryl Boston 38
- Denis Boucher 39
- Oil Can Boyd 39
- Scott Bradley 40
- Glenn Braggs 40
- Jeff Brantley 41
- Sid Bream 41
- George Brett 42
- Greg Briley 42
- Hubie Brooks 43
- Kevin Brown 43
- Jerry Browne 44
- Tom Browning 44
- Tom Brunansky 45
- Steve Buechele 45
- Jay Buhner 46
- Tim Burke 46
- John Burkett 47
- Ellis Burks 47
- Randy Bush 48
- Brett Butler 48
- Francisco Cabrera 49
- Greg Cadaret 49
- Ivan Calderon 50
- Ken Caminiti 50
- Casey Candaele 51
- John Candelaria 51
- Tom Candiotti 52
- Jose Canseco 52
- Cris Carpenter 53
- Mark Carreon 53
- Gary Carter 54
- Joe Carter 54
- Frank Castillo 55
- Rick Cerone 55
- John Cerutti 56
- Wes Chamberlain 56

- Norm Charlton 57
- Steve Chitren 57
- Jack Clark 58
- Jerald Clark 58
- Will Clark 59
- Roger Clemens 59
- Alex Cole 60
- Vince Coleman 60
- Pat Combs 61
- David Cone 61
- Scott Coolbaugh 62
- Joey Cora 62
- Henry Cotto 63
- Danny Cox 63
- Tim Crews 64
- Chuck Crim 64
- Milt Cuyler 65
- Kal Daniels 65
- Ron Darling 66
- Danny Darwin 66
- Doug Dascenzo 67
- Darren Daulton 67
- Alvin Davis 68
- Chili Davis 68
- Eric Davis 69
- Glenn Davis 69
- Mark Davis 70
- Storm Davis 70
- Andre Dawson 71
- Ken Dayley 71
- Steve Decker 72
- Rob Deer 72
- Jose DeJesus 73
- Jose DeLeon 73
- Rich DeLucia 74
- Jim Deshaies 74
- Delino DeShields 75
- Mike Devereaux 75
- Mario Diaz 76
- Rob Dibble 76
- John Dopson 77
- Bill Doran 77
- Brian Downing 78
- Kelly Downs 78
- Doug Drabek 79
- Mariano Duncan 79
- Shawon Dunston 80
- Len Dykstra 80
- Dennis Eckersley 81

CONTENTS

Mark Eichhorn 81	Jason Grimsley 110	Kent Hrbek 139
Jim Eisenreich 82	Marquis Grissom 111	Rex Hudler 140
Kevin Elster 82	Kevin Gross 111	Mike Huff 140
Scott Erickson 83	Kip Gross 112	Tim Hulett 141
Alvaro Espinoza 83	Kelly Gruber 112	Brian Hunter 141
Dwight Evans 84	Mark Gubicza 113	Bruce Hurst 142
Steve Farr 84	Pedro Guerrero 113	Jeff Huson 142
Jeff Fassero 85	Lee Guetterman 114	Pete Incaviglia 143
Mike Felder 85	Ozzie Guillen 114	Jeff Innis 143
Junior Felix 86	Bill Gullickson 115	Bo Jackson 144
Felix Fermin 86	Mark Guthrie 115	Danny Jackson 144
Alex Fernandez 87	Jose Guzman 116	Darrin Jackson 145
Sid Fernandez 87	Juan Guzman 116	Mike Jackson 145
Tony Fernandez 88	Chris Gwynn 117	Brook Jacoby 146
Cecil Fielder 88	Tony Gwynn 117	Chris James 146
Chuck Finley 89	John Habyan 118	Stan Javier 147
Steve Finley 89	Mel Hall 118	Mike Jeffcoat 147
Carlton Fisk 90	Darryl Hamilton 119	Gregg Jefferies 148
Mike Fitzgerald 90	Jeff Hamilton 119	Reggie Jefferson 148
Mike Flanagan 91	Chris Hammond 120	Howard Johnson 149
Tom Foley 91	Chris Haney 120	Jeff Johnson 149
John Franco 92	Eric Hanson 121	Lance Johnson 150
Julio Franco 92	Mike Harkey 121	Randy Johnson 150
Marvin Freeman 93	Pete Harnisch 122	Barry Jones 151
Todd Frohwirth 93	Brian Harper 122	Doug Jones 151
Travis Fryman 94	Greg Harris 123	Jimmy Jones 152
Gary Gaetti 94	Greg Harris 123	Tracy Jones 152
Greg Gagne 95	Lenny Harris 124	Ricky Jordan 153
Andres Galarraga 95	Mike Hartley 124	Felix Jose 153
Dave Gallagher 96	Bryan Harvey 125	Wally Joyner 154
Mike Gallego 96	Billy Hatcher 125	David Justice 154
Ronnie Gant 97	Charlie Hayes 126	Scott Kamieniecki 155
Jim Gantner 97	Von Hayes 126	Ron Karkovice 155
Mike Gardiner 98	Mike Heath 127	Pat Kelly 156
Mark Gardner 98	Neal Heaton 127	Roberto Kelly 156
Scott Garrelts 99	Dave Henderson 128	Terry Kennedy 157
Kirk Gibson 99	Rickey Henderson 128	Jimmy Key 157
Paul Gibson 100	Tom Henke 129	Darryl Kile 158
Bernard Gilkey 100	Mike Henneman 129	Eric King 158
Joe Girardi 101	Tommy Herr 130	Jeff King 159
Dan Gladden 101	Orel Hershier 130	Bob Kipper 159
Tom Glavine 102	Joe Hesketh 131	Joe Klink 160
Jerry Don Gleaton 102	Greg Hibbard 131	Chuck Knoblauch 160
Leo Gomez 103	Ted Higuera 132	Bill Krueger 161
Juan Gonzalez 103	Glenallen Hill 132	John Kruk 161
Luis Gonzalez 104	Ken Hill 133	Steve Lake 162
Dwight Gooden 104	Shawn Hillegas 133	Dennis Lamp 162
Tom Gordon 105	Chris Hoiles 134	Les Lancaster 163
Goose Gossage 105	Dave Hollins 134	Bill Landrum 163
Jim Gott 106	Brian Holman 135	Cedric Landrum 164
Mark Grace 106	Rick Honeycutt 135	Mark Langston 164
Jeff Gray 107	Sam Horn 136	Ray Lankford 165
Craig Grebeck 107	Charlie Hough 136	Carney Lansford 165
Tommy Greene 108	David Howard 137	Barry Larkin 166
Mike Greenwell 108	Tom Howard 137	Gene Larkin 166
Tommy Gregg 109	Steve Howe 138	Mike LaValliere 167
Ken Griffey Jr. 109	Jack Howell 138	Terry Leach 167
Alfredo Griffin 110	Jay Howell 139	Tim Leary 168

CONTENTS

Manny Lee 168	Mike Morgan 197	Pascual Perez 226
Mark Lee 169	Hal Morris 198	Gerald Perry 227
Craig Lefferts 169	Jack Morris 198	Geno Petralli 227
Charlie Leibrandt 170	Lloyd Moseby 199	Gary Pettis 228
Mark Leiter 170	Terry Mulholland 199	Tony Phillips 228
Scott Leius 171	Rance Mulliniks 200	Phil Plantier 229
Mark Lemke 171	Pedro Munoz 200	Dan Plesac 229
Darren Lewis 172	Dale Murphy 201	Luis Polonia 230
Mark Lewis 172	Rob Murphy 201	Mark Portugal 230
Jose Lind 173	Eddie Murray 202	Ted Power 231
Scott Livingstone 173	Greg Myers 202	Kirby Puckett 231
Steve Lyons 174	Randy Myers 203	Carlos Quintana 232
Kevin Maas 174	Chris Nabholz 203	Jamie Quirk 232
Mike Macfarlane 175	Tim Naehring 204	Scott Radinsky 233
Julio Machado 175	Charles Nagy 204	Tim Raines 233
Shane Mack 176	Jaime Navarro 205	Rafael Ramirez 234
Greg Maddux 176	Gene Nelson 205	Willie Randolph 234
Mike Maddux 177	Al Newman 206	Dennis Rasmussen 235
Dave Magadan 177	Rod Nichols 206	Randy Ready 235
Joe Magrane 178	Otis Nixon 207	Jeff Reardon 236
Candy Maldonado 178	Junior Noboa 207	Gary Redus 236
Kirt Manwaring 179	Matt Nokes 208	Jody Reed 237
Carlos Martinez 179	Edwin Nunez 208	Kevin Reimer 237
Carmelo Martinez 180	Charlie O'Brien 209	Mike Remlinger 238
Chito Martinez 180	Pete O'Brien 209	Gil Reyes 238
Dave Martinez 181	Jose Offerman 210	Harold Reynolds 239
Dennis Martinez 181	Bob Ojeda 210	Dave Righetti 239
Edgar Martinez 182	John Olerud 211	Jose Rijo 240
Ramon Martinez 182	Steve Olin 211	Ernest Riles 240
John Marzano 183	Omar Olivares 212	Billy Ripken 241
Don Mattingly 183	Joe Oliver 212	Cal Ripken 241
Kirk McCaskill 184	Francisco Oliveras 213	Wally Ritchie 242
Paul McClellan 184	Greg Olson 213	Luis Rivera 242
Lloyd McClendon 185	Gregg Olson 214	Bip Roberts 243
Ben McDonald 185	Paul O'Neill 214	Don Robinson 243
Jack McDowell 186	Jose Oquendo 215	Jeff Robinson 244
Roger McDowell 186	Jesse Orosco 215	Ron Robinson 244
Chuck McElroy 187	Joe Orsulak 216	Ivan Rodriguez 245
Willie McGee 187	Junior Ortiz 216	Rich Rodriguez 245
Fred McGriff 188	Al Osuna 217	Kenny Rogers 246
Mark McGwire 188	Spike Owen 217	Bruce Ruffin 246
Brian McRae 189	Mike Pagliarulo 218	Scott Ruskin 247
Kevin McReynolds 189	Tom Pagnozzi 218	Jeff Russell 247
Jose Melendez 190	Vicente Palacios 219	Nolan Ryan 248
Bob Melvin 190	Donn Pall 219	Bret Saberhagen 248
Orlando Merced 191	Rafael Palmeiro 220	Chris Sabo 249
Kent Mercker 191	Dean Palmer 220	Luis Salazar 249
Jose Mesa 192	Dave Parker 221	Bill Sampen 250
Hensley Meulens 192	Lance Parrish 221	Juan Samuel 250
Bob Milacki 193	Dan Pasqua 222	Ryan Sandberg 251
Keith Miller 193	Bob Patterson 222	Deion Sanders 251
Randy Milligan 194	Ken Patterson 223	Scott Sanderson 252
Keith Mitchell 194	Bill Pecota 223	Benito Santiago 252
Kevin Mitchell 195	Alejandro Pena 224	Mackey Sasser 253
Paul Molitor 195	Geronimo Pena 224	Steve Sax 253
Jeff Montgomery 196	Tony Pena 225	Bob Scanlan 254
Mike Moore 196	Terry Pendleton 225	Curt Schilling 254
Mickey Morandini 197	Melido Perez 226	Dick Schofield 255

CONTENTS

Mike Schooler 255	Gary Thurman 284	Wilson Alvarez 312
Mike Scioscia 256	Mike Timlin 285	Matt Anderson 313
Scott Scudder 256	Randy Tomlin 285	Johnny Ard 313
Steve Searcy 257	Alan Trammell 286	Marcos Armas 314
David Segui 257	Jeff Treadway 286	Bryan Baar 314
Kevin Seitzer 258	Jose Uribe 287	Willie Banks 315
Mike Sharperson 258	Dave Valle 287	Don Barbara 315
Gary Sheffield 259	Andy Van Slyke 288	Howard Battle 316
Terry Shumpert 259	Gary Varsho 288	Rod Beck 316
Ruben Sierra 260	Greg Vaughn 289	Greg Blosser 317
Doug Simons 260	Mo Vaughn 289	Rod Bolton 317
Joel Skinner 261	Robin Ventura 290	Ricky Bones 318
Don Slaught 261	Frank Viola 290	Bret Boone 318
Heathcliff Slocumb 262	Jose Vizcaino 291	Toby Borland 319
Joe Slusarski 262	Omar Vizquel 291	Ryan Bowen 319
John Smiley 263	Bob Walk 292	Rico Brogna 320
Bryn Smith 263	Chico Walker 292	Jeff Brown 320
Dave Smith 264	Larry Walker 293	Andy Bruce 321
Dwight Smith 264	Tim Wallach 293	Jeromy Burnitz 321
Lee Smith 265	Jerome Walton 294	Darren Burton 322
Lonnie Smith 265	Duane Ward 294	Clayton Byrne 322
Ozzie Smith 266	Bill Wegman 295	Jim Campanis 323
Zane Smith 266	John Wehner 295	Chuck Carr 323
John Smoltz 267	Walt Weiss 296	Larry Casian 324
Luis Sojo 267	Bob Welch 296	Pete Castellano 324
Sammy Sosa 268	David Wells 297	Andujar Cedeno 325
Bill Spiers 268	David West 297	Royce Clayton 325
Ed Sprague 269	Lou Whitaker 298	Greg Colbrunn 326
Mike Stanley 269	Devon White 298	Scott Cooper 326
Mike Stanton 270	Wally Whitehurst 299	Rheal Cormier 327
Terry Steinbach 270	Mark Whiten 299	Tim Costo 327
Dave Stewart 271	Ed Whitson 300	Earl Cunningham 328
Dave Stieb 271	Rick Wilkins 300	Chad Curtis 328
Kurt Stillwell 272	Bernie Williams 301	Brian Deak 329
Todd Stottlemyre 272	Matt Williams 301	Carlos Delgado 329
Darryl Strawberry 273	Mitch Williams 302	John DeSilva 330
Franklin Stubbs 273	Mark Williamson 302	Cesar Devares 330
B.J. Surhoff 274	Carl Willis 303	Lance Dickson 331
Rick Sutcliffe 274	Steve Wilson 303	Jamie Dismuke 331
Dale Sveum 275	Trevor Wilson 304	Kirk Dressendorfer 332
Bill Swift 275	Willie Wilson 304	Cal Eldred 332
Greg Swindell 276	Dave Winfield 305	Donnie Elliott 333
Pat Tabler 276	Herm Winningham 305	John Ericks 333
Frank Tanana 277	Bobby Witt 306	Andy Fairman 334
Kevin Tapani 277	Todd Worrell 306	Hector Fajardo 334
Danny Tartabull 278	Eric Yelding 307	Monty Fariss 335
Wade Taylor 278	Curt Young 307	Dave Fleming 335
Garry Templeton 279	Gerald Young 308	Kevin Flora 336
Walt Terrell 279	Matt Young 308	Ren Frazier 336
Scott Terry 280	Robin Yount 309	Jay Gainer 337
Mickey Tettleton 280	Todd Zeile 309	Rich Garces 337
Tim Teufel 281		Apolinar Garcia 338
Bob Tewksbury 281	**ROOKIE PROFILES 310**	Cheo Garcia 338
Bobby Thigpen 282	Kyle Abbott 310	Ramon Garcia 339
Frank Thomas 282	Scott Aldred 310	Victor Garcia 339
Milt Thompson 283	Manny Alexander 311	Chris Gardner 340
Robby Thompson 283	Moises Alou 311	Darius Gash 340
Dickie Thon 284	Tavo Alvarez 312	Brent Gates 341

CONTENTS

Chris Gies 341	Kerwin Moore 370	Jesus Tavarez 399
Benji Gil 342	Raul Mondesi 371	Brien Taylor 400
Pat Gomez 342	Mike Mongiello 371	Jim Thome 400
Alex Gonzalez 343	Kevin Morton 372	Lee Tinsley 401
Juan Guerrero 343	Jose Munoz 372	Salomon Torres 401
Johnny Guzman 344	Oscar Munoz 373	Ricky Trlicek 402
Greg Hansell 344	Jeff Mutis 373	Todd Van Poppel 402
Shawn Hare 345	Denny Neagle 374	Julian Vasquez 403
Doug Harris 345	Tom Nevers 374	Joe Vitiello 403
Reggie Harris 346	Marc Newfield 375	Kyle Washington 404
Chris Hatcher 346	Dave Nilsson 375	David Weathers 404
Ryan Hawblitzel 347	Rey Noriega 376	Tom Wegmann 405
Pat Hentgen 347	Tom Nuneviller 376	Turk Wendell 405
Carlos Hernandez 348	John O'Donoghue 377	Rondell White 406
Kiki Hernandez 348	Jose Oliva 377	Brian Williams 406
Phil Hiatt 349	Mike Oquist 378	Brandon Wilson 407
Tyrone Hill 349	Donovan Osborne 378	Mark Wohlers 407
Trevor Hoffman 350	Mateo Ozuna 379	Dmitri Young 408
Tyler Houston 350	Lance Painter 379	Kevin Young 408
Pat Howell 351	Elvin Paulino 380	Ed Zinter 409
Rick Huisman 351	Tim Peek 380	Ed Zosky 409
Todd Hundley 352	Dan Peltier 381	
Jon Hurst 352	William Pennyfeather 381	**TEAM OVERVIEWS** 410
Mike Ignasiak 353	Vince Phillips 382	Minnesota Twins 411
Jeff Jackson 353	Mike Piazza 382	Chicago White Sox 412
John Jaha 354	Greg Pirkl 383	Texas Rangers 413
Chipper Jones 354	Paul Quantrill 383	Oakland Athletics 414
Brian Jordan 355	Rafael Quirico 384	Seattle Mariners 415
Jeff Juden 355	Manny Ramirez 384	Kansas City Royals 416
Eric Karros 356	Daryl Ratliff 385	California Angels 417
Steve Karsay 356	John Ray 385	Toronto Blue Jays 418
Mike Kelly 357	Calvin Reese 386	Boston Red Sox 419
Bo Kennedy 357	Arthur Lee Rhodes 386	Detroit Tigers 420
Mark Kiefer 358	Joe Roa 387	Milwaukee Brewers 421
Ryan Klesko 358	Frankie Rodriguez 387	New York Yankees 422
Philip Leftwich 359	John Roper 388	Baltimore Orioles 423
Curtis Leskanic 359	Rich Rowland 388	Cleveland Indians 424
Ron Lockett 360	Stan Royer 389	Atlanta Braves 425
Kenny Lofton 360	Johnny Ruffin 389	Los Angeles Dodgers 426
Pat Mahomes 361	Paul Russo 390	San Diego Padres 427
Ed Martel 361	Roger Salkeld 390	San Francisco Giants 428
Jesus Martinez 362	Tim Salmon 391	Cincinnati Reds 429
Pedro Martinez 362	Rey Sanchez 391	Houston Astros 430
Tino Martinez 363	Reggie Sanders 392	Pittsburgh Pirates 431
Rob Maurer 363	Mo Sanford 392	St. Louis Cardinals 432
Brent Mayne 364	Andres Santana 393	Philadelphia Phillies 433
Terry McFarlin 364	Pete Schourek 393	Chicago Cubs 434
Kevin McGehee 365	Darryl Scott 394	New York Mets 435
Jeff McNeely 365	Gary Scott 394	Montreal Expos 436
Luis Mercedes 366	Frank Seminara 395	
Matt Mieske 366	Basil Shabazz 395	**HALL OF FAME** 437
Sam Militello 367	Ben Shelton 396	
Kurt Miller 367	Dave Silvestri 396	**AWARDS AND HIGHLIGHTS** 473
Mark Mimbs 368	Dan Smith 397	
Michael Mimbs 368	Mark Smith 397	**YEARLY TEAM AND INDIVIDUAL**
Kevin Mmahat 369	Tim Smith 398	**LEADERS** 488
Mike Mohler 369	Dave Staton 398	
Boo Moore 370	Lee Stevens 399	**1991 AWARDS** 672

Current Players and Rookie Prospects

In this section you'll find first 600 current players and then 200 rookie prospects. The current players and rookie prospects are in alphabetical order—players from Jim Abbott to Todd Zeile, rookie prospects from Kyle Abbott to Eddie Zosky.

Full major league statistics are included with the current players. If a player played with two teams in either league in one season, both lines are presented. If the player played with two teams in one league during a season, the statistics were combined to give you accurate information of how each player performed against one league in one season. At the bottom of most of the Major League Registers you'll find a "3 AVE" line. Players who qualified had their last three seasons' statistics averaged for each of the ten categories. For batters to qualify for this line, they had to accumulate 150 at bats in each season. For starters to qualify, they had to pitch at least 60 innings each season. For relievers to qualify, they had to pitch at least 30 innings each season. If the player did not qualify for all three seasons but for only two years out of the last three, you'll find a "2 AVE" line. These lines give you a simple, straightforward way to help you better predict how these players will do in 1992.

The rookie prospects each have a professional register. Included are statistics from each year that the player has been in organized baseball, from the Rookie leagues (**R**), Class-A (**A**), Double-A (**AA**), and Triple-A (**AAA**). If the player has played in the major leagues, each league's performance is also shown (**AL** and **NL**). If during one season a player played with more than one team on one minor league level, or if a player played with more than one AL or NL team, the statistics were combined to give you accurate information of how that player did against one level or against one major league.

The abbreviations for batters are: **BA** = batting average; **G** = games played; **AB** = at bats; **R** = runs scored; **H** = hits; **2B** = doubles; **3B** = triples; **HR** = home runs; **RBI** = runs batted in; **SB** = stolen bases. The abbreviations for pitchers are: **W** = wins; **L** = losses; **ERA** = earned run average; **G** = games; **CG** = complete games; **S** = saves; **IP** = innings pitched; **H** = hits; **ER** = earned runs; **BB** = bases on balls; **SO** = strikeouts.

The "Player Summary" box that accompanies each profile is an at-a-glance look at each player. The "Fantasy Value" line suggests a draft price for any of the fantasy baseball games that have mushroomed around the country. The price range is a guide based on $260 for a 23-player roster. The "Card Value" line is a suggested buying price for a Mint 1992 regular-issue baseball card of that player. It is an investment guide based mostly on the future value gain of that player's card. Any error, variation, or specialty cards are not taken into account.

CURRENT PLAYERS

JIM ABBOTT

Position: Pitcher
Team: California Angels
Born: Sept. 19, 1967 Flint, MI
Height: 6'3" **Weight:** 200 lbs.
Bats: left **Throws:** left
Acquired: First-round pick in 6/88 free-agent draft

Player Summary	
Fantasy Value	$7 to $10
Card Value	5c to 10c
Will	work both sides of plate
Can't	always throw curve for strikes
Expect	victories in double figures
Don't Expect	strikeout crown

After a rocky 1991 start, Abbott went 4-0 with a 1.96 ERA in May. He lost his shot at a 5-0 month when the bullpen blew a lead. Abbott had pitched three four-hit shutouts in his career before holding the Minnesota Twins to three hits in 8⅓ innings last August 7. Through eight innings, all the Twins managed was an infield single. The former University of Michigan star, who never pitched in the minors, split 24 decisions as a 1989 rookie but dropped to 10-14 a year later when he led the AL in hits allowed. Abbott is most effective when he's throwing his curve for strikes. He is working on a forkball and changeup. The winner of the 1987 Golden Spikes Award pitched the U.S. Olympic team to a gold medal a year later—not bad for an athlete born without a right hand. He is a solid fantasy league buy at $7 to $10. His 1991 cards are moderate choices at a nickel to dime each. Abbott is improving with experience and will remain a starter.

Major League Pitching Register

	W	L	ERA	G	CG	IP	H	ER	BB	SO
89 AL	12	12	3.92	29	4	181.1	190	79	74	115
90 AL	10	14	4.51	33	4	211.2	246	106	72	105
91 AL	18	11	2.89	34	5	243.0	222	78	73	158
Life	40	37	3.72	96	13	636.0	658	263	219	378
3 AVE	13	12	3.72	32	4	212.1	219	88	73	126

PAUL ABBOTT

Position: Pitcher
Team: Minnesota Twins
Born: Sept. 15, 1967 Van Nuys, CA
Height: 6'3" **Weight:** 185 lbs.
Bats: right **Throws:** right
Acquired: Third-round pick in 6/85 free-agent draft

Player Summary	
Fantasy Value	$1 to $3
Card Value	5c to 10c
Will	ring up Ks
Can't	throw strikes consistently
Expect	spot starting calls
Don't Expect	big league stardom

Blessed with an exceptional changeup, which he mixes with a fastball and curve, Abbott has been hampered by frequent lapses of control—plus a sore arm in 1989. Abbott had earned two wins in relief before the Twins gave him his first start of the 1991 season on July 1. In 1990, the Twins brought Abbott up from Triple-A Portland as a stopgap hurler. During his short stint in Minnesota, he convinced the team that he has major league stuff, although he had less-than-convincing numbers. Fantasy leaguers shouldn't bet much on Abbott lasting a full season with Minnesota. At Portland in '91, he was 2-3 in eight starts, with a 3.89 ERA, 40 Ks, and 28 walks in 44 innings pitched. He led the Class-A California League with 205 strikeouts and 143 walks in 1988. His 1992 cards are gambles at 5 to 10 cents. A capable fielder, Abbott needs to improve his pickoff move. Abbott spent six seasons on the farm before reaching the majors in 1990. In '91, he allowed batters to have a .396 slugging percentage—earning a return ticket back to Triple-A.

Major League Pitching Register

	W	L	ERA	G	CG	IP	H	ER	BB	SO
90 AL	0	5	5.97	7	0	34.2	37	23	28	25
91 AL	3	1	4.75	15	0	47.1	38	25	36	43
Life	3	6	5.27	22	0	82.0	75	48	64	68

CURRENT PLAYERS

JIM ACKER

Position: Pitcher
Team: Toronto Blue Jays
Born: Sept. 24, 1958 Freer, TX
Height: 6'2" **Weight:** 212 lbs.
Bats: right **Throws:** right
Acquired: Traded from Braves for Tony Castillo and Francisco Cabrera, 8/89

Player Summary	
Fantasy Value	$1 to $3
Card Value	3c to 5c
Will	work frequently
Can't	post big strikeout numbers
Expect	ground-ball outs
Don't Expect	consistent performance

A fastball-and-slider pitcher who has developed his changeup over the years, Acker gets ground-balls rather than strikeouts from rival hitters. He's almost always effective against lefties, but when he isn't getting them out, he is in trouble. He seems to pitch in streaks, being either tough or easy. Though he has had elbow problems in the past, he can work often when healthy. Usually deployed in the middle innings, Acker has appeared in at least 59 games three times but never had more than 14 saves in a season. His status means that he is no better than a $3 fantasy pick. His 1992 cards are commons. He's a decent fielder with an adequate pickoff move. Because he can work several innings per appearance, Acker should continue to serve in his set-up role.

Major League Pitching Register

	W	L	ERA	G	S	IP	H	ER	BB	SO
83 AL	5	1	4.33	38	1	97.2	103	47	38	44
84 AL	3	5	4.38	32	1	72.0	79	35	25	33
85 AL	7	2	3.23	61	10	86.1	86	31	43	42
86 AL	2	4	4.35	23	0	60.0	63	29	22	32
86 NL	3	8	3.79	21	0	95.0	100	40	26	37
87 NL	4	9	4.16	68	14	114.2	109	53	51	68
88 NL	0	4	4.71	21	0	42.0	45	22	14	25
89 NL	0	6	2.67	59	2	97.2	84	29	20	68
89 AL	2	1	1.59	14	0	28.1	24	5	12	24
90 AL	4	4	3.83	59	1	91.2	103	39	30	54
91 AL	3	5	5.20	54	1	88.1	77	51	36	44
Life	33	49	3.92	450	30	873.2	873	381	317	471
3 AVE	3	5	3.65	62	1	101.2	96	41	33	63

JUAN AGOSTO

Position: Pitcher
Team: St. Louis Cardinals
Born: Feb. 23, 1958 Rio Piedras, Puerto Rico
Height: 6'2" **Weight:** 190 lbs.
Bats: left **Throws:** left
Acquired: Signed as a free agent, 12/90

Player Summary	
Fantasy Value	$2 to $4
Card Value	3c to 5c
Will	lead league in games
Can't	throw hard
Expect	ground-ball outs
Don't Expect	deployment as closer

Because he throws a sinker and a big breaking ball, Agosto gets ground-ball outs. He is especially difficult for left-handed hitters but keeps the ball in the park against everyone. He once went 91 innings without throwing a gopher ball. He is a good fielder who keeps runners close. Agosto is baseball's best example of a pitcher with a rubber arm. He has appeared more than 70 times four seasons in a row, including a career-best 82 outings for the 1990 Astros. His rising ERAs may indicate that his arm is overworked. A $3 pitcher, Agosto's ERA is a worry for fantasy leaguers. Deployed almost exclusively as a lefthanded set-up man, Agosto had 16 saves in eight seasons before he signed a three-year pact with the Cardinals before the 1991 campaign. His 1992 cards have no investment appeal.

Major League Pitching Register

	W	L	ERA	G	S	IP	H	ER	BB	SO
81 AL	0	0	4.76	2	0	5.2	5	3	0	3
82 AL	0	0	18.00	1	0	2.0	7	4	0	1
83 AL	2	2	4.10	39	7	41.2	41	19	11	29
84 AL	2	1	3.09	49	7	55.1	54	19	34	26
85 AL	4	3	3.58	54	1	60.1	45	24	23	39
86 AL	1	4	8.64	26	1	25.0	49	24	18	12
87 NL	1	1	2.63	27	2	27.1	26	8	10	6
88 NL	10	2	2.26	75	4	91.2	74	23	30	33
89 NL	4	5	2.93	71	1	83.0	81	27	32	46
90 NL	9	8	4.29	82	4	92.1	91	44	39	50
91 NL	5	3	4.81	72	2	86.0	92	46	39	34
Life	38	29	3.80	498	29	570.1	565	241	236	279
3 AVE	6	5	4.03	75	2	87.0	88	39	37	43

CURRENT PLAYERS

RICK AGUILERA

Position: Pitcher
Team: Minnesota Twins
Born: Dec. 31, 1961 San Gabriel, CA
Height: 6'5" **Weight:** 205 lbs.
Bats: right **Throws:** right
Acquired: Traded from Mets with Kevin Tapani, Tim Drummond, Jack Savage, and David West for Frank Viola, 7/89

Player Summary	
Fantasy Value	$30 to $35
Card Value	5¢ to 10¢
Will	convert most opportunities
Can't	escape elbow problems
Expect	retention of closer job
Don't Expect	more than 60 appearances

Although he has been bothered by occasional elbow problems, Aguilera is one of the premier relief pitchers in the American League. A combination spot starter and reliever during four-plus years with the Mets, he became Minnesota's closer after arriving in the Frank Viola trade. After a great 1990 season, Aguilera was even more impressive in 1991. The arrival of Steve Bedrosian eased Aguilera's short-relief burden in '91, making him more effective. Mucho saves make Aguilera a juicy fantasy league item in the $30 range. His 1992 cards are temptations at a dime or less. He throws a sinking fastball, slider, forkball, and occasional curve. He is a control pitcher whose lone weakness is holding runners on base. Aguilera is not a starter, though, despite his four-pitch mastery. Drafted as a third baseman, he acts like a fifth infielder.

Major League Pitching Register

	W	L	ERA	G	S	IP	H	ER	BB	SO
85 NL	10	7	3.24	21	0	122.1	118	44	37	74
86 NL	10	7	3.88	28	0	141.2	145	61	36	104
87 NL	11	3	3.60	18	0	115.0	124	46	33	77
88 NL	0	4	6.93	11	0	24.2	29	19	10	16
89 NL	6	6	2.34	36	7	69.1	59	18	21	80
89 AL	3	5	3.21	11	0	75.2	71	27	17	57
90 AL	5	3	2.76	56	32	65.1	55	20	19	61
91 AL	4	5	2.35	63	42	69.0	44	18	30	61
Life	49	40	3.33	244	81	683.0	645	253	203	530
3 AVE	6	6	2.67	55	27	93.1	76	28	29	86

MIKE ALDRETE

Position: Outfield; first base
Team: Cleveland Indians
Born: Jan. 29, 1961 Carmel, CA
Height: 5'11" **Weight:** 185 lbs.
Bats: left **Throws:** left
Acquired: Signed as a free agent, 6/91

Player Summary	
Fantasy Value	$1 to $2
Card Value	3¢ to 5¢
Will	deliver as a pinch-hitter
Can't	hit the long ball
Expect	surprisingly good defense
Don't Expect	use as an every-day player

Aldrete's first exposure to American League pitching produced excellent results. He went 15-for-33 (.455) in his first eight starts while serving as first baseman, left fielder, and designated hitter. A career National Leaguer who formerly played for the Giants, Expos, and Pirates, Aldrete has always been considered a competent hitter—especially when called upon as a pinch-hitter. He's hit better than .300 lifetime in that role. A selective hitter who waits for a fastball he can handle, Aldrete draws his share of walks. He also finds himself down in the count. He is a $2 fantasy player. When he connects, he's a spray hitter with little power. Because of that, skip his 1992 commons. His versatility and on-base percentages keep him in the majors. He's a good outfielder with a decent arm at all three positions and can fill in at first. Aldrete is a better hitter against righties, but hits in the .250s against southpaws.

Major League Batting Register

	BA	G	AB	R	H	2B	3B	HR	RBI	SB
86 NL	.250	84	216	27	54	18	3	2	25	1
87 NL	.325	126	357	50	116	18	2	9	51	6
88 NL	.267	139	389	44	104	15	0	3	50	6
89 NL	.221	76	136	12	30	8	1	1	12	1
90 NL	.242	96	161	22	39	7	1	1	18	1
91 NL	.000	12	15	2	0	0	0	0	1	0
91 AL	.262	85	183	20	48	6	1	1	19	1
Life	.268	618	1457	179	391	72	8	17	176	16
2 AVE	.242	97	180	23	44	7	1	1	19	1

CURRENT PLAYERS

GERALD ALEXANDER

Position: Pitcher
Team: Texas Rangers
Born: March 26, 1968 Baton Rouge, LA
Height: 5'11" **Weight:** 190 lbs.
Bats: right **Throws:** right
Acquired: 21st-round pick in 6/89 free-agent draft

Player Summary	
Fantasy Value	$2 to $4
Card Value	10¢ to 20¢
Will	seek starting role
Can't	always throw strikes
Expect	control trouble
Don't Expect	many complete games

Alexander was used as a spot starter and long reliever during the 1991 campaign, his first full year in the major leagues. He won five of his first six decisions while yielding less than a hit per inning but showed an alarming tendency toward wildness. His strikeout-to-walk ratio is 1-to-1, and he pitches about two innings for every strikeout. These are not unusually bad numbers for a rookie hurler. Investors should wait for a good start in '92 before buying his 1992 rookie cards. Alexander had advanced to the Rangers after winning 19 games, an organizational record, in 22 decisions while pitching for two minor-league affiliates in 1990. He had a 2-1 strikeout-to-walk ratio at Triple-A Oklahoma City. He has an outstanding curveball. Fantasy leaguers should gamble a couple bucks on Alexander. The former Tulane University star launched his pro career in 1989 and reached Texas for a three-game September trial a year later. If he solves his control troubles, Alexander could become a starter. If not, his career may remain on a treadmill.

Major League Pitching Register

	W	L	ERA	G	S	IP	H	ER	BB	SO
90 AL	0	0	7.71	3	0	7.0	14	6	5	8
91 AL	5	3	5.24	30	0	89.1	93	52	48	50
Life	5	3	5.42	33	0	96.1	107	58	53	58

ROBERTO ALOMAR

Position: Second base
Team: Toronto Blue Jays
Born: Feb. 5, 1968 Ponce, Puerto Rico
Height: 6' **Weight:** 175 lbs.
Bats: both **Throws:** right
Acquired: Traded from Padres with Joe Carter for Fred McGriff and Tony Fernandez, 12/90

Player Summary	
Fantasy Value	$17 to $20
Card Value	5¢ to 10¢
Will	provide strong defense
Can't	take advantage of SkyDome fences
Expect	annual All-Star selection
Don't Expect	any more trades

After a three-year stint with the Padres, during which he was considered the most promising second baseman in the league, Alomar found himself starting in the All-Star Game for the AL in '91. Though Julio Franco of Texas did not agree, Alomar deserved his 1991 All-Star start. He and brother Sandy Alomar were the seventh brother tandem to appear in the same midseason classic but only the third to start for the same team. A switch-hitter who is more productive from the left side, Roberto's on-base and slugging percentages are superior for league second basemen; he has plenty of time to develop both a better batting eye and more power. Draft him for your fantasy team at $20 or less. His 1992 cards are good additions for a dime or less. He makes a strong contribution defensively. His best asset is an unusually wide range. Alomar still makes some dumb plays in the field but has been improving every year.

Major League Batting Register

	BA	G	AB	R	H	2B	3B	HR	RBI	SB
88 NL	.266	143	545	84	145	24	6	9	41	24
89 NL	.295	158	623	82	184	27	1	7	56	42
90 NL	.287	147	586	80	168	27	5	6	60	24
91 AL	.295	161	637	88	188	41	11	9	69	53
Life	.286	609	2391	334	685	119	23	31	226	143
3 AVE	.293	155	615	83	180	32	6	7	62	40

CURRENT PLAYERS

SANDY ALOMAR

Position: Catcher
Team: Cleveland Indians
Born: June 18, 1966 Salinas, Puerto Rico
Height: 6'5" **Weight:** 200 lbs.
Bats: right **Throws:** right
Acquired: Traded from Padres with Chris James and Carlos Baerga for Joe Carter, 12/89

Player Summary	
Fantasy Value	$7 to $10
Card Value	5¢ to 10¢
Will	nail stealers often
Can't	hit too many long balls
Expect	strong defensive play
Don't Expect	too many throwing errors

Although he is a capable hitter, Alomar is better known for his defense. He has a cannon of a throwing arm, blocks bad pitches, and handles his pitching staff well. Alomar won consecutive Minor League Player of the Year awards before winning AL Rookie of the Year honors with the 1990 Indians. He is a contact hitter who does not strike out often. He probably won't develop more than 15-homer power, but he could approach the 100-RBI level if the Indians had men on base ahead of him. Alomar had 101 RBI in 131 Triple-A games in '89. In his two AL seasons, he's been elected an All-Star starter by the fans twice. It wasn't deserved last year, when he was disabled with rotator cuff problems, but there should be many All-Star games, as well as Gold Gloves, in his future if he stays healthy. Alomar's uncertain health in 1992 limits his fantasy value to $10. His 1992 cards are sound, low-cost buys.

Major League Batting Register

	BA	G	AB	R	H	2B	3B	HR	RBI	SB
88 NL	.000	1	0	0	0	0	0	0	0	0
89 NL	.211	7	19	1	4	1	0	1	6	0
90 AL	.290	132	445	60	129	26	2	9	66	4
91 AL	.217	51	184	10	40	9	0	0	7	0
Life	.267	191	649	71	173	36	2	10	79	4
2 AVE	.269	92	315	35	85	18	1	5	37	2

LARRY ANDERSEN

Position: Pitcher
Team: San Diego Padres
Born: May 6, 1953 Portland, OR
Height: 6'3" **Weight:** 205 lbs.
Bats: right **Throws:** right
Acquired: Signed as a free agent, 12/90

Player Summary	
Fantasy Value	$1 to $3
Card Value	3¢ to 5¢
Will	stifle rivals' rallies
Can't	pitch every day
Expect	good K-to-walk ratio
Don't Expect	any gopher balls

Andersen was one of the game's most successful set-up men before the Padres decided to deploy him as a part-time closer in 1991. He had never had more than seven saves in a season, and he reached a new peak with 13 in '91. A control pitcher whose No. 1 weapon is a nasty slider (which he uses as the majority of his pitches), he almost never yields walks, wild pitches, or home runs. He is especially tough on righthanded hitters. He has notched 21 years in professional baseball, but his age curtails his fantasy appeal to $3. Andersen is an awkward fielder and doesn't keep runners close. A clubhouse prankster, his 1992 commons are good buys because of his possible future as a broadcaster.

Major League Pitching Register

	W	L	ERA	G	S	IP	H	ER	BB	SO
75 AL	0	0	4.76	3	0	5.2	4	3	2	4
77 AL	0	1	3.14	11	0	14.1	10	5	9	8
79 AL	0	0	7.56	8	0	16.2	25	14	4	7
81 AL	3	3	2.66	41	5	67.2	57	20	18	40
82 AL	0	0	5.99	40	1	79.2	100	53	23	32
83 NL	1	0	2.39	17	0	26.1	19	7	9	14
84 NL	3	7	2.38	64	4	90.2	85	24	25	54
85 NL	3	3	4.32	57	3	73.0	78	35	26	50
86 NL	2	1	3.03	48	1	77.1	83	26	26	42
87 NL	9	5	3.45	67	5	101.2	95	39	41	94
88 NL	2	4	2.94	53	5	82.2	82	27	20	66
89 NL	4	4	1.54	60	3	87.2	63	15	24	85
90 NL	5	2	1.95	50	6	73.2	61	16	24	68
90 AL	0	0	1.23	15	1	22.0	18	3	3	25
91 NL	3	4	2.30	38	13	47.0	39	12	13	40
Life	35	34	3.11	572	47	866.0	819	299	267	629
3 AVE	4	3	1.80	54	8	76.1	60	15	21	73

CURRENT PLAYERS

ALLAN ANDERSON

Position: Pitcher
Team: Minnesota Twins
Born: Jan. 7, 1964 Lancaster, OH
Height: 6' **Weight:** 194 lbs.
Bats: left **Throws:** left
Acquired: Second-round pick in 6/82 free-agent draft

Player Summary	
Fantasy Value	$1 to $3
Card Value	3¢ to 5¢
Will	yield more hits than frames
Can't	overpower hitters
Expect	an uncertain future
Don't Expect	another ERA title

In 1988, Anderson went 16-9 and led the AL in ERA; a year later he was 17-10. His pitching declined so steadily over the two following years, however, that he was returned to the minors four months into the 1991 campaign. Even consulting a sports psychologist didn't help. He got into trouble when he lost the razor-sharp control he had in 1988. Card investors should beware of his 1992 commons. Once known as "Little Frankie" because his changeup reminded Minnesota fans of Frank Viola's, Anderson never had a formidable fastball. Instead, he mixed his fastball, change, and curve so well that he kept batters guessing. When he lost the ability to hit the corners and keep his pitches down in the strike zone, Anderson's pitching became extended batting practice for rivals. His downfall should discourage fantasy managers to a $3 limit. He's a good fielder who also keeps runners close.

Major League Pitching Register

	W	L	ERA	G	CG	IP	H	ER	BB	SO
86 AL	3	6	5.55	21	1	84.1	106	52	30	51
87 AL	1	0	10.95	4	0	12.1	20	15	10	3
88 AL	16	9	2.45	30	3	202.1	199	55	37	83
89 AL	17	10	3.80	33	4	196.2	214	83	53	69
90 AL	7	18	4.53	31	5	188.2	214	95	39	82
91 AL	5	11	4.96	29	2	134.1	148	74	42	51
Life	49	54	4.11	148	15	818.2	901	374	211	339
3 AVE	10	13	4.36	31	4	173.2	192	84	45	67

BRADY ANDERSON

Position: Outfield
Team: Baltimore Orioles
Born: Jan. 18, 1964 Silver Spring, MD
Height: 6'1" **Weight:** 195 lbs.
Bats: left **Throws:** left
Acquired: Traded from Red Sox with Curt Schilling for Mike Boddicker, 7/88

Player Summary	
Fantasy Value	$2 to $4
Card Value	3¢ to 5¢
Will	steal when he gets on
Can't	hit the long ball
Expect	stellar defense in center
Don't Expect	acceptable average

Although he was chosen as the AL East's top rookie prospect in 1988 by *Baseball America*, Anderson has never lived up to that prediction. In fact, he's hit so poorly when given a chance to play that 1992 will be a crossroads season for him. Though blessed with great speed and outstanding defensive skills, he has been a complete bust with a bat in his hands. His 1992 commons will not rise in value. Managers keep hoping Anderson will live up to the potential he displayed as a second-year pro, when he hit .319 with 12 homers, 87 RBI, and 44 steals for Double-A Winter Haven in 1986. In his best big league effort, in 1990, Anderson stole 15 bases in 17 tries and went 6-for-18 (.333) as a pinch-hitter—even though he was limited to 55 starts by shoulder and ankle injuries. The emergence of Mike Devereaux in 1991 stopped Anderson from getting more playing time in center field. Other young Oriole flycatchers should reduce Anderson's at bats further, making him a $4 outfielder at best.

Major League Batting Register

	BA	G	AB	R	H	2B	3B	HR	RBI	SB
88 AL	.212	94	325	31	69	13	4	1	21	10
89 AL	.207	94	266	44	55	12	2	4	16	16
90 AL	.231	89	234	24	54	5	2	3	24	15
91 AL	.230	113	256	40	59	12	3	2	27	12
Life	.219	390	1081	139	237	42	11	10	88	53
3 AVE	.222	99	252	36	56	10	2	3	22	14

CURRENT PLAYERS

ERIC ANTHONY

Position: Outfield
Team: Houston Astros
Born: Nov. 8, 1967 San Diego, CA
Height: 6'2" **Weight:** 195 lbs.
Bats: left **Throws:** left
Acquired: 34th-round pick in 6/86 free-agent draft

Player Summary	
Fantasy Value	$2 to $4
Card Value	5¢ to 7¢
Will	provide power plus speed
Can't	avoid frequent Ks
Expect	team lead in homers
Don't Expect	high average

Anthony now has two strikes against him. In each of the last two seasons, Houston has given him extended opportunities to live up to his potential as the organization's top power-hitting prospect. Both times, the team had to return Anthony to the minors. He has great strength and bat speed, but too often that bat does not connect with the ball. Anthony did not hit .200 in either of his extended looks. The power-starved Astros seem willing to wait, though they must be growing impatient since several of their other youngsters are starting to shine. Anthony may have bankrupted a few overzealous fantasy managers in 1991. Don't invest much in him in 1992. His 1992 cards are risky investments, even at 7 cents apiece. He led the Class-A Sally League with 29 homers in 439 at bats in 1988 and the Double-A Southern League with 28 homers in 403 at bats in '89. He hit over .300 against Triple-A pitching in '90. He has a strong throwing arm from right field and has shown steady defensive improvement.

Major League Batting Register

	BA	G	AB	R	H	2B	3B	HR	RBI	SB
89 NL	.180	25	61	7	11	2	0	4	7	0
90 NL	.192	84	239	26	46	8	0	10	29	5
91 NL	.153	39	118	11	18	6	0	1	7	1
Life	.179	148	418	44	75	16	0	15	43	6

KEVIN APPIER

Position: Pitcher
Team: Kansas City Royals
Born: Dec. 6, 1967 Lancaster, CA
Height: 6'2" **Weight:** 190 lbs.
Bats: right **Throws:** right
Acquired: First-round pick in 6/87 free-agent draft

Player Summary	
Fantasy Value	$8 to $11
Card Value	5¢ to 7¢
Will	keep runners off base
Can't	stop runners from stealing
Expect	200 innings pitched
Don't Expect	control problems

Appier was named Rookie Pitcher of the Year by *The Sporting News* with the Royals in 1990. After starting the year in the minors, he moved into the rotation in late May and wound up with a 12-8 record and three shutouts in 24 starts. One of those wins was a one-hitter against Detroit. Appier continued pitching effectively in 1991. A fastball-and-slider pitcher with good control, he is a mediocre fielder who lacks a good pickoff move. Lefthanded hitters give him the most trouble. Due to the Royals' lack of respect, Appier could be a fantasy auction bargain at prices up to $11. He was 8-8 with a 3.95 ERA, 109 Ks, 42 walks, and 141 base hits, in 139 innings for Triple-A Omaha in 1989. In 1988 at Class-A Baseball City, he was 10-9 with a 2.75 ERA. His 1992 cards are latent price gainers at a nickel each. He has made a strong impression on other teams, who tried to trade for him several times in 1991. He's certain to remain a rotation regular and improve with experience.

Major League Pitching Register

	W	L	ERA	G	CG	IP	H	ER	BB	SO
89 AL	1	4	9.14	6	0	21.2	34	22	12	10
90 AL	12	8	2.76	32	3	185.2	179	57	54	127
91 AL	13	10	3.42	34	6	207.2	205	79	61	158
Life	26	22	3.43	72	9	415.0	418	158	127	295
2 AVE	13	9	3.11	33	5	196.2	192	68	58	143

CURRENT PLAYERS

LUIS AQUINO

Position: Pitcher
Team: Kansas City Royals
Born: May 19, 1965 Santurce, Puerto Rico
Height: 6'1" **Weight:** 190 lbs.
Bats: right **Throws:** right
Acquired: Traded from Blue Jays for Juan Beniquez, 7/87

Player Summary	
Fantasy Value	$1 to $3
Card Value	3¢ to 5¢
Will	retain spot starting role
Can't	record high K totals
Expect	results with control
Don't Expect	high ERA

Because Kansas City was disappointing, top performances by individual players on the Royals often were overlooked. Aquino was one of the few beacons in the fog. He was Kansas City Pitcher of the Month in July, when he went 4-1 with two saves and a 1.09 ERA in seven games. Used as both a starter and reliever, Aquino was the most effective pitcher on the staff— even though he occasionally suffers control trouble. He twice saved 20 games in the minors, in 1984 at Class-A Kinston and '85 at Double-A Knoxville. Aquino throws a fastball, curve, and slider, but he does not record high strikeout totals. Therefore, don't consider his 1992 common cards as investments. You can, however, blow a couple bucks drafting Aquino. His combined wins plus saves could surprise other fantasy managers. His versatility makes him especially valuable: He could move into the rotation, remain in the relief corps, or work as a spot starter for the third year in a row.

Major League Pitching Register

	W	L	ERA	G	S	IP	H	ER	BB	SO
86 AL	1	1	6.35	7	0	11.1	14	8	3	5
88 AL	1	0	2.79	7	0	29.0	33	9	17	11
89 AL	6	8	3.50	34	0	141.1	148	55	35	68
90 AL	4	1	3.16	20	0	68.1	59	24	27	28
91 AL	8	4	3.44	38	3	157.0	152	60	47	80
Life	20	14	3.45	106	3	407.0	406	156	129	192
3 AVE	6	4	3.41	31	1	122.1	120	46	36	59

JACK ARMSTRONG

Position: Pitcher
Team: Cleveland Indians
Born: March 7, 1965 Englewood, NJ
Height: 6'5" **Weight:** 220 lbs.
Bats: right **Throws:** right
Acquired: Traded from Reds with Scott Scudder and Joe Turek for Greg Swindell, 11/91

Player Summary	
Fantasy Value	$2 to $4
Card Value	3¢ to 5¢
Will	pitch well in spurts
Can't	win consistently
Expect	another prolonged trial
Don't Expect	guaranteed spot

What happened to Armstrong after starting the 1990 All-Star Game? After taking an 11-3 record into that game, he went 7-16 over two seasons and found himself back in the minors. In 1991, he had the fifth-worst ERA in the NL in the first inning (7.13) among qualifiers, and opponents slugged .491 off of him. He has diminished as a fantasy possibility, even at $3. A sore elbow might be part of the explanation. The Indians hope he returns to the form he showed during 1989 at Triple-A Nashville, when he led the American Association with 13 wins, six shutouts, and a dozen complete games. The University of Oklahoma product has two money pitches, a fastball and a slider, along with a good change-up. Should he regain his touch, Armstrong is certain to be in the rotation in 1992. His 1992 commons are not investments at this point.

Major League Pitching Register

	W	L	ERA	G	CG	IP	H	ER	BB	SO
88 NL	4	7	5.79	14	0	65.1	63	42	38	45
89 NL	2	3	4.64	9	0	42.2	40	22	21	23
90 NL	12	9	3.42	29	2	166.0	151	63	59	110
91 NL	7	13	5.48	27	1	139.2	158	85	54	93
Life	25	32	4.61	79	3	413.2	412	212	172	271
2 AVE	10	11	4.36	28	2	153.1	155	74	57	102

CURRENT PLAYERS

PAUL ASSENMACHER

Position: Pitcher
Team: Chicago Cubs
Born: Dec. 10, 1960 Detroit, MI
Height: 6'3" **Weight:** 200 lbs.
Bats: left **Throws:** left
Acquired: Traded from Braves for Kelly Mann and Pat Gomez, 8/89

Player Summary
Fantasy Value	$3 to $5
Card Value	3¢ to 5¢
Will	use curve as weapon
Can't	muscle heater by hitters
Expect	team lead in games
Don't Expect	return to closer role

Assenmacher is an outstanding relief pitcher who has found success as a middle reliever and a closer. He is a control pitcher who does not throw hard. He is capable of working often and rarely loses time with an injury. A curveball specialist whose fastball is only average, Assenmacher compiles high strikeout totals (a K per inning) by baffling batters with a variety of slow stuff. He is particularly difficult for lefthanded hitters. Cards of relievers are risky investments, and his 1992 commons are no different. He has appeared at least 60 times in four seasons and has managed to prosper while pitching half his games in hitters' parks, for the Braves and Cubs. Therefore, his wins plus saves could help a fantasy team, but for no more than $5. He is an average fielder with an adequate pickoff move. Although he could make a good lefty closer, Assenmacher probably will return to middle relief.

Major League Pitching Register
	W	L	ERA	G	S	IP	H	ER	BB	SO
86 NL	7	3	2.50	61	7	68.1	61	19	26	56
87 NL	1	1	5.10	52	2	54.2	58	31	24	39
88 NL	8	7	3.06	64	5	79.1	72	27	32	71
89 NL	3	4	3.99	63	0	76.2	74	34	28	79
90 NL	7	2	2.80	74	10	103.0	90	32	36	95
91 NL	7	8	3.24	75	15	102.2	85	37	31	117
Life	33	25	3.34	389	39	484.2	440	180	177	457
3 AVE	6	5	3.28	71	8	94.1	83	34	32	97

DON AUGUST

Position: Pitcher
Team: Milwaukee Brewers
Born: July 3, 1963 Inglewood, CA
Height: 6'3" **Weight:** 190 lbs.
Bats: right **Throws:** right
Acquired: Traded from Astros with Mark Knudson for Danny Darwin, 8/86

Player Summary
Fantasy Value	$2 to $4
Card Value	3¢ to 5¢
Will	try to use finesse
Can't	throw 90-mph heat
Expect	OK performance
Don't Expect	guaranteed job

After coming to spring training as a non-roster player in 1991, August pitched his way onto the Milwaukee varsity. A control pitcher with a tendency to throw home run balls, he mixed his fastball, curve, slider, and changeup well enough to win the No. 4 spot in the Brew Crew's starting rotation. His fastball is only average, but his overhand curveball is effective when his placement is on. August silenced skeptics when he went 13-7 with a 3.09 ERA as a 1988 rookie but has done little to keep them quiet since. His 1992 cards have nil promise. He has allowed an average of more than five earned runs per game since—a habit that produced several return tickets to the minors. The ERA would be even worse if he didn't have the ability to keep runners close. August wasn't guaranteed a roster spot in 1991, and his fantasy worth could topple in 1992. Though he was once a first-round draft choice (by the Astros in 1984), August seems unlikely ever to justify that selection.

Major League Pitching Register
	W	L	ERA	G	CG	IP	H	ER	BB	SO
88 AL	13	7	3.09	24	6	148.1	137	51	48	66
89 AL	12	12	5.31	31	2	142.1	175	84	58	51
90 AL	0	3	6.55	5	0	11.0	13	8	5	2
91 AL	9	8	5.47	28	1	138.1	166	84	47	62
Life	34	30	4.64	88	9	440.0	491	227	158	181
2 AVE	11	10	5.39	30	2	140.1	171	84	53	57

CURRENT PLAYERS

STEVE AVERY

Position: Pitcher
Team: Atlanta Braves
Born: April 14, 1970 Trenton, MI
Height: 6'4" **Weight:** 180 lbs.
Bats: left **Throws:** left
Acquired: First-round pick in 6/88 free-agent draft

Player Summary	
Fantasy Value	$8 to $12
Card Value	5¢ to 10¢
Will	become All-Star
Can't	avoid blister woes
Expect	good K-to-walk ratio
Don't Expect	too many losses

Avery was a big reason for Atlanta's resurrection. Rushed to the majors at age 20 in 1990, the rookie lefthander lost 11 of 14 decisions. The half-year of experience obviously helped. In 1991, Avery became the No. 2 starter on the Atlanta staff, behind Tom Glavine. Avery won 18 games, held opponents to a .240 batting average and a .299 on-base average, and gave up 2.78 walks per nine scoreless innings. He pitched an NLCS record 16⅓ innings against the Bucs in '91. He is a strikeout pitcher with good command of a fastball, changeup, and overhand curve. He also has confidence and poise beyond his years. He won't be as affordable in the 1992 fantasy draft as in '91, but he's still a good prospect. If you can, pay no more than $12. He is a capable hitter, getting a .511 average in high school. Bothered only by recurring blisters on his pitching hand, Avery is a budding superstar. His 1992 cards have long-lasting potential up to a dime. He and Glavine give the Braves the best lefthanded duo in baseball.

Major League Pitching Register

	W	L	ERA	G	S	IP	H	ER	BB	SO
90 NL	3	11	5.64	21	1	99.0	121	62	45	75
91 NL	18	8	3.38	35	3	210.1	189	79	65	137
Life	21	19	4.10	56	4	309.1	310	141	110	212
2 AVE	11	10	4.10	28	2	155.1	155	71	55	106

WALLY BACKMAN

Position: Infield
Team: Philadelphia Phillies
Born: Sept. 22, 1959 Hillsboro, OR
Height: 5'9" **Weight:** 168 lbs.
Bats: both **Throws:** right
Acquired: Signed as a free agent, 1/91

Player Summary	
Fantasy Value	$1 to $3
Card Value	3¢ to 5¢
Will	bunt for hits
Can't	hit home runs
Expect	continued back-up role
Don't Expect	many stolen bases

The 1991 Phillies hoped leadoff man Lenny Dykstra and No. 2 hitter Backman would again form the same kind of 1-2 punch that set the table for the 1986 Mets. That was before Dykstra lost two months and before Backman's bat failed to produce. Card investors should steer away from his 1992 commons. A year after hitting .292 for Pittsburgh, he slipped 50 points and lost his job to rookie Mickey Morandini. A switch-hitter with little power, Backman often gets on base with walks, bunts, or infield hits. He's much more productive batting lefthanded and finds himself in platoon situations. In 10 seasons, he's played in more than 128 games only once. He is a $3 fantasy middle infielder who also plays some third. He is a fine fielder at second but so-so at third.

Major League Batting Register

	BA	G	AB	R	H	2B	3B	HR	RBI	SB
80 NL	.323	27	93	12	30	1	1	0	9	2
81 NL	.278	26	36	5	10	2	0	0	0	1
82 NL	.272	96	261	37	71	13	2	3	22	8
83 NL	.167	26	42	6	7	0	1	0	3	0
84 NL	.280	128	436	68	122	19	2	1	26	32
85 NL	.273	145	520	77	142	24	5	1	38	30
86 NL	.320	124	387	67	124	18	2	1	27	13
87 NL	.250	94	300	43	75	6	1	1	23	11
88 NL	.303	99	294	44	89	12	0	0	17	9
89 AL	.231	87	299	33	69	9	2	1	26	1
90 NL	.292	104	315	62	92	21	3	2	28	6
91 NL	.243	94	185	20	45	12	0	0	15	3
Life	.277	1050	3168	474	876	137	19	10	234	116
3 AVE	.258	95	266	38	69	14	2	1	23	3

CURRENT PLAYERS

CARLOS BAERGA

Position: Infield
Team: Cleveland Indians
Born: Nov. 4, 1968 San Juan, Puerto Rico
Height: 5'11" **Weight:** 165 lbs.
Bats: both **Throws:** right
Acquired: Traded from Padres with Sandy Alomar and Chris James for Joe Carter, 12/89

Player Summary	
Fantasy Value	$5 to $8
Card Value	5¢ to 9¢
Will	hit 12 to 15 homers
Can't	get deserved publicity
Expect	best defense at second
Don't Expect	too many walks

Baerga's 5-for-5 performance against Oakland on July 23 was the first five-hit game by an Indian since Joe Carter in 1986. The "fourth player" in the Sandy Alomar deal, Baerga hit .260 with seven homers as a rookie with the 1990 Indians, and showed marked improvement as a sophomore. Since signing at age 17, he has always hit and run well. He had a .305 average and 26 steals at Class-A Charleston as a second-year pro in 1987. He hit .275 with 10 homers and 74 RBI at Triple-A Las Vegas in 1989. Baerga has good range and a good arm and can play three infield positions, though he's best at second and short. His fantasy possibilities are very exciting in the $5 to $8 range. He will open the '92 season at second base, with Jim Thome at third and Mark Lewis switching over to shortstop. Baerga's 1992 cards are modest possibilities at their 7¢ price. He should show more patience at the plate, striking out more than he walks. Baerga shows surprising power for an infielder.

Major League Batting Register

	BA	G	AB	R	H	2B	3B	HR	RBI	SB
90 AL	.260	108	312	46	81	17	2	7	47	0
91 AL	.288	158	593	80	171	28	2	11	69	3
Life	.278	266	905	126	252	45	4	18	116	3
2 AVE	.278	133	453	63	126	23	2	9	58	2

JEFF BAGWELL

Position: First base; third base
Team: Houston Astros
Born: May 27, 1968 Boston, MA
Height: 6' **Weight:** 195 lbs.
Bats: right **Throws:** right
Acquired: Traded from Red Sox for Larry Andersen, 8/90

Player Summary	
Fantasy Value	$10 to $13
Card Value	35¢ to 50¢
Will	hit for average
Can't	steal bases often
Expect	eventual return to third
Don't Expect	many homers in dome

Houston pulled a heist when they landed Bagwell for veteran middle reliever Larry Andersen, who was destined for free agency. Bagwell figures to be a Houston fixture for years. He is a former University of Hartford star that moved from third base to first so that Ken Caminiti could stay in the lineup. Bagwell got off to a slow start but soon established himself as the best candidate for NL Rookie of the Year honors. His 1992 cards have great futures, though they are already priced in a high 50-cent range. He was an important cog in the middle of the Astros batting order. The former Double-A Eastern League MVP (in 1990) even showed surprising power. On May 5, he became the ninth player to hit an upper deck home run (456 feet) at Pittsburgh's Three Rivers Stadium. His fantasy value could increase if the Astros put him back at third base. His $13 high limit is due to his relative youth. Teammate Craig Biggio says Bagwell can hit .340 if he reduces his strikeout frequency.

Major League Batting Register

	BA	G	AB	R	H	2B	3B	HR	RBI	SB
91 NL	.294	156	554	79	163	26	4	15	82	7
Life	.294	156	554	79	163	26	4	15	82	7

CURRENT PLAYERS

SCOTT BAILES

Position: Pitcher
Team: California Angels
Born: Dec. 18, 1962 Chillicothe, OH
Height: 6'2" **Weight:** 171 lbs.
Bats: left **Throws:** left
Acquired: Traded from Indians for Jeff Manto and Colin Charland, 1/90

Player Summary
Fantasy Value	$1 to $2
Card Value	3¢ to 5¢
Will	retire key lefty hitters
Can't	work as effective starter
Expect	frequent short outings
Don't Expect	many wins or saves

Bailes spent the first four years of his major league career moving from the starting rotation to the bullpen. He split 20 decisions as a 1986 rookie, threw two shutouts two years later, but never displayed the effectiveness he had shown as a relief pitcher in the minor leagues. A 1989 shoulder injury also hampered his development. Originally a seventh-round draft choice of Texas in 1982, he was deployed strictly in relief by the Angels in 1991. Because he was often called upon to retire one or two lefthanded hitters, he did not run up a high total of innings pitched. He is a specialized middle reliever who has not had a consistent record of success, thus his 1992 commons are not wise investments. Fading relievers like Bailes aren't viable prospects for fantasy managers. Pay $2 at most. Bailes, who once consulted a sports psychologist to aid his concentration, needs to show better results to protect his big league future.

Major League Pitching Register

	W	L	ERA	G	S	IP	H	ER	BB	SO
86 AL	10	10	4.95	62	7	112.2	123	62	43	60
87 AL	7	8	4.64	39	6	120.1	145	62	47	65
88 AL	9	14	4.90	37	0	145.0	149	79	46	53
89 AL	5	9	4.28	34	0	113.2	116	54	29	47
90 AL	2	0	6.37	27	0	35.1	46	25	20	16
91 AL	1	2	4.18	42	0	51.2	41	24	22	41
Life	34	43	4.76	241	13	578.2	620	306	207	282
3 AVE	3	4	4.62	34	0	66.2	68	34	24	35

HAROLD BAINES

Position: Designated hitter; outfield
Team: Oakland Athletics
Born: March 15, 1959 Easton, MD
Height: 6'2" **Weight:** 195 lbs.
Bats: left **Throws:** left
Acquired: Traded from Rangers for Joe Bitker and Scott Chiamparino, 8/90

Player Summary
Fantasy Value	$12 to $15
Card Value	5¢ to 10¢
Will	still produce frequent power
Can't	run well
Expect	20 homers if healthy
Don't Expect	time in outfield

Knee problems have kept Baines from playing the outfield but have not hampered his hitting. On May 7, he hit three home runs in a game for the second time in his career. Because he's such a threat, pitchers try to keep the ball away from him. He's responded by transforming himself into an opposite-field hitter. The four-time All-Star has good bat speed and is capable of pulling any mistake pitch. His fantasy potential remains good up to $15, providing he's healthy. Pitchers who throw him high, inside fastballs are flirting with disaster. Baines's 1992 cards at a dime could bring small long-term profits. A three-time .300 hitter, Baines ended the longest game in history (a 25-inning 1984 contest that consumed 8:06) with a home run.

Major League Batting Register

	BA	G	AB	R	H	2B	3B	HR	RBI	SB
80 AL	.255	141	491	55	125	23	6	13	49	2
81 AL	.286	82	280	42	80	11	7	10	41	6
82 AL	.271	161	608	89	165	29	8	25	105	10
83 AL	.280	156	596	76	167	33	2	20	99	7
84 AL	.304	147	569	72	173	28	10	29	94	1
85 AL	.309	160	640	86	198	29	3	22	113	1
86 AL	.296	145	570	72	169	29	2	21	88	2
87 AL	.293	132	505	59	148	26	4	20	93	0
88 AL	.277	158	599	55	166	39	1	13	81	0
89 AL	.309	146	505	73	156	29	1	16	72	0
90 AL	.284	135	415	52	118	15	1	16	65	0
91 AL	.295	141	488	76	144	25	1	20	90	0
Life	.289	1704	6266	807	1809	316	46	225	990	29
3 AVE	.297	141	469	67	139	23	1	17	76	0

CURRENT PLAYERS

JEFF BALLARD

Position: Pitcher
Team: Baltimore Orioles
Born: Aug. 13, 1963 Billings, MT
Height: 6'2" **Weight:** 198 lbs.
Bats: left **Throws:** left
Acquired: Seventh-round pick in 6/85 free-agent draft

Player Summary	
Fantasy Value	$1 to $2
Card Value	3¢ to 5¢
Will	rely heavily on location
Can't	throw hard
Expect	slow recovery from surgery
Don't Expect	return to 18-win form

Stanford graduate Ballard was a master of location when he won 18 games for the surprising second-place Orioles of 1989. But he hasn't been the same pitcher since elbow surgery that followed his brilliant season. He slipped so badly in 1991, in fact, that Baltimore returned him to the minors in early August. Because he has not won 40 career games yet, his 1992 commons should not rise in value. Ballard throws only an average fastball and slider. The curve is his best pitch, and also the reason for his elbow problems. A control pitcher, he discovered a sinking fastball in 1989 and mixed it successfully with the slider, curve, and pinpoint location. Though he was one of the AL's top starters that season, rival batters hit .287 against him with 240 hits in 215⅓ innings pitched. His career looks cursed. If you believe in bad luck, sidestep him in fantasy league transactions for more than $2. Perhaps the 1989 Jeff Ballard was a better escape artist than a pitcher.

Major League Pitching Register

	W	L	ERA	G	CG	IP	H	ER	BB	SO
87 AL	2	8	6.59	14	0	69.2	100	51	35	27
88 AL	8	12	4.40	25	6	153.1	167	75	42	41
89 AL	18	8	3.43	35	4	215.1	240	82	57	62
90 AL	2	11	4.93	44	0	133.1	152	73	42	50
91 AL	6	12	5.60	26	0	123.2	153	77	28	37
Life	36	51	4.63	144	10	695.1	812	358	204	217
3 AVE	9	10	4.42	35	1	157.1	182	77	42	50

SCOTT BANKHEAD

Position: Pitcher
Team: Seattle Mariners
Born: July 31, 1963 Raleigh, NC
Height: 5'10" **Weight:** 185 lbs.
Bats: right **Throws:** right
Acquired: Traded from Royals with Steve Shields and Mike Kingery for Danny Tartabull and Rick Luecken, 12/86

Player Summary	
Fantasy Value	$1 to $2
Card Value	3¢ to 5¢
Will	show good control
Can't	avoid shoulder problems
Expect	determined comeback effort
Don't Expect	medical miracle in 1992

Bankhead's long history of shoulder problems has clouded his future. After posting a 14-6 mark and 3.34 ERA in 1989, shoulder problems kept him out almost all of 1990 and 1991. He had a 2-5 record in '91 when Seattle placed him on the 60-day disabled list. The decision was no surprise, because his shoulder problems have forced him onto the list in four of the last five seasons. Several times, he was sidelined twice in one year. His 1992 cards will remain in the commons bins. If he gets healthy, he could win again. Unfortunately, he is too much of a fantasy risk for most managers at more than $2. When healthy, the 1984 U.S. Olympian throws a slider and fastball that move, plus a curve that serves as his changeup. A control pitcher who yields few walks but is susceptible to the long ball, Bankhead helps himself in the field. If he also helped himself in the medical field, the Mariners would be grateful.

Major League Pitching Register

	W	L	ERA	G	CG	IP	H	ER	BB	SO
86 AL	8	9	4.61	24	0	121.0	121	62	37	94
87 AL	9	8	5.42	27	2	149.1	168	90	37	95
88 AL	7	9	3.07	21	2	135.0	115	46	38	102
89 AL	14	6	3.34	33	3	210.1	187	78	63	140
90 AL	0	2	11.08	4	0	13.0	18	16	7	10
91 AL	3	6	4.90	17	0	60.2	73	33	21	28
Life	41	40	4.24	126	7	689.1	682	325	203	469
2 AVE	9	6	3.69	25	2	135.2	130	56	42	84

CURRENT PLAYERS

BRET BARBERIE

Position: Infield
Team: Montreal Expos
Born: Aug. 16, 1967 Long Beach, CA
Height: 5'11" **Weight:** 185 lbs.
Bats: both **Throws:** right
Acquired: Eighth-round pick in 6/88 free-agent draft

Player Summary	
Fantasy Value	$2 to $4
Card Value	10c to 15c
Will	produce power at short
Can't	carry Spike Owen's glove
Expect	improvement with experience
Don't Expect	instant success in majors

When Barberie hit his first two major league home runs during a 6-5 loss to Philadelphia on August 2, he hit one from each side of the plate. The run-starved Expos, who played him at shortstop in that game, hope he provides many similar nights in the future. His 1992 rookie cards are overpriced dangers at more than 15 cents, however. His potential is evident, because he was leading the entire Montreal farm system with 48 runs batted in at the time of his call-up on June 16. His stats in '91 at Triple-A Indianapolis include a .312 average, 10 homers, 10 doubles, 59 bases on balls, and 47 strikeouts in 218 at bats. He hit .260 with seven homers, 56 RBI, and 71 runs scored in 1990 at Double-A Jacksonville. He also had 20 stolen bases and 86 walks against 64 strikeouts that year. He was a member of the 1988 U.S. Olympic team. Unless he beats out Spike Owen at shortstop, Barberie is a $3 fantasy infielder. Barberie's father was a minor league player. The Expos expect Bret to become a baseball rarity: a middle infielder with punch.

Major League Batting Register

	BA	G	AB	R	H	2B	3B	HR	RBI	SB
91 NL	.353	57	136	16	48	12	2	2	18	0
Life	.353	57	136	16	48	12	2	2	18	0

JESSE BARFIELD

Position: Outfield
Team: New York Yankees
Born: Oct. 29, 1959 Joliet, IL
Height: 6'1" **Weight:** 200 lbs.
Bats: right **Throws:** right
Acquired: Traded from Blue Jays for Al Leiter, 4/89

Player Summary	
Fantasy Value	$12 to $15
Card Value	5c to 7c
Will	show off outfield arm
Can't	hit for high average
Expect	considerable long-ball production
Don't Expect	reduced K frequency

Runners think twice about taking an extra base when Barfield is stationed in right field. Armed with the league's best right field arm, he also has a powerful bat that produces power to all fields. When he hit 40 homers for the Blue Jays in 1986, half of them went to the opposite field. Barfield hit 25 homers for the 1990 Yankees but estimates he lost 14 more because of a left-center field fence that stands a distant 399 feet from home plate. A notorious streak hitter, he has recovered from a 1988 wrist injury that threatened his career. His 1992 cards are not buys in the 5- to 7-cent range. A typical slugger, he is basically a pull hitter who strikes out frequently. His decline in run production in '91 should warn fantasy managers to be wary of Barfield's future.

Major League Batting Register

	BA	G	AB	R	H	2B	3B	HR	RBI	SB
81 AL	.232	25	95	7	22	3	2	2	9	4
82 AL	.246	139	394	54	97	13	2	18	58	1
83 AL	.253	128	388	58	98	13	3	27	68	2
84 AL	.284	110	320	51	91	14	1	14	49	8
85 AL	.289	155	539	94	156	34	9	27	84	22
86 AL	.289	158	589	107	170	35	2	40	108	8
87 AL	.263	159	590	89	155	25	3	28	84	3
88 AL	.244	137	468	62	114	21	5	18	56	7
89 AL	.234	150	521	79	122	23	1	23	67	5
90 AL	.246	153	476	69	117	21	2	25	78	4
91 AL	.225	84	284	37	64	12	0	17	48	1
Life	.259	1398	4664	707	1206	214	30	239	709	65
3 AVE	.237	129	427	62	101	19	1	22	64	3

CURRENT PLAYERS

BRIAN BARNES

Position: Pitcher
Team: Montreal Expos
Born: March 25, 1967 Roanoke Rapids, NC
Height: 5'9" **Weight:** 170 lbs.
Bats: left **Throws:** left
Acquired: Fourth-round pick in 6/89 free-agent draft

Player Summary	
Fantasy Value	$4 to $6
Card Value	5¢ to 10¢
Will	throw baffling breaking ball
Can't	depend on hard stuff
Expect	many strikeouts
Don't Expect	wins without experience

Barnes is living proof that a little guy who doesn't throw hard can lead his league in strikeouts. The 5'9" lefty mixed his fastball, curve, and changeup well enough to whiff 213 Double-A Southern League hitters in 201⅓ innings (in 1990). He also proved that he could throw his off-speed pitches for strikes at any time. His 23 major league Ks with his 213 Double-A whiffs combined to lead all pro ball in 1990. That year at Jacksonville, he was 13-7 with a 2.77 ERA, three complete games, and 87 walks. The 1989 All-American Clemson product learned the circle changeup from Pittsburgh reliever Bill Landrum during Barnes's winter workouts at college in '89 before he turned pro. Though he struggled with the last-place 1991 Expos, he should become a successful big league starter as he gains confidence and experience. If Montreal improves, Barnes will, too. Gamble on the youngster's 1992 cards at a dime apiece. His fantasy potential is high, considering that he has a place locked up in Montreal's 1992 rotation. He was 2-0 with a 1.64 ERA for '91 Triple-A Indianapolis.

Major League Pitching Register

	W	L	ERA	G	CG	IP	H	ER	BB	SO
90 NL	1	1	2.89	4	1	28.0	25	9	7	23
91 NL	5	8	4.22	28	1	160.0	135	75	84	117
Life	6	9	4.02	32	2	188.0	160	84	91	140

KEVIN BASS

Position: Outfield
Team: San Francisco Giants
Born: May 12, 1959 Redwood City, CA
Height: 6' **Weight:** 180 lbs.
Bats: both **Throws:** right
Acquired: Signed as a free agent, 11/89

Player Summary	
Fantasy Value	$3 to $5
Card Value	3¢ to 5¢
Will	add speed to lineup
Can't	keep mind off injured knee
Expect	strong outfield defense
Don't Expect	average above .275

Bass was a strong hitter before submitting to knee surgery on May 30, 1990. Sessions with batting coach Dusty Baker helped revive Bass's bat in '91. He had trouble, however, squeezing into an outfield occupied by Kevin Mitchell, Darren Lewis, and Willie McGee. After a season of readjustment, Bass could be a surprise to fantasy managers who gamble $5 or less. He was an NL All-Star in 1986 with Houston, then had two three-hit games in the '86 NLCS. He produces both power and speed when healthy. Because of his injuries, his career stats will never spur long-term movement in his 1992 common-card prices. Defensively, Bass has excellent range and a strong arm. He is a skilled base-runner when not favoring the damaged knee. If healthy, Bass figures to challenge for a regular role.

Major League Batting Register

	BA	G	AB	R	H	2B	3B	HR	RBI	SB
82 AL	.000	18	9	4	0	0	0	0	0	0
82 NL	.042	12	24	2	1	0	0	0	1	0
83 NL	.236	88	195	25	46	7	3	2	18	2
84 NL	.260	121	331	33	86	17	5	2	29	5
85 NL	.269	150	539	72	145	27	5	16	68	19
86 NL	.311	157	591	83	184	33	5	20	79	22
87 NL	.284	157	592	83	168	31	5	19	85	21
88 NL	.255	157	541	57	138	27	2	14	72	31
89 NL	.300	87	313	42	94	19	4	5	44	11
90 NL	.252	61	214	25	54	9	1	7	32	2
91 NL	.233	124	361	43	84	10	4	10	40	7
Life	.270	1132	3710	469	1000	180	34	95	468	120
3 AVE	.261	91	296	37	77	13	3	7	39	7

CURRENT PLAYERS

STEVE BEDROSIAN

Position: Pitcher
Team: Minnesota Twins
Born: Dec. 6, 1957 Methuen, MA
Height: 6'3" **Weight:** 205 lbs.
Bats: right **Throws:** right
Acquired: Traded from Giants for Johnny Ard and Jimmy Williams, 12/90

Player Summary
Fantasy Value	$7 to $10
Card Value	3¢ to 5¢
Will	try to blow batters away
Can't	serve as consistent closer
Expect	lessened work load
Don't Expect	leading role in pen

Bedrosian is one of a handful of relievers who have won a Cy Young Award, doing it in 1987 for the Phillies. Used mostly as a set-up man for Minnesota closer Rick Aguilera in '91, Bedrosian still managed to appear at least 50 times for the sixth year in a row. Since he won't notch many saves if Aguilera continues to be effective, Bedrosian is a shaky draft pick at more than $10. A power pitcher who depends on his fastball and slider, he has had control trouble throughout his career. He usually has a much better ratio of strikeouts to walks. Years of throwing blistering heat have taken a toll, so Bedrosian's best days may be behind him. The 1992 season could determine his future as a closer. Though near 200 career saves, his 1992 cards are unwise investments.

Major League Pitching Register
	W	L	ERA	G	S	IP	H	ER	BB	SO
81 NL	1	2	4.44	15	0	24.1	15	12	15	9
82 NL	8	6	2.42	64	11	137.2	102	37	57	123
83 NL	9	10	3.60	70	19	120.0	100	48	51	114
84 NL	9	6	2.37	40	11	83.2	65	22	33	81
85 NL	7	15	3.83	37	0	206.2	198	88	111	134
86 NL	8	6	3.39	68	29	90.1	79	34	34	82
87 NL	5	3	2.83	65	40	89.0	79	28	28	74
88 NL	6	6	3.75	57	28	74.1	75	31	27	61
89 NL	3	7	2.87	68	23	84.2	56	27	39	58
90 NL	9	9	4.20	68	17	79.1	72	37	44	43
91 AL	5	3	4.42	56	6	77.1	70	38	35	44
Life	70	73	3.39	608	184	1067.1	911	402	474	823
3 AVE	6	6	3.80	64	15	80.1	66	34	39	48

TIM BELCHER

Position: Pitcher
Team: Cincinatti Reds
Born: Oct. 19, 1961 Mount Gilead, OH
Height: 6'3" **Weight:** 210 lbs.
Bats: right **Throws:** right
Acquired: Traded from Dodgers with John Wetteland for Eric Davis and Kip Gross, 11/91

Player Summary
Fantasy Value	$8 to $12
Card Value	3¢ to 5¢
Will	have good K-to-walk ratio
Can't	always finish
Expect	a lively fastball
Don't Expect	recurrence of shoulder trouble

Belcher has had four straight solid seasons as a major league starter. After going 12-6 with a 2.91 ERA in 1988, his first full season, the former Oakland farmhand led the majors with eight shutouts in a 15-12 campaign that included a 2.82 ERA. Though his progress was slowed by shoulder surgery in 1990, he bounced back strong in 1991, cementing a spot as the No. 3 Dodger starter behind Ramon Martinez and Mike Morgan. Belcher should be a solid starter tor the Reds. He throws a fastball, split-fingered fastball, slider, and a curve. He relies heavily on the heater when it's working. He has been timed in the low-90s. He held opponents to a .240 batting average and a .306 on-base percentage in 1991. The hard-throwing righty also helps himself in the field. His 1992 commons aren't buys. His fantasy future looks bright at $10 or so, because if he stays injury-free, Belcher can guarantee anywhere from 12 to 17 wins.

Major League Pitching Register
	W	L	ERA	G	CG	IP	H	ER	BB	SO
87 NL	4	2	2.38	6	0	34.0	30	9	7	23
88 NL	12	6	2.91	36	4	179.2	143	58	51	152
89 NL	15	12	2.82	39	10	230.0	182	72	80	200
90 NL	9	9	4.00	24	5	153.0	136	68	48	102
91 NL	10	9	2.62	33	2	209.1	189	61	75	156
Life	50	38	2.99	138	21	806.0	680	268	261	633
3 AVE	11	10	3.05	32	6	197.0	169	67	68	153

CURRENT PLAYERS

STAN BELINDA

Position: Pitcher
Team: Pittsburgh Pirates
Born: Aug. 6, 1966 Huntington, PA
Height: 6'3" **Weight:** 200 lbs.
Bats: right **Throws:** right
Acquired: 10th-round pick in 6/86 free-agent draft

Player Summary	
Fantasy Value	$5 to $7
Card Value	3¢ to 5¢
Will	top 50 appearances
Can't	succeed without control
Expect	ground-ball outs
Don't Expect	job as top closer

Belinda baffles batters with an unusual delivery that is part sidearm and part submarine. He throws a fastball, forkball, and breaking ball but is not always able to find the plate—a major fault for a relief pitcher. On the plus side, he gets ground-ball outs when he's on because his pitches tend to sink. As a 1990 rookie, Belinda had three wins and eight saves in 55 games as part of Pittsburgh's bullpen-by-committee. Sharing stopper duties caps his fantasy potential to $7. He has never made a start in his professional career, which began in 1986. He was 3-1 with five saves, a 1.90 ERA, 25 strikeouts, and 8 bases on balls in 23⅔ frames for Triple-A Buffalo in 1990. In 1989 he had 13 saves for Double-A Harrisburg and nine for Buffalo. Belinda's 1992 commons aren't high priorities. He has a bright future in the bullpen because batters rarely see such unorthodox style. A problem is his poor defensive positioning caused by his follow-through. He also needs more work on keeping baserunners close.

Major League Pitching Register

	W	L	ERA	G	S	IP	H	ER	BB	SO
89 NL	0	1	6.10	8	0	10.1	13	7	2	10
90 NL	3	4	3.55	55	8	58.1	48	23	29	55
91 NL	7	5	3.45	60	16	78.1	50	30	35	71
Life	10	10	3.67	123	24	147.0	111	60	66	136
2 AVE	5	5	3.49	58	12	68.1	49	27	32	63

DEREK BELL

Position: Outfield
Team: Toronto Blue Jays
Born: Dec. 11, 1968 Tampa, FL
Height: 6'2" **Weight:** 200 lbs.
Bats: right **Throws:** right
Acquired: Second-round pick in 6/87 free-agent draft

Player Summary	
Fantasy Value	$5 to $7
Card Value	10¢ to 15¢
Will	add good RBI bat
Can't	reach fences consistently
Expect	speed and run production
Don't Expect	instant adjustment to AL

Bell had a .375 average, 55 RBI, and 18 stolen bases at Triple-A Syracuse when the Blue Jays promoted him last June 28. He finished the season with a .346 average, 13 homers, and 93 RBI. He was named the No. 1 prospect in the International League by *Baseball America*. Because of him, the Jays traded young outfielders Mark Whiten and Glenallen Hill to Cleveland for veteran starter Tom Candiotti as pennant race insurance. At the plate, Bell reminds some observers of Eric Davis. Bell has a similar physique and depends upon quick wrists to drive the ball. Unlike Davis, however, Bell is more likely to hit a line drive than a home run. His 1992 cards are great buys at 15 cents. His quick start in 1991 was the result of a successful season in the Venezuelan Winter League. He hit .261 at Syracuse in 1990, with seven homers, 56 RBI, and 57 runs in 109 games. He is a good fantasy pick for $8 or less. The owner of a strong outfield arm, Bell could blossom into a star after he improves his overall defensive play.

Major League Batting Register

	BA	G	AB	R	H	2B	3B	HR	RBI	SB
91 AL	.143	18	28	5	4	0	0	0	1	3
Life	.143	18	28	5	4	0	0	0	1	3

CURRENT PLAYERS

GEORGE BELL

Position: Outfield
Team: Chicago Cubs
Born: Oct. 21, 1959 San Pedro de Macoris, Dominican Republic
Height: 6'1" **Weight:** 202 lbs.
Bats: right **Throws:** right
Acquired: Signed as a free agent, 12/90

Player Summary	
Fantasy Value	$20 to $25
Card Value	10¢ to 15¢
Will	thrive in Wrigley Field
Can't	provide strong defense
Expect	excellent run production
Don't Expect	return to MVP form

Switching leagues hardly fazed Bell. He continued to hit 20-plus homers and drive in 80-plus runs. He is Toronto's all-time leader in home runs and RBI, but he wore out his welcome with sloppy defensive play in left field. He was the 1987 American League MVP. With half his games in friendly Wrigley Field, Bell is a good fantasy choice at $25 or less. He has good power to all fields and is a clutch hitter. Though extremely accomplished at bat, his defense is still suspect. He has trouble going back on the ball and often misjudges routine fly balls. He also has limited range. His 1992 cards at less than 15 cents are high priorities for your collection. Though the Cubs knew he was no gazelle in left, they figured Bell would compensate with his bat.

Major League Batting Register

	BA	G	AB	R	H	2B	3B	HR	RBI	SB
81 AL	.233	60	163	19	38	2	1	5	12	3
83 AL	.268	39	112	5	30	5	4	2	17	1
84 AL	.292	159	606	85	177	39	4	26	87	11
85 AL	.275	157	607	87	167	28	6	28	95	21
86 AL	.309	159	641	101	198	38	6	31	108	7
87 AL	.308	156	610	111	188	32	4	47	134	5
88 AL	.269	156	614	78	165	27	5	24	97	4
89 AL	.297	153	613	88	182	41	2	18	104	4
90 AL	.265	142	562	67	149	25	0	21	86	3
91 NL	.285	149	558	63	159	27	0	25	86	2
Life	.286	1330	5086	704	1453	264	32	227	826	61
3 AVE	.283	148	578	73	163	31	1	21	92	3

JAY BELL

Position: Shortstop
Team: Pittsburgh Pirates
Born: Dec. 11, 1965 Eglin Air Force Base, FL
Height: 6'1" **Weight:** 180 lbs.
Bats: right **Throws:** right
Acquired: Traded from Indians for Felix Fermin, 3/89

Player Summary	
Fantasy Value	$4 to $7
Card Value	3¢ to 5¢
Will	lead league in sacrifices
Can't	lift average to .300
Expect	increasing power production
Don't Expect	lots of stolen bases

Bell has developed into one of baseball's best shortstops. A fine No. 2 hitter, whose bunting ability is second only to Brett Butler's, Bell is also adept at the hit-and-run. He showed surprising (and unexpected) power in 1991, often delivering in clutch situations. Before he did it last year, the only Pirate shortstops who had reached a dozen homers in a season were Billy Cox, Glenn Wright, and Arky Vaughn. Bell has long-ball potential and is a sound fantasy addition for $5 or so. Though his average reached a personal peak in 1991, he also had a fine season in 1990, when he led NL shortstops with 159 games played, 260 putouts, and 741 chances. Though he has average range, the strong-armed shortstop has shown himself a vastly improved defensive performer in recent seasons. His 1992 commons probably will not attract investors. He teams with Jose Lind to give the Pirates a fine double-play tandem.

Major League Batting Register

	BA	G	AB	R	H	2B	3B	HR	RBI	SB
86 AL	.357	5	14	3	5	2	0	1	4	0
87 AL	.216	38	125	14	27	9	1	2	13	2
88 AL	.218	73	211	23	46	5	1	2	21	4
89 NL	.258	78	271	33	70	13	3	2	27	5
90 NL	.254	159	583	93	148	28	7	7	52	10
91 NL	.270	157	608	96	164	32	8	16	67	10
Life	.254	510	1812	262	460	89	20	30	184	31
3 AVE	.261	131	487	74	127	24	6	8	49	8

CURRENT PLAYERS

ALBERT BELLE

Position: Outfield
Team: Cleveland Indians
Born: Aug. 25, 1966 Shreveport, LA
Height: 6'2" **Weight:** 200 lbs.
Bats: right **Throws:** right
Acquired: Second-round pick in 6/87 free-agent draft

Player Summary	
Fantasy Value	$16 to $20
Card Value	15¢ to 25¢
Will	hit long home runs
Can't	avoid constant controversy
Expect	good RBI production
Don't Expect	an uneventful season

If Belle could conquer his temper, he could conquer the baseball world. He is not only one of the strongest men in the game but also one of the most headstrong. In 1990, his season was cut short when he checked himself into the Cleveland Clinic to get treatment for alcoholism. In 1991, he was suspended for six games after throwing a ball at a heckler in the stands and sent to the minors for not running out a routine infield grounder. Cleveland missed his power, however, and Belle was recalled after the team went 2-15 immediately after his demotion. Belle's clout will be welcomed by fantasy managers, who can get him for $20 and not have to put up with his attitude. Acquire his 1992 cards, because their quarter prices will climb. He singled off Nolan Ryan in his first major league at bat in 1989. He made the 1991 varsity with a power explosion during spring training. With another slugger behind him, Belle could become one of baseball's most prolific power hitters.

Major League Batting Register

	BA	G	AB	R	H	2B	3B	HR	RBI	SB
89 AL	.225	62	218	22	49	8	4	7	37	2
90 AL	.174	9	23	1	4	0	0	1	3	0
91 AL	.282	123	461	60	130	31	2	28	95	3
Life	.261	194	702	83	183	39	6	36	135	5
2 AVE	.264	93	340	41	90	20	3	18	66	3

RAFAEL BELLIARD

Position: Shortstop
Team: Atlanta Braves
Born: Oct. 24, 1961 Pueblo Nuevo, Mao, Dominican Republic
Height: 5'6" **Weight:** 150 lbs.
Bats: right **Throws:** right
Acquired: Signed as a free agent, 12/90

Player Summary	
Fantasy Value	$2 to $4
Card Value	3¢ to 5¢
Will	provide strong defense
Can't	hit for average or power
Expect	job as defensive replacement
Don't Expect	return to regular duty

Although the Braves projected Belliard as a utility infielder when they collected him from Pittsburgh, Atlanta management changed its thinking when it watched his defense during 1991 spring training. Belliard played every day for almost half the season before his bat caught up with him. He lost his job to the better-hitting Jeff Blauser, then Belliard won it back as the Braves marched into the World Series. After Blauser took over, Belliard's role reverted to the one originally intended for him. He was used as a late-inning defensive replacement, pinch-runner, and infield backup. Belliard is just one of many weak-hitting shortstops from which to choose. Get more for your two bucks by picking a younger streaky infielder. The fact that Belliard made a decade in the bigs attests to his strong defensive skills. Don't invest in his 1992 commons.

Major League Batting Register

	BA	G	AB	R	H	2B	3B	HR	RBI	SB
82 NL	.500	9	2	3	1	0	0	0	0	1
83 NL	.000	4	1	1	0	0	0	0	0	0
84 NL	.227	20	22	3	5	0	0	0	0	4
85 NL	.200	17	20	1	4	0	0	0	1	0
86 NL	.233	117	309	33	72	5	2	0	31	12
87 NL	.207	81	203	26	42	4	3	1	15	5
88 NL	.213	122	286	28	61	0	4	0	11	7
89 NL	.214	67	154	10	33	4	0	0	8	5
90 NL	.204	47	54	10	11	3	0	0	6	1
91 NL	.249	149	353	36	88	9	2	0	27	3
Life	.226	633	1404	151	317	25	11	1	99	38
2 AVE	.239	108	254	23	61	7	1	0	18	4

CURRENT PLAYERS

ANDY BENES

Position: Pitcher
Team: San Diego Padres
Born: Aug. 20, 1967 Evansville, IN
Height: 6'6" **Weight:** 235 lbs.
Bats: right **Throws:** right
Acquired: First-round pick in 6/88 free-agent draft

Player Summary	
Fantasy Value	$12 to $17
Card Value	8¢ to 12¢
Will	show continued improvement
Can't	complete what he starts
Expect	15 victories
Don't Expect	deployment as reliever

A year after he was the first player picked in baseball's 1988 amateur draft, Benes was pitching in the major leagues. He went 6-3 with a 3.51 ERA in 10 starts in 1989. In 1991, however, he staked a claim to fame by out-pitching Tom Glavine three times in their first four meetings. Benes has good command of his fastball, slider, and change and throws them for strikes. When those pitches part the strike zone down the middle, the towering righthander gets hit hard—often over the fence. Although he showed steady improvement down the stretch in 1991, Benes had some games where he resembled a batting-practice pitcher. The lack of minor league experience was telling in some of those games. Benes won several games at the end of '91, and he could get off to a good start in 1992. He is a $15 fantasy choice. He can hit and bunt better than most of his pitching colleagues. He's also a good fielder. His 1992 cards are good pickups at a dime or so.

Major League Pitching Register

	W	L	ERA	G	CG	IP	H	ER	BB	SO
89 NL	6	3	3.51	10	0	66.2	51	26	31	66
90 NL	10	11	3.60	32	2	192.1	177	77	69	140
91 NL	15	11	3.03	33	4	223.0	194	75	59	167
Life	31	25	3.32	75	6	482.0	422	178	159	373
3 AVE	10	8	3.32	25	2	160.1	141	59	53	124

TODD BENZINGER

Position: Outfield; first base
Team: Los Angeles Dodgers
Born: Feb. 11, 1963 Dayton, KY
Height: 6'1" **Weight:** 190 lbs.
Bats: both **Throws:** right
Acquired: Traded from Royals for Chris Gwynn and Domingo Mota, 12/91

Player Summary	
Fantasy Value	$3 to $5
Card Value	3¢ to 5¢
Will	display occasional power
Can't	hit much above .250
Expect	use as DH and back-up
Don't Expect	serious attempts to steal

Benzinger spent nine years in the Red Sox organization after Boston made him a fourth-round draft choice in 1981. He reached the majors six years later and hit eight home runs in 73 games. His best year was 1989, when he led the NL in 628 at bats and paced the Reds in games, hits, runs, and doubles. He was second on the team in both home runs and RBI and had a .995 fielding percentage at first base. A hand injury, plus the play of newcomer Hal Morris, reduced Benzinger's playing time in 1990 and made him expendable. His batting average is above-average, but his homers are few. He could be a fantasy asset at less than $5. He is a spray-hitting switch-hitter who is most productive from the right side. His 1992 cards aren't good investments. Benzinger is an adequate defensive player at both first base and in the outfield. Continued reserve status is probable.

Major League Batting Register

	BA	G	AB	R	H	2B	3B	HR	RBI	SB
87 AL	.278	73	223	36	62	11	1	8	43	5
88 AL	.254	120	405	47	103	28	1	13	70	2
89 NL	.245	161	628	79	154	28	3	17	76	3
90 NL	.253	118	376	35	95	14	2	5	46	3
91 NL	.187	51	123	7	23	3	2	1	11	2
91 AL	.294	78	293	29	86	15	3	2	40	2
Life	.255	601	2048	233	523	99	12	46	286	17
3 AVE	.252	136	473	50	119	20	3	8	58	3

CURRENT PLAYERS

JUAN BERENGUER

Position: Pitcher
Team: Atlanta Braves
Born: Nov. 30, 1954 Aguadulce, Panama
Height: 5'11" **Weight:** 225 lbs.
Bats: right **Throws:** right
Acquired: Signed as a free agent, 1/91

Player Summary	
Fantasy Value	$5 to $8
Card Value	3¢ to 5¢
Will	make many showings
Can't	sit too long
Expect	animated gestures
Don't Expect	30-save season

Berenguer became a short reliever in his 14th major league season. Used almost exclusively as a set-up man before coming to Atlanta, he had accumulated only 14 career saves before 1991. His 1992 commons aren't buys. He had exceeded that total shortly after the All-Star break. He throws a fastball, a forkball, and a curveball, but he usually relies on the hard stuff to overpower opposing hitters. He has a rubber arm, and he is just wild enough to keep hitters off-guard. Berenguer was once the victim of his own emotions. When he got excited, he tended to overthrow and could not throw strikes. If he maintains his closer role in '92, he could be a fantasy buy at $7.

Major League Pitching Register

	W	L	ERA	G	S	IP	H	ER	BB	SO
78 NL	0	2	8.31	5	0	13.0	17	12	11	8
79 NL	1	1	2.93	5	0	30.2	28	10	12	25
80 NL	0	1	5.79	6	0	9.1	9	6	10	7
81 AL	2	11	5.24	20	0	91.0	84	53	51	49
82 AL	0	0	6.75	2	0	6.2	5	5	9	8
83 AL	9	5	3.14	37	1	157.2	110	55	71	129
84 AL	11	10	3.48	31	0	168.1	146	65	79	118
85 AL	5	6	5.59	31	0	95.0	96	59	48	82
86 NL	2	3	2.70	46	4	73.1	64	22	44	72
87 AL	8	1	3.94	47	4	112.0	100	49	47	110
88 AL	8	4	3.96	57	2	100.0	74	44	61	99
89 AL	9	3	3.48	56	3	106.0	96	41	47	93
90 AL	8	5	3.41	51	0	100.1	85	38	58	77
91 NL	0	3	2.24	49	17	64.1	43	16	20	53
Life	63	57	3.79	443	31	1127.1	957	475	568	930
3 AVE	6	4	3.16	52	7	90.1	75	32	42	74

DAVE BERGMAN

Position: First base; designated hitter
Team: Detroit Tigers
Born: June 6, 1953 Evanston, IL
Height: 6'2" **Weight:** 190 lbs.
Bats: left **Throws:** left
Acquired: Traded from Phillies with Willie Hernandez for Glenn Wilson and John Wockenfuss, 3/84

Player Summary	
Fantasy Value	$1 to $2
Card Value	3¢ to 5¢
Will	make good contact
Can't	hit for power
Expect	frequent pinch-hits
Don't Expect	any stolen bases

Because he hits with little power, Bergman has never been a regular. In his first 15 seasons, he played in more than 120 games only when the 1989 Tigers had no one else to play first base. He is a fine defensive first baseman with good range and enough speed to play the outfield on occasion. His 1992 commons are not buys. He is not a fantasy draft, either. He remains a valuable veteran because of his versatility, his lefthanded bat, and his ability to pinch-hit. A selective hitter who makes good contact, Bergman often hits ground balls, a problem for a player whose team plays on natural grass. He is a good hit-and-run man, however.

Major League Batting Register

	BA	G	AB	R	H	2B	3B	HR	RBI	SB
75 AL	.000	7	17	0	0	0	0	0	0	0
77 AL	.250	5	4	1	1	0	0	0	1	0
78 AL	.231	104	186	15	43	5	1	0	12	2
79 NL	.400	13	15	4	6	0	0	1	2	0
80 NL	.256	90	78	12	20	6	1	0	3	1
81 NL	.252	69	151	17	38	9	0	4	14	2
82 NL	.273	100	121	22	33	3	1	4	14	3
83 NL	.286	90	140	16	40	4	1	6	24	2
84 AL	.273	120	271	42	74	8	5	7	44	3
85 AL	.179	69	140	8	25	2	0	3	7	0
86 AL	.231	65	130	14	30	6	1	1	9	0
87 AL	.273	91	172	25	47	7	3	6	22	0
88 AL	.294	116	289	37	85	14	0	5	35	0
89 AL	.268	137	385	38	103	13	1	7	37	1
90 AL	.278	100	205	21	57	10	1	2	26	3
91 AL	.237	86	194	23	46	10	1	7	29	1
Life	.259	1262	2498	295	648	97	16	53	279	18
3 AVE	.263	108	261	27	69	11	1	5	31	2

CURRENT PLAYERS

DAMON BERRYHILL

Position: Catcher
Team: Atlanta Braves
Born: Dec. 3, 1963 Laguna, CA
Height: 6' **Weight:** 210 lbs.
Bats: both **Throws:** right
Acquired: Traded from Cubs with Mike Bielecki for Turk Wendell and Yorkis Perez, 9/91

Player Summary	
Fantasy Value	$2 to $4
Card Value	3¢ to 5¢
Will	face crossroads season
Can't	steal bases or hit homers
Expect	difficulty in coming back
Don't Expect	return to top catching job

Because of recurring shoulder problems, Berryhill has never spent a full season in the major leagues. After unseating incumbent Cub catcher Jody Davis with a .259 average and seven homers in 95 games during the 1988 campaign, Berryhill hit .257 with five homers in 91 contests a year later. If he could come close to those numbers again, he would be worth a $4 draft. Despite the bad shoulder, Berryhill erased 41.7 percent of would-be basestealers that summer. He has had several shoulder operations, including surgery to repair a torn rotator cuff in September 1989. He has not been the same player since. When Berryhill could not boost his average above .200 early in 1991, he was returned to the minors. The Braves obtained Mike Bielecki and Berryhill late in the season for their pennant run. Even when healthy, he lacks speed and power. His strength is defense: calling a game, blocking pitches, and—before his shoulder woes—throwing.

Major League Batting Register

	BA	G	AB	R	H	2B	3B	HR	RBI	SB
87 NL	.179	12	28	2	5	1	0	0	1	0
88 NL	.259	95	309	19	80	19	1	7	38	1
89 NL	.257	91	334	37	86	13	0	5	41	1
90 NL	.189	17	53	6	10	4	0	1	9	0
91 NL	.188	63	160	13	30	7	0	5	14	1
Life	.239	278	884	77	211	44	1	18	103	3
2 AVE	.235	77	247	25	58	10	0	5	28	1

DANTE BICHETTE

Position: Outfield
Team: Milwaukee Brewers
Born: Nov. 18, 1963 West Palm Beach, FL
Height: 6'3" **Weight:** 212 lbs.
Bats: right **Throws:** right
Acquired: Traded from Angels for Dave Parker, 2/91

Player Summary	
Fantasy Value	$3 to $5
Card Value	3¢ to 5¢
Will	impress with throws
Can't	master strike zone
Expect	alarming K totals
Don't Expect	great on-base average

Before his trade to Milwaukee last February, Bichette had a reputation as an outfielder with a great arm but an inconsistent bat. He made a good first impression, however, with six hits in the first 11 at bats during exhibition play. Bichette cooled during the season, though he managed to accumulate the most at bats of his career. As a hitter, he tries to pull every pitch. He had 11 homers in 226 at bats at Triple-A Edmonton in 1989. He does not have patience at the plate, striking out far more often than he walks. He frequently swings at balls that are nowhere near the strike zone. He's a classic first-pitch, fastball hitter, but the word is out. Fantasy managers should be moved for four bucks for his 15 homers a year. Although regular duty may elude Bichette because of his batting problems, his salvation is his defensive ability. His throwing arm may be the AL's best. His 1992 commons aren't good investments.

Major League Batting Register

	BA	G	AB	R	H	2B	3B	HR	RBI	SB
88 AL	.261	21	46	1	12	2	0	0	8	0
89 AL	.210	48	138	13	29	7	0	3	15	3
90 AL	.255	109	349	40	89	15	1	15	53	5
91 AL	.238	134	445	53	106	18	3	15	59	14
Life	.241	312	978	107	236	42	4	33	135	22
2 AVE	.246	122	397	47	98	17	2	15	56	10

CURRENT PLAYERS

MIKE BIELECKI

Position: Pitcher
Team: Atlanta Braves
Born: July 31, 1959 Baltimore, MD
Height: 6'3" **Weight:** 195 lbs.
Bats: right **Throws:** right
Acquired: Traded from Cubs with Damon Berryhill for Turk Wendell and Yorkis Perez, 9/91

Player Summary
Fantasy Value	$3 to $5
Card Value	3¢ to 5¢
Will	mix pitches well
Can't	overpower with heater
Expect	at least 12 wins
Don't Expect	ERA below 4.00

Bielecki joins the Braves to challenge for their No. 4 or No. 5 role in the starting rotation. After several roller-coaster seasons, he was a pleasant surprise for the 1991 Cubs, but his future can't support his common-priced 1992 cards. Returned to the starting rotation, he blossomed into one of the big winners on the staff. He broke into the majors with the 1984 Pirates but did not pitch regularly before posting an 18-7 record for the '89 Cubs. In 1990, however, he slipped while shuttling between the rotation and the bullpen. Bielecki throws a regular and split-fingered fastball, plus a curveball and changeup. An average fielder with a good pickoff move, he is only effective when his control is sharp. His fantasy ability justifies spending $3 to $5. He doesn't get many strikeouts, so he has to average less than a hit per inning to win.

Major League Pitching Register
	W	L	ERA	G	CG	IP	H	ER	BB	SO
84 NL	0	0	0.00	4	0	4.1	4	0	0	1
85 NL	2	3	4.53	12	0	45.2	45	23	31	22
86 NL	6	11	4.66	31	0	148.2	149	77	83	83
87 NL	2	3	4.73	8	2	45.2	43	24	12	25
88 NL	2	2	3.35	19	0	48.1	55	18	16	33
89 NL	18	7	3.14	33	4	212.1	187	74	81	147
90 NL	8	11	4.93	36	0	168.0	188	92	70	103
91 NL	13	11	4.46	41	0	173.2	171	86	56	75
Life	51	48	4.19	184	6	846.2	842	394	349	489
3 AVE	13	10	4.09	37	1	184.1	182	84	69	108

CRAIG BIGGIO

Position: Catcher
Team: Houston Astros
Born: December 14, 1965 Smithtown, NY
Height: 5'11" **Weight:** 180 lbs.
Bats: right **Throws:** right
Acquired: First-round pick in 6/87 free-agent draft

Player Summary
Fantasy Value	$10 to $14
Card Value	3¢ to 5¢
Will	make All-Star team
Can't	throw out runners
Expect	games at second
Don't Expect	great power in Dome

Although he does not have a strong throwing arm, Biggio may be the best all-around catcher in the National League. Houston's best hitter, he was well above .300 for most of the 1991 season before sliding a bit. He had a .358 on-base average. The one-time Seton Hall All-American is a good clutch hitter who also has the speed to collect average-inflating infield hits. He sometimes bunts for hits and is a threat to steal bases. He is a good fantasy choice at $14 or less. Because of his speed and less-than-average arm, the Astros may switch Biggio to second base or center field. That move and his lack of power would hamper the value of his 1992 cards. They are commons for now. Such a switch would probably prolong his career, however. He'll play more games at second in '92. As a catcher, he calls a good game and is regarded as a good handler of pitchers. Biggio made his first All-Star team in 1991.

Major League Batting Register
	BA	G	AB	R	H	2B	3B	HR	RBI	SB
88 NL	.211	50	123	14	26	6	1	3	5	6
89 NL	.257	134	443	64	114	21	2	13	60	21
90 NL	.276	150	555	53	153	24	2	4	42	25
91 NL	.295	149	546	79	161	23	4	4	46	19
Life	.272	483	1667	210	454	74	9	24	153	71
3 AVE	.277	144	515	65	143	23	3	7	49	22

CURRENT PLAYERS

BUD BLACK

Position: Pitcher
Team: San Francisco Giants
Born: June 30, 1957 San Mateo, CA
Height: 6'2" **Weight:** 185 lbs.
Bats: left **Throws:** left
Acquired: Signed as a free agent, 11/90

Player Summary	
Fantasy Value	$7 to $9
Card Value	3¢ to 5¢
Will	seldom miss turn
Can't	always throw hard
Expect	15 wins
Don't Expect	high K totals

Skeptics criticized San Francisco general manager Al Rosen for shelling out big bucks to sign Black for the 1991 season, and the jury is still out. A career .500 AL pitcher, Black joined John Burkett as the only starters who stayed in the rotation all season. Three of Black's first six NL wins were shutouts, and he was a candidate for the All-Star team. He lost steam in the second half and didn't reach the .500 mark. He has good control with all five of his pitches—a slider, curve, change, and two fastballs. His slow curve wrecks the timing of hitters. A $9 fantasy pitcher, Black will never win 20 games. A good fielder who holds hitters close, he also showed an ability to hit during his first NL campaign. His 1992 cards will stay commons.

Major League Pitching Register

	W	L	ERA	G	CG	IP	H	ER	BB	SO
81 AL	0	0	0.00	2	0	1.0	2	0	3	0
82 AL	4	6	4.58	22	0	88.1	92	45	34	40
83 AL	10	7	3.79	24	3	161.1	159	68	43	58
84 AL	17	12	3.12	35	8	257.0	226	89	64	140
85 AL	10	15	4.33	33	5	205.2	216	99	59	122
86 AL	5	10	3.20	56	0	121.0	100	43	43	68
87 AL	8	6	3.60	29	0	122.1	126	49	35	61
88 AL	4	4	5.00	33	0	81.0	82	45	23	63
89 AL	12	11	3.36	33	6	222.1	213	83	52	88
90 AL	13	11	3.57	31	5	206.2	181	82	61	106
91 AL	12	16	3.99	34	3	214.1	201	95	71	104
Life	95	98	3.74	333	30	1681.0	1598	698	499	850
3 AVE	12	13	3.64	33	5	214.1	198	87	61	99

JEFF BLAUSER

Position: Infield
Team: Atlanta Braves
Born: Nov. 8, 1965 Los Gatos, CA
Height: 6'1" **Weight:** 180 lbs.
Bats: right **Throws:** right
Acquired: First-round pick in secondary phase of 6/84 free-agent draft

Player Summary	
Fantasy Value	$4 to $7
Card Value	3¢ to 5¢
Will	hit well in clutch
Can't	hit for high average
Expect	improved defense at short
Don't Expect	shifting to other positions

After starting the 1991 season as a three-position infield reserve, Blauser returned to his natural shortstop spot when Rafael Belliard failed to hit. Blauser played the best defense of his career and added a productive bat to the lineup. In the post-season, however, Braves manager Bobby Cox chose to stay with Belliard's defense over Blauser's offense. Blauser should make a strong bid in '92 to become the full-time shortstop. His 1992 common cards won't appreciate until then. He has become a more selective hitter who has increased his walk totals while reducing his strikeouts. He has also shown an ability to hit inside pitches. His hitting could improve with full-time work, a fact for fantasy managers to mull. He could pay off for $7 at most. A steady shortstop with average range, Blauser makes most of his errors on throws. He has a good arm but sometimes throws lollipops that sail or don't reach their targets on time. He should improve with time.

Major League Batting Register

	BA	G	AB	R	H	2B	3B	HR	RBI	SB
87 NL	.242	51	165	11	40	6	3	2	15	7
88 NL	.239	18	67	7	16	3	1	2	7	0
89 NL	.270	142	456	63	123	24	2	12	46	5
90 NL	.269	115	386	46	104	24	3	8	39	3
91 NL	.259	129	352	49	91	14	3	11	54	5
Life	.262	455	1426	176	374	71	12	35	161	20
3 AVE	.266	129	398	53	106	21	3	10	46	4

CURRENT PLAYERS

MIKE BODDICKER

Position: Pitcher
Team: Kansas City Royals
Born: Aug. 23, 1957 Cedar Rapids, IA
Height: 5'11" **Weight:** 186 lbs.
Bats: right **Throws:** right
Acquired: Signed as a free agent, 11/90

Player Summary	
Fantasy Value	$5 to $7
Card Value	3¢ to 5¢
Will	exceed 200 frames
Can't	whistle heat by hitters
Expect	consistency
Don't Expect	many complete games

Boddicker was a rookie when he helped pitch Baltimore to the 1983 World Championship. He led the league in wins and ERA in 1984. He has never won less than ten games in a season since. Though he owns a good fastball, Boddicker is a breaking-ball artist who throws a vast variety of pitches and changes speeds on all of them. His best delivery, a "foshball," is a dead-fish version of a fastball that acts like a screwball. Boddicker rarely beats himself with walks. His fantasy worth remains in the $6 range. His 1992 cards are commons. He never dies with his own poor defense, because he is a former college third baseman who won a Gold Glove in 1990. Boddicker has the experience and ability to remain a solid No. 2 starter.

Major League Pitching Register

	W	L	ERA	G	CG	IP	H	ER	BB	SO
80 AL	0	1	6.14	1	0	7.1	6	5	5	4
81 AL	0	0	4.76	2	0	5.2	6	3	2	2
82 AL	1	0	3.51	7	0	25.2	25	10	12	20
83 AL	16	8	2.77	27	10	179.0	141	55	52	120
84 AL	20	11	2.79	34	16	261.1	218	81	81	128
85 AL	12	17	4.07	32	9	203.1	227	92	89	135
86 AL	14	12	4.70	33	7	218.1	214	114	74	175
87 AL	10	12	4.18	33	7	226.0	212	105	78	152
88 AL	13	15	3.39	36	5	236.0	234	89	77	156
89 AL	15	11	4.00	34	3	211.2	217	94	71	145
90 AL	17	8	3.36	34	4	228.0	225	85	69	143
91 AL	12	12	4.08	30	1	180.2	188	82	59	79
Life	130	107	3.70	303	62	1983.0	1913	815	669	1259
3 AVE	15	10	3.79	33	3	206.1	210	87	66	122

JOE BOEVER

Position: Pitcher
Team: Philadelphia Phillies
Born: Oct. 4, 1960 St. Louis, MO
Height: 6'1" **Weight:** 200 lbs.
Bats: right **Throws:** right
Acquired: Traded from Braves for Marvin Freeman, 7/90

Player Summary	
Fantasy Value	$2 to $4
Card Value	3¢ to 5¢
Will	rely on palmball
Can't	throw strikes consistently
Expect	use in mop-up role
Don't Expect	return to closer job

Boever is a palmball specialist who is most effective when used frequently. When deployed strictly as a closer, he rarely works enough to keep his control sharp. He led three minor leagues in saves before getting a chance to be the top short man with the '89 Braves. He had 18 saves in his first 21 opportunities but faded, saving only three more games over the final two months. Boever is now a middle reliever, so his fantasy use is limited to $3 or so. He finished 27 games in 1991. He was often called upon to keep the Phils in ballgames. Though he also throws a straight fastball, Boever banks on the palmball to baffle batters. It has a sharp break that looks like an overhand curve, but it is difficult to keep in the strike zone. He had almost a K an inning in '91, but he had too many walks. His 1992 cards are and will remain commons.

Major League Pitching Register

	W	L	ERA	G	S	IP	H	ER	BB	SO
85 NL	0	0	4.41	13	0	16.1	17	8	4	20
86 NL	0	1	1.66	11	0	21.2	19	4	11	8
87 NL	1	0	7.36	14	0	18.1	29	15	12	18
88 NL	0	2	1.77	16	1	20.1	12	4	1	7
89 NL	4	11	3.94	66	21	82.1	78	36	34	68
90 NL	3	6	3.36	67	14	88.1	77	33	51	75
91 NL	3	5	3.84	68	0	98.1	90	42	54	89
Life	11	25	3.70	255	36	345.2	322	142	167	285
3 AVE	3	7	3.71	67	12	89.1	82	37	46	77

CURRENT PLAYERS

WADE BOGGS

Position: Third base
Team: Boston Red Sox
Born: June 15, 1958 Omaha, NE
Height: 6'2" **Weight:** 197 lbs.
Bats: left **Throws:** right
Acquired: Seventh-round pick in 6/76 free-agent draft

Player Summary	
Fantasy Value	$35 to $40
Card Value	10¢ to 20¢
Will	vie for batting crown
Can't	find Fenway fences
Expect	best on-base percentage
Don't Expect	same average on road

Boggs is the most scientific hitter in the AL. He has vast knowledge of the strike zone and will not swing at a bad pitch. With his excellent bat control, he can foul off pitches he doesn't like. Boggs has an inside-out swing perfectly suited for the Green Monster left field wall at Fenway Park. He is more productive at home than on the road. Switching to a lighter bat last year helped him rebound. Because he may be headed to Cooperstown, his 1992 cards are sure bets at less than 20 cents. A six-time All-Star and five-time batting champion, Boggs is the only player of the modern era to produce seven straight 200-hit seasons. His fantasy value is still in the $35 range. In the field, Boggs has limited range but good hands and a strong, accurate arm.

Major League Batting Register

	BA	G	AB	R	H	2B	3B	HR	RBI	SB
82 AL	.349	104	338	51	118	14	1	5	44	1
83 AL	.361	153	582	100	210	44	7	5	74	3
84 AL	.325	158	625	109	203	31	4	6	55	3
85 AL	.368	161	653	107	240	42	3	8	78	2
86 AL	.357	149	580	107	207	47	2	8	71	0
87 AL	.363	147	551	108	200	40	6	24	89	1
88 AL	.366	155	584	128	214	45	6	5	58	2
89 AL	.330	156	621	113	205	51	7	3	54	2
90 AL	.302	155	619	89	187	44	5	6	63	0
91 AL	.332	144	546	93	181	42	2	8	51	1
Life	.345	1482	5699	1005	1965	400	43	78	637	15
3 AVE	.321	152	595	98	191	46	5	6	56	1

TOM BOLTON

Position: Pitcher
Team: Boston Red Sox
Born: May 6, 1962 Nashville, TN
Height: 6'3" **Weight:** 175 lbs.
Bats: left **Throws:** left
Acquired: 20th-round pick in 6/80 free-agent draft

Player Summary	
Fantasy Value	$1 to $3
Card Value	3¢ to 5¢
Will	pitch well in Fenway
Can't	depend on fastball
Expect	wins with control
Don't Expect	Roger Clemens clone

The Red Sox had counted on Bolton to be one of their starters before injuries intervened. He was disabled with a sore left shoulder and back on July 22. He had posted a 10-5 record for the 1990 Red Sox but was only able to get an 8-9 record in '91. Because of his career record, his 1992 commons aren't very good investments. When he's on, he throws a fastball, curveball, and changeup with fairly good control. His fastball sinks, and his curve handcuffs righthanded hitters. He gets hampered, however, when his control wavers. Bolton gave up 16 home runs in '91. He has a knack for pitching well in Fenway Park—regarded as a graveyard for lefthanded pitchers. Bolton's a .500-type pitcher worth a few bucks for your fantasy team. Be wary of his success in Boston, however. That may be fleeting. He's adequate in the field but below average in holding runners. A healthy Bolton would be no more than a fourth or fifth starter.

Major League Pitching Register

	W	L	ERA	G	CG	IP	H	ER	BB	SO
87 AL	1	0	4.38	29	0	61.2	83	30	27	49
88 AL	1	3	4.75	28	0	30.1	35	16	14	21
89 AL	0	4	8.31	4	0	17.1	21	16	10	9
90 AL	10	5	3.38	21	3	119.2	111	45	47	65
91 AL	8	9	5.24	25	0	110.0	136	64	51	64
Life	20	21	4.54	107	3	339.0	386	171	149	208
2 AVE	9	7	4.27	23	2	115.1	124	55	49	65

CURRENT PLAYERS

BARRY BONDS

Position: Outfield
Team: Pittsburgh Pirates
Born: July 24, 1964 Riverside, CA
Height: 6'1" **Weight:** 185 lbs.
Bats: left **Throws:** left
Acquired: First-round pick in 6/85 free-agent draft

Player Summary	
Fantasy Value	$40 to $50
Card Value	15¢ to 25¢
Will	play best left field
Can't	avoid controversy
Expect	30-30 performance
Don't Expect	any batting titles

Bonds is one of baseball's best all-around players. He was National League MVP in 1990, when he became the first big leaguer to hit .300, hit 30 homers, drive in 100 runs, score 100, and steal 50 bases in the same season. He got off to a slow start in 1991 following a spring training shouting match with manager Jim Leyland. Bonds became an important contributor again by midseason, however, and finished with similar numbers. Break the bank at the draft for him, up to $50 (maybe more). He has good power to both alleys and can pull the ball. Part of the only father-and-son tandem in the 30-30 club, Barry is a strong contender for 30-30 honors every year. Eric Davis and Bonds are the only players to hit 30 homers and steal 50 bases in the same season. His 1992 cards are outstanding buys under 25 cents. This perennial Gold Glove candidate is an outstanding defensive player in left field.

Major League Batting Register

	BA	G	AB	R	H	2B	3B	HR	RBI	SB
86 NL	.223	113	413	72	92	26	3	16	48	36
87 NL	.261	150	551	99	144	34	9	25	59	32
88 NL	.283	144	538	97	152	30	5	24	58	17
89 NL	.248	159	580	96	144	34	6	19	58	32
90 NL	.301	151	519	104	156	32	3	33	114	52
91 NL	.292	153	510	95	149	28	5	25	116	43
Life	.269	870	3111	563	837	184	31	142	453	212
3 AVE	.279	154	536	98	150	31	5	26	96	42

BOBBY BONILLA

Position: Outfield; third base
Team: New York Mets
Born: Feb. 23, 1963 New York, NY
Height: 6'3" **Weight:** 230 lbs.
Bats: both **Throws:** right
Acquired: Signed as a free agent, 12/91

Player Summary	
Fantasy Value	$40 to $45
Card Value	15¢ to 25¢
Will	hit for power in any park
Can't	play strong defense at third
Expect	extra-base hits from both sides
Don't Expect	clubhouse controversy

A four-time All-Star, Bonilla was runner-up to teammate Barry Bonds in 1990 MVP voting. Bonilla hit a career-high 32 homers that year. The switch-hitter has good power both ways but is particularly dangerous when he is batting lefthanded. He is a dead fastball hitter who likes the ball down—the opposite approach of most other sluggers. He had a .492 slugging percentage in 1991. Spend up to $45 for him at the fantasy draft. Though he has a strong throwing arm in right field, he has played third base often in recent seasons. In 1991, he played third in 67 games, because of Jeff King's injury. Bonilla looks uncertain on infield grounders and is more comfortable in the outfield. His 1992 cards will be hot, breaking the quarter mark. The cleanup hitter for the 1991 NL All-Stars, he is a durable player who misses very few games. Bonilla is a positive influence in the clubhouse.

Major League Batting Register

	BA	G	AB	R	H	2B	3B	HR	RBI	SB
86 AL	.269	75	234	27	63	10	2	2	26	4
86 NL	.240	63	192	28	46	6	2	1	17	4
87 NL	.300	141	466	58	140	33	3	15	77	3
88 NL	.274	159	584	87	160	32	7	24	100	3
89 NL	.281	163	616	96	173	37	10	24	86	8
90 NL	.280	160	625	112	175	39	7	32	120	4
91 NL	.302	157	577	102	174	44	6	18	100	2
Life	.283	918	3294	510	931	201	37	116	526	28
3 AVE	.287	160	606	103	174	40	8	25	102	5

CURRENT PLAYERS

PAT BORDERS

Position: Catcher
Team: Toronto Blue Jays
Born: May 14, 1963 Columbus, OH
Height: 6'2" **Weight:** 205 lbs.
Bats: right **Throws:** right
Acquired: Sixth-round pick in 6/82 free-agent draft

Player Summary	
Fantasy Value	$2 to $4
Card Value	3¢ to 5¢
Will	challenge base-stealers
Can't	take walks
Expect	continued backup job
Don't Expect	dependable offense

Borders gave Toronto a pleasant surprise in 1990, when he hit .286 with 15 homers in his first major league season as the No. 1 catcher. He had shown only occasional power during a minor league career that began in 1982, and he slipped into that rut again in '91 and lost the top catching job to Greg Myers. As a platoon catcher, Borders won't please card collectors. Skip his 1992 commons. He struck out four times more often than he had walked. An impatient hitter, he chases bad pitches—with frequent whiffs or double-play grounders as a result. He had a .271 on-base percentage and a .354 slugging percentage in 1991. He has the potential to put up some good stats, and he is worth a $3 draft. He does not run well, and is barely adequate on defense (he's a converted third baseman). He could grow into a satisfactory receiver, like Oakland's Terry Steinbach (also a converted third sacker). Because Borders throws well, he'll remain a big league receiver. Maybe he'll hit again.

Major League Batting Register

	BA	G	AB	R	H	2B	3B	HR	RBI	SB
88 AL	.273	56	154	15	42	6	3	5	21	0
89 AL	.257	94	241	22	62	11	1	3	29	2
90 AL	.286	125	346	36	99	24	2	15	49	0
91 AL	.244	105	291	22	71	17	0	5	36	0
Life	.266	380	1032	95	274	58	6	28	135	2
3 AVE	.264	108	293	27	77	17	1	8	38	1

CHRIS BOSIO

Position: Pitcher
Team: Milwaukee Brewers
Born: April 3, 1963 Carmichael, CA
Height: 6'3" **Weight:** 225 lbs.
Bats: right **Throws:** right
Acquired: Second-round pick in 1/82 free-agent draft

Player Summary	
Fantasy Value	$6 to $9
Card Value	3¢ to 5¢
Will	win big for good club
Can't	keep runners close
Expect	15 to 20 victories
Don't Expect	more knee problems

Bosio was a beacon in the fog that shrouded the Milwaukee pitching staff in '91. Rebounding from two knee operations that removed bone spurs and a cyst, he became the Brewers' most dependable starter. With his injury history, his fantasy value is in the $8 range. He was a top starter for the Brewers in ERA. He throws three fastballs—a sinker, riser, and split-fingered variety—plus a slider and changeup. Like many control pitchers, he issues few walks but is often victimized by the home run ball. Opponents had a .244 batting average, a .350 slugging percentage, and a .302 on-base average against him in 1991. A decent fielder with a less-than-decent pickoff move, Bosio needs to avoid physical and emotional problems to succeed. In the past, his game has been hampered by temper tantrums as well as knee problems. His 1992 commons are unattractive. Bosio is a solid big league starter for the Brewers.

Major League Pitching Register

	W	L	ERA	G	CG	IP	H	ER	BB	SO
86 AL	0	4	7.01	10	0	34.2	41	27	13	29
87 AL	11	8	5.24	46	2	170.0	187	99	50	150
88 AL	7	15	3.36	38	9	182.0	190	68	38	84
89 AL	15	10	2.95	33	8	234.2	225	77	48	173
90 AL	4	9	4.00	20	4	132.2	131	59	38	76
91 AL	14	10	3.25	32	5	204.2	187	74	58	117
Life	51	56	3.79	179	28	958.2	961	404	245	629
3 AVE	11	10	3.30	28	6	190.2	181	70	48	122

CURRENT PLAYERS

SHAWN BOSKIE

Position: Pitcher
Team: Chicago Cubs
Born: March 28, 1967 Hawthorne, NV
Height: 6'3" **Weight:** 205 lbs.
Bats: right **Throws:** right
Acquired: First-round pick in 1/86 free-agent draft

Player Summary	
Fantasy Value	$2 to $4
Card Value	5¢ to 10¢
Will	get good velocity
Can't	always throw strikes
Expect	a shot at starting
Don't Expect	end of control woes

Boskie reached Chicago as a starter in 1990, four years after breaking into pro ball. A converted third baseman who throws hard, he had a 3.69 ERA as a rookie but slipped back to the minors after dropping eight of a dozen decisions in 1991. See if he rebounds in '92 before buying his 1992 cards at more than a nickel. He throws a fastball, curve, and changeup. He isn't a power pitcher and needs to paint the corners. He tends to induce fly balls—not a good characteristic for a pitcher whose home park is Wrigley. A converted infielder, he is a good fielder who keeps runners close and helps himself at the plate, but his pitching will determine his future. In 1990, he had a bone chip in his left elbow that ended his season. For $3, a fantasy manager could get a bargain starter. If he steers clear of the arm trouble and control problems that plagued him in the past, Boskie could blossom into a regular third or fourth starter—perhaps in 1992.

League Pitching Register

	W	L	ERA	G	CG	IP	H	ER	BB	SO
90 NL	5	6	3.69	15	1	97.2	99	40	31	49
91 NL	4	9	5.23	28	0	129.0	150	75	52	62
Life	9	15	4.57	43	1	226.2	249	115	83	111
2 AVE	5	8	4.57	22	1	113.1	125	58	42	56

DARYL BOSTON

Position: Outfield
Team: New York Mets
Born: Jan. 4, 1963 Cincinnati, OH
Height: 6'3" **Weight:** 195 lbs.
Bats: left **Throws:** left
Acquired: Signed as a free agent, 4/90

Player Summary	
Fantasy Value	$1 to $3
Card Value	3¢ to 5¢
Will	take extra base
Can't	always hit for power
Expect	continued spot jobs
Don't Expect	much use as regular

The prolonged absence of the injured Vince Coleman in 1991 gave Boston more playing time than expected in the Mets outfield. He repeated his better-than-expected showing of 1990, his first season in the NL. After hitting .273 with 12 homers for the '90 Mets, he again had an average in the .270s but with little power in '91. He is worth a buck or two for fantasy teams. A former free swinger who now hits to all fields, he could utilize his speed more as a bunter or base-stealer. The speed does help in the outfield, where he has good enough range to play a competent center field. He also has a strong throwing arm—certainly better than Coleman's. Boston, even in New York, won't wow card investors. Don't invest in his 1992 commons. With expansion, he may become a starter.

Major League Batting Register

	BA	G	AB	R	H	2B	3B	HR	RBI	SB
84 AL	.169	35	83	8	14	3	1	0	3	6
85 AL	.228	95	232	20	53	13	1	3	15	8
86 AL	.266	56	199	29	53	11	3	5	22	9
87 AL	.258	103	337	51	87	21	2	10	29	12
88 AL	.217	105	281	37	61	12	2	15	31	9
89 AL	.252	101	218	34	55	3	4	5	23	7
90 AL	.000	5	1	0	0	0	0	0	0	1
90 NL	.273	115	366	65	100	21	2	12	45	18
91 NL	.275	137	255	40	70	16	4	4	21	15
Life	.250	752	1972	284	493	100	19	54	189	85
3 AVE	.268	119	280	46	75	13	3	7	30	14

CURRENT PLAYERS

DENIS BOUCHER

Position: Pitcher
Team: Cleveland Indians
Born: March 7, 1968 Montreal, Quebec, Canada
Height: 6'1" **Weight:** 195 lbs.
Bats: right **Throws:** left
Acquired: Traded from Blue Jays with Mark Whiten and Glenallen Hill for Tom Candiotti and Turner Ward, 6/91

Player Summary
Fantasy Value	$2 to $3
Card Value	10¢ to 20¢
Will	win as he matures
Can't	finish what he starts
Expect	youthful inexperience
Don't Expect	big year in 1992

Although he broke into the majors as the fifth starter for the 1991 Blue Jays, Boucher was expecting to be traded. Montreal, anxious to acquire the Quebec native, was hot on his heels when the Indians came up with a better offer. As with any pitcher, he will have lots of chances with Cleveland. His 1992 rookie cards are reasonable gambles at about 15 cents. He began the year as John Cerutti's successor in the Blue Jay rotation, and Boucher got a no-decision in his April 12 debut and then struggled, dropping seven of his first eight decisions. Signed as a nondrafted free agent in 1987, Boucher was a 13-game winner at Class-A Myrtle Beach in his first pro season. In 1988, he won 10 games at Class-A Dunedin. His best year was 1990, when he went 7-0 with a 0.75 ERA and 62 strikeouts in 60 innings for Dunedin, then 8-5 with a 3.85 ERA at Triple-A Syracuse. He is risky for fantasy managers at more than $3. He is the first French-Canadian to pitch in the majors since Claude Raymond.

Major League Pitching Register
	W	L	ERA	G	CG	IP	H	ER	BB	SO
91 AL	1	7	6.05	12	0	58.0	74	39	24	29
Life	1	7	6.05	12	0	58.0	74	39	24	29

DENNIS BOYD

Position: Pitcher
Team: Texas Rangers
Born: Oct. 6, 1959 Meridian, MS
Height: 6'1" **Weight:** 160 lbs.
Bats: right **Throws:** right
Acquired: Traded from Expos for Jonathan Hurst, Joey Eischen, and Travis Buckley, 7/91

Player Summary
Fantasy Value	$1 to $3
Card Value	3¢ to 5¢
Will	try to use finesse
Can't	go all the way
Expect	variety of pitches
Don't Expect	miracle comeback

After missing 120 days of the 1989 season with blood clots in his right shoulder, Boyd resurrected his career with the 1990 Expos, becoming the club's most productive starter. The former power pitcher—who had won at least a dozen games for Boston on three separate occasions—was not as effective with his off-speed deliveries in 1991. Anxious to unload his hefty salary, the Expos shipped him to the Rangers in July. He lost his first four starts, placing his future in jeopardy. His 1992 commons are not buys. When he's right, Boyd throws a sinker, slider, curve, changeup, screwball, and split-fingered fastball—all from various delivery styles and points. His weak fielding and failure to keep runners close hurt his game. Boyd has little merit beyond the past as a fantasy draft for more than $3.

Major League Pitching Register
	W	L	ERA	G	CG	IP	H	ER	BB	SO
82 AL	0	1	5.40	3	0	8.1	11	5	2	2
83 AL	4	8	3.28	15	5	98.2	103	36	23	43
84 AL	12	12	4.37	29	10	197.2	207	96	53	134
85 AL	15	13	3.70	35	13	272.1	273	112	67	154
86 AL	16	10	3.78	30	10	214.1	222	90	45	129
87 AL	1	3	5.89	7	0	36.2	47	24	9	12
88 AL	9	7	5.34	23	1	129.2	147	77	41	71
89 AL	3	2	4.42	10	0	59.0	57	29	19	26
90 NL	10	6	2.93	31	3	190.2	164	62	52	113
91 NL	6	8	3.52	19	1	120.1	115	47	40	82
91 AL	2	7	6.68	12	0	62.0	81	46	17	33
Life	78	77	4.04	214	43	1389.2	1427	624	368	799
2 AVE	9	11	3.74	31	2	186.2	180	78	55	114

CURRENT PLAYERS

SCOTT BRADLEY

Position: Catcher
Team: Seattle Mariners
Born: March 22, 1960 Montclair, NJ
Height: 5'11" **Weight:** 185 lbs.
Bats: left **Throws:** right
Acquired: Traded from White Sox for Ivan Calderon, 6/86

Player Summary
Fantasy Value	$1 to $3
Card Value	3¢ to 5¢
Will	play several positions
Can't	hit long ball
Expect	improvement at bat
Don't Expect	regular status

Bradley was a solid hitter before enduring two off-years in a row. Valued because he's a catcher who hits lefthanded, he also has the advantage of versatility, playing the infield corners and the outfield. Once known as a contact hitter who was tough to strike out, Bradley's game deteriorated when he tried to pull the ball more. Unable to hit the ball out of the park, he watched both his average and power deteriorate, causing headaches for fantasy managers. Pay no more than $3 for him. The former Triple-A International League batting king hit .300 in 77 games for the White Sox and Mariners in 1986, his best year in the majors. He's never appeared in more than 103 games in a season. Part-timers don't inspire card investors. Stay away from his 1992 commons. Should his bat revive, Bradley can be a valuable sub again.

Major League Batting Register
	BA	G	AB	R	H	2B	3B	HR	RBI	SB
84 AL	.286	9	21	3	6	1	0	0	2	0
85 AL	.163	19	49	4	8	2	1	0	1	0
86 AL	.300	77	220	20	66	8	3	5	28	1
87 AL	.278	102	342	34	95	15	1	5	43	0
88 AL	.257	103	335	45	86	17	1	4	33	1
89 AL	.274	103	270	21	74	16	0	3	37	1
90 AL	.223	101	233	11	52	9	0	1	28	0
91 AL	.203	83	172	10	35	7	0	0	11	0
Life	.257	597	1642	148	422	75	6	18	183	3
3 AVE	.239	96	225	14	54	11	0	1	25	0

GLENN BRAGGS

Position: Outfield
Team: Cincinnati Reds
Born: Oct. 17, 1962 San Bernardino, CA
Height: 6'3" **Weight:** 210 lbs.
Bats: right **Throws:** right
Acquired: Traded from Brewers with Billy Bates for Ron Robinson and Bob Sebra, 6/90

Player Summary
Fantasy Value	$4 to $6
Card Value	3¢ to 5¢
Will	hit long ball
Can't	steal regularly
Expect	some work in left
Don't Expect	high average

Though he started out slowly in 1991, Braggs eventually won Cincinnati's left field job with his strong bat. One of a half-dozen players tried at the position, Braggs began to hit with authority around Memorial Day. He is a fastball hitter who sometimes struggles with off-speed pitches. He also hits with much better power against lefthanded pitchers. The former Milwaukee outfielder, who broke into the majors in 1986, has good speed and a powerful throwing arm. He shows off the arm best from right field, where he had been platooned with Paul O'Neill in the past. Draft Braggs at no more than $6 for your fantasy team. He may not get any more at bats in 1992. Don't go for his common-priced 1992 cards, since he is not a full-time player. Though Braggs is not an acceptable fielder or prolific base-stealer, he will stay in the majors because of his bat.

Major League Batting Register
	BA	G	AB	R	H	2B	3B	HR	RBI	SB
86 AL	.237	58	215	19	51	8	2	4	18	1
87 AL	.269	132	505	67	136	28	7	13	77	12
88 AL	.261	72	272	30	71	14	0	10	42	6
89 AL	.247	144	514	77	127	12	3	15	66	17
90 AL	.248	37	113	17	28	5	0	3	13	5
90 NL	.299	72	201	22	60	9	1	6	28	3
91 NL	.260	85	250	36	65	10	0	11	39	11
Life	.260	600	2070	268	538	86	13	62	283	55
3 AVE	.260	113	359	51	93	12	1	12	49	12

CURRENT PLAYERS

JEFF BRANTLEY

Position: Pitcher
Team: San Francisco Giants
Born: Sept. 5, 1963 Florence, AL
Height: 5'11" **Weight:** 180 lbs.
Bats: right **Throws:** right
Acquired: Sixth-round pick in 6/85 free-agent draft

Player Summary	
Fantasy Value	$7 to $10
Card Value	5¢ to 7¢
Will	move batters off plate
Can't	secure bullpen load
Expect	many ground balls
Don't Expect	high K totals

In 1990, his second full big league summer, Brantley had 19 saves and a 1.56 ERA. That performance convinced the Giants they had found a premier righthanded closer. By continuing his solid relief work in 1991, he helped form a fine righty-lefty bullpen tandem with free-agent signee Dave Righetti. Brantley didn't become the sole closer as expected, however, and his save opportunities diminished a bit. Behind Righetti, Brantley is not as attractive as a fantasy draft, peaking at $10. His top pitch is a split-fingered fastball that sinks—producing many ground outs. He also has a fastball and curveball. Opposing hitters had a .225 batting average and a .338 slugging average against him in 1991. A good fielder who keeps runners close, the former Mississippi State All-American (in 1985) can also help himself with a timely bunt. His 1992 cards are lukewarm buys at a nickel each. The victim of shoulder problems in the past, Brantley is protected from overwork by the presence of Righetti.

Major League Pitching Register

	W	L	ERA	G	S	IP	H	ER	BB	SO
88 NL	0	1	5.66	9	1	20.2	22	13	6	11
89 NL	7	1	4.07	59	0	97.1	101	44	37	69
90 NL	5	3	1.56	55	19	86.2	77	15	33	61
91 NL	5	2	2.45	67	15	95.1	78	26	52	81
Life	17	7	2.94	190	35	300.0	278	98	128	222
3 AVE	6	2	2.74	60	11	93.1	85	28	41	70

SID BREAM

Position: First base
Team: Atlanta Braves
Born: Aug. 3, 1960 Carlisle, PA
Height: 6'4" **Weight:** 220 lbs.
Bats: left **Throws:** left
Acquired: Signed as a free agent, 12/90

Player Summary	
Fantasy Value	$5 to $7
Card Value	3¢ to 5¢
Will	provide leadership
Can't	avoid knee problems
Expect	great defense
Don't Expect	injury-free year

Bream gave the pennant-winning Braves much-needed defensive improvement at first base and a winning attitude in the clubhouse when he arrived from Pittsburgh via free agency in 1991. He also supplied a solid lefthanded bat before he submitted to knee surgery on June 26. Bream, who has had previous knee problems, missed much of the season's second half. The injury proved unfortunate for him. He seemed certain to knock in 80 runs had he played a full season. If he's healthy, he will give the Braves strong defense at first, where he'll save the other infielders many potential throwing errors with good scoops and stretches. He is not very fast. His lack of consistent power and history of injury, however, make him a $5 to $7 fantasy draft. Recurring knee problems could shorten Bream's career and hamper his productivity. His 1992 commons are not investments.

Major League Batting Register

	BA	G	AB	R	H	2B	3B	HR	RBI	SB
83 NL	.182	15	11	0	2	0	0	0	2	0
84 NL	.184	27	49	2	9	3	0	0	6	1
85 NL	.230	50	148	18	34	7	0	6	21	0
86 NL	.268	154	522	73	140	37	5	16	77	13
87 NL	.275	149	516	64	142	25	3	13	65	9
88 NL	.264	148	462	50	122	37	0	10	65	9
89 NL	.222	19	36	3	8	3	0	0	4	0
90 NL	.270	147	389	39	105	23	2	15	67	8
91 NL	.253	91	265	32	67	12	0	11	45	0
Life	.262	800	2398	281	629	147	10	71	352	40
2 AVE	.263	119	327	36	86	18	1	13	56	4

CURRENT PLAYERS

GEORGE BRETT

Position: Designated hitter
Team: Kansas City Royals
Born: May 15, 1953 Glendale, WV
Height: 6' **Weight:** 200 lbs.
Bats: left **Throws:** right
Acquired: Second-round pick in 6/71 free-agent draft

Player Summary	
Fantasy Value	$15 to $20
Card Value	15¢ to 25¢
Will	hit well in clutch
Can't	play much at first
Expect	declining power
Don't Expect	more batting crowns

Brett became a full-time designated hitter in 1991. He spent 13 years at third before moving to first in 1987, but also appeared on the disabled list 10 times. Still a dangerous hitter, he is the only player to win batting titles in three decades. AL MVP in 1980, Brett no longer has the same power. A 13-time All-Star, he would have reached 3,000 hits by now without injuries. His 1992 cards are great buys at a quarter. He is a patient hitter with a good eye and ability to make constant adjustments at the plate. He is now a $17 draft as a DH.

Major League Batting Register

	BA	G	AB	R	H	2B	3B	HR	RBI	SB
73 AL	.125	13	40	2	5	2	0	0	0	0
74 AL	.282	133	457	49	129	21	5	2	47	8
75 AL	.308	159	634	84	195	35	13	11	89	13
76 AL	.333	159	645	94	215	34	14	7	67	21
77 AL	.312	139	564	105	176	32	13	22	88	14
78 AL	.294	128	510	79	150	45	8	9	62	23
79 AL	.329	154	645	119	212	42	20	23	107	17
80 AL	.390	117	449	87	175	33	9	24	118	15
81 AL	.314	89	347	42	109	27	7	6	43	14
82 AL	.301	144	552	101	166	32	9	21	82	6
83 AL	.310	123	464	90	144	38	2	25	93	0
84 AL	.284	104	377	42	107	21	3	13	69	0
85 AL	.335	155	550	108	184	38	5	30	112	9
86 AL	.290	124	441	70	128	28	4	16	73	1
87 AL	.290	115	427	71	124	18	2	22	78	6
88 AL	.306	157	589	90	180	42	3	24	103	14
89 AL	.282	124	457	67	129	26	3	12	80	14
90 AL	.329	142	544	82	179	45	7	14	87	9
91 AL	.255	131	505	77	129	40	2	10	61	2
Life	.308	2410	9197	1459	2836	599	129	291	1459	186
3 AVE	.290	132	502	75	146	37	4	12	76	8

GREG BRILEY

Position: Outfield
Team: Seattle Mariners
Born: May 24, 1965 Bethel, NC
Height: 5'8" **Weight:** 165 lbs.
Bats: left **Throws:** right
Acquired: First-round pick in secondary phase of 6/86 free-agent draft

Player Summary	
Fantasy Value	$2 to $4
Card Value	3¢ to 5¢
Will	take advantage of speed
Can't	hit the long ball
Expect	rivals to run on arm
Don't Expect	return of sweet swing

A heavy hitter in the minors, Briley was a disappointment to the 1991 Mariners in his third big league season. Although he was among the team leaders in stolen bases, he didn't improve his batting average much and produced almost no power. His 1992 commons aren't good investments now. In 1991, he had a .260 batting average, a .307 on-base average, and a .336 slugging percentage. A former shortstop and second baseman, he hit .266 with 13 homers in 115 games as a Seattle rookie in 1989 but watched his average shrink steadily in the seasons that followed. He could boost the average simply by bunting for base hits. Briley's biggest strengths are base-running and defense—both because of his outstanding speed. His stolen bases and latent power could benefit poor fantasy teams for $4. Briley compensates for an infielder's throwing arm with great range and the ability to get a good jump on the ball. If he produced power, he would more easily be forgiven for his weak arm.

Major League Batting Register

	BA	G	AB	R	H	2B	3B	HR	RBI	SB
88 AL	.250	13	36	6	9	2	0	1	4	0
89 AL	.266	115	394	52	105	22	4	13	52	11
90 AL	.246	125	337	40	83	18	2	5	29	16
91 AL	.260	139	381	39	99	17	3	2	26	23
Life	.258	392	1148	137	296	59	9	21	111	50
3 AVE	.258	126	371	44	96	19	3	7	36	17

CURRENT PLAYERS

HUBIE BROOKS

Position: Outfield
Team: California Angels
Born: Sept. 24, 1956 Los Angeles, CA
Height: 6' **Weight:** 205 lbs.
Bats: right **Throws:** right
Acquired: Traded from Mets for Dave Gallagher, 12/91

Player Summary	
Fantasy Value	$10 to $15
Card Value	3¢ to 5¢
Will	produce power
Can't	show patience at bat
Expect	frequent Ks
Don't Expect	high average

Brooks was the Mets third baseman during the early 1980s. Though he produced a club-record 24-game hitting streak in 1984, he was traded to the Expos in the Gary Carter deal that winter. Brooks moved to his hometown Dodgers as a 1990 free agent, then was traded back to the Mets as the right field replacement for Darryl Strawberry—who had signed with Los Angeles as a free agent. In Brooks's second New York tour, he showed that age had taken a toll on his skills. The once-feared clutch hitter, still impatient at the plate, struck out far more often than he walked. He was again traded after 1991, this time to California. Fantasy managers will still pay $10 or so for his dingers, but Brooks's 1992 commons don't cut it for card investors.

Major League Batting Register

	BA	G	AB	R	H	2B	3B	HR	RBI	SB
80 NL	.309	24	81	8	25	2	1	1	10	1
81 NL	.307	98	358	34	110	21	2	4	38	9
82 NL	.249	126	457	40	114	21	2	2	40	6
83 NL	.251	150	586	53	147	18	4	5	58	6
84 NL	.283	153	561	61	159	23	2	16	73	6
85 NL	.269	156	605	67	163	34	7	13	100	6
86 NL	.340	80	306	50	104	18	5	14	58	4
87 NL	.263	112	430	57	113	22	3	14	72	4
88 NL	.279	151	588	61	164	35	2	20	90	7
89 NL	.268	148	542	56	145	30	1	14	70	6
90 NL	.266	153	568	74	151	28	1	20	91	2
91 NL	.238	103	357	48	85	11	1	16	50	3
Life	.272	1454	5439	609	1480	263	31	139	750	60
3 AVE	.260	135	489	59	127	23	1	17	70	4

KEVIN BROWN

Position: Pitcher
Team: Texas Rangers
Born: March 14, 1965 McIntyre, GA
Height: 6'4" **Weight:** 188 lbs.
Bats: right **Throws:** right
Acquired: First-round pick in 6/86 free-agent draft

Player Summary	
Fantasy Value	$6 to $8
Card Value	3¢ to 5¢
Will	win 15 games
Can't	finish what he starts
Expect	some control woes
Don't Expect	good K-to-walk ratio

Brown established himself as a real starter by winning a dozen games in each of his first two seasons with Texas. A 1989 rookie, he went 12-9 with a 3.35 ERA—figures that earned him fifth place in that year's AL Rookie of the Year voting. A dozen wins a year won't win his 1992 commons points with card collectors, however. In '90, he became the first Ranger to win his first five starts of the season. Elbow problems later that summer hampered his progress, however. Brown's best pitch is a sinking fastball that coaxes grounders from hitters. He also uses a mid-90s regular fastball. His fantasy value went down to $8 because of his ERA climb in 1991. He's not a great fielder but he keeps runners close when they reach base. The former Georgia Tech star has the potential to justify his selection as the fourth player picked in the 1986 draft. Only Jeff King, Greg Swindell, and Matt Williams were picked ahead of Brown.

Major League Pitching Register

	W	L	ERA	G	CG	IP	H	ER	BB	SO
86 AL	1	0	3.60	1	0	5.0	6	2	0	4
88 AL	1	1	4.24	4	1	23.1	33	11	8	12
89 AL	12	9	3.35	28	7	191.0	167	71	70	104
90 AL	12	10	3.60	26	6	180.0	175	72	60	88
91 AL	9	12	4.40	33	0	210.2	233	103	90	96
Life	35	32	3.82	92	14	610.0	614	259	228	304
3 AVE	11	10	3.81	29	4	194.1	192	82	73	96

CURRENT PLAYERS

JERRY BROWNE

Position: Second base
Team: Cleveland Indians
Born: Feb. 13, 1966 Christiansted, St. Croix, Virgin Islands
Height: 5'10" **Weight:** 170 lbs.
Bats: both **Throws:** right
Acquired: Traded from Rangers with Oddibe McDowell and Pete O'Brien for Julio Franco, 12/88

Player Summary	
Fantasy Value	$3 to $5
Card Value	3¢ to 5¢
Will	show good range
Can't	keep average up
Expect	fewer at bats
Don't Expect	any power

Browne's batting average has declined steadily since hitting a career peak of .299 in 1989. When it fell to .220 last year, he lost his regular position—first to Mark Lewis and later to Carlos Baerga. When Browne lost his starting job, he lost most of his value to fantasy teams. His batting judgement seemed to regress. He struck out more than he walked in '91. His 1992 commons will never tempt investors. His best asset is speed; he stole 27 bases as a rookie for Texas in 1987. He would steal more if his judgement were better. He gets thrown out a lot because he often takes unnecessary chances. As a fielder, he has good range and a strong arm but has never been adept at turning the double-play. Browne will have to improve his hitting to stay in the major leagues. Because he plays only one position, his value as a light-hitting bench player is diminished.

Major League Batting Register

	BA	G	AB	R	H	2B	3B	HR	RBI	SB
86 AL	.417	12	24	6	10	2	0	0	3	0
87 AL	.271	132	454	63	123	16	6	1	38	27
88 AL	.229	73	214	26	49	9	2	1	17	7
89 AL	.299	153	598	83	179	31	4	5	45	14
90 AL	.267	140	513	92	137	26	5	6	50	12
91 AL	.228	107	290	28	66	5	2	1	29	2
Life	.269	617	2093	298	564	89	19	14	182	62
3 AVE	.273	133	467	68	127	21	4	4	41	9

TOM BROWNING

Position: Pitcher
Team: Cincinnati Reds
Born: April 28, 1960 Casper, WY
Height: 6'1" **Weight:** 190 lbs.
Bats: left **Throws:** left
Acquired: Ninth-round pick in 6/82 free-agent draft

Player Summary	
Fantasy Value	$14 to $17
Card Value	5¢ to 8¢
Will	anchor rotation
Can't	avoid gopher balls
Expect	lasting steadiness
Don't Expect	an ERA title

A control pitcher, Browning had an off year in 1991. He has the potential to bounce back, making him a $15 fantasy hurler. He was selected to his first All-Star Game in 1991. In 1985, he became the first rookie since 1954 to win 20 games, and was runner-up in NL Rookie of the Year voting. He cemented his reputation on September 16, 1988, when he pitched the first perfect game in Reds history. Earlier that season, he missed another no-hitter when Tony Gwynn singled with one out in the ninth. On July 4, 1990, a leadoff double by Dickie Thon in the ninth ended another potential perfect game. He is a control fastball pitcher, so he has to paint the corners or he gives up 32 homers (as in '91). He also has a good changeup and a curve. Browning's 1992 cards are modest investments at no more than 8 cents.

Major League Pitching Register

	W	L	ERA	G	CG	IP	H	ER	BB	SO
84 NL	1	0	1.54	3	0	23.1	27	4	5	14
85 NL	20	9	3.55	38	6	261.1	242	103	73	155
86 NL	14	13	3.81	39	4	243.1	225	103	70	147
87 NL	10	13	5.02	32	2	183.0	201	102	61	117
88 NL	18	5	3.41	36	5	250.2	205	95	64	124
89 NL	15	12	3.39	37	9	249.2	241	94	64	118
90 NL	15	9	3.80	35	2	227.2	235	96	52	99
91 NL	14	14	4.18	36	1	230.1	241	107	56	115
Life	107	75	3.80	256	29	1669.1	1617	704	445	889
3 AVE	15	12	3.78	36	4	235.2	239	99	57	111

CURRENT PLAYERS

TOM BRUNANSKY

Position: Outfield
Team: Boston Red Sox
Born: Aug. 20, 1960 Covina, CA
Height: 6'4" **Weight:** 216 lbs.
Bats: right **Throws:** right
Acquired: Traded from Cardinals for Lee Smith, 6/90

Player Summary	
Fantasy Value	$8 to $14
Card Value	3¢ to 5¢
Will	hit some homers
Can't	keep average fit
Expect	mastery in right
Don't Expect	return to regular status

When Brunansky produced the weakest offensive performance of his career in 1991, the Red Sox began platooning him in right field with slugging rookie Phil Plantier. Brunansky early in the year abandoned his stock-still batting stance for a constant wiggling style. He always has been a guess hitter who survives by instinct. He had two 32-homer seasons for Minnesota and topped 20 in six other seasons. He will boost your fantasy team's homers for $12. His 1992 commons are not buys. Though his skills may be starting to erode, Brunansky still thrives in Fenway Park, on defense as well as offense. He is a good right fielder who knows the tendencies of his own pitchers and where to play rival hitters.

Major League Batting Register

	BA	G	AB	R	H	2B	3B	HR	RBI	SB
81 AL	.152	11	33	7	5	0	0	3	6	1
82 AL	.272	127	463	77	126	30	1	20	46	1
83 AL	.227	151	542	70	123	24	5	28	82	2
84 AL	.254	155	567	75	144	21	0	32	85	4
85 AL	.242	157	567	71	137	28	4	27	90	5
86 AL	.256	157	593	69	152	28	1	23	75	12
87 AL	.259	155	532	83	138	22	2	32	85	11
88 AL	.184	14	49	5	9	1	0	1	6	1
88 NL	.245	143	523	69	128	22	4	22	79	16
89 NL	.239	158	556	67	133	29	3	20	85	5
90 NL	.158	19	57	5	9	3	0	1	2	0
90 AL	.267	129	461	61	123	24	5	15	71	5
91 AL	.229	142	459	54	105	24	1	16	70	1
Life	.247	1518	5402	713	1332	256	26	240	782	64
3 AVE	.241	149	511	62	123	27	3	17	76	4

STEVE BUECHELE

Position: Third base
Team: Pittsburgh Pirates
Born: Sept. 26, 1961 Lancaster, CA
Height: 6'2" **Weight:** 190 lbs.
Bats: right **Throws:** right
Acquired: Traded from Texas for Kurt Miler and Hector Fajardo, 8/91

Player Summary	
Fantasy Value	$6 to $8
Card Value	3¢ to 5¢
Will	show some power
Can't	hit for high average
Expect	great glove at third
Don't Expect	any stolen bases

Although he had some woes in the '91 NLCS, Buechele is one of the best-fielding third basemen in the major leagues. He was also one of the game's best-kept secrets until the Pirates nabbed him for their pennant run. He hit 18 home runs in 1986, his first full season, and has hit at least 16 three other times. In 1991, Buechele had a .447 slugging percentage for the Rangers, and he slugged .412 for the Bucs. He's an economical fantasy choice at $7. He does not hit for a high average and is vulnerable to good fastballs—especially from righthanded pitchers. He also hurts himself by not being selective at the plate. Like many third basemen, he does not have good speed. His 1992 commons aren't hot. At third, he has good range and a very respectable arm. Buechele is also capable of playing second base and has handled that spot well on the major league level.

Major League Batting Register

	BA	G	AB	R	H	2B	3B	HR	RBI	SB
85 AL	.219	69	219	22	48	6	3	6	21	3
86 AL	.243	153	461	54	112	19	2	18	54	5
87 AL	.237	136	363	45	86	20	0	13	50	2
88 AL	.250	155	503	68	126	21	4	16	58	2
89 AL	.235	155	486	60	114	22	2	16	59	1
90 AL	.215	91	251	30	54	10	0	7	30	1
91 AL	.267	121	416	58	111	17	2	18	66	0
91 NL	.246	31	114	16	28	5	1	4	19	0
Life	.241	911	2813	353	679	120	14	98	357	14
3 AVE	.242	133	422	55	102	18	2	15	58	1

CURRENT PLAYERS

JAY BUHNER

Position: Outfield
Team: Seattle Mariners
Born: Aug. 13, 1964 Louisville, KY
Height: 6'3" **Weight:** 205 lbs.
Bats: right **Throws:** right
Acquired: Traded from Yankees with Rick Balabon and Troy Evers for Ken Phelps, 7/88

Player Summary
Fantasy Value	$17 to $20
Card Value	5¢ to 10¢
Will	hit 30 homers
Can't	avoid frequent Ks
Expect	tape-measure homers
Don't Expect	average over .270

Buhner has finally realized the promise that once persuaded the Yankees to consider him their top power-hitting prospect. Last August 4, his game-winning three-run homer in the 11th inning was not only his 20th of the year but his fourth in as many games. He often hits the ball for distance. On July 25, for example, his shot over the left-center field bullpen at Yankee Stadium went 479 feet. Batting coach Gene Clines told Buhner that he had enough strength to hit the ball out with a normal swing, and the outfielder became a more productive performer. He hits to the opposite field more and doesn't try to pull every pitch. In 1991, he had a .498 slugging percentage and a .337 on-base average. He is a $17 fantasy bargain. He still strikes out almost three times more than he walks. Buhner is a good right fielder with a strong, accurate arm. His 1992 cards are good buys for less than a dime.

Major League Batting Register
	BA	G	AB	R	H	2B	3B	HR	RBI	SB
87 AL	.227	7	22	0	5	2	0	0	1	0
88 AL	.215	85	261	36	56	13	1	13	38	1
89 AL	.275	58	204	27	56	15	1	9	33	1
90 AL	.276	51	163	16	45	12	0	7	33	2
91 AL	.244	137	406	64	99	14	4	27	77	0
Life	.247	338	1056	143	261	56	6	56	182	4
3 AVE	.259	82	258	36	67	14	2	14	48	1

TIM BURKE

Position: Pitcher
Team: New York Mets
Born: Feb. 19, 1959 Omaha, NE
Height: 6'3" **Weight:** 205 lbs.
Bats: right **Throws:** right
Acquired: Traded from Expos for pitcher Ron Darling, 7/91

Player Summary
Fantasy Value	$8 to $11
Card Value	3¢ to 5¢
Will	suffer dry spells
Can't	ring up many Ks
Expect	role as set-up man
Don't Expect	return to 1989

Burke was one of the NL's best relief pitchers between 1985 and 1990. His 78 appearances in '85 were a record for an NL rookie. He advanced to closer after Montreal traded Jeff Reardon in 1987. Burke hit a career peak with 28 saves in 1989, the only year he was an NL All-Star. He is a control pitcher who throws a sinker, slider, and changeup. He has always had problems with his slider, which is inconsistent, and his sinker, which doesn't always sink. In addition, lefthanded hitters give him a hard time even when all his pitches are working. He became more inconsistent after he broke his leg in May 1990. The Mets had hoped he'd serve as a set-up man for closer John Franco but got a disappointing return on their investment. His reduced role in New York reduces his value to fantasy managers to $10. His 1992 commons are not good ventures. Burke's best days might be behind him.

Major League Pitching Register
	W	L	ERA	G	S	IP	H	ER	BB	SO
85 NL	9	4	2.39	78	8	120.1	86	32	44	87
86 NL	9	7	2.93	68	4	101.1	103	33	46	82
87 NL	7	0	1.19	55	18	91.0	64	12	17	58
88 NL	3	5	3.40	61	18	82.0	84	31	25	42
89 NL	9	3	2.55	68	28	84.2	68	24	22	54
90 NL	3	3	2.52	58	20	75.0	71	21	21	47
91 NL	6	7	3.36	72	6	101.2	96	38	26	59
Life	46	29	2.62	460	102	656.0	572	191	201	429
3 AVE	6	4	2.86	66	18	87.1	78	28	23	53

CURRENT PLAYERS

JOHN BURKETT

Position: Pitcher
Team: San Francisco Giants
Born: Nov. 28, 1964 New Brighton, PA
Height: 6'3" **Weight:** 205 lbs.
Bats: right **Throws:** right
Acquired: Sixth-round pick in 6/83 free-agent draft

Player Summary	
Fantasy Value	$7 to $10
Card Value	3¢ to 5¢
Will	give team 200 innings
Can't	help himself in the field
Expect	streaky performances
Don't Expect	more than 15 victories

Burkett won a big game for the Giants last August 8, when he outpitched Atlanta's Tom Glavine. That was Burkett's fourth consecutive victory—matching the longest win streak of his career. He had already established himself as one of the NL's best young pitchers. He certainly has the confidence of San Francisco manager Roger Craig, who named Burkett the club's Opening Day starter in 1991. He throws a fastball, split-fingered fastball, curveball, and changeup. Because his control is good, he gives up his share of home runs, allowing 19 in '91. Opponents had a .277 batting average, a .392 slugging percentage, and a .332 on-base average against Burkett in 1991. In 1989 at Triple-A Phoenix, he was 10-11 with a 5.05 ERA, 197 Ks, and 59 walks in 167⅔ innings. He was 5-11 with a 5.21 ERA at Phoenix in '88. You should gamble less than $10 in fantasy drafts. He is young enough to improve other aspects of his game. Spend nothing on his 1992 commons.

Major League Pitching Register

	W	L	ERA	G	CG	IP	H	ER	BB	SO
87 NL	0	0	4.50	3	0	6.0	7	3	3	5
90 NL	14	7	3.79	33	2	204.0	201	86	61	118
91 NL	12	11	4.18	36	3	206.2	223	96	60	131
Life	26	18	4.00	72	5	416.2	431	185	124	254
2 AVE	13	9	3.99	35	3	205.1	212	91	61	125

ELLIS BURKS

Position: Outfield
Team: Boston Red Sox
Born: Sept. 11, 1964 Vicksburg, MS
Height: 6'2" **Weight:** 202 lbs.
Bats: right **Throws:** right
Acquired: First-round pick in 1/83 free-agent draft

Player Summary	
Fantasy Value	$25 to $30
Card Value	10¢ to 15¢
Will	generate speed and power
Can't	keep average up
Expect	occasional injuries
Don't Expect	set spot in lineup

Although breaking pitches occasionally give him problems, Burks is a strong hitter who gives the Red Sox both power and speed. In fact, that combination has puzzled Boston managers, who have used him at several different spots in the lineup—including leadoff. With 20 homers and 27 steals as a 1987 rookie, he joined Carl Yastrzemski and Jackie Jensen as the only previous Red Sox in the 20-20 club. Burks had a .422 slugging percentage and a .314 on-base average in 1991; he was caught stealing 11 times. In 1990, he earned a Gold Glove for his play in center field. Because he goes back on the ball so well, he plays a shallow center that enables him to grab many potential base hits. Injuries have slowed his progress, as in 1991. Staying healthy is Burks's biggest challenge. He is a $25 fantasy outfielder. His 1992 cards are fair purchases for a dime apiece. A shortstop and a pitcher as a schoolboy star, Burks became an outfielder after turning pro.

Major League Batting Register

	BA	G	AB	R	H	2B	3B	HR	RBI	SB
87 AL	.272	133	558	94	152	30	2	20	59	27
88 AL	.294	144	540	93	159	37	5	18	92	25
89 AL	.303	97	399	73	121	19	6	12	61	21
90 AL	.296	152	588	89	174	33	8	21	89	9
91 AL	.251	130	474	56	119	33	3	14	56	6
Life	.283	656	2559	405	725	152	24	85	357	88
3 AVE	.283	126	487	73	138	28	6	16	69	12

CURRENT PLAYERS

RANDY BUSH

Position: Outfield; designated hitter
Team: Minnesota Twins
Born: Oct. 5, 1958 Dover, DE
Height: 6'1" **Weight:** 184 lbs.
Bats: left **Throws:** left
Acquired: Second-round pick in 6/79 free-agent draft

Player Summary	
Fantasy Value	$3 to $5
Card Value	3¢ to 5¢
Will	handle reserve role
Can't	hit lefthanders
Expect	designated hitter job
Don't Expect	sudden power

Although he carries a famous last name, Bush was one of the most anonymous players on the first-place Twins in 1991. Though he appeared in fewer than 100 games, he produced the highest batting average of his 10-year career. His power production was down, however. A contact hitter who walks as often as he strikes out, Bush bats almost exclusively against righthanded pitching. He is a $4 fantasy DH. Don't invest in his 1992 commons. Since he's only average in the field and doesn't run well, he's most often used as a designated hitter or pinch-hitter. He throws well enough to play right field and catches anything he can reach, but he doesn't have the range of other outfielders on the team. Bush, who can also play first base, has twice hit 14 homers in a season.

Major League Batting Register

	BA	G	AB	R	H	2B	3B	HR	RBI	SB
82 AL	.244	55	119	13	29	6	1	4	13	0
83 AL	.249	124	373	43	93	24	3	11	56	0
84 AL	.222	113	311	46	69	17	1	11	43	1
85 AL	.239	97	234	26	56	13	3	10	35	3
86 AL	.269	130	357	50	96	19	7	7	45	5
87 AL	.253	122	293	46	74	10	2	11	46	10
88 AL	.261	136	394	51	103	20	3	14	51	8
89 AL	.263	141	391	60	103	17	4	14	54	5
90 AL	.243	73	181	17	44	8	0	6	18	0
91 AL	.303	93	165	21	50	10	1	6	23	0
Life	.254	1084	2818	373	717	144	25	94	384	32
3 AVE	.267	102	246	33	66	12	2	9	32	2

BRETT BUTLER

Position: Outfield
Team: Los Angeles Dodgers
Born: June 15, 1957 Los Angeles, CA
Height: 5'10" **Weight:** 160 lbs.
Bats: left **Throws:** left
Acquired: Signed as a free agent, 12/90

Player Summary	
Fantasy Value	$30 to $40
Card Value	3¢ to 5¢
Will	bunt for hits
Can't	hit home runs
Expect	strong defense
Don't Expect	change in status

Butler's first season as the Dodger center fielder was a roaring success. He gave the Dodgers a bona fide leadoff man, and solidified an outfield also occupied by Kal Daniels and Darryl Strawberry. Butler uncorked the league's longest hitting streak (23 games). Though he plays shallow because of a flimsy arm, he compensates by using excellent judgement along with speed. In 1990 with the Giants, Butler ranked second among NL outfielders in total chances and putouts. He also shared league leadership in hits, with many bunts. A spray hitter who hits the ball on the ground, Butler often drives liners to the opposite field. He's one of the NL's best base-stealers. Butler does everything except hit homers, making him desirable to fantasy teams for up to $40. His lack of power makes his 1992 cards commons.

Major League Batting Register

	BA	G	AB	R	H	2B	3B	HR	RBI	SB
81 NL	.254	40	126	17	32	2	3	0	4	9
82 NL	.217	89	240	35	52	2	0	0	7	21
83 NL	.281	151	549	84	154	21	13	5	37	39
84 AL	.269	159	602	108	162	25	9	3	49	52
85 AL	.311	152	591	106	184	28	14	5	50	47
86 AL	.278	161	587	92	163	17	14	4	51	32
87 AL	.295	137	522	91	154	25	8	9	41	33
88 NL	.287	157	568	109	163	27	9	6	43	43
89 NL	.283	154	594	100	168	22	4	4	36	31
90 NL	.309	160	622	108	192	20	9	3	44	51
91 NL	.296	161	615	112	182	13	5	2	38	38
Life	.286	1521	5616	962	1606	202	88	41	400	396
3 AVE	.296	158	610	107	181	18	6	3	39	40

CURRENT PLAYERS

FRANCISCO CABRERA

Position: First base; catcher
Team: Atlanta Braves
Born: Oct. 10, 1966 Santo Domingo, Dominican Republic
Height: 6'4" **Weight:** 193 lbs.
Bats: right **Throws:** right
Acquired: Traded from Blue Jays with Tony Castillo for Jim Acker, 8/89

Player Summary	
Fantasy Value	$2 to $3
Card Value	3¢ to 5¢
Will	be solid at two spots
Can't	steal bases
Expect	occasional big hits
Don't Expect	high batting average

Even after they acquired him, the Braves did not think much of Cabrera's defensive skills behind the plate, even though he had twice led his minor league in total chances and once tied for the league lead in double-plays. The 1991 arrival of first baseman Sid Bream cut the playing time of the free-swinging Cabrera even more. Returned to Triple-A Richmond to work on his defense, he was recalled after veteran receiver Mike Heath was sidelined in July. In limited playing time behind regular catcher Greg Olson, Cabrera acquitted himself well behind the plate and delivered several timely hits—including two home runs against the Reds on August 21. Because of his versatility, he could be a valuable bench player in 1992. Since he won't start for the Braves, and since Atlanta has several good young prospects at both catcher and first base, Cabrera's fantasy value peaks at $3. His 1992 commons will be good buys only until he finds himself in a starting lineup, in Atlanta or elsewhere.

Major League Batting Register

	BA	G	AB	R	H	2B	3B	HR	RBI	SB
89 AL	.167	3	12	1	2	1	0	0	0	0
89 NL	.214	4	14	0	3	2	0	0	0	0
90 NL	.277	63	137	14	38	5	1	7	25	1
91 NL	.242	44	95	7	23	6	0	4	23	1
Life	.256	114	258	22	66	14	1	11	48	2

GREG CADARET

Position: Pitcher
Team: New York Yankees
Born: Feb. 27, 1962 Detroit, MI
Height: 6'3" **Weight:** 205 lbs.
Bats: left **Throws:** left
Acquired: Traded from Athletics with Eric Plunk and Luis Polonia for Rickey Henderson, 6/89

Player Summary	
Fantasy Value	$2 to $4
Card Value	3¢ to 5¢
Will	bust hitters inside
Can't	keep ahead in count
Expect	great pickoff move
Don't Expect	single role

Cadaret was a middle-innings reliever before the Yankees moved him into their starting rotation last July 15. A power pitcher who also uses a curve and a forkball, he helps himself enormously with his defensive talents. He not only owns one of the league's best pickoff moves but also acquits himself well with the glove. He could return to the bullpen as a long man, middle man, or even a short man. Power pitchers who work inside, such as Cadaret, are ideal for that role. For his potential strikeout value, he should bring a few bucks in the fantasy draft. As a starter, he gets into trouble when he falls behind in the count and has to make cripple pitches. Opponents batted .246 in 1991. Moved from the bullpen to the rotation in each of the last three seasons, Cadaret would be more effective if left in one role for the entire season. His common-priced 1992 cards aren't popular.

Major League Pitching Register

	W	L	ERA	G	S	IP	H	ER	BB	SO
87 AL	6	2	4.54	29	0	39.2	37	20	24	30
88 AL	5	2	2.89	58	3	71.2	60	23	36	64
89 AL	5	5	4.05	46	0	120.0	130	54	57	80
90 AL	5	4	4.15	54	3	121.1	120	56	64	80
91 AL	8	6	3.62	68	3	121.2	110	49	59	105
Life	29	19	3.83	255	9	474.1	457	202	240	359
3 AVE	6	5	3.94	56	2	120.2	120	53	60	88

CURRENT PLAYERS

IVAN CALDERON

Position: Outfield; first base
Team: Montreal Expos
Born: March 19, 1962 Fajardo, Puerto Rico
Height: 6'1" **Weight:** 221 lbs.
Bats: right **Throws:** right
Acquired: Traded from White Sox with Barry Jones for Tim Raines, Jeff Carter, and Mario Brito, 12/90

Player Summary	
Fantasy Value	$20 to $25
Card Value	4¢ to 6¢
Will	produce runs in bunches
Can't	maintain average
Expect	clutch hitting
Don't Expect	great defense

Calderon was a welcome addition to the punchless Expos in 1991. The team's Player of the Month in both April and May, he had a .309 average and 49 RBI by midseason—earning him his first trip to the All-Star Game. Fully recovered from 1988 shoulder surgery, he has some problems with breaking balls and inside pitches but has power to all fields when he connects. Calderon's 1991 explosion means his fantasy value might double, though you should be cautious if bidding gets to $22. He is especially dangerous in the clutch. Calderon used to be known as a free swinger, but he had 53 bases on balls opposed to 64 strikeouts in 1991. He also had a .481 slugging percentage and a .368 on-base percentage. As an outfielder, Calderon has good speed but an average arm. His 1992 cards are not very good buys at their nickel price.

Major League Batting Register

	BA	G	AB	R	H	2B	3B	HR	RBI	SB
84 AL	.208	11	24	2	5	1	0	1	1	1
85 AL	.286	67	210	37	60	16	4	8	28	4
86 AL	.250	50	164	16	41	7	1	2	15	3
87 AL	.293	144	542	93	159	38	2	28	83	10
88 AL	.212	73	264	40	56	14	0	14	35	4
89 AL	.286	157	622	83	178	34	9	14	87	7
90 AL	.273	158	607	85	166	44	2	14	74	32
91 NL	.300	134	470	69	141	22	3	19	75	31
Life	.278	794	2903	425	806	176	21	100	398	92
3 AVE	.285	150	566	79	162	33	5	16	79	23

KEN CAMINITI

Position: Third base
Team: Houston Astros
Born: April 21, 1963 Hanford, CA
Height: 6' **Weight:** 200 lbs.
Bats: both **Throws:** right
Acquired: Third-round pick in 6/84 free-agent draft

Player Summary	
Fantasy Value	$7 to $11
Card Value	3¢ to 5¢
Will	defend hot corner
Can't	hit for average
Expect	occasional homer
Don't Expect	frequent steal attempts

Houston thought so highly of Caminiti's glove work at third base that it shifted highly touted rookie Jeff Bagwell across the diamond during spring training last year. Although he has made more than 20 errors in each of the last three seasons, Caminiti gets to many balls other third basemen can't reach. He has good instincts, good reactions, and a strong throwing arm—though most of his errors come on throws. A .250 hitter at best, he has surprising power that may still be developing. His 1992 commons are not good buys since he has not racked up good career stats. Caminiti reached a career peak in home runs in '91. A switch-hitter with more righthanded power, he fans twice as often as he walks. He had a .383 slugging average and a .312 on-base percentage in '91. If he lifts his batting average, he could be a fantasy bargain at $10. Caminiti is an aggressive runner without much speed. His fielding secures his future.

Major League Batting Register

	BA	G	AB	R	H	2B	3B	HR	RBI	SB
87 NL	.246	63	203	10	50	7	1	3	23	0
88 NL	.181	30	83	5	15	2	0	1	7	0
89 NL	.255	161	585	71	149	31	3	10	72	4
90 NL	.242	153	541	52	131	20	2	4	51	9
91 NL	.253	152	574	65	145	30	3	13	80	4
Life	.247	559	1986	203	490	90	9	31	233	17
3 AVE	.250	155	567	63	142	27	3	9	68	6

CURRENT PLAYERS

CASEY CANDAELE

Position: Infield; outfield
Team: Houston Astros
Born: Jan. 12, 1961 Lompoc, CA
Height: 5'9" **Weight:** 165 lbs.
Bats: both **Throws:** right
Acquired: Traded from Expos for Mark Bailey, 7/88

Player Summary	
Fantasy Value	$3 to $5
Card Value	3¢ to 5¢
Will	play several spots well
Can't	show steady power
Expect	energetic play
Don't Expect	300 average

Candaele is one of baseball's smallest and most versatile players. Though he spends most of his time at second base, he has also played shortstop, third base, and the outfield. His ability to play several positions could pay off for budget-minded fantasy managers at $5 or less. He's a capable fielder who can turn the double-play, a hustler with good speed, and a pinch-hitter with a knack for producing in the clutch. He hits for a better average righthanded but has more power from the left side. Given a chance to play more for the rebuilding Astros of 1991, Candaele reached career highs in home runs and runs batted in. He also had a .362 slugging percentage and a .319 on-base average. He kept his batting average respectable, though not anywhere near his .286 career peak of 1990. His 1992 commons aren't advisable buys. His mentor was his mother, a former standout in the All-American Girls Baseball League.

Major League Batting Register

	BA	G	AB	R	H	2B	3B	HR	RBI	SB
86 NL	.231	30	104	9	24	4	1	0	6	3
87 NL	.272	138	449	62	122	23	4	1	23	7
88 NL	.170	57	147	11	25	8	1	0	5	1
90 NL	.286	130	262	30	75	8	6	3	22	7
91 NL	.262	151	461	44	121	20	7	4	50	9
Life	.258	506	1423	156	367	63	19	8	106	27
2 AVE	.271	141	362	37	98	14	7	4	36	8

JOHN CANDELARIA

Position: Pitcher
Team: Los Angeles Dodgers
Born: Nov. 6, 1953 Brooklyn, NY
Height: 6'6" **Weight:** 225 lbs.
Bats: both **Throws:** left
Acquired: Signed as a free agent, 3/91

Player Summary	
Fantasy Value	$2 to $4
Card Value	3¢ to 5¢
Will	provide firm relief
Can't	return as starter
Expect	heat and sinkers
Don't Expect	control lapses

Candelaria's experience as a premier starter helped him make the transition to middle relief, where he excelled in 1991. He got his chance with the Dodgers after a chance off-season meeting with manager Tommy Lasorda. Lasorda convinced general manager Fred Claire to sign Candelaria. He found plenty of work in the bullpen, and he averaged a strikeout per inning and yielded only three homers. Still, he is a $4 fantasy draft. Card collectors should ignore his 1992 commons. A control pitcher, he is a hard thrower whose best pitch is a sinking fastball that gets grounders.

Major League Pitching Register

	W	L	ERA	G	S	IP	H	ER	BB	SO
75 NL	8	6	2.76	18	0	120.2	95	37	36	95
76 NL	16	7	3.15	32	1	220.0	173	77	60	138
77 NL	20	5	2.34	33	0	230.2	197	60	50	133
78 NL	12	11	3.24	30	1	189.0	191	68	49	94
79 NL	14	9	3.22	33	0	207.0	201	74	41	101
80 NL	11	14	4.01	35	1	233.1	246	104	50	97
81 NL	2	2	3.54	6	0	40.2	42	16	11	14
82 NL	12	7	2.94	31	1	174.2	166	57	37	133
83 NL	15	8	3.23	33	0	197.2	191	71	45	157
84 NL	12	11	2.72	33	2	185.1	179	56	34	133
85 NL	2	4	3.64	37	9	54.1	57	22	14	47
85 AL	7	3	3.80	13	0	71.0	70	30	24	53
86 AL	10	2	2.55	16	0	91.2	68	26	26	81
87 AL	8	6	4.71	20	0	116.2	127	61	20	74
87 NL	2	0	5.84	3	0	12.1	17	8	3	10
88 AL	13	7	3.38	25	0	157.0	150	59	23	121
89 AL	3	3	5.14	10	0	49.0	49	28	12	37
89 NL	0	2	3.31	12	0	16.1	17	6	4	14
90 AL	7	6	3.95	47	5	79.2	87	73	20	63
91 NL	1	1	3.74	59	2	33.2	31	14	11	38
Life	175	114	3.30	526	23	2480.2	2354	909	570	1633
3 AVE	4	4	4.18	43	2	59.2	61	28	16	51

CURRENT PLAYERS

TOM CANDIOTTI

Position: Pitcher
Team: Los Angeles Dodgers
Born: Aug. 31, 1957 Walnut Creek, CA
Height: 6'2" **Weight:** 205 lbs.
Bats: right **Throws:** right
Acquired: Signed as a free agent 12/91

Player Summary	
Fantasy Value	$16 to $20
Card Value	3¢ to 5¢
Will	keep Dodgers in game
Can't	throw good heat
Expect	200 innings
Don't Expect	many physical woes

Candiotti could sue two clubs for nonsupport in 1991. After escaping from Cleveland, he came north convinced Toronto would hit behind him. He was wrong. For example, on August 8, the veteran knuckleballer tied a career high (and Blue Jays record) with 12 strikeouts and pitched seven shutout innings against the hard-hitting Tigers. The Jays, however, gave him nothing to work with and eventually lost 4-0. Candiotti baffles batters with three different types of knucklers (hard, medium, and slow) and often mixes in a curve. He has thrown sliders, fastballs, and cut fastballs in the past but now uses the knuckleball almost exclusively. Now with Los Angeles, Candiotti's stats should blossom, making him an $18 fantasy starter. His 1992 commons suffer from his lack of outstanding career stats. A good fielder, he keeps runners close.

Major League Pitching Register

	W	L	ERA	G	CG	IP	H	ER	BB	SO
83 AL	4	4	3.23	10	2	55.2	62	20	16	21
84 AL	2	2	5.29	8	0	32.1	38	19	10	23
86 AL	16	12	3.57	36	17	252.1	234	100	106	167
87 AL	7	18	4.78	32	7	201.2	193	107	93	111
88 AL	14	8	3.28	31	11	216.2	225	79	53	137
89 AL	13	10	3.10	31	4	206.0	188	71	55	124
90 AL	15	11	3.65	31	3	202.0	207	82	55	128
91 AL	13	13	2.65	34	6	238.0	202	70	73	167
Life	84	78	3.51	213	50	1404.2	1349	548	461	878
3 AVE	14	11	3.11	32	4	215.1	199	74	61	140

JOSE CANSECO

Position: Outfield
Team: Oakland Athletics
Born: July 2, 1964 Havana, Cuba
Height: 6'3" **Weight:** 230 lbs.
Bats: right **Throws:** right
Acquired: 15th-round pick in 6/82 free-agent draft

Player Summary	
Fantasy Value	$40 to $50
Card Value	15¢ to 25¢
Will	challenge for homer crown
Can't	avoid controversy
Expect	long home runs
Don't Expect	another 40-40 season

Although he strikes out often, Canseco is capable of hitting for both power and average. He has enormous strength, great bat speed, and the ability to handle off-speed pitches. A pull hitter who can also hit to the opposite field, Canseco is the only major leaguer to produce a 40-homer and 40-stolen base season. He earned MVP honors for that showing in 1988, two years after he was AL Rookie of the Year. Canseco has already enjoyed five 100-RBI campaigns and hit seven postseason homers. A 1989 ALCS shot at Toronto's SkyDome might have been his longest. His fantasy value is easily $40, probably more. He is a competent right fielder whose best asset is his strong arm. He sometimes struggles on balls hit over his head. He always compensates with his performance at bat, nevertheless. Canseco's 1992 cards are quarter investments. He's controversial and worth every penny.

Major League Batting Register

	BA	G	AB	R	H	2B	3B	HR	RBI	SB
85 AL	.302	29	96	16	29	3	0	5	13	1
86 AL	.240	157	600	85	144	29	1	33	117	15
87 AL	.257	159	630	81	162	35	3	31	113	15
88 AL	.307	158	610	120	187	34	0	42	124	40
89 AL	.269	65	227	40	61	9	1	17	57	6
90 AL	.274	131	481	83	132	14	2	37	101	19
91 AL	.266	154	572	115	152	32	1	44	122	26
Life	.270	853	3216	540	867	156	8	209	647	122
3 AVE	.270	117	427	79	115	18	1	33	93	17

CURRENT PLAYERS

CRIS CARPENTER

Position: Pitcher
Team: St. Louis Cardinals
Born: April 5, 1965 St. Augustine, FL
Height: 6'1" **Weight:** 185 lbs.
Bats: right **Throws:** right
Acquired: First-round pick in 6/87 free-agent draft

Player Summary	
Fantasy Value	$4 to $7
Card Value	3¢ to 5¢
Will	appear often
Can't	always fool hitters
Expect	good K-to-walk ratio
Don't Expect	return to rotation

After three seasons of shuttling between St. Louis and Triple-A Louisville, Carpenter finally made the major leagues to stay in 1991. Though he was used primarily as a starter in the past, he made his contribution strictly as a reliever. Deployed as one of several set-up men for closer Lee Smith, Carpenter won eight of his first 11 decisions. Joe Torre eventually called on Carpenter more than 50 times. Rival batters compiled a .220 batting average, a .365 slugging percentage, and a .278 on-base percentage against him in 1991. He finished 22 games. A former All-American from Georgia, he is a control pitcher who strikes out more than twice as many as he walks. In 1990, he led the Triple-A American Association with fewest walks per nine innings. The fortunes of relievers vary wildly each year. Don't go overboard during the fantasy draft—$7 is the limit. His 1992 commons aren't investments until he becomes a closer. Though he could start, Carpenter should remain a vital member of the pen.

Major League Pitching Register

	W	L	ERA	G	S	IP	H	ER	BB	SO
88 NL	2	3	4.72	8	0	47.2	56	25	9	24
89 NL	4	4	3.18	36	0	68.0	70	24	26	35
90 NL	0	0	4.50	4	0	8.0	5	4	2	6
91 NL	10	4	4.23	59	0	66.0	53	31	20	47
Life	16	11	3.99	107	0	189.2	184	84	57	112
2 AVE	7	4	3.69	48	0	67.0	62	28	23	41

MARK CARREON

Position: Outfield
Team: New York Mets
Born: July 9, 1963 Chicago, IL
Height: 6' **Weight:** 195 lbs.
Bats: right **Throws:** left
Acquired: Seventh-round pick in 6/81 free-agent draft

Player Summary	
Fantasy Value	$2 to $4
Card Value	3¢ to 5¢
Will	deliver long ball in clutch
Can't	provide solid defense
Expect	deployment as pinch-hitter
Don't Expect	average above .300

Before suffering a knee injury that shortened his successful 1990 season, Carreon was one of baseball's best pinch-hitters. Last April 27, he hit his seventh career pinch-homer to break the Mets' club mark previously shared by Rusty Staub and Ed Kranepool. Then Carreon fell on hard times and was not the equal of the player who hit 10 home runs in 188 at bats before injury intervened. The son of former big leaguer Camilo Carreon, Mark gets his cuts but also strikes out twice as much as he walks. After the April 27 homer, he hit only two more over the next four months. He had a .337 slugging percentage and a .291 on-base average in 1991. Carreon could not redeem himself with his outfield play, because he plays all three positions poorly. Next year's expansion could salvage his major league career. His 1992 commons are not buys until he wins a starting job.

Major League Batting Register

	BA	G	AB	R	H	2B	3B	HR	RBI	SB
87 NL	.250	9	12	0	3	0	0	0	1	0
88 NL	.556	7	9	5	5	2	0	1	1	0
89 NL	.308	68	133	20	41	6	0	6	16	2
90 NL	.250	82	188	30	47	12	0	10	26	1
91 NL	.260	106	254	18	66	6	0	4	21	2
Life	.272	272	596	73	162	26	0	21	65	5
2 AVE	.256	94	221	24	57	9	0	7	24	2

CURRENT PLAYERS

GARY CARTER

Position: Catcher
Team: Montreal Expos
Born: April 8, 1954 Culver City, CA
Height: 6'2" **Weight:** 214 lbs.
Bats: right **Throws:** right
Acquired: Signed as a free agent, 11/91

Player Summary	
Fantasy Value	$3 to $5
Card Value	5¢ to 10¢
Will	serve as caddy
Can't	throw like he used to
Expect	occasional long ball
Don't Expect	good speed

Carter is back with the Expos. He did an admirable job as Mike Scioscia's caddy in 1991. When Scioscia was disabled July 5, Carter started 18 of the next 19 games and hit .298 with nine RBI. He also played well defensively—reminding observers that he has won three Gold Gloves. The prime factor in his comeback was a diet-and-exercise regimen that caused him to drop 15 pounds. He is a $4 fantasy catcher. An 11-time All-Star, he has caught more games than anyone in NL history. He's also one of four receivers with 2,000 hits, 1,000 runs, 1,000 RBI, and 300 homers. His 1992 cards are worth up to a dime.

Major League Batting Register

	BA	G	AB	R	H	2B	3B	HR	RBI	SB
74 NL	.407	9	27	5	11	0	1	1	6	2
75 NL	.270	144	503	58	136	20	1	17	68	5
76 NL	.219	91	311	31	68	8	1	6	38	0
77 NL	.284	154	522	86	148	29	2	31	84	5
78 NL	.255	157	533	76	136	27	1	20	72	10
79 NL	.283	141	505	74	143	26	5	22	75	3
80 NL	.264	154	549	76	145	25	5	29	101	3
81 NL	.251	100	374	48	94	20	2	16	68	1
82 NL	.293	154	557	91	163	32	1	29	97	2
83 NL	.270	145	541	63	146	37	3	17	79	1
84 NL	.294	159	596	75	175	32	1	27	106	2
85 NL	.281	149	555	83	156	17	1	32	100	1
86 NL	.255	132	490	81	125	14	2	24	105	1
87 NL	.235	139	523	55	123	18	2	20	83	0
88 NL	.242	130	455	39	110	16	2	11	46	0
89 NL	.183	50	153	14	28	8	0	2	15	0
90 NL	.254	92	244	24	62	10	0	9	27	1
91 NL	.246	101	248	22	61	14	0	6	26	2
Life	.264	2201	7686	1001	2030	353	30	319	1196	39
3 AVE	.234	81	215	20	50	11	0	6	23	1

JOE CARTER

Position: Outfield
Team: Toronto Blue Jays
Born: March 7, 1960 Oklahoma City, OK
Height: 6'3" **Weight:** 215 lbs.
Bats: right **Throws:** right
Acquired: Traded from Padres with Roberto Alomar for Fred McGriff and Tony Fernandez, 12/90

Player Summary	
Fantasy Value	$42 to $47
Card Value	10¢ to 15¢
Will	be top RBI producer
Can't	hit for high average
Expect	many homers at home
Don't Expect	strong outfield throws

Before he made the 1991 All-Star team, Carter was one of baseball's most anonymous stars. He had been traded twice and ignored by fans picking the All-Star lineups and managers picking the reserves. That was unfair, since Carter was not only one of the game's top run producers but one of its most durable players. He took a 426-game playing streak into the '91 All-Star Game. A member of the 30-30 club, he was AL Player of the Month last May. An impatient hitter, Carter should walk more and strike out less, but the results are pretty impressive when he connects. He has good power to all fields. Plus, the SkyDome is a paradise for power-hitters. His long-ball ability will make a fantasy team rich, even for more than $40. For up to 15 cents, his 1992 cards will pick up value.

Major League Batting Register

	BA	G	AB	R	H	2B	3B	HR	RBI	SB
83 NL	.176	23	51	6	9	1	1	0	1	1
84 AL	.275	66	244	32	67	6	1	13	41	2
85 AL	.262	143	489	64	128	27	0	15	59	24
86 AL	.302	162	663	108	200	36	9	29	121	29
87 AL	.264	149	588	83	155	27	2	32	106	31
88 AL	.271	157	621	85	168	36	6	27	98	27
89 AL	.243	162	651	84	158	32	4	35	105	13
90 NL	.232	162	634	79	147	27	1	24	115	22
91 AL	.273	162	638	89	174	42	3	33	108	20
Life	.263	1186	4579	630	1206	234	27	208	754	169
3 AVE	.249	162	641	84	160	34	3	31	109	18

CURRENT PLAYERS

FRANK CASTILLO

Position: Pitcher
Team: Chicago Cubs
Born: April 1, 1969 El Paso, TX
Height: 6'1" **Weight:** 180 lbs.
Bats: right **Throws:** right
Acquired: Sixth-round pick in 6/87 free-agent draft

Player Summary	
Fantasy Value	$3 to $5
Card Value	15¢ to 20¢
Will	take regular turn
Can't	throw blazing fastball
Expect	diet of off-speed pitches
Don't Expect	deployment in bullpen

Castillo pitched eight strong innings in his big league bow last June 27 but lost a 4-3 decision. After holding Pittsburgh scoreless into the ninth, he yielded two hits, then watched the Cub bullpen blow the game. He started the 1991 season in Double-A, then made four starts at Triple-A Iowa before joining the Cubs as a roster replacement for injured veteran Danny Jackson. Castillo, who had an excellent ratio of strikeouts to walks in the minors, continued his strong showing in Chicago. The Cubs had injuries to starters Jackson, Mike Harkey, and Rick Sutcliffe, plus the unexpected slump of Shawn Boskie. If Castillo has a spot in the Chicago rotation coming out of Arizona, you should draft him for about $4. If he finds a spot in the rotation, card investors should pick up his rookie 1992 cards for less than 20 cents. Opponents compiled a .252 batting average, a .351 slugging percentage, and a .304 on-base average against him in 1991. In 1990, Castillo had a 6-6 record, 112 strikeouts, and only 27 walks in 111 innings at Double-A Charlotte.

Major League Pitching Register

	W	L	ERA	G	CG	IP	H	ER	BB	SO
91 NL	6	7	4.35	18	4	111.2	107	54	33	73
Life	6	7	4.35	18	4	111.2	107	54	33	73

RICK CERONE

Position: Catcher
Team: New York Mets
Born: May 19, 1954 Newark, NJ
Height: 5'11" **Weight:** 195 lbs.
Bats: right **Throws:** right
Acquired: Signed as a free agent, 1/91

Player Summary	
Fantasy Value	$1 to $2
Card Value	3¢ to 5¢
Will	be solid backup
Can't	hit long ball
Expect	clutch pinch-hits
Don't Expect	250-plus average

Veteran Cerone was one of the Mets' most pleasant surprises in 1991. After opening the season as the third-stringer behind Mackey Sasser and Charlie O'Brien, Cerone commanded more playing time with superior production. He had a .270-plus batting average all season. The former Seton Hall standout, who broke into the majors with the 1976 Indians, has only had two seasons as a regular. When he makes contact, he goes with the pitch but seldom hits homers. He is a $1 catcher. Cerone is a competent receiver who can still nail base-stealers. His 1992 commons are not wise purchases.

Major League Batting Register

	BA	G	AB	R	H	2B	3B	HR	RBI	SB
75 AL	.250	7	12	1	3	1	0	0	0	0
76 AL	.125	7	16	1	2	0	0	0	1	0
77 AL	.200	31	100	7	20	4	0	1	10	0
78 AL	.223	88	282	25	63	8	2	3	20	0
79 AL	.239	136	469	47	112	27	4	7	61	1
80 AL	.277	147	519	70	144	30	4	14	85	1
81 AL	.244	71	234	23	57	13	2	2	21	0
82 AL	.227	89	300	29	68	10	0	5	28	0
83 AL	.220	80	246	18	54	7	0	2	22	0
84 AL	.208	38	120	8	25	3	0	2	13	1
85 NL	.216	96	282	15	61	9	0	3	25	0
86 AL	.259	68	216	22	56	14	0	4	18	1
87 AL	.243	113	284	28	69	12	1	4	23	0
88 AL	.269	84	264	31	71	13	1	3	27	0
89 AL	.243	102	296	28	72	16	1	4	48	0
90 AL	.302	49	139	12	42	6	0	2	11	0
91 NL	.273	90	227	18	62	13	0	2	16	1
Life	.245	1296	4006	383	981	186	15	58	429	5
2 AVE	.256	96	262	23	67	15	1	3	32	1

CURRENT PLAYERS

JOHN CERUTTI

Position: Pitcher
Team: Detroit Tigers
Born: April 28, 1960 Albany, NY
Height: 6'2" **Weight:** 200 lbs.
Bats: left **Throws:** left
Acquired: Signed as a free agent, 1/91

Player Summary	
Fantasy Value	$1 to $2
Card Value	3¢ to 5¢
Will	get another shot
Can't	recapture old form
Expect	season on brink
Don't Expect	wins in double figures

Although he twice won 11 games in a season as a starter for the Blue Jays, Cerutti was unsuccessful in his efforts to help the pitching-starved Tigers in 1991. Used as both a starter and reliever, he lost a lot more than he won and had a high ERA. His problem was control. He notched more walks than strikeouts. That was unusual for the former Amherst star, who had previously been known as a control pitcher. Opponents compiled a .276 batting average, a .412 slugging percentage, and a .348 on-base average in 1991. Don't gamble more than $2 on his comeback in the fantasy draft. Cerutti's repertoire includes a sinking fastball, curveball, and slider—none of them thrown very hard. When the sinker sinks, he gets many ground balls—an asset in a home run hitter's park. His 1992 commons will remain commons. Cerutti's career has come to a crossroads but he'll get another chance because he is lefthanded.

Major League Pitching Register

	W	L	ERA	G	S	IP	H	ER	BB	SO
85 AL	0	2	5.40	4	0	6.2	10	4	4	5
86 AL	9	4	4.15	34	1	145.1	150	67	47	89
87 AL	11	4	4.40	44	0	151.1	144	74	59	92
88 AL	6	7	3.13	46	1	123.2	120	43	42	65
89 AL	11	11	3.07	33	0	205.1	214	70	53	69
90 AL	9	9	4.76	30	0	140.0	162	74	49	49
91 AL	3	6	4.57	38	2	88.2	94	45	37	29
Life	49	43	3.94	229	4	861.0	894	377	291	398
3 AVE	8	9	3.92	34	1	144.1	157	63	46	49

WES CHAMBERLAIN

Position: Outfield
Team: Philadelphia Phillies
Born: April 13, 1966 Chicago, IL
Height: 6'2" **Weight:** 210 lbs.
Bats: right **Throws:** right
Acquired: Traded from Pirates with Julio Peguero and Tony Longmire for Carmelo Martinez, 8/90

Player Summary	
Fantasy Value	$13 to $17
Card Value	15¢ to 20¢
Will	hit for power
Can't	steal many bases
Expect	continued improvement
Don't Expect	more trips to minors

When he's hot, he's hot: Chamberlain hit .478 (11-for-23) with three homers, six runs scored, and 10 RBI to win NL Player of the Week honors in August last year. He won Philadelphia's left field job after Lenny Dykstra was sidelined by a May 6 car crash. Left fielder Von Hayes shifted to center, creating the opening. Though Chamberlain is sometimes accused of being a hot dog because of his wiggling gyrations at the plate, he is actually a hustling player who is just beginning to tap his potential as a power-hitter. He had a .399 slugging percentage and a .300 on-base average in 1991. You may be able to steal him in fantasy auctions for $20 or less. A capable defensive outfielder, he'll dive for sinking liners or crash into fences if necessary. Chamberlain was a Double-A Eastern League MVP in 1989, when he hit .306 with 21 homers and 87 RBI. At Triple-A Buffalo in 1990, he hit .250 with six homers and 52 RBI. His second-year 1992 cards offer hope for rapid advancement at prices less than 20 cents.

Major League Batting Register

	BA	G	AB	R	H	2B	3B	HR	RBI	SB
90 NL	.283	18	46	9	13	3	0	2	4	4
91 NL	.240	101	383	51	92	16	3	13	50	9
Life	.245	119	429	60	105	19	3	15	54	13

CURRENT PLAYERS

NORM CHARLTON

Position: Pitcher
Team: Cincinnati Reds
Born: Jan. 6, 1963 Fort Polk, LA
Height: 6'3" **Weight:** 195 lbs.
Bats: both **Throws:** left
Acquired: Traded from Expos with Tim Barker for Wayne Krenchicki, 3/86

Player Summary
Fantasy Value ....$5 to $7
Card Value ....3¢ to 5¢
Will ....be top reliever
Can't ....avoid wildness
Expect........................reliance on split-finger
Don't Expect ....job as top closer

Charlton has been successful as both a starter and a reliever for the Reds. After starting the 1990 season as a member of the Nasty Boys bullpen that propelled the Reds to the World Championship, he finished the year in the rotation. He returned to relief in 1991, however, to ease the strain on his left shoulder. The southpaw spent two stints on the disabled list with shoulder tendinitis in '91. Opponents compiled a .236 batting average, a .336 slugging percentage, and a .306 on-base average against him in 1991. As a middle man in 1992, his fantasy value will plunge to $7. Charlton mixes his fastball, curveball, and split-fingered fastball well but sometimes falls victim to wildness. He's a good fielder with an average pickoff move. He rarely helps himself at bat. If he steers clear of shoulder woes, Charlton could continue as one of the NL's better lefthanded relievers. His 1992 cards will not be lucrative until he becomes a starter or a closer.

Major League Pitching Register

	W	L	ERA	G	S	IP	H	ER	BB	SO
88 NL	4	5	3.96	10	0	61.1	60	27	20	39
89 NL	8	3	2.93	69	0	95.1	67	31	40	98
90 NL	12	9	2.74	56	2	154.1	131	47	70	117
91 NL	3	5	2.91	39	1	108.1	92	35	34	77
Life	27	22	3.00	174	3	419.1	350	140	164	331
3 AVE	8	6	2.84	55	1	119.1	97	38	48	97

STEVE CHITREN

Position: Pitcher
Team: Oakland Athletics
Born: June 8, 1967 Tokyo, Japan
Height: 6' **Weight:** 180 lbs.
Bats: right **Throws:** right
Acquired: Sixth-round choice in 6/89 free-agent draft

Player Summary
Fantasy Value ....$1 to $2
Card Value ....8¢ to 12¢
Will ....fan a hitter a frame
Can't..............................become a starter
Expect......................................control lapses
Don't Expect ....promotion to closer

Although he was groomed as a closer in the minor leagues, Chitren was not about to displace Dennis Eckersley with the Oakland Athletics. After Chitren posted a 2-4 record, 1.68 ERA, 27 saves, and 61 strikeouts in 53⅔ innings at Double-A Huntsville in 1990, Chitren advanced to the Athletics as a set-up man. He handled the job well in '91, although his ERA was a little higher than acceptable. Opponents compiled a .258 batting average, a .432 slugging percentage, and a .356 on-base percentage against him in 1991. He also finished 20 games. Chitren, whose curve is better than his fastball, fanned nearly a batter per inning but had a tendency to issue too many free passes—even though he had previously established a reputation for good location. In 1989 at Class-A Madison, he had seven saves and two wins, with 17 Ks and four bases on balls in 22⅔ innings. Should Chitren recapture his former control, he will be used in more crucial roles—possibly closing on occasion. He was on the Stanford squad that won back-to-back College World Series in 1987 and '88.

Major League Pitching Register

	W	L	ERA	G	S	IP	H	ER	BB	SO
90 AL	1	0	1.02	8	0	17.2	7	2	4	19
91 AL	1	4	4.33	56	4	60.1	59	29	32	47
Life	2	4	3.58	64	4	78.0	66	31	36	66

CURRENT PLAYERS

JACK CLARK

Position: Designated hitter; first base
Team: Boston Red Sox
Born: Nov. 10, 1955 New Brighton, PA
Height: 6'3" **Weight:** 205 lbs.
Bats: right **Throws:** right
Acquired: Signed as a free agent, 12/90

Player Summary	
Fantasy Value	$15 to $20
Card Value	5¢ to 7¢
Will	find Fenway friendly
Can't	run well
Expect	RBI production
Don't Expect	stints in field

After hitting a grand slam Opening Day, Clark got off to a slow start in his first season with the Red Sox in 1991. He recaptured his stroke in midseason, however. Batting coach Richie Hebner explained that Clark had been pulling his shoulder toward the third base dugout instead of keeping it in. That mechanical flaw was short-circuiting his natural power, which was perfectly matched with the proximity to home plate of Fenway's left field wall. He is one of baseball's most notorious streak hitters. Clark's late-season injury might worry some fantasy managers for 1992, but his power is worth $15. His 1992 cards are so-so at a nickel each.

Major League Batting Register

	BA	G	AB	R	H	2B	3B	HR	RBI	SB
75 NL	.235	8	17	3	4	0	0	0	2	1
76 NL	.225	26	102	14	23	6	2	2	10	6
77 NL	.252	136	413	64	104	17	4	13	51	12
78 NL	.306	156	592	90	181	46	8	25	98	15
79 NL	.273	143	527	84	144	25	2	26	86	11
80 NL	.284	127	437	77	124	20	8	22	82	2
81 NL	.268	99	385	60	103	19	2	17	53	1
82 NL	.274	157	563	90	154	30	3	27	103	6
83 NL	.268	135	492	82	132	25	0	20	66	5
84 NL	.320	57	203	33	65	9	1	11	44	1
85 NL	.281	126	442	71	124	26	3	22	87	1
86 NL	.237	65	232	34	55	12	2	9	23	1
87 NL	.286	131	419	93	120	23	1	35	106	1
88 AL	.242	150	496	81	120	14	0	27	93	3
89 NL	.242	142	455	76	110	19	1	26	94	6
90 NL	.266	115	334	59	89	12	1	25	62	4
91 AL	.249	140	481	75	120	18	1	28	87	0
Life	.269	1913	6590	1086	1772	321	39	335	1147	76
3 AVE	.251	132	423	70	106	16	1	26	81	3

JERALD CLARK

Position: Outfield
Team: San Diego Padres
Born: Aug. 10, 1963 Crockett, TX
Height: 6'4" **Weight:** 190 lbs.
Bats: right **Throws:** right
Acquired: 12th-round pick in 6/85 free-agent draft

Player Summary	
Fantasy Value	$6 to $9
Card Value	5¢ to 7¢
Will	produce some power
Can't	find .300 stroke
Expect	erratic outfield play
Don't Expect	many attempts to steal

In seven minor league seasons, Clark produced seven .300 campaigns—all with good power. But he's struggled to push his career average above .250 in the majors. Will he ever hit as well in the majors as he did in the minors? A strapping slugger who gave San Diego hope when he hammered two homers in a game against Los Angeles on the last weekend of the 1990 campaign, Clark again failed to live up to his billing in 1991. He is not a patient hitter and strikes out almost three times more than he walks. He had a .352 slugging percentage and a .295 on-base average in '91. His sporadic power could benefit fantasy leaguers for as little as $8. The Padres could find more work for him in '92. His affordable 1992 cards could be sleepers for a nickel each. Perhaps the problem is the lack of the designated hitter rule in the National League. He is a liability in left field and may be worried about making a critical error.

Major League Batting Register

	BA	G	AB	R	H	2B	3B	HR	RBI	SB
88 NL	.200	6	15	0	3	1	0	0	3	0
89 NL	.195	17	41	5	8	2	0	1	7	0
90 NL	.267	53	101	12	27	4	1	5	11	0
91 NL	.228	118	369	26	84	16	0	10	47	2
Life	.232	194	526	43	122	23	1	16	68	2

CURRENT PLAYERS

WILL CLARK

Position: First base
Team: San Francisco Giants
Born: March 13, 1964 New Orleans, LA
Height: 6'1" **Weight:** 190 lbs.
Bats: left **Throws:** left
Acquired: First-round pick in 6/85 free-agent draft

Player Summary	
Fantasy Value	$45 to $50
Card Value	15¢ to 25¢
Will	hit in the clutch
Can't	steal bases
Expect	high RBI total
Don't Expect	home run crown

Many baseball insiders regard Clark as the National League's top all-around player. A proven hitter who delivers both power and average, he is also an outstanding defensive first baseman with good hands, range, and a strong throwing arm. He handles lefthanded pitchers with little difficulty. He homered in his first big league at bat in 1986 against Nolan Ryan, and Clark's offense never stopped. The four-time All-Star was Championship Series MVP in 1989 with a .650 batting average and 1.200 slugging percentage. If there is a guaranteed fantasy selection, select "The Thrill." Four years after earning a berth on the 1984 Olympic team, Clark led the NL in RBI. He remains a constant contender for that title. He benefits by batting third in a lineup anchored by Kevin Mitchell and Matt Williams—thus getting a steady fastball diet. Clark's 1992 cards are bargains for a quarter. His lone weakness is a lack of speed.

Major League Batting Register

	BA	G	AB	R	H	2B	3B	HR	RBI	SB
86 NL	.287	111	408	66	117	27	2	11	41	4
87 NL	.308	150	529	89	163	29	5	35	91	5
88 NL	.282	162	575	102	162	31	6	29	109	9
89 NL	.333	159	588	104	196	38	9	23	111	8
90 NL	.295	154	600	91	177	25	5	19	95	8
91 NL	.301	148	565	84	170	32	7	29	116	4
Life	.302	884	3265	536	985	182	34	146	563	38
3 AVE	.310	154	584	93	181	32	7	24	107	7

ROGER CLEMENS

Position: Pitcher
Team: Boston Red Sox
Born: Aug. 4, 1962 Dayton, OH
Height: 6'4" **Weight:** 220 lbs.
Bats: right **Throws:** right
Acquired: First-round pick in 6/83 free-agent draft

Player Summary	
Fantasy Value	$40 to $45
Card Value	15¢ to 25¢
Will	vie for Cy Young
Can't	avoid controversy
Expect	lofty K totals
Don't Expect	long losing spells

Clemens broke into the majors in 1984 and has dominated hitters since with an explosive fastball, slider, curve, and forkball. He has won Cy Young Awards in 1986, '87, and '91, just missed a fourth, and earned MVP honors in '86. Clemens, who works hitters up-and-down rather than in-and-out, depends upon a conditioning regimen that includes long-distance running. He has led the AL in wins, ERA, completions, and shutouts several times each, has fanned a record 20 hitters in a nine-inning game, and has retired nine NL hitters in a three-inning All-Star start. He set a team record for strikeouts in a season. He is worth $40 or more in fantasy drafts. Clemens has been dogged by shoulder problems and controversies, including a 1990 playoffs outburst that cost him a fine and suspension. Buy his 1992 cards at prices under a quarter.

Major League Pitching Register

	W	L	ERA	G	CG	IP	H	ER	BB	SO
84 AL	9	4	4.32	21	5	133.1	146	64	29	126
85 AL	7	5	3.29	15	3	98.1	83	36	37	74
86 AL	24	4	2.48	33	10	254.0	179	70	67	238
87 AL	20	9	2.97	36	18	281.2	248	93	83	256
88 AL	18	12	2.93	35	14	264.0	217	86	62	291
89 AL	17	11	3.13	35	8	253.1	215	88	93	230
90 AL	21	6	1.93	31	7	228.1	193	49	54	209
91 AL	18	10	2.62	35	13	271.1	219	79	65	241
Life	134	61	2.85	241	78	1784.1	1500	565	490	1665
3 AVE	19	9	2.58	34	9	251.1	209	72	71	227

CURRENT PLAYERS

ALEX COLE

Position: Outfield
Team: Cleveland Indians
Born: August 17, 1965 Fayetteville, NC
Height: 6'2" **Weight:** 175 lbs.
Bats: left **Throws:** left
Acquired: Traded from Padres for Tom Lampkin, 6/90

Player Summary
Fantasy Value ....$7 to $10
Card Value.......................................3¢ to 5¢
Will..................................pose threat to steal
Can't ....hit long ball
Expect ....great range
Don't Expect ....regular role

Cole hopes to steal 100 bases some day. He has the speed, but his bat could stand in the way. Though he hit .300 with 40 steals in 63 games after Cleveland pilfered him from the Padres in 1990, he spent much of 1991 wondering why his success rate was dropping so dramatically, down to about 60 percent. He was caught stealing 17 times in '91. His batting average lacked the punch provided by newcomer Glenallen Hill and he wound up sitting on the bench. Nor can Cole match Hill on defense. Cole is an iffy acquisition for fantasy leaguers for more than $8. A former Cardinal farmhand discarded by Whitey Herzog, Cole has great range but can't always catch or throw it. An opposite-field hitter, he would be more effective if he bunted more. Rod Carew's spring training sessions didn't help much last year. Don't invest in his 1992 commons. Cole could be a regular only for a club willing to sacrifice power for speed. In 1991, he had a .354 slugging percentage and a .386 on-base average.

Major League Batting Register

	BA	G	AB	R	H	2B	3B	HR	RBI	SB
90 AL	.300	63	227	43	68	5	4	0	13	40
91 AL	.295	122	387	58	114	17	3	0	21	27
Life	.296	185	614	101	182	22	7	0	34	67
2 AVE	.296	93	307	51	91	11	4	0	17	34

VINCE COLEMAN

Position: Outfield
Team: New York Mets
Born: September 22, 1961 Jacksonville, FL
Height: 6' **Weight:** 170 lbs.
Bats: both **Throws:** right
Acquired: Signed as a free agent, 12/90

Player Summary
Fantasy Value ....$35 to $40
Card Value......................................5¢ to 10¢
Will...get 100 steals
Can't ....hit homers
Expect ....high strikeout total
Don't Expect..........................great defense

Coleman could steal 200 bases in a season if he could reach base more often. Though he is a natural righthanded batter, he has a better lefthanded swing, but he has a tendency to strike out too frequently. He has little power and would be more effective if he showed more patience at the plate. A walk to Vince Coleman is like a double to anyone else. He can virtually steal at will. He is the only player to reach 100 steals in each of his first three seasons. He also holds the major league record for most successive steals without getting caught, 50 straight from 1988 to '89. He had a hamstring problem in 1991. He is a $35-plus fantasy player. He needs to retake the mantle as the NL's best stolen-base threat for his 1992 cards to rise above their dime ceiling. Defensively, Coleman reaches balls others can't but misjudges balls often and has a below-average arm.

Major League Batting Register

	BA	G	AB	R	H	2B	3B	HR	RBI	SB
85 NL	.267	151	636	107	170	20	10	1	40	110
86 NL	.232	154	600	94	139	13	8	0	29	107
87 NL	.289	151	623	121	180	14	10	3	43	109
88 NL	.260	153	616	77	160	20	10	3	38	81
89 NL	.254	145	563	94	143	21	9	2	28	65
90 NL	.292	124	497	73	145	18	9	6	39	77
91 NL	.255	72	278	45	71	7	5	1	17	37
Life	.264	950	3813	611	1008	113	61	16	234	586
3 AVE	.268	114	446	71	120	15	8	3	28	60

CURRENT PLAYERS

PAT COMBS

Position: Pitcher
Team: Philadelphia Phillies
Born: October 29, 1966 Newport, RI
Height: 6'4" **Weight:** 200 lbs.
Bats: left **Throws:** left
Acquired: First-round pick in 6/88 free-agent draft

Player Summary	
Fantasy Value	$4 to $6
Card Value	4¢ to 6¢
Will	return to rotation
Can't	always throw strikes
Expect	12 wins if healthy
Don't Expect	complete games

The promise of his 1990 rookie season evaporated quickly for Combs. He missed most of 1991 after undergoing surgery to remove a bone spur from his pitching elbow. The former Baylor University star had spent less than a year in the minor leagues before joining the Phillies late in the 1989 campaign. Because he had pitched less than 50 innings, his rookie status remained intact. In his first full season, Combs split 20 decisions. In 1991, batters compiled a .254 batting average, a .389 slugging percentage, and a .365 on-base average against him. When he's healthy, he can mix a fastball, cut fastball, curve, slider, and changeup. He's a competent hitter and fielder who usually keeps runners close. If Combs recovers from the elbow and shoulder problems that plagued him last year, he has a bright future ahead as a starting pitcher. Don't bet more than $6 at the fantasy draft that he will make a full recovery. If you are a gambler, you might want to sink a few dollars into his 1992 commons.

Major League Pitching Register

	W	L	ERA	G	CG	IP	H	ER	BB	SO
89 NL	4	0	2.09	6	1	38.2	36	9	6	30
90 NL	10	10	4.07	32	3	183.1	179	83	86	108
91 NL	2	6	4.90	14	1	64.1	64	35	43	41
Life	16	16	3.99	52	5	286.1	279	127	135	179
2 AVE	6	8	4.29	23	2	124.1	122	59	65	75

DAVID CONE

Position: Pitcher
Team: New York Mets
Born: January 2, 1963 Kansas City, MO
Height: 6'1" **Weight:** 190 lbs.
Bats: left **Throws:** right
Acquired: Traded from Royals with Chris Jelic for Ed Hearn, Mauro Gozzo, and Rick Anderson, 3/87

Player Summary	
Fantasy Value	$14 to $18
Card Value	5¢ to 10¢
Will	win often
Can't	avoid slumps
Expect	high K totals
Don't Expect	bullpen duty

One year Cone is a fastball pitcher, the next year he depends upon the breaking ball. He throws a fastball, split-fingered fastball, slider, and curve—and he throws everything hard. He led the majors with 233 strikeouts in 1990. He posted a club-record .870 winning percentage in 1988, going 20-3. He finished behind Orel Hershiser and Danny Jackson in the NL's Cy Young Award voting that year. Cone is a durable pitcher who is usually among the league leaders in innings pitched and complete games. He tied Tom Seaver and Steve Carlton for most Ks (19) in a nine-inning NL game on October 6, 1991. Cone is a good fantasy option for $15 or so. His 1992 cards are risky investments at their current nickel-plus prices. He helps himself as a hitter, and he is a good fielder. His fatal flaw is an inability to keep base-runners close. Many insiders rate Cone ahead of Doc Gooden as New York's top pitcher.

Major League Pitching Register

	W	L	ERA	G	CG	IP	H	ER	BB	SO
86 AL	0	0	5.56	11	0	22.2	29	14	13	21
87 NL	5	6	3.71	21	1	99.1	87	41	44	68
88 NL	20	3	2.22	35	8	231.1	178	57	80	213
89 NL	14	8	3.52	34	7	219.2	183	86	74	190
90 NL	14	10	3.23	31	6	211.2	177	76	65	233
91 NL	14	14	3.29	34	5	232.2	204	85	73	241
Life	67	41	3.18	166	27	1017.1	858	359	349	966
3 AVE	14	11	3.35	33	6	221.2	188	82	71	221

CURRENT PLAYERS

SCOTT COOLBAUGH

Position: Third base
Team: San Diego Padres
Born: June 13, 1966 Binghamton, NY
Height: 5'11" **Weight:** 185 lbs.
Bats: right **Throws:** right
Acquired: Traded from Rangers for Mark Parent, 12/90

Player Summary
Fantasy Value ....$1 to $2
Card Value ....3¢ to 5¢
Will ....hit the long ball
Can't ....provide much speed
Expect ....good defensive performance
Don't Expect ....average above .270

San Diego traded for Jack Howell in 1991 only after Coolbaugh failed to realize his potential as a power-hitting third baseman. Coolbaugh had a .306 slugging average and a .294 on-base average in 1991. He had hit 18 home runs for Triple-A Oklahoma City and two more for Texas in 1989, the best of his four previous seasons as a pro. Unlike most other sluggers, he generally makes good contact and is selective at the plate. The former University of Texas MVP is also a capable fielder with a strong arm. He turned more double-plays than any Triple-A American Association third baseman in '89. Coolbaugh doesn't run well but few third basemen do. He may be ready to reclaim a major league berth. At this point in his career, he is a $2 fantasy corner man. His 1992 commons will not inflate in value unless he wins a full-time starting job soon. Though he might platoon with a lefthanded hitter, Coolbaugh could claim a full-time position with 1993 expansion.

Major League Batting Register

	BA	G	AB	R	H	2B	3B	HR	RBI	SB
89 AL	.275	25	51	7	14	1	0	2	7	0
90 AL	.200	67	180	21	36	6	0	2	13	1
91 NL	.217	60	180	12	39	8	1	2	15	0
Life	.217	152	411	40	89	15	1	6	35	1
2 AVE	.208	64	180	17	38	7	1	2	14	1

JOEY CORA

Position: Second base
Team: Chicago White Sox
Born: May 14, 1965 Caguas, Puerto Rico
Height: 5'8" **Weight:** 150 lbs.
Bats: both **Throws:** right
Acquired: Traded from Padres with Kevin Garner and Warren Newson for Adam Peterson and Steve Rosenberg, 3/91

Player Summary
Fantasy Value ....$2 to $4
Card Value ....3¢ to 5¢
Will ....make good contact
Can't ....hit the long ball
Expect ....better use of speed
Don't Expect ....return to utility role

Before the White Sox gave him a chance in 1991, Cora had never spent the month of August in the major leagues. One of seven Chicago players under 5'9", he succeeded slumping veteran Scott Fletcher as the regular second baseman. A former Vanderbilt University star, Cora teamed with Ozzie Guillen to give the White Sox strong defense in the middle of the infield. Cora hit well enough to hold the job. He had a .276 slugging percentage and a .313 on-base average in 1991. That wasn't surprising for a player who had a 37-game hitting streak on the Triple-A level in 1989. As he learns AL pitchers, Cora could have a batting average above .300, something he did four times in the minors. Bunting more often would help, because Cora has exceptional speed. His 40 steals in 1989 led the Triple-A Pacific Coast League. He offers fantasy teams many steals at little cost—$4 at most. Cora also had been tried at shortstop and third base during three stints with the Padres.

Major League Batting Register

	BA	G	AB	R	H	2B	3B	HR	RBI	SB
87 NL	.237	77	241	23	57	7	2	0	13	15
89 NL	.316	12	19	5	6	1	0	0	1	1
90 NL	.270	51	100	12	27	3	0	0	2	8
91 AL	.241	100	228	37	55	2	3	0	18	11
Life	.247	240	588	77	145	13	5	0	34	35

CURRENT PLAYERS

HENRY COTTO

Position: Outfield
Team: Seattle Mariners
Born: January 5, 1961 Bronx, NY
Height: 6'2" **Weight:** 178 lbs.
Bats: right **Throws:** right
Acquired: Traded from Yankees with Steve Trout for Lee Guetterman, Clay Parker, and Wade Taylor, 12/87

Player Summary	
Fantasy Value	$3 to $5
Card Value	3¢ to 5¢
Will	add speed and defense
Can't	win regular job
Expect	clutch pinch-hits
Don't Expect	great run production

Cotto had a good-news, bad-news season in 1991. Shortly after AL managers named him the league's third best baserunner, Cotto suffered a torn right rotator cuff that needed surgical repair, missing the final six weeks of the campaign. A superb No. 4 outfielder, he had been leading the league in pinch-hitting, with a 10-for-15 performance, when he went down. Don't overlook his fantasy value, which is good up to $5. He was also hitting over .300 for the first time—even though he's an impatient hitter who fans twice as often as he walks. Though he doesn't have a strong arm, Cotto plays all three outfield positions well. He also can easily steal more than 20 bases a year. He could play regularly for several major league clubs, but has never had the chance to play in more than 133 games. Ignore his 1992 commons.

Major League Batting Register

	BA	G	AB	R	H	2B	3B	HR	RBI	SB
84 NL	.274	105	146	24	40	5	0	0	8	9
85 AL	.304	34	56	4	17	1	0	1	6	1
86 AL	.213	35	80	11	17	3	0	1	6	3
87 AL	.235	68	149	21	35	10	0	5	20	4
88 AL	.259	133	386	50	100	18	1	8	33	27
89 AL	.264	100	295	44	78	11	2	9	33	10
90 AL	.259	127	355	40	92	14	3	4	33	21
91 AL	.305	66	177	35	54	6	2	6	23	16
Life	.263	668	1644	229	433	68	8	34	162	91
3 AVE	.271	98	276	40	75	10	2	6	30	16

DANNY COX

Position: Pitcher
Team: Philadelphia Phillies
Born: September 21, 1959 Northampton, England
Height: 6'4" **Weight:** 225 lbs.
Bats: right **Throws:** right
Acquired: Signed as a free agent, 12/90

Player Summary	
Fantasy Value	$2 to $3
Card Value	3¢ to 5¢
Will	win when healthy
Can't	complete his starts
Expect	gradual recovery
Don't Expect	consistent performance

Cox was a key cog in the starting rotation of the Cardinals before elbow problems began to bother him at the outset of the 1988 campaign. He had a 18-9 record with a 2.88 ERA in 1985, but he had surgery in '88 to remove a bone spur. In 1989, he submitted to the "Tommy John operation" and had a ligament transplanted into his right elbow. After missing all of that season and most of the next, Cox won a job with Philadelphia during 1991 spring training, and made his first start on April 28. Because he's won in double figures three times and pitched in postseason play twice, Cox has the experience to stabilize a young pitching staff. Opponents compiled a .258 batting average, a .426 slugging percentage, and a .323 on-base average against him in 1991. His 1992 commons are far too risky. He is a $2 fantasy hurler, because of his experience and tenacity. If healthy, he can be an important starting pitcher.

Major League Pitching Register

	W	L	ERA	G	CG	IP	H	ER	BB	SO
83 NL	3	6	3.25	12	0	83.0	92	30	23	36
84 NL	9	11	4.03	29	1	156.1	171	70	54	70
85 NL	18	9	2.88	35	10	241.0	226	77	64	131
86 NL	12	13	2.90	32	8	220.0	189	71	60	108
87 NL	11	9	3.88	31	2	199.1	224	86	71	101
88 NL	3	8	3.98	13	0	86.0	89	38	25	47
91 NL	4	6	4.57	23	0	102.1	98	52	39	46
Life	60	62	3.51	175	21	1088.0	1089	424	336	539

CURRENT PLAYERS

TIM CREWS

Position: Pitcher
Team: Los Angeles Dodgers
Born: April 3, 1961 Tampa, FL
Height: 6' **Weight:** 190 lbs.
Bats: right **Throws:** right
Acquired: Traded from Brewers with Tim Leary for Greg Brock, 12/86

Player Summary	
Fantasy Value	$2 to $4
Card Value	3¢ to 5¢
Will	fill many roles
Can't	help himself at bat
Expect	excellent control
Don't Expect	Rob Dibble heat

Crews has joined the ranks of the superstitious, pitching last August after dying his gray hair black and trimming off half his mustache. One of the game's best set-up men, he appeared 66 times for the Dodgers in 1990, his first full season, and was a bullpen workhorse again last year. He did well as a stop-gap closer during Jay Howell's absence but was most effective in his familiar middle-relief role. A control pitcher who relies on a fastball and curve, Crews strikes out more than twice as many as he walks. He fields well and keeps base-runners honest but hasn't shown much ability as a hitter. He accords a reasonable alternative for money-strapped fantasy leaguers. His value is versatility, getting work as a short, middle, and long reliever as well as a starter two full seasons and parts of three others. Although Crews's 1992 commons won't wow card investors, he'll be a vital bullpen hand again in 1992.

Major League Pitching Register

	W	L	ERA	G	S	IP	H	ER	BB	SO
87 NL	1	1	2.48	20	3	29.0	30	8	8	20
88 NL	4	0	3.14	42	0	71.2	77	25	16	45
89 NL	0	1	3.21	44	1	61.2	69	22	23	56
90 NL	4	5	2.77	66	5	107.1	98	33	24	76
91 NL	2	3	3.43	60	6	76.0	75	29	19	53
Life	11	10	3.05	232	15	345.2	349	117	90	250
3 AVE	2	3	3.09	57	4	81.1	81	28	22	62

CHUCK CRIM

Position: Pitcher
Team: California Angels
Born: July 23, 1961 Van Nuys, CA
Height: 6' **Weight:** 190 lbs.
Bats: right **Throws:** right
Acquired: Traded from Brewers for Mike Fetters and Glen Carter, 12/91

Player Summary	
Fantasy Value	$2 to $4
Card Value	3¢ to 5¢
Will	make frequent stints
Can't	always keep ball in park
Expect	many ground balls
Don't Expect	more ineffectiveness

One of the game's true workhorse relievers, Crim has appeared at least 60 times four years in a row. He led the AL in games pitched in both 1988 and 1989 but was used less often last year when his effectiveness declined. His ERA was above the 4.50 mark all season, more than a run per game higher than the lifetime mark he had brought into the 1991 season. The Brewers got rid of him after 1991, trading him to California. He mixes a sinker, slider, and curve in an effort to induce ground balls from hitters. He doesn't get many strikeouts or yield too many walks. In 1991, his biggest problem was throwing too many home run balls (nine). His own poor fielding also hurt. His ERA could scare off fantasy managers unnecessarily. He is worth $3. The hefty workload of recent seasons may have taken its toll on Crim, who was sidelined by shoulder problems in 1990. Stay away from his 1992 commons.

Major League Pitching Register

	W	L	ERA	G	S	IP	H	ER	BB	SO
87 AL	6	8	3.67	53	12	130.0	133	53	39	56
88 AL	7	6	2.91	70	9	105.0	95	34	28	58
89 AL	9	7	2.83	76	7	117.2	114	37	36	59
90 AL	3	5	3.47	67	11	85.2	88	33	23	39
91 AL	8	5	4.63	66	3	91.1	115	47	25	39
Life	33	31	3.47	332	42	529.2	545	204	151	251
3 AVE	7	6	3.57	70	7	98.2	106	39	28	46

CURRENT PLAYERS

MILT CUYLER

Position: Outfield
Team: Detroit Tigers
Born: October 7, 1968 Macon, GA
Height: 5'10" **Weight:** 175 lbs.
Bats: both **Throws:** right
Acquired: Second-round pick in 6/86 free-agent draft

Player Summary
Fantasy Value ....$5 to $7
Card Value.........................5¢ to 10¢
Will.............................steal when on
Can't ....reach Tiger's fences
Expect ....strong play in center
Don't Expect............................good average

On the eve of the 1991 season, Detroit manager Sparky Anderson decided to place rookie speed merchant Cuyler at the top of a lineup anchored by Cecil Fielder, Mickey Tettleton, Pete Incaviglia, and Rob Deer. The switch-hitting Cuyler, who reached the majors four years after signing at age 17, led the Triple-A International League with 52 steals in 1990 and was about to learn Joe Morgan's stealing techniques from Anderson. Cuyler hit .258 at Triple-A Toledo in 1990, with 77 runs scored. He is a $6 fantasy choice, because of his .335 on-base percentage in 1991. His 1992 cards are not good buys at more than a nickel apiece. The Tigers thought Cuyler might be the second coming of Gary Pettis—and they were almost right. Cuyler hits for a higher average but can't match Pettis's Gold Glove play in center field. Cuyler isn't bad, though—especially since he mans the game's deepest center field. He had a game-winning grand slam early last season, and he had a .337 slugging average. He could steal 50 bases if he made better contact.

Major League Batting Register

	BA	G	AB	R	H	2B	3B	HR	RBI	SB
90 AL	.255	19	51	8	13	3	1	0	8	1
91 AL	.257	154	475	77	122	15	7	3	33	41
Life	.257	173	526	85	135	18	8	3	41	42

KAL DANIELS

Position: Outfield
Team: Los Angeles Dodgers
Born: Aug. 20, 1963 Vienna, GA
Height: 5'11" **Weight:** 205 lbs.
Bats: left **Throws:** right
Acquired: Traded from Reds with Lenny Harris for Tim Leary and Mariano Duncan, 7/89

Player Summary
Fantasy Value ....$9 to $12
Card Value.........................3¢ to 5¢
Will ....hit homers to all fields
Can't...............avoid constant knee problems
Expect ....good run production if healthy
Don't Expect.........much defense in left field

Though he has been bothered by knee problems throughout his career, Daniels has never had trouble at the plate. In fact, he is so strong that a majority of his home runs go to the opposite field. He hits with power to all fields but often has trouble against lefthanders who feed him breaking balls. He is unusually selective for a slugger, however, and led the NL with a .402 on-base percentage for a five-year span from 1986 to '90. He had a .337 on-base average in '91. Because he's a below-average left fielder who doesn't throw well and no longer runs well, Daniels would make a great designated hitter. His 1992 cards are commons, albeit promising commons. He stole 53 bases in two years for the Reds, but a half-dozen knee operations have extracted a huge toll. Periodically, he is a offensive force, but his injury history leaves his fantasy value at $12 tops.

Major League Batting Register

	BA	G	AB	R	H	2B	3B	HR	RBI	SB
86 NL	.320	74	181	34	58	10	4	6	23	15
87 NL	.334	108	368	73	123	24	1	26	64	26
88 NL	.291	140	495	95	144	29	1	18	64	27
89 NL	.246	55	171	33	42	3	0	4	17	9
90 NL	.296	130	450	81	133	23	1	27	94	4
91 NL	.249	137	461	54	115	15	1	17	73	6
Life	.289	644	2126	370	615	114	8	98	335	87
3 AVE	.268	107	361	56	97	17	1	16	61	6

CURRENT PLAYERS

RON DARLING

Position: Pitcher
Team: Oakland Athletics
Born: Aug. 19, 1960 Honolulu, HI
Height: 6'3" **Weight:** 195 lbs.
Bats: right **Throws:** right
Acquired: Traded from Expos for Matt Grott and Russell Cormier, 7/91

Player Summary
Fantasy Value	$2 to $4
Card Value	3¢ to 5¢
Will	throw different pitches
Can't	keep ball in park
Expect	reliance on split-finger
Don't Expect	return to '88 form

Darling had a successful career as an NL starter before making his AL debut with seven scoreless innings against the Mariners on August 5. Acquired as stretch drive insurance for the Oakland rotation, Darling had been traded earlier in 1991 by both the Mets and Expos. His pitching had become inconsistent—perhaps because he relied too heavily on the split-fingered fastball—and neither team was willing to dole out the long-term contract the free-agent pitcher wanted. Don't spend more than $4 on him during the fantasy draft. Though he has good control, his fastball and curve are only adequate. When his precision location is off, his pitches become instant homers. His 1992 commons are not going to be price-gainers. An excellent fielder with a good move, Darling can also hit with some power.

Major League Pitching Register

	W	L	ERA	G	CG	IP	H	ER	BB	SO
83 NL	1	3	2.80	5	1	35.1	31	11	17	23
84 NL	12	9	3.81	33	2	205.2	179	87	104	136
85 NL	16	6	2.90	36	4	248.0	214	80	114	167
86 NL	15	6	2.81	34	4	237.0	203	74	81	184
87 NL	12	8	4.29	32	2	207.2	183	99	96	167
88 NL	17	9	3.25	34	7	240.2	218	87	60	161
89 NL	14	14	3.52	33	4	217.1	214	85	70	153
90 NL	7	9	4.50	33	1	126.0	135	63	44	99
91 NL	5	8	4.37	20	0	119.1	121	58	33	69
91 AL	3	7	4.08	12	0	75.0	64	34	38	60
Life	102	79	3.56	272	25	1712.0	1562	678	657	1219
3 AVE	10	13	4.02	33	2	179.1	178	80	62	127

DANNY DARWIN

Position: Pitcher
Team: Boston Red Sox
Born: Oct. 25, 1955 Bonham, TX
Height: 6'3" **Weight:** 190 lbs.
Bats: right **Throws:** right
Acquired: Signed as a free agent, 12/90

Player Summary
Fantasy Value	$6 to $10
Card Value	3¢ to 5¢
Will	keep walks to minimum
Can't	stop gophers
Expect	complete comeback
Don't Expect	return to bullpen

Darwin's first season with the Red Sox was riddled with injuries. He went on the disabled list for the second time with tendinitis of the right shoulder. When healthy, Darwin is one of the game's most effective pitchers. He led the NL with a 2.21 ERA in 1990 and had a 3.40 mark for 13 seasons before his 1991 fiasco. The key to Darwin's success was excellent control. His fastball, slider, and changeup are adequate tools for a pitcher who's always around the plate. He is an $8 pitcher, based mostly on the team's commitment to him. Darwin's fielding is better than his pickoff move, so he's better off keeping the bases empty. Hits against him are often home runs. Don't invest in his 1992 commons.

Major League Pitching Register

	W	L	ERA	G	CG	IP	H	ER	BB	SO
78 AL	1	0	4.15	3	0	8.2	11	4	1	8
79 AL	4	4	4.04	20	1	78.0	50	35	30	58
80 AL	13	4	2.63	53	0	109.2	98	32	50	104
81 AL	9	9	3.64	22	6	146.0	115	59	57	98
82 AL	10	8	3.44	56	0	89.0	95	34	37	61
83 AL	8	13	3.49	28	9	183.0	175	71	62	92
84 AL	8	12	3.94	35	5	223.2	249	98	54	123
85 AL	8	18	3.80	39	11	217.2	212	92	65	125
86 AL	6	8	3.52	27	5	130.1	120	51	35	80
86 NL	5	2	2.32	12	1	54.1	50	14	9	40
87 NL	9	10	3.59	33	3	195.2	184	78	69	134
88 NL	8	13	3.84	44	3	192.0	189	82	48	129
89 NL	11	4	2.36	68	0	122.0	92	32	33	104
90 NL	11	4	2.21	48	3	162.2	136	40	31	109
91 AL	3	6	5.16	12	0	68.0	71	39	15	42
Life	114	115	3.46	500	47	1980.2	1847	761	596	1307
3 AVE	8	5	2.83	43	1	117.1	100	37	26	85

CURRENT PLAYERS

DOUG DASCENZO

Position: Outfield
Team: Chicago Cubs
Born: June 30, 1964 Cleveland, OH
Height: 5'8" **Weight:** 160 lbs.
Bats: both **Throws:** left
Acquired: 12th-round pick in 6/85 free-agent draft

Player Summary	
Fantasy Value	$2 to $4
Card Value	3¢ to 5¢
Will	continue as backup
Can't	produce power
Expect	outstanding defense
Don't Expect	average above .240

Dascenzo is not only a standout defensive center fielder but the game's best emergency relief pitcher. In 1991, he did not allow a run in three pitching appearances. The first position player to work three times out of the pen since Atlanta's Jim Morrison in 1988, Dascenzo is also an accomplished outfielder. He holds the NL record for consecutive errorless games by an outfielder, plus the major league mark for consecutive errorless games from the start of a career. Because he runs well, he has good range in the field and is a threat to steal bases. At the plate, he has little power—especially from the left side. For $3, he will add low-cost speed to your fantasy team. Don't buy his 1992 commons unless he wins a starting center field job. He also needs to exercise more patience, as anyone with a small strike zone should. He makes good contact, but he strikes out as often as he walks. Dascenzo will remain a top reserve.

Major League Batting Register

	BA	G	AB	R	H	2B	3B	HR	RBI	SB
88 NL	.213	26	75	9	16	3	0	0	4	6
89 NL	.165	47	139	20	23	1	0	1	12	6
90 NL	.253	113	241	27	61	9	5	1	26	15
91 NL	.255	118	239	40	61	11	0	1	18	14
Life	.232	304	694	96	161	24	5	3	60	41
2 AVE	.254	116	240	34	61	10	3	1	22	15

DARREN DAULTON

Position: Catcher
Team: Philadelphia Phillies
Born: Jan. 3, 1962 Arkansas City, KS
Height: 6'2" **Weight:** 190 lbs.
Bats: left **Throws:** right
Acquired: 25th-round pick in 6/80 free-agent draft

Player Summary	
Fantasy Value	$4 to $6
Card Value	3¢ to 5¢
Will	remain in lineup
Can't	hit for average
Expect	a dozen homers
Don't Expect	All-Star level

Daulton picked the right time to enjoy his best year. He had career peaks in 1990 while leading NL catchers in games, walks, runs, and doubles. The Phils then gave him a long-term, megabucks contract. Unfortunately, they didn't count on the May 6, 1991, car wreck that sent him and Lenny Dykstra to the disabled list. Daulton was not the same hitter again; he struggled to reach .200. His 1990 success was due to his spot in the order: second behind Dykstra. When Dykstra reached, Daulton got a steady diet of fastballs. He was dropped in the order last year. He is a good fantasy choice for $5. His nickel-priced 1992 cards are taboo. A capable catcher who blocks pitches well and calls a good game, he can also steal a base on occasion. Daulton's major obstacles in 1992 will be recapturing his stroke and avoiding knee problems.

Major League Batting Register

	BA	G	AB	R	H	2B	3B	HR	RBI	SB
83 NL	.333	2	3	1	1	0	0	0	0	0
85 NL	.204	36	103	14	21	3	1	4	11	3
86 NL	.225	49	138	18	31	4	0	8	21	2
87 NL	.194	53	129	10	25	6	0	3	13	0
88 NL	.208	58	144	13	30	6	0	1	12	2
89 NL	.201	131	368	29	74	12	2	8	44	2
90 NL	.268	143	459	62	123	30	1	12	57	7
91 NL	.196	89	285	36	56	12	0	12	42	5
Life	.222	561	1629	183	361	73	4	48	200	21
3 AVE	.228	121	371	42	84	18	1	11	48	5

CURRENT PLAYERS

ALVIN DAVIS

Position: First base; designated hitter
Team: Seattle Mariners
Born: Sept. 9, 1960 Riverside, CA
Height: 6'1" **Weight:** 190 lbs.
Bats: left **Throws:** right
Acquired: Sixth-round pick in 6/82 free-agent draft

Player Summary	
Fantasy Value	$6 to $8
Card Value	3¢ to 5¢
Will	hit for average and power
Can't	steal bases
Expect	high on-base average
Don't Expect	great defense

Davis is a strong hitter with a weak glove. In 1984, Davis was AL Rookie of the Year after hitting .284 with 27 homers and 116 RBI with the Mariners. Three years later, he hit a career-best 29 homers. He's also hit at least .295 three times. When Davis's production slipped in '91, he lost his first base job, initially to Pete O'Brien and later to Tino Martinez. Davis's powerful lefthanded bat remains a valuable commodity. Because he walks more often than he fans, he is a rarity among sluggers. He has received at least 90 walks four different times and always has a high on-base percentage as a result. His 1992 cards are overrated choices at their nickel prices. He could really help a fantasy team for under $10. Davis has little speed and is not agile in the field, but he prefers playing first base to designated hitter.

Major League Batting Register

	BA	G	AB	R	H	2B	3B	HR	RBI	SB
84 AL	.284	152	567	80	161	34	3	27	116	5
85 AL	.287	155	578	78	166	33	1	18	78	1
86 AL	.271	135	479	66	130	18	1	18	72	0
87 AL	.295	157	580	86	171	37	2	29	100	0
88 AL	.295	140	478	67	141	24	1	18	69	1
89 AL	.305	142	498	84	152	30	1	21	95	0
90 AL	.283	140	494	63	140	21	0	17	68	0
91 AL	.221	145	462	39	102	15	1	12	69	0
Life	.281	1166	4136	563	1163	212	10	160	667	7
3 AVE	.271	142	485	62	131	22	1	17	77	0

CHILI DAVIS

Position: Designated hitter
Team: Minnesota Twins
Born: Jan. 17, 1960 Kingston, Jamaica
Height: 6'3" **Weight:** 210 lbs.
Bats: both **Throws:** right
Acquired: Signed as a free agent, 1/91

Player Summary	
Fantasy Value	$22 to $25
Card Value	3¢ to 5¢
Will	generate two-way power
Can't	steal bases anymore
Expect	club highs in homers, RBI
Don't Expect	any appearance in outfield

The Twins decided to replace Gary Gaetti's power during the 1991 season by signing a free agent of their own. Davis, the veteran they selected, turned out to be one of the year's biggest bargains. Used almost exclusively as a designated hitter, he delivered the best home run year of his 10-year career while leading the Twins in both homers and runs batted in. He has more power hitting lefthanded, finding the short right field of the Metrodome an inviting target. Davis was left free to concentrate on his hitting—a good thing for a player whose 19 errors for the '88 Angels were a club record. He strikes out too much and doesn't walk enough, but he compensates with his power production. Recruit him for fantasy play at $25. His 1992 commons are not bad buys.

Major League Batting Register

	BA	G	AB	R	H	2B	3B	HR	RBI	SB
81 NL	.133	8	15	1	2	0	0	0	0	2
82 NL	.261	154	641	86	167	27	6	19	76	24
83 NL	.233	137	486	54	113	21	2	11	59	10
84 NL	.315	137	499	87	157	21	6	21	81	12
85 NL	.270	136	481	53	130	25	2	13	56	15
86 NL	.278	153	526	71	146	28	3	13	70	16
87 NL	.250	149	500	80	125	22	1	24	76	16
88 AL	.268	158	600	81	161	29	3	21	93	9
89 AL	.271	154	560	81	152	24	1	22	90	3
90 AL	.265	113	412	58	109	17	1	12	58	1
91 AL	.277	153	534	84	148	34	1	29	93	5
Life	.268	1452	5254	736	1410	248	26	185	752	113
3 AVE	.272	140	502	74	136	25	1	21	80	3

CURRENT PLAYERS

ERIC DAVIS

Position: Outfield
Team: Los Angeles Dodgers
Born: May 29, 1962 Los Angeles, CA
Height: 6'3" **Weight:** 185 lbs.
Bats: right **Throws:** right
Acquired: Traded from Reds with Kip Gross for Tim Belcher and John Wetteland, 11/91

Player Summary	
Fantasy Value	$32 to $37
Card Value	5¢ to 10¢
Will	deliver power and speed
Can't	stay healthy
Expect	high strikeout ratio
Don't Expect	a .300 average

When he's healthy, Davis can hit, hit with power, run, throw, and field. A healthy Davis, however, is as rare as snow in the Bahamas. Plagued by knee, hamstring, and assorted other problems, he has never played in more than 135 games in a season. A low fastball hitter with power to all fields, he is a good clutch hitter though he strikes out frequently. His great speed has helped him win three Gold Gloves but has not enabled him to hit .300. He could be a fantasy bargain or bust, but he's worth $35 when OK. He is a skilled, strong-armed center fielder who sometimes plays left to reduce the strain on his knees. His 1992 cards are good buys at a nickel. He homered in his first World Series at bat, in 1990, but later suffered a bruised kidney that plagued him in 1991.

GLENN DAVIS

Position: First base
Team: Baltimore Orioles
Born: March 28, 1961 Jacksonville, FL
Height: 6'3" **Weight:** 200 lbs.
Bats: right **Throws:** right
Acquired: Traded from Astros for Steve Finley, Pete Harnisch, and Curt Schilling, 1/91

Player Summary	
Fantasy Value	$20 to $25
Card Value	5¢ to 7¢
Will	challenge for homer crown
Can't	steal much
Expect	comeback from injury
Don't Expect	batting average above .280

The Orioles acquired Davis to give Cal Ripken better protection in the lineup but never got their money's worth. Davis went on the disabled list April 26 with nerve damage in his neck and didn't pick up a bat until taking batting practice before the game on August 7. Normally one of the game's most prolific power hitters, he hit many homers for the Astros though he played half the schedule in the cavernous Astrodome. Before his injury-riddled 1991 campaign, he had reached the 20-homer plateau in all six of his big league seasons. Be careful when spending more than $25 on him in the fantasy draft. His 1992 cards are risky at more than a nickel. He has power to all fields and makes better contact than most other home run hitters. Davis has improved his defense dramatically in recent years.

Major League Batting Register

	BA	G	AB	R	H	2B	3B	HR	RBI	SB
84 NL	.224	57	174	33	39	10	1	10	30	10
85 NL	.246	56	122	26	30	3	3	8	18	16
86 NL	.277	132	415	97	115	15	3	27	71	80
87 NL	.293	129	474	120	139	23	4	37	100	50
88 NL	.273	135	472	81	129	18	3	26	93	35
89 NL	.281	131	462	74	130	14	2	34	101	21
90 NL	.260	127	453	84	118	26	2	24	86	21
91 NL	.235	89	285	39	67	10	0	11	33	14
Life	.268	856	2857	554	767	119	18	177	532	247
3 AVE	.262	116	400	66	105	17	1	23	73	19

Major League Batting Register

	BA	G	AB	R	H	2B	3B	HR	RBI	SB
84 NL	.213	18	61	6	13	5	0	2	8	0
85 NL	.271	100	350	51	95	11	0	20	64	0
86 NL	.265	158	574	91	152	32	3	31	101	3
87 NL	.251	151	578	70	145	35	2	27	93	4
88 NL	.271	152	561	78	152	26	0	30	99	4
89 NL	.269	158	581	87	156	26	1	34	89	4
90 NL	.251	93	327	44	82	15	4	22	64	8
91 AL	.227	49	176	29	40	9	1	10	28	4
Life	.260	879	3208	456	835	159	11	176	546	27
3 AVE	.256	100	361	53	93	17	2	22	60	5

CURRENT PLAYERS

MARK DAVIS

Position: Pitcher
Team: Kansas City Royals
Born: Oct. 19, 1960 Livermore, CA
Height: 6'4" **Weight:** 205 lbs.
Bats: left **Throws:** left
Acquired: Signed as a free agent, 12/89

Player Summary	
Fantasy Value	$2 to $4
Card Value	3¢ to 5¢
Will	try to recapture '89
Can't	keep control of curve
Expect	some experimentation
Don't Expect	return to closer role

Davis was one of baseball's premier closers before leaving the NL to sign with the Royals as a free agent. He has not been the same pitcher since, even though he was reunited with former pitching coach Pat Dobson in 1991. Slowed by an injured index finger on his pitching hand, Davis missed six weeks at midseason and was tried as a starter in the minors. He returned to the Royals as a long reliever. He won the 1989 NL Cy Young Award with 44 saves in 48 opportunities. His three pitches are a curveball, fastball, and split-fingered fastball. Injury and ineffectiveness reduced him from closer to middle man in Kansas City. Davis could return to the rotation, however. He will not pile up saves anymore, so he is a $3 fantasy draft. His 1992 commons are not winning purchases.

Major League Pitching Register

	W	L	ERA	G	S	IP	H	ER	BB	SO
80 NL	0	0	2.57	2	0	7.0	4	2	5	5
81 NL	1	4	7.74	9	0	43.0	49	37	24	29
83 NL	6	4	3.49	20	0	111.0	93	43	50	83
84 NL	5	17	5.36	46	0	174.2	201	104	54	124
85 NL	5	12	3.54	77	7	114.1	89	45	41	131
86 NL	5	7	2.99	67	4	84.1	63	28	34	90
87 NL	9	8	3.99	63	2	133.0	132	59	59	98
88 NL	5	10	2.01	62	28	98.1	70	22	42	102
89 NL	4	3	1.85	70	44	92.2	66	19	31	92
90 AL	2	7	5.11	53	6	68.2	71	39	52	73
91 AL	6	3	3.45	29	1	62.2	55	31	39	47
Life	48	75	3.90	498	92	989.2	884	429	431	874
3 AVE	4	4	3.58	51	17	74.2	64	30	41	71

STORM DAVIS

Position: Pitcher
Team: Baltimore Orioles
Born: Dec. 26, 1961 Dallas, TX
Height: 6'4" **Weight:** 200 lbs.
Bats: right **Throws:** right
Acquired: Traded from Royals for Bob Melvin, 12/91

Player Summary	
Fantasy Value	$1 to $2
Card Value	3¢ to 5¢
Will	be a middle man
Can't	keep ERA respectable
Expect	more hits than frames
Don't Expect	much respect

Davis had won more than a dozen games as a starter four different times before coming to the Royals as a free agent before the 1990 campaign. Two stints on the disabled list ruined his first year in Kansas City. He pitched better after moving to the bullpen in 1991, though. The Royals felt he was best-suited to that role because he had a history of not pitching deep into his starts. A control pitcher who throws a fastball, forkball, and curveball, Davis helps himself as a fielder and also keeps base-runners from taking big leads. His biggest problem is giving up more hits than innings pitched during his career. That's why he has a career ERA of over four per game. In December, Davis was dealt to Baltimore. He is now a $2 fantasy pitcher. His 1992 commons are not good investments.

Major League Pitching Register

	W	L	ERA	G	CG	IP	H	ER	BB	SO
82 AL	8	4	3.49	29	1	100.2	96	39	28	67
83 AL	13	7	3.59	34	6	200.1	180	80	64	125
84 AL	14	9	3.12	35	10	225.0	205	78	71	105
85 AL	10	8	4.53	31	8	175.0	172	88	70	93
86 AL	9	12	3.62	25	2	154.0	166	62	49	96
87 NL	2	7	6.18	21	0	62.2	70	43	36	37
87 AL	1	1	3.26	5	0	30.1	28	11	11	28
88 AL	16	7	3.70	33	1	201.2	211	83	91	127
89 AL	19	7	4.36	31	1	169.1	187	82	68	91
90 AL	7	10	4.74	21	0	112.0	129	59	35	62
91 AL	3	9	4.96	51	1	114.1	140	63	46	53
Life	102	81	4.01	316	30	1545.1	1584	688	569	884
3 AVE	10	9	4.64	34	1	132.1	152	68	50	69

CURRENT PLAYERS

ANDRE DAWSON

Position: Outfield
Team: Chicago Cubs
Born: July 10, 1954 Miami, FL
Height: 6'3" **Weight:** 195 lbs.
Bats: right **Throws:** right
Acquired: Signed as a free agent, 3/87

Player Summary	
Fantasy Value	$33 to $38
Card Value	10¢ to 15¢
Will	hit with power
Can't	play every day
Expect	dramatic clutch hits
Don't Expect	many stolen bases

Dawson became a much better player after he moved from Montreal's ersatz turf to Wrigley's grass. He also found the Cubs' menu of baseball-by-daylight more inviting. The 1987 National League MVP with a career-best 49 homers, Dawson is still a dangerous hitter—even though knee problems sometimes force him to play in pain. He will anchor a fantasy team for under $40. The eight-time All-Star has produced 2,000 hits, 300 homers, and 300 stolen bases—achievements matched only by Willie Mays. Like Mays, Dawson is an excellent outfielder. He now plays right field, where few runners take chances against his strong arm. His 1992 cards are great grabs at 15 cents or less.

Major League Batting Register

	BA	G	AB	R	H	2B	3B	HR	RBI	SB
76 NL	.235	24	85	9	20	4	1	0	7	1
77 NL	.282	139	525	64	148	26	9	19	65	21
78 NL	.253	157	609	84	154	24	8	25	72	28
79 NL	.275	155	639	90	176	24	12	25	92	35
80 NL	.308	151	577	96	178	41	7	17	87	34
81 NL	.302	103	394	71	119	21	3	24	64	26
82 NL	.301	148	608	107	183	37	7	23	83	39
83 NL	.299	159	633	104	189	36	10	32	113	25
84 NL	.248	138	533	73	132	23	6	17	86	13
85 NL	.255	139	529	65	135	27	2	23	91	13
86 NL	.284	130	496	65	141	32	2	20	78	18
87 NL	.287	153	621	90	178	24	2	49	137	11
88 NL	.303	157	591	78	179	31	8	24	79	12
89 NL	.252	118	416	62	105	18	6	21	77	8
90 NL	.310	147	529	72	164	28	5	27	100	16
91 NL	.272	149	563	69	153	21	4	31	104	4
Life	.282	2167	8348	1199	2354	417	92	377	1335	304
3 AVE	.280	138	503	68	141	22	5	26	94	9

KEN DAYLEY

Position: Pitcher
Team: Toronto Blue Jays
Born: Feb. 25, 1959 Jerome, ID
Height: 6' **Weight:** 180 lbs.
Bats: left **Throws:** left
Acquired: Signed as a free agent, 12/90

Player Summary	
Fantasy Value	$3 to $5
Card Value	3¢ to 5¢
Will	destroy lefty hitters
Can't	always find control
Expect	set-up role
Don't Expect	more physical woes

Although many teams sought the services of Dayley when the veteran reliever was on the free-agent market, the Blue Jays did not get the best of the bargain. He was disabled with dizziness caused by a nerve problem of the inner ear on June 12 and was lost for most of the season. When healthy, he is effective because his curve and fastball are both thrown with a three-quarters motion. When he's well, lefthanded hitters shouldn't even show up. Risk up to five bucks in the draft, and you could have a solid reliever. His 1992 commons are not buys. Dayley averages twice as many strikeouts as walks but is subject to occasional wildness. Opponents had a .368 average in '91. He helps himself as a fielder and keeps runners close at first base. He's a quality southpaw set-up man.

Major League Pitching Register

	W	L	ERA	G	S	IP	H	ER	BB	SO
82 NL	5	6	4.54	20	0	71.1	79	36	25	34
83 NL	5	8	4.30	24	0	104.2	100	50	39	70
84 NL	0	5	7.99	7	0	23.2	44	21	11	10
85 NL	4	4	2.76	57	11	65.1	65	20	18	62
86 NL	0	3	3.26	31	5	38.2	42	14	11	33
87 NL	9	5	2.66	53	4	61.0	52	18	33	63
88 NL	2	7	2.77	54	5	55.1	48	17	19	38
89 NL	4	3	2.87	71	12	75.1	63	24	30	40
90 NL	4	4	3.56	58	2	73.1	63	29	30	51
91 AL	0	0	6.23	8	0	4.1	7	3	5	3
Life	33	45	3.64	383	39	573.0	563	232	221	404
2 AVE	4	4	3.21	65	7	74.1	63	27	30	46

CURRENT PLAYERS

STEVE DECKER

Position: Catcher
Team: San Francisco Giants
Born: Oct. 25, 1965 Rock Island, IL
Height: 6'3" **Weight:** 205 lbs.
Bats: right **Throws:** right
Acquired: 21st-round pick in 6/88 free-agent draft

Player Summary	
Fantasy Value	$6 to $9
Card Value	10¢ to 15¢
Will	wipe out runners
Can't	steal many bases
Expect	good power production
Don't Expect	high average

Decker did so well in a September look with the 1990 Giants that the team felt no qualms about releasing veteran receiver Gary Carter. After earning Double-A Texas League All-Star honors with a .295 average, 15 homers, and a 42 percent success ratio in throwing out would-be base-stealers, Decker had a good average and a 41 percent throwing average in a 15-game NL trial. Handed the No. 1 job in 1991, he couldn't hold it. He spent time on the disabled list (he sprained his foot while avoiding an autograph seeker) and more in the minors as the platoon of Terry Kennedy and Kirt Manwaring handled the position. Decker had a .309 slugging percentage and a .262 on-base average in 1991. He had seven errors, and had 44 Ks and 16 walks. His second-year 1992 cards are wise choices in the dime range. He is a smart fantasy pick-up for $10 or less. The Giants still consider Decker their catcher of the future, and that future may begin in 1992. He needs to stay healthy and hit big league pitching.

Major League Batting Register

	BA	G	AB	R	H	2B	3B	HR	RBI	SB
90 NL	.296	15	54	5	16	2	0	3	8	0
91 NL	.206	79	233	11	48	7	1	5	24	0
Life	.223	94	287	16	64	9	1	8	32	0

ROB DEER

Position: Outfield
Team: Detroit Tigers
Born: Sept. 29, 1960 Orange, CA
Height: 6'3" **Weight:** 225 lbs.
Bats: right **Throws:** right
Acquired: Signed as a free agent, 11/90

Player Summary	
Fantasy Value	$6 to $8
Card Value	3¢ to 5¢
Will	threaten strikeout records
Can't	bat his weight
Expect	at least 25 homers
Don't Expect	long hitting streaks

Deer is baseball's best example of an all-or-nothing performer. In his six summers as a big league regular, he has never hit less than 23 home runs or struck out fewer than 147 times per season. Following the 1991 All-Star Game on July 9, he failed to produce a base hit other than a home run until July 23. At the fantasy draft, his power is worth $12, and his average takes at least $4 away. Though he led the Brewers in homers for five straight seasons from 1986 to '90, he also set an AL record for futility with 186 strikeouts in 1987. Had he played more than 134 games that year, he surely would have wiped out Bobby Bonds's 1970 major league mark of 189. In Deer's anxiety to reach the short fences of Tiger Stadium in 1991, he batted .179. Swing and miss on his 1992 commons. Deer's on-base percentage, incredibly, was about 125 points higher.

Major League Batting Register

	BA	G	AB	R	H	2B	3B	HR	RBI	SB
84 NL	.167	13	24	5	4	0	0	3	3	1
85 NL	.185	78	162	22	30	5	1	8	20	0
86 AL	.232	134	466	75	108	17	3	33	86	5
87 AL	.238	134	474	71	113	15	2	28	80	12
88 AL	.252	135	492	71	124	24	0	23	85	9
89 AL	.210	130	466	72	98	18	2	26	65	4
90 AL	.209	134	440	57	92	15	1	27	69	2
91 AL	.179	134	448	64	80	14	2	25	64	1
Life	.218	892	2972	437	649	108	11	173	472	34
3 AVE	.199	133	451	64	90	16	2	26	66	2

CURRENT PLAYERS

JOSE DeJESUS

Position: Pitcher
Team: Philadelphia Phillies
Born: Jan. 6, 1965 Brooklyn, NY
Height: 6'5" **Weight:** 195 lbs.
Bats: right **Throws:** right
Acquired: Traded from Royals for Steve Jeltz, 3/90

Player Summary	
Fantasy Value	$7 to $10
Card Value	3¢ to 5¢
Will	improve with time
Can't	avoid walks
Expect	at least 12 wins
Don't Expect	self-help with hits

After a rocky start punctuated by persistent wildness, DeJesus settled down to become one of Philadelphia's most dependable starters. Winning in double figures in 1991, he had a 3.42 ERA. His numbers would have been better if he had not walked more men than anyone else on the team. A fastball-and-slider pitcher who recently added a changeup to his repertoire, DeJesus intimidates hitters with hard stuff that he can't always control. Opponents regularly post a low batting average against him but score runs, because he doles out more than his share of walks and wild pitches. He allowed opponents to post a .224 batting average, .318 slugging percentage, and a .353 on-base percentage in '91. He was a fantasy bargain in 1991, but good luck getting DeJesus for $10. He may not be worth much more, however. His 1992 commons are pretty good buys. If he learns to strike out more men than he walks, his record will continue to improve.

Major League Pitching Register

	W	L	ERA	G	CG	IP	H	ER	BB	SO
88 AL	0	1	27.00	2	0	2.2	6	8	5	2
89 AL	0	0	4.50	3	0	8.0	7	4	8	2
90 NL	7	8	3.74	22	3	130.0	97	54	73	87
91 NL	10	9	3.42	31	3	181.2	147	69	128	118
Life	17	18	3.77	58	6	322.1	257	135	214	209
2 AVE	9	9	3.55	27	3	156.1	122	62	101	103

JOSE DeLEON

Position: Pitcher
Team: St. Louis Cardinals
Born: Dec. 20, 1960 Rancho Viejo, Dominican Republic
Height: 6'3" **Weight:** 215 lbs.
Bats: right **Throws:** right
Acquired: Traded from White Sox for Rick Horton and Lance Johnson, 2/88

Player Summary	
Fantasy Value	$4 to $7
Card Value	3¢ to 5¢
Will	record strikeouts
Can't	contribute as fielder
Expect	good performance
Don't Expect	another 2-19 season

No matter how well DeLeon pitches, he always seems to lose more than he wins. Twice a 19-game loser, he led St. Louis starters in strikeouts and earned run average last year. That wasn't enough to avoid a losing record for the sixth time in nine seasons, however. A fastball-and-forkball pitcher, he seems to have overcome his past control problems. Being around the plate didn't always help—he was near the top of the staff in throwing home run balls (15). DeLeon is an adequate fielder with an average move but is a weak hitter. As a pitcher, however, he led the NL in strikeouts three years ago and is a candidate to do it again. For $4 to $7, a fantasy team could get many strikeouts from him. His 1992 commons don't appeal to collectors.

Major League Pitching Register

	W	L	ERA	G	CG	IP	H	ER	BB	SO
83 NL	7	3	2.83	15	3	108.0	75	34	47	118
84 NL	7	13	3.74	30	5	192.1	147	80	92	153
85 NL	2	19	4.70	31	1	162.2	138	85	89	149
86 NL	1	3	8.27	9	0	16.1	17	15	17	11
86 AL	4	5	2.96	13	1	79.0	49	26	42	68
87 AL	11	12	4.02	33	2	20>.0	177	92	97	153
88 NL	13	10	3.67	34	3	225.1	198	92	86	208
89 NL	16	12	3.05	36	5	244.2	173	83	80	201
90 NL	7	19	4.43	32	0	182.2	168	90	86	164
91 NL	5	9	2.71	28	1	162.2	144	49	61	118
Life	73	105	3.68	261	21	1579.2	1286	646	697	1343
3 AVE	9	13	3.39	32	2	196.2	162	74	76	161

CURRENT PLAYERS

RICH DeLUCIA

Position: Pitcher
Team: Seattle Mariners
Born: Oct. 7, 1964 Reading, PA
Height: 6′ **Weight:** 180 lbs.
Bats: right **Throws:** right
Acquired: Sixth-round pick in 6/86 free-agent draft

Player Summary	
Fantasy Value	$7 to $10
Card Value	10¢ to 20¢
Will	win 15 with control
Can't	keep balls in park
Expect	job as No. 4 starter
Don't Expect	more walks than Ks

DeLucia was one of four Seattle starters to win in double figures. That made his first full major league season a success—even though too many walks had inflated his ERA. During a minor league career that began in 1986, the former University of Tennessee standout had averaged a 2-1 strikeout-to-walk ratio. He'll need to do that—and to keep the ball in the park more often—to keep his job. DeLucia led all Mariner pitchers in gopher balls last year, with 31. His problem is a fastball that peaks in the mid-80s—slow enough to be timed by enemy hitters whenever he falls behind in the count. He jumped three minor league levels in 1990. He started the season at Class-A San Bernardino, where he went 3-4 with a 2.05 ERA. At Double-A Williamsport, he was 6-6 with a 2.11 ERA. He was 2-2 with a 3.62 ERA at Triple-A Calgary that year. His 1992 cards are fine purchases at 20 cents. He is a $10 fantasy starter. DeLucia is still learning and should be counted on to improve.

Major League Pitching Register

	W	L	ERA	G	CG	IP	H	ER	BB	SO
90 AL	1	2	2.00	5	1	36.0	30	8	9	20
91 AL	12	13	5.09	32	0	182.0	176	103	78	98
Life	13	15	4.58	37	1	218.0	206	111	87	118

JIM DeSHAIES

Position: Pitcher
Team: Houston Astros
Born: June 23, 1960 Massena, NY
Height: 6′4″ **Weight:** 220 lbs.
Bats: left **Throws:** left
Acquired: Traded from Yankees with Neder de Jesus Horta and Dody Rather for Joe Niekro, 9/85

Player Summary	
Fantasy Value	$2 to $4
Card Value	3¢ to 5¢
Will	face fight for job
Can't	recapture 1989 form
Expect	many throws to first
Don't Expect	many strikeouts

DeShaies was a solid starter with the Astros for five years before slipping into a season-long slump in 1991. Once a hard thrower who relied heavily on his fastball, he began using breaking balls, change-ups, and off-speed pitches more often in recent seasons. His strikeouts declined, walks increased, and won-lost record sagged—with predictable results for the ERA. A victim of poor run support in the past, DeShaies made his own nest last year by throwing more home run balls. His old 2-1 strikeout-to-walk ratio evaporated too. He annually leads the league in throwing to first base. DeShaies is a decent fielder with a good move. He is a disaster as a hitter; lately, his pitching has been a disaster as well. Fantasy managers may want to risk $3 that he will comeback. His 1992 commons are not good investments.

Major League Pitching Register

	W	L	ERA	G	CG	IP	H	ER	BB	SO
84 AL	0	1	11.57	2	0	7.0	14	9	7	5
85 NL	0	0	0.00	2	0	3.0	1	0	0	2
86 NL	12	5	3.25	26	1	144.0	124	52	59	128
87 NL	11	6	4.62	26	1	152.0	149	78	57	104
88 NL	11	14	3.00	31	3	207.0	164	69	72	127
89 NL	15	10	2.91	34	6	225.2	180	73	79	153
90 NL	7	12	3.78	34	2	209.1	186	88	84	119
91 NL	5	12	4.98	28	1	161.0	156	89	72	98
Life	61	60	3.72	183	14	1109.0	974	458	430	736
3 AVE	9	11	3.78	32	3	198.1	174	83	78	123

CURRENT PLAYERS

DELINO DeSHIELDS

Position: Second base
Team: Montreal Expos
Born: Jan. 15, 1969 Seaford, DE
Height: 6'1" **Weight:** 170 lbs.
Bats: left **Throws:** right
Acquired: First-round pick in 6/87 free-agent draft

Player Summary	
Fantasy Value	$18 to $22
Card Value	8¢ to 15¢
Will	make use of speed
Can't	reduce errors
Expect	better average
Don't Expect	many home runs

DeShields spent just two and one-half years in the minors before making a major bid for Rookie of the Year honors with the 1990 Expos. The former shortstop, showing tremendous range at second base, hit .289 with 42 steals, filled a vacant role as leadoff man, and eventually finished second to David Justice in voting for the coveted award. DeShields, the former Villanova All-American, uses his wrists to generate line-drive power to all fields. His bat slipped a bit during his sophomore season in '91 but he remained among NL leaders in stolen bases. He needs to increase his average and reduce his errors, however. He strikes out more than he walks—not good for a man at the top of the lineup. If he makes better contact, DeShields will produce the infield hits and Astroturf singles that will boost his average. His base-stealing ability boosts his fantasy worth higher than his actual worth. He is a $20 fantasy second baseman. His 1992 cards are good buys at 10 cents.

Major League Batting Register

	BA	G	AB	R	H	2B	3B	HR	RBI	SB
90 NL	.289	129	499	69	144	28	6	4	45	42
91 NL	.238	151	563	83	134	15	4	10	51	56
Life	.262	280	1062	152	278	43	10	14	96	98
2 AVE	.262	140	531	76	139	22	5	7	48	49

MIKE DEVEREAUX

Position: Outfield
Team: Baltimore Orioles
Born: April 10, 1963 Casper, WY
Height: 6' **Weight:** 191 lbs.
Bats: right **Throws:** right
Acquired: Traded from Dodgers for Mike Morgan, 3/89

Player Summary	
Fantasy Value	$9 to $12
Card Value	3¢ to 5¢
Will	continue improvement
Can't	increase walks
Expect	great defense in center
Don't Expect	more homers than steals

Devereaux developed into a capable leadoff hitter in 1991. He was among all AL leadoff men in homers, even though he had played in fewer games than most. He figures to become a better hitter if he learns to become more selective, striking out twice as often as he walks. The free-swinging Devereaux hits with power to left field but often hits the ball up the middle. His speed helps him on the bases and in center field, where he's quickly developing into one of the league's best. He has good range and an accurate (though not strong) throwing arm. His speed makes him an $8 fantasy outfielder. Devereaux could help his team most by learning patience at the plate, getting on base by walking, and increasing his stolen base totals. He had a .313 on-base percentage in '91. He has the potential to swipe 30 or more per year. Devereaux is just approaching his peak. His 1992 commons will remain at the nickel level.

Major League Batting Register

	BA	G	AB	R	H	2B	3B	HR	RBI	SB
87 NL	.222	19	54	7	12	3	0	0	4	3
88 NL	.116	30	43	4	5	1	0	0	2	0
89 AL	.266	122	391	55	104	14	3	8	46	22
90 AL	.240	108	367	48	88	18	1	12	49	13
91 AL	.260	149	608	82	158	27	10	19	59	16
Life	.251	428	1463	196	367	63	14	39	160	54
3 AVE	.256	126	455	62	117	20	5	13	51	17

CURRENT PLAYERS

MARIO DIAZ

Position: Infield
Team: Milwaukee Brewers
Born: Jan. 10, 1962 Humacao, Puerto Rico
Height: 5'10" **Weight:** 160 lbs.
Bats: right **Throws:** right
Acquired: Signed as a free agent, 12/91

Player Summary	
Fantasy Value	$1 to $2
Card Value	3¢ to 5¢
Will	make good contact
Can't	produce any power
Expect	best play at short
Don't Expect	prolonged regular use

Diaz is one of baseball's best examples of true grit, spending nine years in the minors before getting his first big league trial with the 1987 Mariners. A four-position infielder whose best spot is shortstop, Diaz got more playing time with Texas in 1991 than ever before. He responded well, with a .270-level average most of the season. He also had only seven errors all season. A contact hitter who gets few walks or strikeouts, Diaz makes the most of his hits. For example, he got 20 RBI on his first 40 base hits in '91. He had a .319 slugging percentage and a .318 on-base average in 1991. Stay away from this backup's 1992 commons. He is a $2 fantasy middle infielder. He is often used as a pinch-hitter, defensive replacement, or emergency fill-in. Diaz has almost no power—he usually produces an annual home run—but is valued because of his versatility. He's also one of the best bunters in the league. Diaz will take his utility skills to Milwaukee, which signed him in December.

Major League Batting Register

	BA	G	AB	R	H	2B	3B	HR	RBI	SB
87 AL	.304	11	23	4	7	0	1	0	3	0
88 AL	.306	28	72	6	22	5	0	0	9	0
89 AL	.135	52	74	9	10	0	0	1	7	0
90 NL	.136	16	22	0	3	1	0	0	1	0
91 AL	.264	96	162	24	48	7	0	1	22	0
Life	.241	203	373	43	90	13	1	2	42	0

ROB DIBBLE

Position: Pitcher
Team: Cincinnati Reds
Born: Jan. 24, 1964 Bridgeport, CT
Height: 6'4" **Weight:** 235 lbs.
Bats: left **Throws:** right
Acquired: First pick in the secondary phase of 6/83 free-agent draft

Player Summary	
Fantasy Value	$18 to $25
Card Value	5¢ to 10¢
Will	record high Ks ratio
Can't	control fiery emotions
Expect	outbursts, fines, suspensions
Don't Expect	end to controversy

Dibble devoured rival hitters with his fastball in 1991 but nearly destroyed himself with his temper. He saved 23 of his team's first 44 wins without blowing a single save opportunity. He won NL Pitcher of the Month honors in June with 10 saves and a 1.69 ERA in 15 appearances. His strikeouts per nine innings mark in '91 was 13.55, even better than his 1989 average of 12.8 (which itself was the best in modern baseball history for pitchers who worked at least 25 innings). Opponents compiled a .223 batting average, a .322 slugging percentage, and a .289 on-base average against him in '91. Despite his late slump, he is a premier closer, for up to $25. But the co-MVP of the 1990 playoffs got into trouble for (among other things) injuring a fan with a ball thrown into the stands and throwing behind a batter. Suspended and fined several times, Dibble will have to harness his emotions if he is to remain the game's top closer. His 1992 cards are sleepers at a nickel apiece.

Major League Pitching Register

	W	L	ERA	G	S	IP	H	ER	BB	SO
88 NL	1	1	1.82	37	0	59.1	43	12	21	59
89 NL	10	5	2.09	74	2	99.0	62	23	39	141
90 NL	8	3	1.74	68	11	98.0	62	19	34	136
91 NL	3	5	3.17	67	31	82.1	67	29	25	124
Life	22	14	2.21	246	44	338.2	234	83	119	460
3 AVE	7	4	2.29	70	15	93.0	64	24	33	134

CURRENT PLAYERS

JOHN DOPSON

Position: Pitcher
Team: Boston Red Sox
Born: July 14, 1963 Baltimore, MD
Height: 6'4" **Weight:** 205 lbs.
Bats: left **Throws:** right
Acquired: Traded from Expos with Luis Rivera for Spike Owen and Dan Gakeler, 12/88

Player Summary	
Fantasy Value	$1 to $3
Card Value	3¢ to 5¢
Will	win spot if healthy
Can't	keep ball in park
Expect	a long trial
Don't Expect	quick results

Dopson's 1991 season was a washout following elbow surgery. He was placed on the disabled list April 5. He went 12-8 with a 3.99 ERA for the Red Sox in 1989, but he faces a turning point in his career this spring. Either he shakes off the physical problems that have cost him two seasons or he starts thinking about another profession. He has also had shoulder problems in the past, but Dopson can be an important starting pitcher when he's healthy. He throws a sinker, slider, and changeup, but he gives up frequent gopher balls when the sinker doesn't sink. Dopson doesn't help himself in the field but has a good move to first. Other pitchers have come back from a two-year disability. Dopson will certainly get the opportunity. His health woes make him the classic $1 pitcher. He should have 80 or so victories at his age, instead of 15. His 1992 cards are commons.

Major League Pitching Register

	W	L	ERA	G	CG	IP	H	ER	BB	SO
85 NL	0	2	11.08	4	0	13.0	25	16	4	4
88 NL	3	11	3.04	26	1	168.2	150	57	58	101
89 AL	12	8	3.99	29	2	169.1	166	75	69	95
90 AL	0	0	2.04	4	0	17.2	13	4	9	9
91 AL	0	0	18.00	1	0	1.0	2	2	1	0
Life	15	21	3.75	64	3	369.2	356	154	141	209

BILL DORAN

Position: Second base
Team: Cincinnati Reds
Born: May 28, 1958 Cincinnati, OH
Height: 6' **Weight:** 175 lbs.
Bats: both **Throws:** right
Acquired: Traded from Astros for Butch Henry, Keith Kaiser, and Terry McGriff, 8/90

Player Summary	
Fantasy Value	$4 to $7
Card Value	3¢ to 5¢
Will	play steady defense
Can't	run like he used to
Expect	occasional power
Don't Expect	many strikeouts

Doran expects to be running more in 1992. Taking 196 career steals into the 1991 campaign, he tried only a handful of swipes last year because he was still recuperating from surgery that repaired his ailing back during the previous off-season. The surgery didn't hurt Doran's play at second base; he had a streak of 48 errorless games in '91. Though his range was reduced by the surgery, he remains a good second baseman who turns the double-play well. He is also a patient hitter with some power. Doran walks more often than he strikes out. He is also adept at staying out of double-plays. His 1992 commons will not move. Fantasy managers could get good, cheap ($5) middle infield help from him. Doran may need more rest but there's no reason he shouldn't remain a regular player.

Major League Batting Register

	BA	G	AB	R	H	2B	3B	HR	RBI	SB
82 NL	.278	26	97	11	27	3	0	0	6	5
83 NL	.271	154	535	70	145	12	7	8	39	12
84 NL	.261	147	548	92	143	18	11	4	41	21
85 NL	.287	148	578	84	166	31	6	14	59	23
86 NL	.276	145	550	92	152	29	3	6	37	42
87 NL	.283	162	625	82	177	23	3	16	79	31
88 NL	.248	132	480	66	119	18	1	7	53	17
89 NL	.219	142	507	65	111	25	2	8	58	22
90 NL	.300	126	403	59	121	29	2	7	37	23
91 NL	.280	111	361	51	101	12	2	6	35	5
Life	.269	1293	4684	672	1262	200	37	76	444	201
3 AVE	.262	126	424	58	111	22	2	7	43	17

CURRENT PLAYERS

BRIAN DOWNING

Position: Designated hitter
Team: Texas Rangers
Born: Oct. 9, 1950 Los Angeles, CA
Height: 5'10" **Weight:** 194 lbs.
Bats: right **Throws:** right
Acquired: Signed as a free agent, 4/91

Player Summary	
Fantasy Value	$5 to $8
Card Value	3¢ to 5¢
Will	reach base often
Can't	steal bases
Expect	reduced at bats
Don't Expect	outfield time

After 13 years with California, Downing was turned out to pasture at age 40. The Rangers offered him a last-minute invitation to 1991 spring training. Though he broke his hand three days after arriving, he convinced Bobby Valentine he could help the club. Once activated, Downing proved the point with a home run in his debut and a 19-for-24 tear. His excellent eye and ability to make contact make him a good leadoff hitter even though he does not run well. He is a $6 designated hitter who will provide some power. His 1992 cards aren't the best investments available.

Major League Batting Register

	BA	G	AB	R	H	2B	3B	HR	RBI	SB
73 AL	.178	34	73	5	13	1	0	2	4	0
74 AL	.225	108	293	41	66	12	1	10	39	0
75 AL	.240	138	420	58	101	12	1	7	41	13
76 AL	.256	104	317	38	81	14	0	3	30	7
77 AL	.284	69	169	28	48	4	2	4	25	1
78 AL	.255	133	412	42	105	15	0	7	46	3
79 AL	.326	148	509	87	166	27	3	12	75	3
80 AL	.290	30	93	5	27	6	0	2	25	0
81 AL	.249	93	317	47	79	14	0	9	41	1
82 AL	.281	158	623	109	175	37	2	28	84	2
83 AL	.246	113	403	68	99	15	1	19	53	1
84 AL	.275	156	539	65	148	28	2	23	91	0
85 AL	.263	150	520	80	137	23	1	20	85	5
86 AL	.267	152	513	90	137	27	4	20	95	4
87 AL	.272	155	567	110	154	29	3	29	77	5
88 AL	.242	135	484	80	117	18	2	25	64	3
89 AL	.283	142	544	59	154	25	2	14	59	0
90 AL	.273	96	330	47	90	18	2	14	51	0
91 AL	.278	123	407	76	113	17	2	17	49	1
Life	.267	2237	7533	1135	2010	342	28	265	1034	49
3 AVE	.279	120	427	61	119	20	2	15	53	0

KELLY DOWNS

Position: Pitcher
Team: San Francisco Giants
Born: Oct. 25, 1960 Ogden, UT
Height: 6'4" **Weight:** 200 lbs.
Bats: right **Throws:** right
Acquired: Traded from Phillies with George Riley for Al Oliver and Renie Martin, 9/84

Player Summary	
Fantasy Value	$2 to $4
Card Value	3¢ to 5¢
Will	retain relief role
Can't	help at bat
Expect	erratic control
Don't Expect	return of shoulder woes

Although he had a cloudy medical history, Downs responded well to his deployment as a relief pitcher in 1991. In his first 22 relief outings, he compiled a perfect 7-0 record and 1.25 ERA. With eight straight wins, he became the Giants' first 10-game winner. Though he sometimes suffers lapses of control, Downs throws his fastball, changeup, and split-fingered fastball from an over-the-top delivery that eases the strain on his rotator cuff. He missed most of the 1989 and 1990 campaigns while recuperating from surgery that repaired it. His 1992 cards offer no investment potential. Though he still tops 90 miles an hour, he now changes speeds more than he once did. The varied timing of his pitches has made him much more successful. His fine fielding helps. His stats suggest that he is a $3 fantasy hurler, though he could break through with a big season. A healthy Downs should be one of the league's more reliable relief pitchers.

Major League Pitching Register

	W	L	ERA	G	S	IP	H	ER	BB	SO
86 NL	4	4	2.75	14	0	88.1	78	27	30	64
87 NL	12	9	3.63	41	1	186.0	185	75	67	137
88 NL	13	9	3.32	27	0	168.0	140	62	47	118
89 NL	4	8	4.79	18	0	82.2	82	44	26	49
90 NL	3	2	3.43	13	0	63.0	56	24	20	31
91 NL	10	4	4.19	45	0	111.2	99	52	53	62
Life	46	36	3.65	158	1	699.2	640	284	243	461
3 AVE	6	5	4.20	25	0	85.1	79	40	33	47

CURRENT PLAYERS

DOUG DRABEK

Position: Pitcher
Team: Pittsburgh Pirates
Born: July 25, 1962 Victoria, TX
Height: 6'1" **Weight:** 185 lbs.
Bats: right **Throws:** right
Acquired: Traded from Yankees with Logan Easley and Brian Fisher for Pat Clements, Rick Rhoden, and Cecilio Guante, 11/86

Player Summary	
Fantasy Value	$12 to $17
Card Value	5¢ to 10¢
Will	remain staff ace
Can't	duplicate 1990
Expect	streaky performances
Don't Expect	long losing streaks

Drabek is a control pitcher who throws a fastball, curveball, changeup, and a slider—his best pitch. He used all four pitches to perfection in winning the 1990 NL Cy Young Award, going 22-6 with a 2.76 ERA. He then got off to a slow start in 1991 before recapturing his winning form. He pitched a one-hitter at St. Louis May 27. Drabek labored in the farm systems of the White Sox and Yankees before joining the Pirates. He gives up lots of home runs—most of them with few runners on base—but he is effective against both right- and lefthanded hitters. He helps himself by holding runners close, and he is one of the game's best-fielding pitchers. He is a $15 starter, because the Pirates rely on him so much. Drabek has won at least 14 games four years in a row and is one of the NL's most reliable starters. His 1992 cards are promising nickel buys.

Major League Pitching Register

	W	L	ERA	G	CG	IP	H	ER	BB	SO
86 AL	7	8	4.10	27	0	131.2	126	60	50	76
87 NL	11	12	3.88	29	1	176.1	165	76	46	120
88 NL	15	7	3.08	33	3	219.1	194	75	50	127
89 NL	14	12	2.80	35	8	244.1	215	76	69	123
90 NL	22	6	2.76	33	9	231.1	190	71	56	131
91 NL	15	14	3.07	35	5	234.2	245	80	62	142
Life	84	59	3.19	192	26	1237.2	1135	438	333	719
3 AVE	17	11	2.88	34	7	236.1	217	76	62	132

MARIANO DUNCAN

Position: Infield; outfield
Team: Philadelphia Phillies
Born: March 13, 1963 San Pedro de Macoris, Dominican Republic
Height: 6' **Weight:** 185 lbs.
Bats: right **Throws:** right
Acquired: Signed as a free agent, 12/91

Player Summary	
Fantasy Value	$3 to $6
Card Value	3¢ to 5¢
Will	show world-class speed
Can't	hold everyday job
Expect	erratic defense
Don't Expect	patience at bat

Batting tips from Lou Piniella helped Duncan blossom into a .306 hitter in 1990. That same year, he became the first Red to lead the NL in triples since Vada Pinson in 1967 and the first Red second baseman to hit .300 since Joe Morgan in 1976. He has always had great speed. Relegated to a utility role, he has played shortstop and the outfield, in addition to second base. An impatient hitter, Duncan strikes out three times more than he walks. He can go to the opposite field and usually handles lefthanders well. In December, he signed a free-agent contract with Philadelphia. Duncan's fantasy value will increase with the increase in at bats he should receive in 1992. His 1992 commons are not good buys on the strength of one good season. Duncan's defense leaves much to be desired. He may be best suited to a utility role.\

Major League Batting Register

	BA	G	AB	R	H	2B	3B	HR	RBI	SB
85 NL	.244	142	562	74	137	24	6	6	39	38
86 NL	.229	109	407	47	93	7	0	8	30	48
87 NL	.215	76	261	31	56	8	1	6	18	11
89 NL	.248	94	258	32	64	15	2	3	21	9
90 NL	.306	125	435	67	133	22	11	10	55	13
91 NL	.258	100	333	46	86	7	4	12	40	5
Life	.252	646	2256	297	569	83	24	45	203	124
3 AVE	.276	106	342	48	94	15	6	8	39	9

CURRENT PLAYERS

SHAWON DUNSTON

Position: Shortstop
Team: Chicago Cubs
Born: March 21, 1963 Brooklyn, NY
Height: 6'1" **Weight:** 175 lbs.
Bats: right **Throws:** right
Acquired: First-round pick in 6/82 free-agent draft

Player Summary	
Fantasy Value	$15 to $20
Card Value	5¢ to 7¢
Will	show rifle arm
Can't	hit for high average
Expect	decent production
Don't Expect	reduction in Ks

Dunston could always hit; he hit .790 and stole 37 bases in as many tries as a senior at Brooklyn's Thomas Jefferson High School. Blessed with speed, power, and one of the game's best shortstop arms, Dunston spent three years in the Chicago farm system before reaching the majors in 1985. The Opening Day shortstop that spring, he faltered at bat and returned to Triple-A. After an August recall, Dunston hit .320 in 40 games and earned the right to stay. In 1986, he hit 17 homers, most by a Cub shortstop since Ernie Banks had 29 in 1961, and drove in 68 runs, best by a Cub at his position since Banks had 80 in '61. Dunston also led league shortstops in putouts, total chances, assists, and double-plays. His speed and power make him a $15 fantasy shortstop. You might want to buy a few of his 1992 cards for a nickel apiece. He has been an NL All-Star selection twice.

Major League Batting Register

	BA	G	AB	R	H	2B	3B	HR	RBI	SB
85 NL	.260	74	250	40	65	12	4	4	18	11
86 NL	.250	150	581	66	145	37	3	17	68	13
87 NL	.246	95	346	40	85	18	3	5	22	12
88 NL	.249	155	575	69	143	23	6	9	56	30
89 NL	.278	138	471	52	131	20	6	9	60	19
90 NL	.262	146	545	73	143	22	8	17	66	25
91 NL	.260	142	492	59	128	22	7	12	50	21
Life	.258	900	3260	399	840	154	37	73	340	131
3 AVE	.267	142	503	61	134	21	7	13	59	22

LEN DYKSTRA

Position: Outfield
Team: Philadelphia Phillies
Born: Feb. 10, 1963 Santa Ana, CA
Height: 5'10" **Weight:** 167 lbs.
Bats: left **Throws:** left
Acquired: Traded from Mets with Roger McDowell for Juan Samuel, 6/89

Player Summary	
Fantasy Value	$15 to $25
Card Value	5¢ to 7¢
Will	always play full-throttle
Can't	always hit homers
Expect	September fizzle
Don't Expect	many days on bench

Dykstra was a standout center fielder and leadoff man before suffering a broken collarbone, a broken cheekbone, and three broken ribs in a car crash last May 6. Later charged with drunken driving, he missed 61 games before returning July 15. In his first game back, he singled in the seventh, stole second, and scored on a single to break a 7-7 tie. The healthy Dykstra is one of the most aggressive players in the majors. Though he has a weak throwing arm, he covers considerable ground in center because of good speed coupled with good judgement. His uniform is often dirty from diving catches and head-first slides. A good base-stealer (33 out of 38 in 1990), Dykstra used a new open stance to flirt with a batting title two years ago. A late fade and a broken collarbone stopped his momentum. His ability makes him a $15 to $25 fantasy outfielder. His 1992 cards are average buys at a nickel.

Major League Batting Register

	BA	G	AB	R	H	2B	3B	HR	RBI	SB
85 NL	.254	83	236	40	60	9	3	1	19	15
86 NL	.295	147	431	77	127	27	7	8	45	31
87 NL	.285	132	431	86	123	37	3	10	43	27
88 NL	.270	126	429	57	116	19	3	8	33	30
89 NL	.237	146	511	66	121	32	4	7	32	30
90 NL	.325	149	590	106	192	35	3	9	60	33
91 NL	.297	63	246	48	73	13	5	3	12	24
Life	.283	846	2874	480	812	172	28	46	244	190
3 AVE	.287	119	449	73	129	27	4	6	35	29

CURRENT PLAYERS

DENNIS ECKERSLEY

Position: Pitcher
Team: Oakland Athletics
Born: Oct. 3, 1954 Oakland, CA
Height: 6'2" **Weight:** 195 lbs.
Bats: right **Throws:** right
Acquired: Traded from Cubs with Dan Rohn for Dave Wilder, Brian Guinn, and Mark Leonette, 4/87

Player Summary	
Fantasy Value	$25 to $32
Card Value	5¢ to 7¢
Will	work often
Can't	tolerate losing
Expect	frequent saves
Don't Expect	blown save opportunities

Eckersley is a fastball-and-slider pitcher whose sidearm style is especially difficult for righthanded hitters. He is also one of the game's great control pitchers. The five-time All-Star spent 12 seasons as a starter before Oakland placed him in the bullpen in 1987. Three years later, he had 48 saves in 50 opportunities. He was MVP of the 1988 ALCS. He struggled a bit early in 1991 but started to ring up saves with regularity once the A's started scoring runs. He is a $30 fantasy closer. If he gets into the Hall of Fame, his 1992 cards will appreciate over a nickel.

Major League Pitching Register

	W	L	ERA	G	S	IP	H	ER	BB	SO
75 AL	13	7	2.60	34	2	186.2	147	54	90	152
76 AL	13	12	3.43	36	1	199.1	155	76	78	200
77 AL	14	13	3.53	33	0	247.1	214	97	54	191
78 AL	20	8	2.99	35	0	268.1	258	89	71	162
79 AL	17	10	2.99	33	0	246.2	234	82	59	150
80 AL	12	14	4.28	30	0	197.2	188	94	44	121
81 AL	9	8	4.27	23	0	154.0	160	73	35	79
82 AL	13	13	3.73	33	0	224.1	228	93	43	127
83 AL	9	13	5.61	28	0	176.1	223	110	39	77
84 AL	4	4	5.01	9	0	64.2	71	36	13	33
84 AL	10	8	3.03	24	0	160.1	152	54	36	81
85 NL	11	7	3.08	25	0	169.1	145	58	19	117
86 NL	6	11	4.57	33	0	201.0	226	102	43	137
87 AL	6	8	3.03	54	16	115.2	99	39	17	113
88 AL	4	2	2.35	60	45	72.2	52	19	11	70
89 AL	4	0	1.56	51	33	57.2	32	10	3	55
90 AL	4	2	0.61	63	48	73.1	41	5	4	73
91 AL	5	4	2.96	67	43	76.0	60	25	9	87
Life	174	144	3.47	671	188	2891.1	2685	1116	668	2025
3 AVE	4	2	1.74	60	41	69.1	44	13	5	72

MARK EICHHORN

Position: Pitcher
Team: California Angels
Born: Nov. 21, 1960 San Jose, CA
Height: 6'3" **Weight:** 200 lbs.
Bats: right **Throws:** right
Acquired: Signed as a free agent, 12/89

Player Summary	
Fantasy Value	$2 to $5
Card Value	3¢ to 5¢
Will	keep runners off base
Can't	blow batters away
Expect	great K-to-walk ratio
Don't Expect	control problems

Eichhorn was one of baseball's most effective set-up men last year. He displays exceptional control despite an unorthodox sidearm and submarine style that is especially tough on righthanded hitters. He relied on off-speed deliveries that seemed to magnify the velocity of Bryan Harvey's fastball when the hard-throwing closer followed Eichhorn. He also relied on exceptional control, with about one walk for every 10 innings pitched. His top pitch is a tantalizing changeup designed to spoil the timing of opposing hitters. It usually works: Eichhorn had an ERA below 2.00 last year. In his best year, the veteran reliever went 14-6 with 10 saves and a 1.72 ERA in 157 innings for the 1986 Blue Jays. Middle relievers seldom become stars, so pass up his 1992 commons. Eichhorn's fastball has slowed since, but he survives by outsmarting the hitters. Limit your fantasy bid to $5.

Major League Pitching Register

	W	L	ERA	G	S	IP	H	ER	BB	SO
82 AL	0	3	5.45	7	0	38.0	40	23	14	16
86 AL	14	6	1.72	69	10	157.0	105	30	45	166
87 AL	10	6	3.17	89	4	127.2	110	45	52	96
88 AL	0	3	4.18	37	1	66.2	79	31	27	28
89 NL	5	5	4.35	45	0	68.1	70	33	19	49
90 AL	2	5	3.08	60	13	84.2	98	29	23	69
91 AL	3	3	1.98	70	1	81.2	63	18	13	49
Life	34	31	3.01	377	29	624.0	565	209	193	473
3 AVE	3	4	3.07	58	5	78.2	77	27	18	56

CURRENT PLAYERS

JIM EISENREICH

Position: Outfield; first base
Team: Kansas City Royals
Born: April 18, 1959 St. Cloud, MN
Height: 5'11" **Weight:** 195 lbs.
Bats: left **Throws:** left
Acquired: Signed as a free agent, 10/86

Player Summary	
Fantasy Value	$5 to $8
Card Value	3¢ to 5¢
Will	play strong defense
Can't	reach the outfield fences
Expect	respectable batting average
Don't Expect	everyday play

If Eisenreich had more power, he'd realize his desire to become an everyday player. He does hit for a good average, play good defense, and add speed to the lineup. He broke in with the 1982 Twins but missed most of the next four seasons while suffering from the neurological disease Tourette's Syndrome. He was Kansas City's Player of the Year in 1989, his first full season. He flirted with the .300 mark for most of 1991. Eisenreich has speed (27 steals in 1989) and enough defensive ability to handle all three outfield positions. His .996 fielding percentage led AL outfielders two years ago. He is not a selective hitter and draws few walks, but he doesn't strike out much either. He is a reasonable fantasy commodity for $5 to $8. His 1992 cards will not sell well. Eisenreich is a valuable fourth outfielder who should see plenty of action.

Major League Batting Register

	BA	G	AB	R	H	2B	3B	HR	RBI	SB
82 AL	.303	34	99	10	30	6	0	2	9	0
83 AL	.286	2	7	1	2	1	0	0	0	0
84 AL	.219	12	32	1	7	1	0	0	3	2
87 AL	.238	44	105	10	25	8	2	4	21	1
88 AL	.218	82	202	26	44	8	1	1	19	9
89 AL	.293	134	475	64	139	33	7	9	59	27
90 AL	.280	142	496	61	139	29	7	5	51	12
91 AL	.301	135	375	47	113	22	3	2	47	5
Life			1791	220	499	108	20	23	209	56
3 AVE					130	28	6	5	52	15

KEVIN ELSTER

Position: Shortstop
Team: New York Mets
Born: Aug. 3, 1964 San Pedro, CA
Height: 6'2" **Weight:** 200 lbs.
Bats: right **Throws:** right
Acquired: Second-round pick in 1/84 free-agent draft

Player Summary	
Fantasy Value	$3 to $6
Card Value	3¢ to 5¢
Will	play solid defense
Can't	lift average over .220
Expect	occasional homer
Don't Expect	Ozzie Smith

Good field, no hit: Elster has worn the label for years. In his first three big league seasons, he compiled a .219 average. He was at the same level with six weeks left in his fourth. Though he averages eight home runs a season, he needs to bolster his batting proficiency before he can be assured of holding his job. Even his strong fielding doesn't help. Elster holds the NL record for consecutive errorless games by a shortstop. The fastest road to self-improvement would be better knowledge of the strike zone. Elster is an impatient hitter who strikes out far more often than he walks. He does not hit well in the clutch, most breaking balls give him fits, and he has a history of shoulder problems. Overlook his 1992 common-priced cards as invesiments. He is a $5 fantasy shortstop. The advent of expansion next year might prolong Elster's status as a regular.

Major League Batting Register

	BA	G	AB	R	H	2B	3B	HR	RBI	SB
86 NL	.167	19	30	3	5	1	0	0	0	0
87 NL	.400	5	10	1	4	2	0	0	1	0
88 NL	.214	149	406	41	87	11	1	9	37	2
89 NL	.231	151	458	52	106	25	2	10	55	4
90 NL	.207	92	314	36	65	20	1	9	45	2
91 NL	.241	115	348	33	84	16	2	6	36	2
Life	.224	531	1566	166	351	75	6	34	174	10
3 AVE	.228	119	373	40	85	20	2	8	45	3

CURRENT PLAYERS

SCOTT ERICKSON

Position: Pitcher
Team: Minnesota Twins
Born: Feb. 2, 1968 Long Beach, CA
Height: 6'4" **Weight:** 220 lbs.
Bats: right **Throws:** right
Acquired: Fourth-round pick in 6/89 free-agent draft

Player Summary	
Fantasy Value	$10 to $15
Card Value	15¢ to 20¢
Will	win 20 games
Can't	be defeated easily
Expect	good K-to-walk ratio
Don't Expect	another disabling injury

Erickson became baseball's best pitcher early in 1991, his first full big league season. Between April 20 and June 25, his 12-game winning streak was the biggest factor in Minnesota's rise from worst to first in the AL West. After spending a month on the disabled list with a sore forearm and elbow, he went 3-0 in his first five games back and posted his 15th win—tops in the majors—by August 4. That gave him 20 wins in 23 decisions dating back to September 1, 1990. Erickson's best pitch is a fastball that dives like a sinker but is as unpredictable as a knuckleball. Because his pitches move inside, outside, up, or down, he does not always know where they're going. He was an All-American at Arizona in '89 after an 18-3 season. Draft him for less than $15. While he faltered a bit late in '91, he is a pitcher who will win 12 games. His 1992 cards are good buys at less than 20 cents. If he stays healthy, Erickson should continue his domination of AL hitters.

Major League Pitching Register

	W	L	ERA	G	CG	IP	H	ER	BB	SO
90 AL	8	4	2.87	19	1	113.0	108	36	51	53
91 AL	20	8	3.18	32	5	204.0	189	72	71	108
Life	28	12	3.07	51	6	317.0	297	108	122	161
2 AVE	14	6	3.07	26	3	159.0	149	54	61	81

ALVARO ESPINOZA

Position: Shortstop
Team: New York Yankees
Born: Feb. 19, 1962 Valencia, Venezuela
Height: 6' **Weight:** 170 lbs.
Bats: right **Throws:** right
Acquired: Signed as a free agent, 11/87

Player Summary	
Fantasy Value	$1 to $3
Card Value	3¢ to 5¢
Will	provide good defense
Can't	add power
Expect	bunts when necessary
Don't Expect	high on-base percentage

Espinoza's average has gone up and down like a yo-yo over the last three years, his only full seasons in the majors. A free swinger with little power, he would help the team if he walked more often. Unfortunately, even the return of Frank Howard as Yankee batting coach last year didn't make a dent in that department. Espinoza did lift his average and cut his strikeouts but still refused to confine his swings to pitches in the strike zone. When he hit .282 in 1989, he made contact, hit to the opposite field, and went with the pitch. Howard steered Espinoza back into that pattern last year. Draft him for $2. There are worse-hitting shortstops at higher prices. He does not have great range but does position himself well in the field. He has good hands and a decent throwing arm. His 1992 cards don't deserve investment. If Espinoza keeps his average up, he'll play.

Major League Batting Register

	BA	G	AB	R	H	2B	3B	HR	RBI	SB
84 AL	.000	1	0	0	0	0	0	0	0	0
85 AL	.263	32	57	5	15	2	0	0	9	0
86 AL	.214	37	42	4	9	1	0	0	1	0
88 AL	.000	3	3	0	0	0	0	0	0	0
89 AL	.282	146	503	51	142	23	1	0	41	3
90 AL	.224	150	438	31	98	12	2	2	20	1
91 AL	.256	148	480	51	123	23	2	5	33	4
Life	.254	517	1523	142	387	61	5	7	104	8
3 AVE	.255	148	474	44	121	19	2	2	31	3

CURRENT PLAYERS

DWIGHT EVANS

Position: Designated hitter
Team: Baltimore Orioles
Born: Nov. 3, 1951 Santa Monica, CA
Height: 6'3" **Weight:** 205 lbs.
Bats: right **Throws:** right
Acquired: Signed as a free agent, 12/90

Player Summary	
Fantasy Value	$3 to $6
Card Value	5¢ to 9¢
Will	aim for 400 homers
Can't	play the field
Expect	occasional power
Don't Expect	fountain of youth

Evans began with the 1972 Red Sox, hit 379 home runs over 19 seasons, and then moved to Baltimore. Along the way, Evans had four 100-RBI seasons and topped 30 homers three times. Those days are gone, but he is still a dangerous hitter who coaxes many walks because of his superb knowledge of the strike zone. He won eight Gold Gloves as a right fielder, but his arm is no longer the cannon it once was. A three-time All-Star, he is still dangerous in clutch situations. He is near the end, as his low fantasy price ($5) indicates. His 1992 cards are just beginning to rise in price.

Major League Batting Register

	BA	G	AB	R	H	2B	3B	HR	RBI	SB
72 AL	.263	18	57	2	15	3	1	1	6	0
73 AL	.223	119	282	46	63	13	1	10	32	5
74 AL	.281	133	463	60	130	19	8	10	70	4
75 AL	.274	128	412	61	113	24	6	13	56	3
76 AL	.242	146	501	61	121	34	5	17	62	6
77 AL	.287	73	230	39	66	9	2	14	36	4
77 AL	.247	147	497	75	123	24	2	24	63	8
79 AL	.274	152	489	69	134	24	1	21	58	6
80 AL	.266	148	463	72	123	37	5	18	60	3
81 AL	.296	108	412	84	122	19	4	22	71	3
82 AL	.292	162	609	122	178	37	7	32	98	3
83 AL	.238	126	470	74	112	19	4	22	58	3
84 AL	.295	162	630	121	186	37	8	32	104	3
85 AL	.263	159	617	110	162	29	1	29	78	7
86 AL	.259	152	529	86	137	33	2	26	97	3
87 AL	.305	154	541	109	165	37	2	34	123	4
88 AL	.293	149	559	96	164	31	7	21	111	5
89 AL	.285	146	520	82	148	27	3	20	100	3
90 AL	.249	123	445	66	111	18	3	13	63	3
91 AL	.270	101	270	35	73	9	1	6	38	2
Life	.272	2606	8996	1470	2446	483	73	385	1384	78
3 AVE	.269	123	412	61	111	18	2	13	67	3

STEVE FARR

Position: Pitcher
Team: New York Yankees
Born: Dec. 12, 1956 Cheverly, MD
Height: 5'11" **Weight:** 200 lbs.
Bats: right **Throws:** right
Acquired: Signed as a free agent, 11/90

Player Summary	
Fantasy Value	$8 to $11
Card Value	3¢ to 5¢
Will	use fastball as top pitch
Can't	avoid lapses of control
Expect	a K-per-inning
Don't Expect	fans to forget Righetti

When the Yankees decided to replace departing closer Dave Righetti with newcomer Farr, critics pointed out that he had never served exclusively in short relief. Before a loss on August 4, however, Farr had justified the team's decision with 14 saves in as many opportunities and 27 consecutive scoreless innings. He throws a fastball, slider, and curve but doesn't always get them in the strike zone. He does help himself in the field, however. Farr broke in with the 1984 Indians and went to the Royals a year later. In 1990, his best year, he was 13-7 with one save and a 1.98 ERA in 57 games, with six starts. He isn't a card investor's dream. His 1992 commons will not rise in price. He's an affordable fantasy stopper for $10. He has performed well in a variety of assignments during his career but seems most effective as a reliever.

Major League Pitching Register

	W	L	ERA	G	S	IP	H	ER	BB	SO
84 AL	3	11	4.58	31	1	116.0	106	59	46	83
85 AL	2	1	3.11	16	1	37.2	34	13	20	36
86 AL	8	4	3.13	56	8	109.1	90	38	39	83
87 AL	4	3	4.15	47	1	91.0	97	42	44	88
88 AL	5	4	2.50	62	20	82.2	74	23	30	72
89 AL	2	5	4.12	51	18	63.1	75	29	22	56
90 AL	13	7	1.98	57	1	127.0	99	28	48	94
91 AL	5	5	2.19	60	23	70.0	57	17	20	60
Life	42	40	3.22	380	73	697.0	632	249	269	572
3 AVE	7	6	2.56	56	14	87.0	77	25	30	70

CURRENT PLAYERS

JEFF FASSERO

Position: Pitcher
Team: Montreal Expos
Born: Jan. 5, 1963 Springfield, IL
Height: 6'1" **Weight:** 180 lbs.
Bats: left **Throws:** left
Acquired: Signed as a free agent, 12/90

Player Summary	
Fantasy Value	$2 to $5
Card Value	8¢ to 12¢
Will	fan a hitter a frame
Can't	work into rotation
Expect	frequent outings
Don't Expect	many gopher balls

When Fassero made his major league debut last May 4, he pitched the last two innings of a 13-inning contest against San Diego and yielded a game-winning single to Tony Gwynn. But Fassero, a hard-throwing southpaw, settled down thereafter and proved to be a capable middle man in the Montreal bullpen. Originally signed by St. Louis after the Cards picked him in the 22nd round of the June 1984 free-agent draft, Fassero pitched for the Cleveland organization before coming to Montreal. He is a strikeout pitcher who averaged eight strikeouts per nine innings in the minors. He strikes out twice as many as he walks, and keeps the ball in the park, keeps baserunners close, and holds his own as a fielder. Fassero was Montreal's most effective reliever in 1991. As with many young relievers, Fassero will have overpriced cards in 1992. Wait until he wins the stopper role before investing any money in them. He could notch some saves for your fantasy team for as little as $2. Don't bid more than $5, however.

Major League Pitching Register

	W	L	ERA	G	S	IP	H	ER	BB	SO
91 NL	2	5	2.44	51	8	55.1	39	15	17	42
Life	2	5	2.44	51	8	55.1	39	15	17	42

MIKE FELDER

Position: Outfield
Team: San Francisco Giants
Born: Nov. 18, 1961 Vallejo, CA
Height: 5'8" **Weight:** 160 lbs.
Bats: both **Throws:** right
Acquired: Signed as a free agent, 4/91

Player Summary	
Fantasy Value	$3 to $6
Card Value	3¢ to 5¢
Will	run, run, run
Can't	hit homers
Expect	many reserve roles
Don't Expect	much time at second

In his first full National League season, Felder succeeded Brett Butler as San Francisco's best base-stealer. Though slowed by hamstring problems, Felder made the most of his opportunities as an extra outfielder behind Kevin Mitchell, Darren Lewis, Kevin Bass, and Willie McGee. A contact hitter with little power, Felder doesn't strike out much. Nor does he walk much, which is a problem for a leadoff hitter. A good bunter and hit-and-run man, he is often used as a pinch-hitter or pinch-runner. He's also a fine late-inning defensive replacement—in any outfield position. He can even play second base in a pinch. The switch-hitting utility player is fast enough to be successful on most of his base-stealing attempts. His 1992 cards are commons. He can provide affordable steals for up to $6. With his speed, Felder would be ideal for a team that played home games on synthetic turf.

Major League Batting Register

	BA	G	AB	R	H	2B	3B	HR	RBI	SB
85 AL	.196	15	56	8	11	1	0	0	0	4
86 AL	.239	44	155	24	37	2	4	1	13	16
87 AL	.266	108	289	48	77	5	7	2	31	34
88 AL	.173	50	81	14	14	1	0	0	5	8
89 AL	.241	117	315	50	76	11	3	3	23	26
90 AL	.274	121	237	38	65	7	2	3	27	20
91 NL	.264	132	348	51	92	10	6	0	18	21
Life	.251	587	1481	233	372	37	22	9	117	129
3 AVE	.259	123	300	46	78	9	4	2	23	22

CURRENT PLAYERS

JUNIOR FELIX

Position: Outfield
Team: California Angels
Born: Oct. 3, 1967 Laguna Sabada, Dominican Republic
Height: 5'11" **Weight:** 165 lbs.
Bats: both **Throws:** right
Acquired: Traded from Blue Jays with Luis Sojo and Ken Rivers for Devon White, Willie Fraser, and Marcus Moore, 12/90

Player Summary	
Fantasy Value	$4 to $7
Card Value	3¢ to 5¢
Will	show strong arm
Can't	hit for average
Expect	poor K-to-walk ratio
Don't Expect	Gold Glove defense

Baseball scout Epy Guerrero discovered Felix at a Dominican track meet. Though he had not played baseball since childhood, he showed so much promise during a workout that Guerrero signed him for Toronto. Felix led the Class-A Pioneer League with 37 steals as a first-year pro in '86. He stole 64 in 1987 as a sophomore at Class-A Myrtle Beach, and 40 in 1988 at Double-A Knoxville. He reached the majors in 1989 and immediately showed he could produce some power as well as speed. The Blue Jays gave up on the rifle-armed outfielder because he did not take full advantage of his speed. An impatient hitter, he was not willing to wait for walks that might lead to stolen bases. He strikes out far more often than he walks—negating his potential as a leadoff hitter. He had a .370 slugging percentage and a .321 on-base average in '91. He has stone-cold 1992 cards. He is a fantasy buy at less than $7. When he makes better contact, he will succeed.

Major League Batting Register

	BA	G	AB	R	H	2B	3B	HR	RBI	SB
89 AL	.258	110	415	62	107	14	8	9	46	18
90 AL	.263	127	463	73	122	23	7	15	65	13
91 AL	.283	66	230	32	65	10	2	2	26	7
Life	.265	303	1108	167	294	47	17	26	137	38
3 AVE	.265	101	369	56	98	16	6	9	46	13

FELIX FERMIN

Position: Shortstop
Team: Cleveland Indians
Born: Oct. 9, 1963 Mao Valverde, Dominican Republic
Height: 5'11" **Weight:** 170 lbs.
Bats: right **Throws:** right
Acquired: Traded from Pirates with Denny Gonzales for Jay Bell, 3/89

Player Summary	
Fantasy Value	$1 to $3
Card Value	3¢ to 5¢
Will	hit .250
Can't	steal bases
Expect	strong throws
Don't Expect	any power

Fermin's place in the major leagues is guaranteed by his glove. Never a heavy hitter, he compensates with graceful fielding and skillful bunting. He also makes contact more often than many of his teammates. Hardly an automatic out, he hits better than .250 every season. He doesn't always collect a home run annually, however. When he hit one on April 22, 1990, it was his first in 2,915 times at bat. Fermin also lacks speed. Making contact isn't so great when the ground balls produced result in double-plays. In 1991, "The Cat" had a .302 slugging percentage and a .307 on-base average. That's why Fermin's fielding remains his forte. He makes about two-dozen errors a year, because he reaches balls other shortstops can't. He has a strong arm and plays his position well. He is a $2 fantasy shortstop. His 1992 commons are best left in the bins, because he probably lost his starting job to Mark Lewis.

Major League Batting Register

	BA	G	AB	R	H	2B	3B	HR	RBI	SB
87 NL	.250	23	68	6	17	0	0	0	4	0
88 NL	.276	43	87	9	24	0	2	0	2	3
89 AL	.238	156	484	50	115	9	1	0	21	6
90 AL	.256	148	414	47	106	13	2	1	40	3
91 AL	.262	129	424	30	111	13	2	0	31	5
Life	.253	499	1477	142	373	35	7	1	98	17
3 AVE	.251	144	441	42	111	12	2	0	31	5

CURRENT PLAYERS

ALEX FERNANDEZ

Position: Pitcher
Team: Chicago White Sox
Born: Aug. 13, 1969 Miami Beach, FL
Height: 6'1" **Weight:** 205 lbs.
Bats: right **Throws:** right
Acquired: First-round pick in 6/90 free-agent draft

Player Summary	
Fantasy Value	$4 to $8
Card Value	5¢ to 7¢
Will	throw four pitches
Can't	finish what he starts
Expect	gradual improvement
Don't Expect	Tom Seaver clone

The White Sox wondered last year whether Fernandez was rushed to the majors in 1990. Drafted out of college in June, he reached the majors August 1 after winning six games in eight starts for clubs on all three levels of the minors. He split 10 decisions, fanning almost twice as many as he walked, to justify management's decision to dole out a $350,000 signing bonus to an untested 20-year-old. Inexperience caught up to Fernandez in 1991, when he dropped 11 of his first 17 and became the only member of the staff to yield more than five earned runs per game. Card investors should draw their own conclusions about how quickly he will begin the 1992 season before spending. He was still second on the team in strikeouts, however. When he's right, Fernandez throws four pitches for strikes: a fastball, curve, changeup, and slider. A mediocre fielder with a good pickoff move, Fernandez has the physique and pitching motion of Tom Seaver. The key is getting the results to match. He is a promising fantasy hurler for under $10.

Major League Pitching Register

	W	L	ERA	G	CG	IP	H	ER	BB	SO
90 AL	5	5	3.80	13	3	87.2	89	37	34	61
91 AL	9	13	4.51	34	2	191.2	186	96	88	145
Life	14	18	4.29	47	5	279.1	275	133	122	206
2 AVE	7	9	4.29	24	3	139.2	138	67	61	103

SID FERNANDEZ

Position: Pitcher
Team: New York Mets
Born: Oct. 12, 1962 Honolulu, HI
Height: 6'1" **Weight:** 230 lbs.
Bats: left **Throws:** left
Acquired: Traded from Dodgers with Ross Jones for Carlos Diaz and Bob Bailor, 12/83

Player Summary	
Fantasy Value	$4 to $7
Card Value	3¢ to 5¢
Will	get many Ks
Can't	avoid injury
Expect	few hits allowed
Don't Expect	20 wins

Fernandez missed the first half of the 1991 season after he broke his left arm while trying to field a one-hop smash by Houston's Javier Ortiz during a March exhibition game. A strikeout pitcher who had the NL's lowest batting average against him in 1990, Fernandez always wages a personal Battle of the Bulge. Criticized for carrying too much weight when he reported to spring training last year, he previously had knee problems related to his excess poundage. When healthy, Fernandez throws a riding fastball, slider, changeup, and a hard and slow curve—all from an unorthodox motion that baffles batters. His 1992 commons will not be good investments until he pitches two or so full seasons. He is a promising $5 fantasy hurler. He has good control and helps himself at the plate, but he's slow. Fernandez is a good No. 3 starter.

Major League Pitching Register

	W	L	ERA	G	CG	IP	H	ER	BB	SO
83 NL	0	1	6.00	2	0	6.0	7	4	7	9
84 NL	6	6	3.50	15	0	90.0	74	35	34	62
85 NL	9	9	2.80	26	3	170.1	108	53	80	180
86 NL	16	6	3.52	32	2	204.1	161	80	91	200
87 NL	12	8	3.81	28	3	156.0	130	66	67	134
88 NL	12	10	3.03	31	1	187.0	127	63	70	189
89 NL	14	5	2.83	35	6	219.1	157	69	75	198
90 NL	9	14	3.46	30	2	179.1	130	69	67	181
91 NL	1	3	2.86	8	0	44.0	36	14	9	31
Life	79	62	3.25	207	17	1256.1	930	453	500	1184
2 AVE	12	10	3.12	33	4	199.1	144	69	71	190

CURRENT PLAYERS

TONY FERNANDEZ

Position: Shortstop
Team: San Diego Padres
Born: June 30, 1962 San Pedro de Macoris, Dominican Republic
Height: 6'2" **Weight:** 175 lbs.
Bats: both **Throws:** right
Acquired: Traded from Blue Jays with Fred McGriff for Joe Carter and Roberto Alomar, 12/90

Player Summary
Fantasy Value	$10 to $13
Card Value	5¢ to 7¢
Will	play spectacular defense
Can't	hit for power
Expect	line drives into gaps
Don't Expect	injury-free season

The Padres headed into the 1990 Winter Meetings with one objective, improving their defense at shortstop. With incumbent Garry Templeton suffering from aching knees, the Padres pulled out all the stops to land a top-caliber replacement in Fernandez. He broke into the majors with the 1983 Blue Jays and became the No. 1 shortstop a year later. He has since won four Gold Gloves for fielding excellence but also suffered several serious injuries, including three fractures. In 1991, he had a .360 slugging percentage and a .337 on-base average. His 1992 cards are painless buys for a nickel each. Fewer RBI reduces the fantasy price for him to $13. Fernandez ranks with Ozzie Smith defensively.

Major League Batting Register
	BA	G	AB	R	H	2B	3B	HR	RBI	SB
83 AL	.265	15	34	5	9	1	1	0	2	0
84 AL	.270	88	233	29	63	5	3	3	19	5
85 AL	.289	161	564	71	163	31	10	2	51	13
86 AL	.310	163	687	91	213	33	9	10	65	25
87 AL	.322	146	578	90	186	29	8	5	67	32
88 AL	.287	154	648	76	186	41	4	5	70	15
89 AL	.257	140	573	64	147	25	9	11	64	22
90 AL	.276	161	635	84	175	27	17	4	66	26
91 AL	.272	145	558	81	152	27	5	4	38	23
Life	.287	1173	4510	591	1294	219	66	44	442	161
3 AVE	.268	149	589	76	158	26	10	6	56	24

CECIL FIELDER

Position: First base
Team: Detroit Tigers
Born: Sept. 21, 1963 Los Angeles, CA
Height: 6'3" **Weight:** 230 lbs.
Bats: right **Throws:** right
Acquired: Signed as a free agent, 1/90

Player Summary
Fantasy Value	$40 to $45
Card Value	10¢ to 15¢
Will	show huge power
Can't	steal bases
Expect	challenge to Maris's record
Don't Expect	high average

In 1991, Fielder joined Hank Greenberg as the only Tiger to produce successive 40-homer seasons. A year after becoming the first big leaguer since 1977 to reach 50 homers, Fielder again led the majors in home runs and runs batted in. Playing half the schedule in Tiger Stadium helped, as did his ability to reduce a high strikeout ratio. One of two players to reach the 50-homer plateau in the last 30 years, Fielder has silenced skeptics who condemned the Tigers for giving the former Toronto part-timer a two-year, $3 million contract to leave Japan after the 1989 season. A free swinger who strikes out twice as often as he walks, he has enormous power to all fields—especially against lefties. He is a chancy draft at $45, but he is worth it. Though he lacks speed and has some trouble with pop-ups, Fielder supplies decent defense at first base. Turn his 1992 cards over quickly for short-term profits.

Major League Batting Register
	BA	G	AB	R	H	2B	3B	HR	RBI	SB
85 AL	.311	30	74	6	23	4	0	4	16	0
86 AL	.157	34	83	7	13	2	0	4	13	0
87 AL	.269	82	175	30	47	7	1	14	32	0
88 AL	.230	74	174	24	40	6	1	9	23	0
90 AL	.277	159	573	104	159	25	1	51	132	0
91 AL	.261	162	624	102	163	25	0	44	133	0
Life	.261	541	1703	273	445	69	3	126	349	0
2 AVE	.269	161	599	103	161	25	1	48	133	0

CURRENT PLAYERS

CHUCK FINLEY

Position: Pitcher
Team: California Angels
Born: Nov. 26, 1962 Monroe, LA
Height: 6'6" **Weight:** 212 lbs.
Bats: left **Throws:** left
Acquired: First-round pick in 6/85 free-agent draft

Player Summary	
Fantasy Value	$16 to $21
Card Value	5¢ to 7¢
Will	use four out pitches
Can't	revamp defense
Expect	great changeup
Don't Expect	overpowering pitches

Finley's 10-2 start in 1991 was the fastest in Angel history. The owner of the American League's second-best earned run average in each of the two previous seasons, he developed into a big winner by mixing a fastball, split-fingered fastball, changeup, and occasional curve with usually reliable control. He had developed the curve as a reliever early in his career, then learned the splitter when moved into the regular rotation in 1988. The two-time All-Star was unfairly deprived of a third trip last year. Finley strikes out twice as many as he walks. He has had several good seasons, and his fantasy value reflects that fact. His 1992 cards are not good investments at a nickel apiece. He helps himself with a fine pickoff move but cancels that out with occasional defensive lapses—especially on throws. He joins Jim Abbott and Mark Langston to give the Angels three top southpaw starters.

Major League Pitching Register

	W	L	ERA	G	CG	IP	H	ER	BB	SO
86 AL	3	1	3.30	25	0	46.1	40	17	23	37
87 AL	2	7	4.67	35	0	90.2	102	47	43	63
88 AL	9	15	4.17	31	2	194.1	191	90	82	111
89 AL	16	9	2.57	29	9	199.2	171	57	82	156
90 AL	18	9	2.40	32	7	236.0	210	63	81	177
91 AL	18	9	3.80	34	4	227.1	205	96	101	171
Life	66	50	3.35	186	22	994.1	919	370	412	715
3 AVE	17	9	2.93	32	7	221.1	195	72	88	168

STEVE FINLEY

Position: Outfield
Team: Houston Astros
Born: March 12, 1965 Union City, TN
Height: 6'2" **Weight:** 175 lbs.
Bats: left **Throws:** left
Acquired: Traded from Orioles with Pete Harnisch and Curt Schilling for Glenn Davis, 1/91

Player Summary	
Fantasy Value	$6 to $9
Card Value	3¢ to 5¢
Will	top team in steals
Can't	handle tough lefties
Expect	excellent defense
Don't Expect	consistent power

Finley gave the Astros more than they bargained for. He is a solid leadoff hitter who knows the strike zone, works the count, and hits to all fields. He seems to be improving as he gains experience. He hit .256 with three homers for the 1990 Orioles but improved his numbers significantly in '91. In 1988, he won the Triple-A International League batting crown with a .314 mark. He was selected as that loop's No. 4 prospect in *Baseball America*. He still strikes out slightly more often than he walks but shows signs of becoming more selective—an asset for a leadoff man. A speedy line-drive hitter with power to the gaps, Finley is perfect for the colossal confines of the Astrodome. He has good range and a good arm in center, and rarely makes defensive mistakes. Houston's top base-stealer, Finley should improve as he learns NL pitchers. He has not proved that he can be a $10 fantasy outfielder yet, but he is close. His 1992 cards will probably be commons.

Major League Batting Register

	BA	G	AB	R	H	2B	3B	HR	RBI	SB
89 AL	.249	81	217	35	54	5	2	2	25	17
90 AL	.256	142	464	46	119	16	4	3	37	22
91 NL	.285	159	596	84	170	28	10	8	54	34
Life	.269	382	1277	165	343	49	16	13	116	73
3 AVE	.269	127	426	55	114	16	5	4	39	24

CURRENT PLAYERS

CARLTON FISK

Position: Catcher
Team: Chicago White Sox
Born: Dec. 26, 1947 Bellow Falls, VT
Height: 6'2" **Weight:** 223 lbs.
Bats: right **Throws:** right
Acquired: Signed as a free agent, 3/81

Player Summary	
Fantasy Value	$9 to $12
Card Value	10¢ to 20¢
Will	hit fastballs long
Can't	run as before
Expect	some time at first
Don't Expect	everyday play

Fisk has hit more home runs than any other catcher and will pass Bob Boone in '92 as the all-time leader in games caught. The only receiver with more than 100 steals and 100 home runs, Fisk has made the All-Star team 11 times. His dime-priced 1992 cards are good long-term investments. He still has the arm action to nab a healthy share of base-runners. A disciple of conditioning, Fisk does his hardest work before and after games. He needed surgical repair of both knees before the '91 season.

Major League Batting Register

	BA	G	AB	R	H	2B	3B	HR	RBI	SB
69 AL	.000	2	5	0	0	0	0	0	0	0
71 AL	.313	14	48	7	15	2	1	2	6	0
72 AL	.293	131	457	74	134	28	9	22	61	5
73 AL	.246	135	508	65	125	21	0	26	71	7
74 AL	.299	52	187	36	56	12	1	11	26	5
75 AL	.331	79	263	47	87	14	4	10	52	4
76 AL	.255	134	487	76	124	17	5	17	58	12
77 AL	.315	152	536	106	169	26	3	26	102	7
78 AL	.284	157	571	94	162	39	5	20	88	7
79 AL	.272	91	320	49	87	23	2	10	42	3
80 AL	.289	131	478	73	138	25	3	18	62	11
81 AL	.263	96	338	44	89	12	0	7	45	3
82 AL	.267	135	476	66	127	17	3	14	65	17
83 AL	.289	138	488	85	141	26	4	26	86	9
84 AL	.231	102	359	54	83	20	1	21	43	6
85 AL	.238	153	543	85	129	23	1	37	107	17
86 AL	.221	125	457	42	101	11	0	14	63	2
87 AL	.256	135	454	68	116	22	1	23	71	1
88 AL	.277	76	253	37	70	8	1	19	50	0
89 AL	.293	103	375	47	110	25	2	13	68	1
90 AL	.285	137	452	65	129	21	0	18	65	7
91 AL	.241	134	460	42	111	25	0	18	74	1
Life	.270	2412	8515	1262	2303	417	46	372	1305	125
3 AVE	.272	125	429	51	117	24	1	16	69	3

MIKE FITZGERALD

Position: Catcher
Team: Montreal Expos
Born: July 13, 1960 Long Beach, CA
Height: 5'11" **Weight:** 190 lbs.
Bats: right **Throws:** right
Acquired: Traded from Mets with Hubie Brooks, Floyd Youmans, and Herm Winningham for Gary Carter, 12/84

Player Summary	
Fantasy Value	$1 to $2
Card Value	3¢ to 5¢
Will	get clutch hits
Can't	keep .250 average
Expect	good game-calling
Don't Expect	job as No. 1 catcher

Fitzgerald's inability to keep his average over .200 cost him the top catcher's job with Montreal in '91. Though regarded as a good handler of pitchers, he wound up on the bench with his silent bat. In seven previous seasons, he had produced a .241 average and established a reputation as a better hitter in clutch situations. He even hit a career-high nine home runs in 111 games during the 1990 campaign. Fitzgerald can contribute a stolen base on occasion but invariably strikes out more than he walks. A good defensive backstop, he also finds it difficult to erase potential base-stealers. Versatility could keep him in the big leagues. Fitzgerald can also fill in at first base and the outfield and makes a relatively potent pinch-hitter. He lost some of his fantasy value, and is a $2 catcher. Skip over his 1992 commons.

Major League Batting Register

	BA	G	AB	R	H	2B	3B	HR	RBI	SB
83 NL	.100	8	20	1	2	0	0	1	0	0
84 NL	.242	112	360	20	87	15	1	2	33	1
85 NL	.207	108	295	25	61	7	1	5	34	5
86 NL	.282	73	209	20	59	13	1	6	37	3
87 NL	.240	107	287	32	69	11	0	3	36	3
88 NL	.271	63	155	17	42	6	1	5	23	2
89 NL	.238	100	290	33	69	18	2	7	42	3
90 NL	.243	111	313	36	76	18	1	9	41	8
91 NL	.202	71	198	17	40	5	2	4	28	4
Life	.237	753	2127	201	505	93	9	42	276	29
3 AVE	.231	94	267	29	62	14	2	7	37	5

CURRENT PLAYERS

MIKE FLANAGAN

Position: Pitcher
Team: Baltimore Orioles
Born: Dec. 16, 1951 Manchester, NH
Height: 6' **Weight:** 195 lbs.
Bats: left **Throws:** left
Acquired: Signed as a free agent, 3/91

Player Summary	
Fantasy Value	$1 to $2
Card Value	3¢ to 5¢
Will	work in short spurts
Can't	return to rotation
Expect	great pickoff move
Don't Expect	overpowering stuff

Jim Palmer's ill-fated attempt to return to Baltimore's pitching staff last spring overshadowed the comeback of another Oriole hero, Mike Flanagan. Removed from the publicity spotlight, he succeeded where Palmer failed. Released by Toronto on May 8, 1990, Flanagan sat out the season before winning an Oriole job with a strong spring in '91. He won the Cy Young Award in 1979. He was used as a reliever in 1991. A control pitcher, Flanagan throws a fastball, curveball, slider, and changeup—often with a three-quarters delivery that is tough on lefties. He is a $2 fantasy reliever. His 1992 commons have no investment appeal.

Major League Pitching Register

	W	L	ERA	G	S	IP	H	ER	BB	SO
75 AL	0	1	2.79	2	0	9.2	9	3	6	7
76 AL	3	5	4.13	20	0	85.0	83	39	33	56
77 AL	15	10	3.64	36	1	235.0	235	95	70	149
78 AL	19	15	4.03	40	0	281.1	271	126	87	167
79 AL	23	9	3.08	39	0	265.2	245	91	70	190
80 AL	16	13	4.12	37	0	251.1	278	115	71	128
81 AL	9	6	4.19	20	0	116.0	108	54	37	72
82 AL	15	11	3.97	36	0	236.0	233	104	76	103
83 AL	12	4	3.30	20	0	125.1	135	46	31	50
84 AL	13	13	3.53	34	0	226.2	213	89	81	115
85 AL	4	5	5.13	15	0	86.0	101	49	28	42
86 AL	7	11	4.24	29	0	172.0	179	81	66	96
87 AL	6	8	4.06	23	0	144.0	148	65	51	93
88 AL	13	13	4.18	34	0	211.0	220	98	80	99
89 AL	8	10	3.93	30	0	171.2	186	75	47	47
90 AL	2	2	5.31	5	0	20.1	28	12	8	5
91 AL	2	7	2.38	64	3	98.1	84	26	25	55
Life	167	143	3.84	484	4	2735.1	2756	1168	867	1474
2 AVE	5	9	3.37	47	2	135.2	135	51	36	51

TOM FOLEY

Position: Infield
Team: Montreal Expos
Born: Sept. 9, 1959 Columbus, GA
Height: 6'1" **Weight:** 180 lbs.
Bats: left **Throws:** right
Acquired: Traded from Phillies with Larry Sorensen for Dan Schatzeder and Skeeter Barnes, 7/86

Player Summary	
Fantasy Value	$1 to $3
Card Value	3¢ to 5¢
Will	field with ability
Can't	show power
Expect	use at three spots
Don't Expect	good speed

Foley has been a utility infielder throughout his nine-year career in the majors. Primarily a shortstop, he has also played the other infield positions and even pitched once in a mop-up role. He seems most comfortable at second base, where he played over 100 games in 1989. A contact hitter and good hit-and-run man, Foley sometimes can still tag the ball. He's used almost exclusively against righthanded pitching. He is a good glove man with good range at both second and short but seems destined to remain in his utility role at least until the NL expands next season. The problem is his bat. Foley is a .250 lifetime hitter whose last home run came three years ago. He had a .269 on-base average in 1991. His 1992 cards are commons. Still, he can help a team. He is a $2 fantasy infielder.

Major League Batting Register

	BA	G	AB	R	H	2B	3B	HR	RBI	SB
83 NL	.204	68	98	7	20	4	1	0	9	1
84 NL	.253	106	277	26	70	8	3	5	27	3
85 NL	.240	89	250	24	60	13	1	3	23	2
86 NL	.266	103	263	26	70	15	3	1	30	10
87 NL	.293	106	280	35	82	18	3	5	28	6
88 NL	.265	127	377	33	100	21	3	5	43	2
89 NL	.229	122	375	34	86	19	2	7	39	2
90 NL	.213	73	164	11	35	2	1	0	12	0
91 NL	.208	86	168	12	35	11	1	0	15	2
Life	.248	880	2252	208	558	111	18	26	219	28
3 AVE	.221	94	236	19	52	11	1	2	22	1

CURRENT PLAYERS

JOHN FRANCO

Position: Pitcher
Team: New York Mets
Born: Sept. 17, 1960 Brooklyn, NY
Height: 5'10" **Weight:** 185 lbs.
Bats: left **Throws:** left
Acquired: Traded from Reds with Don Brown for Kip Gross and Randy Myers, 12/89

Player Summary	
Fantasy Value	$37 to $42
Card Value	5¢ to 10¢
Will	keep ball in park
Can't	do Dibble imitation
Expect	frequent outings
Don't Expect	many walks

Although lower back problems bothered him at times during the 1991 season, Franco remained one of the top southpaw relievers in the National League. The veteran short relief specialist passed the 200-save plateau in July. Franco's best pitch remains a screwball that makes him as effective against righties as he is against lefties. Though he mixes the pitch with a fastball, cut fastball, and slider, Franco succeeds primarily because of an ability to change speeds and deliveries. He is a $40 fantasy closer. When he's on, he gets grounders—and iron-gloved Met infielders get ulcers. When Kevin Elster is on the bench, Franco is probably the best fielder out there when he's pitching. He keeps runners close, and he even gets hits occasionally. His 1992 cards won't bring immediate profits, but he is gaining a fair number of career saves.

Major League Pitching Register

	W	L	ERA	G	S	IP	H	ER	BB	SO
84 NL	6	2	2.61	54	4	79.1	74	23	36	55
85 NL	12	3	2.18	67	12	99.0	83	24	40	61
86 NL	6	6	2.94	74	29	101.0	90	33	44	84
87 NL	8	5	2.52	68	32	82.0	76	23	27	61
88 NL	6	6	1.57	70	39	86.0	60	15	27	46
89 NL	4	8	3.12	60	32	80.2	77	28	36	60
90 NL	5	3	2.53	55	33	67.2	66	19	21	56
91 NL	5	9	2.93	52	30	55.1	61	18	18	45
Life	52	42	2.53	500	211	651.0	587	183	249	468
3 AVE	5	7	2.87	56	32	67.2	68	22	25	54

JULIO FRANCO

Position: Second base
Team: Texas Rangers
Born: Aug. 23, 1961 San Pedro de Macoris, Dominican Republic
Height: 6'1" **Weight:** 185 lbs.
Bats: right **Throws:** right
Acquired: Traded from Indians for Oddibe McDowell, Jerry Browne, and Pete O'Brien, 12/88

Player Summary	
Fantasy Value	$25 to $30
Card Value	5¢ to 10¢
Will	hit over .300
Can't	make double-play pivot
Expect	good production
Don't Expect	high K totals

Though he has a unique batting stance, Franco believes it's not wise to mess with success. He won the AL batting crown with his .341 average in '91. He was outspoken in his criticism of the fans for choosing Robby Alomar as the AL's starting All-Star second baseman in 1991. Franco then made a good case for himself with his final statistics. Though he can't match Alomar in the field, Franco is not only the league's best offensive second baseman but a good fielder at the position. A converted shortstop, he has more than adequate range and a strong arm. Franco has good speed, some power, and the ability to hit to the opposite field. He is a fantasy bargain at $25. His nickel-priced 1992 cards are good investments.

Major League Batting Register

	BA	G	AB	R	H	2B	3B	HR	RBI	SB
82 NL	.276	16	29	3	8	1	0	0	3	0
83 AL	.273	149	560	68	153	24	8	8	80	32
84 AL	.286	160	658	82	188	22	5	3	79	19
85 AL	.288	160	636	97	183	33	4	6	90	13
86 AL	.306	149	599	80	183	30	5	10	74	10
87 AL	.319	128	495	86	158	24	3	8	52	32
88 AL	.303	152	613	88	186	23	6	10	54	25
89 AL	.316	150	548	80	173	31	5	13	92	21
90 AL	.296	157	582	96	172	27	1	11	69	31
91 AL	.341	146	589	108	201	27	3	15	78	36
Life	.302	1367	5309	788	1605	242	40	84	671	219
3 AVE	.318	151	573	95	182	28	3	13	80	29

CURRENT PLAYERS

MARVIN FREEMAN

Position: Pitcher
Team: Atlanta Braves
Born: April 10, 1963 Chicago, IL
Height: 6'7" **Weight:** 222 lbs.
Bats: right **Throws:** right
Acquired: Traded from Phillies for Joe Boever, 7/90

Player Summary
Fantasy Value	$2 to $4
Card Value	3¢ to 5¢
Will	throw hard
Can't	shake back woes
Expect	frequent calls
Don't Expect	bouts of wildness

Freeman had just established himself as one of the National League's most reliable set-up men when his 1991 season was curtailed by injury. After surgery August 30 to repair a bulging disc in his back, the towering righthanded reliever was lost for the year. At the time he went down, Freeman had compiled a 3.00 ERA in 34 appearances, spanning 48 innings, and had even picked up his second major league save. He struck out more than twice as many as he walked and kept the ball in the park. In his first full big league campaign after five seasons of bouncing between the majors and minors, he got off to a slow start but came on strong—even though he admitted the back injury bothered him for several months before surgery. His 1992 cards are not recommended investments. He will not get the save opportunities to be more than a $4 fantasy reliever. His showing secured his role as a set-up man for Atlanta.

Major League Pitching Register

	W	L	ERA	G	S	IP	H	ER	BB	SO
86 NL	2	0	2.25	3	0	16.0	6	4	10	8
88 NL	2	3	6.10	11	0	51.2	55	35	43	37
89 NL	0	0	6.00	1	0	3.0	2	2	5	0
90 NL	1	2	4.31	25	1	48.0	41	23	17	38
91 NL	1	0	3.00	34	1	48.0	37	16	13	34
Life	6	5	4.32	74	2	166.2	141	80	88	117
2 AVE	1	1	3.66	30	1	48.2	39	20	15	36

TODD FROHWIRTH

Position: Pitcher
Team: Baltimore Orioles
Born: Sept. 28, 1962 Milwaukee, WI
Height: 6'4" **Weight:** 204 lbs.
Bats: right **Throws:** right
Acquired: Signed as a free agent, 12/90

Player Summary
Fantasy Value	$3 to $5
Card Value	3¢ to 5¢
Will	yield few walks and homers
Can't	use common delivery
Expect	good K-to-walk ratio
Don't Expect	job switch with Gregg Olson

Submariners Ted Abernathy, Dick Hyde, and Dan Quisenberry would be proud of Frohwirth, a Kent Tekulve clone who found success as a set-up man with Baltimore. A true under-hander, Frohwirth had led four minor leagues in saves before the Orioles gave him an extended 1991 audition. He responded with an under-2.00 ERA. He posted a 2-1 ratio of strikeouts to walks and kept the ball in the park. Opponents compiled a .190 batting average, a .267 slugging percentage, and a .255 on-base average against him in 1991. A sidearm pitcher when he first signed, he adapted his underhanded style after watching Tekulve pitch on television. Frohwirth had four stints with Philadelphia but became a minor league free agent after the 1990 campaign. He notched a Triple-A International League-high 21 saves and 67 games at Scranton in '90. His fantasy profile was one of 1991's biggest comebacks. He is a sleeper at $5. His 1992 cards, however, will remain commons.

Major League Pitching Register

	W	L	ERA	G	S	IP	H	ER	BB	SO
87 NL	1	0	0.00	10	0	11.0	12	0	2	9
88 NL	1	2	8.25	12	0	12.0	16	11	11	11
89 NL	1	0	3.59	45	0	62.2	56	25	18	39
90 NL	0	1	18.00	5	0	1.0	3	2	6	1
91 AL	7	3	1.87	51	3	96.1	64	20	29	77
Life	10	6	2.85	123	3	183.0	151	58	66	137
2 AVE	4	2	2.55	48	2	79.2	60	23	24	58

CURRENT PLAYERS

TRAVIS FRYMAN

Position: Third base; shortstop
Team: Detroit Tigers
Born: March 25, 1969 Lexington, KY
Height: 6'2" **Weight:** 190 lbs.
Bats: right **Throws:** right
Acquired: Third-round pick in 6/87 free-agent draft

Player Summary	
Fantasy Value	$24 to $30
Card Value	10¢ to 15¢
Will	hit for power
Can't	master strike zone
Expect	more errors
Don't Expect	dwindling average

In 1991, his first full major league season, Fryman was named the owner of the AL's best infield arm by managers responding to a *Baseball America* poll. Though he is a natural shortstop, he usually plays third when veteran Tiger shortstop Alan Trammell is healthy. Though Fryman was a shortstop when he led several minor leagues in errors, the figures were misleading because he got to balls others couldn't reach. He has excellent range and a strong arm. He is still learning the fundamentals of playing third, however. Most of his team-leading error total in 1991 came while playing that position. At the plate, Fryman is developing into Detroit's typical all-or-nothing mold. He had half the home runs but as many strikeouts as Cecil Fielder. Fryman had a .447 slugging percentage and a .309 on-base average in 1991. He chases too many bad pitches and walks infrequently. On the verge of stardom, try to get his 1992 cards for a dime apiece. He is a fantasy steal for $25.

Major League Batting Register

	BA	G	AB	R	H	2B	3B	HR	RBI	SB
90 AL	.297	66	232	32	69	11	1	9	27	3
91 AL	.259	149	557	65	144	36	3	21	91	12
Life	.270	215	789	97	213	47	4	30	118	15
2 AVE	.270	108	395	49	107	24	2	15	59	8

GARY GAETTI

Position: Third base
Team: California Angels
Born: Aug. 19, 1958 Centralia, IL
Height: 6' **Weight:** 200 lbs.
Bats: right **Throws:** right
Acquired: Signed as a free agent, 1/91

Player Summary	
Fantasy Value	$16 to $20
Card Value	4¢ to 6¢
Will	show Gold Glove defense
Can't	steal bases
Expect	more strikeouts
Don't Expect	more production

If he isn't winning games with home runs, Gaetti is winning them with his glove. A four-time Gold Glove winner, he is still one of the game's premier third basemen even though his power numbers have declined. In the field, he has very good hands and a strong arm. The long-time member of the Twins tried to correct his hitting decline in 1991 by wearing glasses. It's not probable that Gaetti can recapture the stroke that produced two 30-homer, 100-RBI seasons from 1986 to '87. At his peak, he hit with power to all fields. One problem is impatience at bat; he fans three times as much as he walks. Gaetti is a reliable fantasy choice for $20. His 1992 cards are lukewarm investment choices at a nickel apiece.

Major League Batting Register

	BA	G	AB	R	H	2B	3B	HR	RBI	SB
81 AL	.192	9	26	4	5	0	0	2	3	0
82 AL	.230	145	508	59	117	25	4	25	84	0
83 AL	.245	157	584	81	143	30	3	21	78	7
84 AL	.262	162	588	55	154	29	4	5	65	11
85 AL	.246	160	560	71	138	31	0	20	63	13
86 AL	.287	157	596	91	171	34	1	34	108	14
87 AL	.257	154	584	95	150	36	2	31	109	10
88 AL	.301	133	468	66	141	29	2	28	88	7
89 AL	.251	130	498	63	125	11	4	19	75	6
90 AL	.229	154	577	61	132	27	5	16	85	6
91 AL	.246	152	586	58	144	22	1	18	66	5
Life	.255	1513	5575	704	1420	274	26	219	824	79
3 AVE	.241	145	554	61	134	20	3	18	75	6

CURRENT PLAYERS

GREG GAGNE

Position: Shortstop
Team: Minnesota Twins
Born: Nov. 12, 1961 Fall River, MA
Height: 5'11" **Weight:** 172 lbs.
Bats: right **Throws:** right
Acquired: Traded from Yankees with Ron Davis and Paul Boris for Roy Smalley, 4/82

Player Summary	
Fantasy Value	$3 to $5
Card Value	3¢ to 5¢
Will	play solid defense
Can't	wait for walks
Expect	some power
Don't Expect	average above .260

Gagne owns one of the loop's best infield arms. In fact, AL managers said in a survey last year that only Travis Fryman had a better one. Gagne also knows what to do with a glove—he had a 76-game errorless streak last season. Also blessed with great range, Gagne turned in a performance that made him a strong contender for a Gold Glove. On defense, he charges and anticipates well, makes the double-play, and moves well laterally. The Minnesota shortstop has some pop in his bat, consistently reaching the .400 level in slugging percentage during his career. His pop makes him a cheap fantasy extra for $5. He contributes some timely RBI and steals 15 bases a year. He has the speed to swipe more. His common-priced 1992 cards are not high priorities. He still is one of the league's better shortstops.

Major League Batting Register

	BA	G	AB	R	H	2B	3B	HR	RBI	SB
83 AL	.111	10	27	2	3	1	0	0	3	0
84 AL	.000	2	1	0	0	0	0	0	0	0
85 AL	.225	114	293	37	66	15	3	2	23	10
86 AL	.250	156	472	63	118	22	6	12	54	12
87 AL	.265	137	437	68	116	28	7	10	40	6
88 AL	.236	149	461	70	109	20	6	14	48	15
89 AL	.272	149	460	69	125	29	7	9	48	11
90 AL	.235	138	388	38	91	22	3	7	38	8
91 AL	.265	139	408	52	108	23	3	8	42	11
Life	.250	994	2947	399	736	160	35	62	296	73
3 AVE	.258	142	419	53	108	25	4	8	43	10

ANDRES GALARRAGA

Position: First base
Team: St. Louis Cardinals
Born: June 18, 1961 Caracas, Venezuela
Height: 6'3" **Weight:** 235 lbs.
Bats: right **Throws:** right
Acquired: Traded from Expos for Ken Hill, 11/91

Player Summary	
Fantasy Value	$4 to $7
Card Value	3¢ to 5¢
Will	improve in '92
Can't	stop bad swings
Expect	flawless defense
Don't Expect	over 15 steals

When he's healthy, Galarraga hits with power and plays first base as well as anyone in the game. In 1991, however, he missed 42 games after undergoing arthroscopic surgery on his left kneecap on June 9. When he returned, "The Cat" had trouble recapturing the batting stroke that had produced four consecutive seasons of at least 85 runs batted in. He did, however, display the defensive form that earned consecutive Gold Gloves in 1989 and '90. He scoops wild throws, feeds covering pitchers, makes the 3-6-3 double-play, and shows good lateral movement. He is a two-time .300 hitter who reached career peaks with 29 homers and 92 RBI in 1988. He is a $5 fantasy first baseman at this point, though he could rebound. Galarraga has a fatal flaw: a tendency to strike out too often—about four times more than he walks. His 1992 commons have little profit potential.

Major League Batting Register

	BA	G	AB	R	H	2B	3B	HR	RBI	SB
85 NL	.187	24	75	9	14	1	0	2	4	1
86 NL	.271	105	321	39	87	13	0	10	42	6
87 NL	.305	147	551	72	168	40	3	13	90	7
88 NL	.302	157	609	99	184	42	8	29	92	13
89 NL	.257	152	572	76	147	30	1	23	85	12
90 NL	.256	155	579	65	148	29	0	20	87	10
91 NL	.219	107	375	34	82	13	2	9	33	5
Life	.269	847	3082	394	830	168	14	106	433	54
3 AVE	.247	138	509	58	126	24	1	17	68	9

CURRENT PLAYERS

DAVE GALLAGHER

Position: Outfield
Team: New York Mets
Born: Sept. 20, 1960 Trenton, NJ
Height: 6' **Weight:** 180 lbs.
Bats: right **Throws:** right
Acquired: Traded from Angels for Hubie Brooks, 12/91

Player Summary	
Fantasy Value	$1 to $3
Card Value	3c to 5c
Will	play good defense
Can't	steal much
Expect	270-plus average
Don't Expect	much everyday play

Gallagher is a contact hitter who never hits for power but often reaches base. Though he doesn't walk much, he has a good batting stroke that produced a .303 average for the 1988 White Sox. He also has good stamina, as he showed by playing 161 games in 1989. A strong-armed outfielder with good range, Gallagher can play all three positions but is used most often in center. He has a high fielding percentage every year. Though he doesn't steal bases often, he uses his good speed by dropping occasional bunts, taking extra bases, and running down fly balls others might miss. Though he was an Angel last season, California traded him to the Mets in the off-season. Since he doesn't have a starting job, his 1992 commons are not wise investments. Gallagher is an ideal bench player as a pinch-hitter, pinch-runner, and extra outfielder. For a high batting average, spend a couple bucks for him at the draft.

Major League Batting Register

	BA	G	AB	R	H	2B	3B	HR	RBI	SB
87 AL	.111	15	36	2	4	1	1	0	1	2
88 AL	.303	101	347	59	105	15	3	5	31	5
89 AL	.266	161	601	74	160	22	2	1	46	5
90 AL	.254	68	126	12	32	4	1	0	7	1
91 AL	.293	90	270	32	79	17	0	1	30	2
Life	.275	435	1380	179	380	59	7	7	115	15
2 AVE	.274	126	436	53	120	20	1	1	38	4

MIKE GALLEGO

Position: Infield
Team: Oakland Athletics
Born: Oct. 31, 1960 Whittier, CA
Height: 5'8" **Weight:** 160 lbs.
Bats: right **Throws:** right
Acquired: Second-round pick in 6/81 free-agent draft

Player Summary	
Fantasy Value	$4 to $7
Card Value	3c to 5c
Will	play strong second
Can't	swipe bases
Expect	bunts for hits
Don't Expect	average over .250

American League managers rate Gallego right behind Ozzie Guillen as the best bunter in the league, according to a 1991 *Baseball America* poll. Equally at home at second or short, Gallego established career peaks in home runs and RBI when given the chance to be Oakland's everyday second baseman in '91. A skilled fielder, he has outstanding range and good hands at second, where he is adept at turning the double-play. He doesn't have a strong arm from short but fields smoothly and gets rid of the ball in a hurry. As a hitter, Gallego has some pop and can hit to the opposite field. He'll also bunt for a hit on occasion. He has good speed but is thrown out more often than he steals successfully. He is a $5 fantasy middle infielder. His 1992 commons are not great investments. On a team of stars, Gallego is often overlooked and always underrated.

Major League Batting Register

	BA	G	AB	R	H	2B	3B	HR	RBI	SB
85 AL	.208	76	77	13	16	5	1	1	9	1
86 AL	.270	20	37	2	10	2	0	0	4	0
87 AL	.250	72	124	18	31	6	0	2	14	0
88 AL	.209	129	277	38	58	8	0	2	20	2
89 AL	.252	133	357	45	90	14	2	3	30	7
90 AL	.206	140	389	36	80	13	2	3	34	5
91 AL	.247	159	482	67	119	15	4	12	49	6
Life	.232	729	1743	219	404	63	9	23	160	21
3 AVE	.235	144	409	49	96	14	3	6	38	6

CURRENT PLAYERS

RONNIE GANT

Position: Outfield
Team: Atlanta Braves
Born: March 2, 1965 Victoria, TX
Height: 6' **Weight:** 172 lbs.
Bats: right **Throws:** right
Acquired: Fourth-round pick in 6/83 free-agent draft

Player Summary
Fantasy Value	$30 to $35
Card Value	10¢ to 15¢
Will	turn 30-30 trick
Can't	avoid slow starts
Expect	improved defense
Don't Expect	any batting titles

A two-month slump at the start of the 1991 season did not prevent Gant from enjoying his second consecutive 30-30 campaign. Used in several slots in the lineup—including leadoff—he was most productive when utilized as Atlanta's cleanup hitter while David Justice was idled for nearly two months with a bad back. Gant's play in center field, a relatively new position for the former second baseman, improved as the season went on. He became an outfielder in 1989 after the Braves decided to take advantage of his exceptional natural speed. He has the arm for center field, but he has still had some problems adjusting. At bat, he had a .496 slugging percentage and a .338 on-base average in 1991. His 1992 cards are good buys with long-term potential at a dime apiece. Because he has great power, some scouts suggest Gant could soon become the National League's first 40-40 player. You can bust the budget at the fantasy draft. He is a $30-plus outfielder.

Major League Batting Register
	BA	G	AB	R	H	2B	3B	HR	RBI	SB
87 NL	.265	21	83	9	22	4	0	2	9	4
88 NL	.259	146	563	85	146	28	8	19	60	19
89 NL	.177	75	260	26	46	8	3	9	25	9
90 NL	.303	152	575	107	174	34	3	32	84	33
91 NL	.251	154	561	101	141	35	3	32	105	34
Life	.259	548	2042	328	529	109	17	94	283	99
3 AVE	.259	127	465	78	120	26	3	24	71	25

JIM GANTNER

Position: Second base; third base
Team: Milwaukee Brewers
Born: Jan. 5, 1954 Fond Du Lac, WI
Height: 5'11" **Weight:** 175 lbs.
Bats: left **Throws:** right
Acquired: 12th-round pick in 6/74 free-agent draft

Player Summary
Fantasy Value	$1 to $2
Card Value	3¢ to 5¢
Will	help at two spots
Can't	steal bases
Expect	many singles
Don't Expect	over 120 games

Although Gantner recovered from reconstructive knee surgery, he has not recovered from baseball's longest power drought. Between June 14, 1987 and August 28, 1990, Gantner failed to homer in 1,741 at bats, spanning 539 games. The veteran lefthanded hitter broke in with the Brewers in 1976. He spent most of his 1991 season at third base while hot-hitting Willie Randolph played second. A contact hitter who uses all fields, Gantner doesn't strike out much, but he doesn't walk much either. He is a $1 utility infielder. His 1992 commons should be neglected. Gantner is a steady player who holds his own.

Major League Batting Register
	BA	G	AB	R	H	2B	3B	HR	RBI	SB
76 AL	.246	26	69	6	17	1	0	0	7	1
77 AL	.298	14	47	4	14	1	0	1	2	2
78 AL	.216	43	97	14	21	1	0	1	8	2
79 AL	.284	70	208	29	59	10	3	2	22	3
80 AL	.282	132	415	47	117	21	3	4	40	11
81 AL	.267	107	352	35	94	14	1	2	33	3
82 AL	.295	132	447	48	132	17	2	4	43	6
83 AL	.282	161	603	85	170	23	8	11	74	5
84 AL	.282	153	613	61	173	27	1	3	56	6
85 AL	.254	143	523	63	133	15	4	5	44	11
86 AL	.274	139	497	58	136	25	1	7	38	13
87 AL	.272	81	265	37	72	14	0	4	30	6
88 AL	.276	155	539	67	149	28	2	0	47	20
89 AL	.274	116	409	51	112	18	3	0	34	20
90 AL	.263	88	323	36	85	8	5	0	25	18
91 AL	.283	140	526	63	149	27	4	2	47	4
Life	.275	1700	5933	704	1633	250	37	46	550	131
3 AVE	.275	115	419	50	115	18	4	1	35	14

CURRENT PLAYERS

MIKE GARDINER

Position: Pitcher
Team: Boston Red Sox
Born: Oct. 19, 1965 Sarnia, Ontario, Canada
Height: 6' **Weight:** 185 lbs.
Bats: both **Throws:** right
Acquired: Traded from Mariners for Rob Murphy, 4/91

Player Summary	
Fantasy Value	$4 to $7
Card Value	5¢ to 7¢
Will	throw four pitches
Can't	keep ball in park
Expect	high ERA
Don't Expect	complete games

Gardiner had glowing minor league credentials before the Red Sox called him to the majors last May 31. The 1990 Double-A Eastern League Pitcher of the Year, Gardiner notched a 1.90 ERA to go with his 12-8 record. He had 149 strikeouts and 29 walks in 179⅔ innings that year. He won seven of eight decisions in the Triple-A International League early in the 1991 campaign, with a 2.34 ERA and two complete games. He then proceeded to split his first dozen decisions in the majors. Used exclusively as a starter, the 1984 Canadian Olympian had trouble keeping the ball in the park. He yielded 13 gopher balls in his first 14 starts. A control pitcher in the minors, Gardiner throws four pitches for strikes: a fastball, curveball, slider, and changeup. His fastball is only average so he tries to pitch to spots. If his control falters, he can't win. With good support and additional experience, Gardiner could develop into a reliable big league starter. He is a bargain $5 pitcher. His 1992 commons are great buys.

Major League Pitching Register

	W	L	ERA	G	CG	IP	H	ER	BB	SO
90 AL	0	2	10.66	5	0	12.2	22	15	5	6
91 AL	9	10	4.85	22	0	130.0	140	70	47	91
Life	9	12	5.36	27	0	142.2	162	85	52	97

MARK GARDNER

Position: Pitcher
Team: Montreal Expos
Born: March 1, 1962 Los Angeles, CA
Height: 6'1" **Weight:** 190 lbs.
Bats: right **Throws:** right
Acquired: Eighth-round pick in 6/85 free-agent draft

Player Summary	
Fantasy Value	$4 to $7
Card Value	5¢ to 7¢
Will	vie for 15 wins
Can't	muster support
Expect	mastery over righties
Don't Expect	high hit totals

A year after undergoing serious elbow surgery, Gardner proved himself completely recovered by pitching nine no-hit innings against the heavy-hitting Dodgers July 26 before losing, 1-0, in the 10th. A strikeout pitcher, who features an above-average fastball, sweeping overhand curve, and big league changeup, Gardner lacks the wildness that plagues other hard throwers. He allows less than a hit an inning, isn't overly generous with gopher balls, and keeps his ERA respectable. Opposing batters compiled a .230 batting average, a .356 slugging percentage, and a .318 on-base average in '91. Only veteran Dennis Martinez was more effective among Montreal starters. Gardner twice led the Expo farm system in strikeouts and could do the same for the parent club in the near future. He was 12-4 with a 2.37 ERA at Triple-A Indianapolis in '89. Take a chance on him at the fantasy draft for no more than $7. He could win big. His 1992 commons are potentially very good investments. With any support, he should win at least 15 games.

Major League Pitching Register

	W	L	ERA	G	CG	IP	H	ER	BB	SO
89 NL	0	3	5.13	7	0	26.1	26	15	11	21
90 NL	7	9	3.42	27	3	152.2	129	58	61	135
91 NL	9	11	3.85	27	0	168.1	139	72	75	107
Life	16	23	3.76	61	3	347.1	294	145	147	263
2 AVE	8	10	3.64	27	2	160.2	134	65	68	121

CURRENT PLAYERS

SCOTT GARRELTS

Position: Pitcher
Team: San Francisco Giants
Born: Oct. 30, 1961 Urbana, IL
Height: 6'4" **Weight:** 205 lbs.
Bats: right **Throws:** right
Acquired: First-round pick in 6/79 free-agent draft

Player Summary
Fantasy Value	$2 to $4
Card Value	3¢ to 5¢
Will	eat up righties
Can't	be counted on before July
Expect	slow recuperation
Don't Expect	many wins in 1992

A one-time reliever who made a successful conversion to the starting rotation, Garrelts was San Francisco's top pitcher when he went on the shelf with a torn tendon in his right elbow last June 11. Garrelts had the "Tommy John operation" performed by Dr. Frank Jobe on July 18, who said Garrelts would not be available until mid-1992 at the earliest. He is a risk for your fantasy team, even at $3. Garrelts was a reliever before moving into the rotation in 1988. He responded with a 14-5 mark and led the NL with a 2.28 ERA. A year later, he went 12-11 after a slow start. When healthy, Garrelts throws a fastball, slider, and split-fingered fastball and is an excellent fielder. He's an easy out at the plate, however. His 1992 commons aren't worthwhile.

Major League Pitching Register
	W	L	ERA	G	CG	IP	H	ER	BB	SO
82 NL	0	0	13.50	1	0	2.0	3	3	2	4
83 NL	2	2	2.52	5	1	35.2	33	10	19	16
84 NL	2	3	5.65	21	0	43.0	45	27	34	32
85 NL	9	6	2.30	74	0	105.2	76	27	58	106
86 NL	13	9	3.11	53	0	173.2	144	60	74	125
87 NL	11	7	3.22	64	0	106.1	70	38	55	127
88 NL	5	9	3.58	65	0	98.0	80	39	46	86
89 NL	14	5	2.28	30	2	193.1	149	49	46	119
90 NL	12	11	4.15	31	4	182.0	190	84	70	80
91 NL	1	1	6.41	8	0	19.2	25	14	9	8
Life	69	53	3.29	352	9	959.1	815	351	413	703
2 AVE	13	8	3.19	31	3	188.1	170	67	58	100

KIRK GIBSON

Position: Outfield
Team: Kansas City Royals
Born: May 28, 1957 Pontiac, MI
Height: 6'3" **Weight:** 215 lbs.
Bats: left **Throws:** left
Acquired: Signed as a free agent, 12/90

Player Summary
Fantasy Value	$8 to $12
Card Value	5¢ to 7¢
Will	get clutch hits
Can't	provide defense
Expect	stealing success
Don't Expect	return to 25-25

Next to the word intensity in the dictionary is a picture of Gibson. Though he always seems to be injured or playing in pain, he makes the most of his talent. He hits with power and gets more than his share of walks. He's also a savvy base-stealer who succeeds almost every time he tries. As a left fielder, Gibson is a perfect designated hitter. While he earned an "A" for effort, he had weak throws and botched plays last year. Gibson tried to hide his iron glove with his fading speed. His 1992 cards offer unpredictable results at best. He is a good $10 draft. He has been hobbled by hamstring and knee problems that began during his NL MVP season of 1988. He is a team leader.

Major League Batting Register
	BA	G	AB	R	H	2B	3B	HR	RBI	SB
79 AL	.237	12	38	3	9	3	0	1	4	3
80 AL	.263	51	175	23	46	2	1	9	16	4
81 AL	.328	83	290	41	95	11	3	9	40	17
82 AL	.278	69	266	34	74	16	2	8	35	9
83 AL	.227	128	401	60	91	12	9	15	51	14
84 AL	.282	149	531	92	150	23	10	27	91	29
85 AL	.287	154	581	96	167	37	5	29	97	30
86 AL	.268	119	441	84	118	11	2	28	86	34
87 AL	.277	128	487	95	135	25	3	24	79	26
88 NL	.290	150	542	106	157	28	1	25	76	31
89 NL	.213	71	253	35	54	8	2	9	28	12
90 NL	.260	89	315	59	82	20	0	8	38	26
91 AL	.236	132	462	81	109	17	6	16	55	18
Life	.269	1335	4782	809	1287	213	44	208	696	253
3 AVE	.238	97	343	58	82	15	3	11	40	19

CURRENT PLAYERS

PAUL GIBSON

Position: Pitcher
Team: Detroit Tigers
Born: Jan. 4, 1960 Southhampton, NY
Height: 6' **Weight:** 185 lbs.
Bats: right **Throws:** left
Acquired: Signed as a free agent, 11/84

Player Summary	
Fantasy Value	$1 to $3
Card Value	3¢ to 5¢
Will	work 60 games
Can't	always throw strikes
Expect	too many walks
Don't Expect	much closer use

Gibson is hardly the second coming of Willie Hernandez, who won Cy Young and MVP honors with the Champion '84 Tigers. Gibson has given Detroit its best lefthanded relief since Hernandez left, however. Gibson has been a valuable middle man for four straight seasons. After posting a career-best 2.93 ERA in 1988, he hasn't been as stingy with the opposition but his workload has increased. He's appeared more than 60 times in each of the last two seasons. A fastball-and-curveball pitcher who sometimes can't find the strike zone, he also throws too many gophers (10 in '91) to be an effective closer. In spot situations, however, he gives Mike Henneman breathing room. Gibson had a career high in saves in 1991. Opponents compiled a .297 batting average, a .424 slugging percentage, and a .379 on-base average in '91. He's expected to remain in his role during the 1992 campaign. Middle relievers aren't solid fantasy drafts. Stay to $2 for him. His 1992 commons are not good investments.

Major League Pitching Register

	W	L	ERA	G	S	IP	H	ER	BB	SO
88 AL	4	2	2.93	40	0	92.0	83	30	34	50
89 AL	4	8	4.64	45	0	132.0	129	68	57	77
90 AL	5	4	3.05	61	3	97.1	99	33	44	56
91 AL	5	7	4.59	68	8	96.0	112	49	48	52
Life	18	21	3.88	214	11	417.1	423	180	183	235
3 AVE	5	6	4.15	58	4	108.0	113	50	50	62

BERNARD GILKEY

Position: Outfield
Team: St. Louis Cardinals
Born: Sept. 24, 1966 St. Louis, MO
Height: 6' **Weight:** 170 lbs.
Bats: right **Throws:** right
Acquired: Signed as a free agent, 8/84

Player Summary	
Fantasy Value	$2 to $4
Card Value	10¢ to 15¢
Will	provide defense
Can't	hit homers
Expect	steals
Don't Expect	another Lou Brock

Gilkey replaced free agent Vince Coleman as St. Louis left fielder in 1991. Though he not did resemble Coleman as a base-stealer, Gilkey showed the potential to reach base more, strike out less, and play better defense. A broken thumb, suffered when he crashed into the San Diego outfield wall June 13, kept him out for a month. When he returned, his bat sputtered and he was sent to the minors. He hit only .146 at Triple-A Louisville. Gilkey has good speed; he stole 45 bases at Louisville in 1990 and was named best base-runner and most exciting player by American Association managers. After hitting .244 in his first four pro seasons, he tried to improve during off-season workouts. He had three hits in an inning for Louisville in 1990. His speed makes him a great fantasy pick up for $3. His sophomore 1992 cards are a tough call. Stay safe and pick them up only if he gets off to a great start in '92. Gilkey is a definite prospect who will improve with experience. If he bunts enough, he could hit .300.

Major League Batting Register

	BA	G	AB	R	H	2B	3B	HR	RBI	SB
90 NL	.297	18	64	11	19	5	2	1	3	6
91 NL	.216	81	268	28	58	7	2	5	20	14
Life	.232	99	332	39	77	12	4	6	23	20

CURRENT PLAYERS

JOE GIRARDI

Position: Catcher
Team: Chicago Cubs
Born: Oct. 14, 1964 Peoria, IL
Height: 5'11" **Weight:** 195 lbs.
Bats: right **Throws:** right
Acquired: Fifth-round selection in 6/86 free-agent draft

Player Summary	
Fantasy Value	$2 to $4
Card Value	3¢ to 5¢
Will	have good average
Can't	wait for walks
Expect	weak defense
Don't Expect	very much power

Girardi performed well as the everyday receiver for the 1990 Cubs after Damon Berryhill went down with shoulder problems. Girardi was a victim of the injury jinx in 1991, however, when he was disabled with a bulging disc in his back April 17 and did not return until August 6. He had trouble getting untracked but is normally a reliable hitter. In 1990, his first full season, Girardi hit .270 in 133 games. A contact hitter with little power, he would help the team more if he learned to be a selective hitter. Getting on base with walks would compensate for his inability to hit the ball out. He even has the speed to steal after reaching base. A strong-armed receiver who calls a good game, Girardi is also prone to mistakes. He is an unstable fantasy draft pick. While he has potential, he may not get a starting call, so stay under $4. His 1992 commons are not good investments. Light-hitting catchers who allow too many passed balls don't last.

Major League Batting Register

	BA	G	AB	R	H	2B	3B	HR	RBI	SB
89 NL	.248	59	157	15	39	10	0	1	14	2
90 NL	.270	133	419	36	113	24	2	1	38	8
91 NL	.191	21	47	3	9	2	0	0	6	0
Life	.258	213	623	54	161	36	2	2	58	10
2 AVE	.264	96	288	26	76	17	1	1	26	5

DAN GLADDEN

Position: Outfield
Team: Detroit Tigers
Born: July 7, 1957 San Jose, CA
Height: 5'11" **Weight:** 181 lbs.
Bats: right **Throws:** right
Acquired: Signed as a free agent, 12/91

Player Summary	
Fantasy Value	$3 to $6
Card Value	3¢ to 5¢
Will	steal bases
Can't	keep job
Expect	strong throws
Don't Expect	high average

Gladden started slipping as the Minnesota leadoff man, and the Twins let him sign with Detroit after the season. He had been a consistent but unspectacular player. After a four-year career with the Giants (that commenced in 1983), Gladden joined the Twins, who were searching for a dependable offensive aid. He provided the team unanticipated power, as illustrated by his career-high 11 homers and 62 RBI in 1988. He had a .356 slugging percentage in '91. While he was the starting left fielder and leadoff hitter for the World Champions throughout the playoffs, he would have lost his job in '92 to Pedro Munoz or Jarvis Brown. Gladden had a .306 on-base percentage in 1991, below average for a leadoff hitter. His 1992 commons will not sell well outside of Minnesota. He is a risky $5 fantasy outfielder.

Major League Batting Register

	BA	G	AB	R	H	2B	3B	HR	RBI	SB
83 NL	.222	18	63	6	14	2	0	1	9	4
84 NL	.351	86	342	71	120	17	2	4	31	31
85 NL	.243	142	502	64	122	15	8	7	41	32
86 NL	.276	102	351	55	97	16	1	4	29	27
87 AL	.249	121	438	69	109	21	2	8	38	25
88 AL	.269	141	576	91	155	32	6	11	62	28
89 AL	.295	121	461	69	136	23	3	8	46	23
90 AL	.275	136	534	64	147	27	6	5	40	25
91 AL	.247	126	461	65	114	14	9	6	52	15
Life	.272	993	3728	554	1014	167	37	54	348	210
3 AVE	.273	128	485	66	132	21	6	6	46	21

CURRENT PLAYERS

TOM GLAVINE

Position: Pitcher
Team: Atlanta Braves
Born: March 25, 1966 Concord, MA
Height: 6' **Weight:** 175 lbs.
Bats: left **Throws:** left
Acquired: Second-round pick in 6/84 free-agent draft

Player Summary	
Fantasy Value	$15 to $20
Card Value	10¢ to 15¢
Will	be winner
Can't	wait to take mound
Expect	complete games
Don't Expect	bases on balls

When the Braves improved their infield defense by adding Terry Pendleton, Rafael Belliard, and Sid Bream, Glavine was the biggest beneficiary. Armed with better control and a new changeup, Glavine suddenly blossomed into the National League's top lefthander. The first Braves pitcher to start an All-Star Game since Warren Spahn in 1961, Glavine even caused some experts to compare him with the Hall of Fame southpaw. Like Spahn, Glavine is a good hitter, good bunter, and excellent fielder who has a good pickoff move. He throws four pitches but depends most heavily on a fastball and change. He is a $15 to $20 fantasy starter capable of racking up some wins. The 1991 NL Cy Young winner, he was among the major league leaders in victories, complete games, and earned run average. There should be a couple more Cy Young awards in his future. His 1992 cards are good buys, but stay under 15 cents.

Major League Pitching Register

	W	L	ERA	G	CG	IP	H	ER	BB	SO
87 NL	2	4	5.54	9	0	50.1	55	31	33	20
88 NL	7	17	4.56	34	1	195.1	201	99	63	84
89 NL	14	8	3.68	29	6	186.0	172	76	40	90
90 NL	10	12	4.28	33	1	214.1	232	102	78	129
91 NL	20	11	2.55	34	9	246.2	201	70	69	192
Life	53	52	3.81	139	17	892.2	861	378	283	515
3 AVE	15	10	3.45	32	5	215.1	202	83	62	137

JERRY DON GLEATON

Position: Pitcher
Team: Detroit Tigers
Born: Sept. 14, 1957 Brownwood, TX
Height: 6'3" **Weight:** 210 lbs.
Bats: left **Throws:** left
Acquired: Signed as a free agent, 1/90

Player Summary	
Fantasy Value	$1 to $3
Card Value	3¢ to 5¢
Will	provide good relief
Can't	serve as closer
Expect	plate to move
Don't Expect	lots of Ks

Middle reliever Gleaton was one of the unsung heroes of the Detroit surprise success story in 1991. After nine years of riding a yo-yo between the majors and minors, he posted career bests with a 2.94 ERA and 57 appearances for the 1990 Tigers. He even got 13 saves—12 of them when closer Mike Henneman struggled through a slump. Gleaton was less effective last year but remained a Bengals bullpen mainstay. The red-haired lefty used a fastball and curve to throttle opposing hitters. He took the suggestions of pitching coach Billy Muffett early in the 1990 campaign, using some mechanical techniques designed to put extra life on the curveball. The results have revitalized Gleaton's career. He is a $2 fantasy draft. He figures to remain an important set-up man for Henneman in 1992. Gleaton's 1992 commons hold little interest.

Major League Pitching Register

	W	L	ERA	G	S	IP	H	ER	BB	SO
79 AL	0	1	6.52	5	0	9.2	15	7	2	2
80 AL	0	0	2.57	5	0	7.0	5	2	4	2
81 AL	4	7	4.75	20	0	85.1	88	45	38	31
82 AL	0	0	13.50	3	0	4.2	7	7	2	1
84 AL	1	2	3.44	11	2	18.1	20	7	6	4
85 AL	1	0	5.76	31	1	29.2	37	19	13	22
87 AL	4	4	4.26	48	5	50.2	38	24	28	44
88 AL	0	4	3.55	42	3	38.0	33	15	17	29
89 AL	0	0	5.65	15	0	14.1	20	9	6	9
90 AL	1	3	2.94	57	13	82.2	62	27	25	56
91 AL	3	2	4.06	47	2	75.1	74	34	39	47
Life	14	23	4.24	284	26	415.2	399	196	180	247
2 AVE	2	3	3.47	52	8	79.2	68	31	32	52

CURRENT PLAYERS

LEO GOMEZ

Position: Third base
Team: Baltimore Orioles
Born: March 2, 1967 Canovanas, Puerto Rico
Height: 6' **Weight:** 202 lbs.
Bats: right **Throws:** right
Acquired: Signed as free agent, 12/85

Player Summary	
Fantasy Value	$4 to $7
Card Value	10¢ to 15¢
Will	top 20 homers
Can't	steal bases
Expect	high RBI totals
Don't Expect	Brooks's defense

Slick-fielding incumbent Craig Worthington and slugging rookie Gomez fought it out for the O's third base job in the spring. Gomez won the battle, with Worthington returning to Rochester. Gomez had a difficult first season against big league pitching, however. He had led the Triple-A International League with 97 runs batted in, 97 runs scored, and 26 home runs in 1990. Typically, he has good power, can hit to the opposite field, and is a selective hitter who waits for good pitches and often makes contact. At the right price, his 1992 cards will be smart investments. Try not to pay more than 15 cents apiece for them, however, because he is not assured of a starting job. Eventually, he may hit for both power and average, abilities that suggest he'll hit between third and sixth in the lineup. He is still not the most consistent third baseman available. He is not fast and has limited range in the field, though he has a strong arm. Gamble $5 on him, and you may get a good return on your investment. In time, Gomez should be a solid player.

JUAN GONZALEZ

Position: Outfield
Team: Texas Rangers
Born: Oct. 16, 1969 Vega Baja, Puerto Rico
Height: 6'3" **Weight:** 200 lbs.
Bats: right **Throws:** right
Acquired: Signed as free agent, 5/86

Player Summary	
Fantasy Value	$32 to $37
Card Value	10¢ to 15¢
Will	be top run producer
Can't	add base-stealing
Expect	25-plus homers
Don't Expect	return of tantrums

Although arthroscopic surgery on his right knee forced him to miss the start of the 1991 season, Gonzalez made up for lost time in a hurry. The 21-year-old center fielder lived up to his advance billing by staging a season-long offensive and defensive display, including an August 18 grand slam. His quick wrists compensate when he's fooled by a curve, and he made Ranger fans forgive the team for releasing popular slugger Pete Incaviglia in April. Gonzalez had a .479 slugging percentage and a .321 on-base average in 1991. He'd do even better if he were more patient at the plate; he strikes out almost three times as often as he walks. Budget your money to spend up to $37 for him at the draft. Like a young Dale Murphy, Gonzalez does not have exceptional speed but shows a strong arm and good reactions in center field. He shifts to left when Gary Pettis occupies center. Investors should stock up on Gonzalez's 1992 cards. At 15 cents or less, they are fantastic purchases.

Major League Batting Register

	BA	G	AB	R	H	2B	3B	HR	RBI	SB
90 AL	.231	12	39	3	9	0	0	0	1	0
91 AL	.233	118	391	40	91	17	2	16	45	1
Life	.233	130	430	43	100	17	2	16	46	1

Major League Batting Register

	BA	G	AB	R	H	2B	3B	HR	RBI	SB
89 AL	.150	24	60	6	9	3	0	1	7	0
90 AL	.289	25	90	11	26	7	1	4	12	0
91 AL	.264	142	545	78	144	34	1	27	102	4
Life	.258	191	695	95	179	44	2	32	121	4

CURRENT PLAYERS

LUIS GONZALEZ

Position: Outfield
Team: Houston Astros
Born: Sept. 3, 1967 Tampa, FL
Height: 6'2" **Weight:** 180 lbs.
Bats: left **Throws:** right
Acquired: Fourth-round pick in 6/88 free-agent draft

Player Summary	
Fantasy Value	$8 to $11
Card Value	10¢ to 15¢
Will	add power
Can't	show patience at bat
Expect	a 20-20 season
Don't Expect	batting crown

Gonzalez carries a big bat and plays many positions. A high school second baseman who played the infield corners in the minors, he mastered right field in Mexican winter league play before moving to left during 1991 spring training. A 20-20 man in the Double-A Southern League in 1990, Gonzalez started slowly in his first exposure to big league pitching. He proved by midseason that he could hit with power in the majors, though. He batted ahead of Seattle prospect Tino Martinez in high school. Gonzalez hits to all fields but strikes out too frequently. A line-drive hitter, he'll help the team more when he learns the strike zone and starts making better contact. Gonzalez has healed from the rotator cuff surgery that cut short his season in 1989. He has good speed to go with his power. Houston's biggest surprise in 1991, he could surprise faithful fantasy managers in 1992 for ten bucks. His 1992 cards are precarious buys at 10 to 15 cents. Wait until he has another good start in 1992 before putting much money in his cards.

Major League Batting Register

	BA	G	AB	R	H	2B	3B	HR	RBI	SB
90 NL	.190	12	21	1	4	2	0	0	0	0
91 NL	.254	137	473	51	120	28	9	13	69	10
Life	.251	149	494	52	124	30	9	13	69	10

DWIGHT GOODEN

Position: Pitcher
Team: New York Mets
Born: Nov. 16, 1964 Tampa, FL
Height: 6'3" **Weight:** 210 lbs.
Bats: right **Throws:** right
Acquired: First-round pick in 6/82 free-agent draft

Player Summary	
Fantasy Value	$21 to $25
Card Value	7¢ to 10¢
Will	vie for K crown
Can't	avoid shoulder woes
Expect	15-plus wins
Don't Expect	many control lapses

Though he went through a slump early last year, Gooden recaptured his old form by July. He has earned Rookie of the Year and Cy Young (1985) awards, four All-Star selections, and two strikeout crowns. He also has had recurring shoulder woes and a past cocaine problem. The healthy Gooden is one of the game's top pitchers. He often has hot streaks, such as his 16-1 record over a four-month span in 1990. "Doc" throws a fastball, curve, changeup, and cut fastball, but he survives only when either of the first two pitches work. His dime-priced 1992 cards will not be hot buys, but sink a few bucks in them for long-term profits. It will take only one good year for the prices to rise. He is a $21 to $25 fantasy value. He strikes out three times as many as he walks, keeps the ball in the park, and is a strong hitter and fielder.

Major League Pitching Register

	W	L	ERA	G	CG	IP	H	ER	BB	SO
84 NL	17	9	2.60	31	7	218.0	161	63	73	276
85 NL	24	4	1.53	35	16	276.2	198	47	69	268
86 NL	17	6	2.84	33	12	250.0	197	79	80	200
87 NL	15	7	3.21	25	7	179.2	162	64	53	148
88 NL	18	9	3.19	34	10	248.1	242	88	57	175
89 NL	9	4	2.89	19	0	118.0	93	38	47	101
90 NL	19	7	3.83	34	2	232.2	229	99	70	223
91 NL	13	7	3.60	27	3	190.0	185	76	56	150
Life	132	53	2.91	238	57	1713.2	1467	554	505	1541
3 AVE	14	6	3.54	27	2	180.1	169	71	58	158

CURRENT PLAYERS

TOM GORDON

Position: Pitcher
Team: Kansas City Royals
Born: Nov. 18, 1967 Sebring, FL
Height: 5'9" **Weight:** 160 lbs.
Bats: right **Throws:** right
Acquired: Sixth-round pick in 6/86 free-agent draft

Player Summary	
Fantasy Value	$5 to $8
Card Value	3¢ to 5¢
Will	bank on curve
Can't	always throw strikes
Expect	many Ks and walks
Don't Expect	prompt rotation return

Flash Gordon's rocket came down to earth last July 25, when Kansas City manager Hal McRae sent him from the rotation to the bullpen. Gordon had fanned a career-best 13 batters in a game only three months earlier. Always a starter since turning pro, he throws a fastball with good velocity, plus a curve and a slider that breaks in either direction. When he has control of the curve, Gordon is Superman. When he doesn't, he's Clark Kent. Gordon led the Royals pitching staff in walks issued, and he yielded almost four earned runs per game. Even though he led the team in strikeouts, he was nowhere near the 17-9 form that won him Rookie Pitcher of the Year honors in 1989. He was *Baseball America's* minor league player of the year in 1988, going from Class-A Appleton to Kansas City. His 1992 commons aren't foolproof. He is a promising $5 hurler. Gordon needs to work often to be consistent, but he'd prefer to start.

Major League Pitching Register

	W	L	ERA	G	S	IP	H	ER	BB	SO
88 AL	0	2	5.17	5	0	15.2	16	9	7	18
89 AL	17	9	3.64	49	1	163.0	122	66	86	153
90 AL	12	11	3.73	32	0	195.1	192	81	99	175
91 AL	9	14	3.87	45	1	158.0	129	68	87	167
Life	38	36	3.79	131	2	532.0	459	224	279	513
3 AVE	13	11	3.75	42	1	172.0	148	72	91	165

GOOSE GOSSAGE

Position: Pitcher
Team: Texas Rangers
Born: Sept. 5, 1951 Colorado Springs, CO
Height: 6'3" **Weight:** 180 lbs.
Bats: right **Throws:** right
Acquired: Signed as a free agent, 4/91

Player Summary	
Fantasy Value	$2 to $4
Card Value	3¢ to 5¢
Will	throw some heat
Can't	return to closing
Expect	more injuries
Don't Expect	uninterrupted year

One of the greatest short relievers in history, Gossage was considered too old when he left the majors to play Japanese ball in 1990. The detour to the Orient resurrected the career of the once-feared fireballer, however. He returned to the majors after winning a spot in the Texas bullpen. Early in the '91 campaign, he set an unusual record by appearing in the same game as Nolan Ryan; it was the first time a 300-game winner had pitched with a 300-save reliever. Gossage is a $3 sentimental fantasy hurler, and his 1992 commons are long-term buys.

Major League Pitching Register

	W	L	ERA	G	S	IP	H	ER	BB	SO
72 AL	7	1	4.28	36	2	80.0	72	36	44	57
73 AL	0	4	7.43	20	0	49.2	57	41	37	33
74 AL	4	6	4.13	39	1	89.1	92	41	47	64
75 AL	9	8	1.84	62	26	141.2	99	29	70	130
76 AL	9	17	3.94	31	1	224.0	214	98	90	135
77 NL	11	9	1.62	72	26	133.0	78	24	49	151
78 AL	10	11	2.01	63	27	134.1	87	30	59	122
79 AL	5	3	2.62	36	18	58.1	48	17	19	41
80 AL	6	2	2.27	64	33	99.0	74	25	37	103
81 AL	3	2	0.77	32	20	46.2	22	4	14	48
82 AL	4	5	2.23	56	30	93.0	63	23	28	102
83 AL	13	5	2.27	57	22	87.1	82	22	25	90
84 NL	10	6	2.90	62	25	102.1	75	33	36	84
85 NL	5	3	1.82	50	26	79.0	64	16	17	52
86 NL	5	7	4.45	45	21	64.2	69	32	20	63
87 NL	5	4	3.12	40	11	52.0	47	18	19	44
88 NL	4	4	4.33	46	13	43.2	50	21	15	30
89 NL	2	1	2.68	31	4	43.2	32	13	27	24
89 AL	1	0	3.77	11	1	14.1	14	6	3	6
91 AL	4	2	3.57	44	1	40.1	33	16	16	28
Life	117	100	2.94	897	308	1676.1	1372	547	672	1407
2 AVE	4	2	3.20	43	3	49.2	40	18	23	29

JIM GOTT

Position: Pitcher
Team: Los Angeles Dodgers
Born: Aug. 3, 1959 Hollywood, CA
Height: 6'4" **Weight:** 220 lbs.
Bats: right **Throws:** right
Acquired: Signed as a free agent, 12/89

Player Summary	
Fantasy Value	$2 to $4
Card Value	3¢ to 5¢
Will	work often
Can't	return to rotation
Expect	wildness spurts
Don't Expect	freedom from injury

Gott has been used as a starter, closer, and middle reliever during an injury-riddled career that began with the Blue Jays in 1982. He had rotator cuff surgery in 1986 and elbow problems in 1989. In two seasons with the Dodgers, Gott has been used primarily as a set-up man. He was slightly more effective in 1990. He averaged just under a strikeout per inning in '91. Encouragement from Tommy John, a pitcher who previously rebounded from a ruptured elbow ligament, set the psychological stage for Gott's 1990 comeback. A set-up man, his fantasy value peaks at $4. He threw his curve and slider, in addition to his low-90s fastball, without fear of elbow pain. His 1992 cards are never-ending commons. Gott holds his own as a hitter (with some power) but is only average as a fielder.

Major League Pitching Register

	W	L	ERA	G	S	IP	H	ER	BB	SO
82 AL	5	10	4.43	30	0	136.0	134	67	66	82
83 AL	9	14	4.74	34	0	176.2	195	93	68	121
84 AL	7	6	4.02	35	2	109.2	93	49	49	73
85 NL	7	10	3.88	26	0	148.1	144	64	51	78
86 NL	0	0	7.62	9	1	13.0	16	11	13	9
87 NL	1	2	3.41	55	13	87.0	81	33	40	90
88 NL	6	6	3.49	67	34	77.1	68	30	22	76
89 NL	0	0	0.00	1	0	0.2	1	0	1	1
90 NL	3	5	2.90	50	3	62.0	59	20	34	44
91 NL	4	3	2.96	55	2	76.0	63	25	32	73
Life	42	56	3.98	362	55	886.2	854	392	376	647
2 AVE	4	4	2.93	53	3	69.0	61	23	33	59

MARK GRACE

Position: First base
Team: Chicago Cubs
Born: June 28, 1964 Winston-Salem, NC
Height: 6'2" **Weight:** 190 lbs.
Bats: left **Throws:** left
Acquired: 24th-round pick in 6/85 free-agent draft

Player Summary	
Fantasy Value	$22 to $27
Card Value	5¢ to 10¢
Will	reach base frequently
Can't	reach fences regularly
Expect	superlative defense
Don't Expect	many attempts to steal

The 19-game hitting streak uncorked by Grace in 1991 was no fluke. He has been a solid hitter ever since reaching the major leagues in 1988. Because he hits for average but lacks consistent home run power, he swapped lineup spots with Ryne Sandberg in the middle of last season. Grace moved up to No. 2, where his line-drive stroke and gap hits make more sense, while the slugging Sandberg moved in behind him. A contact hitter who walks more frequently than he fans, Grace usually has a high on-base percentage (.346 in '91). He has shown marked improvement against lefthanded pitchers in recent seasons. If he finds a home run stroke, the price of his 1992 cards could jump dramatically. He is a $25 fantasy first baseman. Though he does not have great speed, he's a good base-runner who's improving. Grace is the personification of his name in the field, where he has good range, a good arm, and a good scoop.

Major League Batting Register

	BA	G	AB	R	H	2B	3B	HR	RBI	SB
88 NL	.296	134	486	65	144	23	4	7	57	3
89 NL	.314	142	510	74	160	28	3	13	79	14
90 NL	.309	157	589	72	182	32	1	9	82	15
91 NL	.273	160	619	87	169	28	5	8	58	3
Life	.297	593	2204	298	655	111	13	37	276	35
3 AVE	.297	153	573	78	170	29	3	10	73	11

CURRENT PLAYERS

JEFF GRAY

Position: Pitcher
Team: Boston Red Sox
Born: April 10, 1963 Richmond, VA
Height: 6'1" **Weight:** 190 lbs.
Bats: right **Throws:** right
Acquired: Signed as a free agent, 4/90

Player Summary	
Fantasy Value	$2 to $4
Card Value	3¢ to 5¢
Will	bank on splitter
Can't	erase checkered record
Expect	pinpoint control
Don't Expect	totally clean bill

Gray was a successful set-up reliever for the Red Sox before he suffered a mysterious seizure that caused him to collapse in the locker room on August 4. Had illness not intervened, 1991 would have been Gray's first full season in the majors. At the time he went down, he was Boston's most effective reliever, with a 2.34 ERA in 50 appearances. He had a 2-3 record, one save, and a superlative 4-1 ratio of strikeouts to walks. Gray's top pitch is a split-fingered fastball that he developed in the minor leagues. He also throws a regular fastball and slider. Opponents compiled a .181 batting average, a .338 slugging percentage, and a .219 on-base percentage. He bounced around the minors for six seasons before the Red Sox, needing pitchers for their Triple-A farm club, took a chance. Once he reached the majors, he not only pitched well down the stretch but posted a 2.70 ERA in two playoff appearances. His future is hard to call; postpone his 1992 cards as investments. Limit your fantasy spending to $4.

Major League Pitching Register

	W	L	ERA	G	S	IP	H	ER	BB	SO
88 NL	0	0	3.86	5	0	9.1	12	4	4	5
90 AL	2	4	4.44	41	9	50.2	53	25	15	50
91 AL	2	3	2.34	50	1	61.2	39	16	10	41
Life	4	7	3.33	96	10	121.2	104	45	29	96
2 AVE	2	4	3.28	46	5	56.2	46	21	13	46

CRAIG GREBECK

Position: Infield
Team: Chicago White Sox
Born: Dec. 29, 1964 Johnstown, PA
Height: 5'7" **Weight:** 160 lbs.
Bats: right **Throws:** right
Acquired: Signed as a free agent, 8/86

Player Summary	
Fantasy Value	$2 to $5
Card Value	3¢ to 5¢
Will	see more action
Can't	match Ventura's power
Expect	best defense at third
Don't Expect	great base-stealing

One of the most pleasant surprises for the White Sox in 1991 was the improved hitting performance of Grebeck. After hitting under .200 for both the Sox and Triple-A Vancouver in 1990, he parlayed lengthy sessions with hitting coach Walt Hriniak into one of the best batting averages on the ballclub. Grebeck even hit a few homers. The former Cal State standout, now a three-position infielder, saw most of his action at third last year when Robin Ventura filled in for the injured Frank Thomas at first. Grebeck showed good range, hands, and arm at the position. He had a .460 slugging percentage and a .386 on-base average in '91, fulfilling some promise that he had displayed in the minors. He batted .287 with 80 RBI in 1989 at Double-A Birmingham. He should get more at bats in 1992. He is a good middle infielder for up to $5. The diminutive utility player will retain his role, but he could start with a '93 expansion club. He doesn't have the power to excite collectors. Leave his 1992 commons in the bins.

Major League Batting Register

	BA	G	AB	R	H	2B	3B	HR	RBI	SB
90 AL	.168	59	119	7	20	3	1	1	9	0
91 AL	.281	107	224	37	63	16	3	6	31	1
Life	.242	166	343	44	83	19	4	7	40	1

CURRENT PLAYERS

TOMMY GREENE

Position: Pitcher
Team: Philadelphia Phillies
Born: April 6, 1967 Lumberton, NC
Height: 6'5" **Weight:** 225 lbs.
Bats: right **Throws:** right
Acquired: Traded from Braves with Dale Murphy for Jeff Parrett, Jim Vatcher, and Victor Rosario, 8/90

Player Summary	
Fantasy Value	$12 to $15
Card Value	10¢ to 15¢
Will	help with bat
Can't	always control curve
Expect	high K totals
Don't Expect	many complete games

Greene became the first Phillie to throw consecutive complete-game shutouts since Steve Carlton in 1972. Greene (who had blown three minor league no-hitters with two outs and two strikes in the ninth inning) was Atlanta's first-round draft choice in 1985. He throws a rising fastball, an unpredictable curve, and a newly perfected changeup. When the curve nicks the corner, he's fine. Sometimes it hangs, however; Greene gave up 19 homers in '91. He fields well and has a fair pickoff move. He homered twice in his own games and sometimes pinch-hits for others. His 1992 cards are enticing investments. In 1990 in the Triple-A International League, he was 5-8 with a 3.49 ERA, 69 strikeouts, 67 walks, and 93 hits in 116 innings. He was 9-12 with a 3.61 ERA, 125 strikeouts, 50 walks, and 136 hits in 152 innings at Triple-A Richmond in 1989. Greene led the '91 Phils in strikeouts and fanned more than twice as many as he walked. His strikeouts will fuel your fantasy team for $15.

Major League Pitching Register

	W	L	ERA	G	CG	IP	H	ER	BB	SO
89 NL	1	2	4.10	4	1	26.1	22	12	6	17
90 NL	3	3	5.08	15	0	51.1	50	29	26	21
91 NL	13	7	3.38	36	3	207.2	177	78	66	154
Life	17	12	3.75	55	4	285.1	249	119	98	192
2 AVE	7	4	3.64	21	2	110.2	96	45	38	79

MIKE GREENWELL

Position: Outfield
Team: Boston Red Sox
Born: July 18, 1963 Louisville, KY
Height: 6' **Weight:** 200 lbs.
Bats: left **Throws:** right
Acquired: Third-round pick in 6/82 free-agent draft

Player Summary	
Fantasy Value	$32 to $38
Card Value	10¢ to 15¢
Will	top batting rank
Can't	find Fenway fences
Expect	every fly an adventure
Don't Expect	many walks or Ks

Greenwell prefers runs batted in to home runs. When critics complained that his power numbers were down, he replied that he considered himself the same type of hitter as Don Mattingly or George Brett—line-drive hitters who collect RBI without winning homer crowns. Greenwell, who had winter surgery to repair partially torn cartilage in his right knee, is expected to heal completely by the time the '92 season starts. It's not certain, however, whether the wounds of two fights with teammates will heal over the winter. Greenwell has gap power to all fields but may never return to the form that made him runner-up in the 1988 MVP voting. As a proven .300 hitter, he'll always have a place to play—even though he's an erratic left fielder. He steals a dozen bases, at most. Collectors underrate his cards, and his 1992 issues are good investments at a dime apiece. His fantasy value is a solid $35.

Major League Batting Register

	BA	G	AB	R	H	2B	3B	HR	RBI	SB
85 AL	.323	17	31	7	10	1	0	4	8	1
86 AL	.314	31	35	4	11	2	0	0	4	0
87 AL	.328	125	412	71	135	31	6	19	89	5
88 AL	.325	158	590	86	192	39	8	22	119	16
89 AL	.308	145	578	87	178	36	0	14	95	13
90 AL	.297	159	610	71	181	30	6	14	73	8
91 AL	.300	147	544	76	163	26	6	9	83	15
Life	.311	782	2800	402	870	165	26	82	471	58
3 AVE	.301	150	577	78	174	31	4	12	84	12

CURRENT PLAYERS

TOMMY GREGG

Position: First base; outfield
Team: Atlanta Braves
Born: July 29, 1963 Boone, NC
Height: 6'1" **Weight:** 190 lbs.
Bats: left **Throws:** left
Acquired: Traded from Pirates for Ken Oberkfell, 8/88

Player Summary	
Fantasy Value	$1 to $2
Card Value	3¢ to 5¢
Will	play several spots
Can't	hit lefties
Expect	clutch line drives
Don't Expect	everyday role

After establishing himself as a premier pinch-hitter during the 1990 campaign, Gregg struggled through a season-long slump in 1991. He emerged at times to produce some timely hits, however, as the Braves became contenders. He is a former Double-A Eastern League batting champion (in '87), and he had four pinch-homers while leading the majors in pinch-hits (18) and pinch-RBI (17) while pinch-hitting at a .353 clip in 1990. He struggled to push his average over .200 in '91. A major factor was a 2-1 ratio of strikeouts to walks. Gregg needs to show more patience—especially on 3-1 pitches when his team needs base-runners. Valuable because he can play first base and three outfield spots, Gregg is young enough to become a big league regular—and that could happen for him when the NL expands. He is a $1 fantasy draft. His 1992 commons are dubious investments. He's an adequate first baseman and is better than Lonnie Smith in the outfield.

Major League Batting Register

	BA	G	AB	R	H	2B	3B	HR	RBI	SB
87 NL	.250	10	8	3	2	1	0	0	0	0
88 NL	.295	25	44	5	13	4	0	1	7	0
89 NL	.243	102	276	24	67	8	0	6	23	3
90 NL	.264	124	239	18	63	13	1	5	32	4
91 NL	.187	72	107	13	20	8	1	1	4	2
Life	.245	333	674	63	165	34	2	13	66	9
2 AVE	.252	113	258	21	65	11	1	6	28	4

KEN GRIFFEY JR.

Position: Outfield
Team: Seattle Mariners
Born: Nov. 21, 1969 Donora, PA
Height: 6'3" **Weight:** 195 lbs.
Bats: left **Throws:** left
Acquired: First-round pick in 6/87 free-agent draft

Player Summary	
Fantasy Value	$45 to $50
Card Value	15¢ to 25¢
Will	hit for average plus power
Can't	master base-stealing
Expect	Gold Glove defense
Don't Expect	any prolonged slump

AL managers told *Baseball America* last year that Griffey is the league's top defensive outfielder. The fans obviously agree, because they elected Junior an All-Star starter for the second straight season (he's the only Mariner ever elected). Griffey made the majors at age 19 in 1989, then hit .300 with 22 homers and won a Gold Glove as a sophomore. He had a .527 slugging percentage, a .399 on-base average, and 71 walks in 1991. His improvement can be traced to selectivity; by showing patience at the plate, he now walks almost as often as he strikes out. He has more power against righthanders but is making steady progress against southpaws. In the outfield, he runs, charges, dives, leaps, and throws better than most colleagues. He has the speed and power to become a perennial 30-30 player. He improves every day, and his fantasy value will reflect that. Break the bank and spend up to $50 to secure his services. His 1992 cards are nice investments for prices under a quarter.

Major League Batting Register

	BA	G	AB	R	H	2B	3B	HR	RBI	SB
89 AL	.264	127	455	61	120	23	0	16	61	16
90 AL	.300	155	597	91	179	28	7	22	80	16
91 AL	.327	154	548	76	179	42	1	22	100	18
Life	.299	436	1600	228	478	93	8	60	241	50
3 AVE	.299	145	533	76	159	31	3	20	80	17

CURRENT PLAYERS

ALFREDO GRIFFIN

Position: Shortstop
Team: Los Angeles Dodgers
Born: March 6, 1957 Santo Domingo, Dominican Republic
Height: 5'11" **Weight:** 166 lbs.
Bats: both **Throws:** right
Acquired: Traded from Athletics with Jay Howell for Bob Welch and Matt Young, 12/87

Player Summary	
Fantasy Value	$1 to $2
Card Value	3¢ to 5¢
Will	hack at bad pitches
Can't	generate power
Expect	errors on long throws
Don't Expect	average over .250

Griffin withstood the 1991 challenge of rookie Jose Offerman to retain the regular shortstop job with the Dodgers. While Offerman was returned to the minors, Griffin remained in the lineup. The two switched places in August, however, when the veteran was sidelined for more than a month with a fractured cheekbone. Griffin is an impatient singles hitter who fans twice as often as he walks. He also had more than 20 errors, many of them on throws. Griffin has good range but has trouble throwing from the hole. He is a $1 fantasy infielder. His 1992 commons are terrible buys.

Major League Batting Register

	BA	G	AB	R	H	2B	3B	HR	RBI	SB
76 AL	.250	12	4	0	1	0	0	0	0	0
77 AL	.146	14	41	5	6	1	0	0	3	2
78 AL	.500	5	4	1	2	1	0	0	0	0
79 AL	.287	153	624	81	179	22	10	2	31	21
80 AL	.254	155	653	63	166	26	15	2	41	18
81 AL	.209	101	388	30	81	19	6	0	21	8
82 AL	.241	162	539	57	130	20	8	1	48	10
83 AL	.250	162	528	62	132	22	9	4	47	8
84 AL	.241	140	419	53	101	8	2	4	30	11
85 AL	.270	162	614	75	166	18	7	2	64	24
86 AL	.285	162	594	74	169	23	6	4	51	33
87 AL	.263	144	494	69	130	23	5	3	60	26
88 NL	.199	95	316	39	63	8	3	1	27	7
89 NL	.247	136	506	49	125	27	2	0	29	10
90 NL	.210	141	461	38	97	11	3	1	35	6
91 NL	.243	109	350	27	85	6	2	0	27	5
Life	.250	1853	6535	723	1633	235	78	24	514	189
3 AVE	.233	129	439	38	102	15	2	0	30	7

JASON GRIMSLEY

Position: Pitcher
Team: Philadelphia Phillies
Born: Aug. 7, 1967 Cleveland, TX
Height: 6'3" **Weight:** 180 lbs.
Bats: right **Throws:** right
Acquired: 11th-round pick in 6/85 free-agent draft

Player Summary	
Fantasy Value	$1 to $3
Card Value	3¢ to 5¢
Will	mix heater with curve
Can't	remain as wild
Expect	fine fielding
Don't Expect	surgical strike zone

Grimsley led two minor leagues in walks before reaching the Phillies late in the 1990 campaign. They shouldn't have been surprised when he walked 43 in his first 57⅓ innings. He was slightly better last year, but he still walked only one less than he fanned before going on the disabled list with elbow problems in June. The wildness, more than anything else, contributed to his 1-7 record. In years when he fanned more than he walked, Grimsley found success in the minors. He was Philadelphia's Minor League Pitcher of the Year in 1989, when he pitched a no-hitter in the Double-A Eastern League. He was that loop's No. 6 prospect. His fastball has life and he complements it with a fine curve. Don't expect his 1992 cards to rise much above their commons prices until he finds a regular spot in the rotation. He is a $2 fantasy starter. Mechanical flaws have worked against him. Should he find health and the strike zone, Grimsley should be a big league starter.

Major League Pitching Register

	W	L	ERA	G	CG	IP	H	ER	BB	SO
89 NL	1	3	5.89	4	0	18.1	19	12	19	7
90 NL	3	2	3.30	11	0	57.1	47	21	43	41
91 NL	1	7	4.87	12	0	61.0	54	33	41	42
Life	5	12	4.35	27	0	136.2	120	66	103	90

CURRENT PLAYERS

MARQUIS GRISSOM

Position: Outfield
Team: Montreal Expos
Born: April 17, 1967 Atlanta, GA
Height: 5'11" **Weight:** 190 lbs.
Bats: right **Throws:** right
Acquired: Third-round pick in 6/88 free-agent draft

Player Summary	
Fantasy Value	$25 to $30
Card Value	5¢ to 10¢
Will	vie for swipes crown
Can't	always hit for power
Expect	strong defense
Don't Expect	high average

Grissom is one of the premier speed merchants in the National League. The center fielder of the Expos, who sprints from home to first as fast as anyone in the NL, won the league crown in stolen bases in 1991. He was caught stealing 17 times. His steals could excite any fantasy manager for $25. He had more than two-dozen infield hits and played a strong defensive game. Former Montreal manager Buck Rodgers predicts Grissom will blossom into a speed-plus-power package who could deliver 15 homers a year. During the 1991 campaign, he made a major adjustment in his batting style—moving away from pulling every pitch and learning how to hit the outside pitch to the opposite field. A good contact hitter with good knowledge of the strike zone, he had a .373 slugging percentage and a .310 on-base average in 1991. Grissom also has a strong arm and good range in center field. He had a five-hit game in '91. His 1992 cards are snappy long-range purchases.

Major League Batting Register

	BA	G	AB	R	H	2B	3B	HR	RBI	SB
89 NL	.257	26	74	16	19	2	0	1	2	1
90 NL	.257	98	288	42	74	14	2	3	29	22
91 NL	.267	148	558	73	149	23	9	6	39	76
Life	.263	272	920	131	242	39	11	10	70	99
2 AVE	.264	123	423	58	112	19	6	5	34	49

KEVIN GROSS

Position: Pitcher
Team: Los Angeles Dodgers
Born: June 8, 1961 Downey, CA
Height: 6'5" **Weight:** 215 lbs.
Bats: right **Throws:** right
Acquired: Signed as a free agent, 12/90

Player Summary	
Fantasy Value	$2 to $4
Card Value	3¢ to 5¢
Will	help at bat
Can't	throw critical strikes
Expect	more hits than frames
Don't Expect	removal from middle relief

Although he was a starter before 1991, Gross made the transition to the bullpen when Orel Hershiser rejoined the Dodger rotation in May. Gross even delivered some timely hits, including a pinch-single that he followed by scoring the winning run in extra innings on August 17. As a reliever, he was not very effective. He walked batters in critical situations and yielded about a homer every 11 innings. Because he throws three fastballs—plus a curve, slider, and changeup—Gross is a cross between a power and an off-speed pitcher. He works behind in the count and hurts himself with weak fielding and failure to keep runners close. His 1992 commons will remain commons forever. He'd be a good pitcher on a bad ballclub. On a good one, he's just another arm. He is an affordable fantasy roster filler for $3 or so.

Major League Pitching Register

	W	L	ERA	G	S	IP	H	ER	BB	SO
83 NL	4	6	3.56	17	0	96.0	100	38	35	66
84 NL	8	5	4.12	44	1	129.0	140	59	44	84
85 NL	15	13	3.41	38	0	205.2	194	78	81	151
86 NL	12	12	4.02	37	0	241.2	240	108	94	154
87 NL	9	16	4.35	34	0	200.2	205	97	87	110
88 NL	12	14	3.69	33	0	231.2	209	95	89	162
89 NL	11	12	4.38	31	0	201.1	188	98	88	158
90 NL	9	12	4.57	31	0	163.1	171	83	65	111
91 NL	10	11	3.58	46	3	115.2	123	46	50	95
Life	90	101	3.99	311	4	1585.0	1570	702	633	1091
3 AVE	10	12	4.25	36	1	160.1	161	76	68	121

CURRENT PLAYERS

KIP GROSS

Position: Pitcher
Team: Los Angeles Dodgers
Born: Aug. 24, 1964 Scottsbluff, NE
Height: 6'2" **Weight:** 190
Bats: right **Throws:** right
Acquired: Traded from Reds with Eric Davis for Tim Belcher and John Wetteland, 11/91

Player Summary	
Fantasy Value	$3 to $5
Card Value	10¢ to 20¢
Will	be in rotation and bullpen
Can't	pitch enough
Expect	control lapses
Don't Expect	trips to minors

Gross was used as both a starter and reliever by Cincinnati in 1991. After a rocky start punctuated by bouts of wildness, he settled down. He walked as many as he struck out, however, and yielded more hits than innings. The former University of Nebraska star had been used as a starter throughout his minor league career, which began in 1987. At Triple-A Nashville in '91, he had a 5-3 record with a 2.08 ERA, 28 strikeouts, 16 walks, and 39 hits in 48 innings. He was 12-7 with a 3.33 ERA at Nashville in 1990. As a sophomore, he had a 13-9 record and 2.62 ERA in 27 starts at Class-A St. Lucie in 1988, where he struck out twice as many as he walked. When he has his control, he can be effective. He'd get more chances to pitch on a team that wasn't so top-heavy in veteran talent. If he starts full-time in 1992, he will be a fantasy steal for $4. If it doesn't happen this year, it might when the NL expands in 1993. His 1992 cards are inviting purchases at 15 cents.

Major League Pitching Register

	W	L	ERA	G	S	IP	H	ER	BB	SO
90 NL	0	0	4.26	5	0	6.1	6	3	2	3
91 NL	6	4	3.47	29	0	85.2	93	33	40	40
Life	6	4	3.52	34	0	92.0	99	36	42	43

KELLY GRUBER

Position: Third base
Team: Toronto Blue Jays
Born: Feb. 26, 1962 Bellaire, TX
Height: 6' **Weight:** 185 lbs.
Bats: right **Throws:** right
Acquired: Drafted from Indians, 12/83

Player Summary	
Fantasy Value	$20 to $25
Card Value	5¢ to 7¢
Will	clobber ball
Can't	hurt team in field
Expect	2-1 Ks to walks
Don't Expect	.300 average

After finishing fourth in the voting for 1990 AL MVP, Gruber spent most of 1991 recuperating from a series of first-half injuries, including a chip fracture and ligament sprain of the right thumb. He had trouble recapturing his stroke but returned to the lineup in July because of his Gold Glove-quality defense. A good base-runner who changed his sliding style to avoid jamming fingers and knees, Gruber is a hustling, aggressive player who helps his club several ways. He has good range and a strong arm. He doesn't walk much but gets many hits on pitches out of the strike zone, and he has some opposite-field power. He may not be well-regarded at the draft, but he is choice fantasy fodder for $20 or so. His 1992 cards are not realistic price gainers, even at a nickel apiece. Gruber is young enough to improve on his 1990 performance.

Major League Batting Register

	BA	G	AB	R	H	2B	3B	HR	RBI	SB
84 AL	.063	15	16	1	1	0	0	1	2	0
85 AL	.231	5	13	0	3	0	0	0	1	0
86 AL	.196	87	143	20	28	4	1	5	15	2
87 AL	.235	138	341	50	80	14	3	12	36	12
88 AL	.278	158	569	75	158	33	5	16	81	23
89 AL	.290	135	545	83	158	24	4	18	73	10
90 AL	.274	150	592	92	162	36	6	31	118	14
91 AL	.252	113	429	58	108	18	2	20	65	12
Life	.264	801	2648	379	698	129	21	103	391	73
3 AVE	.273	133	522	78	143	26	4	23	85	12

CURRENT PLAYERS

MARK GUBICZA

Position: Pitcher
Team: Kansas City Royals
Born: Aug. 14, 1962 Philadelphia, PA
Height: 6'5" **Weight:** 220 lbs.
Bats: right **Throws:** right
Acquired: Second-round pick in 6/81 free-agent draft

Player Summary	
Fantasy Value	$5 to $8
Card Value	3¢ to 5¢
Will	throw hard stuff
Can't	help with defense
Expect	many whiffs and walks
Don't Expect	return to 1988

Gubicza is a former 20-game winner who made considerable progress last year in his effort to rebound from arthroscopic surgery on his partially torn rotator cuff. By midseason, he was able to throw his fastball and slider with presurgery velocity but was giving up too many hits. He lost more games than he won in '91, unfamiliar territory for the pitcher who broke in with the 1984 Royals and went 20-8 four years later. A fastball-and-slider pitcher who also throws a curve and changeup, the healthy Gubicza has been among the league leaders in strikeouts. He can handle a heavy workload. For a $7 gamble, he could reap great reward or be a flop on your fantasy team. Nevertheless, he sometimes sabotages his own game with poor control, weak fielding, and failure to hold runners. His unsteady ways clobbered his 1992 card values.

Major League Pitching Register

	W	L	ERA	G	CG	IP	H	ER	BB	SO
84 AL	10	14	4.05	29	4	189.0	172	85	75	111
85 AL	14	10	4.06	29	0	177.1	160	80	77	99
86 AL	12	6	3.64	35	3	180.2	155	73	84	118
87 AL	13	18	3.98	35	10	241.2	231	107	120	166
88 AL	20	8	2.70	35	8	269.2	237	81	83	183
89 AL	15	11	3.04	36	8	255.0	252	86	63	173
90 AL	4	7	4.50	16	2	94.0	101	47	38	71
91 AL	9	12	5.68	26	0	133.0	168	84	42	89
Life	97	86	3.76	241	35	1540.1	1476	643	582	1010
3 AVE	9	10	4.05	26	3	161.0	174	72	48	111

PEDRO GUERRERO

Position: First base
Team: St. Louis Cardinals
Born: June 29, 1956 San Pedro de Macoris, Dominican Republic
Height: 6' **Weight:** 197 lbs.
Bats: right **Throws:** right
Acquired: Traded from Dodgers for John Tudor, 8/88

Player Summary	
Fantasy Value	$20 to $25
Card Value	7¢ to 10¢
Will	deliver extra-base hits
Can't	steal bases
Expect	a solid RBI count
Don't Expect	Gold Glove fielding

A hairline fracture of the right leg knocked Guerrero out of action in the middle of the 1991 season, but the former Dodger swung a potent bat when he played. Always a run-producer, he's had three 100-RBI campaigns, including his first full year with the Cards in 1989. A brittle slugger who's been on the disabled list six times since reaching the majors, Guerrero would produce better power numbers if he played in another ballpark. His speed and defense leave much to be desired but his hitting compensates. He'd be a perfect designated hitter. He is a safe $20 draft, but his 1992 cards are risky at a dime.

Major League Batting Register

	BA	G	AB	R	H	2B	3B	HR	RBI	SB
78 NL	.625	5	8	3	5	0	1	0	1	0
79 NL	.242	25	62	7	15	2	0	2	9	2
80 NL	.322	75	183	27	59	9	1	7	31	2
81 NL	.300	98	347	46	104	17	2	12	48	5
82 NL	.304	150	575	87	175	27	5	32	100	22
83 NL	.298	160	584	87	174	28	6	32	103	23
84 NL	.303	144	535	85	162	29	4	16	72	9
85 NL	.320	137	487	99	156	22	2	33	87	12
86 NL	.246	31	61	7	15	3	0	5	10	0
87 NL	.338	152	545	89	184	25	2	27	89	9
88 NL	.286	103	545	40	104	14	2	10	65	4
89 NL	.311	162	570	60	177	42	1	17	117	2
90 NL	.281	136	498	42	140	31	1	13	80	1
91 NL	.272	115	427	41	116	12	1	8	70	4
Life	.302	1493	5246	720	1586	261	28	214	882	95
3 AVE	.290	138	498	48	144	28	1	13	89	2

CURRENT PLAYERS

LEE GUETTERMAN

Position: Pitcher
Team: New York Yankees
Born: Nov. 22, 1958 Chattanooga, TN
Height: 6'8" **Weight:** 225 lbs.
Bats: left **Throws:** left
Acquired: Traded from Mariners with Clay Parker and Wade Taylor for Steve Trout and Henry Cotto, 12/87

Player Summary	
Fantasy Value	$2 to $4
Card Value	3¢ to 5¢
Will	work 60 games
Can't	be sole closer
Expect	more hits than innings
Don't Expect	many walks or Ks

Guetterman's third year in the Yankee bullpen was his least successful, as far as ERA is concerned. The lanky lefty's problem was yielding more hits than innings pitched. He finished off 37 games in '91. Opponents compiled a .268 batting average, a .388 slugging percentage, and a .320 on-base average against him that year, and he allowed six home runs. A converted starter who throws a sinker, slider, curve, and change, Guetterman usually shows masterful control. That was his forte in 1989, when he went 5-5 with 13 saves and a career-best 2.45 ERA. He also worked 70 games, another personal peak, that summer. He should remain in his role as the lefty set-up man for the Bombers. He is a fantasy pickup for no more than $4. His fielding and pickoff move both need work. Buying his 1992 commons makes no sense.

Major League Pitching Register

	W	L	ERA	G	S	IP	H	ER	BB	SO
84 AL	0	0	4.15	3	0	4.1	9	2	2	2
86 AL	0	4	7.34	41	0	76.0	108	62	30	38
87 AL	11	4	3.81	25	0	113.1	117	48	35	42
88 AL	1	2	4.65	20	0	40.2	49	21	14	15
89 AL	5	5	2.45	70	13	103.0	98	28	26	51
90 AL	11	7	3.39	64	2	93.0	80	35	26	48
91 AL	3	4	3.68	64	6	88.0	91	36	25	35
Life	31	26	4.03	287	21	518.1	552	232	158	231
3 AVE	6	5	3.14	66	7	95.0	90	33	26	45

OZZIE GUILLEN

Position: Shortstop
Team: Chicago White Sox
Born: Jan. 20, 1964 Ocumare del Tuy, Venezuela
Height: 5'11" **Weight:** 150 lbs.
Bats: left **Throws:** right
Acquired: Traded from Padres with Tim Lollar, Bill Long, and Luis Salazar for LaMarr Hoyt, Todd Simmons, and Kevin Kristan, 12/84

Player Summary	
Fantasy Value	$15 to $20
Card Value	3¢ to 5¢
Will	play brilliant shortstop
Can't	provide power
Expect	bunts and infield hits
Don't Expect	walks or whiffs

Guillen is a key player in the success of the White Sox. Managers last year named him the league's best bunter as well as the second-best defensive shortstop in a poll conducted by *Baseball America*. The 1985 AL Rookie of the Year has been an All-Star in three of his seven seasons. An acrobatic fielder who won his first Gold Glove in 1990, Guillen is also a pesky hitter who's extremely difficult to fan. He's even tougher to walk. A first-pitch hitter with little power, his strengths are speed and defense. He has tremendous range, reaches balls others can't, and turns potential base hits into double-plays. As long as he keeps playing shortstop like Luis Aparicio, the White Sox are happy. His $15-plus fantasy value reflects his consistency. His 1992 commons will not start rising in price for years.

Major League Batting Register

	BA	G	AB	R	H	2B	3B	HR	RBI	SB
85 AL	.273	150	491	71	134	21	9	1	33	7
86 AL	.250	159	547	58	137	19	4	2	47	8
87 AL	.279	149	560	64	156	22	7	2	51	25
88 AL	.261	156	566	58	148	16	7	0	39	25
89 AL	.253	155	597	63	151	20	8	1	54	36
90 AL	.279	160	516	61	144	21	4	1	58	13
91 AL	.273	154	524	52	143	20	3	3	49	21
Life	.267	1083	3801	427	1013	139	42	10	331	135
3 AVE	.268	156	546	59	146	20	5	2	54	23

CURRENT PLAYERS

BILL GULLICKSON

Position: Pitcher
Team: Detroit Tigers
Born: Feb. 20, 1959 Marshall, MN
Height: 6'3" **Weight:** 200 lbs.
Bats: right **Throws:** right
Acquired: Signed as a free agent, 12/90

Player Summary	
Fantasy Value	$10 to $14
Card Value	3¢ to 5¢
Will	pitch well enough to win
Can't	keep ball in park
Expect	high-scoring games
Don't Expect	many walks or Ks

The latest Japanese import to make good with the Tigers, Gullickson led the staff in wins last year, his first in Motown. With ample offensive support, he was among the AL leaders in wins in 1991. He showed good control with five pitches, two fastballs, a slider, curve, and occasional changeup. He yielded frequent hits but managed to spread them out. He also threw more than 20 home run balls. If the magic lasts, he will be a hot fantasy property, up to $14. Gullickson jumped to Japan in 1988. Though knee surgery and a pulled groin muscle interfered, he won 21 games over two years and signed with the Astros. After a year, the team decided to unload his big salary. Houston's discard became Detroit's delight. His 1992 commons will not pay off.

Major League Pitching Register

	W	L	ERA	G	CG	IP	H	ER	BB	SO
79 NL	0	0	0.00	1	0	1.0	2	0	0	0
80 NL	10	5	3.00	24	5	141.0	127	47	50	120
81 NL	7	9	2.80	22	3	157.1	142	49	34	115
82 NL	12	14	3.57	34	6	236.2	231	94	61	155
83 NL	17	12	3.75	34	10	242.1	230	101	59	120
84 NL	12	9	3.61	32	3	226.2	230	91	37	100
85 NL	14	12	3.52	29	4	181.1	187	71	47	68
86 NL	15	12	3.38	37	6	244.2	245	92	60	121
87 NL	10	11	4.85	27	3	165.0	172	89	39	89
87 AL	4	2	4.88	8	1	48.0	46	26	11	28
90 NL	10	14	3.82	32	2	193.1	221	82	61	73
91 AL	20	9	3.90	35	4	226.1	256	98	44	91
Life	131	109	3.66	315	47	2063.2	2089	840	503	1080
2 AVE	15	12	3.86	34	3	210.1	239	90	53	82

MARK GUTHRIE

Position: Pitcher
Team: Minnesota Twins
Born: Sept. 22, 1965 Buffalo, NY
Height: 6'4" **Weight:** 202 lbs.
Bats: both **Throws:** left
Acquired: Seventh-round pick in 6/87 free-agent draft

Player Summary	
Fantasy Value	$1 to $2
Card Value	3¢ to 5¢
Will	yield more hits than frames
Can't	avoid control woes
Expect	confusion over role
Don't Expect	many strikeouts

After enjoying some success as a Minnesota starter in 1990, Guthrie moved between the rotation and bullpen in 1991. Sentenced to the bullpen in mid-1991, he is devalued as a fantasy hurler to $1. He yielded 12 hits for every nine innings pitched, resulting in an inflated ERA. Opponents compiled a .303 batting average, a .465 slugging percentage, and a .369 on-base average. Unless he can improve those figures, his future will be cloudy. The pitcher showed great promise as a second-year pro, when he went 12-9 with a 3.31 ERA and 182 strikeouts in 171⅓ innings pitched at Class-A Visalia in 1988. He was also impressive at Double-A Orlando in 1989, going 8-3 with a 1.97 ERA. He was 3-4 with a 3.65 ERA at Triple-A Portland that year. He has yet to live up to that promise on higher levels. A fastball-and-forkball pitcher, Guthrie is an adequate fielder whose biggest asset is a fine pickoff move. He needs it, since he always allows runners to reach first base. His 1992 commons have little impact.

Major League Pitching Register

	W	L	ERA	G	S	IP	H	ER	BB	SO
89 AL	2	4	4.55	13	0	57.1	66	29	21	38
90 AL	7	9	3.79	24	3	144.2	154	61	39	101
91 AL	7	5	4.32	41	0	98.0	116	47	41	72
Life	16	18	4.11	78	3	300.0	336	137	101	211
2 AVE	7	7	4.01	33	2	121.1	135	54	40	87

CURRENT PLAYERS

JOSE GUZMAN

Position: Pitcher
Team: Texas Rangers
Born: April 9, 1963 Santa Isabel, Puerto Rico
Height: 6'3" **Weight:** 198 lbs.
Bats: right **Throws:** right
Acquired: Signed as a free agent, 2/81

Player Summary	
Fantasy Value	$4 to $7
Card Value	3¢ to 5¢
Will	get 10-plus wins
Can't	win K crown
Expect	proficiency when healthy
Don't Expect	bouts of wildness

Guzman went 34 months between major league victories while recuperating from a torn rotator cuff. He had 37 big league wins by age 25 but missed all of the 1989 and 1990 campaigns and part of 1991 before returning to the Rangers in May, two months after Texas released him in spring training. He spurned other organizations to sign a minor league contract with the Rangers and work his way back as a starter. He got his chance when Nolan Ryan, Bobby Witt, and Scott Chiamparino were injured simultaneously. Normally a control pitcher, Guzman walked nine in 3⅔ innings in his first outing May 23. With his fastball back to its former velocity, however, he two-hit the Angels with 10 Ks on June 30. His splendid comeback should thrill pitching-hungry fantasy managers, for up to $7. Stay away from his 1992 commons until he proves that he is all the way back. If he stays healthy, Guzman will be a regular member of the 1992 rotation.

Major League Pitching Register

	W	L	ERA	G	CG	IP	H	ER	BB	SO
85 AL	3	2	2.76	5	0	32.2	27	10	14	24
86 AL	9	15	4.54	29	2	172.1	199	87	60	87
87 AL	14	14	4.67	37	6	208.1	196	108	82	143
88 AL	11	13	3.70	30	6	206.2	180	85	82	157
91 AL	13	7	3.08	25	5	169.2	152	58	84	125
Life	50	51	3.97	126	19	789.2	754	348	322	536

JUAN GUZMAN

Position: Pitcher
Team: Toronto Blue Jays
Born: Oct. 28, 1966 Santo Domingo, Dominican Republic
Height: 5'11" **Weight:** 190 lbs.
Bats: right **Throws:** right
Acquired: Traded from Dodgers for Mike Sharperson, 9/87

Player Summary	
Fantasy Value	$3 to $6
Card Value	10¢ to 15¢
Will	attack with hard stuff
Can't	avoid wild spells
Expect	great hits-to-frames ratio
Don't Expect	more time in minors

In their constant search for quality starting pitching, the Blue Jays gave a rookie a chance when they promoted Guzman from Triple-A Syracuse. Opponents compiled a .197 batting average, a .268 slugging percentage, and a .294 on-base average in 1991. Guzman, whose fastball has been clocked at 94 mph, mixes fastballs, sliders, and changeups. He was 4-5 with a 4.02 ERA, 67 strikeouts, and 42 walks in 67 innings at Syracuse in '91. He had been leading the International League in Ks when summoned by the Blue Jays. The one-time reliever moved to the starting rotation at Double-A Knoxville in 1990. He was 11-9 with a 4.24 ERA and 138 strikeouts, 80 bases on balls, and 145 hits in 157 innings that year. Beware when buying Guzman's dime-priced 1992 cards. With Dave Stieb's physical status uncertain following an injury-riddled 1991 campaign, Guzman's success could play a significant role in Toronto's 1992 season. His rosy future with Toronto makes him a solid $5 fantasy pitcher.

Major League Pitching Register

	W	L	ERA	G	CG	IP	H	ER	BB	SO
91 AL	10	3	2.99	23	1	138.2	98	46	66	123
Life	10	3	2.99	23	1	138.2	98	46	66	123

CURRENT PLAYERS

CHRIS GWYNN

Position: Outfield
Team: Kansas City Royals
Born: Oct. 13, 1964 Los Angeles, CA
Height: 6' **Weight:** 210 lbs.
Bats: left **Throws:** left
Acquired: Traded from Dodgers with Domingo Mota for Todd Benzinger, 12/91

Player Summary	
Fantasy Value	$2 to $4
Card Value	3¢ to 5¢
Will	produce pinch-hits
Can't	swipe like Tony
Expect	use as No. 4 outfielder
Don't Expect	great power

Even though he's never played regularly, Gwynn upholds the family name as a hitter. In 1991, he broke the club record of 15 pinch-hits shared by Manny Mota and Ed Goodson. Though he lacks brother Tony's patience at the plate, Chris has a bit more home run power than his older sibling. Chris is also more of a hacker, much more likely to strike out, and less likely to walk. He had a .410 slugging percentage and a .301 on-base average in '91. When given the chance to play, Gwynn is a good defensive outfielder at all three positions. Though both Gwynns attended San Diego State, Chris holds school season records for runs (95), total bases (243), triples (nine), and RBI (95). He led the Triple-A Pacific Coast League with 10 triples in 1988. He could do some damage as a $3 fantasy outfielder. Many scouts believe Gwynn could be one of the game's most productive hitters if he played regularly. Since he doesn't, his 1992 commons are not buys.

Major League Batting Register

	BA	G	AB	R	H	2B	3B	HR	RBI	SB
87 NL	.219	17	32	2	7	1	0	0	2	0
88 NL	.182	12	11	1	2	0	0	0	0	0
89 NL	.235	32	68	8	16	4	1	0	7	1
90 NL	.284	101	141	19	40	2	1	5	22	0
91 NL	.252	94	139	18	35	5	1	5	22	1
Life	.256	256	391	48	100	12	3	10	53	2

TONY GWYNN

Position: Outfield
Team: San Diego Padres
Born: May 9, 1960 Los Angeles, CA
Height: 5'11" **Weight:** 205 lbs.
Bats: left **Throws:** left
Acquired: Third-round pick in 6/81 free-agent draft

Player Summary	
Fantasy Value	$37 to $44
Card Value	10¢ to 15¢
Will	bid for bat crown
Can't	wait for walks
Expect	Gold Glove defense
Don't Expect	many steals now

Gwynn is the ultimate line-drive hitter. Baseball's best contact hitter, he has won four batting titles. Because he bats third, the seven-time All-Star has had three 70-RBI seasons. At $40, your fantasy squad will get major production. He was batting second when he reached personal peaks in 1987. Blessed with a keen batting eye, Gwynn walks about twice as often as he strikes out. He hits a home run or makes an error once in a blue moon, with only three miscues in '91. A top clutch hitter, Gwynn hit .386 in the 1984 playoffs as the Padres won their only pennant. With better hitters around him, he might make a run at .400. Gwynn is one of baseball's best right fielders, winning five Gold Gloves. His 1992 cards are good buys at a dime apiece.

Major League Batting Register

	BA	G	AB	R	H	2B	3B	HR	RBI	SB
82 NL	.289	54	190	33	55	12	2	1	17	8
83 NL	.309	86	304	34	94	12	2	1	37	7
84 NL	.351	158	606	88	213	21	10	5	71	33
85 NL	.317	154	622	90	197	29	5	6	46	14
86 NL	.329	160	642	107	211	33	7	14	59	37
87 NL	.370	157	589	119	218	36	13	7	54	56
88 NL	.313	133	521	64	163	22	5	7	70	26
89 NL	.336	158	604	82	203	27	7	4	62	40
90 NL	.309	141	573	79	177	29	10	4	72	17
91 NL	.317	134	530	69	168	27	11	4	62	8
Life	.328	1335	5181	765	1699	248	72	53	550	246
3 AVE	.321	144	569	77	183	28	9	4	65	22

CURRENT PLAYERS

JOHN HABYAN

Position: Pitcher
Team: New York Yankees
Born: Jan. 29, 1964 Bayshore, NY
Height: 6'2" **Weight:** 195 lbs.
Bats: right **Throws:** right
Acquired: Traded from Orioles for Stan Jefferson, 7/89

Player Summary	
Fantasy Value	$1 to $3
Card Value	3¢ to 5¢
Will	work often
Can't	get notice in role
Expect	fine K-to-walk ratio
Don't Expect	gopher balls

Habyan had spent a half-dozen seasons bouncing between the majors and minors before blossoming into a quality middle reliever in 1991. It was his first full year in the majors. After going north out of spring training for the first time in seven tries, he was a rare beacon in the fog that enveloped the Yankee pitching staff. Appearing in more than 60 games, he allowed less than a hit per inning pitched, fanned three times more men than he walked, and was among the league's stingiest pitchers with the gopher ball (two). Habyan has excellent command of his fastball, sinker, and slider, plus the temperament to succeed in relief. Opponents compiled a .225 batting average, a .315 slugging percentage, and a .274 on-base average in '91. A pro since 1982, he had spent much of his previous career as a starter. His current status as a middle reliever will not help fantasy teams for more than $3. His 1992 commons are unimportant investments.

Major League Pitching Register

	W	L	ERA	G	S	IP	H	ER	BB	SO
85 AL	1	0	0.00	2	0	2.2	3	0	0	2
86 AL	1	3	4.44	6	0	26.1	24	13	18	14
87 AL	6	7	4.80	27	1	116.1	110	62	40	64
88 AL	1	0	4.30	7	0	14.2	22	7	4	4
90 AL	0	0	2.08	6	0	8.2	10	2	2	4
91 AL	4	2	2.30	66	2	90.0	73	23	20	70
Life	13	12	3.72	114	3	258.2	242	107	84	158

MEL HALL

Position: Outfield
Team: New York Yankees
Born: Sept. 16, 1960 Lyons, NY
Height: 6'1" **Weight:** 218 lbs.
Bats: left **Throws:** left
Acquired: Traded from Indians for Joel Skinner and Turner Ward, 3/89

Player Summary	
Fantasy Value	$10 to $13
Card Value	3¢ to 5¢
Will	pop dramatic homers
Can't	consistently steal
Expect	good average
Don't Expect	a Gold Glove

When the 1991 season opened, Hall was a platoon outfielder and pinch-hitter. That changed after rookie lefthanded-hitting flycatcher Bam-Bam Meulens got off to a slow start. Hall took over and responded very well to playing every day. He hit near the .300 mark all season, and he was among Yankee leaders in homers, RBI, and total bases. He showed more patience at the plate, walking more, fanning less, and making much better contact. Hall erased a former reputation as a one-dimensional player. His play in the outfield corners also improved. Hall's strong arm and speed were superseded in past years by poor play. His satisfying 1991 season gives him fantasy muscle for up to $13. His 1992 commons, however, will not be price gainers.

Major League Batting Register

	BA	G	AB	R	H	2B	3B	HR	RBI	SB
81 NL	.091	10	11	1	1	0	0	1	2	0
82 NL	.262	24	80	6	21	3	2	0	4	0
83 NL	.283	112	410	60	116	23	5	17	56	6
84 NL	.280	48	150	25	42	11	3	4	22	2
84 AL	.257	83	257	43	66	13	1	7	30	1
85 AL	.318	23	66	7	21	6	0	0	12	0
86 AL	.296	140	442	68	131	29	2	18	77	6
87 AL	.280	142	485	57	136	21	1	18	76	5
88 AL	.280	150	515	69	144	32	4	6	71	7
89 AL	.260	113	361	54	94	9	0	17	58	0
90 AL	.258	113	360	41	93	23	2	12	46	0
91 AL	.285	141	492	67	140	23	2	19	80	0
Life	.277	1099	3629	498	1005	193	22	119	534	27
3 AVE	.270	122	404	54	109	18	1	16	61	0

CURRENT PLAYERS

DARRYL HAMILTON

Position: Outfield
Team: Milwaukee Brewers
Born: Dec. 3, 1964 Baton Rouge, LA
Height: 6'1" **Weight:** 180 lbs.
Bats: left **Throws:** right
Acquired: 11th-round pick in 6/86 free-agent draft

Player Summary	
Fantasy Value	$4 to $7
Card Value	3¢ to 5¢
Will	get on base
Can't	hit home runs
Expect	good defense
Don't Expect	many Ks or walks

Hamilton's home run against the Orioles last August 8 was his first since July 8, 1990. It was during a career-high 19-game hitting streak. He compensates for a lack of power with good speed, a high batting average, and strong defensive play in right field. He had only one error and hit at the .300 level all season long. He had a .385 slugging percentage and a .361 on-base average in '91. Hamilton began his pro career by hitting .391 with 34 steals for rookie league Helena in 1986. When he reached Milwaukee to stay four years later, he hit .295. He was a member of Team USA in 1985. Though he strikes out more than he walks, he is a contact hitter who doesn't whiff much. He is basically a singles hitter who works the hit-and-run and steals bases when asked. Hamilton usually hits in the top third of the lineup, sometimes even in the No. 3 slot. He is a capable $5 fantasy reserve outfielder. His 1992 cards are not great investments.

Major League Batting Register

	BA	G	AB	R	H	2B	3B	HR	RBI	SB
88 AL	.184	44	103	14	19	4	0	1	11	7
90 AL	.295	89	156	27	46	5	0	1	18	10
91 AL	.311	122	405	64	126	15	6	1	57	16
Life	.288	255	664	105	191	24	6	3	86	33
2 AVE	.307	106	281	46	86	10	3	1	38	13

JEFF HAMILTON

Position: Third base
Team: Los Angeles Dodgers
Born: March 19, 1964 Flint, MI
Height: 6'3" **Weight:** 207 lbs.
Bats: right **Throws:** right
Acquired: 29th-round pick in 6/82 free-agent draft

Player Summary	
Fantasy Value	$1 to $3
Card Value	3¢ to 5¢
Will	get injured
Can't	hit for average
Expect	dandy defense
Don't Expect	many steals

Hamilton is a standout defensive third baseman with a weak bat and a tendency to fall victim to injury often. In 1991, he went on the 15-day disabled list with a torn ligament in his left knee in June and missed a large chunk of the season. He had past problems with his shoulder, rib cage, and ankle. His injury history keeps his fantasy value at $2 and his 1992 cards below a nickel each. Never a strong hitter, Hamilton had a .235 average for five seasons before 1991. An impatient hitter who strikes out about four times more often than he walks, he struggles against both righty and lefty pitching. In fact, he suggested last year that he should become a pitcher himself. He doesn't hit well enough to hold down the third base job by himself. Hamilton has a fine arm and is such a fine fielder that he'd be a like a fifth infielder on the mound.

Major League Batting Register

	BA	G	AB	R	H	2B	3B	HR	RBI	SB
86 NL	.224	71	147	22	33	5	0	5	19	0
87 NL	.217	35	83	5	18	3	0	0	1	0
88 NL	.236	111	309	34	73	14	2	6	33	0
89 NL	.245	151	548	45	134	35	1	12	56	0
90 NL	.125	7	24	1	3	0	0	0	1	0
91 NL	.223	41	94	4	21	4	0	1	14	0
Life	.234	416	1205	111	282	61	3	24	124	0

CURRENT PLAYERS

CHRIS HAMMOND

Position: Pitcher
Team: Cincinnati Reds
Born: Jan. 21, 1966 Atlanta, GA
Height: 6′ **Weight:** 190 lbs.
Bats: left **Throws:** left
Acquired: Sixth-round pick in 1/86 free-agent draft

Player Summary	
Fantasy Value	$3 to $6
Card Value	5¢ to 7¢
Will	rely on changeup
Can't	rely on fastball
Expect	a dozen wins
Don't Expect	high K totals

Hammond made such an impression as a rookie in 1991 that rival managers in a *Baseball America* poll said his changeup was the league's best behind Frank Viola and Ramon Martinez. Hammond reached the majors after posting a 15-1 record with a 2.17 ERA and 149 strikeouts at Triple-A Nashville in 1990. He led the American Association in wins, strikeouts, and ERA that year. He was 11-7 with a 3.38 ERA, 142 strikeouts, 96 walks, and 144 hits in 157⅓ innings in 1989 at Nashville. A good hitter, bunter, and fielder, he has been hampered in the past by shoulder problems and control lapses. Since his fastball is average, he depends heavily on the changeup. He is a chancy $5 starter. Opposing hitters compiled a .250 batting average, a .340 slugging percentage, and a .339 on-base average in 1991. As he matures, Hammond could blossom into a big winner, especially if given the offensive and defensive support Cincinnati can provide. As the Reds improve, his nickel-priced 1992 cards will rise in value.

Major League Pitching Register

	W	L	ERA	G	CG	IP	H	ER	BB	SO
90 NL	0	2	6.35	3	0	11.1	13	8	12	4
91 NL	7	7	4.06	20	0	99.2	92	45	48	50
Life	7	9	4.30	23	0	111.0	105	53	60	54

CHRIS HANEY

Position: Pitcher
Team: Montreal Expos
Born: Nov. 16, 1968 Baltimore, MD
Height: 6′3″ **Weight:** 185 lbs.
Bats: left **Throws:** left
Acquired: Second-round pick in 6/90 free-agent draft

Player Summary	
Fantasy Value	$2 to $4
Card Value	15¢ to 20¢
Will	work in rotation
Can't	bank on experience
Expect	inconsistent play
Don't Expect	high K totals

Haney comes from good baseball stock; his father Larry was a major league catcher. Chris made his debut last June 21 after Chris Nabholz, another highly regarded young lefthander, went onto the disabled list. Haney almost made the Montreal varsity with a strong showing during spring training. He was so highly regarded by the Expos that he was called up from Double-A Harrisburg, even though several Triple-A prospects also seemed ready to advance. At the time of his recall, Haney had a 5-3 record with a 2.16 earned run average, 68 strikeouts, 31 walks, and 65 hits in 83 innings. He also started two games at Triple-A Indianapolis, going 1-1 with a 4.35 ERA. His Class-A stats combined in 1990 included a 5-4 record with a 1.78 ERA, 71 Ks, and 16 bases on balls in 81 innings. Until he proves himself a little more, he is a $3 fantasy pitcher. With the Expos unloading such high-priced veterans as Oil Can Boyd and Ron Darling, Haney should have a solid future as a starter in Montreal. His rookie 1992 cards are good investment possibilities at 15 cents.

Major League Pitching Register

	W	L	ERA	G	CG	IP	H	ER	BB	SO
91 NL	3	7	4.04	16	0	84.2	94	38	43	51
Life	3	7	4.04	16	0	84.2	94	38	43	51

CURRENT PLAYERS

ERIK HANSON

Position: Pitcher
Team: Seattle Mariners
Born: May 18, 1965 Kinnelon, NJ
Height: 6'6" **Weight:** 210 lbs.
Bats: right **Throws:** right
Acquired: Second-round pick in 6/86 free-agent draft

Player Summary
Fantasy Value	$8 to $10
Card Value	3¢ to 5¢
Will	bank on curve
Can't	stay healthy
Expect	many whiffs
Don't Expect	an ERA over 4.00

After winning 18 games in 1990, Hanson ran into elbow problems that sent him to the disabled list twice in 1991. The Mariners Opening Day starter, Hanson made only 12 starts before the All-Star break. Opponents compiled a .269 batting average, a .414 slugging percentage, and a .323 on-base average in 1991. Injuries also hampered his progress in 1989, when he missed three months with tendinitis of the pitching shoulder. The healthy Hanson has one of baseball's best curveballs, though throwing it too often contributed to his 1991 physical problems. One of the league's top strikeout artists, he has fantasy value up to $10. In 1990, he fell one short of Mark Langston's club record of 19 wins. Hanson was 4-2 at Triple-A Calgary with a 6.87 ERA. He was 12-7 with a 4.23 ERA and a Pacific Coast League-leading 154 strikeouts in 161⅔ innings in 1988 at Calgary. His 1992 commons don't excite collectors, at least yet.

Major League Pitching Register
	W	L	ERA	G	CG	IP	H	ER	BB	SO
88 AL	2	3	3.24	6	0	41.2	35	15	12	36
89 AL	9	5	3.18	17	1	113.1	103	40	32	75
90 AL	18	9	3.24	33	5	236.0	205	85	68	211
91 AL	8	8	3.81	27	2	174.2	182	74	56	143
Life	37	25	3.40	83	8	565.2	525	214	168	465
3 AVE	12	7	3.42	26	3	174.1	163	66	52	143

MIKE HARKEY

Position: Pitcher
Team: Chicago Cubs
Born: Oct. 25, 1966 San Diego, CA
Height: 6'5" **Weight:** 220 lbs.
Bats: right **Throws:** right
Acquired: First-round pick in 6/87 free-agent draft

Player Summary
Fantasy Value	$4 to $6
Card Value	3¢ to 5¢
Will	win when healthy
Can't	avoid injuries
Expect	high K totals
Don't Expect	37 starts

If Harkey ever stays healthy, the Cubs believe he'll develop into a perennial All-Star. His 1991 campaign was ruined when he went on the 60-day disabled list April 27 with torn shoulder cartilage that needed arthroscopic surgery. He also missed most of the '89 season with knee and shoulder woes. Once considered a Bob Gibson clone by scouts who watched him in the minors, Harkey has the potential to develop into a No. 1 starter. He throws a 95 mph fastball, plus a curveball, slider, and changeup—all with good control. The heater rides in on righthanded hitters. At Double-A Pittsfield in 1988, he was 9-2 with a 1.37 ERA, 73 strikeouts, 35 bases on balls, and 66 hits in 85⅔ innings. He was 7-2 with a 3.55 ERA, 62 Ks, 33 walks, and 55 hits in 78⅔ innings that year at Triple-A Iowa. Given good health, plus good offensive and defensive support, he could become a 20-game winner. A talented hurler, he is a $5 fantasy risk. Don't buy his 1992 commons until he has several more major league starts under his belt.

Major League Pitching Register
	W	L	ERA	G	CG	IP	H	ER	BB	SO
88 NL	0	3	2.60	5	0	34.2	33	10	15	18
90 NL	12	6	3.26	27	2	173.2	153	63	59	94
91 NL	0	2	5.30	4	0	18.2	21	11	6	15
Life	12	11	3.33	36	2	227.0	207	84	80	127

CURRENT PLAYERS

PETE HARNISCH

Position: Pitcher
Team: Houston Astros
Born: Sept. 23, 1966 Commack, NY
Height: 6′ **Weight:** 207 lbs.
Bats: right **Throws:** right
Acquired: Traded from Orioles with Steve Finley and Curt Schilling for Glenn Davis, 1/91

Player Summary	
Fantasy Value	$8 to $12
Card Value	3¢ to 5¢
Will	rank with elite starters
Can't	win big with 'Stros
Expect	low-scoring games
Don't Expect	wild spells

Harnisch began 1991 as Houston's third starter behind Mike Scott and Jim Deshaies. That status was short-lived. After going 11-11 with the 1990 Orioles, Harnisch blossomed into a star with the Astros. A power pitcher with good control of his fastball, curveball, changeup, and slider, he was involved in six 1-0 decisions early in the year—two wins, two losses, and two no-decisions. Although he threw harder during his days at Fordham, the O's '87 first-round draft choice was 7-6 with 141 Ks and 52 walks in 132⅓ innings at Double-A Charlotte in 1988. At one point, Harnisch hurled 22 straight scoreless innings. He is a $10 fantasy hurler, a bargain if you think that the Astros are going to score more this year. His 1992 cards are not good investments now, even at their nickel prices. He strikes out twice as many as he walks and is miserly with hits and runs, especially in his home park. The 1991 All-Star may have a Cy Young Award in his future.

Major League Pitching Register

	W	L	ERA	G	CG	IP	H	ER	BB	SO
88 AL	0	2	5.54	2	0	13.0	13	8	9	10
89 AL	5	9	4.62	18	2	103.1	97	53	64	70
90 AL	11	11	4.34	31	3	188.2	189	91	86	122
91 NL	12	9	2.70	33	4	216.2	169	65	83	172
Life	28	31	3.74	84	9	521.2	468	217	242	374
3 AVE	9	10	3.70	27	3	169.2	152	70	78	121

BRIAN HARPER

Position: Catcher
Team: Minnesota Twins
Born: Oct. 16, 1959 Los Angeles, CA
Height: 6′2″ **Weight:** 195 lbs.
Bats: right **Throws:** right
Acquired: Signed as a free agent, 12/87

Player Summary	
Fantasy Value	$10 to $15
Card Value	3¢ to 5¢
Will	hit to all fields
Can't	throw well
Expect	many doubles
Don't Expect	average below .300

Harper blossomed into one of Minnesota's offensive mainstays after taking the advice of batting coach Terry Crowley. The coach got Harper to show more patience at the plate but convinced him he is a better hitter with two strikes. The selectivity paid off, because his ability to reduce his strikeouts fattened his batting average. He whiffed only 22 times in 1991. He had a 25-game hitting streak, longest ever by a catcher, in 1990. He is a contact hitter who hits line drives to all fields. Harper can't match his offense with superior defense. His arm, game-calling, and receiving are more than adequate. He is a $15 fantasy receiver. He proved his toughness in the '91 World Series when he took a big hit by Lonnie Smith. His 1992 commons are poor investments.

Major League Batting Register

	BA	G	AB	R	H	2B	3B	HR	RBI	SB
79 AL	.000	1	2	0	0	0	0	0	0	0
81 AL	.273	4	11	1	3	0	0	0	1	1
82 NL	.276	20	29	4	8	1	0	2	4	0
83 NL	.221	61	131	16	29	4	1	7	20	0
84 NL	.259	46	112	4	29	4	0	2	11	0
85 AL	.250	43	52	5	13	4	0	0	8	0
86 AL	.139	19	36	2	5	1	0	0	3	0
87 AL	.235	11	17	1	4	1	0	0	3	0
88 AL	.295	60	166	15	49	11	1	3	20	0
89 AL	.325	126	385	43	125	24	0	8	57	2
90 AL	.294	134	479	61	141	42	3	6	54	3
91 AL	.311	123	441	54	137	28	1	10	69	1
Life	.292	648	1861	206	543	120	6	38	250	7
3 AVE	.309	128	435	53	134	31	1	8	60	2

CURRENT PLAYERS

GREG HARRIS

Position: Pitcher
Team: Boston Red Sox
Born: Nov. 2, 1955 Lynwood, CA
Height: 5'11" **Weight:** 165 lbs.
Bats: both **Throws:** right
Acquired: Signed as a free agent, 8/89

Player Summary	
Fantasy Value	$7 to $10
Card Value	3¢ to 5¢
Will	rack up Ks
Can't	avoid wildness
Expect	10 to 15 wins
Don't Expect	many complete games

Harris has been used as a starter and reliever during a career that began with the 1981 Mets. He and Roger Clemens were the only Boston starters with both double-figure wins and triple-figure strikeouts. Harris mixes a fastball, cut fastball, and changeup with a curve that serves as his best pitch. He fanned twice as many as he walked last year but usually does not have such a good ratio. He sometimes can't locate the strike zone. He's good at locating anything hit his way, however, and also keeps base-runners close. If he continues to yield less than a hit per inning, Harris should hang onto his job. His wins and Ks look good to fantasy managers for up to $10. His 1992 commons aren't rewarding.

Major League Pitching Register

	W	L	ERA	G	S	IP	H	ER	BB	SO
81 NL	3	5	4.46	16	1	68.2	65	34	28	54
82 NL	2	6	4.83	34	1	91.1	96	49	37	67
83 NL	0	0	27.00	1	0	1.0	2	3	3	1
84 NL	2	2	2.48	34	3	54.1	38	15	25	45
85 AL	5	4	2.47	58	11	113.0	74	31	43	111
86 AL	10	8	2.83	73	20	111.1	103	35	42	95
87 AL	5	10	4.86	42	0	140.2	157	76	56	106
88 NL	4	6	2.36	66	1	107.0	80	28	52	71
89 NL	2	3	3.58	44	1	75.1	64	30	43	51
89 AL	2	2	2.57	15	0	28.0	21	8	15	25
90 AL	13	9	4.00	34	0	184.1	186	82	77	117
91 AL	11	12	3.85	53	2	173.0	157	74	69	127
Life	59	66	3.65	470	40	1148.0	1043	465	490	870
3 AVE	9	8	3.79	49	1	153.1	143	65	68	107

GREG HARRIS

Position: Pitcher
Team: San Diego Padres
Born: Dec. 1, 1963 Greensboro, NC
Height: 6'2" **Weight:** 190 lbs.
Bats: right **Throws:** right
Acquired: Tenth-round pick in 6/85 free-agent draft

Player Summary	
Fantasy Value	$7 to $10
Card Value	3¢ to 5¢
Will	yield few hits
Can't	get timely hits
Expect	fine K-to-walk ratio
Don't Expect	return to bullpen

Had he not spent two months on the disabled list with tendinitis of the elbow, Harris might have been the biggest winner on the San Diego staff. A reliever in all 73 of his 1990 appearances, he made a smooth transition to the rotation. On July 14, he held the Mets hitless before Mackey Sasser hit a leadoff eighth-inning double, the game's only hit. A month later, Harris threw consecutive 1-0 shutouts against the Reds and Braves. He's always had good luck against NL West teams. In his first 81 games against them, his ERA was 1.79. Fantasy managers should take notice of his ability and potential—for up to a ten spot. Bypass his 1992 commons, because his career stats aren't great. Unlike other power pitchers, Harris has excellent control, especially with a curve that he considers his best pitch. He keeps the ball in the park, giving up 16 homers in '91. Harris fields well and keeps runners close but seldom helps himself with a hit.

Major League Pitching Register

	W	L	ERA	G	CG	IP	H	ER	BB	SO
88 NL	2	0	1.50	9	1	18.0	13	3	3	15
89 NL	8	9	2.60	56	0	135.0	106	39	52	106
90 NL	8	8	2.30	73	0	117.1	92	30	49	97
91 NL	9	5	2.23	20	3	133.0	116	33	27	95
Life	27	22	2.34	152	4	403.1	327	105	131	313
3 AVE	8	7	2.38	50	1	128.0	105	34	43	99

CURRENT PLAYERS

LENNY HARRIS

Position: Third base; second base
Team: Los Angeles Dodgers
Born: Oct. 28, 1964 Miami, FL
Height: 5'10" **Weight:** 195 lbs.
Bats: left **Throws:** right
Acquired: Traded from Reds with Kal Daniels for Tim Leary and Mariano Duncan, 7/89

Player Summary
Fantasy Value	$6 to $9
Card Value	3¢ to 5¢
Will	hit near .300
Can't	field flawlessly
Expect	handful of homers
Don't Expect	many walks or Ks

After years of platooning at both second and third base for the Dodgers, Harris became a regular last year when third baseman Jeff Hamilton was injured. Though he could not match Hamilton's defensive skills, Harris more than compensated with his solid hitting. Some observers see Harris as a lefthanded Bill Madlock. Harris has the same build, same line-drive bat, and same fielding deficiencies as the former four-time batting champion. A contact hitter who rarely strikes out or hits for power, Harris hits to all fields and handles all pitchers, except for lefties who feed him a breaking-ball diet. He is a superb addition to your fantasy team for $7. Since he hasn't been a full-time starter, his 1992 cards are not wise buys. He hit .304 in 137 games in 1990, his first full season. Harris's speed helps him in the field, where most of his errors come on throws. Playing mostly third base in '91 helped him improve his defensive game.

Major League Batting Register
	BA	G	AB	R	H	2B	3B	HR	RBI	SB
88 NL	.372	16	43	7	16	1	0	0	8	4
89 NL	.236	115	335	36	79	10	1	3	26	14
90 NL	.304	137	431	61	131	16	4	2	29	15
91 NL	.287	145	429	59	123	16	1	3	38	12
Life	.282	413	1238	163	349	43	6	8	101	45
3 AVE	.279	132	398	52	111	14	2	3	31	14

MIKE HARTLEY

Position: Pitcher
Team: Philadelphia Phillies
Born: Aug. 31, 1961 Hawthorne, CA
Height: 6'1" **Weight:** 197 lbs.
Bats: right **Throws:** right
Acquired: Traded from Dodgers with Braulio Castillo for Roger McDowell, 7/91

Player Summary
Fantasy Value	$2 to $4
Card Value	3¢ to 5¢
Will	appear in set-up roles
Can't	always throw strikes
Expect	a K per inning
Don't Expect	deployment as starter

Hartley's second season in the majors was not as good as his first. The reason was his inability to locate the strike zone. After an impressive rookie year during which he fanned more than twice the number he walked, Hartley found the plate wandering. As his ERA rose, his stock fell, and the displeased Dodgers dispatched him in a late-season deal. In 1989 at Triple-A Albuquerque, he was 7-4 with 18 saves, a 2.79 ERA, 76 strikeouts, 34 walks, and 53 hits in 67⅔ innings. He never found the form that made him a Triple-A standout, however. Opponents compiled a .237 batting average, a .388 slugging percentage, and a .347 on-base percentage in '91. The middle reliever throws a regular fastball, split-fingered fastball, and curveball. He helps himself as a fielder but not as a hitter. Hartley's pickoff move also needs work. His pitching is fine if he finds the plate. He'll get his chances in Philadelphia, making him a $3 fantasy hurler. His common-priced 1992 cards are not good ideas.

Major League Pitching Register
	W	L	ERA	G	S	IP	H	ER	BB	SO
89 NL	0	1	1.50	5	0	6.0	2	1	0	4
90 NL	6	3	2.95	32	1	79.1	58	26	30	76
91 NL	4	1	4.21	58	2	83.1	74	39	47	63
Life	10	5	3.52	95	3	168.2	134	66	77	143
2 AVE	5	2	3.60	45	2	81.1	66	33	39	70

CURRENT PLAYERS

BRYAN HARVEY

Position: Pitcher
Team: California Angels
Born: June 2, 1963 Chattanooga, TN
Height: 6'2" **Weight:** 215 lbs.
Bats: right **Throws:** right
Acquired: Signed as free agent, 8/84

Player Summary	
Fantasy Value	$24 to $30
Card Value	3¢ to 5¢
Will	keep hitters off base
Can't	improve on '91
Expect	blinding heat
Don't Expect	control lapse

When *Baseball America* asked AL managers to name the league's top reliever after the 1990 season, Harvey finished second only to long-time Oakland standout Dennis Eckersley. Those opinions might have changed, because Eckersley struggled a bit in 1991 while Harvey enjoyed his best season. He pared off some excess poundage and managed to locate the strike zone with more consistency. By Labor Day, he had broken Donnie Moore's club record of 31 saves. Harvey, who mixes high, hard fastballs with low forkballs, gave up six homers in 1991. Opposing batters compiled a .178 batting average, a .266 slugging percentage, and a .225 on-base average last summer. Unfortunately, he will be overpriced at this year's fantasy draft. Don't pay more than $30. Though he's a decent fielder with a competent pickoff move, Harvey's pitching overshadows his other contributions. His 1992 commons are still not investment worthy, but they certainly are closer than they were.

Major League Pitching Register

	W	L	ERA	G	S	IP	H	ER	BB	SO
87 AL	0	0	0.00	3	0	5.0	6	0	2	3
88 AL	7	5	2.13	50	17	76.0	59	18	20	67
89 AL	3	3	3.44	51	25	55.0	36	21	41	78
90 AL	4	4	3.22	54	25	64.1	45	23	35	82
91 AL	2	4	1.60	67	46	78.2	51	14	17	101
Life	16	16	2.45	225	113	279.0	197	76	115	331
3 AVE	3	4	2.64	57	32	66.1	44	19	31	87

BILLY HATCHER

Position: Outfield
Team: Cincinnati Reds
Born: Oct. 4, 1960 Williams, AZ
Height: 5'9" **Weight:** 185 lbs.
Bats: right **Throws:** right
Acquired: Traded from Pirates for Mike Roesler and Jeff Richardson, 4/90

Player Summary	
Fantasy Value	$6 to $8
Card Value	3¢ to 5¢
Will	steal more often
Can't	get double-digit homers
Expect	fine fielding
Don't Expect	average over .280

One year after posting the highest average in World Series history (.750), Hatcher had to struggle for playing time with the Reds. Caught in an outfield squeeze also involving Paul O'Neill, Eric Davis, and Glenn Braggs, Hatcher's stolen base production fell dramatically, his success ratio evaporated, and his average and run production also hit the skids. He remains a contact hitter who walks more than he fans and uses all fields when he's right. He poked seven consecutive hits in the 1990 World Series. A fine fielder in both left and center, Hatcher uses his speed in the outfield and on the basepaths. He bunts well and stays out of the doubleplay. Hatcher isn't on base often enough to lead off but is a competent No. 2 hitter. He can contribute to your fantasy squad for $7. Since he isn't full-time, his 1992 commons aren't buys.

Major League Batting Register

	BA	G	AB	R	H	2B	3B	HR	RBI	SB
84 NL	.111	8	9	1	1	0	0	0	0	2
85 NL	.245	53	163	24	40	12	1	2	10	2
86 NL	.258	127	419	55	108	15	4	6	36	38
87 NL	.296	141	564	96	167	28	3	11	63	53
88 NL	.268	145	530	79	142	25	4	7	52	32
89 NL	.231	135	481	59	111	19	3	4	51	24
90 NL	.276	139	504	68	139	28	5	5	25	30
91 NL	.262	138	442	45	116	25	3	4	41	11
Life	.265	886	3112	427	824	152	23	39	278	192
3 AVE	.256	137	476	57	122	24	4	4	39	22

CURRENT PLAYERS

CHARLIE HAYES

Position: Third base
Team: Philadelphia Phillies
Born: May 29, 1965 Hattiesburg, MS
Height: 6' **Weight:** 205 lbs.
Bats: right **Throws:** right
Acquired: Traded from Giants with Terry Mulholland and Dennis Cook for Steve Bedrosian and Rick Parker, 6/89

Player Summary	
Fantasy Value	$5 to $7
Card Value	3¢ to 5¢
Will	show some power
Can't	wait for walks
Expect	solid defense
Don't Expect	average in low .200s

Hayes won't make anyone forget Mike Schmidt, but Hayes is a far better fielder than the butcher who committed 22 errors in 87 games as a 1989 rookie. Losing weight, plus lengthy tutoring from coaches Larry Bowa and John Vukovich, helped. Hayes got off to a slow start with the bat in 1991 but blasted four homers in five games, including his first career grand slam August 27. He had been a major disappointment before the outburst. An impatient hitter who whiffs four times for each walk, Hayes had trouble lifting his average above .220. He compensated with great glove work at third, however. He has a powerful arm plus an ability to flag down potential extra-base hits before they head down the left field line. If his late-season power burst continues and he lifts his average, Hayes will keep the third sack job over Dave Hollins. Since Hayes's job is in jeopardy, his fantasy value stops at $7. His 1992 commons don't have much development capacity.

Major League Batting Register

	BA	G	AB	R	H	2B	3B	HR	RBI	SB
88 NL	.091	7	11	0	1	0	0	0	0	0
89 NL	.257	87	304	26	78	15	1	8	43	3
90 NL	.258	152	561	56	145	20	0	10	57	4
91 NL	.230	142	460	34	106	23	1	12	53	3
Life	.247	388	1336	116	330	58	2	30	153	10
3 AVE	.248	127	442	39	110	19	1	10	51	3

VON HAYES

Position: Outfield; first base
Team: California Angels
Born: Aug. 31, 1958 Stockton, CA
Height: 6'5" **Weight:** 186 lbs.
Bats: left **Throws:** right
Acquired: Traded from Phillies for Kyle Abbott and Ruben Amaro, 12/91

Player Summary	
Fantasy Value	$10 to $15
Card Value	3¢ to 5¢
Will	collect walks
Can't	run with abandon
Expect	play at four positions
Don't Expect	average under .260

Hayes was one of the most productive hitters in the Philadelphia lineup when he suffered a broken right wrist when hit by a Tom Browning pitch on June 14. In 1986, Hayes led the league with 46 doubles and tied for the league lead with 107 runs scored. Hayes, who broke in with the 1981 Indians, has handled all three outfield positions as well as the infield corners. His speed has diminished a bit but he still has good range, plus a throwing arm best suited for right field. Hayes has drawn more than 100 walks in a season twice. He was traded to California in December. Be safe and curb your fantasy bidding to $15. Although he has good career numbers, the sad fact is that his 1992 commons will not rise in value because of his power numbers.

Major League Batting Register

	BA	G	AB	R	H	2B	3B	HR	RBI	SB
81 AL	.257	43	109	21	28	8	2	1	17	8
82 AL	.250	150	527	65	132	25	3	14	82	32
83 NL	.265	124	351	45	93	9	5	6	32	20
84 NL	.292	152	561	85	164	27	6	16	67	48
85 NL	.263	152	570	76	150	30	4	13	70	21
86 NL	.305	158	610	107	186	46	2	19	98	24
87 NL	.277	158	556	84	154	36	5	21	84	16
88 NL	.272	104	367	43	100	28	2	6	45	20
89 NL	.259	154	540	93	140	27	2	26	78	28
90 NL	.261	129	467	70	122	14	3	17	73	16
91 NL	.225	77	284	43	64	15	1	0	21	9
Life	.270	1401	4942	732	1333	265	35	139	667	242
3 AVE	.253	120	430	69	109	19	2	14	57	18

CURRENT PLAYERS

MIKE HEATH

Position: Catcher
Team: Atlanta Braves
Born: Feb. 5, 1955 Tampa, FL
Height: 5'11" **Weight:** 180 lbs.
Bats: right **Throws:** right
Acquired: Signed as a free agent, 1/91

Player Summary	
Fantasy Value	$2 to $4
Card Value	3¢ to 5¢
Will	be weak offensively
Can't	handle NL runners
Expect	back-up status
Don't Expect	strong comeback

After a disappointing 49 games, Heath submitted to arthroscopic surgery on his right elbow July 15. The veteran receiver, who has also played the infield corners and the outfield, missed the remainder of the campaign. The Braves had signed Heath in the hopes of solidifying their catching. He had earned a reputation as a rifle-armed catcher and good handler of pitchers in the AL. He had hit for a respectable average. When he's on his game, he is a spray hitter, though he strikes out too much. He also hits into double-plays with alarming regularity. Even if healthy, his career could be in jeopardy. A fantasy let-down in '91, you should still bid up to $4 for him. Run, don't walk, from his 1992 commons.

Major League Batting Register

	BA	G	AB	R	H	2B	3B	HR	RBI	SB
78 AL	.228	33	92	6	21	3	1	0	8	0
79 AL	.256	74	258	19	66	8	0	3	27	1
80 AL	.243	92	305	27	74	10	2	1	33	3
81 AL	.236	84	301	26	71	7	1	8	30	3
82 AL	.242	101	318	43	77	18	4	3	39	8
83 AL	.281	96	345	45	97	17	0	6	33	3
84 AL	.248	140	475	49	118	21	5	13	64	7
85 AL	.250	138	436	71	109	18	6	13	55	7
86 NL	.205	65	190	19	39	8	1	4	25	2
86 AL	.265	30	98	11	26	3	0	4	11	4
87 AL	.281	93	270	34	76	16	0	8	33	1
88 AL	.247	86	219	24	54	7	2	5	18	1
89 AL	.263	122	396	38	104	16	2	10	43	7
90 AL	.270	122	370	46	100	18	2	7	38	7
91 NL	.209	49	139	4	29	3	1	1	12	0
Life	.252	1325	4212	462	1061	173	27	86	469	54
2 AVE	.266	122	383	42	102	17	2	9	41	7

NEAL HEATON

Position: Pitcher
Team: Pittsburgh Pirates
Born: March 3, 1960 Jamaica, NY
Height: 6'1" **Weight:** 195 lbs.
Bats: left **Throws:** left
Acquired: Traded from Expos for Brett Gideon, 3/89

Player Summary	
Fantasy Value	$2 to $4
Card Value	3¢ to 5¢
Will	throw blistering heat
Can't	recapture early '90
Expect	shoulder woes
Don't Expect	second All-Star Game

One year after making the NL All-Star team, Heaton became the forgotten man of the Pittsburgh pitching staff. He worked 42 times, all but once in middle relief. He has won at least a dozen games three times. His problem was relying too heavily on a fastball that hitters eventually timed. When he added a changeup to his fastball and slider repertoire in 1990, Heaton went 10-2 over the first half. A rotator cuff problem followed, and he finished with a 12-9 mark. A skilled fielder with a good pickoff move, Heaton also helps himself with his hitting and running. Even when Bob Walk went down last year, the Pirates refused to let Heaton join the starting rotation. He has become a middle reliever, spelling death to his fantasy value—down to $3. His 1992 commons are poor investments.

Major League Pitching Register

	W	L	ERA	G	S	IP	H	ER	BB	SO
82 AL	0	2	5.23	8	0	31.0	32	18	16	14
83 AL	11	7	4.16	39	7	149.1	157	69	44	75
84 AL	12	15	5.21	38	0	198.2	231	115	75	75
85 AL	9	17	4.90	36	0	207.2	244	113	80	82
86 AL	7	15	4.08	33	1	198.2	201	90	81	90
87 NL	13	10	4.52	32	0	193.1	207	97	37	105
88 NL	3	10	4.99	32	2	97.1	98	54	43	43
89 NL	6	7	3.05	42	0	147.1	127	50	55	67
90 NL	12	9	3.45	30	0	146.0	143	56	38	68
91 NL	3	3	4.33	42	0	68.2	72	33	21	34
Life	76	95	4.35	332	10	1438.0	1512	695	490	653
3 AVE	7	6	3.46	38	0	120.1	114	46	38	56

CURRENT PLAYERS

DAVE HENDERSON

Position: Outfield
Team: Oakland Athletics
Born: July 21, 1958 Merced, CA
Height: 6'2" **Weight:** 210 lbs.
Bats: right **Throws:** right
Acquired: Signed as a free agent, 12/87

Player Summary	
Fantasy Value	$25 to $30
Card Value	5¢ to 7¢
Will	deliver key hits
Can't	steal many bases
Expect	solid defense
Don't Expect	less run production

Dave is known as "the other Henderson" because he shares the same outfield with Rickey. The Oakland center fielder, Dave broke out with a strong start that included his first five-hit game. After winning a starting spot on the All-Star team, he turned in a fine second half. He hits well in the clutch; his ninth-inning homer propelled Boston in the 1986 playoffs. Henderson draws his share of walks and doesn't fan too much. He has good power to all fields. Two knee operations have slowed him slightly, but he's still a fine outfielder with sound judgement and a reliable arm. He plays a shallow center field but gets away with it. His fantasy value doubled in '91 to $30. His 1992 commons are fair long-term ventures.

Major League Batting Register

	BA	G	AB	R	H	2B	3B	HR	RBI	SB
81 AL	.167	59	126	17	21	3	0	6	13	2
82 AL	.253	104	324	47	82	17	1	14	48	2
83 AL	.269	137	484	50	130	24	5	17	55	9
84 AL	.280	112	350	42	98	23	0	14	43	5
85 AL	.241	139	502	70	121	28	2	14	68	6
86 AL	.265	139	388	59	103	22	4	15	47	2
87 AL	.234	75	184	30	43	10	0	8	25	1
87 NL	.238	15	21	2	5	2	0	0	1	2
88 AL	.304	146	507	100	154	38	1	24	94	2
89 AL	.250	152	579	77	145	24	3	15	80	8
90 AL	.271	127	450	65	122	28	0	20	63	3
91 AL	.276	150	572	86	158	33	0	25	85	6
Life	.263	1355	4487	645	1182	252	16	172	622	48
3 AVE	.265	143	534	76	142	28	1	20	76	6

RICKEY HENDERSON

Position: Outfield
Team: Oakland Athletics
Born: Dec. 25, 1958 Chicago, IL
Height: 5'10" **Weight:** 190 lbs.
Bats: right **Throws:** left
Acquired: Traded from Yankees for Luis Polonia, Greg Cadaret, and Eric Plunk, 6/89

Player Summary	
Fantasy Value	$40 to $50
Card Value	10¢ to 20¢
Will	carry team if happy
Can't	squeeze into 30-30 club
Expect	AL steals crown
Don't Expect	end to controversy

Baseball's ultimate leadoff man, Henderson blends speed with power. He was AL MVP in 1990, notching a .439 on-base percentage and a .577 slugging percentage (second in the AL). The single-season and career leader in steals, he has the ability to excel. The desire is sometimes missing, though. Unhappy that others got fatter contracts, Henderson threatened not to play his best in 1991. After a hamstring problem cut the first month off his season, he still was among the AL leaders in both runs scored and stolen bases. His fantasy value is still at $45. His 1992 cards are great long-term investments at 20 cents. A happy Henderson beats out infield hits, steals at will, walks more than he whiffs, and wins Gold Gloves despite a mediocre arm.

Major League Batting Register

	BA	G	AB	R	H	2B	3B	HR	RBI	SB
79 AL	.274	89	351	49	96	13	3	1	26	33
80 AL	.303	158	591	111	179	22	4	9	53	100
81 AL	.319	108	423	89	135	18	7	6	35	56
82 AL	.267	149	536	119	143	24	4	10	51	130
83 AL	.292	145	513	105	150	25	7	9	48	108
84 AL	.293	142	502	113	147	27	4	16	58	66
85 AL	.314	143	547	146	172	28	5	24	72	80
86 AL	.263	153	608	130	160	31	5	28	74	87
87 AL	.291	95	358	78	104	17	3	17	37	41
88 AL	.305	140	554	118	169	30	2	6	50	93
89 AL	.274	150	541	113	148	26	3	12	57	77
90 AL	.325	136	489	119	159	33	3	28	61	65
91 AL	.268	134	470	105	126	17	1	18	57	58
Life	.291	1742	6483	1395	1888	311	51	184	679	994
3 AVE	.289	140	500	112	144	25	2	19	58	67

CURRENT PLAYERS

TOM HENKE

Position: Pitcher
Team: Toronto Blue Jays
Born: Dec. 21, 1957 Kansas City, MO
Height: 6'5" **Weight:** 225 lbs.
Bats: right **Throws:** right
Acquired: Drafted from Rangers, 1/85

Player Summary	
Fantasy Value	$28 to $33
Card Value	5¢ to 7¢
Will	throw aspirins
Can't	post many wins
Expect	more Ks than frames
Don't Expect	many baserunners

Even before he set a major league record with 25 saves in as many chances last year, Henke was regarded as one of the game's premier short relievers. Called to Toronto in July 1985 after arriving as compensation for the signing of free-agent Cliff Johnson, Henke has always averaged more than a strikeout an inning. His average of 10.38 whiffs per nine innings, into 1991, was the best in baseball history. Though he was sidelined for a month with a groin pull early last year, the bespectacled reliever has been one of the game's more durable and consistent pitchers. A fastball-and-forkball specialist with pinpoint control, Henke became even tougher when he reactivated his slider. Buy his nickel-priced 1992 cards for eventual rewards. The undervalued reliever is a good draft for $30 or so.

Major League Pitching Register

	W	L	ERA	G	S	IP	H	ER	BB	SO
82 AL	1	0	1.15	8	0	15.2	14	2	8	9
83 AL	1	0	3.38	8	1	16.0	16	6	4	17
84 AL	1	1	6.35	25	2	28.1	36	20	20	25
85 AL	3	3	2.03	28	13	40.0	29	9	8	42
86 AL	9	5	3.35	63	27	91.1	63	34	32	118
87 AL	0	6	2.49	72	34	94.0	62	26	25	128
88 AL	4	4	2.91	52	25	68.0	60	22	24	66
89 AL	8	3	1.92	64	20	89.0	66	19	25	116
90 AL	2	4	2.17	61	32	74.2	58	18	19	75
91 AL	0	2	2.32	49	32	50.1	33	13	11	53
Life	29	28	2.68	430	186	567.1	437	169	176	649
3 AVE	3	3	2.10	58	28	71.1	52	17	18	81

MIKE HENNEMAN

Position: Pitcher
Team: Detroit Tigers
Born: Dec. 11, 1961 St. Charles, MO
Height: 6'4" **Weight:** 205 lbs.
Bats: right **Throws:** right
Acquired: Third-round pick in 6/84 free-agent draft

Player Summary	
Fantasy Value	$20 to $25
Card Value	3¢ to 5¢
Will	convert save chances
Can't	reduce walks
Expect	60 appearances
Don't Expect	over 25 saves

Henneman joined the Tigers as a set-up man in 1987, became the top closer a year later, and blossomed into one of the league's best short men in 1991. He was among the top AL relievers in wins in 1991. Unlike other relievers, who use only one or two pitches, Henneman has a fastball, slider, and forkball. He's willing to pitch in pain and doesn't mind the short fences of Tiger Stadium (a 33-6 lifetime record in his first 39 decisions). Opponents compiled a .258 batting average, a .344 slugging percentage, and a .326 on-base average in '91. With thin pitching last year, manager Sparky Anderson's strategy was to get Henneman into any game in which the Tigers had a lead or were tied. Unless he's overworked, Henneman should continue to be one of the AL's most dependable relievers. An underappreciated closer, he is a solid $20 draft. There is little interest in his 1992 commons.

Major League Pitching Register

	W	L	ERA	G	S	IP	H	ER	BB	SO
87 AL	11	3	2.98	55	7	96.2	86	32	30	75
88 AL	9	6	1.87	65	22	91.1	72	19	24	58
89 AL	11	4	3.70	60	8	90.0	84	37	51	69
90 AL	8	6	3.05	69	22	94.1	90	32	33	50
91 AL	10	2	2.88	60	21	84.1	81	27	34	61
Life	49	21	2.90	309	80	456.2	413	147	172	313
3 AVE	10	4	3.22	63	17	89.1	85	32	39	60

CURRENT PLAYERS

TOMMY HERR

Position: Second base
Team: San Francisco Giants
Born: April 4, 1956 Lancaster, PA
Height: 6' **Weight:** 196 lbs.
Bats: both **Throws:** right
Acquired: Signed as a free agent, 8/91

Player Summary	
Fantasy Value	$2 to $4
Card Value	3¢ to 5¢
Will	play solid defense
Can't	hit with power
Expect	dramatic hits
Don't Expect	improvement in offense

Though he's now in the twilight of a fine career, Herr can still provide infield help for a big league ballclub. Once regarded as one of the game's premier defensive second basemen, he now compensates for fading range with superior positioning. He still has good hands and turns the double-play well. The speed that produced four 20-steal seasons has also evaporated, but the veteran knows when to run and usually makes it. Herr is also capable of producing a clutch hit on occasion. Draft the cagey veteran for bench support for $3. A spray hitter with little power, he used to be one of the best hit-and-run practitioners. Don't bother with his 1992 commons. Herr has struggled to keep his average respectable.

Major League Batting Register

	BA	G	AB	R	H	2B	3B	HR	RBI	SB
79 NL	.200	14	10	4	2	0	0	0	1	1
80 NL	.248	76	222	29	55	12	5	0	15	9
81 NL	.268	103	411	50	110	14	9	0	46	23
82 NL	.266	135	493	83	131	19	4	0	36	25
83 NL	.323	89	313	43	101	14	4	2	31	6
84 NL	.276	145	558	67	154	23	2	4	49	13
85 NL	.302	159	596	97	180	38	3	8	110	31
86 NL	.252	152	559	48	141	30	4	2	61	22
87 NL	.263	141	510	73	134	29	0	2	83	19
88 NL	.260	15	50	4	13	0	0	1	3	3
88 AL	.263	86	304	42	80	16	0	1	21	10
89 NL	.287	151	561	65	161	25	6	2	37	10
90 NL	.261	146	547	48	143	26	3	5	60	7
91 NL	.209	102	215	23	45	8	1	1	21	9
Life	.271	1514	5349	676	1450	254	41	28	574	188
3 AVE	.264	133	441	45	116	20	3	3	39	9

OREL HERSHISER

Position: Pitcher
Team: Los Angeles Dodgers
Born: Sept. 16, 1958 Buffalo, NY
Height: 6'3" **Weight:** 192 lbs.
Bats: right **Throws:** right
Acquired: 17th-round pick in 6/79 free-agent draft

Player Summary	
Fantasy Value	$7 to $10
Card Value	5¢ to 7¢
Will	throw strikes
Can't	duplicate '88 season
Expect	big numbers if healthy
Don't Expect	high ERA

When Hershiser won on June 9, the victory was not only the 100th of his career but his first since April 19, 1990. He spent the 14 months between wins recuperating from radical surgery to reconstruct his right shoulder. Even after his return, the former NL Cy Young Award winner could not recapture his old form. His 3.46 ERA was a far cry from his 1988 showing, when he finished the season with a record 59 consecutive scoreless innings, then won MVP honors in both the playoffs and World Series. A control pitcher whose best pitches are a sinking fastball and hard-breaking curve, Hershiser is an intense competitor who often uses charts and computers to track the tendencies of NL batters in certain situations. Be realistic when drafting him. Bid up to $10 only. His 1992 cards aren't good short-term buys, and may not endure long term.

Major League Pitching Register

	W	L	ERA	G	CG	IP	H	ER	BB	SO
83 NL	0	0	3.38	8	0	8.0	7	3	6	5
84 NL	11	8	2.66	45	8	189.2	160	56	50	150
85 NL	19	3	2.03	36	9	239.2	179	54	68	157
86 NL	14	14	3.85	35	8	231.1	213	99	86	153
87 NL	16	16	3.06	37	10	264.2	247	90	74	190
88 NL	23	8	2.26	35	15	267.0	208	67	73	178
89 NL	15	15	2.31	35	8	256.2	226	66	77	178
90 NL	1	1	4.26	4	0	25.1	26	12	4	16
91 NL	7	2	3.46	21	0	112.0	112	43	32	73
Life	106	67	2.77	256	58	1594.1	1378	490	470	1100
2 AVE	11	9	2.66	28	4	184.1	169	55	55	126

CURRENT PLAYERS

JOE HESKETH

Position: Pitcher
Team: Boston Red Sox
Born: Feb. 15, 1959 Lackawanna, NY
Height: 6'2" **Weight:** 170 lbs.
Bats: left **Throws:** left
Acquired: Signed as a free agent, 7/90

Player Summary	
Fantasy Value	$2 to $4
Card Value	3¢ to 5¢
Will	find regular rhythm
Can't	relieve with shoulder
Expect	return to rookie form
Don't Expect	balls to stay in park

Hesketh resurrected his career in 1991 after the Red Sox, desperate for a southpaw starter, squeezed him into their rotation. He won his first four decisions of August and posted a 2.98 ERA over that span. In '91, he posted highly respectable stats for a lefty playing half his games in Fenway Park. Hesketh, released by both the Expos and Braves in 1990, had struggled for five seasons after breaking his leg in a home-plate collision with Mike Scioscia on August 23, 1985. That injury shortened Hesketh's excellent rookie season. He later had shoulder problems. He fans about twice as many as he walks but throws frequent home run balls (19 in '91). He yields less than a hit per inning, however, and is most effective when deployed as a starter. He is a $3 fantasy risk, and his 1992 commons are not buys.

Major League Pitching Register

	W	L	ERA	G	S	IP	H	ER	BB	SO
84 NL	2	2	1.80	11	1	45.0	38	9	15	32
85 NL	10	5	2.49	25	0	155.1	125	43	45	113
86 NL	6	5	5.01	15	0	82.2	92	46	31	67
87 NL	0	0	3.14	18	1	28.2	23	10	15	31
88 NL	4	3	2.85	60	9	72.2	63	23	35	64
89 NL	6	4	5.77	43	3	48.1	54	31	26	44
90 NL	1	2	5.29	33	5	34.0	32	20	14	24
90 AL	0	4	3.51	12	0	25.2	37	10	11	26
91 AL	12	4	3.29	39	0	153.1	142	56	53	104
Life	41	29	3.46	256	19	645.2	606	248	245	505
3 AVE	6	5	4.03	42	3	87.1	88	39	35	66

GREG HIBBARD

Position: Pitcher
Team: Chicago White Sox
Born: Sept. 13, 1964 New Orleans, LA
Height: 6' **Weight:** 190 lbs.
Bats: left **Throws:** left
Acquired: Traded from Royals with John Davis, Chuck Mount, and Melido Perez for Dave Cochrane and Floyd Bannister, 12/87

Player Summary	
Fantasy Value	$5 to $8
Card Value	3¢ to 5¢
Will	win 15 with sinker
Can't	avoid gophers
Expect	few walks or Ks
Don't Expect	exile to minors

Less than a year after he tied for White Sox team leadership with 14 victories, Hibbard found himself back in the minors because his sinker wouldn't sink. The result was too many home runs. When he beat the Yankees 11-3 on August 18, the win was his first since June 29. A finesse pitcher with good control, Hibbard does not record high numbers of strikeouts or walks. He throws his sinker, curveball, and changeup with a delivery that's difficult to decipher, especially for righthanders. In 1991, opponents compiled a .266 batting average, a .402 slugging percentage, and a .320 on-base average. He's a good fielder who keeps runners close. He allowed 23 homers in '91. In 1988 at Triple-A Vancouver, he was 11-11 with a 4.12 ERA and 65 Ks in 144⅓ innings. He figures to be a No. 3 or a No. 4 starter in the Sox rotation. His '91 showing puts his fantasy value at $6 or so. His 1992 commons hold little collector interest.

Major League Pitching Register

	W	L	ERA	G	CG	IP	H	ER	BB	SO
89 AL	6	7	3.21	23	2	137.1	142	49	41	55
90 AL	14	9	3.16	33	3	211.0	202	74	55	92
91 AL	11	11	4.31	32	5	194.0	196	93	57	71
Life	31	27	3.58	88	10	542.1	540	216	153	218
3 AVE	10	9	3.58	29	3	181.0	180	72	51	73

CURRENT PLAYERS

TED HIGUERA

Position: Pitcher
Team: Milwaukee Brewers
Born: Nov. 9, 1958 Los Mochis, Mexico
Height: 5'10" **Weight:** 178 lbs.
Bats: both **Throws:** left
Acquired: Purchased from Juarez of Mexican League, 9/83

Player Summary	
Fantasy Value	$2 to $4
Card Value	3¢ to 5¢
Will	control four pitches
Can't	avoid injury jinx
Expect	gradual recovery
Don't Expect	much this season

Higuera was one of the American League's top pitchers before shoulder problems short-circuited his career. After signing a four-year, $13 million contract, he began the 1991 season on the disabled list with a small tear of the rotator cuff. He went on the shelf again August 6 with a significant tear. Although other pitchers have recovered from similar problems, doctors consider Higuera's latest injury career-threatening. He has also suffered other ailments in his seven-year career but has won in double figures five times. He throws a fastball, slider, curveball, and slow change—all with remarkable control—and has no fear of pitching inside. Higuera's only drawbacks, in addition to his health, are average fielding ability and failure to hold runners. He pitched in the Mexican League from 1979 to 1983. He's not dependable as a fantasy investment; spend no more than $4. Don't invest in his 1992 commons.

Major League Pitching Register

	W	L	ERA	G	CG	IP	H	ER	BB	SO
85 AL	15	8	3.90	32	7	212.1	186	92	63	127
86 AL	20	11	2.79	34	15	248.1	226	77	74	207
87 AL	18	10	3.85	35	14	261.2	236	112	87	240
88 AL	16	9	2.45	31	8	227.1	168	62	59	192
89 AL	9	6	3.46	22	2	135.1	125	52	48	91
90 AL	11	10	3.76	27	4	170.0	167	71	50	129
91 AL	3	2	4.46	7	0	36.1	37	18	10	33
Life	92	56	3.37	188	50	1291.1	1145	484	391	1019
2 AVE	10	8	3.63	25	3	153.1	146	62	49	110

GLENALLEN HILL

Position: Outfield
Team: Cleveland Indians
Born: March 22, 1965 Santa Cruz, CA
Height: 6'2" **Weight:** 205 lbs.
Bats: right **Throws:** right
Acquired: Traded from Blue Jays with Mark Whiten for Tom Candiotti and Turner Ward, 6/90

Player Summary	
Fantasy Value	$7 to $10
Card Value	5¢ to 8¢
Will	hike homer total
Can't	hit for hefty average
Expect	more Ks than walks
Don't Expect	return to bench

Hill was rusting on the Toronto bench before his trade to Cleveland last June. The Indians immediately made him their center fielder. After leading several minor leagues in home runs and strikeouts, he reached the majors late in the '89 season. He can hit, run, and throw, and he has good power to all fields. He has become a more selective hitter in recent seasons. He has the speed to steal 30 bases and uses his running ability well in the outfield, where he was first used as George Bell's caddy. Once hampered by an attitude problem, Hill has started to realize the potential that made him one of the Triple-A International League's top prospects in 1989. That year he hit .321 with 21 homers and 72 RBI in 125 games at Syracuse. All he needs is a chance, and he'll get it with Cleveland. Because of his opportunity, his fantasy value is from $7 to $10. Entrust some money in his nickel-priced 1992 cards. They should rise in value as he drives home some runs.

Major League Batting Register

	BA	G	AB	R	H	2B	3B	HR	RBI	SB
89 AL	.288	19	52	4	15	0	0	1	7	2
90 AL	.231	84	260	47	60	11	3	12	32	8
91 AL	.258	72	221	29	57	8	2	8	25	6
Life	.248	175	533	80	132	19	5	21	64	16
2 AVE	.243	78	241	38	59	10	3	10	29	7

CURRENT PLAYERS

KEN HILL

Position: Pitcher
Team: Montreal Expos
Born: Dec. 14, 1965 Lynn, MA
Height: 6'2" **Weight:** 175 lbs.
Bats: right **Throws:** right
Acquired: Traded from Cardinals for Andres Galarraga, 11/91

Player Summary	
Fantasy Value	$2 to $4
Card Value	3¢ to 5¢
Will	get a dozen wins
Can't	stop walks
Expect	under a hit a frame
Don't Expect	many complete games

Hill's return to the minor leagues in 1990 gave him the boost he needed to reclaim a rotation slot with the Cardinals. He was the Redbirds No. 3 starter and figures to be in the same slot with the Expos. A fastball-and-curveball pitcher with considerable control problems, Hill also fell victim to the gopher ball last year, giving up 15. That wasn't easy at Busch Stadium. He yields less than a hit per inning. Opponents in '91 compiled a .224 batting average, a .346 slugging percentage, and a .299 on-base average. He does help himself as a hitter, fielder, and guardian of base-runners with larceny on their minds. Hill's future success will be directly related to his ability to throw strikes. In 1989, when he led the NL with 99 walks, he tied for the lead with 15 losses. He may never be a 20-game winner, but his strikeouts will boost your fantasy team. They won't boost his common-priced 1992 cards, however.

Major League Pitching Register

	W	L	ERA	G	CG	IP	H	ER	BB	SO
88 NL	0	1	5.14	4	0	14.0	16	8	6	6
89 NL	7	15	3.80	33	2	196.2	186	83	99	112
90 NL	5	6	5.49	17	1	78.2	79	48	33	58
91 NL	11	10	3.57	30	0	181.1	147	72	67	121
Life	23	32	4.03	84	3	470.2	428	211	205	297
3 AVE	8	10	4.00	27	1	152.2	137	68	66	97

SHAWN HILLEGAS

Position: Pitcher
Team: Cleveland Indians
Born: Aug. 21, 1964 Dos Palos, CA
Height: 6'2" **Weight:** 223 lbs.
Bats: right **Throws:** right
Acquired: Traded from White Sox with Eric King for Cory Snyder and Lindsay Foster, 12/90

Player Summary	
Fantasy Value	$2 to $3
Card Value	3¢ to 5¢
Will	get more Ks than walks
Can't	find niche
Expect	big fastball
Don't Expect	respectable ERA

Hillegas got his first chance to be a major league closer in 1991 when veteran Cleveland sinkerballer Doug Jones, unable to shake a season-long slump, was taken out of the role. Hillegas enjoyed only brief success before the experiment was cancelled by Cleveland manager Mike Hargrove. Hillegas was used exclusively as a starter during a six-year career before the White Sox switched him to relief at Triple-A Vancouver in 1990. There he went 5-3 with nine saves, a 1.74 ERA, 52 strikeouts, and 15 walks in 67⅔ innings. He fans nearly a hitter per inning but issues far too many walks. His 1992 commons are not buys. He is beyond the prospect stage and will have to show better results to secure his big league future. Without better numbers this summer, he's likely to show up on a 1993 expansion roster. As a middle reliever, he won't help fantasy managers for more than $3.

Major League Pitching Register

	W	L	ERA	G	S	IP	H	ER	BB	SO
87 NL	4	3	3.57	12	0	58.0	52	23	31	51
88 NL	3	4	4.13	11	0	56.2	54	26	17	30
88 AL	3	2	3.15	6	0	40.0	30	14	18	26
89 AL	7	11	4.74	50	3	119.2	132	63	51	76
90 AL	0	0	0.79	7	0	11.1	4	1	5	5
91 AL	3	4	4.34	51	7	83.0	67	40	46	66
Life	20	24	4.08	137	10	368.2	339	167	168	254
2 AVE	5	8	4.57	51	5	101.1	100	52	49	71

CURRENT PLAYERS

CHRIS HOILES

Position: Catcher
Team: Baltimore Orioles
Born: March 20, 1965 Bowling Green, OH
Height: 6'   **Weight:** 213 lbs.
Bats: right **Throws:** right
Acquired: Traded from Tigers with Cesar Mejia and Robinson Garces for Fred Lynn, 9/88

Player Summary	
Fantasy Value	$4 to $6
Card Value	3¢ to 5¢
Will	learn to hit better
Can't	match minors power
Expect	more playing time
Don't Expect	many steals against him

In the wake of the January 1991 trade that sent Mickey Tettleton to Detroit, Hoiles became the top Baltimore catcher in his first full major league season. Though he shared the position with veteran Bob Melvin early in the campaign, Hoiles got more playing time as his bat began to produce. He had four hits in a game against Minnesota August 30. He has always hit, with a .320 mark at Rookie League Bristol in 1986. He also won a home run crown in the Double-A Eastern League. After hitting .348 with 18 homers and 56 RBI in 74 games at Triple-A Rochester in 1990, Hoiles reached the majors. A late-season shoulder injury slowed his progress, though. When healthy, he is a patient hitter who strikes out only a few more times than he walks. An adequate catcher, his hitting should improve enough to make him a $5 fantasy bet. Don't bet on his 1992 commons, however. He also has a good throwing arm, though he can't match Melvin defensively. Hoiles's bat will guarantee his job.

Major League Batting Register

	BA	G	AB	R	H	2B	3B	HR	RBI	SB
89 AL	.111	6	9	0	1	1	0	0	1	0
90 AL	.190	23	63	7	12	3	0	1	6	0
91 AL	.243	107	341	36	83	15	0	11	31	0
Life	.232	136	413	43	96	19	0	12	38	0

DAVE HOLLINS

Position: Third base
Team: Philadelphia Phillies
Born: May 25, 1966 Buffalo, NY
Height: 6'1" **Weight:** 195 lbs.
Bats: both **Throws:** right
Acquired: Drafted from Padres, 12/89

Player Summary	
Fantasy Value	$2 to $5
Card Value	3¢ to 5¢
Will	destroy lefties
Can't	match minors stats
Expect	good defense
Don't Expect	Mike Schmidt power

Though he spent most of the first half in the minors last year, Hollins took over Philadelphia's third base job when his bat boomed after a July 11 recall. His progress was slowed by a stint on the disabled list with a sore right shoulder on August 16. A switch-hitter with more success against southpaws, Hollins is so selective that he drew more walks than strikeouts in two minor league seasons. He had a .510 slugging average for the '91 Phils. He's best in the clutch, hitting three pinch-homers as a 1990 rookie. Hollins has good hands and a strong arm at third and can play first in a pinch. His speed translates to good range in the field and good tools on the bases. He had a 20-steal season in the minors. Hollins seems ready to emerge as a major league regular. He'll never be Mike Schmidt, but Hollins could be better than Charlie Hayes. He is a potential fantasy bargain at $3 if he wins a full-time job. The value of his nickel-priced 1992 cards won't soar until he's a starter.

Major League Batting Register

	BA	G	AB	R	H	2B	3B	HR	RBI	SB
90 NL	.184	72	114	14	21	0	0	5	15	0
91 NL	.298	56	151	18	45	10	2	6	21	1
Life	.249	128	265	32	66	10	2	11	36	1

CURRENT PLAYERS

BRIAN HOLMAN

Position: Pitcher
Team: Seattle Mariners
Born: Jan. 25, 1965 Denver, CO
Height: 6'4" **Weight:** 185 lbs.
Bats: right **Throws:** right
Acquired: Traded from Expos with Gene Harris and Randy Johnson for Mark Langston and Mike Campbell, 5/89

Player Summary
Fantasy Value	$6 to $9
Card Value	3¢ to 5¢
Will	near 15 wins
Can't	avoid walks
Expect	variety of pitches
Don't Expect	return of injuries

Holman found success after he replaced his slider with an assortment of fastballs, curves, and changeups. The sinker has become his best pitch, but he keeps batters off stride by changing speeds. He came within one out of a perfect game on April 20, 1990, when he held Oakland at bay until Ken Phelps hit a two-out homer in the ninth. Hampered by elbow problems later that season, Holman had the troublesome bone chips removed. The righthanded workhorse of the Seattle staff in 1991, he was overly generous with walks and also yielded more hits than innings pitched. Opposing hitters in '91 compiled a .268 batting average, a .392 slugging percentage, and a .343 on-base percentage. They also homered 16 times. He needs to recapture the form that allowed him to post a 2-1 strikeout-to-walk ratio in 1990. He is a fantasy bargain for less than $9. His 1992 commons are fair acquisitions.

Major League Pitching Register
	W	L	ERA	G	CG	IP	H	ER	BB	SO
88 NL	4	8	3.23	18	1	100.1	101	36	34	58
89 NL	1	2	4.83	10	0	31.2	34	17	15	23
89 AL	8	10	3.44	23	6	159.2	160	61	62	82
90 AL	11	11	4.03	28	3	189.2	188	85	66	121
91 AL	13	14	3.69	30	5	195.1	199	80	77	108
Life	37	45	3.71	109	15	676.2	682	279	254	392
3 AVE	11	12	3.79	30	5	191.2	194	81	73	111

RICK HONEYCUTT

Position: Pitcher
Team: Oakland Athletics
Born: June 29, 1954 Chattanooga, TN
Height: 6'1" **Weight:** 190 lbs.
Bats: left **Throws:** left
Acquired: Traded from Dodgers for Tim Belcher, 8/87

Player Summary
Fantasy Value	$1 to $3
Card Value	3¢ to 5¢
Will	supply solid relief
Can't	return to rotation
Expect	50-plus outings
Don't Expect	overpowering stuff

Honeycutt is a former standout starter who capitalized on a move to the bullpen. Though he was slowed by preseason rotator cuff surgery that sliced 61 games off his season in 1991, he gave Oakland his customary lefthanded middle relief help after his return. The 15-year veteran, who throws sinkers, sliders, and forkballs, gets numerous ground balls when his game is on. He usually strikes out twice as many as he walks and can hit the corners when he wants to. He had worked at least 50 games three years in a row before his physical problems hit. His fantasy value has diminished to a $2 draft. His 1992 commons have no benefit.

Major League Pitching Register
	W	L	ERA	G	S	IP	H	ER	BB	SO
77 AL	0	1	4.34	10	0	29.0	26	14	11	17
78 AL	5	11	4.89	26	0	134.1	150	73	49	50
79 AL	11	12	4.04	33	0	194.0	201	87	67	83
80 AL	10	17	3.94	30	0	203.1	221	89	60	79
81 AL	11	6	3.31	20	0	127.2	120	47	17	40
82 AL	5	17	5.27	30	0	164.0	201	96	54	64
83 AL	14	8	2.42	25	0	174.2	168	47	37	56
83 NL	2	3	5.77	9	0	39.0	46	25	13	18
84 NL	10	9	2.84	29	0	183.2	180	58	51	75
85 NL	8	12	3.42	31	1	142.0	141	54	49	67
86 NL	11	9	3.32	32	0	171.0	164	63	45	100
87 NL	2	12	4.59	27	0	115.2	133	59	45	92
87 AL	1	4	5.32	7	0	23.2	25	14	9	10
88 AL	3	2	3.50	55	7	79.2	74	31	25	47
89 AL	2	2	2.35	64	12	76.2	56	20	26	52
90 AL	2	2	2.70	63	7	63.1	46	19	22	38
91 AL	2	4	3.58	43	0	37.2	37	15	20	26
Life	99	131	3.73	534	27	1959.1	1989	811	600	914
3 AVE	2	3	2.74	57	6	59.2	46	18	23	39

SAM HORN

Position: Designated hitter; first base
Team: Baltimore Orioles
Born: Nov. 2, 1963 Dallas, TX
Height: 6'5" **Weight:** 240 lbs.
Bats: left **Throws:** left
Acquired: Signed as a free agent, 2/90

Player Summary	
Fantasy Value	$12 to $15
Card Value	3¢ to 5¢
Will	hit 20 homers
Can't	field or run
Expect	2-1 Ks to walks
Don't Expect	everyday job

Horn is a one-dimensional player who is best deployed strictly as a designated hitter. He has no speed, little defensive ability, and does not make good contact. He fans twice as often as he walks. Horn does produce runs, however. He had a .502 slugging percentage, a .326 on-base average, 41 walks, and 99 Ks in '91. He had given a hint of things to come in 1987 by hitting 44 homers, 14 with the Red Sox and 30 with Triple-A Pawtucket. His inability to make consistent contact, however, kept sending him back to the minors before earning an outright release. Baltimore, seeking more punch, took a chance. He capitalized when Randy Milligan was hurt. If Horn ever learns to go with the pitch instead of pulling everything, his value will jump. As long as he gets those opportunities, he will be a good fantasy pickup for less than $15. Despite the fact that collectors like bombers, his 1992 commons aren't buys at this point in his career.

Major League Batting Register

	BA	G	AB	R	H	2B	3B	HR	RBI	SB
87 AL	.278	46	158	31	44	7	0	14	34	0
88 AL	.148	24	61	4	9	0	0	2	8	0
89 AL	.148	33	54	1	8	2	0	0	4	0
90 AL	.248	79	246	30	61	13	0	14	45	0
91 AL	.233	121	317	45	74	16	0	23	61	0
Life	.234	303	836	111	196	38	0	53	152	0
2 AVE	.240	100	282	38	68	15	0	19	53	0

CHARLIE HOUGH

Position: Pitcher
Team: Chicago White Sox
Born: Jan. 5, 1948 Honolulu, HI
Height: 6'2" **Weight:** 190 lbs.
Bats: right **Throws:** right
Acquired: Signed as a free agent, 12/90

Player Summary	
Fantasy Value	$2 to $4
Card Value	3¢ to 5¢
Will	baffle with knuckler
Can't	avoid walks
Expect	good pickoff move
Don't Expect	75 mph fastballs

Ten days younger than Carlton Fisk, Hough in '91 hurled his first shutout since 1989. The knuckleballer almost was the only big leaguer to win in double figures for the last 10 years in a row. To win, he needs to control his knuckler. Hough's biggest challenge will be lowering an ERA that has been above 4.00 three straight years. Though the career numbers are lofty, don't speculate on his 1992 commons yet. He is a debatable fantasy pick at $3.

Major League Pitching Register

	W	L	ERA	G	CG	IP	H	ER	BB	SO
70 NL	0	0	5.29	8	0	17.0	18	10	11	8
71 NL	0	0	4.15	4	0	4.1	3	2	3	4
72 NL	0	0	3.38	2	0	2.2	2	1	2	4
73 NL	4	2	2.76	37	0	71.2	52	22	45	70
74 NL	9	4	3.75	49	0	96.0	65	40	40	63
75 NL	3	7	2.95	38	0	61.0	43	20	34	34
76 NL	12	8	2.21	77	0	142.2	102	35	77	81
77 NL	6	12	3.32	70	0	127.1	98	47	70	105
78 NL	5	5	3.28	55	0	93.1	69	34	48	66
79 NL	7	5	4.76	42	0	151.1	152	80	66	76
80 NL	1	3	5.57	19	0	32.1	37	20	21	25
80 AL	2	2	3.96	16	2	61.1	54	27	37	47
81 AL	4	1	2.96	21	2	82.0	61	27	31	69
82 AL	16	13	3.95	34	12	228.0	217	100	72	128
83 AL	15	13	3.18	34	11	252.0	219	89	95	152
84 AL	16	14	3.76	36	17	266.0	260	111	94	164
85 AL	14	16	3.31	34	14	250.1	198	92	83	141
86 AL	17	10	3.79	33	7	230.1	188	97	89	146
87 AL	18	13	3.79	40	13	285.1	238	120	124	223
88 AL	15	16	3.32	34	10	252.0	202	93	126	174
89 AL	10	13	4.35	30	5	182.0	168	88	95	94
90 AL	12	12	4.07	32	5	218.2	190	99	119	114
91 AL	9	10	4.02	31	4	199.1	167	89	94	107
Life	195	179	3.65	776	102	3307.0	2803	1343	1476	2095
3 AVE	10	12	4.14	31	5	200.1	175	92	103	105

CURRENT PLAYERS

DAVID HOWARD

Position: Shortstop
Team: Kansas City Royals
Born: Feb. 26, 1967 Sarasota, FL
Height: 6' **Weight:** 165 lbs.
Bats: both **Throws:** right
Acquired: 32nd-round pick in 6/86 free-agent draft

Player Summary	
Fantasy Value	$1 to $3
Card Value	3¢ to 5¢
Will	improve defense
Can't	add power
Expect	better average
Don't Expect	much offense

Although Howard was the everyday shortstop for Double-A Memphis in 1990, his leap to Kansas City was unexpected. The son of former big leaguer Bruce, David hit .250 with five homers, 44 RBI, and 15 steals in 19 attempts at Memphis in '90. He had 74 strikeouts and 39 walks that year. He jumped over Triple-A by showing a good glove at several positions during spring training. He later won the regular shortstop job when he provided better defense than Kurt Stillwell. Howard is better than Stillwell at going to his left. At Class-A Baseball City in 1989, Howard batted .236 with three homers, 30 RBI, 36 runs, 12 stolen bases, 44 strikeouts, and 23 walks in 267 at bats. He had a .258 slugging percentage and a .267 on-base average for the Royals in '91. He hit at a .280 clip during the second half and is expected to sustain that stroke and utilize his speed more often. He won't add much to your fantasy team, so keep your bid under $3. Don't put any money into his 1992 commons at least until he opens the season at shortstop.

TOM HOWARD

Position: Outfield
Team: San Diego Padres
Born: Dec. 11, 1964 Middletown, OH
Height: 6'2" **Weight:** 200 lbs.
Bats: both **Throws:** right
Acquired: First-round pick in 6/86 free-agent draft

Player Summary	
Fantasy Value	$1 to $3
Card Value	3¢ to 5¢
Will	make better contact
Can't	throw ball well
Expect	good speed
Don't Expect	return of minors stats

Howard got his first extended look in the majors in 1991 but proved to be a disappointment. The switch-hitting outfielder failed to provide either the .300 bat or the blazing speed he had shown in the minors. He is not a power-hitter so could not compensate with long-ball production. A weak hitter from the right side, Howard still produced four .300 campaigns in the San Diego system. In 1990 at Triple-A Las Vegas, he batted .328 with 26 doubles, five homers, 51 RBI, and 27 stolen bases. He batted .300 in 1989. His track record suggested he would make better contact than he did in 1991, when he fanned twice as much as he walked. His outfield play and throwing arm are average at best. Don't spend money on his nickel-priced 1992 cards until he proves himself at the major league level. Until he wins a job, he is a $2 fantasy draft. Unless he recaptures his minor league form, Howard seems destined for a reserve role in the majors, at least until the NL expands next year.

Major League Batting Register

	BA	G	AB	R	H	2B	3B	HR	RBI	SB
91 AL	.216	94	236	20	51	7	0	1	17	3
Life	.216	94	236	20	51	7	0	1	17	3

Major League Batting Register

	BA	G	AB	R	H	2B	3B	HR	RBI	SB
90 NL	.273	20	44	4	12	2	0	0	0	0
91 NL	.249	106	281	30	70	12	3	4	22	10
Life	.252	126	325	34	82	14	3	4	22	10

CURRENT PLAYERS

STEVE HOWE

Position: Pitcher
Team: New York Yankees
Born: March 10, 1958 Pontiac, MI
Height: 6'1" **Weight:** 180 lbs.
Bats: left **Throws:** left
Acquired: Signed as a free agent, 2/91

Player Summary	
Fantasy Value	$6 to $10
Card Value	3¢ to 5¢
Will	appear frequently
Can't	start games
Expect	numerous Ks
Don't Expect	gopher balls

Howe was a University of Michigan standout when the Dodgers made him their top choice in the 1979 free-agent draft. The fastball-and-slider pitcher was NL Rookie of the Year a year later, when he had 17 saves, a Dodger rookie record, to go with seven wins and a 2.65 ERA. His future seemed very bright, before drug problems intervened. Suspended six times, Howe did not pitch in the majors between 1987 and 1991. Then the Yankees, desperate to replace departing lefty closer Dave Righetti, invited Howe to their spring training camp. He earned a Triple-A contract, notched five saves with Columbus, returned to the majors in May, and became the team's most effective pitcher. Opponents compiled a .222 batting average, a .284 slugging percentage, and a .262 on-base average in 1991. He should be the Yankee southpaw closer in 1992. Back from baseball's dead, his fantasy price will rise to $7 or so. His 1992 commons, however, are still moribund.

Major League Pitching Register

	W	L	ERA	G	S	IP	H	ER	BB	SO
80 NL	7	9	2.66	59	17	84.2	83	25	22	39
81 NL	5	3	2.50	41	8	54.0	51	15	18	32
82 NL	7	5	2.08	66	13	99.1	87	23	17	49
83 NL	4	7	1.44	46	18	68.2	55	11	12	52
85 NL	1	1	4.91	19	3	22.0	30	12	5	11
85 AL	2	3	6.16	13	0	19.0	28	13	7	10
87 AL	3	3	4.31	24	1	31.1	33	15	8	19
91 AL	3	1	1.68	37	3	48.1	39	9	7	34
Life	32	32	2.59	305	63	427.1	406	123	96	246

JACK HOWELL

Position: Third base
Team: San Diego Padres
Born: Aug. 18, 1961 Tucson, AZ
Height: 6' **Weight:** 201 lbs.
Bats: left **Throws:** right
Acquired: Traded from Angels for Shawn Abner, 7/91

Player Summary	
Fantasy Value	$2 to $4
Card Value	3¢ to 5¢
Will	show good glove
Can't	handle lefties
Expect	average below .250
Don't Expect	more than platooning

Howell tried to plug the long-standing Padre problem at third base in 1991. He led AL third basemen with a .974 fielding percentage in 1989, and he showed good reflexes, a good arm, and some sting in his bat. He hit an inside-the-park homer against Atlanta on August 16 and two home runs in a game against Los Angeles three days later. He didn't match his usual power figures in '91. He had hit at least 15 homers in a season three times. His fantasy value has declined to the $3 level. His handicaps include impotence against lefties and a tendency to fan more often than he walks. His 1992 commons are not investments. Howell's versatility is a plus: He has played every infield spot and opened one season in left field. He'll probably platoon, pinch-hit, and provide late-inning defensive help.

Major League Batting Register

	BA	G	AB	R	H	2B	3B	HR	RBI	SB
85 AL	.197	43	137	19	27	4	0	5	18	1
86 AL	.272	63	151	26	41	14	2	4	21	2
87 AL	.245	138	449	64	110	18	5	23	64	4
88 AL	.254	154	500	59	127	32	2	16	63	2
89 AL	.228	144	474	56	108	19	4	20	52	0
90 AL	.228	105	316	35	72	19	1	8	33	3
91 AL	.210	32	81	11	17	2	0	2	7	1
91 NL	.206	58	160	24	33	3	1	6	16	0
Life	.236	737	2268	294	535	111	15	84	274	13
3 AVE	.223	113	344	42	77	14	2	12	36	1

CURRENT PLAYERS

JAY HOWELL

Position: Pitcher
Team: Los Angeles Dodgers
Born: Nov. 26, 1955 Miami, FL
Height: 6'3" **Weight:** 205 lbs.
Bats: right **Throws:** right
Acquired: Traded from Athletics with Alfredo Griffin and Jesse Orosco for Bob Welch, Jack Savage, and Matt Young, 12/87

Player Summary	
Fantasy Value	$18 to $24
Card Value	3¢ to 5¢
Will	post high K totals
Can't	pitch every day
Expect	25 saves if healthy
Don't Expect	injury-free season

Howell in '91 went down for a month with a sprained elbow. Before he returned on July 23, the team had gone 12-15 with six losses and just four saves from the bullpen. A healthy Howell has a live fastball, which he augments with an overhand curveball, plus an occasional slider and changeup. A power pitcher who once had elbow surgery, he has also had knee and back problems, making him a player whose health is always suspect. His biggest asset as a reliever is an ability to keep the ball in the park. If he stays healthy, Howell can be a top closer, but only on a staff where he's not required to work every day. He is an adequate draft at $20 or so. His 1992 commons are unfavorable investments.

Major League Pitching Register

	W	L	ERA	G	S	IP	H	ER	BB	SO
80 NL	0	0	13.50	5	0	3.1	8	5	0	1
81 NL	2	0	4.84	10	0	22.1	23	12	10	10
82 AL	2	3	7.71	6	0	28.0	42	24	13	21
83 AL	1	5	5.38	19	0	82.0	89	49	35	61
84 AL	9	4	2.69	61	7	103.2	86	31	34	109
85 AL	9	8	2.85	63	29	98.0	98	31	31	68
86 AL	3	6	3.38	38	16	53.1	53	20	23	42
87 AL	3	4	5.89	36	16	44.1	48	29	21	35
88 NL	5	3	2.08	50	21	65.0	44	15	21	70
89 NL	5	3	1.58	56	28	79.2	60	14	22	55
90 NL	5	5	2.18	45	16	66.0	59	16	20	59
91 NL	6	5	3.18	44	16	51.0	39	18	17	40
Life	50	46	3.41	433	149	696.2	649	264	241	571
3 AVE	5	4	2.20	48	20	65.1	53	16	18	51

KENT HRBEK

Position: First base
Team: Minnesota Twins
Born: May 21, 1960 Minneapolis, MN
Height: 6'4" **Weight:** 250 lbs.
Bats: left **Throws:** right
Acquired: 17th-round pick in 6/78 free-agent draft

Player Summary	
Fantasy Value	$23 to $27
Card Value	5¢ to 7¢
Will	provide great defense
Can't	run enough to steal
Expect	more walks than Ks
Don't Expect	pro wrestling

After getting off to a tough start in 1991, hometown hero Hrbek sparked the Twins to a 15-game winning streak in June. Hrbek's overall power production was down last year, but his average is very respectable. He had a .461 slugging percentage in '91. Since he has little speed, he keeps his average up by being very selective. He has walked more often than he struck out five years in a row, and is a streak hitter with some opposite field power. "T-Rex" scoops, dives, and charges as well as any first baseman and is also adept at turning the tough 3-6-3 double-play. He didn't have a good World Series at bat, but he did make a key defensive play tugging out Ron Gant at first. Hrbek's 1992 commons are sleepers. He is a $25 first baseman.

Major League Batting Register

	BA	G	AB	R	H	2B	3B	HR	RBI	SB
81 AL	.239	24	67	5	16	5	0	1	7	0
82 AL	.301	140	532	82	160	21	4	23	92	3
83 AL	.297	141	515	75	153	41	5	16	84	4
84 AL	.311	149	559	80	174	31	3	27	107	1
85 AL	.278	158	593	78	165	31	2	21	93	1
86 AL	.267	149	550	85	147	27	1	29	91	2
87 AL	.285	143	477	85	136	20	1	34	90	5
88 AL	.312	143	510	75	159	31	0	25	76	0
89 AL	.272	109	375	59	102	17	0	25	84	3
90 AL	.287	143	492	61	141	26	0	22	79	5
91 AL	.284	132	462	72	131	20	1	20	89	4
Life	.289	1431	5132	757	1484	270	17	243	892	28
3 AVE	.281	128	443	64	125	21	0	22	84	4

CURRENT PLAYERS

REX HUDLER

Position: Infield; outfield
Team: St. Louis Cardinals
Born: Sept. 2, 1960 Tempe, AZ
Height: 6′ **Weight:** 180 lbs.
Bats: right **Throws:** right
Acquired: Traded from Expos for John Costello, 4/90

Player Summary	
Fantasy Value	$2 to $4
Card Value	3¢ to 5¢
Will	play anywhere
Can't	provide much power
Expect	ability off bench
Don't Expect	average under .250

One of the most versatile players in the majors, Hudler has done everything but catch and pitch since breaking in with the 1984 Yankees. His wife has even sung the National Anthem. Though he has little power, Hudler is a hustler with enough speed to lead off. His career-best .282 average in 1990 was inflated by bunt hits and infield singles. Two years earlier, he stole 29 bases in only 77 games. A fine spot performer, Hudler will pinch-run at any time and provide surprising punch as a pinch-hitter against lefties. A natural second baseman, Hudler handles himself well at the other infield spots but seems most comfortable in the outfield. He cuts off balls in the gaps, makes diving catches, and throws well enough to get several assists a year. He is well-liked in St. Louis, but his 1992 commons are not hot sellers. He is a $3 utility player.

Major League Batting Register

	BA	G	AB	R	H	2B	3B	HR	RBI	SB
84 AL	.143	9	7	2	1	1	0	0	0	0
85 AL	.157	20	51	4	8	0	1	0	1	0
86 AL	.000	14	1	1	0	0	0	0	0	1
88 NL	.273	77	216	38	59	14	2	4	14	29
89 NL	.245	92	155	21	38	7	0	6	13	15
90 NL	.282	93	220	31	62	11	2	7	22	18
91 NL	.227	101	207	21	47	10	2	1	15	12
Life	.251	406	857	118	215	43	7	18	65	75
3 AVE	.253	95	194	24	49	9	1	5	17	15

MIKE HUFF

Position: Outfield
Team: Chicago White Sox
Born: Aug. 11, 1963 Honolulu, HI
Height: 6′1″ **Weight:** 180 lbs.
Bats: right **Throws:** right
Acquired: Signed as a free agent, 6/91

Player Summary	
Fantasy Value	$2 to $5
Card Value	3¢ to 5¢
Will	steal bases
Can't	produce power
Expect	stalwart defense
Don't Expect	.250 average

As a 1991 rookie, Huff lived up to his advance billing as an exceptional defensive outfielder with good speed. He struck out about as much as he walked and kept his average above the .250 level while filling in well at all three outfield positions. He also plays second base, and he made virtually no mistakes in the outfield. In 1990 at Triple-A Albuquerque, he hit .325 with seven homers, 28 doubles, 99 runs scored, and 84 RBI in 138 games. He hit .318 with 10 homers and 78 RBI in Albuquerque in '89. He was drafted out of the Dodger organization by the Indians in 1990, but they gave up on him. Given more playing time, Huff's offensive numbers should rise—though it's improbable he'll ever duplicate his 1990 Albuquerque numbers. Because his speed gives him exceptional range, he can contribute best as a center fielder. He has a good throwing arm, and is a fine fourth outfielder who could probably hold his own if he played regularly. He is a $3 fantasy choice mainly for his stolen bases. Disregard his 1992 commons.

Major League Batting Register

	BA	G	AB	R	H	2B	3B	HR	RBI	SB
89 NL	.200	12	25	4	5	1	0	1	2	0
91 AL	.251	102	243	42	61	10	2	3	25	14
Life	.246	114	268	46	66	11	2	4	27	14

CURRENT PLAYERS

TIM HULETT

Position: Second base; third base
Team: Baltimore Orioles
Born: Jan. 12, 1960 Springfield, IL
Height: 6' **Weight:** 185 lbs.
Bats: right **Throws:** right
Acquired: Signed as a free agent, 11/88

Player Summary
Fantasy Value	$1 to $3
Card Value	3¢ to 5¢
Will	sub at two spots
Can't	hit for average
Expect	so-so defense
Don't Expect	prolonged use

Hulett is a typical utility infielder. He's a capable fill-in at second or third and provides occasional pop when called upon to pinch-hit. A former free swinger who still overreacts when he sees a fastball, Hulett fans three times more than he walks. He has no speed and, not surprisingly, limited range in the field. His versatility definitely keeps him in the majors, however. So does his bat; his power was up but his average was down in '91, with a .350 slugging percentage and a .255 on-base average. Hulett hit 17 homers in 1986 as the regular third baseman for the White Sox but hasn't had more than seven in a season since. He is a low-cost fantasy utility player, but don't count on more than 150 at bats. His 1992 commons have no relevance. Only the advent of 1993 expansion guarantees Hulett a place in the majors.

Major League Batting Register
	BA	G	AB	R	H	2B	3B	HR	RBI	SB
83 AL	.200	6	5	0	1	0	0	0	0	1
84 AL	.000	8	7	1	0	0	0	0	0	1
85 AL	.268	141	395	52	106	19	4	5	37	6
86 AL	.231	150	520	53	120	16	5	17	44	4
87 AL	.217	68	240	20	52	10	0	7	28	0
89 AL	.278	33	97	12	27	5	0	3	18	0
90 AL	.255	53	153	16	39	7	1	3	16	1
91 AL	.204	79	206	29	42	9	0	7	18	0
Life	.238	538	1623	183	387	66	10	42	161	13
2 AVE	.226	66	180	23	41	8	1	5	17	1

BRIAN HUNTER

Position: First base; outfield
Team: Atlanta Braves
Born: March 4, 1968 El Toro, CA
Height: 6' **Weight:** 195 lbs.
Bats: right **Throws:** left
Acquired: Eighth-round pick in free-agent draft, 6/87

Player Summary
Fantasy Value	$6 to $10
Card Value	15¢ to 20¢
Will	swing big RBI bat
Can't	add stealing
Expect	higher average
Don't Expect	return of fielding woes

The Braves initially deployed David Justice as a platoon first baseman in 1990. Hunter began his big league career last May 31 the same way. Like Justice, Hunter was more comfortable in the outfield but willing to play anywhere. When both Justice and Sid Bream were sidelined for two months, manager Bobby Cox—desperate for offense—permitted Hunter to play full time. The rookie promptly improved both his hitting and his fielding. He drove in runs late in '91 on a pace that projects to about 100 RBI a year. In a half season at Triple-A Richmond in '91, he hit .260 with 10 homers and 30 RBI. He hit .241 with 14 homers, 55 RBI, 43 walks, and 62 strikeouts in 320 at bats at Double-A Greenville in 1990. Moved up to Richmond that year, he seemed overmatched, hitting .197 with five homers and 16 RBI. Hunter will get plenty of playing time in 1992 as a first baseman, outfielder, and power-hitting pinch-hitter. He could be a low-cost find for $8 at the fantasy draft. His 1992 cards are extremely promising buys at 20 cents or less.

Major League Batting Register
	BA	G	AB	R	H	2B	3B	HR	RBI	SB
91 NL	.251	97	271	32	68	16	1	12	50	0
Life	.251	97	271	32	68	16	1	12	50	0

CURRENT PLAYERS

BRUCE HURST

Position: Pitcher
Team: San Diego Padres
Born: March 24, 1958 St. George, UT
Height: 6'3" **Weight:** 214 lbs.
Bats: left **Throws:** left
Acquired: Signed as a free agent, 12/88

Player Summary	
Fantasy Value	$16 to $21
Card Value	4¢ to 6¢
Will	win 15 with support
Can't	count on heat
Expect	consistency
Don't Expect	poor K-to-walk ratio

Hurst has been one of baseball's most consistent starting pitchers since breaking into the big leagues with Boston. For nine years in a row, he's won at least 11 games—including 15 or more three times in the last four seasons. He shared the NL lead in shutouts (four) in 1990 and complete games in 1989. He fans more than twice as many as he walks. He suffers every control pitcher's dilemma, however; when he puts pitches in the strike zone, often they become home runs (17 in '91). Hurst throws a forkball, slider, slow curve, and occasional fastball, and he succeeds by changing speeds and pitching to spots. He's a good fielder with a fine pickoff move. He rarely helps himself as a hitter. He shouldn't be overlooked by collectors; his 1992 commons are good buys. He is a $18 fantasy draft.

Major League Pitching Register

	W	L	ERA	G	CG	IP	H	ER	BB	SO
80 AL	2	2	9.10	12	0	30.2	39	31	16	16
81 AL	2	0	4.30	5	0	23.0	23	11	12	11
82 AL	3	7	5.77	28	0	117.0	161	75	40	53
83 AL	12	12	4.09	33	6	211.2	241	96	62	115
84 AL	12	12	3.92	33	9	218.0	232	95	88	136
85 AL	11	13	4.51	35	6	229.1	243	115	70	189
86 AL	13	8	2.99	25	11	174.1	169	58	50	167
87 AL	15	13	4.41	33	15	238.2	239	117	76	190
88 AL	18	6	3.66	33	7	216.2	222	88	65	166
89 NL	15	11	2.69	33	10	244.2	214	73	66	179
90 NL	11	9	3.14	33	9	223.2	188	78	63	162
91 NL	15	8	3.29	31	4	221.2	201	81	59	141
Life	129	101	3.84	334	77	2149.0	2172	918	667	1525
3 AVE	14	9	3.03	32	8	229.2	201	77	63	161

JEFF HUSON

Position: Infield
Team: Texas Rangers
Born: Aug. 15, 1964 Scottsdale, AZ
Height: 6'3" **Weight:** 170 lbs.
Bats: left **Throws:** right
Acquired: Traded from Expos for Drew Hall, 4/90

Player Summary	
Fantasy Value	$1 to $3
Card Value	3¢ to 5¢
Will	use speed if healthy
Can't	hit for average
Expect	a part-time role
Don't Expect	many walks or Ks

Huson's development was slowed by a knee injury in 1991. He was the regular Ranger shortstop in 1990, when he hit .240 with 12 stolen bases in 145 games. He contributed even less as his playing time fell. He has yet to realize his minor league promise as a wide-ranging shortstop, base-stealer, and productive leadoff man. Huson even had 16 homers as a first-year pro in 1986, but has hit only a half-dozen in five seasons since. He had an unassisted triple play for Montreal in 1989. Speed is his biggest asset. He stole 56 bases to lead the Double-A Southern League in 1988 and had several 30-plus years in the minors. Not a full-time performer, he doesn't warrant more than $3 at the draft, and his 1992 commons are not investments. With 15 errors, his defense was not up to par. Unless Huson shows more life at the plate and improves his disappointing defense of recent seasons, he's unlikely to shed his image as a utility player.

Major League Batting Register

	BA	G	AB	R	H	2B	3B	HR	RBI	SB
88 NL	.310	20	42	7	13	2	0	0	3	2
89 NL	.162	32	74	1	12	5	0	0	2	3
90 AL	.240	145	396	57	95	12	2	0	28	12
91 AL	.213	119	268	36	57	8	3	2	26	8
Life	.227	316	780	101	177	27	5	2	59	25
2 AVE	.229	132	332	47	76	10	3	1	27	10

CURRENT PLAYERS

PETE INCAVIGLIA

Position: Outfield
Team: Detroit Tigers
Born: April 2, 1964 Pebble Beach, CA
Height: 6'1" **Weight:** 220 lbs.
Bats: right **Throws:** right
Acquired: Signed as a free agent, 4/91

Player Summary	
Fantasy Value	$7 to $10
Card Value	3¢ to 5¢
Will	hit ball far
Can't	add speed
Expect	many Ks
Don't Expect	high average

Incaviglia was the designated hitter on *The Sporting News* 1985 College All-America team and that is exactly where he should play. Despite a strong arm and a willingness to hustle after balls hit in his direction, he is far below average as a big league left fielder. He's also below average as a hitter, since he's a one-dimensional player with embarrassingly high strikeout totals. Though he knocked in 80-plus runs in four of his first five seasons, Incaviglia was a bust in his lone season with the Tigers last year. His average and power were way off their norms, and he wasn't drawing enough walks to compensate. His homers draw mild interest from fantasy league managers, but he will be overpriced at $10. Despite his big bat, his 1992 cards are commons. The former Ranger, who went directly to the majors from the Oklahoma State campus, fans three times more than he walks anyway.

JEFF INNIS

Position: Pitcher
Team: New York Mets
Born: July 5, 1962 Decatur, IL
Height: 6' **Weight:** 170 lbs.
Bats: right **Throws:** right
Acquired: 13th-round pick in 6/83 free-agent draft

Player Summary	
Fantasy Value	$2 to $4
Card Value	3¢ to 5¢
Will	appear frequently
Can't	intimidate hitters
Expect	more middle relief
Don't Expect	starting or closing

Innis was one of the busiest middle relievers in the National League last season. In his first full year with the Mets, the sidewheeling righthander appeared in more than 60 games yet kept his ERA respectable by keeping the ball in the park (only two gophers). Innis fans twice as many as he walks and yields considerably less than a hit per inning. In '91, opponents compiled a .219 batting average, a .291 slugging percentage, and a .270 on-base average. His motion is difficult for righthanded batters but also bothersome to southpaws. The former University of Illinois star began his pro career with an 8-0 record and 1.37 ERA at rookie league Little Falls in 1983. He led the Double-A Texas League in saves with 25 in 1986. He reached the Mets for the first time in 1987. Without the saves to interest fantasy managers, he is a $3 draft. Bypass his 1992 commons. If he keeps throwing the ball the way he did in '91, Innis will have a secure job.

Major League Batting Register

	BA	G	AB	R	H	2B	3B	HR	RBI	SB
86 AL	.250	153	540	82	135	21	2	30	88	3
87 AL	.271	139	509	85	138	26	4	27	80	9
88 AL	.249	116	418	59	104	19	3	22	54	6
89 AL	.236	133	453	48	107	27	4	21	81	5
90 AL	.233	153	529	59	123	27	0	24	85	3
91 AL	.214	97	337	38	72	12	1	11	38	1
Life	.244	791	2786	371	679	132	14	135	426	27
3 AVE	.229	128	440	48	101	22	2	19	68	3

Major League Pitching Register

	W	L	ERA	G	S	IP	H	ER	BB	SO
87 NL	0	1	3.16	17	0	25.2	29	9	4	28
88 NL	1	1	1.89	12	0	19.0	19	4	2	14
89 NL	0	1	3.18	29	0	39.2	38	14	8	16
90 NL	1	3	2.39	18	1	26.1	19	7	10	12
91 NL	0	2	2.66	69	0	84.2	66	25	23	47
Life	2	8	2.72	145	1	195.1	171	59	47	117
2 AVE	0	2	2.82	49	0	62.2	52	20	16	32

CURRENT PLAYERS

BO JACKSON

Position: Outfield
Team: Chicago White Sox
Born: Nov. 30, 1962 Bessemer, AL
Height: 6'1" **Weight:** 225 lbs.
Bats: right **Throws:** right
Acquired: Signed as a free agent, 4/91

Player Summary	
Fantasy Value	$25 to $30
Card Value	10¢ to 20¢
Will	hit long homers
Can't	avoid many, many Ks
Expect	sensational throws
Don't Expect	an injury-free season

Bo Jackson's ability to play two sports, not to mention his career, nearly came to a crushing halt when he suffered a severe hip injury in a 1991 NFL playoff game. After the Royals released him, the White Sox grabbed him, then waited until September 2, the fifth anniversary of his debut, to activate him. He played well upon his 1991 return, notching a .408 slugging percentage. When healthy, Bo can top 30 homers and 100 RBI, even though he fans frequently and is notorious for chasing bad pitches. His homers often travel a long way—sometimes to the opposite field. His power potential makes his fantasy value $25 to $30. Jackson also had the speed to become a 30-30 contender, if only injuries don't interfere. He has great range and a strong but inaccurate arm. Center field could be his best spot, if he has his speed back. Regardless of his play, his 1992 cards will remain expensive. Be prepared to pay up to 20 cents apiece.

Major League Batting Register

	BA	G	AB	R	H	2B	3B	HR	RBI	SB
86 AL	.207	25	82	9	17	2	1	2	9	3
87 AL	.235	116	396	46	93	17	2	22	53	10
88 AL	.246	124	439	63	108	16	4	25	68	27
89 AL	.256	135	515	86	132	15	6	32	105	26
90 AL	.272	111	405	74	110	16	1	28	78	15
91 AL	.225	23	71	8	16	4	0	3	14	0
Life	.249	534	1908	286	476	70	14	112	327	81
2 AVE	.263	123	460	80	121	16	4	30	92	21

DANNY JACKSON

Position: Pitcher
Team: Chicago Cubs
Born: Jan. 5, 1962 San Antonio, TX
Height: 6' **Weight:** 205 lbs.
Bats: right **Throws:** left
Acquired: Signed as a free agent, 11/90

Player Summary	
Fantasy Value	$2 to $5
Card Value	3¢ to 5¢
Will	win big minus injuries
Can't	avoid gopher balls
Expect	hit an inning
Don't Expect	full season

Although he's a quality starter when healthy, Jackson endured two stints on the disabled list during his first season with the Cubs last year and was banished to the bullpen. He is no stranger to injury, visiting the DL nine times in as many seasons. Jackson, who has pitched well in postseason play, is a fastball-and-slider pitcher with a good glove and a fine move to first base. He often has trouble controlling his slider, a flaw that invariably results in a flurry of base hits. Though he has fairly good control, Jackson sometimes allows more hits than innings pitched. The Cubs sank so much money into him that he will get every opportunity to turn his career around. If he does, some fantasy manager who bid only $3 for him is going to be happy. His 1992 commons are not buys.

Major League Pitching Register

	W	L	ERA	G	CG	IP	H	ER	BB	SO
83 AL	1	1	5.21	4	0	19.0	26	11	6	9
84 AL	2	6	4.26	15	1	76.0	84	36	35	40
85 AL	14	12	3.42	32	4	208.0	209	79	76	114
86 AL	11	12	3.20	32	4	185.2	177	66	79	115
87 AL	9	18	4.02	36	11	224.0	219	100	109	152
88 NL	23	8	2.73	35	15	260.2	206	79	71	161
89 NL	6	11	5.60	20	1	115.2	122	72	57	70
90 NL	6	6	3.61	22	0	117.1	119	47	40	76
91 NL	1	5	6.75	17	0	70.2	89	53	48	31
Life	73	79	3.83	213	36	1277.0	1251	543	521	768
3 AVE	4	7	5.10	20	0	101.2	110	57	48	59

CURRENT PLAYERS

DARRIN JACKSON

Position: Outfield
Team: San Diego Padres
Born: Aug. 22, 1963 Los Angeles, CA
Height: 6' **Weight:** 185 lbs.
Bats: right **Throws:** right
Acquired: Traded from Cubs with Calvin Schiraldi and Phil Stephenson for Luis Salazar and Marvell Wynne, 8/89

Player Summary	
Fantasy Value	$6 to $9
Card Value	3¢ to 5¢
Will	show surprising power
Can't	reduce K-to-walk ratio
Expect	good glove in center
Don't Expect	too many walks

Though he had worked in Mike Schooler's shadow, Jackson got a chance to pitch more short relief when Schooler was sidelined for the first half of 1991. The results were so good that managers polled by *Baseball America* said Jackson threw the best slider in the AL. His fastball isn't too shabby, being timed in the mid-90s. Working more than 60 games for the fourth year in a row, he set a career high in saves. He fans twice as many as he walks, keeps the ball in the park, and yields less than a hit per inning. His fielding prowess also helps. In December, Jackson was traded to the Giants, where he'll be used as a set-up man. His stats will drop, as will his fantasy allure to $6. He needs to get more saves before his 1992 commons will inflate.

Major League Batting Register

	BA	G	AB	R	H	2B	3B	HR	RBI	SB
85 NL	.091	5	11	0	1	0	0	0	0	0
87 NL	.800	7	5	2	4	1	0	0	0	0
88 NL	.266	100	188	29	50	11	3	6	20	4
89 NL	.218	70	170	17	37	7	0	4	20	1
90 NL	.257	58	113	10	29	3	0	3	9	3
91 NL	.262	122	359	51	94	12	1	21	49	5
Life	.254	362	846	109	215	34	4	34	98	13
2 AVE	.248	96	265	34	66	10	1	13	35	3

MIKE JACKSON

Position: Pitcher
Team: San Francisco Giants
Born: Dec. 22, 1964 Houston, TX
Height: 6' **Weight:** 185 lbs.
Bats: right **Throws:** right
Acquired: Traded from Mariners with Bill Swift and Dave Burba for Kevin Mitchell and Mike Remlinkger, 12/91

Player Summary	
Fantasy Value	$5 to $7
Card Value	3¢ to 5¢
Will	throw blue darters
Can't	always find strike zone
Expect	under a hit a frame
Don't Expect	few gophers

Though he usually works in Mike Schooler's shadow, Jackson got a chance to pitch more short relief when Schooler was sidelined for the first half of 1991. The results were so good that managers polled by *Baseball America* said Jackson threw the best slider in the AL. His fastball isn't too shabby, being timed in the mid-90s. Working more than 60 games for the fourth year in a row, he set a career high in saves. He fans twice as many as he walks, keeps the ball in the park, and yields less than a hit per inning. His fielding prowess also helps. If he steers clear of past shoulder and knee problems, not to mention the bouts of wildness that have plagued him, Jackson could be an effective set-up man. With Schooler returning, his stats will drop, as will his fantasy allure to $6. He needs to get more saves before his 1992 commons will inflate.

Major League Pitching Register

	W	L	ERA	G	S	IP	H	ER	BB	SO
86 NL	0	0	3.38	9	0	13.1	12	5	4	3
87 NL	3	10	4.20	55	1	109.1	88	51	56	93
88 AL	6	5	2.63	62	4	99.1	74	29	43	76
89 AL	4	6	3.17	65	7	99.1	81	35	54	94
90 AL	5	7	4.54	63	3	77.1	64	39	44	69
91 AL	7	7	3.25	72	14	88.2	64	32	34	74
Life	25	35	3.53	326	29	487.1	383	191	235	409
3 AVE	5	7	3.60	67	8	88.1	70	35	44	79

CURRENT PLAYERS

BROOK JACOBY

Position: Third base; first base
Team: Oakland Athletics
Born: Nov. 23, 1959 Philadelphia, PA
Height: 5'11" **Weight:** 195 lbs.
Bats: right **Throws:** right
Acquired: Traded from Indians for Lee Tinsley and Apolinar Garcia, 7/91

Player Summary	
Fantasy Value	$2 to $5
Card Value	3¢ to 5¢
Will	lift average
Can't	run or steal
Expect	solid defense
Don't Expect	return of '87 power

Jacoby got off to a wretched start with the Indians before his late-summer swap to Oakland. One of his problems was a 2-1 ratio of strikeouts to walks. Valuable because of his versatility, he filled in for injured third baseman Carney Lansford after arriving in Oakland. Jacoby also is a fine defensive player at first. A former free swinger, he's learned to be more selective over the years and has topped the .290 mark twice as a result. He has hit at least 20 homers in a season twice and knocked in at least 75 runs three times. Jacoby handles off-speed pitches well and often aims for the opposite field with two strikes. He also bangs into frequent double-plays. Unless a starting job for him turns up, don't invest more than $3. His 1992 commons don't look promising.

Major League Batting Register

	BA	G	AB	R	H	2B	3B	HR	RBI	SB
81 NL	.200	11	10	0	2	0	0	0	1	0
83 NL	.000	4	8	0	0	0	0	0	0	0
84 AL	.264	126	439	64	116	19	3	7	40	3
85 AL	.274	161	606	72	166	26	3	20	87	2
86 AL	.288	158	583	83	168	30	4	17	80	2
87 AL	.300	155	540	73	162	26	4	32	69	2
88 AL	.241	152	552	59	133	25	0	9	49	2
89 AL	.272	147	519	49	141	26	5	13	64	2
90 AL	.293	155	553	77	162	24	4	14	75	1
91 AL	.224	122	419	28	94	21	1	4	44	2
Life	.271	1191	4229	505	1144	197	24	116	509	16
3 AVE	.266	141	497	51	132	24	3	10	61	2

CHRIS JAMES

Position: Designated hitter; outfield
Team: Cleveland Indians
Born: Oct. 4, 1962 Rusk, TX
Height: 6'1" **Weight:** 190 lbs.
Bats: right **Throws:** right
Acquired: Traded from Padres with Carlos Baerga and Sandy Alomar for Joe Carter, 12/89

Player Summary	
Fantasy Value	$5 to $8
Card Value	3¢ to 5¢
Will	boost average
Can't	steal bases
Expect	12 homers and 60 RBI
Don't Expect	spectacular defense

James had his day in the sun with the Indians last May 4. He drove in nine runs with two homers and two singles as the Tribe trounced Oakland, 20-6. That turned out to be the outfielder's whole season, however. After breaking Earl Averill's club record of eight RBI in a game, James encountered the malaise that swamped Cleveland's ship in 1991. His power production has dropped four years in a row following a career-best 19 homers for the 1988 Phillies. James fans more than twice as much as he walks, doesn't steal much, and plays a shaky outfield despite a good throwing arm. He's a streak hitter with a fondness for fastballs. If his skid is temporary, he could be a fantasy steal for $7. He is still young enough to reverse his fortunes. James will have to do just that if he wants to get any more playing time. Don't go for his 1992 commons, however.

Major League Batting Register

	BA	G	AB	R	H	2B	3B	HR	RBI	SB
86 NL	.283	16	46	5	13	3	0	1	5	0
87 NL	.293	115	358	48	105	20	6	17	54	3
88 NL	.242	150	566	57	137	24	1	19	66	7
89 NL	.243	132	482	55	117	17	2	13	65	5
90 AL	.299	140	528	62	158	32	4	12	70	4
91 AL	.238	115	437	31	104	16	2	5	41	3
Life	.262	668	2417	258	634	112	15	67	301	22
3 AVE	.262	129	482	49	126	22	3	10	59	4

CURRENT PLAYERS

STAN JAVIER

Position: Outfield
Team: Los Angeles Dodgers
Born: Sept. 1, 1965 San Pedro de Macoris, Dominican Republic
Height: 6' **Weight:** 185 lbs.
Bats: both **Throws:** right
Acquired: Traded from Athletics for Willie Randolph, 6/90

Player Summary
Fantasy Value	$2 to $4
Card Value	3¢ to 5¢
Will	provide great defense
Can't	produce runs
Expect	use as late-inning sub
Don't Expect	1990's .304 form

Javier is a superior defensive center fielder who would probably hit better with more playing time. He proved that point in 1990, when he hit .304 in 104 games. The average plunged to the Mendoza Line in 1991 after the free agent signings of Darryl Strawberry and Brett Butler. The switch-hitting son of former Cardinal second baseman Julian Javier, Stan has never been able to shake the tag of being just a utility player since breaking into the majors with the 1984 Yankees. Though he has proven himself a gifted outfielder, he has never received 400 at bats. A better righthanded hitter, he has little power but compensates by adding speed. Javier has the arm, range, and judgement to play all three outfield positions well. His reserve status alters his fantasy possibilities downward to $3. His 1992 commons suffer the same fate.

Major League Batting Register
	BA	G	AB	R	H	2B	3B	HR	RBI	SB
84 AL	.143	7	7	1	1	0	0	0	0	0
86 AL	.202	59	114	13	23	8	0	0	8	8
87 AL	.185	81	151	22	28	3	1	2	9	3
88 AL	.257	125	397	49	102	13	3	2	35	20
89 AL	.248	112	310	42	77	12	3	1	28	12
90 AL	.242	19	33	4	8	0	2	0	3	0
90 NL	.304	104	276	56	84	9	4	3	24	15
91 NL	.205	121	176	21	36	5	3	1	11	7
Life	.245	628	1464	208	359	50	16	9	118	65
3 AVE	.258	119	265	41	68	9	4	2	22	11

MIKE JEFFCOAT

Position: Pitcher
Team: Texas Rangers
Born: Aug. 3, 1959 Pine Bluff, AR
Height: 6'2" **Weight:** 189 lbs.
Bats: left **Throws:** left
Acquired: Signed as a free agent, 12/86

Player Summary
Fantasy Value	$1 to $3
Card Value	3¢ to 5¢
Will	work 60 games
Can't	dominate righty hitters
Expect	2-1 K-to-walk ratio
Don't Expect	return to rotation

Jeffcoat carved a unique niche in baseball history last year when he delivered an RBI double last August 2. The last AL pitcher to produce a hit had been Ferguson Jenkins on October 2, 1974. Jeffcoat's pitching was even more of a conversation piece than his hitting. He worked more than 60 times for the first time and gave the Rangers strong middle relief. He is a control artist who succeeds by changing speeds on his curveball and split-fingered fastball. He's especially effective against lefthanded hitters. Jeffcoat strikes out twice the number he walks, keeps the ball in the ballpark, and knows what to do with a glove. Though he had some success as a starter in 1989, he's more likely to retain his present role. His stats give him the look of a $2 fantasy pitcher. Avoid his 1992 commons.

Major League Pitching Register
	W	L	ERA	G	S	IP	H	ER	BB	SO
83 AL	1	3	3.31	11	0	32.2	32	12	13	9
84 AL	5	2	2.99	63	1	75.1	82	25	24	41
85 AL	0	0	2.79	9	0	9.2	8	3	6	4
85 NL	0	2	5.32	19	0	22.0	27	13	6	10
87 AL	0	1	12.86	2	0	7.0	11	10	4	1
88 AL	0	2	11.70	5	0	10.0	19	13	5	5
89 AL	9	6	3.58	22	0	130.2	139	52	33	64
90 AL	5	6	4.47	44	5	110.2	122	55	28	58
91 AL	5	3	4.63	70	1	79.2	104	41	25	43
Life	25	25	4.22	245	7	477.2	544	224	144	235
3 AVE	6	5	4.15	45	2	106.2	122	49	29	55

CURRENT PLAYERS

GREGG JEFFERIES

Position: Third base
Team: Kansas City Royals
Born: Aug. 1, 1967 Burlingame, CA
Height: 5'10" **Weight:** 180 lbs.
Bats: both **Throws:** right
Acquired: Traded from Mets with Kevin McReynolds and Keith Miller for Bret Saberhagen and Bill Pecota, 12/91

Player Summary	
Fantasy Value	$20 to $25
Card Value	5¢ to 15¢
Will	steal bases
Can't	avoid errors
Expect	him to play third
Don't Expect	All-Star bat

Jefferies has been a disappointment in his three big league seasons. He was projected as a .300-hitting All-Star after winning consecutive Minor League Player of the Year awards. He has often struggled at bat, on the field, and even in the clubhouse. In the off-season, he was dealt to Kansas City, where he's expected to play third base. Jefferies was called up in 1988 and hit .321 to help the Mets win the NL East. That performance fueled extremely high expectations. He also hit at a .294 clip from June 6 to the end of his rookie year in 1989 but hasn't done as well since. Love him or hate him, he still has enough potential to command $20 at the draft. His dime-priced 1992 cards may be wonderful long-term investments. Jefferies has good speed and good range but is not adept at making the double-play. He has some power, plus some base-stealing ability.

Major League Batting Register

	BA	G	AB	R	H	2B	3B	HR	RBI	SB
87 NL	.500	6	6	0	3	1	0	0	2	0
88 NL	.321	29	109	19	35	8	2	6	17	5
89 NL	.258	141	508	72	131	28	2	12	56	21
90 NL	.283	153	604	96	171	40	3	15	68	11
91 NL	.272	136	486	59	132	19	2	9	62	26
Life	.276	465	1713	246	472	96	9	42	205	63
3 AVE	.272	143	533	76	145	29	2	12	62	19

REGGIE JEFFERSON

Position: First base
Team: Cleveland Indians
Born: Sept. 25, 1968 Tallahassee, FL
Height: 6'4" **Weight:** 210 lbs.
Bats: both **Throws:** left
Acquired: Traded from Reds for Tim Costo, 6/91

Player Summary	
Fantasy Value	$2 to $5
Card Value	10¢ to 15¢
Will	homer from both sides
Can't	avoid injuries
Expect	fine fielding
Don't Expect	DH role

Jefferson's advance to the major leagues has been slowed by an assortment of ailments. The slugging switch-hitter had a fractured right shin as a first-year pro in 1987, back problems in 1990, and both pneumonia and a pulled chest muscle in '91. Jefferson did manage to make his major league debut on May 18 and homered against Andy Benes in his first start the next day. His Cincinnati career was short-lived before when a front-office snafu forced his trade to Cleveland, however. Though he eventually returned to the minors, he could become an impact player. A contact hitter with more power from his natural left side, at Double-A Chattanooga in 1989, he hit .287 with 19 doubles, 17 homers, and 80 RBI in 135 games. He hit .288 with 18 homers and 90 RBI at Class-A Cedar Rapids in '88. He was a Midwest League All-Star and the No. 8 prospect that year. Jefferson is also a good first baseman who once led a minor league in assists. His power potential merits $5 at the fantasy draft. His rookie 1992 cards are good investments at a dime.

Major League Batting Register

	BA	G	AB	R	H	2B	3B	HR	RBI	SB
91 NL	.143	5	7	1	1	0	0	0	1	0
91 AL	.198	26	101	10	20	3	0	2	12	0
Life	.194	31	108	11	21	3	0	3	13	0

CURRENT PLAYERS

HOWARD JOHNSON

Position: Third base; outfield
Team: New York Mets
Born: Nov. 29, 1960 Clearwater, FL
Height: 5'10" **Weight:** 195 lbs.
Bats: both **Throws:** right
Acquired: Traded from Tigers for Walt Terrell, 12/84

Player Summary	
Fantasy Value	$35 to $45
Card Value	10¢ to 20¢
Will	vie for homer crown
Can't	find position
Expect	stolen bases
Don't Expect	Gold Glove at third

Johnson is a regular member of the 30-30 club, but in 1991 he became a member of the 30-30-30 club. The triple 30 means he hit that many homers, stole that many bases, and made that many errors. Still bothered by a surgically repaired shoulder in cold weather, he started the 1991 season at shortstop before returning to third. In September, he moved to the outfield. His bat should be more productive if he doesn't have to worry about his defense. Johnson is one of the league's best run producers, and he is now the central component of the Mets' offense. His annual games at shortstop push his fantasy value through the roof. His power and production dictate that you break the bank at the draft. His 1992 cards are very good investments at a dime.

Major League Batting Register

	BA	G	AB	R	H	2B	3B	HR	RBI	SB
82 AL	.316	54	155	23	49	5	0	4	14	7
83 AL	.212	27	66	11	14	0	0	3	5	0
84 AL	.248	116	355	43	88	14	1	12	50	10
85 NL	.242	126	389	38	94	18	4	11	46	6
86 NL	.245	88	220	30	54	14	0	10	39	8
87 NL	.265	157	554	93	147	22	1	36	99	32
88 NL	.230	148	495	85	114	21	1	24	68	23
89 NL	.287	153	571	104	164	41	3	36	101	41
90 NL	.244	154	590	89	144	37	3	23	90	34
91 NL	.259	156	564	108	146	34	4	38	117	30
Life	.256	1179	3959	624	1014	206	17	197	629	191
3 AVE	.263	154	575	100	151	37	3	32	103	35

JEFF JOHNSON

Position: Pitcher
Team: New York Yankees
Born: Aug. 4, 1966 Durham, NC
Height: 6'3" **Weight:** 200 lbs.
Bats: right **Throws:** left
Acquired: Sixth-round pick in 6/88 free-agent draft

Player Summary	
Fantasy Value	$2 to $4
Card Value	7¢ to 15¢
Will	yield more hits than frames
Can't	keep ball in park
Expect	2-1 ratio of Ks to walks
Don't Expect	many complete games

In the space of one year, Johnson rose from Class-A Fort Lauderdale to the New York rotation. Before his June 5 call to the majors, Johnson had a 4-0 mark, a 2.61 ERA, and 40 strikeouts in 62 innings pitched at Triple-A Columbus. He fanned Joe Carter twice in his debut. Johnson took the roster spot created by Pascual Perez' placement on the disabled list. A University of North Carolina product, Johnson had a respectable ERA in the bigs until his last several starts. He turned pro in 1988 and immediately showed promise by winning six of seven at Class-A Oneonta, with a 2.89 ERA and 91 Ks in 87⅔ innings. He was 4-10 with a 2.92 ERA and 99 Ks in 138⅔ frames at Class-A Prince William in '89. At Fort Lauderdale in 1990, he was 6-8 with a 3.65 ERA, 84 strikeouts, 25 walks, and 101 hits in 103⅔ innings. Johnson promises to be an important member of the Yankee rotation for a long time. His 1992 cards are overpriced; try to pay no more than a dime apiece. He is a $3 fantasy hurler at this point in his career.

Major League Pitching Register

	W	L	ERA	G	CG	IP	H	ER	BB	SO
91 AL	6	11	5.95	23	0	127.0	156	84	33	62
Life	6	11	5.95	23	0	127.0	156	84	33	62

CURRENT PLAYERS

LANCE JOHNSON

Position: Outfield
Team: Chicago White Sox
Born: July 7, 1963 Cincinnati, OH
Height: 5'11" **Weight:** 159 lbs.
Bats: left **Throws:** left
Acquired: Traded from Cardinals with Ricky Horton for Jose DeLeon, 2/88

Player Summary	
Fantasy Value	$6 to $9
Card Value	3¢ to 5¢
Will	play good defense
Can't	win a steady job
Expect	a better average
Don't Expect	even an ounce of power

Though he doesn't have a strong arm, Johnson is one of baseball's better defensive center fielders. He went 116 games without an error before making a miscue last August 30. He uses his speed to run down balls many others couldn't reach. He also uses it while running the bases, though he still gets nailed too many times. He was caught stealing 11 times in '91. His speed gives him $7 fantasy consideration. Because Johnson's average has fallen steadily over the last three seasons, his job could be in jeopardy. He generates no power, and there are better-hitting candidates for his position. Consider his 1992 cards risky investments. Johnson fanned three times more than he walked last year but has shown patience at the plate in the past. Unless he walks more, his on-base average won't be high enough to justify his presence at the top of the lineup. He had a .304 on-base percentage and 26 walks in '91.

Major League Batting Register

	BA	G	AB	R	H	2B	3B	HR	RBI	SB
87 NL	.220	33	59	4	13	2	1	0	7	6
88 AL	.185	33	124	11	23	4	1	0	6	6
89 AL	.300	50	180	28	54	8	2	0	16	16
90 AL	.285	151	541	76	154	18	9	1	51	36
91 AL	.274	159	588	72	161	14	13	0	49	26
Life	.271	426	1492	191	405	46	26	1	129	90
3 AVE	.282	120	436	59	123	13	8	0	39	26

RANDY JOHNSON

Position: Pitcher
Team: Seattle Mariners
Born: Sept. 10, 1963 Walnut Creek, CA
Height: 6'10" **Weight:** 225 lbs.
Bats: right **Throws:** left
Acquired: Traded from Expos with Gene Harris and Brian Holman for Mark Langston and Mike Campbell, 5/89

Player Summary	
Fantasy Value	$10 to $12
Card Value	4¢ to 7¢
Will	keep hitters off base
Can't	curtail wild spells
Expect	top rank in walks
Don't Expect	lower ERA without control

Johnson is not only baseball's tallest player but one of its biggest achievers. He was the author of a 1990 no-hitter and a 1991 one-hitter. Mike Gallego ended Johnson's bid for a second no-hitter with a leadoff ninth-inning single. He found consolation because he fanned a dozen to match his career high. Johnson is especially effective against lefthanded hitters, who have hit under .200 against him during his big league career. He is a strikeout pitcher, notching well over a K an inning. When the towering lefty loses, he usually beats himself by issuing free passes. He gives up almost a walk an inning. Opponents compiled a .213 batting average, a .325 slugging percentage, and a .358 on-base average in 1991. Don't overlook his fantasy potential; his Ks make him a $10 pitcher. Sink a buck or so into his 1992 commons, because if he should ever find control, he'll be a perennial All-Star.

Major League Pitching Register

	W	L	ERA	G	CG	IP	H	ER	BB	SO
88 NL	3	0	2.42	4	1	26.0	23	7	7	25
89 NL	0	4	6.67	7	0	29.2	29	22	26	26
89 AL	7	9	4.40	22	2	131.0	118	64	70	104
90 AL	14	11	3.65	33	5	219.2	174	89	120	194
91 AL	13	10	3.98	33	2	201.1	151	89	152	228
Life	37	34	4.01	99	10	607.2	495	271	375	577
3 AVE	11	11	4.08	32	3	193.2	157	88	123	184

CURRENT PLAYERS

BARRY JONES

Position: Pitcher
Team: Montreal Expos
Born: Feb. 15, 1963 Centerville, IN
Height: 6'4" **Weight:** 225 lbs.
Bats: right **Throws:** right
Acquired: Traded from Expos for Darrin Fletcher, 12/91

Player Summary
Fantasy Value	$3 to $6
Card Value	3¢ to 5¢
Will	trick with soft stuff
Can't	avoid walks
Expect	frequent work
Don't Expect	heavy use as a closer

Jones was more effective as a set-up man than he was as a closer. He preserved 30 leads—by far the most in the majors—when he went 11-4 with a 2.31 ERA for the 1990 White Sox. His ERA jumped nearly a full run when he crossed league lines in '91, however. He sabotaged his own record by issuing too many walks and throwing too many home run balls (eight) to NL hitters. In December, he was dealt to Philadelphia, where he'll remain a $5 fantasy hurler. His 1992 cards are beyond help, though. Working more than 60 games for the second year in a row, Jones was the president in the Expos' closer-by-committee. He mixes a curveball, changeup, and sinker to keep batters off base. He doesn't have the same success against lefties that he does against righthanded hitters. Without a dynamic out pitch, Jones seems more suited for his customary middle relief role.

Major League Pitching Register
	W	L	ERA	G	S	IP	H	ER	BB	SO
86 NL	3	4	2.89	26	3	37.1	29	12	21	29
87 NL	2	4	5.61	32	1	43.1	55	27	23	28
88 NL	1	1	3.04	42	2	56.1	57	19	21	31
88 AL	3	2	2.42	17	1	26.0	15	7	17	17
89 AL	3	2	2.37	22	1	30.1	22	8	8	17
90 AL	11	4	2.31	65	1	74.0	62	19	33	45
91 NL	4	9	3.35	77	13	88.2	76	33	33	46
Life	26	26	3.16	281	22	356.0	316	125	156	213
2 AVE	8	7	2.88	71	7	81.1	69	26	33	46

DOUG JONES

Position: Pitcher
Team: Cleveland Indians
Born: June 24, 1957 Covina, CA
Height: 6'2" **Weight:** 195 lbs.
Bats: right **Throws:** right
Acquired: Signed as a free agent, 4/85

Player Summary
Fantasy Value	$10 to $12
Card Value	3¢ to 5¢
Will	respond to frequent work
Can't	rely on fastball
Expect	bid to reclaim closer role
Don't Expect	another minors sojourn

Jones slipped into a season-long slump in 1991. Exiled to the minors with a 1-7 mark, 7.47 ERA, and five blown saves in 11 chances, he got his act together by using his fastball to set up his changeup. In his first 30 innings at Triple-A Colorado Springs, he fanned 22 and walked only five. It was not unfamiliar territory for Jones, who spent 10 years in the bushes before 1987. He had more than 30 saves three years in a row and even made the All-Star team twice before his ship ran aground. See why relievers are risky fantasy and card choices? Look for him as a $10 hurler in 1992. Don't look for his 1992 commons. When he's right, he fans more than twice the number he walks and keeps the ball in the park. He notched several starts for the Tribe in '91, but he probably will get every chance to win back his closer role.

Major League Pitching Register
	W	L	ERA	G	S	IP	H	ER	BB	SO
82 AL	0	0	10.13	4	0	2.2	5	3	1	1
86 AL	1	0	2.50	11	1	18.0	18	5	6	12
87 AL	6	5	3.15	49	8	91.1	101	32	24	87
88 AL	3	4	2.27	51	37	83.1	69	21	16	72
89 AL	7	10	2.34	59	32	80.2	76	21	13	65
90 AL	5	5	2.56	66	43	84.1	66	24	22	55
91 AL	4	8	5.54	36	7	63.1	87	39	17	48
Life	26	32	3.08	276	128	423.2	422	145	99	340
3 AVE	5	8	3.31	54	27	76.1	76	28	17	56

CURRENT PLAYERS

JIMMY JONES

Position: Pitcher
Team: Houston Astros
Born: April 20, 1964 Dallas, TX
Height: 6'2" **Weight:** 190 lbs.
Bats: right **Throws:** right
Acquired: Signed as a free agent, 3/91

Player Summary	
Fantasy Value	$3 to $5
Card Value	3¢ to 5¢
Will	get shot at rotation
Can't	pitch deep into starts
Expect	over a hit a frame
Don't Expect	many whiffs

Although he broke into the majors with the 1986 Padres, Jones had only one complete season in the big leagues before spending the entire 1991 campaign as an Astro starter. He made the Houston varsity after going to spring training as a non-roster player. With his opportunity, he acquired a No. 4 or No. 5 spot in the rotation, though he posted mediocre stats. Opponents compiled a .270 batting average, a .374 slugging percentage, and a .336 on-base percentage in 1991. Unless the 'Stros find somebody better down on the farms, Jones should retain his rotation spot. Even though he usually fans twice as many as he walks, Jones often finds that the hits prove fatal. In a pro career that stretches back to 1982, he has never won in double figures. With better offensive support, the righthander could get that chance in '92. Don't take his 1992 cards seriously, but seriously consider him for your fantasy team for $4.

Major League Pitching Register

	W	L	ERA	G	CG	IP	H	ER	BB	SO
86 NL	2	0	2.50	3	1	18.0	10	5	3	15
87 NL	9	7	4.14	30	2	145.2	154	67	54	51
88 NL	9	14	4.12	29	3	179.0	192	82	44	82
89 AL	2	1	5.25	11	0	48.0	56	28	16	25
90 AL	1	2	6.30	17	0	50.0	72	35	23	25
91 NL	6	8	4.39	26	1	135.1	143	66	51	88
Life	29	32	4.42	116	7	576.0	627	283	191	286
2 AVE	4	5	4.90	22	1	93.1	108	51	37	57

TRACY JONES

Position: Outfield
Team: Seattle Mariners
Born: March 31, 1961 Hawthorne, CA
Height: 6'3" **Weight:** 220 lbs.
Bats: right **Throws:** right
Acquired: Traded from Tigers for Darnell Coles, 6/90

Player Summary	
Fantasy Value	$1 to $3
Card Value	3¢ to 5¢
Will	find utility work
Can't	run well anymore
Expect	good contact
Don't Expect	extended outfield use

Jones has moaned for years about playing every day but never received the chance. He hit .349 in 46 games as a rookie with the 1986 Reds and .290 in 117 games a year later. He hasn't played more than 100 games since. Five stints on the disabled list haven't helped. Slowed by weak knees (three operations), Jones no longer runs the way he once did. That has reduced his range in the outfield and eliminated him as a threat to steal, even though he had a career-best 31 steals. Since Jones has little power, he's forced to wear a utility tag. As a designated hitter or pinch-hitter, he has value because he makes good contact. More patience at the plate would hike his on-base percentage, however. Draft a younger, speedier, more powerful reserve outfielder than him. His 1992 commons are not buys. No longer a prospect, Jones must prove completely sound to be considered for more playing time.

Major League Batting Register

	BA	G	AB	R	H	2B	3B	HR	RBI	SB
86 NL	.349	46	86	16	30	3	0	2	10	7
87 NL	.290	117	359	53	104	17	3	10	44	31
88 NL	.295	90	224	29	66	6	1	3	24	18
89 NL	.186	40	97	5	18	4	0	0	12	2
89 AL	.259	46	158	17	41	10	0	3	26	1
90 AL	.260	75	204	23	53	8	1	6	24	1
91 AL	.251	79	175	30	44	8	1	3	24	2
Life	.273	493	1303	173	356	56	6	27	164	62
3 AVE	.246	80	211	25	52	10	1	4	29	2

CURRENT PLAYERS

RICKY JORDAN

Position: First base
Team: Philadelphia Phillies
Born: May 26, 1965 Richmond, CA
Height: 6'3" **Weight:** 210 lbs.
Bats: right **Throws:** right
Acquired: First-round pick in 6/83 free-agent draft

Player Summary	
Fantasy Value	$7 to $10
Card Value	3¢ to 5¢
Will	hammer lefties
Can't	win awards for glove
Expect	power to the gaps
Don't Expect	good K-to-walk ratio

Although he spent much of last year platooning with John Kruk, Jordan saw considerably more action when his bat began producing in late summer. He showed a .270-level average with some gap power and run-producing ability when given the chance in '91. Hiking his average after successive declines over three seasons revived Jordan's reputation, which had evaporated after his .308 rookie season. He is far more productive against left-handed pitchers. He had a .452 slugging percentage and a .304 on-base average in '91. He had been a strong hitter during his minor league days. He'd get more playing time if he showed more patience at the plate. A free swinger, he is unsuccessful in trying to emulate Hank Aaron's tactic of generating power from his wrists. Jordan fans two and one-half times per walk. He's still not a polished first baseman but has improved in recent seasons. Due to his power collapse, his 1992 card values have faded. Don't dismiss him from your fantasy team for $8, however.

Major League Batting Register

	BA	G	AB	R	H	2B	3B	HR	RBI	SB
88 NL	.308	69	273	41	84	15	1	11	43	1
89 NL	.285	144	523	63	149	22	3	12	75	4
90 NL	.241	92	324	32	78	21	0	5	44	2
91 NL	.272	101	301	38	82	21	3	9	49	0
Life	.277	406	1421	174	393	79	7	37	211	7
3 AVE	.269	112	383	44	103	21	2	9	56	2

FELIX JOSE

Position: Outfield
Team: St. Louis Cardinals
Born: May 8, 1965 Santo Domingo, Dominican Republic
Height: 6'1" **Weight:** 190 lbs.
Bats: both **Throws:** right
Acquired: Traded from Athletics with Stan Royer and Daryl Green for Willie McGee, 8/90

Player Summary	
Fantasy Value	$15 to $20
Card Value	5¢ to 10¢
Will	produce runs
Can't	master stealing techniques
Expect	strong throws
Don't Expect	NL's Jose Canseco

Jose got off to such a hot start for the Cardinals last season that he made the National League All-Star team. Though he cooled a bit, he actually enjoyed his best game September 1, when he had two homers and five RBI in a 14-1 romp at San Francisco. A free swinger whose power is still developing, he reminds some observers of Bobby Bonilla. Both have better power from the left side plus strong right field arms. Both have line-drive swings that produce plenty of doubles. Though Jose fans twice as often as he walks, his increased patience paid off last year when he compiled one of the league's top averages. Fantasy owners who bought Jose for $10 in 1991 may brag now. He is a $17 fantasy player, and his 1992 cards are good buys under a dime. He's still thrown out too often on the bases (12 times in 1991), but the Cards anticipate improvement as he learns the pitchers.

Major League Batting Register

	BA	G	AB	R	H	2B	3B	HR	RBI	SB
88 AL	.333	8	6	2	2	1	0	0	1	1
89 AL	.193	20	57	3	11	2	0	0	5	0
90 AL	.264	101	341	42	90	12	0	8	39	8
90 NL	.271	25	85	12	23	4	1	3	13	4
91 NL	.305	154	568	69	173	40	6	8	77	20
Life	.283	308	1057	128	299	59	7	19	135	33
2 AVE	.288	140	497	62	143	28	4	10	65	16

CURRENT PLAYERS

WALLY JOYNER

Position: First base
Team: Kansas City Royals
Born: June 16, 1962 Atlanta, GA
Height: 6'2" **Weight:** 198 lbs.
Bats: left **Throws:** left
Acquired: Signed as a free agent, 12/91

Player Summary	
Fantasy Value	$30 to $38
Card Value	5¢ to 10¢
Will	hit for average
Can't	count on steals
Expect	superior defense
Don't Expect	return of '87 power

Joyner broke in with such a bang in 1986 that he contested Jose Canseco's selection as AL Rookie of the Year. Joyner not only hit .290 with 22 homers and 100 RBI but played far better defense than predecessor Rod Carew. In 1991, Joyner's bat boomed from the start. He hit at the .300 level, and he provided some power and run-producing ability. He had a .488 slugging average in '91. He hits to all fields but concentrates on hitting to left against southpaws who pitch him outside. A contact hitter who walks as much as he fans, he is proficient at the hit-and-run and more likely to hit a ball in the gap than over the fence. While enjoying his third 20-homer season in '91, he took the RBI lead on the California squad. In December, he signed a free-agent contract with Kansas City. He is a $30-plus fantasy buy. His 1992 cards may be good investments at a nickel or less.

Major League Batting Register

	BA	G	AB	R	H	2B	3B	HR	RBI	SB
86 AL	.290	154	593	82	172	27	3	22	100	5
87 AL	.285	149	564	100	161	33	1	34	117	8
88 AL	.295	158	597	81	176	31	2	13	85	8
89 AL	.282	159	593	78	167	30	2	16	79	3
90 AL	.268	83	310	35	83	15	0	8	41	2
91 AL	.301	143	551	79	166	34	3	21	96	2
Life	.288	846	3208	455	925	170	11	114	518	28
3 AVE	.286	128	485	64	139	26	2	15	72	2

DAVID JUSTICE

Position: Outfield
Team: Atlanta Braves
Born: April 14, 1966 Cincinnati, OH
Height: 6'3" **Weight:** 200 lbs.
Bats: left **Throws:** left
Acquired: Fourth-round pick in 6/85 free-agent draft

Player Summary	
Fantasy Value	$28 to $35
Card Value	10¢ to 15¢
Will	top 30 homers and 100 RBI
Can't	play hero every night
Expect	annual All-Star bid
Don't Expect	more than 10 steals

After winning 1990 rookie honors with a late-summer power explosion, Justice was determined to avoid the sophomore jinx. Had he avoided a severe back sprain on June 27, he would have succeeded. The NL's top RBI man at the time, he did not play again until late August. He led the Braves to the World Series when he came back, though. A feared slugger who is usually more productive against left-handed pitchers, Justice should have a long career as Atlanta's right fielder and clean-up man, roles previously filled by two-time MVP Dale Murphy. The long, looping Justice swing has been compared to the swings of both Ted Williams and Billy Williams. Justice had a .503 slugging percentage and a .377 on-base average in '91. He teams with Ronnie Gant to give the Braves one of the game's most devastating lefty-righty tandems. Justice has a powerful throwing arm and good speed, though he needs some more experience. Now's the time to draft Justice, even at the $30 level. His dime-priced 1992 cards are adequate investments.

Major League Batting Register

	BA	G	AB	R	H	2B	3B	HR	RBI	SB
89 NL	.235	16	51	7	12	3	0	1	3	2
90 NL	.282	127	439	76	124	23	2	28	78	11
91 NL	.275	109	396	67	109	25	1	21	87	8
Life	.277	252	886	150	245	51	3	50	168	21
2 AVE	.279	118	418	72	117	24	2	25	83	10

CURRENT PLAYERS

SCOTT KAMIENIECKI

Position: Pitcher
Team: New York Yankees
Born: April 19, 1964 Mt. Clemens, MI
Height: 6′ **Weight:** 195 lbs.
Bats: right **Throws:** right
Acquired: 14th-round pick in 6/86 free-agent draft

Player Summary
Fantasy Value	$4 to $7
Card Value	10¢ to 15¢
Will	yield a hit a frame
Can't	avoid walks or homers
Expect	lower ERA as he learns
Don't Expect	immediate winning record

RON KARKOVICE

Position: Catcher
Team: Chicago White Sox
Born: Aug. 8, 1963 Union, NJ
Height: 6′1″ **Weight:** 215 lbs.
Bats: right **Throws:** right
Acquired: First-round pick in 6/82 free-agent draft

Player Summary
Fantasy Value	$3 to $5
Card Value	3¢ to 5¢
Will	gun down base-stealers
Can't	finagle more work
Expect	continued hitting progress
Don't Expect	less than great defense

In the first full season without George Steinbrenner at the helm, the Yankees inserted three promising rookies into their pitching rotation. Kamieniecki, who made his big league bow with a 4-2 win over the Blue Jays on June 18, was one of them, along with Jeff Johnson and Wade Taylor. Kamieniecki is a former University of Michigan star (who roomed with Jim Abbott), and he struggled somewhat over the remainder of the '91 campaign. Nevertheless, Kamieniecki showed flashes of brilliance that suggested he might emerge as one of the American League's best young pitchers within the next year or two. He had only a few more strikeouts than walks for the Yankees, but he had a better than 3-1 ratio of Ks to bases on balls at Triple-A Columbus in 1991. He finished at 6-3 with a 2.36 ERA and three complete games in 11 starts there. He was 10-9 with a 3.20 ERA, 99 strikeouts, 61 walks, and 113 hits in 132 innings at Double-A Albany in 1990. His 1992 cards will be hot investments; invest up to 15 cents. He is a promising $5 fantasy draft.

With Carlton Fisk still going strong, Karkovice doesn't play as often as he would like. But rival managers like what they see, naming Karko the AL's top defensive receiver in a 1991 *Baseball America* poll. Former Sox skipper Jeff Torborg, a former catcher himself, let Karkovice call his own game all year. The receiver never lost his cool, rarely made a mistake, and showed an uncanny ability to settle down his pitcher. Detroit manager Sparky Anderson even called Karkovice the best defensive catcher since Hall of Famer Johnny Bench. Karkovice blocks wild pitches and handles his staff well. He has an outstanding arm, and erases enemy base-stealers with great regularity. With help from Walt Hriniak, Karkovice has also improved his average and power in recent seasons. He is a good reserve fantasy pick for $4. His 1992 commons are not the best investments you can make.

Major League Pitching Register
	W	L	ERA	G	CG	IP	H	ER	BB	SO
91 AL	4	4	3.90	9	0	55.1	54	24	22	34
Life	4	4	3.90	9	0	55.1	54	24	22	34

Major League Batting Register
	BA	G	AB	R	H	2B	3B	HR	RBI	SB
86 AL	.247	37	97	13	24	7	0	4	13	1
87 AL	.071	39	85	7	6	0	0	2	7	3
88 AL	.174	46	115	10	20	4	0	3	9	4
89 AL	.264	71	182	21	48	9	2	3	24	0
90 AL	.246	68	183	30	45	10	0	6	20	2
91 AL	.246	75	167	25	41	13	0	5	22	0
Life	.222	336	829	106	184	43	2	23	95	10
3 AVE	.252	71	177	25	45	11	1	5	22	1

CURRENT PLAYERS

PAT KELLY

Position: Third base; second base
Team: New York Yankees
Born: Oct. 10, 1967 Philadelphia, PA
Height: 6′ **Weight:** 180 lbs.
Bats: right **Throws:** right
Acquired: Ninth-round pick in 6/88 free-agent draft

Player Summary	
Fantasy Value	$3 to $6
Card Value	10¢ to 15¢
Will	succeed swiping bases
Can't	yield steady power
Expect	a return to second
Don't Expect	a ticket to Columbus

Kelly was drafted as a shortstop and converted to second in his first pro season. But he was brought to the major leagues in a continuing Yankee quest to find a reliable everyday third baseman. When he first arrived in the majors in May, the plan was to shift veteran Steve Sax from second to third and put the rookie at second. Within a week, however, the two had exchanged places. Though Kelly did not supply the power expected of the position, he provided a better bat and defense at the new position than the previous 1991 occupants. Kelly, who averaged 30 steals a year in the minors, was hitting .366 at Triple-A Columbus when promoted. At Double-A Albany in 1990, he hit .270 with eight homers, 44 RBI, 67 runs scored, and 31 stolen bases. He was named the Eastern League's top defensive second baseman that year. He doubled off Tom Candiotti for his first major league hit. His rookie 1992 cards look like options for card investors up to 15 cents. Fantasy managers could get a bargain by drafting him for $5.

Major League Batting Register

	BA	G	AB	R	H	2B	3B	HR	RBI	SB
91 AL	.242	96	298	35	72	12	4	3	23	12
Life	.242	96	298	35	72	12	4	3	23	12

ROBERTO KELLY

Position: Outfield
Team: New York Yankees
Born: Oct. 1, 1964 Panama City, Panama
Height: 6′4″ **Weight:** 185 lbs.
Bats: right **Throws:** right
Acquired: Signed as a free agent, 2/82

Player Summary	
Fantasy Value	$22 to $27
Card Value	3¢ to 5¢
Will	steal bases
Can't	apply selectivity at bat
Expect	respectable average
Don't Expect	strong throws

Kelly missed more than a month of the 1991 season with a sprained right wrist that sent him to the disabled list July 7. He suffered the injury when he crashed into the outfield wall in pursuit of a double by Cal Ripken. Most other center fielders couldn't have reached the ball, but Kelly has enormous speed that permits him free range into the gaps and latitude on the bases. He had 77 steals over two years before '91. A free swinger with no patience to wait for walks, he fans too often to bat first but produces good results when he connects. He had a .288 career average before 1991 and had 15 homers when he played the full 162-game schedule in '90. He can help your fantasy team in several categories for $25. His 1992 commons are good investments. Kelly was unhappy about moving to left after his return last season, but he faces a major challenge from Bernie Williams to regain the center field spot for the Yankees.

Major League Batting Register

	BA	G	AB	R	H	2B	3B	HR	RBI	SB
87 AL	.269	23	52	12	14	3	0	1	7	9
88 AL	.247	38	77	9	19	4	1	1	7	5
89 AL	.302	137	441	65	133	18	3	9	48	35
90 AL	.285	162	641	85	183	32	4	15	61	42
91 AL	.267	126	486	68	130	22	2	20	69	32
Life	.282	486	1697	239	479	79	10	46	192	123
3 AVE	.284	142	523	73	149	24	3	15	59	36

CURRENT PLAYERS

TERRY KENNEDY

Position: Catcher
Team: San Francisco Giants
Born: June 4, 1956 Euclid, OH
Height: 6'4" **Weight:** 230 lbs.
Bats: left **Throws:** right
Acquired: Traded from Orioles for Bob Melvin, 1/89

Player Summary	
Fantasy Value	$1 to $2
Card Value	3¢ to 5¢
Will	show punch
Can't	run or throw well
Expect	less catching
Don't Expect	return of power

Kennedy has bad knees, a mediocre throwing arm, no speed, and statistics that have declined steadily over the last four seasons. He's in the bigs because lefty-hitting catchers are hard to find. Kennedy has hit at least a dozen homers five times in his career but hasn't had more than five in any of the last four years. A selective hitter who makes contact, Kennedy hits into a number of double-plays. On occasion, however, he hits balls into the gaps or even down the line of the opposite field. His knowledge of opposing hitters helps his game-calling but his mechanics are mediocre. Keep your fantasy buck unless you're desperate. His 1992 commons are unfortunate.

Major League Batting Register

	BA	G	AB	R	H	2B	3B	HR	RBI	SB
78 NL	.172	10	29	0	5	0	0	0	2	0
79 NL	.284	33	109	11	31	7	0	2	17	0
80 NL	.254	84	248	28	63	12	3	4	34	0
81 NL	.301	101	382	32	115	24	1	2	41	0
82 NL	.295	153	562	75	166	42	1	21	97	1
83 NL	.284	149	549	47	156	27	2	17	98	1
84 NL	.240	148	530	54	127	16	1	14	57	1
85 NL	.261	143	532	54	.139	27	1	10	74	0
86 NL	.264	141	432	46	114	22	1	12	57	0
87 AL	.250	143	512	51	128	13	1	18	62	1
88 AL	.226	85	265	20	60	10	0	3	16	0
89 NL	.239	125	355	19	85	15	0	5	34	1
90 NL	.277	107	303	25	84	22	0	2	26	1
91 NL	.234	69	171	12	40	7	1	3	13	0
Life	.264	1491	4979	474	1313	244	12	113	628	6
3 AVE	.252	100	276	19	70	15	0	3	24	1

JIMMY KEY

Position: Pitcher
Team: Toronto Blue Jays
Born: April 22, 1961 Huntsville, AL
Height: 6'1" **Weight:** 190 lbs.
Bats: right **Throws:** left
Acquired: Third-round pick in 6/82 free-agent draft

Player Summary	
Fantasy Value	$10 to $15
Card Value	3¢ to 5¢
Will	win 15
Can't	blow heat by hitters
Expect	crafty change of speeds
Don't Expect	bouts of wildness

Managers in a *Baseball America* survey said Key has the best changeup and best pickoff move in the AL. When he got his 100th win on August 26, Key joined Dave Stieb and Jim Clancy as the only Toronto pitchers with triple-figure wins. Key had arthroscopic rotator cuff surgery after the 1989 season, and it took him a few years to make it back. An All-Star for the first time in 1991, he uses a sinker as his No. 1 pitch. He also throws a curveball, slider, and changeup. Key varies speeds well and has the added advantage of excellent control. He whiffs three times more men than he walks. He allowed 12 homers in '91. He is a good fielder who keeps his teammates alert by working at a brisk pace. As a fantasy hurler, he's durable, dependable, and cheap (at $12). His 1992 commons aren't as promising.

Major League Pitching Register

	W	L	ERA	G	CG	IP	H	ER	BB	SO
84 AL	4	5	4.65	63	0	62.0	70	32	32	44
85 AL	14	6	3.00	35	3	212.2	188	71	50	85
86 AL	14	11	3.57	36	4	232.0	222	92	74	141
87 AL	17	8	2.76	36	8	261.0	210	80	66	161
88 AL	12	5	3.29	21	2	131.1	127	48	30	65
89 AL	13	14	3.88	33	5	216.0	226	93	27	118
90 AL	13	7	4.25	27	0	154.2	169	73	22	88
91 AL	16	12	3.05	33	2	209.1	207	71	44	125
Life	103	68	3.41	284	24	1479.0	1419	560	345	827
3 AVE	14	11	3.68	31	2	193.1	201	79	31	110

CURRENT PLAYERS

DARRYL KILE

Position: Pitcher
Team: Houston Astros
Born: Dec. 2, 1968 Garden Grove, CA
Height: 6'5" **Weight:** 185 lbs.
Bats: right **Throws:** right
Acquired: 30th-round pick in 6/87 free-agent draft

Player Summary	
Fantasy Value	$2 to $5
Card Value	5¢ to 10¢
Will	throw heat
Can't	prevent walks
Expect	poor K-to-walk ratio
Don't Expect	many complete games

Kile spent three years as a starter in the minors before advancing to the Astros as a reliever in 1991. One of several youngsters imported to fill bullpen vacancies created by departed free agents Juan Agosto, Larry Andersen, and Dave Smith, Kile showed enough promise to be given a slot in the regular rotation. He walked too many batters but he kept his ERA at a respectable level, especially considering his youth. He was Houston's youngest rotation regular since Floyd Bannister and Mark Lemongello in 1977. Kile, ordered to drop his slider out of fears it might injure his elbow, throws a 90 mph fastball, curve, and changeup. His best pro season was 1989, when he won 11 of his last 15 at Double-A Columbus and had a 1.64 ERA during that streak. He had a rough time at Triple-A in 1990, going 5-10 with a 6.64 ERA at Tucson. Houston expects Kile to be a key 1992 starter. He will be a surprise for your fantasy team for $3. There should be some interest in his 1992 cards; invest at prices less than a dime.

Major League Pitching Register

	W	L	ERA	G	CG	IP	H	ER	BB	SO
91 NL	7	11	3.69	37	0	153.2	144	63	84	100
Life	7	11	3.69	37	0	153.2	144	63	84	100

ERIC KING

Position: Pitcher
Team: Cleveland Indians
Born: April 10, 1964 Oxnard, CA
Height: 6'2" **Weight:** 218 lbs.
Bats: right **Throws:** right
Acquired: Traded from White Sox with Shawn Hillegas for Cory Snyder and Lindsay Foster, 12/90

Player Summary	
Fantasy Value	$2 to $4
Card Value	3¢ to 5¢
Will	win a dozen games
Can't	seem to finish
Expect	complete comeback
Don't Expect	many walks or Ks

When he's healthy, King is one of the game's most promising young pitchers. Disabled in each of the past three years, he had rebounded with strong performances. In '91, however, he wasn't so fortunate. King struggled through much of the season. His number of losses and lofty ERA was atypical for a pitcher with previous 11-4 and 12-4 seasons. King's problem was yielding more hits than innings pitched. In 1991, opposing batters compiled a .279 batting average, a .384 slugging percentage, and a .328 on-base average. A fastball-and-curveball pitcher, he doesn't get many strikeouts but usually has pretty good control. He gets a high number of grounders. He fields well and keeps runners close. If King's shoulder stays healthy, he should be a successful starter again. He's a modest risk at $3 for your fantasy team. His 1992 commons are huge risks.

Major League Pitching Register

	W	L	ERA	G	CG	IP	H	ER	BB	SO
86 AL	11	4	3.51	33	3	138.1	108	54	63	79
87 AL	6	9	4.89	55	0	116.0	111	63	60	89
88 AL	4	1	3.41	23	0	68.2	60	26	34	45
89 AL	9	10	3.39	25	1	159.1	144	60	64	72
90 AL	12	4	3.28	25	2	151.0	135	55	40	70
91 AL	6	11	4.60	25	2	150.2	166	77	44	59
Life	48	39	3.85	186	8	784.0	724	335	305	414
3 AVE	9	8	3.75	25	2	153.1	148	64	49	67

CURRENT PLAYERS

JEFF KING

Position: Third base
Team: Pittsburgh Pirates
Born: Dec. 26, 1964 Marion, IN
Height: 6'1" **Weight:** 180 lbs.
Bats: right **Throws:** right
Acquired: First-round pick in 6/86 free-agent draft

Player Summary	
Fantasy Value	$2 to $4
Card Value	3¢ to 5¢
Will	make contact
Can't	evade injury jinx
Expect	some pop in bat
Don't Expect	defensive lapses

King had earned Pittsburgh's everyday third base job before going on the disabled list with back problems on June 14. Surgery to repair the bulging disc in his lower back ended his season prematurely. Even if that injury heals, King's history of shoulder problems clouds his future as a third baseman. He has played first in the past and could shift across the diamond. There's nothing wrong with King's defense at third, where he shows good instincts, excellent reactions, and a surprisingly strong throwing arm. His bat will get him into the lineup somewhere. He had 14 homers and 53 RBI in 127 games in 1990, his only uninterrupted season. King doesn't strike out as much as other power-hitters. His hot second half in 1990 suggests that he could hit 20 to 25 homers over a full year. He was the first player picked in the nation in 1986. He needs to reprove his potential to card investors; don't purchase his 1992 commons until he does. He is a $3 fantasy draft.

Major League Batting Register

	BA	G	AB	R	H	2B	3B	HR	RBI	SB
89 NL	.195	75	215	31	42	13	3	5	19	4
90 NL	.245	127	371	46	91	17	1	14	53	3
91 NL	.239	33	109	16	26	1	1	4	18	3
Life	.229	235	695	93	159	31	5	23	90	10
2 AVE	.227	101	293	39	67	15	2	10	36	4

BOB KIPPER

Position: Pitcher
Team: Minnesota Twins
Born: July 8, 1964 Aurora, IL
Height: 6'2" **Weight:** 182 lbs.
Bats: right **Throws:** left
Acquired: Signed as a free agent, 12/91

Player Summary	
Fantasy Value	$1 to $3
Card Value	3¢ to 5¢
Will	surrender gophers
Can't	find strike zone
Expect	success against lefties
Don't Expect	switch to closer

Kipper's efforts to supply solid southpaw middle relief for the Pirates in 1991 were unsuccessful because he yielded more hits than innings pitched. He was clipped for an ERA of more than four and one-half, the worst on the Pittsburgh staff. In December, he signed on with Minnesota. A fastball-and-slider pitcher who also throws a changeup, Kipper has problems finding the strike zone and keeping the ball in the park. When he's right, he's adept at retiring lefthanded hitters—something he did very effectively in 1990. A good fielder, he keeps runners close. He's no help at all as an emergency starter, however. That has been tried. Kipper hopes to recapture the effectiveness he showed in both 1989 and '90. Don't do anything about his fantasy prospects unless you have no other choice. Don't bother with his 1992 commons.

Major League Pitching Register

	W	L	ERA	G	S	IP	H	ER	BB	SO
85 AL	0	1	21.60	2	0	3.1	7	8	3	0
85 NL	1	2	5.11	5	0	24.2	21	14	7	13
86 NL	6	8	4.03	20	0	114.0	123	51	34	81
87 NL	5	9	5.94	24	0	110.2	117	73	52	83
88 NL	2	6	3.74	50	0	65.0	54	27	26	39
89 NL	3	4	2.93	52	4	83.0	55	27	33	58
90 NL	5	2	3.02	41	3	62.2	41	21	26	35
91 NL	2	2	4.65	52	4	60.0	66	31	22	38
Life	24	34	4.33	246	11	523.1	487	252	203	347
3 AVE	3	3	3.46	48	4	68.1	55	26	27	44

CURRENT PLAYERS

JOE KLINK

Position: Pitcher
Team: Oakland Athletics
Born: Feb. 3, 1962 Johnstown, PA
Height: 5'11" **Weight:** 175 lbs.
Bats: left **Throws:** left
Acquired: Traded from Twins for Russ Kibler, 3/88

Player Summary	
Fantasy Value	$4 to $6
Card Value	3¢ to 5¢
Will	get crucial lefties out
Can't	take over as closer
Expect	lots of curves
Don't Expect	many gopher balls

Klink's fine 1991 sophomore season was impeded only by a broken foot, an injury incurred in June. With veteran Rick Honeycutt out of action early, Klink saw considerably more action and got more frequent calls as he won the confidence of Oakland manager Tony LaRussa. Klink is a sinking curveball specialist who doesn't bring heat but paints the corners. Often used to retire one or two key lefthanded hitters, he succeeds by allowing less than a hit per inning and keeping the ball in the park. Opponents compiled a .260 batting average, a .364 slugging percentage, and a .335 on-base average. He fans twice as many as he walks. Klink's best pro season was 1989, when he was used as a closer for Double-A Huntsville. He had a 4-4 record, 26 saves, and 2.82 ERA in 57 outings while fanning near one per inning. Even though he had good numbers in '91, he is a middle reliever on Oakland, spelling doom for his fantasy value. His nickel-priced 1992 cards are not good purchases.

Major League Pitching Register

	W	L	ERA	G	S	IP	H	ER	BB	SO
87 AL	0	1	6.65	12	0	23.0	37	17	11	17
90 AL	0	0	2.04	40	1	39.2	34	9	18	19
91 AL	10	3	4.35	62	2	62.0	60	30	21	34
Life	10	4	4.04	114	3	124.2	131	56	50	70
2 AVE	5	2	3.45	51	2	51.1	47	20	20	27

CHUCK KNOBLAUCH

Position: Second base
Team: Minnesota Twins
Born: July 7, 1968 Houston, TX
Height: 5'9" **Weight:** 175 lbs.
Bats: right **Throws:** right
Acquired: First-round pick in 6/89 free-agent draft

Player Summary	
Fantasy Value	$15 to $20
Card Value	15¢ to 25¢
Will	show great glove
Can't	hit the long ball
Expect	a rising average
Don't Expect	more Ks than walks

After beating out veteran Al Newman for Minnesota's second base job during 1991 spring training, Knoblauch lived up to manager Tom Kelly's confidence by notching a very respectable batting average, taking walks, stealing bases, and providing exceptional defense around the bag. In fact, Knoblauch played well enough to capture AL Rookie of the Year honors. Knoblauch's insertion into the lineup was one of the main reasons Minnesota won the World Championship. He had eight hits in the World Series. The former Texas A&M star is ideal at No. 2. A contact hitter who rarely strikes out, he is patient at the plate, has a good eye, and is adept at the hit-and-run. He also has good speed and good instincts. He hit .289 with two homers, 53 RBI, 23 swipes, and 74 runs scored at Double-A Orlando in 1990. He faces the sophomore jinx, so invest carefully, up to $20. Knoblauch's 1992 cards are deals at a quarter apiece. He comes from a baseball family; his father, Ray, and uncle Ed both played in the minors.

Major League Batting Register

	BA	G	AB	R	H	2B	3B	HR	RBI	SB
91 AL	.281	151	565	78	159	24	6	1	50	25
Life	.281	151	565	78	159	24	6	1	50	25

CURRENT PLAYERS

BILL KRUEGER

Position: Pitcher
Team: Seattle Mariners
Born: April 24, 1958 Waukegan, IL
Height: 6'5" **Weight:** 205 lbs.
Bats: left **Throws:** left
Acquired: Signed as a free agent, 12/90

Player Summary	
Fantasy Value	$6 to $8
Card Value	3¢ to 5¢
Will	often escape trouble
Can't	win without curve
Expect	lots of hits
Don't Expect	job in bullpen

Krueger has always done better as a starter than as a reliever. After breaking in with Oakland in 1983, he was released twice and traded twice before Seattle signed him as an extra bullpen arm. That was before the Mariners learned that Krueger works better when he develops a pitching plan in advance. Once known as a curveball specialist, he now gets outs by moving fastballs in and out and mixing pitches. He had a successful season though he yielded more than a hit per inning and failed to complete all but one of his starts. Krueger is adept at working with men on base and knows how to escape jams. He is a good fielder with a fine pickoff move. Get him cheaply at the draft for $7. His 1992 commons are not good investments.

Major League Pitching Register

	W	L	ERA	G	CG	IP	H	ER	BB	SO
83 AL	7	6	3.61	17	2	109.2	104	44	53	58
84 AL	10	10	4.75	26	1	142.0	156	75	85	61
85 AL	9	10	4.52	32	2	151.1	165	76	69	56
86 AL	1	2	6.03	11	0	34.1	40	23	13	10
87 AL	0	3	9.53	9	0	5.2	9	6	8	2
87 NL	0	0	0.00	2	0	2.1	3	0	1	2
88 NL	0	0	11.57	1	0	2.1	4	3	2	1
89 AL	3	2	3.84	34	0	93.2	96	40	33	72
90 AL	6	8	3.98	30	0	129.0	137	57	54	64
91 AL	11	8	3.60	35	1	175.0	194	70	60	91
Life	47	49	4.19	197	6	845.1	908	394	378	417
3 AVE	7	6	3.78	33	0	132.1	142	56	49	76

JOHN KRUK

Position: Outfield; first base
Team: Philadelphia Phillies
Born: Feb. 9, 1961 Charleston, WV
Height: 5'10" **Weight:** 204 lbs.
Bats: left **Throws:** left
Acquired: Traded from Padres with Randy Ready for Chris James, 6/89

Player Summary	
Fantasy Value	$23 to $28
Card Value	3¢ to 5¢
Will	hit to opposite field
Can't	avoid double-plays
Expect	run production
Don't Expect	regular All-Star play

Kruk's RBI bat boomed early last season, tying Mike Schmidt's mark for most RBI in the opening month (20). Three months later, Kruk was the lone Philadelphia representative on the NL All-Star squad. Kruk hit .309 as a rookie with the 1986 Padres and has been a quality hitter since. The owner of an inside-out swing that produces opposite-field power, he has little trouble with lefthanders. Because he thrives in clutch situations, he displaced Dale Murphy as Philadelphia's cleanup hitter in '91. Kruk doesn't have great speed but runs well enough to play left or right field, steal a dozen bases, and take an extra base on occasion. He's used most often as a first baseman or left fielder and is a good defensive player at both positions. Pay generously for his fantasy assistance, up to $28. Pay little for his undiscovered common-priced 1992 cards.

Major League Batting Register

	BA	G	AB	R	H	2B	3B	HR	RBI	SB
86 NL	.309	122	278	33	86	16	2	4	38	2
87 NL	.313	138	447	72	140	14	2	20	91	18
88 NL	.241	120	378	54	91	17	1	9	44	5
89 NL	.300	112	357	53	107	13	6	8	44	3
90 NL	.291	142	443	52	129	25	8	7	67	10
91 NL	.294	152	538	84	158	27	6	21	92	7
Life	.291	786	2441	348	711	112	25	69	376	45
3 AVE	.294	135	446	63	131	22	7	12	68	7

CURRENT PLAYERS

STEVE LAKE

Position: Catcher
Team: Philadelphia Phillies
Born: March 14, 1957 Inglewood, CA
Height: 6'1" **Weight:** 199 lbs.
Bats: right **Throws:** right
Acquired: Traded from Cardinals with Curt Ford for Milt Thompson, 12/88

Player Summary	
Fantasy Value	$1 to $2
Card Value	3¢ to 5¢
Will	play great defense
Can't	run or hit well
Expect	continued reserve role
Don't Expect	any power

If Lake could hit, he'd be an All-Star catcher every year. One of the best defensive receivers in the game, he had erased an amazing 50 percent plus of would-be base-stealers in his career. A career .240 hitter, Lake couldn't lift his average above that level in '91. He seldom bunts, never steals, and can't fatten his average with infield hits. Nor can he hit the ball over the fence. On the other hand, Lake's defense is the reverse of his offense. He knows enemy hitters, handles his pitchers well, and couples the cannon arm with a quick release. What more could a manager ask? He's never played in more than 74 games a year. His defense won't help your fantasy team much. He is a $1 catcher. His 1992 commons are not buys.

Major League Batting Register

	BA	G	AB	R	H	2B	3B	HR	RBI	SB
83 NL	.259	38	85	9	22	4	1	1	7	0
84 NL	.222	25	54	4	12	4	0	2	7	0
85 NL	.151	58	119	5	18	2	0	1	11	1
86 NL	.294	36	68	8	20	2	0	2	14	0
87 NL	.251	74	179	19	45	7	2	2	19	0
88 NL	.278	36	54	5	15	3	0	1	4	0
89 NL	.252	58	155	9	39	5	1	2	14	0
90 NL	.250	29	80	4	20	2	0	0	6	0
91 NL	.228	58	158	12	36	4	1	1	11	0
Life	.238	412	952	75	227	33	5	12	93	1
2 AVE	.240	58	157	11	38	5	1	2	13	0

DENNIS LAMP

Position: Pitcher
Team: Boston Red Sox
Born: Sept. 23, 1952 Los Angeles, CA
Height: 6'3" **Weight:** 215 lbs.
Bats: right **Throws:** right
Acquired: Signed as a free agent, 1/87

Player Summary	
Fantasy Value	$1 to $2
Card Value	3¢ to 5¢
Will	keep his team in game
Can't	throw as hard anymore
Expect	rivals to run and bunt
Don't Expect	return to 1985 form

Though he spent five years as a starter for the Cubs early in his career, Lamp has been used as a middle reliever for most of his 15 years in the majors. He went 11-0 for the first-place Blue Jays of 1985. A sinker-and-slider pitcher usually noted for good control, Lamp's flame flickered a bit in 1991. Lamp fans twice as many as he walks and allows about a hit per inning. He threw harder earlier in his career, but he still has a sound arm that allows him to work often. Lamp should provide some help in the middle innings. He is not a good fantasy investment, even at a couple of bucks. His 1992 commons will stay in the box.

Major League Pitching Register

	W	L	ERA	G	S	IP	H	ER	BB	SO
77 NL	0	2	6.30	11	0	30.0	43	21	8	12
78 NL	7	15	3.30	37	0	223.2	221	82	56	73
79 NL	11	10	3.50	38	0	200.1	223	78	46	86
80 NL	10	14	5.20	41	0	202.2	259	117	82	83
81 AL	7	6	2.41	27	0	127.0	103	34	43	71
82 AL	11	8	3.99	44	5	189.2	206	84	59	78
83 AL	7	7	3.71	49	15	116.1	123	48	29	44
84 AL	8	8	4.55	56	9	85.0	97	43	38	45
85 AL	11	0	3.32	53	2	105.2	96	39	27	68
86 AL	2	6	5.05	40	2	73.0	93	41	23	30
87 AL	1	3	5.08	36	0	56.2	76	32	22	36
88 AL	7	6	3.48	46	0	82.2	92	32	19	49
89 AL	4	2	2.32	42	2	112.1	96	29	27	61
90 AL	3	5	4.68	47	0	105.2	114	55	30	49
91 AL	6	3	4.70	51	0	92.0	100	48	31	57
Life	95	95	3.91	618	35	1802.2	1942	783	540	842
3 AVE	4	3	3.83	47	1	103.1	103	44	29	56

CURRENT PLAYERS

LES LANCASTER

Position: Pitcher
Team: Chicago Cubs
Born: April 21, 1962 Dallas, TX
Height: 6'2" **Weight:** 200 lbs.
Bats: right **Throws:** right
Acquired: Signed as a free agent, 6/85

Player Summary	
Fantasy Value	$6 to $8
Card Value	3¢ to 5¢
Will	top 50 games
Can't	seesaw from pen to rotation
Expect	excellent K-to-walk ratio
Don't Expect	dramatic ERA improvement

During his five-year career with the Cubs, Lancaster has been tried as both a starter and reliever. In 1991, he was used both ways. He started 10 games before the Cubs stuck him back in the bullpen. A control pitcher who fans three times more than he walks, Lancaster also throws more than his share of home run balls, though pitching in Wrigley Field doesn't help. He also has occasional control trouble, though he's a tough pitcher when he has good location of his fastball, slider, and changeup. He helps himself by holding base-runners close and fielding anything hit near him. Lancaster requires a pinch-hitter when his batting turn comes up in close ballgames. According to some scouts, Lancaster's performance will improve when and if he finds a steady role. His 1992 commons will not rise in value as long as he shuttles from the bullpen to the rotation. But he can offer some fantasy stats for $7.

Major League Pitching Register

	W	L	ERA	G	S	IP	H	ER	BB	SO
87 NL	8	3	4.90	27	0	132.1	138	72	51	78
88 NL	4	6	3.78	44	5	85.2	89	36	34	36
89 NL	4	2	1.36	42	8	72.2	60	11	15	56
90 NL	9	5	4.62	55	6	109.0	121	56	40	65
91 NL	9	7	3.52	64	0	156.0	150	61	49	102
Life	34	23	3.82	232	22	555.2	558	236	189	337
3 AVE	7	5	3.41	54	6	112.1	110	43	35	74

BILL LANDRUM

Position: Pitcher
Team: Pittsburgh Pirates
Born: Aug. 17, 1958 Columbia, SC
Height: 6'2" **Weight:** 185 lbs.
Bats: right **Throws:** right
Acquired: Signed as a free agent, 1/89

Player Summary	
Fantasy Value	$15 to $20
Card Value	3¢ to 5¢
Will	perform well as closer
Can't	carry relief load alone
Expect	3-1 K-to-walk ratio
Don't Expect	hitters to take him deep

Landrum was discarded by the Reds, Cubs, and White Sox before blossoming into a closer with the 1989 Pirates. He saved 26 games to go with a 2-3 record and 1.67 ERA for that team. He succeeds by working fast, changing speeds, and throwing strikes. He mixes his cut fastball with a hard forkball that destroys righthanded hitters. He also throws a curveball and changeup. Landrum is a good fielder with a so-so pickoff move and a weak bat. Sharing closer chores with Stan Belinda in 1991, Landrum got off to a fast start, converting his first nine save opportunities. His ERA was too high for a sole closer role, but the Pirates don't like to rely on a single relief ace. Opponents compiled a .252 batting average, a .329 slugging percentage, and a .296 on-base percentage in '91. Landrum's stubble makes him easily recognizable on the bullpen bench. His 1992 commons don't measure up. He is worth $15 for your fantasy team.

Major League Pitching Register

	W	L	ERA	G	S	IP	H	ER	BB	SO
86 NL	0	0	6.75	10	0	13.1	23	10	4	14
87 NL	3	2	4.71	44	2	65.0	68	34	34	42
88 NL	1	0	5.84	7	0	12.1	19	8	3	6
89 NL	2	3	1.67	56	26	81.0	60	15	28	51
90 NL	7	3	2.13	54	13	71.2	69	17	21	39
91 NL	4	4	3.18	61	17	76.1	76	27	19	45
Life	17	12	3.13	232	58	319.2	315	111	109	197
3 AVE	4	3	2.32	57	19	76.1	68	20	23	45

CURRENT PLAYERS

CEDRIC LANDRUM

Position: Outfield
Team: Chicago Cubs
Born: Sept. 3, 1963 Butler, AL
Height: 5'9" **Weight:** 165 lbs.
Bats: left **Throws:** right
Acquired: Signed as a free agent, 11/85

Player Summary
Fantasy Value	$4 to $7
Card Value	10¢ to 15¢
Will	steal bases in bunches
Can't	produce any power
Expect	strong defense
Don't Expect	a return to minors

Before the May 28 promotion of Landrum, the Cubs had seldom been accused of utilizing speed as an offensive weapon. He has the potential to change that tradition. He was leading the Triple-A American Association in steals when the Cubs called him up. His final stats for Iowa in 1991 were: a .336 batting average, one homer, 11 RBI, five walks, 21 strikeouts, 131 at bats, 14 runs scored, and 13 stolen bases. Landrum got his chance when Jim Essian became the Chicago manager in May. The rookie provided the Cubs with good defense and great base-running. In 1990 at Iowa, he batted .296 with 46 stolen bases, 71 runs scored, 43 walks, and 63 strikeouts in 372 at bats. He led four minor leagues in stolen bases. Should he improve his hitting, he could win an everyday berth. He had a .279 slugging percentage and a .313 on-base percentage for Chicago in '91. He was caught stealing only five times. Landrum has the speed to become a solid leadoff man. His dime-priced 1992 cards aren't savory investments yet. With his speed, though, he has a fantasy future at $6.

Major League Batting Register
	BA	G	AB	R	H	2B	3B	HR	RBI	SB
91 NL	.233	56	86	28	20	2	1	0	6	27
Life	.233	56	86	28	20	2	1	0	6	27

MARK LANGSTON

Position: Pitcher
Team: California Angels
Born: Aug. 20, 1960 San Diego, CA
Height: 6'2" **Weight:** 190 lbs.
Bats: right **Throws:** left
Acquired: Signed as a free agent, 12/89

Player Summary
Fantasy Value	$25 to $30
Card Value	5¢ to 10¢
Will	win 15
Can't	keep ball in park
Expect	lots of Ks
Don't Expect	ERA over 4.00

Langston won three strikeout crowns before California gave him a five-year, $16 million contract during the 1989 winter meetings. Although the Angels were generous with the money, they hardly provided sufficient support. Langston got only 18 runs in his 17 losses of 1990, though he hurt himself by walking 104 hitters. Determined to be more aggressive in '91, he sharpened his control while taking 12 of his first 14. The club's improved offense and defense helped. In addition to throwing a fastball, slider, and changeup, Langston changes speeds on his curveball. Guessing which one he's going to use is almost as distracting to batters as the leg-kick in his windup. The hard-throwing lefthander has won several Gold Gloves for his defense. His nickel-priced 1992 cards are reasonable purchases. His Ks give him a higher fantasy standing, up to $30.

Major League Pitching Register
	W	L	ERA	G	CG	IP	H	ER	BB	SO
84 AL	17	10	3.40	35	5	225.0	188	85	118	204
85 AL	7	14	5.47	24	2	126.2	122	77	91	72
86 AL	12	14	4.85	37	9	239.1	234	129	123	245
87 AL	19	13	3.84	35	14	272.0	242	116	114	262
88 AL	15	11	3.34	35	9	261.1	222	97	110	235
89 AL	4	5	3.56	10	2	73.1	60	29	19	60
89 NL	12	9	2.39	24	6	176.2	138	47	93	175
90 AL	10	17	4.40	33	5	223.0	215	109	104	195
91 AL	19	8	3.00	34	7	246.1	190	82	96	183
Life	115	101	3.76	267	59	1843.2	1611	771	868	1631
3 AVE	15	13	3.34	34	7	239.1	201	89	104	204

CURRENT PLAYERS

RAY LANKFORD

Position: Outfield
Team: St. Louis Cardinals
Born: June 5, 1967 Modesto, CA
Height: 5'11" **Weight:** 180 lbs.
Bats: left **Throws:** left
Acquired: Third-round pick in 6/87 free-agent draft

Player Summary
Fantasy Value	$22 to $28
Card Value	10¢ to 15¢
Will	vie for steals title
Can't	create consistent power
Expect	a better average
Don't Expect	less than strong defense

Lankford responded well when asked to become the Cardinal leadoff man on July 29. Using his bat and speed to spark the St. Louis offense, he cracked a league high in triples. He also crashed the 40-steal plateau despite an average that was struggling to reach .250. Manager Joe Torre believes Lankford will develop into a premier base-stealer who will swipe 70 per year, putting him into contention for league leadership. He strikes out three times more than he walks, a fallacy the Cards want to correct. Lankford's gap power is suited to his home ballpark and he should hit more homers now that the St. Louis fences have been moved in. In 1990 at Triple-A Louisville, he hit .260 with 10 homers, 25 doubles, 29 stolen bases, 72 RBI, and 61 runs scored. He was named the No. 3 prospect in the American Association by *Baseball America*. Pay a dime for his second-year 1992 cards. Make him a fantasy draft at $30 or less. If his hitting rises to the level of his defense and base-running, Lankford will be an All-Star.

Major League Batting Register
	BA	G	AB	R	H	2B	3B	HR	RBI	SB
90 NL	.286	39	126	12	36	10	1	3	12	8
91 NL	.251	151	566	83	142	23	15	9	69	44
Life	.257	190	692	95	178	33	16	12	81	52

CARNEY LANSFORD

Position: Third base
Team: Oakland Athletics
Born: Feb. 7, 1957 San Jose, CA
Height: 6'2" **Weight:** 195 lbs.
Bats: right **Throws:** right
Acquired: Traded from Red Sox with Garry Hancock and Jerry King for Jeff Newman and Tony Armas, 12/82

Player Summary
Fantasy Value	$12 to $16
Card Value	3¢ to 5¢
Will	reclaim job
Can't	recapture power
Expect	fine defense
Don't Expect	anything to slow him

Lansford, the regular third baseman of the Athletics, missed most of the 1991 season while recuperating from a knee injury suffered in a New Year's Eve snowmobile accident. He was unsuccessful in a July comeback bid and returned to the disabled list. The healthy Lansford is a defensive stalwart who swings a line-drive bat. He remains a peerless fielder, however, with only nine errors charged against him in 1990. He was one of the game's toughest hitters to fan. He hits to all fields and is adept at moving runners along. A tough ballplayer, he is a good-looking fantasy gamble at $14. His 1992 commons are not good investments in the short term.

Major League Batting Register
	BA	G	AB	R	H	2B	3B	HR	RBI	SB
78 AL	.294	121	453	63	133	23	2	8	52	20
79 AL	.287	157	654	114	188	30	5	19	79	20
80 AL	.261	151	602	87	157	27	3	15	80	14
81 AL	.336	102	399	61	134	23	3	4	52	15
82 AL	.301	128	482	65	145	28	4	11	63	9
83 AL	.308	80	299	43	92	16	2	10	45	3
84 AL	.300	151	597	70	179	31	5	14	74	9
85 AL	.277	98	401	51	111	18	2	13	46	2
86 AL	.284	151	591	80	168	16	4	19	72	16
87 AL	.289	151	554	89	160	27	4	19	76	27
88 AL	.279	150	556	80	155	20	2	7	57	29
89 AL	.336	148	551	81	185	28	2	2	52	37
90 AL	.268	134	507	58	136	15	1	3	50	16
91 AL	.063	5	16	0	1	0	0	0	1	0
Life	.292	1727	6662	942	1944	302	39	144	799	217
2 AVE	.303	141	529	70	161	22	2	3	51	27

CURRENT PLAYERS

BARRY LARKIN

Position: Shortstop
Team: Cincinnati Reds
Born: April 28, 1964 Cincinnati, OH
Height: 6' **Weight:** 185 lbs.
Bats: right **Throws:** right
Acquired: First-round pick in 6/85 free-agent draft

Player Summary	
Fantasy Value	$33 to $38
Card Value	10¢ to 15¢
Will	bid for 30-30 club
Can't	oust All-Star Ozzie Smith
Expect	fine average and speed
Don't Expect	defensive lapses

Most scouts agree that Larkin has a stronger arm than Ozzie Smith, that his range and agility are just as good, and that he's a better hitter with more power. Smith, who makes fewer errors, always beats Larkin in the fan voting for the All-Star team. NL managers voted Larkin the league's most exciting player. His bat produced five home runs in two games early in the '91 campaign and an 18-game hitting streak late. The two-time All-American (from Michigan University) and four-time All-Star had career bests in home runs and RBI. He compiled a .506 slugging percentage and a .378 on-base average in '91. The Cincinnati native stole 30 times in 35 tries in 1990 and went on to hit .353 in the World Series. He has a good eye and walks as often as he strikes out. For $40 or less, he's a fantasy gift. His 1992 cards are just as inviting, especially for a dime.

Major League Batting Register

	BA	G	AB	R	H	2B	3B	HR	RBI	SB
86 NL	.283	41	159	27	45	4	3	3	19	8
87 NL	.244	125	439	64	107	16	2	12	43	21
88 NL	.296	151	588	91	174	32	5	12	56	40
89 NL	.342	97	325	47	111	14	4	4	36	10
90 NL	.301	158	614	85	185	25	6	7	67	30
91 NL	.302	123	464	88	140	27	4	20	69	24
Life	.294	695	2589	402	762	118	24	58	290	133
3 AVE	.311	126	468	73	145	22	5	10	57	21

GENE LARKIN

Position: Outfield; designated hitter
Team: Minnesota Twins
Born: Oct. 24, 1962 Astoria, NY
Height: 6'3" **Weight:** 205 lbs.
Bats: both **Throws:** right
Acquired: 20th-round pick in 6/84 free-agent draft

Player Summary	
Fantasy Value	$2 to $3
Card Value	3¢ to 5¢
Will	hit to all fields
Can't	steal bases
Expect	good defense
Don't Expect	average under .270

Though Larkin hit well over .300 in all four of his minor league seasons, he has missed that plateau in five big league campaigns. After breaking Lou Gehrig's hitting records at Columbia University, Larkin was heralded as a can't-miss prospect. He made the majors, but hardly lived up to the hype. Instead, he's been a designated hitter, back-up first baseman, fill-in outfielder, and occasional pinch-hitter. He has never played in 150 games, topped 70 RBI, or hit home runs in double figures. He is a $2 fantasy player and a commons-priced 1992 card buy. He was 2 for 4 in the Series with an RBI. The switch-hitting Larkin bats for a higher average righthanded but has more power as a lefty. A contact hitter who uses all fields, he walks more often than he strikes out. Because he doesn't deliver power in a ballpark conducive to the long ball, Larkin is likely to be backup again.

Major League Batting Register

	BA	G	AB	R	H	2B	3B	HR	RBI	SB
87 AL	.266	85	233	23	62	11	2	4	28	1
88 AL	.267	149	505	56	135	30	2	8	70	3
89 AL	.267	136	446	61	119	25	1	6	46	5
90 AL	.269	119	401	46	108	26	4	5	42	5
91 AL	.286	98	255	34	73	14	1	2	19	2
Life	.270	587	1840	220	497	106	10	25	205	16
3 AVE	.272	118	367	47	100	22	2	4	36	4

CURRENT PLAYERS

MIKE LaVALLIERE

Position: Catcher
Team: Pittsburgh Pirates
Born: Aug. 18, 1960 Charlotte, NC
Height: 5'10" **Weight:** 205 lbs.
Bats: left **Throws:** right
Acquired: Traded from Cardinals with Mike Dunne and Andy Van Slyke for Tony Pena, 4/87

Player Summary	
Fantasy Value	$3 to $5
Card Value	3¢ to 5¢
Will	play good defense
Can't	get homers or swipes
Expect	platoon against righties
Don't Expect	more Ks than walks

Before the 1991 season started, LaValliere followed a conditioning regimen that included running, lifting weights, and reducing his body fat. That routine paid off in more playing time and a better batting average. A contact hitter who walks more often than he strikes out, he doesn't hit homers or steal bases but does supply defensive strength (including a fine throwing arm) that would merit a Gold Glove if Benito Santiago weren't in the league. LaValliere has a strong, accurate arm and handles pitchers well. A two-time .300 hitter, he murders righthanded pitching and seldom faces anything else. The notorious fastball hitter gets a steady diet of breaking balls. He is a former high school and college hockey player. A platoon catcher, he is worth $4 at the draft. His 1992 commons are not investments.

Major League Batting Register

	BA	G	AB	R	H	2B	3B	HR	RBI	SB
84 NL	.000	6	7	0	0	0	0	0	0	0
85 NL	.147	12	34	2	5	1	0	0	6	0
86 NL	.234	110	303	18	71	10	2	3	30	0
87 NL	.300	121	340	33	102	19	0	1	36	0
88 NL	.261	120	352	24	92	18	0	2	47	3
89 NL	.316	68	190	15	60	10	0	2	23	0
90 NL	.258	96	279	27	72	15	0	3	31	0
91 NL	.289	108	336	25	97	11	2	3	41	2
Life	.271	641	1841	144	499	84	4	14	214	5
3 AVE	.284	91	268	22	76	12	1	3	32	1

TERRY LEACH

Position: Pitcher
Team: Minnesota Twins
Born: March 13, 1954 Selma, AL
Height: 6' **Weight:** 191 lbs.
Bats: right **Throws:** right
Acquired: Signed as a free agent, 4/90

Player Summary	
Fantasy Value	$1 to $2
Card Value	3¢ to 5¢
Will	work 40 games
Can't	return to rotation
Expect	a confusing windup
Don't Expect	lots of free passes

One of the unsung heroes of Minnesota's miraculous Summer of '91, submarining reliever Leach is another example of a pitcher who recovered from rotator cuff surgery. He began his career with the 1981 Mets, pitching a 10-inning one-hitter in '82. A middle reliever through most of his career, Leach made a career-high 12 starts during his strong 1987 campaign. Because he doesn't have much velocity on his sinker or curve, he depends upon location and his unorthodox windup to confuse enemy hitters. He's most effective against righties. Leach keeps the ball in the park. His lone '91 weakness was yielding more than a hit per inning. Though he's a good fielder, Leach is an easy mark for would-be base-stealers. He is of little use to fantasy managers or card investors.

Major League Pitching Register

	W	L	ERA	G	S	IP	H	ER	BB	SO
81 NL	1	1	2.55	21	0	35.1	26	10	12	16
82 NL	2	1	4.17	21	3	45.1	46	21	18	30
85 NL	3	4	2.91	22	1	55.2	48	18	14	30
86 NL	0	0	2.70	6	0	6.2	6	2	3	4
87 NL	11	1	3.22	44	0	131.1	132	47	29	61
88 NL	7	2	2.54	52	3	92.0	95	26	24	51
89 NL	0	0	4.22	10	0	21.1	19	10	4	2
89 AL	5	6	4.15	30	0	73.2	78	34	36	34
90 AL	2	5	3.20	55	2	81.2	84	29	21	46
91 AL	1	2	3.61	50	0	67.1	82	27	14	32
Life	32	22	3.30	311	9	610.1	616	224	175	306
3 AVE	3	4	3.69	48	1	81.2	88	33	25	38

CURRENT PLAYERS

TIM LEARY

Position: Pitcher
Team: New York Yankees
Born: Dec. 23, 1958 Santa Monica, CA
Height: 6'3" **Weight:** 205 lbs.
Bats: right **Throws:** right
Acquired: Traded from Reds with Van Snider for Hal Morris and Rodney Imes, 12/89

Player Summary
Fantasy Value	$2 to $4
Card Value	3¢ to 5¢
Will	yield too many hits
Can't	shake loser tag
Expect	one last comeback
Don't Expect	return of 1988 form

If Leary can hang on, maybe an expansion team will take him. His figures, declining steadily over four years since his best year with the 1988 Dodgers, hit rock bottom last year. Even the pitching-poor Yankees couldn't take the risk of using him. He had made 18 starts before New York put him in the bullpen. He had an embarrassing ERA near six and one-half. Too many walks was a problem, but too many hits per inning—especially of the four-base variety—was the biggest one. Leary throws a fastball, slider, curve, and split-fingered fastball but seemed to have lost confidence in 1991. He has some strikeout potential but needs to revitalize before fantasy managers should move on him. He has a lower than 4.00 lifetime ERA, so he is likely to get another chance. His 1992 commons aren't promising.

Major League Pitching Register
	W	L	ERA	G	CG	IP	H	ER	BB	SO
81 NL	0	0	0.00	1	0	2.0	0	0	1	3
83 NL	1	1	3.38	2	1	10.2	15	4	4	9
84 NL	3	3	4.02	20	0	53.2	61	24	18	29
85 AL	1	4	4.05	5	0	33.1	40	15	8	29
86 AL	12	12	4.21	33	2	188.1	216	88	53	110
87 NL	3	11	4.76	39	0	107.2	121	57	36	61
88 NL	17	11	2.91	35	9	228.2	201	74	56	180
89 NL	8	14	3.52	33	2	207.0	205	81	68	123
90 AL	9	19	4.11	31	6	208.0	202	95	78	138
91 AL	4	10	6.49	28	1	120.2	150	87	57	83
Life	58	85	4.07	227	22	1160.0	1211	525	379	765
3 AVE	7	14	4.42	31	3	178.2	186	88	68	115

MANNY LEE

Position: Shortstop
Team: Toronto Blue Jays
Born: June 17, 1965 San Pedro de Macoris, Dominican Republic
Height: 5'9" **Weight:** 161 lbs.
Bats: both **Throws:** right
Acquired: Drafted from Astros, 12/84

Player Summary
Fantasy Value	$3 to $6
Card Value	3¢ to 5¢
Will	play solid shortstop
Can't	hit for power
Expect	return to bench
Don't Expect	bat to wake up

When Toronto traded Tony Fernandez in the December 1990 deal that landed Roberto Alomar, they knew they had a fine replacement in Lee. Though he does not hit like Fernandez, Lee carries a capable glove. As a second baseman, he led the league in fielding percentage. He even hit .291 in 116 games despite experiencing shoulder problems in 1988. Lee's 1991 campaign was not so fortunate. His average hovered below .240 much of the season, he failed to generate any power, and he struck out four times more often than he walked. Yet he was the shortstop on a pennant-contender because he has the quickness to reach balls others can't. Sometimes, he doesn't handle them cleanly or make accurate off-balance throws. The best thing about Lee's hitting is that it's the same from both sides. His lack of power keeps his fantasy value peaked at $6. His 1992 commons aren't likely to rise in value much.

Major League Batting Register
	BA	G	AB	R	H	2B	3B	HR	RBI	SB
85 AL	.200	64	40	9	8	0	0	0	0	1
86 AL	.205	35	78	8	16	0	1	1	7	0
87 AL	.256	56	121	14	31	2	3	1	11	2
88 AL	.291	116	381	38	111	16	3	2	38	3
89 AL	.260	99	300	27	78	9	2	3	34	4
90 AL	.243	117	391	45	95	12	4	6	41	3
91 AL	.234	138	445	41	104	18	3	0	29	7
Life	.252	625	1756	182	443	57	16	13	160	20
3 AVE	.244	118	379	38	92	13	3	3	35	5

CURRENT PLAYERS

MARK LEE

Position: Pitcher
Team: Milwaukee Brewers
Born: July 20, 1964 Williston, ND
Height: 6'3" **Weight:** 200 lbs.
Bats: left **Throws:** left
Acquired: Signed as a free agent, 5/90

Player Summary	
Fantasy Value	$1 to $3
Card Value	5¢ to 10¢
Will	keep hits down
Can't	always keep ball in park
Expect	more middle relief
Don't Expect	many walks or whiffs

Lee broke into pro ball in 1985 and has been used exclusively as a reliever since, except for one unfortunate season as a minor league starter. The hard-throwing southpaw assumed his heaviest workload in 1991, when he appeared more than 50 times for Milwaukee in his first full big league campaign. Used most often as a set-up man, Lee responded well despite occasional lapses of control and a tendency to throw too many home run balls. He yielded less than a hit per inning, and opponents compiled a .283 batting average, a .453 slugging percentage, and a .362 on-base percentage against him in 1991. Lee had given hint of things to come at Triple-A Denver in 1990, when he fanned 35 hitters in 28 innings pitched. He always had excellent control during his minor league apprenticeship. Lee is likely to continue in his 1991 role as a lefthanded middle-innings reliever. Skip his overpriced rookie 1992 cards. Fantasy managers should view his early relief career with suspicion when rating his fantasy outlook.

Major League Pitching Register

	W	L	ERA	G	S	IP	H	ER	BB	SO
88 AL	0	0	3.60	4	0	5.0	6	2	1	0
90 AL	1	0	2.11	11	0	21.1	20	5	4	14
91 AL	2	5	3.86	62	1	67.2	72	29	31	43
Life	3	5	3.45	77	1	94.0	98	36	36	57

CRAIG LEFFERTS

Position: Pitcher
Team: San Diego Padres
Born: Sept. 29, 1957 Munich, West Germany
Height: 6'1" **Weight:** 210 lbs.
Bats: left **Throws:** left
Acquired: Signed as a free agent, 12/89

Player Summary	
Fantasy Value	$20 to $23
Card Value	3¢ to 5¢
Will	trim ERA
Can't	yield as many hits
Expect	pinpoint control
Don't Expect	nightmare to continue

Lefferts was a solid southpaw reliever before experiencing the worst season of his nine-year career in 1991. He is unique with his headlong dash from the bullpen, but he had nothing else to distinguish himself in 1991. He yielded more than a hit per inning and didn't fan too many batters. No wonder he blew as many saves as he did. Lefferts did manage to save more than 20 games, but he's had much better success in other years. Perhaps the strain of working at least 50 games every season is taking a toll. It's not surprising that he had elbow and shoulder problems in the past. A screwball specialist who also throws a slider and fastball, Lefferts helps himself as a good fielder with a fine pickoff move. He's an underpriced fantasy closer, available for $20. His 1992 cards should stay at their commons prices.

Major League Pitching Register

	W	L	ERA	G	S	IP	H	ER	BB	SO
83 NL	3	4	3.13	56	1	89.0	80	31	29	60
84 NL	3	4	2.13	62	10	105.2	88	25	24	56
85 NL	7	6	3.35	60	2	83.1	75	31	30	48
86 NL	9	8	3.09	83	4	107.2	98	37	44	72
87 NL	5	5	3.83	77	6	98.2	92	42	33	57
88 NL	3	8	2.92	64	11	92.1	74	30	23	58
89 NL	2	4	2.69	70	20	107.0	93	32	22	71
90 NL	7	5	2.52	56	23	78.2	68	22	22	60
91 NL	1	6	3.91	54	23	69.0	74	30	14	48
Life	40	50	3.03	582	100	831.1	742	280	241	530
3 AVE	3	5	2.97	60	22	85.1	78	28	19	60

CURRENT PLAYERS

CHARLIE LEIBRANDT

Position: Pitcher
Team: Atlanta Braves
Born: Oct. 4, 1956 Chicago, IL
Height: 6'3" **Weight:** 200 lbs.
Bats: right **Throws:** left
Acquired: Traded from Royals with Rick Luecken for Gerald Perry and Jim Lemasters, 12/89

Player Summary	
Fantasy Value	$5 to $8
Card Value	3¢ to 5¢
Will	supply quality
Can't	prevent gophers
Expect	frequent off-speed stuff
Don't Expect	many walks

Leibrandt's ability to keep batters off stride by changing speeds paid big dividends for the Braves in 1991. A control pitcher who does not throw hard, he uses savvy and off-speed pitches to succeed. The slider is his best pitch but he also uses a fastball, curve, and baffling changeup designed to throttle batters' timing. He had a tough Series, including throwing an off-speed pitch in the wheelhouse of Kirby Puckett. A fine example to the young but sometimes erratic Atlanta pitching staff, Leibrandt fanned two batters for every walk in '91. He seldom went all the way but worked deep into most of his starts. He will help any fantasy team for $6. His 1992 commons, however, are about as cold as they come.

Major League Pitching Register

	W	L	ERA	G	CG	IP	H	ER	BB	SO
79 NL	0	0	0.00	3	0	4.1	2	0	2	1
80 NL	10	9	4.25	36	5	173.2	200	82	54	62
81 NL	1	1	3.60	7	1	30.0	28	12	15	9
82 NL	5	7	5.10	36	0	107.2	130	61	48	34
84 NL	11	7	3.63	23	0	143.2	158	58	38	53
85 AL	17	9	2.69	33	8	237.2	223	71	68	108
86 AL	14	11	4.09	35	8	231.1	238	105	63	108
87 AL	16	11	3.41	35	8	240.1	235	91	74	151
88 AL	13	12	3.19	35	7	243.0	244	86	62	125
89 AL	5	11	5.14	33	3	161.0	196	92	54	73
90 NL	9	11	3.16	24	5	162.1	164	57	35	76
91 NL	15	13	3.49	36	1	229.2	212	89	56	128
Life	116	102	3.68	336	46	1964.2	2030	804	569	928
3 AVE	10	12	3.87	31	3	184.1	191	79	48	92

MARK LEITER

Position: Pitcher
Team: Detroit Tigers
Born: April 13, 1963 Joliet, IL
Height: 6'3" **Weight:** 210 lbs.
Bats: right **Throws:** right
Acquired: Traded from Yankees for Torey Lovullo, 4/91

Player Summary	
Fantasy Value	$2 to $4
Card Value	3¢ to 5¢
Will	keep hitters off base
Can't	prevent gophers
Expect	more wins
Don't Expect	bouts of wildness

Leiter's stock wasn't very high when the pitching-short Yankees let him go in a spring training trade. Only the Tigers—just as desperate for bodies to populate their pitching staff—were willing to take a flyer on the marginal prospect. Their timing couldn't have been better. Given a chance to pitch, Leiter caught fire as the summer heated up. Opponents compiled a .245 batting average, a .397 slugging percentage, and a .316 on-base average in '91. He whiffs twice the number he walks and allows less than a hit per inning. His major problem is a tendency to yield too many gopher balls (16 in '91). He started his career as a promising righty for the Yankees, but he could not stay healthy. Between being on the disabled list and the Columbus-New York shuttle, he could not nail down a spot. He figures to be a key man in Detroit's 1992 rotation. He is not a sure thing, so keep your fantasy bids to $4. His 1992 commons are not good buys yet.

Major League Pitching Register

	W	L	ERA	G	S	IP	H	ER	BB	SO
90 AL	1	1	6.84	8	0	26.1	33	20	9	21
91 AL	9	7	4.21	38	1	134.2	125	63	50	103
Life	10	8	4.64	46	1	161.0	158	83	59	124

CURRENT PLAYERS

SCOTT LEIUS

Position: Third base
Team: Minnesota Twins
Born: Sept. 24, 1965 Yonkers, NY
Height: 6'3" **Weight:** 185 lbs.
Bats: right **Throws:** right
Acquired: 13th-round pick in 6/86 free-agent draft

Player Summary
Fantasy Value	$3 to $6
Card Value	3¢ to 5¢
Will	play solid defense
Can't	utilize Homerdome fences
Expect	platooning at third
Don't Expect	return ticket to farms

Although shortstop is his natural position, rookie Leius formed a righty-lefty third base platoon with Mike Pagliarulo in 1991. Leius, who had one strong minor league season to go with one decent campaign and three weak ones, proved to be a pleasant surprise in the majors. He hit .357 with a homer in the Series. He had a .417 slugging percentage and a .286 batting average in '91. Not unfamiliar with a glove, he was the managers' choice as the best defensive shortstop in the Double-A Southern League in 1989. He hit .303 with four homers, 22 doubles, and 45 RBI at Orlando that year. At Triple-A Portland in 1991, he hit .229, with two homers, 13 doubles, 23 RBI, 34 runs scored, 35 walks, and 66 strikeouts. Leius has good range, a strong throwing arm, and good reactions. He played the new position well. As a hitter, he doesn't have much power but compensates by making good contact. If his hitting improves, Leius is likely to receive more playing time. He is a $4 fantasy corner man and middle infielder, and his 1992 commons are not bad endeavors.

Major League Batting Register
	BA	G	AB	R	H	2B	3B	HR	RBI	SB
90 AL	.240	14	25	4	6	1	0	1	4	0
91 AL	.286	109	199	35	57	7	2	5	20	5
Life	.281	123	224	39	63	8	2	6	24	5

MARK LEMKE

Position: Infield
Team: Atlanta Braves
Born: Aug. 13, 1965 Utica, NY
Height: 5'9" **Weight:** 167 lbs.
Bats: both **Throws:** right
Acquired: 27th-round pick in 6/83 free-agent draft

Player Summary
Fantasy Value	$1 to $3
Card Value	3¢ to 5¢
Will	produce great glove
Can't	restore minors power
Expect	solid pinch-running
Don't Expect	average over .250

As Jack Buck referred to him, "the incredible Lemke" had an outstanding World Series. "Dirt" hit .417 with three triples and a double during the affair. He spent last season platooning at second base with lefty-hitting Jeff Treadway and serving as a defensive replacement and occasional pinch-hitter. Since Lemke was vastly superior as a fielder and Treadway was clearly the better hitter, critics joked that the two could be fused into a single All-Star. Lemke, who can also play third, played outstanding defense at second. In the pinch, however, he delivered with the precision of a seasoned veteran. He was Atlanta's most prolific pinch-hitter during the '91 campaign. A contact hitter who walks as often as he strikes out, he enjoys much more success against left-handed pitching. Because of the Series, his 1992 cards will enjoy a slight surge of interest before settling back to their commons level. He is a $2 part-time fantasy second baseman.

Major League Batting Register
	BA	G	AB	R	H	2B	3B	HR	RBI	SB
88 NL	.224	16	58	8	13	4	0	0	2	0
89 NL	.182	14	55	4	10	2	1	2	10	0
90 NL	.226	102	239	22	54	13	0	0	21	0
91 NL	.234	136	269	36	63	11	2	2	23	1
Life	.225	268	621	70	140	30	3	4	56	1
2 AVE	.230	119	254	29	59	12	1	1	22	1

DARREN LEWIS

Position: Outfield
Team: San Francisco Giants
Born: Aug. 28, 1967 Berkeley, CA
Height: 6' **Weight:** 175 lbs.
Bats: right **Throws:** right
Acquired: Traded from Athletics with Pedro Pena for Ernest Riles, 12/90

Player Summary	
Fantasy Value	$4 to $6
Card Value	10¢ to 15¢
Will	play superb center
Can't	hit homers yet
Expect	more steals
Don't Expect	many strikeouts

When Willie McGee was disabled last July, the Giants went to Lewis for a replacement. He responded so well that manager Roger Craig predicted Lewis would be the team's leadoff hitter for a dozen years. He was able to take a base on balls and show some speed on the base paths. He notched a .311 slugging percentage and a .358 on-base average. When he learns NL pitchers and masters base-stealing techniques, he may contend for leadership in steals. At Phoenix in '91, he hit .340, with 32 stolen bases, 52 RBI, 41 walks, and 36 strikeouts in 315 at bats. He hit .296 with 21 stolen bases at Double-A Huntsville in 1990, and hit .291 with 16 swipes at Triple-A Tacoma that year. When McGee returned, Craig decided to move him to right field and leave Lewis in center. He makes good contact and has the ability to pull the ball. Though he doesn't throw well, he's an absolute gazelle in center. Once he becomes a starter, his fantasy stats will justify an bid of $6. His 1992 cards' outlook is sunny at a dime apiece.

Major League Batting Register

	BA	G	AB	R	H	2B	3B	HR	RBI	SB
90 AL	.229	25	35	4	8	0	0	0	1	2
91 NL	.248	72	222	41	55	5	3	1	15	13
Life	.245	97	257	45	63	5	3	1	16	15

MARK LEWIS

Position: Shortstop; second base
Team: Cleveland Indians
Born: Nov. 30, 1969 Hamilton, OH
Height: 6'1" **Weight:** 190 lbs.
Bats: right **Throws:** right
Acquired: First-round pick in 6/88 free-agent draft

Player Summary	
Fantasy Value	$4 to $6
Card Value	7¢ to 12¢
Will	hit for power
Can't	master curveball
Expect	quick hitting improvement
Don't Expect	further exile to minors

Cleveland's top prospect, Lewis had a .431 batting average and 13 RBI in 13 games at Triple-A Colorado Springs when he was called up on April 26. He continued that hot streak in the majors, with a walk, single, and two-run double in his first game. Lewis hit .355 in May before slipping into a long slump. After successive .144 and .150 averages in June and July, he returned to the minors. Lewis is eventually expected to hit more consistently and with power. He had been preceded to the majors by his reputation. In 1990, Double-A Eastern League managers named him the top prospect. He has quick wrists and makes good contact. A Barry Larkin fan as a youth and an All-Star shortstop in the minors, Lewis has great range and a strong arm. He may stay at second base in the majors for the Tribe. He is a $5 fantasy draft at this point in his career, though that number could double by year's end. His 1992 cards are attractive choices at a dime or less apiece.

Major League Batting Register

	BA	G	AB	R	H	2B	3B	HR	RBI	SB
91 AL	.264	84	314	29	83	15	1	0	30	2
Life	.264	84	314	29	83	15	1	0	30	2

CURRENT PLAYERS

JOSE LIND

Position: Second base
Team: Pittsburgh Pirates
Born: May 1, 1964 Toabaja, Puerto Rico
Height: 5'11" **Weight:** 170 lbs.
Bats: right **Throws:** right
Acquired: Signed as a free agent, 12/82

Player Summary	
Fantasy Value	$5 to $8
Card Value	3¢ to 5¢
Will	slap hits to all fields
Can't	deliver high average
Expect	acrobatic defense
Don't Expect	walks or swipes

Though he uses a tiny glove that's more than 10 years old, Lind emerged in 1991 as a strong challenger to Ryne Sandberg's string of consecutive Gold Gloves. Lind has exceptional range and an ability to leap high into the air without a running start. He steals some half-dozen potential hits each year that other second basemen can't reach. He makes the double-play, throws well, and tracks down bloops between the infield and outfield. Lind's offense is average but the Pirates would settle for less because his defense is so exceptional. He's a smart selection for fantasy managers at less than a ten spot. His 1992 commons, however, are suspect investments at this point. A .260 hitter without power, he doesn't walk or strike out much but is one of the league's best bunters. There's no adequate defense against him, since he's been known to pull the ball, go up the middle, and hit to the opposite field.

Major League Batting Register

	BA	G	AB	R	H	2B	3B	HR	RBI	SB
87 NL	.322	35	143	21	46	8	4	0	11	2
88 NL	.262	154	611	82	160	24	4	2	49	15
89 NL	.232	153	578	52	134	21	3	2	48	15
90 NL	.261	152	514	46	134	28	5	1	48	8
91 NL	.265	150	502	53	133	16	6	3	54	7
Life	.259	644	2348	254	607	97	22	8	210	47
3 AVE	.252	152	531	50	134	22	5	2	50	10

SCOTT LIVINGSTONE

Position: Third base
Team: Detroit Tigers
Born: July 15, 1965 Dallas, TX
Height: 6' **Weight:** 190 lbs.
Bats: left **Throws:** right
Acquired: Second-round pick in 6/88 free-agent draft

Player Summary	
Fantasy Value	$4 to $7
Card Value	15¢ to 20¢
Will	produce runs
Can't	cut poor K-to-walk ratio
Expect	more playing time
Don't Expect	many steal attempts

Livingstone was the RBI leader in the Triple-A International League when the Tigers promoted him on July 19. In his first game, he went 3-for-5 and scored four runs. His instant success pleased Detroit manager Sparky Anderson, who had been looking for infield help after veteran shortstop Alan Trammell suffered knee, wrist, and back ailments that forced the transfer of third baseman Travis Fryman to shortstop. Livingstone is a line-drive hitter who had been hitting .296 with 44 runs scored and 56 RBI at Toledo. With Trammell on the downside of a great career, Livingstone is likely to see considerable infield action for Detroit in 1992. The Texas A&M grad hit .272 at Toledo in 1990, with six home runs, 36 RBI, 44 runs scored, 40 strikeouts, and 21 walks in 345 at bats. He led Double-A Eastern League third basemen with 360 total chances in 1989. He had 14 homers, 71 RBI, and 52 walks to go with his .217 batting average that year. His prospects for 1992 make him a solid $5 fantasy choice. His rookie 1992 cards are good buys at 15 cents apiece.

Major League Batting Register

	BA	G	AB	R	H	2B	3B	HR	RBI	SB
91 AL	.291	44	127	19	37	5	0	2	11	2
Life	.291	44	127	19	37	5	0	2	11	2

CURRENT PLAYERS

STEVE LYONS

Position: Infield; outfield
Team: Boston Red Sox
Born: June 3, 1960 Tacoma, WA
Height: 6'3" **Weight:** 195 lbs.
Bats: left **Throws:** right
Acquired: Signed as a free agent, 4/91

Player Summary	
Fantasy Value	$1 to $3
Card Value	3¢ to 5¢
Will	sub at nine spots
Can't	hit with power
Expect	sense of humor
Don't Expect	regular job

Lyons has played every position, including pitcher, since reaching the majors with the 1985 Red Sox. He even led AL third basemen in double-plays with 36 in 1988. He also hit 17 home runs at Triple-A Pawtucket in 1984. He has played both second and third base regularly, but is a better fielder as a first baseman or outfielder. He has some speed and a decent bat but does not hit with power, produce runs, or play any position well enough to man it every day. His main claims to fame are an even-up trade for Tom Seaver in 1986 and dropped drawers at Detroit in 1990. Lyons will keep his pants on in '92; that should be worth $2 at the draft. Because of his ability to fill in anywhere, he should have a big league job again this summer. His 1992 commons have slight potential if he finds a post-baseball career as a sportscaster.

Major League Batting Register

	BA	G	AB	R	H	2B	3B	HR	RBI	SB
85 AL	.264	133	371	52	98	14	3	5	30	12
86 AL	.227	91	247	30	56	9	3	1	20	4
87 AL	.280	76	193	26	54	11	1	1	19	3
88 AL	.269	146	472	59	127	28	3	5	45	1
89 AL	.264	140	443	51	117	21	3	2	50	9
90 AL	.192	94	146	22	28	6	1	1	11	1
91 AL	.241	87	212	15	51	10	1	4	17	10
Life	.255	777	2084	255	531	99	15	19	192	40
2 AVE	.256	114	328	33	84	16	2	3	34	10

KEVIN MAAS

Position: First base; outfield
Team: New York Yankees
Born: Jan. 20, 1965 Castro Valley, CA
Height: 6'3" **Weight:** 205 lbs.
Bats: left **Throws:** left
Acquired: 22nd-round pick in 6/86 free-agent draft

Player Summary	
Fantasy Value	$20 to $23
Card Value	5¢ to 10¢
Will	fight for job
Can't	play great outfield
Expect	walk, whiff, or homer
Don't Expect	repeat of 1990

During the 1990 season, Maas assuaged Yankee fans distressed over Don Mattingly's back problems. Called up June 28, he hit 10 homers in his first 77 at bats, a major league record. With Mattingly healthy again in '91, Maas became New York's designated hitter. His trying to pull every pitch led to trouble, and he led the club in strikeouts. Maas did not produce in the clutch and was roundly booed by fans who had cheered him the year before. He notched a .390 slugging percentage and a .310 on-base average in '91. At Triple-A Columbus in 1990, he hit .284 with 13 homers, 38 RBI, and 15 doubles in 194 at bats. He missed half of the '89 season with a knee injury, but he hit .320 with six homers and 45 RBI at Columbus. He hit .263 at Double-A Albany in 1988, with 16 homers and 55 RBI; he was the Eastern League All-Star first baseman. While his batting average should concern you, pop $20 on his fantasy stats at the draft. His 1992 cards are mediocre investments at more than a nickel apiece.

Major League Batting Register

	BA	G	AB	R	H	2B	3B	HR	RBI	SB
90 AL	.252	79	254	42	64	9	0	21	41	1
91 AL	.220	148	500	69	110	14	1	23	63	5
Life	.231	227	754	111	174	23	1	44	104	6
2 AVE	.231	114	377	56	87	12	1	22	52	3

CURRENT PLAYERS

MIKE MACFARLANE

Position: Catcher
Team: Kansas City Royals
Born: April 12, 1964 Stockton, CA
Height: 6'1" **Weight:** 200 lbs.
Bats: right **Throws:** right
Acquired: Fourth-round pick in 6/85 free-agent draft

Player Summary	
Fantasy Value	$10 to $15
Card Value	3¢ to 5¢
Will	show some power
Can't	make hard throws
Expect	continued improvement
Don't Expect	a lost job

The No. 1 catcher of the Kansas City Royals, Macfarlane went on the shelf with a torn ligament in his left knee on July 16. He suffered the injury in a home-plate collision with Joe Carter the day before. Macfarlane had shown dramatic improvement in his defense over the past few seasons, and he credited his turnaround to the 1989 signing of Gold Glove free agent Bob Boone. A year-long lesson in catching mechanics and strategy followed as the veteran Boone spent long hours working with his heir apparent. Macfarlane also adopted the weight training methods of Carlton Fisk. The extra strength helped, because he hit double-digits in round-trippers in 1991, more than double his 1990 total of six in 124 games. Even though he doesn't have a strong arm, Macfarlane is a capable defensive catcher whose bat will keep him in the lineup. He is a solid $12 fantasy receiver because of his power, but his 1992 commons are fairly shaky.

Major League Batting Register

	BA	G	AB	R	H	2B	3B	HR	RBI	SB
87 AL	.211	8	19	0	4	1	0	0	3	0
88 AL	.265	70	211	25	56	15	0	4	26	0
89 AL	.223	69	157	13	35	6	0	2	19	0
90 AL	.255	124	400	37	102	24	4	6	58	1
91 AL	.277	84	267	34	74	18	2	13	41	1
Life	.257	355	1054	109	271	64	6	25	147	2
3 AVE	.256	92	275	28	70	16	2	7	39	1

JULIO MACHADO

Position: Pitcher
Team: Milwaukee Brewers
Born: Dec. 1, 1965 Zulia, Venezuela
Height: 5'9" **Weight:** 165 lbs.
Bats: right **Throws:** right
Acquired: Traded from Mets with Kevin Brown for Charlie O'Brien and Kevin Carmody, 9/90

Player Summary	
Fantasy Value	$2 to $4
Card Value	3¢ to 5¢
Will	throw heat for strikes
Can't	prevent walks
Expect	many Ks and homers
Don't Expect	him as closer

Machado made a favorable impression in Milwaukee during a September trial in 1990, when he had three saves and an 0.69 ERA in 10 appearances, spanning 13 innings. He continued his good work as a middle reliever in 1991, his first full season. A hard-throwing fastball-and-slider pitcher who likes to challenge the hitters, Machado sometimes loses control because his motion has a lot of arm and leg movement. He compensates by averaging a strikeout per inning and allowing considerably less than a hit per inning. Opponents compiled a .211 batting average, a .364 slugging percentage, and a .334 on-base percentage in '91. Too many of those he does allow leave the park (12 in '91). If you can, pass spending any money at the fantasy draft for him this year. He may be a better draft next year. His 1992 commons are not buys. Machado is not only unique on the field but off. He answers to the nickname "Iguana Man." He considers the lizard a culinary delicacy.

Major League Pitching Register

	W	L	ERA	G	S	IP	H	ER	BB	SO
89 NL	0	1	3.27	10	0	11.0	9	4	3	14
90 NL	4	1	3.15	27	0	34.1	32	12	17	27
90 AL	0	0	0.69	10	3	13.0	9	1	8	12
91 AL	3	3	3.45	54	3	88.2	65	34	55	98
Life	7	5	3.12	101	6	147.0	115	51	83	151
2 AVE	4	2	3.11	46	3	68.2	53	24	40	69

CURRENT PLAYERS

SHANE MACK

Position: Outfield
Team: Minnesota Twins
Born: Dec. 7, 1963 Los Angeles, CA
Height: 6' **Weight:** 190 lbs.
Bats: right **Throws:** right
Acquired: Drafted from Padres, 12/89

Player Summary	
Fantasy Value	$20 to $25
Card Value	3¢ to 5¢
Will	produce runs
Can't	hit righties well
Expect	strong defense
Don't Expect	good-field, no-hit rep

Before he hit .326 in 125 games for Minnesota in 1990, Mack had always been considered a better fielder than a hitter. He continued his strong hitting in 1991, when he produced the first four-hit game of his career against Detroit on July 30. He lifted his average from .175 early to .310. He showed power with double-digit homers. The 1984 Olympian succeeded because he became more selective as a hitter, though he still fans twice as often as he walks. He notched a .529 slugging percentage and a .363 on-base average in '91. He tied his career high with five RBI August 21, giving him 28 RBI, 24 extra-base hits, and a .410 average over a 35-game stretch. Mack has some speed, good range in the outfield, and a decent throwing arm. He didn't have a good Series until the last game, but he certainly helped the Twins get to the Big Show. Winning the starting job propelled him from $5 fantasy draft territory to $20 range. His 1992 cards still are not good investments.

Major League Batting Register

	BA	G	AB	R	H	2B	3B	HR	RBI	SB
87 NL	.239	105	238	28	57	11	3	4	25	4
88 NL	.244	56	119	13	29	3	0	0	12	5
90 AL	.326	125	313	50	102	10	4	8	44	13
91 AL	.310	143	442	79	137	27	8	18	74	13
Life	.292	429	1112	170	325	51	15	30	155	35
2 AVE	.317	134	378	65	120	19	6	13	59	13

GREG MADDUX

Position: Pitcher
Team: Chicago Cubs
Born: April 14, 1966 San Angelo, TX
Height: 6' **Weight:** 170 lbs.
Bats: right **Throws:** right
Acquired: Second-round pick in 6/84 free-agent draft

Player Summary	
Fantasy Value	$10 to $15
Card Value	3¢ to 5¢
Will	win often
Can't	prevent gophers
Expect	heavy workload
Don't Expect	wild spells

Maddux is one of the game's most dependable starters. He has exceeded 200 innings pitched and 10 wins four years in a row. An annual contender for the strikeout crown, he throws a sinking fastball, hard slider, curveball, and circle change. He has fine control—usually fanning three times more men than he walks—but often falls victim to the gopher ball. Since he averages less than a hit per inning and doesn't yield many walks, those home runs often come with nobody on base. Still, they make Maddux mad, and he shows it. He'd be a better pitcher if he conquered his temper. Maddux gets extra points for hitting, fielding, and keeping runners close; he's better than most of his colleagues in all three departments. Collectors don't like the fact that he seems bent on a .500 career, keeping his 1992 cards commons. Fantasy managers should pay $12 for double-digit win production.

Major League Pitching Register

	W	L	ERA	G	CG	IP	H	ER	BB	SO
86 NL	2	4	5.52	6	1	31.0	44	19	11	20
87 NL	6	14	5.61	30	1	155.2	181	97	74	101
88 NL	18	8	3.18	34	9	249.0	230	88	81	140
89 NL	19	12	2.95	35	7	238.1	222	78	82	135
90 NL	15	15	3.46	35	8	237.0	242	91	71	144
91 NL	15	11	3.35	37	7	263.0	232	98	66	198
Life	75	64	3.61	177	33	1174.0	1151	471	385	738
3 AVE	16	13	3.25	36	7	246.0	232	89	73	159

CURRENT PLAYERS

MIKE MADDUX

Position: Pitcher
Team: San Diego Padres
Born: Aug. 27, 1961 Dayton, OH
Height: 6'2" **Weight:** 180 lbs.
Bats: right **Throws:** right
Acquired: Signed as a free agent, 3/91

Player Summary	
Fantasy Value	$1 to $3
Card Value	3¢ to 5¢
Will	work often
Can't	win with erratic use
Expect	few hits or walks
Don't Expect	an embarrassing ERA

Maddux was a pleasant surprise in his first season with the Padres last year. The older brother of Chicago's Greg Maddux, Mike proved he had overcome shoulder and elbow problems that had plagued him three years earlier. He broke in with the 1986 Phillies and lost to his brother in baseball's first match of rookie siblings on September 29. Now regarded as a middle relief specialist, in 1991 he worked in more than 60 games, by far the most of his pro career. He allowed less than a hit per inning, kept the ball in the park, and fanned twice the number he walked. He even made an emergency start for San Diego. With a career 10-14 record and 4.68 ERA before 1991, Maddux thrived when given regular work. Opponents compiled a .221 batting average, a .300 slugging percentage, and a .277 on-base percentage in 1991. You may want to take advantage of his low $2 draft price. You will want to take a furlough from his 1992 commons.

Major League Pitching Register

	W	L	ERA	G	S	IP	H	ER	BB	SO
86 NL	3	7	5.42	16	0	78.0	88	47	34	44
87 NL	2	0	2.65	7	0	17.0	17	5	5	15
88 NL	4	3	3.76	25	0	88.2	91	37	34	59
89 NL	1	3	5.15	16	1	43.2	52	25	14	26
90 NL	0	1	6.53	11	0	20.2	24	15	4	11
91 NL	7	2	2.46	64	5	98.2	78	27	27	57
Life	17	16	4.05	139	6	346.2	350	156	118	212
2 AVE	4	3	3.29	40	3	71.2	65	26	21	42

DAVE MAGADAN

Position: First base; third base
Team: New York Mets
Born: Sept. 30, 1962 Tampa, FL
Height: 6'3" **Weight:** 195 lbs.
Bats: left **Throws:** right
Acquired: Second-round pick in 6/83 free-agent draft

Player Summary	
Fantasy Value	$10 to $15
Card Value	3¢ to 5¢
Will	hit to all fields
Can't	run a lick
Expect	decent defense
Don't Expect	first base power

Before a season-long slump in 1991, Magadan had always compensated for his lack of power with a line-drive stroke that produced a high batting average. Adept at the hit-and-run, he is an ideal No. 2 hitter when he's producing. He wasn't in 1991, though. He had a .258 average, four homers, and 51 RBI in 124 games before submitting to arthroscopic surgery on both shoulders in September. A contact hitter who's unusually selective, he had a .378 on-base percentage in 1991. He walks much more often than he strikes out. One year earlier, when Magadan hit .328, his on-base average reached .417, second in the league. In the field, he has little range but good hands, good instincts, and an unusually strong arm (he could play third base in 1992). He has had a drop in fantasy value, but he could be a bargain at $10. His 1992 commons suffer because of his power scarcity.

Major League Batting Register

	BA	G	AB	R	H	2B	3B	HR	RBI	SB
86 NL	.444	10	18	3	8	0	0	0	3	0
87 NL	.318	85	192	21	61	13	1	3	24	0
88 NL	.277	112	314	39	87	15	0	1	35	0
89 NL	.286	127	374	47	107	22	3	4	41	1
90 NL	.328	144	451	74	148	28	6	6	72	2
91 NL	.258	124	418	58	108	23	0	4	51	1
Life	.294	602	1767	242	519	101	10	18	226	4
3 AVE	.292	132	414	60	121	24	3	5	55	1

CURRENT PLAYERS

JOE MAGRANE

Position: Pitcher
Team: St. Louis Cardinals
Born: July 2, 1964 Des Moines, IA
Height: 6'6" **Weight:** 230 lbs.
Bats: right **Throws:** left
Acquired: First-round pick in 6/85 free-agent draft

Player Summary	
Fantasy Value	$5 to $7
Card Value	3¢ to 5¢
Will	lead staff if healthy
Can't	worry about elbow
Expect	a strong return
Don't Expect	ERA over 3.00

The season-long absence of pitching ace Magrane hurt the 1991 pennant chances of the Cardinals. The star lefthander submitted to elbow surgery and was placed on the 60-day disabled list on March 19. When healthy, he is one of the game's top pitchers. He led the Cards with 18 wins three years ago, one season after topping the National League in ERA. Magrane normally has excellent control of his fastball, curve, and slider. He yields less than a hit per inning, keeps the ball in the park, and fans about twice the number he walks. He's also an accomplished hitter who's often used as a pinch-hitter for other pitchers. Magrane is also adept with a glove and has one of the game's better pickoff moves. He's also quick with a quip. The former University of Arizona star could be a cheap $6 draft pick primed for a comeback. Don't consider his 1992 commons until he has several good starts.

Major League Pitching Register

	W	L	ERA	G	CG	IP	H	ER	BB	SO
87 NL	9	7	3.54	27	4	170.1	157	67	60	101
88 NL	5	9	2.18	24	4	165.1	133	40	51	100
89 NL	18	9	2.91	34	9	234.2	219	76	72	127
90 NL	10	17	3.59	31	3	203.1	204	81	59	100
Life	42	42	3.07	116	20	773.2	713	264	242	428
2 AVE	14	13	3.25	33	6	219.0	212	79	62	114

CANDY MALDONADO

Position: Outfield
Team: Toronto Blue Jays
Born: Sept. 5, 1960 Humacao, Puerto Rico
Height: 6' **Weight:** 195 lbs.
Bats: right **Throws:** right
Acquired: Traded from Brewers for William Suero and Rob Wishnevski, 8/91

Player Summary	
Fantasy Value	$8 to $10
Card Value	3¢ to 5¢
Will	produce power
Can't	steal or field well
Expect	designated hitter role
Don't Expect	high on-base average

Although Maldonado missed more than two months of the 1991 season with a broken bone in his right foot, he is a productive power-hitter when healthy. After having a career year with the 1990 Indians, he signed with the Brewers in 1991. They traded him to the Blue Jays for their pennant run. Maldonado does not show much patience at the plate and tries to pull too much. Because he likes the ball over the plate, pitchers work him inside until he adjusts. Then they go outside. Maldonado does not usually make good contact. Because he's a below-average outfielder who lacks speed and a great arm, he's often used in left field. A better spot for him is designated hitter. Grab him at $10 for his 15-plus homer capacity. His 1992 commons won't grab you, however.

Major League Batting Register

	BA	G	AB	R	H	2B	3B	HR	RBI	SB
81 NL	.083	11	12	0	1	0	0	0	0	0
82 NL	.000	6	4	0	0	0	0	0	0	0
83 NL	.194	42	62	5	12	1	1	1	6	0
84 NL	.268	116	254	25	68	14	0	5	28	0
85 NL	.225	121	213	20	48	7	1	5	19	1
86 NL	.252	133	405	49	102	31	3	18	85	4
87 NL	.292	118	442	69	129	28	4	20	85	8
88 NL	.255	142	499	53	127	23	1	12	68	6
89 NL	.217	129	345	39	75	23	0	9	41	4
90 AL	.273	155	590	76	161	32	2	22	95	3
91 AL	.250	86	288	37	72	15	0	12	48	4
Life	.255	1059	3114	373	795	174	12	104	475	30
3 AVE	.252	123	408	51	103	23	1	14	61	4

CURRENT PLAYERS

KIRT MANWARING

Position: Catcher
Team: San Francisco Giants
Born: July 15, 1965 Elmira, NY
Height: 5'11" **Weight:** 190 lbs.
Bats: right **Throws:** right
Acquired: Second-round pick in 6/86 free-agent draft

Player Summary	
Fantasy Value	$1 to $3
Card Value	3¢ to 5¢
Will	nail stealers
Can't	produce power
Expect	good-field, no-hit rep
Don't Expect	more than bench duty

Manwaring became a better hitter in 1991 when he began wearing contact lenses. He got a chance to play during spring training when heralded rookie prospect Steve Decker fouled a ball off his foot and missed a few games. Manwaring made the ballclub and became Terry Kennedy's righthanded platoon partner when Decker was returned to the minors with a silent bat. Though Manwaring is a good receiver with a strong throwing arm, he also failed to produce at the plate. He didn't do any worse than did Kennedy, though. Manwaring wasn't expected to hit home runs or steal bases but he pilfered a base anyway, perhaps just to say he could do it. He notched a .275 slugging percentage and a .271 on-base average in '91. His performance, coupled with a previous .220 average compiled over parts of four seasons, doesn't suggest he'll play every day. His fantasy value stops at a couple of bucks, and his 1992 cards are commons.

Major League Batting Register

	BA	G	AB	R	H	2B	3B	HR	RBI	SB
87 NL	.143	6	7	0	1	0	0	0	0	0
88 NL	.250	40	116	12	29	7	0	1	15	0
89 NL	.210	85	200	14	42	4	2	0	18	2
90 NL	.154	8	13	0	2	0	1	0	1	0
91 NL	.225	67	178	16	40	9	0	0	19	1
Life	.222	206	514	42	114	20	3	1	53	3
2 AVE	.217	76	189	15	41	7	1	0	19	2

CARLOS MARTINEZ

Position: First base; designated hitter
Team: Cleveland Indians
Born: Aug. 11, 1965 La Guaira, Venezuela
Height: 6'5" **Weight:** 175 lbs.
Bats: right **Throws:** right
Acquired: Signed as a free agent, 3/91

Player Summary	
Fantasy Value	$4 to $6
Card Value	5¢ to 10¢
Will	notch good average
Can't	generate power
Expect	success with fastballs
Don't Expect	patience at bat

After spending the first half of 1991 in the minors, Martinez returned to the bigs as designated hitter for the Indians on July 12. The former White Sox first baseman had hit .329 with 11 homers, 48 runs scored, 78 RBI, and 11 stolen bases in 80 games at Double-A Canton-Akron in '91. Martinez continued to hit at the big league level and was AL Player of the Week for the period ending July 29. During that time, he hit .520 with two homers, six RBI, a .500 on-base average, and an .800 slugging percentage. One of the least patient hitters in the game, he fans more than four times as often as he walks. He makes contact, however, consistently hitting over .280. He notched a .397 slugging percentage and a .346 on-base average in '91. He will get some early opportunities with the Tribe, making him a $4 fantasy draft. Martinez runs and fields poorly, factors that explain his shift from first baseman to designated hitter. His 1992 cards are overpriced at a dime apiece.

Major League Batting Register

	BA	G	AB	R	H	2B	3B	HR	RBI	SB
88 AL	.164	17	55	5	9	1	0	0	0	1
89 AL	.300	109	350	44	105	22	0	5	32	4
90 AL	.224	92	272	18	61	6	5	4	24	0
91 AL	.284	72	257	22	73	14	0	5	30	3
Life	.266	290	934	89	248	43	5	14	86	8
3 AVE	.272	91	293	28	80	14	2	5	29	2

CURRENT PLAYERS

CARMELO MARTINEZ

Position: First base; outfield
Team: Cincinnati Reds
Born: July 28, 1960 Dorado, Puerto Rico
Height: 6'2" **Weight:** 211 lbs.
Bats: right **Throws:** right
Acquired: Traded from Royals for Todd Benzinger, 7/91

Player Summary	
Fantasy Value	$1 to $3
Card Value	3¢ to 5¢
Will	hit long ball
Can't	play defense or run
Expect	one dimension
Don't Expect	use every day

With enough at bats, Martinez would produce about 20 homers and knock in 70 runs. That hasn't happened in the last three seasons, however, as he has bounced to five different ballclubs. His playing time is decreasing, and he is beginning to acquire an unwanted reputation as a one-dimensional slugger. His problem is patience, or lack of it. He fans twice as often as he walks and feels the pressure to produce big power numbers every time he's traded. He's a last-ditch option for fantasy leaguers only. A natural first baseman who plays left field, his 1992 cards are eternal commons. Martinez is a mediocre first baseman but an abominable outfielder whose lack of speed is a glaring weakness. His best option for a future is to find an AL team that needs a designated hitter.

Major League Batting Register

	BA	G	AB	R	H	2B	3B	HR	RBI	SB
83 NL	.258	29	89	8	23	3	0	6	16	0
84 NL	.250	149	488	64	122	28	2	13	66	1
85 NL	.253	150	514	64	130	28	1	21	72	0
86 NL	.238	113	244	28	58	10	0	9	25	1
87 NL	.273	139	447	59	122	21	2	15	70	5
88 NL	.236	121	365	48	86	12	0	18	65	1
89 NL	.221	111	267	23	59	12	2	6	39	0
90 NL	.240	83	217	26	52	9	0	10	35	2
91 AL	.207	44	121	17	25	6	0	4	17	0
91 NL	.234	64	154	13	36	5	0	6	19	0
Life	.245	1003	2906	350	713	134	7	108	424	10
3 AVE	.226	97	248	26	56	11	1	9	37	1

CHITO MARTINEZ

Position: Outfield
Team: Baltimore Orioles
Born: Dec. 19, 1965 Belize
Height: 5'10" **Weight:** 180 lbs.
Bats: left **Throws:** left
Acquired: Signed as a free agent, 11/90

Player Summary	
Fantasy Value	$10 to $12
Card Value	15¢ to 25¢
Will	hit for power
Can't	steal bases
Expect	better stats with patience
Don't Expect	sophomore jinx

After trying natural first basemen David Segui and Randy Milligan in left field, Baltimore called Martinez to the majors on July 5. He showed considerable power potential. Martinez was hammering Triple-A International League pitching when the Orioles called. He had a .324 batting average at Rochester and was leading the club in home runs, RBI, and slugging. He spent six years in the Royals organization before coming to Baltimore. He had a .264 batting average with 21 homers and 67 RBI, 54 walks, and 129 strikeouts at Triple-A Omaha in 1990. He has a strong arm, averaging 20 outfield assists from 1988 to '90 in the minors. The O's needed a hitter to take up the slack when Glenn Davis went down. Martinez fanned four times for every walk last year and will increase his value if he learns to become a more selective hitter. He had a .514 slugging percentage and a .303 on-base average for the O's in '91. He could increase his power significantly in '92, making him a $10 fantasy draft. His rookie 1992 cards are average investments at 15 cents to a quarter apiece.

Major League Batting Register

	BA	G	AB	R	H	2B	3B	HR	RBI	SB
91 AL	.269	67	216	32	58	12	1	13	33	1
Life	.269	67	216	32	58	12	1	13	33	1

CURRENT PLAYERS

DAVE MARTINEZ

Position: Outfield
Team: Cincinnati Reds
Born: Sept. 26, 1964 New York, NY
Height: 5'10" **Weight:** 170 lbs.
Bats: left **Throws:** left
Acquired: Traded from Expos with Scott Ruskin and Willie Green for John Wetteland and Bill Risley, 12/91

Player Summary
Fantasy Value	$6 to $9
Card Value	3¢ to 5¢
Will	play strong defense
Can't	generate consistent power
Expect	line drives and steals
Don't Expect	frequent walks

Martinez is an outstanding defensive center fielder who can run, throw, and judge fly balls better than most of his contemporaries. He's also a competent hitter coming off his best season since his rookie year of 1987. Though he strikes out twice as often as he walks, he is basically a contact hitter who hits line drives. He is a fantasy budget saver for $7. He has never exceeded 11 homers or 50 RBI in a season but is considered a good clutch hitter. He notched a .419 slugging percentage and a .332 on-base average in 1991. Often platooned in the past, Martinez has improved his hitting against lefthanders in recent seasons. He's a pesky base-runner with enough speed to steal. He has stolen 23 in a season twice. Because his arm is strong enough for right field, Martinez sometimes plays there too, giving him the unwanted image of defensive replacement. His 1992 commons are not ripe for investment.

Major League Batting Register

	BA	G	AB	R	H	2B	3B	HR	RBI	SB
86 NL	.139	53	108	13	15	1	1	1	7	4
87 NL	.292	142	459	70	134	18	8	8	36	16
88 NL	.255	138	447	51	114	13	6	6	46	23
89 NL	.274	126	361	41	99	16	7	3	27	23
90 NL	.279	118	391	60	109	13	5	11	39	13
91 NL	.295	124	396	47	117	18	5	7	42	16
Life	.272	701	2162	282	588	79	32	36	197	95
3 AVE	.283	123	383	49	108	16	6	7	36	17

DENNIS MARTINEZ

Position: Pitcher
Team: Montreal Expos
Born: May 14, 1955 Granada, Nicaragua
Height: 6'1" **Weight:** 180 lbs.
Bats: right **Throws:** right
Acquired: Traded from Orioles for Rene Gonzales, 6/86

Player Summary
Fantasy Value	$10 to $15
Card Value	3¢ to 5¢
Will	win 15 with no trouble
Can't	help himself at bat
Expect	control and a low ERA
Don't Expect	many walks or homers

Martinez could not be blamed for Montreal's disappointing 1991 campaign. He appeared in the All-Star Game, pitched a perfect game against Los Angeles on July 28, and was named the NL's best curveball pitcher in a Baseball America managers poll. He rated second in both control and pickoff move. He was third as the best all-around pitcher. In addition to the hard curve, Martinez throws strikes with a fastball, sinker, and changeup. He's a good fielder with a good move but a weak hitter. He is an attractive fantasy hurler for $12. His 1992 cards are short-term commons.

Major League Pitching Register

	W	L	ERA	G	CG	IP	H	ER	BB	SO
76 AL	1	2	2.60	4	1	27.2	23	8	8	18
77 AL	14	7	4.10	42	5	166.2	157	76	64	107
78 AL	16	11	3.52	40	15	276.1	257	108	93	142
79 AL	15	16	3.66	40	18	292.1	279	119	78	132
80 AL	6	4	3.97	25	2	99.2	103	44	44	42
81 AL	14	5	3.32	25	9	179.0	173	66	62	88
82 AL	16	12	4.21	40	10	252.0	262	118	87	111
83 AL	7	16	5.53	32	4	153.0	209	94	45	71
84 AL	6	9	5.02	34	2	141.2	145	79	37	77
85 AL	13	11	5.15	33	3	180.0	203	103	63	68
86 AL	0	0	6.75	4	0	6.2	11	5	2	2
86 NL	3	6	4.59	19	1	98.0	103	50	28	63
87 NL	11	4	3.30	22	2	144.2	133	53	40	84
88 NL	15	13	2.72	34	9	235.1	215	71	55	120
89 NL	16	7	3.18	34	5	232.0	227	82	49	142
90 NL	10	11	2.95	32	7	226.0	191	74	49	156
91 NL	14	11	2.39	31	9	222.0	187	59	62	123
Life	177	145	3.71	491	102	2933.0	2878	1209	866	1546
3 AVE	13	10	2.85	32	7	227.0	202	72	53	140

CURRENT PLAYERS

EDGAR MARTINEZ

Position: Third base
Team: Seattle Mariners
Born: January 2, 1963 New York, NY
Height: 5'11" **Weight:** 175 lbs.
Bats: right **Throws:** right
Acquired: Signed as a free agent, 12/82

Player Summary	
Fantasy Value	$15 to $20
Card Value	3¢ to 5¢
Will	show some power
Can't	leg out infield hits
Expect	on-base average over .400
Don't Expect	shoddy defense

Ken Griffey Sr. says Martinez reminds him of Joe Torre: A high-average hitter who has a good eye, hits to all fields, shows occasional power, but doesn't run well enough to fatten his average with bunts or infield singles. Martinez had a .452 slugging percentage and a .405 on-base average in '91. He had a 15-game hitting streak in April. Corrective surgery on his sore right knee cut his errors in half from 1990 to '91. A weight-lifting regimen gave him more agility by strengthening his legs. Martinez, who once made four miscues in a game, took hours of third base drills to improve his defense. Though his range is limited, he charges and throws well and has good reactions. Martinez is one of the best all-around players at his position. Grab him for your team after better-known third sackers are taken, and he will produce for you. His 1992 commons will continue to suffer, however, from his lack of exposure.

RAMON MARTINEZ

Position: Pitcher
Team: Los Angeles Dodgers
Born: March 22, 1968 Santo Domingo, Dominican Republic
Height: 6'4" **Weight:** 173 lbs.
Bats: right **Throws:** right
Acquired: Signed as a free agent, 9/84

Player Summary	
Fantasy Value	$35 to $40
Card Value	5¢ to 10¢
Will	keep ERA down
Can't	always keep ball in park
Expect	wins and shutouts
Don't Expect	walks to distort record

Early last season, NL managers polled by *Baseball America* said Martinez is the best pitcher in the league. They also said his fastball is second only to Rob Dibble's, while the Martinez change is second only to Frank Viola's. Martinez had a 20-6 record in 1990, his first full season, and approached the 20-win circle again in '91, even though he was still working to perfect his curve. Martinez, who once fanned 18 in a game, strikes out more than twice the number he walks. He also allows far less than a hit per inning. Opponents compiled a .229 batting average, a .337 slugging percentage, and a .293 on-base average in 1991. He is a $40 fantasy value, though he may be overpriced in many drafts. He does yield more homers than any other Dodger, however (18 in '91). Martinez knows how to field and drop a bunt but doesn't help himself as a hitter. His 1992 cards are very good investments at a dime apiece.

Major League Batting Register

	BA	G	AB	R	H	2B	3B	HR	RBI	SB
87 AL	.372	13	43	6	16	5	2	0	5	0
88 AL	.281	14	32	0	9	4	0	0	5	0
89 AL	.240	65	171	20	41	5	0	2	20	2
90 AL	.302	144	487	71	147	27	2	11	49	1
91 AL	.307	150	544	98	167	35	1	14	52	0
Life	.298	386	1277	195	380	76	5	27	131	3
3 AVE	.295	120	401	63	118	22	1	9	40	1

Major League Pitching Register

	W	L	ERA	G	CG	IP	H	ER	BB	SO
88 NL	1	3	3.79	9	0	35.2	27	15	22	23
89 NL	6	4	3.19	15	2	98.2	79	35	41	89
90 NL	20	6	2.92	33	12	234.1	191	76	67	223
91 NL	17	13	3.27	33	6	220.1	190	80	69	150
Life	44	26	3.15	90	20	589.0	487	206	199	485
3 AVE	14	8	3.11	27	7	184.1	153	64	59	154

CURRENT PLAYERS

JOHN MARZANO

Position: Catcher
Team: Boston Red Sox
Born: Feb. 14, 1963 Philadelphia, PA
Height: 5'11" **Weight:** 197 lbs.
Bats: right **Throws:** right
Acquired: First-round pick in 6/84 free-agent draft

Player Summary
Fantasy Value	$1 to $2
Card Value	3¢ to 5¢
Will	serve as OK back-up
Can't	hit for average or power
Expect	good defense
Don't Expect	strong arm

Marzano has spent all five of his big league seasons as back-up catcher for Boston. The 1984 Olympian is a good defensive performer with an average arm. Unfortunately, he is a punchless hitter who usually hits between .240 and .250. Marzano, who once showed some power potential as a college star at Temple, began his pro career in 1985 and advanced to the Red Sox two years later. He hit five homers in 52 games for Boston as a rookie but has hit only one in the last three years. He is an impatient hitter who strikes out far more often than he walks. That fact, coupled with his low average and power output, explains why he has never played in more than 52 big league games in a season. Next year's expansion could give him his first shot at daily duty. He is not a very good choice as a fantasy backstop, and his 1992 commons are not good investments.

Major League Batting Register

	BA	G	AB	R	H	2B	3B	HR	RBI	SB
87 AL	.244	52	168	20	41	11	0	5	24	0
88 AL	.138	10	29	3	4	1	0	0	1	0
89 AL	.444	7	18	5	8	3	0	1	3	0
90 AL	.241	32	83	8	20	4	0	0	6	0
91 AL	.263	49	114	10	30	8	0	0	9	0
Life	.250	150	412	46	103	27	0	6	43	0

DON MATTINGLY

Position: First base
Team: New York Yankees
Born: April 20, 1961 Evansville, IN
Height: 6' **Weight:** 192 lbs.
Bats: left **Throws:** left
Acquired: 19th-round pick in 6/79 free-agent draft

Player Summary
Fantasy Value	$23 to $28
Card Value	10¢ to 20¢
Will	play great defense
Can't	rouse hibernating power
Expect	leadership by example
Don't Expect	many Ks or stolen bases

Mattingly was widely regarded as the AL's top star before he missed most of 1990 with back problems. The 1986 MVP and five-time Gold Glove winner recovered his .300 stroke last year but suffered a puzzling power shortage. His homer April 23 was his first in 312 at bats, the longest drought of his career. The Yankee captain even suggested that he should hit second or fifth rather than third, a spot reserved for run-producers. Mattingly still walks more than he fans and always seems to make good contact. He's an exceptional fielder who scoops low throws, plays hitters well, and moves well around the first base bag. With questions about his health cleared up, his fantasy stock has risen to $25. If his power output would return, his fantasy value and his 15-cent 1992 cards would rise even more.

Major League Batting Register

	BA	G	AB	R	H	2B	3B	HR	RBI	SB
82 AL	.167	7	12	0	2	0	0	0	1	0
83 AL	.283	91	279	34	79	15	4	4	32	0
84 AL	.343	153	603	91	207	44	2	23	110	1
85 AL	.324	159	652	107	211	48	3	35	145	2
86 AL	.352	162	677	117	238	53	2	31	113	0
87 AL	.327	141	569	93	186	38	2	30	115	1
88 AL	.311	144	599	94	186	37	0	18	88	1
89 AL	.303	158	631	79	191	37	2	23	113	3
90 AL	.256	102	394	40	101	16	0	5	42	1
91 AL	.288	152	587	64	169	35	0	9	68	2
Life	.314	1269	5003	719	1570	323	15	178	827	11
3 AVE	.286	137	537	61	154	29	1	12	74	2

CURRENT PLAYERS

KIRK McCASKILL

Position: Pitcher
Team: California Angels
Born: April 9, 1961 Kapuskasing, Ontario, Canada
Height: 6'1" **Weight:** 196 lbs.
Bats: right **Throws:** right
Acquired: Fourth-round pick in 6/82 free-agent draft

Player Summary	
Fantasy Value	$6 to $9
Card Value	3¢ to 5¢
Will	post double-digit wins
Can't	prevent walks or homers
Expect	many baserunners
Don't Expect	high ERA

McCaskill deserved a better fate in 1991. Though he yielded more hits than innings pitched, threw too many home run balls, and suffered the embarrassment of a 1-1 ratio of strikeouts to walks, his earned run average did not warrant such a lopsided won-lost record. After getting nine runs of support in his first 14 losses, he almost became the AL's first 20-game loser since Oakland's Brian Kingman in 1980. McCaskill is a former power pitcher who now depends upon a slider and curveball as his primary pitches. He also has a fastball and changeup. When he gets the pitches up, McCaskill gets clobbered. That hasn't happened much over the years. He has won at least a dozen games four times in seven seasons. Strong fielding and a fine pickoff move helped. Give him a fantasy tryout for less than $10. Neglect McCaskill's 1992 commons.

Major League Pitching Register

	W	L	ERA	G	CG	IP	H	ER	BB	SO
85 AL	12	12	4.70	30	6	189.2	189	99	64	102
86 AL	17	10	3.36	34	10	246.1	207	92	92	202
87 AL	4	6	5.67	14	1	74.2	84	47	34	56
88 AL	8	6	4.31	23	4	146.1	155	70	61	98
89 AL	15	10	2.93	32	6	212.0	202	69	59	107
90 AL	12	11	3.25	29	2	174.1	161	63	72	78
91 AL	10	19	4.26	30	1	177.2	193	84	66	71
Life	78	74	3.86	192	30	1221.0	1191	524	448	714
3 AVE	12	13	3.45	30	3	188.1	185	72	66	85

PAUL McCLELLAN

Position: Pitcher
Team: San Francisco Giants
Born: Feb. 8, 1966 San Mateo, CA
Height: 6'2" **Weight:** 180 lbs.
Bats: right **Throws:** right
Acquired: First-round pick in 1/86 free-agent draft

Player Summary	
Fantasy Value	$2 to $4
Card Value	10¢ to 15¢
Will	bid to retain spot
Can't	keep doling out walks
Expect	lower ERA over time
Don't Expect	1990's 7-16 Triple-A mark

After making one start and three relief outings for the 1990 Giants, McClellan proved himself a valuable addition to the starting rotation when he returned on July 23, 1991. He yielded two singles in seven scoreless innings against Philadelphia in his first start, then one run in a route-going 8-1 win over Cincinnati. He got his third win in four decisions August 15 when he retired the first 15 Reds and allowed one hit in seven and one-third innings. The hard-throwing righthander allowed less than a hit per inning but yielded too many home run balls (12). He also needs to improve his control. At Triple-A Phoenix in '91, he was 2-2 with a 2.82 ERA, two complete games in five starts, 21 walks, and 18 strikeouts in 38 innings. He was 7-16 with a 5.17 ERA, 102 strikeouts, 78 bases on balls, and 192 hits in 172⅓ innings at Phoenix in 1990. McClellan's potential is enormous. As a second-year pro at Class-A Clinton in 1987, he fanned 209 in 177⅓ innings pitched. His rookie 1992 cards aren't celebrated at their dime prices. His fantasy chances at $3 are decent.

Major League Pitching Register

	W	L	ERA	G	CG	IP	H	ER	BB	SO
90 NL	0	1	11.74	4	0	7.2	14	10	6	2
91 NL	3	6	4.56	13	1	71.0	68	36	25	44
Life	3	7	5.26	17	1	78.2	82	46	31	46

CURRENT PLAYERS

LLOYD McCLENDON

Position: Catcher; first base; outfield
Team: Pittsburgh Pirates
Born: July 11, 1959 Gary, IN
Height: 5'11" **Weight:** 195 lbs.
Bats: right **Throws:** right
Acquired: Traded from Cubs for Mike Pomeranz, 9/90

Player Summary
Fantasy Value	$3 to $6
Card Value	3¢ to 5¢
Will	provide power
Can't	run enough to steal
Expect	service at five spots
Don't Expect	over 100 games

McClendon is one of the most valuable bit players in baseball. A versatile performer who swings a potent bat, he can come off the bench cold and hit the ball over the fence. He plays many games as a pinch-hitter with a single at bat, but he produced last year when called upon. A patient hitter who walks almost as often as he strikes out, McClendon usually makes good contact, especially against lefthanded pitchers. Righties can usually retire him, however. He notched a .460 slugging percentage and a .366 on-base average in 1991. Speed is not an asset—he's swiped 14 bases in five years—but versatility is. He can play the infield or outfield corners or even catch without too much embarrassment. He broke in as a catcher when he launched his pro career in 1980. He could yield a fantasy discount for $5. His 1992 commons, however, won't be as lucky.

BEN McDONALD

Position: Pitcher
Team: Baltimore Orioles
Born: Nov. 24, 1967 Baton Rouge, LA
Height: 6'7" **Weight:** 212 lbs.
Bats: right **Throws:** right
Acquired: First-round pick in 6/89 free-agent draft

Player Summary
Fantasy Value	$7 to $9
Card Value	5¢ to 10¢
Will	win often if healthy
Can't	keep ball in park
Expect	more strikeouts
Don't Expect	continued control woes

When McDonald learns to throw strikes consistently, he's likely to become one of the top pitchers in the American League. His fastball is so lively that he can often get by with that pitch alone on days when his curve isn't working. He was a two-pitch pitcher before adding a changeup last year. He didn't get much chance to experiment with the expanded repertoire because of elbow problems that sent him to the disabled list twice. When he returned July 1, McDonald held the heavy-hitting Tigers to two hits in eight shutout innings. Even after that game, the former Louisiana State star didn't enjoy clear sailing. McDonald yielded a hit per inning, threw too many home run balls, and had a strikeout-to-walk ratio of less than 2-to-1. His "off" year can give a daring fantasy manager a great opportunity to slip in while prices dip; he is a bargain for less than $10. His 1992 cards are good buys for a dime apiece.

Major League Batting Register
	BA	G	AB	R	H	2B	3B	HR	RBI	SB
87 NL	.208	45	72	8	15	5	0	2	13	1
88 NL	.219	72	137	9	30	4	0	3	14	4
89 NL	.286	92	259	47	74	12	1	12	40	6
90 NL	.164	53	110	6	18	3	0	2	12	1
91 NL	.288	85	163	24	47	7	0	7	24	2
Life	.248	347	741	94	184	31	1	26	103	14
2 AVE	.287	89	211	36	61	10	1	10	32	4

Major League Pitching Register
	W	L	ERA	G	CG	IP	H	ER	BB	SO
89 AL	1	0	8.59	6	0	7.1	8	7	4	3
90 AL	8	5	2.43	21	3	118.2	88	32	35	65
91 AL	6	8	4.84	21	1	126.1	126	68	43	85
Life	15	13	3.82	48	4	252.1	222	107	82	153
2 AVE	7	7	3.67	21	2	122.2	107	50	39	75

CURRENT PLAYERS

JACK McDOWELL

Position: Pitcher
Team: Chicago White Sox
Born: January 16, 1966 Van Nuys, CA
Height: 6'5" **Weight:** 179 lbs.
Bats: right **Throws:** right
Acquired: First-round pick in 6/87 free-agent draft

Player Summary	
Fantasy Value	$16 to $22
Card Value	5¢ to 10¢
Will	rank among AL leaders
Can't	avoid occasional homer
Expect	complete games and Ks
Don't Expect	long bouts of wildness

McDowell became a 1991 All-Star by harnessing his control. He pitched 7⅓ hitless innings before settling for a three-hitter June 25, then hurled a one-hitter July 14. McDowell has full command of his fastball, curveball, and split-fingered fastball. He's one of the league leaders in strikeouts and averages two and one-half whiffs per walk. Opponents compiled a .228 batting average, a .347 slugging percentage, and a .292 on-base average in 1991. He also notched three shutouts. A fine fielder who keeps base-runners close, the former Stanford pitcher rates as one of the game's premier pitchers. He's been the leader of the White Sox staff for two straight years and figures to remain the team's No. 1 starter for the foreseeable future. The wins and Ks make him a bargain $18 hurler. His 1992 cards will continue to increase as he gains more wins. McDowell is the lead singer and guitarist for a rock group called V.I.E.W.

Major League Pitching Register

	W	L	ERA	G	CG	IP	H	ER	BB	SO
87 AL	3	0	1.93	4	0	28.0	16	6	6	15
88 AL	5	10	3.97	26	1	158.2	147	70	68	84
90 AL	14	9	3.82	33	4	205.0	189	87	77	165
91 AL	17	10	3.41	35	15	253.2	212	96	82	191
Life	39	29	3.61	98	20	645.1	564	259	233	455
2 AVE	16	10	3.59	34	10	229.1	201	92	80	178

ROGER McDOWELL

Position: Pitcher
Team: Los Angeles Dodgers
Born: Dec. 21, 1960 Cincinnati, OH
Height: 6'1" **Weight:** 185 lbs.
Bats: right **Throws:** right
Acquired: Traded from Phillies for Mike Hartley and Braulio Castillo, 7/91

Player Summary	
Fantasy Value	$8 to $12
Card Value	3¢ to 5¢
Will	bank on sinker
Can't	help himself with defense
Expect	grounders not gophers
Don't Expect	high ERA

When McDowell's sinker sinks, he's one of the best relief pitchers in the National League. Because he induces opposing hitters to hit the ball on the ground, he's at his best on a team with strong infield defense. McDowell, who also throws a fastball, had four 20-save seasons and a career ERA of 3.05 before struggling a bit early in the '91 campaign. He doesn't get many strikeouts but keeps the ball in the park. He does have occasional control trouble, however, and gives up almost a hit per innings pitched. In 1991, opponents compiled a .262 batting average, a .357 slugging percentage, and a .346 on-base average. McDowell can hit and bunt but has trouble fielding and keeping runners close. Blessed with a rubber arm, he has worked more than 55 games in all seven of his big league seasons. A mildly promising fantasy choice, he shouldn't cost more than $12. His 1992 cards are duds.

Major League Pitching Register

	W	L	ERA	G	S	IP	H	ER	BB	SO
85 NL	6	5	2.83	62	17	127.1	108	40	37	70
86 NL	14	9	3.02	75	22	128.0	107	43	42	65
87 NL	7	5	4.16	56	25	88.2	95	41	28	32
88 NL	5	5	2.63	62	16	89.0	80	26	31	46
89 NL	4	8	1.96	69	23	92.0	79	20	38	47
90 NL	6	8	3.86	72	22	86.1	92	37	35	39
91 NL	9	9	2.93	71	10	101.3	100	33	48	50
Life	51	49	3.03	467	135	712.2	661	240	259	349
3 AVE	6	8	2.90	71	18	93.2	90	30	40	45

CHUCK McELROY

Position: Pitcher
Team: Chicago Cubs
Born: Oct. 1, 1967 Galveston, TX
Height: 6' **Weight:** 160 lbs.
Bats: left **Throws:** left
Acquired: Traded from Phillies with Bob Scanlan for Mitch Williams, 4/91

Player Summary	
Fantasy Value	$3 to $6
Card Value	5¢ to 10¢
Will	work often
Can't	always harness control
Expect	a whiff per inning
Don't Expect	many hits allowed

In his first major league season, McElroy lived up to the potential he had flashed for five seasons in the Philadelphia organization. Used primarily in middle relief, the hard-throwing lefthander yielded less than a hit per inning in 1991. His lone problem was periodic lapses of control. A fastball-and-curveball pitcher who began his career as a starter, McElroy throws strikes early in the count, trying to get ahead of opposing batters. He can sometimes get burned with this strategy. Nevertheless, he secured his 1992 bullpen spot with his superior rookie season. Philadelphia's second-round draft choice in 1986, McElroy had several cups of coffee with the Phils before they included him in the Mitch Williams trade last spring. In 1990 at Triple-A Scranton, McElroy was 6-8 with a 2.72 ERA, 78 strikeouts, 34 walks, 68 hits, 62 innings pitched, and seven saves. He had 12 saves for Double-A Reading in '89. His low ERA and high strikeouts can buoy needy fantasy teams for $5. Hold out on purchasing his dime-priced 1992 cards.

Major League Pitching Register

	W	L	ERA	G	S	IP	H	ER	BB	SO
89 NL	0	0	1.74	11	0	10.1	12	2	4	8
90 NL	0	1	7.71	16	0	14.0	24	12	10	16
91 NL	6	2	1.95	71	3	101.1	73	22	57	92
Life	6	3	2.58	98	3	125.2	109	36	71	116

WILLIE McGEE

Position: Outfield
Team: San Francisco Giants
Born: Nov. 2, 1958 San Francisco, CA
Height: 6'1" **Weight:** 195 lbs.
Bats: both **Throws:** right
Acquired: Signed as a free agent, 12/90

Player Summary	
Fantasy Value	$18 to $24
Card Value	5¢ to 7¢
Will	steal 30 bases
Can't	belt many homers
Expect	regular opposite-field hits
Don't Expect	fourth Gold Glove

McGee injured his right rib cage muscle while taking batting practice last July 2. The two-time batting champion had difficulty finding his stroke when he first returned, but he picked up the pace near the close of the season. He fanned twice as often as he walked. McGee still has the speed to play center but moved to right after rookie Darren Lewis made a strong impression as McGee's understudy. Though his throwing arm is not exceptional, he has used his speed to win three Gold Gloves. If he's healthy, the four-time All-Star can be expected to steal 30 bases. McGee was the NL MVP in 1985 for the Cardinals. Count on him as a solid fantasy pick for $20. His 1992 cards, priced at a nickel each, hold mild investor interest.

Major League Batting Register

	BA	G	AB	R	H	2B	3B	HR	RBI	SB
82 NL	.296	123	422	43	125	12	8	4	56	24
83 NL	.286	147	601	75	172	22	8	5	75	39
84 NL	.291	145	571	82	166	19	11	6	50	43
85 NL	.353	152	612	114	216	26	18	10	82	56
86 NL	.256	124	497	65	127	22	7	7	48	19
87 NL	.285	153	620	76	177	37	11	11	105	16
88 NL	.292	137	562	73	164	24	6	3	50	41
89 NL	.236	58	199	23	47	10	2	3	17	8
90 NL	.335	125	501	76	168	32	5	3	62	28
90 AL	.274	29	113	23	31	3	2	0	15	3
91 NL	.312	131	497	67	155	30	3	4	43	17
Life	.298	1324	5195	717	1548	237	81	56	603	294
3 AVE	.306	114	437	63	134	25	4	3	46	19

CURRENT PLAYERS

FRED McGRIFF

Position: First base
Team: San Diego Padres
Born: Oct. 31, 1963 Tampa, FL
Height: 6'3" **Weight:** 215 lbs.
Bats: left **Throws:** left
Acquired: Traded from Blue Jays with Tony Fernandez for Joe Carter and Roberto Alomar, 12/90

Player Summary	
Fantasy Value	$40 to $45
Card Value	10¢ to 15¢
Will	hit for power
Can't	steal a base
Expect	high on-base average
Don't Expect	decline in production

Though McGriff was overlooked for a berth on the NL All-Star squad in 1991, he was not overlooked by NL pitchers. In his first season in the league, he showed moving across league lines did not stifle his power. "Crime Dog" not only led the Padres in homers but tied a major league mark with grand slams in consecutive games, on August 13 and 14. McGriff was among the league leaders in home runs, RBI, slugging, and strikeouts. Though his average hovered below .280 most of the summer, his on-base percentage was .396 because he led the league in intentional walks and also had the patience to receive many unintentional passes. A fine fielder, McGriff's lack of speed is his one weakness. He has good hands, good reactions, and makes a good target. A cornerstone for your fantasy team, he is worth at least $40. His 1992 cards are good buys at a dime each.

Major League Batting Register

	BA	G	AB	R	H	2B	3B	HR	RBI	SB
86 AL	.200	3	5	1	1	0	0	0	0	0
87 AL	.247	107	295	58	73	16	0	20	43	3
88 AL	.282	154	536	100	151	35	4	34	82	6
89 AL	.269	161	551	98	148	27	3	36	92	7
90 AL	.300	153	557	91	167	21	1	35	88	5
91 NL	.278	153	528	84	147	19	1	31	106	4
Life	.278	731	2472	432	687	118	9	156	411	25
3 AVE	.282	156	545	91	154	22	2	34	95	5

MARK McGWIRE

Position: First base
Team: Oakland Athletics
Born: Oct. 1, 1963 Pomona, CA
Height: 6'5" **Weight:** 225 lbs.
Bats: right **Throws:** right
Acquired: First-round pick in 6/84 free-agent draft

Player Summary	
Fantasy Value	$20 to $24
Card Value	5¢ to 10¢
Will	hit for distance
Can't	hit for average
Expect	exceptional defense
Don't Expect	repeat of '87 or '91

McGwire hit a record 49 homers as a 1987 rookie, then became the only player to hit 30 homers in each of his first four seasons. Nagging injuries prevented him from hitting his weight in 1991, however. One wag even joked that his glove was keeping him in the lineup. Although the strong-armed McGwire is one of the game's best first basemen, his team counts on him most for long ball production. He had 22 homers in 483 at bats, but he also struck out 116 times, leading to his low batting average. He was among the league leaders with 93 walks and only four errors in the field. A big man with great bat speed, McGwire hammers mistakes and hits breaking balls well. On the negative side, he bangs into double-plays frequently. His nickel-priced 1992 cards are questionable buys. His fantasy value has declined, but he is a bargain draft for anything under $20.

Major League Batting Register

	BA	G	AB	R	H	2B	3B	HR	RBI	SB
86 AL	.189	18	53	10	10	1	0	3	9	0
87 AL	.289	151	557	97	161	28	4	49	118	1
88 AL	.260	155	550	87	143	22	1	32	99	0
89 AL	.231	143	490	74	113	17	0	33	95	1
90 AL	.235	156	523	87	123	16	0	39	108	2
91 AL	.201	154	483	62	97	22	0	22	75	2
Life	.244	777	2656	417	647	106	5	178	504	6
3 AVE	.223	151	499	74	111	18	0	31	93	2

CURRENT PLAYERS

BRIAN McRAE

Position: Outfield
Team: Kansas City Royals
Born: Aug. 27, 1967 Bradenton, FL
Height: 6' **Weight:** 180 lbs.
Bats: both **Throws:** right
Acquired: First-round pick in 6/85 free-agent draft

Player Summary	
Fantasy Value	$0 to $14
Card Value	10¢ to 15¢
Will	add defense
Can't	power ball consistently
Expect	average to rise
Don't Expect	drop off in defense

McRae won't soon forget his first full major league season. He led the Royals with a 22-game hitting streak and got the chance to play for his father when Hal McRae replaced John Wathan as manager. Brian, who hit .386 during his streak, gave the Royals one of the league's top leadoff men. He even delivered an inside-the-park home run, something his dad had done for the Royals more than a dozen years earlier. A switch-hitter who murders lefthanders, McRae has the speed to steal 30 bases a year. He also has some power, thanks to the bulging biceps on his wiry frame. He notched a .372 slugging percentage and a .288 on-base average in '91. McRae was AL Player of the Month in May after producing 29 hits, 17 runs, 15 RBI, and five steals. The one-time infielder supplies strong defense in center field. He hit .268 with 10 homers, 24 doubles, 64 RBI, 72 runs scored, and 21 stolen bases at Double-A Memphis in 1990. He is a phenomenal fantasy choice at $12. Likewise, his 1992 cards are great pickups at 15 cents.

Major League Batting Register

	BA	G	AB	R	H	2B	3B	HR	RBI	SB
90 AL	.286	46	168	21	48	8	3	2	23	4
91 AL	.261	152	629	86	164	28	9	8	64	20
Life	.266	198	797	107	212	36	12	10	87	24
2 AVE	.266	99	399	54	106	18	6	5	44	12

KEVIN McREYNOLDS

Position: Outfield
Team: Kansas City Royals
Born: Oct. 16, 1959 Little Rock, AR
Height: 6'1" **Weight:** 215 lbs.
Bats: right **Throws:** right
Acquired: Traded from Mets with Gregg Jeffries and Keith Miller for Bret Saberhagen and Bill Pecota, 12/91

Player Summary	
Fantasy Value	$12 to $16
Card Value	3¢ to 5¢
Will	provide good defense
Can't	reach .300 plateau
Expect	clutch run production
Don't Expect	many walks or whiffs

After topping 20 home runs and 80 RBI for five straight seasons, the power production of McReynolds fell sharply in 1991. Counted on to fill the void created by the free-agent desertion of Darryl Strawberry, McReynolds hit several clutch homers, all in the first half of the season. McReynolds did produce his normal batting average, and he also notched a .416 slugging percentage and a .332 on-base average. His fantasy value has fallen to $14 or so. His 1992 common-priced cards are intriguing gambles. He played solid defense—especially in left field, his best position. He wasn't happy when asked to play right and center. The Mets traded the disgruntled outfielder to Kansas City in December.

Major League Batting Register

	BA	G	AB	R	H	2B	3B	HR	RBI	SB
83 NL	.221	39	140	15	31	3	1	4	14	2
84 NL	.278	147	525	68	146	26	6	20	75	3
85 NL	.234	152	564	61	132	24	4	15	75	4
86 NL	.287	158	560	89	161	31	6	26	96	8
87 NL	.276	151	590	86	163	32	5	29	95	14
88 NL	.288	147	552	82	159	30	2	27	99	21
89 NL	.272	148	545	74	148	25	3	22	85	15
90 NL	.269	147	521	75	140	23	1	24	82	9
91 NL	.259	143	522	65	135	32	1	16	74	6
Life	.269	1232	4519	615	1215	226	29	183	695	82
3 AVE	.266	146	529	71	141	27	2	21	80	10

CURRENT PLAYERS

JOSE MELENDEZ

Position: Pitcher
Team: San Diego Padres
Born: Sept. 2, 1965 Naguabo, Puerto Rico
Height: 6'2" **Weight:** 175 lbs.
Bats: right **Throws:** right
Acquired: Acquired from Mariners through waiver claim, 3/91

Player Summary	
Fantasy Value	$2 to $4
Card Value	10¢ to 15¢
Will	post good K-to-walk ratio
Can't	start as well as he relieves
Expect	heavier workload
Don't Expect	inflated ERA

Melendez found his niche after moving from the rotation to the bullpen last July 4. In his first 13 relief outings, spanning 25⅔ innings, he went 3-0 with a 1.05 ERA. Melendez got his first save August 24 with two hitless innings against the Cubs. He started eight games and had one relief appearance for Triple-A Las Vegas in '91, going 7-0 with a 3.99 ERA, 45 strikeouts, and 11 walks in 59 innings. He began his pro career in 1984. In 1990 at Triple-A Calgary, he was 11-4 with a 3.90 ERA and two saves. He struck out 95, and allowed 44 bases on balls and 119 hits in 124⅔ innings. He saw no big league action before Seattle gave him a brief trial at the end of the 1990 campaign. In 1991, he showed good control, fanning more than twice the number he walked, and yielded less than a hit per inning. His undoing was the gopher ball. He allowed 11 homers. Melendez has proven he can pitch in the majors. He is a $3 fantasy draft pick at this point in his career. His 1992 cards are overpriced at 15 cents a pop.

Major League Pitching Register

	W	L	ERA	G	S	IP	H	ER	BB	SO
90 AL	0	0	11.81	3	0	5.1	8	7	3	7
91 NL	8	5	3.27	31	3	93.2	77	34	24	60
Life	8	5	3.73	34	3	99.0	85	41	27	67

BOB MELVIN

Position: Catcher
Team: Kansas City Royals
Born: Oct. 28, 1961 Palo Alto, CA
Height: 6'4" **Weight:** 210 lbs.
Bats: right **Throws:** right
Acquired: Traded from Orioles for Storm Davis, 12/91

Player Summary	
Fantasy Value	$1 to $3
Card Value	3¢ to 5¢
Will	call a great game
Can't	hit for power
Expect	him to throw well
Don't Expect	high on-base percentage

Though he may not hit much, Melvin will remain in the majors because of his glove. One of the game's best defensive catchers, he handles pitchers well, knows enemy hitters, has a very strong arm, presents a good target, and blocks potential wild pitches. An impatient hitter who rarely walks, Melvin has some pop in his bat. He hit 19 homers over a two-year span for the 1987 and '88 Giants. He posted the best average of his seven-year career in 1991. A spray hitter often used in a strict platoon against lefthanded pitching, Melvin hits better in clutch situations. He has no speed, however, so he can't pad his average with infield hits. He notched a .307 slugging percentage and a .279 on-base average in '91. He is a $2 receiver. His 1992 commons are not buys. Melvin was delat to the Royals in December.

Major League Batting Register

	BA	G	AB	R	H	2B	3B	HR	RBI	SB
85 AL	.220	41	82	10	18	4	1	0	4	0
86 NL	.224	89	268	24	60	14	2	5	25	3
87 NL	.199	84	246	31	49	8	0	11	31	0
88 NL	.234	92	273	23	64	13	1	8	27	0
89 AL	.241	85	278	22	67	10	1	1	32	1
90 AL	.243	93	301	30	73	14	1	5	37	0
91 AL	.250	79	228	11	57	10	0	1	23	0
Life	.232	563	1676	151	388	73	6	31	179	4
3 AVE	.244	86	269	21	66	11	1	2	31	0

CURRENT PLAYERS

ORLANDO MERCED

Position: First base
Team: Pittsburgh Pirates
Born: Nov. 2, 1966 San Juan, PR
Height: 5'11" **Weight:** 170 lbs.
Bats: both **Throws:** right
Acquired: Signed as free agent, 2/85

Player Summary
Fantasy Value	$3 to $7
Card Value	15¢ to 20¢
Will	devour lefthanders
Can't	play other positions
Expect	walks and hits
Don't Expect	Sid Bream's power

The final Pittsburgh cut of 1991 spring training, Merced returned 10 days later and quickly became a contender for NL Rookie of the Year. He filled the dual role of replacing popular free-agent defector Sid Bream at first base and batting leadoff for the first time in his career. Merced's on-base percentage against lefthanded pitchers was over .400. He notched a .399 slugging percentage and a .373 on-base average in '91. A switch-hitter who's usually more potent from the left side, he is expected to move into an RBI spot eventually. He batted .262 with nine homers, 55 RBI, and 14 stolen bases at Triple-A Buffalo in 1990. The former neighbor of the late Pirate great Roberto Clemente, Merced has some speed and good range at first base. He can also play third base, the outfield, or catch in an emergency. An offensive plus to a fantasy team is his moving to the outfield to leave your first base position in more power-conscious hands. His 1992 cards look good at 15 cents apiece.

Major League Batting Register
	BA	G	AB	R	H	2B	3B	HR	RBI	SB
90 NL	.208	25	24	3	5	1	0	0	0	0
91 NL	.275	120	411	83	113	17	2	10	50	8
Life	.271	145	435	86	118	18	2	10	50	8

KENT MERCKER

Position: Pitcher
Team: Atlanta Braves
Born: Feb. 1, 1968 Dublin, OH
Height: 6'2" **Weight:** 195 lbs.
Bats: left **Throws:** left
Acquired: First-round pick in 6/86 free-agent draft

Player Summary
Fantasy Value	$4 to $8
Card Value	3¢ to 5¢
Will	blaze fastball by hitters
Can't	avoid control lapses
Expect	good hits-to-frames ratio
Don't Expect	quick return to relief

Mercker made 44 relief appearances for the 1991 Braves before he won the team's No. 5 starting job on September 6. A starter in the minors, Mercker has always had a live arm. He throws a hopping fastball, curve, and changeup, but sometimes has trouble finding the strike zone. He compensates by getting lots of strikeouts, helping himself at the plate, and fielding his position well. He fanned twice as many as he walked in 1991, and he allowed fewer hits than innings pitched. Opponents compiled a .211 batting average, a .316 slugging percentage, and a .303 on-base average in '91. If he maintains those levels, he will be a successful starter. In 1990 at Triple-A Richmond, he was 5-4 with a 3.55 ERA, one save, 69 strikeouts, and 27 walks in 58⅓ innings. He led the International League with 144 strikeouts and 95 walks at Richmond in '89, going 9-12 with a 3.20 ERA and four complete games. His more defined role in '91 should make his fantasy value rise to $6. His 1992 cards are not going to rise above commons prices right away.

Major League Pitching Register
	W	L	ERA	G	S	IP	H	ER	BB	SO
89 NL	0	0	12.46	2	0	4.1	8	6	6	4
90 NL	4	7	3.17	36	7	48.1	43	17	24	39
91 NL	5	3	2.58	50	6	73.1	56	21	35	62
Life	9	10	3.14	88	13	126.0	107	44	65	105
2 AVE	5	5	2.81	43	7	61.1	50	19	30	51

CURRENT PLAYERS

JOSE MESA

Position: Pitcher
Team: Baltimore Orioles
Born: May 22, 1966 Azua, Dominican Republic
Height: 6'3" **Weight:** 219 lbs.
Bats: right **Throws:** right
Acquired: Traded from Blue Jays with Oswaldo Peraza for Mike Flanagan, 8/87

Player Summary	
Fantasy Value	$1 to $2
Card Value	3¢ to 5¢
Will	seek rotation spot
Can't	avoid walks or homers
Expect	blazing speed if healthy
Don't Expect	good K-to-walk ratio

After bouncing around in the minors for 10 years, Mesa received his first extended tour in the AL last season. He allowed more than a hit per inning, walked as many men as he struck out, and threw too many home run balls (11). Opponents compiled a .307 batting average, a .449 slugging percentage, and a .385 on-base average in '91. Yet he showed enough raw ability to remain in the rotation. A hard thrower who missed nearly two years after a pair of elbow operations, Mesa mixes a curveball and changeup with a fastball once timed at 94 miles per hour. He also throws a slider. Once compared favorably with Jose Rijo, Mesa has never won more than 10 games in a season but could erase that dubious distinction if he gets adequate support and good health. At Triple-A Rochester in '91, he was 3-3 with a 3.86 ERA, eight starts, 48 strikeouts, and 30 walks in 51 innings. He is not a good $1 fantasy gamble. His 1992 commons don't have much potential.

HENSLEY MEULENS

Position: Outfield
Team: New York Yankees
Born: June 23, 1967 Curacao, Netherlands Antilles
Height: 6'3" **Weight:** 212 lbs.
Bats: right **Throws:** right
Acquired: Signed as a free agent, 10/85

Player Summary	
Fantasy Value	$3 to $6
Card Value	3¢ to 5¢
Will	get five Ks per walk
Can't	make contact
Expect	sporadic homers
Don't Expect	much team patience

Meulens was the Triple-A International League Player of the Year in 1990 but a Rookie of the Year candidate gone bust in 1991. A former third baseman moved to left field to hide his glove, he failed to generate the same power in New York, but he fanned just as often. He had a .319 slugging average, a .276 on-base average, and 97 Ks in 288 at bats in 1991. "Bam-Bam" hits the ball hard when he connects, but he doesn't make contact with enough frequency to hold a job on a team overloaded with outfielders. He could return to third. Meulens played eight games there in 1989 but failed to field or hit. A year later, manager Clete Boyer coaxed Meulens into the great year at Triple-A Columbus. He batted .285 with 26 homers, 20 doubles, 96 RBI, and 81 walks. He followed by topping the Venezuelan Winter League with a .338 average. In 1987, he had 28 homers and 105 RBI at Class-A Prince William. Still young, Meulens needs to capitalize on his power-hitting potential.

Major League Pitching Register

	W	L	ERA	G	CG	IP	H	ER	BB	SO
87 AL	1	3	6.03	6	0	31.1	38	21	15	17
90 AL	3	2	3.86	7	0	46.2	37	20	27	24
91 AL	6	11	5.97	23	2	123.2	151	82	62	64
Life	10	16	5.49	36	2	201.2	226	123	104	105

Major League Batting Register

	BA	G	AB	R	H	2B	3B	HR	RBI	SB
89 AL	.179	8	28	2	5	0	0	0	1	0
90 AL	.241	23	83	12	20	7	0	3	10	1
91 AL	.222	96	288	37	64	8	1	6	29	3
Life	.223	127	399	51	89	15	1	9	40	4

CURRENT PLAYERS

BOB MILACKI

Position: Pitcher
Team: Baltimore Orioles
Born: July 28, 1964 Trenton, NJ
Height: 6'4" **Weight:** 225 lbs.
Bats: right **Throws:** right
Acquired: Second-round pick in 6/83 free-agent draft

Player Summary	
Fantasy Value	$6 to $8
Card Value	3¢ to 5¢
Will	win with support
Can't	prevent gophers
Expect	good K-to-walk ratio
Don't Expect	further bullpen work

Milacki was the biggest winner on the Baltimore staff in 1991. His best game came on July 13, when he was the first of four Orioles who threw a no-hitter at Oakland. Milacki lasted six innings before leaving with a hand injury. He had three complete games in 1991, with one shutout. He has good control of his fastball, curve, slider, and changeup but is prone to throwing gopher balls. He strikes out twice the number he walks and allows less than a hit per inning. Oriole confusion over how to use him last year hurt his effectiveness. He came out of spring training as a reliever, moving to the rotation after five games. He played well enough to start for the remainder. He won 14 games in 1989, his best season, when he was strictly a starting pitcher. That is the role he'll fill in 1992. If his draft price is an affordable $7, give him a chance on your fantasy team. His 1992 commons are limited.

KEITH MILLER

Position: Second base; outfield
Team: Kansas City Royals
Born: June 12, 1963 Midland, MI
Height: 5'11" **Weight:** 180 lbs.
Bats: right **Throws:** right
Acquired: Traded from Mets with Kevin McReynolds and Gregg Jeffries for Bret Saberhagen and Bill Peota, 12/91

Player Summary	
Fantasy Value	$3 to $5
Card Value	3¢ to 5¢
Will	make contact
Can't	produce extra-base hits
Expect	line drives
Don't Expect	return to utility job

Miller began the 1991 campaign as a supersub but finished it as the leadoff man and regular second baseman. His 7-for-14 explosion in a Labor Day weekend series against the Reds sparked a rare New York sweep. He had a game-winning single August 30 and a game-winning homer—against flame-throwing Rob Dibble—the next night. A spray hitter who can bunt, Miller doesn't walk as much as a typical leadoff man and could drop to the No. 2 slot in 1992. On the plus side, he doesn't strike out much either. Miller was traded to Kansas City in the off-season and is scheduled to start at second base. He will keep that job if his offense holds up. Miller has some power, as well as some speed, and should improve his production with more playing time. His fantasy value will top out at $5, and his 1992 cards will remain commons, at least until he has a break-through season.

Major League Pitching Register

	W	L	ERA	G	CG	IP	H	ER	BB	SO
88 AL	2	0	0.72	3	1	25.0	9	2	9	18
89 AL	14	12	3.74	37	3	243.0	233	101	88	113
90 AL	5	8	4.46	27	1	135.1	143	67	61	60
91 AL	10	9	4.01	31	3	184.0	175	82	53	108
Life	31	29	3.86	98	8	587.1	560	252	211	299
3 AVE	10	10	4.00	32	2	187.0	184	83	67	94

Major League Batting Register

	BA	G	AB	R	H	2B	3B	HR	RBI	SB
87 NL	.373	25	51	14	19	2	2	0	1	8
88 NL	.214	40	70	9	15	1	1	1	5	0
89 NL	.231	57	143	15	33	7	0	1	7	6
90 NL	.258	88	233	42	60	8	0	1	12	16
91 NL	.280	98	275	41	77	22	1	4	23	14
Life	.264	308	772	121	204	40	4	7	48	44
2 AVE	.270	93	254	42	69	15	1	3	18	15

CURRENT PLAYERS

RANDY MILLIGAN

Position: First base; outfield
Team: Baltimore Orioles
Born: Nov. 27, 1961 San Diego, CA
Height: 6'2" **Weight:** 225 lbs.
Bats: right **Throws:** right
Acquired: Traded from Pirates for Pete Blohm, 11/88

Player Summary	
Fantasy Value	$15 to $20
Card Value	5¢ to 7¢
Will	coax walks
Can't	help on defense
Expect	more RBI if he plays
Don't Expect	average under .260

Milligan played more but produced less in 1991 than he had the year before. He had 20 homers and 60 RBI before he dislocated his shoulder in a home-plate collision on August 7, 1990. He didn't approach those figures in 1991. Perhaps uncertainty over his role played a part in the power plunge. He was used as a first baseman, left fielder, designated hitter, and pinch-hitter, with mixed results. Given the confidence that accompanies a steady position, Milligan figures to be a better run producer. He draws a large number of walks (84 in '91) and doesn't strike out as often (108 in '91) as other sluggers. He had a .406 slugging percentage and a .373 on-base average in 1991. Fantasy managers should note that he is a low-cost power source at $15. His nickel-priced 1992 cards don't generate much heat, though. Defensively, designated hitter is his best position. But he tries, and he brings a good attitude with him into the clubhouse.

Major League Batting Register

	BA	G	AB	R	H	2B	3B	HR	RBI	SB
87 NL	.000	3	1	0	0	0	0	0	0	0
88 NL	.220	40	82	10	18	5	0	3	8	1
89 AL	.268	124	365	56	98	23	5	12	45	9
90 AL	.265	109	362	64	96	20	1	20	60	6
91 AL	.263	141	483	57	127	17	2	16	70	0
Life	.262	417	1293	187	339	65	8	51	183	16
3 AVE	.265	125	403	59	107	20	3	16	58	5

KEITH MITCHELL

Position: Outfield
Team: Atlanta Braves
Born: Aug. 6, 1969 San Diego, CA
Height: 5'10" **Weight:** 180 lbs.
Bats: right **Throws:** right
Acquired: Fourth-round pick in 6/87 free-agent draft

Player Summary	
Fantasy Value	$5 to $8
Card Value	15¢ to 20¢
Will	have high average
Can't	stay on the bench
Expect	good defense
Don't Expect	cousin Kevin's power

Although he is the second cousin of slugger Kevin Mitchell, Keith Mitchell is not expected to produce as many home runs, even in a cozy home park like Atlanta-Fulton County Stadium. He is, however, expected to hit for a high average, steal more bases than his cousin, and play strong defense in the outfield. In his major league debut July 23, Mitchell had three hits, a stolen base, and an RBI. He finished the season with a .409 slugging percentage and a .392 on-base average. In the World Series, he made an unfortunate mistake, losing a fly ball in the Metrodome ceiling. He will challenge for Atlanta's regular left field job in 1992. He also batted .326 with two homers, 17 RBI, 13 strikeouts, and nine walks in 55 at bats at Triple-A Richmond in 1991. At Double-A Greenville in '91, he batted .327 with 10 homers, 47 RBI, 15 doubles, 12 stolen bases, 29 strikeouts, and 29 walks in 214 at bats. He was the Southern League's No. 8 prospect. His stats hint of big rewards for fantasy managers up to $8. His 1992 cards are choice picks at 15 cents each.

Major League Batting Register

	BA	G	AB	R	H	2B	3B	HR	RBI	SB
91 NL	.318	48	66	11	21	0	0	2	5	3
Life	.318	48	66	11	21	0	0	2	5	3

CURRENT PLAYERS

KEVIN MITCHELL

Position: Outfield
Team: Seattle Mariners
Born: Jan. 13, 1962 San Diego, CA
Height: 5'11" **Weight:** 210 lbs.
Bats: right **Throws:** right
Acquired: Traded from Giants with Mike Remlinger for Bill Swift, Mike Jackson and Dave Burba, 12/91

Player Summary
Fantasy Value	$35 to $40
Card Value	5¢ to 10¢
Will	show tremendous power
Can't	play strong defense
Expect	a good average
Don't Expect	injuries to cut playing time

Although bothered by bone chips in his right wrist plus a sore knee that required arthroscopic surgery, Mitchell remained one of the most prolific run producers in the major leagues in 1991. He was the NL MVP with 47 homers and 125 RBI in 1989. He doesn't strike out as much as most other sluggers, and he's patient enough to work pitchers for walks. He notched a .515 slugging percentage and a .338 on-base average in '91. A hustling, aggressive player, Mitchell runs well but doesn't steal much. He catches anything hit his way in left field but has to compensate for a mediocre arm with accurate throws. In December, Mitchell was traded to Seattle, where he'll thrive in the Kingdome. An offensive force, he still brings $35 to $40 in fantasy drafts. His dime-priced 1992 cards are great purchases.

Major League Batting Register

	BA	G	AB	R	H	2B	3B	HR	RBI	SB
84 NL	.214	7	14	0	3	0	0	0	1	0
86 NL	.277	108	328	51	91	22	2	12	43	3
87 NL	.280	131	328	68	130	20	2	22	70	9
88 NL	.251	148	505	60	127	25	7	19	80	5
89 NL	.291	154	543	100	158	34	6	47	125	3
90 NL	.290	140	524	90	152	24	2	35	93	4
91 NL	.256	113	371	52	95	13	1	27	69	2
Life	.275	801	2749	421	756	138	20	162	481	26
3 AVE	.282	136	479	81	135	24	3	36	96	3

PAUL MOLITOR

Position: Infield
Team: Milwaukee Brewers
Born: Aug. 22, 1956 St. Paul, MN
Height: 6' **Weight:** 185 lbs.
Bats: right **Throws:** right
Acquired: First-round pick in 6/77 free-agent draft

Player Summary
Fantasy Value	$23 to $30
Card Value	5¢ to 10¢
Will	make contact
Can't	avoid the disabled list
Expect	good speed and some pop
Don't Expect	play anywhere but first

Molitor is one of the game's best hitters but one of its most brittle stars. He hit for the cycle for the first time in his career on May 15. He continued to swing a potent bat, getting a .489 slugging percentage in 1991, with a .399 on-base average. He also plays a decent defensive game at first base, a position he tried in 1990 to ease the strain on his troublesome shoulder. He was a second baseman when he came up, and he has also played third base. His injury history curbs higher fantasy bids than $30. Molitor has landed on the disabled list a dozen times in his 14-year career. The four-time All-Star's nickel-priced 1992 cards have some long-term attraction.

Major League Batting Register

	BA	G	AB	R	H	2B	3B	HR	RBI	SB
78 AL	.273	125	521	73	142	26	4	6	45	30
79 AL	.322	140	584	88	188	27	16	9	62	33
80 AL	.304	111	450	81	137	29	2	9	37	34
81 AL	.267	64	251	45	67	11	0	2	19	10
82 AL	.302	160	666	136	201	26	8	19	71	41
83 AL	.270	152	608	95	164	28	6	15	47	41
84 AL	.217	13	46	3	10	1	0	0	6	1
85 AL	.297	140	576	93	171	28	3	10	48	21
86 AL	.281	105	437	62	123	24	6	9	55	20
87 AL	.353	118	465	114	164	41	5	16	75	45
88 AL	.312	154	609	115	190	34	6	13	60	41
89 AL	.315	155	615	84	194	35	4	11	56	27
90 AL	.285	103	418	64	119	27	6	12	45	18
91 AL	.325	158	665	133	216	32	13	17	75	19
Life	.302	1698	6911	1186	2086	369	79	148	701	381
3 AVE	.312	139	566	94	176	31	8	13	59	21

195

CURRENT PLAYERS

JEFF MONTGOMERY

Position: Pitcher
Team: Kansas City Royals
Born: Jan. 7, 1962 Wellston, OH
Height: 5'11" **Weight:** 180 lbs.
Bats: right **Throws:** right
Acquired: Traded from Reds for Van Snider, 2/88

Player Summary	
Fantasy Value	$33 to $40
Card Value	3¢ to 5¢
Will	throw heat by batters
Can't	always escape control lapses
Expect	60-plus calls
Don't Expect	gophers to expand ERA

Even after the Royals signed Mark Davis for the 1990 season, Montgomery did not relinquish his role as the club's top closer. When Davis did little to defend his NL Cy Young Award, Montgomery moved in and never let go. He began 1991 with a flourish, winning Royal Pitcher of the Month honors in April with a 1-1 record, five saves, and 1.74 ERA. He retired 33 of the 40 hitters he faced. Montgomery wins by throwing strikes. He uses his fastball, curve, and slider to fan three times more men than he walks. He keeps the ball in the park and makes a habit of finishing games in which he appears. Opponents compiled a .246 batting average, a .355 slugging percentage, and a .305 on-base percentage in '91. Montgomery has a good glove and a sound pickoff move. He's one of the highest ranking relievers in the game. His fantasy lot has soared to $40. His 1992 commons, though, remain in the boxes.

Major League Pitching Register

	W	L	ERA	G	S	IP	H	ER	BB	SO
87 NL	2	2	6.52	14	0	19.1	25	14	9	13
88 AL	7	2	3.45	45	1	62.2	54	24	30	47
89 AL	7	3	1.37	63	18	92.0	66	14	25	94
90 AL	6	5	2.39	73	24	94.1	81	25	34	94
91 AL	4	4	2.90	67	33	90.0	83	29	28	77
Life	26	16	2.66	262	76	358.1	309	106	126	325
3 AVE	6	4	2.21	68	25	92.0	77	23	29	88

MIKE MOORE

Position: Pitcher
Team: Oakland Athletics
Born: Nov. 26, 1959 Eakly, OK
Height: 6'4" **Weight:** 205 lbs.
Bats: right **Throws:** right
Acquired: Signed as a free agent, 11/88

Player Summary	
Fantasy Value	$10 to $14
Card Value	3¢ to 5¢
Will	win 15 games
Can't	always keep ERA low
Expect	under a hit a frame
Don't Expect	pinpoint control

In his third season with Oakland in 1991, Moore became the top starter on the staff. While Dave Stewart and Bob Welch slumped, Moore won the most games for the A's, plus he notched three complete games and one shutout. He ranked first on the A's in strikeouts. His only weak spot was a tendency to issue too many walks. Moore mixes a sinker, slider, and split-fingered fastball with great success. The former first-round draft choice (by Seattle in 1981) helps himself with his fielding and ability to keep runners close. A cross between a power and a finesse pitcher, Moore gets grounders with his sinker and strikeouts with his other pitches. He should be at the peak of his game. A solid $12 fantasy hurler, his 1992 commons don't have a chance to appreciate.

Major League Pitching Register

	W	L	ERA	G	CG	IP	H	ER	BB	SO
82 AL	7	14	5.36	28	1	144.1	159	86	79	73
83 AL	6	8	4.71	22	3	128.0	130	67	60	108
84 AL	7	17	4.97	34	6	212.0	236	117	85	158
85 AL	17	10	3.46	35	14	247.0	230	95	70	155
86 AL	11	13	4.30	38	11	266.0	279	127	94	146
87 AL	9	19	4.71	33	12	231.0	268	121	84	115
88 AL	9	15	3.78	37	9	228.2	196	96	63	182
89 AL	19	11	2.61	35	6	241.2	193	70	83	172
90 AL	13	15	4.65	33	3	199.1	204	103	84	73
91 AL	17	8	2.96	33	4	210.0	176	69	105	153
Life	115	130	4.06	328	68	2108.0	2071	951	807	1335
3 AVE	16	11	3.35	34	4	217.1	191	81	91	133

CURRENT PLAYERS

MICKEY MORANDINI

Position: Second base
Team: Philadelphia Phillies
Born: April 22, 1966 Kittanning, PA
Height: 5'11" **Weight:** 170 lbs.
Bats: left **Throws:** right
Acquired: Fifth-round pick in 6/88 free-agent draft

Player Summary	
Fantasy Value	$3 to $0
Card Value	5¢ to 10¢
Will	slap hits to all fields
Can't	produce runs
Expect	good defense
Don't Expect	substantial power

Morandini may not hit many home runs but his defense will keep him in the big leagues. He had six errors at second, a small number for someone with so little experience. Once he learns how to position himself for all the batters in all the situations, he should be able to cut down on that number. Since Morandini is a converted shortstop, he has a good arm and good range at second base. He is adept at turning the double-play. He also managed to steal 13 bases in 15 tries, even though his .313 on-base average did not allow him to reach base frequently. He proved himself to be a contact hitter who strikes out just a few more times than he walks. He also notched a .317 slugging percentage in '91. As his knowledge of pitchers grows, his walk total—and his stolen bases—should expand. His stolen bases boost his fantasy value to $4. His dime-priced 1992 cards are slightly overpriced. The 1988 Olympian is a good bunter who sprays hits to all fields. He'll lose playing time in 1992 since the Phillies have signed Mariano Duncan.

Major League Batting Register

	BA	G	AB	R	H	2B	3B	HR	RBI	SB
90 NL	.241	25	79	9	19	4	0	1	3	3
91 NL	.249	98	325	38	81	11	4	1	20	13
Life	.248	123	404	47	100	15	4	2	23	16

MIKE MORGAN

Position: Pitcher
Team: Chicago Cubs
Born: Oct. 8, 1959 Tulare, CA
Height: 6'2" **Weight:** 215 lbs.
Bats: right **Throws:** right
Acquired: Traded from Orioles for Mike Devereaux, 3/89

Player Summary	
Fantasy Value	$6 to $8
Card Value	3¢ to 5¢
Will	pitch 200-plus innings
Can't	post decent won-lost mark
Expect	ground-ball outs
Don't Expect	ERA over 4.00

Morgan strikes out twice as many men as he walks but doesn't consider himself a strikeout pitcher. He prefers to get ground-ball outs. A sinker-and-slider pitcher who uses a four-seam fastball and split-fingered fastball as changeups, he relies on control—and his infield—to retire rival hitters. A 1991 All-Star, he was second on the staff to Ramon Martinez with five complete games. Morgan then signed a free-agent contract with the Cubs after the season. He doesn't hit well but does keep runners close and field his position respectably. He keeps his team in the game and gives his manager more than 200 innings a year. He isn't a great fantasy pick, $8 at most. His 1992 cards will remain commons. Morgan's winning record in 1991 was the first in his major league career.

Major League Pitching Register

	W	L	ERA	G	CG	IP	H	ER	BB	SO
78 AL	0	3	7.30	3	1	12.1	19	10	8	0
79 AL	2	10	5.94	13	2	77.1	102	51	50	17
82 AL	7	11	4.37	30	2	150.1	167	73	67	71
83 AL	0	3	5.16	16	0	45.1	48	26	21	22
85 AL	1	1	12.00	2	0	6.0	11	8	5	2
86 AL	11	17	4.53	37	9	216.1	243	109	86	116
87 AL	12	17	4.65	34	8	207.0	245	107	53	85
88 AL	1	6	5.43	22	2	71.1	70	43	23	29
89 NL	8	11	2.53	40	0	152.2	130	43	33	72
90 NL	11	15	3.75	33	6	211.0	216	88	60	106
91 NL	14	10	2.78	34	5	236.1	197	73	61	140
Life	67	104	4.10	264	35	1386.0	1448	631	467	660
3 AVE	11	12	3.06	36	4	200.1	181	68	51	106

CURRENT PLAYERS

HAL MORRIS

Position: First base
Team: Cincinnati Reds
Born: April 9, 1965 Fort Rucker, AL
Height: 6'4" **Weight:** 215 lbs.
Bats: left **Throws:** left
Acquired: Traded from Yankees with Rodney Imes for Tim Leary and Van Snider, 12/89

Player Summary	
Fantasy Value	$10 to $14
Card Value	5¢ to 10¢
Will	hit line drives
Can't	compete for Gold Glove
Expect	sporadic power
Don't Expect	much time in outfield

After hitting .340 as a rookie in 1990, Morris knew he had established a lofty standard of excellence. He smashed the sophomore jinx, however, with another strong performance. A student of hitting whose boyhood hero was Rod Carew, Morris got off to a great start in 1991. During one week in May, he hit .533 with a home run, five RBI, two stolen bases, and six walks. He competed for the batting title all the way to the last game of the season. A contact hitter who walks almost as often as he strikes out, Morris has also improved his defense at first base. His sparking offense translates into a $12 fantasy bid. His dime-priced 1992 cards are overpriced, however. He led the Triple-A International League with a .326 batting average in 1989. The former Michigan star was a college teammate of Barry Larkin and Jim Abbott. Morris has a good baseball background; his great uncle is Buddy Lewis, a former All-Star.

Major League Batting Register

	BA	G	AB	R	H	2B	3B	HR	RBI	SB
88 AL	.100	15	20	1	2	0	0	0	0	0
89 AL	.278	15	18	2	5	0	0	0	4	0
90 NL	.340	107	309	50	105	22	3	7	36	9
91 NL	.318	136	478	72	152	33	1	14	59	10
Life	.320	273	825	125	264	55	4	21	99	19
2 AVE	.327	122	394	61	129	28	2	11	48	10

JACK MORRIS

Position: Pitcher
Team: Toronto Blue Jays
Born: May 16, 1955 St. Paul, MN
Height: 6'3" **Weight:** 200 lbs.
Bats: right **Throws:** right
Acquired: Signed as a free agent, 12/91

Player Summary	
Fantasy Value	$17 to $22
Card Value	5¢ to 10¢
Will	pitch 200-plus frames
Can't	avoid gopher balls
Expect	at least 15 wins
Don't Expect	frequent control lapses

Morris was masterful in the World Series, earning the MVP nod. After growing up watching Harmon Killebrew and Tony Oliva, Morris had always wanted to play for Minnesota. After spending 14 years with the Tigers, he got his wish in 1991. He is a classic power pitcher, employing a forkball, fastball, hard slider, and change. He was struck by two line drives last year—including one in the All-Star Game—but remained in the rotation. Morris is an intense competitor who screams at himself. Former coach Roger Craig calls him "the Will Clark of pitching." Morris's fantasy value flourished, but deliberate before paying more than $22 for him. Morris signed a free-agent contract with Toronto in December.

Major League Pitching Register

	W	L	ERA	G	CG	IP	H	ER	BB	SO
77 AL	1	1	3.74	7	1	45.2	38	19	23	28
78 AL	3	5	4.33	28	0	106.0	107	51	49	48
79 AL	17	7	3.28	27	9	197.2	179	72	59	113
80 AL	16	15	4.18	36	11	250.0	252	116	87	112
81 AL	14	7	3.05	25	15	198.0	153	67	78	97
82 AL	17	16	4.06	37	17	266.1	247	120	96	135
83 AL	20	13	3.34	37	20	293.2	257	109	83	232
84 AL	19	11	3.60	35	9	240.1	221	96	87	148
85 AL	16	11	3.33	35	2	257.0	212	95	110	191
86 AL	21	8	3.27	35	15	267.0	229	97	82	223
87 AL	18	11	3.38	34	13	266.0	227	100	93	208
88 AL	15	13	3.94	34	10	235.0	225	103	83	168
89 AL	6	14	4.86	24	10	170.1	189	92	59	115
90 AL	15	18	4.51	36	11	249.2	231	125	97	162
91 AL	18	12	3.43	35	10	246.2	226	94	92	163
Life	216	162	3.71	465	164	3289.1	2993	1356	1178	2143
3 AVE	13	15	4.20	32	10	222.2	215	104	83	147

CURRENT PLAYERS

LLOYD MOSEBY

Position: Outfield
Team: Detroit Tigers
Born: Nov. 5, 1959 Portland, AK
Height: 6'3" **Weight:** 200 lbs.
Bats: left **Throws:** right
Acquired: Signed as a free agent, 12/89

Player Summary	
Fantasy Value	$3 to $6
Card Value	3¢ to 5¢
Will	punish righties
Can't	make contact
Expect	continued decline
Don't Expect	strong outfield throws

Moseby had his best major league seasons for the Blue Jays, but remained an important contributor to the Tigers in 1991. On August 4, he singled home the winning run in the 10th inning for Detroit while completing his first four-hit game since 1987. He had hit home runs in double figures for eight straight years before his playing time was drastically reduced in 1991. Moseby is still a respectable hitter with some power and decent speed. In 1991, he had a .396 slugging percentage and a .321 on-base average. He will never steal 30 bases in a season again, though. Moseby can't play right because of his weak arm and he's only average in center or left. Back problems over the years have taken their toll. His fantasy value stops at $6. His 1992 commons are suspect investments.

Major League Batting Register

	BA	G	AB	R	H	2B	3B	HR	RBI	SB
80 AL	.229	114	389	44	89	24	1	9	46	4
81 AL	.233	100	378	36	88	16	2	9	43	11
82 AL	.236	147	487	51	115	20	9	9	52	11
83 AL	.315	151	539	104	170	31	7	18	81	27
84 AL	.280	158	592	97	166	28	15	18	92	39
85 AL	.259	152	584	92	151	30	7	18	70	37
86 AL	.253	152	589	89	149	24	5	21	86	32
87 AL	.282	155	592	106	167	27	4	26	96	39
88 AL	.239	128	472	77	113	17	7	10	42	31
89 AL	.221	135	502	72	111	25	3	11	43	24
90 AL	.248	122	431	64	107	16	5	14	51	17
91 AL	.262	74	260	37	68	15	1	6	35	8
Life	.257	1588	5815	869	1494	273	66	169	737	280
3 AVE	.240	110	398	58	95	19	3	10	43	16

TERRY MULHOLLAND

Position: Pitcher
Team: Philadelphia Phillies
Born: March 9, 1963 Uniontown, PA
Height: 6'3" **Weight:** 200 lbs.
Bats: right **Throws:** left
Acquired: Traded from Giants with Dennis Cook and Charlie Hayes for Steve Bedrosian and Rick Parker, 6/89

Player Summary	
Fantasy Value	$7 to $10
Card Value	3¢ to 5¢
Will	win 15 with support
Can't	prevent steals
Expect	many groundouts
Don't Expect	control problems

Mulholland proved in 1991 that his no-hitter two years ago was no fluke. In a 5-0 three-hitter against Houston September 8, he retired 19 of the last 20 hitters, including the final 14. It was his sixth route-going effort, and he finished the season with eight, third in the National League. A sinker-and-slider pitcher who maintains his stamina through a rigorous conditioning program, Mulholland strikes out three times as many as he walks and allows about a hit per inning. He was in the league's top ten in innings pitched in 1991. He does have a problem with the home run ball, an occupational hazard for control pitchers. He doesn't help himself as a hitter or fielder but his pitching has progressed so well that it hardly matters. Mulholland is one of the premier southpaws in the National League. He is a promising fantasy choice for $10 or less. The outlook on his 1992 commons isn't so favorable, however.

Major League Pitching Register

	W	L	ERA	G	CG	IP	H	ER	BB	SO
86 NL	1	7	4.94	15	0	54.2	51	30	35	27
88 NL	2	1	3.72	9	2	46.0	50	19	7	18
89 NL	4	7	4.92	25	2	115.1	137	63	36	66
90 NL	9	10	3.34	33	6	180.2	172	67	42	75
91 NL	16	13	3.61	34	8	232.0	231	93	49	142
Life	32	38	3.89	116	18	628.2	641	272	169	328
3 AVE	10	10	3.80	31	5	176.1	180	74	42	94

CURRENT PLAYERS

RANCE MULLINIKS

Position: Infield
Team: Toronto Blue Jays
Born: Jan. 15, 1956 Tulare, CA
Height: 6' **Weight:** 175 lbs.
Bats: left **Throws:** right
Acquired: Traded from Royals for Phil Huffman, 3/82

Player Summary	
Fantasy Value	$1 to $3
Card Value	3¢ to 5¢
Will	find way to reach base
Can't	run well
Expect	pinch-hitting duty
Don't Expect	return of .300 stroke

Mulliniks has spent most of his major league career as Toronto's platoon third baseman, used only against lefthanded pitching. When Kelly Gruber claimed full-time dominion over the bag in 1990, Mulliniks was reduced to pinch-hitter, lefty designated hitter, and understudy. A veteran who began his big league career as a shortstop for the 1977 Angels, he still manages a high on-base percentage because he walks more often than he strikes out. He hits to the opposite field and occasionally pokes one over the fence. Mulliniks has little speed. He was a part-timer his entire career, and thus his 1992 cards will remain commons. He is a mediocre fantasy pick.

Major League Batting Register

	BA	G	AB	R	H	2B	3B	HR	RBI	SB
77 AL	.269	78	271	36	73	13	2	3	21	1
78 AL	.185	50	119	6	22	3	1	1	6	2
79 AL	.147	22	68	7	10	0	0	1	8	0
80 AL	.259	36	54	8	14	3	0	0	6	0
81 AL	.227	24	44	6	10	3	0	0	5	0
82 AL	.244	112	311	32	76	25	0	4	35	3
83 AL	.275	129	364	54	100	34	3	10	49	0
84 AL	.324	125	343	41	111	21	5	3	42	2
85 AL	.295	129	366	55	108	26	1	10	57	2
86 AL	.259	117	348	50	90	22	0	11	45	1
87 AL	.310	124	332	37	103	28	1	11	44	1
88 AL	.300	119	337	49	101	21	1	12	48	1
89 AL	.238	103	273	25	65	11	2	3	29	0
90 AL	.289	57	97	11	28	4	0	2	16	2
91 AL	.250	97	240	27	60	12	1	2	24	0
Life	.272	1322	3567	444	971	226	17	73	435	15
2 AVE	.244	100	257	26	63	12	2	3	27	0

PEDRO MUNOZ

Position: Outfield
Team: Minnesota Twins
Born: Sept. 19, 1968 Ponce, Puerto Rico
Height: 5'11" **Weight:** 170 lbs.
Bats: right **Throws:** right
Acquired: Traded from Blue Jays with Nelson Liriano for John Candelaria, 7/90

Player Summary	
Fantasy Value	$5 to $8
Card Value	10¢ to 20¢
Will	slap liners everywhere
Can't	show patience at bat
Expect	some stolen bases
Don't Expect	strong defense

Munoz returned to Minnesota from Triple-A Portland with a bang in 1991. His pinch-single won a game on September 7, the day of his recall, and his three-run homer sparked a win the next day. At Portland, he hit .316 with five homers, 28 RBI, nine stolen bases, and 19 doubles in 312 at bats. He has a right field throwing arm and enough speed to steal 30 bases a season. For Minnesota in '91, he compiled a .500 slugging percentage and a .327 on-base average. He hit .318 with five homers and 21 RBI at Portland in 1990. He also hit .319 with seven homers and 56 RBI at Triple-A Syracuse that year. Drafted by the Blue Jays at age 16, Munoz began his pro career in 1985. He was a solid hitter and run producer throughout his minor league career but once led the Class-A Florida State League with 15 errors—too many for an outfielder. Munoz might become a designated hitter. Invest a couple of bucks in his rookie 1992 cards at 20 cents apiece or less. He is a fantasy bargain for $6.

Major League Batting Register

	BA	G	AB	R	H	2B	3B	HR	RBI	SB
90 AL	.271	22	85	13	23	4	1	0	5	3
91 AL	.283	51	138	15	39	7	1	7	26	3
Life	.278	73	223	28	62	11	2	7	31	6

CURRENT PLAYERS

DALE MURPHY

Position: Outfield
Team: Philadelphia Phillies
Born: March 12, 1956 Portland, OR
Height: 6'4" **Weight:** 215 lbs.
Bats: right **Throws:** right
Acquired: Traded from Braves with Tommy Greene for Jeff Parrett, Jim Vatcher, and Victor Rosario, 8/90

Player Summary
Fantasy Value	$15 to $20
Card Value	5¢ to 10¢
Will	slam southpaws
Can't	show patience
Expect	platooning possibility
Don't Expect	average to reach .250

Murphy is only a shadow of the player who won consecutive MVP awards in 1982 and '83, but he's still capable of winning games with timely home runs. He still murders lefthanded pitching but has become an impotent giant against righties. His patience evaporated, he lunges after bad pitches, often losing his grip on the bat. His fantasy value is between $15 and $20. His nickel-priced 1992 cards are good long-term investments. Still a standout right fielder with a powerful arm and good reactions but declining speed, Murphy might become a platoon player. He lost his cleanup job last year.

Major League Batting Register
	BA	G	AB	R	H	2B	3B	HR	RBI	SB
76 NL	.262	19	65	3	17	6	0	0	9	0
77 NL	.316	18	76	5	24	8	1	2	14	0
78 NL	.226	151	530	66	120	14	3	23	79	11
79 NL	.276	104	384	53	106	7	2	21	57	6
80 NL	.281	156	569	98	160	27	2	33	89	9
81 NL	.247	104	369	43	91	12	1	13	50	14
82 NL	.281	162	598	113	168	23	2	36	109	23
83 NL	.302	162	589	131	178	24	4	36	121	30
84 NL	.290	162	607	94	176	32	8	36	100	19
85 NL	.300	162	616	118	185	32	2	37	111	10
86 NL	.265	160	614	89	163	29	7	29	83	7
87 NL	.295	159	566	115	167	27	1	44	105	16
88 NL	.226	156	592	77	134	35	4	24	77	3
89 NL	.228	154	574	60	131	16	0	20	84	3
90 NL	.245	154	563	60	138	23	1	24	83	9
91 NL	.252	153	544	66	137	33	1	18	81	1
Life	.267	2136	7856	1191	2095	348	39	396	1252	161
3 AVE	.242	154	560	62	135	24	1	21	83	4

ROB MURPHY

Position: Pitcher
Team: Seattle Mariners
Born: May 26, 1960 Miami, FL
Height: 6'2" **Weight:** 215 lbs.
Bats: left **Throws:** left
Acquired: Traded from Red Sox for Mark Gardiner, 3/91

Player Summary
Fantasy Value	$1 to $3
Card Value	3¢ to 5¢
Will	throw hard with control
Can't	always control his emotions
Expect	frequent use
Don't Expect	many hits or homers

Murphy is one of baseball's busiest and best middle relievers. He had appeared more than 60 times four years in a row and once answered 87. In addition to his rubber arm, he has good control of three pitches—a fastball, slider, and forkball. He finished 26 games in his 57 appearances in 1991. Murphy allows less than a hit per inning and keeps the ball in the park. He's not a strong fielder but holds base-runners well. His strong showing last year convinced insiders that his 1990 fiasco in Fenway Park was an aberration. Since he was used so frequently by both the Reds and the BoSox, Murphy may not have been able to get any velocity on his heater. He is best used as a situational reliever mainly against lefthanded batters. He notches a few saves a year, which benefits fantasy teams for $2 or so. His 1992 commons are not top-drawer commodities.

Major League Pitching Register
	W	L	ERA	G	S	IP	H	ER	BB	SO
85 NL	0	0	6.00	2	0	3.0	2	2	2	1
86 NL	6	0	0.72	34	1	50.1	26	4	21	36
87 NL	8	5	3.04	87	3	100.2	91	34	32	99
88 NL	0	6	3.08	76	3	84.2	69	29	38	74
89 NL	5	7	2.74	74	9	105.0	97	32	41	107
90 AL	0	6	6.32	68	7	57.0	85	40	32	54
91 AL	0	1	3.00	57	4	48.0	47	16	19	34
Life	19	25	3.15	398	27	448.2	417	157	185	405
3 AVE	2	5	3.77	66	7	70.0	76	29	31	65

CURRENT PLAYERS

EDDIE MURRAY

Position: First base
Team: New York Mets
Born: Feb. 24, 1956 Los Angeles, CA
Height: 6'2" **Weight:** 224 lbs.
Bats: both **Throws:** right
Acquired: Signed as a free agent, 11/91

Player Summary	
Fantasy Value	$20 to $25
Card Value	5¢ to 10¢
Will	hit with clutch power
Can't	produce with mastery
Expect	decent defense
Don't Expect	return of .300 stroke

After watching Murray's performance in 1991, some scouts wondered whether the slugger's 1990 showing was a veteran's last hurrah. A heavy workload could be taking its toll on the switch-hitting slugger; he has played at least 150 games nine times in 10 years. Although he drove in 96 runs, his batting average, slugging average (.403), and on-base average (.321) were down in '91. He also fanned more than he walked, something he didn't do in good years. The eight-time All-Star and three-time Gold Glover ranks second to Mickey Mantle in homers by a switch-hitter. Murray's nickel-priced 1992 cards have great promise. His fantasy value continues at the $25 level.

Major League Batting Register

	BA	G	AB	R	H	2B	3B	HR	RBI	SB
77 AL	.283	160	611	81	173	29	2	27	88	0
78 AL	.285	161	610	85	174	32	3	27	95	6
79 AL	.295	159	606	90	179	30	2	25	99	10
80 AL	.300	158	621	100	186	36	2	32	116	7
81 AL	.294	99	378	57	111	21	2	22	78	2
82 AL	.316	151	550	87	174	30	1	32	110	7
83 AL	.306	156	582	115	178	30	3	33	111	5
84 AL	.306	162	588	97	180	26	3	29	110	10
85 AL	.297	156	583	111	173	37	1	31	124	5
86 AL	.305	137	495	61	151	25	1	17	84	3
87 AL	.277	160	618	89	171	28	3	30	91	1
88 AL	.284	161	603	75	171	27	2	28	84	5
89 NL	.247	160	594	66	147	29	1	20	88	7
90 NL	.330	155	558	96	184	22	3	26	95	8
91 NL	.260	153	576	69	150	23	1	19	96	10
Life	.292	2288	8573	1279	2502	425	30	398	1469	86
3 AVE	.278	156	576	77	160	25	2	22	93	8

GREG MYERS

Position: Catcher
Team: Toronto Blue Jays
Born: April 14, 1966 Riverside, CA
Height: 6'2" **Weight:** 206 lbs.
Bats: left **Throws:** right
Acquired: Third-round pick in 6/84 free-agent draft

Player Summary	
Fantasy Value	$3 to $5
Card Value	3¢ to 5¢
Will	make good contact
Can't	hit righthanders
Expect	some power in platoon
Don't Expect	walks or strikeouts

Myers teamed with Pat Borders to give Toronto a lefty-righty catching platoon last year. Myers, who had been second fiddle to Borders the summer before, proved more productive. Myers produced a .411 slugging percentage and a .306 on-base average in '91. He acquitted himself well behind the plate. He doesn't strike out often but doesn't walk enough either. He also hits into too many double-plays; lack of speed is a contributing factor. Myers is a decent defensive catcher who handles pitchers well and has a good arm, despite previous problems with his left elbow and shoulder. He had rotator cuff surgery in 1988, which limited his playing time. In his last minor league season with 300-plus at bats, he batted .246 at Triple-A Syracuse in 1987 with 10 homers and 47 RBI. He only has one full season under his belt and should improve with experience. He will provide some offense for your fantasy squad at $5. His 1992 commons aren't good buys.

Major League Batting Register

	BA	G	AB	R	H	2B	3B	HR	RBI	SB
87 AL	.111	7	9	1	1	0	0	0	0	0
89 AL	.114	17	44	0	5	2	0	0	1	0
90 AL	.236	87	250	33	59	7	1	5	22	0
91 AL	.262	107	309	25	81	22	0	8	36	0
Life	.239	218	612	59	146	31	1	13	59	0
2 AVE	.250	97	280	29	70	15	1	7	29	0

CURRENT PLAYERS

RANDY MYERS

Position: Pitcher
Team: San Diego Padres
Born: Sept. 19, 1962 Vancouver, WA
Height: 6'1" **Weight:** 210 lbs.
Bats: left **Throws:** left
Acquired: Traded from Reds for Bip Roberts, 12/91

Player Summary
Fantasy Value ....$23 to $28
Card Value..3¢ to 5¢
Will ....ring up Ks
Can't..............................avoid control lapses
Expect.........................move back to bullpen
Don't Expect............ERA to remain inflated

In 1990, Cincinnati had the best one-two bullpen punch in Rob Dibble and Myers. When injuries struck the Cincinnati pitching staff in 1991, Myers was put in the starting rotation, after 293 career relief appearances. A fastball-and-slider pitcher who usually has good control (despite repeated lapses in 1991), he had saved at least two dozen games in three straight years before becoming a starter. Opponents compiled a .242 batting average, a .342 slugging percentage, and a .347 on-base average in '91. His inflated '91 3.55 ERA was almost a full run above his career mark. In December, Myers was dealt to San Diego, where he'll be the stopper. He can get key strikeouts in late innings, especially against lefties. As closer material, he remains in the upper reaches of the fantasy draft at $25. His 1992 cards, however, scrape the depths of the commons box.

Major League Pitching Register

	W	L	ERA	G	S	IP	H	ER	BB	SO
85 NL	0	0	0.00	1	0	2.0	0	0	1	2
86 NL	0	0	4.22	10	0	10.2	11	5	9	13
87 NL	3	6	3.96	54	6	75.0	61	33	30	92
88 NL	7	3	1.72	55	26	68.0	45	13	17	69
89 NL	7	4	2.35	65	24	84.1	62	22	40	88
90 NL	4	6	2.08	66	31	86.2	59	20	38	98
91 NL	6	13	3.55	58	6	132.0	116	52	80	108
Life	27	32	2.85	309	93	458.2	354	145	215	470
3 AVE	6	8	2.79	63	20	101.1	79	31	53	98

CHRIS NABHOLZ

Position: Pitcher
Team: Montreal Expos
Born: Jan. 5, 1967 Harrisburg, PA
Height: 6'5" **Weight:** 210 lbs.
Bats: left **Throws:** left
Acquired: Third-round pick in 6/88 free-agent draft

Player Summary
Fantasy Value ....$2 to $4
Card Value..3¢ to 5¢
Will ....win 10 if healthy
Can't ....avoid wildness
Expect ....few gophers
Don't Expect.....................over a hit a frame

Nabholz enjoyed a fine first season with Montreal in 1990 before injuries interfered with his progress in 1991. The lefty starter was disabled June 17 with tendinitis of the left shoulder. He seemed to find his rookie form after his return. He fanned a career-high 11 batters September 1 to lead a 6-1 win. The former Towson State University star throws a sinker, curve, and change-up—usually with good location. He allows less than a hit per inning and keeps the ball from leaving the park (five homers in '91). Opponents compiled a .237 batting average, a .336 slugging percentage, and a .307 on-base average in '91. Nabholz is weak at bat and average in the field but seems to have a strong future on the mound—especially if he displays the same form as his stint with the Expos late in '90. He was 2-2 with a 1.86 ERA, 16 Ks, five walks, and 13 hits in 19 innings at Triple-A Indianapolis in 1991. Because of his shoulder considerations, though, his fantasy value culminates at $5, and his 1992 commons are not hot commodities.

Major League Pitching Register

	W	L	ERA	G	CG	IP	H	ER	BB	SO
90 NL	6	2	2.83	11	1	70.0	43	22	32	53
91 NL	8	7	3.63	24	1	153.2	134	62	57	99
Life	14	9	3.38	35	2	223.2	177	84	89	152
2 AVE	7	5	3.38	18	1	112.1	89	42	45	76

CURRENT PLAYERS

TIM NAEHRING

Position: Shortstop
Team: Boston Red Sox
Born: Feb. 1, 1967 Cincinnati, OH
Height: 6'2" **Weight:** 190 lbs.
Bats: right **Throws:** right
Acquired: Eighth-round pick in 6/88 free-agent draft

Player Summary	
Fantasy Value	$2 to $4
Card Value	3¢ to 5¢
Will	throw well
Can't	show great range
Expect	line drives
Don't Expect	Ks or walks

Although Boston had expected Naehring to be their regular shortstop in 1991, he suffered serious back problems that forced the Sox to place him on the disabled list May 18. He submitted to surgery on July 3. He will get another crack at a varsity job in 1992 if he gets a clean bill of health. In 1990, he impressed Boston brass by hitting 15 home runs at Triple-A Pawtucket. A line-drive hitter who makes good contact, Naehring walks almost as often as he strikes out. He fields and throws well but has limited range, usually the makeup of a third baseman. But not when Wade Boggs is a teammate. Naehring also has a problem at shortstop, because Luis Rivera had a good season at bat for Boston. Naehring has a long, hard road to travel before he gets a starting job. He should prove both that he is healed and can win a starting job before you spend much money on him. Don't bid more than $4 for him this year, and stay away from his 1992 commons.

CHARLES NAGY

Position: Pitcher
Team: Cleveland Indians
Born: May 5, 1967 Bridgeport, CT
Height: 6'3" **Weight:** 200 lbs.
Bats: left **Throws:** right
Acquired: First-round pick in 6/88 free-agent draft

Player Summary	
Fantasy Value	$2 to $5
Card Value	5¢ to 7¢
Will	win with maturity
Can't	count on teammates
Expect	fewer men on
Don't Expect	more control woes

Nagy's first full season in 1991 didn't have many highlights but there was one big exception: a six-hit, 3-0 shutout, the first of his career, against Milwaukee on July 4. The 1988 Olympic standout mixes a fastball, slider, curve, and changeup. He experienced the jitters of on-the-job training as a rookie last season, however. He led the Tribe with 10 wins, but his ERA was much too high. He yielded more than a hit per inning and walked more men than any of his teammates. Playing without much offensive or defensive support didn't help Nagy maintain his minor league reputation for keeping baserunners to a minimum. Nagy had averaged a strikeout per inning in the minors and may approach that ratio once he gains experience. In 1990 at Double-A Canton-Akron, he was 13-8 with a 2.52 ERA, nine complete games, 99 strikeouts, 39 walks, and 132 hits in 175 innings. Nagy was named the No. 7 prospect in the Eastern League that year. He is a good fantasy draft for $5, tops. His 1992 cards, at a nickel apiece, could move up quickly.

Major League Batting Register

	BA	G	AB	R	H	2B	3B	HR	RBI	SB
90 AL	.271	24	85	10	23	6	0	2	12	0
91 AL	.109	20	55	1	6	1	0	0	3	0
Life	.207	44	140	11	29	7	0	2	15	0

Major League Pitching Register

	W	L	ERA	G	CG	IP	H	ER	BB	SO
90 AL	2	4	5.91	9	0	45.2	58	30	21	26
91 AL	10	15	4.13	33	6	211.1	228	97	66	109
Life	12	19	4.45	42	6	257.0	286	127	87	135

CURRENT PLAYERS

JAIME NAVARRO

Position: Pitcher
Team: Milwaukee Brewers
Born: March 27, 1967 Bayamon, Puerto Rico
Height: 6'4" **Weight:** 210 lbs.
Bats: right **Throws:** right
Acquired: Third-round pick in 6/87 free-agent draft

Player Summary	
Fantasy Value	$5 to $9
Card Value	3¢ to 5¢
Will	win 15 with help
Can't	avoid walks or homers
Expect	improvement over time
Don't Expect	ERA over 4.00

Navarro found success in 1991, his first full major league season, by learning to control his slider. A fastball-and-slider pitcher who recently perfected a change-up, he fanned twice as many as he walked in 1991 but was often sabotaged by a shoddy defense. He yielded 15 unearned runs in his 34 starts. Navarro gives up more than a hit per inning but knows how to work out of jams. His Achilles' heel is a tendency to throw gopher balls. He gave up 18 homers in 1991. Opponents compiled a .261 batting average, a .370 slugging percentage, and a .318 on-base average. At Triple-A Denver in 1990, he was 2-3 with a 4.20 ERA, 41 strikeouts and 14 walks in 40⅔ innings. He was 5-2 with a 2.47 ERA and 78 Ks in 76⅔ innings at Double-A El Paso in 1989. Navarro is long on talent but short on experience and should get much better. Investors should stand by for more before investing in his common-priced 1992 cards. His workhorse season boosts his fantasy bid to the $7 range, which may look cheap next year.

Major League Pitching Register

	W	L	ERA	G	CG	IP	H	ER	BB	SO
89 AL	7	8	3.12	19	1	109.2	119	38	32	56
90 AL	8	7	4.46	32	3	149.1	176	74	41	75
91 AL	15	12	3.92	34	10	234.0	237	102	73	114
Life	30	27	3.91	85	14	493.0	532	214	146	245
3 AVE	10	9	3.91	28	5	164.1	177	71	49	82

GENE NELSON

Position: Pitcher
Team: Oakland Athletics
Born: Dec. 3, 1960 Tampa, FL
Height: 6' **Weight:** 174 lbs.
Bats: right **Throws:** right
Acquired: Traded from White Sox with Bruce Tanner for Donnie Hill, 12/86

Player Summary	
Fantasy Value	$2 to $4
Card Value	3¢ to 5¢
Will	improve with health
Can't	erase '91 numbers
Expect	complete return to role
Don't Expect	many walks or saves

Nelson was minding his own business when he got hurt last spring. He broke a finger on his pitching hand when struck by a foul ball while sitting in the Oakland dugout. The injury ruined Nelson's season. Instead, he had a fat ERA, finished only 11 games, and had the same number of walks as strikeouts. Given a fresh (and healthy) start, Nelson should rejoin the ranks of the respectable relievers. He is an accomplished middle man who thrives on a fastball-and-slider diet, with an occasional forkball as a side dish. He's never had more than five saves in a season and will maintain that tradition as a middle man. He could rebound and notch a few wins and saves, making him a $3 dare. Don't be so brave with his 1992 commons.

Major League Pitching Register

	W	L	ERA	G	S	IP	H	ER	BB	SO
81 AL	3	1	4.81	8	0	39.1	40	21	23	16
82 AL	6	9	4.62	22	0	122.2	133	63	60	71
83 AL	0	3	7.87	10	0	32.0	38	28	21	11
84 AL	3	5	4.46	20	1	74.2	72	37	17	36
85 AL	10	10	4.26	46	2	145.2	144	69	67	101
86 AL	6	6	3.85	54	6	114.2	118	49	41	70
87 AL	6	5	3.93	54	3	123.2	120	54	35	94
88 AL	9	6	3.06	54	3	111.2	93	38	38	67
89 AL	3	5	3.26	50	3	80.0	60	29	30	70
90 AL	3	3	1.57	51	5	74.2	55	13	17	38
91 AL	1	5	6.84	44	0	48.2	60	37	23	23
Life	50	58	4.07	413	23	967.2	933	438	372	597
3 AVE	2	4	3.50	48	3	67.1	58	26	23	44

CURRENT PLAYERS

AL NEWMAN

Position: Infield
Team: Minnesota Twins
Born: June 30, 1960 Kansas City, MO
Height: 5'9" **Weight:** 183 lbs.
Bats: both **Throws:** right
Acquired: Traded from Expos for Mike Shade, 2/87

Player Summary	
Fantasy Value	$1 to $2
Card Value	3¢ to 5¢
Will	scratch and claw at bat
Can't	hit for average or power
Expect	service at several spots
Don't Expect	many walks or whiffs

After two seasons as a semiregular at second base, Newman returned to fulltime utility status after Chuck Knoblauch reached Minnesota in 1991. The light-hitting Newman, who has hit only one home run in seven seasons, is a baseball rarity because his on-base percentage exceeds his slugging percentage. He accumulated a .211 slugging percentage and a .260 on-base average in '91. He walks more often than he strikes out and drops occasional bunts to reach base. He's also adept at laying down a sacrifice bunt. Newman has good speed, once stealing 25 bases in a season. A three-position infielder who also plays the outfield when needed, he has enough adequate defensive skills at every spot but is best at second, his original position. Newman has good hands and turns the double-play well. His lack of at bats has taken the fantasy merit from him. Stay away from his 1992 commons.

Major League Batting Register

	BA	G	AB	R	H	2B	3B	HR	RBI	SB
85 NL	.172	25	29	7	5	1	0	0	1	2
86 NL	.200	95	185	23	37	3	0	1	8	11
87 AL	.221	110	307	44	68	15	5	0	29	15
88 AL	.223	105	260	35	58	7	0	0	19	12
89 AL	.253	141	446	62	113	18	2	0	38	25
90 AL	.242	144	388	43	94	14	0	0	30	13
91 AL	.191	118	246	25	47	5	0	0	19	4
Life	.227	738	1861	239	422	63	7	1	144	82
3 AVE	.235	134	360	43	85	12	1	0	29	14

ROD NICHOLS

Position: Pitcher
Team: Cleveland Indians
Born: Dec. 29, 1964 Burlington, IA
Height: 6'2" **Weight:** 190 lbs.
Bats: right **Throws:** right
Acquired: Fifth-round pick in 6/85 free-agent draft

Player Summary	
Fantasy Value	$1 to $3
Card Value	3¢ to 5¢
Will	win more
Can't	continue bad luck
Expect	good control
Don't Expect	poor K-to-walk ratio

Long losing streaks will make players superstitious. After going 0-13 in 16 starts between September 1989 and the 1991 All-Star break, Nichols resorted to wearing the hats, uniforms, and underwear of teammates. When he finally got a win, beating Oakland on July 20, he wore Greg Swindell's socks while Dave Otto wore Nichols's socks. The righthander had bad luck last year. He lost his first eight decisions of the season, despite having a 3.91 ERA at the time, one of the best on the staff. His 2-11 record belies the fact that he had one shutout, one save, and four games finished. He throws few gopher balls (six in '91). Nichols has the time and potential to improve. If the Indians would place him in the starting rotation, he probably could hold his own in the No. 3 or No. 4 spot. Because of his low win total, don't sink too much money into him at the draft. His 1992 commons likewise don't have much appeal.

Major League Pitching Register

	W	L	ERA	G	S	IP	H	ER	BB	SO
88 AL	1	7	5.06	11	0	69.1	73	39	23	31
89 AL	4	6	4.40	15	0	71.2	81	35	24	42
90 AL	0	3	7.87	4	0	16.0	24	14	6	3
91 AL	2	11	3.54	31	1	137.1	145	54	30	76
Life	7	27	4.34	61	1	294.1	323	142	83	152
2 AVE	3	9	3.83	23	1	104.2	113	45	27	59

CURRENT PLAYERS

OTIS NIXON

Position: Outfield
Team: Atlanta Braves
Born: Jan. 9, 1959 Evergreen, NC
Height: 6'2" **Weight:** 180 lbs.
Bats: both **Throws:** right
Acquired: Traded from Expos for Jimmy Kremers, 4/91

Player Summary
Fantasy Value ....$1 to $20
Card Value ....3¢ to 5¢
Will ....steal bases
Can't ....generate power
Expect ....bunts and infield hits
Don't Expect ......Braves fans' sympathy

When Montreal shopped Nixon at the end of 1991 spring training, only Atlanta, desperate to add speed and defense, was interested. Nixon then batted over .300 most of the season, had a record-tying six steals in a single game, and was leading the NL with 72 stolen bases on September 15. On September 16, he was suspended for 60 days for failing his drug test. Nixon fields well at all three outfield spots. A premier base-stealer, it remains to be seen whether any clubs will take a chance on a 33-year-old multiple drug culprit with one good year at bat; the guess is more than likely. His fantasy value goes from a buck up to $20, depending on whether he will get another shot, whether he will get a shot at starting, and whether he can repeat his successes of 1991. His 1992 cards are lousy investments.

Major League Batting Register

	BA	G	AB	R	H	2B	3B	HR	RBI	SB
83 AL	.143	13	14	2	2	0	0	0	0	2
84 AL	.154	49	91	16	14	0	0	0	1	12
85 AL	.235	104	162	34	38	4	0	3	9	20
86 AL	.263	105	95	33	25	4	1	0	8	23
87 AL	.059	19	17	2	1	0	0	0	1	2
88 NL	.244	90	271	47	66	8	2	0	15	46
89 NL	.217	126	258	41	56	7	2	0	21	37
90 NL	.251	119	231	46	58	6	2	1	20	50
91 NL	.297	124	401	81	119	10	1	0	26	72
Life	.246	749	1540	302	379	39	8	4	101	264
3 AVE	.262	123	297	56	78	8	2	0	22	53

JUNIOR NOBOA

Position: Infield
Team: New York Mets
Born: Nov. 10, 1964 Azua, Dominican Republic
Height: 5'9" **Weight:** 160 lbs.
Bats: right **Throws:** right
Acquired: Signed as a free agent, 10/91

Player Summary
Fantasy Value ....$1 to $2
Card Value ....3¢ to 5¢
Will ....spray singles
Can't ....deliver extra-base power
Expect ....good defense
Don't Expect ....a starting job

In his brief big league career, Noboa has played three infield positions, the outfield, and even tried his hand as a pitcher. He has also delivered frequently as a pinch-hitter. Noboa could always hit, leading the Triple-A American Association with a .340 average and 159 hits in 1989. A spray hitter who rarely strikes out, he is much more likely to get an infield hit than hit a ball over the fence. The former Expo has the speed to drop bunts or leg out infield hits but doesn't steal many bases. A natural second baseman, Noboa is also reasonably competent at his other positions. He notched a .305 slugging percentage and a .250 on-base average in 1991 with Montreal. He's likely to retain his old role with his new club as a valuable bench player who fills in well whenever he's called. No longer a prospect, he is a $1 fantasy value, and his 1992 commons aren't beneficial.

Major League Batting Register

	BA	G	AB	R	H	2B	3B	HR	RBI	SB
84 AL	.364	23	11	3	4	0	0	0	0	1
87 AL	.225	39	80	7	18	2	1	0	7	1
88 AL	.063	21	16	4	1	0	0	0	0	0
89 NL	.227	21	44	3	10	0	0	0	1	0
90 NL	.266	81	158	15	42	7	2	0	14	4
91 NL	.242	67	95	5	23	3	0	1	2	2
Life	.243	252	404	37	98	12	3	1	24	8

CURRENT PLAYERS

MATT NOKES

Position: Catcher
Team: New York Yankees
Born: Oct. 31, 1963 San Diego, CA
Height: 6'1" **Weight:** 191 lbs.
Bats: left **Throws:** right
Acquired: Traded from Tigers for Clay Parker and Lance McCullers, 6/90

Player Summary	
Fantasy Value	$16 to $20
Card Value	3¢ to 5¢
Will	hit for power
Can't	wait for walks
Expect	improved defense
Don't Expect	any surrender to southpaws

The Tigers traded Nokes because his defensive skills had deteriorated so much that they considered him nothing more than a designated hitter. Private tutoring sessions from former big league catcher Marc Hill, the Yankee bullpen coach in '91, resurrected Nokes's career behind the plate. Deployed every day at catcher, he began to hit with the same authority he had shown when he hit 32 homers in 1987. Between July 3 and August 30, he hit two home runs in a game five times. His 24 homers were the most by a Yankee catcher since Elston Howard in 1963. A good clutch hitter who hits lefties well, Nokes has blossomed into one of the league's top catchers. He handles pitchers well, knows the hitters, blocks errant tosses, and erases potential base-stealers. He came through in '91, and $17 is an investment that he'll do it again. His 1992 commons are not ready to generate sufficient collector interest.

Major League Batting Register

	BA	G	AB	R	H	2B	3B	HR	RBI	SB
85 NL	.208	19	53	3	11	2	0	2	5	0
86 AL	.333	7	24	2	8	1	0	1	2	0
87 AL	.289	135	461	69	133	14	2	32	87	2
88 AL	.251	122	382	53	96	18	0	16	53	0
89 AL	.250	87	268	15	67	10	0	9	39	1
90 AL	.248	136	351	33	87	9	1	11	40	2
91 AL	.268	135	456	52	122	20	0	24	77	3
Life	.263	641	1995	227	524	74	3	95	303	8
3 AVE	.257	119	358	33	92	13	0	15	52	2

EDWIN NUNEZ

Position: Pitcher
Team: Milwaukee Brewers
Born: May 27, 1963 Humacao, Puerto Rico
Height: 6'5" **Weight:** 240 lbs.
Bats: right **Throws:** right
Acquired: Signed as a free agent, 12/90

Player Summary	
Fantasy Value	$2 to $4
Card Value	3¢ to 5¢
Will	post 2-1 K-to-walk ratio
Can't	hold base-runners
Expect	injury jinx to interfere
Don't Expect	inflated ERA

Nunez was on the verge of becoming Milwaukee's top closer in 1991 before he was sidelined by back surgery. When he notched three saves in five days after his return, he showed he might still justify the team's decision to sign him as a free agent. He'll have to stay off the disabled list first, though. He has been on it nine times in 10 years. A strikeout pitcher who combines a regular fastball with a split-fingered fastball, Nunez yields less than a hit per inning. He always strikes out more men than he walks but falls victim to occasional control problems. He's also sabotaged by his own poor fielding and inability to hold runners on. Nunez finished 18 games in '91, despite his lofty ERA. He is a low-cost, $3 fantasy choice, but don't choose his 1992 commons.

Major League Pitching Register

	W	L	ERA	G	S	IP	H	ER	BB	SO
82 AL	1	2	4.58	8	0	35.1	36	18	16	27
83 AL	0	4	4.38	14	0	37.0	40	18	22	35
84 AL	2	2	3.19	37	7	67.2	55	24	21	57
85 AL	7	3	3.09	70	16	90.1	79	31	34	58
86 AL	1	2	5.82	14	0	21.2	25	14	5	17
87 AL	3	4	3.80	48	12	47.1	45	20	18	34
88 AL	1	4	7.98	14	0	29.1	45	26	14	19
88 NL	1	0	4.50	10	0	14.0	21	7	3	8
89 AL	3	4	4.17	27	1	54.0	49	25	36	41
90 AL	3	1	2.24	42	6	80.1	65	20	37	66
91 AL	2	1	6.04	23	8	25.1	28	17	13	24
Life	24	27	3.94	307	50	502.1	488	220	219	386
2 AVE	3	3	3.01	35	4	67.1	57	23	37	54

CURRENT PLAYERS

CHARLIE O'BRIEN

Position: Catcher
Team: New York Mets
Born: May 1, 1961 Tulsa, OK
Height: 6'2" **Weight:** 190 lbs.
Bats: right **Throws:** right
Acquired: Traded from Brewers for Julio Machado and Kevin Brown, 8/90

Player Summary	
Fantasy Value	$1 to $2
Card Value	3¢ to 5¢
Will	play strong defense
Can't	produce power or runs
Expect	patience at plate
Don't Expect	respectable average

O'Brien is one of baseball's best examples of a good-field, no-hit catcher. He compiled a .209 batting average over his first five seasons, and he didn't even come close to hitting at that level in 1991. Six of his 10 career homers came in a single season, so it's safe to say he's not a power hitter. On the plus side, O'Brien is a good game-caller who handles pitchers well, knows enemy hitters, blocks balls in the dirt, and makes runners think twice about stealing. He has never stolen a base himself. O'Brien doesn't strike out much and is willing to work pitchers for walks, one reason why he flirted with a .300 on-base percentage in '91. He is, however, more likely to ground into a double-play than to produce a key base hit. Such glove men as O'Brien won't woo fantasy managers for more than a buck or increase 1992 commons values.

PETE O'BRIEN

Position: First base; outfield
Team: Seattle Mariners
Born: Feb. 9, 1958 Santa Monica, CA
Height: 6'2" **Weight:** 195 lbs.
Bats: left **Throws:** left
Acquired: Signed as a free agent, 12/89

Player Summary	
Fantasy Value	$10 to $14
Card Value	3¢ to 5¢
Will	make contact
Can't	stop slow decline
Expect	less action at first
Don't Expect	former slugging form

Before he signed a four-year deal to play for Seattle in 1990, O'Brien had averaged 17 homers and 76 RBI over seven previous seasons. Things went sour in '90, however, when he went onto the disabled list for the first time in his career. He finished with embarrassing numbers. O'Brien managed a comeback in 1991, with a .402 slugging percentage and a .300 on-base average. He still wasn't delivering as advertised, though. O'Brien doesn't strike out much and actually walked more often than he fanned in 1990. But good contact doesn't overcome a .248 average. Finding a place to play is also tough. O'Brien was crowded out of Seattle's first base picture last year. If you want to invest in the cards of an M's first sacker, pick Tino Martinez's issues, not O'Brien's 1992 commons. He is a $12 fantasy draft.

Major League Batting Register

	BA	G	AB	R	H	2B	3B	HR	RBI	SB
85 AL	.273	16	11	3	3	1	0	0	1	0
87 AL	.200	10	35	2	7	3	1	0	0	0
88 AL	.220	40	118	12	26	6	0	2	9	0
89 AL	.234	62	188	22	44	10	0	6	35	0
90 AL	.186	46	145	11	27	7	2	0	11	0
90 NL	.162	28	68	6	11	3	0	0	9	0
91 NL	.185	69	168	16	31	6	0	2	14	0
Life	.203	271	733	72	149	36	3	10	79	0
3 AVE	.199	68	190	18	38	9	1	3	23	0

Major League Batting Register

	BA	G	AB	R	H	2B	3B	HR	RBI	SB
82 AL	.239	20	67	13	16	4	1	4	13	1
83 AL	.237	154	524	53	124	24	5	8	53	5
84 AL	.287	142	520	57	149	26	2	18	80	3
85 AL	.267	159	573	69	153	34	3	22	92	5
86 AL	.290	156	551	86	160	23	3	23	90	4
87 AL	.286	159	569	84	163	26	1	23	88	0
88 AL	.272	156	547	57	149	24	1	16	71	1
89 AL	.260	155	554	75	144	24	1	12	55	3
90 AL	.224	108	366	32	82	18	0	5	27	0
91 AL	.248	152	560	58	139	29	3	17	88	0
Life	.265	1361	4831	584	1279	232	20	148	657	22
3 AVE	.247	138	493	55	122	24	1	11	57	1

CURRENT PLAYERS

JOSE OFFERMAN

Position: Shortstop
Team: Los Angeles Dodgers
Born: Nov. 8, 1968 San Pedro de Macoris, Dominican Republic
Height: 6' **Weight:** 160 lbs.
Bats: both **Throws:** right
Acquired: Signed as a free agent, 7/86

Player Summary	
Fantasy Value	$3 to $6
Card Value	5¢ to 10¢
Will	run wild on basepaths
Can't	reduce errors
Expect	bunts and infield hits
Don't Expect	patience with poor stats

After winning Minor League Player of the Year honors in 1990, Offerman was projected as the preseason favorite to be NL Rookie of the Year in 1991. Nonetheless, he failed to make the varsity out of spring training, then fared poorly when recalled to fill in for Alfredo Griffin. Offerman had hit .326 with 104 runs, 56 RBI, and 60 steals at Triple-A Albuquerque in 1990 but played a defensive game that was as erratic as it was spectacular (36 errors in 117 games). He made 10 more miscues in 52 NL games in '91. The Dodgers wanted Offerman to charge more aggressively and throw in a single motion. He batted .298 with eight doubles, 29 RBI, 58 runs, and 32 stolen bases. Named the Pacific Coast League's No. 3 prospect, he had no homers. Though his star has been tarnished, Offerman still has a great arm, great range, and enough speed to steal 50 bases. The question is, when? With his future clouded, be safe and spend only $5 on him in the draft. Hold off on buying his nickel-priced cards until he wins the starting job.

Major League Batting Register

	BA	G	AB	R	H	2B	3B	HR	RBI	SB
90 NL	.155	29	58	7	9	0	0	1	7	1
91 NL	.195	52	113	10	22	2	0	0	3	3
Life	.181	81	171	17	31	2	0	1	10	4

BOB OJEDA

Position: Pitcher
Team: Los Angeles Dodgers
Born: Dec. 17, 1957 Los Angeles, CA
Height: 6'1" **Weight:** 195 lbs.
Bats: left **Throws:** left
Acquired: Traded from Mets with Greg Hansell for Hubie Brooks, 12/90

Player Summary	
Fantasy Value	$4 to $8
Card Value	3¢ to 5¢
Will	yield under a hit a frame
Can't	avoid walks or gophers
Expect	10-plus wins
Don't Expect	return to relief

Ojeda celebrated his return to the rotation in 1991 by winning in double figures for the sixth time in his career. Unhappy in the bullpen of the Mets, he found life in Los Angeles so appealing that he enjoyed his best year since his career-best 18-5 season in 1986. He gets many of his outs with a changeup that rates as his best pitch. The veteran lefthander also throws a fastball, curveball, and slider. He did not display the control of 1988, when he fanned four times more than he walked, but yielded less than a hit per inning. A good glove man with an adequate pickoff move, Ojeda has a pretty fair bat. Don't overestimate his fantasy value; he is a $6 item. Stay away from his common-priced 1992 cards.

Major League Pitching Register

	W	L	ERA	G	CG	IP	H	ER	BB	SO
80 AL	1	1	6.92	7	0	26.0	39	20	14	12
81 AL	6	2	3.12	10	2	66.1	50	23	25	28
82 AL	4	6	5.63	22	0	78.1	95	49	29	52
83 AL	12	7	4.04	29	5	173.2	173	78	73	94
84 AL	12	12	3.99	33	8	216.2	211	96	96	137
85 AL	9	11	4.00	39	5	157.2	166	70	48	102
86 NL	18	5	2.57	32	7	217.1	185	62	52	148
87 NL	3	5	3.88	10	0	46.1	45	20	10	21
88 NL	10	13	2.88	29	5	190.1	158	61	33	133
89 NL	13	11	3.47	31	5	192.0	179	74	78	95
90 NL	7	6	3.66	38	0	118.0	123	48	40	62
91 NL	12	9	3.18	31	2	189.1	181	67	70	120
Life	107	88	3.60	311	39	1672.0	1605	668	568	1004
3 AVE	11	9	3.41	33	2	166.0	161	63	63	92

CURRENT PLAYERS

JOHN OLERUD

Position: First base
Team: Toronto Blue Jays
Born: Aug. 5, 1968 Seattle, WA
Height: 6'5" **Weight:** 205 lbs.
Bats: left **Throws:** left
Acquired: Third-round pick in 6/89 free-agent draft

Player Summary	
Fantasy Value	$22 to $27
Card Value	5¢ to 10¢
Will	improve all facets
Can't	run well
Expect	liners with some power
Don't Expect	further pitching talk

The sophomore jinx did not swallow Olerud. Instead, the former Washington State University standout showed steady improvement in power production while switching from designated hitter to everyday first baseman. He had a strong .438 slugging percentage in 1991, and his team-leading 68 walks helped contribute to a .353 on-base average. He struck out only slightly more often than he drew a free pass. Taking over first full-time upped his fantasy value to about $25. Olerud, who never played in the minors, hits line drives to all fields and seldom swings at a bad pitch. His lack of speed limits his range at first base but he has quick reactions, good hands, and a long stretch. He also has a strong throwing arm, as any former pitcher should. Olerud went 26-4 as a college pitcher and had a 15-0 mark in 1988. His collegiate batting average (with an aluminum bat) was .434. He had a near-fatal brain aneurysm in 1989 but has no ill-effects. Provide up to a dime for each of his 1992 cards.

Major League Batting Register

	BA	G	AB	R	H	2B	3B	HR	RBI	SB
89 AL	.375	6	8	2	3	0	0	0	0	0
90 AL	.265	111	358	43	95	15	1	14	48	0
91 AL	.256	139	454	64	116	30	1	17	68	0
Life	.261	256	820	109	214	45	2	31	116	0
2 AVE	.260	125	406	54	106	23	1	16	58	0

STEVE OLIN

Position: Pitcher
Team: Cleveland Indians
Born: Oct. 10, 1965 Portland, OR
Height: 6'2" **Weight:** 190 lbs.
Bats: right **Throws:** right
Acquired: 16th-round pick in 6/87 free-agent draft

Player Summary	
Fantasy Value	$5 to $9
Card Value	3¢ to 5¢
Will	baffle batters
Can't	contain lefty hitters
Expect	chance to be closer
Don't Expect	many walks or gophers

Most submarine pitchers develop their unorthodox styles to prolong fading careers. Olin is different, having pitched from down under since high school. A sinker-and-slider sidewinder just beginning to benefit from a newly perfected changeup, Olin rode to the rescue in '91 after a long line of Cleveland closers failed and finished 32 games. He was sent to Triple-A Colorado Springs during the season to sharpen his effectiveness against lefty hitters. There he had a 3-2 record with a 4.47 ERA, 22 games, 10 walks, 36 strikeouts, 44 innings, and six saves. He usually gets into trouble when his sinking fastball doesn't sink. Batters know they'll eventually receive a flat slider and wait for the pitch. Olin began his career in 1987 and led the Triple-A Pacific Coast League with 24 saves in 1989. If he can show that form in the majors, he could become a No. 1 closer. With this chance, he could pay off big with a bid of less than $10. His 1992 cards, on the other hand, will maintain their status as commons.

Major League Pitching Register

	W	L	ERA	G	S	IP	H	ER	BB	SO
89 AL	1	4	3.75	25	1	36.0	35	15	14	24
90 AL	4	4	3.41	50	1	92.1	96	35	26	64
91 AL	3	6	3.36	48	17	56.1	61	21	23	38
Life	8	14	3.46	123	19	184.2	192	71	63	126
3 AVE	3	5	3.46	41	6	61.1	64	24	21	42

CURRENT PLAYERS

OMAR OLIVARES

Position: Pitcher
Team: St. Louis Cardinals
Born: July 6, 1967 Mayaguez, Puerto Rico
Height: 6'1" **Weight:** 185 lbs.
Bats: right **Throws:** right
Acquired: Traded from Padres for Alex Cole and Steve Peters, 2/90

Player Summary	
Fantasy Value	$4 to $7
Card Value	10¢ to 15¢
Will	help with bat
Can't	surmount K-to-walk ratio
Expect	10-plus wins
Don't Expect	removal from rotation

Olivares secured his berth in the St. Louis rotation in 1991 with a solid August showing that included a 4-2 record and 2.12 ERA. A sinker-and-slider pitcher who gets lots of ground-ball outs, he gives up less than a hit per inning but often gets taken deep, especially away from Busch Memorial Stadium. He allowed 13 homers in '91. Wild spells have hurt Olivares, whose ratio of strikeouts to walks was only slightly better than 1-to-1 in 1991. Bid up to $7 for him, but beware if going higher. His 1992 cards are acceptable investments at a dime apiece. At Triple-A Louisville in 1990, he was 10-11 with a 2.82 ERA and five complete games. His bat has been a major plus. One of the NL's best-hitting pitchers, Olivares actually hit .370 at Triple-A Tuscson in 1989. He's a good fielder with a better-than-average pickoff move. Olivares earned a regular rotation berth with his second-half showing last year and should have no trouble keeping it. He figures to keep improving as he gains experience.

Major League Pitching Register

	W	L	ERA	G	CG	IP	H	ER	BB	SO
90 NL	1	1	2.92	9	0	49.1	45	16	17	20
91 NL	11	7	3.71	28	0	167.1	148	69	61	91
Life	12	8	3.53	37	0	216.2	193	85	78	111

JOE OLIVER

Position: Catcher
Team: Cincinnati Reds
Born: July 24, 1965 Memphis, TN
Height: 6'3" **Weight:** 210 lbs.
Bats: right **Throws:** right
Acquired: Second-round pick in 6/83 free-agent draft

Player Summary	
Fantasy Value	$4 to $8
Card Value	3¢ to 5¢
Will	throw pretty well
Can't	hit breaking balls
Expect	very good defense
Don't Expect	high batting average

A shoulder injury slowed Oliver's development in 1991. Though he hammered 11 home runs, his batting average about matched his weight. A pull hitter who has trouble with breaking balls, he would make a major improvement in his performance if he learned to hit outside pitches to the opposite field. Cutting his strikeouts wouldn't hurt either. He comes up empty three times more than he walks. He can't even pad his average with infield hits because he has the speed of an icewagon. Good receivers don't have to win the 100-yard dash, however. Oliver wears the tools of ignorance well, blocking potential wild pitches, handling his battery-mates, and throwing with the best in the league. At Triple-A Nashville in 1989, he hit .292 with six homers and 31 RBI. If he can stop a three-year downward spiral in his batting average, Oliver could even contend for an All-Star berth. If his average returns, he'll be an economical fantasy booster, for up to $8. His 1992 cards are weak.

Major League Batting Register

	BA	G	AB	R	H	2B	3B	HR	RBI	SB
89 NL	.272	49	151	13	41	8	0	3	23	0
90 NL	.231	121	364	34	84	23	0	8	52	1
91 NL	.216	94	269	21	58	11	0	11	41	0
Life	.233	264	784	68	183	42	0	22	116	1
3 AVE	.233	88	261	23	61	14	0	7	39	0

CURRENT PLAYERS

FRANCISCO OLIVERAS

Position: Pitcher
Team: San Francisco Giants
Born: Jan. 31, 1963 Santurce, Puerto Rico
Height: 5'10" **Weight:** 180 lbs.
Bats: right **Throws:** right
Acquired: Traded from Twins for Ed Gustafson, 5/90

Player Summary	
Fantasy Value	$2 to $4
Card Value	5¢ to 7¢
Will	maintain tidy ERA
Can't	find defined role
Expect	under a hit a frame
Don't Expect	problem with control

Oliveras played several roles as a relief pitcher for the Giants in 1991. Used primarily as a middle man, he also saved three games and finished 17. Working more than 50 games for the first time in a career that began in 1981, he pitched quite effectively. He allowed less than a hit per inning and showed good control, with an average of two and one-half strikeouts for every walk. He is a fastball-and-slider pitcher who also throws a split-fingered fastball. Opponents compiled a .242 batting average, a .400 slugging percentage, and a .296 on-base average. Oliveras helps his cause with a glove but not with a bat. He also needs work at holding runners on base. Despite these problems, he's now had two good years in a row. There's still doubt about how he should be used, however. In 1990, Oliveras made two starts among his 33 outings but also earned two saves. He also made a start in '91. His 1992 commons will stay that way, but he is a $5 hurler.

GREG OLSON

Position: Catcher
Team: Atlanta Braves
Born: Sept. 6, 1960 Marshall, MN
Height: 6' **Weight:** 200 lbs.
Bats: right **Throws:** right
Acquired: Signed as a free agent, 11/89

Player Summary	
Fantasy Value	$3 to $5
Card Value	3¢ to 5¢
Will	provide strong defense
Can't	avoid double-plays
Expect	clutch hits and walks
Don't Expect	many errors or Ks

After making major improvements in his catching skills, Olson became one of the best all-around receivers in the National League in 1991. In his second big league season, he did a masterful job of calming the young Atlanta pitching staff, blocking balls in the dirt, and nabbing potential base-stealers. He committed only four errors, and he donned the tools of ignorance in more than 30 consecutive games down the stretch for the pennant-winning Braves. In addition to his stellar defense, Olson also produced more clutch hits than a .241 average would suggest. A patient hitter who makes good contact, he had about the same number of walks and strikeouts. He is especially dangerous against lefthanded pitching but is not overmatched by righties. He compiled a .345 slugging percentage and a .316 on-base average in '91. Olson bangs into a lot of double-plays but also produces 20 or so extra-base hits. A mild fantasy pick-up, don't spend more than $5. Don't trust his 1992 commons.

Major League Pitching Register

	W	L	ERA	G	S	IP	H	ER	BB	SO
89 AL	3	4	4.53	12	0	55.2	64	28	15	24
90 NL	2	2	2.77	33	2	55.1	47	17	21	41
91 NL	6	6	3.86	55	3	79.1	69	34	22	48
Life	11	12	3.74	100	5	190.1	180	79	58	113
2 AVE	4	4	3.41	44	3	67.1	58	26	22	45

Major League Batting Register

	BA	G	AB	R	H	2B	3B	HR	RBI	SB
89 AL	.500	3	2	0	1	0	0	0	0	0
90 NL	.262	100	298	36	78	12	1	7	36	1
91 NL	.241	133	411	46	99	25	0	6	44	1
Life	.250	236	711	82	178	37	1	13	80	2
2 AVE	.250	117	355	41	89	19	1	7	40	1

CURRENT PLAYERS

GREGG OLSON

Position: Pitcher
Team: Baltimore Orioles
Born: Oct. 11, 1966 Omaha, NE
Height: 6'4" **Weight:** 210 lbs.
Bats: right **Throws:** right
Acquired: First-round pick in 6/88 free-agent draft

Player Summary	
Fantasy Value	$24 to $30
Card Value	3¢ to 5¢
Will	curve batters into oblivion
Can't	raise saves
Expect	K per frame
Don't Expect	control lapses

The Orioles didn't give Olson many save opportunities in 1991 but he capitalized on the few he received. Even with his team buried in the divisional depths, he performed like an All-Star. He worked more than 60 times for the third straight year and kept the ball in the yard (only one home run allowed in '91). The former Auburn University closer used his fastball and several types of curves to average a strikeout an inning, a ratio he has maintained since coming into the league in 1988. Olson also showed he has not yet mastered the art of fielding or holding runners. But few men reach when he's pitching. On a good club, he'd top 40 saves a year, a level he would have reached in 1990 if he hadn't suffered a late-summer elbow injury. As with almost all other closers' cards, you should leave Olson's nickel-priced 1992 cards alone. A blue-chip fantasy investment, pay up to $30 for his saves and more.

Major League Pitching Register

	W	L	ERA	G	S	IP	H	ER	BB	SO
88 AL	1	1	3.27	10	0	11.0	10	4	10	9
89 AL	5	2	1.69	64	27	85.0	57	16	46	90
90 AL	6	5	2.42	64	37	74.1	57	20	31	74
91 AL	4	6	3.18	72	31	73.2	74	26	29	72
Life	16	14	2.43	210	95	244.0	198	66	116	245
3 AVE	5	4	2.39	67	32	77.1	63	21	35	79

PAUL O'NEILL

Position: Outfield
Team: Cincinnati Reds
Born: Feb. 25, 1963 Columbus, OH
Height: 6'4" **Weight:** 210 lbs.
Bats: left **Throws:** left
Acquired: Fourth-round pick in 6/81 free-agent draft

Player Summary	
Fantasy Value	$20 to $25
Card Value	3¢ to 5¢
Will	top 30 homers
Can't	avoid frequent Ks
Expect	strong outfield throws
Don't Expect	return to platooning

Lou Piniella made O'Neill his personal project with the Reds last spring. The manager used his skills as a hitting coach to change O'Neill's stance, then pronounced him ready to hit 30 home runs. It almost happened. The Reds right fielder, once overmatched by southpaws, got off to a strong start, made the All-Star team for the first time, and tied with Darryl Strawberry for seventh in the National League with 28 homers. O'Neill also had more walks and strikeouts than any of his teammates. His speed enables him to steal a dozen bases and translates into good range in right field. He is a fine defensive outfielder with a strong, accurate arm. He was even used as a mop-up pitcher in a 1987 game against Atlanta. His '91 numbers pushed his fantasy value up to the $20-plus range. His career numbers still do not add up to an investment in his 1992 commons.

Major League Batting Register

	BA	G	AB	R	H	2B	3B	HR	RBI	SB
85 NL	.333	5	12	1	4	1	0	0	1	0
86 NL	.000	3	2	0	0	0	0	0	0	0
87 NL	.256	84	160	24	41	14	1	7	28	2
88 NL	.252	145	485	58	122	25	3	16	73	8
89 NL	.276	117	428	49	118	24	2	15	74	20
90 NL	.270	145	503	59	136	28	0	16	78	13
91 NL	.256	152	532	71	136	36	0	28	91	12
Life	.262	651	2122	262	557	128	6	82	345	55
3 AVE	.267	138	488	60	130	29	1	20	81	15

CURRENT PLAYERS

JOSE OQUENDO

Position: Second base
Team: St. Louis Cardinals
Born: July 4, 1963 Rio Piedras, Puerto Rico
Height: 5'10" **Weight:** 160 lbs.
Bats: both **Throws:** right
Acquired: Traded from Mets with Mark Davis for Argenis Salazar and John Young, 4/85

Player Summary
Fantasy Value	$2 to $5
Card Value	3¢ to 5¢
Will	supply defense
Can't	hit long ball
Expect	more walks than Ks
Don't Expect	use of versatility

Oquendo is an outstanding defensive second baseman who is equally at home at shortstop. He made only three errors in 1990, when he set records for the highest fielding percentage (.996) and fewest miscues by a second baseman playing at least 150 games. Because he has a shortstop's arm, he makes unusually strong throws from second base. He reacts well and is almost as acrobatic as Ozzie Smith. Oquendo was once regarded as a good-field, no-hit utility player, but he has worked hard to make himself a competent contact hitter. He doesn't hit homers or steal bases but has extraordinary patience at the plate and walks much more often than he strikes out. He has more power as a righthanded hitter. Oquendo has played all nine positions in the major leagues. Stop at five bucks at the draft. Leave his 1992 commons in the bins.

Major League Batting Register
	BA	G	AB	R	H	2B	3B	HR	RBI	SB
83 NL	.213	120	328	29	70	7	0	1	17	8
84 NL	.222	81	189	23	42	5	0	0	10	10
86 NL	.297	76	138	20	41	4	1	0	13	2
87 NL	.286	116	248	43	71	9	0	1	24	4
88 NL	.277	148	451	36	125	10	1	7	46	4
89 NL	.291	163	556	59	162	28	7	1	48	3
90 NL	.252	156	469	38	118	17	5	1	37	1
91 NL	.240	127	366	37	88	11	4	1	26	1
Life	.261	987	2745	285	717	91	18	12	221	33
3 AVE	.265	149	464	45	123	19	5	1	37	2

JESSE OROSCO

Position: Pitcher
Team: Cleveland Indians
Born: April 21, 1957 Santa Barbara, CA
Height: 6'2" **Weight:** 185 lbs.
Bats: right **Throws:** left
Acquired: Signed as a free agent, 12/88

Player Summary
Fantasy Value	$1 to $3
Card Value	3¢ to 5¢
Will	supply middle relief
Can't	handle closer role
Expect	short but frequent stints
Don't Expect	much diligence

Orosco gave Cleveland effective middle relief pitching last season. He no longer appears in save situations, and his 1991 deployment did little to stop his downward spiral in that department. In his heyday with the 1984 Mets, Orosco had 31 saves, but those days are long gone. He's often used now to retire one or two tough left-handed hitters. A fastball-and-slider pitcher, Orosco still strikes out twice as many as he walks but allows more than a hit per inning. Some scouts believe a bigger problem for him is failure to concentrate when he's not working in crucial situations. Orosco does concentrate in the field. He handles a glove well and keeps base-runners close. Avoid his 1992 commons, and bid only a couple of bucks on him.

Major League Pitching Register
	W	L	ERA	G	S	IP	H	ER	BB	SO
79 NL	1	2	4.89	18	0	35.0	33	19	22	22
81 NL	0	1	1.56	8	1	17.1	13	3	6	18
82 NL	4	10	2.72	54	4	109.1	92	33	40	89
83 NL	13	7	1.47	62	17	110.0	76	18	38	84
84 NL	10	6	2.59	60	31	87.0	58	25	34	85
85 NL	8	6	2.73	54	17	79.0	66	24	34	68
86 NL	8	6	2.33	58	21	81.0	64	21	35	62
87 NL	3	9	4.44	58	16	77.0	78	38	31	78
88 NL	3	2	2.72	55	9	53.0	41	16	30	43
89 AL	3	4	2.08	69	3	78.0	54	18	26	79
90 AL	5	4	3.90	55	2	64.2	58	28	38	55
91 AL	2	0	3.74	47	0	45.2	52	19	15	36
Life	60	57	2.82	598	121	837.0	685	262	349	719
3 AVE	3	3	3.11	57	2	62.1	55	22	26	57

CURRENT PLAYERS

JOE ORSULAK

Position: Outfield
Team: Baltimore Orioles
Born: May 31, 1962 Glen Ridge, NJ
Height: 6'1" **Weight:** 196 lbs.
Bats: left **Throws:** left
Acquired: Traded from Pirates for Terry Crowley Jr. and Rico Rossy, 11/87

Player Summary	
Fantasy Value	$3 to $6
Card Value	3¢ to 5¢
Will	slap hits to all fields
Can't	provide power
Expect	strong game in right
Don't Expect	many errors or Ks

When Orsulak's 21-game hitting streak ended last August 27, the outfielder was one shy of the Baltimore club record shared by Eddie Murray and Doug DeCinces. Orsulak's bat merely took a breather. On August 30, he enjoyed his first five-hit game with a 5-for-5, 3-RBI performance. A contact hitter who strikes out infrequently, he hits line drives to all fields but seldom hits the ball out of the park. His 11 home runs in 1990 were the exception rather than the rule. Orsulak is usually consistent, taking a .276 lifetime average into 1991 and finishing at just two points above that level. Though not blessed with abundant speed, Orsulak plays a strong right field. He deserves more publicity; he's one of baseball's steadiest but most anonymous performers. He is losing luster as a fantasy reserve—pay less than $6. His 1992 commons lacked glory from the start.

Major League Batting Register

	BA	G	AB	R	H	2B	3B	HR	RBI	SB
83 NL	.182	7	11	0	2	0	0	0	1	0
84 NL	.254	32	67	12	17	1	2	0	3	3
85 NL	.300	121	397	54	119	14	6	0	21	24
86 NL	.249	138	401	60	100	19	6	2	19	24
88 AL	.288	125	379	48	109	21	3	8	27	9
89 AL	.285	123	390	59	111	22	5	7	55	5
90 AL	.269	124	413	49	111	14	3	11	57	6
91 AL	.278	143	486	57	135	22	1	5	43	6
Life	.277	813	2544	339	704	113	26	33	226	77
3 AVE	.277	130	430	55	119	19	3	8	52	6

JUNIOR ORTIZ

Position: Catcher
Team: Minnesota Twins
Born: Oct. 24, 1959 Humacao, Puerto Rico
Height: 5'11" **Weight:** 176 lbs.
Bats: right **Throws:** right
Acquired: Traded from Pirates with Orlando Lind for Mike Pomerantz, 4/90

Player Summary	
Fantasy Value	$1 to $3
Card Value	3¢ to 5¢
Will	start hitting again
Can't	block pitches
Expect	job in danger
Don't Expect	100-point improvement

After a brilliant .335 showing in 1990, his first year as backup catcher for Minnesota, Ortiz lost his stroke in 1991. Inability to oust regular receiver Brian Harper may have been a contributing factor. Ortiz, whose average has ridden a roller-coaster from .198 to .336 during a 10-year career, came up empty in both home runs and stolen bases for the season. That wasn't surprising, since he had only five homers and six steals in his entire career going in. When his sleeping bat awakens, Ortiz slaps singles to the opposite field and makes good contact, but he doesn't have the patience to wait for walks. Behind the plate, he shows a strong throwing arm and enjoys a good rapport with his pitchers. He is not adept at blocking balls in the dirt. His 1992 commons are not worth consideration. He is a $1 catcher.

Major League Batting Register

	BA	G	AB	R	H	2B	3B	HR	RBI	SB
82 NL	.200	7	15	1	3	1	0	0	0	0
83 NL	.249	73	193	11	48	5	0	0	12	1
84 NL	.198	40	91	6	18	3	0	0	11	1
85 NL	.292	23	72	4	21	2	0	1	5	1
86 NL	.336	49	110	11	37	6	0	0	14	0
87 NL	.271	75	192	16	52	8	1	1	22	0
88 NL	.280	49	118	8	33	6	0	2	18	1
89 NL	.217	91	230	16	50	6	1	1	22	2
90 AL	.335	71	170	18	57	7	1	0	18	0
91 AL	.209	61	134	9	28	5	1	0	11	0
Life	.262	539	1325	100	347	49	4	5	133	6
2 AVE	.268	81	200	17	54	7	1	1	20	1

CURRENT PLAYERS

AL OSUNA

Position: Pitcher
Team: Houston Astros
Born: Aug. 10, 1965 Inglewood, CA
Height: 6'3" **Weight:** 200 lbs.
Bats: right **Throws:** left
Acquired: 16th-round pick in 6/87 free-agent draft

Player Summary	
Fantasy Value	$7 to $12
Card Value	15¢ to 20¢
Will	rely on splitter
Can't	always throw strikes
Expect	few hits or homers
Don't Expect	less than 60 calls

Osuna became Houston's chief 1991 closer in the wake of the off-season free agent exodus by veterans Dave Smith, Juan Agosto, and Larry Andersen. Osuna responded well, appearing in more than 60 games for the first time in his career. He had seven wins and 12 saves, accounting for 29 percent of Houston's wins—impressive statistics for a pitcher on a last-place ballclub. The rookie left-hander allowed less than a hit per inning and kept the ball in the park (five in '91), though he had occasional problems with his control. Opponents compiled a .201 batting average, a .304 slugging percentage, and a .311 on-base average. He banks heavily on a split-fingered fastball but also throws a traditional fastball, curve, and screwball. Osuna's fastball has been timed at 91 miles per hour. He could solidify his hold on the closer role, making him a fantasy bargain at less than $12. The former Stanford star led the Double-A Southern League with 60 appearances in 1990, going 7-5 with a 3.38 ERA and six saves. His rookie 1992 cards are good risks at a quarter apiece.

Major League Pitching Register

	W	L	ERA	G	S	IP	H	ER	BB	SO
90 NL	2	0	4.76	12	0	11.1	10	6	6	6
91 NL	7	6	3.42	71	12	81.2	59	31	46	68
Life	9	6	3.58	83	12	93.0	69	37	52	74

SPIKE OWEN

Position: Shortstop
Team: Montreal Expos
Born: April 19, 1961 Cleburne, TX
Height: 5'10" **Weight:** 170 lbs.
Bats: both **Throws:** right
Acquired: Traded from Red Sox with Dan Gakeler for Luis Rivera and John Dopson, 12/88

Player Summary	
Fantasy Value	$1 to $3
Card Value	3¢ to 5¢
Will	keep errors to minimum
Can't	survive rookie challenge
Expect	good defense
Don't Expect	high average or power

Owen is a switch-hitter who's much more productive from the right side, but he is basically a .240 hitter with little power. He is in the lineup for his glove rather than his bat. In 1990, he went 63 consecutive games without an error, a National League record. He lacks great range or a Shawon Dunston arm but handles everything cleanly and throws with accuracy. He has led NL shortstops in fielding several times. Owen maintains a decent on-base percentage by showing patience at the plate. He strikes out only a few more times than he walks and draws more walks than a .240 hitter should. He doesn't run much because he's usually thrown out when he tries to steal. He is in danger of losing his job to Wil Cordero. Owen is a $2 fantasy risk, and his 1992 commons are dubious.

Major League Batting Register

	BA	G	AB	R	H	2B	3B	HR	RBI	SB
83 AL	.196	80	306	36	60	11	3	2	21	10
84 AL	.245	152	530	67	130	18	8	3	43	16
85 AL	.259	118	352	41	91	10	6	6	37	11
86 AL	.231	154	528	67	122	24	7	1	45	4
87 AL	.259	132	437	50	113	17	7	2	48	11
88 AL	.249	89	257	40	64	14	1	5	18	0
89 NL	.233	142	437	52	102	17	4	6	41	3
90 NL	.234	149	453	55	106	24	5	5	35	8
91 NL	.255	139	424	39	108	22	8	3	26	2
Life	.241	1155	3724	447	896	157	49	33	314	65
3 AVE	.240	143	438	49	105	21	6	5	34	4

CURRENT PLAYERS

MIKE PAGLIARULO

Position: Third base
Team: Minnesota Twins
Born: March 15, 1960 Medford, MA
Height: 6'2" **Weight:** 195 lbs.
Bats: left **Throws:** right
Acquired: Signed as a free agent, 1/91

Player Summary	
Fantasy Value	$3 to $6
Card Value	3¢ to 5¢
Will	make contact
Can't	avoid 3-1 K-to-walk ratio
Expect	decent defense
Don't Expect	many steals

Ever since hitting 28 and 32 home runs early in his career, Pagliarulo has had to explain what became of his power. The explaining stopped last year, when he produced the highest batting average of his eight-year career by swinging for base hits instead of home runs. His fantasy value stops at $6, however, because of his lessening power. His 1992 commons suffer from the same problem. Used in a lefty-righty platoon with Scott Leius, Pagliarulo also played a decent defensive game at third. Despite limited range, he positioned himself well, picked the ball cleanly, and showed a knack for grabbing bunts and rollers with his throwing hand. Although most of his errors came on throws, Pags was able to throw hard. Minnesota got more than it bargained for when it signed him to plug the gap created by Gary Gaetti's defection.

Major League Batting Register

	BA	G	AB	R	H	2B	3B	HR	RBI	SB
84 AL	.239	67	201	24	48	15	3	7	34	0
85 AL	.239	138	380	55	91	16	2	19	62	0
86 AL	.238	149	504	71	120	24	3	28	71	4
87 AL	.234	150	522	76	122	26	3	32	87	1
88 AL	.216	125	444	46	96	20	1	15	67	1
89 AL	.197	74	223	19	44	10	0	4	16	1
89 NL	.196	50	148	12	29	7	0	3	14	2
90 NL	.254	128	398	29	101	23	2	7	38	1
91 AL	.279	121	365	38	102	20	0	6	36	1
Life	.236	1002	3185	370	753	161	14	121	425	11
3 AVE	.243	124	378	33	92	20	1	7	35	2

TOM PAGNOZZI

Position: Catcher
Team: St. Louis Cardinals
Born: July 30, 1962 Tucson, AZ
Height: 6'1" **Weight:** 190 lbs.
Bats: right **Throws:** right
Acquired: Eighth-round pick in 6/83 free-agent draft

Player Summary	
Fantasy Value	$4 to $8
Card Value	3¢ to 5¢
Will	make powerful throws
Can't	hit for power
Expect	No.1 catcher job
Don't Expect	poor contact

When former catcher Joe Torre became Cardinal manager midway through the 1990 season, he decided backup catcher Pagnozzi would make a better defensive backstop than rookie Todd Zeile. Taking a page from his own career, he switched the hard-hitting Zeile to third and made Pagnozzi the No. 1 catcher. The moves paid their first dividends in 1991. Pagnozzi, playing more than 100 games for the first time in his five-year career, topped .250 and even stole more than a half-dozen bases. He compiled a .351 slugging percentage and a .319 on-base average. As expected, he provided dynamite defense, with strong throws, few errors, and expert blocking of potential wild pitches. He also provided expert guidance for the pitching staff. So what if he only contributed a pair of homers to the attack? It hurts the future value of his 1992 commons, but he still is a $6 fantasy catcher.

Major League Batting Register

	BA	G	AB	R	H	2B	3B	HR	RBI	SB
87 NL	.188	27	48	8	9	1	0	2	9	1
88 NL	.282	81	195	17	55	9	0	0	15	0
89 NL	.150	52	80	3	12	2	0	0	3	0
90 NL	.277	69	220	20	61	15	0	2	23	1
91 NL	.264	140	459	38	121	24	5	2	57	9
Life	.257	369	1002	86	258	51	5	6	107	11
2 AVE	.268	105	340	29	91	20	3	2	40	5

CURRENT PLAYERS

VICENTE PALACIOS

Position: Pitcher
Team: Pittsburgh Pirates
Born: July 19, 1963 Mataloma, Mexico
Height: 6'3" **Weight:** 180 lbs.
Bats: right **Throws:** right
Acquired: Purchased from Brewers, 4/87

Player Summary	
Fantasy Value	$2 to $4
Card Value	3¢ to 5¢
Will	have to prove health
Can't	avoid shoulder problems
Expect	uncertainty over role
Don't Expect	over a hit a frame

After getting off to a good start as a member of Pittsburgh's starting rotation in 1991, Palacios was slowed by a strained rotator cuff. His traditional and split-fingered fastballs, which he mixes with a variety of breaking balls, are his best pitches. In 1991, opponents compiled a .228 batting average, a .386 slugging percentage, and a .315 on-base percentage. He is adept at keeping runners close. On the down side, he gives up too many home run balls, allowing 12 in 1991. Staying healthy is something else. He has had rotator cuff problems, missing much of 1988 and all of 1989. Palacios remains a puzzle. If he's sound, there could be confusion over how to use him. He's been effective as both a starter and reliever during a pro career that began in 1982. As a starter with Triple-A Buffalo in 1990, he was 13-7 with a 3.43 ERA, 53 walks, 137 strikeouts, and 173 hits in 183⅔ innings. He is a reasonable fantasy draft for up to $4. His 1992 commons should be avoided until he notches a few more career wins.

Major League Pitching Register

	W	L	ERA	G	S	IP	H	ER	BB	SO
87 NL	2	1	4.30	6	0	29.1	27	14	9	13
88 NL	1	2	6.66	7	0	24.1	28	18	15	15
90 NL	0	0	0.00	7	3	15.0	4	0	2	8
91 NL	6	3	3.75	36	3	81.2	69	34	38	64
Life	9	6	3.95	56	6	150.1	128	66	64	100

DONN PALL

Position: Pitcher
Team: Chicago White Sox
Born: Jan. 11, 1962 Chicago, IL
Height: 6'1" **Weight:** 180 lbs.
Bats: right **Throws:** right
Acquired: 23rd-round pick in 6/85 free-agent draft

Player Summary	
Fantasy Value	$2 to $4
Card Value	3¢ to 5¢
Will	relieve well
Can't	remain in long
Expect	double plays
Don't Expect	frequent walks

Pall is coming off the best of his four big league seasons as a middle reliever, all with the Sox. He is especially effective in short stints. He has relatively good control of his fastball, curve, and split-fingered fastball and keeps the ball in the park. He gave up seven gophers in '91. His 2-1 ratio of strikeouts to walks is fine for a set-up man. In 1991, opponents accrued a .231 batting average, a .337 slugging percentage, and a .295 on-base percentage. Pall succeeds by getting batters to hit the ball on the ground, often setting up double-plays that stifle opposition rallies. He starts some of those twin-killings himself and is generally agile with the glove. Preventing rivals from stealing is another matter, however. Pall needs more work in that department. The former University of Illinois standout is a home-grown product. He is a $3 fantasy reliever until he starts accumulating some saves, and his 1992 cards are commons.

Major League Pitching Register

	W	L	ERA	G	S	IP	H	ER	BB	SO
88 AL	0	2	3.45	17	0	28.2	39	11	8	16
89 AL	4	5	3.31	53	6	87.0	90	32	19	58
90 AL	3	5	3.32	56	2	76.0	63	28	24	39
91 AL	7	2	2.41	51	0	71.0	59	19	20	40
Life	14	14	3.08	177	8	262.2	251	90	71	153
3 AVE	5	4	3.04	53	3	78.0	71	26	21	46

CURRENT PLAYERS

RAFAEL PALMEIRO

Position: First base
Team: Texas Rangers
Born: Sept. 24, 1964 Havana, Cuba
Height: 6' **Weight:** 180 lbs.
Bats: left **Throws:** left
Acquired: Traded from Cubs with Drew Hall and Jamie Moyer for Curtis Wilkerson, Steve Wilson, Mitch Williams, Paul Kilgus, Luis Benitez, and Pablo Delgado, 12/88

Player Summary	
Fantasy Value	$36 to $42
Card Value	5¢ to 10¢
Will	produce high average
Can't	play great defense
Expect	bid for batting crown
Don't Expect	prolonged slumps

Palmeiro has always been a high-average hitter. Even he was surprised at his showing after the 1991 All-Star Game, notching a .455 average (45-for-99) in the first month after action resumed. He finished the season at .322, though he didn't lead the team (that went to AL champ Julio Franco). In 1990, Palmeiro finished at .319, then the best average by a Ranger in 10 years. When he's hot, he is almost impossible to retire. He does not have good speed and is only average on defense. He prefers the ball down and away but knows how to go with the pitch. He is a selective hitter with a short stroke who has abandoned previous efforts to hit every ball out of the park. He had a .532 slugging percentage and a .389 on-base average. He is a $40 fantasy draft. His 1992 cards are good buys at a nickel apiece.

Major League Batting Register

	BA	G	AB	R	H	2B	3B	HR	RBI	SB
86 NL	.247	22	73	9	18	4	0	3	12	1
87 NL	.276	84	221	32	61	15	1	14	30	2
88 NL	.307	152	580	75	178	41	5	8	53	12
89 AL	.275	156	559	76	154	23	4	8	64	4
90 AL	.319	154	598	72	191	35	6	14	89	3
91 AL	.322	159	631	115	203	49	3	26	88	4
Life	.302	727	2662	379	805	167	19	73	336	26
3 AVE	.306	156	596	88	183	36	4	16	80	4

DEAN PALMER

Position: Third base; outfield
Team: Texas Rangers
Born: Dec. 27, 1968 Tallahassee, FL
Height: 6'1" **Weight:** 190 lbs.
Bats: right **Throws:** right
Acquired: Third-round pick in 6/86 free-agent draft

Player Summary	
Fantasy Value	$5 to $10
Card Value	5¢ to 10¢
Will	power home runs
Can't	hit for average
Expect	Steve Buechele's glove
Don't Expect	many steals

Palmer had difficulty adjusting to major league pitching after his recall from the minors last June. Scouts insist he'll become one of the game's premier power-hitters, however. He blasted an American Association-leading 22 homers at Triple-A Oklahoma City before his recall, then hit his first big league shot June 27. He has shown some discipline at the plate, plus an ability to hit to right field with two strikes. Drafted at age 17, Palmer is blessed with great bat speed and a strong throwing arm. Defensively, he won't make Ranger fans forget popular third baseman Steve Buechele, but Palmer won't embarrass himself either. Before Buechele was traded to Pittsburgh, Palmer played left field for Texas and handled the position well. The half-year of experience, plus the chance to start the year as a big league third baseman, should boost his confidence as well as production. Stay safe before investing heavily in his 1992 cards. Buy for a dime apiece until he has some success on the major league level. He is a $10 fantasy draft.

Major League Batting Register

	BA	G	AB	R	H	2B	3B	HR	RBI	SB
89 AL	.105	16	19	0	2	2	0	0	1	0
91 AL	.187	81	268	38	50	9	2	15	37	0
Life	.181	97	287	38	52	11	2	15	38	0

CURRENT PLAYERS

DAVE PARKER

Position: Designated hitter
Team: Toronto Blue Jays
Born: June 9, 1951 Jackson, MS
Height: 6'5" **Weight:** 230 lbs.
Bats: left **Throws:** right
Acquired: Signed as a free agent, 9/91

Player Summary	
Fantasy Value	$8 to $12
Card Value	5¢ to 10¢
Will	swing with power
Can't	play every day
Expect	frequent strikeouts
Don't Expect	great mobility

Parker was a disappointment in his one year as an Angel, but the Jays wasted little time in signing him after he drew his release from California. Because of chronic knee problems, he is best utilized as a designated hitter but can play first. A physically imposing lefthanded hitter, Parker still has power in his swing, though his strikeout frequency seems to be increasing with age. His lifetime average and power totals are quite respectable. He is a fantasy gamble at $10, but one that could pay off. His nickel-priced 1992 cards are good long-term buys.

Major League Batting Register

	BA	G	AB	R	H	2B	3B	HR	RBI	SB
73 NL	.288	54	139	17	40	9	1	4	14	1
74 NL	.282	73	220	27	62	10	3	4	29	3
75 NL	.308	148	558	75	172	35	10	25	101	8
76 NL	.313	138	537	82	168	28	10	13	90	19
77 NL	.338	159	637	107	215	44	8	21	88	17
78 NL	.334	148	581	102	194	32	12	30	117	20
79 NL	.310	158	622	109	193	45	7	25	94	20
80 NL	.295	139	518	71	153	31	1	17	79	10
81 NL	.258	67	240	29	62	14	3	9	48	6
82 NL	.270	73	244	41	66	19	3	6	29	7
83 NL	.279	144	552	68	154	29	4	12	69	12
84 NL	.285	156	607	73	173	28	0	16	94	11
85 NL	.312	160	635	88	198	42	4	34	125	5
86 NL	.273	162	637	89	174	31	3	31	116	1
87 NL	.253	153	589	77	149	28	0	26	97	7
88 AL	.257	101	377	43	97	18	1	12	55	0
89 AL	.264	144	553	56	146	27	0	22	97	0
90 AL	.289	157	610	71	176	30	3	21	92	4
91 AL	.239	132	502	47	120	26	2	11	59	3
Life	.290	2466	9358	1272	2712	526	75	339	1493	154
3 AVE	.265	144	555	58	147	28	2	18	83	2

LANCE PARRISH

Position: Catcher
Team: California Angels
Born: June 15, 1956 Clairton, PA
Height: 6'3" **Weight:** 220 lbs.
Bats: right **Throws:** right
Acquired: Traded from Phillies for David Holdridge, 10/88

Player Summary	
Fantasy Value	$10 to $15
Card Value	3¢ to 5¢
Will	bludgeon southpaws
Can't	explain production drop
Expect	platoon status
Don't Expect	any speed

Parrish proved he still swings a potent bat when he smacked his 300th career home run in '91. The eight-time All-Star backstop seems to be in the twilight of his career. He wore out his welcome with the Angels in '91 by failing to hit his weight or throw out runners at his usual rate. He had led the league by wiping out 47 percent of would-be stealers in 1990. The 15-year veteran strikes out three times more than he walks. A pull hitter without much patience, Parrish still punishes lefthanders, a trait that could convince management to make him a platoon player. He is a deserving fantasy draft at $10. His 1992 commons, though, are not great purchases.

Major League Batting Register

	BA	G	AB	R	H	2B	3B	HR	RBI	SB
77 AL	.196	12	46	10	9	2	0	3	7	0
78 AL	.219	85	288	37	63	11	3	14	41	0
79 AL	.276	143	493	65	136	26	3	19	65	6
80 AL	.286	144	553	79	158	34	6	24	82	6
81 AL	.244	96	348	39	85	18	2	10	46	2
82 AL	.284	133	486	75	138	19	2	32	87	3
83 AL	.269	155	605	80	163	42	3	27	114	1
84 AL	.237	147	578	75	137	16	2	33	98	2
85 AL	.273	140	549	64	150	27	1	28	98	2
86 AL	.257	91	327	53	84	6	1	22	62	0
87 NL	.245	130	466	42	114	21	0	17	67	0
88 NL	.215	123	424	44	91	17	2	15	60	0
89 AL	.238	124	433	48	103	12	1	17	50	1
90 AL	.268	133	470	54	126	14	0	24	70	2
91 AL	.216	119	402	38	87	12	0	19	51	0
Life	.254	1775	6468	803	1644	277	26	304	998	25
3 AVE	.242	125	435	47	105	13	0	20	57	1

221

CURRENT PLAYERS

DAN PASQUA

Position: Outfield; first base
Team: Chicago White Sox
Born: Oct. 17, 1961 Yonkers, NY
Height: 6' **Weight:** 203 lbs.
Bats: left **Throws:** left
Acquired: Traded from Yankees with Mark Salas and Steve Rosenberg for Richard Dotson and Scott Nielsen, 11/87

Player Summary	
Fantasy Value	$8 to $12
Card Value	3¢ to 5¢
Will	assault righties
Can't	play great left field
Expect	15 to 20 homers
Don't Expect	everyday status

Pasqua plays first base, the outfield corners, and serves as a designated hitter and pinch-hitter with power. He's used almost exclusively against righthanded pitching, primarily because he's been an automatic out any time he's been given a crack at lefties. Pasqua's power gets him playing time. He had a personal peak of 20 homers in 129 games in 1988 and is always a threat to reach that level again. Pasqua is also a patient hitter who had a 1-1 ratio of walks to RBI in 1991. He compiled a .465 slugging percentage and a .358 on-base average in 1991. He hits well in the clutch. Pasqua would probably play more if not for his lack of speed. When Bo Jackson surfaced last September, Frank Thomas moved from designated hitter to first and cut Pasqua's time. He is a solid $10 fantasy draft, but his 1992 cards remain commons.

Major League Batting Register

	BA	G	AB	R	H	2B	3B	HR	RBI	SB
85 AL	.209	60	148	17	31	3	1	9	25	0
86 AL	.293	102	280	44	82	17	0	16	45	2
87 AL	.233	113	318	42	74	7	1	17	42	0
88 AL	.227	129	422	48	96	16	2	20	50	1
89 AL	.248	73	246	26	61	9	1	11	47	1
90 AL	.274	112	325	43	89	27	3	13	58	1
91 AL	.259	134	417	71	108	22	5	18	66	0
Life	.251	723	2156	291	541	101	13	104	333	5
3 AVE	.261	106	329	47	86	19	3	14	57	1

BOB PATTERSON

Position: Pitcher
Team: Pittsburgh Pirates
Born: May 16, 1959 Jacksonville, FL
Height: 6'2" **Weight:** 192 lbs.
Bats: right **Throws:** left
Acquired: Traded from Padres for Marvell Wynne, 4/86

Player Summary	
Fantasy Value	$2 to $4
Card Value	3¢ to 5¢
Will	work often
Can't	help at bat
Expect	fine ratio of Ks to walks
Don't Expect	many walks or homers

Patterson has been a relief pitcher for most of his professional career. He has appeared in more than 50 games two years in a row but has never worked more than 95 innings in any of his five big league seasons. One of the game's most versatile pitchers, he has been used in short, middle, and long relief and has even made a few starts, including one in the 1987 season opener. A fastball-and-curveball pitcher with good control, Patterson averages almost a strikeout an inning. He maintains an excellent strikeout-to-walk ratio of 4-to-1. He keeps the ball in the park, knows what to do with a glove, and doesn't let runners get good jumps against him. He finished 19 games in 1991. His save totals warrant a $4 fantasy bid, at most. His 1992 commons don't authorize amassing. He's mismatched with a bat in his hands, however. Patterson could be attractive for one of the expansion clubs.

Major League Pitching Register

	W	L	ERA	G	S	IP	H	ER	BB	SO
85 NL	0	0	24.75	3	0	4.0	13	11	3	1
86 NL	2	3	4.95	11	0	36.1	49	20	5	20
87 NL	1	4	6.70	15	0	43.0	49	32	22	27
88 NL	0	0	4.20	2	1	26.2	23	12	8	20
89 NL	4	3	4.05	12	1	26.2	23	12	8	20
90 NL	8	5	2.95	55	5	94.2	88	31	21	70
91 NL	4	3	4.11	54	2	65.2	67	30	15	57
Life	19	18	4.53	150	8	270.1	289	136	74	195
2 AVE	6	4	3.42	55	4	80.2	78	31	18	64

CURRENT PLAYERS

KEN PATTERSON

Position: Pitcher
Team: Chicago White Sox
Born: July 8, 1964 Costa Mesa, CA
Height: 6'4" **Weight:** 210 lbs.
Bats: left **Throws:** left
Acquired: Traded from Yankees with Jeff Pries for Jerry Royster and Mike Soper, 8/87

Player Summary
Fantasy Value	$2 to $4
Card Value	3¢ to 5¢
Will	retire tough lefties
Can't	stop righties from homering
Expect	respectable ERA
Don't Expect	good K-to-walk ratio

Although the plate tended to wander on Patterson in 1991, the southpaw relief specialist enjoyed his third straight successful season for the White Sox. He proved to be one of the most effective pitchers on the staff. He had allowed less than a hit per inning. He also gave up only one walk for every two innings pitched. Before last season, Patterson had often been used to retire one or two key lefthanded hitters. In 1991, his stints tended to lengthen in direct proportion to his strong performance. A fastball pitcher, he overpowers most lefties but gives up occasional long balls to righthanded hitters. He didn't notch many strikeouts, however. In 1991, opponents compiled a .214 batting average, a .330 slugging percentage, and a .321 on-base average. There's nothing wrong with his fielding or ability to hold runners close. He's sure to have a job in 1992. A three buck fantasy bid, he doesn't start or save, so his 1992 commons are not good buys.

Major League Pitching Register
	W	L	ERA	G	S	IP	H	ER	BB	SO
88 AL	0	2	4.79	9	1	20.2	25	11	7	8
89 AL	6	1	4.52	50	0	65.2	64	33	28	43
90 AL	2	1	3.39	43	2	66.1	58	25	34	40
91 AL	3	0	2.83	43	1	63.2	48	20	35	32
Life	11	4	3.70	145	4	216.1	195	89	104	123
3 AVE	4	1	3.59	46	1	65.2	57	26	32	38

BILL PECOTA

Position: Third base
Team: New York Mets
Born: Feb. 16, 1960 Redwood City, CA
Height: 6'2" **Weight:** 190 lbs.
Bats: right **Throws:** right
Acquired: Traded from Royals with Bret Saberhagen for Gregg Jefferies, Kevin McReynolds, and Keith Miller, 12/91

Player Summary
Fantasy Value	$3 to $6
Card Value	3¢ to 5¢
Will	play strong defense
Can't	hit for power
Expect	solid average
Don't Expect	minor league

Once they gave him a chance to play, the Royals learned that Pecota can bunt, squeeze, hit-and-run, steal bases, and play a solid defensive game at third base. Once nicknamed I-29 because he was on a constant shuttle between Kansas City and Omaha, Pecota has played every position in the majors but stopped the merry-go-round by winning the third base job from Kevin Seitzer in '91. The strong-armed Pecota not only showed better hands and better range at third but also wielded a more potent bat. The beneficiary of long tutoring sessions with batting coach John Mayberry, Pecota had a batting average 20 points above Seitzer's. In December, he was dealt to the Mets, where he'll get significant playing time. His power deficiency caps the bidding at $6 and precludes investment in his 1992 commons.

Major League Batting Register
	BA	G	AB	R	H	2B	3B	HR	RBI	SB
86 AL	.207	12	29	3	6	2	0	0	2	0
87 AL	.276	66	156	22	43	5	1	3	14	5
88 AL	.208	90	178	25	37	3	3	1	15	7
89 AL	.205	65	83	21	17	4	2	3	5	5
90 AL	.242	87	240	43	58	15	2	5	20	8
91 AL	.286	125	398	53	114	23	2	6	45	16
Life	.254	445	1084	167	275	52	10	18	101	41
2 AVE	.270	106	319	48	86	19	2	6	33	12

CURRENT PLAYERS

ALEJANDRO PENA

Position: Pitcher
Team: Atlanta Braves
Born: June 25, 1959 Cambiaso, Dominican Republic
Height: 6'1" **Weight:** 203 lbs.
Bats: right **Throws:** right
Acquired: Traded from Mets for Tony Castillo and Joe Roa, 8/91

Player Summary	
Fantasy Value	$4 to $8
Card Value	3¢ to 5¢
Will	work 50 games
Can't	hold runners on
Expect	career ERA under 3.00
Don't Expect	many walks or homers

Pena pumped new life into the Braves bullpen after he was acquired for last year's stretch drive. Helping fill the breach created by Juan Berenguer's arm injury, Pena worked as both a set-up man and part-time closer. He was perfect in all save opportunities down the stretch. A fastball-and-slider pitcher who also has a changeup, he is a former starter who became a reliever in 1986 after recovering from shoulder problems. He yields less than a hit per inning, keeps the ball in the park, and strikes out triple the number he walks. Although he's a fine pitcher, Pena doesn't help himself as a hitter, fielder, or guardian of base-runners. He will notch more saves with the Braves, so his fantasy value is $6 or so. His 1992 cards will stay at commons prices.

Major League Pitching Register

	W	L	ERA	G	S	IP	H	ER	BB	SO
81 NL	1	1	2.84	14	2	25.1	18	8	11	14
82 NL	0	2	4.79	29	0	35.2	37	19	21	20
83 NL	12	9	2.75	34	1	177.0	152	54	51	120
84 NL	12	6	2.48	28	0	199.1	186	55	46	135
85 NL	0	1	8.31	2	0	4.1	7	4	3	2
86 NL	1	2	4.89	24	1	70.0	74	38	30	46
87 NL	2	7	3.50	37	11	87.1	82	34	37	76
88 NL	6	7	1.91	60	12	94.1	75	20	27	83
89 NL	4	3	2.13	53	5	76.0	62	18	18	75
90 NL	3	3	3.20	52	5	76.0	71	27	22	76
91 NL	8	1	2.40	59	15	82.1	74	22	22	62
Life	49	42	2.90	392	52	927.2	838	299	288	709
3 AVE	5	2	2.57	55	8	78.0	69	22	21	71

GERONIMO PENA

Position: Second base
Team: St. Louis Cardinals
Born: March 29, 1967 Distrito Nacional, Dominican Republic
Height: 6'1" **Weight:** 170 lbs.
Bats: both **Throws:** right
Acquired: Signed as free agent, 8/84

Player Summary	
Fantasy Value	$3 to $6
Card Value	15¢ to 20¢
Will	give strong defense
Can't	curtail his free-swinging
Expect	a .250 average
Don't Expect	starting job

The Cardinals lost little when Pena, normally a second baseman, replaced Bernard Gilkey (exiled to the minors) in left field. A natural second baseman who can also play shortstop and third base, Pena needs to reach base more often to be considered for an everyday job. He's a wild swinger who strikes out far more often than he walks, one reason why he failed to hit .250 in a year of Triple-A and two years in the majors. For St. Louis in 1991, he compiled a .400 slugging percentage and a .322 on-base average. At Triple-A Louisville in 1990, he hit .249 with six homers, 35 RBI, 65 runs, and 24 stolen bases. His speed and defense will keep in the big leagues. Pena is an acrobatic infielder with a good arm, range, and hands. He led the Class-A South Atlantic League with 80 stolen bases in 1987. As a shortstop in 1987, he led the loop in putouts, assists, and fielding percentage. When he gets a starting spot, the value of his rookie 1992 cards will multiply beyond 15 cents. He is a $4 fantasy draft.

Major League Batting Register

	BA	G	AB	R	H	2B	3B	HR	RBI	SB
90 NL	.244	18	45	5	11	2	0	0	2	1
91 NL	.243	104	185	38	45	8	3	5	17	15
Life	.243	122	230	43	56	10	3	5	19	16

CURRENT PLAYERS

TONY PENA

Position: Catcher
Team: Boston Red Sox
Born: June 4, 1957 Monte Cristi, Dominican Republic
Height: 6' **Weight:** 184 lbs.
Bats: right **Throws:** right
Acquired: Signed as a free agent, 11/89

Player Summary	
Fantasy Value	$5 to $8
Card Value	3¢ to 5¢
Will	vie for Gold Glove
Can't	exploit Fenway fences
Expect	better production
Don't Expect	another 140 games

Pena won three Gold Glove awards in the NL, and he has taken two seasons to establish himself as one of the finest defensive receivers in the AL. He not only handles his pitchers well but calls intelligent games, blocks balls in the dirt, and makes runners think twice about stealing. Pena even runs better than any catcher in the AL. He normally hits too, but he's coming off his worst season, an injury-riddled 1987 campaign. After catching 140-plus games three years in a row, Pena hit more than 30 points below the 11-year average of .273 that he took into the 1991 season. The five-time All-Star should be able to add power in '92. Get him for $7. His 1991 commons are not great deals, however.

Major League Batting Register

	BA	G	AB	R	H	2B	3B	HR	RBI	SB
80 NL	.429	8	21	1	9	1	1	0	1	0
81 NL	.300	66	210	16	63	9	1	2	17	1
82 NL	.296	138	497	53	147	28	4	11	63	2
83 NL	.301	151	542	51	163	22	3	15	70	6
84 NL	.286	147	546	77	156	27	2	15	78	12
85 NL	.249	147	546	53	136	27	2	10	59	12
86 NL	.288	144	510	56	147	26	2	10	52	9
87 NL	.214	116	384	40	82	13	4	5	44	6
88 NL	.263	149	505	55	133	23	1	10	51	6
89 NL	.259	141	424	36	110	17	2	4	37	5
90 AL	.263	143	491	62	129	19	1	7	56	8
91 NL	.231	141	464	45	107	23	2	5	48	8
Life	.269	1491	5140	545	1382	235	25	94	576	75
3 AVE	.251	142	460	48	115	20	2	5	47	7

TERRY PENDLETON

Position: Third base
Team: Atlanta Braves
Born: July 16, 1960 Los Angeles, CA
Height: 5'9" **Weight:** 195 lbs.
Bats: both **Throws:** right
Acquired: Signed as a free agent, 12/90

Player Summary	
Fantasy Value	$22 to $30
Card Value	5¢ to 10¢
Will	deliver in clutch
Can't	run as well
Expect	Gold Glove defense
Don't Expect	repetition of 1991

The Braves knew they were getting defense and leadership when they signed Pendleton. They didn't know they were also adding a batting champion. One year after hitting .230 for St. Louis, he produced career highs in almost every batting category. Overlooked for the All-Star squad, he had the last laugh when he led the Braves to their first divisional title since 1982. Flashing the form that won several Gold Gloves, he prevented doubles down the line, threw out runners from the outfield grass, and used his range and reactions to grab balls others couldn't reach. His addition boosted the confidence of the young pitchers and made a bad team a champion. That's the reason Pendleton won the 1991 NL Most Valuable Player Award. He is a fantasy bargain at less than $30. His 1992 cards may see immediate, small gains to a dime.

Major League Batting Register

	BA	G	AB	R	H	2B	3B	HR	RBI	SB
84 NL	.324	67	262	37	85	16	3	1	33	20
85 NL	.240	149	559	56	134	16	3	5	69	17
86 NL	.239	159	578	56	138	26	5	1	59	24
87 NL	.286	159	583	82	167	29	4	12	96	19
88 NL	.253	110	391	44	99	20	2	6	53	3
89 NL	.264	162	613	83	162	28	5	13	74	9
90 NL	.230	121	447	46	103	20	2	6	58	7
91 NL	.319	153	586	94	187	34	8	22	86	10
Life	.267	1080	4019	498	1075	189	32	66	528	109
3 AVE	.275	145	549	74	151	27	5	14	73	9

CURRENT PLAYERS

MELIDO PEREZ

Position: Pitcher
Team: Chicago White Sox
Born: Feb. 15, 1966 San Cristobal, Dominican Republic
Height: 6'4" **Weight:** 180 lbs.
Bats: right **Throws:** right
Acquired: Traded from Royals with Greg Hibbard, John Davis, and Chuck Mount for Dave Cochrane and Floyd Bannister, 12/87

Player Summary	
Fantasy Value	$2 to $4
Card Value	3¢ to 5¢
Will	keep batters at bay
Can't	avoid trouble as starter
Expect	good control
Don't Expect	return of high ERA

After the White Sox moved Perez from the rotation to the relief corps in 1991, he turned into a better pitcher. The hard-throwing Perez notched almost a K per inning and finished 16 of his 41 relief games. His 3.12 ERA was by far the best of his four-year career. He succeeds by keeping runners off base. He allows far less than a hit per inning, gets two and one-half strikeouts per walk, and has a better ratio of strikeouts to innings pitched than anyone else on the staff. Perez is a fastball-and-curveball pitcher who also throws a hard split-fingered fastball that is one of the league's best when it's sinking. He handles a glove well and keeps runners close. Though he fought it at first, Perez now realizes relief pitching is the best thing for him. His fantasy value has dropped to a $4 ceiling, and his 1992 commons will remain there unless he regains a spot in the rotation.

Major League Pitching Register

	W	L	ERA	G	S	IP	H	ER	BB	SO
87 AL	1	1	7.84	3	0	10.1	18	9	5	5
88 AL	12	10	3.79	32	0	197.0	186	83	72	138
89 AL	11	14	5.01	31	0	183.1	187	102	90	141
90 AL	13	14	4.61	35	0	197.0	177	101	86	161
91 AL	8	7	3.12	49	1	135.2	111	47	52	128
Life	45	46	4.26	150	1	723.1	679	342	305	573
3 AVE	11	12	4.36	38	0	172.1	158	83	76	143

PASCUAL PEREZ

Position: Pitcher
Team: New York Yankees
Born: May 17, 1957 San Cristobal, Dominican Republic
Height: 6'3" **Weight:** 180 lbs.
Bats: right **Throws:** right
Acquired: Signed as a free agent, 11/89

Player Summary	
Fantasy Value	$1 to $2
Card Value	3¢ to 5¢
Will	win 15 if healthy
Can't	wait to vindicate
Expect	3-1 ratio of Ks to walks
Don't Expect	year on bench

After signing a three-year, $5.7 million contract to pitch for the Yankees, Perez suffered shoulder problems that forced him to miss most of his first two years in the Bronx. The partially torn rotator cuff finally healed in time for him to leave the disabled list and rejoin the rotation on August 16, 1991. A fastball-and-slider pitcher who compiled a 3.45 career ERA over a 10-year career before 1991, Perez is a flamboyant performer whose antics have not only annoyed rivals but also sparked beanball wars. When he's winning, such shenanigans are almost tolerable. He once had a suspension for substance abuse. That problem is solved, but his shoulder remains a question mark. Don't hazard much money at the fantasy draft on his right arm, and waste none buying his 1992 commons.

Major League Pitching Register

	W	L	ERA	G	CG	IP	H	ER	BB	SO
80 NL	0	1	3.75	2	0	12.0	15	5	2	7
81 NL	2	7	3.96	17	2	86.1	92	38	34	46
82 NL	4	4	3.06	16	0	79.1	85	27	17	29
83 NL	15	8	3.43	33	7	215.1	213	82	51	144
84 NL	14	8	3.74	30	4	211.2	208	88	51	145
85 NL	1	13	6.14	22	0	95.1	115	65	57	57
87 NL	7	0	2.30	10	2	70.1	52	18	16	58
88 NL	12	8	2.44	27	4	188.0	133	51	44	131
89 NL	9	13	3.31	33	2	198.1	178	73	45	152
90 AL	1	2	1.29	3	0	14.0	8	2	3	12
91 AL	2	4	3.18	14	0	73.2	68	26	24	41
Life	67	68	3.44	.207	21	1244.1	1167	475	344	822
2 AVE	6	9	3.28	24	1	136.2	123	50	35	97

CURRENT PLAYERS

GERALD PERRY

Position: First base; outfield
Team: St. Louis Cardinals
Born: Oct. 30, 1960 Savannah, GA
Height: 6' **Weight:** 190 lbs.
Bats: left **Throws:** right
Acquired: Signed as a free agent, 12/90

Player Summary
Fantasy Value	$2 to $4
Card Value	3¢ to 5¢
Will	use speed as weapon
Can't	generate consistent power
Expect	bunts and infield hits
Don't Expect	strong defense

Although he has been a big league regular before, Perry got only seven starts for St. Louis in the first half of 1991 before succeeding the injured Pedro Guerrero on July 7. Perry has the speed to sweeten his average with infield hits, and he made the most of his opportunity. A streak hitter who eats righthanded pitchers for breakfast, he doesn't have the power usually associated with his position but compensates with a line-drive stroke and an ability to steal bases. He contended for the 1988 NL batting title before a September snooze sent the mercury back to .300. Perry has since perfected a running game that was once laced with mistakes. He's still imperfect in the field, however, and would be better off as a designated hitter. He is a $3 fantasy hitter. His 1992 cards will remain commons as long as he remains grounded.

Major League Batting Register
	BA	G	AB	R	H	2B	3B	HR	RBI	SB
83 NL	.359	27	39	5	14	2	0	1	6	0
84 NL	.265	122	347	52	92	12	2	7	47	15
85 NL	.214	110	238	22	51	5	0	3	13	9
86 NL	.271	29	70	6	19	2	0	2	11	0
87 NL	.270	142	533	77	144	35	2	12	74	42
88 NL	.300	141	547	61	164	29	1	8	74	29
89 NL	.252	72	266	24	67	11	0	4	21	10
90 AL	.254	133	465	57	118	22	2	8	57	17
91 NL	.240	109	242	29	58	8	4	6	36	15
Life	.265	885	2747	333	727	126	11	51	339	137
3 AVE	.250	105	324	37	81	14	2	6	38	14

GENO PETRALLI

Position: Catcher
Team: Texas Rangers
Born: Sept. 25, 1959 Sacramento, CA
Height: 6'2" **Weight:** 180 lbs.
Bats: left **Throws:** right
Acquired: Signed as a free agent, 5/85

Player Summary
Fantasy Value	$1 to $2
Card Value	3¢ to 5¢
Will	make contact
Can't	hit for power
Expect	continued backup service
Don't Expect	strikeouts or infield hits

When Petralli hit a three-run home run against the Yankees last August 26, it was his first since June 20, 1989, a span of 223 games and 544 at bats. A contact hitter who took a .279 career mark into the '91 campaign, the lefty-hitting catcher walks almost as often as he strikes out. He's basically a singles hitter who uses the opposite field often. His defense improved dramatically in the wake of the trade that made knuckleballer Charlie Hough an ex-Ranger. Petralli throws well enough to be a platoon catcher but no one will deny daily duty to strong-armed sophomore Ivan Rodriguez in Texas. If Petralli remains a Ranger, he'll serve as a pinch-hitter, DH, and sub. Ignore his 1992 commons, and spend only a buck for him at the draft.

Major League Batting Register
	BA	G	AB	R	H	2B	3B	HR	RBI	SB
82 AL	.364	16	44	3	16	2	0	0	1	0
83 AL	.000	6	4	0	0	0	0	0	0	0
84 AL	.000	3	3	0	0	0	0	0	0	0
85 AL	.270	42	100	7	27	2	0	0	11	1
86 AL	.255	69	137	17	35	9	3	2	18	3
87 AL	.302	101	202	28	61	11	2	7	31	0
88 AL	.282	129	351	35	99	14	2	7	36	0
89 AL	.304	70	184	18	56	7	0	4	23	0
90 AL	.255	133	325	28	83	13	1	0	21	0
91 AL	.271	87	199	21	54	8	1	2	20	2
Life	.278	656	1549	157	431	66	9	22	161	6
3 AVE	.273	97	236	22	64	9	1	2	21	1

CURRENT PLAYERS

GARY PETTIS

Position: Outfield
Team: Texas Rangers
Born: April 3, 1958 Oakland, CA
Height: 6'1" **Weight:** 160 lbs.
Bats: both **Throws:** left
Acquired: Signed as a free agent, 11/89

Player Summary	
Fantasy Value	$2 to $6
Card Value	3¢ to 5¢
Will	run like a deer
Can't	hit with power
Expect	infield hits
Don't Expect	daily job

Pettis is a weak-hitting outfielder with an exceptionally gifted glove. The center fielder had won the Gold Glove for fielding excellence five times in nine years before the 1991 campaign and might have won it again had he played more often. He often appears as a pinch-runner or defensive replacement. He stole 29 bases in limited action in '91. A patient hitter who draws dozens of walks, Pettis still strikes out twice as often as he reaches on free passes. That makes him a bad risk as a leadoff man. His weak arm isn't so risky, because he plays a shallow center to compensate and runs back on the ball better than anyone else. His 1992 cards will always be commons. His stolen bases, however, will continue to be a treat helpful to any fantasy team.

TONY PHILLIPS

Position: Infield; outfield
Team: Detroit Tigers
Born: April 15, 1959 Atlanta, GA
Height: 5'10" **Weight:** 175 lbs.
Bats: both **Throws:** right
Acquired: Signed as a free agent, 12/89

Player Summary	
Fantasy Value	$10 to $15
Card Value	3¢ to 5¢
Will	wait for walks
Can't	explain sudden power
Expect	competence at several spots
Don't Expect	higher average

Detroit manager Sparky Anderson called Phillips his most valuable player in 1991. In his first year in the Motor City, the versatile switch-hitter played everywhere but catcher, pitcher, and first base. He also hit everything in sight—reaching career peaks in home runs and RBI. The 10-year veteran proved to be a potent leadoff man, even pulling the ball against righthanded pitchers. Winter workouts with White Sox hitting coach Walt Hriniak helped. Phillips is a spray hitter who is patient at bat. In 1991, he compiled a .438 slugging percentage and a .371 on-base average. He is a natural at second, and he also played well at several other spots. Good speed and a strong arm helped. He can help a fantasy team in many categories, and he is a $10-plus draft. His 1992 commons are to be avoided.

Major League Batting Register

	BA	G	AB	R	H	2B	3B	HR	RBI	SB
82 AL	.200	10	5	5	1	0	0	1	1	0
83 AL	.294	22	85	19	25	2	3	3	6	8
84 AL	.227	140	397	63	90	11	6	2	29	48
85 AL	.257	125	443	67	114	10	8	1	32	56
86 AL	.258	154	539	93	139	23	4	5	58	50
87 AL	.208	133	394	49	82	13	2	1	17	24
88 AL	.210	129	458	65	96	14	4	3	36	44
89 AL	.257	119	444	77	114	8	6	1	18	43
90 AL	.239	136	423	66	101	16	8	3	31	38
91 AL	.216	137	282	37	61	7	5	0	19	29
Life	.237	1105	3470	541	823	104	46	20	247	340
3 AVE	.240	131	383	60	92	10	6	1	23	37

Major League Batting Register

	BA	G	AB	R	H	2B	3B	HR	RBI	SB
82 AL	.210	40	81	11	17	2	2	0	8	2
83 AL	.248	148	412	54	102	12	3	4	35	16
84 AL	.266	154	451	62	120	24	3	4	37	10
85 AL	.280	42	161	23	45	12	2	4	17	3
86 AL	.256	118	441	76	113	14	5	5	52	15
87 AL	.240	111	379	48	91	20	0	10	46	7
88 AL	.203	79	212	32	43	8	4	2	17	0
89 AL	.262	143	451	48	118	15	6	4	47	3
90 AL	.251	152	573	97	144	23	5	8	55	19
91 AL	.284	146	564	87	160	28	4	17	72	10
Life	.256	1133	3725	538	953	158	34	58	386	85
3 AVE	.266	147	529	77	141	22	5	10	58	11

CURRENT PLAYERS

PHIL PLANTIER

Position: Outfield
Team: Boston Red Sox
Born: Jan. 27, 1969 Manchester, NH
Height: 6' **Weight:** 175 lbs.
Bats: left **Throws:** right
Acquired: 11th-round pick in 6/87 free-agent draft

Player Summary	
Fantasy Value	$10 to $14
Card Value	10¢ to 15¢
Will	supply lefty power
Can't	play strong defense
Expect	new stance to help
Don't Expect	lofty average to last

After leading the minors with 33 home runs at Triple-A Pawtucket in 1990, Plantier thought he would advance directly to the majors. The Red Sox, however, wanted him to gain better knowledge of the strike zone first. The rookie returned with a new stance that helped him see the ball better. The result was a decrease in strikeouts and an increase in productivity. He had a .615 slugging percentage, a .331 batting average, and a .420 on-base percentage in 53 games for the BoSox in '91, and actually walked (23) almost as often as he struck out (38). He hit .305 with 16 homers and 61 RBI in '91 at Pawtucket. Plantier even showed he was a better outfielder than scouting reports had indicated. The converted third baseman has a strong arm that seems more suitable for right field than left. His range is limited by average speed but he's not in the majors to run. Fantasy managers will want to spend up to $14 for him, though he may go higher. Card sharks will want to stock up on his 1992 issues at 15 cents apiece.

Major League Batting Register

	BA	G	AB	R	H	2B	3B	HR	RBI	SB
90 AL	.133	14	15	1	2	1	0	0	3	0
91 AL	.331	53	148	27	49	7	1	11	35	1
Life	.313	67	163	28	51	8	1	11	38	1

DAN PLESAC

Position: Pitcher
Team: Milwaukee Brewers
Born: Feb. 4, 1962 Gary, IN
Height: 6'5" **Weight:** 215 lbs.
Bats: left **Throws:** left
Acquired: First-round pick in 6/83 free-agent draft

Player Summary	
Fantasy Value	$6 to $10
Card Value	3¢ to 5¢
Will	improve K-to-walk ratio
Can't	shuttle from starter to pen
Expect	almost a K a frame
Don't Expect	ERA much over 3.00

When Plesac reached the major leagues in 1986, he hoped to break into the starting rotation. Instead, he became one of the game's best short relievers, before a starting vacancy sent him back to the rotation in 1991. He beat Texas 5-2 in his first big league start August 10. After that, he encountered lack of support from teammates. He yields about a hit per inning and fans more men than he walks. Plesac also passes more than he should for a closer, and he throws too many gopher balls (12 in '91). The three-time All-Star, who's especially effective against lefty hitters, is a fastball-and-slider pitcher who had four straight 20-save seasons before switching to the rotation. He recently added a changeup to his repertoire. He never had hot cards, and his 1992 commons are no different. He may provide some surprises in 1992, but bet only $8 that occurs.

Major League Pitching Register

	W	L	ERA	G	S	IP	H	ER	BB	SO
86 AL	10	7	2.97	51	14	91.0	81	30	29	75
87 AL	5	6	2.61	57	23	79.1	63	23	23	89
88 AL	1	2	2.41	50	30	52.1	46	14	12	52
89 AL	3	4	2.35	52	33	61.1	47	16	17	52
90 AL	3	7	4.43	66	24	69.0	67	34	31	65
91 AL	2	7	4.29	45	8	92.1	92	44	39	61
Life	24	33	3.25	321	132	445.1	396	161	151	394
3 AVE	3	6	3.80	54	22	74.1	69	31	29	59

CURRENT PLAYERS

LUIS POLONIA

Position: Outfield
Team: California Angels
Born: Oct. 12, 1964 Santiago City, Dominican Republic
Height: 5'8" **Weight:** 155 lbs.
Bats: left **Throws:** left
Acquired: Traded from Yankees for Claudell Washington, 4/90

Player Summary	
Fantasy Value	$20 to $25
Card Value	5¢ to 7¢
Will	hit .300 with many walks
Can't	play strong defense
Expect	three-dozen steals
Don't Expect	much power

Polonia compiled a .304 average over his first four seasons and came within a whisker of matching that mark in 1991. A slap hitter with speed but no power, he powders righthanded pitching but often struggles against southpaws. He's an accomplished hit-and-run artist who can take a pitch to the opposite field. He also has enough patience to work pitchers for walks. A high on-base percentage (.352 in 1991), coupled with 40-steal potential, make Polonia a good leadoff man. He is nailed too frequently trying to steal (he previously led two minor leagues in caught stealing). Polonia's left field defense also needs work, though not much can be done to strengthen a poor throwing arm. He did reduce his errors last year but still made every fly ball an adventure. His nickel-priced 1992 cards aren't big sellers. However, he is a high-demand fantasy outfielder, especially his stolen bases.

Major League Batting Register

	BA	G	AB	R	H	2B	3B	HR	RBI	SB
87 AL	.287	125	435	78	125	16	10	4	49	29
88 AL	.292	84	288	51	84	11	4	2	27	24
89 AL	.300	125	433	70	130	17	6	3	46	22
90 AL	.335	120	403	52	135	7	9	2	35	21
91 AL	.296	150	604	92	179	28	8	2	50	48
Life	.302	604	2163	343	653	79	37	13	207	144
3 AVE	.308	132	480	71	148	17	8	2	44	30

MARK PORTUGAL

Position: Pitcher
Team: Houston Astros
Born: Oct. 30, 1962 Los Angeles, CA
Height: 6' **Weight:** 190 lbs.
Bats: right **Throws:** right
Acquired: Traded from Twins for Todd McClure, 12/88

Player Summary	
Fantasy Value	$8 to $11
Card Value	3¢ to 5¢
Will	win more often
Can't	keep ball in park
Expect	self-help with bat
Don't Expect	many control lapses

For the second year in a row, Portugal was a double-figure winner on a weak Houston ballclub. Armed with control that far exceeds anything he showed during earlier days with Minnesota, he handcuffs hitters by mixing his fine curve with a fastball, change, and slider. He yields less than a hit per inning and fans two times more hitters than he walks. Control pitchers often fall victim to gopher balls, however, and Portugal is no exception. Although he is prone to streaks as a pitcher, he is consistent as a hitter and fielder. He swings the bat exceptionally well and is the toughest pitcher to fan in the majors. He's also a fine fielder who keeps runners from straying. With a contending club, Portugal would be a certain 15-game winner. He should be at the peak of his career. Fantasy managers can count on him for $10. Have faith in his 1992 cards remaining commons.

Major League Pitching Register

	W	L	ERA	G	CG	IP	H	ER	BB	SO
85 AL	1	3	5.55	6	0	24.1	24	15	14	12
86 AL	6	10	4.31	27	3	112.2	112	54	50	67
87 AL	1	3	7.77	13	0	44.0	58	38	24	28
88 AL	3	3	4.53	26	0	57.2	60	29	17	31
89 NL	7	1	2.75	20	2	108.0	91	33	37	86
90 NL	11	10	3.62	32	1	196.2	187	79	67	136
91 NL	10	12	4.49	32	1	168.1	163	84	59	120
Life	39	42	4.20	156	7	711.2	695	332	268	480
3 AVE	9	8	3.73	28	1	157.1	147	65	54	114

CURRENT PLAYERS

TED POWER

Position: Pitcher
Team: Cincinnati Reds
Born: Jan. 31, 1955 Guthrie, OK
Height: 6'4" **Weight:** 220 lbs.
Bats: right **Throws:** right
Acquired: Signed as a free agent, 12/90

Player Summary	
Fantasy Value	$1 to $3
Card Value	3¢ to 5¢
Will	throw hard
Can't	count on control
Expect	many bullpen calls
Don't Expect	further starting jobs

After four seasons of relative inactivity, Power resumed his old workhorse role in the Cincinnati bullpen in 1991. His 78 appearances for the '84 Reds led the NL. In '91, he allowed a hit per inning, was not overly generous with the home run ball, and compiled a respectable ERA, finishing 22 games. He also issued too many bases on balls. Though he relies heavily on his fastball, Power also throws a curveball, slider, and changeup—none of them worth writing home about. His hitting isn't worth a mention either. He doesn't have much value, either as a fantasy draft ($2) or a 1992 card subject (commons). He is competent with a glove and pickoff move. Power is content as a middle man who can also go long when necessary. He has made more than 80 big league starts (none in '91).

Major League Pitching Register

	W	L	ERA	G	S	IP	H	ER	BB	SO
81 NL	1	3	3.14	5	0	14.1	16	5	7	7
82 NL	1	1	6.68	12	0	33.2	38	25	23	15
83 NL	5	6	4.54	49	2	111.0	120	56	49	57
84 NL	9	7	2.82	78	11	108.2	93	34	46	81
85 NL	8	6	2.70	64	27	80.0	65	24	45	42
86 NL	10	6	3.70	56	1	129.0	115	53	52	95
87 NL	10	13	4.50	34	0	204.0	213	102	71	133
88 AL	6	7	5.91	26	0	99.0	121	65	38	57
89 NL	7	7	3.71	23	0	97.0	96	40	21	43
90 NL	1	3	3.66	40	7	51.2	50	21	17	42
91 NL	5	3	3.62	68	3	87.0	87	35	31	51
Life	63	62	4.08	455	51	1015.1	1014	460	400	623
3 AVE	4	4	3.67	44	3	78.1	78	32	23	45

KIRBY PUCKETT

Position: Outfield
Team: Minnesota Twins
Born: March 14, 1961 Chicago, IL
Height: 5'8" **Weight:** 213 lbs.
Bats: right **Throws:** right
Acquired: First-round pick in 6/82 free-agent draft

Player Summary	
Fantasy Value	$36 to $45
Card Value	10¢ to 20¢
Will	vie for bat title
Can't	sustain power stroke
Expect	superb defense
Don't Expect	many walks or steals

Puckett is not only the best righthanded hitter in the AL but one of the game's defensive stars. A four-time Gold Glove center fielder, he also won a batting title with a .339 mark in 1989. His best year, however, was 1988, when his .356 average was the AL's best by a righthander since Joe DiMaggio hit .357 in 1941. Puckett, who leads the majors in hits over the last six years, has also made the All-Star team six times. Though he's primarily a line-drive hitter, he once hit 31 homers in a season. Puckett is baseball's best bad-ball hitter. He rarely walks, but who cares? He makes leaping catches, steals a dozen bases, and knocks in 80 runs. He is at the peak of his career. His 1992 cards are in demand, and collectors should pay up to 20 cents for them. He is a fantasy bonanza at $40.

Major League Batting Register

	BA	G	AB	R	H	2B	3B	HR	RBI	SB
84 AL	.296	128	557	63	165	12	5	0	31	14
85 AL	.288	161	691	80	199	29	13	4	74	21
86 AL	.328	161	680	119	223	37	6	31	96	20
87 AL	.332	157	624	96	207	32	5	28	99	12
88 AL	.356	158	657	109	234	42	5	24	121	6
89 AL	.339	159	635	75	215	45	4	9	85	11
90 AL	.298	146	551	82	164	40	3	12	80	5
91 AL	.319	152	611	92	195	29	6	15	89	11
Life	.320	1222	5006	716	1602	266	47	123	675	100
3 AVE	.319	152	599	83	191	38	4	12	85	9

CURRENT PLAYERS

CARLOS QUINTANA

Position: First base; outfield
Team: Boston Red Sox
Born: Aug. 26, 1965 Estado Miranda, Venezuela
Height: 6'2" **Weight:** 195 lbs.
Bats: right **Throws:** right
Acquired: Signed as a free agent, 11/84

Player Summary
Fantasy Value	$13 to $20
Card Value	5¢ to 10¢
Will	make contact
Can't	always reach fences
Expect	good defense
Don't Expect	infield hits or swipes

Though he is a natural outfielder, Quintana was Boston's everyday first baseman before Mo Vaughn was recalled from the minors at midseason last year. Quintana didn't like his new role in a righty-lefty platoon but made the most of it. On July 30, he knocked in six runs in an inning during an 11-6 win over Texas, the first AL player to do that since Jim Lemon in 1959. A line-drive hitter with good instincts, Quintana pushed his .287 rookie average to .295 in 1991. He did it by becoming a more patient hitter, getting a 1-1 ratio of walks to strikeouts. He also delivered a .412 slugging percentage and a .375 on-base percentage. Quintana also became so proficient at first base that he saved the infield an average of an error per week. If he keeps hitting, Quintana could force his way back into a full-time job, perhaps in left or right field. He offers good stats for $15 or so. Stock up on his nickel-priced 1992 cards.

Major League Batting Register
	BA	G	AB	R	H	2B	3B	HR	RBI	SB
88 AL	.333	5	6	1	2	0	0	0	2	0
89 AL	.208	34	77	6	16	5	0	0	6	0
90 AL	.287	149	512	56	147	28	0	7	67	1
91 AL	.295	149	478	69	141	21	1	11	71	1
Life	.285	337	1073	132	306	54	1	18	146	2
2 AVE	.291	149	495	63	144	25	1	9	69	1

JAMIE QUIRK

Position: Catcher; third base
Team: Oakland Athletics
Born: Oct. 22, 1954 Whittier, CA
Bats: left **Throws:** right
Height: 6'4" **Weight:** 200 lbs.
Acquired: Signed as a free agent, 11/90

Player Summary
Fantasy Value	$1 to $3
Card Value	3¢ to 5¢
Will	deliver in clutch
Can't	generate much power
Expect	use at six positions
Don't Expect	high average

In a career that began with Kansas City in 1975, Quirk has played every position, including pitcher. He is considered a valuable commodity because of his versatility. He can play the infield corners and outfield as well as catch, and he fills in whenever his team needs a lefthanded pinch-hitter or DH. He's a decent defensive catcher with a good arm, but he isn't a great infielder or outfielder. He comes through in the clutch. He even hit .448 with runners in scoring position in 1990. Quirk makes good contact and goes with the pitch, often hitting to the opposite field. He is not a good bet for your backup catcher, and his 1992 commons will see no appreciation.

Major League Batting Register
	BA	G	AB	R	H	2B	3B	HR	RBI	SB
75 AL	.256	14	39	2	10	0	0	1	5	0
76 AL	.246	64	114	11	28	6	0	1	15	0
77 AL	.217	93	221	16	48	14	1	3	13	0
78 AL	.207	17	29	3	6	2	0	0	2	0
79 AL	.304	51	79	8	24	6	1	1	11	0
80 AL	.276	62	163	13	45	5	0	5	21	3
81 AL	.250	46	100	8	25	7	0	0	10	0
82 AL	.231	36	78	8	18	3	0	1	5	0
83 NL	.209	48	86	3	18	2	1	2	11	0
84 AL	.333	4	3	1	1	0	0	1	2	0
85 AL	.281	19	57	3	16	3	1	0	4	0
86 AL	.215	80	219	24	47	10	0	8	26	0
87 AL	.236	109	296	24	70	17	0	5	33	1
88 AL	.240	84	196	22	47	7	1	8	25	1
89 AL	.176	47	85	6	15	2	0	1	10	0
90 AL	.281	56	121	12	34	5	1	3	26	0
91 AL	.261	76	203	16	53	4	0	1	17	0
Life	.242	906	2089	180	505	93	6	41	236	5

CURRENT PLAYERS

SCOTT RADINSKY

Position: Pitcher
Team: Chicago White Sox
Born: March 3, 1968 Glendale, CA
Height: 6'3" **Weight:** 190 lbs.
Bats: left **Throws:** left
Acquired: Third-round pick in 6/86 free-agent draft

Player Summary
Fantasy Value	$3 to $6
Card Value	3¢ to 5¢
Will	lasso lefty hitters
Can't	always maintain curve
Expect	many short stints
Don't Expect	batters to reach often

Radinsky made a radical improvement in his game plan in 1991, reducing the number of free passes he was giving opposing hitters. He was plagued by bouts of wildness as a 1990 rookie, but he held rivals to less than three walks per nine innings in '91. He also blossomed into the most effective pitcher on the White Sox staff. He finished 19 games, gave up only four homers, and held opponents to a .206 batting average, a .288 slugging percentage, and a .270 on-base percentage. Often used to retire one or two lefthanded hitters at critical moments, Radinsky usually rears back and fires his fastball. He mixes in breaking pitches to keep batters off-stride. His strong 1991 season was a combination of allowing less than a hit per inning, keeping the ball in the park, and striking out three times more than he walked. He had 31 saves for Class-A South Bend in 1989. His future is bright. Bid up to $6 for this reliever, and you'll get solid results. His 1992 commons don't rate as assets.

Major League Pitching Register
	W	L	ERA	G	S	IP	H	ER	BB	SO
90 AL	6	1	4.82	62	4	52.1	47	28	36	46
91 AL	5	5	2.02	67	8	71.1	53	16	23	49
Life	11	6	3.20	129	12	123.2	100	44	59	95
2 AVE	6	3	3.20	65	6	62.1	50	22	30	48

TIM RAINES

Position: Outfield
Team: Chicago White Sox
Born: Sept. 16, 1959 Sanford, FL
Height: 5'8" **Weight:** 185 lbs.
Bats: both **Throws:** right
Acquired: Traded from Expos with Jeff Carter and Mario Brito for Barry Jones and Ivan Calderon,12/90

Player Summary
Fantasy Value	$22 to $28
Card Value	5¢ to 10¢
Will	get on base
Can't	make strong throws
Expect	better average in '92
Don't Expect	under 50 swipes

In his first year with the White Sox, Raines had a disappointing batting average, but he scored over 100 runs and gave Chicago a legit leadoff man. He brought four stolen base crowns, one batting title, and a lifetime .301 average to Chicago. He blamed a three-year decline on Montreal's decision to bat him in the third spot, rather than first. Raines walked more than he fanned but had trouble getting untracked against AL pitching. He managed to ignite the attack, however, and play decent defense despite a weak arm. He will shine in '92, making him a $25 fantasy buy. His nickel-priced 1992 cards are savory commodities.

Major League Batting Register
	BA	G	AB	R	H	2B	3B	HR	RBI	SB
79 NL	.000	6	0	3	0	0	0	0	0	2
80 NL	.050	15	20	5	1	0	0	0	0	5
81 NL	.304	88	313	61	95	13	7	5	37	71
82 NL	.277	156	647	90	179	32	8	4	43	78
83 NL	.298	156	615	133	183	32	8	11	71	90
84 NL	.309	160	622	106	192	38	9	8	60	75
85 NL	.320	150	575	115	184	30	13	11	41	70
86 NL	.334	151	580	91	194	35	10	9	62	70
87 NL	.330	139	530	123	175	34	8	18	68	50
88 NL	.270	109	429	66	116	19	7	12	48	33
89 NL	.286	145	517	76	148	29	6	9	60	41
90 NL	.287	130	457	65	131	11	5	9	62	49
91 AL	.268	155	609	102	163	20	6	5	50	51
Life	.298	1560	5914	1036	1761	293	87	101	602	685
3 AVE	.279	143	528	81	147	20	6	8	57	47

CURRENT PLAYERS

RAFAEL RAMIREZ

Position: Shortstop; second base
Team: Houston Astros
Born: Feb. 18, 1959 San Pedro de Macoris, Dominican Republic
Height: 5'11" **Weight:** 190 lbs.
Bats: right **Throws:** right
Acquired: Traded from Braves for Mike Stoker and Ed Whited, 12/87

Player Summary
Fantasy Value	$1 to $2
Card Value	3¢ to 5¢
Will	serve as backup
Can't	hit for average or power
Expect	more Ks than walks
Don't Expect	strong defense

When Ramirez led NL shortstops in errors for five straight years from 1981 to '85, apologists blamed the rocky Atlanta infield. When he led the league again while playing for Houston in 1989, they ran out of excuses. Astro management also ran out of patience. Until he became a utility player last year, he had totaled more errors than walks in each of his 11 seasons. He still strikes out three times more often than he walks. In his heyday, Ramirez had enough speed to compensate by getting to balls others couldn't reach. He led the league in chances and double-plays several times. You don't need Ramirez on your fantasy team. His 1992 commons generate little interest.

Major League Batting Register
	BA	G	AB	R	H	2B	3B	HR	RBI	SB
80 NL	.267	50	165	17	44	6	1	2	11	2
81 NL	.218	95	307	30	67	16	2	2	20	7
82 NL	.278	157	609	74	169	24	4	10	52	27
83 NL	.297	152	622	82	185	13	5	7	58	16
84 NL	.266	145	591	51	157	22	4	2	48	14
85 NL	.248	138	568	54	141	25	4	5	58	2
86 NL	.240	134	496	57	119	21	1	8	33	19
87 NL	.263	56	179	22	47	12	0	1	21	6
88 NL	.276	155	566	51	156	30	5	6	59	3
89 NL	.246	151	537	46	132	20	2	6	54	3
90 NL	.261	132	445	44	116	19	3	2	37	10
91 NL	.236	101	233	17	55	10	0	1	20	3
Life	.261	1466	5318	545	1388	218	31	52	471	112
3 AVE	.249	128	405	36	101	16	2	3	37	5

WILLIE RANDOLPH

Position: Second base
Team: New York Mets
Born: July 6, 1954 Holly Hill, SC
Height: 5'11" **Weight:** 163 lbs.
Bats: right **Throws:** right
Acquired: Signed as a free agent, 12/91

Player Summary
Fantasy Value	$2 to $5
Card Value	3¢ to 5¢
Will	wait for walks
Can't	steal often
Expect	team leadership
Don't Expect	defensive decline

Determined to prove he was not washed up, Randolph became a surprise contender for the batting crown in 1991. In his first season with the Brewers, he hit for the highest average of his 17-year career. An excellent contact hitter, he walks much more often than he strikes out. The rest of the time, he singles pitchers to death. Randolph still has enough speed to steal an occasional base and show decent range at second base. He knows the hitters, reacts quickly, and still turns the double-play pivot well. In December, Randolph signed with the Mets. At $3, he is a keepsake for fantasy teams. His 1992 commons are not buys.

Major League Batting Register
	BA	G	AB	R	H	2B	3B	HR	RBI	SB
75 NL	.164	30	61	9	10	1	0	0	3	1
76 AL	.267	125	430	59	115	15	4	1	40	37
77 AL	.274	147	551	91	151	28	11	4	40	13
78 AL	.279	134	499	87	139	18	6	3	42	36
79 AL	.270	153	574	98	155	15	13	5	61	33
80 AL	.294	138	513	99	151	23	7	7	46	30
81 AL	.232	93	357	59	83	14	3	2	24	14
82 AL	.280	144	553	85	155	21	4	3	36	16
83 AL	.279	104	420	73	117	21	1	2	38	12
84 AL	.287	142	564	86	162	24	2	2	31	10
85 AL	.276	143	497	75	137	21	2	5	40	16
86 AL	.276	141	492	76	136	15	2	5	50	15
87 AL	.305	120	449	96	137	24	2	7	67	11
88 AL	.230	110	404	43	93	20	1	2	34	8
89 AL	.282	145	549	62	155	18	0	2	36	7
90 NL	.271	26	96	15	26	4	0	1	9	1
90 AL	.257	93	292	37	75	9	3	1	21	6
91 AL	.327	124	431	60	141	14	3	0	54	4
Life	.277	2112	7732	1210	2138	305	64	52	672	270
3 AVE	.290	129	456	58	132	15	2	1	40	6

CURRENT PLAYERS

DENNIS RASMUSSEN

Position: Pitcher
Team: San Diego Padres
Born: April 18, 1959 Los Angeles, CA
Height: 6'7" **Weight:** 233 lbs.
Bats: left **Throws:** left
Acquired: Traded from Reds for Candy Sierra, 6/88

Player Summary	
Fantasy Value	$2 to $6
Card Value	3¢ to 5¢
Will	win more with defense
Can't	avoid walks or gophers
Expect	more than 12 wins
Don't Expect	20 wins

Rasmussen could sue for nonsupport. Padre defenders allowed 11 unearned runs while he was pitching. He also had a bad shoulder that ended his five-year streak of throwing at least 180 innings. He had averaged 14 wins during that span. The 6'7" southpaw, who is not a power pitcher despite his size, wins without blowing hitters away. A fastball-and-curveball pitcher who holds opponents to less than a hit per inning, Rasmussen hurts himself by allowing too many walks and home runs. Neither his fielding nor his pickoff move help either. On the other hand, he is one of the league's best-hitting pitchers. With health and support, he might regain his 16-win form of 1988. His fantasy value is less than $6 until he proves he is injury-free. Risk no money on his 1992 commons.

RANDY READY

Position: Second base; outfield
Team: Philadelphia Phillies
Born: Jan. 8, 1960 San Mateo, CA
Height: 5'11" **Weight:** 180 lbs.
Bats: right **Throws:** right
Acquired: Traded from Padres with John Kruk for Chris James, 6/89

Player Summary	
Fantasy Value	$1 to $3
Card Value	3¢ to 5¢
Will	make contact
Can't	stop decline in average
Expect	utility work
Don't Expect	many homers or steals

After entering the season as a potential platoon partner at second for veteran Wally Backman or rookie Mickey Morandini, Ready couldn't revive his dormant bat. By season's end, the slumbering lumber did nothing to stop a five-year downward spiral in his batting average. Ready didn't hit for power, steal bases, or hit with enough consistency to fill Philadelphia's holes at the top of the lineup. The only thing he did well was make contact, a 2-1 ratio of walks to strikeouts and only 25 whiffs. Ready did supply stop-gap defense at two positions but doesn't have great range at either. He can throw, however. Ready is less of a liability at second and should see most of his '92 action there. He isn't much of a fantasy prospect at $3. His 1992 commons are not sound buys.

Major League Pitching Register

	W	L	ERA	G	CG	IP	H	ER	BB	SO
83 NL	0	0	1.98	4	0	13.2	10	3	8	13
84 AL	9	6	4.57	24	1	147.2	127	75	60	110
85 AL	3	5	3.98	22	2	101.2	97	45	42	63
86 AL	18	6	3.88	31	3	202.0	160	87	74	131
87 AL	9	7	4.75	26	2	146.0	145	77	55	89
87 NL	4	1	3.97	7	0	45.1	39	20	12	39
88 NL	16	10	3.43	31	7	204.2	199	78	58	112
89 NL	10	10	4.26	33	1	183.2	190	87	72	87
90 NL	11	15	4.51	32	3	187.2	217	94	62	86
91 NL	6	13	3.74	24	1	146.2	155	61	49	75
Life	86	73	4.09	234	20	1379.0	1339	627	492	805
3 AVE	9	13	4.20	30	2	172.2	187	81	61	83

Major League Batting Register

	BA	G	AB	R	H	2B	3B	HR	RBI	SB
83 AL	.405	12	37	8	15	3	2	1	6	0
84 AL	.187	37	123	13	23	6	1	3	13	0
85 AL	.265	48	181	29	48	9	5	1	21	0
86 AL	.190	23	79	8	15	4	0	1	4	2
86 NL	.000	1	3	0	0	0	0	0	0	0
87 NL	.309	124	350	69	108	26	6	12	54	7
88 NL	.266	114	331	43	88	16	2	7	39	6
89 NL	.264	100	254	37	67	13	2	8	24	4
90 NL	.244	101	217	26	53	9	1	1	26	3
91 NL	.249	76	205	32	51	10	1	1	20	2
Life	.263	636	1780	265	468	96	20	35	209	24
3 AVE	.253	92	225	32	57	11	1	3	24	3

CURRENT PLAYERS

JEFF REARDON

Position: Pitcher
Team: Boston Red Sox
Born: Oct. 1, 1955 Dalton, MA
Height: 6' **Weight:** 200 lbs.
Bats: right **Throws:** right
Acquired: Signed as a free agent, 12/89

Player Summary	
Fantasy Value	$28 to $35
Card Value	5¢ to 10¢
Will	use five pitches
Can't	fret over back woes
Expect	30 to 40 saves
Don't Expect	any control trouble

Reardon is the only pitcher to save 40 games in both leagues, he notched his 300th career save, and joined Dennis Eckersley as the only pitchers with three 40-save seasons. Reardon rattled rivals with a sidearm delivery he hadn't used since 1985. That gave him two fastballs—a riser and a sinker—to go with his curveball, changeup, and cut fastball. He is neither a good glove man nor adept at keeping runners close. The only reliever ever to record five straight 30-save seasons, Reardon survived a scare in 1990 when he underwent surgery to repair a ruptured disc in his back. Bid up to $35 knowing that he will get plenty of opportunities. His 1992 cards are good investments because of his outstanding number of career saves.

Major League Pitching Register

	W	L	ERA	G	S	IP	H	ER	BB	SO
79 NL	1	2	1.74	18	2	20.2	12	4	9	10
80 NL	8	7	2.61	61	6	110.1	96	32	47	101
81 NL	3	0	2.18	43	8	70.1	48	17	21	49
82 NL	7	4	2.06	75	26	109.0	87	25	36	86
83 NL	7	9	3.03	66	21	92.0	87	31	44	78
84 NL	7	7	2.90	68	23	87.0	70	28	37	79
85 NL	2	8	3.18	63	41	87.2	68	31	26	67
86 NL	7	9	3.94	62	35	89.0	83	39	26	67
87 AL	8	8	4.48	63	31	80.1	70	40	28	83
88 AL	2	4	2.47	63	42	73.0	68	20	15	56
89 AL	5	4	4.07	65	31	73.0	68	33	12	46
90 AL	5	3	3.16	47	21	51.1	39	18	19	33
91 AL	1	4	3.03	57	40	59.1	54	20	16	44
Life	63	69	3.03	751	327	1003.0	850	338	336	799
3 AVE	4	4	3.48	56	31	61.1	54	24	16	41

GARY REDUS

Position: First base; outfield
Team: Pittsburgh Pirates
Born: Nov. 1, 1956 Tanner, AL
Height: 6'1" **Weight:** 185 lbs.
Bats: right **Throws:** right
Acquired: Traded from White Sox for Mike Diaz, 8/88

Player Summary	
Fantasy Value	$3 to $5
Card Value	3¢ to 5¢
Will	use power against lefties
Can't	budge average over .250
Expect	continued platooning
Don't Expect	good defense at first

Before Orlando Merced broke through in 1991, Redus was his righthanded alter ego at first base. The Redus-Merced platoon had been projected to fill the void created by Sid Bream's free agent defection to Atlanta. Instead, Redus finished the year as a part-time first baseman, fourth outfielder, and pinch-hitter—the same status he had held during two previous Pirate campaigns. Redus hasn't played in 100 games since coming to Pittsburgh in 1988. At this point in his career that doesn't figure to change. Righties own Redus but he hits with power to all fields against southpaws. He is a decent outfielder but mediocre first baseman. Don't spend more than $5 on him for your fantasy team. His 1992 commons are not great investments.

Major League Batting Register

	BA	G	AB	R	H	2B	3B	HR	RBI	SB
82 NL	.217	20	83	12	18	3	2	1	7	11
83 NL	.247	125	453	90	112	20	9	17	51	39
84 NL	.254	123	394	69	100	21	3	7	22	48
85 NL	.252	101	246	51	62	14	4	6	28	48
86 NL	.247	90	340	62	84	22	4	11	33	25
87 AL	.236	130	475	78	112	26	6	12	48	52
88 AL	.263	77	262	42	69	10	4	6	34	26
88 NL	.197	30	71	12	14	2	0	2	4	5
89 NL	.283	98	279	42	79	18	7	6	33	25
90 NL	.247	96	227	32	56	15	3	6	23	11
91 NL	.246	98	252	45	62	12	2	7	24	17
Life	.249	988	3082	535	768	163	44	81	307	307
3 AVE	.260	97	253	40	66	15	4	6	27	18

CURRENT PLAYERS

JODY REED

Position: Second base; shortstop
Team: Boston Red Sox
Born: July 26, 1962 Tampa, FL
Height: 5'9" **Weight:** 160 lbs.
Bats: right **Throws:** right
Acquired: Eighth-round pick in 6/84 free-agent draft

Player Summary	
Fantasy Value	$5 to $7
Card Value	3¢ to 5¢
Will	work hit-and-run
Can't	hit homers
Expect	doubles off Green Monster
Don't Expect	more Ks than walks

Because he plays on a team of stars, Reed does not get the publicity he deserves. Rival managers know who he is, however; They named him the AL's top hit-and-run man in a 1991 *Baseball America* survey. A contact hitter who bats second in the Boston lineup, Reed knows how to reach base. He's patient enough to wait for walks and receives them more often than he strikes out. Reed reached often enough to have a more than respectable .349 on-base percentage. He also had a .382 slugging percentage. It was not surprising that he finished second on the team to Wade Boggs in runs scored. Reed is a also a major contributor on defense. He makes the double-play pivot and handles the glove better than most of his peers. He's one of the finest second basemen in the league. He is a solid investment at $5 to $8 for your fantasy squad. His 1992 cards are reasonable commons.

Major League Batting Register

	BA	G	AB	R	H	2B	3B	HR	RBI	SB
87 AL	.300	9	30	4	9	1	1	0	8	1
88 AL	.293	109	338	60	99	23	1	1	28	1
89 AL	.288	146	524	76	151	42	2	3	40	4
90 AL	.289	155	598	70	173	45	0	5	51	4
91 AL	.283	153	618	87	175	42	2	5	60	6
Life	.288	572	2108	297	607	153	6	14	187	16
3 AVE	.287	151	580	78	166	43	1	4	50	5

KEVIN REIMER

Position: Designated hitter; outfield
Team: Texas Rangers
Born: June 28, 1964 Macon, GA
Height: 6'2" **Weight:** 215 lbs.
Bats: left **Throws:** right
Acquired: 11th-round pick in 6/85 free-agent draft

Player Summary	
Fantasy Value	$8 to $11
Card Value	3¢ to 5¢
Will	develop into run-producer
Can't	steal bases
Expect	respectable average
Don't Expect	Gold Glove award

With nine home runs last August, Reimer fell one shy of the Texas club month-long record shared by Mike Hargrove and Dave Hostetler. Though Reimer was also used as a designated hitter, he got most of his playing time in left field, especially after the Steve Buechele trade allowed the Rangers to bring power-hitting prospect Dean Palmer back to the infield. That alignment gave Texas a slugging outfield trio of Reimer, Juan Gonzalez, and Ruben Sierra from left to right. Reimer was a 1984 Canadian Olympian (he was raised in British Columbia). He strikes out three times more than he walks and doesn't steal bases. Nevertheless, he plays a better left field and makes better contact than predecessor Pete Incaviglia. Reimer in 1990 hit .283 with four homers, 18 doubles, 33 RBI in 51 games at Triple-A Oklahoma City. In 1989 there, he hit .267 with 10 homers and 73 RBI. He is a clutch hitter who produces when asked to pinch-hit. He makes sense for fantasy managers for $10, but purchasing his 1992 commons defies logic.

Major League Batting Register

	BA	G	AB	R	H	2B	3B	HR	RBI	SB
88 AL	.120	12	25	2	3	0	0	1	2	0
89 AL	.000	3	5	0	0	0	0	0	0	0
90 AL	.260	64	100	5	26	9	1	2	15	0
91 AL	.269	136	394	46	106	22	0	20	69	0
Life	.258	215	524	53	135	31	1	23	86	0

MIKE REMLINGER

Position: Pitcher
Team: Seattle Mariners
Born: March 23, 1966 Middletown, NY
Height: 6' **Weight:** 195 lbs.
Bats: left **Throws:** left
Acquired: Traded from Giants with Kevin Mitchell for Bill Swift, Dave Burba, and Mike Jackson, 12/91

Player Summary	
Fantasy Value	$2 to $4
Card Value	5¢ to 7¢
Will	try to better control
Can't	find Dartmouth poise
Expect	walks and homers
Don't Expect	winning record

After taking the rotation spot of the injured Scott Garrelts, Remlinger made a brilliant big league debut with a three-hit, 4-0 shutout over Pittsburgh on June 15. He fizzled after that, however, and wound up back in the minors. The Dartmouth product throws a fastball, curveball, and straight change, but he has been slow to regain his confidence following 1988 elbow problems. San Francisco traded him to Seattle after the 1991 season. Remlinger has had control trouble throughout his career and did little to reverse that trend when he reached the majors. At Triple-A Phoenix in 1991, Remlinger was 5-5 with a 6.39 ERA, 19 starts, 68 strikeouts, 59 bases on balls, and 134 hits allowed in 109 innings pitched. In 1990, he was 9-11 with a 3.90 ERA, 75 strikeouts, and 72 walks in 147⅔ innings at Double-A Shreveport. He was also guilty of throwing the home run ball too often. Big league opponents had a .451 slugging percentage against him in '91. He is not a sure thing for 1992, so limit your draft to $4. Don't buy his nickel-priced 1992 cards

Major League Pitching Register

	W	L	ERA	G	CG	IP	H	ER	BB	SO
91 NL	2	1	4.37	8	1	35.0	36	17	20	19
Life	2	1	4.37	8	1	35.0	36	17	20	19

GILBERTO REYES

Position: Catcher
Team: Montreal Expos
Born: Dec. 10, 1963 Santo Domingo, Dominican Republic
Height: 6'2" **Weight:** 200 lbs.
Bats: right **Throws:** right
Acquired: Traded from Dodgers for Jeff Fischer, 3/89

Player Summary	
Fantasy Value	$1 to $2
Card Value	3¢ to 5¢
Will	display dynamite arm
Can't	hit for power or run
Expect	well-timed pinch-hits
Don't Expect	everyday deployment

Few base-stealers ply their trade against the rifle arm for Reyes. He throws out some 55 percent of those who try to run on him. That's a career figure, and it is one of the best in the business. He doesn't play more often because he is a classic good-field, no-hit receiver. He hit only .184 in parts of five big league seasons before 1991 and less than .220 last year. Since he adds neither power nor speed to the equation, managers can't afford to use him with regularity. An impatient hitter who fans three times more than he walks, Reyes rarely produces an extra-base hit. He had a .261 slugging percentage and a .285 on-base average in 1991. Perhaps if he played he'd find the stroke that produced two nine-homer years for Triple-A Indianapolis. Even a team that's crying for catchers can't afford to take that chance. His 1992 commons don't generate interest, and he is a $2 catcher.

Major League Batting Register

	BA	G	AB	R	H	2B	3B	HR	RBI	SB
83 NL	.161	19	31	1	5	2	0	0	0	0
84 NL	.000	4	5	0	0	0	0	0	0	0
85 NL	.000	6	1	0	0	0	0	0	0	0
87 NL	.000	1	0	0	0	0	0	0	0	0
88 NL	.111	5	9	1	1	0	0	0	0	0
89 NL	.200	4	5	0	1	0	0	0	1	0
91 NL	.217	83	207	11	45	9	0	0	13	2
Life	.202	122	258	13	52	11	0	0	14	2

CURRENT PLAYERS

HAROLD REYNOLDS

Position: Second base
Team: Seattle Mariners
Born: Nov. 26, 1960 Eugene, OR
Height: 5'11" **Weight:** 165 lbs.
Bats: both **Throws:** right
Acquired: First-round pick in secondary phase of 6/80 free-agent draft

Player Summary	
Fantasy Value	$7 to $10
Card Value	3¢ to 5¢
Will	use speed as weapon
Can't	reach Kingdome's fences
Expect	bunts and leg hits
Don't Expect	flawless fielding

A two-time All-Star and three-time Gold Glove winner, Reynolds added to his awards in 1991 by winning the 21st Roberto Clemente Award, given annually to the player who best exemplifies the game on and off the field. Reynolds is a clutch hitter, with an AL best .426 batting average with two outs and men in scoring position in '91. A patient hitter who makes good contact, he walks more often than he strikes out, drops bunts for base hits, and is so good at the hit-and-run that he was lowered from leadoff to second in the lineup. He also runs well, leading the league with 60 steals in 1987 and 11 triples in '88. Reynolds reaches more ground balls than any other AL second baseman. His 1992 commons are suitable buys in the nickel range. With his swipes, he is a $8 fantasy buy.

Major League Batting Register

	BA	G	AB	R	H	2B	3B	HR	RBI	SB
83 AL	.203	20	59	8	12	4	1	0	1	0
84 AL	.300	10	10	3	3	0	0	0	0	1
85 AL	.144	67	104	15	15	3	1	0	6	3
86 AL	.222	126	445	46	99	19	4	1	24	30
87 AL	.275	160	530	73	146	31	8	1	35	60
88 AL	.283	158	598	61	169	26	11	4	41	35
89 AL	.300	153	613	87	184	24	9	0	43	25
90 AL	.252	160	642	100	162	36	5	5	55	31
91 AL	.254	161	631	95	160	34	6	3	57	28
Life	.262	1015	3632	488	950	177	45	14	262	213
3 AVE	.268	158	629	94	169	31	7	3	52	28

DAVE RIGHETTI

Position: Pitcher
Team: San Francisco Giants
Born: Nov. 28, 1958 San Jose, CA
Height: 6'4" **Weight:** 210 lbs.
Bats: left **Throws:** left
Acquired: Signed as a free agent, 12/90

Player Summary	
Fantasy Value	$20 to $25
Card Value	3¢ to 5¢
Will	work often
Can't	fan as many as he had
Expect	20-plus saves
Don't Expect	more control woes

Righetti readily agreed to compensate for lost velocity by adding a split-fingered fastball to his fastball-and-slider repertoire in 1991. He also has a changeup. He got off to a slow start in the NL but eventually became the closer the Giants had expected. The team failed to provide few opportunities, however. Working more than 50 times for the eighth straight year, he allowed less than a hit per inning and kept the ball in the park. He allowed only four home runs in 1991. He had a disappointing strikeout-to-walk ratio. Righetti's left arm has provided a lot of innings. How much it can help a good NL team remains to be seen. He should come through for your fantasy team for $25 or less. Don't gamble on his nickel-priced 1992 cards.

Major League Pitching Register

	W	L	ERA	G	S	IP	H	ER	BB	SO
79 AL	0	1	3.63	3	0	17.1	10	7	10	13
81 AL	8	4	2.05	15	0	105.1	75	24	38	89
82 AL	11	10	3.79	33	1	183.0	155	77	108	163
83 AL	14	8	3.44	31	0	217.0	194	83	67	169
84 AL	5	6	2.34	64	31	96.1	79	25	37	90
85 AL	12	7	2.78	74	29	107.0	96	33	45	92
86 AL	8	8	2.45	74	46	106.2	88	29	35	83
87 AL	8	6	3.51	60	31	95.0	95	37	44	77
88 AL	5	4	3.52	60	25	87.0	86	34	37	70
89 AL	2	6	3.00	55	25	69.0	73	23	26	51
90 AL	1	1	3.57	53	36	53.0	48	21	26	43
91 NL	2	7	3.39	61	24	71.2	64	27	28	51
Life	76	68	3.13	583	248	1208.1	1063	420	501	991
3 AVE	2	5	3.30	56	28	64.1	62	24	27	48

CURRENT PLAYERS

JOSE RIJO

Position: Pitcher
Team: Cincinnati Reds
Born: May 13, 1965 San Cristobal, Dominican Republic
Height: 6'2" **Weight:** 210 lbs.
Bats: right **Throws:** right
Acquired: Traded from Athletics with Tim Birtsas for Dave Parker, 12/87

Player Summary	
Fantasy Value	$10 to $15
Card Value	3¢ to 5¢
Will	get more Ks than hits
Can't	avoid injuries
Expect	high win percentage
Don't Expect	bouts of wildness

After Rijo two-hit the Mets 7-0 last August 24, Gregg Jefferies called the performance the best pitching effort he had ever seen. Rijo's '91 record would have been better if the pitcher hadn't lost six weeks recuperating from an ankle injury incurred when he attempted to steal. The 1990 World Series MVP has never realized his full potential; nagging injuries have plagued him four years in a row. Rushed to the majors at age 18, Rijo has matured into one of the game's top pitchers. He throws a fastball, slider, forkball, and changeup. Opponents had a .219 batting average and a .272 on-base average. He helps himself by being an agile fielder and a reliable batter. If Rijo could stay healthy, he could be a candidate for the Cy Young. He will command up to $15 at the draft. His 1992 commons will remain cheap.

ERNEST RILES

Position: Infield; outfield
Team: Oakland Athletics
Born: Oct. 2, 1960 Bainbridge, GA
Height: 6'1" **Weight:** 175 lbs.
Bats: left **Throws:** right
Acquired: Traded from Giants for Darren Lewis and Pedro Pena, 12/90

Player Summary	
Fantasy Value	$2 to $5
Card Value	3¢ to 5¢
Will	play several spots
Can't	rekindle bat
Expect	continued utility role
Don't Expect	old Milwaukee stroke

Carney Lansford's snowmobile accident could have been a career opportunity for Riles, but he failed to take advantage. After hitting .264 in seven big league seasons, Riles blew the chance to shake a utility tag and become the starting third baseman for the American League champions. Instead he flirted with the Mendoza Line most of the year and finished under a cloud of uncertainty. Riles, who spent two seasons as Milwaukee's shortstop before settling into the utility role, suddenly stopped hitting in 1990. He did get a few pinch-hits, but they did little to keep his average afloat. Riles has the patience to wait for walks and usually puts the ball into play. He is a natural second baseman with good range and good hands. He is not a starter, so his 1992 cards are not purchases. He is a $3 utility fantasy draft.

Major League Pitching Register

	W	L	ERA	G	CG	IP	H	ER	BB	SO
84 AL	2	8	4.76	24	0	62.1	74	33	33	47
85 AL	6	4	3.53	12	0	63.2	57	25	28	65
86 AL	9	11	4.65	39	4	193.2	172	100	108	176
87 AL	2	7	5.90	21	1	82.1	106	54	41	67
88 NL	13	8	2.39	49	0	162.0	120	43	63	160
89 NL	7	6	2.84	19	1	111.0	101	35	48	86
90 NL	14	8	2.70	29	7	197.0	151	59	78	152
91 NL	15	6	2.51	30	3	204.1	165	57	55	172
Life	68	58	3.39	223	16	1076.1	946	406	454	925
3 AVE	12	7	2.65	26	4	171.0	139	50	60	137

Major League Batting Register

	BA	G	AB	R	H	2B	3B	HR	RBI	SB
85 AL	.286	116	448	54	128	12	7	5	45	2
86 AL	.252	145	524	69	132	24	2	9	47	7
87 AL	.261	83	276	38	72	11	1	4	38	3
88 AL	.252	41	127	7	32	6	1	1	9	2
88 NL	.294	79	187	26	55	7	2	3	28	1
89 NL	.278	122	302	43	84	13	2	7	40	0
90 NL	.200	92	155	22	31	2	1	8	21	0
91 AL	.214	108	281	30	60	8	4	5	32	3
Life	.258	786	2300	289	594	83	20	42	260	18
3 AVE	.237	107	246	32	58	8	2	7	31	1

CURRENT PLAYERS

BILLY RIPKEN

Position: Second base
Team: Baltimore Orioles
Born: Dec. 16, 1964 Havre de Grace, MD
Height: 6'1" **Weight:** 185 lbs.
Bats: right **Throws:** right
Acquired: 11th-round pick in 6/82 free-agent draft

Player Summary	
Fantasy Value	$2 to $4
Card Value	3¢ to 5¢
Will	contend for Gold Glove
Can't	notch steals or homers
Expect	fair contact
Don't Expect	consistency at bat

Ripken may not hit like brother Cal, but he does provide the same strong defense. Billy hit under .240 for the third time in four years in 1991 but played his usual strong game at second base. In 1990, his best overall season, Ripken led the Orioles in batting average, sacrifices, and doubles. He batted .316 after the All-Star break. Blessed with quick hands, Ripken learned to stand still in the batter's box, a technique that enabled him to see the ball longer and better. He fouled off pitches he didn't like and began to draw more walks. Ripken reverted to old patterns last year but still made good contact. He has Cal's "speed" but not his power. In the field, Billy ranges well to both sides, dives and leaps without hesitation, and forms a strong double-play tandem with his brother. Billy is a $3 fantasy second sacker. Almost all his cards are commons, and his 1992 cards should be as well.

Major League Batting Register

	BA	G	AB	R	H	2B	3B	HR	RBI	SB
87 AL	.308	58	234	27	72	9	0	2	20	4
88 AL	.207	150	512	52	106	18	1	2	34	8
89 AL	.239	115	318	31	76	11	2	2	26	1
90 AL	.291	129	406	48	118	28	1	3	38	5
91 AL	.216	104	287	24	62	11	1	0	14	0
Life	.247	556	1757	182	434	77	5	9	132	18
3 AVE	.253	116	337	34	85	17	1	2	26	2

CAL RIPKEN

Position: Shortstop
Team: Baltimore Orioles
Born: Aug. 24, 1960 Havre de Grace, MD
Height: 6'4" **Weight:** 220 lbs.
Bats: right **Throws:** right
Acquired: Second-round pick in 6/78 free-agent draft

Player Summary	
Fantasy Value	$38 to $48
Card Value	10¢ to 20¢
Will	play full schedule
Can't	bunt or steal
Expect	walks and extra bases
Don't Expect	fielding errors

When Ripken roared into the 1991 All-Star break with a .348 average, he became the first shortstop to lead a league in midseason since Lou Boudreau in 1947. Starting the midseason classic for the eighth straight time, Ripken won MVP honors with a three-run homer. Ripken's robust hitting invariably overshadows his achievements in the field. In 1990, he went a record 95 straight games without an error. He hasn't missed a game since July 1, 1982. Barring injury or labor dispute, Ripken will break Lou Gehrig's record of 2,130 consecutive games played in 1995. Fantasy teams who took Ripken last year for $30 or less, take a bow. His draft prices are up to near $50, but these are deserved increases. His 1992 cards are great long-term investments under 20 cents.

Major League Batting Register

	BA	G	AB	R	H	2B	3B	HR	RBI	SB
81 AL	.128	23	39	1	5	0	0	0	0	0
82 AL	.264	160	598	90	158	32	5	28	93	3
83 AL	.318	162	663	121	211	47	2	27	102	0
84 AL	.304	162	641	103	195	37	7	27	86	2
85 AL	.282	161	642	116	181	32	5	26	110	2
86 AL	.282	162	627	98	177	35	1	25	81	4
87 AL	.252	162	624	97	157	28	3	27	98	3
88 AL	.264	161	575	87	152	25	1	23	81	2
89 AL	.257	162	646	80	166	30	0	21	93	3
90 AL	.250	161	600	78	150	28	4	21	84	3
91 AL	.323	162	650	99	210	46	5	34	114	6
Life	.279	1638	6305	970	1762	340	33	259	942	28
3 AVE	.277	162	632	86	175	35	3	25	97	4

CURRENT PLAYERS

WALLY RITCHIE

Position: Pitcher
Team: Philadelphia Phillies
Born: July 12, 1965 Glendale, CA
Height: 6'2" **Weight:** 180 lbs.
Bats: left **Throws:** left
Acquired: Fifth-round pick in 6/85 free-agent draft

Player Summary	
Fantasy Value	$2 to $5
Card Value	10¢ to 15¢
Will	throw hard
Can't	always find strike zone
Expect	frequent calls
Don't Expect	use as closer

Although Ritchie pitched effective middle relief for the Phillies in 1991, his season will be best remembered for his encounter with the flying spikes of Otis Nixon. The Atlanta outfielder, believing Ritchie was throwing at his legs, charged the mound and took a flying, spikes-first leap at him. The pitcher emerged with bleeding flesh wounds and a stint on the 15-day disabled list. On the mound, Ritchie yields less than a hit per inning and is extremely stingy with the home run ball. In 1991, opponents got four homers and compiled a .234 batting average, a .346 slugging percentage, and a .299 on-base average. His main problem is allowing too many bases on balls. He should have a solid major league future. At Triple-A Scranton in '91, he was 1-0 with a 2.42 ERA and two saves. A strong year in middle relief this season could gain him a look as a closer with an expansion team a year from now. Invest only up to $5 during the draft. His 1992 cards are good products up to 15 cents.

Major League Pitching Register

	W	L	ERA	G	S	IP	H	ER	BB	SO
87 NL	3	2	3.75	49	3	62.1	60	26	29	45
88 NL	0	0	3.12	19	0	26.0	19	9	17	8
91 NL	1	2	2.50	39	0	50.1	44	14	17	26
Life	4	4	3.18	107	3	138.2	123	49	63	79

LUIS RIVERA

Position: Shortstop
Team: Boston Red Sox
Born: Jan. 3, 1964 Cidra, Puerto Rico
Height: 5'10" **Weight:** 170 lbs.
Bats: right **Throws:** right
Acquired: Traded from Expos with John Dopson for Spike Owen and Dan Gakeler, 12/88

Player Summary	
Fantasy Value	$2 to $5
Card Value	3¢ to 5¢
Will	deliver in clutch
Can't	show patience at bat
Expect	strong throws
Don't Expect	another '91 at bat

Rivera played a solid shortstop for the Red Sox in 1991 even though his performance was hampered by physical problems in his left shoulder. Surgery corrected the situation in time for the 1992 campaign. That may make him a better player, but he wasn't bad before. He has good range, a strong throwing arm, and some pop in his bat. He's usually good for a .250 average and half-dozen homers a year. He showed more patience at the plate last year, increasing his walk total, but he still isn't selective enough. He's a good bunter, however, and is often called upon to sacrifice. In the clutch, though, the Red Sox let him swing away. He probably had a career year in '91. Rivera doesn't steal much but few Boston players do. His main job is to supply defense. Don't bet more than $5 that his success will continue in 1992. Don't hazard any coin on his 1992 commons.

Major League Batting Register

	BA	G	AB	R	H	2B	3B	HR	RBI	SB
86 NL	.205	55	166	20	34	11	1	0	13	1
87 NL	.156	18	32	0	5	2	0	0	1	0
88 NL	.224	123	371	35	83	17	3	4	30	3
89 AL	.257	93	323	35	83	17	1	5	29	2
90 AL	.225	118	346	38	78	20	0	7	45	4
91 AL	.258	129	414	64	107	22	3	8	40	4
Life	.236	536	1652	192	390	89	8	24	158	14
3 AVE	.247	113	361	46	89	20	1	7	38	3

CURRENT PLAYERS

BIP ROBERTS

Position: Infield; outfield
Team: Cincinnati Reds
Born: Oct. 27, 1963 Berkeley, CA
Height: 5'7" **Weight:** 165 lbs.
Bats: both **Throws:** right
Acquired: Traded from Padres for Randy Myers, 12/91

Player Summary	
Fantasy Value	$12 to $16
Card Value	...3¢ to 5¢
Will	run rivals ragged
Can't	show routine power
Expect	twice as many Ks as walks
Don't Expect	strong throws

In 1991, Roberts suffered torn cartilage in his left knee when caught in an August rundown and was unable to play at full strength. San Diego was counting on him. In 1990, he joined MVPs Barry Bonds and Rickey Henderson as the only men to hit .300, steal 40 bases, and get 40 extra-base hits. The 5'7" San Diego leadoff man had a below average year, but he notched a .342 on-base average and a .347 slugging percentage. The versatile speed merchant enjoyed a 4-for-4, two-homer game against Cincinnati. He is not really a home run hitter—even though he hit nine in 1990 after a winter of weight training. Speed is the reason Roberts remains a regular. Though his range is impressive, his arm is not. Second base, where strong throws aren't required, is his best position. In December, he was traded to the Reds. If his speed isn't greatly impaired, he will be worth a $14 fantasy draft. His 1992 commons are not good buys.

Major League Batting Register

	BA	G	AB	R	H	2B	3B	HR	RBI	SB
86 NL	.253	101	241	34	61	5	2	1	12	14
88 NL	.333	5	9	1	3	0	0	0	0	0
89 NL	.301	117	424	81	99	15	8	3	25	21
90 NL	.309	149	556	104	172	36	3	9	44	46
91 NL	.281	117	424	66	119	13	3	3	32	26
Life	.291	489	1559	286	454	69	16	16	113	107
3 AVE	.298	128	436	84	130	21	5	5	34	31

DON ROBINSON

Position: Pitcher
Team: San Francisco Giants
Born: June 8, 1957 Ashland, KY
Height: 6'4" **Weight:** 231 lbs.
Bats: right **Throws:** right
Acquired: Traded from Pirates for Mackey Sasser and cash, 7/87

Player Summary	
Fantasy Value	$1 to $3
Card Value	3¢ to 5¢
Will	help self with big bat
Can't	keep ball in park
Expect	uncertainty over role
Don't Expect	injury-free season

Robinson is a decent pitcher who would probably be a lot better if he could escape an injury bug that follows him around like a shadow. He has had more than 100 cortisone shots and nine stints on the disabled list in his 14-year career. Primarily a starter, he is a sinker-and-slider pitcher who also throws a curveball and change-up. His control, usually good, was not sharp last year. It's not too late for the strong-hitting pitcher to satisfy a stated urge to become a first baseman. Robinson pinch-hits on days he's not pitching. He's had two years of 4.00-plus ERAs; don't bet more than $2 that 1992 won't be No. 3. His career numbers are mediocre, so don't buy his 1992 commons.

Major League Pitching Register

	W	L	ERA	G	S	IP	H	ER	BB	SO
78 NL	14	6	3.47	35	1	228.1	203	88	57	135
79 NL	8	8	3.87	29	0	160.2	171	69	52	96
80 NL	7	10	3.99	29	1	160.1	157	71	45	103
81 NL	0	3	5.87	16	2	38.1	47	2=	23	17
82 NL	15	13	4.28	38	0	227.0	213	108	103	165
83 NL	2	2	4.46	9	0	36.1	43	18	21	28
84 NL	5	6	3.02	51	10	122.0	99	41	49	110
85 NL	5	11	3.87	44	3	95.1	95	41	42	65
86 NL	3	4	3.38	50	14	69.1	61	26	27	53
87 NL	11	7	3.42	67	19	108.0	105	41	40	79
88 NL	10	5	2.45	51	6	176.2	152	48	49	122
89 NL	12	11	3.43	34	0	197.0	184	75	37	96
90 NL	10	7	4.57	26	0	157.2	173	80	41	78
91 NL	5	9	4.38	34	1	121.1	123	59	50	78
Life	107	102	3.75	513	57	1898.1	1826	790	636	1225
3 AVE	9	9	4.05	31	0	158.1	160	71	43	

CURRENT PLAYERS

JEFF ROBINSON

Position: Pitcher
Team: California Angels
Born: Dec. 13, 1960 Santa Ana, CA
Height: 6'4" **Weight:** 200 lbs.
Bats: right **Throws:** right
Acquired: Signed as a free agent, 1/91

Player Summary
Fantasy Value	$1 to $3
Card Value	3¢ to 5¢
Will	work over 50 games
Can't	erase memory of '91
Expect	work in middle relief
Don't Expect	return to 1987 and '88

Robinson appeared in more than 50 games five years in a row before suffering through his worst big league season in 1991. He had career highs with 14 saves in 1987 and 11 wins a year later, but he never got untracked with the '91 Angels and allowed opponents to bat .259 and slug .444. A sinker-and-slider pitcher who also throws a curve and split-fingered fastball, Robinson usually maintains a 2-1 ratio of strikeouts to walks and allows less than a hit per inning. His fielding helped him compile that record. He handles a glove well and keeps runners close. Even with expansion around the corner, Robinson will have to make a comeback to keep his grip on a big league job. There are plenty of righthanded middle relievers who earn less money. Without many saves, his fantasy worth stops at $3. His 1992 commons hold no appeal.

Major League Pitching Register
	W	L	ERA	G	S	IP	H	ER	BB	SO
84 NL	7	15	4.56	34	0	171.2	195	87	52	102
85 NL	0	0	5.11	8	0	12.1	16	7	10	8
86 NL	6	3	3.36	64	8	104.1	92	39	32	90
87 NL	8	9	2.85	81	14	123.1	89	39	54	101
88 NL	11	5	3.03	75	9	124.2	113	42	39	87
89 NL	7	13	4.58	50	4	141.1	161	72	59	95
90 AL	3	6	3.45	54	0	88.2	82	34	34	43
91 AL	0	3	5.37	39	3	57.0	56	34	29	57
Life	42	54	3.87	405	38	823.1	804	354	309	583
3 AVE	3	7	4.39	48	2	95.1	100	47	41	65

RON ROBINSON

Position: Pitcher
Team: Milwaukee Brewers
Born: March 24, 1962 Woodlake, CA
Height: 6'4" **Weight:** 235 lbs.
Bats: right **Throws:** right
Acquired: Traded from Reds with Bob Sebra for Glenn Braggs and Billy Bates, 6/90

Player Summary
Fantasy Value	$2 to $4
Card Value	3¢ to 5¢
Will	bid for rotation berth
Can't	win without mixing pitches
Expect	good chance of comeback
Don't Expect	many gophers

Robinson was the top pitcher on the 1990 Brewers but a persistent presence on the disabled list in '91. After doctors found bone chips in his right elbow, Robinson was placed on the disabled list. He started only once before he was shunted to the sidelines. In seven previous seasons, he had a respectable ERA. Robinson doesn't pile up strikeouts but averages about two whiffs per walk. He also keeps the ball in the park. Robinson throws a fastball, slider, curve, and changeup—all of which are ordinary. He mixes pitches and changes speeds with the poise of a veteran, however. He helps himself in the field and watches baserunners carefully. He is young enough and strong enough to stage a comeback. If he has a good spring, you will want to bid up to $4 for him. His 1992 commons will never be movers.

Major League Pitching Register
	W	L	ERA	G	CG	IP	H	ER	BB	SO
84 NL	1	2	2.72	12	1	39.2	35	12	13	24
85 NL	7	7	3.99	33	0	108.1	107	48	32	76
86 NL	10	3	3.24	70	0	116.2	110	42	43	117
87 NL	7	5	3.68	48	0	154.0	148	63	43	99
88 NL	3	7	4.12	17	0	78.2	88	36	26	38
89 NL	5	3	3.35	15	0	83.1	80	31	28	36
90 NL	2	2	4.88	6	0	31.1	36	17	14	14
90 AL	12	5	2.91	22	7	148.1	158	48	37	57
91 AL	0	1	6.23	1	0	4.1	6	3	3	0
Life	47	35	3.53	224	8	764.2	768	300	239	461
2 AVE	10	5	3.29	22	4	131.2	137	48	40	54

CURRENT PLAYERS

IVAN RODRIGUEZ

Position: Catcher
Team: Texas Rangers
Born: Nov. 30, 1971 Vega Baja, Puerto Rico
Height: 5'9" **Weight:** 165 lbs.
Bats: right **Throws:** right
Acquired: Signed as a free agent, 7/88

Player Summary	
Fantasy Value	$9 to $12
Card Value	15¢ to 25¢
Will	gun down runners
Can't	wait for walks
Expect	some run production
Don't Expect	consistency (yet)

When Texas promoted Rodriguez from Double-A Tulsa on June 20, he became the sixth teenager ever to play for the club. He showed off his throwing arm, nabbing two would-be base-stealers. Many scouts insist he has a better arm than those of All-Stars Sandy Alomar and Benito Santiago. Rodriguez's throws to second have been timed at 85 mph. He had thrown out 61 percent of the runners in the minors before his promotion. He bunts and works the hit-and-run like a veteran. Rodriguez had a .354 slugging percentage and a .276 on-base average in '91. On August 30, he became the youngest Texas player (19 years, 9 months) to hit a home run. He also batted .274 with three homers, seven doubles, and 28 RBI in 175 at bats at Tulsa in '91. He was named the No. 1 prospect in the Class-A Florida State League in 1990. His nickname is Pudge for idol Carlton Fisk. His rookie 1992 cards will be hot; spend up to a quarter apiece on them. He will be a hot item at the fantasy draft, but try not to pay more than $12.

Major League Batting Register

	BA	G	AB	R	H	2B	3B	HR	RBI	SB
91 AL	.264	88	280	24	74	16	0	3	27	0
Life	.264	88	280	24	74	16	0	3	27	0

RICH RODRIGUEZ

Position: Pitcher
Team: San Diego Padres
Born: March 1, 1963 Los Angeles, CA
Height: 5'11" **Weight:** 200 lbs.
Bats: left **Throws:** left
Acquired: Traded from Mets for Brad Pounders and Bill Stevenson, 1/89

Player Summary	
Fantasy Value	$2 to $4
Card Value	10¢ to 15¢
Will	lean on breaking balls
Can't	always show control
Expect	occasional gophers
Don't Expect	great K-to-walk ratio

So much for the sophomore jinx: Rodriguez enjoyed his second straight banner year out of the San Diego bullpen in 1991. He worked a team-high 64 times. Though he often finds the plate wandering (44 walks and 40 strikeouts) and has a tendency toward gopher balls (eight in '91), Rodriguez succeeds by yielding less than a hit per inning. He specializes in breaking balls and owns several varieties. Opponents compiled a .234 batting average, a .365 slugging percentage, and a .335 on-base average. A good fielder who keeps runners close, Rodriguez rarely gets to swing the bat. It's a good thing, too. In 1990 at Triple-A Las Vegas, he had a 3-4 record with a 3.51 ERA, eight saves, 46 strikeouts, 22 walks, and 50 hits in 59 innings. The pitcher began his pro career at Class-A Little Falls in 1984. Rodriguez should have little trouble retaining his role as a lefthanded middle reliever. Don't invest in his dime-priced 1992 cards so early in his career. If he gets a shot at closing, his fantasy value, now at $3, will climb.

Major League Pitching Register

	W	L	ERA	G	S	IP	H	ER	BB	SO
90 NL	1	1	2.83	32	1	47.2	52	15	16	22
91 NL	3	1	3.26	64	0	80.0	66	29	44	40
Life	4	2	3.10	96	1	127.2	118	44	60	62
2 AVE	2	1	3.10	48	1	64.1	59	22	30	31

CURRENT PLAYERS

KENNY ROGERS

Position: Pitcher
Team: Texas Rangers
Born: Nov. 10, 1964 Savannah, GA
Height: 6'1" **Weight:** 200 lbs.
Bats: left **Throws:** left
Acquired: 39th-round pick in 6/82 free-agent draft

Player Summary	
Fantasy Value	$3 to $5
Card Value	3¢ to 5¢
Will	improve as workhorse
Can't	avoid gophers
Expect	improved stats
Don't Expect	shuttle from rotation to pen

Rogers began the 1991 season as a starter but finished it in the bullpen, where he began his big league career three years ago. After going 13-10 with 17 saves and a 3.05 ERA in his first two seasons, Rogers seemed to have a bright future ahead as a lefthanded reliever. But Ranger management doesn't subscribe to the theory that says, "Don't fix what ain't broke." It took Rogers only nine starts to convince them. He had given up too many hits, too many homers (14 in '91), and too many walks. He has a good move to first. A fastball-and-slider pitcher who usually has good control, Rogers seems to fare better when he doesn't know he's pitching. He worked 142 times (all but three in relief) in his first two seasons and wants to return to that schedule. In 1991, opponents compiled a .281 batting average, a .444 slugging percentage, and a .375 on-base average. Be a gambler, and draft him for up to $5. But know when to walk away from his 1992 commons.

Major League Pitching Register

	W	L	ERA	G	S	IP	H	ER	BB	SO
89 AL	3	4	2.93	73	2	73.2	60	24	42	63
90 AL	10	6	3.13	69	15	97.2	93	34	42	74
91 AL	10	10	5.42	63	5	109.2	121	66	61	73
Life	23	20	3.97	205	22	281.0	274	124	145	210
3 AVE	8	7	3.97	68	7	93.2	91	41	48	70

BRUCE RUFFIN

Position: Pitcher
Team: Milwaukee Brewers
Born: Oct. 4, 1963 Lubbock, TX
Height: 6'2" **Weight:** 213 lbs.
Bats: right **Throws:** left
Acquired: Traded from Phillies for Dale Sveum, 12/91

Player Summary	
Fantasy Value	$1 to $3
Card Value	3¢ to 5¢
Will	be in '92 rotation
Can't	win more than he loses
Expect	better results
Don't Expect	another Steve Carlton

When Ruffin finally found the strike zone in 1991, he snapped a five-year string of ERAs that almost matched the federal deficit. Flashing his best form since his 1986 rookie year, the hard-throwing lefthander had a 3.78 ERA. He fanned more than twice the number he walked, kept the ball in the park (six homers), and allowed only a little more than a hit per inning. Though the team was pleased with his turnaround, the pitcher was a victim of nonsupport. He lost six of his first nine to clinch his fifth straight losing season. A sinker-and-slider pitcher who was once compared to Steve Carlton, Ruffin has been treated like a ruffian in recent years. His 1991 performance suggests he might yet salvage his career. He was traded to Milwaukee in December. He is an inexpensive but ordinary fantasy B-list pitcher. His 1992 commons aren't selling.

Major League Pitching Register

	W	L	ERA	G	S	IP	H	ER	BB	SO
86 NL	9	4	2.46	21	0	146.1	138	40	44	70
87 NL	11	14	4.35	35	0	204.2	236	99	73	93
88 NL	6	10	4.43	55	3	144.1	151	71	80	82
89 NL	6	10	4.44	24	0	125.2	152	62	62	70
90 NL	6	13	5.38	32	0	149.0	178	89	62	79
91 NL	4	7	3.78	31	0	119.0	125	50	38	85
Life	42	58	4.16	198	3	889.0	980	411	359	479
3 AVE	5	10	4.60	29	0	131.1	152	67	54	78

CURRENT PLAYERS

SCOTT RUSKIN

Position: Pitcher
Team: Cincinnati Reds
Born: June 6, 1963 Jacksonville, FL
Height: 6'2" **Weight:** 185 lbs.
Bats: right **Throws:** left
Acquired: Traded from Expos with Dave Martinez and Willie Green for John Wetteland and Bill Risley, 12/91

Player Summary	
Fantasy Value	$2 to $4
Card Value	3¢ to 5¢
Will	lean on curve
Can't	survive K-to-walk ratio
Expect	return to middle relief
Don't Expect	Reds patience

The sophomore jinx swallowed Ruskin whole in 1991, chewed him up, and spit him out. A year after making a strong debut as a curveballing middle reliever, he contributed to the bullpen collapse that plunged the Expos to the divisional depths. His problem was an inability to throw his curve over the plate. He yielded less than a hit per inning but had a poor ratio of strikeouts to walks. Ruskin, who fashioned a 2.75 ERA while working 67 times as a rookie, is learning on the job. He's a former outfielder who became a pitcher four years ago. He was a pitcher and an outfielder at the University of Florida, though. Not surprisingly, Ruskin swings the bat well. He also helps himself in the field. Ruskin's return to form depends upon his ability to find the strike zone. His fastball keeps batters off-stride. He is a secondary reliever with some fantasy lure, because of his few saves. Don't procure his 1992 commons unless he would win a closer job somewhere.

Major League Pitching Register

	W	L	ERA	G	S	IP	H	ER	BB	SO
90 NL	3	2	2.75	67	2	75.1	75	23	38	57
91 NL	4	4	4.24	64	6	63.2	57	30	30	4>
Life	7	6	3.43	131	8	139.0	132	53	68	103
2 AVE	4	3	3.43	66	4	70.0	66	27	34	52

JEFF RUSSELL

Position: Pitcher
Team: Texas Rangers
Born: Sept. 2, 1961 Cincinnati, OH
Height: 6'3" **Weight:** 210 lbs.
Bats: right **Throws:** right
Acquired: Traded from Reds with Duane Walker for Buddy Bell, 7/85

Player Summary	
Fantasy Value	$15 to $20
Card Value	3¢ to 5¢
Will	throw heat
Can't	duplicate 1989
Expect	25 saves
Don't Expect	many walks or homers

Russell wasted little time last year proving that he had fully recovered from 1990 surgery that removed bone spurs from his pitching elbow. A fastball-and-slider pitcher who also throws a changeup, Russell won the AL's Rolaids Relief Man Award for May with 21 points. Russell yields less than a hit per inning and fans twice as many men as he walks. But he doesn't seem to have the velocity he showed when he fanned more than a batter per inning in 1989 while leading the AL with 38 saves. Opponents compiled a .236 batting average, a .365 slugging percentage, and a .295 on-base average in 1991. The former Cincinnati starter is a good fielder with an adequate pickoff move. But few runners reach when he's pitching. He is a solid fantasy selection for $20 or less. The prices of his 1992 commons aren't substantial, however.

Major League Pitching Register

	W	L	ERA	G	S	IP	H	ER	BB	SO
83 NL	4	5	3.03	10	0	68.1	58	23	22	40
84 NL	6	18	4.26	33	0	181.2	186	86	65	101
85 AL	3	6	7.55	13	0	62.0	85	52	27	44
86 AL	5	2	3.40	37	2	82.0	74	31	31	54
87 AL	5	4	4.44	52	3	97.1	109	48	52	56
88 AL	10	9	3.82	34	0	188.2	183	80	66	88
89 AL	6	4	1.98	71	38	72.2	45	16	24	77
90 AL	1	5	4.26	27	10	25.1	23	12	16	16
91 AL	6	4	3.29	68	30	79.1	71	29	26	52
Life	46	57	3.96	345	83	857.1	834	377	329	528
2 AVE	6	4	2.66	70	34	76.2	58	23	25	65

CURRENT PLAYERS

NOLAN RYAN

Position: Pitcher
Team: Texas Rangers
Born: Jan. 31, 1947 Refugio, TX
Height: 6'2" **Weight:** 210 lbs.
Bats: right **Throws:** right
Acquired: Signed as a free agent, 12/88

Player Summary	
Fantasy Value	$30 to $40
Card Value	25¢ to 50¢
Will	still blaze heater
Can't	avoid injury jinx
Expect	exceptional control
Don't Expect	Father Time to visit

After coming off the disabled list for the second time in 1991, Ryan encountered problems with his mechanics. Working with a slower windup, he became the second pitcher to win in double figures 20 different times. Ryan's biggest win of 1991, however, was his seventh career no-hitter against Toronto May 1, extending his own record. The career strikeout leader is a blessing to any fantasy team. Grab his 1992 cards at any price under 50 cents.

Major League Pitching Register

	W	L	ERA	G	CG	IP	H	ER	BB	SO
66 NL	0	1	15.00	2	0	3.0	5	5	3	6
68 NL	6	9	3.09	21	3	134.0	93	46	75	133
69 NL	6	3	3.53	25	2	89.1	60	35	53	92
70 NL	7	11	3.42	27	5	131.2	86	50	97	125
71 NL	10	14	3.97	30	3	152.0	125	67	116	137
72 AL	19	16	2.28	39	20	284.0	166	72	157	329
73 AL	21	16	2.87	41	26	326.0	238	104	162	383
74 AL	22	16	2.89	42	26	332.2	221	107	202	367
75 AL	14	12	3.45	28	10	198.0	152	76	132	186
76 AL	17	18	3.36	39	21	284.1	193	106	183	327
77 AL	19	16	2.77	37	22	299.0	198	92	204	341
78 AL	10	13	3.72	31	14	234.2	183	97	148	260
79 AL	16	14	3.60	34	17	222.2	169	89	114	223
80 NL	11	10	3.35	35	4	233.2	205	87	98	200
81 NL	11	5	1.69	21	5	149.0	99	28	68	140
82 NL	16	12	3.16	35	10	250.1	196	88	109	245
83 NL	14	9	2.98	29	5	196.1	134	65	101	183
84 NL	12	11	3.04	30	5	183.2	143	62	69	197
85 NL	10	12	3.80	35	4	232.0	205	98	95	209
86 NL	12	8	3.34	30	1	178.0	119	66	82	194
87 NL	8	16	2.76	34	0	211.2	154	65	87	270
88 NL	12	11	3.52	33	4	220.0	186	86	87	228
89 AL	16	10	3.20	32	6	239.1	162	85	98	301
90 AL	13	9	3.44	30	5	204.0	137	78	74	232
91 AL	12	6	2.91	27	2	173.0	102	56	72	203
Life	314	278	3.16	767	220	5162.1	3731	1810	2686	5511
3 AVE	14	8	3.20	30	4	205.0	134	73	81	245

BRET SABERHAGEN

Position: Pitcher
Team: New York Mets
Born: April 11, 1964 Chicago Heights, IL
Height: 6'1" **Weight:** 195 lbs.
Bats: right **Throws:** right
Acquired: Traded from Royals with Bill Pecota for Kevin McReynolds, Gregg Jefferies, and Keith Miller, 12/91

Player Summary	
Fantasy Value	$10 to $15
Card Value	5¢ to 10¢
Will	get double-figure wins
Can't	end on-and-off pattern
Expect	great control
Don't Expect	walks or gophers

Though Saberhagen missed a month of the 1991 season with tendinitis of the right rotator cuff, he pitched so well when he returned that he resembled the pitcher who won two previous Cy Young awards. On August 26, Saberhagen pitched a 7-0 no-hitter against the White Sox. He has developed a pattern of winning seasons in odd-numbered years but losing seasons in even-numbered years, but the Mets—to whom he was traded in December—hope he breaks that trend in 1992. He has been the victim of previous elbow, shoulder, and foot problems, so limit your fantasy bid to $15. Saberhagen was the AL's youngest Cy Young Award winner in 1985, and he won the trophy again in 1989. A control pitcher with a fastball, curve, and changeup, Saberhagen is a fine fielder with a good move. The values of his nickel-priced 1992 cards will rise when he has another top season.

Major League Pitching Register

	W	L	ERA	G	CG	IP	H	ER	BB	SO
84 AL	10	11	3.48	38	2	157.2	138	61	36	73
85 AL	20	6	2.87	32	10	235.1	211	75	38	158
86 AL	7	12	4.15	30	4	156.0	165	72	29	112
87 AL	18	10	3.36	33	15	257.0	246	96	53	163
88 AL	14	16	3.80	35	9	260.2	271	110	59	171
89 AL	23	6	2.16	36	12	262.1	209	63	43	193
90 AL	5	9	3.27	20	5	135.0	146	49	28	87
91 AL	13	8	3.07	28	7	196.1	165	67	45	136
Life	110	78	3.21	252	64	1660.1	1551	593	331	1093
3 AVE	14	8	2.71	28	8	198.1	173	60	39	139

CURRENT PLAYERS

CHRIS SABO

Position: Third base
Team: Cincinnati Reds
Born: Jan. 19, 1962 Detroit, MI
Height: 6'1" **Weight:** 185 lbs.
Bats: right **Throws:** right
Acquired: Second-round pick in 6/83 free-agent draft

Player Summary	
Fantasy Value	$25 to $30
Card Value	4¢ to 7¢
Will	hit and throw well
Can't	always control emotions
Expect	two-dozen homers
Don't Expect	batting title bid

Sabo not only swung a potent bat for Cincinnati in 1991, he swung his fists. Sabo scuffled with an autograph hound in St. Louis and with teammate Jose Rijo in the dugout. He didn't let his second career as a fighter interfere with baseball, however. While the rest of the ballclub rested on the laurels of its 1990 World Championship, Sabo hit career peaks in batting, home runs, and runs batted in. The .300 finish was the first of his four-year career. An All-Star starter for the second straight summer, Sabo continued to capitalize on hitting tips provided by manager Lou Piniella prior to the start of the 1990 campaign. He also ran the bases well, though his steals were far from his rookie-year peak. A good third baseman who makes less than a dozen errors a year, Sabo owns a strong arm. He helps in four categories and is a good fantasy candidate at $25. Don't spend more than 7 cents for his 1992 cards.

Major League Batting Register

	BA	G	AB	R	H	2B	3B	HR	RBI	SB
88 NL	.271	137	538	74	146	40	2	11	44	46
89 NL	.260	82	304	40	79	21	1	6	29	14
90 NL	.270	148	567	95	153	38	2	25	71	25
91 NL	.301	153	582	91	175	35	3	26	88	19
Life	.278	520	1991	300	553	134	8	68	232	104
3 AVE	.280	128	484	75	136	31	2	19	63	19

LUIS SALAZAR

Position: Infield; outfield
Team: Chicago Cubs
Born: May 19, 1956 Barcelona, Venezuela
Height: 5'9" **Weight:** 180 lbs.
Bats: right **Throws:** right
Acquired: Traded from Padres with Marvell Wynne for Calvin Schiraldi, Phil Stephenson, and Darrin Jackson, 8/89

Player Summary	
Fantasy Value	$5 to $8
Card Value	3¢ to 5¢
Will	provide some power
Can't	steal anymore
Expect	utility play
Don't Expect	many errors

The failure of heralded prospect Gary Scott to stick with the Cubs gave versatile Salazar considerable playing time at third base in 1991. He responded with a typical season. The 12-year veteran is remarkably consistent—over the last four years, his statistics are extremely comparable. A free-swinging contact hitter who rarely walks or strikes out, Salazar has slowed considerably since putting together consecutive 20-steal seasons in 1982 and '83. That speed loss has limited his range at third base, his best position. His arm is still strong, though, and he doesn't mangle many plays. With his double-digits in homers every year, he is a solid $6 fantasy corner man. His 1992 commons, though, are empty investments.

Major League Batting Register

	BA	G	AB	R	H	2B	3B	HR	RBI	SB
80 NL	.337	44	169	28	57	4	7	1	25	11
81 NL	.303	109	400	37	121	19	6	3	38	11
82 NL	.242	145	524	55	127	15	5	8	62	32
83 NL	.258	134	481	52	124	16	2	14	45	24
84 NL	.241	93	228	20	55	7	2	3	17	11
85 AL	.245	122	327	39	80	18	2	10	45	14
86 AL	.143	4	7	1	1	0	0	0	0	0
87 NL	.254	84	189	13	48	5	0	3	17	3
88 AL	.270	130	452	61	122	14	1	12	62	6
89 NL	.282	121	326	34	92	12	2	9	34	1
90 NL	.254	115	410	44	104	13	3	12	47	3
91 NL	.258	103	333	34	86	14	1	14	38	0
Life	.264	1204	3846	418	1017	137	31	89	430	116
3 AVE	.264	113	356	37	94	13	2	12	40	1

BILL SAMPEN

Position: Pitcher
Team: Montreal Expos
Born: Jan. 18, 1963 Lincoln, IL
Height: 6'1" **Weight:** 185 lbs.
Bats: right **Throws:** right
Acquired: Drafted from Pirates, 4/89

Player Summary	
Fantasy Value	$1 to $3
Card Value	3¢ to 5¢
Will	win with control
Can't	stay in rotation
Expect	fine breaking balls
Don't Expect	as many walks

Sampen has succeeded as both a starter and reliever in his two seasons with the Expos. Last September 2, he stepped in as an emergency starter when ace Dennis Martinez begged off with a lower back sprain. The result was a 4-3 win over Tom Glavine. Sampen is a power pitcher who mixes his heater with a slider and change. He struggled with his control as a sophomore in 1991. He allowed about a hit per inning but barely managed to avoid a 1-1 ratio of strikeouts to walks. Opponents compiled a .273 batting average, a .452 slugging percentage, and a .358 on-base average. He allowed 13 homers. He was much more effective as a 1990 rookie, when he went 12-7 with a 2.99 ERA in 59 outings (four of them starts). In 1989 at Double-A Harrisburg, he was 11-9 with a 3.33 ERA, 134 strikeouts, only 40 walks, and 148 hits in 165⅔ innings. He'd be better off if he settled into one role and stayed there. His fantasy value would be better than $2 if he started. Don't accumulate his 1992 commons.

Major League Pitching Register

	W	L	ERA	G	S	IP	H	ER	BB	SO
90 NL	12	7	2.99	59	2	90.1	94	30	33	69
91 NL	9	5	4.00	43	0	92.1	96	41	46	52
Life	21	12	3.50	102	2	182.2	190	71	79	121
2 AVE	11	6	3.50	51	1	91.1	95	36	40	61

JUAN SAMUEL

Position: Second base
Team: Los Angeles Dodgers
Born: Dec. 9, 1960 San Pedro do Macoris, Dominican Republic
Height: 5'11" **Weight:** 170 lbs.
Bats: right **Throws:** right
Acquired: Traded from Mets for Mike Marshall, 12/89

Player Summary	
Fantasy Value	$12 to $16
Card Value	3¢ to 5¢
Will	show some power
Can't	turn double play
Expect	frequent Ks
Don't Expect	strong defense

The dog days of August hit Samuel hard. After enjoying a big first half that included his third trip to the All-Star Game, Samuel slid into an August funk. Samuel's slide was an enigma; he had done so well over the first three months that many considered him the team's MVP. He was among the first-half league leaders in batting, hits, runs, and total bases. By season's end, his streak of seven straight 30-steal seasons had ended, but he still finished with his best batting average in four years. With his run production and speed far from his former Philadelphia form and his fielding far from flawless, Samuel has probably seen his best days. Since he succeeds at the four fantasy categories, his standing at $14 is solid. His 1992 commons suffer from his lack of all-around superiority.

Major League Batting Register

	BA	G	AB	R	H	2B	3B	HR	RBI	SB
83 NL	.277	18	65	14	18	1	2	2	5	3
84 NL	.272	160	701	105	191	36	19	15	69	72
85 NL	.264	161	663	101	175	31	13	19	74	53
86 NL	.266	145	591	90	157	36	12	16	78	42
87 NL	.272	160	655	113	178	37	15	28	100	35
88 NL	.243	157	629	68	153	32	9	12	67	33
89 NL	.235	137	532	69	125	16	2	11	48	42
90 NL	.242	143	492	62	119	24	3	13	52	38
91 NL	.271	153	594	74	161	22	6	12	58	23
Life	.259	1234	4922	696	1277	235	81	128	551	341
3 AVE	.250	144	539	68	135	21	4	12	53	34

CURRENT PLAYERS

RYNE SANDBERG

Position: Second base
Team: Chicago Cubs
Born: Sept 18, 1959 Spokane, WA
Height: 6'2" **Weight:** 180 lbs.
Bats: right **Throws:** right
Acquired: Traded from Phillies with Larry Bowa for Ivan DeJesus, 1/82

Player Summary	
Fantasy Value	$40 to $50
Card Value	10¢ to 20¢
Will	bid for MVP
Can't	carry club alone
Expect	Gold Glove
Don't Expect	production outage

A Sandberg miscue is a rare baseball event. When his 47-game errorless streak ended last August 20, it was the seventh time in his career that he had compiled streaks of at least 40 games without an error. One of them lasted 123 games, a major league record. Sandberg has won nine straight Gold Gloves, a Most Valuable Player Award, and a home run crown. With 40 homers in 1990, he became the first second baseman to lead the league in 65 years. Sandberg is the only second baseman in the league who bats third in the order. He walks as much as he strikes out and consistently ranks among the league leaders in hits and runs. Bust the budget and spend up to $50 to get him on your team. Break the bank and stockpile his 1992 cards at 20 cents apiece.

Major League Batting Register

	BA	G	AB	R	H	2B	3B	HR	RBI	SB
81 NL	.167	13	6	2	1	0	0	0	0	0
82 NL	.271	156	635	103	172	33	5	7	54	32
83 NL	.261	158	633	94	165	25	4	8	48	37
84 NL	.314	156	636	114	200	36	19	19	84	32
85 NL	.305	153	609	113	186	31	6	26	83	54
86 NL	.284	154	627	68	178	28	5	14	76	34
87 NL	.294	132	523	81	154	25	2	16	59	21
88 NL	.264	155	618	77	163	23	8	19	69	25
89 NL	.290	157	606	104	176	25	5	30	76	15
90 NL	.306	155	615	116	188	30	3	40	100	25
91 NL	.291	158	585	104	170	32	2	26	100	22
Life	.288	1547	6093	976	1753	288	59	205	749	297
3 AVE	.296	157	602	108	178	29	3	32	92	21

DEION SANDERS

Position: Outfield
Team: Atlanta Braves
Born: Aug. 9, 1967 Fort Myers, FL
Height: 6'1" **Weight:** 195 lbs.
Bats: left **Throws:** left
Acquired: Signed as a free agent, 1/91

Player Summary	
Fantasy Value	$2 to $4
Card Value	5¢ to 10¢
Will	sit on bench
Can't	concentrate on two sports
Expect	bunts and steals
Don't Expect	high average

Just before he left the Atlanta Braves for the football training camp of the Atlanta Falcons to play cornerback and punt returner last August 1, Sanders received some fatherly advice from Braves general manager John Schuerholz. The veteran executive strongly suggested that Sanders's dual role was preventing him from realizing his potential as a baseball star. In brief major league stints, Sanders has shown occasional power, great speed on the bases, strong defensive ability in the outfield, and a flair for the dramatic. Though he hit only .191 for the 1991 Braves, Sanders stole 11 bases in 14 tries. He also ended his stay with a three-run homer that beat the Pirates on July 31. That blast prompted his first standing ovation as a baseball player. Scouts say there could be many more. He also has a problem with the crowded Atlanta outfield. His two-sport routine guarantees that his 1992 cards will sell for more than a nickel. His fantasy value, though, will remain low because of his short season.

Major League Batting Register

	BA	G	AB	R	H	2B	3B	HR	RBI	SB
89 AL	.234	14	47	7	11	2	0	2	7	1
90 AL	.158	57	133	24	21	2	2	3	9	8
91 NL	.191	54	110	16	21	1	2	4	13	11
Life	.183	125	290	47	53	5	4	9	29	20

CURRENT PLAYERS

SCOTT SANDERSON

Position: Pitcher
Team: New York Yankees
Born: July 22, 1956 Dearborn, MI
Height: 6'5" **Weight:** 200 lbs.
Bats: right **Throws:** right
Acquired: Purchased from Athletics, 1/91

Player Summary	
Fantasy Value	$8 to $14
Card Value	3¢ to 5¢
Will	remain big winner
Can't	stop gophers
Expect	pinpoint control
Don't Expect	bad K-to-walk ratio

An All-Star for the first time in 1991, Sanderson started well, winning 10 of his first 13 decisions as a first-year Yankee. He combined with Greg Cadaret for a one-hitter April 10 and hurled his own one-hitter July 15. Sanderson, known for exceptional control, is a fastball-and-curveball pitcher who added a forkball only recently. The new pitch must have helped, since Sanderson's last two seasons were the best of his career. His lone weakness is a tendency to throw too many gopher balls (22 in '91). Sanderson helps himself with strong fielding and gets help from his strong-hitting team, allowing him to win with a high ERA. He'll get plenty of opportunity to tally wins and strikeouts, so his fantasy value is $10. Don't spend anything for his 1992 commons.

Major League Pitching Register

	W	L	ERA	G	CG	IP	H	ER	BB	SO
78 NL	4	2	2.51	10	1	61.0	52	17	21	50
79 NL	9	8	3.43	34	5	168.0	148	64	54	138
80 NL	16	11	3.11	33	7	211.1	206	73	56	125
81 NL	9	7	2.95	22	4	137.1	122	45	31	77
82 NL	12	12	3.46	32	7	224.0	212	86	58	158
83 NL	6	7	4.65	18	0	81.1	98	42	20	55
84 NL	8	5	3.14	24	3	140.2	140	49	24	76
85 NL	5	6	3.12	19	2	121.0	100	42	27	80
86 NL	9	11	4.19	37	1	169.2	165	79	37	124
87 NL	8	9	4.29	32	0	144.2	156	69	50	106
88 NL	1	2	5.28	11	0	15.1	13	9	3	6
89 NL	11	9	3.94	37	2	146.1	155	64	31	86
90 AL	17	11	3.88	34	2	206.1	205	89	66	128
91 AL	16	10	3.81	34	2	208.0	200	88	29	130
Life	131	110	3.61	377	36	2035.0	1972	816	507	1339
3 AVE	15	10	3.87	35	2	187.1	187	80	42	115

BENITO SANTIAGO

Position: Catcher
Team: San Diego Padres
Born: March 9, 1965 Ponce, Puerto Rico
Height: 6'1" **Weight:** 185 lbs.
Bats: right **Throws:** right
Acquired: Signed as a free agent, 9/82

Player Summary	
Fantasy Value	$11 to $14
Card Value	5¢ to 10¢
Will	show off arm
Can't	lift average
Expect	at least 12 homers
Don't Expect	better K-to-walk ratio

Although he uncorked a 34-game hitting streak, a record for a rookie, during his first big league season in 1987, Santiago is best known for his defensive skills. He not only has an accurate, powerful arm but delights in making snap throws to first and throwing from his knees. The value of the arm is obvious: Santiago took out a $5 million insurance policy against a career-ending injury. The only thing injured in 1991 was Santiago's pride. He suffered the embarrassment of flinging his batting helmet in anger and striking manager Greg Riddoch. He also criticized San Diego fans and asked to be traded. The free-swinging Santiago had made the mistake of hitting .300 as a rookie but never coming close since. He still has good power and good speed for a catcher, plus the fabled arm. Now is the time to draft him—for up to $14. His nickel-priced 1992 cards are suitable bets.

Major League Batting Register

	BA	G	AB	R	H	2B	3B	HR	RBI	SB
86 NL	.290	17	62	10	18	2	0	3	6	0
87 NL	.300	146	546	64	164	33	2	18	79	21
88 NL	.248	139	492	49	122	22	2	10	46	15
89 NL	.236	129	462	50	109	16	3	16	62	11
90 NL	.270	100	344	42	93	8	5	11	53	5
91 NL	.267	152	580	60	155	22	3	17	87	8
Life	.266	683	2486	275	661	103	15	75	333	60
3 AVE	.258	127	462	51	119	15	4	15	67	8

CURRENT PLAYERS

MACKEY SASSER

Position: Catcher; outfield
Team: New York Mets
Born: Aug. 3, 1962 Fort Gaines, GA
Height: 6'1" **Weight:** 210 lbs.
Bats: left **Throws:** right
Acquired: Traded from Pirates with Tim Drummond for Randy Milligan and Scott Henion, 3/88

Player Summary	
Fantasy Value	$2 to $5
Card Value	3¢ to 5¢
Will	produce timely hits
Can't	throw well
Expect	more outfield time
Don't Expect	many walks

Although he has trouble throwing as a catcher, Sasser has little difficulty in the outfield. He notched three assists in his first eight games as a right fielder, made some difficult catches, and showed good reactions on balls that came his way—even though his range is limited by lack of speed. The outfield performance could influence Sasser's playing time, which had been limited to pinch-hitting and spot duty because he was considered a defensive liability. No one questions his hitting, however. A free-swinging lefthanded batter who murders righthanders, Sasser often serves as a pinch-hitter with power. He took a four-year average of .292 into the '91 campaign before reaching a career low last year. He had a .417 slugging percentage and a .298 on-base average. He could be a minor fantasy help by catching and playing in the outfield at $4. Overlook his 1992 commons, however.

Major League Batting Register

	BA	G	AB	R	H	2B	3B	HR	RBI	SB
87 NL	.185	12	27	2	5	0	0	0	2	0
88 NL	.285	60	123	9	35	10	1	1	17	0
89 NL	.291	72	182	17	53	14	2	1	22	0
90 NL	.307	100	270	31	83	14	0	6	41	0
91 NL	.272	96	228	18	62	14	2	5	35	0
Life	.287	342	830	77	238	52	5	13	117	0
3 AVE	.291	89	227	22	66	14	1	4	33	0

STEVE SAX

Position: Second base
Team: New York Yankees
Born: Jan. 29, 1960 West Sacramento, CA
Height: 6' **Weight:** 182 lbs.
Bats: right **Throws:** right
Acquired: Signed as a free agent, 11/88

Player Summary	
Fantasy Value	$33 to $40
Card Value	5¢ to 10¢
Will	make contact
Can't	erase stone hands tag
Expect	good defense
Don't Expect	more home runs

Sax raised his batting average in '91 to .304 after reaching rock bottom with a .231 mark May 27. The five-time All-Star, among the leaders in fielding percentage at his position, also added to his ranking among the half-dozen active players with 400 career steals. He led the Yankees in stolen bases and hit a personal peak in home runs. He led the club in multihit games, thanks to his uncanny ability to wait for a pitch he likes. He is a contact hitter who walks more than he strikes out. His fielding has also come a long way, turning Sax from the league leader in errors into one of the best at his position. Pay up to $40 for him at the draft. His nickel-priced 1992 cards could see some short-term profits.

Major League Batting Register

	BA	G	AB	R	H	2B	3B	HR	RBI	SB
81 NL	.277	31	119	15	33	2	0	2	9	5
82 NL	.282	150	638	88	180	23	7	4	47	49
83 NL	.281	155	623	94	175	18	5	5	41	56
84 NL	.243	145	569	70	138	24	4	1	35	34
85 NL	.279	136	488	62	136	8	4	1	42	27
86 NL	.332	157	633	91	210	43	4	6	56	40
87 NL	.280	157	610	84	171	22	7	6	46	37
88 NL	.277	160	632	70	175	19	4	5	57	42
89 AL	.315	158	651	88	205	26	3	5	63	43
90 AL	.260	155	615	70	160	24	2	4	42	43
91 AL	.304	158	652	85	198	38	2	10	56	31
Life	.286	1562	6230	817	1781	247	42	49	494	407
3 AVE	.294	157	639	81	188	29	2	6	54	39

CURRENT PLAYERS

BOB SCANLAN

Position: Pitcher
Team: Chicago Cubs
Born: Aug. 9, 1966, Los Angeles, CA
Height: 6'7" **Weight:** 215 lbs.
Bats: right **Throws:** right
Acquired: Traded from Phillies with Chuck McElroy for Mitch Williams, 4/91

Player Summary	
Fantasy Value	$2 to $4
Card Value	10¢ to 15¢
Will	spot start
Can't	prevent walks
Expect	improvement with changeup
Don't Expect	worse K-to-walk ratio

A strikeout pitcher who sometimes suffers from occasional lapses of control, Scanlan surfaced in Chicago May 7 after posting a 2-0 record and 2.95 ERA in three starts at Triple-A Iowa. A slider-and-fastball pitcher who figures to improve steadily as he perfects his changeup, Scanlan was exclusively a starter during his seven-year apprenticeship in the minors but deployed as both a starter and reliever by the Cubs. His ability to perform well in both roles makes him a valuable member of the team's 1992 staff. He was once known as Beverly Hills Flop because of his inability to escape the farm system of the Phillies. In 1990 at Triple-A Scranton, he was 8-11 with a 4.85 ERA, 74 strikeouts, 59 walks, and 128 hits in 130 innings. He was named the No. 5 prospect in the Double-A Eastern League in 1987, going 15-5 with a 5.10 ERA. Scanlan traces his success to an Oriental exercise-meditation discipline called Tai Chi. Since he doesn't have an established pitching role, you should limit your bidding to $4. His 1992 cards will be overpriced; don't spend 15 cents apiece.

Major League Pitching Register

	W	L	ERA	G	S	IP	H	ER	BB	SO
91 NL	7	8	3.89	40	1	111.0	114	48	40	44
Life	7	8	3.89	40	1	111.0	114	48	40	44

CURT SCHILLING

Position: Pitcher
Team: Houston Astros
Born: Nov. 14, 1966 Anchorage, AK
Height: 6'4" **Weight:** 215 lbs.
Bats: right **Throws:** right
Acquired: Traded from Orioles with Steve Finley and Pete Harnisch for Glenn Davis, 1/91

Player Summary	
Fantasy Value	$3 to $6
Card Value	3¢ to 5¢
Will	win with control
Can't	allow so many walks
Expect	return to bullpen
Don't Expect	3-1 K-to-walk ratio

Before the start of the 1991 season, Houston had projected Schilling as their closer. But NL hitters had other ideas. They manhandled him for more than a hit per inning and waited out walks so frequently that the team had to send Schilling back to Triple-A Tucson. He was improved when he returned, whittling his ERA from 4.00-plus down to 3.81. At Tucson, he was 0-1 with a 3.42 ERA, three saves, 21 Ks, 12 walks, and 16 hits in 24 innings. A power pitcher who throws a fastball, slider, and split-fingered fastball, Schilling has the right tools for short relief but has yet to master command and location. He might even start, a role he relished after leading the Triple-A International League with 13 wins, nine complete games, and three shutouts in 1989. There's no doubt he has a great arm. Don't plan on investing in many of his 1992 common-priced cards. Note, however, that he averaged nearly one strikeout per inning, making him an unsung fantasy possibility for $4.

Major League Pitching Register

	W	L	ERA	G	S	IP	H	ER	BB	SO
88 AL	0	3	9.82	4	0	14.2	22	16	10	4
89 AL	0	1	6.23	5	0	8.2	10	6	3	6
90 AL	1	2	2.54	35	3	46.0	38	13	19	32
91 NL	3	5	3.81	56	8	75.2	79	32	39	71
Life	4	11	4.16	100	11	145.0	149	67	71	113
2 AVE	2	4	3.33	46	6	61.1	59	23	29	52

CURRENT PLAYERS

DICK SCHOFIELD

Position: Shortstop
Team: California Angels
Born: Nov. 21, 1962 Springfield, IL
Height: 5'10" **Weight:** 175 lbs.
Bats: right **Throws:** right
Acquired: First-round pick in 6/81 free-agent draft

Player Summary	
Fantasy Value	$2 to $4
Card Value	3¢ to 5¢
Will	reach base
Can't	hit for power
Expect	solid defense
Don't Expect	average over .255

Schofield compiled a .233 batting average over eight seasons but didn't hit that in '91. Since he failed to supply any power, his presence in the lineup can be traced to strong defense and the absence of anyone better. A three-time leader in fielding percentage at his position, he has good range, a decent arm, and a knack for turning the double-play. He used to run well enough to steal 20 times a year but that's no longer true. Because Schofield draws frequent walks, he also ranked among team leaders in on-base percentage. The son of a big league shortstop with the same name, Schofield avoided the injury jinx that has disabled him five times in the past. With that history of injuries and little power, he is a $3 fantasy shortstop. His 1992 commons are unpopular with collectors.

Major League Batting Register

	BA	G	AB	R	H	2B	3B	HR	RBI	SB
83 AL	.204	21	54	4	11	2	0	3	4	0
84 AL	.192	140	400	39	77	10	3	4	21	5
85 AL	.219	147	438	50	96	19	3	8	41	11
86 AL	.249	139	458	67	114	17	6	13	57	23
87 AL	.251	134	479	52	120	17	3	9	46	19
88 AL	.239	155	527	61	126	11	6	6	34	20
89 AL	.228	91	302	42	69	11	2	4	26	9
90 AL	.255	99	310	41	79	8	1	1	18	3
91 AL	.225	134	427	44	96	9	3	0	31	8
Life	.232	1060	3395	400	788	104	27	48	278	98
3 AVE	.235	108	346	42	81	9	2	2	25	7

MIKE SCHOOLER

Position: Pitcher
Team: Seattle Mariners
Born: Aug. 10, 1962 Anaheim, CA
Height: 6'3" **Weight:** 220 lbs.
Bats: right **Throws:** right
Acquired: Second-round pick in 6/85 free-agent draft

Player Summary	
Fantasy Value	$10 to $20
Card Value	3¢ to 5¢
Will	use heat and control
Can't	insure OK shoulder
Expect	3-to-1 Ks to walks
Don't Expect	walks or homers

The Seattle Mariners were without their top reliever during the first half of the 1991 season because Schooler was disabled with an inflamed right shoulder. Activated on July 8, he showed that the lengthy stint on the sidelines had not stifled his ability to throw a sharp breaking ball. He converted all five of his save opportunities before August 22, when the Twins beat him with two home runs. Prior to that outburst, Schooler had converted 63 of 74 save chances over two seasons. He became Seattle's career leader in saves by throwing his fastball and slider with precision control, allowing less than a hit per inning, keeping the ball in the park, and serving as his own fifth infielder while on the mound. He's good for at least 30 saves if he stays healthy. He is possibly the cheapest fantasy stopper around. He may become one of the best in 1992, so you should spend up to $20 on him. His 1992 commons are not hot buys.

Major League Pitching Register

	W	L	ERA	G	S	IP	H	ER	BB	SO
88 AL	5	8	3.54	40	15	48.1	45	19	24	54
89 AL	1	7	2.81	67	33	77.0	81	24	19	69
90 AL	1	4	2.25	49	30	56.0	47	14	16	45
91 AL	3	3	3.67	34	7	34.1	25	14	10	31
Life	10	22	2.96	190	85	215.2	198	71	69	199
3 AVE	2	5	2.80	50	23	56.0	51	17	15	48

CURRENT PLAYERS

MIKE SCIOSCIA

Position: Catcher
Team: Los Angeles Dodgers
Born: Nov. 27, 1958 Upper Darby, PA
Height: 6'2" **Weight:** 223 lbs.
Bats: left **Throws:** right
Acquired: First-round pick in 6/76 free-agent draft

Player Summary	
Fantasy Value	$2 to $5
Card Value	3¢ to 5¢
Will	provide great defense
Can't	avoid injuries
Expect	hit-and-runs
Don't Expect	any speed

When *Baseball America* asked National League managers to pick the top players in all departments in 1991, Scioscia was named the top hit-and-run artist and the third best defensive catcher. On May 13, he caught his 1,200th game to surpass John Roseboro as the Los Angeles career leader in games caught. Scioscia catches as often as possible because he handles pitchers well, calls a good game, prevents wild pitches, and blocks the plate better than anyone in the game. He also has a good arm and a capable bat. He walks twice as often as he strikes out and hits well in the clutch. Consistency is Scioscia's calling card. He is a steady $4 fantasy catcher. Unless you live in Los Angeles, don't buy his 1992 commons.

Major League Batting Register

	BA	G	AB	R	H	2B	3B	HR	RBI	SB
80 NL	.254	54	134	8	34	5	1	1	8	1
81 NL	.276	93	290	27	80	10	0	2	29	0
82 NL	.219	129	365	31	80	11	1	5	38	2
83 NL	.314	12	35	3	11	3	0	1	7	0
84 NL	.273	114	341	29	93	18	0	5	38	2
85 NL	.296	141	429	47	127	26	3	7	53	3
86 NL	.251	122	374	36	94	18	1	5	26	3
87 NL	.265	142	461	44	122	26	1	6	38	7
88 NL	.257	130	408	29	105	18	0	3	35	0
89 NL	.250	133	408	40	102	16	0	10	44	0
90 NL	.264	135	435	46	115	25	0	12	66	4
91 NL	.264	119	345	39	91	16	2	8	40	4
Life	.262	1324	4025	379	1054	192	9	65	422	26
3 AVE	.259	129	396	42	103	19	1	10	50	3

SCOTT SCUDDER

Position: Pitcher
Team: Cleveland Indians
Born: Feb. 14, 1968 Paris, TX
Height: 6'2" **Weight:** 180 lbs.
Bats: right **Throws:** right
Acquired: Traded from Reds with Jack Armstrong and Joe Turek for Greg Swindell, 11/91

Player Summary	
Fantasy Value	$2 to $4
Card Value	3¢ to 5¢
Will	mix four pitches
Can't	find plate
Expect	some fine outings
Don't Expect	good K-to-walk ratio

Though Scudder missed six weeks with shoulder tendinitis last season, the Indians still expect him to help their starting rotation. He'll have to find home plate first, however. Opponents compiled a .246 batting average, a .362 slugging percentage, and a .352 on-base average in '91. Even though he allows less than a hit per inning, Scudder walks as many men as he strikes out. Scudder owns the standard repertoire of a fastball, curveball, slider, and change. He also fields well and has a decent pickoff move. But he's never found the success in three major league seasons that he had in the minors. There were three reasons why: location, location, location. Because he'd been the target of other clubs in trade talks, Scudder was an enigma to Cincinnati management. The Indians want to be the recipients when he finally harnesses his control. He will make a smaller impact as a $3 fantasy pitcher if he doesn't get a spot in the rotation. Keep your investments in his 1992 commons small, too.

Major League Pitching Register

	W	L	ERA	G	CG	IP	H	ER	BB	SO
89 NL	4	9	4.49	23	0	100.1	91	50	61	66
90 NL	5	5	4.90	21	0	71.2	74	39	30	42
91 NL	6	9	4.35	27	0	101.1	91	49	56	51
Life	15	23	4.54	71	0	273.1	256	138	147	159
3 AVE	5	8	4.54	24	0	91.1	85	46	49	53

CURRENT PLAYERS

STEVE SEARCY

Position: Pitcher
Team: Philadelphia Phillies
Born: June 4, 1964 Knoxville, TN
Height: 6'1" **Weight:** 195 lbs.
Bats: left **Throws:** left
Acquired: Signed as a free agent, 7/91

Player Summary	
Fantasy Value	$1 to $2
Card Value	3¢ to 5¢
Will	prove shoulder
Can't	always find plate
Expect	bid for bullpen
Don't Expect	good glove

Like Humpty Dumpty, Searcy once sat on a wall, tried to get off but had a great fall. The darling of the Detroit system after winning Triple-A International League Pitcher of the Year honors in 1988, Searcy needed arthroscopic shoulder surgery before reaching the varsity. He hasn't been the same since. After the Tigers threw in the towel, the pitching-poor Phils took a chance. The lefty responded with a respectable performance as a middle reliever. But he wasn't the same pitcher who had more strikeouts than innings three times in the minors. For the second straight year, he walked almost as many as he fanned. NL batters compiled a .252 batting average, a .400 slugging percentage, and a .328 on-base percentage in 1991. His fielding needs work too. The only thing saving Searcy from another minor league exile is the fact that he throws lefthanded. You should find a spot for him, provided you don't spend more than $2. His 1992 commons are unpopular investments.

Major League Pitching Register

	W	L	ERA	G	S	IP	H	ER	BB	SO
88 AL	0	2	5.63	2	0	8.0	8	5	4	5
89 AL	1	1	6.04	8	0	22.1	27	15	12	11
90 AL	2	7	4.66	16	0	75.1	76	39	51	66
91 AL	1	2	8.41	16	0	40.2	52	38	30	32
91 NL	2	1	4.15	18	0	30.1	29	14	14	21
Life	6	13	5.65	60	0	176.2	192	111	111	135
2 AVE	3	5	5.60	25	0	73.2	79	46	48	60

DAVID SEGUI

Position: Outfield; first base
Team: Baltimore Orioles
Born: July 19, 1966 Kansas City, KS
Height: 6'1" **Weight:** 195 lbs.
Bats: both **Throws:** left
Acquired: 18th-round pick in 6/87 free-agent draft

Player Summary	
Fantasy Value	$3 to $5
Card Value	5¢ to 10¢
Will	defend best at first
Can't	generate power
Expect	line drives everywhere
Don't Expect	more Ks than walks

Segui's dad Diego pitched in the majors from 1962 to 1977, then lasted in the Mexican League until 1985. The switch-hitting David is far more proficient in the batter's box than Diego was on the mound. He had three straight .300 years in the minors before *Baseball America* named him the second best prospect in the Triple-A International League for 1990. He hit .336 with two homers, 51 RBI, and 55 runs scored in 307 at bats that year. Young Segui has no speed and only modest power but owns a line-drive stroke that makes frequent contact. He rarely whiffs and walks more often than he strikes out. He had a .340 slugging percentage and a .316 on-base average in 1991 at Baltimore. A first baseman by trade, Segui has also had a look in the outfield. Because he doesn't have his dad's arm, he's better off in the infield. He has to win an everyday spot in the lineup before his dime-priced 1992 cards will have the sizzle needed to captivate investors. He is a $4 first baseman and outfielder.

Major League Batting Register

	BA	G	AB	R	H	2B	3B	HR	RBI	SB
90 AL	.244	40	123	14	30	7	0	2	15	0
91 AL	.278	86	212	15	59	7	0	2	22	1
Life	.266	126	335	29	89	14	0	4	37	1

CURRENT PLAYERS

KEVIN SEITZER

Position: Third base
Team: Kansas City Royals
Born: March 26, 1962 Springfield, IL
Height: 5'11" **Weight:** 180 lbs.
Bats: right **Throws:** right
Acquired: 11th-round pick in 6/83 free-agent draft

Player Summary	
Fantasy Value	$5 to $8
Card Value	3¢ to 5¢
Will	try to reclaim job
Can't	hit long ball
Expect	average descent to end
Don't Expect	frequent strikeouts

Seitzer was Kansas City's regular third baseman before new manager Hal McRae, opting for better defense, replaced him with Bill Pecota last July 7. Seitzer, suffering from knee problems, had limited lateral movement, a problem corrected by off-season arthroscopic surgery. There's little doubt about his hitting. Seitzer went 5-for-5 (all singles) July 4. A spray hitter who goes with the pitch, he also waits out walks. Contact is his game. He seldom fans and almost always puts the ball into play. Now that his knee has been repaired, he might fatten his average with infield hits. Playing on good knees three years ago, Seitzer swiped 17 bases. Surgery should also improve his defense, no matter where he's stationed. He's played every infield position but is most comfortable at third. After he lost his position in 1991, he squandered much of his fantasy and card respect. Think hard before bidding more than $8 for him or paying anything for his 1992 commons.

Major League Batting Register

	BA	G	AB	R	H	2B	3B	HR	RBI	SB
86 AL	.323	28	96	16	31	4	1	2	11	0
87 AL	.323	161	641	105	207	33	8	15	83	12
88 AL	.304	149	559	90	170	32	5	5	60	10
89 AL	.281	160	597	78	168	17	2	4	48	17
90 AL	.275	158	622	91	171	31	5	6	38	7
91 AL	.265	85	234	28	62	11	3	1	25	4
Life	.294	741	2749	408	809	128	24	33	265	50
3 AVE	.276	134	484	66	134	20	3	4	37	9

MIKE SHARPERSON

Position: Infield
Team: Los Angeles Dodgers
Born: Oct. 4, 1961 Orangeburg, SC
Height: 6'3" **Weight:** 190 lbs.
Bats: right **Throws:** right
Acquired: Traded from Blue Jays for Juan Guzman, 9/87

Player Summary	
Fantasy Value	$3 to $7
Card Value	3¢ to 5¢
Will	keep utility role
Can't	yield high average
Expect	good contact
Don't Expect	strong defense

Sharperson doesn't hit .300 or smash home runs but does play several positions, put the ball in play, and deliver in the clutch. He also finds ways to reach base, as explained by an on-base percentage (.355 in '91) that matched Darryl Strawberry's. Usually used as a platoon player, Sharperson spent most of '91 sharing third base with lefty-hitting Lenny Harris. He also served as Juan Samuel's understudy at second, Sharperson's natural position. The five-year veteran matched his .276 career average and made contact when it counted. His patience at the plate paid off when he walked more often than he struck out. A spray hitter who hammers lefthanded pitching, Sharperson also has the ability to steal when necessary. Sharperson's defense is only adequate. Platooning doesn't help his stats and makes him a capable fantasy filler at $4. Investors should stay away from his 1992 commons.

Major League Batting Register

	BA	G	AB	R	H	2B	3B	HR	RBI	SB
87 AL	.208	32	96	4	20	4	1	0	9	2
87 NL	.273	10	33	7	9	2	0	0	1	0
88 NL	.271	46	59	8	16	1	0	0	4	0
89 NL	.250	27	28	2	7	3	0	0	5	0
90 NL	.297	129	357	42	106	14	2	3	36	15
91 NL	.278	105	216	24	60	11	2	2	20	1
Life	.276	349	789	87	218	35	5	5	75	18
2 AVE	.290	117	287	33	83	13	2	3	28	8

CURRENT PLAYERS

GARY SHEFFIELD

Position: Third base
Team: Milwaukee Brewers
Born: Nov. 18, 1968 Tampa, FL
Height: 5'11" **Weight:** 190 lbs.
Bats: right **Throws:** right
Acquired: First-round pick in 6/86 free-agent draft

Player Summary	
Fantasy Value	$7 to $10
Card Value	5¢ to 7¢
Will	hit and run when right
Can't	avoid controversy
Expect	best season with health
Don't Expect	return of huge power

Sheffield's 1991 production was hampered by a sore shoulder and sore left wrist. Playing less than a third of the schedule, he barely hit his weight and homered only twice. He made a bad season worse by criticizing general manager Harry Dalton. What Sheffield may need is a fresh start. The nephew of Mets pitcher Dwight Gooden, Sheffield had improved in each of his three seasons before 1991. But he has yet to capitalize on the potential suggested when he won 1988 Minor League Player of the Year honors. He had 32 homers and 131 RBI while making three stops during that 1988 campaign. Though he uses a strange stance, Sheffield is a natural hitter who topped .300 three times in the minors. Moved to third because he lacks suitable range, he's often voiced a desire to return to short. His 1991 ordeal could provide both fantasy managers and card collectors with abundance in 1992. Bid up to $10 for him and drop a few bucks on his 1992 commons.

Major League Batting Register

	BA	G	AB	R	H	2B	3B	HR	RBI	SB
88 AL	.237	24	80	12	19	1	0	4	12	3
89 AL	.247	95	368	34	91	18	0	5	32	10
90 AL	.294	125	487	67	143	30	1	10	67	25
91 AL	.194	50	175	25	34	12	2	2	22	5
Life	.259	294	1110	138	287	61	3	21	133	43
3 AVE	.260	90	343	42	89	20	1	6	40	13

TERRY SHUMPERT

Position: Second base
Team: Kansas City Royals
Born: Aug. 16, 1966 Paducah, KY
Height: 5'11" **Weight:** 190 lbs.
Bats: right **Throws:** right
Acquired: Second-round pick in 6/87 free-agent draft

Player Summary	
Fantasy Value	$4 to $7
Card Value	3¢ to 5¢
Will	try to keep job
Can't	hit for power
Expect	frequent strikeouts
Don't Expect	another Frank White

Shumpert may not hit much but he has a good batting eye. Before he was hit by a pitch last September 2, he had walked six straight times, one short of the major league record for consecutive walks. The University of Kentucky product replaced eight-time Gold Glove winner Frank White as Kansas City's second baseman in 1990 but missed half his rookie year after tearing a ligament in his thumb. Shumpert won't win friends or influence people with his bat. He is a singles hitter who strikes out three times more than he walks. He does have limited power but he's three times more likely to steal than homer. In 1991, he had a .322 slugging percentage and a .283 on-base average. Shumpert's impotence is not unexpected. His three-year minor league average before '91 was only in the .240s. In the majors primarily for defense, Shumpert has the arm, range, and reactions to succeed. His steals could help a fantasy team for up to $7. His common-priced 1992 cards need time to develop into profits.

Major League Batting Register

	BA	G	AB	R	H	2B	3B	HR	RBI	SB
90 AL	.275	32	91	7	25	6	1	0	8	3
91 AL	.217	144	369	45	80	16	4	5	34	17
Life	.226	176	460	52	105	22	5	5	42	20

CURRENT PLAYERS

RUBEN SIERRA

Position: Outfield
Team: Texas Rangers
Born: Oct. 6, 1965 Rio Piedras, Puerto Rico
Height: 6'1" **Weight:** 175 lbs.
Bats: both **Throws:** right
Acquired: Signed as a free agent, 11/82

Player Summary	
Fantasy Value	$40 to $48
Card Value	10¢ to 15¢
Will	top 100 RBI
Can't	steal much
Expect	solid average
Don't Expect	sloppy defense

Sierra's 1991 season silenced skeptics who said he wasn't making maximum use of his skills. He uncorked an 18-game hitting streak in June and later joined Rafael Palmeiro as the only Texas teammates ever to score 100 runs in the same season. He also knocked in at least 90 runs for the fifth consecutive year out of six. Though he led the AL with 119 RBI in 1989, Sierra finished second in the MVP voting. Since then, he has worked hard to improve his all-around play, especially in right field. The switch-hitting slugger, who had more errors than assists in 1990, paid special attention to his fielding last spring. He has a bad knee that prevents him from running much. Sierra was an All-Star for the second time in 1991. He has everything that you would want in a fantasy outfielder. He will go high—bid up to $50. His 1992 cards are good purchases at 10 to 15 cents.

Major League Batting Register

	BA	G	AB	R	H	2B	3B	HR	RBI	SB
86 AL	.264	113	382	50	101	13	10	16	55	7
87 AL	.263	158	643	97	169	35	4	30	109	16
88 AL	.254	156	615	77	156	32	2	23	91	18
89 AL	.306	162	634	101	194	35	14	29	119	8
90 AL	.280	159	608	70	170	37	2	16	96	9
91 AL	.307	161	661	110	203	44	5	25	116	16
Life	.280	909	3543	505	993	196	37	139	586	74
3 AVE	.298	161	634	94	189	39	7	23	110	11

DOUG SIMONS

Position: Pitcher
Team: New York Mets
Born: Sept. 15, 1966 Bakersfield, CA
Height: 6' **Weight:** 160 lbs.
Bats: left **Throws:** left
Acquired: Drafted from Twins, 12/90

Player Summary	
Fantasy Value	$1 to $3
Card Value	10¢ to 15¢
Will	yield under hit a frame
Can't	always find plate
Expect	bullpen job
Don't Expect	unlimited patience

Lefthanded middle relievers are hard to find. The Mets, thinking they could convert Simons from the starting rotation to that role, took him in the Rule 5 draft at the 1990 winter meetings. Simons responded by posting the best earned run average in exhibition play and making the New York varsity. He pitched two scoreless innings and picked up a win in his first game on April 9. A ninth-round draft pick of the Twins in 1988, Simons started his pro career in 1988 and was used exclusively as a starter. His best season was 1990, when he led the Double-A Southern League with 15 wins (against 12 losses), five of them shutouts. He also had a 2.54 ERA, 109 strikeouts, 43 walks, and 160 hits in 188 innings that year. He was 7-3 at Double-A Orlando in 1989, with a 3.81 ERA, 58 strikeouts, and 38 walks in 87⅔ innings. Simons, who once fanned 16 hitters in a minor league game, could become a starter if a rotation vacancy develops but will otherwise remain in the bullpen. His dime-priced 1992 cards are overpriced. He's a reasonably priced fantasy hurler for $3.

Major League Pitching Register

	W	L	ERA	G	S	IP	H	ER	BB	SO
91 NL	2	3	5.19	42	1	60.2	55	35	19	38
Life	2	3	5.19	42	1	60.2	55	35	19	38

CURRENT PLAYERS

JOEL SKINNER

Position: Catcher
Team: Cleveland Indians
Born: Feb. 21, 1961 La Jolla, CA
Height: 6'4" **Weight:** 205 lbs.
Bats: right **Throws:** right
Acquired: Traded from Yankees with Turner Ward for Mel Hall, 3/89

Player Summary	
Fantasy Value	$1 to $2
Card Value	3¢ to 5¢
Will	supply good defense
Can't	hit or produce power
Expect	adequate arm
Don't Expect	respectable average

Skinner will never follow father Bob to the All-Star Game. Joel took an eight-year average of .225 into the 1991 season and did little to change prevailing opinion. He has little power, less speed, and a knack for striking out four times more often than he walks. Yet he lasts because of a reputation for playing good defense. He can't hold a candle to Sandy Alomar but does have a good arm, an ability to block balls in the dirt, and game-calling skills. Injuries to Alomar allowed Skinner to see his most playing time in six years last season but there was no discernible improvement in his performance. He could be ripe for one of the expansion teams. A good second-string receiver, he is a $1 fantasy reserve. Reserves don't offer good card investments, though, as his 1992 commons demonstrate.

Major League Batting Register

	BA	G	AB	R	H	2B	3B	HR	RBI	SB
83 AL	.273	6	11	2	3	0	0	0	1	0
84 AL	.213	43	80	4	17	2	0	0	3	1
85 AL	.341	22	44	9	15	4	1	1	5	0
86 AL	.232	114	315	23	73	9	1	5	37	1
87 AL	.137	64	139	9	19	4	0	3	14	0
88 AL	.227	88	251	23	57	15	0	4	23	0
89 AL	.230	79	178	10	41	10	0	1	13	1
90 AL	.252	49	139	16	35	4	1	2	16	0
91 AL	.243	99	284	23	69	14	0	1	24	0
Life	.228	564	1441	119	329	62	3	17	136	3
2 AVE	.238	89	231	17	55	12	0	1	19	1

DON SLAUGHT

Position: Catcher
Team: Pittsburgh Pirates
Born: Sept. 11, 1958 Long Beach, CA
Height: 6'1" **Weight:** 190 lbs.
Bats: right **Throws:** right
Acquired: Traded from Yankees for Willie Smith and Jeff Robinson, 12/89

Player Summary	
Fantasy Value	$1 to $3
Card Value	3¢ to 5¢
Will	fill platoon role
Can't	hammer homers
Expect	decent defense
Don't Expect	poor contact

For the last two years, Slaught has teamed with Mike LaValliere to give the Pirates a potent right-left catching platoon. Slaught, a 10-year veteran who began his career with the 1982 Royals, suffered a surprise power shortage in 1991 but still contributed a solid batting average. A contact hitter who doesn't walk or strike out often, he handles clutch situations well. He is often called upon as a pinch-hitter. Though he's a decent receiver who handles pitchers well, he can't match the rifle-armed LaValliere on defense. Slaught had five errors in his 77 games last year while LaValliere had one in his first 108 games. Slaught has career highs of 13 homers (1986) and a .300 average (1990) but is unlikely to exceed either. He is a modest fantasy contributor for up to $3. His 1992 commons aren't credible deals.

Major League Batting Register

	BA	G	AB	R	H	2B	3B	HR	RBI	SB
82 AL	.278	43	115	14	32	6	0	3	8	0
83 AL	.312	83	276	21	86	13	4	0	28	3
84 AL	.264	124	409	48	108	27	4	4	42	0
85 AL	.280	102	343	34	96	17	4	8	35	5
86 AL	.264	95	314	39	83	17	1	13	46	3
87 AL	.224	95	237	25	53	15	2	8	16	0
88 AL	.283	97	322	33	91	25	1	9	43	1
89 AL	.251	117	350	34	88	21	3	5	38	1
90 NL	.300	84	230	27	69	18	3	4	29	0
91 NL	.295	77	220	19	65	17	1	1	29	1
Life	.274	917	2816	294	771	176	23	55	314	14
3 AVE	.278	93	267	27	74	19	2	3	32	1

CURRENT PLAYERS

HEATHCLIFF SLOCUMB

Position: Pitcher
Team: Chicago Cubs
Born: June 7, 1966 Jamaica, NY
Height: 6'3" **Weight:** 180 lbs.
Bats: right **Throws:** right
Acquired: Drafted from Mets, 12/86

Player Summary	
Fantasy Value	$1 to $3
Card Value	10¢ to 15¢
Will	assume heavy bullpen workload
Can't	maintain good K-to-walk ratio
Expect	low 90s fastball, control lapses
Don't Expect	high save total in middle relief

Slocumb spent seven years in the minors—the last three as a reliever—before making the major leagues with the Chicago Cubs in 1991. He retired all three batters he faced in his April 11 debut. He had career peaks with 22 saves and a 1.78 ERA in 49 games at Class-A Peoria in 1989. He was used primarily as a middle reliever and set-up man for the Cubs, though he made occasional late appearances after closer Dave Smith was sidelined by injury. Slocumb has a resilient arm and is able to pitch frequently, a strong attribute on a staff that seems to be hit with injuries often. Slocumb is also valuable because he is stingy with the long ball; at Double-A Charlotte in 1990, he did not permit a home run to any of the 232 hitters he faced. He has a 2.15 ERA with 12 saves and 37 strikeouts in 50⅓ innings there. He allowed only three home runs for the Cubs in 1991, an excellent number considering Wrigley is his home park. He doesn't hold fantasy managers spellbound from his role of long reliever. Avoid his dime-priced 1992 cards until he gets a starting or closing position.

Major League Pitching Register

	W	L	ERA	G	S	IP	H	ER	BB	SO
91 NL	2	1	3.45	52	1	62.2	53	24	30	34
Life	2	1	3.45	52	1	62.2	53	24	30	34

JOE SLUSARSKI

Position: Pitcher
Team: Oakland Athletics
Born: Dec. 19, 1966 Indianapolis, IN
Height: 6'4" **Weight:** 195 lbs.
Bats: right **Throws:** right
Acquired: Second-round pick in 6/88 free-agent draft

Player Summary	
Fantasy Value	$2 to $4
Card Value	10¢ to 15¢
Will	try for rotation
Can't	yield as many hits
Expect	better results
Don't Expect	great ERA

A 1988 Olympian who spent only two years in the minors before advancing to the Athletics, Slusarski pitched seven scoreless innings to beat the Twins in his April 11 debut. He lost four of his next six decisions, however. Slusarski, one of several promising young pitchers advancing through the A's system, should remain in Oakland once he conquers a tendency toward wildness. He walked 34 hitters in his first 70 major league innings. The Athletics hope he will do for them what he did for Class-A Modesto in 1989, his first pro season. He went 13-10 with a 3.18 ERA for a bad ballclub. That season, he struck out 160 hitters in 184 innings. He went 6-8 at Double-A Huntsville in 1990, with a 4.47 ERA, 75 Ks, and 35 walks in 109 innings. He was 4-2 with a 3.40 ERA at Triple-A Tacoma that year. The University of New Orleans product has to prove he is over the shoulder problems that bothered him most of last season. Fantasy managers should remember him for $2, because he could win big. His dime-priced 1992 cards aren't ready for immediate price climbs.

Major League Pitching Register

	W	L	ERA	G	CG	IP	H	ER	BB	SO
91 AL	5	7	5.27	20	1	109.1	121	64	52	60
Life	5	7	5.27	20	1	109.1	121	64	52	60

CURRENT PLAYERS

JOHN SMILEY

Position: Pitcher
Team: Pittsburgh Pirates
Born: March 17, 1965 Phoenixville, PA
Height: 6'4" **Weight:** 200 lbs.
Bats: left **Throws:** left
Acquired: 12th-round pick in 6/83 free-agent draft

Player Summary	
Fantasy Value	$11 to $15
Card Value	3¢ to 5¢
Will	stay top lefty
Can't	worry about elbow
Expect	wins and strikeouts
Don't Expect	control lapses

Smiley was a pleasant surprise for the Pirates in 1991. No Pirate southpaw had won 15 games since John Candelaria and Larry McWilliams both hit that number in 1983. Smiley left them in the dust as he roared toward a 20-win season. He had never won more than 13 games before, and gave hint of good things to come with a 4-0 one-hitter against the Mets April 17. He never looked back. Smiley succeeds because he fans three times more men than he walks and allows less than a hit per inning. Those figures proved he was fully healed from the elbow problems that hampered his performance in 1990. Smiley is a power pitcher who throws a sinking fastball, curveball, slider, and change-up—all with excellent control. A fantasy steal in 1991, he is priced higher at up to $15, but he is still an attractive buy for fantasy managers. His 1992 commons are fine purchases.

Major League Pitching Register

	W	L	ERA	G	CG	IP	H	ER	BB	SO
86 NL	1	0	3.86	12	0	11.2	4	5	4	9
87 NL	5	5	5.76	63	0	75.0	69	48	50	58
88 NL	13	11	3.25	34	5	205.0	185	74	46	129
89 NL	12	8	2.81	28	8	205.1	174	64	49	123
90 NL	9	10	4.64	26	2	149.1	161	77	36	86
91 NL	20	8	3.08	33	2	207.2	194	71	44	129
Life	60	42	3.57	196	17	854.0	787	339	229	534
3 AVE	14	9	3.39	29	4	187.1	176	71	43	113

BRYN SMITH

Position: Pitcher
Team: St. Louis Cardinals
Born: Aug. 11, 1955 Marietta, GA
Height: 6'2" **Weight:** 205 lbs.
Bats: right **Throws:** right
Acquired: Signed as a free agent, 11/89

Player Summary	
Fantasy Value	$8 to $12
Card Value	3¢ to 5¢
Will	bank on control
Can't	blow heat by hitters
Expect	good fielding
Don't Expect	many hits or walks

Smith's second year in the St. Louis rotation was much more successful than his first. Fully recovered from his 1990 shoulder problems, he led the staff in victories. He allowed less than a hit per inning, struck out twice as many as he walked, and kept his ERA at respectable levels even though he threw frequent gopher balls. Smith, who has also had past elbow problems, features finesse rather than fireballs. He blends a sinker and a palmball with one of the most intelligent minds in the majors. He's won in double figures six times in 11 seasons. He does the little things that help: hitting, bunting, and fielding his position. He won't repeat his '85 season but should be able to fashion a winning record. He is a dependable $10 pitcher. His common-priced 1992 cards are not significant.

Major League Pitching Register

	W	L	ERA	G	CG	IP	H	ER	BB	SO
81 NL	1	0	2.77	7	0	13.0	14	4	3	9
82 NL	2	4	4.20	47	0	79.1	81	37	23	50
83 NL	6	11	2.49	49	5	155.1	142	43	43	101
84 NL	12	13	3.32	28	4	179.0	178	66	51	101
85 NL	18	5	2.91	32	4	222.1	193	72	41	127
86 NL	10	8	3.94	30	1	187.1	182	82	63	105
87 NL	10	9	4.37	26	2	150.1	164	73	31	94
88 NL	12	10	3.00	32	1	198.0	179	66	32	122
89 NL	10	11	2.84	33	3	215.2	177	68	54	129
90 NL	9	8	4.27	26	0	141.1	160	67	30	78
91 NL	12	9	3.85	31	3	198.2	188	85	45	94
Life	102	88	3.43	341	23	1740.1	1658	663	416	1010
3 AVE	10	9	3.56	30	2	185.2	175	73	43	100

CURRENT PLAYERS

DAVE SMITH

Position: Pitcher
Team: Chicago Cubs
Born: Jan. 21, 1955 San Francisco, CA
Height: 6'1" **Weight:** 195 lbs.
Bats: right **Throws:** right
Acquired: Signed as a free agent, 12/90

Player Summary	
Fantasy Value	$15 to $20
Card Value	3¢ to 5¢
Will	try for top closer role
Can't	expect miracles
Expect	20 saves
Don't Expect	return to glory

After signing a megabucks free-agent contract to pitch for the Cubs, long-time Houston relief ace Smith suffered through an injury-riddled initial season with Chicago in 1991. He strained ligaments in his knee June 25 and tried to pitch with the pain before submitting to arthroscopic surgery July 22. Staging a full comeback at his age could be difficult but Smith has a history of consistency. When he's right, the two-time All-Star throws two fastballs plus a split-fingered fastball and a curve, all with pinpoint control. He fans twice the number he walks, keeps the ball in the park, and yields less than a hit per inning. Don't spend wildly banking on a comeback. He is a $15 to $20 closer. Don't overestimate his cold 1992 commons.

Major League Pitching Register

	W	L	ERA	G	S	IP	H	ER	BB	SO
80 NL	7	5	1.93	57	10	102.2	90	22	32	85
81 NL	5	3	2.76	42	8	75.0	54	23	23	52
82 NL	5	4	3.84	49	11	63.1	69	27	31	28
83 NL	3	1	3.10	42	6	72.2	72	25	36	41
84 NL	5	4	2.21	53	5	77.1	60	19	20	45
85 NL	9	5	2.27	64	27	79.1	69	20	17	40
86 NL	4	7	2.73	54	33	56.0	39	17	22	46
87 NL	2	3	1.65	50	24	60.0	39	11	21	73
88 NL	4	5	2.67	51	27	57.1	60	17	19	38
89 NL	3	4	2.64	52	25	58.0	49	17	19	31
90 NL	6	6	2.39	49	23	60.1	45	16	20	50
91 NL	0	6	6.00	35	17	33.0	39	22	19	16
Life	53	53	2.67	598	216	795.0	685	236	279	545
3 AVE	3	5	3.27	45	22	50.0	44	18	19	32

DWIGHT SMITH

Position: Outfield
Team: Chicago Cubs
Born: Nov. 8, 1963 Tallahassee, FL
Height: 5'11" **Weight:** 175 lbs.
Bats: left **Throws:** right
Acquired: Third-round pick in secondary phase of 6/84 free-agent draft

Player Summary	
Fantasy Value	$3 to $7
Card Value	3¢ to 5¢
Will	stop falling average
Can't	supply defense
Expect	improvement
Don't Expect	frequent steals

Because Smith's batting average declined for the third consecutive season in 1991, he finished the year on the bench. He'll have to prove he still has the potential he showed when he hit .324 and finished second to teammate Jerome Walton in the 1989 Rookie of the Year voting. Smith's main problem in 1991 was impatience. He struck out three times more than he walked, which was considerably worse than his ratio of the year before. Poor defense is another blot on Smith's record. He has a weak arm and his judgement is not much better. He also has limited range despite decent speed. He has the motor for good base-running but is not great on the paths. Smith would be perfect as a designated hitter if given enough playing time to keep his stroke sharp. He has enough pop in his bat to regain the form that produced two minor league seasons with double figures in triples and homers. He may be a sleeper fantasy buy at $5 or so. His 1992 commons, though, are tiresome.

Major League Batting Register

	BA	G	AB	R	H	2B	3B	HR	RBI	SB
89 NL	.324	109	343	52	111	19	6	9	52	9
90 NL	.262	117	290	34	76	15	0	6	27	11
91 NL	.228	90	167	16	38	7	2	3	21	2
Life	.281	316	800	102	225	41	8	18	100	22
3 AVE	.281	105	267	34	75	14	3	6	33	7

CURRENT PLAYERS

LEE SMITH

Position: Pitcher
Team: St. Louis Cardinals
Born: Dec. 4, 1957 Jamestown, LA
Height: 6'6" **Weight:** 250 lbs.
Bats: right **Throws:** right
Acquired: Traded from Red Sox for Tom Brunansky, 5/90

Player Summary	
Fantasy Value	$40 to $45
Card Value	5¢ to 7¢
Will	lead league in saves
Can't	worry about knees
Expect	All-Star stats
Don't Expect	decrease in skill

Smith has saved 25-plus games nine straight times, a major league record. The flame-throwing closer became even more effective in '91 when he added an off-speed forkball to a repertoire that already included a fastball and slider. He discovered the pitch while throwing with fellow reliever Frank DiPino and began using it at DiPino's urging. Smith got off to his best start, enjoyed his first 40-save season, and broke Bruce Sutter's NL record for saves. Smith got his 300th save August 25 and is a cinch to surpass Rollie Fingers's 341 this season. Though Smith has been troubled by knee problems, he has an elastic arm perfectly suited for his heavy workload. He is a top-notch fantasy draft at $40. His 1992 commons may bring long-term rewards.

Major League Pitching Register

	W	L	ERA	G	S	IP	H	ER	BB	SO
80 NL	2	0	2.91	18	0	21.2	21	7	14	17
81 NL	3	6	3.51	40	1	66.2	57	26	31	50
82 NL	2	5	2.69	72	17	117.0	105	35	37	99
83 NL	4	10	1.65	66	29	103.1	70	19	41	91
84 NL	9	7	3.65	69	33	101.0	98	41	35	86
85 NL	7	4	3.04	65	33	97.2	87	33	32	112
86 NL	9	9	3.09	66	31	90.1	69	31	42	93
87 NL	4	10	3.12	62	36	83.2	84	29	32	96
88 AL	4	5	2.80	64	29	83.2	72	26	37	96
89 AL	6	1	3.57	64	25	70.2	53	28	33	96
90 AL	2	1	1.88	11	4	14.1	13	3	9	17
90 NL	3	4	2.10	53	27	68.2	58	16	20	70
91 NL	6	3	2.34	67	47	73.0	70	19	13	67
Life	61	65	2.84	717	312	991.2	857	313	376	990
3 AVE	6	3	2.62	65	34	75.2	65	22	25	83

LONNIE SMITH

Position: Outfield
Team: Atlanta Braves
Born: Dec. 22, 1955 Chicago, IL
Height: 5'9" **Weight:** 170 lbs.
Bats: right **Throws:** right
Acquired: Signed as a free agent, 3/88

Player Summary	
Fantasy Value	$4 to $8
Card Value	3¢ to 5¢
Will	hit for OK average
Can't	throw or steal
Expect	atrocious defense
Don't Expect	everyday play

Smith proved again last year that he is a designated hitter disguised in left fielder's clothing. Easily the worst defensive outfielder in the NL, his poor judgement and pathetically weak throwing arm made him a major liability in the lineup—especially since he was only a shadow of the player who won 1989 Comeback of the Year honors. Smith ballooned out of shape after that season and has not been the same since. He doesn't run well anymore, seldom hits the ball out of the park (except for his three homers in the '91 Series), and shows an tendency toward nonchalance in the field. He is not a very good base-runner, either. Smith is an ordinary fantasy choice at $6. His 1992 cards are not acquisitions.

Major League Batting Register

	BA	G	AB	R	H	2B	3B	HR	RBI	SB
78 NL	.000	17	4	6	0	0	0	0	0	4
79 NL	.167	17	30	4	5	2	0	0	3	2
80 NL	.339	100	298	69	101	14	4	3	20	33
81 NL	.324	62	176	40	57	14	3	2	11	21
82 NL	.307	156	592	120	182	35	8	8	69	68
83 NL	.321	130	492	83	158	31	5	8	45	43
84 NL	.250	145	504	77	126	20	4	6	49	50
85 NL	.260	28	96	15	25	2	2	0	7	12
85 AL	.257	120	448	77	115	23	4	6	41	40
86 AL	.287	134	508	80	146	25	7	8	44	26
87 AL	.251	48	167	26	42	7	1	3	8	9
88 NL	.237	43	114	14	27	3	0	3	9	4
89 NL	.315	134	482	89	152	34	4	21	79	25
90 NL	.305	135	466	72	142	27	9	9	42	10
91 NL	.275	122	353	58	97	19	1	7	44	9
Life	.291	1391	4730	830	1375	256	52	84	471	356
3 AVE	.301	130	434	73	130	27	5	12	55	15

CURRENT PLAYERS

OZZIE SMITH

Position: Shortstop
Team: St. Louis Cardinals
Born: Dec. 26, 1954 Mobile, AL
Height: 5'10" **Weight:** 160 lbs.
Bats: both **Throws:** right
Acquired: Traded from Padres for Garry Templeton, 2/82

Player Summary	
Fantasy Value	$20 to $27
Card Value	5¢ to 10¢
Will	dazzle with defense
Can't	hit homers
Expect	All-Star start
Don't Expect	75 RBI

Smith is a baseball rarity, a player whose defense is so exceptional that his fielding should eventually lead to Cooperstown. The acrobatic shortstop has not only won a dozen straight Gold Gloves but has improved as a hitter over the years. His average last year was the second best of his 14-year career, and he topped 30 steals for the eighth time. Smith is a patient hitter who makes good contact and walks twice as often as he strikes out. So what if he rarely homers? He is still a defensive star even though his range has declined from superhuman to All-Star standards. He compensates with superior positioning. Draft him for $27 tops. File his nickel-priced 1992 cards in your future Hall of Fame drawer.

Major League Batting Register

	BA	G	AB	R	H	2B	3B	HR	RBI	SB
78 NL	.258	159	590	69	152	17	6	1	46	40
79 NL	.211	156	587	77	124	18	6	0	27	28
80 NL	.230	158	609	67	140	18	5	0	35	57
81 NL	.222	110	450	53	100	11	2	0	21	22
82 NL	.248	140	488	58	121	24	1	2	43	25
83 NL	.243	159	552	69	134	30	6	3	50	34
84 NL	.257	124	412	53	106	20	5	1	44	35
85 NL	.276	158	537	70	148	22	3	6	54	31
86 NL	.280	153	514	67	144	19	4	0	54	31
87 NL	.303	158	600	104	182	40	4	0	75	43
88 NL	.270	153	575	80	155	27	1	3	51	57
89 NL	.273	155	593	82	162	30	8	2	50	29
90 NL	.254	143	512	61	130	21	1	1	50	32
91 NL	.285	150	550	96	157	30	3	3	50	35
Life	.258	2076	7569	1006	1955	327	55	22	650	499
3 AVE	.271	149	552	80	150	27	4	2	50	32

ZANE SMITH

Position: Pitcher
Team: Pittsburgh Pirates
Born: Dec. 28, 1960 Madison, WI
Height: 6'2" **Weight:** 195 lbs.
Bats: left **Throws:** left
Acquired: Traded from Expos for Scott Ruskin, Moises Alou, and Willie Greene, 8/90

Player Summary	
Fantasy Value	$10 to $15
Card Value	3¢ to 5¢
Will	keep ERA down
Can't	help with fielding
Expect	fine K-to-walk ratio
Don't Expect	control lapses

The acquisition of Smith enabled the Pirates to win consecutive NL East titles over the last two years. He went 6-2 after arriving in 1990 as the Bucs edged the second-place Mets by four games. He had a stretch-drive ERA of 1.30, giving him a seasonal mark of 2.55 that ranked second in the league. Smith continued his strong pitching in 1991, when he pitched his second career one-hitter May 29. A sinker-and-slider pitcher who also owns a good changeup, Smith became a top-flight starter after former backstop Ted Simmons accelerated his delivery. The transformation turned Smith from one of the league's slowest workers to one of its fastest and improved his control, ERA, and record. He's now the league's leading control artist. His 1992 commons offer no promise, but as a fantasy draft, he fills managers with hope at $10.

Major League Pitching Register

	W	L	ERA	G	CG	IP	H	ER	BB	SO
84 NL	1	0	2.25	3	0	20.0	16	5	13	16
85 NL	9	10	3.80	42	2	147.0	135	62	80	85
86 NL	8	16	4.05	38	3	204.2	209	92	105	139
87 NL	15	10	4.09	36	9	242.0	245	110	91	130
88 NL	5	10	4.30	23	3	140.1	159	67	44	59
89 NL	1	13	3.49	48	0	147.0	141	57	52	93
90 NL	12	9	2.55	33	4	215.1	196	61	50	130
91 NL	16	10	3.20	35	6	228.0	234	81	29	120
Life	67	78	3.58	258	27	1344.1	1335	535	464	772
3 AVE	10	11	3.03	39	3	197.0	190	66	44	114

CURRENT PLAYERS

JOHN SMOLTZ

Position: Pitcher
Team: Atlanta Braves
Born: May 15, 1967 Detroit, MI
Height: 6'3" **Weight:** 185 lbs.
Bats: right **Throws:** right
Acquired: Traded from Tigers for Doyle Alexander, 8/87

Player Summary	
Fantasy Value	$9 to $12
Card Value	5¢ to 7¢
Will	overpower foes
Can't	avoid walks
Expect	200 innings
Don't Expect	under 15 wins

After establishing himself as Atlanta's No.1 pitcher with a 14-win season for a bad ballclub in 1990, Smoltz struggled through a difficult season with a good Braves team in 1991. After pitching well but getting little support early in the year, he began pressing, and losing. After taking a 2-11 record into the All-Star break, Smoltz consulted a sports psychologist and got good results. His fastball, control, and confidence returned as he helped pitch the Braves into the NL title with 10 wins in his first dozen decisions over the second half. Smoltz, who also throws a slider, curveball, and changeup, pitched so well that Sparky Anderson said he regretted trading Smoltz in 1987. He still yields too many walks and home runs but allows less than a hit an inning and is overpowering when his pitches are working. Just as 1991 was Tom Glavine's year, Smoltz will smoke in 1992. Draft him for your fantasy team at $10. His 1992 commons are shrewd investments.

Major League Pitching Register

	W	L	ERA	G	CG	IP	H	ER	BB	SO
88 NL	2	7	5.48	12	0	64.0	74	39	33	37
89 NL	12	11	2.94	29	5	208.0	160	68	72	168
90 NL	14	11	3.85	34	6	231.1	206	99	90	170
91 NL	14	13	3.80	36	5	229.2	206	97	77	148
Life	42	42	3.72	111	16	733.0	646	303	272	523
3 AVE	13	12	3.55	33	5	223.1	191	88	80	162

LUIS SOJO

Position: Infield
Team: California Angels
Born: Jan. 3, 1966 Barquisimeto, Venezuela
Height: 5'11" **Weight:** 174 lbs.
Bats: right **Throws:** right
Acquired: Traded from Blue Jays with Junior Felix and Ken Rivers for Devon White, Willie Fraser, and Marcus Moore, 12/90

Player Summary	
Fantasy Value	$2 to $4
Card Value	3¢ to 5¢
Will	play adequate defense
Can't	wait for walks
Expect	good range
Don't Expect	high average

Though he's a natural shortstop, Sojo spent his first full big league season as the regular second baseman of the Angels. He showed much better range than predecessor Johnny Ray but did not supply the same offense. Though Sojo is a contact hitter who's tough to strike out, he proved to be little more than a so-so hitter, as a punchless .260 mark suggests. He had a .327 slugging percentage. He needs to boost his .295 on-base average by becoming a more selective hitter and learning to wait for walks. Since Sojo steals only a handful of bases per year, his sole contribution to the club is defense. He reaches balls others wouldn't and turns the double-play with facility but has little job security. That might change if he recaptures the minor league batting stroke that produced a .296 average in his last year at Triple-A Syracuse in 1990. He also had six homers, 25 RBI, and 10 swipes that year. He isn't a prime choice for fantasy managers, even at his $4 price. Disregard his 1992 commons.

Major League Batting Register

	BA	G	AB	R	H	2B	3B	HR	RBI	SB
90 AL	.225	33	80	14	18	3	0	1	9	1
91 AL	.258	113	364	38	94	14	1	3	20	4
Life	.252	146	444	52	112	17	1	4	29	5

CURRENT PLAYERS

SAMMY SOSA

Position: Outfield
Team: Chicago White Sox
Born: Nov. 10, 1968 San Pedro Je Macoris, Dominican Republic
Height: 6′ **Weight:** 175 lbs.
Bats: right **Throws:** right
Acquired: Traded from Rangers with Scott Fletcher and Wilson Alvarez for Harold Baines and Fred Manique, 7/89

Player Summary	
Fantasy Value	$5 to $10
Card Value	5¢ to 7¢
Will	show power and speed
Can't	coax walks
Expect	strong defense
Don't Expect	respectable average

After homering twice as the White Sox right fielder on Opening Day of the 1991 season, Sosa suffered a severe batting slump that resulted in his July return to the minor leagues. He rejoined the team after posting a .358 on-base percentage in 32 Triple-A games. The slump was somewhat of a mystery for him. Even though he barely kept his average above the Mendoza line last year, Sosa showed enough power and speed to warrant another long look. If he masters the art of hitting the curve, he should be a mainstay in the White Sox lineup. Showing more selectivity would help; Sosa fans five times more than he walks. Defensively, he owns a powerful right field throwing arm and uses his speed to good advantage. While his fantasy value has dropped, don't expect his slump to last. Sosa remains a strong consideration at the draft for $7. His 1992 cards are attractive investments at a nickel apiece.

Major League Batting Register

	BA	G	AB	R	H	2B	3B	HR	RBI	SB
89 AL	.257	58	183	27	47	8	0	4	13	7
90 AL	.233	153	532	72	124	26	10	15	70	32
91 AL	.203	116	316	39	64	10	1	10	33	13
Life	.228	327	1031	138	235	44	11	29	116	52
3 AVE	.228	109	344	46	78	15	4	10	39	17

BILL SPIERS

Position: Shortstop
Team: Milwaukee Brewers
Born: June 5, 1966 Orangeburg, SC
Height: 6′2″ **Weight:** 190 lbs.
Bats: left **Throws:** right
Acquired: First-round pick in 6/87 free-agent draft

Player Summary	
Fantasy Value	$8 to $11
Card Value	3¢ to 5¢
Will	show some pop
Can't	vie for bat title
Expect	good defense
Don't Expect	All-Star nod

Spiers refused to let elbow problems interfere with his performance in 1991. He hit two home runs in a game for the first time in his career September 20 and also collected his first grand-slam. He finished with career peaks in games, home runs, RBI, and batting average, cementing his position as Milwaukee's regular shortstop. Spiers, who hits better in his home ballpark, makes decent contact. In 1991, he had a .401 slugging percentage and a .337 on-base average. He is a line-drive spray hitter who drives in his fair share of runs. In the field, he shows good range, good hands, and an adequate throwing arm. Keeping Gary Sheffield at third base has been Spiers's toughest play. The 1987 Clemson All-American, who played all four infield positions as a 1989 AL rookie, will get the most playing time of his career if he stays healthy this season. He was a fantasy bargain in 1991, and he looks satisfactory at an increased rate of $10. His 1992 commons may catch on later.

Major League Batting Register

	BA	G	AB	R	H	2B	3B	HR	RBI	SB
89 AL	.255	114	345	44	88	9	3	4	33	10
90 AL	.242	112	363	44	88	15	3	2	36	11
91 AL	.283	133	414	71	117	13	6	8	54	14
Life	.261	359	1122	159	293	37	12	14	123	35
3 AVE	.261	120	374	53	98	12	4	5	41	12

CURRENT PLAYERS

ED SPRAGUE

Position: Catcher; third base
Team: Toronto Blue Jays
Born: July 25, 1967 Castro Valley, CA
Height: 6'2" **Weight:** 215 lbs.
Bats: right **Throws:** right
Acquired: First-round pick in 6/88 free-agent draft

Player Summary	
Fantasy Value	$2 to $6
Card Value	5¢ to 8¢
Will	play in four spots
Can't	vie for Gold Glove
Expect	some power
Don't Expect	more walks than Ks

Kelly Gruber's first-half injury allowed Sprague to advance to Toronto for the first time in 1991. The son of a former big league pitcher, Sprague made good contact and hit a handful of homers in limited action. He had a .394 slugging percentage and a .361 on-base average. He also showed his versatility by filling in as a catcher, third baseman, first baseman, and designated hitter. A 1988 Stanford graduate and U.S. Olympian, Sprague showed his power potential with 20 homers in 1990 at Triple-A Syracuse. He struck out three times more often than he walked that year, but he rapped 48 extra-base hits. He reduced his K-to-walk ratio in Toronto and reached a career high in batting average as a result. He hit .364 with five homers and 25 RBI at Syracuse in '91. Sprague, who has a strong arm, should improve defensively as a catcher as he gains experience. He added the position to his repertoire in 1990. He has limited fantasy value at this point—no more than $6. His 1992 commons are interesting purchases.

Major League Batting Register

	BA	G	AB	R	H	2B	3B	HR	RBI	SB
91 AL	.275	61	160	17	44	7	0	4	20	0
Life	.275	61	160	17	44	7	0	4	20	0

MIKE STANLEY

Position: Catcher; third base
Team: Texas Rangers
Born: June 25, 1963 Fort Lauderdale, FL
Height: 6' **Weight:** 190 lbs.
Bats: right **Throws:** right
Acquired: 16th-round pick in 6/85 free-agent draft

Player Summary	
Fantasy Value	$2 to $4
Card Value	3¢ to 5¢
Will	play at several spots
Can't	hit for average
Expect	at bats against lefties
Don't Expect	swipes or homers

Before minor league phenom Ivan Rodriguez was promoted to Texas, Stanley shared the top Texas catching job with lefty-hitting Geno Petralli. Stanley was behind the plate last May 1, when Nolan Ryan pitched his record seventh no-hitter, but he has also filled in at first, second, and third base. A contact hitter who walks almost as often as he strikes out, Stanley delivered respectable numbers in limited action, usually against lefty pitching. Though he seldom exhibits much power, Stanley once hit .335 with 13 homers on the Triple-A level. Since he's only gotten into 100 games once in five years, Stanley has never had the chance to duplicate that showing in the majors. Stanley's below-average defensive skills won't keep him in the lineup. He fills many needs, but none of them remarkably. Put him on your fantasy bench for no more than $4. Put off purchasing his 1992 commons.

Major League Batting Register

	BA	G	AB	R	H	2B	3B	HR	RBI	SB
86 AL	.333	15	30	4	10	3	0	1	1	1
87 AL	.273	78	216	34	59	8	1	6	37	3
88 AL	.229	94	249	21	57	8	0	3	27	0
89 AL	.246	67	122	9	30	3	1	1	11	1
90 AL	.249	103	189	21	47	8	1	2	19	1
91 AL	.249	95	181	25	45	13	1	3	25	0
Life	.251	452	987	114	248	43	4	16	120	6
2 AVE	.249	99	185	23	46	11	1	3	22	1

CURRENT PLAYERS

MIKE STANTON

Position: Pitcher
Team: Atlanta Braves
Born: June 2, 1967 Houston, TX
Height: 6'1" **Weight:** 190 lbs.
Bats: left **Throws:** left
Acquired: 13th-round pick in 6/87 free-agent draft

Player Summary	
Fantasy Value	$4 to $7
Card Value	3¢ to 5¢
Will	throw hard
Can't	always find plate
Expect	under hit a frame
Don't Expect	poor K-to-walk ratio

Stanton showed in 1991 that he had recovered from the shoulder problems that kept him sidelined virtually all of the previous season. After a slow start, he posted his first big league win May 28, then waited two days before notching his first save since April 22, 1990. Stanton had been projected as Atlanta's 1990 closer after a brilliant 1989 campaign that featured 34 saves in three stops (including the majors). Between June 18 and August 18, 1991, he had a 1-1 record, three saves, and 0.94 ERA in 25 outings, spanning 28⅔ innings. Opponents compiled a .217 batting average, a .325 slugging percentage, and a .273 on-base average. A strikeout pitcher who blends a sinking fastball with a curve, Stanton sometimes struggles with his control. He does help his own cause with his fielding, however. If the price is right (up to $7), you should take a shot on his saves for your fantasy team. Fly away from his 1992 commons, though, at least until he becomes a closer.

Major League Pitching Register

	W	L	ERA	G	S	IP	H	ER	BB	SO
89 NL	0	1	1.50	20	7	24.0	17	4	8	27
90 NL	0	3	18.00	7	2	7.0	16	14	4	7
91 NL	5	5	2.88	74	7	78.0	62	25	21	54
Life	5	9	3.55	101	16	109.0	95	43	33	88

TERRY STEINBACH

Position: Catcher
Team: Oakland Athletics
Born: March 2, 1962 New Ulm, MN
Height: 6'1" **Weight:** 195 lbs.
Bats: right **Throws:** right
Acquired: Ninth-round pick in 6/83 free-agent draft

Player Summary	
Fantasy Value	$7 to $12
Card Value	3¢ to 5¢
Will	knock in runs
Can't	wait for walks
Expect	strong throws
Don't Expect	frequent homers

Steinbach survived the general malaise that engulfed the Oakland Athletics in 1991. Though his home run total was down, the two-time All-Star reached a career high in RBI and produced the second-best average of his six-year career. He out-hits many AL catchers, making him a $10 fantasy backstop. Steinbach stumbled a bit on defense but is still regarded as one of the best all-around catchers in the American League. His strong arm and quick release reinforce that reputation. Oakland would like Steinbach to recapture the power stroke that produced 24 homers and 132 RBI (along with a .325 average) for Double-A Huntsville in 1986. He has never reached double figures since '87. In 1991, he had a .386 slugging average and a .312 on-base percentage. His 1992 commons are uninspiring buys at this point. He hasn't reached double figures in steals either, getting seven in six years.

Major League Batting Register

	BA	G	AB	R	H	2B	3B	HR	RBI	SB
86 AL	.333	6	15	3	5	0	0	2	4	0
87 AL	.284	122	391	66	111	16	3	16	56	1
88 AL	.265	104	351	42	93	19	1	9	51	3
89 AL	.273	130	454	37	124	13	1	7	42	1
90 AL	.251	114	379	32	95	15	2	9	57	0
91 AL	.274	129	456	50	125	31	1	6	67	2
Life	.270	605	2046	230	553	94	8	49	277	7
3 AVE	.267	124	430	40	115	20	1	7	55	1

CURRENT PLAYERS

DAVE STEWART

Position: Pitcher
Team: Oakland Athletics
Born: Feb. 19, 1957 Oakland, CA
Height: 6'2" **Weight:** 200 lbs.
Bats: right **Throws:** right
Acquired: Signed as a free agent, 5/86

Player Summary	
Fantasy Value	$10 to $12
Card Value	3¢ to 5¢
Will	aim for comeback
Can't	avoid walks or homers
Expect	better results
Don't Expect	return to peak

Stewart has been playoff MVP twice, World Series MVP once, and is the only pitcher to post two wins in the same year's Championship Series and World Series. In 1990, he had a no-hitter against Toronto. But the model of consistency still failed to win a Cy Young Award. Winning became more difficult in 1991, when Stewart used his curveball as frequently as his fastball and forkball. Inability to throw the forkball for strikes hurt him, however. Stewart was also slowed by a pulled rib cage muscle that ended a string of 166 consecutive starts. Consider him a draft risk at $10; his downfall may be a one-year slump or the beginning of the end. His 1992 commons probably will not bring long-term rewards.

Major League Pitching Register

	W	L	ERA	G	CG	IP	H	ER	BB	SO
78 NL	0	0	0.00	1	0	2.0	1	0	0	1
81 NL	4	3	2.49	32	0	43.1	40	12	14	29
82 NL	9	8	3.81	45	0	146.1	137	62	49	80
83 NL	5	2	2.96	46	0	76.0	67	25	33	54
83 AL	5	2	2.14	8	2	59.0	50	14	17	24
84 AL	7	14	4.73	32	3	192.1	193	101	87	119
85 AL	0	6	5.42	42	0	81.1	86	49	37	64
85 NL	0	0	6.23	4	0	4.1	5	3	4	2
86 NL	0	0	6.57	8	0	12.1	15	9	4	9
86 AL	9	5	3.74	29	4	149.1	137	62	65	102
87 AL	20	13	3.68	37	8	261.1	224	107	105	205
88 AL	21	12	3.23	37	14	275.2	240	99	110	192
89 AL	21	9	3.32	36	8	257.2	260	95	69	155
90 AL	22	11	2.56	36	11	267.0	226	76	83	166
91 AL	11	11	5.18	35	2	226.0	245	130	105	144
Life	134	96	3.70	428	52	2054.0	1926	844	782	1346
3 AVE	18	10	3.61	36	7	250.1	244	100	86	155

DAVE STIEB

Position: Pitcher
Team: Toronto Blue Jays
Born: July 22, 1957 Santa Ana, CA
Height: 6'1" **Weight:** 195 lbs.
Bats: right **Throws:** right
Acquired: Fifth-round pick in 6/78 free-agent draft

Player Summary	
Fantasy Value	$10 to $15
Card Value	5¢ to 7¢
Will	top rotation if healthy
Can't	always hide emotions
Expect	strong effort
Don't Expect	more walks than Ks

Stieb was one of the game's most successful pitchers before shoulder tendinitis and a herniated disc idled him last May 23. In 1990, the seven-time All-Star became the only Toronto pitcher to author a no-hitter. That was poetic justice since Stieb had finished 1988 with consecutive one-hitters—both of them no-hitters broken up with two outs and 2-2 counts in the ninth. Stieb had tossed another one-hitter earlier that year, then produced two more in 1989, including an April gem that was his third one-hitter in four starts. Stieb has good control of his fastball, slider, curve, and changeup. He's a fine fielder who can hit. He should rebound enough to satisfy managers willing to bid $10. His 1992 cards are good items at a nickel apiece.

Major League Pitching Register

	W	L	ERA	G	CG	IP	H	ER	BB	SO
79 AL	8	8	4.31	18	7	129.1	139	62	48	52
80 AL	12	15	3.71	34	14	242.2	232	100	83	108
81 AL	11	10	3.19	25	11	183.2	148	65	61	89
82 AL	17	14	3.25	38	19	288.1	271	104	75	141
83 AL	17	12	3.04	36	14	278.0	223	94	93	187
84 AL	16	8	2.83	35	11	267.0	215	84	88	198
85 AL	14	13	2.48	36	8	265.0	206	73	96	167
86 AL	7	12	4.74	37	1	205.0	239	108	87	127
87 AL	13	9	4.09	33	3	185.0	164	84	87	115
88 AL	16	8	3.04	32	8	207.1	157	70	79	147
89 AL	17	8	3.35	33	3	206.2	164	77	76	101
90 AL	18	6	2.93	33	2	208.2	179	68	64	125
91 AL	4	3	3.17	9	1	59.2	52	21	23	29
Life	170	126	3.33	399	102	2726.1	2389	1010	960	1586
2 AVE	18	7	3.14	33	3	207.2	172	73	70	113

CURRENT PLAYERS

KURT STILLWELL

Position: Shortstop; second base
Team: Kansas City Royals
Born: June 4, 1965 Glendale, CA
Height: 5'11" **Weight:** 175 lbs.
Bats: both **Throws:** right
Acquired: Traded from Reds with Ted Power for Danny Jackson and Angel Salazar, 11/87

Player Summary	
Fantasy Value	$3 to $6
Card Value	3¢ to 5¢
Will	play average defense
Can't	avoid errors
Expect	strong throws
Don't Expect	many home runs

Stillwell was Kansas City's starting shortstop before new manager Hal McRae, opting for defense over offense, gave the job to rookie David Howard last July 7. Stillwell is no better than average at the position and no better than average at bat. He compiled a .251 average over his first five seasons and was slightly over that mark again in 1991. He averages a half-dozen homers and half-dozen steals a year. Though he doesn't run well, his range in the field is still average. His above-average arm is neutralized by below-average hands, bringing Stillwell back to the average rating as a shortstop. Many scouts feel he'd do better at second base, and he could wind up there with a new club in 1992. He might be better at turning the double-play from second than he is at short. He is an acceptable fantasy choice at $5. His 1992 cards are common-priced puzzlers.

TODD STOTTLEMYRE

Position: Pitcher
Team: Toronto Blue Jays
Born: May 20, 1965 Sunnyside, WA
Height: 6'3" **Weight:** 190 lbs.
Bats: left **Throws:** right
Acquired: First-round pick in secondary phase of 6/85 free-agent draft

Player Summary	
Fantasy Value	$10 to $15
Card Value	5¢ to 7¢
Will	work 200 innings, win 12-15
Can't	avoid bases on balls, gophers
Expect	better K-to-walk ratio
Don't Expect	a hit per inning by rivals

Stottlemyre became a successful starter in 1991 after learning to change speeds on his fastball. The son of former big league starter Mel Stottlemyre, Todd won more than he lost for the first time in four seasons. He still allowed almost four earned runs per game because of occasional control lapses and home run balls (21 in '91). Stottlemyre managed to pitch more than 200 innings for the second year in a row. When he's right, the strong-armed righthander not only has command of his fastball, curve, and slider but changes speeds on all three. He is a potential 20-game winner who should pay off at a $10 to $15 bid. He still needs to improve a strikeout-to-walk ratio that was less than 2-to-1, however. He yields less than a hit per inning but gets into trouble when he falls behind in the count. Failure to keep runners close is another area Stottlemyre must address. His 1992 commons are appealing investments.

Major League Batting Register

	BA	G	AB	R	H	2B	3B	HR	RBI	SB
86 NL	.229	104	279	31	64	6	1	0	26	6
87 NL	.258	131	395	54	102	20	7	4	33	4
88 AL	.251	128	459	63	115	28	5	10	53	6
89 AL	.261	130	463	52	121	20	7	7	54	9
90 AL	.249	144	506	60	126	35	4	3	51	0
91 AL	.265	122	385	44	102	17	1	6	51	3
Life	.253	759	2487	304	630	126	25	30	268	28
3 AVE	.258	132	451	52	116	24	4	5	52	4

Major League Pitching Register

	W	L	ERA	G	CG	IP	H	ER	BB	SO
88 AL	4	8	5.69	28	0	98.0	109	62	46	67
89 AL	7	7	3.88	27	0	127.2	137	55	44	63
90 AL	13	17	4.34	33	4	203.0	214	98	69	115
91 AL	15	8	3.78	34	1	219.0	194	92	75	116
Life	39	40	4.27	122	5	647.2	654	307	234	361
3 AVE	12	11	4.01	31	2	183.1	182	82	63	98

CURRENT PLAYERS

DARRYL STRAWBERRY

Position: Outfield
Team: Los Angeles Dodgers
Born: March 12, 1962 Los Angeles, CA
Height: 6'6" **Weight:** 200 lbs.
Bats: left **Throws:** left
Acquired: Signed as a free agent, 11/90

Player Summary	
Fantasy Value	$40 to $48
Card Value	10¢ to 25¢
Will	thrill crowds
Can't	avoid strikeouts
Expect	run production
Don't Expect	good defense

After a slow start in his first year as a Dodger, Strawberry delivered during the stretch. He had his best day as a Dodger August 21 with two homers (one a grandslam) and seven RBI. His power is frightening. He has hit the roof of Olympic Stadium, the clock at Busch Stadium, and the center field scoreboard at Shea Stadium twice. Once intimidated by lefthanded pitchers, Strawberry now hits them with regularity. Without a bat in his hands, however, the eight-time All-Star is an ordinary mortal. He uses his speed mainly to compensate for defensive blunders (poor jumps, poor judgement) in right field. Strawberry's arm is strong but inaccurate. For clutch power, he is as close to a guaranteed draft as you can get. He is worth more than $40. Wager on his 1992 cards for up to a quarter apiece.

Major League Batting Register

	BA	G	AB	R	H	2B	3B	HR	RBI	SB
83 NL	.257	122	420	63	108	15	7	26	74	19
84 NL	.251	147	522	75	131	27	4	26	97	27
85 NL	.277	111	393	78	109	15	4	29	79	26
86 NL	.259	136	475	76	123	27	5	27	93	28
87 NL	.284	154	532	108	151	32	5	39	104	36
88 NL	.269	153	543	101	146	27	3	39	101	29
89 NL	.225	134	476	69	107	26	1	29	77	11
90 NL	.277	152	542	92	150	18	1	37	108	15
91 NL	.265	139	505	86	134	22	4	28	99	10
Life	.263	1248	4408	748	1159	209	34	280	832	201
3 AVE	.257	142	508	82	130	22	2	31	95	12

FRANKLIN STUBBS

Position: First base; outfield
Team: Milwaukee Brewers
Born: Oct. 21, 1960 Laurinburg, NC
Height: 6'2" **Weight:** 209 lbs.
Bats: left **Throws:** left
Acquired: Signed as a free agent, 12/90

Player Summary	
Fantasy Value	$7 to $10
Card Value	3¢ to 5¢
Will	contribute power
Can't	hit lefthanders
Expect	a homer or K
Don't Expect	strong defense

Stubbs was a major disappointment as a first-year American Leaguer in 1991. After producing two 23-homer campaigns in five previous seasons, he was expected to replace departing free agent Rob Deer in Milwaukee's lineup. Stubbs succeeded in supplying the high strikeout frequency and low batting average but not the home run power. By season's end, he was sitting on the bench. He fans twice as often as he walks and doesn't supply strong outfield defense, even though he has enough speed to steal more than a dozen bases. The owner of a throwing arm best suited to left field, Stubbs plays best when at first base. He'd also be a competent designated hitter if he recaptured the power stroke that produced so handsomely for Houston in '90. After a year's adjustment, his presence will aid fantasy managers for less than $10. His common-priced 1992 cards aren't hot.

Major League Batting Register

	BA	G	AB	R	H	2B	3B	HR	RBI	SB
84 NL	.194	87	217	22	42	2	3	8	17	2
85 NL	.222	10	9	0	2	0	0	0	2	0
86 NL	.226	132	420	55	95	11	1	23	58	7
87 NL	.233	129	386	48	90	16	3	16	52	8
88 NL	.223	115	242	30	54	13	0	8	34	11
89 NL	.291	69	103	11	30	6	0	4	15	3
90 NL	.261	146	448	59	117	23	2	23	71	19
91 AL	.213	103	362	48	77	16	2	11	38	13
Life	.232	791	2187	273	507	87	11	93	287	63
2 AVE	.240	125	405	54	97	20	2	17	55	16

273

CURRENT PLAYERS

B.J. SURHOFF

Position: Catcher
Team: Milwaukee Brewers
Born: Aug. 4, 1964 Bronx, NY
Height: 6'1" **Weight:** 200 lbs.
Bats: left **Throws:** right
Acquired: First-round pick in 6/85 free-agent draft

Player Summary	
Fantasy Value	$5 to $8
Card Value	3¢ to 5¢
Will	slash liners
Can't	hit for power
Expect	adequate defense
Don't Expect	many strikeouts

Better control of his emotions helped Surhoff engineer a strong comeback in the second half of the 1991 season. He hit .330 between the All-Star break and Labor Day. Surhoff's surge was surprising for a player with a four-year .266 average before the season. The 1984 Olympian and 1985 University of North Carolina All-American had hit .299 as a 1987 rookie but went downhill since. Surhoff has enough speed to sweeten his average with bunts and infield hits. A contact hitter who hits lefties and uses all fields, Surhoff is no slugger, hitting about a half-dozen homers a year. Because he's much more likely to steal a base, some scouts insist he's the AL's answer to Benito Santiago, another catcher who can run. Santiago has a much better arm, though. Surhoff is decent defensively but could move to third if rookie Dave Nilsson sticks. Surhoff defended his catching job with improved hitting and is an $8 or less draft. Don't buy many of his 1992 commons.

Major League Batting Register

	BA	G	AB	R	H	2B	3B	HR	RBI	SB
87 AL	.299	115	395	50	118	22	3	7	68	11
88 AL	.245	139	493	47	121	21	0	5	38	21
89 AL	.248	126	436	42	108	17	4	5	55	14
90 AL	.276	135	474	55	131	21	4	6	59	18
91 AL	.289	143	505	57	146	19	4	5	68	5
Life	.271	658	2303	251	624	100	15	28	288	69
3 AVE	.272	135	472	51	128	19	4	5	61	12

RICK SUTCLIFFE

Position: Pitcher
Team: Chicago Cubs
Born: June 21, 1956 Independence, MO
Height: 6'7" **Weight:** 215 lbs.
Bats: left **Throws:** right
Acquired: Traded from Indians with Ron Hassey and George Frazier for Mel Hall, Joe Carter, Don Schulze, and Darryl Banks, 6/84

Player Summary	
Fantasy Value	$3 to $7
Card Value	3¢ to 5¢
Will	try to comeback
Can't	find old velocity
Expect	injuries to continue
Don't Expect	medical miracle

After winning the NL's Cy Young Award in 1984, his first season with the Cubs, Sutcliffe has spent considerable time on the shelf. He was disabled last June with a tired right shoulder and mulled retirement while out of action. Those thoughts evaporated after Sutcliffe proved himself sound in late summer. Because of persistent shoulder problems, he no longer throws as hard as he once did but still gets good velocity on his fastball, curve, and slider. He throws in a changeup to keep batters honest. Optimistic managers should bid $7 for his return. Sutcliffe often helps his own cause with solid fielding. His 1992 commons are not good buys.

Major League Pitching Register

	W	L	ERA	G	CG	IP	H	ER	BB	SO
76 NL	0	0	0.00	1	0	5.0	2	0	1	3
78 NL	0	0	0.00	2	0	1.2	2	0	1	0
79 NL	17	10	3.46	39	5	242.0	217	93	97	117
80 NL	3	9	5.56	42	1	110.0	122	68	55	59
81 NL	2	2	4.02	14	0	47.0	41	21	20	16
82 AL	14	8	2.96	34	6	216.0	174	71	98	142
83 AL	17	11	4.29	36	10	243.1	251	116	102	160
84 AL	4	5	5.15	15	2	94.1	111	54	46	58
84 NL	16	1	2.69	20	7	150.1	123	45	39	155
85 NL	8	8	3.18	20	6	130.0	119	46	44	102
86 NL	5	14	4.64	28	4	176.2	166	91	96	122
87 NL	18	10	3.68	34	6	237.1	223	97	106	174
88 NL	13	14	3.86	32	12	226.0	232	97	70	144
89 NL	16	11	3.66	35	5	229.0	202	93	69	153
90 NL	0	2	5.91	5	0	21.1	25	14	12	7
91 NL	6	5	4.10	19	0	96.2	96	44	45	52
Life	139	110	3.84	376	64	2226.2	2106	950	901	1464
2 AVE	11	8	3.79	27	3	163.1	149	69	57	103

CURRENT PLAYERS

DALE SVEUM

Position: Infield
Team: Philadelphia Phillies
Born: Nov. 23, 1963 Richmond, CA
Height: 6'3" **Weight:** 185 lbs.
Bats: both **Throws:** right
Acquired: Traded from Phillies for Bruce Ruffin, 12/91

Player Summary	
Fantasy Value	$1 to $3
Card Value	3¢ to 5¢
Will	play several positions
Can't	regain power
Expect	another comeback
Don't Expect	walks or fair average

Sveum is still searching for the stroke that he used to slam 25 home runs for the Brewers in 1987. He failed to reach double figures either before or since in a pro career that began in 1982. The biggest factor in Sveum's slide was a broken leg suffered in September 1988. It kept him out all of the following season and reduced his role from regular to utility infielder. A shortstop who can also play second and third, Sveum is a good news-bad news fielder; limited range cancels out a strong arm. Lack of speed doesn't help. Sveum was sent home from an August road trip with a back injury. The Brewers didn't miss his low batting average or sporadic power production. He finished the year with a poor ratio of strikeouts to walks and a clouded future as a regular. A utility infielder with some pop, he is a $3 fantasy choice at best. His 1992 commons will remain that way.

BILL SWIFT

Position: Pitcher
Team: San Francisco Giants
Born: Oct. 27, 1961 South Portland, ME
Height: 6' **Weight:** 180 lbs.
Bats: right **Throws:** right
Acquired: Traded from Mariners with Dave Burba and Mike Jackson for Kevin Mitchell and Mike Remlinger, 12/91

Player Summary	
Fantasy Value	$8 to $15
Card Value	3¢ to 5¢
Will	throw hard
Can't	return to rotation
Expect	frequent grounders
Don't Expect	job as sole closer

In five major league seasons before 1991, Swift was tried as both a starter and reliever by the Mariners. He found his niche in the bullpen in 1990 but bronzed it in 1991. Working exclusively in relief, Swift enjoyed his finest season. He appeared in more than 60 games for the first time in his career, posted the best ERA on the team, and helped fill the void created by the first-half injury to closer Mike Schooler. Swift is a sinker-and-slider pitcher with good control. He strikes out twice as many as he walks, allows less than a hit per inning, and keeps the ball in the park. His defensive skills serve him well. He is a fifth infielder who gobbles up the grounders his pitches produce. In December, he was traded to the Giants, who will give him a lot of work in 1992. He is a super draft for under $15. Don't acquire many of his 1992 commons.

Major League Batting Register

	BA	G	AB	R	H	2B	3B	HR	RBI	SB
86 AL	.246	91	317	35	78	13	2	7	35	4
87 AL	.252	153	535	86	135	27	3	25	95	2
88 AL	.242	129	467	41	113	14	4	9	51	1
90 AL	.197	48	117	15	23	7	0	1	12	0
91 AL	.241	90	266	33	64	19	1	4	43	2
Life	.243	511	1702	210	413	80	10	46	236	9

Major League Pitching Register

	W	L	ERA	G	S	IP	H	ER	BB	SO
85 AL	6	10	4.77	23	0	120.2	131	64	48	55
86 AL	2	9	5.46	29	0	115.1	148	70	55	55
88 AL	8	12	4.59	38	0	174.2	199	89	65	47
89 AL	7	3	4.43	37	1	130.0	140	64	38	45
90 AL	6	4	2.39	55	6	128.0	135	34	21	42
91 AL	1	2	1.99	71	17	90.1	74	20	26	48
Life	30	40	4.04	253	24	759.0	827	341	253	292
3 AVE	5	3	3.05	54	8	116.0	116	39	28	45

CURRENT PLAYERS

GREG SWINDELL

Position: Pitcher
Team: Cincinnati Reds
Born: Jan. 2, 1965 Fort Worth, TX
Height: 6'3" **Weight:** 225 lbs.
Bats: both **Throws:** left
Acquired: Traded from Indians for Jack Armstrong, Scott Scudder, and Joe Turek, 11/91.

Player Summary	
Fantasy Value	$9 to $12
Card Value	5¢ to 7¢
Will	win big some day
Can't	avoid gophers
Expect	pinpoint control
Don't Expect	15-plus wins

Though he seldom received adequate support, Swindell is widely regarded as one of the game's most effective pitchers. His lopsided record last season was caused by an anemic attack that produced two runs or less in 14 of his first 25 starts. Swindell was also sabotaged by his club's porous defense. The hard-throwing left-hander peaked with an 18-14 record and 3.20 ERA in 1988 but has won less often in each of the three seasons since. It's hardly his fault. He suffers from the typical control pitcher's problem, however: Too many balls leave the park. Swindell's best pitch is a slider, though he also throws a fastball, curve, and changeup. He helps himself by fielding his position well and keeping runners close. His high strikeouts and innings pitched totals signal his hidden value to fantasy managers, who can pilfer him at the draft for under $12. His 1992 commons are bargains.

Major League Pitching Register

	W	L	ERA	G	CG	IP	H	ER	BB	SO
86 AL	5	2	4.23	9	1	61.2	57	29	15	46
87 AL	3	8	5.10	16	4	102.1	112	58	37	97
88 AL	18	14	3.20	33	12	242.0	234	86	45	180
89 AL	13	6	3.37	28	5	184.1	170	69	51	129
90 AL	12	9	4.40	34	3	214.2	245	105	47	135
91 AL	9	16	3.48	33	7	238.0	241	92	31	169
Life	60	55	3.79	153	32	1043.0	1059	439	226	756
3 AVE	11	10	3.76	32	5	212.1	219	89	43	144

PAT TABLER

Position: Infield; outfield
Team: New York Mets
Born: Feb. 2, 1958 Hamilton, OH
Height: 6'2" **Weight:** 200 lbs.
Bats: right **Throws:** right
Acquired: Signed as a free agent, 12/90

Player Summary	
Fantasy Value	$1 to $3
Card Value	3¢ to 5¢
Will	deliver with bases loaded
Can't	run very well
Expect	hike in average
Don't Expect	homers or strong defense

Though Tabler is short on press clippings, he's long on ability in clutch situations. He's a virtuoso with the bases loaded. When he delivered again last August 25, he improved his lifetime mark in bases-loaded situations to 42 hits and 102 RBI in 85 at bats. Except when the bases are loaded, he is an ordinary fantasy choice at $3. Though he finished with the lowest average of his career in 1991, Tabler performed well in pinch-hit situations. He is too slow to help much defensively at the infield or outfield corners. As a hitter, he lacks power but compensates with a good batting eye. He walks more often than he strikes out and puts the ball into play. He's valuable against lefties. Stocking up on his 1992 commons cards is not recommended.

Major League Batting Register

	BA	G	AB	R	H	2B	3B	HR	RBI	SB
81 NL	.188	35	101	11	19	3	1	1	5	0
82 NL	.235	25	85	9	20	4	2	1	7	0
83 AL	.291	124	430	56	125	23	5	6	65	2
84 AL	.290	144	473	66	137	21	3	10	68	3
85 AL	.275	117	404	47	111	18	3	5	59	0
86 AL	.326	130	473	61	154	29	2	6	48	3
87 AL	.307	151	553	66	170	34	3	11	86	5
88 AL	.282	130	444	53	124	23	3	2	66	3
89 AL	.259	123	390	36	101	11	1	2	42	0
90 AL	.272	75	195	12	53	14	0	1	19	0
90 NL	.279	17	43	6	12	1	1	1	10	0
91 AL	.216	82	185	20	40	5	1	1	21	0
Life	.283	1153	3776	443	1067	185	25	47	496	16
3 AVE	.253	99	271	25	69	10	1	2	31	0

CURRENT PLAYERS

FRANK TANANA

Position: Pitcher
Team: Detroit Tigers
Born: July 3, 1953 Detroit, MI
Height: 6'3" **Weight:** 195 lbs.
Bats: left **Throws:** left
Acquired: Traded from Rangers for Duane James, 6/85

Player Summary	
Fantasy Value	$3 to $5
Card Value	3¢ to 5¢
Will	fool batters
Can't	keep ball in park
Expect	decent control
Don't Expect	low ERA

A former power pitcher who relies on finesse, Tanana was one of the most effective pitchers on the Tiger staff, even though he led the team in throwing homers. He used his variety of off-speed pitches to throw two shutouts. Tanana still expects to hang onto his starting berth. If conditioning is a barometer, he should succeed; he's in great shape. Though he can't throw hard anymore, the veteran southpaw uses experience to compensate. His 1992 commons aren't prime investments, but he might spark a fantasy team for $4.

Major League Pitching Register

	W	L	ERA	G	CG	IP	H	ER	BB	SO
73 AL	2	2	3.08	4	2	26.1	20	9	8	22
74 AL	14	19	3.12	39	12	268.2	262	93	77	180
75 AL	16	9	2.62	34	16	257.1	211	75	73	269
76 AL	19	10	2.43	34	23	288.1	212	78	73	261
77 AL	15	9	2.54	31	20	241.1	201	68	61	205
78 AL	18	12	3.65	33	10	239.0	239	97	60	137
79 AL	7	5	3.89	18	2	90.1	93	39	25	46
80 AL	11	12	4.15	32	7	204.0	223	94	45	113
81 AL	4	10	4.01	24	5	141.1	142	63	43	78
82 AL	7	18	4.21	30	7	194.1	199	91	55	87
83 AL	7	9	3.16	29	3	159.1	144	56	49	108
84 AL	15	15	3.25	35	9	246.1	234	89	81	141
85 AL	12	14	4.27	33	4	215.0	220	102	57	159
86 AL	12	9	4.16	32	3	188.1	196	87	65	119
87 AL	15	10	3.91	34	5	218.2	216	95	56	146
88 AL	14	11	4.21	32	2	203.0	213	95	64	127
89 AL	10	14	3.58	33	6	223.2	227	89	74	147
90 AL	9	8	5.31	34	1	176.1	190	104	66	114
91 AL	13	12	3.77	33	3	217.1	217	91	78	107
Life	220	208	3.59	574	140	3799.0	3659	1515	1110	2566
3 AVE	11	11	4.14	33	3	205.1	211	95	73	123

KEVIN TAPANI

Position: Pitcher
Team: Minnesota Twins
Born: Feb. 18, 1964 Des Moines, IA
Height: 6' **Weight:** 180 lbs.
Bats: right **Throws:** right
Acquired: Traded from Mets with David West, Jack Savage, Rick Aguilera, and Tim Drummond for Loy McBride and Frank Viola, 7/89

Player Summary	
Fantasy Value	$10 to $15
Card Value	5¢ to 7¢
Will	use five pitches
Can't	avoid gophers
Expect	compact ERA
Don't Expect	many walks

After getting off to a 2-6 start in 1991, Tapani went 11-1 with a 2.35 ERA and uncorked a nine-game winning streak that made him a candidate for the AL's Cy Young Award. Before the streak ended in September, he had succeeded teammate Scott Erickson as the Twins' top pitcher. Tapani was AL Pitcher of the Month in August with a 5-0 record, 2.63 ERA, 10 walks, and 35 hits in 48 innings pitched. He throws a four-seam fastball, two-seamer, breaking ball, changeup, and split-fingered fastball, all with exceptional control. He fans three times more than he walks and allows less than a hit per inning. Like other control pitchers, however, he's prone to throwing gopher balls. He was 1-1 with a 4.50 ERA in the World Series. Tapani had given hint of things to come with a strong rookie year in 1990, despite shin and shoulder injuries. He is at least a $10 hurler; bid up to $15. His 1992 cards are fair buys at a nickel apiece.

Major League Pitching Register

	W	L	ERA	G	CG	IP	H	ER	BB	SO
89 NL	0	0	3.68	3	0	7.1	5	3	4	2
89 AL	2	2	3.86	5	0	32.2	34	14	8	21
90 AL	12	8	4.07	28	1	159.1	164	72	29	101
91 AL	16	9	2.99	34	4	244.0	225	81	40	135
Life	30	19	3.45	70	5	443.1	428	170	81	259
3 AVE	9	6	3.42	22	2	137.1	131	52	24	79

CURRENT PLAYERS

DANNY TARTABULL

Position: Outfield
Team: Kansas City Royals
Born: Oct. 30, 1962 San Juan, Puerto Rico
Height: 6'1" **Weight:** 205 lbs.
Bats: right **Throws:** right
Acquired: Traded from Mariners with Rick Luecken for Scott Bankhead, Mike Kingery, and Steve Shields, 12/86

Player Summary	
Fantasy Value	$35 to $45
Card Value	5¢ to 10¢
Will	hit for power and average
Can't	steal much
Expect	30 homers
Don't Expect	great defense

After surviving a winter of trade rumors, Tartabull became the Royals' best player in 1991. Hal McRae's appointment as manager helped. He got Tartabull to start hitting the ball up the middle. The right fielder responded by winning team Player of the Month honors in both June and July, hitting three homers in a game against Oakland on July 6, and making the All-Star team for the first time. The son of big leaguer Jose Tartabull, Danny began his career as a second baseman but moved to the outfield as a rookie in 1986. A notorious streak hitter, his 30-homer season entailed numerous timely hits, including an 11th-inning grand-slam. His 1992 cards are acceptable purchases at prices up to a dime. He is a hot fantasy grab, but remember that his 1991 probably won't occur again.

Major League Batting Register

	BA	G	AB	R	H	2B	3B	HR	RBI	SB
84 AL	.300	10	20	3	6	1	0	2	7	0
85 AL	.328	19	61	8	20	7	1	1	7	1
86 AL	.270	137	511	76	138	25	6	25	96	4
87 AL	.309	158	582	95	180	27	3	34	101	9
88 AL	.274	146	507	80	139	38	3	26	102	8
89 AL	.268	133	441	54	118	22	0	18	62	4
90 AL	.268	88	313	41	84	19	0	15	60	1
91 AL	.316	132	484	78	153	35	3	31	100	6
Life	.287	823	2919	435	838	174	16	152	535	33
3 AVE	.287	118	413	58	118	25	1	21	74	4

WADE TAYLOR

Position: Pitcher
Team: New York Yankees
Born: Oct. 19, 1965 Mobile, AL
Height: 6'1" **Weight:** 185 lbs.
Bats: right **Throws:** right
Acquired: Traded from Mariners with Lee Guetterman and Clay Parker for Steve Trout and Henry Cotto, 12/87

Player Summary	
Fantasy Value	$4 to $8
Card Value	10¢ to 20¢
Will	keep rotation role
Can't	handle lefties
Expect	improvement
Don't Expect	ERA over 5.00

Taylor spurned drafts by the Blue Jays and Dodgers to attend the University of Miami. Eventually drafted by the Mariners, who had signed him as a free agent in 1987, Taylor never pitched for that club. Instead, he made his major league debut for the Yankees last June 2. A fastball-and-slider pitcher, Taylor had won four of five decisions at Triple-A Columbus, completing three of nine starts (one of them a shutout) and notching a 3.54 ERA and 36 strikeouts in 61 innings when he was promoted to the Yankees. In 1990 at Columbus, he was 6-4 with a 2.19 ERA. Although he was a shortstop, as well as a pitcher, while attending junior college, Taylor is strictly a pitcher now. He will win more when he learns how to pitch lefties. Collectors might benefit from short-term gains if he starts off hot in '92. Buy his cards at a dime apiece and sell if the price gets up to 50 cents. Draft him for $6 or so, because he seems to have a rotation spot locked up.

Major League Pitching Register

	W	L	ERA	G	CG	IP	H	ER	BB	SO
91 AL	7	12	6.27	23	0	116.1	144	81	53	72
Life	7	12	6.27	23	0	116.1	144	81	53	72

CURRENT PLAYERS

GARRY TEMPLETON

Position: Infield
Team: New York Mets
Born: March 24, 1956 Lockey, TX
Height: 6' **Weight:** 192 lbs.
Bats: both **Throws:** right
Acquired: Traded from Padres for Tim Teufel, 5/91

Player Summary	
Fantasy Value	$2 to $4
Card Value	3¢ to 5¢
Will	play several spots
Can't	run well
Expect	less playing time
Don't Expect	power or speed

Templeton made the switch from regular to utility infielder in 1991. The switch-hitter even played first base for the first time. The deal did little to revive his bat, but Templeton demonstrated enough versatility to keep his job. A three-time All-Star whose speed has been neutralized by age and arthritic knees, he no longer has great range in the field. He compensates by knowing the hitters and making strong throws on balls he reaches. He has occasional pop at the plate and is far more likely to produce as a righthanded batter. Templeton hasn't tempered his free-swinging ways in his old age. He has a fantasy value of $4. His 1992 commons have little investment value.

Major League Batting Register

	BA	G	AB	R	H	2B	3B	HR	RBI	SB
76 NL	.291	53	213	32	62	8	2	1	17	11
77 NL	.322	153	621	94	200	19	18	8	79	28
78 NL	.280	155	647	82	181	31	13	2	47	34
79 NL	.314	154	672	105	211	32	19	9	62	26
80 NL	.319	118	504	83	161	19	9	4	43	31
81 NL	.288	80	333	47	96	16	8	1	33	8
82 NL	.247	141	563	76	139	25	8	6	64	27
83 NL	.263	126	460	39	121	20	2	3	40	16
84 NL	.258	148	493	40	127	19	3	2	35	8
85 NL	.282	148	546	63	154	30	2	6	55	16
86 NL	.247	147	510	42	126	21	2	2	44	10
87 NL	.222	148	510	42	113	13	5	5	48	14
88 NL	.249	110	362	35	90	15	7	3	36	8
89 NL	.255	142	506	43	129	26	3	6	40	1
90 NL	.248	144	505	45	125	25	3	9	59	1
91 NL	.221	112	276	25	61	10	2	3	26	3
Life	.271	2079	7721	893	2096	329	106	70	728	242
3 AVE	.245	133	429	38	105	20	3	6	42	2

WALT TERRELL

Position: Pitcher
Team: Detroit Tigers
Born: May 11, 1958, Jeffersonville, IN
Height: 6'1" **Weight:** 215 lbs.
Bats: right **Throws:** right
Acquired: Signed as a free agent, 7/90

Player Summary	
Fantasy Value	$2 to $4
Card Value	3¢ to 5¢
Will	pitch many innings
Can't	keep hit total low
Expect	ground balls
Don't Expect	frequent Ks

Terrell's strong second-half showing helped turn the Tigers into surprise AL East contenders last year. He took eight of his first nine decisions after the All-Star Game to solidify his spot in the Detroit rotation. His 5-0 whitewash of the White Sox August 20 was his second shutout in 10 days. A sinkerballer who produces ground balls, he enjoyed his best season in 1991 since his 1987 campaign. Though he yielded more than a hit per inning and walked almost as many men as he fanned, Terrell led the team in complete games and innings pitched. He helps himself by keeping base-runners close but is not an agile fielder. Terrell is a solid No. 3 or No. 4 pitcher, especially for a team that plays on grass. His fantasy value peaks at $4, and his 1992 commons don't sell well.

Major League Pitching Register

	W	L	ERA	G	CG	IP	H	ER	BB	SO
82 NL	0	3	3.43	3	0	21.0	22	8	14	8
83 NL	8	8	3.57	21	4	133.2	123	53	55	59
84 NL	11	12	3.52	33	3	215.0	232	84	80	114
85 AL	15	10	3.85	34	5	229.0	221	98	95	130
86 AL	15	12	4.56	34	9	217.1	199	110	98	93
87 AL	17	10	4.05	35	10	244.2	254	110	94	143
88 AL	7	16	3.97	29	11	206.1	199	91	78	84
89 NL	5	13	4.01	19	4	123.1	134	55	26	63
89 AL	6	5	5.20	13	1	83.0	102	48	24	30
90 NL	2	7	5.88	16	0	82.2	98	54	33	34
90 AL	6	4	4.54	13	0	75.1	86	38	24	30
91 AL	12	14	4.24	35	8	218.2	257	103	79	80
Life	104	114	4.14	285	55	1850.0	1927	852	700	868
3 AVE	10	14	4.60	32	4	194.2	226	99	62	79

CURRENT PLAYERS

SCOTT TERRY

Position: Pitcher
Team: St. Louis Cardinals
Born: Nov. 21, 1959 Hobbs, NM
Height: 5'11" **Weight:** 195 lbs.
Bats: right **Throws:** right
Acquired: Traded from Reds for Pat Perry, 9/87

Player Summary	
Fantasy Value	$2 to $4
Card Value	3¢ to 5¢
Will	set-up Smith
Can't	worry about shoulder
Expect	self-help with bat
Don't Expect	lapses of control

After healing from off-season arthroscopic surgery on his pitching shoulder, Terry proved a perfect set-up man for star St. Louis closer Lee Smith. Working in the most games of his career, Terry allowed less than a hit per inning, proved extremely stingy with the gopher ball, and struck out almost twice as many men as he walked. His fine season was predictable. He had a fine finish in 1990 after pitching coach Mike Roarke initiated some changes in his pitching motion. Terry has a fastball, slider, and a changeup. A converted outfielder who often helps his own cause with his bat, he is also a fine fielder with good reflexes. He even holds runners well for a righthander. He should have little difficulty keeping his job. His stat totals don't inspire more than a $3 fantasy bid. Cards of middle relievers rarely inspire hobbyists, and his 1992 commons are no different.

Major League Pitching Register

	W	L	ERA	G	S	IP	H	ER	BB	SO
86 NL	1	2	6.14	28	0	55.2	66	38	32	32
87 NL	0	0	3.38	11	0	13.1	13	5	8	9
88 NL	9	6	2.92	51	3	129.1	119	42	34	65
89 NL	8	10	3.57	31	2	148.2	142	59	43	69
90 NL	2	6	4.75	50	2	72.0	75	38	27	35
91 NL	4	4	2.80	65	1	80.1	76	25	32	52
Life	24	28	3.73	236	8	499.1	491	207	176	262
3 AVE	5	7	3.65	49	2	100.1	98	41	34	52

MICKEY TETTLETON

Position: Catcher
Team: Detroit Tigers
Born: Sept. 16, 1960 Oklahoma, OK
Height: 6'2" **Weight:** 214 lbs.
Bats: both **Throws:** right
Acquired: Traded from Orioles for Jeff Robinson, 1/91

Player Summary	
Fantasy Value	$23 to $28
Card Value	3¢ to 5¢
Will	hit homers often
Can't	produce high average
Expect	decent defense
Don't Expect	poor power output

Tettleton's ability to reduce his strikeout frequency boosted his power production in 1991. He not only became the fifth player to hit two or more balls out of Tiger Stadium but the first Tiger to clear the roof twice in the same year since Jason Thompson in 1977. Tettleton performed the feat within a six-day span of June. By season's end, he had reached career highs in both home runs and RBI. The switch-hitting catcher reduced his strikeouts sharply and ranked second among the league leaders in walks. Tettleton now plays in a ballpark perfectly suited to his power. His homers drive his fantasy worth to $23 or more. He's neither a Gold Glove catcher nor a defensive liability. He has a decent arm, handles pitchers well, blocks most balls in the dirt, and even has some speed. His 1992 commons are not priorities with investors.

Major League Batting Register

	BA	G	AB	R	H	2B	3B	HR	RBI	SB
84 AL	.263	33	76	10	20	2	1	1	5	0
85 AL	.251	78	211	23	53	12	0	3	15	2
86 AL	.204	90	211	26	43	9	0	10	35	7
87 AL	.194	82	211	19	41	3	0	8	26	1
88 AL	.261	86	283	31	74	11	1	11	37	0
89 AL	.258	117	411	72	106	21	2	26	65	3
90 AL	.223	135	444	68	99	21	2	15	51	2
91 AL	.263	154	501	85	132	17	2	31	89	3
Life	.242	775	2348	334	568	96	8	105	323	18
3 AVE	.249	135	452	75	112	20	2	24	68	3

CURRENT PLAYERS

TIM TEUFEL

Position: Infield
Team: San Diego Padres
Born: July 7, 1958 Greenwich, CT
Height: 6' **Weight:** 175 lbs.
Bats: right **Throws:** right
Acquired: Traded from Mets for Garry Templeton, 5/91

Player Summary	
Fantasy Value	$3 to $6
Card Value	3¢ to 5¢
Will	show some pop
Can't	play shortstop
Expect	use against lefties
Don't Expect	another low average

Teufel played both second and third base for San Diego after arriving from New York in 1991. He has always swung the bat. He was a regular for two years after coming to the majors with Minnesota in 1984 but has been a platoon player for six seasons since. Teufel normally thrives against lefthanded pitching but suffered a season-long slump last year. A patient hitter who usually makes good contact, Teufel mixes some speed with his power. He's good for about a dozen homers and half-dozen steals a year. For $4, his homers will entice fantasy managers in need of a bench. He's also a capable pinch-hitter and can even drop a bunt on occasion. Teufel doesn't have the range for short but handles himself well at all three bases (he was an All-American at second in 1980). His 1992 commons don't hold interest.

Major League Batting Register

	BA	G	AB	R	H	2B	3B	HR	RBI	SB
83 AL	.308	21	78	11	24	7	1	3	6	0
84 AL	.262	157	568	76	149	30	3	14	61	1
85 AL	.260	138	434	58	113	24	3	10	50	4
86 NL	.247	93	279	35	69	20	1	4	31	1
87 NL	.308	97	299	55	92	29	0	14	61	3
88 NL	.234	90	273	35	64	20	0	4	31	0
89 NL	.256	83	219	27	56	7	2	2	15	1
90 NL	.246	80	175	28	43	11	0	10	24	0
91 NL	.217	117	341	41	74	16	0	12	44	9
Life	.257	876	2666	366	684	164	10	73	323	19
3 AVE	.235	93	245	32	58	11	1	8	28	3

BOB TEWKSBURY

Position: Pitcher
Team: St. Louis Cardinals
Born: Nov. 30, 1960 Concord, NH
Height: 6'4" **Weight:** 200 lbs.
Bats: right **Throws:** right
Acquired: Signed as a free agent, 12/88

Player Summary	
Fantasy Value	$4 to $7
Card Value	3¢ to 5¢
Will	finesse batters
Can't	prevent many hits
Expect	few walks or Ks
Don't Expect	fastball to smoke

Off the field, Tewksbury is a talented artist who spends free moments sketching his teammates. On the field, he's a talented pitcher. With the 1991 Cardinals, he won in double figures for the second year in a row and produced the best ERA of his five-year career. The stellar St. Louis defense helped. Tewksbury gets relatively few strikeouts. He still fans twice as many as he walks, however, because he's an excellent control pitcher. He throws occasional gophers on the road but few at spacious Busch Stadium. Tewksbury carries a capable glove and keeps base-runners close but doesn't help himself with a bat. He blends a variety of curves and changeups with a "fastball" to keep hitters off-stride. Velocity of the Tewksbury fastball is often less than 80 miles an hour. He will go for $5 at the draft, and that is a bargain. His 1992 cards are not bargains, even at their commons prices.

Major League Pitching Register

	W	L	ERA	G	CG	IP	H	ER	BB	SO
86 AL	9	5	3.31	23	2	130.1	144	48	31	49
87 AL	1	4	6.75	8	0	33.1	47	25	7	12
87 NL	0	4	6.50	7	0	18.0	32	13	13	10
88 NL	0	0	8.10	1	0	3.1	6	3	2	1
89 NL	1	0	3.30	7	1	30.0	25	11	10	17
90 NL	10	9	3.47	28	3	145.1	151	56	15	50
91 NL	11	12	3.25	30	3	191.0	206	69	38	75
Life	32	34	3.67	104	9	551.1	611	225	116	214
2 AVE	11	11	3.34	29	3	168.1	179	63	27	63

CURRENT PLAYERS

BOBBY THIGPEN

Position: Pitcher
Team: Chicago White Sox
Born: July 17, 1963 Tallahassee, FL
Height: 6'3" **Weight:** 195 lbs.
Bats: right **Throws:** right
Acquired: Fourth-round pick in 6/85 free-agent draft

Player Summary	
Fantasy Value	$30 to $40
Card Value	3¢ to 5¢
Will	get 30 saves
Can't	stay sharp without use
Expect	occasional control woes
Don't Expect	repeat of 1990

Had Thigpen saved his big year for 1991, the White Sox would have won the AL West title. Instead, the hard-throwing righthander followed his record 57-save season with a mere mortal campaign. Though Thigpen reached the 30-save plateau for the fourth straight season, his strikeouts were down while his walks and homers were up. He still yielded less than a hit per inning but his ERA jumped more than one and one-half runs per game. Thigpen staggered at the start in '91 and never caught up. Working less frequently than the year before, he endured bouts of wildness and failed to maintain the sharpness of his four pitches: fastball, curveball, changeup, and slider (flat sliders sail over the fence). A sharp Thigpen is an imposing pitcher and a fine fielder who keeps runners close. He is dependable for 30 saves, making him a $30-plus fantasy man. His 1992 cards are commons in the short term.

Major League Pitching Register

	W	L	ERA	G	S	IP	H	ER	BB	SO
86 AL	2	0	1.77	20	7	35.2	26	7	12	20
87 AL	7	5	2.73	51	16	89.0	86	27	24	52
88 AL	5	8	3.30	68	34	90.0	96	33	33	62
89 AL	2	6	3.76	61	34	79.0	62	33	40	47
90 AL	4	6	1.83	77	57	88.2	60	18	32	70
91 AL	7	5	3.49	67	30	69.2	63	27	38	47
Life	27	30	2.89	344	178	452.0	393	145	179	298
3 AVE	4	6	2.96	68	40	79.1	62	26	37	55

FRANK THOMAS

Position: First base
Team: Chicago White Sox
Born: May 27, 1968 Columbus, GA
Height: 6'5" **Weight:** 240 lbs.
Bats: right **Throws:** right
Acquired: First-round pick in 6/89 free-agent draft

Player Summary	
Fantasy Value	$40 to $55
Card Value	20¢ to 50¢
Will	produce runs
Can't	throw or steal
Expect	MVP bid
Don't Expect	shoulder woes to linger

Shoulder tendinitis did not prevent Thomas from assaulting AL pitching in 1991, his first full season in the majors. A very selective hitter who combined Walt Hriniak's coaching with his own strengths to develop his powerful, compact swing, Thomas made a strong bid for MVP honors. He could be even more devastating in 1992 following a winter of weight work designed to restore full strength in the ailing shoulder. Thomas was August Player of the Month with a .373 average, eight homers, and 27 RBI. By season's end, he had scored and knocked in 100 runs and become the first 100-RBI White Sox player in six years. He's a definite threat to Zeke Bonura's 1936 club RBI record of 138. A big man, Thomas is an agile first baseman with good hands and decent range. Only his throwing arm is below average. He doesn't figure to steal much. He will go high at the fantasy draft, deservedly so. Plan on bidding up to $55 for his services. His 1992 cards are exceptional buys up to 50 cents each.

Major League Batting Register

	BA	G	AB	R	H	2B	3B	HR	RBI	SB
90 AL	.330	60	191	39	63	11	3	7	31	0
91 AL	.318	158	559	104	178	31	2	32	109	1
Life	.321	218	710	143	241	42	5	39	140	1
2 AVE	.321	109	375	72	121	21	3	20	70	1

CURRENT PLAYERS

MILT THOMPSON

Position: Outfield
Team: St. Louis Cardinals
Born: Jan. 5, 1959 Washington, DC
Height: 5'11" **Weight:** 170 lbs.
Bats: left **Throws:** right
Acquired: Traded from Phillies for Steve Lake and Curt Ford, 12/88

Player Summary	
Fantasy Value	$8 to $12
Card Value	3¢ to 5¢
Will	pinch-hit
Can't	handle top lefties
Expect	good speed
Don't Expect	over six homers

After losing his job with a .218 batting average in 1990, Thompson started well in 1991. He finished with the highest mark on the Cardinals and the best of his eight-year career. He responded well when rookie left fielder Bernard Gilkey slumped. He also backed up the other outfield positions and served as a productive pinch-hitter. Thompson uses an inside-out swing to hit to all fields and beats out bunts and infield hits. He makes good contact but also coaxes his share of walks, keeping his on-base percentage tops on the team. He had reached 25 steals three times in four years before failing to swipe 20 in '91. Thompson is a good outfielder with fine range but a weak arm. One of baseball's top fourth outfielders, he is a fantasy gem for $10. His 1992 commons, like those of other part-timers, are not important.

Major League Batting Register

	BA	G	AB	R	H	2B	3B	HR	RBI	SB
84 NL	.303	25	99	16	30	1	0	2	4	14
85 NL	.302	73	182	17	55	7	2	0	6	9
86 NL	.251	96	299	38	75	7	1	6	23	19
87 NL	.302	150	527	86	159	26	9	7	43	46
88 NL	.288	122	378	53	109	16	2	2	33	17
89 NL	.290	155	545	60	158	28	8	4	68	27
90 NL	.218	135	418	42	91	14	7	6	30	25
91 NL	.307	115	326	55	100	16	5	6	34	16
Life	.280	871	2774	367	777	115	34	33	241	173
3 AVE	.271	135	430	52	116	19	7	5	44	23

ROBBY THOMPSON

Position: Second base
Team: San Francisco Giants
Born: May 10, 1962 West Palm Beach, FL
Height: 5'11" **Weight:** 170 lbs.
Bats: right **Throws:** right
Acquired: First-round pick in secondary phase of 6/83 free-agent draft

Player Summary	
Fantasy Value	$15 to $22
Card Value	3¢ to 5¢
Will	play good defense
Can't	avoid frequent Ks
Expect	surprising power
Don't Expect	more walks than Ks

Although he is one of the NL's best second basemen, Thompson is also one of the league's most underrated players. Overshadowed by sluggers in San Francisco, he is among his team's most durable and reliable performers. A good all-around player, he became the seventh player in Giant history to hit for the cycle last April 22. He also played so well in the field that NL managers in a *Baseball America* survey said he ranked behind only Ryne Sandberg and Jose Lind at his position. He is a powerful middle infielder, with the stats for a $15-plus bid. As a leadoff man, however, Thompson was found wanting because of his tendency to fan frequently. He did walk more in 1991, however. Thompson has both power and speed. He stole his usual dozen bases. He turns the double-play well and has a strong arm. At this point, his 1992 commons don't have much future.

Major League Batting Register

	BA	G	AB	R	H	2B	3B	HR	RBI	SB
86 NL	.271	149	549	73	149	27	3	7	47	12
87 NL	.262	132	420	62	110	26	5	10	44	16
88 NL	.264	138	477	66	126	24	6	7	48	14
89 NL	.241	148	547	91	132	26	11	13	50	12
90 NL	.245	144	498	67	122	22	3	15	56	14
91 NL	.262	144	492	74	129	24	5	19	48	14
Life	.257	855	2983	433	768	149	33	71	293	82
3 AVE	.249	145	512	77	128	24	6	16	51	13

CURRENT PLAYERS

DICKIE THON

Position: Shortstop
Team: Texas Rangers
Born: June 20, 1958 South Bend, IN
Height: 5'11" **Weight:** 175 lbs.
Bats: right **Throws:** right
Acquired: Signed as a free agent, 12/91

Player Summary
Fantasy Value	$4 to $8
Card Value	3¢ to 5¢
Will	hit in streaks
Can't	run like before
Expect	limited range
Don't Expect	guaranteed spot

Thon was a key player in Philadelphia's August awakening in 1991. He topped .300 during the month. He compiled a .351 slugging percentage and a .283 on-base average in '91. He left Philly after the season, signed with Texas, and could be their starter in 1992. Thon has more power than most shortstops but has never come close to repeating the 20-homer, 34-steal season that won him a trip to the 1983 All-Star Game. Eye problems that resulted from a Mike Torrez beaning in April 1984 almost ruined his career and certainly curtailed his development. Since then, Thon has homered in double figures only once and hasn't had a 20-steal season. With some 45 errors in the last two years, he might have played his way off the position. He might move to second base. With his power, he is a good $6 infielder. His 1992 commons don't rate, however.

Major League Batting Register
	BA	G	AB	R	H	2B	3B	HR	RBI	SB
79 AL	.339	35	56	6	19	3	0	0	8	0
80 AL	.255	80	267	32	68	12	2	0	15	7
81 NL	.274	49	95	13	26	6	0	0	3	6
82 NL	.276	136	496	73	137	31	10	3	36	37
83 NL	.286	154	619	81	177	28	9	20	79	34
84 NL	.353	5	17	3	6	0	1	0	1	0
85 NL	.251	84	251	26	63	6	1	6	29	8
86 NL	.248	106	278	24	69	13	1	3	21	6
87 NL	.212	32	66	6	14	1	0	1	3	3
88 NL	.264	95	258	36	68	12	2	1	18	19
89 NL	.271	136	435	45	118	18	4	15	60	6
90 NL	.255	149	552	54	141	20	4	8	48	12
91 NL	.252	146	539	44	136	18	4	9	44	11
Life	.265	1207	3929	443	1042	168	38	66	365	149

GARY THURMAN

Position: Outfield
Team: Kansas City Royals
Born: Nov. 12, 1964 Indianapolis, IN
Height: 5'10" **Weight:** 175 lbs.
Bats: right **Throws:** right
Acquired: First-round pick in 6/83 free-agent draft

Player Summary
Fantasy Value	$2 to $5
Card Value	3¢ to 5¢
Will	steal often
Can't	hit homers
Expect	shot as regular
Don't Expect	poor defense

Before a knee injury interfered with Thurman's development in 1991, he was making a major impression in his first full season with the Kansas City Royals. Thurman had a .290 average with a dozen steals in his first 69 games but went on the shelf after tearing a ligament in his right knee August 6. If the knee heals fully and Thurman's bat keeps producing, he has a shot at the starting center fielder job. Among other things, he offers world-class speed. After leading two minor leagues in stolen bases, he swiped 16-for-16 with the 1989 Royals to tie an AL record for most steals without getting caught. Thurman's speed also gives him tremendous range in the outfield and he sweetens the picture by possessing a powerful throwing arm. His main weakness is impatience at the plate; more walks mean more steals. Without a guaranteed job, his fantasy value remains stuck at less than $5. His 1992 commons will remain in the box until he wins a job.

Major League Batting Register
	BA	G	AB	R	H	2B	3B	HR	RBI	SB
87 AL	.296	27	81	12	24	2	0	0	5	7
88 AL	.167	35	66	6	11	1	0	0	3	5
89 AL	.195	72	87	24	17	2	1	0	5	16
90 AL	.233	23	60	5	14	3	0	0	3	1
91 AL	.277	80	184	24	51	9	0	2	13	15
Life	.245	237	478	71	117	17	1	2	28	44

CURRENT PLAYERS

MIKE TIMLIN

Position: Pitcher
Team: Toronto Blue Jays
Born: March 10, 1966 Midland, TX
Height: 6'4" **Weight:** 205 lbs.
Bats: right **Throws:** right
Acquired: Fifth-round pick in 6/87 free-agent draft

Player Summary	
Fantasy Value	$4 to $8
Card Value	10¢ to 15¢
Will	work often as set-up reliever
Can't	win if sinker doesn't sink
Expect	2-1 K-to-walk ratio
Don't Expect	assignments in rotation

Timlin was a pleasant surprise as a rookie in 1991. He made his major league debut as a middle reliever on April 8 and remained a relief mainstay the rest of the season. After posting an 8-4 record and 30 saves for two Toronto farm clubs in 1990, the hard-throwing sinkerballer effectively replaced veteran John Candelaria (who signed with the Dodgers as a free agent) in the Blue Jay bullpen. By season's end, Timlin had made more than 60 appearances, including three starts. Timlin, who converted from starter to reliever in 1989, had earned a promotion with two strong years of relief work in the minors. He fans twice as many as he walks, yields less than a hit per inning, and keeps the ball in the park. Timlin's fine rookie season assures his return to his role as a set-up man for closers Tom Henke and Duane Ward. Don't overestimate his 1992 card prospects based solely on his first-year relief record. You should pay no more than 15 cents apiece. He is a fantasy pickup at $6 or so.

Major League Pitching Register

	W	L	ERA	G	S	IP	H	ER	BB	SO
91 AL	11	6	3.16	63	3	108.1	94	38	50	85
Life	11	6	3.16	63	3	108.1	94	38	50	85

RANDY TOMLIN

Position: Pitcher
Team: Pittsburgh Pirates
Born: June 14, 1966 Bainbridge, MD
Height: 5'11" **Weight:** 179 lbs.
Bats: left **Throws:** left
Acquired: 18th-round pick in 6/88 free-agent draft

Player Summary	
Fantasy Value	$6 to $10
Card Value	5¢ to 7¢
Will	baffle batters
Can't	blow hitters away
Expect	good control
Don't Expect	self-help at bat

Tomlin is the prototypical crafty lefthander. He throws across his body, usually has good location, and is particularly effective against lefthanded hitters. When he hurled consecutive shutouts last July, he became the first Pirate to do that since Rick Reuschel in 1987. On August 6, Tomlin beat the New York Mets for the third time without a loss. Teammates call him "Whispers" because he is naturally soft-spoken. His pitches seem soft-spoken too. He doesn't blow batters away with his fastball, slider, curve, or change-up but baffles them by changing speeds and placing pitches in certain zones. He was one of the most effective pitchers on the Pittsburgh staff. Opponents compiled a .254 batting average, a .354 slugging percentage, and a .315 on-base average in 1991. Draft him for no more than $10 for a deal. Tomlin's unorthodox motion not only fools hitters but base-runners. Few try to steal against him. Tomlin is a fine fielder but can't hit. Stash a few of his nickel-priced 1992 cards for the future.

Major League Pitching Register

	W	L	ERA	G	CG	IP	H	ER	BB	SO
90 NL	4	4	2.55	12	2	77.2	62	22	12	42
91 NL	8	7	2.98	31	4	175.0	170	58	54	104
Life	12	11	2.85	43	6	252.2	232	80	66	146
2 AVE	6	6	2.85	22	3	126.1	116	40	33	73

CURRENT PLAYERS

ALAN TRAMMELL

Position: Shortstop
Team: Detroit Tigers
Born: Feb. 21, 1958 Garden Grove, CA
Height: 6' **Weight:** 180 lbs.
Bats: right **Throws:** right
Acquired: Second-round pick in 6/76 free-agent draft

Player Summary	
Fantasy Value	$9 to $12
Card Value	5¢ to 7¢
Will	show powerful bat
Can't	offset slowness
Expect	strong comeback
Don't Expect	back woes to vanish

When Trammell hit .304 for the Tigers in 1990, he joined a group of five other shortstops who produced at least six .300 seasons: Luke Appling, Joe Sewell, Joe Cronin, Arky Vaughn, and Honus Wagner. Trammell's cards will appreciate only if he follows that select group to Cooperstown. If you believe he has a shot, invest in his nickel-priced 1992 issues. A six-time All-Star with four Gold Gloves, Trammell was runner-up to George Bell in the MVP voting in 1987. Trammell was bothered by ankle, wrist, knee, and back problems in '91. He is still a fine contact hitter who walks almost as often as he strikes out. At $10, his fantasy value is reasonable, considering his career twilight.

Major League Batting Register

	BA	G	AB	R	H	2B	3B	HR	RBI	SB
77 AL	.186	19	43	6	8	0	0	0	0	0
78 AL	.268	139	448	49	120	14	6	2	34	3
79 AL	.276	142	460	68	127	11	4	6	50	17
80 AL	.300	146	560	107	168	21	5	9	65	12
81 AL	.258	105	392	52	101	15	3	2	31	10
82 AL	.258	157	489	66	126	34	3	9	57	19
83 AL	.319	142	505	83	161	31	2	14	66	30
84 AL	.314	139	555	85	174	34	5	14	69	19
85 AL	.258	149	605	79	156	21	7	13	57	14
86 AL	.277	151	574	107	159	33	7	21	75	25
87 AL	.343	151	597	109	205	34	3	28	105	21
88 AL	.311	128	466	73	145	24	1	15	69	7
89 AL	.243	121	449	54	109	20	3	5	43	10
90 AL	.304	146	559	71	170	37	1	14	89	12
91 AL	.248	100	375	57	93	20	0	9	55	11
Life	.286	1936	7077	1066	2022	349	50	161	865	210
3 AVE	.269	123	461	61	124	26	1	9	62	11

JEFF TREADWAY

Position: Second base
Team: Atlanta Braves
Born: Jan. 22, 1963 Columbus, GA
Height: 5'11" **Weight:** 170 lbs.
Bats: left **Throws:** right
Acquired: Purchased from Reds, 3/89

Player Summary	
Fantasy Value	$5 to $10
Card Value	3¢ to 5¢
Will	make contact
Can't	play strong defense
Expect	fewer at bats
Don't Expect	injuries to hinder

Treadway's average has climbed steadily in each of his four major league seasons. But his error total has climbed at the same rate. Limited to just over 100 games by a series of injuries in '91, the lefthanded contact hitter made 15 miscues—a total that so alarmed Atlanta manager Bobby Cox that he played light-hitting but better-fielding Mark Lemke down the stretch last fall. Lemke than exploded in the World Series. A contact hitter who walks more often than he strikes out, Treadway spent much of last year in platoon with Lemke. The see-saw arrangement might have interfered with Treadway's power, which vanished overnight after a career-best 11 homers (three in one game) in 1990. The platoon arrangement might not persist. The question is not Treadway's ability to hit lefties (he hit .303 against them in '90) but his ability in the field. He still looks sound to fantasy managers at drafts less than $10, but investing in his 1992 commons is unheard-of.

Major League Batting Register

	BA	G	AB	R	H	2B	3B	HR	RBI	SB
87 NL	.333	23	84	9	28	4	0	2	4	1
88 NL	.252	103	301	30	76	19	4	2	23	2
89 NL	.277	134	473	58	131	18	3	8	40	3
90 NL	.283	128	474	56	134	20	2	11	59	3
91 NL	.320	106	306	41	98	17	2	3	32	2
Life	.285	494	1638	194	467	78	11	26	158	11
3 AVE	.290	123	418	52	121	18	2	7	44	3

CURRENT PLAYERS

JOSE URIBE

Position: Shortstop
Team: San Francisco Giants
Born: Jan. 21, 1960 San Cristobal, Dominican Republic
Height: 5'10" **Weight:** 165 lbs.
Bats: both **Throws:** right
Acquired: Traded from Cardinals with Dave LaPoint, David Green, and Gary Rajsich for Jack Clark, 2/85

Player Summary	
Fantasy Value	$1 to $2
Card Value	3¢ to 5¢
Will	play good defense
Can't	hit enough
Expect	job challenge
Don't Expect	hits from left side

Uribe's glove keeps him in the major leagues but his bat sometimes adds another dimension. Though his 1991 season was disappointing, he had shown some ability at the plate in seven previous seasons. He had career bests with 22 swipes in 1986 and a .291 average in '87. He also led NL shortstops in double-plays in 1989. A switch-hitter who's better from the right side, Uribe usually makes decent contact and manages to inflate his on-base percentage by drawing a few walks. His forte is fielding, however. Good hands, good positioning, and a strong arm compensate for his somewhat limited range. Uribe has decent speed. He's in danger of losing his job to a better batter. His terrifying hitting should frighten most fantasy managers for more than $1 and scare investors from his 1992 commons.

Major League Batting Register

	BA	G	AB	R	H	2B	3B	HR	RBI	SB
84 NL	.211	8	19	4	4	0	0	0	3	1
85 NL	.237	147	476	46	113	20	4	3	26	8
86 NL	.223	157	453	46	101	15	1	3	43	22
87 NL	.291	95	309	44	90	16	5	5	30	12
88 NL	.252	141	493	47	124	10	7	3	35	14
89 NL	.221	151	453	34	100	12	6	1	30	6
90 NL	.248	138	415	35	103	8	6	1	24	5
91 NL	.221	90	231	23	51	8	4	1	12	3
Life	.241	927	2849	279	686	89	33	17	203	71
3 AVE	.231	126	366	31	85	9	5	1	22	5

DAVID VALLE

Position: Catcher
Team: Seattle Mariners
Born: Oct. 30, 1960 Bayside, NY
Height: 6'2" **Weight:** 200 lbs.
Bats: right **Throws:** right
Acquired: Second-round pick in 6/78 free-agent draft

Player Summary	
Fantasy Value	$1 to $3
Card Value	3¢ to 5¢
Will	play strong defense
Can't	avoid disabled list
Expect	better batting average
Don't Expect	very costly suds

Though he compiled a .236 average in seven seasons before 1991, Valle was unprepared for the nightmare that followed. His average hovered so low at times that a Seattle bar continually changed its beer price to match Valle's average of the day. As a result, patrons encouraged him to perform poorly. He didn't listen, surging in the second half to send the price of beer to almost $2 a glass. Valle is a selective hitter who knows the strike zone and walks almost as often as he strikes out. He can't pad his average with infield hits because his speed is negligible. Valle keeps his varsity job because of his defensive skills. He owns a cannon arm, handles pitchers well, and always posts a fine fielding percentage. His paltry batting average counteracts his slight power, making him a $2 catcher. His 1992 commons are more futile.

Major League Batting Register

	BA	G	AB	R	H	2B	3B	HR	RBI	SB
84 AL	.296	13	27	4	8	1	0	1	4	0
85 AL	.157	31	70	2	11	1	0	0	4	0
86 AL	.340	22	53	10	18	3	0	5	15	0
87 AL	.256	95	324	40	83	16	3	12	53	2
88 AL	.231	93	290	29	67	15	2	10	50	0
89 AL	.237	94	316	32	75	10	3	7	34	0
90 AL	.214	107	308	37	66	15	0	7	33	1
91 AL	.194	132	324	38	63	8	1	8	32	0
Life	.228	587	1712	192	391	69	9	50	225	3
3 AVE	.215	111	316	36	68	11	1	7	33	0

CURRENT PLAYERS

ANDY VAN SLYKE

Position: Outfield
Team: Pittsburgh Pirates
Born: Dec. 21, 1960 Utica, NY
Height: 6'2" **Weight:** 192 lbs.
Bats: left **Throws:** right
Acquired: Traded from Cardinals with Mike Dunne and Mike LaValliere for Tony Pena, 4/87

Player Summary	
Fantasy Value	$20 to $25
Card Value	5¢ to 7¢
Will	hit for average and power
Can't	steal as much
Expect	rocket throws
Don't Expect	less than Gold Glove

Van Slyke was the anchor of the NL's best defensive outfield for the last several seasons. He won four straight Gold Gloves as center fielder for the Pirates, who usually flanked him with Bobby Bonds in left and Bobby Bonilla in right. Van Slyke can also hit; he finished 1988 with 25 homers, 100 RBI, and a .288 average. A .270 lifetime hitter, Van Slyke was once regarded as a platoon player who could not hit lefthanders. He's erased that label with a respectable performance against southpaws. In addition, he maintains a high on-base percentage because of willingness to wait for walks. Van Slyke's speed translates into excellent range in center, where he also charges, dives, leaps, and throws better than other center fielders. His fantasy value remains at $25 or so, while his nickel-priced 1992 cards are not bad buys.

Major League Batting Register

	BA	G	AB	R	H	2B	3B	HR	RBI	SB
83 NL	.262	101	309	51	81	15	5	8	38	21
84 NL	.244	137	361	45	88	16	4	7	50	28
85 NL	.259	146	424	61	110	25	6	13	55	34
86 NL	.270	137	418	48	113	23	7	13	61	21
87 NL	.293	157	564	93	165	36	11	21	82	34
88 NL	.288	154	587	101	169	23	15	25	100	30
89 NL	.237	130	476	64	113	18	9	9	53	16
90 NL	.284	136	493	67	140	26	6	17	77	14
91 NL	.265	138	491	87	130	24	7	17	83	10
Life	.269	1236	4123	617	1109	206	70	130	599	208
3 AVE	.262	135	487	73	128	23	7	14	71	13

GARY VARSHO

Position: First base; outfield
Team: Pittsburgh Pirates
Born: June 20, 1961 Marshfield, WI
Height: 5'11" **Weight:** 190 lbs.
Bats: left **Throws:** right
Acquired: Traded from Cubs for Steve Carter, 3/91

Player Summary	
Fantasy Value	$1 to $3
Card Value	3¢ to 5¢
Will	poke key pinch-hits
Can't	play every day
Expect	use against righties
Don't Expect	high average

Varsho was a valuable sub for the NL East Champion Pirates in 1991. A lefthanded batter who served as a platoon first baseman, reserve outfielder, and pinch-hitter, he enjoyed his finest major league season. Though he saw only limited action, Varsho stole more than a half-dozen bases and collected his first big league homers, including two in one game. His lack of at bats corks his fantasy value at $3. His 1992 commons are forgettable. He often hits outside pitches to the opposite field. Though he strikes out twice as often as he walks, Varsho can coax walks in key situations. In 1991, he had a .417 slugging percentage and a .344 on-base average. Varsho had a .302 average for Triple-A Iowa in 1987. He can also make any necessary throws from the outfield, where his speed yields adequate range. He started his pro career as a second baseman. Varsho is a career benchwarmer but his productive lefthanded bat will be a welcome addition to a big league club.

Major League Batting Register

	BA	G	AB	R	H	2B	3B	HR	RBI	SB
88 NL	.274	46	73	6	20	3	0	0	5	6
89 NL	.184	61	87	10	16	4	2	0	6	3
90 NL	.250	46	48	10	12	4	0	0	1	2
91 NL	.273	99	187	23	51	11	2	4	23	9
Life	.251	252	395	49	99	22	4	4	35	19

CURRENT PLAYERS

GREG VAUGHN

Position: Outfield
Team: Milwaukee Brewers
Born: July 3, 1965 Sacramento, CA
Height: 6′ **Weight:** 195 lbs.
Bats: right **Throws:** right
Acquired: Fourth-round pick in 6/86 free-agent draft

Player Summary	
Fantasy Value	$16 to $22
Card Value	5¢ to 10¢
Will	produce runs
Can't	avoid Ks
Expect	better defense
Don't Expect	high average

Vaughn not only survived the sophomore jinx in 1991 but helped engineer Milwaukee's last-season revival with several key contributions, including the first four-hit game of his career on August 25. The owner of a short, compact swing, he left no doubt about his power with a 17-homer season as a 1990 rookie. His defense in left field, though, left a bad impression. Long sessions with coach Duffy Dyer helped. Vaughn made only two miscues in his first 131 games of 1991. Dyer couldn't do much about Vaughn's weak arm, however. Milwaukee can't do without his 30-homer power, a level he might have reached last year if not for a tender knee. Vaughn still wound up leading the Brewers in home runs, RBI, and strikeouts. He whiffs twice as often as he walks but the ball goes a long way when he connects. His growth as a ballplayer is encouraging to fantasy managers, who should bid up to $22 for him. His nickel-priced 1992 cards are uninspiring investments.

Major League Batting Register

	BA	G	AB	R	H	2B	3B	HR	RBI	SB
89 AL	.265	38	113	18	30	3	0	5	23	4
90 AL	.220	120	382	51	84	26	2	17	61	7
91 AL	.244	145	542	81	132	24	5	27	98	2
Life	.237	303	1037	150	246	53	7	49	182	13
2 AVE	.234	133	462	66	108	25	4	22	80	5

MO VAUGHN

Position: First base
Team: Boston Red Sox
Born: Dec. 15, 1967 Norwalk, CT
Height: 6′1″ **Weight:** 225 lbs.
Bats: left **Throws:** right
Acquired: First-round pick in 6/89 free-agent draft

Player Summary	
Fantasy Value	$10 to $16
Card Value	10¢ to 15¢
Will	hit for power
Can't	master lefties
Expect	fine glovework
Don't Expect	frequent steals

After leading the Triple-A International League in walks (60) and placing second in both homers (14) and RBI (50) by mid-1991, Vaughn made his big league debut June 27 against the Yankees. Starting at first base, he walked in his first at bat, then collected his first big league hit with a ninth-inning single. Initially used in platoon with Carlos Quintana, Vaughn figures to win full-time status soon because of his immense power potential. He hit two 430-foot homers during his first week in the majors, six RBI in his first five games, and three homers in his first eight. Vaughn holds Seton Hall career records with 57 homers and 218 RBI. He is prepared to explode, but must win an everyday position to be worth more than $16 for fantasy teams. His 1992 cards, at a dime or more, are hot buys. He is surprisingly agile on defense, where some scouts compare him to former Gold Glove winner George Scott. Since he's already been compared to Dave Parker at the plate, the combination isn't bad.

Major League Batting Register

	BA	G	AB	R	H	2B	3B	HR	RBI	SB
91 AL	.260	74	219	21	57	12	0	4	32	2
Life	.260	74	219	21	57	12	0	4	32	2

CURRENT PLAYERS

ROBIN VENTURA

Position: Third base
Team: Chicago White Sox
Born: July 14, 1967 Santa Maria, CA
Height: 6'1" **Weight:** 185 lbs.
Bats: left **Throws:** right
Acquired: First-round pick in 6/88 free-agent draft

Player Summary	
Fantasy Value	$24 to $30
Card Value	5¢ to 10¢
Will	show great glove
Can't	wait to hit
Expect	All-Star bid
Don't Expect	more 0-for-41 slumps

Ventura has shown in two major league seasons that his 58-game hitting streak for Oklahoma State was no fluke. Winner of the 1988 Golden Spikes Award as the top collegian, he hit 26 homers in his last collegiate season. He moved into the second slot in the White Sox batting order last June 5 and immediately took to the change. He benefits from positioning between Tim Raines and Frank Thomas. When Raines is on base, Ventura sees more fastballs. That helps him get on base ahead of Thomas. With 12 homers in July, Ventura fell one short of Dick Allen's club record. After hitting five homers in 150 games as a rookie, he has recaptured his collegiate home run stroke. He had a .442 slugging percentage and a .367 on-base average in '91. He's a fine performer in the field, where he is regarded as one of the AL's top third basemen. He is the most promising fantasy third sacker in the AL. Bid up to $30 for him. His nickel-priced 1992 cards are excellent investments.

Major League Batting Register

	BA	G	AB	R	H	2B	3B	HR	RBI	SB
89 AL	.178	16	45	5	8	3	0	0	7	0
90 AL	.249	150	493	48	123	17	1	5	54	1
91 AL	.284	157	606	92	172	25	1	23	100	2
Life	.265	323	1144	145	303	45	2	28	161	3
2 AVE	.268	154	550	70	148	21	1	14	77	2

FRANK VIOLA

Position: Pitcher
Team: Boston Red Sox
Born: April 19, 1960 Hempstead, NY
Height: 6'4" **Weight:** 209 lbs.
Bats: left **Throws:** left
Acquired: Signed as a free agent, 12/91

Player Summary	
Fantasy Value	$10 to $15
Card Value	5¢ to 10¢
Will	resurrect changeup
Can't	return to '88
Expect	strong comeback
Don't Expect	so many homers

During 1991 spring training, Viola contemplated undergoing surgery to repair chips in his pitching elbow. By season's end, he was probably sorry he decided against it. Viola staggered through one of his worst years, losing seven straight for the first time in his career. Viola's famous changeup, voted the NL's best in a *Baseball America* poll of managers, simply wasn't effective over the second half. That made his fastball, curve, and slider seem more ordinary and made him vulnerable to getting hit. After the season, he signed as a free agent with Boston. Enjoy the lower draft bids while they last, and try to get him for under $15. His nickel-priced 1992 cards could be good short-term investments.

Major League Pitching Register

	W	L	ERA	G	CG	IP	H	ER	BB	SO
82 AL	4	10	5.21	22	3	126.0	152	73	38	84
83 AL	7	15	5.49	35	4	210.0	242	128	92	127
84 AL	18	12	3.21	35	10	257.2	225	92	73	149
85 AL	18	14	4.09	36	9	250.2	262	114	68	135
86 AL	16	13	4.51	37	7	245.2	257	123	83	191
87 AL	17	10	2.90	36	7	251.2	230	81	66	197
88 AL	24	7	2.64	35	7	255.1	236	75	54	193
89 AL	8	12	3.79	24	7	175.2	171	74	47	138
89 NL	5	5	3.38	12	2	85.1	75	32	27	73
90 NL	20	12	2.67	35	7	249.2	227	74	60	182
91 NL	13	15	3.97	35	3	231.1	259	102	54	132
Life	150	125	3.72	342	66	2339.0	2336	968	662	1601
3 AVE	15	15	3.42	35	6	247.2	244	94	63	175

CURRENT PLAYERS

JOSE VIZCAINO

Position: Shortstop; second base
Team: Chicago Cubs
Born: March 26, 1968 Palenque, Dominican Republic
Height: 6'1" **Weight:** 150 lbs.
Bats: both **Throws:** right
Acquired: Traded from Dodgers for Greg Smith, 12/90

Player Summary	
Fantasy Value	$1 to $3
Card Value	3¢ to 5¢
Will	make contact
Can't	wait out walks
Expect	steady defense
Don't Expect	Dunston's arm

A year before the Cubs thought they might lose Shawon Dunston to free agency, they acquired a potential replacement in Vizcaino. At the time of the deal, he was a second baseman, after moving there to clear shortstop for fellow Dodger farmhand Jose Offerman. In his brief career, Vizcaino had led two minor leagues in double-plays and one in total chances, all as a shortstop. A steady, sure-handed fielder with a good arm and good range, he is expected to be a solid major league player. He hit well in limited action during the 1991 season, when he revealed himself to be a free-swinging hitter who rarely walks but makes contact. The switch-hitting Vizcaino has little power but enough speed to steal 15 to 20 bases a year. He was voted best defensive second baseman in the Triple-A Pacific Coast League in 1990. He doesn't have much of a shot of starting this year, making his 1992 cards commons value. His draft value is a low $3.

Major League Batting Register

	BA	G	AB	R	H	2B	3B	HR	RBI	SB
89 NL	.200	7	10	2	2	0	0	0	0	0
90 NL	.275	37	51	3	14	1	1	0	2	1
91 NL	.262	93	145	7	38	5	0	0	10	2
Life	.262	137	206	12	54	6	1	0	12	3

OMAR VIZQUEL

Position: Shortstop
Team: Seattle Mariners
Born: April 24, 1967 Caracas, Venezuela
Height: 5'9" **Weight:** 165 lbs.
Bats: both **Throws:** right
Acquired: Signed as a free agent, 4/84

Player Summary	
Fantasy Value	$2 to $4
Card Value	3¢ to 5¢
Will	make few miscues
Can't	hit for average or power
Expect	potential for 20 swipes
Don't Expect	skill against righties

Vizquel is a .230 hitter with little power. His saving graces as a hitter are an uncanny ability to make contact and a willingness to wait for walks. Vizquel actually walks more than he strikes out. A natural righthanded hitter, he's still learning to hit from the left side. He had a .293 slugging percentage and a .302 on-base average in '91. Because he can run, Vizquel would help his offense immensely by occasionally dropping bunts for hits. He doesn't run much but could steal 15 to 20 bases if he did. He hit .233 with 18 runs, no homers, 13 RBI, and four stolen bases in 150 at bats at Triple-A Calgary in 1990. In fact, Vizquel doesn't excel anywhere but in the field. He's a fine defensive player with good hands and a strong arm. He made only 13 errors in '91, a low figure for a shortstop. Whether Seattle can afford to carry his weak bat will be a question to be answered every year. Don't bid more than $4 on him. His 1992 commons don't merit investment.

Major League Batting Register

	BA	G	AB	R	H	2B	3B	HR	RBI	SB
89 AL	.220	143	387	45	85	7	3	1	20	1
90 AL	.247	81	255	19	63	3	2	2	18	4
91 AL	.230	142	426	42	98	16	4	1	41	7
Life	.230	366	1068	106	246	26	9	4	79	12
3 AVE	.230	122	356	35	82	9	3	1	26	4

CURRENT PLAYERS

BOB WALK

Position: Pitcher
Team: Pittsburgh Pirates
Born: Nov. 26, 1955 Van Nuys, CA
Height: 6'4" **Weight:** 217 lbs.
Bats: right **Throws:** right
Acquired: Signed as a free agent, 4/84

Player Summary
Fantasy Value	$4 to $8
Card Value	3¢ to 5¢
Will	shine in clutch spots
Can't	pitch many innings
Expect	good control
Don't Expect	much bullpen duty

Walk was sorely missed when he missed a major chunk of the 1991 season with a strained right hamstring. His replacements failed to fill the void in his absence. He is a control pitcher who throws a fastball, curveball, slider, and changeup. Walk allows almost a hit per inning, gives up his share of home run balls, but fans twice as many as he walks. He's at his best in clutch situations, holding opponents to a low average with runners on base. While he's on the mound, Walk is a good fielder with a fine pickoff move. He also bunts and hits better than most of his opponents. He tires easily, however, and seldom lasts late into games. He is a stable $6 fantasy hurler. Don't procure his 1992 commons.

Major League Pitching Register
	W	L	ERA	G	CG	IP	H	ER	BB	SO
80 NL	11	7	4.57	27	2	151.2	163	77	71	94
81 NL	1	4	4.57	12	0	43.1	41	22	23	16
82 NL	11	9	4.87	32	3	164.1	179	89	59	84
83 NL	0	0	7.36	1	0	3.2	7	3	2	4
84 NL	1	1	2.61	2	0	10.1	8	3	4	10
85 NL	2	3	3.68	9	1	58.2	60	24	18	40
86 NL	7	8	3.75	44	1	141.2	129	59	64	78
87 NL	8	2	3.31	39	1	117.0	107	43	51	78
88 NL	12	10	2.71	32	1	212.2	183	64	65	81
89 NL	13	10	4.41	33	2	196.0	208	96	65	83
90 NL	7	5	3.75	26	1	129.2	136	54	36	73
91 NL	9	2	3.60	25	0	115.0	104	46	35	67
Life	82	61	3.88	282	12	1344.0	1325	580	493	708
3 AVE	10	6	4.00	28	1	147.1	149	65	45	74

CHICO WALKER

Position: Third base; outfield
Team: Chicago Cubs
Born: Nov. 25, 1957 Jackson, MS
Height: 5'9" **Weight:** 170 lbs.
Bats: both **Throws:** right
Acquired: Signed as a free agent, 4/90

Player Summary
Fantasy Value	$4 to $6
Card Value	5¢ to 7¢
Will	return to utility role
Can't	always show power
Expect	pinch-hits and steals
Don't Expect	regular play at third

The failure of rookie third baseman Gary Scott gave Walker considerable playing time with the 1991 Cubs. He rarely gets to play second base, his best position, but Walker also performed well as an outfielder and pinch-hitter. He had 12 hits, including a homer, in his first 23 at bats (.522) as a pinch-hitter. A pro since 1976, Walker only had a .218 average and two homers in 161 big league games (with three clubs) before 1991. He had demonstrated his speed, power, and versatility in the minors. As recently as 1986 at Triple-A Iowa, Walker had 16 homers. He also had 158 base hits and 67 steals that year, which tied him for the lead in the American Association that year. His stolen bases help boost his fantasy value to the $5 level. Don't stock up on his nickel-priced 1992 cards unless he wins a starting spot in the bigs.

Major League Batting Register
	BA	G	AB	R	H	2B	3B	HR	RBI	SB
80 AL	.211	19	57	3	12	0	0	1	5	3
81 AL	.353	6	17	3	6	0	0	0	2	0
83 AL	.400	4	5	2	2	0	2	0	1	0
84 AL	.000	3	2	0	0	0	0	0	1	0
85 NL	.083	21	12	3	1	0	0	0	0	1
86 NL	.277	28	101	21	28	3	2	1	7	15
87 NL	.200	47	105	15	21	4	0	0	7	11
88 AL	.154	33	78	8	12	1	0	0	2	2
91 NL	.257	124	374	51	96	10	1	6	34	13
Life	.237	285	751	106	178	18	5	8	59	45

CURRENT PLAYERS

LARRY WALKER

Position: Outfield; first base
Team: Montreal Expos
Born: Dec. 1, 1966 Maple Ridge, British Columbia, Canada
Height: 6'2" **Weight:** 205 lbs.
Bats: left **Throws:** right
Acquired: Signed as a free agent, 11/84

Player Summary	
Fantasy Value	$12 to $18
Card Value	5¢ to 7¢
Will	achieve 20-20 status
Can't	avoid streaks
Expect	NL's best defense in right
Don't Expect	great power at home

Many baseball insiders believe Walker is the NL's best defensive right fielder. Andre Dawson fans may argue, but Walker has an outstanding arm. On April 26, he tied a major league record with two outfield assists in one inning. As a 1990 rookie, he had ranked second to Bobby Bonilla in assists by an NL outfielder. Walker has enough speed to get a great jump on the ball, giving him excellent range. He also played some first base when Andres Galarraga was sidelined in 1991. Walker's strong lefthanded bat makes major contributions to the offense. After opening his stance in '91, he became more comfortable with his swing, though Montreal hurts his stats. He collected 18 RBI in 21 games through August 12 and won NL Player of the Month honors with a .376 average, four homers, and 12 RBI. With power and speed, he can help in four categories. His fantasy value is in the $15 range. His nickel-priced 1992 cards will rise in value if he begins turning in several 155-game seasons.

Major League Batting Register

	BA	G	AB	R	H	2B	3B	HR	RBI	SB
89 NL	.170	20	47	4	8	0	0	0	4	1
90 NL	.241	133	419	59	101	18	3	19	51	21
91 NL	.290	137	487	59	141	30	2	16	64	14
Life	.262	290	953	122	250	48	5	35	119	36
2 AVE	.267	135	453	59	121	24	3	18	58	18

TIM WALLACH

Position: Third base
Team: Montreal Expos
Born: Sept. 14, 1957 Huntington Park, CA
Height: 6'3" **Weight:** 200 lbs.
Bats: right **Throws:** right
Acquired: First-round pick in 6/79 free-agent draft

Player Summary	
Fantasy Value	$12 to $17
Card Value	3¢ to 5¢
Will	play great defense
Can't	duplicate '87
Expect	declining skills
Don't Expect	more cleanup duty

Wallach hit a home run in his first plate appearance as a pro and also homered in his first official big league at bat in '80. He has topped 20 homers four times. His best season was 1987, when he had a league-high 42 doubles. He hit three home runs in a game during the 1987 season. Though that was his only 100-RBI campaign, Wallach has contributed with his glove as well as his bat. He has won the Gold Glove Award three times. Montreal's team captain and three-time Player of the Year, Wallach is a durable performer who often plays through pain. Fantasy managers are often tempted to pay more than $17 because of Wallach's periodic power bursts, but don't you. His 1992 commons just miss being investments by that much.

Major League Batting Register

	BA	G	AB	R	H	2B	3B	HR	RBI	SB
80 NL	.182	5	11	1	2	0	0	1	2	0
81 NL	.236	71	212	19	50	9	1	4	13	0
82 NL	.268	158	596	89	160	31	3	28	97	6
83 NL	.269	156	581	54	156	33	3	19	70	0
84 NL	.246	160	582	55	143	25	4	18	72	3
85 NL	.260	155	569	70	148	36	3	22	81	9
86 NL	.233	134	480	50	112	22	1	18	71	8
87 NL	.298	153	593	89	177	42	4	26	123	9
88 NL	.257	159	592	52	152	32	5	12	69	2
89 NL	.277	154	573	76	159	42	0	13	77	3
90 NL	.296	161	626	69	185	37	5	21	98	6
91 NL	.225	151	577	60	130	22	1	13	73	2
Life	.263	1617	5992	684	1574	331	30	195	846	48
3 AVE	.267	155	592	68	158	34	2	16	83	4

CURRENT PLAYERS

JEROME WALTON

Position: Outfield
Team: Chicago Cubs
Born: July 8, 1965 Newman, GA
Height: 6'1" **Weight:** 175 lbs.
Bats: right **Throws:** right
Acquired: Second-round pick in 6/86 free-agent draft

Player Summary
Fantasy Value	$3 to $6
Card Value	3¢ to 5¢
Will	provide good defense
Can't	wait for walks
Expect	average to rise
Don't Expect	extra-base hits

Two years after winning NL Rookie of the Year honors, Walton became the forgotten man of the Cubs. He lost some 70 points off his freshman average, didn't try for many steals, and found himself the third-string center fielder behind Doug Dascenzo and Ced Landrum. Walton's best assets are speed and defense. Because he runs well, he has good range and plays a strong center field, with his weak arm the primary handicap. He's certainly capable of stealing two-dozen bases, his rookie total, again. Reaching base more often would help, however. After showing good selectivity in his first two seasons, he began chasing bad balls in '91, giving him a poor 3-1 ratio of strikeouts to walks. Walton can fatten his average with bunts and leg hits. He'll have to show more patience. He can't help your fantasy team while he is sitting on the pines. His value has dropped to a $6 bid, max. His 1992 commons will stay in the box as long as he is on the bench.

Major League Batting Register

	BA	G	AB	R	H	2B	3B	HR	RBI	SB
89 NL	.293	116	475	64	139	23	3	5	46	24
90 NL	.263	101	392	63	103	16	2	2	21	14
91 NL	.219	123	270	42	59	13	1	5	17	7
Life	.265	340	1137	169	301	52	6	12	84	45
3 AVE	.265	113	379	56	100	17	2	4	28	15

DUANE WARD

Position: Pitcher
Team: Toronto Blue Jays
Born: May 28, 1964 Parkview, NM
Height: 6'4" **Weight:** 205 lbs.
Bats: right **Throws:** right
Acquired: Traded from Braves for Doyle Alexander, 7/86

Player Summary
Fantasy Value	$20 to $24
Card Value	3¢ to 5¢
Will	blaze heater
Can't	stay sharp without work
Expect	more Ks than frames
Don't Expect	control trouble

Ward has a resilient right arm. The only reliever to throw more than 100 innings in each of the last three seasons, he has learned to get ahead of the hitters by throwing his heater for strikes. Thus, his strikeouts went up while his walks went down. He served as Toronto's top closer when Tom Henke was idled for parts of 1991, and Ward rarely lets a save opportunity escape. He yields considerably less than a hit per inning, fans four times more men than he walks, and is one of very few pitchers who has more strikeouts than innings pitched. A fastball-and-slider pitcher who started for five years before moving to the pen, Ward throws such a heavy ball that it seldom leaves the park. He's fully capable of becoming the No. 1 closer. He helped some fantasy teams win the saves category in '91. He is a $20-plus reliever in this draft. Don't accumulate his 1992 commons, however.

Major League Pitching Register

	W	L	ERA	G	S	IP	H	ER	BB	SO
86 NL	0	1	7.31	10	0	16.0	22	13	8	8
86 AL	0	1	13.50	2	0	2.0	3	3	4	1
87 AL	1	0	6.94	12	0	11.2	14	9	12	10
88 AL	9	3	3.30	64	15	111.2	101	41	60	91
89 AL	4	10	3.77	66	15	114.2	94	48	58	122
90 AL	2	8	3.45	73	11	127.2	101	49	42	112
91 AL	7	6	2.77	81	23	107.1	80	33	33	132
Life	23	29	3.59	308	64	491.0	415	196	217	476
3 AVE	4	8	3.35	73	16	116.2	92	43	44	122

CURRENT PLAYERS

BILL WEGMAN

Position: Pitcher
Team: Milwaukee Brewers
Born: Dec. 19, 1962 Cincinnati, OH
Height: 6'5" **Weight:** 220 lbs.
Bats: right **Throws:** right
Acquired: Fifth-round pick in 6/81 free-agent draft

Player Summary	
Fantasy Value	$9 to $12
Card Value	3¢ to 5¢
Will	throw three pitches
Can't	worry about elbow
Expect	15 wins
Don't Expect	over a hit a frame

After his 1990 season ended in June with elbow surgery, Wegman had a lot to prove in 1991. He came off the disabled list April 20 and wasted little time. With 10 strikeouts in eight innings against Oakland September 4, Wegman became the first Brewer since 1986 to win five straight starts. His ERA was the best among Brewer starters. Wegman has good command of his fastball, curve, and change-up, though he doesn't throw very hard. He yields less than a hit per inning and strikes more than twice the number he walks. The inept Milwaukee defense hurt him last year but he helped himself with good glovework and a fine pickoff move. Wegman is a former infielder who knows how to handle himself in the field. His 1991 season reminds fantasy managers why they should pay attention to $1 pitchers at the draft. He will go as high as $12 in this year's auction. Don't worry about his 1992 commons.

Major League Pitching Register

	W	L	ERA	G	CG	IP	H	ER	BB	SO
85 AL	2	0	3.57	3	0	17.2	17	7	3	6
86 AL	5	12	5.13	35	2	198.1	217	113	43	82
87 AL	12	11	4.24	34	7	225.0	229	106	53	102
88 AL	13	13	4.12	32	4	199.0	207	91	50	84
89 AL	2	6	6.71	11	0	51.0	69	38	21	27
90 AL	2	2	4.85	8	1	29.2	37	16	6	20
91 AL	15	7	2.84	28	7	193.1	176	61	40	89
Life	51	51	4.25	151	21	914.0	952	432	216	410

JOHN WEHNER

Position: Third base
Team: Pittsburgh Pirates
Born: June 29, 1967 Pittsburgh, PA
Height: 6'3" **Weight:** 204 lbs.
Bats: right **Throws:** right
Acquired: Seventh-round pick in 6/88 free-agent draft

Player Summary	
Fantasy Value	$3 to $6
Card Value	10¢ to 15¢
Will	thrill hometown fans
Can't	show consistent power
Expect	sterling defense
Don't Expect	another Don Hoak

Wehner is the classic example of the hometown boy who made good. When incumbent Pittsburgh third baseman Jeff King was sidelined by injury, the club first tried Bobby Bonilla, then Joe Redfield. That was before Wehner came up and gave the Pirates the best defense they had seen at the position in years. The Indiana University product even reminded some observers of the late Don Hoak. Though he does not produce third base power, Wehner is a capable hitter. He had a .304 average at Triple-A Buffalo when called to the majors July 17. He had only one homer in 112 at bats, but had more walks than Ks. He hit .288 at Double-A Harrisburg in 1990, with four homers, 62 RBI, 72 runs scored, and 24 stolen bases. He was sidelined by sciatica, a painful nerve condition. Wehner underwent September surgery to repair a ruptured disc in his lower back, the same injury that had kayoed King. With Wehner's injury and the challenge of Steve Buechele, Wehner's value stops at $6. His 1992 cards are average investments at a dime.

Major League Batting Register

	BA	G	AB	R	H	2B	3B	HR	RBI	SB
91 NL	.340	37	106	15	36	7	0	0	7	3
Life	.340	37	106	15	36	7	0	0	7	3

CURRENT PLAYERS

WALT WEISS

Position: Shortstop
Team: Oakland Athletics
Born: Nov. 28, 1963 Tuxedo, NY
Height: 6' **Weight:** 175 lbs.
Bats: both **Throws:** right
Acquired: First-round pick in 6/85 free-agent draft

Player Summary	
Fantasy Value	$2 to $4
Card Value	3¢ to 5¢
Will	play fine defense
Can't	post high average
Expect	bunts and infield hits
Don't Expect	injury-free season

Weiss has been a brilliant but brittle performer since breaking into the majors in 1988. The AL Rookie of the Year that season, he has had a string of injuries since, including a ruptured tendon in his ankle that disabled him last June 6. Weiss, out earlier in the 1991 campaign with a hamstring pull, missed the rest of the year while recuperating from ankle surgery. Some scouts suggest his range might have been reduced by the injury. The switch-hitting shortstop doesn't share their skepticism, because he's rebounded from three knee operations, a severe hamstring pull, and a pulled rib cage muscle. When healthy, Weiss is a contact hitter who walks as often as he strikes out, hits to the opposite field, and sometimes bunts for hits. He has lost most of his fantasy value, though, and is a $3 middle infielder now. He has speed, range, consistency, a good glove, and an exceptional arm. His 1992 cards are and will remain commons.

Major League Batting Register

	BA	G	AB	R	H	2B	3B	HR	RBI	SB
87 AL	.462	16	26	3	12	4	0	0	1	1
88 AL	.250	147	452	44	113	17	3	3	39	4
89 AL	.233	84	236	30	55	11	0	3	21	6
90 AL	.265	138	445	50	118	17	1	2	35	9
91 AL	.226	40	133	15	30	6	1	0	13	6
Life	.254	425	1292	142	328	55	5	8	109	26
2 AVE	.254	111	341	40	87	14	1	3	28	8

BOB WELCH

Position: Pitcher
Team: Oakland Athletics
Born: Nov. 3, 1956 Detroit, MI
Height: 6'3" **Weight:** 195 lbs.
Bats: right **Throws:** right
Acquired: Traded from Dodgers with Matt Young for Alfredo Griffin and Jay Howell, 12/87

Player Summary	
Fantasy Value	$13 to $20
Card Value	3¢ to 5¢
Will	shake off jinx
Can't	avoid walks
Expect	at least 15 wins
Don't Expect	another '90

One year after winning the 1990 Cy Young Award, Welch fell upon hard times. While splitting 25 decisions, he threw more than two-dozen home run balls, issued an atypical number of walks, and suffered a sharp decline in strikeouts. He succeeded in '90 by using his forkball to set up his fastball, curve, and cut fastball, and he spent all of 1991 trying to resurrect that formula. Nothing worked, resulting in the worst earned run average of his career. He is unlikely to duplicate his 1990 career year but is virtually certain to bounce back from his first bad year since 1986. He should do better in 1992, justifying a $15 bid. Don't tender an offer on his 1992 commons.

Major League Pitching Register

	W	L	ERA	G	CG	IP	H	ER	BB	SO
78 NL	7	4	2.02	23	4	111.1	92	25	26	66
79 NL	5	6	3.98	25	1	81.1	82	36	32	64
80 NL	14	9	3.29	32	3	213.2	190	78	79	141
81 NL	9	5	3.44	23	2	141.1	141	54	41	88
82 NL	16	11	3.36	36	9	235.2	199	88	81	176
83 NL	15	12	2.65	31	4	204.0	164	60	72	156
84 NL	13	13	3.78	31	3	178.2	191	75	58	126
85 NL	14	4	2.31	23	8	167.1	141	43	35	96
86 NL	7	13	3.28	33	7	235.2	227	86	55	183
87 NL	15	9	3.22	35	6	251.2	204	90	86	196
88 AL	17	9	3.64	36	4	244.2	237	99	81	158
89 AL	17	8	3.00	33	1	209.2	191	70	78	137
90 AL	27	6	2.95	35	2	238.0	214	78	77	127
91 AL	12	13	4.58	35	2	220.0	220	112	91	101
Life	188	122	3.27	431	61	2733.0	2493	994	892	1815
3 AVE	19	9	3.50	34	3	222.1	208	87	82	122

CURRENT PLAYERS

DAVID WELLS

Position: Pitcher
Team: Toronto Blue Jays
Born: May 20, 1963 Torrance, CA
Height: 6'4" **Weight:** 225 lbs.
Bats: left **Throws:** left
Acquired: Second-round pick in 6/82 free-agent draft

Player Summary	
Fantasy Value	$10 to $12
Card Value	3¢ to 5¢
Will	win 12 as starter
Can't	avoid gophers
Expect	good control
Don't Expect	over hit a frame

Although he had his best season as a Toronto starter in 1991, Wells was dogged all year by the gopher ball. He reached the 15-win plateau for the first time but would have won more had he not led the Blue Jays in allowing enemy home runs, with 24. The problem became so severe in late summer that he was bounced from the starting rotation. With good command of his fastball, curve, and changeup, Wells whiffs twice as many as he walks and allows less than a hit per inning. He's especially adept at pitching his way out of crucial situations. His fielding is passable, which is more than scouts say about his pickoff move. The hard-throwing Wells, who broke in with the 1987 Blue Jays as an extra left arm in the bullpen, could reclaim his rotation berth if he stops being so generous to rivals. Count on him as a $10 fantasy hurler. His 1992 cards should remain commons, however.

Major League Pitching Register

	W	L	ERA	G	CG	IP	H	ER	BB	SO
87 AL	4	3	3.99	18	0	29.1	37	13	12	32
88 AL	3	5	4.62	41	0	64.1	65	33	31	56
89 AL	7	4	2.40	54	0	86.1	66	23	28	78
90 AL	11	6	3.14	43	0	189.0	165	66	45	115
91 AL	15	10	3.72	40	2	198.1	188	82	49	106
Life	40	28	3.44	196	2	567.1	521	217	165	387
3 AVE	11	7	3.25	46	1	158.1	140	57	41	100

DAVID WEST

Position: Pitcher
Team: Minnesota Twins
Born: Sept. 1, 1964 Memphis, TN
Height: 6'6" **Weight:** 220 lbs.
Bats: left **Throws:** left
Acquired: Traded from Mets with Rick Aguilera, Kevin Tapani, Jack Savage, and Tim Drummond for Loy McBride and Frank Viola, 7/89

Player Summary	
Fantasy Value	$2 to $4
Card Value	3¢ to 5¢
Will	win with health
Can't	control great stuff
Expect	struggle for job
Don't Expect	to meet potential

After missing the first three months of the 1991 season with an elbow problem and an abdominal muscle injury, West made his return felt by yielding two hits in seven innings of a 1-0 win over Toronto July 4. He complements his fastball with a slider and changeup, but he did not maintain the lofty standard he had set. He split eight decisions and threw 13 home run balls in '91. Once the prized prospect of the Mets, West has yet to deliver on his promise. He yields less hits than innings pitched but has battled injuries as well as mechanical problems during his four-year career. Control has also posed problems for West: he led three minor leagues in bases on balls and has never managed a 2-1 ratio of strikeouts to walks. To succeed in the majors, he'll have to have better location. Don't overbid on him at the draft. He is a $3 starter at this point. His 1992 cards will remain commons.

Major League Pitching Register

	W	L	ERA	G	CG	IP	H	ER	BB	SO
88 NL	1	0	3.00	2	0	6.0	6	2	3	3
89 NL	0	2	7.40	11	0	24.1	25	20	14	19
89 AL	3	2	6.41	10	0	39.1	48	28	19	31
90 AL	7	9	5.10	29	2	146.1	142	83	78	92
91 AL	4	4	4.54	15	0	71.1	66	36	28	52
Life	15	17	5.29	67	2	287.1	287	169	142	197
3 AVE	5	6	5.34	22	1	93.1	94	56	46	65

CURRENT PLAYERS

LOU WHITAKER

Position: Second base
Team: Detroit Tigers
Born: May 12, 1957 Brooklyn, NY
Height: 5'11" **Weight:** 180 lbs.
Bats: left **Throws:** right
Acquired: Fifth pick in 6/75 free-agent draft

Player Summary	
Fantasy Value	$18 to $24
Card Value	5¢ to 10¢
Will	have good power
Can't	handle lefties
Expect	strong defense
Don't Expect	many strikeouts

Whitaker has held the second baseman job since 1978, when he began his record 15-year partnership with shortstop Alan Trammell. Whitaker's bat keeps the Tigers from contemplating any changes. Before he was stopped last August 7, he reached base in 50 consecutive games. By season's end, the five-time All-Star had gained 40 points on his 1990 average. An extremely patient contact hitter who walks twice as often as he strikes out, Whitaker struggles against southpaws but hammers righthanders. He has a strong arm and good range, turns the double-play well, and makes few errors. His nickel-priced 1992 cards will have long-term profits. His offense will reward fantasy teams immediately for $20 or so.

Major League Batting Register

	BA	G	AB	R	H	2B	3B	HR	RBI	SB
77 AL	.250	11	32	5	8	1	0	0	2	2
78 AL	.285	139	484	71	138	12	7	3	58	7
79 AL	.286	127	423	75	121	14	8	3	42	20
80 AL	.233	145	477	68	111	19	1	1	45	8
81 AL	.263	109	335	48	88	14	4	5	36	5
82 AL	.286	152	560	76	160	22	8	15	65	11
83 AL	.320	161	643	94	206	40	6	12	72	17
84 AL	.289	143	558	90	161	25	1	13	56	6
85 AL	.279	152	609	102	170	29	8	21	73	6
86 AL	.269	144	584	95	157	26	6	20	73	13
87 AL	.265	149	604	110	160	38	6	16	59	13
88 AL	.275	115	403	54	111	18	2	12	55	2
89 AL	.251	148	509	77	128	21	1	28	85	6
90 AL	.237	132	472	75	112	22	2	18	60	8
91 AL	.279	138	470	94	131	26	2	23	78	4
Life	.274	1965	7163	1134	1962	327	62	190	859	128
3 AVE	.256	139	484	82	124	23	2	23	74	6

DEVON WHITE

Position: Outfield
Team: Toronto Blue Jays
Born: Dec. 29, 1962 Kingston, Jamaica
Height: 6'2" **Weight:** 178 lbs.
Bats: both **Throws:** right
Acquired: Traded from Angels with Willie Fraser and Marcus Moore for Junior Felix, Luis Sojo, and Ken Rivers, 12/90

Player Summary	
Fantasy Value	$25 to $32
Card Value	3¢ to 5¢
Will	exhibit speed
Can't	reduce strikeouts
Expect	Gold Glove defense
Don't Expect	exile to minors

White uses his exceptional speed to reach balls hit into the gaps on either side of his center field position. The three-time Gold Glove winner resurrected his career in '91 after arriving in Toronto. In addition to playing his usual stalwart defense, White began to resemble the player who had 32 steals and 24 homers in 1987. Managers polled by *Baseball America* even named him the AL's fastest baserunner, a designation that upset Rickey Henderson fans. Thriving in Toronto's leadoff slot, White collected 40 doubles, and led AL outfielders in fielding. The rifle-armed center fielder finished with the best batting average of his seven-year career. He has more than doubled his fantasy worth; go over the $25 limit only if you think he will come close to 1991's stats. Don't go over a nickel for each of his 1992 cards.

Major League Batting Register

	BA	G	AB	R	H	2B	3B	HR	RBI	SB
85 AL	.143	21	7	7	1	0	0	0	0	3
86 AL	.235	29	51	8	12	1	1	1	3	6
87 AL	.263	159	639	103	168	33	5	24	87	32
88 AL	.259	122	455	76	118	22	2	11	51	17
89 AL	.245	156	636	86	156	18	13	12	56	44
90 AL	.217	125	443	57	96	17	3	11	44	21
91 AL	.282	156	642	110	181	40	10	17	60	33
Life	.255	768	2873	447	732	131	34	76	301	156
3 AVE	.252	146	574	84	144	25	9	13	53	33

CURRENT PLAYERS

WALLY WHITEHURST

Position: Pitcher
Team: New York Mets
Born: April 11, 1964 Shreveport, LA
Height: 6'3" **Weight:** 185 lbs.
Bats: right **Throws:** right
Acquired: Traded from Athletics with Kevin Tapani and Jack Savage for Jesse Orosco, 12/87

Player Summary	
Fantasy Value	$1 to $3
Card Value	3¢ to 5¢
Will	try to rebound
Can't	avoid hits or homers
Expect	search for role
Don't Expect	better won-lost record

Whitehurst wasn't wildly successful after moving into the Mets' rotation last July 15 following the trade of Ron Darling. At one point, Whitehurst had lost five straight starts. He ended his first full major league season with a losing record and bloated earned run average. A curveball specialist who also throws a fastball and slider, Whitehurst maintained his reputation as a control pitcher in '91. He allowed a dozen gophers, though. Opponents compiled a .274 batting average, a .409 slugging percentage, and a .311 on-base average. Whitehurst never had great minor league numbers but impressed management with his aggressive pitching style. At Triple-A Tidewater in 1989, he was 8-7 with a 3.25 ERA. A pitching economist, Whitehurst averages less pitches per inning than his teammates. He can't hit but is a decent fielder who keeps base-runners close. There are better $2 fantasy risks on which to gamble than this unspectacular hurler. Don't sink any money on his 1992 commons, either.

Major League Pitching Register

	W	L	ERA	G	S	IP	H	ER	BB	SO
89 NL	0	1	4.50	9	0	14.0	17	7	5	9
90 NL	1	0	3.29	38	2	65.2	63	24	9	46
91 NL	7	12	4.18	36	1	133.1	142	62	25	87
Life	8	13	3.93	83	3	213.0	222	93	39	142
2 AVE	4	6	3.89	37	2	99.2	103	43	17	67

MARK WHITEN

Position: Outfield
Team: Cleveland Indians
Born: Nov. 25, 1966 Pensacola, FL
Height: 6'3" **Weight:** 215 lbs.
Bats: both **Throws:** right
Acquired: Traded from Blue Jays with Glenallen Hill and Denis Boucher for Tom Candiotti and Turner Ward, 6/91

Player Summary	
Fantasy Value	$10 to $14
Card Value	5¢ to 10¢
Will	make great throws
Can't	quite realize potential
Expect	occasional power
Don't Expect	another Bo Jackson

After getting limited playing time in Toronto, Whiten began realizing his potential in a Cleveland uniform. Last August 5, the switch-hittin' Whiten hit two homers in a game for the first time. One of them was a 418-footer over the center field wall in Arlington. He also made major contributions on defense. The owner of a stronger, more accurate arm than Cory Snyder's, Whiten recorded seven assists (four of them at home plate) between his June 27 arrival in Cleveland and August 12. Whiten's speed translates into good range on defense and base-stealing potential on offense. Reaching base more would help but he fans twice as often as he walks. He has yet to justify his 1990 selection as *Baseball America's* top International League prospect, but Whiten showed flashes of fine all-around skills in '91. At Syracuse in '90, he hit .290 with 14 homers, 48 RBI, 65 runs, and 14 stolen bases. He was also named the loop's Best Defensive Outfielder. Draft him for $14 or less if you can, and accumulate his 1992 cards quickly for a dime or less.

Major League Batting Register

	BA	G	AB	R	H	2B	3B	HR	RBI	SB
90 AL	.273	33	88	12	24	1	1	2	7	2
91 AL	.243	116	407	46	99	18	7	9	45	4
Life	.248	149	495	58	123	19	8	11	52	6

CURRENT PLAYERS

ED WHITSON

Position: Pitcher
Team: San Diego Padres
Born: May 19, 1955 Johnson City, TN
Height: 6'3" **Weight:** 195 lbs.
Bats: right **Throws:** left
Acquired: Traded from Yankees for Tim Stoddard, 7/86

Player Summary	
Fantasy Value	$3 to $6
Card Value	3¢ to 5¢
Will	win, with OK elbow
Can't	blaze fastball
Expect	good control
Don't Expect	gopher balls

After establishing himself as San Diego's top pitcher in 1990, Whitson suffered bone spurs in his right elbow and had to be placed on the disabled list last July 6. He had arthroscopic surgery nine days later and didn't return until late September. Since Whitson had won 30 games in the two preceding seasons, his loss was a major blow to San Diego's quest for the NL West title. When he's right, he throws a fastball, slider, curve, and changeup with great control and is a master of changing speeds. He should have little difficulty recapturing his old form. Make sure that his elbow is sound before bidding $6 for him. His 1992 commons will not attract hobbyists.

Major League Pitching Register

	W	L	ERA	G	CG	IP	H	ER	BB	SO
77 NL	1	0	3.45	5	0	15.2	11	6	9	10
78 NL	5	6	3.27	43	0	74.1	66	27	37	64
79 NL	7	11	4.10	37	2	158.0	151	72	75	93
80 NL	11	13	3.10	34	6	211.2	222	73	56	90
81 NL	6	9	4.02	22	2	123.0	130	55	47	65
82 AL	4	2	3.26	40	1	107.2	91	39	58	61
83 NL	5	7	4.30	31	2	144.1	143	69	50	81
84 NL	14	8	3.24	31	1	189.0	181	68	42	103
85 AL	10	8	4.88	30	2	158.2	201	86	43	89
86 AL	5	2	7.54	14	0	37.0	54	31	23	27
86 NL	1	7	5.59	17	0	75.2	85	47	37	46
87 NL	10	13	4.73	36	3	205.2	197	108	64	135
88 NL	13	11	3.77	34	3	205.1	202	86	45	118
89 NL	16	11	2.66	33	5	227.0	198	67	48	117
90 NL	14	9	2.60	32	6	228.2	215	66	47	127
91 NL	4	6	5.03	13	2	78.2	93	44	17	40
Life	126	123	3.79	452	35	2240.1	2240	944	698	1266
3 AVE	11	9	2.98	26	4	178.1	169	59	37	95

RICK WILKINS

Position: Catcher
Team: Chicago Cubs
Born: July 4, 1967 Jacksonville, FL
Height: 6'2" **Weight:** 210 lbs.
Bats: left **Throws:** right
Acquired: 23rd-round pick in 6/86 free-agent draft

Player Summary	
Fantasy Value	$2 to $4
Card Value	10¢ to 15¢
Will	show off arm
Can't	hit for average
Expect	occasional power
Don't Expect	return to minors

Although the Cubs expected catching to be their deepest department in 1991, they found themselves forced to reach into the minors for help when the season was only two months old. With Damon Berryhill struggling to shake off an old injury and Joe Girardi sidelined with a new one, rookie Erik Pappas was unable to plug the gap. Wilkins, preceded by his reputation as a strong defensive receiver, rode to the rescue. In his third big league game, he went 3-for-3 against Los Angeles. Later, he delivered several timely home runs. Wilkins was hitting .271 at Triple-A Iowa with five homers and 14 RBI when promoted on June 6. He hit .227 with 17 homers and 71 RBI at Double-A Charlotte in 1990. He also threw out a Southern-League high 41.5 percent of runners attempting to steal that year. He also displayed an exceptional throwing arm in the majors. He's expected to remain a regular catcher in Chicago unless his bat suddenly falls silent. His uncertain status keeps his fantasy value at a low $3; his dime-priced 1992 cards also suffer.

Major League Batting Register

	BA	G	AB	R	H	2B	3B	HR	RBI	SB
91 NL	.222	86	203	21	45	9	0	6	22	3
Life	.222	86	203	21	45	9	0	6	22	3

CURRENT PLAYERS

BERNIE WILLIAMS

Position: Outfield
Team: New York Yankees
Born: Sept. 13, 1968 San Juan, Puerto Rico
Height: 6'2" **Weight:** 180 lbs.
Bats: both **Throws:** right
Acquired: Signed as a free agent, 9/85

Player Summary	
Fantasy Value	$4 to $8
Card Value	10¢ to 15¢
Will	play great defense
Can't	hit long ball
Expect	better results
Don't Expect	ticket to minors

Williams reached the big leagues sooner than anyone anticipated, making it to New York when the Yankees needed a center fielder to replace the injured Roberto Kelly (sprained wrist). Williams made his big league bow on July 7 in the last game before the All-Star break and collected two runs batted in against Baltimore. He finished the year with a .350 slugging percentage and a .336 on-base average in '91. New York's top prospect, Williams is an exceptional defensive center fielder with both speed and power. He had been hitting .294 at Triple-A Columbus when he was called, leading the club in at bats (306), runs (52), hits (90), and triples (six). He was named the International League's No. 6 prospect in '91. In 1990, he hit .281 at Double-A Albany with eight homers, 28 doubles, 54 RBI, 91 runs scored, and 39 stolen bases. He was named the Eastern League's No. 2 prospect that year. The Yankees have persistently resisted other clubs' bids for Williams in trade talks. He is a $6 fantasy draft at this point. His dime-priced 1992 cards are very good investments.

Major League Batting Register

	BA	G	AB	R	H	2B	3B	HR	RBI	SB
91 AL	.237	85	320	43	76	19	4	3	34	10
Life	.237	85	320	43	76	19	4	3	34	10

MATT WILLIAMS

Position: Third base
Team: San Francisco Giants
Born: Nov. 28, 1965 Bishop, CA
Height: 6'2" **Weight:** 205 lbs.
Bats: right **Throws:** right
Acquired: First-round pick in 6/86 free-agent draft

Player Summary	
Fantasy Value	$40 to $45
Card Value	10¢ to 15¢
Will	provide great power
Can't	avoid Ks
Expect	great defense
Don't Expect	return to short

Williams is not only the most prolific power producer among NL third basemen but arguably the best fielder. An intense player who wasn't satisfied after leading the league with 122 RBI in 1990, he registered another landmark in 1991 by smashing Jim Ray Hart's 1966 club record for home runs by a third baseman. Though Williams strikes out four times as much as he walks, he is a feared run producer who's virtually certain to compile his third consecutive 30-homer campaign. His homer totals make him a $40-plus corner man. He would contend for league leadership if he were selective at the plate or if another slugger followed him in the lineup. He had a .499 slugging average and a .310 on-base average in '91. Williams also played shortstop for the first time in two years, but that didn't last long. Williams has great hands, quick reactions, and a powerful arm from the hot corner. His 1992 cards are fine buys at 15 cents.

Major League Batting Register

	BA	G	AB	R	H	2B	3B	HR	RBI	SB
87 NL	.188	84	245	28	46	9	2	8	21	4
88 NL	.205	52	156	17	32	6	1	8	19	0
89 NL	.202	84	292	31	59	18	1	18	50	1
90 NL	.277	159	617	87	171	27	2	33	122	7
91 NL	.268	157	589	72	158	24	5	34	98	5
Life	.245	536	1899	235	466	84	11	101	310	17
3 AVE	.259	133	499	63	129	23	3	28	90	4

CURRENT PLAYERS

MITCH WILLIAMS

Position: Pitcher
Team: Philadelphia Phillies
Born: Nov. 17, 1964 Santa Ana, CA
Height: 6'4" **Weight:** 205 lbs.
Bats: left **Throws:** left
Acquired: Traded from Cubs for Bob Scanlan and Chuck McElroy, 4/91

Player Summary	
Fantasy Value	$30 to $35
Card Value	3¢ to 5¢
Will	throw very hard
Can't	stop "Wild Thing" tag
Expect	strikeouts and walks
Don't Expect	self-help fielding

Williams enjoyed a fine comeback season in his first year with the Phillies. He was NL Player of the Month for August with an 8-1 record (one short of Christy Mathewson's NL mark for wins in a month), five saves, and a 1.21 ERA in 15 games. Williams had good velocity on his fastball, split-fingered fastball, slider, and curve. He doesn't always know where they're going, however. He underwent 1990 knee surgery and fell out of favor in Chicago. Before he left, he had earned the nickname "Wild Thing" for such antics as walking the bases loaded before striking out the side. Still wild with the Phils, Williams yielded fewer hits than innings and kept the ball in the park. Working more than 60 times for the fifth time in six years, he saved 30 and had his best ERA. He is a good $30 fantasy bid to rack up saves. No one is going wild over his 1992 commons.

Major League Pitching Register

	W	L	ERA	G	S	IP	H	ER	BB	SO
86 AL	8	6	3.58	80	8	98.0	69	39	79	90
87 AL	8	6	3.23	85	6	108.2	63	39	94	129
88 AL	2	7	4.63	67	18	68.0	48	35	47	61
89 NL	4	4	2.76	76	36	81.2	71	25	52	67
90 NL	1	8	3.93	59	16	66.1	60	29	50	55
91 NL	12	5	2.34	69	30	88.1	56	23	62	84
Life	35	36	3.35	436	114	511.0	367	190	384	486
3 AVE	6	6	2.93	68	27	78.1	62	26	55	69

MARK WILLIAMSON

Position: Pitcher
Team: Baltimore Orioles
Born: July 21, 1959 Corpus Christi, TX
Height: 6' **Weight:** 172 lbs.
Bats: right **Throws:** right
Acquired: Traded from Padres with Terry Kennedy for Storm Davis, 10/86

Player Summary	
Fantasy Value	$2 to $4
Card Value	3¢ to 5¢
Will	continue to set up
Can't	win without control
Expect	better command
Don't Expect	long stints

After three straight strong seasons as a set-up reliever for the Orioles, Williamson struggled to recapture his old form in '91. He never found it. Though he worked more than 60 times for the third time in five seasons, he yielded more hits than innings pitched, threw too many gopher balls (nine), and suffered spells of control trouble. He finished 21 games. That was unusual for the veteran righthander, who fanned three times more than he walked in 1990 and had little trouble keeping the ball in the park. Williamson throws a fastball, palmball, curve, and slider but can't win without throwing them for strikes. Usually a master of changing speeds, he started badly early in '91 and never recovered. A decent fielder who keeps runners close, Williamson will focus his attention on resurrecting his rating as a relief pitcher in 1992. His fantasy stock fell in 1991 to $4, and it may go lower. His 1992 commons also have no where to go but up.

Major League Pitching Register

	W	L	ERA	G	S	IP	H	ER	BB	SO
87 AL	8	9	4.03	61	3	125.0	122	56	41	73
88 AL	5	8	4.90	37	2	117.2	125	64	40	69
89 AL	10	5	2.93	65	9	107.1	105	35	30	55
90 AL	8	2	2.21	49	1	85.1	65	21	28	60
91 AL	5	5	4.48	65	4	80.1	87	40	35	53
Life	36	29	3.77	277	19	515.2	504	216	174	310
3 AVE	8	4	3.16	60	5	91.1	86	32	31	56

CURRENT PLAYERS

CARL WILLIS

Position: Pitcher
Team: Minnesota Twins
Born: Dec. 28, 1960 Danville, VA
Height: 6'4" **Weight:** 212 lbs.
Bats: left **Throws:** right
Acquired: Signed as a free agent, 12/90

Player Summary	
Fantasy Value	$3 to $5
Card Value	3¢ to 5¢
Will	utilize fine forkball
Can't	get much attention
Expect	set-up role extensive
Don't Expect	many hits or walks

Although Sparky Anderson predicted in 1984 that Willis would become a big league star, he has had a checkered career in three organizations since leaving the Tiger system. Armed with the forkball taught to him by former Detroit pitching coach Roger Craig, Willis finally capitalized on his promise in 1991. Deployed in long and middle relief, he won eight of 11 while keeping his earned run average low. On July 30, he went 4⅓ shutout innings against Detroit while lowering the ERA to 2.16. His ERA shrank to 1.88 when he extended his scoreless innings streak to 24 in early August. Signed as a minor league free agent at age 30, Willis has matured into a pitcher who fans three times more than he walks, yields less hits than innings pitched, and keeps the ball in the park (only four homers in '91). He's a fine set-up man. Rescued from oblivion, he could be a fantasy find for less than $5. His 1992 commons are still lost, however.

Major League Pitching Register

	W	L	ERA	G	S	IP	H	ER	BB	SO
84 AL	0	2	7.31	10	0	16.0	25	13	5	4
84 NL	0	1	3.72	7	1	9.2	8	4	2	3
85 NL	1	0	9.22	11	1	13.2	21	14	5	6
86 NL	1	3	4.47	29	0	52.1	54	26	32	24
88 AL	0	0	8.25	6	0	12.0	17	11	7	6
91 AL	8	3	2.63	40	2	89.0	76	26	19	53
Life	10	9	4.39	103	4	192.2	201	94	70	96

STEVE WILSON

Position: Pitcher
Team: Los Angeles Dodgers
Born: Dec. 13, 1964 Victoria, British Columbia, Canada
Height: 6'4" **Weight:** 195 lbs.
Bats: left **Throws:** left
Acquired: Claimed from Cubs on waivers, 8/91

Player Summary	
Fantasy Value	$1 to $2
Card Value	3¢ to 5¢
Will	handle tough lefties
Can't	return to rotation
Expect	frequent stints
Don't Expect	low ERA, many wins

Wilson was used almost exclusively as a starting pitcher during his first four years in professional baseball. As a 1989 rookie with the Cubs, however, his role changed. Wilson worked 53 times, all but eight of them out of the bullpen, to help Chicago secure a divisional title. He was involved in another title fight in 1991 after arriving in Los Angeles via a late-summer waiver deal. He relies on a fastball and change-up, and did reasonably well in more than a dozen appearances for the Dodgers. In most of those outings, he was asked to retire tough lefthand hitters. Wilson's lone weakness with the Blue Crew was a tendency to issue too many walks. Wilson would have been more effective had he maintained the 2-1 ratio of strikeouts to walks that he brought into 1991. He'll try to find it this year with a team noted for developing hurlers. His 1992 commons and draft values are scraping the bottom of the barrel.

Major League Pitching Register

	W	L	ERA	G	S	IP	H	ER	BB	SO
88 AL	0	0	5.87	3	0	7.2	7	5	4	1
89 NL	6	4	4.20	53	2	85.2	83	40	31	65
90 NL	4	9	4.79	45	1	139.0	140	74	43	95
91 NL	0	0	2.61	19	2	20.2	14	6	9	14
Life	10	13	4.45	120	5	253.0	244	125	87	175
2 AVE	5	7	4.57	49	2	112.1	112	57	37	80

CURRENT PLAYERS

TREVOR WILSON

Position: Pitcher
Team: San Francisco Giants
Born: June 7, 1966 Torrance, CA
Height: 6′ **Weight:** 175 lbs.
Bats: left **Throws:** left
Acquired: Eighth-round pick in 6/85 free-agent draft

Player Summary	
Fantasy Value	$9 to $12
Card Value	5¢ to 7¢
Will	throw four strikes
Can't	count on bullpen
Expect	15 wins
Don't Expect	return to bullpen

Wilson was the most effective starter on the San Francisco staff in 1991, his first full season in the big leagues. A fastball-and-slider pitcher who also throws a curve and changeup, Wilson reached a dozen wins for the first time and was the only Giant starter to yield an average of less than four earned runs per game. Wilson's winning formula includes fanning twice as many as he walks, allowing less hits than innings pitched, and keeping the ball in the park. The team's third busiest starter behind Bud Black and John Burkett, Wilson also worked in relief (15 appearances). The young lefthander helps his own cause with good fielding, a fine pick-off move, and a bat that makes surprising contact. Based upon his late-season success in 1991, he figures to return as a regular member of the rotation. His slow, steady improvements point to dividends for managers bidding up to $12 for him at the 1992 draft. His 1992 commons have surprising potential.

Major League Pitching Register

	W	L	ERA	G	CG	IP	H	ER	BB	SO
88 NL	0	2	4.09	4	0	22.0	25	10	8	15
89 NL	2	3	4.35	14	0	39.1	28	19	24	22
90 NL	8	7	4.00	27	3	110.1	87	49	49	66
91 NL	13	11	3.56	44	2	202.0	173	80	77	139
Life	23	23	3.81	89	5	373.2	313	158	158	242
3 AVE	8	7	3.79	28	2	117.1	96	49	50	76

WILLIE WILSON

Position: Outfield
Team: Oakland Athletics
Born: July 9, 1955 Montgomery, AL
Height: 6′3″ **Weight:** 200 lbs.
Bats: both **Throws:** right
Acquired: Signed as a free agent, 12/90

Player Summary	
Fantasy Value	$3 to $7
Card Value	3¢ to 5¢
Will	try many roles
Can't	throw well
Expect	maximum use of speed
Don't Expect	regular outfield spot

Wilson had spent 15 years as a Kansas City regular before joining Oakland as a sub in 1991. He responded with 20 steals in limited playing time but hit some 50 points below the .289 career average he brought into 1991. The switch-hitting Wilson received less than 300 at bats for the first time since his 1978 rookie campaign. A two-time All-Star who abhors the understudy role, he delivers more often as a pinch-runner than he does as a pinch-hitter. He still runs well (though not up to his old standards) and has enough speed left to serve as a capable outfield sub. Forget his 1992 commons, but draft him at $7 or less and get a line on some of his steals.

Major League Batting Register

	BA	G	AB	R	H	2B	3B	HR	RBI	SB
76 AL	.167	12	6	0	1	0	0	0	0	2
77 AL	.324	13	34	10	11	2	0	0	1	6
78 AL	.217	127	198	43	43	8	2	0	16	46
79 AL	.315	154	588	113	185	18	13	6	49	83
80 AL	.326	161	705	133	230	28	15	3	49	79
81 AL	.303	102	439	54	133	10	7	1	32	34
82 AL	.332	136	585	87	194	19	15	3	46	37
83 AL	.276	137	576	90	159	22	8	2	33	59
84 AL	.301	128	541	81	163	24	9	2	44	47
85 AL	.278	141	605	87	168	25	21	4	43	43
86 AL	.269	156	631	77	170	20	7	9	44	34
87 AL	.279	146	610	97	170	18	15	4	30	59
88 AL	.262	147	591	81	155	17	11	1	37	35
89 AL	.253	112	383	58	97	17	7	3	43	24
90 AL	.290	115	307	49	89	13	3	2	42	24
91 AL	.238	113	294	38	70	14	4	0	28	20
Life	.287	1900	7093	1098	2038	255	137	40	537	632
3 AVE	.260	113	328	48	85	15	5	2	38	23

CURRENT PLAYERS

DAVE WINFIELD

Position: Outfield
Team: Toronto Blue Jays
Born: Oct. 3, 1951 St. Paul, MN
Height: 6'6" **Weight:** 220 lbs.
Bats: right **Throws:** right
Acquired: Signed as a free agent, 12/91

Player Summary	
Fantasy Value	$14 to $19
Card Value	10¢ to 15¢
Will	pull ball
Can't	steal bases
Expect	home runs and walks
Don't Expect	huge decline in defense

A 12-time All-Star and seven-time Gold Glover since his 1973 debut, Winfield has been one of baseball's most durable and consistent players, with the exception of back trouble that cost him the entire 1989 campaign. He doesn't run as well as he once did, but the Blue Jays (with whom he signed in December) covet his power. Winfield, always anxious to debunk critics who claim he's too old, changes his stance periodically in an effort to stay ahead of the pitchers. For the most part, he's done that, getting his 400th career homer in '91. Acquire his 1992 cards for 15 cents or less. He is a draft under $20.

Major League Batting Register

	BA	G	AB	R	H	2B	3B	HR	RBI	SB
73 NL	.277	56	141	9	39	4	1	3	12	0
74 NL	.265	145	498	57	132	18	4	20	75	9
75 NL	.267	143	509	74	136	20	2	15	76	23
76 NL	.283	137	492	81	139	26	4	13	69	26
77 NL	.275	157	615	104	169	29	7	25	92	16
78 NL	.308	158	587	88	181	30	5	24	97	21
79 NL	.308	159	597	97	184	27	10	34	118	15
80 NL	.276	162	558	89	154	25	6	20	87	23
81 AL	.294	105	388	52	114	25	1	13	68	11
82 AL	.280	140	539	84	151	24	8	37	106	5
83 AL	.283	152	598	99	169	26	8	32	116	15
84 AL	.340	141	567	106	193	34	4	19	100	6
85 AL	.275	155	633	105	174	34	6	26	114	19
86 AL	.262	154	565	90	148	31	5	24	104	6
87 AL	.275	156	575	83	158	22	1	27	97	5
88 AL	.322	149	559	96	180	37	2	25	107	9
90 AL	.267	132	475	70	127	21	2	21	78	0
91 AL	.262	150	568	75	149	27	4	28	86	7
Life	.285	2551	9464	1459	2697	460	80	406	1602	216
2 AVE	.265	141	522	73	138	24	3	25	82	4

HERM WINNINGHAM

Position: Outfield
Team: Cincinnati Reds
Born: Dec. 1, 1961 Orangeburg, SC
Height: 5'11" **Weight:** 175 lbs.
Bats: left **Throws:** right
Acquired: Traded from Expos with Jeff Reed and Randy St. Claire for Pat Pacillo and Tracy Jones, 7/88

Player Summary	
Fantasy Value	$1 to $2
Card Value	3¢ to 5¢
Will	serve as backup
Can't	produce good average
Expect	adequate defense
Don't Expect	100 games

Winningham played on a bad right knee throughout the 1991 season and needed arthroscopic surgery during the off-season. He wouldn't have played much anyway. Winningham doesn't hit enough to hold down a full-time outfield job. He finished the 1991 season almost 20 points off his career .242 average. If Winningham were more patient at the plate, he could hike his value by boosting his on-base percentage and taking advantage of his speed. His running ability helps him only on defense, where he's a substitute center fielder with above-average range but below-average throwing ability. Winningham has little hope of cracking the lineup. At this point in his career, he is not a good fantasy risk; bid up to $2 only. His cards are and have been commons, and his 1992 issues are no different.

Major League Batting Register

	BA	G	AB	R	H	2B	3B	HR	RBI	SB
84 NL	.407	14	27	5	11	1	1	0	5	2
85 NL	.237	125	312	30	74	6	5	3	21	20
86 NL	.216	90	185	23	40	6	3	4	11	12
87 NL	.239	137	347	34	83	20	3	4	41	29
88 NL	.232	100	203	16	47	3	4	0	21	12
89 NL	.251	115	251	40	63	11	3	3	13	14
90 NL	.256	84	160	20	41	8	5	3	17	6
91 NL	.225	98	169	17	38	6	1	1	4	4
Life	.240	763	1654	185	397	61	25	18	133	99
3 AVE	.245	99	193	26	47	8	3	2	11	8

CURRENT PLAYERS

BOBBY WITT

Position: Pitcher
Team: Texas Rangers
Born: May 11, 1964 Arlington, VA
Height: 6'2" **Weight:** 205 lbs.
Bats: right **Throws:** right
Acquired: First-round pick in 6/85 free-agent draft

Player Summary	
Fantasy Value	$3 to $7
Card Value	3¢ to 5¢
Will	win with health
Can't	resume walking 100
Expect	explosive fastball
Don't Expect	empty bases

Witt missed most of the first half of the 1991 campaign while recuperating from a tear in his rotator cuff. Even after he returned, he pitched with pain in his right elbow and had an arthrogram in September. He wasn't able to maintain his improvement in 1991. Opponents compiled a .254 batting average, a .356 slugging average, and a .388 on-base percentage. The flame-throwing righty had entered the season on the heels of a 17-10 campaign (entailing a club-record dozen straight wins) that included 221 strikeouts, second in the AL. He's led the league in walks three times and passed more than 100 in all five of his full seasons. A power pitcher with a 95 mph fastball, Witt uses a slider and curve to confuse the hitters. He'll reclaim his rotation spot if he's healthy. Unpredictable, he went backward in '91. Bet up to $8 that he regains some of his 1990 prowess. His common-priced 1992 cards are not good investments.

Major League Pitching Register

	W	L	ERA	G	CG	IP	H	ER	BB	SO
86 AL	11	9	5.48	31	0	157.2	130	96	143	174
87 AL	8	10	4.91	26	1	143.0	114	78	140	160
88 AL	8	10	3.92	22	13	174.1	134	76	101	148
89 AL	12	13	5.14	31	5	194.1	182	111	114	166
90 AL	17	10	3.36	33	7	222.0	197	83	110	221
91 AL	3	7	6.09	17	1	88.2	84	60	74	82
Life	59	59	4.63	160	27	980.0	841	504	682	951
3 AVE	11	10	4.53	27	4	168.1	154	85	99	156

TODD WORRELL

Position: Pitcher
Team: St. Louis Cardinals
Born: Sept. 28, 1959 Arcadia, CA
Height: 6'5" **Weight:** 210 lbs.
Bats: right **Throws:** right
Acquired: First-round pick in 6/82 free-agent draft

Player Summary	
Fantasy Value	$1 to $3
Card Value	3¢ to 5¢
Will	throw blazing heat
Can't	rely on fastball
Expect	low ERA
Don't Expect	instant return

Worrell was one of the game's top closers before suffering ligament damage in his elbow late in the 1989 season. He missed all of the last two seasons while allowing the surgically repaired elbow to heal. The former Rookie of the Year posted three straight 30-save seasons from 1986 to '88. A power pitcher who deploys a fastball, slider, and rare changeup, Worrell throws as hard as he can for as long as he can. He fans twice as many as he walks, averages close to a strikeout an inning, and allows less hits than innings pitched. Worrell can't hit, field, or hold runners on base but rarely has to worry about those aspects of the game. When he's on, batters have a hard time connecting. If his elbow is sound, he's still young enough to pick up where he left off. He is not a bad $2 gamble, because of the talent he displayed before his injury. His 1992 commons are not healthy risks, however.

Major League Pitching Register

	W	L	ERA	G	S	IP	H	ER	BB	SO
85 NL	3	0	2.91	17	5	21.2	17	7	7	17
86 NL	9	10	2.08	74	36	103.2	86	24	41	73
87 NL	8	6	2.66	75	33	94.2	86	28	34	92
88 NL	5	9	3.00	68	32	90.0	69	30	34	78
89 NL	3	5	2.96	47	20	51.2	42	17	26	41
Life	28	30	2.64	281	126	361.2	300	106	142	301

CURRENT PLAYERS

ERIC YELDING

Position: Shortstop; outfield
Team: Houston Astros
Born: Feb. 22, 1965 Montrose, AL
Height: 5'11" **Weight:** 165 lbs.
Bats: right **Throws:** right
Acquired: Drafted from Cubs, 4/89

Player Summary	
Fantasy Value	$1 to $3
Card Value	3¢ to 5¢
Will	show great speed
Can't	wait for walks
Expect	good arm
Don't Expect	permanent position

Yelding did not enjoy the 1991 season. After winning Houston's regular shortstop job during spring training, he struggled defensively and lost the position to rookie Andujar Cedeno. Sent to the minors to regain his confidence, Yelding suffered a broken cheekbone when hit in the face by an Adam Peterson pitch August 12. Yelding also broke his nose when he crashed to the ground. That mishap ended his season prematurely. He will be back, because his versatility and speed make him a valuable commodity. A three-position infielder who also plays the outfield, he has good range and a strong arm but is still too erratic defensively to play an infield position every day. His fielding was so erratic in 1991 that the Astros sacrificed his speed (64 steals in 1990) when they sent him out. In '91, he had a .301 slugging percentage and a .276 on-base average. If Yelding bats .250 he'll stick in the big leagues. Make sure he has a good spring before drafting him for $2 or so. His 1992 commons aren't good purchases.

Major League Batting Register

	BA	G	AB	R	H	2B	3B	HR	RBI	SB
89 NL	.233	70	90	19	21	2	0	0	9	11
90 NL	.254	142	511	69	130	9	5	1	28	64
91 NL	.243	78	276	19	67	11	1	1	20	11
Life	.249	290	877	107	218	22	6	2	57	86
2 AVE	.250	110	394	44	99	10	3	1	24	38

CURT YOUNG

Position: Pitcher
Team: Oakland Athletics
Born: April 16, 1960 Saginaw, MI
Height: 6'1" **Weight:** 180 lbs.
Bats: right **Throws:** left
Acquired: Fourth-round pick in 6/81 free-agent draft

Player Summary	
Fantasy Value	$1 to $2
Card Value	3¢ to 5¢
Will	get grounders
Can't	keep ball in park
Expect	return to rotation
Don't Expect	so many walks

After spending six years in the starting rotation of the Athletics, Young spent all of 1991 in the bullpen as the replacement for injured veteran Rick Honeycutt, another southpaw set-up man. Young caught the general malaise that struck the Oakland staff and stumbled through his worst season. A sinkerballer who also throws a forkball, curve, and slider, Young sabotaged his own efforts by allowing more than a hit per inning and walking more men than he struck out. The former power pitcher also threw too many home run balls for a middle reliever who doesn't get much work. He kept a bad situation from getting worse by fielding his position well and keeping base-runners close. Young may return to the rotation or resurrect his career as a reliever. Now is not the time to draft him. Don't accumulate his 1992 commons.

Major League Pitching Register

	W	L	ERA	G	S	IP	H	ER	BB	SO
83 AL	0	1	16.00	8	0	9.0	17	16	5	5
84 AL	9	4	4.06	20	0	108.2	118	49	31	41
85 AL	0	4	7.24	19	0	46.0	57	37	22	19
86 AL	13	9	3.45	29	0	198.0	176	76	57	116
87 AL	13	7	4.08	31	0	203.0	194	92	44	124
88 AL	11	8	4.14	26	0	156.1	162	72	50	69
89 AL	5	9	3.73	25	0	111.0	117	46	47	55
90 AL	9	6	4.85	26	0	124.1	124	67	53	56
91 AL	4	2	5.00	41	0	68.1	74	38	34	27
Life	64	50	4.33	225	0	1024.2	1039	493	343	512
3 AVE	6	6	4.48	31	0	101.1	105	50	45	46

CURRENT PLAYERS

GERALD YOUNG

Position: Outfield
Team: Houston Astros
Born: Oct. 22, 1964 Tela, Honduras
Height: 6'2" **Weight:** 185 lbs.
Bats: both **Throws:** right
Acquired: Traded from Mets with Manny Lee and Mitch Cook for Ray Knight, 8/84

Player Summary	
Fantasy Value	$2 to $4
Card Value	3¢ to 5¢
Will	hit under .250
Can't	show discipline at bat
Expect	Gold Glove defense
Don't Expect	another minors trip

Young's gift of speed is a mixed blessing. He stole 65 bases for Houston in 1988 and made a league-leading 412 putouts in center a year later. He also failed to heed advice that would also make swiftness an asset at the plate. As a result, Young has spent most of the last two years playing in the minors or riding the bench in the majors. After hitting a respectable .257 in '88, Young followed with .233 and .175 years that led to his exile. Like Otis Nixon, a speed merchant who became a regular by adding 70 points to his career average in 1991, Young could play every day by dropping bunts, beating out infield rollers, spraying hits to all fields, and working pitchers for walks. There's no doubt about his speed or his arm. His 15 assists and .998 fielding percentage led NL outfielders in 1988. He can run, but he can't hit—spend only $2 at the draft. His 1992 commons are not attractive commodities.

MATT YOUNG

Position: Pitcher
Team: Boston Red Sox
Born: Aug. 9, 1958 Pasadena, CA
Height: 6'3" **Weight:** 205 lbs.
Bats: left **Throws:** left
Acquired: Signed as a free agent, 12/90

Player Summary	
Fantasy Value	$1 to $3
Card Value	3¢ to 5¢
Will	show one of league's best curves
Can't	justify contract, avoid injuries
Expect	batters to get frequent hits, walks
Don't Expect	many wins, low ERA

Young's 1991 season was shortened by two-and-one-half months when he suffered a slight tear of the rotator cuff May 30. Young, in his first year with the Red Sox after signing a megabucks free-agent contract, didn't come close to justifying the team's investment. He was winless between May 20 and September 12, a dry spell that sealed the club's fate as a bridesmaid to Toronto in the AL East. The curveball specialist had a record consistent with a career that includes one winning season. Young suffers control problems, can't field his position, and has a shaky medical history (1988 and '89 elbow problems before the '91 shoulder woes). He isn't much of a fantasy candidate, but he could get plenty of opportunities if he has a good spring since the BoSox blew a wad by signing him. His 1992 commons will not get any breaks with collectors, though.

Major League Batting Register

	BA	G	AB	R	H	2B	3B	HR	RBI	SB
87 NL	.321	71	274	44	88	9	2	1	15	26
88 NL	.257	149	576	79	148	21	9	0	37	65
89 NL	.233	146	533	71	124	17	3	0	38	34
90 NL	.175	57	154	15	27	4	1	0	4	6
91 NL	.218	108	142	26	31	3	1	1	11	16
Life	.249	531	1679	235	418	54	16	3	105	147
2 AVE	.220	102	344	43	76	11	2	1	21	20

Major League Pitching Register

	W	L	ERA	G	CG	IP	H	ER	BB	SO
83 AL	11	15	3.27	33	5	203.2	178	74	79	130
84 AL	6	8	5.72	22	1	113.1	141	72	57	73
85 AL	12	19	4.91	37	5	218.1	242	119	76	136
86 AL	8	6	3.82	65	1	103.2	108	44	46	82
87 NL	5	8	4.47	47	0	54.1	62	27	17	42
89 AL	1	4	6.75	26	0	37.1	42	28	31	27
90 AL	8	18	3.51	34	7	225.1	198	88	107	176
91 AL	3	7	5.18	19	0	88.2	92	51	53	69
Life	54	85	4.33	283	19	1044.2	1063	503	466	735
3 AVE	4	10	4.28	26	2	117.1	111	56	64	91

CURRENT PLAYERS

ROBIN YOUNT

Position: Outfield
Team: Milwaukee Brewers
Born: Sept. 16, 1955 Danville, IL
Height: 6' **Weight:** 180 lbs.
Bats: right **Throws:** right
Acquired: First-round pick in 6/73 free-agent draft

Player Summary	
Fantasy Value	$17 to $22
Card Value	5¢ to 10¢
Will	play strong defense
Can't	slow power slide
Expect	run production
Don't Expect	return of 1989

Although Yount is no longer the player who won two MVP awards, he is still a capable player when healthy. In 1991, however, he missed 32 games at midseason with kidney stone problems. He's still a contact hitter who fans only slightly more than he walks. Yount remains a fine center fielder with good range, good judgement, and a strong, accurate throwing arm. He's as good there as he was at short, where he starred from 1974 to '84 before hurting his shoulder. His power has declined, coloring his fantasy value to $20. His nickel-priced 1992 cards will hit long-term jackpots.

Major League Batting Register

	BA	G	AB	R	H	2B	3B	HR	RBI	SB
74 AL	.250	107	344	48	86	14	5	3	26	7
75 AL	.267	147	558	67	149	28	2	8	52	12
76 AL	.252	161	638	59	161	19	3	2	54	16
77 AL	.288	154	605	66	174	34	4	4	49	16
78 AL	.293	127	502	66	147	23	9	9	71	16
79 AL	.267	149	577	72	154	26	5	8	51	11
80 AL	.293	143	611	121	179	49	10	23	87	20
81 AL	.273	96	377	50	103	15	5	10	49	4
82 AL	.331	156	635	129	210	46	12	29	114	14
83 AL	.308	149	578	102	178	42	10	17	80	12
84 AL	.298	160	624	105	186	27	7	16	80	14
85 AL	.277	122	466	76	129	26	3	15	68	10
86 AL	.312	140	522	82	163	31	7	9	46	14
87 AL	.312	158	635	99	198	25	9	21	103	19
88 AL	.306	162	621	92	190	38	11	13	91	22
89 AL	.318	160	614	101	195	38	9	21	103	19
90 AL	.247	158	587	98	145	17	5	17	77	15
91 AL	.260	130	503	66	131	20	4	10	77	6
Life	.288	2579	9997	1499	2878	518	120	235	1278	247
3 AVE	.276	149	568	88	157	25	6	16	86	13

TODD ZEILE

Position: Third base
Team: St. Louis Cardinals
Born: Sept. 9, 1965 Van Nuys, CA
Height: 6'1" **Weight:** 190 lbs.
Bats: right **Throws:** right
Acquired: Third-round pick in 6/86 free-agent draft

Player Summary	
Fantasy Value	$12 to $18
Card Value	5¢ to 10¢
Will	master new position
Can't	avoid errors
Expect	run production
Don't Expect	another Joe Torre

One of the major reasons for the surprising success of the 1991 Cardinals was Zeile's smooth transfer from catcher to third base. Playing for manager Joe Torre, who had made the same switch as a player, Zeile relaxed more at the new position and became a more potent hitter. On August 3, he led off the 10th inning with a home run that beat Pittsburgh, 6-5. Zeile, the top power-hitter on a punchless team, would hit many more if not relegated to playing half his schedule in spacious Busch Memorial Stadium. Though Zeile was a more prolific RBI man as a sophomore, his home run total actually fell. His homers should multiply, making him a $15 fantasy corner man. He had a .412 slugging percentage and a .353 on-base average in '91. The novice third baseman did emerge as a base-stealing threat, and also showed improved defensive skills when he uncorked a 22-game errorless streak. He'll get better as he gains experience. Pay up to a dime apiece for his 1992 cards.

Major League Batting Register

	BA	G	AB	R	H	2B	3B	HR	RBI	SB
89 NL	.256	28	82	7	21	3	1	1	8	0
90 NL	.244	144	495	62	121	25	3	15	57	2
91 NL	.280	155	565	76	158	36	3	11	81	17
Life	.263	327	1142	145	300	64	7	27	146	19
2 AVE	.263	150	530	69	140	31	3	13	69	10

ROOKIE PROSPECTS

KYLE ABBOTT

Position: Pitcher
Team: Philadelphia Phillies
Born: Feb. 18, 1968 Newbury Port, MA
Height: 6'4" **Weight:** 195 lbs.
Bats: left **Throws:** left
Acquired: Traded from Angels with Ruben Amaro for Von Hayes, 12/91

Player Summary	
Fantasy Value	$2 to $4
Card Value	5¢ to 10¢
Will	throw heat
Can't	finish what he starts
Expect	other teams to covet him
Don't Expect	much time at Triple-A

You've heard of the comedy team of Abbott and Costello? Well, the Phillies may soon have an Abbott of their own, and opposing hitters may not find it very funny. Kyle Abbott is one of the Phillies' finest pitching prospects. Kyle pitched for the Angels' top farm team at Triple-A Edmonton in 1991, and was among the organization's leaders in victories, strikeouts and earned run average. He was the ninth pick overall in the 1989 draft, and wasted little time justifying this lofty opinion of his abilities. He pitched for Class-A Quad City, going 5-4 with a 2.57 ERA. In 1990, Abbott jumped two rungs, pitching both in the Double-A and Triple-A. He allowed two earned runs or less in 14 of his 27 starting jobs. He is a good fantasy choice at $3, considering that he could crack the 1992 Phillies rotation. His 1992 cards are intelligent investments at a nickel or so.

SCOTT ALDRED

Position: Pitcher
Team: Detroit Tigers
Born: June 12, 1968 Flint, MI
Height: 6'4" **Weight:** 215 lbs.
Bats: left **Throws:** left
Acquired: 16th-round pick in 6/86 free-agent draft

Player Summary	
Fantasy Value	$1 to $3
Card Value	5¢ to 10¢
Will	become fan favorite
Can't	avoid walks
Expect	lots of patience
Don't Expect	15 wins

Aldred has many things going for him, including size, stuff, and youth. When he adds control to this equation, he is going to be a popular figure in Detroit for a long time, especially considering he is a home state product. He was winless in his first three major league starts of 1991, giving up eight walks in 10⅓ innings. He made his major league debut on September 9, 1990, and earned a victory. He went five innings, combining with Edwin Nunez on a six-hitter in a 5-0 triumph over Milwaukee. Aldred turned in another impressive outing later in 1990, going six innings and allowing one run in a 2-0 loss to Scott Erickson and the Twins. Aldred's best pro season came in 1989 when, despite a midseason hand injury, he posted a 10-6 mark for Double-A London of the Eastern League. Batters hit just .221 off Aldred, the fourth-best figure in the league. He is not that high a priority for either card investors or fantasy managers yet.

Professional Pitching Register

	W	L	ERA	G	CG	IP	H	ER	BB	SO
89 A	5	4	2.57	13	0	73.2	55	21	30	95
90 AA	6	9	4.14	24	2	128.1	124	59	73	91
90 AAA	1	0	14.81	3	0	10.1	26	17	4	14
91 AAA	14	10	3.99	27	4	180.1	173	80	46	120
91 AL	1	2	4.58	5	0	19.2	22	10	13	12

Professional Pitching Register

	W	L	ERA	G	CG	IP	H	ER	BB	SO
87 A	4	9	3.57	21	0	111.0	101	44	69	91
88 A	8	7	3.56	25	1	131.1	122	52	72	102
89 AA	10	6	3.84	20	3	122.0	98	52	59	97
90 AAA	6	15	4.90	29	2	158.0	145	86	81	133
90 AL	1	2	3.77	4	0	14.1	13	6	10	7
91 AAA	8	8	3.92	22	2	135.1	127	59	72	95
91 AL	2	4	5.18	11	1	57.1	58	33	30	35

ROOKIE PROSPECTS

MANNY ALEXANDER

Position: Shortstop
Team: Baltimore Orioles
Born: March 20, 1971 San Pedro de Macoris, Dominican Republic
Height: 5'10" **Weight:** 150 lbs.
Bats: right **Throws:** right
Acquired: Signed as a free agent, 2/88

Player Summary	
Fantasy Value	$1 to $3
Card Value	5¢ to 10¢
Will	be compared to Ozzie
Can't	hit long ball
Expect	long apprenticeship
Don't Expect	Ripken to be moving

Alexander looks like he may one day fit in with the Orioles' tradition of fine defensive infielders. Everything about his glove has inspired raves. *Baseball America* rated him the best defensive shortstop, the best infield arm, and the most exciting player in the Class-A Carolina League in 1991. That honor came one year after the same publication named him the Class-A Appalachian League's best prospect and the best shortstop in all five rookie leagues. Alexander was also named by *The Sporting News* as among the more interesting shortstop prospects. He may never hit much of a long ball, but he has enough speed to steal more than 20 bases. Alexander spent a huge hunk of his 1990 season on the disabled list with a sore back, and hit .178 in 44 games for Wausau. He played the 1988 season in the Dominican Summer League, then batted .310 with 34 RBI and 19 steals with Class-A Bluefield in 1989. His fantasy future at a couple bucks, and his 1992 card investment growth looks modest.

Professional Batting Register

	BA	G	AB	R	H	2B	3B	HR	RBI	SB
89 R	.310	65	274	49	85	13	2	2	34	19
90 A	.178	44	152	16	27	3	1	0	11	8
91 A	.261	134	548	81	143	17	3	3	42	47
91 AA	.333	3	9	3	3	1	0	0	2	0

MOISES ALOU

Position: Outfield
Team: Montreal Expos
Born: July 3, 1966 Atlanta, GA
Height: 6'3" **Weight:** 180 lbs.
Bats: right **Throws:** right
Acquired: Traded from Pirates with Scott Ruskin and Willie Greene for Zane Smith, 8/90

Player Summary	
Fantasy Value	$1 to $3
Card Value	5¢ to 7¢
Will	face long rehab
Can't	be rushed
Expect	loss of power
Don't Expect	majors before 1993

Reaching the majors can be challenge enough, but Alou faces a tougher test than most. Not only did he get a late start on his baseball career, but he also suffered an injury—a torn labrum in the right shoulder—that kept him out for the 1991 season. Fortunately for the son of former major leaguer Felipe Alou, Moises is still young enough to put his gifts to use. These include some speed and power, plus an ability to hit for average. Drafted by Pittsburgh in '86, Alou was slow to develop because he never played organized ball until college. He seemed to find himself in 1989. In August of '90, he was the player to be named in the deal that sent lefty Zane Smith to the Pirates. Fantasy managers should wait for Alou's shoulder to be completely healed before they invest more than a couple of bucks. His 1992 cards are iffy at more than a nickel.

Professional Batting Register

	BA	G	AB	R	H	2B	3B	HR	RBI	SB
86 A	.236	69	254	30	60	9	8	6	35	14
87 A	.208	43	125	21	26	6	2	4	18	6
88 A	.313	105	358	58	112	23	5	7	62	24
89 A	.302	86	321	50	97	29	2	14	53	12
89 AA	.293	54	205	36	60	5	2	3	19	8
90 AA	.295	36	132	19	39	12	2	3	22	7
90 AAA	.264	90	326	44	86	5	6	5	37	8
90 NL	.200	16	20	4	4	0	1	0	0	0

ROOKIE PROSPECTS

TAVO ALVAREZ

Position: Pitcher
Team: Montreal Expos
Born: Nov. 25, 1971 Obregon, MX
Height: 6'3" **Weight:** 183 lbs.
Bats: right **Throws:** right
Acquired: Second-round pick in 6/90 free-agent draft

Player Summary
Fantasy Value	$1 to $2
Card Value	4¢ to 6¢
Will	keep batters off-balance
Can't	afford to rush
Expect	majors by '93
Don't Expect	under a K a frame

Alvarez has already proven quite a find for the Expos, especially since major league clubs find it very difficult to acquire players from Mexico. Montreal, however, spotted him attending high school in Tucson, Arizona, and made him part of a draft in which they had 10 of the first 51 picks. Instead of going to the University of Arizona, Alvarez reported to Montreal's club in the rookie Gulf Coast League, and now he is considered the organization's top pitching prospect. He picked up an unorthodox breaking ball from Class-A Sumter pitching coach Gary Lance in 1991, and it is already considered to be of major league caliber. Alvarez added it to a repertoire that included a fastball and changeup. Alvarez was one of the top starters in the Class-A South Atlantic League, and led the Expos' chain in strikeouts by a wide margin. He has a chance to move up to Double-A in 1991. He is a few years away, but not a bad fantasy gamble at $2. Buy his current cards for a nickel apiece.

Professional Pitching Register
	W	L	ERA	G	CG	IP	H	ER	BB	SO
90 R	5	2	2.60	11	0	52.0	42	15	16	47
91 A	12	10	3.24	25	3	152.2	152	55	58	158

WILSON ALVAREZ

Position: Pitcher
Team: Chicago White Sox
Born: March 24, 1970 Maracaibo, Venezuela
Height: 6'1" **Weight:** 175 lbs.
Bats: left **Throws:** left
Acquired: Traded from Rangers with Scott Fletcher and Sammy Sosa for Harold Baines and Fred Manrique, 7/89

Player Summary
Fantasy Value	$2 to $4
Card Value	5¢ to 7¢
Will	make 1992 rotation
Can't	rest on his no-hitter
Expect	another no-hitter in his career
Don't Expect	20-win season

What a difference a start makes. In his first major league start, in 1989, Alvarez pitched to five batters and retired none. More than two years later, with a different club, he started again, and this time pitched a no-hitter against Baltimore. He may prove to be the most interesting of the players acquired by the White Sox when they sent Harold Baines and Fred Manrique to the Rangers. He arrived with Scott Fletcher and Sammy Sosa, and neither has the future Alvarez does. Alvarez, though still very young, has been dominant both in international and pro competition, and there's no reason he can't do the same in the majors. Alvarez was one of the organization's top hurlers in 1991. He is not an great choice for fantasy managers—keep your bid under $4. His 1992 cards are only fair at a nickel.

Professional Pitching Register
	W	L	ERA	G	CG	IP	H	ER	BB	SO
87 R	2	5	5.24	10	0	44.2	41	26	21	46
87 A	1	5	6.47	8	0	32.0	39	23	23	19
88 A	4	11	2.98	23	1	127.0	113	42	49	134
88 AAA	1	1	3.78	5	0	16.2	17	7	6	9
89 A	7	4	2.11	13	3	81.0	68	19	21	51
89 AA	4	3	2.47	13	1	83.2	72	23	32	47
89 AL	0	1	0.00	1	0	0.0	3	3	2	0
90 AA	5	1	4.27	7	1	46.1	44	22	25	36
90 AAA	7	7	6.00	17	1	75.0	91	50	51	35
91 AA	10	6	1.83	23	3	152.1	109	31	74	165
91 AL	3	2	3.51	10	2	56.1	47	22	29	32

ROOKIE PROSPECTS

MATT ANDERSON

Position: Pitcher
Team: Baltimore Orioles
Born: June 3, 1971 Glendale, CA
Height: 6'3" **Weight:** 180 lbs.
Bats: left **Throws:** left
Acquired: Fifth-round pick in 6/89 free-agent draft

Player Summary	
Fantasy Value	$2 to $4
Card Value	10¢ to 15¢
Will	be around the plate
Can't	rely on Ks
Expect	lots of decisions
Don't Expect	move to bullpen

Anderson became the ace of the Class-A Kane County starting rotation in 1991 in just his second full pro season. He is big and can strike out a batter, but is the kind of lefty who catches your eye because he can throw strikes. Anderson walked just 42 in his first 122 innings. He also looks like the kind of pitcher who enjoys getting involved, collecting 10 wins and six losses in his first 19 starts. His hits ratio also was excellent. Anderson's father, Bud, played in the Boston organization. Matt graduated from Buena High School in 1989, and shortly thereafter was in pro ball. He had a rough time, losing his first four decisions, but righted himself in '90. Pitching for Bluefield, he fanned 88 to lead the rookie Appalachian League. His 2.71 ERA placed him ninth. Anderson went 6-4 in 12 starts, then went to Class-A Wausau, which used him mostly in relief. The O's could consider this strikeout sultan soon. He's an investment at $4 or less. His current cards are fine buys at a dime each.

Professional Pitching Register

	W	L	ERA	G	CG	IP	H	ER	BB	SO
89 R	0	4	8.66	14	0	35.1	60	34	18	35
90 R	6	4	2.71	12	2	83.0	74	25	21	88
90 A	1	3	4.43	18	0	42.2	49	21	24	39
91 A	13	9	3.14	27	5	174.2	142	61	68	166

JOHNNY ARD

Position: Pitcher
Team: San Francisco Giants
Born: June 1, 1967 Las Vegas, NE
Height: 6'5" **Weight:** 220 lbs.
Bats: right **Throws:** right
Acquired: Traded from Twins with Jimmy Williams for Steve Bedrosian, 12/90

Player Summary	
Fantasy Value	$2 to $4
Card Value	10¢ to 15¢
Will	be taught splitter
Can't	produce ERA under 3.50
Expect	Giants to rush him
Don't Expect	move to work

Traded for a player nicknamed "Bedrock," Ard may be a building block in the next big San Francisco rotation. He came to the Giants in December of 1990 with Jimmy Williams for Steve "Bedrock" Bedrosian. Ard had some trouble at Triple-A Phoenix, but won his first three starts for San Francisco's Double-A Texas League club in Shreveport. A first-round pick of the Twins and the 20th overall selection in 1988, Ard was sent to Elizabethton, where he went 4-1 and finished fifth in the rookie Appalachian League with a 1.97 ERA. He went 3-0 with a 1.05 ERA in four appearances after being promoted to Class-A Kenosha, and was named Minnesota's Minor League Pitcher of the Month for August. Ard went to Class-A Visalia in 1989 and led the California League with 28 starts and 13 wins. He made the All-Star team. Don't depend on him yet—limit your bid to $4. His 1992 cards, though, are outstanding choices at less than a dime apiece.

Professional Pitching Register

	W	L	ERA	G	CG	IP	H	ER	BB	SO
88 R	4	1	1.97	9	1	59.1	40	13	26	71
88 A	3	0	1.05	4	1	25.2	14	3	4	16
89 A	13	7	3.29	28	4	186.0	155	68	84	153
90 AA	12	9	3.79	29	4	180.1	167	76	85	101
91 AA	9	3	2.74	13	4	88.2	77	27	36	58
91 AAA	3	5	5.78	10	1	62.1	76	40	33	30

ROOKIE PROSPECTS

MARCOS ARMAS

Position: First base; outfield
Team: Oakland Athletics
Born: Aug. 5, 1969 Puerto Pirtu, Venezuela
Height: 6'5" **Weight:** 190 lbs.
Bats: right **Throws:** right
Acquired: Signed as a free agent, 12/87

Player Summary	
Fantasy Value	$1 to $3
Card Value	5¢ to 10¢
Will	strike out every third at bat
Can't	hit .300
Expect	another year at Double-A
Don't Expect	spot in Oakland

The A's can only hope Marcos Armas is like his brother Tony, a power hitter who was part of the franchise's renaissance in the early 1980s. So far, Marcos has shown some of his sibling's punch, but he had trouble adjusting to Double-A in 1991 and was demoted from Huntsville of the Southern League to Class-A Modesto of the California League with a .230 average. Still, Tony didn't really hit his stride until he was about 26 years old, so there's time for his little brother at age 22. Also, Marcos' combined 1991 totals get your attention; he ranked among the top home run and RBI men in the Oakland organization for 1991. He has improved his power totals in each of his four pro seasons, which could indicate a filling out of his physique, combined with more experience. His career progression is a bit stalled, however. He needs a strong 1992 at Double-A before card collectors or fantasy managers should consider him a good risk.

Professional Batting Register

	BA	G	AB	R	H	2B	3B	HR	RBI	SB
88 R	.293	17	58	14	17	2	1	0	10	0
89 A	.316	36	136	18	43	5	2	3	22	1
90 A	.238	75	260	32	62	13	0	7	33	3
91 A	.279	36	140	21	39	7	0	8	33	0
91 AA	.226	81	305	40	69	16	1	8	53	2

BRYAN BAAR

Position: Catcher
Team: Los Angeles Dodgers
Born: April 10, 1968 Zeeland, MI
Height: 6'3" **Weight:** 205 lbs.
Bats: right **Throws:** right
Acquired: Seventh-round pick in 6/89 free-agent draft

Player Summary	
Fantasy Value	$1 to $3
Card Value	5¢ to 10¢
Will	dent the wall
Can't	afford another slump
Expect	20 home runs
Don't Expect	1992 call-up

Baar ran into some problems at the plate as he moved up a notch in 1991, but still made the Double-A Texas League All-Star squad. Projected as the Dodgers' catcher of the future, he has both the size and power to make it in the majors, though he must still work on his contact. Baar, who attended Western Michigan University, began his pro career in 1989, and immediately established his power at Great Falls of the rookie Pioneer League. He hit .288 and added 10 homers with 38 RBI. Half of his 40 hits went for extra bases. Baar's promotion to Class-A Bakersfield of the California League in 1990 netted him a berth on the All-Star team. He maintained his average, hitting .285 and adding 20 homers and 71 RBI. But he also struck out 114 times. The question is whether Baar's 1991 slump indicates a stall, or whether he can adjust. As he continues to improve behind the plate, he gets closer to the big club. His fantasy value, though, stops at $3. His dime-priced 1992 cards should stay on the shelves.

Professional Batting Register

	BA	G	AB	R	H	2B	3B	HR	RBI	SB
89 R	.288	48	139	31	40	9	1	10	38	1
90 A	.285	111	389	53	111	23	1	20	71	1
91 AA	.224	101	348	33	78	19	0	10	51	3

ROOKIE PROSPECTS

WILLIE BANKS

Position: Pitcher
Team: Minnesota Twins
Born: Feb. 27, 1969 Jersey City, NJ
Height: 6'1" **Weight:** 190 lbs.
Bats: right **Throws:** right
Acquired: First-round pick in 6/87 free-agent draft

Player Summary	
Fantasy Value	$3 to $6
Card Value	10¢ to 15¢
Will	record 200 Ks
Can't	rely on fastball
Expect	full year in majors
Don't Expect	20 wins soon

Banks seems to have collected an unusual amount of distinctions even for a pro athlete. An extremely hard thrower, he dominated hitters in the amateur ranks and is learning to win in the pros. At St. Anthony's High School, he twice fanned 19 men in a seven-inning game. He also hurled three no-hitters. No wonder the Twins made him the third overall pick of the 1987 draft, the first pitcher taken, and the highest pick ever from New Jersey. Wildness contributed to Banks's poor stats at his first pro stop, in '87, but he was rated by *Baseball America* the top pitching prospect in the rookie Appalachian League. In 1989 at Class-A Visalia, Banks no-hit Palm Springs, becoming the youngest man to hurl a nine-inning no hitter in the California League. Managers said Banks owned the league's top fastball. He first appeared on a 1991 Upper Deck card. His dime-priced 1992 cards are great investments. He's a fantasy hopeful for up to $6.

Professional Pitching Register

	W	L	ERA	G	CG	IP	H	ER	BB	SO
87 R	1	8	6.99	13	0	65.2	73	51	62	71
88 A	10	10	3.72	24	0	125.2	109	52	107	113
89 A	12	9	2.59	27	7	174.0	122	50	85	173
89 AA	1	0	5.14	1	0	7.0	10	4	0	9
90 AA	7	9	3.93	28	1	162.2	161	71	98	114
91 AAA	9	8	4.55	25	1	146.1	156	74	76	63
91 AL	1	1	5.71	5	0	17.1	21	11	12	16

DON BARBARA

Position: First base
Team: California Angels
Born: Oct. 27, 1968 Long Beach, CA
Height: 6'2" **Weight:** 215 lbs.
Bats: left **Throws:** left
Acquired: 23rd-round pick in 6/90 free-agent draft

Player Summary	
Fantasy Value	$1 to $3
Card Value	5¢ to 10¢
Will	drive home 100 runs
Can't	steal a base
Expect	promotion to Triple-A
Don't Expect	call-up soon

Barbara is a player who leaves California well-stocked at first base, building stats even as he had Wally Joyner and Lee Stevens ahead of him in 1991. Barbara looks big, maybe a little too big, but the size doesn't seem to get in the way of his game. He's no speed demon, but he was the top fielding first baseman in the Class-A Midwest League in 1991 with just two errors in 66 games. A good contact hitter and among the RBI leaders in the California system, Barbara, who attended Long Beach State, becomes especially dangerous with men on base. He shows an ability to carry a team, and he nearly led Quad City to the first-half title in 1991. Barbara is very mature for his age, and a leader type who is admired by his teammates. Another encouraging fact is that he hit even better after his promotion to Double-A, notching a .554 slugging average. His ability at bat is promising for fantasy investors, who will want to sink a few bucks in him. His 1992 cards are good buys at a nickel each.

Professional Batting Register

	BA	G	AB	R	H	2B	3B	HR	RBI	SB
90 A	.291	66	220	22	64	8	0	4	39	1
91 A	.288	66	226	29	65	15	2	5	48	2
91 AA	.362	63	224	43	81	13	0	10	40	0

ROOKIE PROSPECTS

HOWARD BATTLE

Position: Infield
Team: Toronto Blue Jays
Born: March 25, 1972 Ocean Springs, MS
Height: 6'1" **Weight:** 197 lbs.
Bats: right **Throws:** right
Acquired: Fifth-round pick in 6/90 free-agent draft

Player Summary	
Fantasy Value	$1 to $3
Card Value	4¢ to 6¢
Will	improve power numbers
Can't	stay down on grounders
Expect	20 homers
Don't Expect	Gold Glove

Ballclubs like to put power on their corners and Toronto may be able to do that in a few years with Battle. Rated by *Baseball America* the eighth-best prospect in the rookie Pioneer League in 1990, Battle made the All-Star team in the Class-A South Atlantic League in 1991. He looks like he may provide extra-base power, high batting average, and even a little speed at third base. As August approached in '91, Battle ranked among the leaders in all the minors with 44 extra-base hits. He was hitting .282 for Myrtle Beach, tops among regulars. He led all Toronto farmhands with his 26 doubles, and had four triples and 12 homers with 61 RBI. He finished the year with a .345 on-base average and a .477 slugging percentage. He worked on defense with Garth Iorg, Myrtle Beach manager. Battle knows that he has to be more consistent and that he needs to stay down on grounders that he comes up on now. He also puts many balls out of parks that pitchers wish would stay in. He is a $2 fantasy choice, and his current cards are risks at a nickel.

Professional Batting Register

	BA	G	AB	R	H	2B	3B	HR	RBI	SB
90 R	.266	61	233	25	62	17	1	5	32	5
91 A	.283	138	520	82	147	33	4	20	86	15

ROD BECK

Position: Pitcher
Team: San Francisco Giants
Born: Aug. 3, 1968 Burbank, CA
Height: 6'1" **Weight:** 215 lbs.
Bats: right **Throws:** right
Acquired: Traded from Athletics for Charlie Corbell, 3/88

Player Summary	
Fantasy Value	$2 to $4
Card Value	10¢ to 15¢
Will	not walk batters
Can't	stay down
Expect	low ERA
Don't Expect	defined role

Beck not only was born in California and grew up there, but he was also drafted by a California team and then traded to one. In between, he also made the All-Star team in the Class-A California League. Beck graduated from high school in 1986 and became Oakland's 13th pick in the draft. It took him a while to get established in the pros, and the A's traded him across the bay on March 23, 1988. Beck's career seemed to take off at that point. He went 12-7 with a 3.00 ERA for Class-A Clinton of the Midwest League. In 1989, Beck made the California League All-Star squad with an 11-2 mark for San Jose. He carried the sharpness with him to Double-A Shreveport, going 7-3 to cap a cumulative 18-5 mark. A dependable middle reliever, he is no fantasy standout and will go for about $3. His 1992 cards are a bit overpriced at more than a dime.

Professional Pitching Register

	W	L	ERA	G	CG	IP	H	ER	BB	SO
86 A	1	3	5.23	13	0	32.2	47	19	11	21
87 A	5	8	5.18	17	2	92.0	106	53	26	69
88 A	12	7	3.00	28	5	177.0	177	59	27	123
89 A	11	2	2.40	13	4	97.1	91	26	26	88
89 AA	7	3	3.55	16	4	99.0	108	39	16	74
90 AA	10	3	2.23	14	2	93.0	85	23	17	71
90 AAA	4	7	4.93	12	2	76.2	100	42	18	43
91 AAA	4	3	2.02	23	3	71.1	56	16	13	35
91 NL	1	1	3.78	31	0	52.1	53	22	13	38

ROOKIE PROSPECTS

GREG BLOSSER

Position: Outfield
Team: Boston Red Sox
Born: June 26, 1971 Bradenton, FL
Height: 6'3" **Weight:** 200 lbs.
Bats: left **Throws:** left
Acquired: First-round pick in 6/89 free-agent draft

Player Summary	
Fantasy Value	$2 to $4
Card Value	5¢ to 10¢
Will	swing at bad balls
Can't	afford long slumps
Expect	20 homers
Don't Expect	300 average

The Red Sox may have gained something when Bruce Hurst left as a free agent. Using a compensation pick, they made Blosser—a big lefty with potential to hit for both power and average—the 16th overall selection. He showed what he could do in just his second pro season, batting .282 for Class-A Lynchburg and making the Carolina League All-Star team. His 18 homers led the league, and his .459 slugging percentage tied him for third. Blosser had to fight a slump in 1991 Double-A New Britain. He said that the problems he had were mechanical and not because he was overmatched. In 1988, Blosser was the MVP of the USA Junior National Team that played in Australia. The following season, he went from a state and national championship high school team that went 32-1 to the pros. He swings at pitches outside of the strike zone. He debuted in the 1991 Upper Deck set. His 1992 cards are iffy buys at a dime apiece. His fantasy worth is limited to $4.

Professional Batting Register

	BA	G	AB	R	H	2B	3B	HR	RBI	SB
89 R	.288	40	146	17	42	7	3	2	20	3
89 A	.255	28	94	6	24	1	1	2	14	1
90 A	.282	119	447	63	126	23	1	18	62	5
91 AA	.217	134	452	48	98	21	3	8	46	9

ROD BOLTON

Position: Pitcher
Team: Chicago White Sox
Born: Sept. 23, 1968 Chattanooga, TN
Height: 6'2" **Weight:** 190 lbs.
Bats: right **Throws:** right
Acquired: 13th-round pick in 6/90 free-agent draft

Player Summary	
Fantasy Value	$3 to $6
Card Value	15¢ to 20¢
Will	go the distance
Can't	make White Sox yet
Expect	3-1 K-to-walk ratio
Don't Expect	many no-decisions

Baseball America named Bolton the top pitching prospect in the Class-A Florida State league, but the poll must have been taken quickly. After all, he wasn't there very long. Continuing his quick rise through the Chicago system, he went 7-6 with a 1.91 ERA for Sarasota before being promoted. He won his first start for Double-A Birmingham of the Southern League with a seven-inning three-hitter. That made four stops for Bolton in less than two years. He split his rookie season between Class-A Utica and Class-A South Bend, going 5-1 in both places, and striking out 95 in as many innings. Of Bolton's 13 starts, four were complete games and two were shutouts. Only once did he fail to get a decision. Bolton holds a bachelor's degree in marketing from the University of Kentucky, but his pitches do lots of advertising for him these days. He could see a major league debut and his first baseball cards in 1992. His rookie issues are worth up to 20 cents apiece. He is a $4 fantasy draft.

Professional Pitching Register

	W	L	ERA	G	CG	IP	H	ER	BB	SO
90 A	10	2	1.23	13	4	95.0	61	13	23	95
91 A	7	6	1.91	15	5	103.2	81	22	23	77
91 AA	8	4	1.62	12	3	89.0	73	16	21	57

ROOKIE PROSPECTS

RICKY BONES

Position: Pitcher
Team: San Diego Padres
Born: April 7, 1969 Salinas, PR
Height: 5'10" **Weight:** 175 lbs.
Bats: right **Throws:** right
Acquired: Signed as a free agent, 5/86

Player Summary	
Fantasy Value	$3 to $6
Card Value	15¢ to 20¢
Will	stay at Triple-A
Can't	keep runners off base
Expect	San Diego in '92
Don't Expect	ERA under 3.00

Bones enjoyed a solid year at the top rung of the minor leagues in 1991, serving as the ace of the Triple-A Las Vegas starting rotation. His ratio of hits to innings pitched was not exceptional, but he kept walks to a minimum. Bones has been over .500 at several stops since joining the pros in 1986 at the tender age of 17. He went 12-5 with a 3.65 ERA with Class-A Charleston in 1987, then helped Riverside to the Class-A California League title the following year. In 1989, Bones had some trouble with his ERA (5.74) at Double-A Wichita, but still managed a 10-9 mark. He earned still another promotion in 1990, jumping in midseason to the Pacific Coast League. Bones opened with Wichita, going 6-4 and sharing Wichita Player of the Year honors. The value of his issues will keep rising, bringing good news those who invest in his 1992 cards. Fantasy managers will want to spend $5 on his services.

Professional Pitching Register

	W	L	ERA	G	CG	IP	H	ER	BB	SO
86 A	1	3	5.59	18	0	58.0	63	36	29	46
87 A	12	5	3.65	26	4	170.1	183	69	45	130
88 A	15	6	3.64	25	5	175.1	162	71	64	129
89 AA	10	9	5.74	24	2	136.1	162	87	47	88
90 AA	6	4	3.48	21	2	137.0	138	53	45	96
90 AAA	2	1	3.47	5	0	36.1	45	14	10	25
91 AAA	8	6	4.22	23	1	136.1	155	64	43	95
91 NL	4	6	4.83	11	0	54.0	57	29	18	31

BRET BOONE

Position: Second base
Team: Seattle Mariners
Born: April 6, 1969 El Cajon, CA
Height: 5'10" **Weight:** 180 lbs.
Bats: right **Throws:** right
Acquired: Fifth-round pick in 6/90 free-agent draft

Player Summary	
Fantasy Value	$4 to $8
Card Value	15¢ to 25¢
Will	hit 20 homers
Can't	avoid Sandberg comparison
Expect	third generation in majors
Don't Expect	quick promotion

The name of Boone seems destined to be in major league circles for many more years. Long-time catcher Bob Boone, himself the son of Ray Boone, has produced an offspring who looks like a sure big leaguer. Bret was the regular second baseman at Double-A Jacksonville of the Southern League in 1991, showing an ability to hit for above-average power for a middle infielder. He also made the All-Star team, playing second and batting second for the American League Double-A farmhands. Bret attended the University of Southern California and was named a preseason all-American in his sophomore and junior years. He set USC records with 166 runs, 51 doubles, 12 triples, and 160 RBI. He never missed a game. He also feels that being around baseball all his life can do nothing but help him in the future. His baseball heritage and power potential makes his 1992 cards investment gems even at their dime prices. He shows good fantasy potential at $6, and he could even move to shortstop and be in Seattle by the middle of 1992.

Professional Batting Register

	BA	G	AB	R	H	2B	3B	HR	RBI	SB
90 A	.267	74	255	42	68	13	2	8	38	5
91 AA	.255	139	475	64	121	18	1	19	75	9

ROOKIE PROSPECTS

TOBY BORLAND

Position: Pitcher
Team: Philadelphia Phillies
Born: May 29, 1969 Quitman, LA
Height: 6'6" **Weight:** 180 lbs.
Bats: right **Throws:** right
Acquired: 27th-round pick in 6/87 free-agent draft

Player Summary	
Fantasy Value	$2 to $5
Card Value	15¢ to 20¢
Will	pitch into trouble
Can't	pitch down middle
Expect	promotion to Triple-A
Don't Expect	catchers to have it easy

His size alone tells you there must be an element of intimidation when Borland goes to the mound. He certainly used his size and stuff to good advantage in 1991, leading Double-A Reading in saves. Borland also made an appearance in the All-Star Game, pitching one-third of an inning. He sometimes can be wild, but a little wildness does nothing to decrease the intimidation factor, either. He has been a reliever since the day he set foot in the pros. He saved 12 games for Martinsville in 1988, striking out 45 in 49 innings. He was the Phils' Minor League Pitcher of the Month for August, and won the Rolaids Relief Man Award for the rookie Appalachian League. Borland added nine saves the following year in Spartanburg. In 1990, he saved five games in 44 outings for Class-A Clearwater, earning a berth on the Florida State League All-Star Team. He may be Philadelphia's next stopper. His 1992 cards are encouraging investments for 15 cents. He is a $3 fantasy draft.

Professional Pitching Register

	W	L	ERA	G	S	IP	H	ER	BB	SO
88 R	2	3	4.04	34	12	49.0	42	22	29	43
89 A	4	5	2.97	47	9	66.2	62	22	35	48
90 A	1	2	2.26	44	5	59.2	44	15	35	44
90 AA	4	1	1.44	14	0	25.0	16	4	11	26
91 AA	8	3	2.70	59	24	76.2	68	23	56	72

RYAN BOWEN

Position: Pitcher
Team: Houston Astros
Born: Feb. 10, 1968 Hanford, CA
Height: 6' **Weight:** 180 lbs.
Bats: right **Throws:** right
Acquired: First-round pick in 6/86 free-agent draft

Player Summary	
Fantasy Value	$3 to $7
Card Value	15¢ to 25¢
Will	stay in Houston
Can't	keep walking people
Expect	high ERA
Don't Expect	12 wins

A man named Ryan used to throw hard and bring no-hit excitement to the Astrodome. Nolan Ryan is gone and can't be replaced, but Ryan Bowen may create some dramatics of his own. He made an impressive debut in 1991 after being called to fill in for the injured Mark Portugal. Bowen pitched five hitless innings against the Cardinals before being roughed up in the sixth and taking the loss. Bowen was 5-5 with a 4.38 ERA in 18 games for Triple-A Tucson of the Pacific Coast League at the time of the call. The 13th player taken in the 1986 draft, Bowen made his pro debut for Class-A Asheville of the South Atlantic League, going 12-5 in 26 starts. A shoulder ailment virtually ruined his 1988 season, and Bowen rebounded slowly in 1989. He finally got hot in July and August, going 5-2 during those two months with a 3.34 ERA. His 1992 cards could surprise you for 15 cents apiece. He is a safe $4 draft for the future.

Professional Pitching Register

	W	L	ERA	G	CG	IP	H	ER	BB	SO
87 A	12	5	4.04	26	6	160.1	143	72	78	126
88 A	1	0	3.95	4	0	13.2	12	6	10	12
89 AA	8	6	4.25	27	1	139.2	123	66	116	136
90 AA	8	4	3.74	18	2	113.0	103	47	49	109
90 AAA	1	3	9.35	10	0	34.2	41	36	38	29
91 AAA	5	5	4.38	18	2	98.2	114	48	56	78
91 NL	6	4	5.15	14	0	71.2	73	41	36	49

ROOKIE PROSPECTS

RICO BROGNA
Position: First baseman
Team: Detroit Tigers
Born: April 18, 1970 Watertown, CT
Height: 6'2" **Weight:** 190 lbs.
Bats: left **Throws:** left
Acquired: First-round pick in 6/88 free-agent draft

Player Summary	
Fantasy Value	$2 to $5
Card Value	10¢ to 15¢
Will	improve power numbers
Can't	displace Cecil Fielder
Expect	return to Triple-A
Don't Expect	280 average

Brogna has a chance to become the classic first baseman—a smooth-fielding lefty with power. So far in the minors, he has led his league in fielding, played on an All-Star team, won a home run title and helped capture a league championship. He suffered a bit of a reversal in 1991, starting the season with Detroit's top farm team at Triple-A Toledo, but getting sent back to Double-A London. He still was the No. 4 prospect in the Eastern League in '91. He was rated Detroit's top prospect two years in a row by *Baseball America*, which also tabbed him the Class-A Florida State League's top fielding first baseman in 1989. In 1990, he hit a career-high 21 homers to lead the Eastern League, and helped London to a title. He hit two grand slams, one off Ben McDonald, and also led the league in several defensive categories. Brogna had a .447 slugging average that year. At this point, Brogna is a moderate fantasy draft at $3. His 1992 cards are not great purchases for a dime apiece.

Professional Batting Register

	BA	G	AB	R	H	2B	3B	HR	RBI	SB
88 R	.254	60	209	37	53	11	2	7	33	3
89 A	.235	128	459	47	108	20	7	5	51	2
90 AA	.262	137	488	70	128	21	3	21	77	1
91 AA	.273	77	293	40	80	13	1	13	51	0
91 AAA	.220	41	132	13	29	5	1	2	13	2

JEFF BROWN
Position: Pitcher
Team: San Diego Padres
Born: Sept. 8, 1970 Smithville, MO
Height: 6' **Weight:** 165 lbs.
Bats: left **Throws:** left
Acquired: Fourth-round pick in 6/90 free-agent draft

Player Summary	
Fantasy Value	$1 to $4
Card Value	10¢ to 20¢
Will	average K per inning
Can't	understand 1990
Expect	promotion to Double-A
Don't Expect	backslide

Brown may have benefited from exposure to Bruce Tanner, son of former big league manager Chuck Tanner. Bruce was the pitching coach when Brown arrived at Class-A Charleston for his second pro year. Brown was coming off a 1-7 mark in the rookie Arizona League in 1990, but found himself among the South Atlantic League's elite with 10 wins in his first 14 starts. It remains to be seen whether Brown or Tanner is the wizard. The Padres, of course, hope that it's both of them. Whatever the cause, the effects for Brown were wondrous. He ranked among the leaders in the Padres' chain in wins, strikeouts and earned run average. He struck out nine in a 7-0 victory over Gastonia July 18 to raise his record to 10-3 with a 2.11 ERA. Brown's numbers weren't all that bad even in that first difficult pro year. He fanned 59 batters in 58⅓ innings, and walked just 12. He is two seasons away from San Diego, and is a year away for fantasy managers. His 1992 cards are future buys at a dime apiece.

Professional Pitching Register

	W	L	ERA	G	CG	IP	H	ER	BB	SO
90 R	1	7	5.86	16	0	58.1	71	38	12	59
91 A	13	8	2.45	28	4	165.0	134	45	45	152

ROOKIE PROSPECTS

ANDY BRUCE

Position: Infield
Team: St. Louis Cardinals
Born: April 15, 1969 Marietta, GA
Height: 6'1" **Weight:** 205 lbs.
Bats: right **Throws:** right
Acquired: Fourth-round pick in 6/91 free-agent draft

Player Summary	
Fantasy Value	$3 to $5
Card Value	10¢ to 15¢
Will	homer anywhere
Can't	steal bases
Expect	better contact
Don't Expect	majors before late '93

The distances of vast Busch Stadium are forbidding indeed, but the Cardinals have drafted a player who may one day be able to bridge them with one stroke. Bruce is a power and RBI man who earned laurels in college and then went about doing the same in the pros. Part of a draft in which the Cardinals led all major league teams in percentage of college players taken (69), Bruce was the ACC Player of the Year in 1991 at Georgia Tech. His pro career started with Johnson City of the rookie Appalachian League. In July, he was the Player of the Month in the St. Louis chain, the first time a player from that franchise had done that. Bruce may not be a third baseman of major league caliber, and it's possible he would play somewhere else, perhaps first. He definitely showed his power, however, and responded nicely in clutch situations. He had a .530 slugging percentage and a .330 on-base average at Johnson City. A promising third baseman, Bruce is a $4 future fantasy draft. He's not a likely inclusion among 1992 sets. His current cards are fair buys at a dime.

Professional Batting Register

	BA	G	AB	R	H	2B	3B	HR	RBI	SB
91 R	.288	50	198	34	57	21	0	9	42	1
91 A	.184	20	76	6	14	5	0	1	6	0

JEROMY BURNITZ

Position: Outfield
Team: New York Mets
Born: April 14, 1969 Westminster, CA
Height: 6' **Weight:** 190 lbs.
Bats: left **Throws:** right
Acquired: First-round pick in 6/90 free-agent draft

Player Summary	
Fantasy Value	$3 to $6
Card Value	5¢ to 10¢
Will	reach 30-30 again
Can't	make contact
Expect	fast move
Don't Expect	miracles

The Mets began hearing a lot of overtures about Burnitz in 1991, but you couldn't blame them for just smiling and dreaming of the day he arrives in Shea Stadium. He was named the top power hitter in the Double-A Eastern League by *Baseball America*, and he also has the speed to make him the club's next 30-homer, 30-steal man. By the time Burnitz reached 25 homers in late July, no one in the Mets' minor league system had more than 18. He had a little trouble translating all those homers into RBI, as he possessed just 61 at that juncture. Still, hitting with men on base can come with experience, but the ability to run fast and lose baseballs is another matter. Playing with Williamsport in '91, Burnitz put together one stretch in which he hit four homers in five games, going 8-for-24 with nine RBI. Like many power hitters, he strikes out a lot. Found originally in 1991 Score, his 1992 cards will be enticing to collectors for a dime apiece. Fantasy managers will draft him for $4.

Professional Batting Register

	BA	G	AB	R	H	2B	3B	HR	RBI	SB
90 A	.156	11	32	6	5	1	0	0	3	1
90 A	.278	62	205	43	57	7	5	6	25	13
91 AA	.225	135	457	80	103	16	10	31	85	31

ROOKIE PROSPECTS

DARREN BURTON

Position: Outfield
Team: Kansas City Royals
Born: Sept. 16, 1972 Somerset, KY
Height: 6'2" **Weight:** 175 lbs.
Bats: right **Throws:** right
Acquired: Fifth-round pick in 6/90 free-agent draft

Player Summary	
Fantasy Value	$1 to $3
Card Value	5¢ to 10¢
Will	steal 50 bases
Can't	steal first
Expect	more bunting
Don't Expect	Brian McRae to move

The Royals may have found themselves a thoroughbred from Kentucky, one who can show a sprinter's speed while roaming the pastures of center field. Considered one of the Royals' top prospects, Burton in 1990 found himself at the rookie Gulf Coast League, where he stole the first six bases of his pro career. He was also one of six outfielders who took part in the Royals' Instructional League. Burton played for Class-A Appleton of the Midwest League in 1991, and showed both his potential and some of what he has to learn. On the plus side, Burton hit in the .270 range while ranking among the top basestealers in the chain. However, he also struck out too much (122) and walked too seldom for a player who must rely on speed. If Burton can translate some of those whiffs into bunt singles or infield hits, he will race to the bigs. He had a .324 on-base average, and was caught stealing 12 times in 49 attempts, in '91. He will put his speed to use for a fantasy team for $2. His current cards are not hot buys just yet.

Professional Batting Register

	BA	G	AB	R	H	2B	3B	HR	RBI	SB
90 R	.207	15	58	10	12	0	1	0	2	6
91 A	.269	134	532	78	143	32	6	2	51	37

CLAYTON BYRNE

Position: Shortstop
Team: Baltimore Orioles
Born: Feb. 12, 1972 Guildford, Australia
Height: 6'1" **Weight:** 180 lbs.
Bats: right **Throws:** right
Acquired: Signed as a free agent, 12/90

Player Summary	
Fantasy Value	$1 to $2
Card Value	5¢ to 10¢
Will	hit .280
Can't	produce runs
Expect	improved power
Don't Expect	fast progress

This man from Down Under may come out on top in the Orioles' future. Byrne received praise from Baltimore assistant general manager Doug Melvin and was promoted to Class-A Kane County of the Midwest League from extended spring training. He eventually was dropped a notch to Bluefield of the rookie Appalachian League, where he hit .355 in his first 76 at bats. Byrne has shown little power in the low minors, but his size may allow him to do a bit more damage eventually. He compiled a .439 slugging average at Bluefield in '91. He played for the Perth Heat of the Australian Baseball League in 1990, and also represented his native land in the World Youth Series in Cuba. Byrne's father, Rodney, coached Western Australia to numerous Claxton Shield titles, the equivalent of the World Series of amateur baseball. Byrne likes to surf, but the Orioles hope he skims through their chain. He had a great beginning, but he is several years away from being a real fantasy possibility. Spend no more than $2. His current cards are not realistic buys at a nickel apiece.

Professional Batting Register

	BA	G	AB	R	H	2B	3B	HR	RBI	SB
91 R	.321	54	221	39	71	9	4	3	25	8
91 A	.212	26	104	14	22	6	0	0	3	2

ROOKIE PROSPECTS

JIM CAMPANIS

Position: Catcher
Team: Seattle Mariners
Born: Aug. 27, 1967 Fullerton, CA
Height: 6'1" **Weight:** 200 lbs.
Bats: right **Throws:** right
Acquired: Third-round pick in 6/88 free-agent draft

Player Summary	
Fantasy Value	$5 to $12
Card Value	15¢ to 25¢
Will	hit 20 homers
Can't	run well
Expect	call-up in '92
Don't Expect	long stint in Triple-A

Like Double-A Jacksonville teammate Bret Boone, Campanis has a chance to be a third-generation major leaguer. His father, Jim Sr., was a major league catcher, and his grandfather, Al, played and was an executive in the majors. Jim Jr. and Boone were also teammates at the University of Southern California and in the 1991 Double-A All-Star Game. Campanis was also named to the postseason All-Star team, even though he had to compete with Dan Wilson. Campanis put together a long hitting streak that he extended by breaking up a combined no-hitter. A member of Team USA in 1988, he began his pro career in 1989, leading all Class-A California League catchers with 11 homers and 58 RBI. He was also named to the All-Star team. Campanis spent 1990 with Class-A Peninsula, leading all Carolina League catchers with 87 assists. He threw out 42.3 percent of runners trying to steal. He will be in Seattle in 1992, making him a $7 fantasy pick. His 1992 cards are good buys at 15 cents apiece.

Professional Batting Register

	BA	G	AB	R	H	2B	3B	HR	RBI	SB
89 A	.255	133	455	49	116	26	0	11	58	0
90 A	.250	112	364	47	91	22	0	14	60	3
91 AA	.248	118	387	36	96	10	0	15	49	0

CHUCK CARR

Position: Outfield
Team: New York Mets
Born: Aug. 10, 1968 San Bernardino, CA
Height: 5'10" **Weight:** 165 lbs.
Bats: both **Throws:** right
Acquired: Traded from Mariners for Reggie Dobie, 11/88

Player Summary	
Fantasy Value	$2 to $4
Card Value	5¢ to 10¢
Will	chase anything down
Can't	blow this chance
Expect	Triple-A play
Don't Expect	40 RBI

Carr is known as one of the fastest runners in organized baseball, but he must be speedy in putting it to good use. Named by *Baseball America* as the fastest man in the International League in 1991, he was nevertheless fighting to keep his average above .200. Only eight of his first 46 hits were for extra bases, and he drove in just 11 runs in his first 224 at bats. Carr must put his game together in a hurry or risk getting caught from behind by a younger prospect. Carr was originally picked by Cincinnati in the ninth round of the '86 draft but was released a year later. He signed as a free agent with Seattle and got to Double-A but was traded to New York for pitcher Reggie Dobie. Carr is worth a small bid—no more than $3. His nickel-priced 1992 cards are so-so buys.

Professional Batting Register

	BA	G	AB	R	H	2B	3B	HR	RBI	SB
86 R	.171	44	123	13	21	5	0	0	10	9
87 A	.242	44	165	31	40	1	1	1	11	20
88 A	.299	82	304	58	91	14	2	6	30	41
88 AA	.245	41	159	26	39	4	2	1	13	21
89 AA	.241	116	444	45	107	13	1	0	22	47
90 AA	.258	93	360	60	93	20	9	3	24	47
90 AAA	.259	20	81	13	21	5	1	0	8	6
90 NL	.000	4	2	0	0	0	0	0	0	1
91 AAA	.195	64	246	34	48	6	1	1	11	27
91 NL	.182	12	11	1	2	0	0	0	1	1

ROOKIE PROSPECTS

LARRY CASIAN

Position: Pitcher
Team: Minnesota Twins
Born: Oct. 28, 1965 Lynwood, CA
Height: 6' **Weight:** 170 lbs.
Bats: right **Throws:** left
Acquired: Sixth-round pick in 6/87 free-agent draft

Player Summary	
Fantasy Value	$2 to $4
Card Value	5¢ to 10¢
Will	pick off runners
Can't	dominate a hitter
Expect	more Triple-A
Don't Expect	50 Ks

A starter for most of his career, Casian got his first pro save in four years on Aug. 4, 1991, when he nailed down Portland's 7-3 victory over Edmonton. A fine defensive player with a good pickoff move, Casian may one day fit in as a reliever and spot starter. He's not overpowering but can throw the ball over the plate. Casian spent his first pro season in Class-A Visalia, picking up 10 wins and two saves in 18 appearances. He had 27 pickoffs in 18 games, and once was named the organization's Player of the Week. Casian was tabbed a Double-A Southern League All-Star in 1988 and also jumped to the Triple-A Pacific Coast League. In 1989, Casian seemed to stall, but he bounced back with a 9-9 campaign in 1990, and also got his first shot at the majors. He will be a decent middle reliever, but nothing for either fantasy managers or collectors to go nuts over.

Professional Pitching Register

	W	L	ERA	G	S	IP	H	ER	BB	SO
87 A	10	3	2.51	18	2	97.0	89	27	49	96
88 AA	9	9	2.95	27	0	174.0	165	57	62	104
88 AAA	0	1	0.00	1	0	2.2	5	0	0	2
89 AAA	7	12	4.52	28	0	169.1	201	85	63	65
90 AAA	9	9	4.48	31	0	156.2	171	78	59	89
90 AL	2	1	3.22	5	0	22.1	26	8	4	11
91 AAA	3	2	3.46	34	2	52.0	51	20	16	24
91 AL	0	0	7.36	15	0	18.1	28	15	7	6

PETE CASTELLANO

Position: Infielder
Team: Chicago Cubs
Born: March 11, 1970 Lara, Venezuela
Height: 6'1" **Weight:** 175 lbs.
Bats: right **Throws:** right
Acquired: Signed as a free agent, 4/88

Player Summary	
Fantasy Value	$2 to $5
Card Value	10¢ to 15¢
Will	hit .280
Can't	jump to Triple-A
Expect	.400 on-base percentage
Don't Expect	under 70 walks

The Cubs can merely smile as they dream of what this young slugger might someday do in the Friendly Confines of Wrigley Field. Castellano has already established himself as an offensive force in the minors, and added weight may increase his home run totals. *Baseball America* rated him the top power prospect in the Carolina League. For good measure, the publication also tabbed him the best defensive third baseman. Castellano played at Class-A Peoria in 1990, hitting .276 with two homers and 44 RBI, but moved to Class-A Winston-Salem of the Carolina League when Gary Scott was promoted to Double-A Charlotte. Castellano remained with Winston-Salem to open 1991, playing short. He eventually returned to third, where he may be more comfortable. Castellano made the All-Star team and led his team with 88 RBI. A limited fantasy option, he may inherit the Cubs third base job, making him a $4 risk. Investors should wait until he makes it to the bigs before investing in his current cards.

Professional Batting Register

	BA	G	AB	R	H	2B	3B	HR	RBI	SB
89 R	.311	66	244	55	76	17	4	9	42	5
90 A	.265	136	483	67	128	27	4	3	52	8
91 A	.303	129	459	59	139	25	3	10	88	11
91 AA	.421	7	19	2	8	0	0	0	2	0

ROOKIE PROSPECTS

ANDUJAR CEDENO

Position: Shortstop
Team: Houston Astros
Born: Aug. 21, 1969 La Romana, Dominican Republic
Height: 6'1" **Weight:** 168 lbs.
Bats: right **Throws:** right
Acquired: Signed as a free agent, 10/86

Player Summary	
Fantasy Value	$2 to $6
Card Value	5¢ to 10¢
Will	become regular shortstop
Can't	homer in Astrodome
Expect	extra-base pop
Don't Expect	high on-base percentage

Cedeno showed a little of what he can do in the Triple-A All-Star Game, hitting a home run to help the NL farmhands to victory. Cedeno reached the majors on Sept. 2, 1990, and had more than a cup of coffee in 1991. Cedeno played in the Dominican Summer League in 1987, and spent the following year in the United States. He ranked second on the Gulf Coast Astros in average (.285) and in RBI (20). Cedeno blossomed in 1989, making the Class-A South Atlantic League's All-Star team and getting named No. 5 prospect by *Baseball America*. In 1990, Cedeno led the Double-A Southern League with 11 triples. He has the look of a .300 hitter who may be able to add some punch. His rookie '91 cards are wise choices, and his 1992 issues are good buys up to a dime apiece. He will have a full year as the Astros shortstop, so bid up to $6 for his services.

ROYCE CLAYTON

Position: Shortstop
Team: San Francisco Giants
Born: Jan. 2, 1970 Burbank, CA
Height: 6' **Weight:** 175 lbs.
Bats: right **Throws:** right
Acquired: First-round pick in 6/88 free-agent draft

Player Summary	
Fantasy Value	$4 to $10
Card Value	5¢ to 10¢
Will	lead off
Can't	strike out so much
Expect	full year at Triple-A
Don't Expect	12 homers

If Clayton can play anywhere near what the plaudits on his resume indicate, he should be a regular in the majors before very long. He was named the best defensive shortstop and the most exciting player in the Texas League by *Baseball America* in 1991. In 1990, Clayton hit .267 with seven homers and 71 RBI for Class-A San Jose. He made the California League All-Star team and was considered one of that circuit's top prospects. When he arrives in the majors for good, Clayton will give his team speed, a solid average and a little power at the top of the lineup. He still strikes out a bit too much for a leadoff man but he offers a payoff in extra-base hits. He also can draw a walk. Clayton put together a 16-game hitting streak for Double-A Shreveport in 1991. He also had a .361 on-base average and a .390 slugging percentage. He will be a highlight at the draft; try to get him for less than $10. His 1992 cards are great deals at a dime or less.

Professional Batting Register

	BA	G	AB	R	H	2B	3B	HR	RBI	SB
88 R	.285	46	165	25	47	5	2	1	20	10
89 A	.300	126	487	76	146	23	6	14	93	23
90 AA	.240	132	495	57	119	21	11	19	64	6
90 NL	.000	7	8	0	0	0	0	0	0	0
91 AAA	.303	93	347	49	105	19	6	7	55	5
91 NL	.243	67	251	27	61	13	2	9	36	4

Professional Batting Register

	BA	G	AB	R	H	2B	3B	HR	RBI	SB
88 A	.259	60	212	35	55	4	0	3	29	10
89 A	.214	132	477	44	102	15	3	0	28	38
90 A	.267	123	460	80	123	15	10	7	71	33
91 AA	.280	126	485	84	136	22	8	5	68	36
91 NL	.115	9	26	0	3	1	0	0	2	0

ROOKIE PROSPECTS

GREG COLBRUNN

Position: Catcher
Team: Montreal Expos
Born: July 26, 1969 Fontana, CA
Height: 6′ **Weight:** 190 lbs.
Bats: right **Throws:** right
Acquired: Sixth-round pick in 6/87 free-agent draft

Player Summary	
Fantasy Value	$2 to $5
Card Value	5¢ to 10¢
Will	bounce back
Can't	throw like he used to
Expect	extended spring training
Don't Expect	1992 call-up

Here's a name to keep in mind as a long-range possibility. You didn't hear much of Colbrunn in 1991 because he underwent reconstructive surgery on his right elbow in April, and missed the whole year. The Expos said they weren't planning on him playing before spring training of 1992. But before the injury, he looked like one of the Expos' better catching prospects since Gary Carter. In 1990, Colbrunn played for Double-A Jacksonville and hit .301 with 29 doubles, 13 homers, and 76 RBI, making the Southern League All-Star team and being rated the top offensive catcher in the minor leagues. Signed to his first pro contract Aug. 18, 1987, Colbrunn reported to the Florida Instructional League. He spent his first season at Class-A Rockford and hit .266 with seven homers and 46 RBI. He worked out with the Expos late in 1990. Because of his injury, he is a top catching prospect affordable to fantasy managers. Spend no more than $5. A 1991 Donruss Rated Rookie, his 1992 cards look good, too, for a dime or less.

Professional Batting Register

	BA	G	AB	R	H	2B	3B	HR	RBI	SB
88 A	.266	115	417	55	111	18	2	7	46	5
89 A	.237	59	228	20	54	8	0	0	25	3
89 AA	.275	55	178	21	49	11	1	3	18	0
90 AA	.301	125	458	57	138	29	1	13	76	1

SCOTT COOPER

Position: Third base
Team: Boston Red Sox
Born: Oct. 13, 1967 St. Louis, MO
Height: 6′3″ **Weight:** 200 lbs.
Bats: left **Throws:** right
Acquired: Third-round pick in 6/86 free-agent draft

Player Summary	
Fantasy Value	$3 to $6
Card Value	5¢ to 10¢
Will	be in trade rumors
Can't	move Wade Boggs
Expect	extra-base pop
Don't Expect	20 homers

In many organizations, Cooper might already be in the majors to stay. He has shown some punch with the bat, and twice has been named by *Baseball America* as the top fielding third baseman in the Triple-A International League. However, the incumbent at that position is Wade Boggs, so Cooper must get some kind of a break to show what he can do. He had one of his best seasons in 1991, making an appearance in the Triple-A All-Star game and producing an RBI double in one trip to the plate. It was his best season since 1988, where he was picked to the final Class-A Carolina League All-Star team, and hit .393 in seven playoff games. Cooper moved up to Double-A New Britain in 1989 and rebounded from a slow start to hit .247. He showed that he could help some team. Draft him for $4. His nickel-priced 1992 cards are good investments.

Professional Batting Register

	BA	G	AB	R	H	2B	3B	HR	RBI	SB
86 A	.288	51	191	23	55	9	0	9	43	1
87 A	.251	119	370	52	93	21	2	15	63	1
88 A	.298	130	497	90	148	45	7	9	73	0
89 AA	.247	124	421	50	104	24	2	7	39	1
90 AAA	.266	124	433	56	115	17	1	12	44	2
90 AL	.000	2	1	0	0	0	0	0	0	0
91 AAA	.277	137	483	55	134	21	2	15	72	3
91 AL	.457	14	35	6	16	4	2	0	7	0

ROOKIE PROSPECTS

RHEAL CORMIER

Position: Pitcher
Team: St. Louis Cardinals
Born: April 23, 1967 Moneton, New Brunswick, Canada
Height: 5'10" **Weight:** 185 lbs.
Bats: left **Throws:** left
Acquired: Sixth-round pick in 6/88 free-agent draft

Player Summary	
Fantasy Value	$2 to $4
Card Value	5¢ to 10¢
Will	throw strikes
Can't	give up long ball
Expect	lower ERA
Don't Expect	quick development

Can a lumberjack from a coastal province of Canada find happiness in middle America? Absolutely—especially if he gets people out. Actually, Cormier has played as much baseball as most of his colleagues, maybe more. He has, however, worked as a lumberjack during the offseason. If he pitches many games like his major league debut, though, he'll be able to take off during the winter. Cormier went six innings against the Mets, allowing one earned run and picking up the win. Some of his subsequent starts didn't go quite that smoothly, but he got your attention by walking just four men over his first six outings. Cormier was a member of the Canadian Olympic team in the summer of 1988, and pitched for the Cards' Instructional League club. In his first pro season, 1989, Cormier finished third in the Class-A Florida State League in ERA and showed outstanding control. He is a medium fantasy bid at $3, and his nickel-priced 1992 cards are fair investments.

Professional Pitching Register

	W	L	ERA	G	CG	IP	H	ER	BB	SO
89 A	12	7	2.23	26	4	169.2	141	42	33	122
90 AAA	1	1	2.25	4	0	24.0	18	6	3	9
90 AA	5	12	5.04	22	3	121.1	133	68	30	102
91 AAA	7	9	4.23	21	3	127.2	140	60	31	74
91 NL	4	5	4.12	11	2	67.2	74	31	8	38

TIM COSTO

Position: Infield
Team: Cincinnati Reds
Born: Feb. 16, 1969 Glen Ellyn, IL
Height: 6'5" **Weight:** 220 lbs.
Bats: right **Throws:** right
Acquired: Traded from Indians for Reggie Jefferson, 6/91

Player Summary	
Fantasy Value	$2 to $4
Card Value	5¢ to 10¢
Will	improve power
Can't	hit .300
Expect	move to Triple-A
Don't Expect	Cincinnati in '92

Costo was involved in one of the most controversial trades of the 1991 season. It came about because of a front-office snafu that forced Cincinnati to trade top prospect Reggie Jefferson or risk losing him. The Reds found a taker in the Indians, and Costo was the player who arrived in return. Reds players criticized the front office at the time, but the deal may yet prove to be a good one. Costo was Cleveland's No. 1 pick in the 1990 draft, and the eighth overall selection. He was a first-team All-America shortstop at the University of Iowa, but now plays first base. Costo hit .316 with four homers and 42 RBI in '90 at Class-A Kinston. He played the first part of the 1991 season at Double-A Canton-Akron and hit .275 with one homer and 24 RBI in 51 games. At Double-A Chattanooga in 1991, he had a .416 slugging average and a .332 on-base percentage. Scouts credit him with big league pop and better-than-average fielding. A familiar face in 1991 sets, skip his 1992 cards—even at their nickel prices. He is a long-term $3 fantasy draft.

Professional Batting Register

	BA	G	AB	R	H	2B	3B	HR	RBI	SB
90 A	.316	56	206	34	65	13	1	4	42	4
91 AA	.280	137	485	59	134	29	6	6	53	13

ROOKIE PROSPECTS

EARL CUNNINGHAM

Position: Outfield
Team: Chicago Cubs
Born: June 3, 1970 Lancaster, SC
Height: 6'2" **Weight:** 225 lbs.
Bats: right **Throws:** right
Acquired: First-round pick in 6/89 free-agent draft

Player Summary	
Fantasy Value	$2 to $4
Card Value	10¢ to 15¢
Will	hit with power
Can't	swing at everything
Expect	more walks
Don't Expect	polished hitter

Cunningham has a long way to go, especially in his knowledge of the strike zone, but he has begun to show why he was the eighth overall pick in the 1989 draft. He has the power to hit home runs and to drive in runs, and possesses outstanding speed. Cunningham is improving as an outfielder, and the Cubs still consider his potential enormous. The most glaring part of his game right now is a huge discrepancy between his walks and his strikeouts. You expect a slugger to whiff a lot, but you also hope that hurlers will pitch around him now and then. Also, Cunningham has some weaknesses in his approach. He began to put things together in August of 1991, and he supplemented his other skills by adding the bunt. He had a .438 slugging average at Class-A Peoria in 1991. During his first pro year, he was named the No. 4 prospect in the rookie Appalachian League by *Baseball America*. He looks at least a year away, so invest in his dime-priced current cards accordingly. Fantasy managers will want to limit their bidding to $4.

Professional Batting Register

	BA	G	AB	R	H	2B	3B	HR	RBI	SB
89 R	.258	49	182	20	47	6	2	7	38	3
90 A	.216	78	269	24	58	9	0	5	26	2
91 A	.239	101	381	50	91	17	1	19	70	5

CHAD CURTIS

Position: Infield
Team: California Angels
Born: Nov. 6, 1968 Benson, AZ
Height: 5'10" **Weight:** 175 lbs.
Bats: right **Throws:** right
Acquired: 45th-round pick in 6/89 free-agent draft

Player Summary	
Fantasy Value	$3 to $7
Card Value	15¢ to 20¢
Will	hit .300
Can't	move Gary Gaetti
Expect	return to outfield
Don't Expect	Anaheim in '92

Curtis has come a long way quickly. Then again, quickness is his style and his best shot at the majors. He stole 63 bases in 1990 for Class-A Quad City, earning him a trip to Triple-A the following year. He hit .328 with 32 steals in 37 attempts in his first 65 games in the Pacific Coast League. He must work on finding a position; he is listed at an outfielder in the Angels' press guide, having been drafted as a center fielder out of Grand Canyon University. He made the Triple-A All-Star Game as a second baseman, and also played third and the outfield in Edmonton. He probably will not play much middle infield in the bigs. Curtis was married in his baseball uniform, showing up for the service at the Davenport, Iowa, courthouse at 1:30 then going to the park for batting practice. He spent some time on the disabled list in 1991, but still ranked among league leaders in steals. Bid up to $7 for him. His 1992 cards are promising investments at 20 cents apiece.

Professional Batting Register

	BA	G	AB	R	H	2B	3B	HR	RBI	SB
89 R	.303	32	122	30	37	4	4	3	20	17
89 A	.244	23	78	7	19	3	0	2	11	7
90 A	.307	135	492	87	151	28	1	14	65	63
91 AAA	.316	115	431	81	136	28	7	9	61	46

ROOKIE PROSPECTS

BRIAN DEAK

Position: Catcher
Team: Atlanta Braves
Born: Oct. 25, 1967 Harrisburg, PA
Height: 6' **Weight:** 183 lbs.
Bats: right **Throws:** right
Acquired: Third-round pick in 1/86 free-agent draft

Player Summary
Fantasy Value	$1 to $3
Card Value	5¢ to 10¢
Will	get power back
Can't	hit .270
Expect	more Double-A
Don't Expect	regular big leaguer

An injury stalled Deak on the verge of a major league job in 1989, and he has had a hard time reassembling the numbers that made him so alluring back then. He had 21 homers and 64 RBI for Class-A Durham, went to the Carolina League All-Star Game and received postseason honors as well. He would have been promoted to Atlanta in September, but broke a finger on his throwing hand Aug. 24. He hit .218 with three homers in 66 games for Double-A Greenville in 1990, and was sent back to Durham, where the slump continued. Deak wound up with six homers. His power came back in 1991, as Deak hit 10 homers in his first 193 at bats. Another injury sent him to the disabled list. Never a high average hitter, Deak will likely have to rely on power and fine defensive skills to reach the majors and stick. His 1992 cards peak at a dime apiece. He is a questionable fantasy draft for $2.

Professional Batting Register
	BA	G	AB	R	H	2B	3B	HR	RBI	SB
86 R	.325	62	197	45	64	15	2	12	43	12
87 A	.202	92	252	50	51	6	0	15	49	7
88 A	.246	119	345	58	85	19	1	20	59	3
89 A	.235	113	327	44	77	10	0	21	64	3
90 A	.188	43	133	14	25	3	1	3	16	2
90 AA	.218	66	188	24	41	13	0	3	26	2
91 AA	.201	73	204	31	41	9	0	10	41	0

CARLOS DELGADO

Position: Catcher
Team: Toronto Blue Jays
Born: June 25, 1972 Aguadilla, PR
Height: 6'2" **Weight:** 206 lbs.
Bats: left **Throws:** right
Acquired: Signed as a free agent, 10/88

Player Summary
Fantasy Value	$4 to $8
Card Value	10¢ to 20¢
Will	provide long ball
Can't	be held back
Expect	Double-A in '92
Don't Expect	rush to Toronto

You won't need many fingers if you start counting up the true lefthanded, power-hitting catchers in baseball these days. But that's what the Blue Jays may have in this prospect who has accomplished a great deal while still in his teens. Delgado was MVP of St. Catherines of the Class-A New York-Penn League in 1990, leading the team with 13 doubles and 39 RBI and tying for the lead with 30 runs. Delgado improved on that performance with Myrtle Beach in 1991, making the Class-A South Atlantic League All-Star team. His 18 homers were in second place among Toronto farmhands. Delgado also had 71 RBI, placing him in the thick of that scramble, too. He had a .458 slugging percentage and a .395 on-base average. Like most power hitters, he strikes out some but he isn't an undue offender. Right now he is considered to be more advanced in his offensive game than his defensive. Invest smartly in his current cards for a dime each. Draft him for less than $8—he could move up to Toronto quickly.

Professional Batting Register
	BA	G	AB	R	H	2B	3B	HR	RBI	SB
89 A	.180	31	89	9	16	5	0	0	11	0
90 A	.283	67	226	29	64	13	0	6	39	2
91 A	.286	132	441	72	126	18	2	18	71	9
91 AAA	.000	1	3	0	0	0	0	0	0	0

ROOKIE PROSPECTS

JOHN DeSILVA

Position: Pitcher
Team: Detroit Tigers
Born: Sept. 30, 1967 Fort Bragg, CA
Height: 6' **Weight:** 193 lbs.
Bats: right **Throws:** right
Acquired: Eight-round pick in 6/89 free-agent draft

Player Summary	
Fantasy Value	$2 to $4
Card Value	10¢ to 15¢
Will	average K per inning
Can't	sustain rapid progress
Expect	more Triple-A
Don't Expect	call-up in '92

For some players, the constant packing and unpacking of a suitcase can be a sign of mediocrity or of a journeyman. In DeSilva's case, however, his travels merely represent a fast track to success. He attended Brigham Young University, where he was the Western Athletic Conference's Baseball Player of the Year in 1989. After the draft, DeSilva made his first pro appearance for Class-A Niagara Falls, where he went 3-0 with a 1.88 ERA in his first four starts. The Tigers quickly moved him to Class-A Fayetteville, where he split four decisions while allowing just 40 hits in 52⅔ innings. In 1990, DeSilva went to Class-A Lakeland and responded with an 8-1 mark. The next stop was Double-A London, where DeSilva fanned 76 in 89 innings. In 28 starts at Lakeland and London, DeSilva posted a combined 13-7 mark. He was in Triple-A in 1991, and went 2-2 in his first six starts. He doesn't offer to fantasy managers a stunning draft, even for $4. His 1992 cards also lack excitement at a dime apiece.

Professional Pitching Register

	W	L	ERA	G	CG	IP	H	ER	BB	SO
89 A	5	2	2.47	13	1	76.2	55	21	29	78
90 A	8	1	1.48	14	0	91.0	54	15	25	113
90 AA	5	6	3.74	14	1	89.0	87	37	27	76
91 AA	5	4	2.81	11	2	73.2	51	23	24	80
91 AAA	5	4	4.60	11	1	58.2	62	30	21	56

CESAR DEVARES

Position: Catcher
Team: Baltimore Orioles
Born: Sept. 22, 1969 San Francisco de Macoris, Dominican Republic
Height: 5'10" **Weight:** 175 lbs.
Bats: right **Throws:** right
Acquired: Signed as a free agent, 2/88

Player Summary	
Fantasy Value	$1 to $3
Card Value	5¢ to 10¢
Will	improve average
Can't	drive in 50
Expect	frustrated baserunners
Don't Expect	quick promotion

Devares made some progress on his offensive game in 1991, but lost some continuity when he went on the disabled list July 21. He is an interesting case: He is not big as catchers go, and he may never develop into the classic power-hitting catcher, but switch-hitting plus a rifle of a throwing arm may take him far in the game. He played for Class-A Frederick of the Carolina League in 1991 and, at one point, had thrown out about 65 percent of the runners who tried him. He also hit .251, an improvement over previous years. Devares was signed in February 1988 and played the following summer in the Dominican league. He made his pro debut in the United States with Bluefield of the rookie Appalachian League in 1989, but hit just .214 in 12 games. In 1990, Devares played for Class-A Wausau, batting .199. He produced three RBI in his first game but couldn't sustain it. Don't go overboard at the draft on him, limiting your bid to $3. His nickel-priced 1992 cards don't excite many investors.

Professional Batting Register

	BA	G	AB	R	H	2B	3B	HR	RBI	SB
89 R	.214	12	42	3	9	4	0	0	7	0
90 A	.199	56	171	7	34	4	1	3	19	2
91 A	.251	74	235	25	59	13	2	3	29	2

ROOKIE PROSPECTS

LANCE DICKSON

Position: Pitcher
Team: Chicago Cubs
Born: Oct. 19, 1969 Fullerton, CA
Height: 6'1" **Weight:** 185 lbs.
Bats: right **Throws:** left
Acquired: First-round pick in 6/90 free-agent draft

Player Summary	
Fantasy Value	$4 to $7
Card Value	10¢ to 15¢
Will	cut down on walks
Can't	be a one-pitch man
Expect	return to Wrigley
Don't Expect	12 wins

Dickson is a top prospect who has used an outstanding curveball to breeze through the minors and get a taste of the majors. Now the question is whether that pitch, combined with a fastball that may not yet have reached a peak, can give him success in the big leagues. Dickson's fastball is said to be short, but not that short. Furthermore, it's possible that he may gain a foot or two, as sometimes happens to pitchers who go to school at the University of Arizona. Dickson suffered a foot injury in May of 1991, but still led the league in strikeouts for most of the season. Opponents compiled a .237 batting average against him that year. In 1990, he pitched at four levels of pro ball, having more strikeouts than innings at three of them. He rocketed to the majors based on need, and made three starts, but didn't have much. He has plenty of time to excel, provided he stays healthy. He is a good fantasy draft at $5. His 1992 cards are appealing investments at a nickel or so.

JAMIE DISMUKE

Position: Infield
Team: Cincinnati Reds
Born: Oct. 17, 1969 Syracuse, NY
Height: 6'1" **Weight:** 215 lbs.
Bats: left **Throws:** right
Acquired: 12th-round pick in 6/89 free-agent draft

Player Summary	
Fantasy Value	$1 to $3
Card Value	5¢ to 10¢
Will	hit 30 doubles
Can't	bat .300
Expect	logjam ahead
Don't Expect	whirlwind ascent

Being a lefty swinger with some size and some pop in his bat, Dismuke has the chance to be a prototypical first baseman. But first he must get some at bats and in 1991, that's just what he did. In his first full pro year, Dismuke responded by becoming a bonafide run producer. He battled for the lead in RBI among Reds' farmhands. He also led Class-A Cedar Rapids of the Midwest League in doubles and was tied for second on the club with eight homers. Dismuke signed out of high school in Syracuse in 1989, but it took him two years to experience the test of a long season. He made his pro debut with rookie ball Plant City and hit .184 in just 34 games. In 1990, he played in only 39 games in the Gulf Coast League, batting 124 times, but got some attention. Dismuke batted .355 with eight doubles, four triples, and seven homers. Wait for a few years before drafting this prospect at $3. His current cards are inferior buys at a nickel apiece.

Professional Pitching Register

	W	L	ERA	G	CG	IP	H	ER	BB	SO
90 A	5	2	1.20	8	1	52.2	27	7	15	73
90 AA	2	1	0.38	3	1	23.2	13	1	3	28
90 NL	0	3	7.24	3	0	13.2	20	11	4	4
91 AAA	4	4	3.11	18	1	101.1	85	35	57	101

Professional Batting Register

	BA	G	AB	R	H	2B	3B	HR	RBI	SB
89 R	.184	34	98	6	18	1	0	1	5	0
90 R	.355	39	124	22	44	8	4	7	28	3
91 A	.254	133	492	56	125	35	1	8	72	4

ROOKIE PROSPECTS

KIRK DRESSENDORFER

Position: Pitcher
Team: Oakland Athletics
Born: April 8, 1969 Houston, TX
Height: 5'11" **Weight:** 190 lbs.
Bats: right **Throws:** right
Acquired: First-round pick in 6/90 free-agent draft

Player Summary	
Fantasy Value	$2 to $4
Card Value	10¢ to 15¢
Will	throw heat
Can't	fit name on jersey
Expect	seasoning in minors
Don't Expect	injury-free year

Dressendorfer likely will never forget the 1991 season, a campaign marred by an ear infection and by ineffective performances. However, this top prospect has an arm that no one should give up on. He was taken as Oakland's first-round supplemental choice for the loss of free agent Dave Parker, and though hampered by tendinitis, Dressendorfer struck out 22 in his first 19⅓ innings. He was named the No. 2 prospect in the Class-A Northwest League in '90. He was a star at the University of Texas, selected as a first-team All-America all three years there. He went 45-8 with a 2.56 ERA, and struck out 462 men in 429⅔ innings. He broke Greg Swindell's freshman marks for wins, complete games, and innings, and was named the Southwest Conference Player of the Year. Dressendorfer was drafted out of high school by the Orioles in the 34th round in 1987 but elected to attend college. He may have stalled, but he has the talent. He is a good fantasy pick up to $4, and his dime-priced 1992 cards are tempting buys.

Professional Pitching Register

	W	L	ERA	G	CG	IP	H	ER	BB	SO
90 A	0	1	2.33	7	0	19.1	18	5	2	22
91 AAA	1	3	10.88	8	0	24.0	31	29	20	19
91 AL	3	3	5.45	7	0	34.2	33	21	21	17

CAL ELDRED

Position: Pitcher
Team: Milwaukee Brewers
Born: Nov. 24, 1967 Cedar Rapids, IA
Height: 6'4" **Weight:** 215 lbs.
Bats: right **Throws:** right
Acquired: First-round pick in 6/89 free-agent draft

Player Summary	
Fantasy Value	$4 to $8
Card Value	15¢ to 20¢
Will	average K a frame
Can't	allow so many walks
Expect	'92 start at Triple-A
Don't Expect	full year in minors

Eldred made an impression at Triple-A Denver in 1991 because, despite suffering a six-game losing streak, he displayed the air of confidence so necessary in baseball. At one point, he was having trouble with walks and with escaping jams, but he rebounded to the point where the Zephyrs expected a win whenever Eldred went out there. He can be overpowering, can dominate a game, and led the American Association in strikeouts. Eldred's control is not textbook variety, but it isn't bad, either. Originally drafted by the Mets in 1986, Eldred attended the University of Iowa, where he finished fourth on that school's all-time strikeout list. Eldred was the 17th overall pick in the 1989 draft and would have been higher but for injuries. He was termed the second-best college prospect by *Collegiate Baseball*. He has only had two full years of pro ball, and may be fearsome when he adds experience. His 1992 cards will be hot buys at 20 cents apiece. He is a $6 fantasy pick.

Professional Pitching Register

	W	L	ERA	G	CG	IP	H	ER	BB	SO
89 A	2	1	2.30	8	0	31.1	23	8	11	32
90 A	4	2	1.62	7	3	50.0	31	9	19	75
90 AA	5	4	4.49	19	0	110.1	126	55	47	93
91 AAA	13	9	3.75	29	3	185.0	161	77	84	168
91 AL	2	0	4.50	3	0	16.0	20	8	6	10

ROOKIE PROSPECTS

DONNIE ELLIOTT

Position: Pitcher
Team: Philadelphia Phillies
Born: Sept. 20, 1968 Pasadena, TX
Height: 6'4" **Weight:** 190 lbs.
Bats: right **Throws:** right
Acquired: Seventh-round pick in 6/87 free-agent draft

Player Summary
Fantasy Value	$1 to $2
Card Value	5¢ to 10¢
Will	post low ERA
Can't	let control regress
Expect	heat
Don't Expect	fast progress

Elliott was named Class-A Florida State Pitcher of the Week midway through 1991 when he shut out Fort Lauderdale and Port Charlotte. He was among the organization's leaders in victories and led all Phillie farmhands in strikeouts with 184. Pitching for Spartanburg on May 25, Elliott fanned 17 in seven and two-thirds innings against Sumter. He was named by *Baseball America* as having the Class-A South Atlantic League's best fastball. Elliott pitched for both Spartanburg and Clearwater in 1991. He entered the pros in '88, a year after being drafted. Used both as a starter and in relief, he went 4-2 at Martinsville in the rookie Appalachian League. In 1989, Elliott opened with Batavia of the Class-A New York-Penn League and went 4-1 in eight starts. The Phils moved him to the Sally League, where he was 2-3 with a 2.47 ERA. He stayed at Spartanburg all of '90. He is not a worthy investment yet, and his current cards are nickel priced. He is a risky $1 fantasy pitcher at this point.

Professional Pitching Register
	W	L	ERA	G	CG	IP	H	ER	BB	SO
88 R	4	2	3.66	15	0	59.0	47	24	31	77
89 A	6	4	1.88	15	1	100.2	91	21	28	84
90 A	4	8	3.50	20	0	105.1	101	41	46	109
91 A	11	9	2.78	28	1	158.0	120	57	87	184

JOHN ERICKS

Position: Pitcher
Team: St. Louis Cardinals
Born: Sept. 16, 1967 Oaklawn, IL
Height: 6'7" **Weight:** 220 lbs.
Bats: right **Throws:** right
Acquired: First-round pick in 6/88 free-agent draft

Player Summary
Fantasy Value	$1 to $3
Card Value	5¢ to 10¢
Will	double win total
Can't	walk as many
Expect	more Double-A
Don't Expect	ERA below 3.50

This Stephen King fan experienced every pitcher's horror story when he had arm trouble and underwent surgery to remove bone chips from his right elbow. Ericks made a slow recovery, and now the Cardinals are hoping he can again be the pitcher he was in 1989, when he led the Class-A South Atlantic League with 211 strikeouts and was named the league's second-best pitching prospect by *Baseball America*. He began the 1990 season with Class-A St. Petersburg of the Florida State League and went 2-1 in four starts. He was promoted to Double-A Arkansas to the Texas League but was not himself. He went on the disabled list May 19 and was lost for the season. Ericks lost his first eight decisions of 1991 at Arkansas, then began to put things together. Wait for success at the Double-A level before sinking a buck in Ericks's fantasy future. His current cards are risky, even at a nickel apiece. He was included in the '91 Upper Deck set.

Professional Pitching Register
	W	L	ERA	G	CG	IP	H	ER	BB	SO
88 R	3	2	3.73	9	1	41.0	27	17	27	41
89 A	11	10	2.04	28	1	167.1	90	38	101	211
90 A	2	1	1.57	4	0	23.0	16	4	6	25
90 AA	1	2	9.39	4	1	15.1	17	16	19	19
91 AA	5	14	4.77	25	1	139.2	138	74	84	103

ROOKIE PROSPECTS

ANDY FAIRMAN

Position: First base
Team: Milwaukee Brewers
Born: April 9, 1970 Royal Oak, MI
Height: 6'2" **Weight:** 210 lbs.
Bats: left **Throws:** left
Acquired: 24th-round pick in 6/91 free-agent draft

Player Summary	
Fantasy Value	$1 to $2
Card Value	5¢ to 10¢
Will	pound 30 doubles
Can't	keep up same pace
Expect	100 RBI
Don't Expect	100 K

Fairman may be the strongest man to prowl the Northwest since Paul Bunyan. He posted numbers in the rookie Pioneer League that catch attention, numbers that would make him a rich man if he could sustain them to the majors. Fairman, who attended the University of Michigan, forged two career nights early in his pro career. He went 3-for-4 with two doubles and five RBI against Medicine Hat, then the next night went 3-for-5 with a triple, two home runs, and six RBI against Great Falls. His numbers may partially result from playing in a hitter's park, but he also showed a good knowledge of the strike zone. In 268 at bats, he had walked (48) more than twice as much as he struck out (27). At that point, he also owned 22 doubles, a triple, and eight homers. He had a .552 slugging percentage and a .463 on-base average. He may become a power hitter who can also make consistent contact, though he didn't kill rookie pitching. He is a reasonable fantasy future risk at a buck. His current cards, though, are illogical at a nickel each.

Professional Batting Register

	BA	G	AB	R	H	2B	3B	HR	RBI	SB
91 R	.373	70	268	57	100	22	1	8	62	3

HECTOR FAJARDO

Position: Pitcher
Team: Texas Rangers
Born: Nov. 6, 1970 Michoacan, Mexico
Height: 6'4" **Weight:** 185 lbs.
Bats: right **Throws:** right
Acquired: Traded from Pirates with Kurt Miller for Steve Buechele, 8/91

Player Summary	
Fantasy Value	$2 to $5
Card Value	5¢ to 10¢
Will	improve K-to-walk ratio
Can't	get ERA below 3.50
Expect	long look
Don't Expect	Steel City Opening Day

Focus and poise, not to mention a 98-mph fastball, helped Fajardo skyrocket through the Bucs' minor league system and reach the big leagues in 1991. Though he didn't enter the season as a top prospect, and even though he was just 20, he was 4-3 with a 2.69 ERA for Class-A Augusta of the South Atlantic League. He made one start for Class-A Salem of the Carolina League and won it, then graduated to Double-A, then Triple-A, then finally the big leagues. Little of what Fajardo accomplished in his first two years in the Pirates' chain suggested the success to come. In 1989, he went 0-5 with Bradenton of the rookie Gulf Coast League. He had a 3-3 mark in 1990, starting at Bradenton and moving up to Augusta. Though he made it to the bigs already, don't place unreasonably high expectations on his future. Wait until he has some success in 1992 before spending a dime on his 1992 cards. He is a $3 fantasy future draft.

Professional Pitching Register

	W	L	ERA	G	CG	IP	H	ER	BB	SO
89 R	0	5	5.97	10	0	34.2	38	23	20	19
90 R	1	1	3.86	5	0	21.0	23	9	8	17
90 A	2	2	3.86	7	0	39.2	41	17	15	28
91 A	4	1	2.65	12	2	68.0	48	20	25	86
91 AA	3	4	4.13	10	1	61.0	55	28	24	53
91 AAA	1	0	0.96	8	0	9.1	6	1	3	12
91 NL	0	0	9.95	2	0	6.1	10	7	7	8
91 AL	0	2	5.68	4	0	19.0	25	12	4	15

ROOKIE PROSPECTS

MONTY FARISS

Position: Infield
Team: Texas Rangers
Born: Oct. 13, 1967 Cordell, OK
Height: 6'4" **Weight:** 200 lbs.
Bats: right **Throws:** right
Acquired: First-round pick in 6/88 free-agent draft

Player Summary	
Fantasy Value	$3 to $5
Card Value	5¢ to 10¢
Will	hit .275
Can't	be tops with glove
Expect	talk of moving Franco to short
Don't Expect	continued power

Fariss may have a chance to hit his way onto a 1992 berth with the Rangers coming off the most productive year of his pro career. He made the Triple-A All-Star team and was among the home run and RBI leaders in the Texas chain in 1991. His glove, however, may not be up to that standard, though a switch from short to second might help. A star at Oklahoma State University, Fariss hit .330 with 65 homers and 247 RBI in three years. He ranked third behind Pete Incaviglia and Robin Ventura in home runs and RBI on the school's all-time list. In 1988, Fariss hit .397 with 30 homers and 114 RBI, becoming an All-America selection. He was the sixth overall pick in the 1988 draft. In 1989, Fariss led Texas League shortstops with 51 errors. He reached Triple-A in 1990 and started his conversion to second base. Getting only a brief shot at Texas in 1991 reduced his fantasy value to $4. His 1992 cards are fair investments at a nickel.

Professional Batting Register

	BA	G	AB	R	H	2B	3B	HR	RBI	SB
88 R	.396	17	53	16	21	1	0	4	22	2
88 AA	.224	49	165	21	37	6	6	3	31	2
89 AA	.272	132	497	72	135	27	2	5	52	12
90 AA	.299	71	244	45	73	15	6	7	34	8
90 AAA	.302	62	225	30	68	12	3	4	31	1
91 AAA	.271	137	494	84	134	31	9	13	73	4
91 AL	.258	19	31	6	8	1	0	1	6	0

DAVE FLEMING

Position: Pitcher
Team: Seattle Mariners
Born: Nov. 7, 1969 Queens, NY
Height: 6' **Weight:** 190 lbs.
Bats: left **Throws:** left
Acquired: Third-round pick in 6/90 free-agent draft

Player Summary	
Fantasy Value	$2 to $4
Card Value	10¢ to 15¢
Will	take the ball
Can't	open '92 in Seattle
Expect	5-1 K-to-walk ratio
Don't Expect	prolonged time in minors

Fleming looks like one of the very best lefthanded prospects in all of baseball. He has control that sets any pitcher, much less a young lefty, apart. He distinguished himself in the Double-A Southern League in 1991 by allowing two or fewer walks in 16 of his first 17 starts. Fleming attended the University of Georgia and also played for Team USA in 1989. He led Georgia to the 1990 College World Series championship, saving the title game with three scoreless innings against Oklahoma State and striking out the side in the ninth. Earlier that season, he ended Mississippi State's 177-game scoring streak by hurling a 9-0 shutout. Straight from college ball, Fleming was a standout for Class-A San Bernardino of the California League. He went 7-3 with four complete games. In 1991, he became Double-A Jacksonville's first 10-game winner of the season with a 3-0 whitewash of Knoxville. He is an ordinary fantasy draft at $3. Don't stock up on his dime-priced 1992 cards until he finds a spot in the Seattle rotation.

Professional Pitching Register

	W	L	ERA	G	CG	IP	H	ER	BB	SO
90 A	7	3	2.60	12	4	79.2	64	23	30	77
91 AAA	2	0	1.13	3	1	16.0	10	2	3	16
91 AA	10	6	2.70	21	6	140.0	129	42	25	109
91 AL	1	0	6.62	9	0	17.2	19	13	3	11

ROOKIE PROSPECTS

KEVIN FLORA

Position: Infield
Team: California Angels
Born: June 10, 1969 Fontana, CA
Height: 6' **Weight:** 180 lbs.
Bats: right **Throws:** right
Acquired: Second-round pick in 6/87 free-agent draft

Player Summary	
Fantasy Value	$1 to $2
Card Value	5¢ to 10¢
Will	steal 30 bases
Can't	reach 60 RBI
Expect	more triples than homers
Don't Expect	blossoming in Anaheim

Four years after being drafted, Flora finally stepped forward at the plate in 1991, and did so while learning a new position. This reestablished him as a prospect, but there is still some sentiment his search for a defensive slot may not yet be over. He had been a shortstop but switched to second, where he proved to be of average Double-A caliber. He is both quick and fast, but has some thing to learn there. He had some trouble getting the ball out of his glove, but became better over the course of the year at turning the double play. It's possible Flora's best position might be center, where his arm might suffice and he could use his speed. Flora may be the fastest man in the chain. His strikeout-to-walk ratio has been poor most of his career. But in 1991 at Double-A Midland, he had a .338 on-base average and a .450 slugging percentage. He is a couple of years away, so keep your bid to $1. Don't stock up on his current cards

RON FRAZIER

Position: Pitcher
Team: New York Yankees
Born: June 13, 1969 Berlin, VT
Height: 6'2" **Weight:** 175 lbs.
Bats: right **Throws:** right
Acquired: 12th-round pick in 6/90 free-agent draft

Player Summary	
Fantasy Value	$3 to $5
Card Value	10¢ to 15¢
Will	keep ERA below 3.50
Can't	jump to Double-A
Expect	3-1 K-to-walk ratio
Don't Expect	fast trip

This son of New England may end up being a big part of the plans for those hated rivals of the Boston Red Sox. Frazier, who was born in Vermont, went to high school in Connecticut and lists his home as Otis, Massachusetts, has been consistently effective as a pro. He followed up a pleasing debut year in the New York-Penn League with an even more impressive one in the South Atlantic League. All the right ratios—hits to innings and walks to innings—seem to be in the right place. Frazier, who attended Clemson University, broke into the pros with Class-A Oneonta in 1990, going 6-2 with a 2.46 ERA in 13 starts. In 80⅓ innings, he allowed just 67 hits and 33 walks while striking out 67. Bumped up the chain to Class-A Greensboro in 1991, Frazier won 12, walking just 42 in 169 innings. He ranked among the leaders in New York's chain with a 2.40 ERA. A long-shot fantasy buy at $3, he has the arm to make that bid pay off. His current cards are tempting at a dime.

Professional Batting Register

	BA	G	AB	R	H	2B	3B	HR	RBI	SB
87 A	.273	35	88	17	24	5	1	0	12	8
88 A	.217	48	152	19	33	3	4	0	15	5
89 A	.218	120	372	46	81	8	4	1	21	30
90 AA	.228	71	232	35	53	16	5	5	32	11
91 AA	.285	124	484	97	138	14	15	12	67	40
91 AL	.125	3	8	1	1	0	0	0	0	1

Professional Pitching Register

	W	L	ERA	G	CG	IP	H	ER	BB	SO
90 A	6	2	2.46	13	0	80.1	67	22	33	67
91 A	12	6	2.40	25	3	169.0	140	45	42	127

ROOKIE PROSPECTS

JAY GAINER

Position: First base
Team: San Diego Padres
Born: Oct. 8, 1966 Panama City, FL
Height: 6' **Weight:** 188 lbs.
Bats: left **Throws:** left
Acquired: 24th-round pick in 6/90 free-agent draft

Player Summary	
Fantasy Value	$2 to $6
Card Value	10¢ to 20¢
Will	drive in 100 runs
Can't	understand low draft spot
Expect	promotion to Double-A
Don't Expect	unseating of McGriff

Gainer has a chance to become one of the better-known players ever taken in the 24th round of any draft. From this relatively low status, the first baseman stepped into the Class-A Northwest League in 1990 with a league-leading .356 average. With 21 doubles and 10 homers, Gainer produced 31 extra-base hits among his 100 safeties. He also drove in 54 runs. He was even more astonishing in his 1991 promotion to Class-A High Desert of the California League. Gainer led all San Diego farmhands with 32 homers, and had 120 RBI, beating out teammate Matt Mieske by one. Gainer had a pair of home runs and five RBI in a victory over Modesto August 5. He hit a 430-foot home run and another off the top of a light pole. Estimates place its length at 460 feet had it not been stopped. He went 4-for-5 with six RBI in a game against Bakersfield. He is a strong fantasy draft for $2, but he is iffy nearer the $6 range. His current cards are fine purchases at a dime or so apiece.

RICH GARCES

Position: Pitcher
Team: Minnesota Twins
Born: May 18, 1971 Maracay, Venezuela
Height: 6' **Weight:** 215 lbs.
Bats: right **Throws:** right
Acquired: Signed as a free agent, 12/87

Player Summary	
Fantasy Value	$2 to $4
Card Value	5¢ to 10¢
Will	need time to recover
Can't	go AWOL again
Expect	another chance
Don't Expect	quick progress

For a reliever, Garces certainly found no relief from ill fortune in 1991. The season began with a bout with tendinitis, included a suspension for leaving the Twins' Triple-A affiliate in Portland, and ended with an elbow injury. Garces enters the 1992 season hoping to have recovered from a displaced nerve in his pitching elbow. The injury occurred in a game against Birmingham, when he fell to the ground in pain after striking out Carl Sullivan. Garces's fantasy value also slipped a bit, down to $3. In 1990, he made his way from Class-A Visalia to the majors, compiling 38 saves. He had 28 with Visalia of the California League, added eight for Double-A Orlando, and wound up with two for the Twins. Garces has been a reliever for most of his pro career, the exception coming in '89 when he went 9-10 for Kenosha in 24 starts. His 1992 cards are holds until he comes back from injury and has some good numbers during the season.

Professional Batting Register

	BA	G	AB	R	H	2B	3B	HR	RBI	SB
90 A	.356	74	281	41	100	21	0	10	54	4
91 A	.263	127	499	83	131	17	0	32	120	4

Professional Pitching Register

	W	L	ERA	G	S	IP	H	ER	BB	SO
88 R	5	4	2.29	17	5	59.0	51	15	27	69
89 A	9	10	3.41	24	0	142.2	117	54	62	84
90 A	2	2	1.81	47	28	54.2	33	11	16	75
90 AA	2	1	2.08	15	8	17.1	17	4	14	22
90 AL	0	0	1.59	5	2	5.2	4	1	4	1
91 AA	2	1	3.31	10	0	16.1	12	6	14	17
91 AAA	0	1	4.85	10	3	13.0	10	7	8	13

ROOKIE PROSPECTS

APOLINAR GARCIA

Position: Pitcher
Team: Cleveland Indians
Born: Jan. 30, 1968 Bonao, Dominican Republic
Height: 5'11" **Weight:** 165 lbs.
Bats: right **Throws:** right
Acquired: Traded from Athletics with Lee Tinsley for Brook Jacoby, 7/91

Player Summary
Fantasy Value	$2 to $4
Card Value	15¢ to 20¢
Will	be around plate
Can't	rely on strikeouts
Expect	time at Triple-A
Don't Expect	Indians to wait on him

Garcia came to the Indians in the Brook Jacoby deal. Garcia was assigned to Cleveland's Double-A affiliate in Canton-Akron of the Eastern League. With the A's, Garcia had pitched for Double-A Huntsville of the Southern League, winning six of nine decisions. He stretched his winning streak to six with a complete-game, 4-2 victory over Knoxville. Signed by Juan Marichal with the Oakland organization in 1987, Garcia played his first pro ball in the Dominican Republic. He worked in the United States in 1988, making three stops. Garcia spent 1989 in the rotation for Class-A Madison of the Midwest League, going 5-14 with a 4.60 ERA. He opened 1990 in the Class-A California League, pitching better than his 3-11 mark indicates. He is a tempting selection for fantasy managers speculating on the future for $3. His 1992 cards should be stocked at 20 cents or less.

Professional Pitching Register
	W	L	ERA	G	CG	IP	H	ER	BB	SO
88 R	1	1	8.31	2	0	13.0	19	12	4	8
88 A	2	4	8.10	10	0	36.2	49	33	16	17
88 AAA	0	0	9.00	1	0	5.0	6	5	4	1
89 A	5	14	4.60	27	3	139.0	146	71	65	110
90 A	3	11	3.59	20	1	123.0	113	49	41	96
90 AA	5	1	3.50	7	2	54.0	45	21	18	29
91 AA	8	4	2.40	17	3	97.2	98	26	35	50
91 AAA	0	4	10.92	7	0	29.2	49	36	20	12

CHEO GARCIA

Position: Third base
Team: Minnesota Twins
Born: April 27, 1968 Maracaibo, Venezuela
Height: 5'11" **Weight:** 165 lbs.
Bats: both **Throws:** right
Acquired: Signed as a free agent, 6/88

Player Summary
Fantasy Value	$3 to $6
Card Value	10¢ to 20¢
Will	drive in key runs
Can't	rely just on defense
Expect	.25 doubles
Don't Expect	100 Ks

Managers named Garcia the best defensive third baseman in the Southern League in 1991 and, more importantly for him, he may have been the best at his position in the Minnesota organization. His reflexes are quick, he has very good range, and he has a cannon for an arm. A contact hitter, Garcia was also doing his part at the plate. At midsummer, he was hitting .318, third-best in the league, and had nine homers and 58 RBI. He finished at fifth in the batting race. His RBI total placed him among the leaders both in the league and in the Twins' minor league system. He had a .349 on-base average and a .401 slugging percentage in 1991. He was named to the loop's postseason All-Star Team. That followed a 1990 campaign in which Garcia hit .274 with 10 homers and 71 RBI for Visalia of the Class-A California League. If Scott Leius falters in development, Garcia may get a look at third for the Twins, making him a $4 fantasy possibility. His current cards are good buys at a dime or so.

Professional Batting Register
	BA	G	AB	R	H	2B	3B	HR	RBI	SB
88 R	.259	59	228	31	59	9	3	2	27	9
89 A	.235	123	468	58	110	24	4	6	49	16
90 A	.274	137	486	68	133	29	4	10	71	10
91 AA	.282	137	496	57	140	24	4	9	75	13

ROOKIE PROSPECTS

RAMON GARCIA

Position: Pitcher
Team: Chicago White Sox
Born: Dec. 9, 1969 Guanare, Venezuela
Height: 6'2" **Weight:** 200 lbs.
Bats: right **Throws:** right
Acquired: Signed as a free agent, 6/87

Player Summary	
Fantasy Value	$2 to $4
Card Value	10¢ to 15¢
Will	throw strikes
Can't	keep ball in park
Expect	one walk per three innings
Don't Expect	low ERA

Garcia stepped into the White Sox rotation in 1991. He performed adequately considering his age, going 4-4 with a 5.40 ERA in his 15 starts and one relief appearance. He had some trouble keeping the ball in the park; there were 13 dingers off him in his 78⅓ innings. The White Sox have made Garcia into a starter after he spent his first two seasons working out of the bullpen for Sarasota of the rookie Gulf Coast League. In 1989, Garcia split 14 appearances between starting and relief. He tied for the Gulf Coast League lead with two complete games. He had a no-hitter against the Mets' rookie squad in which Garcia fanned 11. He started all 26 appearances in 1990 with Sarasota—this time in the Class-A Florida State League—and led with 130 Ks. He went 9-4 with a 3.95 ERA and was promoted to Vancouver of the Pacific Coast League. He is a good fantasy draft at $3, and his 1992 cards are impressive buys at a dime each.

Professional Pitching Register

	W	L	ERA	G	CG	IP	H	ER	BB	SO
89 R	6	4	3.06	14	2	53.0	34	18	17	52
90 A	9	14	3.95	26	1	157.1	155	69	45	130
90 AAA	0	0	0.00	1	0	1.0	2	0	0	1
91 AA	4	0	0.93	6	2	38.2	27	4	11	38
91 AAA	2	2	4.05	4	0	26.2	24	12	7	17
91 AL	4	4	5.40	16	0	78.1	79	47	31	40

VICTOR GARCIA

Position: Pitcher
Team: Cincinnati Reds
Born: Sept. 15, 1969 Bonao, Dominican Republic
Height: 6'2" **Weight:** 190 lbs.
Bats: right **Throws:** right
Acquired: Signed as a free agent, 2/88

Player Summary	
Fantasy Value	$2 to $4
Card Value	10¢ to 15¢
Will	blow away hitters
Can't	go back to starting
Expect	Triple-A to start '92
Don't Expect	many hits

Garcia arrived on the scene too late to be one of the "Nasty Boys," but his stuff is nasty even if he can't have the nickname. He has the ability to blow away hitters, and he may get better with experience. The Reds used him as a starter in his first exposure to pro ball, when he led the Gulf Coast League Reds with 13 starts, but the bullpen has been his office ever since. Garcia's best year came in 1990 with Class-A Cedar Rapids of the Midwest League, when he went 8-3 with a 1.52 ERA and 15 saves in 49 appearances. Garcia's most devastating weapon was his strikeout pitch; he whiffed 106 in 71 innings. Even more spectacular was his amount of runners allowed. Garcia gave up 36 hits, about one for every two innings, and walked just 18. In the Double-A Southern League, Garcia continued to excel in '91. He went 5-3 with a 1.98 ERA and five saves over 40 outings. He is a promising fantasy hurler for no more than $4. His 1992 cards are good possibilities at a dime each.

Professional Pitching Register

	W	L	ERA	G	S	IP	H	ER	BB	SO
88 R	4	4	2.27	13	0	71.1	60	18	30	47
89 A	10	1	2.75	43	5	85.0	54	26	39	108
90 A	8	3	1.52	49	15	71.0	36	12	18	106
91 AA	5	3	1.98	25	5	50.0	41	11	20	51
91 AAA	2	0	2.63	15	0	24.0	15	7	14	12

ROOKIE PROSPECTS

CHRIS GARDNER

Position: Pitcher
Team: Houston Astros
Born: March 30, 1969 Paso Robles, CA
Height: 6' **Weight:** 175 lbs.
Bats: right **Throws:** right
Acquired: Sixth-round pick in 6/88 free-agent draft

Player Summary
Fantasy Value	$2 to $5
Card Value	10¢ to 15¢
Will	start year at Triple-A
Can't	walk so many
Expect	some ugly outings
Don't Expect	many strikeouts

If this Gardner can figure a way to trim his bases on balls, then he could enjoy a fruitful career. He raised his game a notch in 1991, his fourth year in the pros. A member of the Double-A Texas League All-Star Team, he hurled three innings of one-hit ball in the loop's midseason classic. He also set a career high in victories and was a key member of Jackson's starting rotation. He has shown an ability to keep his hits near or under his innings pitched. However, he has had trouble with his control, walking 75 in 131⅓ innings. Gardner broke into the pros with the Astros of the rookie Gulf Coast League in 1988, going 4-3 with a 1.42 ERA. Promoted to Class-A Asheville in 1989, he won just three of 11 decisions. He remained at Asheville in 1990, finishing seventh in the South Atlantic League with a 2.62 ERA. But his won-lost mark was a disappointing 5-10. He's a realistic fantasy prospect at $4. Spend a dime or so on his 1992 cards.

Professional Pitching Register
	W	L	ERA	G	CG	IP	H	ER	BB	SO
88 R	4	3	1.46	12	0	55.1	37	9	23	41
89 A	3	8	3.84	15	2	77.1	76	33	58	49
90 A	5	10	2.62	23	3	134.0	102	39	69	81
91 AA	13	5	3.15	22	1	131.1	116	46	75	72
91 NL	1	2	4.01	5	0	24.2	19	11	14	12

DARIUS GASH

Position: Outfield
Team: San Diego Padres
Born: June 15, 1967 Cleveland, TN
Height: 6' **Weight:** 175 lbs.
Bats: both **Throws:** right
Acquired: 32nd-round pick in 6/90 free-agent draft

Player Summary
Fantasy Value	$1 to $3
Card Value	5¢ to 10¢
Will	have to make better contact
Can't	be as inconsistent
Expect	.30 steals
Don't Expect	majors in '92

The only negative you can cite on Gash is that, entering the 1992 season at 24 years of age, he's a little older than the average prospect out of Class-A. Otherwise, this player and his potential are meant to be enjoyed. Not only did Gash excel at the plate in almost every aspect except pure power, he was also named by *Baseball America* the top defensive outfielder in the Midwest League in 1991. He ranked among the organization's leaders in average and stolen bases. He also scored his share of runs. Gash went 5-for-5 against Cedar Rapids June 21, as part of a string of five multiple-hit games. He had a 19-game batting streak that put his average to .331, tops in the league at that time. Gash's big season came as somewhat of a surprise considering his .236 average in 1990 with Class-A Spokane of the Northwest League. However, he did show his speed. Wait to invest any money in his current cards until he takes off at the Double-A level. He is an iffy $2 fantasy draft.

Professional Batting Register
	BA	G	AB	R	H	2B	3B	HR	RBI	SB
90 A	.236	64	254	47	60	7	6	2	26	20
91 A	.307	130	501	84	154	27	2	5	60	31

ROOKIE PROSPECTS

BRENT GATES

Position: Infielder
Team: Oakland Athletics
Born: March 14, 1970 Grand Rapids, MI
Height: 6'1" **Weight:** 180 lbs.
Bats: both **Throws:** right
Acquired: First-round pick in 6/91 free-agent draft

Player Summary	
Fantasy Value	$1 to $3
Card Value	5¢ to 10¢
Will	hit for average
Can't	play shortstop in bigs
Expect	.280 average
Don't Expect	12 homers

The A's have no illusions about Gates; they know he doesn't project as a Walt Weiss-type in the field. Gates lacks an outstanding arm or range and it's likely he will wind up as a second baseman. The A's, however, also believe they found one of the best-hitting middle infielders in the country when they addressed a hole in the system by grabbing this former Team USA and University of Minnesota star. His college coach, John Anderson, praised Gates's instincts and first step. Oakland assigned Gates to Class-A Southern Oregon in the Northwest League, where he hit .288. He had a .375 on-base average and a .379 slugging average. At one point of the season, he went 10-for-22 during a six-game hitting streak. He went 3-for-4 as Southern Oregon took an 11-10 slugfest from Everett July 23. He was the loop's postseason shortstop on the All-Star Team. He also saw action at Class-A Madison in the Midwest League, hitting .333 with a couple of doubles. Gates is a $2 fantasy prospect. His current cards are attractive long-term buys at a nickel each.

CHRIS GIES

Position: Pitcher
Team: Texas Rangers
Born: Oct. 8, 1968 Philadelphia, PA
Height: 6'3" **Weight:** 190 lbs.
Bats: right **Throws:** right
Acquired: 38th-round pick in 6/90 free-agent draft

Player Summary	
Fantasy Value	$2 to $5
Card Value	10¢ to 15¢
Will	throw strikes
Can't	pitch in AL yet
Expect	complete games
Don't Expect	over two walks a game

If they don't already, batters will soon understand that to reach base against Gies, they've got to hit the ball. He just doesn't walk that many people. And that certainly complicates things, because his stuff isn't easy to hit. That's why he won 10 of his 13 decisions for Class-A Gastonia of the South Atlantic League in 1991. In his 19 starts, Gies walked just 20. He assembled one four-game win streak in which he hurled three complete games, two shutouts, and a 12-strikeout game. He walked one batter or fewer in nine straight outings. Gies was promoted to Double-A Tulsa and notched his first win with a six-inning start against Jackson. Shortly after being moved up, Gies led all Texas farmhands in wins and strikeouts and was second in ERA. He entered pro ball with Butte in 1990, and led the rookie Pioneer League with five complete games. He went 6-2 with a 3.77 ERA. Be ready to invest now, when prices are lowest, in his current cards, priced at a dime. He is a $3 fantasy candidate.

Professional Batting Register

	BA	G	AB	R	H	2B	3B	HR	RBI	SB
91 A	.290	62	231	45	67	17	2	3	26	9

Professional Pitching Register

	W	L	ERA	G	CG	IP	H	ER	BB	SO
90 R	6	2	3.77	15	5	88.1	86	37	27	64
91 A	10	3	2.54	19	5	138.1	122	39	20	124
91 AA	2	2	4.82	8	0	37.1	51	20	13	25

ROOKIE PROSPECTS

BENJI GIL

Position: Shortstop
Team: Texas Rangers
Born: June 10, 1972 Tijuana, Mexico
Height: 6'2" **Weight:** 180 lbs.
Bats: right **Throws:** right
Acquired: First-round pick in 6/91 free-agent draft

Player Summary	
Fantasy Value	$1 to $4
Card Value	15¢ to 20¢
Will	make throw from hole
Can't	reach bigs before '94
Expect	300 average
Don't Expect	15 homers

Gil had enough tools to become the 19th overall pick in the draft, and earn a signing bonus reported at $310,000. The Rangers don't view him as a player who will step right out of the draft and help the big club within a year or two. They love his raw ability. He is a shortstop with good range, but his best asset is his throwing arm, and he was a pitcher in high school. Texas projects Gil as a major league hitter, with perhaps a little bit of power. His speed is said to be not bad, maybe a little above average. Signed out of high school, Gil had a scholarship offer to the University of Miami, but passed it up to turn professional. He was among the last 10 first-round picks to agree to terms, then began his pro career with Texas' rookie affiliate in the Pioneer League. He had some problems at shortstop, getting 14 errors in 163 total chances. Offensively, he had a .354 on-base average and a .411 slugging percentage. His 1992 first-round cards will be steady price gainers at 20 cents or less. He is a $2 fantasy prospect at this point.

Professional Batting Register

	BA	G	AB	R	H	2B	3B	HR	RBI	SB
91 R	287	32	129	25	37	4	3	2	15	9

PAT GOMEZ

Position: Pitcher
Team: Atlanta Braves
Born: March 17, 1968 Roseville, CA
Height: 5'11" **Weight:** 185 lbs.
Bats: left **Throws:** left
Acquired: Traded from Cubs with Kelly Mann for Paul Assenmacher, 8/89

Player Summary	
Fantasy Value	$1 to $3
Card Value	8¢ to 12¢
Will	lower hits ratio
Can't	pitch in NL yet
Expect	stiff competition
Don't Expect	ERA below 3.50

By helping the Chicago Cubs win a division in 1989, the Braves may have captured themselves a piece of the '90s. And that future may have begun arriving in 1991. After spending parts of three seasons in Double-A, Gomez pitched his way to the Triple-A level. He was obtained by the Braves as the first of two players to be named later in a deal that sent reliever Paul Assenmacher to the Cubs. At the time of the trade, Gomez was one of the top prospects in baseball, having made the Class-A Carolina League All-Star squad. He went 11-6 with a 2.75 ERA for Winston-Salem, and was named the eighth-best prospect in the league by *Baseball America*. Gomez was promoted to Charlotte and went 1-0 in two starts. He hasn't adjusted to Triple-A yet. His '91 stats indicate that his fantasy value stops at $3. His 1992 cards are a little overpriced at a dime.

Professional Pitching Register

	W	L	ERA	G	CG	IP	H	ER	BB	SO
86 R	3	6	5.17	11	0	54.0	57	31	46	55
87 A	3	6	4.31	20	17	94.0	88	45	71	95
88 A	2	7	5.38	36	0	78.2	75	47	52	97
89 A	11	6	2.75	23	3	137.2	115	42	60	127
89 AA	1	0	2.51	2	0	14.1	14	4	3	11
90 AA	6	8	4.49	23	0	124.1	126	62	71	94
90 AAA	1	1	8.80	4	0	15.1	19	15	10	8
91 AA	5	2	1.81	13	0	79.2	58	16	31	71
91 AAA	2	9	4.39	16	0	82.0	99	40	41	41

ROOKIE PROSPECTS

ALEX GONZALEZ

Position: Shortstop
Team: Toronto Blue Jays
Born: April 8, 1973 Miami, FL
Height: 6' **Weight:** 185 lbs.
Bats: right **Throws:** right
Acquired: 13th-round pick in 6/91 free-agent draft

Player Summary	
Fantasy Value	$1 to $2
Card Value	5¢ to 10¢
Will	improve average
Can't	hit long ball
Expect	low Class-A in '92
Don't Expect	fast progression

Every club enters the draft looking for that little something that may give them an edge. It's very possible the Blue Jays have "engineered" a bit of a coup in taking Gonzalez. A graduate of Killian High School in Miami, he was an all-Florida shortstop, but he also had the option of attending and playing ball at the University of Miami. Furthermore, his father is a professor of electrical engineering at the school, and that made the likelihood of Alex attending seem even greater. The Blue Jays, however, took a chance well into the draft and got Gonzalez. Not every club agreed with the Blue Jays' opinion. One veteran baseball man said his team rated Gonzalez as fringe when they considered his ability and his "signability." In his first pro year, he didn't show much offensively except some speed. Defensively, he had 21 errors in 247 total chances, but a low fielding percentage is not that unusual for a young player in his first year of pro baseball. He is too young to make an assessment whether you should spend a buck on his future. His current cards, at a nickel, are also holds until he shows something at bat.

Professional Batting Register

	BA	G	AB	R	H	2B	3B	HR	RBI	SB
91 R	.208	53	192	29	40	5	4	0	10	7

JUAN GUERRERO

Position: Infielder
Team: San Francisco Giants
Born: Feb. 1, 1967 Los Llanos, Dominican Republic
Height: 5'11" **Weight:** 160 lbs.
Bats: right **Throws:** right
Acquired: Signed as a free agent, 9/86

Player Summary	
Fantasy Value	$3 to $6
Card Value	10¢ to 20¢
Will	have 50 extra-base hits
Can't	move Matt Williams
Expect	power numbers
Don't Expect	bigs in '92

What would you say about a player who was just voted his team's MVP? A player who has played for two consecutive championship squads? A player who has competed for an organization's Triple Crown? You'd say he was headed for the big leagues. There's a hitch. Guerrero is a third baseman, and there's a fellow named Matt Williams holding down that position for the Giants right now. Still, there may have to be room somewhere for a player who has hung up the kind of numbers Guerrero has. In 1991, he led Double-A Shreveport to its second straight Texas League title. He paced the Giants' chain with a .334 average, and finished second in both homers and RBI. All those figures represented highs for his four-year minor league career. He played in the Double-A All-Star Game and went 1-for-4. He also made the league's postseason All-Star squad. He is a top prospect, making him a $5 fantasy draft. Stock up on his dime-priced 1992 cards.

Professional Batting Register

	BA	G	AB	R	H	2B	3B	HR	RBI	SB
87 R	.210	34	81	13	17	5	1	1	7	1
88 A	.275	111	385	57	106	17	3	13	54	7
89 A	.281	108	409	61	115	24	2	13	78	7
90 AA	.241	118	390	55	94	21	1	16	47	4
91 AA	.334	128	479	78	160	40	2	19	94	14

ROOKIE PROSPECTS

JOHNNY GUZMAN

Position: Pitcher
Team: Oakland Athletics
Born: Jan. 21, 1971 Hatillo Palma, Dominican Republic
Height: 5'11" **Weight:** 185 lbs.
Bats: right **Throws:** left
Acquired: Signed as a free agent, 6/88

Player Summary	
Fantasy Value	$1 to $3
Card Value	5¢ to 10¢
Will	be around plate
Can't	get key out
Expect	Triple-A in '92
Don't Expect	80 Ks

The A's thought enough of this lefthander to bring him to the big leagues early in 1991. It was quite a spot for Guzman, and he was hit hard. Oakland optioned him to Triple-A Tacoma, where he also had some problems, and eventually Guzman was returned to Double-A Huntsville of the Southern League to regain his confidence. The setback may only be temporary, as he has the necessary pitches and a knowledge of the craft. He throws a sinking fastball with a good breaking ball and change. Guzman could probably sharpen his control, but it is not particularly bad for someone his age, and many pitchers feel they have to be too fine as they advance. Without a great deal of size, and lacking a strikeout pitch, he will likely have to rely on location and setting up hitters. He faces another season before he'll be a serious fantasy draft; stay under $3. His 1992 cards are fair investments at a nickel apiece.

Professional Pitching Register

	W	L	ERA	G	CG	IP	H	ER	BB	SO
88 R	0	2	8.61	16	0	23.0	37	22	8	18
89 A	3	5	4.04	14	1	62.1	64	28	34	48
90 A	7	4	1.91	13	1	84.2	67	18	23	58
90 AA	5	6	3.58	16	0	105.2	89	42	54	63
91 AA	2	1	3.48	7	0	44.0	46	17	25	23
91 AAA	2	5	6.78	17	0	79.2	113	60	51	40
91 AL	1	0	9.00	5	0	5.0	11	5	2	5

GREG HANSELL

Position: Pitcher
Team: Los Angeles Dodgers
Born: March 12, 1971 Bellflower, CA
Height: 6'4" **Weight:** 200 lbs.
Bats: right **Throws:** right
Acquired: Traded from Mets with Bob Ojeda for Hubie Brooks, 12/90

Player Summary	
Fantasy Value	$3 to $5
Card Value	15¢ to 25¢
Will	jump a rung
Can't	finish what he starts
Expect	good K-to-walk ratio
Don't Expect	another trade

Hansell has very likely found a home with the Dodgers after moving around a bit in his young career. Assigned to Class-A Bakersfield of the California League in 1991, Hansell made the postseason All-Star team and finished second only to Pedro Martinez in wins among the Los Angeles minor leaguers. Hansell was one of the top pitchers on a squad that puts together first- and second-place finishes. All of his ratios are in the right place, as he allowed fewer hits than innings pitched, and walked just two and one-half every nine innings. Opponents notched only five homers against Hansell in 1991. He has made at least 25 starts two straight years. Originally drafted by the Red Sox, he came to the Mets as part of the Mike Marshall deal. The Mets shipped Hansell to Los Angeles in a package that also netted them Hubie Brooks. Now that Hansell has established himself with the Dodgers, it is time for a move up. Be prepared to draft him for up to $5. His current cards are a bit overpriced at a quarter apiece.

Professional Pitching Register

	W	L	ERA	G	CG	IP	H	ER	BB	SO
89 R	3	2	2.53	10	0	57.0	51	16	23	44
90 A	9	14	3.35	27	2	153.1	129	57	79	95
91 A	14	5	2.87	25	0	150.2	142	48	42	132

ROOKIE PROSPECTS

SHAWN HARE

Position: Outfield; first base
Team: Detroit Tigers
Born: March 26, 1967 St. Louis, MO
Height: 6'2" **Weight:** 190 lbs.
Bats: left **Throws:** left
Acquired: Signed as a free agent, 8/88

Player Summary	
Fantasy Value	$4 to $8
Card Value	10¢ to 20¢
Will	get long look
Can't	wait much longer
Expect	some power
Don't Expect	stolen bases

The Tigers front office is very enthusiastic about Hare's chances of hitting in the big leagues. He is said to take instruction well in addition to being a natural. Hare started 1991 with Triple-A Toledo of the International League, was sent to the Double-A Eastern League, and came back to Triple-A. He hit .400 with seven homers and 22 RBI in his first 85 at bats upon his return. Some of the credit may go to adjustments that Toledo manager Joe Sparks made in Hare's style and hand position. Hare attended Central Michigan University, where he played on three Mid-American Conference championship teams. His .324 average led Class-A Lakeland in 1989, and he didn't seem to suffer from jumping two levels to Triple-A, making the All-Star Team. His stats once suggested extra-base punch rather than home run power, but that may be changing a bit. Hare even steals an occasional base. He is a fantasy draft attraction for $6. Buy up his dime-priced 1992 cards.

Professional Batting Register

	BA	G	AB	R	H	2B	3B	HR	RBI	SB
89 A	.324	93	290	32	94	16	4	2	36	11
90 AAA	.254	127	429	53	109	25	4	9	55	9
91 AA	.272	31	125	20	34	12	0	4	28	2
91 AAA	.310	80	252	44	78	18	2	9	42	1
91 AL	.053	9	19	0	1	1	0	0	0	0

DOUG HARRIS

Position: Pitcher
Team: Kansas City Royals
Born: Sept. 27, 1969 Carlisle, PA
Height: 6'4" **Weight:** 185 lbs.
Bats: right **Throws:** right
Acquired: Fourth-round pick in 6/90 free-agent draft

Player Summary	
Fantasy Value	$1 to $2
Card Value	5¢ to 10¢
Will	increase strikeouts
Can't	pitch in bigs yet
Expect	few baserunners
Don't Expect	tired arm

Harris has what the Royals call a "young" arm, because he wasn't the No. 1 pitcher at James Madison University and therefore wasn't overused. The Royals give the school credit for identifying him as a pitching prospect and putting him on the mound. So far Harris has not looked out of place in pro ball, and was a regular member of the rotation in his first two pro stops. He has exhibited above-average control, and improved his hits-to-innings ratio in 1991. He not only was one of the stalwarts for Class-A Baseball City of the Florida State League, he also ranked among the leaders in the Kansas City farm system in wins and earned run average. Harris held FSL batters to a .214 average. He moved up to Appleton of the Midwest League, where he notched a 2.20 ERA. He already is a four-pitch pitcher, with an average fastball that has above-average sink, so he has a chance to get the double play and keep the ball in the park. Delay investing in his nickel-priced current cards until he conquers Double-A. His projected fantasy values stop at $2.

Professional Pitching Register

	W	L	ERA	G	CG	IP	H	ER	BB	SO
90 A	4	5	4.41	15	0	69.1	74	34	28	46
91 A	12	8	2.39	26	4	161.2	133	43	37	123

ROOKIE PROSPECTS

REGGIE HARRIS

Position: Pitcher
Team: Oakland Athletics
Born: Aug. 12, 1968 Waynesboro, VA
Height: 6'1" **Weight:** 190 lbs.
Bats: right **Throws:** right
Acquired: Drafted from Red Sox, 12/89

Player Summary	
Fantasy Value	$3 to $6
Card Value	5¢ to 10¢
Will	drop ERA
Can't	match Dave Stewart
Expect	berth in rotation
Don't Expect	big win percentage

A first-round draft pick of the Red Sox in 1987, Harris has failed to live up to expectations. He is a hard thrower but never had a winning record at any level as a pro until he went 1-0 in limited time with Oakland in 1990. As a Rule 5 draftee that year, he had to remain with the Athletics through August. However, a bout with hepatitis had a bit of a bright side; it allowed him to be placed on the disabled list and got him some rehab starts at Double-A Huntsville of the Southern League. Though he owned the best fastball in the Pacific Coast League, injuries and inconsistency limited his effectiveness at Triple-A Tacoma in 1991. He allowed Triple-A batters to hit .264 in 1991. A comment on Harris's progress is the fact that despite all the injuries to their staff, the A's didn't exactly run to Harris for help. His 1991 cards are strong investments, and his nickel-priced 1992 cards look just as strong. He is a solid $5 draft.

Professional Pitching Register

	W	L	ERA	G	CG	IP	H	ER	BB	SO
87 A	2	3	5.01	9	1	46.2	50	26	22	25
88 A	4	14	6.47	27	0	118.1	142	85	62	94
89 A	10	13	3.99	29	1	153.1	144	68	77	85
90 AA	0	2	3.03	5	0	29.2	26	10	16	34
90 AL	1	0	3.48	16	0	41.1	25	16	21	31
91 AAA	5	4	4.99	16	0	83.0	83	46	58	72
91 AL	0	0	12.00	2	0	3.0	5	4	3	2

CHRIS HATCHER

Position: Outfield
Team: Houston Astros
Born: Jan. 7, 1969 Anaheim, CA
Height: 6'3" **Weight:** 220 lbs.
Bats: right **Throws:** right
Acquired: Third-round pick in 6/90 free-agent draft

Player Summary	
Fantasy Value	$1 to $2
Card Value	5¢ to 10¢
Will	raise average
Can't	make contact
Expect	moonshots
Don't Expect	long slumps

The Astros, ever searching for power hitters who can cover the vast distances in the Astrodome, may have a prospect in Hatcher. The former University of Iowa star was named the Class-A Midwest League's best batting prospect and most exciting player by *Baseball America*. Managers around the circuit were no doubt impressed by the tape-measure homers he hit at Burlington. He was named the Most Valuable Player in the league's All-Star Game after hitting two home runs, including a mammoth shot to straightaway center. Like most power hitters, though, Hatcher needs to be more disciplined at the plate. He hit .183 in July with 45 strikeouts in 120 official trips. Still, major league clubs are willing to take that trade-off, and power hitters can make lots of money. Hatcher has made strides in right field after spending much of his college career as a designated hitter. He has to explode at Double-A for his fantasy potential to be worth more than $1. His current cards are overpriced at this time, even at a nickel.

Professional Batting Register

	BA	G	AB	R	H	2B	3B	HR	RBI	SB
90 A	.247	72	259	37	64	10	0	9	45	8
91 A	.235	129	497	69	117	23	6	13	65	10

ROOKIE PROSPECTS

RYAN HAWBLITZEL

Position: Pitcher
Team: Chicago Cubs
Born: April 30, 1971 West Palm Beach, FL
Height: 6'2" **Weight:** 170 lbs.
Bats: right **Throws:** right
Acquired: Second-round pick in 6/89 free-agent draft

Player Summary	
Fantasy Value	$2 to $4
Card Value	5¢ to 10¢
Will	go the route
Can't	sustain numbers
Expect	craftsmanship
Don't Expect	Cubs in '92

Cub fans may get to know a lot more about Hawblitzel in the future because even at this early stage of his career he is a possibility to alleviate their chronic need for pitching. Already, he is a bit more well-known than other Class-A players because he was a prominent member of *Baseball America's* Player of the Year Watch in 1991, with numbers to back it up. Despite his youth, his 15 wins at Winston-Salem tied for the Carolina League lead, and his 16 victories overall made him the leader in the Cubs' chain. His ERA ranked him second. One factor in particular makes Hawblitzel a prospect to watch. He doesn't walk many, which comes in handy in Wrigley, where every runner is a candidate to score ahead of a homer. Hawblitzel continued his command of the strike zone upon being boosted a notch, walking fewer than three per game. His nickel current cards are promising buys, especially if he stays in Double-A. He is worth about $3 in the fantasy futures market.

Professional Pitching Register

	W	L	ERA	G	CG	IP	H	ER	BB	SO
90 R	6	5	3.93	14	2	75.2	72	33	25	71
91 A	15	2	2.28	20	5	134.0	110	34	47	103
91 AA	1	2	3.21	5	1	33.2	31	12	12	25

PAT HENTGEN

Position: Pitcher
Team: Toronto Blue Jays
Born: Sept. 13, 1968 Detroit, MI
Height: 6'2" **Weight:** 200 lbs.
Bats: right **Throws:** right
Acquired: Fifth-round pick in 6/86 free-agent draft

Player Summary	
Fantasy Value	$2 to $4
Card Value	7¢ to 12¢
Will	lower ERA
Can't	get by on speed
Expect	work on third pitch
Don't Expect	complete games

A converted shortstop who had been offered a baseball scholarship at Western Michigan, Hentgen has slowed down slightly after making progress for most of five years through the Toronto system. His fastball was rated the best in the Triple-A International League by managers—not because of velocity but because of movement. He has also developed a big breaking curve, but needs to improve his changeup. A pitcher supposedly on a track to the majors should have acquired a little better control by this stage, and in his six years of pro ball Hentgen hasn't improved his walks-to-innings ratio. His record also shows a distinct dearth of complete games. On the plus side, Hentgen has repeated only one stop on his rise through the system (Class-A Dunedin in both 1988 and '89), and since 1991 was a Triple-A job, next year he may stay in Toronto. He is a solid $3 fantasy draft. His 1992 cards are good values at a dime.

Professional Pitching Register

	W	L	ERA	G	CG	IP	H	ER	BB	SO
86 A	0	4	4.50	13	0	40.0	38	20	30	30
87 A	11	5	2.35	32	2	188.0	145	49	60	131
88 A	3	12	3.45	31	0	151.1	139	58	65	125
89 A	9	8	2.68	29	0	151.1	123	45	71	148
90 AA	9	5	3.05	28	0	153.1	121	52	68	142
91 AAA	8	9	4.47	31	1	171.0	146	85	90	155
91 AL	0	0	2.45	3	0	7.1	5	2	3	3

ROOKIE PROSPECTS

CARLOS HERNANDEZ

Position: Catcher
Team: Los Angeles Dodgers
Born: May 24, 1967 San Felix, Venezuela
Height: 5'11" **Weight:** 185 lbs.
Bats: right **Throws:** right
Acquired: Signed as a free agent, 10/84

Player Summary	
Fantasy Value	$3 to $6
Card Value	15¢ to 25¢
Will	fatten RBI
Can't	beat out Scioscia
Expect	300 average
Don't Expect	power

Hernandez has come on strong in the last couple of years and is now considered the heir-apparent to Mike Scioscia. Possessor of a strong arm, Hernandez won the Venezuela high school title in the javelin throw. He was ranked the best defensive catcher in the Triple-A Pacific Coast League by *Baseball America*. Originally signed as an infielder, he made the switch to catcher in 1986 and has made slow but steady progress. He was named the team MVP at Class-A Bakersfield in 1988 and rated the third-best defensive catcher by California League managers. After being tabbed a Double-A Texas League All-Star in 1989, he had two tours with the Dodgers in 1990. Power does not appear to be part of Hernandez's repertoire, but he makes consistent contact. He is a promising $4 fantasy catcher. His 1992 cards are fine purchases for 20 cents apiece.

Professional Batting Register

	BA	G	AB	R	H	2B	3B	HR	RBI	SB
85 R	.245	22	49	3	12	1	0	0	6	0
86 R	.312	57	205	19	64	7	0	1	31	1
87 A	.228	48	162	22	37	6	1	3	22	8
88 A	.309	92	333	37	103	15	2	5	52	3
88 AAA	.125	3	8	0	1	0	0	0	1	0
89 AA	.300	99	370	37	111	16	3	8	41	2
89 AAA	.214	4	14	1	3	0	0	0	1	0
90 AAA	.315	52	143	11	45	8	1	0	16	2
90 NL	.200	10	20	2	4	1	0	0	1	0
91 AAA	.345	95	345	60	119	24	2	8	44	5
91 NL	.214	15	14	1	3	1	0	0	1	0

KIKI HERNANDEZ

Position: Catcher
Team: New York Yankees
Born: Oct. 3, 1969 Arecibo, PR
Height: 5'11" **Weight:** 195 lbs.
Bats: right **Throws:** right
Acquired: Signed as a free agent, 7/88

Player Summary	
Fantasy Value	$1 to $2
Card Value	4¢ to 7¢
Will	make big jump
Can't	maintain high average
Expect	further improvement
Don't Expect	prolonged slump

In his fourth year of pro baseball, Hernandez blossomed into one of the top hitters in the Yankee organization. He had never hit higher than .250 in his previous minor league campaigns, but suddenly came near to winning the Triple Crown among New York farmhands. His average, compiled mainly with Class-A Greensboro of the South Atlantic League, led the Yankee chain. His home run and RBI totals placed him second. Hernandez was named Most Valuable Player in the league, as well as the All-Star catcher. He had a .530 slugging percentage with Greensboro. An off-season conditioning program allowed him to lose 24 pounds before the campaign, and that helped him to operate better both offensively and defensively. However, there is more to being a catching prospect than swinging a bat, and so it may be significant that Hernandez, despite his hitting exploits, did not make *Baseball America's* top 10 prospects in the Sally League. He is a $2 fantasy prospect, and his current cards are holds at 5 cents.

Professional Batting Register

	BA	G	AB	R	H	2B	3B	HR	RBI	SB
88 R	.160	9	25	2	4	1	0	0	0	0
89 A	.223	29	94	12	21	4	0	2	21	0
90 A	.250	107	360	39	90	20	2	6	47	0
91 A	.328	115	415	58	136	29	2	16	83	2

ROOKIE PROSPECTS

PHIL HIATT

Position: Third base
Team: Kansas City Royals
Born: May 1, 1969 Pensacola, FL
Height: 6'3" **Weight:** 187 lbs.
Bats: right **Throws:** right
Acquired: Eighth-round pick in 6/90 free-agent draft

Player Summary	
Fantasy Value	$1 to $2
Card Value	5¢ to 10¢
Will	mesh with ballpark
Can't	hit it out
Expect	position switch
Don't Expect	awestruck rookie

Hiatt enjoyed a successful 1991 campaign, so much so that he was named by *Baseball America* as the top Class-A Florida State League prospect. He has shown an ability to hit for average, and has potential as a run producer. To cross the gap between prospect and major leaguer, though, he still has some work to do, especially on his command of the strike zone. His ratio of walks to strikeouts is poor, which hurts him in two ways. First, by neglecting to walk, Hiatt deprives himself of the chance to show his speed. Second, he loses the benefit of putting the ball in play on an artificial surface such as the one at Royals Stadium. He was among Class-A Northwest League leaders in doubles and triples his first pro year. Hiatt's chances may depend on producing that kind of offense without giving up too many at bats. He needs to provide more evidence of power before his fantasy futures value will increase beyond its $2 cap. His current cards are not good buys.

Professional Batting Register

	BA	G	AB	R	H	2B	3B	HR	RBI	SB
90 A	.294	73	289	33	85	18	5	2	44	15
91 A	.298	81	315	41	94	21	6	5	33	28
91 AA	.228	56	206	29	47	7	1	6	33	6

TYRONE HILL

Position: Pitcher
Team: Milwaukee Brewers
Born: March 7, 1972 Yucaipa, CA
Height: 6'5" **Weight:** 195 lbs.
Bats: left **Throws:** left
Acquired: First-round pick in 6/91 free-agent draft

Player Summary	
Fantasy Value	$2 to $4
Card Value	10¢ to 15¢
Will	keep Brewers' attention
Can't	rely on limited repertoire
Expect	heat
Don't Expect	rush job

One season doesn't make a career, of course, but it must be reassuring to a ballclub to see its first-round draft pick step into the pros and perform. That's exactly what Hill did. After being tabbed 15th overall in the draft—and third lefty after the Yanks' Brien Taylor and Mariners' Shawn Estes—Hill gave rookie Pioneer League hitters some heat for those chilly Northwest evenings. He moved right into the Helena rotation, winning four of his six decisions. In his 60 innings, Hill fanned 76. Batters hit only .206 against him. He is a little rough around the edges, and the Brewers may have drafted him above where some other clubs might have. He must cut down on his walks and develop another pitch. He also needs to improve his fielding (.813 percentage in '91). Hill led Yucaipa High School to the Southern California Sectional championship, posting an 11-1 record and 0.35 ERA. With the Brewers' pitching problems, the temptation may be to rush him. Move fast if he becomes available in the future fantasy draft for up to $4. His current cards are top-drawer investments.

Professional Pitching Register

	W	L	ERA	G	CG	IP	H	ER	BB	SO
91 R	4	2	3.15	11	0	60.0	43	21	35	76

ROOKIE PROSPECTS

TREVOR HOFFMAN

Position: Pitcher
Team: Cincinnati Reds
Born: Oct. 13, 1967 Bellflower, CA
Height: 6′ **Weight:** 195 lbs.
Bats: right **Throws:** right
Acquired: 11th-round pick in 6/89 free-agent draft

Player Summary	
Fantasy Value	$1 to $2
Card Value	4¢ to 7¢
Will	throw hard
Can't	go over two frames
Expect	another Nasty Boy
Don't Expect	return to infield

Brother of former big leaguer Glenn Hoffman, Trevor was an infielder just as his sibling was. However, two years of pro ball strongly suggested that his bat would not get Trevor to the majors. So he tried pitching, and produced a degree of success that makes him one of the interesting stories to watch. Described as having a "phenomenal" arm, Trevor wound up among the save leaders in the Cincinnati chain. After being named MVP of the Class-A Cedar Rapids club in the Midwest League, Hoffman took on Double-A hitters with the same effectiveness. Using a fastball said to be in the low 90s, Hoffman fanned 19 batters in his first 11⅔ innings. From this improbable beginning, it's possible he could wind up on the Reds' 40-man roster before long. As he moves higher in the chain, it will be interesting to see if his repertoire grows. But a 90 mph fastball covers many flaws. He is not a good fantasy candidate at this point, and his current cards are way too risky for speculation.

Professional Pitching Register

	W	L	ERA	G	S	IP	H	ER	BB	SO
91 A	1	1	1.87	27	12	33.2	22	7	13	52
91 AA	1	0	1.93	14	8	14.0	10	3	7	23

TYLER HOUSTON

Position: Catcher
Team: Atlanta Braves
Born: Jan. 17, 1968 Las Vegas, NV
Height: 6′2″ **Weight:** 210 lbs.
Bats: left **Throws:** right
Acquired: First-round pick in 6/89 free-agent draft

Player Summary	
Fantasy Value	$1 to $3
Card Value	5¢ to 10¢
Will	play good defense
Can't	justify draft rank
Expect	more Class-A
Don't Expect	many more chances

Houston has reached a stage where only he can decide how far he will go in his pro career. He possesses size and skills, but so far he has not established much offensively, even in three years in the low minors. There is also some question about his attitude. Houston is prone to slumps, seems to get down on himself, and is inconsistent. He was the second pick in the country in the '89 draft. Houston is a fine defensive player with an above-average arm, and he makes major league plays. On one sequence, he received a bruised nose and stitches in his lip but held the ball in a home-plate collision. One measure of his ability is that he made the Class-A South Atlantic League midseason All-Star Team in 1991 even though he was hitting only .215 at the time. He ended the season with a .362 slugging percentage. Houston still has time to find a spark. He is too young to spend any more than $3 on his fantasy prospects. His current cards are good buys, however, at a nickel apiece.

Professional Batting Register

	BA	G	AB	R	H	2B	3B	HR	RBI	SB
89 R	.244	50	176	30	43	11	0	4	24	4
90 A	.210	117	442	58	93	14	3	13	56	6
91 A	.231	107	351	41	81	16	3	8	47	10

ROOKIE PROSPECTS

PAT HOWELL

Position: Outfield
Team: New York Mets
Born: Aug. 31, 1968 Mobile, AL
Height: 5'11" **Weight:** 155 lbs.
Bats: both **Throws:** right
Acquired: Ninth-round pick in 6/87 free-agent draft

Player Summary	
Fantasy Value	$2 to $4
Card Value	10¢ to 15¢
Will	steal 50 bases
Can't	hit long ball
Expect	electricity
Don't Expect	uncaught flyballs

The Twins thought enough of Howell's tools to take him in the Rule 5 draft during the winter meetings in 1990, but returned him to New York when they felt they couldn't keep him on their roster for all of 1991. Howell was voted the fastest baserunner, best defensive outfielder, and most exciting player in the Class-A Florida State League in '91, but slumped until he was promoted to Double-A Williamsport of the Eastern League. Howell is a natural righty, and is still trying to catch up from the left side. A line drive hitter with virtually no power, he must make some offensive adjustments, such as working the count. He has cut down on his strikeouts, though his stolen bases were down from 1990. Howell showed his defensive ability in 1990, leading Class-A Sally League outfielders with 334 total chances. When he starts taking some walks, his fantasy value will go through the roof. Wait for a good '92 before buying his dime-priced current cards.

Professional Batting Register

	BA	G	AB	R	H	2B	3B	HR	RBI	SB
87 R	.217	34	92	14	20	2	0	1	5	8
88 R	.267	66	251	43	67	6	3	0	16	27
89 A	.290	56	231	41	67	4	3	1	26	45
90 A	.264	135	573	97	151	15	5	1	37	79
91 A	.220	62	246	36	54	8	2	0	10	37
91 AA	.281	70	274	43	77	5	1	1	26	27

RICK HUISMAN

Position: Pitcher
Team: San Francisco Giants
Born: May 17, 1969 Bensenville, IL
Height: 6'3" **Weight:** 200 lbs.
Bats: right **Throws:** right
Acquired: Sixth-round pick in 6/90 free-agent draft

Player Summary	
Fantasy Value	$3 to $6
Card Value	15¢ to 25¢
Will	dominate hitters
Can't	lose command
Expect	hot streaks
Don't Expect	major leagues in '92

Huisman's pitching in 1991 left the Giants with only one problem: How would they ever get him to match it? In his second pro season, he surpassed his achievements of the previous year. He was a Class-A All-Star as named by *Baseball America*, as well as the California League's third-best prospect as tabbed by that publication. Huisman was selected to the league's postseason All-Star squad. He wound up in a three-way tie for most wins in San Francisco's minor-league system, led the farmhands in strikeouts, and finished second in ERA. Huisman averaged well below one hit per inning, and well over a strikeout per game. He could use work on his control, because in his expected promotion he will be facing more selective hitters. In 1990, Huisman set a Class-A Midwest League mark by opening a game with eight strikeouts. He will get a long look by the 1992 Giants, and his heat makes investing $4 in his fantasy prospects worthwhile. His current cards are good buys at 15 cents each.

Professional Pitching Register

	W	L	ERA	G	CG	IP	H	ER	BB	SO
90 A	6	5	2.11	15	0	81.0	60	19	35	105
91 A	16	4	1.83	26	7	182.1	126	37	73	216

ROOKIE PROSPECTS

TODD HUNDLEY

Position: Catcher
Team: New York Mets
Born: May 27, 1969 Martinsville, VA
Height: 5'11" **Weight:** 185 lbs.
Bats: both **Throws:** right
Acquired: Second-round pick in 6/87 free-agent draft

Player Summary
Fantasy Value	$3 to $7
Card Value	15¢ to 25¢
Will	start for Mets
Can't	worry about offense
Expect	lots of assists
Don't Expect	20 homers

Hundley has been viewed as New York's catcher of the future and, based on the Mets' disappointing 1991 campaign, the future may have already begun. As the rebuilding proceeds, there may be no better way than to install a young catcher and acquaint him with the pitching staff. The son of former major league catcher Randy Hundley, Todd enjoyed his best season at the plate in '91, ranking among the leaders in the Mets' farm system in home runs and RBI. He played in the Triple-A All-Star Game. He can be deadly on baserunners; in 1990 while in the Double-A Texas League, he threw out 48 percent of the runners who tested him. The league average was 34 percent. In 1989, Hundley was named to the midseason and postseason All-Star teams in the Class-A South Atlantic League. He could also play third base in a pinch. He is a certain $5 draft, and his 1992 cards are good buys at a quarter.

Professional Batting Register
	BA	G	AB	R	H	2B	3B	HR	RBI	SB
87 A	.146	34	103	12	15	4	0	1	10	0
88 A	.186	53	177	23	33	8	0	2	18	1
89 A	.269	125	439	67	118	23	4	11	66	6
90 AA	.265	81	279	27	74	12	2	1	35	5
90 NL	.209	36	67	8	14	6	0	0	2	0
91 AAA	.273	125	454	62	124	24	4	14	66	1
91 NL	.133	21	60	5	8	0	1	1	7	0

JON HURST

Position: Pitcher
Team: Montreal Expos
Born: Oct. 20, 1966 New York, NY
Height: 6'3" **Weight:** 175 lbs.
Bats: right **Throws:** right
Acquired: Traded from Rangers with Joey Eischen and Travis Buckley for Dennis Boyd, 7/91

Player Summary
Fantasy Value	$2 to $4
Card Value	10¢ to 15¢
Will	make fans look good
Can't	complete games
Expect	start at Double-A
Don't Expect	return to bullpen

Hurst had given the Expos' brass an eyeful long before the July 21 deal that made Oil Can Boyd a Ranger. He no-hit Montreal's Class-A West Palm Beach club for eight and two-thirds innings in June. So when Texas sought pitching help after being in contention in July, Montreal acquired Hurst as part of the transaction. He won five of his six starts with Double-A Harrisburg of the Eastern League with an 0.86 ERA, averaging almost a strikeout per inning. Hurst has an above average fastball and a plus curve, with the makings of a changeup. He is a good athlete who holds runners and fields his position well. Hurst had pitched in relief for some of 1990 and '91. The Expos are building a young and promising rotation, and Hurst before long could be part of it. His odds look good for fantasy investments at $3. His current cards are mediocre purchases at 20 cents.

Professional Pitching Register
	W	L	ERA	G	CG	IP	H	ER	BB	SO
87 R	4	3	1.88	12	0	57.1	34	12	32	59
88 R	1	0	0.59	5	0	15.1	5	1	4	13
88 A	1	0	1.69	7	0	16.0	8	3	6	20
88 AAA	0	0	10.80	1	0	1.2	1	2	5	2
89 A	4	6	4.45	19	0	58.2	67	29	32	37
90 A	9	1	2.57	21	0	73.2	56	21	24	57
90 AA	0	2	9.47	8	0	25.2	29	27	16	23
91 A	8	2	2.90	15	0	99.1	89	32	31	91
91 AA	7	1	1.34	11	2	67.0	44	10	18	51

ROOKIE PROSPECTS

MIKE IGNASIAK

Position: Pitcher
Team: Milwaukee Brewers
Born: March 12, 1966 Mt. Clemens, NC
Height: 5'11" **Weight:** 175 lbs.
Bats: both **Throws:** right
Acquired: Eighth-round pick in 6/88 free-agent draft

Player Summary	
Fantasy Value	$2 to $4
Card Value	7¢ to 12¢
Will	give you innings
Can't	keep ball in park
Expect	long look in spring
Don't Expect	fancy stats

Ignasiak is not an imposing physical specimen, especially for a righthander, but the fact he has held his own in two tough ballparks may signal his readiness for a major league job. Ignasiak worked in Double-A El Paso for part of 1990 and in Triple-A Denver in 1991, and neither facility is famous for holding the ball in the park. Yet Ignasiak has climbed his way to the majors and did OK. You won't find him among the leaders in any of the glamor categories, and there isn't one part of his game that is compelling, but he takes the ball. At Denver, batters hit only .228 against him. A starter for most of his pro career, Ignasiak can be expected to fit in as a swingman for the Brewers, though he may get a shot at the starting rotation in spring training of 1992. He is not a wonderful fantasy pick—limit your bid to $3. His 1992 cards are fair buys at a dime each.

Professional Pitching Register

	W	L	ERA	G	CG	IP	H	ER	BB	SO
88 R	2	0	3.09	7	0	11.2	10	4	7	18
88 A	2	4	2.72	9	1	56.1	52	17	12	66
89 A	11	6	2.72	28	4	179.0	140	54	97	142
90 A	3	1	3.94	6	1	32.0	18	14	17	23
90 AA	6	3	4.35	15	1	82.2	96	40	34	39
91 AAA	9	5	4.25	24	1	137.2	119	65	57	103
91 AL	2	1	5.68	4	0	12.2	7	8	8	10

JEFF JACKSON

Position: Outfield
Team: Philadelphia Phillies
Born: Jan. 2, 1972 Chicago, IL
Height: 6'2" **Weight:** 185 lbs.
Bats: right **Throws:** right
Acquired: First-round pick in 6/89 free-agent draft

Player Summary	
Fantasy Value	$1 to $3
Card Value	5¢ to 10¢
Will	run the bases
Can't	steal first
Expect	strikeouts
Don't Expect	infinite patience

Jackson suffered through his third weak offensive year in as many pro seasons, and 1992 may loom as a time for him to show whether his game will ever come around. He did show some improvement, especially in stolen bases, but still strikes out way too much for a player whose game is speed. Jackson swings at too many bad pitches and must work at keeping his hands back and being patient. A gap hitter as opposed to a home run slugger, Jackson hasn't offered a great deal of extra-base punch in any variety. He did, however, turn a bloop 20 feet behind second into a double. In 1991 at Class-A Spartanburg, he had a .305 slugging percentage and a .315 on-base average. In the outfield, his coverage area is exceptional. He could use some work going back on balls, but he isn't afraid to dive. Jackson's status as a former first pick will probably earn him an extra look or two, but he must produce soon. He still is not at the point where it would be wise to draft him. His nickel-priced current cards should be left alone.

Professional Batting Register

	BA	G	AB	R	H	2B	3B	HR	RBI	SB
89 R	.227	48	163	16	37	5	1	2	21	11
90 A	.198	63	227	30	45	11	3	3	22	12
91 A	.225	121	440	73	99	18	1	5	33	29

ROOKIE PROSPECTS

JOHN JAHA

Position: First base
Team: Milwaukee Brewers
Born: May 27, 1966 Portland, OR
Height: 6'1" **Weight:** 195 lbs.
Bats: right **Throws:** right
Acquired: 14th-round pick in 6/84 free-agent draft

Player Summary	
Fantasy Value	$4 to $7
Card Value	15¢ to 20¢
Will	pound the ball
Can't	crack Brewers lineup
Expect	60 extra base hits
Don't Expect	same stats in AL

A man who nearly wrecked his career by running on stairs has resumed his climb to the majors. Jaha, out most of 1990 with knee surgery stemming from a tear, experienced a spectacular year at Double-A in 1991. He benefits in part from a park where the ball seems to jump, but he appears to have regained some of the momentum that resulted in a standout season in the Class-A California League in 1989. Jaha was voted the best power hitter in the Double-A Texas League and also its best defensive first baseman, but he needs work on some fielding techniques, including scooping balls. He was among the top minor league players in homers and RBI. Jaha went 2-for-2 with an RBI in the Double-A All-Star Game. Had it not been for the knee surgery, Jaha might well have a regular job in the majors now. Invest in him up to $7. His 1992 cards are fine investments up to 20 cents.

Professional Batting Register

	BA	G	AB	R	H	2B	3B	HR	RBI	SB
85 R	.265	24	68	13	18	3	0	2	14	4
86 A	.318	73	258	65	82	13	2	15	67	9
87 A	.269	122	376	68	101	22	0	7	47	10
88 A	.255	99	302	58	77	14	6	8	54	10
89 A	.292	140	479	83	140	26	5	25	91	8
90 A	.262	26	84	12	22	5	0	4	19	0
91 AA	.344	130	486	121	167	38	3	30	134	12

CHIPPER JONES

Position: Shortstop
Team: Atlanta Braves
Born: April 24, 1972 Deland, GA
Height: 6'3" **Weight:** 185 lbs.
Bats: both **Throws:** right
Acquired: First-round pick in 6/90 free-agent draft

Player Summary	
Fantasy Value	$5 to $10
Card Value	10¢ to 20¢
Will	jump a notch
Can't	win Gold Glove
Expect	power and speed
Don't Expect	short apprenticeship

This Georgia product has a chance to be a part of the Braves' scheme for a long time. In 1991, Jones was named to the Class-A South Atlantic League's postseason All-Star Team and was tabbed as the league's most outstanding prospect. He did it by posting numbers that mark him as one of the finest offensive middle infield prospects in baseball. Playing for Macon, he did all of the things that a batter can do: run, hit, and hit for power. Jones took the Triple Crown among Atlanta farmhands, and only one of the categories—home runs—was even close. He also ranked among the Braves' leaders in stolen base. His extra-base pop can go into the alleys or over the fence, which could help him thrive in Atlanta. He had a .516 slugging percentage and a .405 on-base average in 1991. *The Sporting News* named Jones on its list of shortstops to watch. If Jones improves his defense, he could be a major leaguer of stature. He's a great choice for fantasy managers up to $10. His current cards are fine buys at a dime.

Professional Batting Register

	BA	G	AB	R	H	2B	3B	HR	RBI	SB
90 R	.229	44	140	20	32	1	1	1	18	5
91 A	.323	136	473	104	153	24	11	15	98	39

ROOKIE PROSPECTS

BRIAN JORDAN

Position: Outfield
Team: St. Louis Cardinals
Born: March 29, 1967 Baltimore, MD
Height: 6'1" **Weight:** 205 lbs.
Bats: right **Throws:** right
Acquired: First-round pick in 6/88 free-agent draft

Player Summary	
Fantasy Value	$1 to $3
Card Value	5¢ to 10¢
Will	start at Triple-A
Can't	be two-sport star
Expect	power surge
Don't Expect	polish

This two-sport man finally got his baseball career going in 1991 after a series of injuries. Entering the season, Jordan had played in just 55 pro games. He showed some of his potential with the Cards' top farm team, exhibiting some punch and speed. He met up with Atlanta Falcons defensive backfield partner Deion Sanders in a June 10 game, and each went 1-for-4. Jordan broke into pro baseball with some nice stats in 18 games in 1988, but suffered a bone bruise in his right heel and played in only one game thereafter. In 1989 he was limited to 11 games by an ankle injury he suffered in the Senior Bowl football game. In 1990, Jordan broke the navicular bone in his right wrist. Drafted by the Buffalo Bills, Jordan was released and picked up on waivers by the Falcons. Though he's not Bo Jackson, Jordan has some power. A good draft possibility for 1993, pass on him for over $2 this year. Sink a few bucks in his nickel-priced current cards, however.

Professional Batting Register

	BA	G	AB	R	H	2B	3B	HR	RBI	SB
88 A	.310	19	71	12	22	3	1	4	12	3
89 A	.349	11	43	7	15	4	1	2	11	0
90 A	.167	9	30	3	5	0	1	0	1	0
90 AA	.160	16	50	4	8	1	0	0	0	0
91 AAA	.264	61	212	35	56	11	4	4	24	10

JEFF JUDEN

Position: Pitcher
Team: Houston Astros
Born: Jan. 19, 1971 Salem, MA
Height: 6'7" **Weight:** 245 lbs.
Bats: right **Throws:** right
Acquired: First-round pick in 6/89 free-agent draft

Player Summary	
Fantasy Value	$5 to $10
Card Value	5¢ to 10¢
Will	dominate hitters
Can't	neglect nuances
Expect	a K a frame
Don't Expect	long stay in minors

Juden made more progress in 1991 than can be measured by statistics or even by the level of ball he played. By reaching the majors when he did, he also got a peek of the pennant race when the Astros played the Braves late in the season. He started against Atlanta and went six and one-third innings, allowing three earned runs. Juden's arrival in the majors capped a spirited rise through the Houston chain. *Baseball America* tabbed him the second-best prospect in the Class-A Florida State League in 1990. Juden appeared in the Double-A All-Star Game in 1991, hurling two innings and allowing one run on three hits. With his size, he can be an intimidator on the mound. He has shown the ability to strike batters out. He will be part of Houston's rebuilding effort. He is a card veteran by now, but his nickel-priced 1992 cards will still sell. He is a promising fantasy draft up to $10.

Professional Pitching Register

	W	L	ERA	G	CG	IP	H	ER	BB	SO
89 R	1	4	3.40	9	0	39.2	33	15	17	49
90 A	10	1	2.27	15	2	91.0	72	23	42	85
90 AA	1	3	5.37	11	0	52.0	55	31	42	40
91 AA	6	3	3.10	16	0	95.2	84	33	44	75
91 AAA	3	2	3.18	10	0	56.2	56	20	25	51
91 AL	0	2	6.00	4	0	18.0	19	12	7	11

ROOKIE PROSPECTS

ERIC KARROS

Position: First base
Team: Los Angeles Dodgers
Born: Nov. 4, 1967 Hakensack, NJ
Height: 6'4" **Weight:** 205 lbs.
Bats: right **Throws:** right
Acquired: Sixth-round pick in 6/88 free-agent draft

Player Summary	
Fantasy Value	$5 to $12
Card Value	10¢ to 20¢
Will	slug over .500
Can't	stay down much longer
Expect	trade rumors
Don't Expect	Albuquerque

Your first impulse upon seeing Karros's numbers is to say that Triple-A Pacific Coast League numbers can be deceiving. Then you look back and see that he has torn apart a variety of leagues, always hitting for average and power. A walk-on for UCLA in 1986, Karros became an All-American and helped the Bruins to the NCAA tournament. With the exception of the 1989 season, he has achieved his offensive production without the strikeouts you might expect. In 1990, he led Double-A San Antonio in several offensive categories—including slugging percentage with a .554—and helped the club into the Texas League finals. The kind of hitter who can tear apart a pitching staff, Karros has some explosive days in 1991. He had four hits, including a double and two homers, and seven RBI in a contest against Tucson. He also had two homers and six RBI against Colorado Springs. He is a classic fantasy draft for a dozen bucks. His 1992 cards are great investments under a quarter apiece.

Professional Batting Register

	BA	G	AB	R	H	2B	3B	HR	RBI	SB
88 R	.366	66	268	68	98	12	1	12	55	9
89 A	.303	142	545	86	165	40	1	15	86	18
90 AA	.352	131	509	90	179	45	2	18	78	8
91 AAA	.316	132	488	88	154	33	8	22	101	3
91 NL	.071	14	14	0	1	1	0	0	1	0

STEVE KARSAY

Position: Pitcher
Team: Toronto Blue Jays
Born: March 24, 1972 College Point, NY
Height: 6'3" **Weight:** 185 lbs.
Bats: right **Throws:** right
Acquired: First-round pick in 6/90 free-agent draft

Player Summary	
Fantasy Value	$2 to $5
Card Value	15¢ to 25¢
Will	cut down walks
Can't	keep developing blisters
Expect	improvement
Don't Expect	big numbers

Karsay learned something about baseball's ups and downs in 1991. One year removed from being Toronto's top pick, he endured a rough season with Class-A Myrtle Beach of the South Atlantic League. He posted mediocre numbers, possibly due in part to a persistent blister problem. He also ended the season with a bad arm. However, when healthy Karsay is a hard thrower with a changeup. Although his walk total was not particularly high, sometimes he struggled with his location. Opponents compiled a .240 batting average against him in 1991. A very competitive pitcher, he is nevertheless a down-to-earth type with no ego problem over his high draft status. He is considered willing to learn. The blister was a bit of a mystery, seeming to be healed then opening up again. However, he did take his share of starts. Karsay's ERA and hits-to-innings ratio suggest that if his arm problems are not serious, he will advance in 1992. His 1992 cards will be golden buys at up to 25 cents. He is a $3 fantasy draft for the future.

Professional Pitching Register

	W	L	ERA	G	CG	IP	H	ER	BB	SO
90 A	1	1	0.79	5	0	22.2	11	2	12	25
91 A	4	9	3.58	20	1	110.2	96	44	48	100

ROOKIE PROSPECTS

MIKE KELLY

Position: Outfield
Team: Atlanta Braves
Born: June 2, 1970 Los Angeles, CA
Height: 6'4" **Weight:** 195 lbs.
Bats: right **Throws:** right
Acquired: First-round pick in 6/91 free-agent draft

Player Summary	
Fantasy Value	$2 to $5
Card Value	15¢ to 20¢
Will	crush pitches
Can't	sit on fastballs
Expect	30 homers
Don't Expect	Atlanta until '93

Kelly was the second overall pick in the 1991 draft, and the Braves are hoping it won't be long before his raw power and his run production get him to the big leagues. He attended Arizona State, and in fact has been compared to another product of that school—Barry Bonds. Kelly runs well, and his coverage in the outfield is good. The Braves think he simply needs to get adjusted to pro ball, where he will see breaking balls in spots where he would have gotten fastballs in college. Signed for $575,000, he was sent to Class-A Durham of the Carolina League. He started a bit slowly, going 1-for-15 with seven strikeouts, but two of his first five pro hits were homers. He finished the year with a .356 on-base average and a .460 slugging percentage. If Kelly were to develop quickly, he would help form one of the better outfields of this era, along with David Justice and Ron Gant. Kelly's first-round 1992 cards will be great investments. While young, he will be a great long-term addition to the reserve roster for up to $5.

Professional Batting Register

	BA	G	AB	R	H	2B	3B	HR	RBI	SB
91 A	.250	35	124	29	31	6	1	6	17	6

BO KENNEDY

Position: Pitcher
Team: Chicago White Sox
Born: Jan. 4, 1968 Fredericktown, MO
Height: 5'11" **Weight:** 185 lbs.
Bats: right **Throws:** right
Acquired: Sixth-round pick in 6/86 free-agent draft

Player Summary	
Fantasy Value	$1 to $3
Card Value	5¢ to 10¢
Will	do the job
Can't	overpower hitters
Expect	10 wins
Don't Expect	pretty innings

Kennedy must now prove that he can overcome what was a distinctly unimpressive boost to the Triple-A level. Until he reached Vancouver of the Pacific Coast League, he had been a steady member of the White Sox chain, reaching double figures in wins for four consecutive years. But the PCL, not exactly a pitcher's league, was rough on Kennedy. His control, never of the pinpoint variety, was poor. He also allowed one and one-half hits per inning. His role also changed in Triple-A; formerly a starter, he made most of his appearances in relief. Unfortunately, he has been in the chain for six years. And he may be judged a little on the small side. He could bounce back and win in double figures again. He also has a shot at a middle relief role with Chicago, which keeps his fantasy value capped at $3. His nickel-priced 1992 cards are not buys.

Professional Pitching Register

	W	L	ERA	G	CG	IP	H	ER	BB	SO
86 R	0	4	6.38	10	0	36.2	47	26	32	35
87 R	4	2	2.72	9	0	53.0	45	16	19	50
87 A	0	1	6.62	15	0	50.1	57	37	44	43
88 A	10	8	3.48	27	5	176.0	158	68	71	109
89 A	14	7	3.01	25	3	161.2	137	54	57	86
90 AA	11	12	4.73	30	3	175.0	175	92	89	121
91 AA	10	3	2.32	15	0	93.0	88	24	48	52
91 AAA	3	4	7.85	17	0	36.2	56	32	29	25

ROOKIE PROSPECTS

MARK KIEFER

Position: Pitcher
Team: Milwaukee Brewers
Born: Nov. 13, 1968 Orange, CA
Height: 6'4" **Weight:** 175 lbs.
Bats: right **Throws:** right
Acquired: 21st-round pick in 6/87 free-agent draft

Player Summary	
Fantasy Value	$3 to $5
Card Value	15¢ to 20¢
Will	get ERA under 4.00
Can't	notch key K
Expect	more seasoning
Don't Expect	consistency

Kiefer gets attention not only because of his high win total, but also because his progress accelerated in 1991. And this happened despite his pitching in two parks that are not pitchers' paradises: El Paso's Cohen Stadium and Denver's Mile High Stadium. He made a particularly impressive adjustment to Triple-A, rebounding from an inconsistent start to put together a four-game stretch. After going 5-5 with a 6.33 ERA, Kiefer suddenly was 9-5 with a 4.66. He can sometimes overpower a hitter, especially when his breaking ball is working. His control was excellent in his first three pro seasons, but he had a little trouble with walks in Double- and Triple-A. Often that's just a matter of learning confidence in your own style. Kiefer made his Triple-A debut against Iowa and tossed a two-hitter. In August, he and Greg Mathews hurled back-to-back shutouts. Kiefer is a low-profile prospect with some draft appeal. His 1992 cards, though, have allure up to 20 cents.

Professional Pitching Register

	W	L	ERA	G	CG	IP	H	ER	BB	SO
88 R	4	4	2.65	15	2	68.0	76	20	17	51
89 A	9	6	2.32	30	7	131.2	106	34	32	100
90 R	0	0	3.86	1	0	2.1	3	1	1	2
90 A	5	2	3.30	11	0	60.0	65	22	17	37
91 AA	7	1	3.33	12	0	75.2	62	28	43	72
91 AAA	9	5	4.62	17	3	101.1	104	52	41	68

RYAN KLESKO

Position: First base
Team: Atlanta Braves
Born: June 12, 1971 Westminster, CA
Height: 6'3" **Weight:** 220 lbs.
Bats: left **Throws:** left
Acquired: Sixth-round pick in 6/89 free-agent draft

Player Summary	
Fantasy Value	$6 to $11
Card Value	15¢ to 25¢
Will	hit
Can't	lay off balls
Expect	some errors
Don't Expect	return to mound

Klesko may turn out to be one of those classic cases of former pitchers converted into sluggers. He is described as a raw-boned, thick-bodied first baseman who is a pure hitter. He needs work in his overall game, particularly defense and baserunning. But his strength is hitting, and the Braves like the fact that he knows he can hit and does so with confidence. He doesn't get cheated at the plate, and he will leave his feet to hit a ball. In spite of this aggressiveness, he doesn't have a particularly high rate of strikeouts, and he also can take a walk. He had a .404 on-base average and a .458 slugging percentage in '91. Klesko was drafted as a pitcher, but had arm troubles and was shifted to first because of his bat. It took a while for the pitching bug to leave his system. If he continues to develop, Klesko may soon join what promises to be a bruising lineup. Priced at 15 cents, his 1992 cards are deserving investments. He is a good fantasy draft for your reserves at $8.

Professional Batting Register

	BA	G	AB	R	H	2B	3B	HR	RBI	SB
89 R	.404	17	57	14	23	5	4	1	16	4
89 A	.289	25	90	17	26	6	0	1	12	1
90 A	.274	140	523	81	165	31	2	17	85	23
91 AA	.291	126	419	64	122	22	3	14	67	14

ROOKIE PROSPECTS

PHILIP LEFTWICH

Position: Pitcher
Team: California Angels
Born: May 19, 1969 Lynchburg, VA
Height: 6'5" **Weight:** 205 lbs.
Bats: right **Throws:** left
Acquired: Second-round pick in 6/90 free-agent draft

Player Summary	
Fantasy Value	$2 to $4
Card Value	5¢ to 10¢
Will	complete a game
Can't	live on fastball
Expect	big numbers
Don't Expect	exceptional heat

Leftwich is one of the jewels of a California system that has done a nice job of grooming lefthanders, including Jim Abbott and Chuck Finley. Leftwich is a while from joining them as a major league starter, but he has turned in two straight impressive seasons on the pro level. The Angels' top pick in the draft, he can strike out hitters and possesses good control, especially for a young lefthander. He not only was the strikeout king by far in California's minor league system in 1991, Leftwich also ranked among the leaders in wins and ERA. Class-A opponents compiled a .245 batting average in '91. His fastball is said to be above average, though not exceptional, in the 87 to 90 mph range. He is a smart individual who enhances his skills with a knowledge of the game. Leftwich studies the hitters and gets ahead in the count. He was called to Double-A Midland at season's end. He is a good fantasy choice for $3. Pass on his current cards, however, until he dominates Double-A.

Professional Pitching Register

	W	L	ERA	G	CG	IP	H	ER	BB	SO
90 A	8	2	1.86	15	0	92.0	88	19	23	81
91 A	11	9	3.28	26	5	173.0	158	63	59	163
91 AA	1	0	3.00	1	0	6.0	5	2	5	3

CURTIS LESKANIC

Position: Pitcher
Team: Cleveland Indians
Born: April 2, 1968 Homestead, PA
Height: 6' **Weight:** 180 lbs.
Bats: right **Throws:** right
Acquired: Eighth-round pick in 6/89 free-agent draft

Player Summary	
Fantasy Value	$2 to $4
Card Value	5¢ to 10¢
Will	be a winner
Can't	finish starts
Expect	big repertoire
Don't Expect	many hits

Leskanic has three pitches and has done well enough to become a top winner in the Indians' farm system, and the feeling is he can do even better. His concentration is said to be imperfect at times, and this affects his control. Leskanic has a fastball, slider, and a curve, and he is being urged to use the slider more, especially to set up the fastball. Sometimes he gets pumped and overthrows his heater, losing his control. He must also learn to go to his other pitches when the fastball isn't working, but this is part of experience. He is a hard worker, a good player to have on a team. He keeps the other players loose, and is the go-to guy when there is a tough game. However, there is still a sense that Leskanic can have more good outings than he does, and he needs to improve consistency. Opponents in the Class-A Carolina League compiled a .226 batting average in 1991. He is a good fantasy draft for up to $4. His nickel-priced current cards are risky until he clobbers Double-A.

Professional Pitching Register

	W	L	ERA	G	CG	IP	H	ER	BB	SO
90 A	6	5	3.68	14	2	73.1	61	30	30	71
91 A	15	8	2.79	28	0	174.1	143	54	91	163

ROOKIE PROSPECTS

RON LOCKETT

Position: First base
Team: Philadelphia Phillies
Born: Sept. 5, 1969 Chicago, IL
Height: 6'1" **Weight:** 189 lbs.
Bats: left **Throws:** left
Acquired: Eighth-round pick in 6/90 free-agent draft

Player Summary	
Fantasy Value	$1 to $2
Card Value	5¢ to 10¢
Will	take extra base
Can't	make contact
Expect	offense
Don't Expect	Gold Glove

Lockett is an outfielder by trade who played first base with Class-A Clearwater of the Florida State League in 1991, and who may return to the outfield in 1992. Right now, though, his main appeal doesn't stem from defensive play. He is a lefty power hitter, a commodity always desirable in the majors. He was Clearwater's MVP in 1991, leading the team in homers and finishing fifth in the league in RBI. He had a .364 on-base average and a .392 slugging percentage in '91. Batting from the third hole, Lockett missed just three games all season. He has a good eye at the plate. Even though he strikes out too much, they are aggressive swings, and he doesn't chase too many bad balls. He has decent speed, and it shows up in the triples and stolen base columns. His doubles total was a little short, though. Lockett was the Phils' Player of the Month in July of 1990. He needs to develop his all-around play before he will make a great fantasy pick for more than $2. His nickel-priced current cards are not good choices yet.

Professional Batting Register

	BA	G	AB	R	H	2B	3B	HR	RBI	SB
90 R	.310	63	229	32	71	12	5	6	34	10
91 A	.268	128	459	81	123	13	7	10	71	10

KENNY LOFTON

Position: Outfield
Team: Cleveland Indians
Born: May 31, 1967 East Chicago, IN
Height: 6' **Weight:** 180 lbs.
Bats: left **Throws:** left
Acquired: Traded from Astros with Dave Rohde for Ed Taubensee and Willie Blair, 12/91

Player Summary	
Fantasy Value	$3 to $6
Card Value	15¢ to 20¢
Will	strike out
Can't	hit homers
Expect	start in Triple-A
Don't Expect	starting job

Lofton can run and hit, and that always makes someone an interesting prospect. He will open the 1992 season at 24 years of age, which is a little late in the game for a speed player. Houston traded Lofton to Cleveland in December. Lofton's tools, however, still demand some attention. He led off for the National League farmhands in the 1991 Triple-A All-Star Game and went the whole way in center field, going 1-for-4 with a stolen base. A 5-for-30 slump in August diminished what was an outstanding batting average, but Lofton still managed to be a standout hitter and basestealer for Houston. On the minus side, Lofton walks too seldom and strikes out too often for a leadoff man. He doesn't get enough extra-base hits to justify that kind of swinging. He should start the season in Triple-A to work on his strike zone. His 1992 card chances are excellent up to 20 cents. He is a $4 fantasy draft.

Professional Batting Register

	BA	G	AB	R	H	2B	3B	HR	RBI	SB
88 A	.214	48	187	23	40	6	1	1	14	26
89 A	.264	56	192	35	56	5	1	0	17	40
90 A	.331	124	481	98	159	15	5	2	35	62
91 AAA	.308	130	545	93	168	19	17	2	50	40
91 NL	.203	20	74	9	15	1	0	0	0	2

ROOKIE PROSPECTS

PAT MAHOMES

Position: Pitcher
Team: Minnesota Twins
Born: Aug. 9, 1970 Bryan, TX
Height: 6'1" **Weight:** 175 lbs.
Bats: right **Throws:** right
Acquired: Sixth-round pick in 6/88 free-agent draft

Player Summary	
Fantasy Value	$2 to $4
Card Value	10¢ to 15¢
Will	trim ERA
Can't	lapse on control
Expect	strikeouts
Don't Expect	rattled pitcher

Mahomes was a winner on both the Double-A and Triple-A levels in 1991, and it won't be long before he does it in the majors. His size isn't particularly imposing, but he throws a good, hard fastball and has excellent control. He also possesses a good slider and changeup, and these pitches combine to give him fearsome strikeout capabilities. Mahomes put his talents on display in the Double-A All-Star Game, hurling two hitless innings and striking out two in gaining the victory. At the time, Mahomes was working for Orlando of the Southern League and owned 121 strikeouts in 107 innings. Promoted to Triple-A Portland of the Pacific Coast League, he stepped right into the rotation, though his control suffered a bit. He is described as a focused pitcher who doesn't get rattled on the mound. All this stamps Mahomes as one of the Twins' top hopes. He is a future fantasy grab at $3. His dime-priced 1992 cards are lethargic investment vehicles currently.

ED MARTEL

Position: Pitcher
Team: New York Yankees
Born: March 2, 1969 Mount Clemens, MI
Height: 6'1" **Weight:** 190 lbs.
Bats: right **Throws:** right
Acquired: 11th-round pick in 6/87 free-agent draft

Player Summary	
Fantasy Value	$3 to $6
Card Value	15¢ to 20¢
Will	limit runners
Can't	pitch in AL yet
Expect	berth at Triple-A
Don't Expect	15 wins

Martel is still so young it's hard to believe he's completed five years in the Yankee farm system. He signed right out of high school in 1987 and has opted to continue his education at Northwestern in the off-season. Martel has made his way through the chain, and, based on his performance at the end of 1991 at Double-A, he may soon have a shot at a job in the Yankee rotation. He had an award-winning week late in August, moving into second place among Yankee farmhands in victories, and keeping position among the leading strikeout artists. Working for Double-A Albany-Colonie of the Eastern League, Martel hurled consecutive shutouts, first beating New Britain 1-0 on August 20, allowing just two hits and fanning 10. He came back five days later to stifle Harrisburg on three hits with nine Ks. In 1989, he was a Florida State League All-Star. He could hurl in '92 pinstripes, giving him up to a $6 fantasy value. His 1992 cards are positive investments.

Professional Pitching Register

	W	L	ERA	G	CG	IP	H	ER	BB	SO
88 R	6	3	3.69	13	3	78.0	66	32	51	93
89 A	13	7	3.28	25	3	156.1	120	57	100	167
90 A	11	11	3.30	28	5	185.1	136	68	118	178
91 AA	8	5	1.78	18	2	116.0	77	23	57	136
91 AAA	3	5	3.44	9	2	55.0	50	21	36	41

Professional Pitching Register

	W	L	ERA	G	CG	IP	H	ER	BB	SO
87 A	1	0	3.00	2	0	3.0	2	1	3	2
88 A	2	2	3.02	9	0	41.2	53	14	8	24
89 A	10	8	4.04	26	4	144.2	151	65	39	86
90 A	8	13	4.08	25	2	143.1	134	65	65	95
91 AA	13	6	2.81	25	3	163.1	129	51	55	141

ROOKIE PROSPECTS

JESUS MARTINEZ

Position: Pitcher
Team: Los Angeles Dodgers
Born: March 13, 1974 Santo Domingo, Dominican Republic
Height: 6'2" **Weight:** 145 lbs.
Bats: left **Throws:** left
Acquired: Signed as a free agent, 8/90

Player Summary	
Fantasy Value	$1 to $2
Card Value	5¢ to 7¢
Will	throw hard
Can't	avoid comparisons
Expect	patience from Dodgers
Don't Expect	quick arrival

Jesus is unlike many other fine players who come from the Dominican Republic in that North American sports fans already have an idea who he is. That's because of the success of his brother Ramon, a star for the Dodgers, and his brother Pedro, a big winner in the minors in 1991. Whether Jesus will feel this scrutiny and the pressure of living up to his brothers is a question that can only be answered with time. Right now he needs experience; he played in the Dominican Republic in 1991, his first pro year. He is similar to Ramon in build, though a little shorter. Jesus also has the obvious difference of being left-handed. He throws a fastball considered good for his age, plus a curve and a changeup. Like his brothers, Jesus is described as hard-working with an excellent baseball attitude. Since he has no professional experience in the United States, he is not a fantasy draft. His cards will be buys just because of the family connection.

No minor league experience

PEDRO MARTINEZ

Position: Pitcher
Team: Los Angeles Dodgers
Born: July 25, 1971 Manoguayabo, Dominican Republic
Height: 5'11" **Weight:** 150 lbs.
Bats: right **Throws:** right
Acquired: Signed as a free agent, 8/88

Player Summary	
Fantasy Value	$5 to $10
Card Value	15¢ to 25¢
Will	throw heat
Can't	avoid comparisons
Expect	Triple-A
Don't Expect	call-up in '92

Pedro is the shortest of the three Martinez brothers in the Dodgers organization, but he certainly didn't pitch small in 1991. He was perhaps the top pitching prospect in the system, posting standout totals in wins, ERA, and strikeouts. His pitching coach at Triple-A Albuquerque, Von Joshua, said that he was impressed with Martinez's poise on the rubber for a little guy. Pedro's brother Ramon described Pedro as a competitor. He spent some time with Double-A San Antonio of the Texas League in '91 and delivered some fine performances. He beat 1990 first-round draft pick Donovan Osborne with a two-hitter. Martinez was then promoted to Triple-A Albuquerque in the Pacific Coast League. He has a fastball in the 90s and is reported to have better command of the curve than does Ramon. Pedro may also adjust to the United States more easily than Ramon because Pedro's English is not bad. His 1992 card potential, at a quarter apiece, are unlimited. He is a $8 fantasy buy.

Professional Pitching Register

	W	L	ERA	G	CG	IP	H	ER	BB	SO
90 R	8	3	3.62	14	0	77.0	74	31	40	82
91 A	8	0	2.05	10	0	61.1	41	14	19	83
91 AAA	3	3	3.66	6	0	39.1	28	16	16	35
91 AA	7	5	1.76	12	4	76.2	57	15	31	74

ROOKIE PROSPECTS

TINO MARTINEZ

Position: First base
Team: Seattle Mariners
Born: Dec. 7, 1967 Tampa, FL
Height: 6'2" **Weight:** 205 lbs.
Bats: left **Throws:** left
Acquired: First-round pick in 6/88 free-agent draft

Player Summary	
Fantasy Value	$10 to $16
Card Value	20¢ to 30¢
Will	hit .300
Can't	go back to minors
Expect	line-drive power
Don't Expect	home runs

One of the most highly touted prospects in baseball, Martinez returned to Seattle in August of 1991, probably for good. He has all the look of a major leaguer who can drive in runs without giving up the contact many power hitters do. Martinez was a star on the 1988 Team USA, the seventh-best prospect in the Double-A Eastern League in 1989, and was *USA Today*'s Minor League Player of the Year in 1990. *Baseball America* placed Martinez on its Player of the Year Watch in 1991. Though known as a hitter, Martinez led Eastern League first basemen in five fielding categories in 1989. He has slammed at least 29 doubles in all three of his pro years. Owner of a good eye, Martinez usually has more walks than strikeouts. There's a chance he may never be a homer man, especially with the Kingdome wall rising 23 feet in right, but if the RBI keep coming no one will mind. He is a $12 fantasy venture, and his 1992 cards are bargains at 20 cents apiece.

Professional Batting Register

	BA	G	AB	R	H	2B	3B	HR	RBI	SB
89 AA	.257	137	509	51	131	29	2	13	64	7
90 AAA	.320	128	453	83	145	28	1	17	93	8
90 AL	.221	24	68	4	15	4	0	0	5	0
91 AAA	.326	122	442	94	144	34	5	18	86	7
91 AL	.205	36	112	11	23	2	0	4	9	0

ROB MAURER

Position: First base
Team: Texas Rangers
Born: Jan. 7, 1967 Evansville, IN
Height: 6' **Weight:** 215 lbs.
Bats: left **Throws:** left
Acquired: Sixth-round pick in 6/88 free-agent draft

Player Summary	
Fantasy Value	$3 to $6
Card Value	5¢ to 10¢
Will	hit 20 homers
Can't	move Rafael Palmeiro
Expect	outfield experiment
Don't Expect	regular job

Maurer is a player with major league ability and an obstacle to match. A first baseman, he may have his path to a regular big league job blocked by Rafael Palmeiro. Maurer has hit for average throughout his career and definitely shows some pop. He is considered a pretty good defensive player, but still would not uproot Palmeiro. With Triple-A Oklahoma City of the American Association in 1991, Maurer was voted the league's Batter of the Week by hitting .417 in seven games, with two homers and seven RBI. He was also named to the Triple-A All-Star Game. In 1990, he led the Double-A Texas League with his .578 slugging percentage and was second with his 21 homers. He homered once every 17.48 at bats, best ratio in the circuit. His .391 average in 1988 was the highest by any Ranger in a short-season league. He should be in the majors in '92—wait until he has a position before investing in his 1992 cards. He is a $4 fantasy draft.

Professional Batting Register

	BA	G	AB	R	H	2B	3B	HR	RBI	SB
88 R	.391	63	233	65	91	18	3	8	60	0
89 A	.276	132	456	69	126	18	9	6	51	3
90 AA	.300	104	367	55	110	31	4	21	78	4
91 AAA	.301	132	459	76	138	41	3	20	77	2
91 AL	.063	13	16	0	1	1	0	0	2	0

ROOKIE PROSPECTS

BRENT MAYNE

Position: Catcher
Team: Kansas City Royals
Born: April 19, 1968 Loma Linda, CA
Height: 6'1" **Weight:** 190 lbs.
Bats: left **Throws:** right
Acquired: First-round pick in 6/89 free-agent draft

Player Summary	
Fantasy Value	$3 to $5
Card Value	5¢ to 10¢
Will	receive well
Can't	crush ball
Expect	a role
Don't Expect	everyday status

A combination of talent and circumstance has helped Mayne to come a long way in a short period of time. A veteran of the College World Series, he wound up with a hefty portion of the Royals' catching duties in 1991. This high draft choice was seeing spot duty when regular receiver Mike Macfarlane was injured, and thereafter shared work with Tim Spehr. Mayne has not been an especially fearsome hitter as a pro, and he may never be a power man, especially in Royals Stadium. He puts the bat on the ball, however, can get a hit with a man in scoring position, and has the potential to drive in 60 runs—perhaps as the lefty part of a platoon. He had a .315 on-base average in 1991. It's possible his defensive game may remain ahead of his offense. Kansas City made Mayne the 13th overall pick in the draft. A back strain cut short his first pro season. At this point, he is no more than a $4 fantasy backstop. His nickel-priced 1992 cards offer little excitement.

Professional Batting Register

	BA	G	AB	R	H	2B	3B	HR	RBI	SB
89 A	.542	7	24	5	13	3	1	0	8	0
90 AA	.267	115	412	48	110	16	3	2	61	5
90 AL	.231	5	13	2	3	0	0	0	1	0
91 AL	.251	85	231	22	58	8	0	3	31	2

TERRY McFARLIN

Position: Pitcher
Team: Los Angeles Dodgers
Born: April 6, 1969 Brooklyn, NY
Height: 6' **Weight:** 160 lbs.
Bats: both **Throws:** right
Acquired: Signed as a free agent, 9/90

Player Summary	
Fantasy Value	$1 to $2
Card Value	5¢ to 10¢
Will	jump to Double-A
Can't	return to bullpen
Expect	lots of Ks
Don't Expect	unlimited progress

McFarlin lost an extra-curricular activity but gained a career. He was born in the same place that the Dodgers were, and he attended the same high school that Sandy Koufax did. McFarlin enrolled at the Borough of Manhattan Community College. The school dropped baseball, though. He went to a sandlot team on Long Island and led his team through the tournament with three shutouts. The Dodgers then signed him, and he became a hot prospect within a year. When the 1991 season began, he was at extended spring training, but then Class-A Bakersfield of the California League needed a pitcher, and he was assigned there. McFarlin began in the bullpen but was so effective that he quickly was inserted into the rotation. He became one of the chain's biggest winners. He possesses a good fastball and curve. Opponents compiled a .245 batting average against McFarlin, and he allowed six homers. He does not get rattled on the mound. He opened some fantasy managers' eyes, but he is still too far away to be worth more than $1. His current cards, at a nickel each, are holds.

Professional Pitching Register

	W	L	ERA	G	CG	IP	H	ER	BB	SO
91 A	14	6	2.66	26	0	152.0	139	45	56	128

ROOKIE PROSPECTS

KEVIN McGEHEE

Position: Pitcher
Team: San Francisco Giants
Born: Jan. 18, 1969 Pineville, LA
Height: 6' **Weight:** 190 lbs.
Bats: right **Throws:** right
Acquired: 11th-round pick in 6/90 free-agent draft

Player Summary	
Fantasy Value	$3 to $5
Card Value	10¢ to 15¢
Will	keep hits down
Can't	struggle with control
Expect	move to Double-A
Don't Expect	ERA over 3.50

McGehee is one of a group of young pitchers who may be bolstering the Giants within two or three years. He was one of two Class-A San Jose righthanders named by *Baseball America* among the California League's Top 10 prospects, Rich Huisman being the other. McGehee, a hard thrower, was tabbed as the ninth-best hopeful. He was also one of three starters, and four pitchers overall, to reach double figures in wins for the club. McGehee was among the organizational leaders in ERA and in strikeouts, and tied for fourth in victories. He posted an excellent ratio of hits to innings in 1991, but he has showed in both pro seasons that his control needs work. McGehee, who attended Louisiana Tech, finished fifth in strikeouts in the Class-A Northwest League in 1990. His performance at a high Class-A level in 1991 suggests that in 1992 he will go to Double-A or even better. Spend $3 for your fantasy reserves, just in case. His current cards are good buys at a dime apiece.

JEFF McNEELY

Position: Outfield
Team: Boston Red Sox
Born: Oct. 18, 1970 Monroe, NC
Height: 6'2" **Weight:** 190 lbs.
Bats: right **Throws:** right
Acquired: Second-round pick in 6/89 free-agent draft

Player Summary	
Fantasy Value	$1 to $2
Card Value	5¢ to 10¢
Will	steal 40 bases
Can't	hit for power
Expect	fewer Ks
Don't Expect	Fenway until '93

The Red Sox have often been criticized for lacking speed and an ignitor who could shake up a defense. That's what makes McNeely's exploits so intriguing. At Class-A Lynchburg of the Carolina League in 1991, McNeely was voted the circuit's fastest baserunner by *Baseball America*. He hit for average, including .394 in July (making him the Carolina League Player of the Month). He also stole bases and drew walks. He was named the loop's best defensive outfielder. He has made such an impact that he has become a reference point for the draft. One Red Sox official described a 1991 draftee as a "Jeff McNeely type." McNeely played for Spartanburg Methodist College in 1989, earning JUCO All-American honors. After a stint in the Florida Instructional League in 1989, he was a New York-Penn League All-Star in 1990. His 39 swipes led the league. His power shortage may slow his ascent, making his fantasy value a $2 bet at best. His current cards probably won't appreciate that quickly, either.

Professional Pitching Register

	W	L	ERA	G	CG	IP	H	ER	BB	SO
90 A	4	8	4.76	15	1	73.2	74	39	38	86
91 A	13	6	2.33	26	2	174.0	129	45	87	171

Professional Batting Register

	BA	G	AB	R	H	2B	3B	HR	RBI	SB
89 R	.406	9	32	10	13	1	1	0	4	5
89 A	.250	61	208	20	52	7	0	2	21	16
90 A	.282	89	308	44	87	4	5	6	40	46
91 A	.322	106	382	58	123	16	5	4	38	38

ROOKIE PROSPECTS

LUIS MERCEDES

Position: Outfield
Team: Baltimore Orioles
Born: Feb. 20, 1968 San Pedro de Macoris, Dominican Republic
Height: 6' **Weight:** 180 lbs.
Bats: right **Throws:** right
Acquired: Signed as a free agent, 2/87

Player Summary	
Fantasy Value	$3 to $7
Card Value	15¢ to 20¢
Will	post high average
Can't	crack Baltimore's infield
Expect	.30 steals
Don't Expect	five homers

Mercedes registered his third straight year with a batting average over the .300 mark, and he did it at the Triple-A level, which indicates that very soon he could be swinging in the majors to stay. Mercedes is an infielder and outfielder, but his speed makes him most suitable for the outfield. He is not bashful at the plate, striking out quite often for such a high-average hitter. In 1990, he was .402 in at bats when he put the ball in play. Mercedes enjoyed a 15-game stretch near the end of August 1991 when he went 24-for-57 to raise his average to .330. He ranked among the leading base stealers on the Orioles' farm. He was involved in an incident in which he slid hard into second, and then argued with third baseman Tom Quinlan while returning to the dugout. Mercedes then hit Quinlan in the face with his batting helmet. Mercedes will be used somewhere, making him a $4 fantasy possibility. His 1992 cards are good purchases for 15 cents each.

MATT MIESKE

Position: Outfield
Team: San Diego Padres
Born: Feb. 13, 1968 Midland, MI
Height: 6' **Weight:** 185 lbs.
Bats: right **Throws:** right
Acquired: 17th-round pick in 6/90 free-agent draft

Player Summary	
Fantasy Value	$3 to $6
Card Value	10¢ to 15¢
Will	hit for power
Can't	jump to Triple-A
Expect	100 RBI
Don't Expect	100 K

Mieske has been among the dominant players in his league during his first two pro seasons. He has combined power and speed, placing him among team leaders in total bases and steals two straight years. In 1990 in the Class-A Northwestern League, he took two of three Triple Crown categories with 12 homers and 63 RBI. A 1991 move to high Class-A didn't bother him at all. A poll in *Baseball America* named him the Most Exciting Player in the California League, and he won MVP and Rookie of the Year awards—plus a berth on the All-Star Team. He was the loop's Player of the Month for July, the third time he has taken such an honor. He had a .530 slugging percentage and a .431 on-base average. It should be noted that Mieske played in Maverick Stadium, a definite hitter's park. His speed and the fact that he doesn't strike out much (82 Ks in 1991) suggest Mieske could succeed anywhere, however. It won't take him long to reach the NL, and he is a $4 fantasy draft. His current cards are great buys at a dime.

Professional Batting Register

	BA	G	AB	R	H	2B	3B	HR	RBI	SB
88 R	.274	59	215	36	59	8	4	0	20	16
89 A	.309	108	401	62	124	12	5	3	36	29
90 AA	.334	108	416	71	139	12	4	3	37	38
91 AAA	.334	102	374	68	125	14	5	2	36	23
91 AL	.204	19	54	10	11	2	0	0	2	0

Professional Batting Register

	BA	G	AB	R	H	2B	3B	HR	RBI	SB
90 A	.340	76	291	59	99	20	0	12	63	25
91 A	.341	133	492	108	168	36	6	15	119	39

ROOKIE PROSPECTS

SAM MILITELLO

Position: Pitcher
Team: New York Yankees
Born: Nov. 26, 1969 Tampa, FL
Height: 6'3" **Weight:** 200 lbs.
Bats: right **Throws:** right
Acquired: Sixth-round pick in 6/90 free-agent draft

Player Summary	
Fantasy Value	$1 to $3
Card Value	5¢ to 10¢
Will	win 10 games
Can't	match '91 numbers
Expect	strikeout an inning
Don't Expect	Yankees in '92

Right now, Militello can say he went to the same high school as Fred McGriff and Tony LaRussa. Maybe one day, they'll say they attended the same high school as Militello. He has become one of the best—and perhaps the best—pitching prospect in an organization that used to trade youngsters for established stars. Militello has an average or slightly better fastball but a very good slider he considers his out pitch. He says he tries to get ahead of the hitters, hit spots, and then set up his slider. The combination was too much for the Class-A Carolina League in 1991. Militello was 10-1 with an 0.88 ERA after just 13 starts. Batters hit just .180 off him. He received a call-up to Double-A Albany-Colonie during the second half of the season. That placed him not far from New York City, literally and figuratively. In 1990, he was named Star of Stars in the Class-A New York-Penn League. He is worth a $2 fantasy pick. His current cards are good buys at a nickel each.

KURT MILLER

Position: Pitcher
Team: Texas Rangers
Born: Aug. 24, 1972 Tucson, AZ
Height: 6'5" **Weight:** 200 lbs.
Bats: right **Throws:** right
Acquired: Traded from Pirates with Hector Fajardo for Steve Buechele, 8/91

Player Summary	
Fantasy Value	$1 to $2
Card Value	5¢ to 10¢
Will	improve percentage
Can't	always find plate
Expect	some rough innings
Don't Expect	rush job

Miller came to the Texas chain in August as part of a deal that sent third baseman Steve Buechele to the Pirates. Miller had somewhat of a disappointing season in 1991, but he is a former first-round draft pick, and is still very young, and so the Rangers can assume they have picked up some interesting tools until Miller proves otherwise. As a member of Class-A Welland in the New York-Penn League in 1990, Miller pitched respectably, mostly as a starter. In 1991, he worked for Class-A Augusta of the South Atlantic League and posted a won-lost mark that didn't measure up to the high quality of his ERA. However, his control was not textbook, accounting for some of the bad luck. Opponents compiled a .208 average against him, and he allowed six home runs. He needs work on his fielding. Miller should have a better shot in Texas than in Pittsburgh, and '92 is a big year. Don't gamble on his fantasy future at this point. Wait until he has a good year in Double-A before purchasing his current cards.

Professional Pitching Register

	W	L	ERA	G	CG	IP	H	ER	BB	SO
90 A	8	2	1.22	13	3	88.2	53	12	24	119
91 AA	2	2	2.35	7	0	46.0	40	12	19	55
91 A	12	2	1.22	16	1	103.1	65	14	27	113

Professional Pitching Register

	W	L	ERA	G	CG	IP	H	ER	BB	SO
90 A	3	2	3.29	14	0	65.2	59	24	37	61
91 A	6	7	2.50	21	2	115.1	89	32	57	103

ROOKIE PROSPECTS

MARK MIMBS

Position: Pitcher
Team: Los Angeles Dodgers
Born: Feb. 13, 1969 Macon, GA
Height: 6'2" **Weight:** 180 lbs.
Bats: left **Throws:** left
Acquired: 25th-round pick in 6/90 free-agent draft

Player Summary	
Fantasy Value	$2 to $4
Card Value	15¢ to 20¢
Will	throw strikes
Can't	go the distance
Expect	jump to Double-A
Don't Expect	reunion with brother

It would be extraordinary if the Dodgers one day had a pair of low-round draft picks in their rotation. Still more unusual would be if those pitchers were identical twins. Mark and his brother Mike are trying to become the third set to reach the majors, and only the second to play on the same team. Mark, drafted one round after his brother, caught the eye of Class-A California League managers, who judged him to have the best control in the circuit. He also had an outstanding strikeout-to-inning ratio, and opponents batted .216 against him. He spent 1991 on the West Coast while his brother was in Florida. Mark finished with the fifth-best ERA in Bakersfield history. He was second among Dodger farmhands in strikeouts, and he has shown he can throw the ball over the plate. In 1990 at Great Falls in the rookie Pioneer League, he allowed a .234 average. Mimbs is said to be the first to volunteer when the team needs someone for a personal appearance. He is a $3 draft, and his current cards are hot items at 15 cents each.

MICHAEL MIMBS

Position: Pitcher
Team: Los Angeles Dodgers
Born: Feb. 13, 1969 Macon, GA
Height: 6'2" **Weight:** 180 lbs.
Bats: left **Throws:** left
Acquired: 24th-round pick in 6/90 free-agent draft

Player Summary	
Fantasy Value	$2 to $4
Card Value	15¢ to 20¢
Will	post low ERA
Can't	throw heat
Expect	20 wins
Don't Expect	LA in '92

Michael is the other half of the brother act trying to reach the majors. Like the three Martinez brothers, the Mimbs boys will inevitably be viewed as somewhat of a novelty, and there may be an element of distraction to that. But the stats are there to support hopes for a trip to the majors. Like his brother Mark, Michael is out of Mercer University in Georgia, and is stingy with base hits. Among his victories was a three-hitter against Fort Lauderdale, his first complete-game shutout in the pros. Michael was the winning pitcher in the Florida State League All-Star Game in 1991, giving up one earned run in two innings. He was also one of two lefties named to the postseason squad. Michael finished tied for fourth in the Dodgers minor league system in strikeouts, and was fifth in ERA. Batters compiled a .241 average against Mimbs in 1991. There are some who think that the fastball of both brothers is a little short. He is a $3 draft, and his current cards are hot items at 15 cents each.

Professional Pitching Register

	W	L	ERA	G	CG	IP	H	ER	BB	SO
90 R	7	4	3.23	14	0	78.0	69	28	29	94
91 A	12	6	2.22	27	0	170.0	134	42	59	164

Professional Pitching Register

	W	L	ERA	G	CG	IP	H	ER	BB	SO
90 R	0	0	4.05	3	0	6.2	4	3	5	7
90 A	4	3	3.88	12	0	67.1	58	29	39	72
91 A	12	4	2.67	24	1	141.2	124	42	70	132

ROOKIE PROSPECTS

KEVIN MMAHAT

Position: Pitcher
Team: New York Yankees
Born: Nov. 9, 1964 Memphis, TN
Height: 6'5" **Weight:** 220 lbs.
Bats: left **Throws:** left
Acquired: Purchased from Texas, 6/88

Player Summary
Fantasy Value	$1 to $3
Card Value	5¢ to 10¢
Will	rebound
Can't	produce same velocity
Expect	another year in Triple-A
Don't Expect	another no-hitter

There was a time not long ago when a torn rotator cuff meant a death sentence to any pitcher's career. Fortunately for Mmahat, times have changed. Not only did the big lefty rebound from surgery, he did so with a flourish, hurling Triple-A Columbus to a no-hit victory over Louisville (for some belated fireworks) on July 5, 1991. Mmahat had turned in a respectable year with the Clippers in 1990, even though he seldom went past the sixth inning. He also played winter ball before his injury was diagnosed and he underwent surgery in November. Mmahat played with Wally Whitehurst and Gene Harris at Tulane, and he opposed Will Clark in high school. Mmahat was the Rangers' 31st-round pick in the June 1987 draft. His nickname is "Hat" given by a football coach who could not pronounce his name. Find out if he has come back from his injury before bidding more than $3 for him. His dime-priced 1992 cards are overpriced.

Professional Pitching Register
	W	L	ERA	G	CG	IP	H	ER	BB	SO
87 R	3	3	3.21	12	1	53.1	37	19	30	60
88 A	7	7	4.13	17	3	102.1	95	47	57	78
88 AA	2	3	3.99	6	0	38.1	30	17	24	32
89 AA	5	1	1.58	8	1	51.1	35	9	19	48
89 AAA	3	4	3.84	15	1	82.0	70	35	49	50
89 AL	0	2	12.91	4	0	7.2	13	11	8	3
90 AAA	11	5	3.76	20	1	115.0	99	48	61	81
91 AAA	3	3	3.58	12	2	65.1	54	26	34	59

MIKE MOHLER

Position: Pitcher
Team: Oakland Athletics
Born: July 26, 1968 Dayton, OH
Height: 6'2" **Weight:** 195 lbs.
Bats: right **Throws:** left
Acquired: 42nd-round pick in 6/88 free-agent draft

Player Summary
Fantasy Value	$1 to $3
Card Value	3¢ to 5¢
Will	be around plate
Can't	overpower hitters
Expect	low ERA
Don't Expect	100 K

Mohler is an accounting major who may prove that the 42nd draft pick was a profitable investment for the A's. A reliever turned into a starter, he came out of nowhere in 1991 to become one of Oakland's top pitching prospects. An off-speed type of pitcher who has enough fastball to keep the hitters honest, he knows how to pitch. He has an average fastball with good movement. He also has a very good curve and change. Mohler didn't immediately begin play upon his signing out of Nicholls State University, and his first pro assignment came in the Class-A Midwest League, where he relieved in all but two of his 42 appearances. He attended the Instructional League after the season and did well. He wound up as one of the top winners in the system in 1991 at Class-A Modesto of the California League. He was then promoted to Double-A Huntsville, where his ERA rose. He is a $2 fantasy reserve at this point. His current cards are in the commons bins.

Professional Pitching Register
	W	L	ERA	G	CG	IP	H	ER	BB	SO
90 A	1	1	3.41	42	0	63.1	56	24	32	72
91 A	9	4	2.86	21	1	122.2	106	39	45	98
91 AA	4	2	3.57	8	0	53.0	55	21	20	27

ROOKIE PROSPECTS

RAUL MONDESI

Position: Outfield
Team: Los Angeles Dodgers
Born: March 12, 1971 San Cristobal, Dominican Republic
Height: 5'11" **Weight:** 150 lbs.
Bats: right **Throws:** right
Acquired: Signed as a free agent, 6/88

Player Summary	
Fantasy Value	$1 to $2
Card Value	5¢ to 10¢
Will	cover ground
Can't	lay off bad balls
Expect	speed on bases
Don't Expect	bases on balls

Mondesi really knows how to celebrate an occasion. Upon being promoted from the Class-A California League to the Double-A Texas League in 1991, Mondesi homered in his first two games. That's all the better because his talent may earn him another couple of moves up the ladder. Mondesi is a speed player with surprising pop for his slim frame. Just 21 entering the 1992 season, when Mondesi gains more experience, he may emerge as an all-around offensive weapon. He also was voted the top outfield arm in the California League and there's very few balls he can't reach. In fact, it's said he covered so much ground he was taking balls from the left and right fielders. Mondesi is a free swinger who must learn the strike zone. He has the speed to beat out plenty of infield hits. He had a .307 on-base average and a .437 slugging percentage at Double-A in 1991. You might see him in the bigs some time in 1992. Don't invest in him for your fantasy reserves yet. His nickel-priced current cards are fair investments.

Professional Batting Register

	BA	G	AB	R	H	2B	3B	HR	RBI	SB
90 R	.303	44	175	35	53	10	4	8	31	30
91 A	.283	28	106	23	30	7	2	3	13	9
91 AA	.272	53	213	32	58	10	5	5	26	7
91 AAA	.333	2	9	3	3	0	1	0	0	1

MIKE MONGIELLO

Position: Pitcher
Team: Chicago White Sox
Born: Jan. 19, 1968 Hoboken, NJ
Height: 6'2" **Weight:** 215 lbs.
Bats: right **Throws:** right
Acquired: Seventh-round pick in 6/89 free-agent draft

Player Summary	
Fantasy Value	$1 to $2
Card Value	3¢ to 5¢
Will	cut down walks
Can't	keep men off base
Expect	25 saves
Don't Expect	return to starting

Mongiello's outstanding 1991 campaign certainly merits him a closer look, even though his stuff is not quite in the high-octane class of major league stoppers. Not only was he in the top five in saves in the Florida State League, but his ERA would be even lower than it was except for just two or three bad outings. Opponents compiled just a .202 batting average against him in 1991. Mongiello throws mostly three-quarters, but also goes to sidearm, especially to righthanded hitters. His fastball is not devastating but, together with the curve, it gets the job done. Mongiello needs to develop more consistency on the all-important first batter, and must sharpen his control. He attended the Instructional League after the season. Mongiello has apparently settled into the bullpen after being both a starter and reliever his first two pro seasons. His 13 saves in 1990 made him first for Class-A South Bend of the Midwest League. He is a good fantasy reserve at $1. Don't purchase his nickel-priced current cards, though.

Professional Pitching Register

	W	L	ERA	G	S	IP	H	ER	BB	SO
89 R	1	3	3.58	8	2	32.2	28	13	13	28
90 A	6	6	3.30	38	13	106.1	98	39	54	89
91 A	4	4	2.25	55	23	68.0	51	17	34	62

ROOKIE PROSPECTS

BOO MOORE

Position: Outfield
Team: Boston Red Sox
Born: Jan. 23, 1970 Augusta, GA
Height: 6'4" **Weight:** 200 lbs.
Bats: right **Throws:** right
Acquired: 10th-round pick in 6/88 free-agent draft

Player Summary	
Fantasy Value	$1 to $3
Card Value	3¢ to 5¢
Will	drive the ball
Can't	make contact
Expect	15 homers
Don't Expect	high average

Moore is a big man who may one day fit a familiar Red Sox role as a righthanded slugger who can take aim on the Green Monster in Fenway Park. First, however, he must take aim on the ball. In a move to the Class-A Carolina League in 1991, Moore raised his power numbers but also struck out more than once a game. Right now the Red Sox are trying to give him as many at bats as they can, because he doesn't have much baseball experience. He had only 200 at bats in his first two seasons, and didn't even play much in high school. Moore isn't speedy in the outfield, and if he played there in the majors it would be in left. The Red Sox are toying with the idea of moving him to first. His future really depends on how quickly he can learn his way around the strike zone. Moore compiled a .404 slugging percentage and a .306 on-base average in 1991. He is a $2 fantasy reserve. His current cards, at a nickel each, are not investments.

Professional Batting Register

	BA	G	AB	R	H	2B	3B	HR	RBI	SB
88 R	.276	28	87	12	24	2	2	0	5	6
89 R	.267	28	86	10	23	4	1	2	13	2
89 A	.074	12	27	0	2	0	0	0	0	1
90 A	.255	123	431	46	110	19	7	4	33	17
91 A	.249	132	502	63	125	30	3	14	69	7

KERWIN MOORE

Position: Outfield
Team: Kansas City Royals
Born: Oct. 29, 1970 Detroit, MI
Height: 6'1" **Weight:** 190 lbs.
Bats: both **Throws:** right
Acquired: 16th-round pick in 6/88 free-agent draft

Player Summary	
Fantasy Value	$1 to $3
Card Value	3¢ to 5¢
Will	raise average
Can't	steal first
Expect	stolen bases
Don't Expect	RBI

Moore has had his problems at the plate for all four pro seasons, but the Royals remain high on him because so many of his other tools are at the major league standard. Mentioned as a Vince Coleman type of player, Moore is considered a "seven" runner, the top rank given on a scouting system. He is viewed as a potential 80-steal man in the majors, someone who can bunt his way on and steal around to third. His play in the outfield is also of high quality. That means if Moore can add some hits to the high amount of walks he receives, he could be an ideal leadoff man. The Royals have made him a switch-hitter, trying to get him a step closer to first base. Moore's bunting is not yet polished, but it has improved. He had a .322 on-base average and a .254 slugging percentage in 1991. He had 77 walks. He needs to hit more to have his fantasy value reach higher than two bucks. Don't buy his nickel-priced current cards until he hits.

Professional Batting Register

	BA	G	AB	R	H	2B	3B	HR	RBI	SB
88 R	.176	53	165	19	29	5	0	0	14	20
89 A	.228	69	237	47	54	9	2	3	27	20
90 A	.222	128	451	93	100	17	7	2	36	57
91 A	.210	130	485	67	102	14	2	1	23	61

ROOKIE PROSPECTS

KEVIN MORTON

Position: Pitcher
Team: Boston Red Sox
Born: Aug. 3, 1968 Norwalk, CT
Height: 6'2" **Weight:** 185 lbs.
Bats: right **Throws:** left
Acquired: First-round pick in 6/89 free-agent draft

Player Summary	
Fantasy Value	$3 to $7
Card Value	10¢ to 20¢
Will	cut down walks
Can't	keep men off base
Expect	return to starting
Don't Expect	bullpen duty

If Morton's pitches move as quickly as he did through the Red Sox system, he should be successful indeed. He had already played at five levels, including three in 1989, when injuries to the big club helped bring him to the majors. With Matt Young and Mike Gardiner out, Morton started against Detroit and retired the first eight batters. He wound up with a 7-1 win, and earned 15 starts over the course of the season. Sometimes a quick route to the bigs can keep young pitchers from learning enough on the way. Morton attended Seton Hall and went 27-5. In 1989 he was named the Big East Pitcher of the Year. He spent all of 1990 with Double-A New Britain of the Eastern League, a change after all his moving the previous season. Morton's victories included a seven-inning perfecto. He may have found a place in the Boston rotation, making him a $5 fantasy hurler. His 1992 cards are good buys at a dime apiece.

Professional Pitching Register

	W	L	ERA	G	CG	IP	H	ER	BB	SO
89 R	1	0	0.00	2	0	6.0	2	0	1	11
89 A	5	6	2.23	11	6	89.0	53	22	23	100
90 AA	8	14	3.81	26	7	163.0	151	69	48	131
91 AAA	7	3	3.49	16	1	98.0	91	38	30	80
91 AL	6	5	4.59	16	1	86.1	93	44	40	45

JOSE MUNOZ

Position: Infield
Team: Los Angeles Dodgers
Born: Nov. 11, 1967 Chicago, IL
Height: 5'11" **Weight:** 165 lbs.
Bats: both **Throws:** right
Acquired: 20th-round pick in 6/87 free-agent draft

Player Summary	
Fantasy Value	$1 to $3
Card Value	5¢ to 10¢
Will	get uniform dirty
Can't	hit long ball
Expect	high average
Don't Expect	regular playing time

Munoz is an interesting prospect in that he may turn out to be a supersub instead of superstar. Stalled in the lower minors for four years, he blossomed in 1991 and climbed through Double-A into the Triple-A Pacific Coast League. For an insight into Munoz's style of play, take a look at his home run numbers against his RBI figures; they reflect a knack for clutch hitting. He is called a gamer with great baseball sense. In 1991 at San Antonio, he helped create a run by running hard to first on a dropped third strike. He can play third, second, and right. His ability to switch hit and to steal a base add even more to the package. At Triple-A Albuquerque in '91, he had a .358 on-base average and a .393 slugging percentage. He has been likened to veteran Jose Oquendo as a player for whom you've got to find a slot. Munoz's power deficit caps his fantasy value at $3. Don't purchase his 1992 cards until he makes the big club out of spring training.

Professional Batting Register

	BA	G	AB	R	H	2B	3B	HR	RBI	SB
87 R	.321	54	187	31	60	7	0	0	22	6
88 A	.248	105	347	35	86	6	0	0	24	7
89 A	.257	105	300	39	77	15	1	0	24	6
90 A	.284	127	436	60	124	19	3	2	53	30
91 AA	.317	31	123	25	39	6	2	0	13	4
91 AAA	.326	101	389	49	127	18	4	0	65	15

ROOKIE PROSPECTS

OSCAR MUNOZ

Position: Pitcher
Team: Cleveland Indians
Born: Sept. 25, 1969 Hialeah, FL
Height: 6'2" **Weight:** 205 lbs.
Bats: right **Throws:** right
Acquired: Fifth-round pick in 6/90 free-agent draft

Player Summary
Fantasy Value	$1 to $2
Card Value	3¢ to 5¢
Will	improve ERA
Can't	stay ahead in count
Expect	tryout in Cleveland
Don't Expect	good K-to-walk ratio

Munoz has come a long way in just two pro seasons, and seems to have overcome the only thing that really challenged him in 1991. After dominating with Kinston in the Carolina League, Munoz ran into trouble upon being promoted to Double-A. He was pitching behind in the count and lost a little command. He slipped badly enough that you should not draft him or purchase his current cards, even at a nickel. He eventually ironed out some of the flaws, however, and put together a string of impressive outings that kept him on track for arrival in the majors sometime in 1993. Munoz is a four-pitch pitcher who can throw a fastball into the high 80s. He has two kinds of breaking ball, an overhand curve that breaks top to bottom, and a traditional side-to-side slider. He uses a split-finger fastball as his change of speed pitch and his out pitch. Despite the jump and the necessary adjustments, Munoz was a top strikeout whiz. He also no-hit Prince William 1-0 in May.

Professional Pitching Register
	W	L	ERA	G	CG	IP	H	ER	BB	SO
90 A	8	1	2.29	11	2	74.2	51	19	21	64
91 A	6	3	1.44	14	2	93.2	60	15	36	111
91 AA	3	8	5.72	15	2	85.0	88	54	51	71

JEFF MUTIS

Position: Pitcher
Team: Cleveland Indians
Born: Dec. 20, 1966 Allentown, PA
Height: 6'2" **Weight:** 185 lbs.
Bats: left **Throws:** left
Acquired: First-round pick in 6/88 free-agent draft

Player Summary
Fantasy Value	$2 to $4
Card Value	15¢ to 20¢
Will	keep batters off balance
Can't	rely on fastball
Expect	big league job
Don't Expect	instant success

The Indians had three of the top 27 picks in the 1988 draft, and they turned the third one into one of their top pitching prospects. Mutis was named the best of all the Eastern League's pitching hopefuls by *Baseball America* early in 1991. The publication also tabbed him as having the best control in that league. Mutis justified the praise, not only briefly reaching the big leagues but also assembling a solid year at Double-A. Mutis throws an average-to-plus fastball, and overhand curve, and a circle change. He is also working on a cut fastball. In his second straight year in Double-A, Mutis led Canton-Akron in ERA. He fired a two-hit shutout against New Britain on Aug. 25, dropping his ERA to 1.90. He is a prospect, but must increase his physical strength. Grab his 1992 cards quickly at a dime, because he looks like a starter for the Tribe. He is a good $3 fantasy candidate.

Professional Pitching Register
	W	L	ERA	G	CG	IP	H	ER	BB	SO
88 R	3	0	0.41	3	0	22.0	8	1	6	20
88 A	1	0	1.59	1	0	5.2	6	1	3	2
89 A	7	3	2.62	16	5	99.2	87	29	20	68
90 AA	11	10	3.16	26	7	165.0	178	58	44	94
91 AA	11	5	1.80	25	7	169.2	138	34	51	89
91 AL	0	3	11.68	3	0	12.1	23	16	7	6

ROOKIE PROSPECTS

DENNY NEAGLE

Position: Pitcher
Team: Minnesota Twins
Born: Sept. 13, 1968 Prince Georges County, MD
Height: 6'4" **Weight:** 200 lbs.
Bats: left **Throws:** left
Acquired: Third-round pick in 6/89 free-agent draft

Player Summary	
Fantasy Value	$4 to $8
Card Value	15¢ to 20¢
Will	stick with Twins
Can't	dominate hitters
Expect	10 wins
Don't Expect	15 wins

Neagle is another reason why the Twins can savor their 1991 success all the more. They did it mostly without the help of one of their top prospects. Neagle managed to get his feet wet in Minnesota's runaway regular season, and that experience can only help him as he bids for a major league job in 1992. He is a young lefthander who can throw the ball over the plate all day long. Furthermore, he has enjoyed a high winning percentage over the last two years. In 1990, while pitching both in Class-A and Double-A, Neagle became the first minor leaguer since 1986 to reach 20 wins in a season. He was named Minnesota minor league player of the year. In 1991, *Baseball America* named him the best pitching prospect in the Triple-A Pacific Coast League. He was a starting pitcher in the Triple-A All-Star Game. His is a good $6 fantasy grab. His 1992 cards are hot buys at a dime.

Professional Pitching Register

	W	L	ERA	G	CG	IP	H	ER	BB	SO
89 R	1	2	4.50	6	0	22.0	20	11	8	32
89 A	2	1	1.65	6	1	43.2	25	8	16	40
90 AA	12	3	2.45	17	4	121.1	94	33	31	94
90 A	8	0	1.43	10	0	63.0	39	10	16	92
91 AAA	9	4	3.27	19	1	104.2	101	38	32	94
91 AL	0	1	4.05	7	0	20.0	28	9	7	14

TOM NEVERS

Position: Infield
Team: Houston Astros
Born: Sept. 13, 1971 Edina, MN
Height: 6'1" **Weight:** 175 lbs.
Bats: right **Throws:** right
Acquired: First-round pick in 6/90 free-agent draft

Player Summary	
Fantasy Value	$1 to $3
Card Value	5¢ to 7¢
Will	raise average
Can't	make contact
Expect	position switch
Don't Expect	rapid progress

Nevers comes from hockey country and plays that sport well enough to have been a fifth-round pick of the NHL Pittsburgh Penguins. But the Astros may have seen a little more in him, making him the 21st overall selection. He is a power-hitting infielder who has a great deal to learn about baseball, but his manager at Class-A Asheville, Frank Cacciatore, predicts Nevers will make the majors. He broke into the pros in 1990 and was named the 10th-best prospect in the rookie Gulf Coast League. He was tabbed best defensive shortstop in the Class-A South Atlantic League by *Baseball America*, even though he made plenty of errors. Nevers may end up at third. Cacciatore worked with Nevers on infield play. Nevers ranked among the home run and RBI leaders in the Houston chain in 1991, and had the strikeout totals to prove it. He is a tempting $2 fantasy futures pick, especially if he can stay in the middle infield. His current cards are iffy buys at a nickel each.

Professional Batting Register

	BA	G	AB	R	H	2B	3B	HR	RBI	SB
90 R	.238	50	185	23	44	10	5	2	32	13
91 A	.252	129	441	59	111	26	2	16	71	10

ROOKIE PROSPECTS

MARC NEWFIELD

Position: Outfield
Team: Seattle Mariners
Born: Oct. 19, 1972 Sacramento, CA
Height: 6'4" **Weight:** 205 lbs.
Bats: right **Throws:** right
Acquired: First-round pick in 6/90 free-agent draft

Player Summary	
Fantasy Value	$2 to $4
Card Value	5¢ to 10¢
Will	improve muscles
Can't	throw out runners
Expect	Double-A
Don't Expect	Seattle until '93

The Mariners may have themselves a big-time prospect in Newfield, who did everything you could expect in his first full season of pro ball. Newfield made the Class-A California League All-Star team as an outfielder. *Baseball America* named him the second-best prospect, and the top position player, in the loop. Despite his extreme youth, he hit for average and power, and showed some speed. It was the second straight season in which Newfield won laurels. He was the All-Star first baseman and MVP of the Arizona complex league in 1990, and was tabbed as the No. 2 prospect in that circuit. The sixth overall pick in the 1990 grab bag, Newfield hit a 500-foot homer in his first pro game. He was also a Player of the Month. Everything suggests he should be ready for Double-A, at least, in the 1992 season. His cards appeared in several national 1991 sets. His current cards are great buys at a nickel each. Pay up to $4 to get him in your fantasy organization.

Professional Batting Register

	BA	G	AB	R	H	2B	3B	HR	RBI	SB
90 R	.324	49	185	34	60	13	2	6	38	4
91 A	.300	125	440	64	132	22	3	11	68	12
91 AA	.231	6	26	4	6	3	0	0	2	0

DAVE NILSSON

Position: Catcher
Team: Milwaukee Brewers
Born: Dec. 14, 1969 Queensland, Australia
Height: 6'3" **Weight:** 185 lbs.
Bats: both **Throws:** right
Acquired: Signed as a free agent, 1/87

Player Summary	
Fantasy Value	$2 to $5
Card Value	7¢ to 12¢
Will	post high average
Can't	catch in majors yet
Expect	line-drive power
Don't Expect	flawless throwing

Nilsson comes from a long way, being one of the few natives of Australia to play pro ball in America. *Baseball America* placed him on its Player of the Year list, and named him the top hitting prospect in the Double-A Texas League. However, 1992 looks like a crucial year for Nilsson. He will be coming off an operation to fix a nagging problem in his left shoulder. He needs a healthy spring before his fantasy value will be more than $5. His 1992 cards will stay at 12 cents until his health returns. Nilsson's defensive game also needs some work, even though he was named second-best defensive catcher in the California League in 1990. His arm is average to above-average, but he hasn't really taken command behind the plate. After a promotion to Triple-A, Nilsson underwent surgery and returned home. Not a pure power hitter, he can hit for average, and uses the whole field. He had a .473 on-base average and a .598 slugging percentage at Double-A in 1991.

Professional Batting Register

	BA	G	AB	R	H	2B	3B	HR	RBI	SB
87 R	.394	55	188	36	74	13	0	1	21	0
88 A	.223	95	332	28	74	15	2	4	41	2
89 A	.244	125	472	59	115	16	6	5	56	2
90 A	.290	107	359	70	104	22	3	7	47	6
91 AA	.418	65	249	52	104	24	3	5	57	4
91 AAA	.232	28	95	10	22	8	0	1	14	1

ROOKIE PROSPECTS

REY NORIEGA

Position: Infield
Team: New York Yankees
Born: March 15, 1968 Miami Beach, FL
Height: 6'1" **Weight:** 175 lbs.
Bats: both **Throws:** right
Acquired: 60th-round pick in 6/89 free-agent draft

Player Summary	
Fantasy Value	$1 to $2
Card Value	5¢ to 10¢
Will	hit 15 homers
Can't	win Gold Glove
Expect	position switch
Don't Expect	quick jump

Noriega began to hit with some power with Class-A Ft. Lauderdale of the Florida State League in 1991, a development that made his overall package all the more attractive. Even without the power, Noriega is a switch-hitter who can steal a base and who has played three infield positions. He has a quick bat, and is a line-drive hitter who sends the ball to all fields. A cleanup hitter, Noriega set a career high in RBI in '91 and was among the top home run hitters on the farm. He spent two years in the same league, and was named to the All-Star team the second time around. His batting average declined toward the end of the year, as will happen to batters who strike out a lot. He had 134 strikeouts in 1991, but he notched a .424 slugging percentage and a .366 on-base average. As a defensive player, Noriega is adequate at third, and it's possible a better position for him might be second. He is just too far away to put on your reserves list. His nickel-priced current cards are also too risky.

Professional Batting Register

	BA	G	AB	R	H	2B	3B	HR	RBI	SB
89 R	.296	39	125	29	37	4	6	0	16	7
90 A	.226	84	305	52	69	17	3	3	28	7
91 A	.249	126	429	67	107	19	7	14	68	12

TOM NUNEVILLER

Position: Outfield
Team: Philadelphia Phillies
Born: May 15, 1969 Sellersville, PA
Height: 6'3" **Weight:** 210 lbs.
Bats: right **Throws:** right
Acquired: Fifth-round pick in 6/90 free-agent draft

Player Summary	
Fantasy Value	$1 to $2
Card Value	4¢ to 6¢
Will	hit .280
Can't	jump to Triple-A
Expect	30 doubles
Don't Expect	10 homers

This Pennsylvania product may one day fit in well in Veterans Stadium, a park that is very kind to batters with some pop. Nuneviller is a left and right fielder who can run and throw. The Phils say he can hit the ball in the gaps and will hit for average. With Class-A Clearwater in the Florida State League, he showed some pop in 1991, leading his team in doubles by a wide margin. He also demonstrated an ability to take a walk and can steal a base. Nuneviller's home run total was nothing to get excited about, but people don't hit very many homers in that league. He had a .388 slugging percentage and a .360 on-base average in '91. Some of that power potential was on display with Class-A Batavia in 1990, when he hit nine homers in 259 at bats. Nuneviller went to Pennridge High School in Perkasie, Pennsylvania, not far from Philadelphia, and attended West Chester University, so he will have a lot of friends to watch him if he makes it. His fantasy value peaks at $2, and his current cards top out at a nickel each.

Professional Batting Register

	BA	G	AB	R	H	2B	3B	HR	RBI	SB
90 A	.232	71	259	36	60	10	0	9	31	15
91 A	.283	124	446	77	126	31	5	2	54	16

ROOKIE PROSPECTS

JOHN O'DONOGHUE

Position: Pitcher
Team: Baltimore Orioles
Born: May 26, 1969 Wilmington, DE
Height: 6'6" **Weight:** 198 lbs.
Bats: left **Throws:** left
Acquired: Signed as a free agent, 6/90

Player Summary	
Fantasy Value	$1 to $3
Card Value	5¢ to 10¢
Will	up win percentage
Can't	overpower hitters
Expect	jump to Double-A
Don't Expect	an ace

If O'Donoghue reaches the big leagues with the Orioles, it would mark two generations of his family to have done so. His father appeared for Baltimore in 1968 as part of a career that stretched from 1963 to '71. John has a superstition of pitching with his father's baseball card in his back pocket. He doesn't throw as hard as you'd expect from someone with his size, his fastball being average or just a tad below. He also throws a sinker and a slider, and is working on a changeup. O'Donoghue moves the ball around on the mound and has good command of his pitches. A righthander with similar stuff would probably not be a prospect, but there are lefties who get the job done with this type of repertoire. A member of the Class-A Frederick rotation in 1991, O'Donoghue more than doubled his innings from the previous year. Opponents compiled a .255 batting average in '91. He was a college mate of Ben McDonald. O'Donoghue's current cards are mediocre buys at a nickel apiece, and he is an uninspiring $2 fantasy reserve.

Professional Pitching Register

	W	L	ERA	G	CG	IP	H	ER	BB	SO
90 A	0	1	4.50	1	0	4.0	5	2	0	3
90 R	4	2	2.01	10	2	49.1	49	11	10	67
91 A	7	8	2.90	22	2	133.2	131	43	50	128

JOSE OLIVA

Position: Infield
Team: Texas Rangers
Born: March 3, 1971 San Pedro de Macoris, Dominican Republic
Height: 6'1" **Weight:** 150 lbs.
Bats: right **Throws:** right
Acquired: Signed as a free agent, 11/87

Player Summary	
Fantasy Value	$2 to $3
Card Value	10¢ to 15¢
Will	add muscle
Can't	hit .300
Expect	15 homers
Don't Expect	Tony Oliva

Oliva has not produced the kind of batting average that baseball fans associate with his famous name. Jose is still young and even if he doesn't knock out anyone's eyes with high batting average, he may be developing as a power hitter. Over the past two seasons, he has moved into double figures in home runs. With Class-A Charlotte of the Florida State League in 1991, he ranked among the leaders in that category in the Texas farm system. Oliva had 11 homers by July 14; the club record was 12 set by Gar Millay in 1987. Oliva has a nice looking swing and a quick bat, and his physique should allow for the addition of muscle. In what might seem like heresy for someone coming from the shortstop capital of the world, San Pedro de Macoris, Oliva moved from shortstop to third base. That move will take advantage of his strong arm. He's a little quicker there, too. He is a $2 fantasy hopeful. His current cards are good gambles at a dime each.

Professional Batting Register

	BA	G	AB	R	H	2B	3B	HR	RBI	SB
88 R	.214	27	70	5	15	3	0	1	11	0
89 R	.211	41	114	18	24	2	3	4	13	4
90 A	.209	119	383	44	80	24	1	10	52	9
91 R	.091	3	11	0	1	1	0	0	1	0
91 A	.240	108	384	55	92	17	4	14	59	9

ROOKIE PROSPECTS

MIKE OQUIST

Position: Pitcher
Team: Baltimore Orioles
Born: May 30, 1968 La Junta, CO
Height: 6'2" **Weight:** 170 lbs.
Bats: right **Throws:** right
Acquired: 13th-round pick in 6/89 free-agent draft

Player Summary	
Fantasy Value	$2 to $5
Card Value	10¢ to 15¢
Will	take the ball
Can't	pitch in AL yet
Expect	some craftsmanship
Don't Expect	big heat

Oquist has come along more quickly than some thought. In 1991, he pitched for Baltimore's Double-A team in Hagerstown of the Carolina League, leading the team in starts. He is a dependable pitcher who has topped 150 innings two straight years. He throws an average fastball, somewhere in the 85 mph range, plus a slider and a change. He has command of his pitches and mixes them. Oquist doesn't get rattled during games and he has an idea of how to pitch. His strikeout ratio declined a bit in 1991, but that isn't surprising considering he moved up a notch. He still has struck out at least 100 in all three pro seasons. Oquist attended the University of Arkansas, pitching in the College World Series in 1986 and '89. He finished second in the Class-A New York-Penn League in Ks in 1989 and was named to the midseason Class-A Carolina League All-Star Team in '90. He is a good bet for your fantasy team at a $5 or less bid. His 1992 cards are satisfactory buys at a dime each.

Professional Pitching Register

	W	L	ERA	G	CG	IP	H	ER	BB	SO
89 A	7	4	3.59	15	1	97.2	86	39	25	109
90 A	9	8	2.81	25	3	166.1	134	52	48	170
91 AA	10	9	4.06	27	1	166.1	168	75	62	136

DONOVAN OSBORNE

Position: Pitcher
Team: St. Louis Cardinals
Born: June 21, 1969 Roseville, CA
Height: 6'2" **Weight:** 195 lbs.
Bats: both **Throws:** left
Acquired: First-round pick in 6/90 free-agent draft

Player Summary	
Fantasy Value	$2 to $4
Card Value	10¢ to 15¢
Will	post many Ks
Can't	race up ladder
Expect	better '92
Don't Expect	spring in St. Louis

Osborne's numbers didn't exactly light up the sky in 1991. But part of that stems from a decision the Cardinals made to throw him into tough Double-A competition. Coming off just 10 starts in the low minors, he was assigned to the Texas League, just two steps away from the majors. He lost most of his early decisions, but, just as you'd hope a first-round pick would, Osborne responded and made the necessary adjustments. He finished second in strikeouts among St. Louis farmhands, was throwing strikes, and had a respectable ERA. Originally drafted by the Expos in 1987, Osborne did not sign. He attended UNLV, where he broke the school strikeout record as a freshman. In his first pro year, Osborne won game two of the Class-A Sally League playoffs. Now that he's been tested against a tough level, Osborne must concentrate on turning strikeouts and ERA into victories. Bid a couple of bucks on him, and you might see him in your rotation soon. His current cards are buys at a dime.

Professional Pitching Register

	W	L	ERA	G	CG	IP	H	ER	BB	SO
90 A	2	2	2.93	10	1	61.1	61	20	12	42
91 AA	8	12	3.63	26	3	166.0	177	67	43	130

ROOKIE PROSPECTS

MATEO OZUNA

Position: Infield
Team: St. Louis Cardinals
Born: Jan. 1, 1971 LaRomana, Dominican Republic
Height: 5'11" **Weight:** 165 lbs.
Bats: right **Throws:** right
Acquired: Signed as a free agent, 12/88

Player Summary	
Fantasy Value	$1 to $2
Card Value	5¢ to 7¢
Will	draw a walk
Can't	win defensive award
Expect	50 steals
Don't Expect	10 homers

This New Year's Day baby is the kind of player who can turn a base on balls into a party. Ozuna, named the best baserunner in the Class-A Midwest League, has stolen at least 65 bases two straight years. His speed fits right into the kind of game that the Cards play, so if they can smooth out the rest of his game, they will have something special. Right now, though, Ozuna isn't in the St. Louis mold of fine defensive players. A second baseman, he has trouble with the routine play, isn't the best at reading balls, and must improve his range. Ozuna has occasional power, though no one expects him to dent the walls at Busch Stadium. Ozuna should work on hitting the gaps or keeping it on the ground. He strikes out just once in every 10 official trips, and he must stay close to that ratio to keep advancing. He had 46 bases on balls in '91, pushing his on-base average to .325. He is not quite a fantasy draft yet, and his nickel-priced current cards should be shelved for now.

LANCE PAINTER

Position: Pitcher
Team: San Diego Padres
Born: July 21, 1967 Bedford, England
Height: 6'1" **Weight:** 195 lbs.
Bats: left **Throws:** left
Acquired: 25th-round pick in 6/90 free-agent draft

Player Summary	
Fantasy Value	$2 to $4
Card Value	5¢ to 10¢
Will	throw strikes
Can't	jump to Triple-A
Expect	command
Don't Expect	wild streaks

Painter has registered two winning seasons in the low minors, and he has shown the ability to advance quickly to higher classifications. He is a three-pitch man, throwing a fastball, curveball and change-up. What sets him apart from many on his level is the ability to throw any of them for a strike anywhere in the count. Painter owns above-average command and control. At one point in 1991, he went 6-2 with a 1.32 ERA over nine starts for Class-A Waterloo of the Midwest League. He led all Padres farmhands in strikeouts, and was among the leaders in wins and ERA as well. Averaging roughly one strikeout per inning, Painter allowed so few hits and walks that his ratio of baserunners to innings was outstanding. Opponents compiled a .256 average against him in '91. The same pattern held true in his first pro season, when Painter fanned six times as many as he walked. His current cards are fair purchases up to a dime each. If he is another Andy Benes, you had better get your wallet out now and bid up to $4.

Professional Batting Register

	BA	G	AB	R	H	2B	3B	HR	RBI	SB
89 A	.208	114	365	46	76	9	2	0	25	24
90 A	.236	121	449	65	106	8	2	2	29	65
91 A	.252	115	437	68	110	11	4	3	35	78

Professional Pitching Register

	W	L	ERA	G	CG	IP	H	ER	BB	SO
90 A	7	3	1.51	23	0	71.2	45	12	16	104
91 A	14	8	2.30	28	7	200.0	162	51	57	201

ROOKIE PROSPECTS

ELVIN PAULINO

Position: First base
Team: Chicago Cubs
Born: Nov. 6, 1967 Moca, Dominican Republic
Height: 6'1" **Weight:** 190 lbs.
Bats: left **Throws:** left
Acquired: Signed as a free agent, 4/86

Player Summary	
Fantasy Value	$2 to $4
Card Value	10¢ to 15¢
Will	hit 25 homers
Can't	move Mark Grace
Expect	50 extra-base hits
Don't Expect	300 average

Paulino continued his development in 1991, showing power, production, and an ability to hit for a decent average. Trouble for him is that the Cubs already have a pretty good hitting first baseman at the major league level in Mark Grace. Paulino had hit 14 homers his previous year, and might have hit more if not for a broken leg. He has hit the breaking ball, and shown some power to the opposite field. Paulino is described as having a quick bat—he says he uses a 37-ouncer—and as being a decent first baseman. Among the outstanding power hitters in the minors, Paulino helped Double-A Charlotte enjoy a fine year at the gate. He led the Southern League with 24 homers and 81 RBI. Paulino played first base for the National League farmhands in the Double-A All-Star Game and went 1-for-3. His power makes him a $4 fantasy future bid. His dime-priced current cards are wise ventures.

Professional Batting Register

	BA	G	AB	R	H	2B	3B	HR	RBI	SB
87 A	.205	49	117	22	24	2	0	1	13	1
87 R	.314	55	185	42	58	11	2	8	40	4
88 A	.233	122	404	44	94	19	5	2	40	3
89 A	.295	119	414	57	122	29	2	8	72	5
90 A	.262	109	409	69	107	23	2	14	63	5
91 AA	.257	132	460	67	118	27	1	24	81	9

TIM PEEK

Position: Pitcher
Team: Oakland Athletics
Born: Jan. 23, 1968 Elkhart, IN
Height: 6'2" **Weight:** 195 lbs.
Bats: right **Throws:** right
Acquired: Signed as a free agent, 4/90

Player Summary	
Fantasy Value	$1 to $3
Card Value	5¢ to 10¢
Will	get key outs
Can't	return to rotation
Expect	Phils to regret release
Don't Expect	A's closer job

Good teams keep coming up with good players, and the A's have found a discarded player who may become a big part of their bullpen. Originally drafted by the Phils in 1986, Peek kicked around in their farm system for three years without inspiring any awe. The Phils tried him both in starting and relief, then released him after he picked up four wins and three saves deep in their chain in 1989. Signed by the A's in April of 1990, Peek proceeded to make himself a prospect again. He went to Class-A Madison of the Midwest League, where he threw strikes and got people out. He made the Double-A All-Star Game in 1991. Opponents compiled a .256 batting average against him in '91. Peek throws an average fastball, but his out pitch is a split-fingered fastball. With Dennis Eckersley as Oakland's closer, Peek could not expect to take that job. Headed toward middle relief in Oakland, he is a $2 fantasy hurler. His 1992 cards are inferior buys at a dime each.

Professional Pitching Register

	W	L	ERA	G	S	IP	H	ER	BB	SO
87 A	3	4	2.65	14	0	81.2	70	24	23	52
88 A	6	3	1.87	37	9	105.2	77	22	30	80
89 A	4	1	3.11	27	3	63.2	55	22	26	55
90 A	5	3	2.70	39	7	56.2	41	17	10	70
91 AA	2	4	3.26	56	26	66.1	65	24	15	52

ROOKIE PROSPECTS

DAN PELTIER

Position: Outfield
Team: Texas Rangers
Born: June 30, 1968 Clifton Park, NY
Height: 6'1" **Weight:** 200 lbs.
Bats: left **Throws:** left
Acquired: Third-round pick in 6/89 free-agent draft

Player Summary	
Fantasy Value	$2 to $4
Card Value	5¢ to 10¢
Will	hike numbers
Can't	crack Texas outfield
Expect	live bat
Don't Expect	lots of power

A second-team academic All-America from Notre Dame in 1989, Peltier is smart money to win a big league job before too long. He was slowed in 1991 with a strained wrist, which helps account for some of his disappointing stats at Triple-A Oklahoma City. He is, however, a line-drive hitter with quick hands who makes the ball jump off his bat. Peltier was a sensation in his first year of pro ball, making the rookie Pioneer League All-Star team despite playing just 33 games. He was leading the league in batting when sidelined for the rest of the season with a fractured collarbone. He set a Butte team record by hitting safely in 22 straight games, and was just four games short of Gary Sheffield's league mark. Peltier batted .391 in his last 28 games of the 1990 season at Double-A Tulsa, then missed the last eight games to return to Notre Dame for the fall semester. Wait to see if he's healthy before sinking your $3 into him. His current cards are also holds.

Professional Batting Register

	BA	G	AB	R	H	2B	3B	HR	RBI	SB
89 R	.402	33	122	35	49	7	1	7	28	10
90 AA	.279	117	448	66	125	19	4	11	57	8
91 AAA	.229	94	345	38	79	16	4	3	31	6

WILLIAM PENNYFEATHER

Position: Outfield
Team: Pittsburgh Pirates
Born: May 25, 1968 Perth Amboy, NJ
Height: 6'2" **Weight:** 195 lbs.
Bats: right **Throws:** right
Acquired: Signed as a free agent, 7/88

Player Summary	
Fantasy Value	$1 to $3
Card Value	5¢ to 10¢
Will	swing at bad balls
Can't	hit for power
Expect	more steals
Don't Expect	disciplined hitting

Pennyfeather may bring a big payoff as a diamond in the rough, but the emphasis still is on rough. A great athlete, he played football at Syracuse University and didn't have much of a baseball background. Pennyfeather has played both center and right, and may have the tools to do both on a big league level. Pennyfeather was having some trouble at the plate in 1991, pulling his head out, but this is something most hitters battle from time to time. A line-drive, gap hitter, Pennyfeather hasn't shown much power. He may get stronger, but he will never be in the mold of the Pittsburgh bashers of the past. The Pirates sent him to the Instructional League after the 1991 season to work on his baserunning, on taking leads, and on his bunting. It also wouldn't hurt him to take some pitches and walk a bit more. In 1991, he had a .310 on-base average at Double-A Carolina, and a .285 on-base average at Class-A Salem. If he puts it all together, your $2 fantasy gamble will look great. His nickel-priced current cards are somewhat risky, though.

Professional Batting Register

	BA	G	AB	R	H	2B	3B	HR	RBI	SB
88 R	.282	33	131	17	37	4	1	2	12	10
89 A	.190	75	289	34	55	10	1	3	26	18
90 A	.262	122	465	69	122	14	4	4	48	21
91 A	.266	81	319	35	85	17	3	8	46	11
91 AA	.275	42	149	13	41	5	0	0	9	3

ROOKIE PROSPECTS

VINCE PHILLIPS

Position: Outfield
Team: New York Yankees
Born: April 9, 1969 Pasadena, CA
Height: 6'1" **Weight:** 190 lbs.
Bats: left **Throws:** left
Acquired: 13th-round pick in 6/87 free-agent draft

Player Summary
Fantasy Value	$2 to $4
Card Value	10¢ to 15¢
Will	double homers total
Can't	dominate with arm
Expect	line drives
Don't Expect	flawless baserunning

Phillips showed the ability to turn on the ball in 1991, making him a valuable part of the Yankee future because of their cozy dimensions in right field. He has also improved his hitting to left; he used to hit lazy fly balls there, but now is producing line drives. With a little more power, he would be a great $4 fantasy draft. Phillips has also upgraded his performance against lefthanded pitching and may now be kept in the middle of the lineup against them. Phillips drove in 85 runs for Double-A Albany-Colonie in 1991, tying Jeromy Burnitz of Williamsport for the Eastern League lead. Phillips's arm has not proven as strong as expected, especially since he was recruited as a quarterback at Southern Cal, but he has improved in the field. Phillips is susceptible to lapses on the base paths. He does have pretty good speed, though. He has a chance to play in Triple-A or higher in 1992. His current cards are good buys at a dime apiece.

Professional Batting Register
	BA	G	AB	R	H	2B	3B	HR	RBI	SB
88 A	.267	106	356	44	95	11	1	1	42	9
89 A	.265	132	437	63	116	19	2	6	60	22
90 AA	.241	117	402	49	97	20	5	2	46	6
91 AA	.274	130	482	71	132	26	1	8	85	12

MIKE PIAZZA

Position: Catcher
Team: Los Angeles Dodgers
Born: Sept. 4, 1968 Norristown, PA
Height: 6'3" **Weight:** 200 lbs.
Bats: right **Throws:** right
Acquired: 62nd-round pick in 6/88 free-agent draft

Player Summary
Fantasy Value	$2 to $4
Card Value	10¢ to 15¢
Will	hit 25 homers
Can't	run very well
Expect	logjam behind plate
Don't Expect	fast progress

If Piazza is an example of what happens when an infielder is converted to a catcher, then the line will form behind home plate. However, his position change is no magic formula, just some good instincts on the part of the Dodgers. Signed as a first baseman out of Miami-Dade College, Piazza attended a tryout at Dodger Stadium. He not only hit the ball, but impressed the brass with his throws from home to second. Since then, he has learned more about catching and has developed into one of the top power prospects in the game. He led Class-A Bakersfield in home runs in 1991 and trailed only Jay Gainer for the California League lead. Piazza also delivered good extra-base power and didn't strike out as often as you might expect from a slugger. His RBI totals were a little short for someone who hits that many homers. Behind the plate, Piazza still needs work on his throwing mechanics. He is a $3 fantasy backstop. His current cards are popular, 10-cent items.

Professional Batting Register
	BA	G	AB	R	H	2B	3B	HR	RBI	SB
89 A	.268	57	198	22	53	11	0	8	25	0
90 A	.250	88	272	27	68	20	0	6	45	0
91 A	.277	117	448	71	124	27	2	29	80	0

ROOKIE PROSPECTS

GREG PIRKL

Position: Catcher; first base
Team: Seattle Mariners
Born: Aug. 7, 1970 Long Beach, CA
Height: 6'5" **Weight:** 225 lbs.
Bats: right **Throws:** right
Acquired: Second-round pick in 6/88 free-agent draft

Player Summary	
Fantasy Value	$2 to $4
Card Value	5¢ to 10¢
Will	concentrate on catching
Can't	match Johnny Bench
Expect	strong bat
Don't Expect	fast adjustments

Right now Pirkl is an offensive player who is trying to develop as a catcher. He has power, can hit for average and drive the ball well. He needs to play and find a position, whether it be behind the plate or at first. He owns an average major league arm, and seems to like catching. Sometimes he loses concentration, but he is an aggressive player who is learning the job. It's offense that will get Pirkl to the majors if he reaches there. He ranked with the leaders in the Seattle chain in both homers and RBI in 1991 in what was really his first full year of pro ball. He notched a .552 slugging percentage at Class-A San Bernardino, and a .401 slugging average at Class-A Peninsula in '91. Pirkl began 1990 at Class-A San Bernardino, but a strained knee limited him to 56 games. Whether he excels at catching or not, his acquaintance with the position may help him reach the bigs. He isn't ready yet, but he is a $3 future backstop. Don't invest in his current cards until he has a great season at Double-A.

Professional Batting Register

	BA	G	AB	R	H	2B	3B	HR	RBI	SB
88 A	.240	65	246	22	59	6	0	6	35	1
89 A	.257	70	265	31	68	6	0	8	36	4
90 A	.295	58	207	37	61	10	0	5	28	3
91 A	.264	127	478	52	138	29	1	20	94	4

PAUL QUANTRILL

Position: Pitcher
Team: Boston Red Sox
Born: Nov. 3, 1968 London, Ontario, Canada
Height: 6'1" **Weight:** 165 lbs.
Bats: left **Throws:** right
Acquired: Sixth-round pick in 6/89 free-agent draft

Player Summary	
Fantasy Value	$2 to $4
Card Value	10¢ to 15¢
Will	lower ERA
Can't	get key strikeout
Expect	return to pen
Don't Expect	100 Ks

The Red Sox have found a righthander from the north who throws a fastball that goes south. Quantrill's bread-and-butter pitch is a hard, heavy sinker in the high 80s. This sinker has helped him rise quickly through the Red Sox system, and come within a phone call of a major league job. He started his pro career as a reliever and saved his first two appearances. He eventually became a starter but has not had exceptional success in that role. It's possible Quantrill's future may be in the bullpen, because he has very good control, loves to throw, and can bounce back quickly. He does not show the high strikeout totals normally associated with a short reliever, and there were plans to work on that part of his game. Sink a few bucks in him at the draft; he may get some Ws for you this year. His 1992 cards will be steady gainers at a dime each.

Professional Pitching Register

	W	L	ERA	G	CG	IP	H	ER	BB	SO
89 R	0	0	0.00	2	0	5.0	2	0	0	5
89 A	5	4	3.43	20	5	76.0	90	29	12	57
90 A	2	5	4.14	7	1	45.2	46	21	6	14
90 AA	7	11	3.53	22	1	132.2	149	52	23	53
91 AA	2	1	2.06	5	1	35.0	32	8	8	18
91 AAA	10	7	4.45	25	6	155.2	169	77	30	75

ROOKIE PROSPECTS

RAFAEL QUIRICO

Position: Pitcher
Team: New York Yankees
Born: Sept. 7, 1969 Santo Domingo, Dominican Republic
Height: 6'2" **Weight:** 185 lbs.
Bats: left **Throws:** left
Acquired: Signed as a free agent, 5/87

Player Summary
Fantasy Value	$1 to $3
Card Value	5¢ to 10¢
Will	take the ball
Can't	relax
Expect	strikeouts
Don't Expect	control

Quirico has a world of talent, and in 1991 he posted the best ratio of strikeouts to innings of his entire career. He ranked among the top Yankee farmhands in wins, strikeouts, and ERA. However, he needs to cut down on his bases on balls, and he must also harness some of his enthusiasm on the mound. Quirico tends to get hyped up, and sometimes an error behind him will rattle him a bit. A starter with a good curveball and fastball, he is also developing a changeup. He fired a 2-0 no-hitter against Charleston while pitching for Class-A Greensboro of the South Atlantic League. His development quickened in 1991, and he attributed that to pitching coach Mark Shiflett. Quirico was voted the best lefthander in the Sally League by coaches and managers. Quirico will have a good shot at the Carolina League in 1992 and it's possible he could even skip up to Double-A. He is a decent fantasy bet at $2. His current cards are long-term buys at a nickel each.

Professional Pitching Register
	W	L	ERA	G	CG	IP	H	ER	BB	SO
89 R	2	2	3.82	17	0	63.2	61	27	20	55
90 A	8	9	3.21	27	2	159.0	143	71	69	121
91 A	12	8	2.26	26	1	155.1	103	39	80	162

MANNY RAMIREZ

Position: Outfield
Team: Cleveland Indians
Born: May 30, 1972 Santiago, Dominican Republic
Height: 6' **Weight:** 195 lbs.
Bats: right **Throws:** right
Acquired: First-round pick in 6/91 free-agent draft

Player Summary
Fantasy Value	$1 to $2
Card Value	5¢ to 10¢
Will	hit 25 homers
Can't	throw with best
Expect	high average
Don't Expect	bigs before '94

An immigrant to the United States at the age of 13, Ramirez settled in the Washington Heights section of New York and then in the Bronx. He was one of the top high school hitters in the draft class of 1991. He hit over .600 in his last two years at George Washington High in the Bronx, the same school that produced Hall of Famer Rod Carew. The Indians made him what they hope will be the lucky 13th pick of the draft, and signed him for $250,000. His prowess extended into the pro ranks, where Ramirez had three homers with seven RBI in his first 58 pro at bats and contended for the rookie Appalachian League Triple Crown all season. There are elements of Gary Sheffield in Ramirez's batting style. Ramirez has good speed in center, but his arm is only average. Although he dominated at the rookie-league level in 1991, he is too young to take a fantasy risk for more than $2. His dime-priced current cards have high risk, but they also could have high reward.

Professional Batting Register
	BA	G	AB	R	H	2B	3B	HR	RBI	SB
91 R	.326	59	215	44	70	11	4	19	63	7

ROOKIE PROSPECTS

DARYL RATLIFF

Position: Outfield
Team: Pittsburgh Pirates
Born: Oct. 15, 1969 Santa Cruz, CA
Height: 6'1" **Weight:** 180 lbs.
Bats: right **Throws:** right
Acquired: Fifth-round pick in 6/89 free-agent draft

Player Summary	
Fantasy Value	$1 to $3
Card Value	5¢ to 10¢
Will	steal 45 bases
Can't	find the gaps
Expect	open at Double-A
Don't Expect	five homers

Ratliff was slowed a bit by a thumb injury in 1991, which is a bit of a surprise in itself—there aren't many things that can slow down one of the top speedsters in the organization. He has increased his stolen base total as he moves up the ladder, and played well enough to receive a midseason promotion from the Class-A Carolina League to the Double-A Southern League. He notched a .342 on-base average and a .355 slugging percentage at Class-A Salem. Ratliff's speed will serve him well in the outfield, and his arm is considered at least major league average. Though he has not shown much power in his pro career—not even extra-base power—that aspect of his game may yet emerge. He's learned to hit the ball the other way, and is concentrating on making contact, two skills that help avoid prolonged slumps. He can learn how to turn on a ball later. Ratliff had hit .362 over one 14-game stretch. He is a $2 fantasy choice. Don't stock up on his current cards yet.

JOHN RAY

Position: Pitcher
Team: Cincinnati Reds
Born: Oct. 28, 1967 Collierville, TN
Height: 6'3" **Weight:** 215 lbs.
Bats: right **Throws:** right
Acquired: Signed as a free agent, 6/89

Player Summary	
Fantasy Value	$1 to $2
Card Value	5¢ to 10¢
Will	pile up innings
Can't	throw heat
Expect	lots of decisions
Don't Expect	Triple-A

If numbers were all that were involved in stamping somewhat a prospect, Ray would be among the top futures in baseball. He has been a pro for three years and has been an impressive winner all three times. However, Ray has spent his career in low Class-A ball. He throws a change, a decent slider, and a fastball. He's one of those pitchers who must have good control, and he does. Ray pitched at Class-A Charleston, West Virginia, of the South Atlantic League in 1991, and his 16th victory enabled him to break the team record set one year earlier. His 30 wins over two years made him Charleston's all-time leader. Ray is a competitor who likes to have a piece of the game; he owns a high percentage of decisions per start throughout his career. Opponents compiled a .250 batting average against him in 1991. He gave up eight homers. If you spend a buck on him in the draft, it will be a few years before you see returns. His current nickel-priced cards are not buys.

Professional Batting Register

	BA	G	AB	R	H	2B	3B	HR	RBI	SB
89 R	.245	66	208	28	51	2	0	0	21	10
90 A	.295	122	417	70	123	11	6	1	55	24
91 A	.293	88	352	60	103	8	4	2	23	35
91 AA	.215	24	93	10	20	3	0	0	9	7

Professional Pitching Register

	W	L	ERA	G	CG	IP	H	ER	BB	SO
89 R	6	2	2.72	11	0	56.1	55	17	13	28
90 A	14	7	2.93	30	3	153.2	147	50	48	81
91 A	16	9	3.36	28	3	171.1	161	64	57	120

ROOKIE PROSPECTS

CALVIN REESE

Position: Infield
Team: Cincinnati Reds
Born: Nov. 21, 1971 Moore County, NC
Height: 5'11" **Weight:** 160 lbs.
Bats: right **Throws:** right
Acquired: First-round pick in 6/91 free-agent draft

Player Summary	
Fantasy Value	$1 to $2
Card Value	5¢ to 10¢
Will	cover ground
Can't	put zip on throws
Expect	improved average
Don't Expect	bigs before '95

Comparisons can be a curse; people are doing Reese no favors when they mention his name in the same breath with Ozzie Smith's. Especially since Reese's game needs so much polish. The 20th pick in the draft, he has great range and quickness, but his biggest gift is said to be for anticipation. Reese gets a good jump on the ball and doesn't get caught out of position. His arm is rated only above-average, so a move to second base may be in his future. Like most other players, Reese struggled a bit at the plate, but contributed some speed and even a touch of extra-base pop. His numbers are the type you'll take from an outstanding defensive shortstop. He had a .338 slugging percentage and a .305 on-base average in '91. Being a top athlete, Reese may get even better. He accepted a grid scholarship to Arizona but failed to produce the test scores necessary for frosh eligibility. His struggles at bat show that he is not a fantasy draft in the foreseeable future. His current cards are not good investments at a nickel each.

Professional Batting Register

	BA	G	AB	R	H	2B	3B	HR	RBI	SB
91 R	.238	62	231	30	55	8	3	3	27	10

ARTHUR LEE RHODES

Position: Pitcher
Team: Baltimore Orioles
Born: Oct. 24, 1969 Waco, TX
Height: 6'2" **Weight:** 190 lbs.
Bats: left **Throws:** left
Acquired: Second-round pick in 6/88 free-agent draft

Player Summary	
Fantasy Value	$3 to $5
Card Value	15¢ to 20¢
Will	bring heat
Can't	finesse hitters
Expect	a K a frame
Don't Expect	return to minors

It has been said there are too many finesse lefties and not enough hard throwers, but Rhodes certainly provides the heat scouts love to see. His fastball has been clocked at 93 mph, and it shouldn't be long before he joins Ben McDonald on the Orioles' staff. Rhodes's delivery has reminded some of a young Vida Blue, though he doesn't throw as hard as Blue did. However, Rhodes's heater does move, which is just as important. He has also developed a curveball to complement the heat, but must improve command. The combination helped him become a top strikeout pitcher in the minors. Despite missing three weeks with shoulder stiffness, Rhodes won seven straight starts at Double-A Hagerstown after losing the season opener. Rhodes has been brought along slowly, so he may click quickly in the majors. His fantasy value is going to explode soon, so bid up to $5 for him now. Stock up on his 1992 cards at 15 cents apiece or less.

Professional Pitching Register

	W	L	ERA	G	CG	IP	H	ER	BB	SO
88 R	3	4	3.31	11	0	35.1	29	13	15	44
89 A	2	2	2.93	12	1	55.1	32	18	29	73
90 A	4	6	2.12	13	4	80.2	62	19	21	103
90 AA	3	4	3.73	12	0	72.1	62	30	39	60
91 AA	7	4	2.70	19	2	106.2	73	32	47	115
91 AL	0	3	8.00	8	0	36.0	47	32	23	23

ROOKIE PROSPECTS

JOE ROA

Position: Pitcher
Team: New York Mets
Born: Oct. 11, 1971 Southfield, MI
Height: 6'2" **Weight:** 180 lbs.
Bats: right **Throws:** right
Acquired: Traded from Braves with Tony Castillo for Alejandro Pena, 8/91

Player Summary	
Fantasy Value	$1 to $2
Card Value	5¢ to 10¢
Will	keep hits low
Can't	jump to Triple-A
Expect	strikeouts
Don't Expect	relief work

Roa was the player to be named later in a deal that sent Alejandro Pena to the Braves for Tony Castillo. Fitting the bill of being a young prospect that the Mets wanted included, Roa looks as if he could be a major part of rebuilding what once was a vaunted Mets pitching staff. He enjoyed a great deal of success at Class-A Macon of the South Atlantic League in 1991. He is described as being as good a competitor as there was in the Atlanta organization and is a fighter who will keep a ballclub in a game. Roa throws a lively fastball, has good control, and an outstanding ratio of hits to innings. In 1991, he ranked with the best in the Atlanta farm system in victories, ERA, and strikeouts. Opponents batted only .206 against him, and he allowed only six home runs in 141 innings pitched. Roa has worked both in the rotation and from the bullpen, but look for him to start. He is too far away from the Mets to put on your fantasy reserves now. His current cards are not buys yet, either.

Professional Pitching Register

	W	L	ERA	G	CG	IP	H	ER	BB	SO
89 R	2	2	2.89	13	0	37.1	40	12	10	21
90 R	4	2	2.97	14	3	75.2	55	25	26	49
91 A	13	3	2.11	30	4	141.0	106	33	33	96

FRANKIE RODRIGUEZ

Position: Shortstop
Team: Boston Red Sox
Born: Dec. 11, 1972 Brooklyn, NY
Height: 6' **Weight:** 175 lbs.
Bats: right **Throws:** right
Acquired: Second-round pick in 6/90 free-agent draft

Player Summary	
Fantasy Value	$1 to $3
Card Value	5¢ to 10¢
Will	gun ball
Can't	carry team
Expect	more extra-base hits
Don't Expect	20 homers

Quick, name a shortstop with a 98 mph fastball. Well, maybe Shawon Dunston. OK, name another one. Rodriguez is a pitcher turned shortstop. He was among the best two-way prospects in the draft, but held out and spent a season in junior college before signing just hours before the 1991 grab bag. Using that fastball, Rodriguez struck out 17 in the final of the Junior College World Series leading Howard (Texas) to the title. In his talks with the Red Sox, though, Rodriguez insisted he be allowed to begin his pro career as a shortstop. Naturally, that arm can come in handy on plays from the hole, but there is more to the position than that. There has been some question about Rodriguez's maturity, one reason the Red Sox let him go to junior college. He has shown some ability at the plate (he hit .450 at Howard), however, and can drive in a run. He is a $2 fantasy flyer, since he has two positions to find success. His current cards are interesting investments at 5 cents each.

Professional Batting Register

	BA	G	AB	R	H	2B	3B	HR	RBI	SB
91 R	.500	3	14	3	7	0	1	0	3	0
91 A	.271	67	255	36	69	5	3	6	31	3

ROOKIE PROSPECTS

JOHN ROPER

Position: Pitcher
Team: Cincinnati Reds
Born: Nov. 21, 1971 Moore County, NC
Height: 6' **Weight:** 170 lbs.
Bats: right **Throws:** right
Acquired: 12th-round pick in 6/90 free-agent draft

Player Summary	
Fantasy Value	$1 to $2
Card Value	5¢ to 10¢
Will	go nine
Can't	rely on knuckle-curve
Expect	ERA below 3.50
Don't Expect	many hits

The mention of Roper will increasingly recall memories of Burt Hooton, who made himself a nice major league career by throwing a knuckle-curve. Roper is an effective practitioner of this pitch, and it helped him become the ace of the Class-A Charleston, West Virginia, staff in only his second pro season. He throws a fastball that is average to plus, and is also working on a changeup. If he comes up with a good one, he could be even tougher than he was in 1991, when South Atlantic League batters found him baffling. Opponents compiled a .200 batting average against him. He contended for the organization's pitching triple crown, ranking among the top in ERA, wins, and strikeouts. He can also pile up the innings, and was a leader in that department, too. Roper's quick rise in the pros is more impressive because he did not enroll in college, signing right out of high school. He won seven of his first nine professional decisions. Don't draft him until Double-A, and hold off on getting his current cards.

Professional Pitching Register

	W	L	ERA	G	CG	IP	H	ER	BB	SO
90 R	7	2	0.97	13	0	74.0	41	8	31	76
91 A	14	9	2.31	27	5	186.2	133	48	67	189

RICH ROWLAND

Position: Catcher
Team: Detroit Tigers
Born: Feb. 25, 1967 Cloverdale, CA
Height: 6'1" **Weight:** 210 lbs.
Bats: right **Throws:** right
Acquired: 17th-round pick in 6/88 free-agent draft

Player Summary	
Fantasy Value	$3 to $6
Card Value	10¢ to 20¢
Will	call good game
Can't	match Mickey Tettleton
Expect	12 homers
Don't Expect	three triples

A catcher with good defensive skills, a strong arm, and some power can usually count on a job in the majors, which is why you should be hearing Rowland's name more often in the future. He is described as having excellent catching skills, with a strong arm. Rowland is also said to call a good game, and his power—while not on the level of Mickey Tettleton's—will do some damage in Tiger Stadium. He ranked among the top Detroit farmhands in both homers and RBI in 1991, and knows how to draw a walk. With the exception of his 1989 campaign with Class-A Fayetteville of the South Atlantic League, Rowland has not struck out much, either. His first major league start in 1990 resulted in a combined six-hit shutout by Scott Aldred and Ed Nunez. Rowland will enjoy a more extended stay in 1992. He is a solid $4 fantasy choice. His dime-priced 1992 cards are good purchases.

Professional Batting Register

	BA	G	AB	R	H	2B	3B	HR	RBI	SB
88 R	.274	56	186	29	51	10	1	4	41	1
89 A	.272	108	375	43	102	17	1	9	59	4
90 AA	.286	47	161	22	46	10	0	8	30	1
90 AAA	.260	62	192	28	50	12	0	7	22	2
90 AL	.158	7	19	3	3	1	0	0	0	0
91 AAA	.272	109	383	56	104	25	0	13	68	4
91 AL	.250	4	4	0	1	0	0	0	1	0

ROOKIE PROSPECTS

STAN ROYER

Position: Third base
Team: St. Louis Cardinals
Born: Aug. 31, 1967 Olney, IL
Height: 6'3" **Weight:** 195 lbs.
Bats: right **Throws:** right
Acquired: Traded from Athletics with Felix Jose and Daryl Green for Willie McGee, 8/90

Player Summary	
Fantasy Value	$2 to $4
Card Value	15¢ to 20¢
Will	drive in runs
Can't	budge Zeile
Expect	shot at first
Don't Expect	regular role

An experiment that proved so successful for Todd Zeile and the Cardinals has doubled the challenge for Royer. Zeile, who came to the majors as a catcher, has settled in nicely at third. Unfortunately for Royer, that's the one position where he might have made an impact. Acquired from Oakland in 1990 in the trade that sent Willie McGee to the A's, Royer played his first full year of Triple-A in 1991, and topped Louisville in many offensive categories. He led all St. Louis farmhands in RBI and was among the tops in homers. It was the second straight year Royer has led a minor league chain in RBI, having paced the Oakland system in 1990. Royer doesn't have the speed that the Cardinals value so much. His offense suggests a niche at one of the infield corners, and now he must make something open up. Choose his 1992 cards at 15 cents apiece for investment. He is a $3 fantasy draft.

Professional Batting Register

	BA	G	AB	R	H	2B	3B	HR	RBI	SB
88 A	.318	73	286	47	91	19	3	6	48	1
89 A	.252	127	476	54	120	28	1	11	69	3
89 AAA	.263	6	19	2	5	1	0	0	2	0
90 AA	.258	137	527	69	136	29	3	14	89	4
90 AAA	.267	4	15	1	4	1	0	0	4	0
91 AAA	.254	138	523	48	133	29	6	14	74	1
91 NL	.286	9	21	1	6	1	0	0	1	0

JOHNNY RUFFIN

Position: Pitcher
Team: Chicago White Sox
Born: July 29, 1971 Butler, AL
Height: 6'3" **Weight:** 172 lbs.
Bats: right **Throws:** right
Acquired: Fourth-round pick in 6/88 free-agent draft

Player Summary	
Fantasy Value	$1 to $3
Card Value	5¢ to 10¢
Will	finish games
Can't	be consistent
Expect	more strikeouts
Don't Expect	ERA below 3.00

Ruffin has the kind of numbers that excite the imagination, and we're not talking just about stats, either. He was once clocked at 97 miles an hour, though in 1991 the figure was closer to 92 mph. He so far has failed to completely harness this gift, but he gave a hint of what he can do. He hurled a no-hitter for Class-A Sarasota of the Florida State League, allowing a run as the result of a walk. Ruffin was toting an ERA of about 7.00 in May, then went 10 starts permitting three or fewer earned runs. In nine of those starts, he gave up no more than one earned run. Opponents compiled a .217 batting average, and he allowed nine home runs. Now a top pitching prospect for the White Sox, Ruffin advanced slowly until '91. He may be headed for Double-A or higher. Besides the fastball, he also throws a breaking ball that needs work, and is developing a change. He needs some time to develop, so pass on his current cards and a fantasy draft.

Professional Pitching Register

	W	L	ERA	G	CG	IP	H	ER	BB	SO
88 R	4	2	2.30	13	1	58.2	43	15	22	31
89 A	4	8	3.36	15	0	88.1	67	33	46	92
90 A	7	6	4.17	24	0	123.0	117	57	82	92
91 A	11	4	3.23	26	6	158.2	126	57	62	117

ROOKIE PROSPECTS

PAUL RUSSO

Position: Third base
Team: Minnesota Twins
Born: Aug. 26, 1969 Tampa, FL
Height: 6′ **Weight:** 215 lbs.
Bats: left **Throws:** left
Acquired: 19th-round pick in 6/90 free-agent draft

Player Summary	
Fantasy Value	$2 to $4
Card Value	10¢ to 15¢
Will	cut down Ks
Can't	win Gold Glove
Expect	20 homers
Don't Expect	great range

Part of good drafting involves "slotting," that is, envisioning a player in a certain round and hoping he is still there. That's what the Twins did with Russo, and they may have emerged with a bona fide power prospect. He led the Class-A Midwest League in both home runs and RBI. He had a .475 slugging percentage and a .369 on-base average. He apparently was available in a lower round because he lacked a position. Russo came out of the University of Tampa as a third baseman-catcher, but the Twins used him exclusively at third in '91. He will never be a Brooks Robinson, but time and experience have made Russo more at ease, and his arm is adequate. He doesn't have great quickness, but if he reaches a ball he makes the play. Besides, if a player keeps bringing home two-thirds of the Triple Crown, you find a place for him. Russo went to the Instructional League to work on defense and on cutting down strikeouts. His power makes him a $3 fantasy draft. His current cards are winners at a dime apiece.

Professional Batting Register

	BA	G	AB	R	H	2B	3B	HR	RBI	SB
90 R	.335	62	221	58	74	9	3	22	67	4
91 A	.271	125	421	60	114	20	3	20	100	4

ROGER SALKELD

Position: Pitcher
Team: Seattle Mariners
Born: March 6, 1971 Burbank, CA
Height: 6′5″ **Weight:** 215 lbs.
Bats: right **Throws:** right
Acquired: First-round pick in 6/90 free-agent draft

Player Summary	
Fantasy Value	$8 to $15
Card Value	15¢ to 25¢
Will	dominate in majors
Can't	miss
Expect	more seasoning
Don't Expect	full year in minors

The Mariners made Salkeld the third overall pick in the '90 draft, and they hope it's the last time he'll be third in anything. They are projecting him to the big leagues as early as 1992, and see him as a No. 1 or 2 starter within three or four years. Salkeld spent much of the 1991 season in Double-A but finished with Triple-A Calgary of the Pacific Coast League. He is a power pitcher with a plus-plus fastball, meaning in the mid-90s. He has command of a slider and change. Salkeld is an aggressive and confident pitcher who shows no fear on the mound. He was the No. 6 prospect in the Double-A Southern League in '91. Hitters managed just a .234 average off him. In 1990, Salkeld was a Class-A California League All-Star. Batters hit .240 against him that year. Figure him to start at Triple-A in '92, though he'll have a shot at the big club. He will make some fantasy manager happy for a $10 draft. Entrust some money into his 1992 cards.

Professional Pitching Register

	W	L	ERA	G	CG	IP	H	ER	BB	SO
89 A	2	2	1.29	8	0	42.0	27	6	10	55
90 A	11	5	3.40	25	2	153.1	140	58	83	167
91 AA	8	8	3.05	23	5	153.2	131	52	55	159
91 AAA	2	1	5.12	4	0	19.1	18	11	13	21

ROOKIE PROSPECTS

TIM SALMON

Position: Outfield
Team: California Angels
Born: Aug. 24, 1968 Long Beach, CA
Height: 6'3" **Weight:** 200 lbs.
Bats: left **Throws:** left
Acquired: Third-round pick in 6/89 free-agent draft

Player Summary	
Fantasy Value	$3 to $6
Card Value	15¢ to 20¢
Will	fatten average
Can't	work pitcher
Expect	40 extra-base hits
Don't Expect	100 RBI

Salmon's spectacular numbers in 1991 must be perceived with some caution. For one thing, the Double-A Texas League is a hitter's league. Even more importantly, Salmon struck out a great deal, more than once every three at bats. Yet there is much to commend Salmon. He is making a comeback from being hit in the face with pitched balls not once but twice. Second, his problem with strikeouts may be addressed by having him take fewer pitches. Salmon gets himself in a hole and instructors are working with him on being more aggressive. He also has some trouble with the breaking ball, but few prospects don't. As an outfielder, Salmon owned one of the best arms in the loop, and had assists both at third and home. He covers ground in right, and runs well for a big man. Salmon's past injuries have cut into playing time, so he needs more at bats. His homers look good to fantasy managers for $4. His current cards are promising buys at 15 cents.

Professional Batting Register

	BA	G	AB	R	H	2B	3B	HR	RBI	SB
89 A	.245	55	196	37	48	6	5	6	31	2
90 A	.288	36	118	19	34	6	0	2	21	11
90 AA	.268	27	97	17	26	3	1	3	16	1
91 AA	.245	131	465	100	114	26	4	23	94	12

REY SANCHEZ

Position: Infield
Team: Chicago Cubs
Born: Oct. 5, 1967 Rio Piedras, PR
Height: 5'10" **Weight:** 180 lbs.
Bats: right **Throws:** right
Acquired: Traded from Rangers for Brian House, 1/90

Player Summary	
Fantasy Value	$2 to $4
Card Value	10¢ to 15¢
Will	play everyday
Can't	match Dunston's numbers
Expect	chemistry
Don't Expect	power

Sanchez was an All-Star shortstop at Triple-A Iowa in 1991 but may never have the chance to repeat that distinction, because he could be in the majors in 1992. He is a consistent player with good hands and good range. He can catch the ball and throw it. He may never be the offensive player that Shawon Dunston is; if Sanchez gets to the big leagues and stays there, it will be on account of his defensive ability. He is a singles hitter who projects to a .240 average. He won't turn into a home run man, even in the inviting winds of Wrigley Field. It's not impossible for Sanchez to produce some extra base hits, and he can run a bit, as shown by his stolen base and triples totals. He should quietly serve as the glue to a team. If he breaks into the bigs in '92, spend up to 15 cents on his 1992 cards. His bat keeps his fantasy value at $4.

Professional Batting Register

	BA	G	AB	R	H	2B	3B	HR	RBI	SB
86 R	.290	52	169	27	49	3	1	0	23	10
87 R	.365	49	189	36	69	10	6	0	25	22
87 A	.219	50	160	19	35	1	2	1	10	6
88 A	.306	128	418	60	128	6	5	0	38	29
89 AAA	.224	134	464	38	104	10	4	1	39	4
91 AAA	.290	126	417	60	121	16	5	2	46	13
91 NL	.261	13	23	1	6	0	0	0	2	0

ROOKIE PROSPECTS

REGGIE SANDERS

Position: Outfield
Team: Cincinnati Reds
Born: Dec. 1, 1967 Florence, SC
Height: 6'1" **Weight:** 180 lbs.
Bats: right **Throws:** right
Acquired: Seventh-round pick in 6/87 free-agent draft

Player Summary	
Fantasy Value	$3 to $6
Card Value	10¢ to 15¢
Will	hit for average
Can't	stay healthy
Expect	year at Triple-A
Don't Expect	Davis-like power

Sanders, "The Next Eric Davis," is blessed with many similar skills but among them, apparently, is the knack for getting hurt. Three of Sanders's four pro seasons have been marred by injury, including a separated shoulder that cut short the look the Reds were taking at him late in 1991. Just up from Double-A, he tripped over the catcher on a play at the plate in his second game. The Reds were scrutinizing Sanders because they were trying to make some decisions on Davis. A shoulder injury limited Sanders to 17 games in his pro debut with Billings of the rookie Pioneer League in 1988. He fractured an ankle in July of 1989 and was out for the season. At the time, Sanders was leading Class-A Greensboro in several offensive categories, and was the MVP of the South Atlantic League All-Star Game. Like Davis, Sanders is a converted shortstop who was moved to the outfield. He is a $4 fantasy bargain. His 1992 cards are appealing at 10 cents each.

MO SANFORD

Position: Pitcher
Team: Cincinnati Reds
Born: Dec. 24, 1966 Americus, GA
Height: 6'6" **Weight:** 220 lbs.
Bats: right **Throws:** right
Acquired: 32nd-round pick in 6/88 free-agent draft

Player Summary	
Fantasy Value	$5 to $8
Card Value	15¢ to 20¢
Will	collect strikeouts
Can't	stay more in minors
Expect	a K a frame
Don't Expect	ERA above 3.50

There's no need to ask Sanford what color is significant in his life—he was four years with the Crimson Tide before signing with the Reds. In his fourth pro season, he pitched primarily at the Double-A level in 1991, but also made it to the big leagues for a few starts. Sanford made his debut by allowing just one unearned run over seven innings in a victory over the Padres. He throws the fastball at about 90 mph, owns a sharp breaking curve, and is learning a straight change. He averaged more than one strikeout per inning over his minor league career, and his arrival in the big leagues didn't change the pattern. He fanned Bip Roberts, Tony Fernandez, and Tony Gwynn, the first three men Sanford faced. He hurled one shutout in the Class-A South Atlantic League in 1989—a no-hitter. With a spot in the rotation, he is a $6 fantasy hurler. His 1992 cards are lukewarm purchases at 15 cents.

Professional Batting Register

	BA	G	AB	R	H	2B	3B	HR	RBI	SB
88 R	.234	17	64	11	15	1	1	0	3	10
89 A	.289	81	315	53	91	18	5	9	53	21
90 A	.285	127	466	89	133	21	4	17	63	40
91 AA	.315	86	302	50	95	15	8	8	49	15
91 NL	.200	9	40	6	8	0	0	1	3	1

Professional Pitching Register

	W	L	ERA	G	CG	IP	H	ER	BB	SO
88 R	3	4	3.23	14	0	53.0	34	19	25	64
89 A	12	6	2.81	25	3	153.2	112	48	64	160
90 A	13	4	2.74	25	2	157.2	112	48	55	180
91 AA	7	4	2.74	16	1	95.1	69	29	55	124
91 AAA	3	0	1.60	5	2	33.2	19	6	22	38
91 NL	1	2	3.86	5	0	28.0	19	12	15	31

ROOKIE PROSPECTS

ANDRES SANTANA

Position: Infield
Team: San Francisco Giants
Born: March 19, 1968 San Pedro de Macoris, Dominican Republic
Height: 5'11" **Weight:** 160 lbs.
Bats: both **Throws:** right
Acquired: Signed as free agent, 1/86

Player Summary	
Fantasy Value	$2 to $6
Card Value	5¢ to 10¢
Will	steal 40 bases
Can't	go deep
Expect	shot at bigs
Don't Expect	ball in alleys

Nicknamed "Santini," Santana enjoyed a 1991 season that could be described as magical. Playing for Triple-A Phoenix of the Pacific Coast League, Santana hit .316 with 45 steals, ranking among the leaders in the San Francisco farm system in both departments. He was named to the postseason All-Star Team as a second baseman. He has come back much of the way from a fractured fibula he suffered just 18 games into the 1989 season. He was operated on and back playing in the Instructional League by October. Before the injury, Santana had led two leagues in stolen bases and had notched a career-high 88. Since then, the numbers aren't quite that gaudy, but Santana has now topped 30 for two straight years. Possessing virtually no power, he would have to ride his speed to a regular major league job. His switch-hitting gives him a chance to add versatility to a lineup. He is a $4 middle infielder. His 1992 cards are good purchases at a nickel.

Professional Batting Register

	BA	G	AB	R	H	2B	3B	HR	RBI	SB
87 R	.262	67	256	51	67	2	3	0	9	45
88 A	.280	118	450	77	126	4	1	0	24	88
88 AA	.167	11	36	3	6	0	0	0	3	3
89 A	.261	18	69	14	18	3	0	0	3	10
90 AA	.292	92	336	50	98	5	4	0	24	31
90 NL	.000	6	2	0	0	0	0	0	1	0
91 AAA	.316	113	456	84	144	7	5	1	35	45

PETE SCHOUREK

Position: Pitcher
Team: New York Mets
Born: May 10, 1969 Falls Church, VA
Height: 6'5" **Weight:** 195 lbs.
Bats: left **Throws:** left
Acquired: Third-round pick in 6/87 free-agent draft

Player Summary	
Fantasy Value	$2 to $5
Card Value	15¢ to 20¢
Will	join rotation
Can't	overpower anyone
Expect	better ERA
Don't Expect	step backwards

Schourek reached the big leagues by making the team out of spring training in 1991, an exceptional feat considering that the Mets were supposed to have one of the best pitching staffs in baseball. The staff wasn't as good as people thought. Although he didn't have an overpowering year, the experience of being in the big leagues can only do him good. Schourek throws an average to above-average fastball, and also has a curve and change. The Mets like his poise and emotional control on the mound, particularly the fact that an error behind him doesn't faze him. Schourek served as a middle reliever for most of the season, though he did make the odd start. With the Mets looking for answers, it's not impossible that he could be a member of their 1992 rotation. Wait until he does before you invest in his 15-cent 1992 cards. He is a $3 fantasy hurler.

Professional Pitching Register

	W	L	ERA	G	CG	IP	H	ER	BB	SO
87 R	4	5	3.68	12	2	78.1	70	32	34	57
89 A	5	9	2.83	29	5	140.0	123	44	68	135
90 A	4	1	0.97	5	2	37.0	29	4	8	28
90 AA	11	4	3.04	19	1	124.1	109	42	39	94
90 AAA	1	0	2.57	2	1	14.0	9	4	5	14
91 AAA	1	1	2.52	4	0	25.0	18	7	10	17
91 NL	5	4	4.27	35	1	86.1	82	41	43	67

ROOKIE PROSPECTS

DARRYL SCOTT

Position: Pitcher
Team: California Angels
Born: Aug. 6, 1968 Fresno, CA
Height: 6'1" **Weight:** 185 lbs.
Bats: right **Throws:** right
Acquired: Signed as a free agent, 6/90

Player Summary	
Fantasy Value	$1 to $2
Card Value	5¢ to 10¢
Will	save 20 games
Can't	duplicate K ratio
Expect	low ERA
Don't Expect	many baserunners

Scott dominated hitters in the Class-A Midwest League in 1991 the way few pitchers at any level did. Batters were hitting just .137 off him, he was averaging an incredible 14.7 strikeouts per nine innings, and allowed just two earned runs in the second half. He began the season as one of Quad City's two closers, but took over the job as the season went along. Scott was 9-for-9 in save opportunities in July. He did it with a split-fingered fastball that helps him on the Class-A level but which may be a bit of a problem as he progresses. The splitter is a strike when batters see it, but a ball when they swing. Batters in Class-A won't always lay off, but better hitters might. And if Scott falls behind in the count, he'll have to come in with a fastball described as being below average. But Scott looks ripe to jump at least one rung. In 1990 at Boise, Class-A Northwest League batters hit .200 against the former Loyola Marymount righthander. He is not a fantasy draft yet, and his current cards are not buys.

Professional Pitching Register

	W	L	ERA	G	S	IP	H	ER	BB	SO
90 A	2	1	1.34	27	5	53.2	40	8	19	57
91 A	4	3	1.55	47	19	75.1	35	13	26	123

GARY SCOTT

Position: Third base
Team: Chicago Cubs
Born: Aug. 22, 1968 New Rochelle, NY
Height: 6' **Weight:** 175 lbs.
Bats: left **Throws:** left
Acquired: Second-round pick in 6/89 free-agent draft

Player Summary	
Fantasy Value	$2 to $4
Card Value	10¢ to 15¢
Will	bounce back
Can't	get rushed again
Expect	double hit total
Don't Expect	another flop

Scott was one of the first components to go awry as the Cubs' 1991 season fell short of expectations. He seized the third base job as a nonroster player in spring training and hopes were that he could fill a hole there. He failed to hit and soon he was back in the minors, trying to rebuild after the setback. Scott never did recover in 1991 while playing at Triple-A Iowa of the American Association, and was hurt at the end of the year. Scott had homered in double figures in his first two seasons, and never hit below .280 in three different stops. He led the Class-A New York-Penn League with a .520 slugging average in 1989, was the Class-A Carolina League's MVP in 1990, and was also tabbed as the Cubs' Minor League Player of the Year. Scott is young enough to bounce back. He had a .447 slugging percentage and a .361 on-base average at Class-A Winston-Salem. Buy low, sell high. His 1992 cards are good purchases at a dime each. He is a fantasy draft for less than $4.

Professional Batting Register

	BA	G	AB	R	H	2B	3B	HR	RBI	SB
89 A	.280	48	175	33	49	10	1	10	42	4
90 A	.295	102	380	63	112	22	0	12	70	17
90 AA	.308	35	143	21	44	9	0	4	17	3
91 AAA	.208	63	231	21	48	10	2	3	34	0
91 NL	.165	31	79	8	13	3	0	1	5	0

ROOKIE PROSPECTS

FRANK SEMINARA

Position: Pitcher
Team: San Diego Padres
Born: May 16, 1967 Brooklyn, NY
Height: 6'2" **Weight:** 195 lbs.
Bats: right **Throws:** right
Acquired: Drafted from Yankees, 12/90

Player Summary	
Fantasy Value	$2 to $4
Card Value	10¢ to 15¢
Will	go the distance
Can't	return to bullpen
Expect	promotion to Triple-A
Don't Expect	K per inning

Seminara pitched for Double-A Wichita of the Texas League in 1991, after being plucked by the Padres in a Rule 5 draft at the winter meetings. The Yankees may have made a mistake in exposing the righthander, especially after a season in which he had 16 wins. He has been likened to Roger McDowell because of his very hard type of sinker. Seminara can vary the speed of this pitch, but needs a better breaking ball. His pro career took one peculiar turn: He has been a starter for most of his career, but was used only in relief upon being promoted to Class-A Prince William midway through 1989. By 1990, he was back in the rotation and was named Pitcher of the Year in the Class-A Carolina League. He isn't a devastating strikeout man, but has decent control. Opponents compiled a .258 batting average in 1991. He is a top candidate for promotion in '92. He is a reasonable fantasy draft for $3 or less. His 1992 cards are holds at a dime unless he breaks into the Padres rotation.

Professional Pitching Register

	W	L	ERA	G	CG	IP	H	ER	BB	SO
88 A	4	7	4.37	16	0	78.1	86	38	32	60
89 A	9	6	2.62	32	3	106.2	77	31	40	93
90 A	16	8	1.90	25	4	170.1	136	36	52	132
91 AA	15	10	3.38	27	6	176.0	173	66	68	107

BASIL SHABAZZ

Position: Outfield
Team: St. Louis Cardinals
Born: Jan. 31, 1972
Height: 6'1" **Weight:** 195 lbs.
Bats: right **Throws:** right
Acquired: Third-round pick in 6/91 free-agent draft

Player Summary	
Fantasy Value	$1 to $2
Card Value	5¢ to 10¢
Will	terrorize basepaths
Can't	be consistent
Expect	improved average
Don't Expect	overnight success

Because of his overwhelming speed, Shabazz has the potential to be one of the most exciting players in organized baseball. Blessed with enough talent to make him a fine all-around athlete, he is nevertheless trying to make it in his fourth-best sport because he can play longer. Shabazz owns 4.1 or 4.2 speed in the 40, making him a perfect fit with the tradition of speedsters in St. Louis. He turned down football, basketball, and track scholarship offers to play baseball. On his first night with Johnson City of the rookie Appalachian League, he beat out a routine one-hopper to second. He had a .231 slugging percentage, and his 16 walks pushed his on-base average to .309. He has also mastered the difficult bank they have in right field at Howard Johnson Field. Johnson City Manager Chris Maloney considered Shabazz's arm good enough to play him in right field. Shabazz has played very little organized ball, so he will need lots of at bats. Until he masters the game, pass on his current cards. He is not a fantasy choice.

Professional Batting Register

	BA	G	AB	R	H	2B	3B	HR	RBI	SB
91 R	.205	40	117	18	24	3	0	0	11	4

ROOKIE PROSPECTS

BEN SHELTON

Position: First base
Team: Pittsburgh Pirates
Born: Sept. 21, 1969 Chicago, IL
Height: 6'3" **Weight:** 210 lbs.
Bats: right **Throws:** left
Acquired: Second-round pick in 6/87 free-agent draft

Player Summary	
Fantasy Value	$1 to $3
Card Value	5¢ to 10¢
Will	drive the ball
Can't	take too many strikes
Expect	15 HR
Don't Expect	high average

Sometimes a power hitter can strike out too frequently because he flails at pitches. Shelton is just the opposite—he often stands and watches as a hittable delivery goes by. The Pirates are trying to get him to jump on these pitches to make use of his power. In his fifth pro season, he had his best year in terms of production, and was among the top homer and RBI men in the organization in 1991. He was leading the Class-A Carolina League in RBI when boosted to Double-A, and he toasted his new surroundings by slamming the first pitch for a triple. Shelton also fanned a great deal, often looking. Paradoxically, his selectivity may make Shelton a better hitter at a higher level. He is a good first baseman, and may play some outfield. Wait until his power translates to success on the Double-A level before bidding on him or buying his nickel-priced current cards.

Professional Batting Register

	BA	G	AB	R	H	2B	3B	HR	RBI	SB
87 R	.286	38	119	22	34	8	3	4	16	7
88 R	.221	63	204	34	45	7	3	4	20	8
88 A	.195	38	128	25	25	2	2	5	20	3
89 A	.246	122	386	67	95	16	4	8	50	18
90 A	.206	109	320	44	66	10	2	10	36	1
91 A	.261	65	203	37	53	10	2	14	56	3
91 AA	.231	55	169	19	39	8	3	1	19	2

DAVE SILVESTRI

Position: Shortstop
Team: New York Yankees
Born: Sept. 29, 1967 St. Louis, MO
Height: 6' **Weight:** 180 lbs.
Bats: right **Throws:** right
Acquired: Traded from Astros for Orlando Miller and Daven Bond, 3/90

Player Summary	
Fantasy Value	$2 to $5
Card Value	15¢ to 20¢
Will	star in majors
Can't	make consistent contact
Expect	20 steals
Don't Expect	20 homers

Silvestri blossomed as a hitter one year after arriving in a trade that may go down as one of the more solid in recent Yankee history. A former member of the 1988 United States Olympic team, he registered a spectacular 1991 in the Double-A Eastern League—a circuit where it's not easy to hit. Silvestri was among the top Yankee farmhands in homers and RBI. If he reduces his strikeouts, he will be in the bigs soon. He was the starting shortstop and leadoff man for the American League minor leaguers in the Double-A All-Star Game, going 2-for-4 with two stolen bases and a run scored. Silvestri can do more than hit, having led the Class-A Carolina League in several defensive stats in '90. Houston drafted the University of Missouri product in the second round of the 1988 June draft, and he was the starting shortstop for the U.S. team in Seoul. His power makes him a $3 or so fantasy draft. His 1992 cards are tempting at 15 cents.

Professional Batting Register

	BA	G	AB	R	H	2B	3B	HR	RBI	SB
89 A	.254	129	437	67	111	20	1	2	50	28
90 A	.258	131	465	74	120	30	7	5	56	37
90 AA	.286	2	7	0	2	0	0	0	2	0
91 AA	.262	140	512	97	134	31	8	19	83	20

ROOKIE PROSPECTS

DAN SMITH

Position: Pitcher
Team: Texas Rangers
Born: April 20, 1969 St. Paul, MN
Height: 6'5" **Weight:** 190 lbs.
Bats: left **Throws:** left
Acquired: First-round pick in 6/90 free-agent draft

Player Summary	
Fantasy Value	$1 to $2
Card Value	3¢ to 5¢
Will	slash runs
Can't	pitch ahead
Expect	10 wins
Don't Expect	another rush job

Don't be misled by those 1991 stats; Smith was gaining some experience on the job. He was just two years out of college and 1991 was really his first full pro season. The fact that Smith pitched at Triple-A was testimony to how highly the Rangers must regard him, but now we must see if being rushed to the highest level of the minors will have any adverse effect. It's said that the slider is Smith's best pitch, and he throws a fastball and a decent change. His high walk total no doubt contributed to some of his problems at Triple-A Oklahoma City, and he probably pitched behind in the count often. Smith attended Creighton University and pitched three seasons there, going 30-12. In 1990, he went 14-3, and earned first-team All-American honors from *Baseball America*. He pitched for the United States national team in 1989, going 4-2 and leading the squad in ERA. He has to rebound in Triple-A before his fantasy value and cards prices rise beyond their low levels.

Professional Pitching Register

	W	L	ERA	G	CG	IP	H	ER	BB	SO
90 R	2	0	3.65	5	0	24.2	23	10	6	27
90 AA	3	2	3.76	7	0	38.1	27	16	16	32
91 AAA	4	17	5.52	28	3	151.2	195	93	75	85

MARK SMITH

Position: Outfield
Team: Baltimore Orioles
Born: May 7, 1970 Pasadena, CA
Height: 6'3" **Weight:** 200 lbs.
Bats: right **Throws:** right
Acquired: First-round pick in 6/91 free-agent draft

Player Summary	
Fantasy Value	$1 to $3
Card Value	10¢ to 15¢
Will	hit .300
Can't	start in bigs yet
Expect	late '92 call-up
Don't Expect	miracles

Smith was the ninth overall pick in the draft, the third outfielder, and the first position player taken by the Orioles in the first round since 1980. An all-around player, he is a good outfielder with a strong and accurate arm. The Orioles showed their high opinion of his ability by placing him in the Class-A Carolina League, where he never quite caught up with everyone. He still managed to flash some power, though. Baltimore is projecting Smith as a right fielder who could hit in the .270 to .280 range. With some good stats, he can make Baltimore by late 1992. The Birds were impressed with the way he handled the wood bat in the Cape Cod League in 1990, hitting over .400. Like some other first-rounders, Smith signed late, for $350,000, and had to get his timing back after missing time. Part of his contract with the Birds was that he would finish school (Southern Cal), so he didn't attend Instructional League. His 1992 first-round card will be an immediate investment at a dime. He is a $2 future draft.

Professional Batting Register

	BA	G	AB	R	H	2B	3B	HR	RBI	SB
91A	.250	48	148	20	37	5	1	4	29	1

ROOKIE PROSPECTS

TIM SMITH

Position: Pitcher
Team: Boston Red Sox
Born: Aug. 9, 1968 Melrose, MA
Height: 6'4" **Weight:** 190 lbs.
Bats: right **Throws:** right
Acquired: 24th-round pick in 6/90 free-agent draft

Player Summary	
Fantasy Value	$1 to $2
Card Value	5¢ to 10¢
Will	provide innings
Can't	blow people away
Expect	low ERA
Don't Expect	long games

Smith is a New England product who would be especially popular as a hometown boy in Fenway Park. He would have to make it to the majors without an overpowering fastball, but that isn't impossible. He is a sinker-and-slider pitcher who relies on spotting the ball, and this style gave him a top ERA among Boston farmhands. Opponents compiled a .229 batting average against him in 1991. Smith is a hustling pitcher with good habits, a manager's delight who can give you a complete game now and then. He helps himself by being a fast-working pitcher, which tends to keep the infielders on their toes. Batters often try to step out of the box on him. Smith missed some time at the end of the 1991 season with either bursitis or tendinitis in the shoulder, but it is not believed to be serious. Smith graduated from Boston College with a marketing degree and was a Big East Academic All-Star. His future is intriguing, but don't draft him yet. His nickel-priced current cards are also holds.

DAVE STATON

Position: Infield
Team: San Diego Padres
Born: April 12, 1968 Seattle, WA
Height: 6'5" **Weight:** 215 lbs.
Bats: right **Throws:** right
Acquired: Fifth-round pick in 6/89 free-agent draft

Player Summary	
Fantasy Value	$2 to $4
Card Value	15¢ to 20¢
Will	go deep
Can't	budge Fred McGriff
Expect	position switch
Don't Expect	.300 hitter

Staton has been described as being the best pure hitter in the San Diego organization, quite a compliment considering what Matt Mieske and Jay Gainer have done in their careers. In fact, Staton may be able to hit the ball farther than Gainer can. However, Staton may find his road to the majors slowed by the defensive side of the game. He needs a position, and must make progress. If he can do that, then you're looking at an interesting prospect. He opened his pro career with a Triple Crown at Class-A Spokane of the Northwest League, and has advanced level by level. In 1991, he played first base for San Diego's Triple-A club in Las Vegas, and led the team in both homers and RBI. He had a .499 slugging percentage and a .346 on-base average. Staton will strike out more than a bit, but he will also walk. He shows no evidence of speed. He has earned a shot on your squad for up to $4. His 1992 cards are good bets under 20 cents each.

Professional Pitching Register

	W	L	ERA	G	CG	IP	H	ER	BB	SO
90 A	4	6	3.68	23	2	66.0	62	27	25	52
91 A	12	9	2.16	25	8	174.2	149	42	34	103

Professional Batting Register

	BA	G	AB	R	H	2B	3B	HR	RBI	SB
89 A	.362	70	260	52	94	18	0	17	72	1
90 A	.290	92	335	56	97	16	1	20	64	4
90 AA	.305	45	164	26	50	11	0	6	31	0
91 AAA	.267	107	375	61	100	19	1	22	74	1

ROOKIE PROSPECTS

LEE STEVENS

Position: Outfield
Team: California Angels
Born: July 10, 1967 Kansas City, MO
Height: 6'4" **Weight:** 219 lbs.
Bats: left **Throws:** left
Acquired: First-round pick in 6/86 free-agent draft

Player Summary	
Fantasy Value	$9 to $16
Card Value	5¢ to 10¢
Will	get extra-base hits
Can't	create an opening
Expect	long look
Don't Expect	another year in minors

With his path to the majors blocked at first base by Wally Joyner, Stevens played most of three straight years in the Triple-A Pacific Coast League, making the All-Star team twice. He has made All-Star teams at both first base and the outfield. He played only at first base in his 67-game stint with the Angels in 1990. However, he played the outfield for Edmonton in 1991. He had a .505 slugging percentage that year. The 22nd overall draft pick, Stevens is a power hitter who usually strikes out twice as often as he walks, and would be more effective if he drew more bases on balls. He got a big break in December when Joyner bolted the Angels as a free agent. Stevens could finally inherit the starting job. He is a fantasy coup waiting to happen at $16 or less. His 1992 cards are fair investments until he wins a starting job in the bigs.

Professional Batting Register

	BA	G	AB	R	H	2B	3B	HR	RBI	SB
86 A	.281	72	267	45	75	18	2	6	47	13
87 A	.244	140	532	82	130	29	2	19	97	1
88 AA	.297	116	414	79	123	26	2	23	76	0
89 AAA	.247	127	446	72	110	29	9	14	74	5
90 AAA	.293	90	338	57	99	31	2	16	66	1
90 AL	.214	67	248	28	53	10	0	7	32	1
91 AAA	.314	123	481	75	151	29	3	19	96	4
91 AL	.293	18	58	8	17	7	0	0	9	1

JESUS TAVAREZ

Position: Outfield
Team: Seattle Mariners
Born: March 26, 1971 Santo Domingo, Dominican Republic
Height: 6' **Weight:** 170 lbs.
Bats: right **Throws:** right
Acquired: Signed as a free agent, 6/89

Player Summary	
Fantasy Value	$1 to $3
Card Value	5¢ to 10¢
Will	steal 50 bases
Can't	get glove down
Expect	higher average
Don't Expect	much slugging

Tavarez is already an exciting player and he may prove to be even more so when he gets a bit stronger. He is a fast runner, with steal home kind of speed, and he may well give Seattle an ignitor one of these years. Right now, though, Tavarez needs some more endurance so as to take fullest advantage of his gifts. This added strength has nothing to do with power at the plate, although Tavarez showed some pop at Class-A San Bernardino of the California league in 1991. He had a .352 slugging percentage and a .343 on-base average. There is stamina necessary in the running game, which involves taking leads, diving back into bases, and sliding and getting tagged. He is learning how to bunt and to put the ball in play a little more. Tavarez is a good defensive player with an average arm. In 1989, he played with the Mariners' club in the Dominican League and won the batting title with a .394 mark. Give him another year, then draft him for $2. His current cards are good purchases at a nickel each.

Professional Batting Register

	BA	G	AB	R	H	2B	3B	HR	RBI	SB
90 A	.237	108	379	39	90	10	1	0	32	40
91 A	.283	124	466	80	132	11	3	5	41	69

ROOKIE PROSPECTS

BRIEN TAYLOR

Position: Pitcher
Team: New York Yankees
Born: Dec. 26, 1971 Beaufort, NC
Height: 6'3" **Weight:** 195 lbs.
Bats: left **Throws:** left
Acquired: First-round pick in 6/91 free-agent draft

Player Summary	
Fantasy Value	$1 to $4
Card Value	50¢ to $1
Will	throw smoke
Can't	escape scrutiny
Expect	frustrated batters
Don't Expect	lightning ascent

If Taylor shows any of the stuff that his mom did during his contract negotiations, he is going to be a very tough customer out on the mound. She helped win Brien a contract worth $1.55 million over three years. That's a lot of money, but the Yankees thought Taylor was something special because they made him the top overall pick in the draft out of high school. He made the scouts drool, being a lefty with a 98 mph fastball, a big overhand curve, and a change. He also has the confidence of a top-notch pitcher. Taylor will no doubt need all of them, and more. The expectations that come with being a top draft pick are tough enough. In Taylor's case, they are made greater by a contract that caught the attention of all baseball. Taylor's first stop was the fall Instructional League. His assignment in 1992 is a key because the Yankees will want to remove some pressure. His 1992 cards are very hot, but don't pay more than $1 apiece. You'll probably have to draft him this year, but don't pay too much.

No minor league experience

JIM THOME

Position: Third base
Team: Cleveland Indians
Born: Aug. 27, 1970 Peoria, IL
Height: 6'3" **Weight:** 200 lbs.
Bats: left **Throws:** right
Acquired: 13th-round pick in 6/89 free-agent draft

Player Summary	
Fantasy Value	$3 to $7
Card Value	15¢ to 25¢
Will	pile up doubles
Can't	go downtown
Expect	line drives
Don't Expect	speed game

Thome is a blue-chip prospect who has made what are termed "gigantic" strides in his three-year pro career. He is said to have everything you look for in a player. He's a line drive contact hitter from the lefthand side who is beginning to produce power. It's possible that he may still grow a bit. He's big, but has very quick feet, and has improved his play at third. The Indians love the fact that when promoted during the 1991 season, Thome was leading the Double-A Eastern League in hitting. He had an ordinary first year in pro ball. He blossomed in 1990, however, working his way up to high Class-A and earning awards. He tied for third in the rookie Appalachian League in homers despite playing just 34 games. He also captured the Lou Boudreau Award as top farmhand in the organization. Thome is a $7 fantasy third baseman, because of his youth. His 1992 cards are great buys for prices less than a quarter each.

Professional Batting Register

	BA	G	AB	R	H	2B	3B	HR	RBI	SB
89 R	.237	55	186	22	44	5	0	0	22	6
90 R	.373	34	118	31	44	7	1	12	34	6
90 A	.308	33	117	19	36	4	1	4	16	4
91 AA	.337	84	294	47	99	20	2	5	45	8
91 AAA	.285	41	151	20	43	7	3	2	28	0
91 A	.255	27	98	7	25	4	2	1	9	1

ROOKIE PROSPECTS

LEE TINSLEY

Position: Outfield
Team: Cleveland Indians
Born: March 4, 1969 Shelbyville, KY
Height: 5'10" **Weight:** 180 lbs.
Bats: both **Throws:** right
Acquired: Traded from Athletics with Apolinar Garcia for Brook Jacoby, 7/91

Player Summary	
Fantasy Value	$1 to $2
Card Value	5¢ to 10¢
Will	be running threat
Can't	steal first
Expect	better average
Don't Expect	regular job

Tinsley is so new to Cleveland that the organization is still getting to know him. He came to the Indians as part of a deal that sent third baseman Brook Jacoby to the Athletics. Tinsley has great tools, beginning with what the ballclub calls "impact speed." In other words, he can fly. A switch-hitter, he also has bat speed from both sides of the plate. Tinsley is described as a green, raw player, some of which comes from his not having played very much baseball in high school. He has shown signs of starting to hit, and has even flashed a bit of power. Tinsley was a first-round pick of the A's, the 11th selection, in 1987. A four-sport star in high school, he turned down a football scholarship at Purdue to play baseball. He has been in the minors for five years now and needs to make a move. His current cards are interesting investments at 5 cents apiece. He is a $2 future fantasy pick.

Professional Batting Register

	BA	G	AB	R	H	2B	3B	HR	RBI	SB
87 A	.174	45	132	22	23	3	2	0	13	9
88 A	.250	72	256	56	64	8	2	3	28	42
89 A	.181	123	397	51	72	10	2	6	31	19
90 A	.251	132	482	88	121	14	11	12	59	44
91 AA	.295	38	139	26	41	7	2	3	8	18
91 AA	.224	130	442	73	109	14	8	5	32	54

SALOMON TORRES

Position: Pitcher
Team: San Francisco Giants
Born: March 11, 1972 San Pedro de Macoris, Dominican Republic
Height: 5'11" **Weight:** 150 lbs.
Bats: right **Throws:** right
Acquired: Signed as a free agent, 9/89

Player Summary	
Fantasy Value	$1 to $3
Card Value	5¢ to 10¢
Will	post lean ERA
Can't	repeat '91
Expect	bright future
Don't Expect	immediate impact

Torres shows that there are more than shortstops in San Pedro de Macoris. This top-level pitching prospect has delivered two astonishing seasons in his first two cracks at pro ball, and now the only question is how quickly and how far he will advance. As the ace of Class-A Clinton in the Midwest League in 1991, Torres showed everything you like to see from a pitcher: He took the ball, finished what he started, struck out four times as many batters as he walked, and allowed roughly one baserunner per inning. Opponents compiled a .195 batting average against him. He was 11-1 in the Dominican League in '90. He was the league's Player of the Month for May, and started the league's All-Star Game June 24, going two shutout innings and leaving with a 2-0 lead. *Baseball America* listed Torres as the league's best pitching prospect, as well as its best fastball and top control artist. He allowed only four homers in 210⅔ innings pitched. All this before turning 20. He is a top future draft for $2. His current cards are safe at a nickel.

Professional Pitching Register

	W	L	ERA	G	CG	IP	H	ER	BB	SO
91 A	16	5	1.41	28	8	210.2	148	33	47	214

ROOKIE PROSPECTS

RICKY TRLICEK

Position: Pitcher
Team: Toronto Blue Jays
Born: April 26, 1969 Houston, TX
Height: 6'2" **Weight:** 200 lbs.
Bats: right **Throws:** right
Acquired: Traded from Braves for Ernie Whitt and Kevin Batiste, 12/89

Player Summary	
Fantasy Value	$1 to $3
Card Value	5¢ to 10¢
Will	sharpen control
Can't	return to rotation
Expect	time in majors
Don't Expect	another Tom Henke

Trlicek has experienced quite a bit of change in his short career. For one thing, he is already on his third major league organization. For another, he has made a successful transition from the starting rotation to the bullpen. Trlicek's success as a reliever may be what gets him to the majors after four years of pro ball. He led Double-A Knoxville of the Southern League in saves, flashing improved control and increased domination of hitters. Trlicek was drafted by Philadelphia in the fourth round of the June 1987 draft and released two years later. Atlanta picked him up 10 days later, and he pitched respectably in the Class-A Sally League in 1989. The Braves then sent him to Toronto in a deal that netted them Ernie Whitt, but Trlicek enjoyed little success for Toronto's club in the Class-A Florida State League. He isn't hot enough to warrant a fantasy draft at more than $3. His current cards are questionable investments at a nickel each.

Professional Pitching Register

	W	L	ERA	G	CG	IP	H	ER	BB	SO
87 A	2	5	4.10	10	0	37.1	43	17	31	22
88 A	2	3	7.39	8	0	31.2	27	26	31	26
89 A	6	5	2.48	16	0	101.2	76	28	41	76
90 A	5	8	3.73	26	0	154.1	128	64	72	125
91 AA	2	5	2.45	41	16	51.1	36	14	22	55

TODD VAN POPPEL

Position: Pitcher
Team: Oakland Athletics
Born: Dec. 9, 1971 Hinsdale, IL
Height: 6'5" **Weight:** 210 lbs.
Bats: right **Throws:** right
Acquired: First-round pick in 6/90 free-agent draft

Player Summary	
Fantasy Value	$3 to $6
Card Value	20¢ to 30¢
Will	throw hard
Can't	win in bigs yet
Expect	more strikes
Don't Expect	stats to match contract

Van Poppel has already made an impact on baseball history simply with a signature. He hopes to prove he can do more with his arm than sign his name. He would likely have been a top draft pick of the Atlanta Braves in 1990, but he indicated he wanted to go to college. After the Braves passed, the A's took a gamble and made Van Poppel the 14th overall pick. He then signed a lucrative contract, a contract that was cited by the family of 1991 top draft pick Brien Taylor in his own talks with the Yankees. Van Poppel pitched at Huntsville of the Southern League in 1991 and did well for a 19-year-old at Double-A, even though the won-loss record wasn't there. He also got a taste of the bigs. Van Poppel throws an overpowering fastball, an outstanding curve, and a good change. He must work on command of the strike zone, but his stuff is major league. His 1992 cards are top-drawer investments at a quarter. His fantasy value stops at $6, though.

Professional Pitching Register

	W	L	ERA	G	CG	IP	H	ER	BB	SO
90 A	3	2	2.15	8	0	37.2	18	9	19	49
91 AA	6	13	3.47	24	1	132.1	118	51	90	115
91 AL	0	0	9.64	1	0	4.2	7	5	2	6

ROOKIE PROSPECTS

JULIAN VASQUEZ

Position: Pitcher
Team: New York Mets
Born: May 24, 1968 Puerta Plata, Dominican Republic
Height: 6'3" **Weight:** 165 lbs.
Bats: right **Throws:** right
Acquired: Signed as a free agent, 7/86

Player Summary	
Fantasy Value	$1 to $3
Card Value	5¢ to 10¢
Will	dominate hitters
Can't	jump to majors
Expect	strikeouts
Don't Expect	perfect command

Vasquez's lanky frame helps produce "loose arm action." He uses his whole body in pitching, and the result is tremendous velocity and movement on the fastball, and near-total domination. He threw as hard as anyone in the Class-A Florida State League, and he did not allow an earned run for the entire first half of St. Lucie's season. Vasquez also throws a slider, and hitters were baffled to the extent that his ERA was well below one per nine innings. All this gives him a bright future as a closer, especially if he sharpens his control a bit. He broke the club record for saves by June, and was named to the league's All-Star team. He ranked in the top 10 of all minor league pitchers in batting average against. Opponents batted just .163 off his pitching. Vasquez may still be a step or two away from the majors, but he could take those steps quickly. Don't draft him yet, but sink a few bucks in his 5-cent current cards.

Professional Pitching Register

	W	L	ERA	G	S	IP	H	ER	BB	SO
87 R	2	3	3.29	25	3	41.0	36	15	22	36
88 R	0	1	3.19	19	10	31.0	19	11	13	30
89 A	1	5	3.88	37	7	58.0	47	25	32	61
90 A	1	4	2.17	25	9	29.0	28	7	17	37
91 A	3	2	0.28	56	25	64.0	35	2	39	56

JOE VITIELLO

Position: Outfield
Team: Kansas City Royals
Born: April 11, 1970 Cambridge, MA
Height: 6'3" **Weight:** 215 lbs.
Bats: right **Throws:** right
Acquired: First-round pick in 6/91 free-agent draft

Player Summary	
Fantasy Value	$1 to $3
Card Value	10¢ to 15¢
Will	hit .280
Can't	handle bigs yet
Expect	more muscle
Don't Expect	dull at bats

The Royals hope that the seventh overall pick will prove to be a lucky one for them, although Vitiello's success would be due more to skill than to fortune. Kansas City likes his bat speed, and the feeling is that Vitiello could be a middle of the order type of player. The front office calls his bat "hitterish," meaning that the ball has a different type of sound (solid and loud) when it hits wood. Signed for $345,000, Vitiello was assigned to Class-A Eugene of the Northwest League. He went 1-for-2 with an RBI in his professional debut, and dazzled thereafter. He hit .333 with five homers and 19 RBI in his first 15 games, including a two-homer game against Everett. He ended his tour there with a .641 slugging percentage. This performance, plus a makeup the ballclub liked, helped earn Vitiello a huge promotion to the Royals' Double-A club in Memphis. He hit .219 on 7-for-32 right after the move, but drove in six runs with those seven hits. He needs a few years before he is a fantasy draft. His current cards are purchases, though, at a dime each.

Professional Batting Register

	BA	G	AB	R	H	2B	3B	HR	RBI	SB
91 AA	.211	36	128	15	27	4	1	0	18	0
91 A	.328	19	64	16	21	2	0	6	21	1

ROOKIE PROSPECTS

KYLE WASHINGTON

Position: Outfield
Team: Cleveland Indians
Born: Dec. 9, 1969 Chicago Heights, IL
Height: 6'2" **Weight:** 190 lbs.
Bats: right **Throws:** right
Acquired: Signed as a free agent, 4/91

Player Summary	
Fantasy Value	$1 to $2
Card Value	5¢ to 10¢
Will	steal his share
Can't	hit breaking ball
Expect	extra-base pop
Don't Expect	cleanup-type RBI

Cleveland scored a coup by signing Washington after the Mets let him go. He went to the Indians' Class-A farm team in Columbus, Georgia, and captured the South Atlantic League batting title. Washington has above-average speed, which has translated into stolen bases, and great baseball instincts. He is a true center fielder, able to cover the territory. His arm is average at best, but it may get better as the Indians work with him on throwing mechanics. Washington is like most young hitters in that he loves the fastball but has problems with the breaking pitch. The adjustments he makes will likely determine whether he reaches the bigs or not. Washington was released by the Mets in spring training after several mediocre years. Cleveland had good reports on him and made the sign. He may just be a one-year wonder, so don't draft him until '93. His nickel-priced current cards are not good buys right now. Wait until he repeats his success before you buy.

DAVID WEATHERS

Position: Pitcher
Team: Toronto Blue Jays
Born: Sept. 25, 1969 Lawrenceburg, TN
Height: 6'3" **Weight:** 205 lbs.
Bats: right **Throws:** right
Acquired: Third-round pick in 6/88 free-agent draft

Player Summary	
Fantasy Value	$1 to $3
Card Value	5¢ to 10¢
Will	take the ball
Can't	be consistent
Expect	10 wins
Don't Expect	15 wins

Weathers has shown a capacity for work since turning pro in 1988. His 31 starts for Class-A Myrtle Beach in 1989 are particularly impressive for the minor leagues, where the seasons are shorter than in the majors. Among Weathers's gifts is a stingy attitude about the long ball. In his first three pro seasons, he surrendered just eight gopher balls. Even in the majors, he continued this knack, which will help prevent him from getting hurt until he gets better command of the strike zone. Weathers must also learn to minimize some of the mistakes that can hurt—such as wild pitches, balks, and hit batsmen. A spectacular athlete, he pitched a no-hitter in high school and added three home runs. His favorite pitchers growing up were Dwight Gooden and Todd Worrell, so it will be interesting to see if any elements of their game surface in his. Weathers is a good fantasy pick for $3 or less. His 1992 cards are good investments at a nickel each.

Professional Batting Register

	BA	G	AB	R	H	2B	3B	HR	RBI	SB
88 R	.202	52	129	14	26	3	0	1	6	4
89 R	.222	62	185	28	41	6	1	6	20	11
90 A	.265	63	226	42	60	7	3	2	23	31
91 A	.342	121	444	87	152	31	13	8	58	51

Professional Pitching Register

	W	L	ERA	G	CG	IP	H	ER	BB	SO
88 A	4	4	3.02	15	0	62.2	58	21	26	36
89 A	11	13	3.86	31	2	172.2	163	74	86	111
90 A	10	7	3.70	27	2	158.0	158	65	59	96
91 AA	10	7	2.45	24	5	139.1	121	38	49	114
91 AL	1	0	4.91	15	0	14.2	15	8	17	13

ROOKIE PROSPECTS

TOM WEGMANN

Position: Pitcher
Team: New York Mets
Born: Aug. 29, 1968 Dyersville, IA
Height: 6' **Weight:** 190 lbs.
Bats: right **Throws:** right
Acquired: Signed as a free agent, 6/90

Player Summary	
Fantasy Value	$1 to $2
Card Value	3¢ to 5¢
Will	throw strikes
Can't	blow people away
Expect	good K-to-walk ratio
Don't Expect	many baserunners

Wegmann's troubles in his senior year of college may translate into success for the Mets. He did not enjoy a good year at Middle Tennessee State, which may explain why the Mets were able to get him outside of the draft. Pitching at Class-A St. Lucie of the Florida State League in 1991, Wegmann established himself as a great future for a franchise whose pitching staff has fallen from the ranks of baseball's best. He ranked among the top Met farmhands in strikeouts, ERA, and winning percentage. His walks and hits combined were well below his innings pitched. In 1991, Florida State League opponents batted .208 against him, while Class-A Sally League hitters compiled a .130 average. Wegmann does all this with a below-average fastball, but he has great command of his off-speed stuff. He suffered two injuries in 1991, one a muscle problem in his side, and the other a broken bone in his hand. Wegmann is described as a fierce competitor and is said to own a good pitching makeup. He is not a draft yet, and his current cards are holds.

Professional Pitching Register

	W	L	ERA	G	CG	IP	H	ER	BB	SO
90 R	5	4	2.53	15	4	85.1	53	24	30	106
91 A	9	3	1.65	20	1	109.0	67	20	23	138

TURK WENDELL

Position: Pitcher
Team: Chicago Cubs
Born: May 19, 1967 Pittsfield, MA
Height: 6'2" **Weight:** 175 lbs.
Bats: left **Throws:** right
Acquired: Traded from Braves with Yorkis Perez for Damon Berryhill and Mike Bielecki, 9/91

Player Summary	
Fantasy Value	$3 to $5
Card Value	15¢ to 20¢
Will	get people out
Can't	be sideshow
Expect	less bullpen work
Don't Expect	double-figure wins

Steven John "Turk" Wendell has a chance to be one of baseball's best-known players, a combination of personality and talent. Running everywhere, hustling to pick up a ground ball, chewing licorice on the mound, and generally adding a refreshing presence, that's all part of Wendell's game. But when the action starts, he is said to be all business. Wendell pitched for Double-A Greenville of the Southern League in 1991, and was among the top strikeout artists in the Braves' organization. He was the starting pitcher in the Double-A All-Star Game. He throws a sinker and slider and a good change. After entering the Atlanta chain as a starting pitcher, Wendell has recently appeared in both starting and relief roles. The bleacher bums in Wrigley will appreciate his personality in proportion to how many people he retires. His quirky character alone will buoy his 1992 card values up to 20 cents. He is a $4 fantasy draft.

Professional Pitching Register

	W	L	ERA	G	CG	IP	H	ER	BB	SO
88 R	3	8	3.83	14	6	101.0	85	43	30	87
89 A	11	11	2.07	25	10	183.0	140	42	47	180
89 AA	0	0	9.82	1	0	3.2	7	4	1	3
90 A	1	3	1.86	6	1	38.2	24	8	15	26
90 AA	4	9	5.74	36	1	91.0	105	58	48	85
91 AAA	0	2	3.43	3	1	21.0	20	8	16	18
91 AA	11	3	2.56	25	1	147.2	130	42	51	122

ROOKIE PROSPECTS

RONDELL WHITE

Position: Outfield
Team: Montreal Expos
Born: Feb. 23, 1972 Milledgeville, GA
Height: 6'1" **Weight:** 205 lbs.
Bats: right **Throws:** right
Acquired: First-round pick in 6/90 free-agent draft

Player Summary	
Fantasy Value	$3 to $7
Card Value	10¢ to 20¢
Will	challenge catchers
Can't	throw people out
Expect	better average
Don't Expect	big-time pop

White was the Expos' second pick in the draft and in just two pro seasons he has justified that high opinion. Playing in the Class-A South Atlantic League in 1991, he showed both power and speed and enjoyed his second consecutive honors-filled season. He had a .413 slugging percentage and a .349 on-base average in '91. He made the All-Star team, the second year in a row he has done so. One year after being named Player of the Month for July, White batted .345 with three homers and 13 RBI in August, collecting 11 multiple-hit games. He led the Expos chain in stolen bases by a wide margin, and could one day reach double figures in doubles, triples, and homers. White is described as an outstanding outfielder with a work ethic to match, but is quite bluntly said to have a poor arm. Some of that can be addressed through work on mechanics. But the more he hits, the better his arm gets. His fantasy value stops at $7 at this point. His current cards are fine buys at prices less than 20 cents.

Professional Batting Register

	BA	G	AB	R	H	2B	3B	HR	RBI	SB
90 R	.297	57	222	33	66	8	4	5	34	10
91 A	.260	123	465	80	121	23	6	12	67	51

BRIAN WILLIAMS

Position: Pitcher
Team: Houston Astros
Born: Feb. 15, 1969 Lancaster, SC
Height: 6'2" **Weight:** 195 lbs.
Bats: right **Throws:** right
Acquired: First-round pick in 6/90 free-agent draft

Player Summary	
Fantasy Value	$1 to $3
Card Value	5¢ to 10¢
Will	cut down walks
Can't	go the route
Expect	'92 at Triple-A
Don't Expect	stingy ERA

Williams made extraordinary strides in 1991, more than making up for a 1990 campaign that essentially was a bust. He pitched only six and two-thirds innings before his arm got tender that year, and the organization shut him down rather than risk damage to such a high pick. Williams attended the Instructional League to make sure his arm was sound and to get innings. In 1991, he then made a meteoric jump through the system, and may be in the majors to stay before very long. Williams has a live arm and is a power pitcher now, though he may drop down a bit after he goes to his breaking ball a little more. He throws a fastball, curve, and straight change. Williams attended South Carolina and not only excelled on the mound, but hit .309 in his career. Williams played for Team USA in 1989. He needs to win at Double-A or higher before he will be a fantasy draft. His current cards are good buys, though.

Professional Pitching Register

	W	L	ERA	G	CG	IP	H	ER	BB	SO
90 A	0	0	4.05	3	0	6.2	6	3	6	7
91 A	6	4	2.91	15	0	89.2	72	29	40	67
91 AA	2	1	4.20	3	0	15.0	17	7	7	15
91 AAA	0	1	4.93	7	0	38.1	39	21	22	29
91	0	1	3.75	2	0	12.0	11	5	4	4

ROOKIE PROSPECTS

BRANDON WILSON

Position: Shortstop
Team: Chicago White Sox
Born: Feb. 26, 1969 Owensboro, KY
Height: 6'1" **Weight:** 170 lbs.
Bats: right **Throws:** right
Acquired: 18th-round pick in 6/90 free-agent draft

Player Summary	
Fantasy Value	$1 to $3
Card Value	5¢ to 7¢
Will	hit .300
Can't	jump to Triple-A
Expect	100 runs
Don't Expect	power

In only his second year of pro ball, Wilson emerged as a candidate for the White Sox infield of the future. He played for Class-A South Bend of the Midwest League and showed high offensive potential, especially to be the catalyst in a lineup. Making sure that his speed was put to good use, Wilson both drew walks and hit for average. The result was an impressive pile of stolen bases and runs. Wilson, who played baseball at the University of Kentucky, also ranked among the leaders in all of the minor leagues in batting average in 1991. An extremely consistent hitter, at one point Wilson batted safely in 35 of 41 games, for a .357 average. He had a .391 slugging average and a .392 on-base percentage at South Bend in '91. A member of a state championship team in high school, he has shown virtually no power as a pro. Based on 1991, Wilson could be headed for high Class-A or Double-A in 1992. He is too far away to put a bid in. His cards are not good buys yet.

Professional Batting Register

	BA	G	AB	R	H	2B	3B	HR	RBI	SB
90 R	.268	11	41	4	11	1	0	0	5	3
90 A	.248	53	165	31	41	2	0	0	14	14
91 A	.313	125	463	75	145	18	6	2	49	41
91 AA	.400	2	10	3	4	1	0	0	2	0

MARK WOHLERS

Position: Pitcher
Team: Atlanta Braves
Born: Jan. 23, 1970 Holyoke, MA
Height: 6'4" **Weight:** 207 lbs.
Bats: right **Throws:** right
Acquired: 10th-round pick in 6/88 free-agent draft

Player Summary	
Fantasy Value	$6 to $12
Card Value	15¢ to 25¢
Will	be Atlanta's closer
Can't	finesse hitters
Expect	30 saves
Don't Expect	contact

If Wohlers goes on to make a name for himself as a big league closer, it will be interesting to look back and reflect that he didn't even earn a save until his third pro season. In fact, only 10 of his first 41 appearances came out of the bullpen. But in 1990, Wohlers became almost exclusively a reliever, was the outstanding pitcher in the Braves' minor league system, and now he may be baseball's next dominating closer. Owner of a fastball that has been clocked at or near 100 mph, Wohlers contributed to the Braves' fine season in 1991. He was on the mound for two innings of a combined 1-0 no-hitter over San Diego, though he got neither a win nor a save. Wohlers was at three different rungs in '91, and succeeded on all three. Lock Wohlers in for your fantasy team at up to $12, and stockpile his 1992 cards up to a quarter each.

Professional Pitching Register

	W	L	ERA	G	S	IP	H	ER	BB	SO
88 R	5	3	3.32	13	0	59.2	47	22	50	49
89 R	1	1	5.48	14	0	46.0	48	28	28	50
89 A	2	7	6.49	14	0	68.0	74	49	59	51
90 A	5	4	1.88	37	5	52.2	27	11	20	85
90 AA	0	1	4.02	14	6	15.2	14	7	14	20
91 AA	0	0	0.57	28	21	31.1	9	2	13	44
91 AAA	1	0	1.03	23	11	26.1	23	3	12	22
91 NL	3	1	3.20	17	2	19.2	17	7	13	13

ROOKIE PROSPECTS

DMITRI YOUNG

Position: Infield
Team: St. Louis Cardinals
Born: Oct. 11, 1973 Vicksburg, MS
Height: 6'2" **Weight:** 215 lbs.
Bats: both **Throws:** right
Acquired: First-round pick in 6/91 free-agent draft

Player Summary	
Fantasy Value	$1 to $3
Card Value	5¢ to 10¢
Will	increase power
Can't	be rushed
Expect	300 plateau
Don't Expect	rapid rise

Young accomplished some extraordinary feats for a 17-year-old. Maybe the best tribute came from his fellow players at Johnson City of the rookie Appalachian League, who would watch him take batting practice. Young made quite a debut, singling home a run in his first at bat. In his third trip to the plate, he drove a ball over the gap in right. It not only cleared the baseball park, but passed over the bleachers on an adjoining football field, a shot estimated at 450 feet. Rated the best high school hitter in the country, Young was the fourth overall pick in the draft and signed for $385,000. A switch-hitter, he has great power and some speed, especially for someone of his size. He compiled a .380 slugging percentage and a .364 on-base average in 1991. He had 21 walks against 28 strikeouts. So far, Young has shown ability at third base, playing the bunt well and defending down the line. He is not ready for a fantasy draft yet, but he will be one of the top futures taken in 1993. His current cards are fine buys at a nickel each.

Professional Batting Register

	BA	G	AB	R	H	2B	3B	HR	RBI	SB
91 R	.256	37	129	22	33	10	0	2	22	2

KEVIN YOUNG

Position: Infield
Team: Pittsburgh Pirates
Born: June 16, 1969 Kansas City, MO
Height: 6'3" **Weight:** 210 lbs.
Bats: right **Throws:** right
Acquired: Seventh-round pick in 6/90 free-agent draft

Player Summary	
Fantasy Value	$1 to $3
Card Value	5¢ to 10¢
Will	get his hits
Can't	win Gold Glove
Expect	25 doubles
Don't Expect	jump to majors

A career in the majors could be all in the numbers for Young, who wore No. 22 during his 1991 stint with Class-A Carolina of the Southern League. The previous owner of that numeral was John Wehner, who made the jump to the Pirates in 1991. If Young keeps hitting the way he can, it shouldn't be long before he follows Wehner to the bigs. After being summoned from Class-A in June, Young batted .406 for July, narrowly missing Player of the Month honors. The only reason he didn't claim the batting title was because he didn't spend enough time there. Young, a consistent hitter who avoids strikeouts, assembled two 10-game streaks and never went more than two games without a base hit. With his size, he may eventually hit with power. That size should also help him knock down some balls at third. He's had some trouble with throws, but should improve with time. He is a sleeper pick for your fantasy reserves at $3. His current cards are priced right at a nickel each.

Professional Batting Register

	BA	G	AB	R	H	2B	3B	HR	RBI	SB
90 A	.244	72	238	46	58	93	2	5	30	10
91 A	.313	56	201	38	63	11	4	6	28	3
91 AA	.342	75	263	36	90	19	6	3	33	9
91 AAA	.222	4	9	1	2	1	0	0	2	0

ROOKIE PROSPECTS

ED ZINTER

Position: Pitcher
Team: San Diego Padres
Born: Nov. 27, 1967 Denver, CO
Height: 6'3" **Weight:** 210 lbs.
Bats: right **Throws:** right
Acquired: 38th-round pick in 6/89 free-agent draft

Player Summary	
Fantasy Value	$1 to $2
Card Value	5¢ to 10¢
Will	cut ERA in half
Can't	stay out of jams
Expect	20 saves
Don't Expect	control artist

Zinter has found himself a niche as one of the minor leagues' top closers. He has pitched three years in the pros, and has reached double figures in saves the last two. Zinter worked both as a starter and reliever upon entering pro ball with Class-A Spokane of the Northwest League in 1989, but became a reliever the following season. He worked for Class-A High Desert of the California League in 1991, and tied for the league lead in saves. His size gives him a presence on the mound and his stuff is considered to be of major league caliber. Zinter throws a fastball and slider, but has problems with consistency and control. If another year of experience gives him that total command, look out. The question is where the next level will be and what exactly will be his role. Wait until he harnesses his location before you draft him for your fantasy reserves. His current cards, at a nickel or so, should remain on the shelves until then, too.

Professional Pitching Register

	W	L	ERA	G	S	IP	H	ER	BB	SO
89 A	6	4	2.70	17	2	73.1	64	22	37	89
90 A	3	2	2.20	45	17	57.1	43	14	23	65
91 A	6	6	5.49	50	18	59.0	55	36	53	72

ED ZOSKY

Position: Shortstop
Team: Toronto Blue Jays
Born: Feb. 10, 1968 Whittier, CA
Height: 6' **Weight:** 175 lbs.
Bats: right **Throws:** right
Acquired: First-round pick in 6/89 free-agent draft

Player Summary	
Fantasy Value	$4 to $8
Card Value	15¢ to 25¢
Will	start for Jays
Can't	hit long ball
Expect	fine glove
Don't Expect	Tony Fernandez numbers

Zosky's presence in the wings was one reason the Blue Jays dealt Tony Fernandez to the Padres after the 1991 season. However, Zosky didn't make the Blue Jays right away, instead going to Triple-A Syracuse of the International League. There he made his share of errors, possibly an indication that the extra stint in the minors wasn't such a bad idea. He was called to the Blue Jays in September and should be there for good. Zosky was voted to the IL All-Star team, the second time in his minor league career he achieved league All-Star status. He had been named to the Double-A Southern League squad in 1990. The 19th overall pick in the draft, Zosky was a *Sporting News* and *Baseball America* All-America in 1989 while with Fresno State. He may never rival Fernandez as a hitter, but shortstops maybe are best judged by the chemistry they bring, and it will take time before Zosky can be evaluated. His 1992 cards are locks as 15-cent investments. Draft him for $8 tops.

Professional Batting Register

	BA	G	AB	R	H	2B	3B	HR	RBI	SB
89 AA	.221	56	208	21	46	5	3	2	14	1
90 AA	.271	115	450	53	122	20	7	3	45	3
91 AAA	.264	119	511	69	135	18	4	6	39	9
91 AL	.148	18	27	2	4	1	1	0	2	0

Team Overviews

You'll find an overview of each of the 26 major league organizations in this section. The section is arranged by the finish each club had in 1991, starting with the AL West, followed by the AL East, the NL West, and the NL East.

The teams are ordered as follows: Minnesota Twins, Chicago White Sox, Texas Rangers, Oakland Athletics, Seattle Mariners, Kansas City Royals, and California Angels in the AL West; Toronto Blue Jays, Boston Red Sox, Detroit Tigers, Milwaukee Brewers, New York Yankees, Baltimore Orioles, and Cleveland Indians in the AL East; Atlanta Braves, Los Angeles Dodgers, San Diego Padres, San Francisco Giants, Cincinnati Reds, and Houston Astros in the NL West; and the Pittsburgh Pirates, St. Louis Cardinals, Philadelphia Phillies, Chicago Cubs, New York Mets, and Montreal Expos in the NL East.

Each team overview begins with an analysis of that club's key players (not all of each ballclub's players were mentioned); the team's '91 season is examined as well. The manager section includes the skipper's overall record, including each major league ballclub he has managed, his overall record with his current team, and his record in 1991. The abbreviations for managers are: **W** = wins; **L** = losses; **PCT** = winning percentage. The executives listed make up the ownership and baseball structure for each organization.

The "Five-Year Finishes" show in what place each organization finished in its division in the last five years and their overall record. If two or more clubs were tied for a position—such as the Chicago Cubs and the Philadelphia Phillies, who tied for third in the 1991 NL East—each ballclub gets a "T" designation; the Cubs and the Phillies received a 3T. The ballparks that the franchise has occupied, plus the years that the organization was there, are shown. If more than one ballpark is listed for a season, the franchise occupied both parks that year. The seating capacity, attendance, and the dimensions of the present ballpark are included with the team's address. A brief history of each organization is presented with an emphasis on how each franchise has done over the last 15 to 20 years.

AMERICAN LEAGUE WEST

Minnesota Twins
95-67, .586 Manager: Tom Kelly

The World Champion 1991 Twins were a baseball fairy tale, rising from a basement finish in 1990 to join the Atlanta Braves as the only teams ever to go from last place to the World Series in just one year. The Twins blended a potent offense (.280 team average) with a spectacular starting pitching troika to dust all comers in the AL West and Toronto in the ALCS. Kirby Puckett was again sensational (.319, 15 HR, 89 RBI), and his supporting cast of catcher Brian Harper (.311), outfielder Shane Mack (.310), and first baseman Kent Hrbek (.284, 20 HR, 89 RBI) was strong all year. Free-agent acquisition Chili Davis (.277, 29 HR, 93 RBI) performed beyond anyone's expectations at designated hitter, and '91 AL Rookie of the Year Chuck Knoblauch was a revelation at second. Scott Erickson (20-8) was the staff ace in his first full year in the majors, while free-agent signee Jack Morris (18-12) was strong all year. He was the World Series MVP. Kevin Tapani (16-9) rebounded from a dreadful first half. Rick Aguilera (42 saves) and Carl Willis (8-3) were bullpen stalwarts.

Manager Tom Kelly	W	L	PCT
Major League record	437	396	.525
With Twins, 1986-91	437	396	.525
1991 record	95	67	.586

Coaches: Terry Crowley, Ron Gardenhire, Tony Oliva, Dick Such, Rick Stelmaszek, Wayne Terwilliger

Five-Year Finishes
91	90	89	88	87
1	7	5	2	1

Five-Year Record: 425-385, .527

Ballparks

Washington: American League Park 1901-1910; Griffith Stadium 1911-1960. **Minnesota:** Metropolitan Stadium 1961-1981; Hubert H. Humphrey Metrodome 1982-present

Owner: Carl R. Pohlad
President: Jerry Bell
Executive Vice President, General Manager: Andy MacPhail
Director of Minor Leagues: Jim Rantz
Director of Scouting: Terry Ryan

Capacity: 55,883
1991 Attendance: 2,293,842
Surface: artificial turf
Stationary Dome
Left field fence: 343 feet
Center field fence: 408 feet
Right field fence: 327 feet
Left-center fence: 385 feet
Right-center fence: 367 feet

Address
501 Chicago Avenue So.
Minneapolis, MN 55415

Team History

As the Washington Senators, this franchise mixed a few highs—three pennants, a 1924 World Championship—with years of deep lows. After a move to the Twin Cities in 1960, the team won the 1965 pennant but slid out of contention for most of the next two decades. The team moved indoors in 1982 and captured the World Series in '87 with a young team of sluggers, and the championship again in 1991.

AMERICAN LEAGUE WEST

Chicago White Sox
87-75, .534, 8 Manager: Jeff Torborg

The Sox moved into "new" Comiskey Park in 1991 but didn't adjust quickly to their new surroundings. A slow start doomed Chicago, which brimmed with potential following last year's run at the AL West title. Despite challenging during the second half, the Sox were again runners-up, eight games out. And they'll begin the 1992 season without manager Jeff Torborg, who defected to the Mets. Still, the emergence of slugging second-year first baseman Frank Thomas (.318, 32 HR, 109 RBI) was a pretty good consolation prize. So was the performance of sophomore third baseman Robin Ventura (.284, 23 HR, 100 RBI). Center fielder Lance Johnson (.274), slick-fielding shortstop Ozzie Guillen (.273), and reliable catcher Carlton Fisk (18 HR, 74 RBI) were valuable offensive weapons. But leadoff man Tim Raines slumped somewhat. Pitching highlights included rookie Wilson Alvarez's no-hitter in August and Jack McDowell's 17-10 (191 strikeouts) record. But other Sox starters—Charlie Hough (9-10), Greg Hibbard (11-11) and Alex Fernandez (9-13)—were inconsistent. Closer Bobby Thigpen (37 saves) fell well off his major league record pace of 1990.

Manager Gene LaMont	W	L	PCT
Major League record	0	0	.000
With White Sox, 1991	0	0	.000
1991 record	0	0	.000

Coaches: Terry Bevington, Walt Hriniak, Joe Nossak, Doug Mansolini, Mike Squires, Jackie Brown

Five-Year Finishes

91	90	89	88	87
2	2	7	5	5

Five-Year Record: 398-410, .493

Ballparks
South Side Park 1901-1910; Comiskey Park 1911-1990; New Comiskey Park 1991-present

Capacity: 44,702
1991 Attendance: 2,934,154
Surface: natural grass
Left field fence: 347 feet
Center field fence: 400 feet
Right field fence: 347 feet
Left-center fence: 375 feet
Right-center fence: 375 feet

Chairman: Jerry Reinsdorf
Vice Chairman: Eddie Einhorn
Executive Vice President: Howard Pizer
Senior Vice President, Major League Operations: Ron Schueler
Director of Minor League Operations: Steve Noworyta
Director of Scouting: Duane Shaffer

Address
333 W. 35th Street
Chicago, IL 60616

Team History

A stepchild to the cross-town rival Cubs, the White Sox have had a disappointing history. They won the AL pennant in their first year (1901) and captured World Championships in 1906 and 1917. Chicago is infamous for throwing the 1919 World Series and didn't win another pennant until 1959, with the Go-Go Sox. An AL West title in 1983 is the extent of the Sox's recent success.

AMERICAN LEAGUE WEST

Texas Rangers
85-77, .525, 10 Manager: Bobby Valentine

The Rangers were exciting, thanks to a club-record 14-game winning streak in May, a potent offense and the 44-year-old arm of Nolan Ryan. That added up to a third-place finish, eight games above .500. The Rangers scored more runs than any other team in baseball (829) and were fueled by a host of big hitters. Second baseman Julio Franco (.341, 15 HR, 78 RBI) won the batting title, while first sacker Rafael Palmeiro (.322, 26 HR, 88 RBI) and right fielder Ruben Sierra (.307 25 HR, 116 RBI) were deadly. Left fielder Juan Gonzalez (27 HR, 102 RBI) starred in his first full big league season, while first-year DH Kevin Reimer showed promise. The pitching staff was not so effective. Ryan (12-6, 2.91 ERA, 203 strikeouts) was overpowering, Jose Guzman (13-7, 3.08 ERA) rebounded impressively from a shoulder injury, and Jeff Russell (30 saves) was an impressive closer. But Kevin Brown (9-12, 4.40 ERA) struggled, Bobby Witt was injured, and Oil Can Boyd fizzled.

Manager
Bobby Valentine	W	L	PCT
Major League record	536	564	.487
With Rangers, 1985-1991	536	564	.487
1991 record:	85	77	.525

Coaches: Orlando Gomez, Toby Harrah, Tom House, Dave Oliver, Tom Robson, Ray Burris

Five-Year Finishes
91	90	89	88	87
3	3	4	6	7

Five-Year Record: 396-413, .490

Ballparks

Washington: Griffith Stadium 1961; Robert F. Kennedy Stadium 1962-1971 **Texas:** Arlington Stadium 1972-present

Capacity: 43,521
1991 Attendance: 2,297,718
Surface: natural grass
Left field fence: 330 feet
Center field fence: 400 feet
Right field fence: 330 feet
Left-center fence: 380 feet
Right-center fence: 380 feet

General Partner: George W. Bush
General Partner: Edward W. "Rusty" Rose
President: J. Thomas Schieffer
Vice President, General Manager: Thomas A. Grieve
Assistant G.M., Player Personnel, and Scouting: Sandy Johnson

Address
P.O. Box 91111
1250 Copeland Road
Arlington, TX 76004

Team History

What can you expect from a team that began as the reincarnation of the Washington Senators? In the three decades since its inception in 1961 in the nation's capital, this franchise has won no titles and has rarely snuck above .500. Since their 1972 move to Arlington, the Rangers have been a perennial also-ran in the AL West, contending rarely.

AMERICAN LEAGUE WEST

Oakland Athletics
84-78, .519, 11 Manager: Tony LaRussa

Instead of making their expected late-season charge, the A's stayed mired in the middle of the AL West and finished 11 games off the pace. The three-time AL champions' demise was caused by the disintegration of its pitching staff. Dave Stewart won only 11 games, and 1990 Cy Young winner Bob Welch slipped to 12-13. Mike Moore (17-8, 2.96 ERA) was the staff ace, but no other starter had a winning record. Even bullpen terminator Dennis Eckersley (43 saves, 2.96 ERA) looked mortal at times. The A's offense wasn't much better, ranking next-to-last in the league in team average. Dave Henderson (.276, 25 HR, 85 RBI) started fast, but cooled quickly, and Rickey Henderson (.258, 18 HR, 58 steals) was disappointing. Jose Canseco made headlines with his bat (44 HR, 122 RBI) and his mouth, criticizing Oakland's fans, and Mark McGwire (.201, 22 HR) swung for the fences with poor results. Harold Baines (.295) and Terry Steinbach (.274) were steady, but an early season injury to shortstop Walter Weiss hurt the team's defense.

Manager Tony LaRussa	W	L	PCT
Major League record	1038	883	.540
With A's, 1986-90	516	373	.580
1991 record	84	78	.519

Coaches: Rick Burleson, Dave Duncan, Art Kusnyer, Rene Lachemann, Dave McKay, Tommie Reynolds, Doug Radar

Five-Year Finishes

91	90	89	88	87
4	1	1	1	3

Five-Year Record: 471-339, .582

Owner/Managing General Partner: Walter A. Haas, Jr.
President/Chief Operating Officer: Walter J. Haas
Vice President, Baseball Operations: Sandy Alderson
Director of Player Development: Karl Kuehl
Director of Scouting: Dick Bogard
Director of Baseball Administration: Walt Jocketty

Ballparks

Philadelphia: Columbia Park 1901-1908; Shibe Park 1909-1954. **Kansas City:** Municipal Stadium 1955-1967. **Oakland:** Oakland-Alameda County Stadium 1968-present

Capacity: 47,313
1991 Attendance: 2,713,463
Surface: natural grass
Left field fence: 330 feet
Center field fence: 400 feet
Right field fence: 330 feet
Left-center fence: 375 feet
Right-center fence: 375 feet

Address
Oakland-Alameda County Coliseum
Oakland, CA 94621

Team History

Fans of the A's are able to point to four periods of glory. Formed in 1901 in Philadelphia, the A's captured World Championships in 1910, 1911, and '13, and 1929 and 1930, before embarking on a dismal period that saw the franchise move to Kansas City and then to Oakland. More world titles came in 1972 to '74, and recent history includes pennants from 1988 to '90 and the 1989 World Championship.

AMERICAN LEAGUE WEST

Seattle Mariners
83-79, .512, 12 Manager: Jim Lefebrve

Champagne corks might well have been popping all over Seattle last October when the Mariners clinched the franchise's first-ever above-.500 finish. Still, the 83-79 record was well off the AL West division leader, Minnesota, and Jim Lefebvre got the axe following the season. Ken Griffey, Jr. (.327, 22 HR, 100 RBI) had a huge season, and for once, he got some support. Third baseman Edgar Martinez (.307, 14 HR) had another good year, while first baseman Pete O'Brien (17 HR, 88 RBI) and right fielder Jay Buhner (27 HR, 77 RBI) provided some power. Second-year shortstop Omar Vizquel showed promise, but the Mariners could have used more from catcher Dave Valle. Seattle's pitching staff boasted a team ERA of 3.79, fourth-best in the American League. Free-agent acquisition Bill Krueger (11-8) and Randy Johnson (13-10, 228 strikeouts) bolstered the starting rotation, and Brian Holman and rookie Rich DeLucia each won more than 10 games. Bill Swift, Rob Murphy, Russ Swan, and Mike Jackson comprised a formidable bullpen.

Manager Bill Plummer	W	L	PCT
Major League record	0	0	.000
With Mariners, 1992	0	0	.000
1991 record	0	0	.000
Coaches: Gene Clines, Rusty Kuntz, Russ Nixon			

Five-Year Finishes

91	90	89	88	87
5	5	6	7	4

Five-Year Record: 379-430, .469

Ballparks

Kingdome 1977-present

Capacity: 57,748
1991 Attendance: 2,147,905
Surface: artificial turf
Stationary Dome
Left field fence: 331 feet
Center field fence: 405 feet
Right field fence: 312 feet
Left-center fence: 372 feet
Right-center fence: 349 feet

Chairman: Jeff Smulyan
President: Gary Kaseff
Vice President, Baseball Operations: Woody Woodward
Vice President, Scouting & Player Development: Roger Jongewaard
Director of Baseball Administration: Lee Pelekoudas

Address
P.O. Box 4100
Seattle, WA 98104

Team History

As one of only two teams—the Rangers are the other—never to win a division championship or a pennant, the Mariners have brought little joy to fans in the Pacific Northwest. Since its birth in 1977, Seattle had never been above .500 or finished in the top half of the AL West. The M's enjoyed their first winning year in 1991.

AMERICAN LEAGUE WEST

Kansas City Royals
82-80, .506, 13 Managers: John Wathan (16-22), Hal McRae (66-58)

For the second consecutive season, a poor start doomed the Royals—and cost manager John Wathan his job after just 38 games. Hal McRae took over and helped the Royals to an 82-80 finish. The Royals' offense was hurt before the season even began by Bo Jackson's celebrated hip injury, and though Danny Tartabull (.316, 31 HR, 100 RBI) assumed the power mantle well, he had little help in the run producing department. George Brett slumped to .255, and Kirk Gibson hit just .236. But Jim Eisenreich (.301), Todd Benzinger (.294) and Bill Pecota (.286) had good seasons. The starting pitching was again a problem, despite a good recovery by Bret Saberhagen (13-8, 3.07 ERA), who threw a no-hitter in August. Second-year man Kevin Appier (13-10, 158 strikeouts) was again steady, but free-agent acquisition Mike Boddicker (12-12) didn't duplicate his big 1990 season with Boston. Mark Gubicza (9-12) was a big disappointment, though Mark Davis showed some potential in a few late starts. Jeff Montgomery led the bullpen with 33 saves.

Manager Hal McRae	W	L	PCT
Major League record	66	58	.532
With Royals, 1991	66	58	.532
1991 record:	66	58	.532

Coaches: Lee May, Bruce Kison, Lynn Jones, Adrian Garrett, Glenn Ezell, Guy Hansen

Five-Year Finishes

91	90	89	88	87
6	6	2	3	2

Five-Year Record: 404-392, .508

Ballparks
Municipal Stadium 1969-1972; Royals Stadium 1973-present

Chairman of the Board/Owner: Ewing Kauffman
President: Joe Burke
Executive Vice President & General Manager: Herk Robinson
Vice President-Director of Player Personnel: Joe Klein
Director of Scouting: Art Stewart

Capacity: 40,625
1991 Attendance: 2,161,537
Surface: artificial turf
Left field fence: 330 feet
Center field fence: 410 feet
Right field fence: 330 feet
Left-center fence: 385 feet
Right-center fence: 385 feet

Address
1 Royal Way
Kansas City, MO 64129

Team History
Born in 1968 to fill a void left by the departed A's, the Royals moved quickly to the top of the AL West, winning divisional titles from 1976 to '78. The team took its first pennant in 1980, and after another West crown in 1984, finally won a World Championship in 1985, overcoming 3-1 deficits in the playoffs and World Series.

AMERICAN LEAGUE WEST

California Angels
81-81, .500, 14 Managers: Doug Rader (60-63), Buck Rodgers (21-18)

The 1991 Angels had the dubious distinction of finishing last in the only division ever to have all its members finish .500 or better. The Angels started well, then fell apart, forcing management to replace manager Doug Rader with Buck Rodgers. Despite the last-place finish, the Angels did boast three starters—Mark Langston (19-8, 3.00 ERA, 183 strikeouts), Jim Abbott (18-11, 2.89 ERA, 158 Ks), and Chuck Finley (18-9, 171 strikeouts)—among the league leaders in wins. California also featured the American League's top reliever, fireballer Bryan Harvey (46 saves, 1.60 ERA, 101 strikeouts). But the rest of the rotation struggled, particularly Kirk McCaskill (10-19). The offense just didn't score enough runs, despite some fine performances. First baseman Wally Joyner (.301, 21 HR, 96 RBI) rebounded big, and right fielder Dave Winfield (28 HR, 86 RBI) was productive. Luis Polonia (.296, 48 steals) was dangerous at the top of the lineup, and free-agent acquisition Gary Gaetti (18 HR, 66 RBI) was solid at third base. Luis Sojo showed promise in his first full year at second base.

Manager

Buck Rodgers	W	L	PCT
Major League record	695	648	.517
With Angels, 1991	21	18	.538
1991 record	21	18	.538

Coaches: John Wathan, Ken Macha, Rod Carew, Deron Johnson, Bruce Hines, Bobby Knoop, Marcel Lachemann, Frank Reberger, Jimmie Reese

Five-Year Finishes

91	90	89	88	87
7	4	3	4	6

Five-Year Record: 402-408, .496

Ballparks

Los Angeles: Wrigley Field 1961; Dodger Stadium 1962-1965. **Anaheim:** Anaheim Stadium 1966-present

Chairman of the Board: Gene Autry
President & CEO: Richard M. Brown
Senior Vice President, Director of Player Personnel: Whitey Herzog
Senior Vice President, Baseball Operations: Daniel F. O'Brien
Director, Minor League Operations: Bill Bavasi
Director of Scouting: Bob Fontaine, Jr.

Capacity: 64,593
1991 Attendance: 2,416,236
Surface: natural grass
Left field fence: 333 feet
Center field fence: 404 feet
Right field fence: 333 feet
Left-center fence: 386 feet
Right-center fence: 386 feet

Address
P.O. Box 2000
Anaheim, CA 92803

Team History

Cowboy singer Gene Autry gave birth to the Angels in Los Angeles in 1961, and he has yet to enjoy an American League pennant. Though third in 1964, the Angels faltered for the next 14 years. California won the AL West in 1979 and 1982, and came within one pitch of the pennant in 1986, losing to Boston.

AMERICAN LEAGUE EAST

Toronto Blue Jays
91-71, .562 Manager: Cito Gaston

They said it wouldn't happen, but it did. After surviving its traditional September swoon to win the AL East, Toronto dropped three straight home games in the ALCS and blew another World Series shot. Despite the playoff stumble, Toronto treated 4 million-plus Skydome fans to a big season, featuring speed, not power, and great pitching. Gene Tenace filled in for ailing skipper Cito Gaston and went 19-14. Second baseman Roberto Alomar (.295, 53 steals) and center fielder Devon White (.282, 33 steals) triggered the Jays, while newcomer Joe Carter (33 HR, 108 RBI) provided the pop. First baseman John Olerud (17 HR) had a fine season, as did third bagger Kelly Gruber (20 HR). Rance Mulliniks was a valuable in the infield, and second-year catcher Greg Myers showed promise. Though perennial ace Dave Steib missed most of the year with an injury, Jimmy Key (16-12), surprising rookie Juan Guzman (10-3), David Wells (15-10), Todd Stottlemyre (15-8), and Tom Candiotti (13-13, 2.65 ERA) comprised a formidable rotation. Tom Henke (32 saves) and Duane Ward (23 saves) were the league's most imposing bullpen tandem.

Manager
Cito Gaston	W	L	PCT
Major League record	227	176	.563
With Blue Jays, 1989-91	227	176	.563
1991 record	72	57	.558

Coaches: Galen Cisco, John Sullivan, Rich Hacker, Gene Tenace

Five-Year Finishes
91	90	89	88	87
1	2	1	3	2

Five-Year Record: 449-361, .554

Ballparks

Exhibition Stadium 1977-1989; The Skydome 1989-present

Chairman: William R. Ferguson
Vice Chairman & Chief Executive Officer: P.N.T. Widdrington
President & Chief Operation Officer: Paul Beeston
Executive Vice President, Baseball: Pat Gillick
Vice President, Baseball: Bob Mattick
Vice President, Baseball: Al LaMacchia

Capacity: 50,516
1991 Attendance: 4,001,526
Surface: artificial turf
Retractable Dome
Left field fence: 328 feet
Center field fence: 400 feet
Right field fence: 328 feet
Left-center fence: 375 feet
Right-center fence: 375 feet

Address
The Skydome
300 Bremner Blvd.
Toronto, Ontario M5V 3B3

Team History

Unlike their 1977 expansion siblings, Seattle, the Blue Jays have had some success. Toronto asserted itself in the early 1980s and became a contender. The Jays won the 1985 AL East crown but choked away the '87 title, losing their last seven games. Toronto rebounded to win the division again in 1989 and 1991.

AMERICAN LEAGUE EAST

Boston Red Sox
84-78, .519, 7 Manager: Joe Morgan

Despite rallying from an 11-game August deficit, the Sox couldn't overtake Toronto for the AL East crown. The disappointing finish led the Sox to replace manager Joe Morgan with former Sox player Butch Hobson. He'll have some big expectations, just as Morgan did in '91 when management brought high-priced free-agent slugger Jack Clark and pitchers Matt Young and Danny Darwin to Beantown and appeased pitching staff ace Roger Clemens with a giant contract. Except for a midseason slump, 1991 Cy Young Award winner Clemens was again great, (18-10, 2.62 ERA, 241 strikeouts), and he got some help from Joe Hesketh (12-4). But Young and Darwin were awful, and last year's surprise, Greg Harris, slumped to 11-12. Though he started slowly, Clark (28 HR, 87 RBI) keyed the late-season resurgence. Third baseman Wade Boggs (.332) got hot at midseason, and Mike Greenwell (.300, 83 RBI) and Carlos Quintana (.295, 71 RBI) were strong down the stretch. Rookies Mo Vaughn and Phil Plantier (.331) showed promise in August and September.

Manager Butch Hobson	W	L	PCT
Major League record	0	0	.000
With Red Sox, 1992	0	0	.000
1991 record	0	0	.000

Coaches: Don Zimmer, Rich Gale, Al Bumbry, Dick Berardino, Bill Fischer, John McLaren

Ballparks

Huntington Avenue Grounds 1901-1911; Fenway Park 1912-present

Capacity: 34,142
1991 Attendance: 2,562,438
Surface: natural grass
Left field fence: 315 feet
Center field fence: 390 feet
Right field fence: 302 feet
Left-center fence: 379 feet
Right-center fence: 380 feet

Five-Year Finishes

91	90	89	88	87
T2	1	3	1	5

Five-Year Record: 422-388, .521

Majority Owner and Chairwoman of the Board: Jean R. Yawkey
President: John L. Harrrington
Owner and General Partner: Haywood C. Sullivan
Senior Vice President & General Manager: James "Lou" Gorman
Director of Scouting: Edward M. Kasko
Assistant General Manager: Elaine C. Weddington

Address
4 Yawkey Way
Boston, MA 02215

Team History

Long-suffering Beantown fans wish they could be transported back to the early 1900s, when the BoSox were winners—five pennants, four world titles. But after selling Babe Ruth to the Yankees in 1920, the franchise fell fast. The Sox rebounded in the 1940s and '50s, but despite pennants in 1946, 1967, 1975, and 1986, the Sox couldn't win the World Series.

AMERICAN LEAGUE EAST

Detroit Tigers
84-78, .519, 7 Manager: Sparky Anderson

The 1991 Tigers were one of the strangest baseball teams in history. Last in the American league in team pitching, next-to-last in team batting average, Detroit nonetheless contended for the AL East crown until mid-September. The reason? Power. The Tigers mashed 209 homers in '91, but also struck out a league-record 1,184 times. Huge first baseman Cecil Fielder proved his big 1990 season was no fluke with 44 homers and 133 RBI. He had plenty of help. Catcher Mickey Tettleton (31 homers), outfielder Rob Deer (25 homers, 175 strikeouts), second baseman Lou Whitaker (.279, 23 homers), third baseman Travis Fryman (21 homers, 91 RBI) and utilityman Tony Phillips (.284, 17 homers, 72 RBI) provided the rest of the power surge. Since Detroit scored 817 runs (second in the majors), Tiger pitchers didn't need to be precise. Bill Gullickson went 20-9 with a 3.90 ERA. Closer Mike Henneman was 10-2 with 21 saves, while other double-figure winners were veteran Frank Tanana (13-12) and Walt Terrell (12-14).

Manager Sparky Anderson	W	L	PCT
Major League record	1921	1524	.558
With Tigers, 1979-91	1058	938	.530
1991 record	84	78	.519
Coaches: Larry Herndon, Billy Consolo, Billy Muffett, Dick Tracewski			

Five-Year Finishes

91	90	89	88	87
T2	3	7	2	1

Five-Year Record: 408-402, .504

Ballparks

Bennett Park 1901-1911; Tiger Stadium 1912-present

Owner: Thomas S. Monaghan
Chairman-Chief Executive Officer: James A. Campbell
President-Chief Operating Officer: Glenn (Bo) Schembechler
Senior Vice President-Player Procurement & Development: Joseph A. McDonald
Director-Scouting: Jax Robertson

Capacity: 52,416
1991 Attendance: 1,641,661
Surface: natural grass
Left field fence: 340 feet
Center field fence: 440 feet
Right field fence: 325 feet
Left-center fence: 365 feet
Right-center fence: 375 feet

Address
Tiger Stadium
Detroit, MI 48216

Team History

With a winning percentage of well over .500, the Tigers have been perennial contenders since their inception in 1901. They have finished last only four times and have never had more than four consecutive losing seasons. The franchise has won 11 titles and brought World Championships to the Motor City in 1935, 1945, 1968, and 1984.

AMERICAN LEAGUE EAST

Milwaukee Brewers
83-79, .512, 8 Manager: Tom Trebelhorn

It was another tale of disappointment in Brew Town in 1991. Injuries and unproductive free agents mired Milwaukee in the middle of the AL East and cost manager Tom Trebelhorn his job. Hard-luck pitcher Ted Higuera saw limited action, thanks to injuries. But a trio of Brewer starters won 14 or more games apiece, led by surprising Bill Wegman (15-7, 2.84 ERA). Chris Bosio (14-10) and Jaime Navarro (15-12) were also impressive, but closer Dan Plesac saved only eight games and was made a starter late in the season. Rookie Doug Henry (2-1, 1.00 ERA, 15 saves) helped pick up some of the bullpen slack. The Brewers did have a potent offense, led by first baseman Paul Molitor (.325, 17 homers, 75 RBI, 216 hits). Veteran second baseman Willie Randolph (.327) was a pleasant surprise, as was second-year outfielder Darryl Hamilton (.311). Infielders Jim Gantner (.283) and Bill Spiers (.283) had good seasons, but center fielder Robin Yount had his second consecutive down year, and free-agent outfielder Franklin Stubbs (.213) was a flop.

Manager Phil Garner	W	L	PCT
Major League record	0	0	.000
With Brewers, 1992	0	0	.000
1991 record	0	0	.000

Coaches: Larry Hisle, Bob Bailor, Toby Oldham, Bill Castro, Duffy Dyer, Mike Easler, Tim Foli, Dan Rowe

Five-Year Finishes

91	90	89	88	87
4	6	4	4	3

Five-Year Record: 416-394, .514

Ballparks

Seattle: Sicks' Stadium 1969; **Milwaukee:** County Stadium 1970-present

President, Chief Executive Officer: Allan H. (Bud) Selig
Senior Vice President, Baseball Operations: Sal Bando
Senior Vice President: Harry Dalton
Assistant Vice Persident, Baseball Operations: Bruce Manno
Vice President of Scouting: Al Goldis

Capacity: 53,192
1991 Attendance: 1,478,814
Surface: natural grass
Left field fence: 315 feet

Center field fence: 402 feet
Right field fence: 315 feet
Left-center fence: 392 feet
Right-center fence: 392 feet

Address
201 S. 46th Street
Milwaukee, WI 53214

Team History

After a one-year stint as the dreadful Seattle Pilots, this franchise brought baseball back to Milwaukee in 1970. The Brewers floundered in the AL East for much of the next decade but came alive in the early 1980s. The Brew Crew won the division's second-half title in strike-shortened 1981 and took their only AL pennant in 1982.

AMERICAN LEAGUE EAST

New York Yankees
71-91, .438, 20 Manager: Stump Merrill

A season without Steinbrenner didn't change much for the Bronx Bombers in 1991. The Yankees climbed out of the basement but played inconsistent baseball. They had their moments, like a mid-season flirtation with .500, but slumped thereafter. Former third base coach and new manager Buck Showalter has his work cut out for him. Second baseman Steve Sax (.304, 85 runs) rebounded from a lackluster 1990 campaign, and Mel Hall improved to .285, with 19 homers and 80 RBI. First baseman Don Mattingly caused more commotion with his long hair and sore back than his bat (.288, 9 HR, 68 RBI). Catcher Matt Nokes (24 homers, 77 RBI) and outfielder Roberto Kelly (20 homers, 69 RBI) had good seasons, as did rookie third bagger Pat Kelly. Kevin Maas, a rookie sensation in '90, slumped in '91 (.220). Free-agent acquisition Scott Sanderson (16-10, 3.81 ERA) was the ace of a young pitching staff, which included struggling rookies Wade Taylor and Jeff Johnson. Pascual Perez was again hampered by injuries, but Steve Howe (1.68 ERA) rebounded from substance abuse to form an effective bullpen trio with Steve Farr (23 saves, 2.19 ERA) and John Habyan.

Manager Buck Showalter	W	L	PCT
Major League record	0	0	.000
With Yankees, 1992	0	0	.000
1991 record	0	0	.000

Coaches: Frank Howard, Mark Connor, Clete Boyer, Ed Napoleon, Tony Cloninger, Russ Meyer

Five-Year Finishes

91	90	89	88	87
5	7	5	5	4

Five-Year Record: 386-422, .478

Managing General Partner: Robert E. Nederlander
Executive VP & Chief Operating Officer: Leonard L. Kleinman
Senior Vice President: Arthur Richman
Vice President and General Manager: Gene Michael
Vice President, Player Development and Scouting: Brian Sabean
Director of Minor League Operations: Mitch Lukevics

Ballparks

American League Park 1901-1902; Hilltop Park 1903-1912; Polo Grounds 1913-1922; Shea Stadium 1974-1975; Yankee Stadium 1923-1973, 1976-present

Capacity: 57,545
1991 Attendance: 1,863,731
Surface: natural grass
Left field fence: 318 feet
Center field fence: 408 feet
Right field fence: 314 feet
Left-center fence: 399 feet
Right-center fence: 385 feet

Address
Yankee Stadium
Bronx, NY 10451

Team History

Easily baseball's showcase franchise, the Yankees have won a record 22 World Championships and have fielded some of the game's greatest teams, players, and managers. The 1927 Murderer's Row unit featured immortals Babe Ruth and Lou Gehrig, while Hall of Famers like Joe DiMaggio, Yogi Berra and Whitey Ford dotted the rosters in the 1930s, '40s and '50s. The 1977 and '78 championship squads boasted Reggie Jackson and Catfish Hunter.

AMERICAN LEAGUE EAST

Baltimore Orioles

67-95, .414, 24 Managers: Frank Robinson (13-24), Johnny Oates (54-71)

Baltimore bid farewell to venerable Memorial Stadium in 1991 with a sixth-place finish. Fans can only hope the move to the new ballpark at Camden Yards will invigorate the young Orioles, who ranked last in the AL in pitching and near the bottom in hitting. You can't blame Cal Ripken Jr. He turned in MVP numbers (.323, 34 homers, 114 RBI), silencing those who thought playing every day was hurting his production. Joe Orsulak (.278) was again steady in the outfield, and the Orioles got power from Sam Horn (23 homers), Randy Milligan (16 homers, 70 RBI), and Mike Devereaux (19 homers). Starter Bob Milacki (10-9) was one of the few pitching highlights for Baltimore, and he combined with Mark Williamson, Gregg Olson, and Mike Flanagan on a no-hitter in August. Ben McDonald (6-8) was again plagued by arm troubles, but Olson (31 saves) and Todd Frohwirth (1.87 ERA) anchored a solid bullpen.

Manager Johnny Oates	W	L	PCT
Major League record	54	71	.432
With Orioles, 1991	54	71	.432
1991 record	54	71	.432

Coaches: Davey Lopes, Dick Bosman, Greg Biagini, Elrod Hendricks, Cal Ripken Sr.

Five-Year Finishes

91	90	89	88	87
6	5	2	7	6

Five-Year Record: 351-457, .434

Ballparks

Milwaukee: Lloyd Street Grounds 1901. **St. Louis:** Sportsman's Park 1902-1953. **Baltimore:** Memorial Stadium 1954-1991; Oriole Park 1992

Capacity: 46,500
1991 Attendance: 2,552,808
Surface: natural grass
Left field fence: 335 feet
Center field fence: 397 feet
Right field fence: 319 feet
Left-center fence: 410 feet
Right-center fence: 386 feet

Chairman: Eli S. Jacobs
President: Lawrence Lucchino
Executive Vice President and General Manager: Roland A. Helmond
Asst. General Manager, Director of Player Personnel: R. Douglas Melvin
Director of Scouting: Gary Nickels

Address
Oriole Park at Camden Yards
Baltimore, MD 21230

Team History

For nearly 45 years, futility in American League baseball had a home in St. Louis. There the Browns, founded in 1902, wallowed until winning the AL pennant in 1944, though they lost the series to the cross-town Cardinals. The team moved to Baltimore in 1953, became the Orioles and won seven division titles, six pennants and world titles in 1966, 1970, and 1983.

AMERICAN LEAGUE EAST

Cleveland Indians

57-105, .352, 34 Managers: John McNamara (25-52), Mike Hargrove (32-53)

The problems continued in 1991 for the team on Lake Erie—the only AL East team never to win a division title. The Tribe stumbled to a team record 105 losses, dashing the hopes of anyone encouraged by 1990's fourth-place finish. That included skipper John McNamara, who was replaced by Mike Hargrove in mid-season. The Indians sorely lacked power hitting, got a subpar performance from pitching staff ace Greg Swindell (9-16, 3.48 ERA) and had no bullpen consistency. There were some bright spots, however. Speedy Alex Cole hit .295 in his first full year in the outfield, and Albert Belle hit .282 with 28 homers and 95 RBI, despite early season trouble with his temper. Still, he was the only Indian to reach double-figures in home runs. Sandy Alomar was injured early. Infielders Carlos Baerga, Jim Thome, and Felix Fermin showed promise, and young starter Charles Nagy (10-15) showed flashes of becoming a big-time pitcher.

Manager Mike Hargrove	W	L	PCT
Major League record	32	53	.376
With Indians, 1991	32	53	.376
1991 record	32	53	.376

Coaches: Dave Nelson, Jeff Newman, Rick Adair, Ron Clark, Ken Bolek, Dave Chiti

Five-Year Finishes

91	90	89	88	87
7	4	6	6	7

Five-Year Record: 346-464, .427

Ballparks

League Park 1901-1946; Cleveland Stadium 1932-present

Chairman of the Board & CEO: Richard E. Jacobs
President and COO: Hank Peters
Vice President: Rick Bay
Director of Baseball Operations: John Hart
Director of Scouting: Mickey White

Capacity: 74,483
1991 Attendance: 1,051,863
Surface: natural grass
Left field fence: 320 feet
Center field fence: 415 feet
Right field fence: 320 feet
Left-center fence: 400 feet
Right-center fence: 400 feet

Address
Boudreau Blvd.
Cleveland, OH 44114

Team History

Current Indian boosters would find it tough to believe the Tribe was once an AL power. Cleveland won the World Series in 1920 and 1948 and set a league record for wins (111), en route to the 1954 pennant. Since then, there has been little to cheer about. The Indians are the only team never to win the AL East title.

NATIONAL LEAGUE WEST

Atlanta Braves
94-68, .580 Manager: Bobby Cox

Baseball fans waited for Rod Serling to appear magically during the 1991 season and report that the Braves had transported all of us into the Twilight Zone. After seven years of baseball bungling, Atlanta tomahawk-chopped its way to the NL pennant, winning three NLCS games in Pittsburgh along the way. A slew of heroes thrilled the Braves' fans. Free-agent third baseman Terry Pendleton (.319, 22 homers, 86 RBI) emerged as the team leader and won the 1991 NL MVP Award. Center fielder Ron Gant (32 HR, 105 RBI) again was a main power source. Right fielder David Justice (.275, 21 HR, 87 RBI), left fielder Otis Nixon (.297, 72 steals), second baseman Jeff Treadway (.320) and many others made big plays all season long. The pitching staff improved greatly—to third in the league. Tom Glavine (20-11, 2.55 ERA, 192 strikeouts) was the league's top starter and '91 NL Cy Young Award winner, while Steve Avery (18-8) shone in his first full major league season. John Smoltz (14-13) and Charlie Liebrandt (15-13) were both very solid, while Juan Berenguer (17 saves, 2.24 ERA) and Alejandro Pena (15 saves) were the top guns in a solid bullpen.

Manager Bobby Cox	W	L	PCT
Major League record	755	740	.505
With Braves, 1978-81, 1990-91	400	448	.472
1991 record	94	68	.580

Coaches: Pat Corrales, Jimy Williams, Leo Mazzone, Clarence Jones, Jim Beauchamp, Ned Yost

Five-Year Finishes

91	90	89	88	87
1	6	6	6	5

Five-Year Record: 345-460, .429

Ballparks

Boston: South End Grounds 1871-1914; Braves Field 1914-1952. **Milwaukee:** County Stadium 1953-1965. **Atlanta:** Fulton County Stadium 1966-present

Chairman of the Board: William C. Batholomay
President: Stanley H. Kasten
Senior Vice President and Assistant to the President: Henry L. Aaron
Executive Vice President and General Manager: John Schuerholz
Director of Scouting & Player Development: Chuck LaMar

Capacity: 52,007
1991 Attendance: 2,140,217
Surface: natural grass
Left field fence: 330 feet
Center field fence: 420 feet
Right field fence: 330 feet
Left-center fence: 385 feet
Right-center fence: 385 feet

Address
521 Capitol Avenue SW
Atlanta, GA 30312

Team History

Born in 1871 in Boston, this franchise dominated 1890s baseball and won the 1914 World Series. The Braves were a weak sister to the Red Sox for the next 39 years, despite a pennant in 1948, and moved to Milwaukee in 1953. Though they won the 1957 Series, poor attendance forced a move to Atlanta in '66. The Braves won the NL West in 1969 and 1982.

NATIONAL LEAGUE WEST

Los Angeles Dodgers
93-69, .574, 1 Manager: Tommy LaSorda

An active off-season that brought Darryl Strawberry, Brett Butler, Bob Ojeda, and Gary Carter to Tinseltown was supposed to yield another NL West title. But the talented Dodgers fell apart down the stretch and finished a disappointing second. Three straight losses in October spoiled a quick start and made LA a runner-up to the miracle Atlanta Braves. Strawberry was strong in September, finishing with 28 homers and 99 RBI. Equally impressive was center fielder Butler (.296, 38 steals), who keyed the team's offense. Infielder Lenny Harris (.287) and first baseman Eddie Murray (19 homers, 96 RBI) were potent weapons, but Kal Daniels was well off his big 1990 numbers, and Juan Samuel followed a hot start with an abysmal second half. Ramon Martinez (17-13, 3.27) anchored the league's best pitching staff, though he slipped some after the All-Star break. Mike Morgan (14-10) had his first-ever winning season, Ojeda won 12 games, Tim Belcher notched 10 wins, and Orel Hershiser returned from shoulder surgery to finish 7-2.

Manager			
Tommy LaSorda	W	L	PCT
Major League record	1278	1102	.537
With Dodgers, 1976-91	1278	1102	.537
1991 record	93	69	.574

Coaches: Joe Amalfitano, Mark Cresse, Ben Hines, Ron Perronski

Five-Year Finishes

91	90	89	88	87
2	2	4	1	4

Five-Year Record: 423-384, .524

Ballparks

Brooklyn: Union Grounds 1876; Washington Park 1891-1897; Ebbett's Field 1913-1957. **Los Angeles:** Memorial Coliseum 1958-1961; Dodger Stadium 1962-present

President: Peter O'Malley
Executive Vice President, Player Personnel: Fred Claire
Vice President Communications: Tommy Hawkins
Director, Minor League Operations: Charlie Blaney
Director, Scouting: Terry Reynolds

Capacity: 56,000
1991 Attendance: 3,348,170
Surface: natural grass
Left field fence: 330 feet
Center field fence: 395 feet
Right field fence: 330 feet
Left-center fence: 385 feet
Right-center fence: 385 feet

Address
1000 Elysian Park Avenue
Los Angeles, CA 90012

Team History

The National League's most successful franchise got its start in Brooklyn in 1884, named for the borough's Trolley Dodgers. Flatbush fans suffered until "next year" finally brought a World Championship in 1955. They cried two years later when Walter O'Malley moved the team to Los Angeles, where the Dodgers won World Series in 1959, 1963, 1965, 1977, and 1988.

NATIONAL LEAGUE WEST

San Diego Padres
84-78, .519, 10 Manager: Greg Riddoch

It was another of those years for the Padres—preseason contention hopes followed by a middle-of-the-pack finish. San Diego settled into third place and never challenged for the division title. The Padres finished near the bottom of the league in hitting and scored fewer runs than all but two NL teams. Second-year pitcher Andy Benes started slow but finished 15-11 with a 3.03 ERA, and Bruce Hurst (15-8, 3.29 ERA) also had a good second half. Ed Whitson missed most of the year with an injury, and Atlee Hammaker only pitched once. Though Craig Lefferts saved 23 games, his ERA was 3.91. Fred McGriff, acquired from Toronto in the Joe Carter deal, had 31 homers, 106 RBI, and 105 walks. Tony Gwynn hit "only" .317, and Bip Roberts hit .281 and stole 26 bases. Outfielder Darrin Jackson had 21 homers, but only 49 RBI. Catcher Benito Santiago (17 homers, 87 RBI) was stellar, and new shortstop Tony Fernandez (.272) helped solidify the infield.

Manager Greg Riddoch	W	L	PCT
Major League record	122	122	.500
With Padres, 1990-91	122	122	.500
1991 record	84	78	.519

Coaches: Bruce Kimm, Rob Picciolo, Merv Rettenmund, Mike Roarke, Jim Snyder

Five-Year Finishes

91	90	89	88	87
3	5	2	3	6

Five-Year Record: 396-413, .490

Chairman/Managing Partner: Tom Werner
President: Dick Freeman
Executive Vice President/Baseball Operations & General Manager: Joe McIlvaine
Assistant Vice President/Baseball Operations & Assistant General Manager: John Barr
Director/Minor Leagues: Ed Lynch
Director/Scouting: Reggie Waller

Ballparks
Jack Murphy Stadium 1969-present

Capacity: 59,022
1991 Attendance: 1,804,289
Surface: natural grass
Left field fence: 327 feet
Center field fence: 405 feet
Right field fence: 327 feet
Left-center fence: 370 feet
Right-center fence: 370 feet

Address
P.O. Box 2000
San Diego, CA 92112

Team History

A product of the 1969 expansion with Montreal, the Padres struggled below .500 for their first 15 seasons. Their first winning year—1984—was also a pennant winner, but the Padres fell to Detroit in the World Series. The rest of the decade featured middle-division finishes that dashed preseason hopes.

NATIONAL LEAGUE WEST

San Francisco Giants
75-87, .463, 19 Manager: Roger Craig

The Giants' 1991 slide to fourth place in the West exposed a dreadful (last in league ERA) pitching staff and an offense that waits for the long ball. No wonder manager Roger Craig had heart problems by season's end. Trevor Wilson (13-11, 3.56 ERA) was the best of a mediocre starting rotation. Expensive free-agent import Bud Black (12-16) was a huge disappointment, as was John Burkett, who followed up a promising rookie year with a 12-11 record. Kelly Downs was 10-4, former ace Rick Reuschel never pitched, and newcomer Dave Rhigetti managed only 24 saves—down 11 from 1990. The offense had some pop, but it missed Brett Butler. Will Clark (.301, 29 homers, 116 RBI) was again thrilling, but Kevin Mitchell was erratic (27 HR, 69 RBI). Third sacker Matt Williams added 34 homers and 98 RBI to the mix, free-agent import Willie McGee hit .312, and second baseman Robby Thompson had 19 homers and knocked in 48 runs.

Manager Roger Craig	W	L	PCT
Major League record	656	657	.499
With Giants, 1985-91	504	486	.509
1991 record	75	87	.463

Coaches: Dusty Baker, Bill Fahey, Wendell Kim, Bob Lillis

Ballparks
New York: Polo Grounds 1883-1888, 1891-1957; St. George Cricket Grounds 1889-1890. **San Francisco:** Seals Stadium 1958-1959; Candlestick Park 1960-present

Capacity: 58,000
1991 Attendance: 1,737,479
Surface: natural grass
Left field fence: 335 feet
Center field fence: 400 feet
Right field fence: 335 feet
Left-center fence: 365 feet
Right-center fence: 365 feet

Five-Year Finishes

91	90	89	88	87
4	3	1	4	1

Five-Year Record: 425-385, .525

Chairman of the Board: Bob Lurie
President and General Manager: Al Rosen
Vice President & Assistant General Manager: Ralph Nelson
Vice President, Baseball Operations: Bob Kennedy
Vice President, Scouting: Bob Fontaine
Director of Minor League Operations: Tony Seigle
Director of Player Development: Carlos Alfonso

Address
Candlestick Park
San Francisco, CA 94124

Team History

Few dispute the economic reasons for moving this proud franchise west from New York, but many believe the Giants were never the same after coming to San Francisco. The Giants dominated the NL before 1900 and won 15 pennants and five World Championships from 1904 to 1954. Though they enjoyed 14 consecutive winning seasons after their 1958 move, the Giants won only two more pennants—1962 and '89.

Cincinnati Reds
74-88, .457, 20 Manager: Lou Pinella

So Lou Pinella thought he could stand pat and win another World Series, did he? Wrong. The Reds led the NL West early and stayed in contention for much of the summer but finally collapsed in a heap of injuries and controversy. Slugger Eric Davis complained of a variety of maladies—including fatigue—all year and played just half the season. Flamethrowing closer Rob Dibble couldn't control his temper, despite his 31 saves, and bullpen mate Norm Charlton had discipline troubles of his own. Ace Jose Rijo (15-6, 2.51 ERA) sparkled again, but Tom Browning (14-14, 4.18 ERA) struggled, Jack Armstrong (7-13) fizzled, and the Randy Myers (6-13, 3.55 ERA) starting experiment failed. Hal Morris (.318) came within one point of winning the NL batting title, and Barry Larkin (.302, 20 homers, 69 RBI) and Chris Sabo (.301, 26 HR, 88 RBI) were again solid. Paul O'Neill (28 HR, 91 RBI) picked up some of Davis's slack (11 HR, 33 RBI), but the Reds missed the center fielder's bat.

Manager
Lou Pinella

	W	L	PCT
Major League record	389	352	.524
With Reds, 1990-91	165	159	.509
1991 record	74	88	.457

Coaches: John McClaren, Sam Perlozzo, Tony Perez, Jackie Moore, Larry Rothschild

Five-Year Finishes
91	90	89	88	87
5	1	5	2	2

Five-Year Record: 411-398, .508

Ballparks
Lincoln Park Grounds 1876; Avenue Grounds 1876-1879; Bank Street Grounds 1880; League Park 1890-1901; Palace of the Fans 1902-1911: Crosley Field 1912-1970; Riverfront Stadium 1970-present

President and CEO: Marge Schott
Vice President and General Manager: Bob Quinn
Director Player Development: Howie Bedell
Director Scouting: Julian Mock

Capacity: 52,952
1991 Attendance: 2,372,377
Surface: artificial turf
Left field fence: 330 feet
Center field fence: 404 feet
Right field fence: 330 feet
Left-center fence: 375 feet
Right-center fence: 375 feet

Address
100 Riverfront Stadium
Cincinnati, OH, 45202

Team History

Baseball's first professional team has enjoyed recent decades more than the past. The Reds won the tainted 1919 World Series but didn't top the baseball world again until 1939. A 1961 pennant was followed by the Big Red Machine which won the 1975 and '76 World Series. The Reds won another World Championship in 1990.

NATIONAL LEAGUE WEST

Houston Astros
65-97, .401, 29 Manager: Art Howe

Following a fire sale of high-priced veterans and a campaign by owner John McMullen to sell the team, the Astros made good on predictions for a sixth-place finish—despite showcasing some young talent. The pitching staff was stung by an injury to Mike Scott, who started—and lost—only two games all year. Second-year pitcher Pete Harnisch, acquired from Baltimore in the Glenn Davis trade, became the team's ace (12-9, 172 strikeouts, 2.70 ERA). But the rest of the rotation was poor, and so was the bullpen. Mark Portugal was 10-12, but no other starter approached double figures in wins. Third-year catcher Craig Biggio hit .295, and '91 NL Rookie of the Year first baseman Jeff Bagwell replaced Davis nicely, hitting .294 slamming 15 home runs, and knocking in 82 runs. Outfielder Steve Finley hit .285 and stole 34 bases, while third baseman Ken Caminiti knocked in 80 runs. Rookie shortstop Andujar Cedeno (.243) looked like a future star.

Manager
Art Howe	W	L	PCT
Major League record	226	260	.465
With Astros, 1989-91	226	260	.465
1991 Record	65	97	.401

Coaches: Matt Galante, Bob Cluck, Ed Ott, Rudy Jaramillo, Tom Spencer

Five-Year Finishes
91	90	89	88	87
6	4	3	5	3

Five-Year Record: 384-426, .474

Ballparks
Colt Stadium 1962-1964; The Astrodome 1965-present

Chairman of the Board: Dr. John J. McMullen
General Manager: Bill Wood
Assistant General Manager: Bob Watson
Director of Minor League Operations: Fred Nelson
Director of Scouting: Dan O'Brien

Capacity: 54,816
1991 Attendance: 1,196,152
Surface: artificial turf
Stationary Dome
Left field fence: 330 feet
Center field fence: 400 feet
Right field fence: 330 feet
Left-center fence: 380 feet
Right-center fence: 380 feet

Address
P.O Box 288
Houston, TX 77001

Team History

Baseball purists may curse the arrival of baseball in Texas. After three years outdoors as the Colt .45s, the franchise became the first to play indoors when it moved into the Astrodome in 1965. Astro-Turf arrived the next year, but Houston's play hasn't matched its innovation. The Astros won division titles in 1980 and 1986 but no pennants.

NATIONAL LEAGUE EAST

Pittsburgh Pirates
98-64, .605 Manager: Jim Leyland

Despite some preseason acrimony, the Pirates had another outstanding season. A spring training shouting match between 1990 MVP Barry Bonds and manager Jim Leyland, and speculation about Bobby Bonilla's free-agent value didn't matter. Pittsburgh persevered and won its second straight NL East title. But the Buc offense fell quiet in the playoffs, and Pittsburgh dropped a disappointing seven-game decision to Atlanta, losing the final two games at home. The Bucs assumed control of first place in the NL East on April 20 and didn't let go. Bonds started slowly but posted some big numbers—.292, 25 HR, 116 RBI, while Bonilla was also potent (.302, 18 homers, 100 RBI). Though Andy Van Slyke slumped a little, catcher Mike LaValliere (.289) showed some spark at the plate, and rookie Orlando Merced slugged 10 homers—seven of them game-winners. Despite an early stumble by ace winner Doug Drabek, the Pirate starters were again strong. John Smiley won 20 games, Zane Smith 16, and Drabek notched 15. Bill Landrum (17 saves) and Stan Belinda (16 saves) led the bullpen.

Manager			
Jim Leyland	W	L	PCT
Major League record	499	474	.513
With Pirates, 1986-91	499	474	.513
1991 record	98	64	.605

Coaches: Rich Donnelly, Ray Miller, Milt May, Tommy Sandt, Terry Collins

Five-Year Finishes

91	90	89	88	87
1	1	5	2	T4

Five-Year Record: 432-376, .535

Ballparks

Exposition Park 1891-1909; Forbes Field 1909-1970; Three Rivers Stadium 1970-present

Chairman of the Board: Douglas D. Danforth
President & CEO: Mark Sauer
Senior Vice President and General Manager for Baseball Operations: Larry Doughty
Director of Minor League Operations: Chet Montgomery
Director of Scouting: Jack Zduriencik

Capacity: 58,729
1991 Attendance: 2,065,302
Surface: artificial turf
Left field fence: 335 feet
Center field fence: 400 feet
Right field fence: 335 feet
Left-center fence: 375 feet
Right-center fence: 375 feet

Address
P.O. Box 7000
Pittsburgh, PA 15212

Team History

From the early 1900s, Pirate fans have enjoyed much success. Pittsburgh won five pennants and two World Series—1909 and '25—from 1900 to '30. After sagging throughout the '40s and '50s, the Bucs stunned the Yankees in the 1960 fall classic. The Bucs captured the 1971 Series as well and were on top again in 1979. Pittsburgh regained some luster in 1990 and '91 with the NL East title.

NATIONAL LEAGUE EAST

St. Louis Cardinals
84-78, .519, 14 Manager: Joe Torre

In a baseball season filled with surprises, the Cardinals stood out. Picked by many to wallow in NL East's recesses, St. Louis put together its usual assortment of speedsters, mixed in some solid pitching and added big-time closer Lee Smith (NL record 47 saves) to challenge for the title. Though the Cards folded in mid-September, the season was a huge success. Six St. Louis regulars hit .260 or over, with outfielders Milt Thompson (.307) and Felix Jose (.305, 77 RBI) and ageless shortstop Ozzie Smith (.285) leading the way. Todd Zeile had 81 RBI, but Pedro Guerrero was injured and managed only 70. Though they only hit 68 homers as a team, the Cards were able to manufacture runs—as always—and keep things close until Lee Smith could close the door. The rest of the pitching staff wasn't too bad, either. Five Cardinals won 10 games or more, with starters Bryn Smith (12-9), rookie Omar Olivares (11-7), and Ken Hill (11-10) leading the way.

Manager			
Joe Torre	W	L	PCT
Major League record	652	761	.461
With Cardinals, 1990-91	129	122	.514
1991 record	84	78	.519

Coaches: Don Baylor, Joe Coleman, Dave Collins, Bucky Dent, Gaylen Pitts, Red Schoendienst

Five-Year Finishes

91	90	89	88	87
2	6	3	5	1

Five-Year Record: 411-399, .507

Chairman of the Board: August A. Busch III
President & CEO: Fred L. Kuhlmann
Executive Vice President, COO: Mark Sauer
Vice President/General Manager: Dal Maxvill
Director of Player Development: Ted Simmons
Director of Scouting: Fred McAlister

Ballparks

Robison Field 1893-1920; Sportsman's Park 1920-1966; Busch Stadium 1966-present

Capacity: 56,227
1991 Attendance: 2,449,537
Surface: artificial turf
Left field fence: 330 feet
Center field fence: 414 feet
Right field fence: 330 feet
Left-center fence: 383 feet
Right-center fence: 383 feet

Address
250 Stadium Plaza
St. Louis, MO 63102

Team History

Born the Browns in 1884, St. Louis enjoyed some glory in the early days of organized baseball. The Cards won six World Championships from 1926 to 1946, thanks mostly to Branch Rickey's fine farm system. St. Louis was back on top in 1964 and '67, and following weak showings throughout the 1970s, captured a World Series in 1982.

NATIONAL LEAGUE EAST

Philadelphia Phillies
78-84, .481, 20 Managers: Nick Leyva (4-9), Jim Fregosi (74-75)

The 1991 Phillies season featured upheaval and turmoil, beginning when Jim Fregosi replaced manager Nick Leyva after just 13 games. The Phils responded, but their minimal momentum was terminated in early May when center fielder and an offensive sparkplug Lenny Dykstra wrapped his Mercedes around a tree, injuring him and his passenger, catcher Darren Daulton. The Phils slid into the basement until Dykstra's return, but they embarked on a 13-game winning streak in August. Though Dykstra was injured again, the Phils climbed into a tie for third place and showed some flashes of promise. First baseman John Kruk (.294, 21 homers, 92 RBI) led an inconsistent offense. Rookie outfielder Wes Chamberlain added some pop, Dave Hollins was promising at third base, and Dale Murphy (18 homers) helped in right. Philadelphia's young pitching staff included three double-figure winners, ace Terry Mulholland (16-13), hard-throwing Tommy Greene (13-7, including a no-hitter) and second-year flamethrower Jose DeJesus (10-9). Closer Mitch Williams (30 saves, 12-5) was also impressive.

Manager Jim Fregosi	W	L	PCT
Major League record	528	549	.490
With Phillies, 1991	74	75	.497
1991 record	74	75	.497

Coaches: Mike Ryan, John Vukovich, Larry Bowa, Dennis Menke, Johnny Podres, Mel Roberts

Five-Year Finishes

91	90	89	88	87
T3	T4	6	6	4

Five-Year Record: 367-442, .454

Ballparks

Philadelphia Base Ball Grounds 1887-1894; Baker Bowl 1895-1938; Shibe Park 1938-1970; Veterans Stadium 1971-present

Capacity: 62,382
1991 Attendance: 2,050,012
Surface: artificial turf
Left field fence: 330 feet
Center field fence: 408 feet
Right field fence: 330 feet
Left-center fence: 371 feet
Right-center fence: 371 feet

President & General Partner: Bill Giles
Executive Vice President: David Montgomery
Vice President, General Manager: Lee Thomas
Director, Player Development: Del Unser
Director, Scouting: Jay Hankins

Address
P.O. Box 7575
Philadelphia, PA 19148

Team History

The Phillies have won just one World Championship in 108 years. The 1915 pennant winners lost in the Series to Boston, while the 1950 NL champion Whiz Kids were dropped by the Yankees. The Phils won the NL East from 1976 to '78 but didn't reach the Series again until 1980, when they finally won. A 1983 Series appearance was not so fruitful.

NATIONAL LEAGUE EAST

Chicago Cubs
77-83, .481, 20 Managers: Don Zimmer (18-20), Jim Essian (59-63)

The optimism was high around the Friendly Confines when the 1991 season began, thanks to a trio of free-agents—pitchers Danny Jackson and Dave Smith, and slugger George Bell—who were supposed to help Chicago challenge for the NL East title. It didn't happen, as the Cubs finished tied for third. Lovable Cub manager Don Zimmer was dumped in May and replaced by Jim Essian, who was dumped in October. And the high-priced newcomers received mixed reviews. Bell was productive (25 homers, 86 RBI), but Smith and Jackson were dreadful, each registering ERAs over 6.00 while struggling with injuries. Ryne Sandberg didn't disappoint, following up a stellar 1990 with a .291 average, 26 HRs, and 100 RBI. Andre Dawson was again dangerous (31 homers, 104 RBI), but Mark Grace's numbers fell. Chicago's pitching improved some, with Greg Maddux (15-11) and Mike Bielecki (who was traded to Atlanta in September), but Smith's poor showing hurt the bullpen, despite surprise performances from Paul Assenmacher and Chuck McElroy.

Manager Jim Lefebvre	W	L	PCT
Major League record	233	253	.479
With Cubs, 1991	0	0	.000
1991 record (with Mariners)	83	79	.512

Coaches: Chuck Cottier, Jose Martinez, Billy Connors, Sammy Ellis, Tom Trebelhorn

Ballparks

Union Base-Ball Grounds, 23rd Street Grounds, LakeFront Park, South Side Park pre-1916; Wrigley Field 1916-present

Capacity: 38,710
1991 Attendance: 2,314,250
Surface: natural grass
Left field fence: 355 feet
Center field fence: 400 feet
Right field fence: 353 feet
Left-center fence: 368 feet
Right-center fence: 368 feet

Five-Year Finishes

91	90	89	88	87
3	4	1	4	6

Five-Year Record: 400-407, .496

Executive Vice President: Jim Frey
Vice President, Baseball Operations: Larry Himes
Vice President, Business Operations: Mark E. McGuire
Vice President, Scouting & Player Development: Richard P. Balderson
Director, Baseball Administration: Ned L. Colletti
Director, Minor League Operations: William J. Harford, Jr.

Address
Clark & Addison Streets
Chicago, IL 60613

Team History

The Cubs are notorious for having baseball's longest championship drought. Born the White Stockings in 1870, the franchise dominated NL play during the late 1800s. Chicago won the 1906 pennant and captured World Championships in 1907 and 1908. Despite seven NL pennants from 1910 to 1945, the Cubs couldn't win the Series. Chicago never won another pennant, though they did take the NL East in 1984 and 1989.

NATIONAL LEAGUE EAST

New York Mets
77-84, .478, 20½ Managers: Bud Harrelson (74-80), Mike Cubbage (3-4)

With just a week left in the season, Bud Harrelson became the NL East's fourth managing casualty—a punishment for leading the Mets to their worst finish since 1983. Though the Mets trailed Pittsburgh by only five games heading into August, they finished the month 14 back and ended up in fifth place. An early season injury to pitcher Sid Fernandez and Dwight Gooden's late-season arm troubles decimated the starting rotation, as did lackluster performances by Frank Viola (13-15, 3.97 ERA) and David Cone (14-14, including a no-hitter). The loss of slugger Darryl Strawberry to free agency was another blow. Howard Johnson switched to shortstop and back to third, and responded with a 30-30 season (38 HR, 31 errors), with 117 RBI. Speedster Vince Coleman (37 swipes), lured away from St. Louis during the off-season to ignite the offense, spent much of the year on the disabled list. Gregg Jefferies was again productive (.272, 62 RBI), but Kevin McReynolds managed only 16 homers and 74 RBI, and Hubie Brooks slumped even further.

Manager
Jeff Torborg

	W	L	PCT
Major League record	407	436	.482
With Mets, 1992	0	0	.000
1991 record (with White Sox)	87	75	.537

Coaches: Mike Cubbage, Tom McCraw, Mel Stottlemyre

Five-Year Finishes

91	90	89	88	87
5	2	2	1	2

Five-Year Record: 447-360, .554

Ballparks
Polo Grounds 1962-1963; Shea Stadium 1964-present

Chairman of the Board: Nelson Doubleday
President & CEO: Fred Wilpon
Chief Operating Officer/Senior. Executive Vice President: Frank Cashen
General Manager: Al Harazin
Director of Baseball Operations: Gerald Hunsicker

Capacity: 55,601
1991 Attendance: 2,284,484
Surface: natural grass
Left field fence: 338 feet
Center field fence: 410 feet
Right field fence: 338 feet
Left-center fence: 371 feet
Right-center fence: 371 feet

Address
126th Street & Roosevelt Ave.
Flushing, NY 11368

Team History

The 30-year history of the Big Apple's "other" franchise has been filled with meteoric highs and laughable lows. New York debuted in 1962 and lost 120 games, but the Miracle Mets stunned the baseball world in 1969 with a storybook World Series title. New York won another pennant in 1973 but was inept until a 1980s renaissance that included the 1986 World Championship.

NATIONAL LEAGUE EAST

Montreal Expos
71-90, .441, 26½ Managers: Buck Rodgers (50-58), Tom Runnels (21-32)

The Expos' 1991 futility was illustrated in mid-September when the roof—or 55 concrete tons of it—actually fell in on Olympic Stadium, forcing Montreal to play its remaining home games on the road. Les Expos were poor from the start, featuring an anemic offense and weak pitching staff that led management to can Buck Rodgers June 3 and replace him with Tom Runnels. The off-season trade of Tim Raines hurt the top of the lineup, though newcomer Ivan Calderon did post some good numbers (.300, 19 homers, 75 RBI). Dave Martinez hit for average (.295) but little else, and the speedy tandem of outfielder Marquis Grissom (.267, 76 stolen bases) and second baseman Delino DeShields (.238, 56 SBs) was dangerous at times. Larry Walker knocked in 64 runs, but Tim Wallach and Andres Galarraga slumped. Sharp veteran Dennis Martinez (14-11, 2.39 ERA) provided the team's undeniable pitching highlight with an August perfect game. Mark Gardner (9-11) and Chris Nabholz gave some hope for the future, while Barry Jones saved 13 games.

Manager Tom Runnels	W	L	PCT
Major League record	21	32	.396
With Expos, 1991	21	32	.396
1991 record	21	32	.396

Coaches: Felipe Alou, Jerry Manuel, Tommy Harper, Jay Ward

Five-Year Finishes

91	90	89	88	87
6	3	4	3	3

Five-Year Record: 409-400, .506

President & CEO: Claude R. Brochu
Vice President, Baseball Operations: Bill Stoneman
Executive Advisor, Baseball Operations: Eddie Haas
Vice President, Player Personnel and General Manager: Dan Duquette
Director of Minor League Operations: Kent Qualls
Director of Scouting: Kevin Malone

Ballparks

Jarry Park 1969-1976; Stade Olympique 1977-present

Capacity: 60,011
1991 Attendance: 978,045
Retractable Dome
Surface: artificial turf
Left field fence: 325 feet
Center field fence: 404 feet
Right field fence: 325 feet
Left-center fence: 375 feet
Right-center fence: 375 feet

Address
P.O. Box 500, Station M
Montreal, Quebec
H1V 3P2 Canada

Team History

Named for the city's world exposition in the late 1960s, the Expos have given French Canadians few highlights. Their humble beginnings in tiny Jarry Park were matched by equally modest performances. Les Expos did not contend for the NL East title until the late 1970s, and captured the division crown in 1981—their only championship of any kind.

Hall of Famers

Profiles of the players, managers, umpires, and executives who have been inducted into the National Baseball Museum Hall of Fame comprise this section. The profiles are presented in alphabetical order.

While the rules governing election to the Hall of Fame have varied in specifics over the years, in general the criteria has remained the same. One must be named on 75 percent of ballots cast by members of the Baseball Writers' Association of America. To be eligible, players must have played for at least 10 years. The players have to be retired for at least five years but not more than 20 years. A player is eligible for 15 years in the BBWAA vote.

If the player is not named on 75 percent of the ballots in 15 years, his name becomes eligible to be considered by the Committee on Baseball Veterans. This committee also considers managers, umpires, and executives for induction to Cooperstown. The same 75 percent rule applies.

The Committee on the Negro Leagues had been added to the selection process in 1971. This board considered players who had 10 years of service in the pre-1946 Negro Leagues, and also those who made the major leagues. The Negro League board dissolved into the Veterans' Committee in 1977.

In preparation for baseball's centennial in 1939, a National Baseball Museum was proposed, first as a matter of civic pride, and later as memorial for the greatest of those who have ever played the game.

HANK AARON
Outfielder (1954-1976)
Aaron is baseball's all-time leader in home runs with 755 and in RBI with 2,297. During a 23-year career with the Braves and the Brewers, Hammerin' Hank stood out as one of the game's most complete and consistent performers. He was the NL MVP in 1957 when he hit .322 with 44 home runs and 132 RBI. Inducted in 1982, Aaron hit 40 home runs or more eight times and had more than 100 RBI 11 different seasons.

GROVER ALEXANDER
Pitcher (1911-1930)
Despite battles against alcohol and epilepsy, Alexander's 373 wins is tied for the NL record. While pitching with Philadelphia in 1916, he recorded a major league record 16 shutouts on his way to a 33-12 record. Inducted in 1938, "Pete's" 90 shutouts are second on the all-time list.

HALL OF FAME

WALTER ALSTON
Manager (1954-1976)
"Smokey" Alston struck out in his only big league at bat. In 23 years as manager of the Dodgers, however, all under one-year contracts, Alston led the club to seven pennants and four world championships. Under his patient leadership, the Dodgers made pitching and defense a winning combination. Inducted in 1983, his career record is 2,040 wins and 1,613 losses for a .558 winning percentage.

CAP ANSON
First baseman (1871-1897)
Manager (1879-1898)
A baseball pioneer, as player, manager, and part-owner of NL Chicago, "Pop" Anson was the game's most influential figure in the 19th century. He hit .300 or better in 20 consecutive seasons, won five pennants, and is often credited with developing the hit-and-run and other strategies. Inducted in 1939, he reached 3,000 base hits. But, in 1887, he intimidated organized baseball into banning blacks.

LUIS APARICIO
Shortstop (1956-1973)
No man played more games at shortstop—2,581—than Aparicio. The swift, sure-handed infielder played a vital role in championship seasons for the White Sox in 1959 and the Orioles in 1966. Inducted in 1984, the winner of nine Gold Gloves led the AL in stolen bases nine times en route to 506 career thefts.

LUKE APPLING
Shortstop (1930-1943; 1945-1950)
Known better for his bat than his glove, Appling nonetheless played shortstop for the White Sox for 20 seasons, finishing with a career average of .310. Nicknamed "Old Aches and Pains," Appling led the AL in batting twice. Inducted in 1964, he finished his career with 1,116 RBI and 1,319 runs scored. In 1936, he hit .388 and collected 128 RBI, despite hitting only six home runs.

EARL AVERILL
Outfielder (1929-1941)
The only outfielder selected to baseball's first six All-Star games, Averill didn't turn pro until age 23, and didn't make the major leagues, with Cleveland, until age 26. In his first 10 seasons he was one of the game's best sluggers. In a 1933 doubleheader, he hit four home runs, three consecutively. Inducted in 1975, Averill had more than 90 RBI in nine seasons and ended his career with 1,165 runs batted in. A congenital back condition cut short his career.

FRANK BAKER
Third baseman (1908-1922)
Despite never hitting more than 12 home runs in a season, during baseball's dead-ball era Baker was a slugger supreme. He led the AL in home runs from 1911 to 1914, and his two 1911 World Series home runs earned him his "Home Run" nickname. In six World Series with the A's and Yankees, he hit .363. Inducted in 1955, Baker had 1,013 RBI in his career.

DAVE BANCROFT
Shortstop (1915-1930)
One of the best fielding shortstops of all-time, Bancroft set a major league record in 1922 when he handled 984 chances. A heady

ballplayer, "Beauty" was named captain of the Giants in 1920 and led them to four straight pennants. Inducted in 1971, he batted over .300 five times in his career.

ERNIE BANKS
Shortstop; first baseman (1953-1971)
"Mr. Cub," the irrepressible Banks combined unbridled enthusiasm with remarkable talent to become one of the most popular players of his era. As a shortstop he won back-to-back NL MVP awards in 1958 and 1959 before switching to first base. Despite 512 career home runs and 11 All-Star appearances, the Cubs failed to win a pennant during Banks's tenure. Inducted in 1977, he had 2,583 lifetime hits and 1,636 RBI.

AL BARLICK
Umpire (1940-1971)
One of the most respected arbiters in baseball, Barlick began his career in the NL in 1940 when old-timer Bill Klem was injured. He worked in Jackie Robinson's first game. Inducted in 1989, Barlick also umpired in seven All-Star contests and in seven World Series.

ED BARROW
Executive
In 1918, Barrow was named manager of the Red Sox and led them to a World Series victory. Credited with transferring Babe Ruth from the mound to the outfield, Barrow followed Ruth to the Yankees as business manager. Under "Cousin Ed's" direction, the Yankee dynasty became legend. Inducted in 1953, he was in charge of the Bronx Bombers from 1920 to 1947.

JAKE BECKLEY
First baseman (1888-1907)
One of baseball's earliest stars, Beckley played more games at first base than any man in history. Inducted in 1971, he had 2,931 hits, 1,600 runs scored, and 1,575 RBI. His dashing handle-bar mustache made him a fan favorite. "St. Jacob's" 246 career triples are fourth on the all-time list.

COOL PAPA BELL
Outfielder (1922-1946)
Perhaps the fastest man to ever play the game, for more than two decades Bell starred as an outfielder in the Negro Leagues. Satchel Paige claimed Bell was so fast he could switch off the light and leap into bed before the room got dark. Often credited with scoring from second on a sacrifice fly, Bell (who was inducted in 1974) hit .392 against organized major league competition.

JOHNNY BENCH
Catcher (1967-1983)
Upon his arrival in the big leagues in 1967, Bench was heralded as baseball's best defensive catcher. After his NL MVP year in 1970 at age 22, with 48 home runs and 148 RBI, he was baseball's best catcher, period. He won his second MVP in 1972. With Bench behind the plate, the Reds won four pennants and two World Series. In the 1976 Series against the Yankees, he hit .533. Inducted in 1989, he had 389 homers and 1,376 RBI.

CHIEF BENDER
Pitcher (1903-1917; 1925)
An alumni of the Carlisle Indian School, the half-Chippewa Bender overcame a series of racial slights

HALL OF FAME

to become one of the Philadelphia A's most valued members. In 10 World Series appearances, Bender went 6-4. Inducted in 1953, he led the AL in winning percentage three times, including a 17-3 mark in 1914.

YOGI BERRA
Catcher (1946-1965)
If championships are the best measure of success, then Berra stands second to no one. His 14 World Series appearances, 75 Series games played, and 71 Series hits are all records. A three-time MVP, the Yankee hit 20 homers in 10 consecutive seasons. Known as well for his way with words, Berra will be remembered for the oft-quoted "it's never over till it's over." Inducted in 1972, he had 1,430 lifetime RBI to go with his 358 home runs.

JIM BOTTOMLEY
First baseman (1922-1937)
One of the first products of the famous Cardinals' farm system, Bottomley was named NL MVP in 1928 for hitting .325, 31 homers, and driving in 136 runs. On September 16, 1924, "Sunny Jim" knocked in 12 runs with six hits against Brooklyn. Inducted in 1974, Bottomley had a career .310 batting average and 1,422 RBI.

LOU BOUDREAU
Shortstop (1938-1952)
Both as a fielder and a hitter, Boudreau was one of the game's great shortstops. He was named Cleveland's player-manager in 1942 at age 24. In 1948, he led the club to the AL pennant, hitting .355, scoring 116 runs, while driving in 106, easily capturing the AL MVP Award. Inducted in 1970, he led AL shortstops in fielding eight times. As a manager, he won 1,162 games.

ROGER BRESNAHAN
Catcher (1897; 1900-1915)
The first catcher elected to the Hall of Fame, Bresnahan is most famous for pioneering the use of shin guards and batting helmets. A solid hitter, Bresnahan hit .350 with the Giants in 1903. Inducted in 1945, he possessed rare speed for a catcher, stealing 34 bases in 1903 and finishing his career with 212 stolen bases.

LOU BROCK
(1961-1979)
Brock's career totals of 938 stolen bases and 3,023 career hits, coupled with a .293 batting average, gained him admittance to the Hall. In 1974, at age 35, he stole 118 bases. In three World Series for the Cardinals he excelled, hitting .391 and scoring 16 runs. Inducted in 1985, Brock had more than 200 hits four times.

DAN BROUTHERS
First baseman (1879-1896; 1904)
Baseball's premier 19th century slugger, Brouthers toiled for nine different clubs, in three different major leagues, for 21 seasons. He was the first man to win back-to-back batting titles, in 1882 and 1883. Inducted in 1945, he hit over .300 in 16 consecutive seasons, reaching .374 in 1883.

THREE FINGER BROWN
Pitcher (1903-1916)
A farm accident in a corn grinder mutilated Brown's right hand, severing most of his index finger, mangling his middle finger, and paralyzing his little finger. The injuries,

however, gave his pitches a natural sink and curve. While pitching with the Cubs, between 1904 and 1910 Brown's highest ERA was 1.86, helping Chicago to four pennants. Inducted in 1949, he had a career 239-129 record, with a 2.06 ERA and 57 shutouts.

MORGAN BULKELEY
NL President (1876)
Bulkeley's notoriety is in his almost complete anonymity. In 1876, Bulkeley was named the first President of the new National League, primarily because of his respectable standing in the business world. He served one year without distinction and resigned. He was inducted in 1937.

JESSE BURKETT
Outfielder (1890-1905)
In the 1890s, the lefthanded-hitting Burkett hit over .400 two times. A fine baserunner and bunter, the third-strike foul-bunt rule was created due to Burkett's prowess at the art. "Crab" won three batting titles in his career. Inducted in 1946, he scored 1,718 runs and notched 2,853 base hits in his 16-year career.

ROY CAMPANELLA
Catcher (1948-1957)
Campanella, one of the great athletes of his time, had a .312 average, 41 homers, 103 runs scored, and 142 RBI in 1953—amazing marks for a backstop. In 1951, 1953, and 1955 the Dodger catcher was named the NL's MVP. Inducted in 1969, he led his team to five pennants in 10 years. A 1958 automobile accident left Campanella paralyzed, and his struggle to remain active has served as a continuing inspiration.

ROD CAREW
First baseman; second baseman (1967-1985)
An infielder with Minnesota and California, Carew was one of baseball's premiere singles hitters, slapping 3,053 hits and registering a lifetime .328 batting average. Inducted in 1991, he topped .300 in 15 consecutive seasons on his way to seven batting titles, a mark surpassed only by Ty Cobb's 12 batting titles. Carew's 1977 MVP year consisted of a .388 batting average, 239 hits, 16 triples, 128 runs scored, and an on-base percentage of .415.

MAX CAREY
Outfielder (1910-1929)
A tremendous defensive center fielder, primarily with Pittsburgh, Carey took advantage of his speed and instincts to swipe 738 bases. In 1925, despite two broken ribs, "Scoops" batted .458 in the World Series as the Pirates defeated Washington. In game seven, his four hits and three runs scored beat the great Walter Johnson. Inducted in 1961, Carey scored 1,545 runs and had 2,665 base hits in his 20-year career.

ALEXANDER CARTWRIGHT
Executive
On September 23, 1845, Alexander Cartwright formed the Knickerbocker Base Ball Club and formalized a set of 20 rules that gave baseball its basic shape. While Cartwright's involvement with the game lasted only a few years, he is the man

most responsible for the game that is played, and loved, today. Our national pastime is his legacy. He was inducted in 1938.

HENRY CHADWICK
Writer-Statistician
While Alexander Cartwright is baseball's inventor, Chadwick is the first man to chronicle the game. The only sportswriter enshrined in the Hall itself (in 1938), as opposed to the Writers Wing, he was the first baseball writer. Chadwick's guides and instructional booklets helped popularize the game, and his method of scoring led to the game's wealth of statistics.

FRANK CHANCE
First baseman (1898-1914)
Anchor of the Cubs' "Tinker-to-Evers-to-Chance" double-play combo, Chance helped Chicago win four pennants. While he was hardly a dominant player, he nevertheless hit .296 during his career and hit .310 in Series play. Chance's career was cut short by repeated beanings, which eventually left him deaf in one ear. Inducted in 1946, "The Peerless Leader" managed the Cubs for seven years and won at least 100 games four times.

HAPPY CHANDLER
Commissioner (1945-1951)
The former governor and U.S. senator from Kentucky, Chandler succeeded Judge Kenesaw Mountain Landis as the second Commissioner of baseball. Despite the opposition of most baseball owners, Chandler backed Branch Rickey's signing of Jackie Robinson and prevented a player strike by threatening to ban any striking player for life. Preferring a "yes-man," the owners voted Chandler out in 1951. He was inducted in 1982.

OSCAR CHARLESTON
Outfielder (1915-1941)
Blessed with speed and power in abundance, center fielder Charleston is thought by many to be greatest of all Negro League players. Superb defensively, on offense he could both steal a base and hit a home run. In 1932 he became player-manager of the Pittsburgh Crawfords, whose lineup, including Charleston, included five Hall of Famers. The team went 99-36 that year, and Charleston hit .363. He was enshrined in 1976.

JACK CHESBRO
Pitcher (1899-1909)
Chesbro's 41 victories in 454⅔ innings in 1904 stand as one of the game's more remarkable single-season achievements. A master of the spitball, his wild pitch, however, in the next to the last game of the 1904 season against Boston cost New York the AL pennant. The winner of 199 games, "Happy Jack" (inducted in 1946) led his league in winning percentage in three different seasons.

FRED CLARKE
Outfielder (1894-1915)
Manager (1897-1915)
For 19 of his 21 big league seasons, Clarke was a manager as well as a player, all for the NL Louisville-Pittsburgh franchise. As a player, he hit .312 with 2,675 base hits and 1,621 runs scored. As manager he won one World Series in 1910, four pennants, including three in row from 1901 to 1903, and finished second five times. Inducted

HALL OF FAME

in 1945, "Cap" finished his managing career with 1,602 wins against 1,181 losses.

JOHN CLARKSON
Pitcher (1882-1894)
An early master of the curveball, Clarkson excelled during the years when the pitching distance was a mere 50 feet. Six times he hurled more than 400 innings, twice more than 600. In 1885 with the White Stockings, he went 53-16. With the Beaneaters in 1889, Clarkson's record was 49-19 in an incredible 73 appearances. Winner of 326 games for his career, he had 485 complete games and led the NL in strikeouts four times. He was inducted in 1963.

ROBERTO CLEMENTE
Outfielder (1955-1972)
Clemente won four NL batting titles and also possessed one of the strongest outfield arms in baseball history. Intensely proud of his Puerto Rican heritage, it was not until the 1971 World Series, when Clemente led Pittsburgh to victory with a .414 average, that he began to receive his due. In 13 of his 18 seasons he hit .300 or better, topping the .350 mark three times. On New Year's Eve, 1972, Clemente died in a plane crash bringing supplies to earthquake-ravaged Nicaragua. The normal five-year waiting period was waived, and in 1973 Clemente became the first Hispanic elected to the Hall of Fame.

TY COBB
Outfielder (1905-1928)
The first man elected to the Hall of Fame, Cobb received more votes than any of his counterparts. Intense beyond belief, the daring Cobb epitomized the "scientific" style of play that dominated baseball in the first quarter of the 20th century. In 23 of his 24 seasons Cobb hit over the .320 mark, and his lifetime .367 average is still the all-time best. Inducted in 1936, he led the AL in batting average 12 seasons. The "Georgia Peach's" 2,245 runs scored are the most in history, while his 4,191 hits and 892 stolen bases rank second and third respectively.

MICKEY COCHRANE
Catcher (1925-1937)
An exceptional defensive catcher and dangerous hitter, Cochrane led the Athletics and Tigers to five pennants, including two as Detroit manager. "Black Mike" cracked the .300 mark in eight seasons, and his lifetime .320 batting average is the highest of any catcher. Inducted in 1947, Mickey was twice AL MVP. In 1937 Cochrane was beaned by Yankee pitcher Bump Hadley and suffered a fractured skull, ending his career at a relatively young age of 34.

EDDIE COLLINS
Second baseman (1906-1930)
As Connie Mack's on-field manager, Collins led the Athletics to four pennants in five years. Traded to the White Sox, he helped that club to two more. An accomplished all-around ballplayer, Collins smacked 3,311 hits for a career average of .333, yet never won a batting title. A consummate base-stealer, he ranks fourth on the all-time list with 743 career swipes. Inducted in 1939, "Cocky" scored 1,818 runs and drove in 1,299 runs in his 25-year career.

JIMMY COLLINS
Third baseman (1895-1908)
Inducted in 1945, Collins revolutionized the third base position by moving around, charging in, and fielding bunts bare-handed. Playing primarily for both the Boston Beaneaters in the National League and the Boston Pilgrims in the AL, Collins hit a robust .294, topping the .300 mark five times and driving in over 100 RBI four times.

EARLE COMBS
Outfielder (1924-1935)
While Babe Ruth and Lou Gehrig cleaned up at the plate, Combs set the table. As the leadoff man and center fielder for the Yankees, Combs scored 100 or more runs in eight straight seasons. Inducted in 1970, "The Kentucky Colonel" lifetime had a .325 average and scored 1,186 runs. A collision with an outfield fence in 1934 forced his retirement a year later.

CHARLES COMISKEY
Executive
Comiskey parlayed modest field success into managerial brilliance, later becoming the first former player to be sole owner of a major league franchise. Inducted in 1939, the "Old Roman" assisted Ban Johnson in the formation of the American League. As owner of the White Sox, Comiskey earned a reputation as a cheapskate, and some historians feel that his parsimonious spending habits indirectly led to the 1919 "Black Sox" scandal.

JOCKO CONLAN
Umpire (1941-1964)
A long-time minor leaguer, Conlan started umpiring by accident. In a 1935 game, when one of the regular umpires was overcome by the heat, Conlan was rushed in to pinch-ump. Remembered for his trademark polka dot tie, Conlan utilized a sharp tongue to keep order. Inducted in 1974, he umpired in six World Series and six All-Star Games.

TOMMY CONNOLLY
Umpire (1898-1931)
Although born in England, Connolly fell in love with baseball as a teenager and became an NL umpire in 1898. Frustrated with the circuit by 1900, he signed on to the AL in 1901. Thirty years later he was named chief of AL umpires, his position for another 23 years. Connolly and Bill Klem became the first umpires named to the Hall of Fame, in 1953. Connolly umpired in eight World Series, including the first in 1903.

ROGER CONNOR
First baseman (1880-1897)
Until Babe Ruth broke the mark in 1921, Connor held the lifetime record for home runs with 136. A career .317 hitter, the Giant first baseman was a bona fide dead-ball era slugger, smacking 233 triples, fifth all time. Inducted in 1976, he scored 1,620 runs and had 1,125 RBI in his career.

STAN COVELESKI
Pitcher (1912; 1916-1928)
A coal miner at age 13, Coveleski didn't reach the majors to stay until 1916, when he was age 27. The spitball artist had his best years with Cleveland from 1918 to 1921, winning 20 games or more each season. Inducted in 1969, Coveleski won 215 games, while his brother

Harry won 81. Stan lost only 142 games and retired with a lifetime 2.88 ERA.

SAM CRAWFORD
Outfielder (1899-1917)
Crawford played outfield for Detroit alongside Ty Cobb. The powerful Crawford is baseball's all-time leader in triples with 312. A native of Wahoo, Nebraska, "Wahoo Sam" retired only 36 hits shy of 3,000. Inducted in 1957, he hit .309 lifetime, with 1,393 runs scored and 1,525 RBI. He later returned to baseball as an umpire in the Pacific Coast League.

JOE CRONIN
Shortstop (1926-1945)
Manager (1933-1947)
AL President (1959-1973)
For 50 years, Cronin excelled as a player, manager, and executive. A hard-hitting shortstop, he made baseball history in 1934 when Red Sox owner Tom Yawkey purchased him from Washington owner (and Cronin's uncle-in-law) Clark Griffith for $225,000. Cronin was a .301 career batter, and he had 1,233 runs scored and 1,424 RBI to go with his 515 doubles. As a manager, Cronin led the Senators to a pennant in 1934 and the Red Sox to one in 1946. From 1959 to 1973, he served as AL President. He was inducted in 1956.

CANDY CUMMINGS
Pitcher (1872-1877)
Baseball's legendary inventor of the curveball, Cummings allegedly discovered the pitch while tossing clam shells as a youngster. Despite standing 5'9" and never weighing more than 120 pounds, from 1872 to 1877, he won 146 games before overwork forced him to retire. Inducted in 1939, he pitched for the Excelsior Club of Brooklyn before becoming a professional in the National Association.

KIKI CUYLER
Outfielder (1921-1938)
Pronounced "Cuy-Cuy," Kiki Cuyler hit a robust .354 as a Pirate rookie in 1924 and was heralded as "the next Ty Cobb." Kiki hit over .300 ten times and topped the .350 mark four times. He accumulated 2,299 hits for a lifetime mark of .321. Inducted in 1968, he had 1,305 runs, 1,065 RBI, and 328 swipes in his career.

RAY DANDRIDGE
Third baseman (1933-1944)
Dandridge excelled at third base in the Negro and Mexico Leagues, hitting for power and average while fielding with precision. He accumulated a .347 average against white big league pitching. In 1949, he signed with the Giants and tore apart the American Association for Minneapolis, but at age 36 never received a call to the majors. He was inducted in 1987.

DIZZY DEAN
Pitcher (1930-1941; 1947)
Baseball's most colorful pitcher, Dean threw smoke, spoke in homespun hyperbole, and by age 26 had won 134 games for the Cardinals. After breaking his toe in the 1937 All-Star game, Dean altered his motion, hurt his arm, and never approached his previous record. Inducted in 1953, he had a 150-83 career record with a 3.02 ERA. Dizzy was the last NL pitcher to notch 30 wins in a season when he went 30-7 in 1934. His brother Paul

also pitched for the Cardinals. Later a broadcaster, Dizzy's folksy, broken grammar attracted the ire of English teachers and the devotion of listeners everywhere.

ED DELAHANTY
Outfielder (1888-1903)
One of five brothers to play in the majors, Delahanty was perhaps baseball's premier hitter of the 1890s. He hit .400 three times, and his .346 career mark is fourth all time. Unfortunately, he lived as hard as he played. In 1903, Delahanty was suspended for drinking. En route to his home, Big Ed (age 35) was kicked off a train, fell into the Niagara River, and was swept over the falls to his death. He was inducted in 1945.

BILL DICKEY
Catcher (1928-1943; 1946)
Catcher of 100 or more games for 13 consecutive seasons, in 1936 Dickey hit .363, still a record for the position. He accumulated a .313 batting average and 1,209 RBI in his career. During his 17 years, the Yankees won nine pennants and captured eight world championships. Inducted in 1954, Dickey is also credited with developing the receiving skills of Yogi Berra.

MARTIN DIHIGO
Pitcher; outfielder (1923-1950)
The first Cuban elected to the Hall, Dihigo starred as a pitcher and outfielder in Negro and Caribbean baseball from 1923 to 1950. Winner of more than 250 games from the mound, he hit over .400 three times. He was one of the most versatile players in the game's recent history; he was able to play all of the infield positions, as well as being one of the best hurlers in history. Inducted in 1977, Dihigo is also in the Cuban and Mexican Halls of Fame.

JOE DiMAGGIO
Outfielder (1936-1942; 1946-1951)
The best of the DiMaggio brothers, "Joltin' Joe" led the Yankees to nine pennants while making 13 All-Star teams in 13 seasons. A three-time MVP, the quiet, graceful center fielder is often credited with being the best player of his generation. In 1941, "The Yankee Clipper" hit in a record 56 consecutive games. He led the AL in batting average twice, slugging average twice, triples once, home runs twice, runs scored once, and RBI twice. Inducted in 1955, he retired with a .325 batting average, a .579 slugging average, 361 home runs, 1,390 runs scored, and 1,537 RBI.

BOBBY DOERR
Second baseman (1937-1944; 1946-1951)
Doerr was known for his reliable defensive play and potent bat. For 14 seasons he was one of the best second baseman in baseball, spending his entire career with the Red Sox, and never playing a game at another position. In 1944, Doerr was the AL MVP, leading the loop in slugging at .528. Inducted in 1986, Doerr had a career .288 average, 223 homers, and 1,247 RBI.

DON DRYSDALE
Pitcher (1956-1969)
In the early 1960s, Drysdale and teammate Sandy Koufax gave the Dodgers baseball's best pitching tandem. The intimidating Drysdale led the NL in Ks three times. He was 25-9 with a 2.83 ERA and a

league-best 232 strikeouts in 1962, winning the Cy Young Award. In 1968, "Big D" hurled six shutouts in a row on his way to 58 consecutive scoreless innings. Inducted in 1984, he was 209-166 with a 2.95 ERA and 2,486 strikeouts in his 14-year career.

HUGH DUFFY
Outfielder (1888-1906)
In 1894, the diminutive Duffy hit .438 for NL Boston, the highest mark ever recorded under current rules. He also captured the first-ever Triple Crown that year, with 18 homers and 145 RBI. Never again approaching .400, Duffy still compiled a career .324 average, 1,551 runs, and 1,299 RBI. Inducted in 1945, he led the NL in homers twice despite playing at 165 pounds. After his retirement, he served another 48 seasons as manager, coach, owner, and scout.

BILLY EVANS
Umpire (1906-1927)
Inducted in 1973, Evans got his start as a sportswriter and then became what many writers have always thought they could do better—an umpire. He was one of the best in the AL, working six World Series.

JOHNNY EVERS
Second baseman (1902-1917; 1922; 1929)
Perhaps the best of the "Tinker-to-Evers-to-Chance" double play combination, second baseman Evers relied on a steady glove and just enough hitting to help lead his club to five pennants in 16 seasons. Although he played most of his career with the Cubs, in 1914 he was the NL MVP while with the "Miracle" Boston Braves. Inducted in 1946, "The Trojan" retired with 919 runs scored and 324 stolen bases.

BUCK EWING
Catcher (1880-1897)
Connie Mack called Ewing "the greatest catcher of all time." He eclipsed the .300 mark in 10 seasons, including a string of eight straight times. Inducted in 1939, Ewing had a lifetime .303 batting average and scored 1,129 runs.

RED FABER
Pitcher (1914-1933)
The last AL pitcher allowed to throw the spitball, Faber spent his entire 20-year career with the White Sox, posting a 254-213 record. An illness and injury in 1919 kept him out of the World Series, and left him untouched by the infamous "Black Sox" scandal. He led the AL in ERA and in complete games in two years. Inducted in 1964, Faber posted a career 3.15 ERA in 4,087⅔ innings, with 274 complete games.

BOB FELLER
Pitcher (1936-1941; 1945-1956)
Phenom Feller left the farm at age 17 and struck out 15 in his first official big league appearance. Feller's fastball, once timed at over 98 mph, may have been the fastest of all time. "Rapid Robert" led the AL seven times in strikeouts, six seasons in wins, and four times in shutouts. Inducted in 1962, Feller won 266 games, all for Cleveland, and three no-hitters.

RICK FERRELL
Catcher (1929-1947)
One of the few players inducted (in 1984) primarily for his defense, Fer-

rell nonetheless hit .300 four times. He was a career .281 hitter and drew 931 walks. With the Red Sox, for four seasons Ferrell teamed with pitching brother Wes to form one of baseball's few brothers batteries.

ELMER FLICK
Outfielder (1898-1910)
A slick fielding, speedy outfielder for the Phillies and Indians, in 1905 Flick won the AL batting crown with a then record low average of .306. In the spring of 1907 Detroit thought so much of Flick they offered Ty Cobb in trade. The Indians turned Detroit down. That season Flick hit .302 in his last full season, Cobb hit .350 in his first. Inducted in 1963, Flick compiled a .313 career batting average.

WHITEY FORD
Pitcher (1950; 1953-1967)
Ford's winning percentage of .690 is the best of any 200-game winner. The Yankee pitcher led the AL in wins three times and ERA twice. Ford holds eight World Series pitching records, including wins (10) and strikeouts (94). His 25-4 record in 1961 earned him the Cy Young Award. Inducted in 1974, "The Chairman of the Board" was 236-106 with a 2.75 ERA and 156 complete games.

RUBE FOSTER
Executive; pitcher
As a star pitcher for a number of early black teams, and later as the first president of the Negro National League, Foster earned the title "Father of Black Baseball." Foster's efforts in organizing the NNL gave black baseball needed stability. He in effect saved the Negro League and made it a popular game. Foster was enshrined to the Hall of Fame in 1981.

JIMMIE FOXX
First baseman (1925-1942; 1944-1945)
For 12 consecutive seasons with the Athletics and Red Sox, Foxx slammed 30 or more home runs and knocked in more than 100 runs. In 1933, Foxx hit .356, 48 homers, and knocked in 163 RBI to win the Triple Crown. A three-time MVP, "Double X" had a lifetime slugging average of .609, fourth all time. Inducted in 1951, Foxx had 534 career homers, 1,921 RBI, and a .325 average.

FORD FRICK
NL President (1934-1951)
Commissioner (1951-1965)
Frick served as Babe Ruth's ghost writer before being named NL President in 1934. In 1951, he was elected Commissioner. During his executive tenure he helped establish the Hall of Fame, supported Branch Rickey's signing of Jackie Robinson, and presided over baseball's busiest period of expansion before retiring. He was inducted in 1970.

FRANKIE FRISCH
Second baseman (1919-1937)
A member of more NL pennant winners than any other player, Frisch played in four fall classics with the Giants and four with the Cardinals. He cracked the .300 mark 13 times, scored 100 runs seven times, and was the 1931 NL MVP. Named player-manager in 1933, "The Fordham Flash" led the "Gashouse Gang" to the world championship in 1934. Inducted in 1947, he scored

1,532 runs in his career while batting .316.

PUD GALVIN
Pitcher (1875; 1879-1892)
Nicknamed "Pud" because he made pudding out of hitters, Galvin was pitcher supreme for NL Buffalo in the 1880s. On his way to 361 career victories, Galvin pitched more than 400 innings nine times, and won 46 games in both 1883 and 1884. "Gentle Jeems" is 10th on the all-time list with 57 shutouts. Inducted in 1965, he is also second all time with 639 complete games and 5,941⅓ innings pitched.

LOU GEHRIG
First baseman (1923-1939)
"The Iron Horse," Gehrig played in a record 2,130 consecutive games for the Yankees. Usually batting cleanup behind Babe Ruth, Gehrig knocked 46 home runs and set the AL record for RBI with 184 in 1931. He had more than 40 home runs in five seasons, more than 150 RBI in seven seasons, and a .600 slugging percentage in nine seasons. "Columbia Lou" had a .632 career slugging percentage, a .340 batting average, 493 home runs, 1,990 RBI, and 1,888 runs scored. Although fatally ill with amyotrophic lateral sclerosis, in 1939 he bid farewell to 61,000 fans at Yankee Stadium by saying "Today I consider myself the luckiest man on the face of the earth." The waiting period for the Hall was waived, and Gehrig was admitted in 1939.

CHARLIE GEHRINGER
Second baseman (1924-1942)
His efficient and dependable play at second base for the Tigers earned Gehringer the appellation "The Mechanical Man." He regularly led the league in fielding and hit over .300 in 13 of 16 seasons. He had over 100 RBI and 200 or more hits in seven seasons. In 1937, his loop-high .371 average made him AL MVP. Inducted in 1949, he retired with a career .320 batting average, 2,839 hits, 1,774 runs scored, and 1,427 RBI.

BOB GIBSON
Pitcher (1959-1975)
In 1968, Gibson had the lowest ERA in NL history, a stingy 1.12, while winning both Cy Young and MVP honors. He also won the Cy Young Award in 1970. In the 1967 World Series, he led St. Louis to victory over Boston, winning three times while giving up only 14 hits. A consummate power-pitcher, Gibson's intimidating blend of speed and control resulted in 251 career wins. Inducted in 1981, "Hoot" had a career 2.91 ERA, 3,117 strikeouts, and 255 complete games.

JOSH GIBSON
Catcher (1930-1946)
For 16 seasons Gibson reigned as the Negro Leagues' supreme slugger, perhaps smacking nearly 1,000 home runs and as many as 90 in a single season. The powerful catcher was often called the black Babe Ruth; in another time, Ruth may have been referred to as the poor man's Josh Gibson. One of the most dedicated players ever, Gibson would play 200 games in summer and winter leagues in a single season. In 1947, with Jackie Robinson on the verge of breaking the big league color line, Gibson, only age 36, died of a brain hemorrhage. He was inducted in 1972.

HALL OF FAME

WARREN GILES
NL President (1951-1969)
Giles's career started as president of minor league Moline in 1919 and ended 50 years later when he retired as president of the NL. During his tenure, from 1951 to 1969, he oversaw the transfer of the Giants and Dodgers to California, and the addition of franchises in New York (Mets), Houston, San Diego, and Montreal. He was inducted in 1979.

LEFTY GOMEZ
Pitcher (1930-1943)
Gomez's sense of humor was matched only by his skill on the mound. A 20-game winner four times for the Yankees of the 1930s, Gomez went undefeated in six World Series decisions. He led the AL in Ks three times and in ERA twice. His secret to success? Quipped Lefty, "Clean living and a fast outfield." Inducted in 1972, "Goofy" was 189-102 with a 3.34 ERA in his career.

GOOSE GOSLIN
Outfielder (1921-1938)
The best hitter ever to play for the Senators, Goslin led Washington to its only three appearances in the World Series. In both the 1924 and 1925 fall classics, he slugged three home runs. Goose had 100 RBI or more and batted over .300 in 11 seasons. Inducted in 1968, he excelled in the clutch in 18 seasons had 1,609 RBI, 2,735 hits, and a .316 average.

HANK GREENBERG
First baseman (1930; 1933-1941; 1945-1947)
Despite playing only nine full seasons, Greenberg smacked 331 home runs and captured AL MVP honors in 1935 and 1940 for the Tigers. He lost three years to World War II, but came back in 1946 to lead the AL in homers and RBI. He had league- and career-high totals of 58 dingers (1938) and 183 RBI (1937). Inducted in 1956, "Hammerin' Hank" had a career .313 batting average, a .605 slugging percentage, and 1,276 RBI.

CLARK GRIFFITH
Manager (1901-1920)
A leading pitcher of the 1890s, Griffith won 20 games six straight seasons with the White Stockings. He won 240 games in his career. Over 20 years the cagey "Old Fox" managed, in turn, the White Sox, Yankees, Reds, and Senators. He had a 1,491-1,367 record and won but one pennant. Inducted in 1946, he was also president of the Senators from 1920 to 1955.

BURLEIGH GRIMES
Pitcher (1916-1934)
In 1934, Grimes threw the last legal spitter in baseball history. Over the preceding 19 seasons, he won 270 games with seven different teams. One of a handful of pitchers allowed to throw the spitter after its ban in 1920, Grimes was by far the most successful. Inducted in 1964, "Ol' Stubblebeard" won more than 20 games in five seasons, and led the NL in complete games four times.

LEFTY GROVE
Pitcher (1925-1941)
In an era dominated by hitting, the lefthanded Grove was almost unhittable, winning 20 games or more seven straight seasons with Connie Mack's Philadelphia A's, including a remarkable 31-4 mark in 1931. That

year, Grove was the AL MVP. On his way to 300 wins, he led the AL in strikeouts seven times, in ERA nine times, in complete games three times, and in winning percentage five times. "Mose" was inducted in 1947.

CHICK HAFEY
Outfielder (1924-1937)
Hafey's misfortune was to play before the advent of the batting helmet. Several beanings and a chronic sinus condition affected his vision, forcing him to wear glasses in an effort to correct the damage. Nevertheless, Chick (inducted in 1971) hit over .300 in nine seasons and captured the NL title in 1931 with a .349 mark. Ill health and vision problems forced the career .317 batter to retire.

JESSE HAINES
Pitcher (1918; 1920-1937)
Knuckleballer Haines didn't make the big leagues for good until he was age 26. However, he stuck around until he was 45, winning 20 games three times and finishing with 210 victories for the Cardinals, including a no-hitter against the Braves in 1924. In 1927, he racked up a 24-10 record, leading the NL with 25 complete games and six shutouts. Inducted in 1970, "Pop" had a career .571 winning percentage and 209 complete games.

BILLY HAMILTON
Outfielder (1888-1901)
While playing with Philadelphia and Boston in the NL, "Sliding Billy" Hamilton ran into the records. He was credited with 915 stolen bases, although for most of his career a runner received credit for a base theft by advancing an extra base on a hit. Inducted in 1961, his lifetime .344 mark is the eighth best all time. In 1894, his ability on the bases brought him home a record 196 times.

WILL HARRIDGE
AL President (1931-1959)
AL President from 1931 until 1959, Harridge stayed out of the limelight and quietly led the league from the era of Babe Ruth to the era of Mickey Mantle. An early supporter of the All-Star game and night baseball, Harridge was a tough, conservative executive who insisted on order. He was inducted in 1972.

BUCKY HARRIS
Manager (1924-1943; 1947-1948; 1950-1956)
An above average second baseman for the Senators, Harris was a natural leader who had his greatest success as manager. In his first season as player-manager in 1924, he led the Senators to their only world championship. He went on to manage another 28 seasons with five other clubs, going 2,157-2,218. Inducted in 1975, Harris usually had little talent but was a respected strategist who drove his players to play their best.

GABBY HARTNETT
Catcher (1922-1941)
From 1922 through 1940, Hartnett was likely the NL's best catcher. A fine defensive catcher, his best season was 1930, when he hit .339 with 37 home runs and 122 RBI. He hit .344 as the NL MVP in 1935. His late-season, ninth-inning "homer in the gloaming" against Pittsburgh won the 1938 pennant for the Cubs.

inducted in 1955, he had a .297 career batting average, with 236 homers and 1,179 RBI.

HARRY HEILMANN
Outfielder (1914; 1916-1930; 1932)
In the four seasons that Heilmann won the AL batting crown, his lowest average was .393. Inducted in 1952, he batted over .300 in 12 seasons and hit an amazing .403 in 1923. Playing mostly for Detroit, the slow-footed outfielder (nicknamed "Slug") wielded a line-drive bat that resulted in 2,660 hits, including 542 doubles, for a .342 batting average.

BILLY HERMAN
Second baseman (1931-1943; 1946-1947)
A 10-time All-Star, Herman's 227 hits and 57 doubles in 1935 were tops in the NL. The best defensive second baseman in the loop, he hit .300 or better eight times in his career. After playing most of his career for the Cubs, in 1941 he was traded to Brooklyn, prompting Dodger owner Larry MacPhail to pronounce, accurately, "I just bought a pennant." Inducted in 1975, Herman had a career .304 batting average and 486 doubles.

HARRY HOOPER
Outfielder (1909-1925)
A right field star, Hooper's arm was legendary (he averaged 20 assists a year) as he teamed with Duffy Lewis and Tris Speaker to give the BoSox the best outfield of the era. A lifetime .281 hitter, he scored 1,429 runs. He was inducted in 1971.

ROGERS HORNSBY
Second baseman (1915-1937)
Perhaps the greatest righthanded hitter of all-time, Hornsby's career .358 average is second only to Ty Cobb's .367. "Rajah's" .424 mark in 1924 is the best of the century. His greatest success came with the Cardinals, where between 1920 and 1925 he collected six straight batting titles, as well as two Triple Crowns. Inducted in 1942, Hornsby's fierce demeanor made him one of the most disliked players of his time.

WAITE HOYT
Pitcher (1918-1938)
The Yankee pitching ace of the 1920s, Hoyt won 20 games only twice, but compiled a 6-4 record in the World Series with a 1.83 ERA. In 1927, "Schoolboy" led the AL in wins (22), winning percentage (.759), and ERA (2.63). Inducted in 1969, he won in double figures 12 seasons and had a career 237-182 record. He was one of the first ex-ballplayers to work in broadcasting.

CAL HUBBARD
Umpire (1936-1951; 1954-1962)
Hubbard is the only man in the baseball, college football, and pro football Halls of Fame. While starring as a football tackle, Cal umpired in his off-seasons, and when he retired from football became an AL umpire. He weighed 250 pounds, and few players chose to argue with Hubbard. He was inducted in 1976.

CARL HUBBELL
Pitcher (1928-1943)
Hubbell used the screwball to notch 253 career wins and a 2.97 ERA, all for the Giants. From 1933 to 1937,

HALL OF FAME

he posted five straight 20-win seasons, and was NL MVP in '33 and '36. Inducted in 1947, "King Carl" led the NL in wins three times, ERA three times, and in strikeouts once. In the 1934 All-Star game, the left-handed "Meal Ticket" struck out five straight Hall-of-Famers—Babe Ruth, Lou Gehrig, Jimmie Foxx, Al Simmons, and Joe Cronin.

MILLER HUGGINS
Manager (1913-1929)
A decent second baseman with the Reds and Cardinals, Huggins is best remembered as the Yankee manager of the 1920s. Standing only 5'6", he was the one man able to temper the boisterous Babe Ruth. "The Mighty Mite's" 1927 Yankees team is widely consider the best of all time. "Hug" was 1,413-1,134 in his career, including five seasons with mediocre Cardinal clubs. Inducted in 1964, he won six pennants and three world championships in his 12 years with the Yankees.

CATFISH HUNTER
Pitcher (1965-1979)
Given his nickname by A's owner Charlie Finley, Hunter went directly from high school to the major leagues. Beginning in 1971, Catfish won 20 games or more five straight seasons and earned the Cy Young Award in 1974 with a 25-12 record. After three A's world championships (1972 to 1974), Hunter signed with the Yankees for $3.75 million in 1975, then the biggest contract in baseball history. Inducted in 1987, he had a 224-166 career record with a 3.26 ERA and 2,958 strikeouts.

MONTE IRVIN
Outfielder (Negro Leagues years 1939-1943; 1945-1948; NL years 1949-1956)
Despite twice leading the Negro National League in hitting, it was 1949 before 30-year-old Irvin was signed by the Giants. He began his Negro League career in 1939, and he also played in the Mexican League, where he won a triple crown in 1940. In eight NL seasons, he hit .293, leading the league in RBI with 121 in 1951. He was enshrined in 1973.

TRAVIS JACKSON
Shortstop (1922-1936)
A solid defensive shortstop for the Giants of the 1920s and 1930s, Jackson helped the Giants to four pennants. "Stonewall" also batted over .300 in six seasons, and he had more than 90 RBI in three seasons. Inducted in 1982, he accumulated a career average of .291, peaking at .339 in 1930.

FERGUSON JENKINS
Pitcher (1965-1983)
After being traded from the Phillies to the Cubs in early 1966, Jenkins embarked on a string of six consecutive 20-plus win seasons. He won only 14 in 1973 and was traded to Texas, where he won the 1974 Cy Young Award with a 25-12 record. One of the game's most durable pitchers, Jenkins had a career 284-226 record, with a a 3.34 ERA and 3,192 Ks. He was inducted in 1991.

HUGHIE JENNINGS
Shortstop (1891-1903; 1907; 1909; 1912; 1918)
Manager (1907-1920; 1924)
From 1894 to 1896 as shortstop and captain of NL Baltimore, Jen-

nings led the club to pennants. In his five years with Baltimore, "Hustling Hughie" never hit below .328 and was a lifetime .312 hitter. In his first three years as Detroit's manager, Jennings won pennants, from 1907 to 1909. Inducted in 1945, he was 1,163-984 as a manager.

BAN JOHNSON
AL President (1901-1927)
The founder of the American League, Johnson was arguably the most powerful man in baseball during the first quarter of the 20th century. When the minor Western League folded in 1893, Johnson revived it. He put it on solid footing and made it a major league in 1901. The Black Sox scandal of 1920 undermined his power, however, and led to the Commissioner system, leading to Johnson's retirement in 1927. He was inducted in 1937.

JUDY JOHNSON
Third baseman (1919-1936)
The greatest third baseman in Negro League history, Johnson combined steady defensive play with stellar batting performances. A line-drive hitter, Johnson hit .390 and .406 in two of his seasons with the Philadelphia Hilldales, leading them to two black World Series appearances. In later years, Judy scouted for the Philadelphia A's and Phillies. He was inducted in 1975.

WALTER JOHNSON
Pitcher (1907-1927)
One of the first five men elected to the Hall, Johnson's legendary fastball and pinpoint control enabled him to win 416 games (second on the all-time list) with the usually inferior Senators. In his 20-year career, "The Big Train" led the AL in strikeouts 12 times, shutouts seven times, and in victories six times. His 110 shutouts are the most in history. Inducted in 1936, "Barney's" 2.17 career ERA is seventh lowest, his 531 complete games rank fifth, and his 5,923 innings pitched are the third most in baseball.

ADDIE JOSS
Pitcher (1902-1910)
In only nine seasons with Cleveland, Joss won 160 games with a winning percentage of .623 and an ERA of 1.88 (second all time). A side-armer, Joss hurled two no-hitters. He struck out 926 batters and walked only 370 in 2,336 innings pitched. In 1911, he died of tubercular meningitis at age 31. Due to his spectacular record, the Hall's usual 10-year career requirement was waived for Joss, in 1978.

AL KALINE
Outfielder (1953-1974)
As a 20-year-old outfielder with Detroit in 1955, Kaline won the batting title, hitting .340, to become the youngest champion ever. Although he never duplicated that figure, he played in 18 All-Star games, won 11 Gold Gloves, and accumulated 3,007 hits. Inducted in 1980, he also had 498 doubles, 399 home runs, 1,583 RBI, 1,622 runs scored, and 1,277 bases on balls. In his only World Series, in 1968, Kaline hit .379 and had two homers.

TIM KEEFE
Pitcher (1880-1893)
In only 14 seasons, Keefe won 342 games, one of six 19th century pitchers to top the 300 mark. Remarkably, after overhand pitching was legalized in 1884, Keefe continued to pitch—and win—underhand-

HALL OF FAME

ed. Inducted in 1964, "Sir Timothy" pioneered the use of the changeup to notch a career 2.62 ERA with 557 complete games. He led his league in ERA in three seasons.

WEE WILLIE KEELER
Outfielder (1892-1910)
Keeler said, "I hit 'em where they ain't." Utilizing his good speed and batting skills, he developed the "Baltimore chop" to bounce the ball over and between infielders. From 1894 to 1901, he collected a major league record 200 hits each season. Inducted in 1939, he had 2,947 career hits, 1,727 runs, and a .343 batting average. In 1897, he hit in 44 consecutive games.

GEORGE KELL
Third baseman (1943-1957)
An excellent third baseman and career .306 hitter, Kell excelled for five different clubs in the 1940s and 1950s. In 1949, he edged out Ted Williams for his only batting crown, hitting .3429 to Williams's .3427. Inducted in 1983, Kell scored a lifetime 881 runs and drove in 870 runs.

JOE KELLEY
Outfielder (1891-1906; 1908)
Kelley played for the great Baltimore teams of the 1890s, and later went to star with Brooklyn and Cincinnati. He batted over .300 in 11 straight years. In 1894, he hit .393 and batted a perfect 9 for 9 in a doubleheader. Kelley had a lifetime .317 average, with 194 triples, 1,424 runs scored, and 1,193 RBI. He was inducted in 1971.

GEORGE KELLY
First baseman (1915-1917; 1919-1930; 1932)
After failing in his first three seasons in the bigs, Kelly came into his own for the Giants in 1919. From 1921 to 1926, Kelly hit over .300 and averaged 108 RBI, helping the Giants capture four pennants. Inducted in 1973, he was a .297 hitter and totaled 1,020 RBI.

KING KELLY
Outfielder; catcher (1878-1993)
Baseball's first celebrity, Kelly was the subject of the popular song, "Slide, Kelly, Slide"; recited "Casey At The Bat" on stage; and off the field played the role of dandy to a tee. On field, he perfected the hit-and-run and developed the hook and head-first slides. Inducted in 1945, he hit .308 lifetime and scored 1,357 runs.

HARMON KILLEBREW
First baseman; third baseman (1954-1975)
Killebrew hit 573 home runs; only Babe Ruth hit more in AL history. Killebrew led the league in homers five times, each time hitting more than 40. "Killer" had 40 or more homers in eight different seasons. The 1969 AL MVP also drove in more than 100 RBI in nine years, pacing the AL three times. Inducted in 1984, he hit only .256 lifetime but had 1,559 bases on balls.

RALPH KINER
Outfielder (1946-1955)
Joining Pittsburgh after World War II, in his first seven seasons Kiner led or tied for the NL lead in homers. Inducted in 1975, he had 369 lifetime dingers (for an incredible 7.1 home run percentage),

1,015 RBI, and 1,011 bases on balls in 10 years. Kiner has enjoyed a second career as a broadcaster for the Mets.

CHUCK KLEIN
Outfielder (1928-1944)
Playing five and one-half seasons in Philadelphia's cozy Baker Bowl, Klein led the NL in homers four times and never hit below .337. He was the 1932 NL MVP and won the Triple Crown in 1933 (.368 average, 28 homers, 120 RBI). Klein set an all-time record for outfield assists with 44 in 1930. Traded to the Cubs in 1934, he remained productive but didn't approach his earlier performances. Inducted in 1980, lifetime he had a .320 batting average, 300 homers, and 1,202 RBI.

BILL KLEM
Umpire (1905-1941)
Baseball's best-known umpire, Klem was active from 1905 to 1941. He revolutionized the position, and is credited with being the first to employ hand signals and don a chest protector. Inducted in 1953, he worked a record 18 World Series, and he was the umpire at the first All-Star Game in 1933.

SANDY KOUFAX
Pitcher (1955-1966)
Koufax had two careers. His best record in his first six years was an 11-11 mark. But, between 1961 and 1966, the lefty led the NL in wins and shutouts three times each and Ks four times. Koufax paced the Dodgers to pennants in '63, '65, and '66 while winning the Cy Young Award each year. His 25-5 record in 1963 earned him the NL MVP. Pitching in excruciating pain due to arthritis, Koufax led the NL in ERA his final five seasons, culminating with a 1.73 mark while going 27-9 in 1966. He retired at the peak of his profession. Inducted in 1972, he had a 165-87 record with a 2.76 career ERA and 2,396 strikeouts to only 817 walks.

NAP LAJOIE
Second baseman (1896-1916)
One of the best righty batters in history, Lajoie was the best second baseman of his era and became the first man at his position to be elected to the Hall. A graceful fielder, he hit over .300 16 times in his career. Inducted in 1937, he won the Triple Crown in 1901, the American League's debut season; he batted .422 with 14 homers and 125 RBI. His presence and outstanding performance gave the AL much-neeed attention and respect. Lajoie had a career .339 average, 3,251 hits, and 658 doubles.

KENESAW MOUNTAIN LANDIS
Commissioner (1920-1944)
Baseball's first Commissioner, Landis left his job as a federal judge in 1920 to take complete control of the major leagues. In cleaning up the Black Sox scandal, he restored the public's confidence in the integrity of baseball. His rule was law, and nobody dared challenge his authority. A champion of player rights, he unsuccessfully tried to halt the farm system. He died in 1944, eight days after his election for another seven-year term as "Baseball Czar." He was inducted in 1944.

TONY LAZZERI
Second baseman (1926-1939)
The second baseman on the Murderer's Row Yankee teams of the

1920s and '30s, Lazzeri combined power, high average, and slick fielding. A career .292 hitter who socked 178 homers, "Poosh 'Em Up" topped the .300 mark five times, and hit .354 in 1929. He was inducted in 1991.

BOB LEMON
Pitcher (1941-1942; 1946-1958)
Lemon made the big leagues as a third baseman, but he made the Hall of Fame as a pitcher. Turned into a pitcher during World War II, Lemon won 20 games for the Indians seven times from 1948 to 1956. He led the AL in wins three times and complete games five times. Inducted in 1976, he had a career 207-128 record for a .618 winning percentage. As manager, he took over the Yankees in mid-1978, overtaking the bumbling Red Sox from 10½ games back and leading the Bombers to a world championship.

BUCK LEONARD
First baseman (1934-1948)
In the Negro Leagues, Walter Leonard played Lou Gehrig to teammate Josh Gibson's Babe Ruth. Leonard played for the Homestead Grays and helped lead them to nine consecutive pennants. He was a lefthanded power hitter and clutch RBI man who hit for a high average. Inducted in 1972, he twice led the NNL in hitting, peaking at .410 in 1947. In 1952, at age 45, Leonard turned down an offer from Bill Veeck to play for the St. Louis Browns.

FREDDIE LINDSTROM
Third baseman (1924-1936)
Playing in the World Series for the Giants as an 18-year-old rookie in 1924, Lindstrom survived two bad hop ground balls that helped beat New York to become one of the NL's best third basemen. He topped the .300 mark seven times, including a .379 average in 1930. A year later an injury led to a switch to the outfield. He retired in 1936, at age 31, with a .311 career batting average, 301 doubles, and 895 runs scored. He was inducted in 1976.

POP LLOYD
Shortstop (1905-1932)
The finest shortstop in Negro baseball, Lloyd's stellar performance in a 1909 exhibition series against Ty Cobb's Tigers so embarrassed Cobb he vowed never to play blacks again. In 1928, despite being age 44, Lloyd led the Negro National League in batting with an eye-popping .564 average. From his time in Cuba, his nickname was *"El Cuchara,"* which means "scoop" in Spanish. Lloyd was inducted in 1977.

ERNIE LOMBARDI
Catcher (1931-1947)
Called "Schnozz" because of his enormous nose, Lombardi was a slow, awkward-looking catcher who could hit a ton. He surpassed the .300 mark 10 times. In 1938 his league-leading .342 average with Cincinnati earned him the NL MVP Award. Five years later with the Braves, Lombardi again led the league with a .330 average, becoming the only catcher to do so twice. Inducted in 1986, he had a career .306 batting average and 990 RBI.

AL LOPEZ
Manager (1951-1965; 1968-1969)
Catcher (1928; 1930-1947)
A workhorse behind the plate, until 1987 Lopez held the major league

HALL OF FAME

record for games caught. He turned manager in 1951, and in 1954 led Cleveland to 111 wins. In 1959 he won another pennant with the White Sox. Inducted in 1977, he drove his 17 teams to a 1,410-1,004 record for a .584 winning percentage, eighth all time. Usually losing the pennant to the Yankees, Lopez's clubs finished second in the AL ten times.

TED LYONS
Pitcher (1923-1942; 1946)
Lyons had the misfortune of pitching for the White Sox during some of the worst years in the history of the franchise. Inducted in 1955, he won 260 games lifetime, with 356 complete games and 27 shutouts. He led the AL in shutouts twice and wins twice. In 1942, he led the AL with a 2.10 ERA. At age 42, he served three years in the Marines during World War II, then returned to baseball for one last season in 1946, going 1-4 despite a 2.32 ERA.

CONNIE MACK
Manager (1894-1896; 1901-1950)
As player, manager, and owner, Mack had a career that spanned an incredible eight decades. Manager of the Athletics from 1901 to 1950, Mack built then tore apart several championship clubs. His first dynasty was from 1910 to 1914, when the Athletics won four pennants and three world championships. He sold off many of those players and finished in last place from 1915 to 1921. His second dynasty was the 1929 to 1931 clubs—three pennants and two world champs. Known to all as "Mr. Mack," he was the last man to manage out of uniform, preferring to wear formal attire. Inducted in 1937, he was 3,731-3,948 in his 53 years as a manager.

LARRY MacPHAIL
Executive
As general manager of the Reds and Dodgers, and part-owner of the Yankees, MacPhail played a part in virtually every major baseball development between the wars. He brought air travel and lights to the major leagues with Cincinnati in 1935, and radio broadcasts to Brooklyn in 1938. He was inducted in 1978. MacPhail's son and grandson, Lee and Andy, followed him into positions as baseball executives.

MICKEY MANTLE
Outfielder (1951-1968)
Named after Mickey Cochrane by his baseball-loving father, Mutt, Mantle was taught to switch hit and became baseball's leading switch-hitter. Succeeding Joe DiMaggio as Yankee center fielder, all Mantle did was match Joe's three MVP Awards (1956, 1957, 1962). "The Commerce Comet" hit .353, 52 homers, and drove in 130 RBI to win the Triple Crown in 1956. He led the AL in home runs four times, RBI once, runs scored six times, and walks five times. If not for a series of knee injuries, Mantle may have been the best all time. He had the most all-time World Series homers, RBI, and runs. Inducted in 1974, lifetime he had a .298 batting average, 536 homers, 1,509 RBI, 1,677 runs scored, and 1,734 walks.

HEINIE MANUSH
Outfielder (1923-1939)
Often overlooked today, Manush was one of the best hitters in base-

ball during his era. Topping the .300 mark 11 times, he compiled a career average of .330. Playing for the Tigers, Browns, Senators, Braves, Pirates, and Dodgers, he led his league in hits twice. Inducted in 1964, Manush notched 1,173 career RBI and 1,287 runs.

RABBIT MARANVILLE
Shortstop (1912-1933; 1935)
A top defensive shortstop and consummate showman, Maranville was the kind of player that did the little things, on and off the field, to make his team better. A superior fielder, he ranks first among all shortstops in putouts (5,139). Inducted in 1954, Maranville managed to collect 2,605 hits and score 1,255 runs in 23 NL seasons.

JUAN MARICHAL
Pitcher (1960-1975)
In the mid-1960s, the Giants' Marichal was one of the best and most consistent pitchers in the game. His patented high leg kick masked a multitude of pitches. A six-time 20-game winner, Marichal somehow failed to win the Cy Young Award. His 243 career wins more than made up for that omission. He led the league in shutouts and in complete games twice. Inducted in 1983, "The Dominican Dandy" had a career 243-142 record, a 2.89 ERA, 2,303 Ks, and 52 shutouts.

RUBE MARQUARD
Pitcher (1908-1925)
In 1912, Marquard won his first 19 decisions for the Giants on his way to a 26-11 record. Although he won 23 games the following season, he never again matched his earlier play. He and Christy Mathewson gave the Giants a one-two punch few teams could match. Inducted in 1971, Marquard had a 201-177 career record with 197 complete games.

EDDIE MATHEWS
Third baseman (1952-1968)
Mathews combined with Hank Aaron to form one of the best power combos ever. For 14 consecutive years, Mathews hit 23 or more home runs, hitting 40 or more four times. A steady defensive player, he was an All-Star nine times. He led the NL in bases on balls in four seasons to retire with a total of 1,444. Inducted in 1978, he also tallied 512 career homers, 1,453 RBI, and 1,509 runs scored.

CHRISTY MATHEWSON
Pitcher (1900-1916)
As baseball's most popular player in his day, Mathewson dispelled the prevalent notion at the time that ballplayers need be crude and uneducated. "Big Six" was also perhaps the game's best pitcher. For 12 consecutive seasons he won 20 or more games for the Giants, as his trademark "fadeaway," a screwball, baffled a generation of batters. In the 1905 World Series, he hurled three shutouts in six days. He led the NL in ERA in five seasons, in Ks five times, and in shutouts four times. Inducted in 1936, "Matty" had a 373-188 career record, with a 2.13 ERA and 80 shutouts.

WILLIE MAYS
Outfielder (1951-1952; 1954-1973)
Mays could do everything: hit, field, and run. While his 660 home runs rank third all time, his magnificent over-the-shoulder catch of Vic Wertz's blast to center field in the

1954 World Series has become the standard against which all other catches are compared. Inducted in 1979, "The Say Hey Kid" led the NL in slugging percentage five times, homers and stolen bases four times, triples three times, and runs scored twice. He had 3,283 career hits, a .302 batting average, a .557 slugging percentage, 1,903 RBI, and 2,062 runs scored.

JOE McCARTHY
Manager (1926-1946; 1948-1950)
While McCarthy never played a game in the majors, in 24 years as manager he collected seven world championships and nine pennants. Inducted in 1957, his 2,125-1,333 record gives him an all-time best .615 winning percentage. Most of his success came with the Yankees, where he won four straight World Series from 1936 to 1939. After winning the NL pennant with the Cubs in 1929, McCarthy piloted the Yankees to a pennant in 1932 to become the first manager to win a pennant in both leagues.

TOMMY McCARTHY
Outfielder (1884-1896)
McCarthy made a lasting mark on the game when he perfected the flyball trap in order to throw out the lead runner of a double play, leading to the infield fly rule. Although he was known for his defense, in 1893 he hit a robust .361, helping Boston to the NL title. Inducted in 1946, he was a career .292 hitter and topped the .300 mark four times.

WILLIE McCOVEY
First baseman (1959-1980)
Willie McCovey joined Giants teammate Willie Mays to give opposing pitchers the willies. McCovey smashed 30 or more home runs seven times, leading the NL in dingers three times, in home run percentage five times, and in RBI twice. In 1969, "Stretch" was NL MVP with a .320 average, 45 homers, and 126 RBI. Inducted in 1986, "Big Mac" notched 521 homers, 1,555 RBI, 1,229 runs scored, and 1,350 walks in his career.

JOE McGINNITY
Pitcher (1899-1908)
While McGinnity's nickname "Iron Man" was derived from his off-season occupation in a foundry, it well described his mound efforts. For nine straight years he pitched 300-plus innings, topping 400 twice and leading the league five times. Inducted in 1946, he had a career 247-144 record with a 2.64 ERA and 314 complete games. He pitched another 17 seasons in the minors, finally retiring at age 54.

JOHN McGRAW
Manager (1899; 1901-1932)
As third baseman for Baltimore in the 1890s, McGraw was talented enough to make the Hall on his merits as a player. As the Giants manager from 1902 to 1932, he dominated baseball during it's "scientific" era, and successfully made the transition to the power game of the 1920s. Despite capturing 10 pennants, the "Little Napoleon" won the World Series only three times. A manager for 33 years, McGraw racked up 2,784 victories in 4,801 games, both second on the all-time list to Connie Mack.

BILL McKECHNIE
Manager (1915; 1922-1926; 1928-1946)

McKechnie may have been the best-liked manager ever. Winning pennants with three different teams, the gentlemanly McKechnie refuted Leo Durocher's notion that "nice guys finish last." McKechnie's best effort, though, might have been with the fifth-place 1937 Braves, enough to win "The Deacon" Manager of the Year. Inducted in 1962, he won two world championships and was 1,899-1,724 in 25 years.

JOE MEDWICK
Outfielder (1932-1948)

Medwick provided the power to light up the 1930s Cardinals' "Gashouse Gang." He led the NL in RBI three consecutive years and in hits twice. In 1937, "Ducky" (a nickname he loathed) batted .374 with 31 homers and 154 RBI to capture the Triple Crown. Inducted in 1968, "Muscles" was a brawler who had a career .324 average, 1,383 RBI, and 540 doubles. In the 1934 World Series against Detroit, his hard slide into third earned him the wrath of Tiger fans, who pelted him with garbage until Commissioner Landis ordered him from the field for his own safety.

JOHNNY MIZE
First baseman (1936-1942; 1946-1953)

Despite losing three prime years to World War II, Mize still connected for 359 home runs, primarily with the Cardinals and Giants. He led the NL in homers four times and RBI three times. Sold to the Yankees in 1949, Mize played in five World Series, hitting three home runs in the 1952 classic. Inducted in 1981, lifetime "The Big Cat" batted .312, slugged .562 (eighth highest in history), and drove in 1,337.

JOE MORGAN
Second baseman (1963-1984)

Where Morgan played, championships followed. After leading Cincinnati's "Big Red Machine" of the mid-1970s to two World Series victories, Morgan led the 1980 Astros to a division title. He then helped Philadelphia capture the pennant in 1983. Inducted in 1990, "Little Joe" won back-to-back NL MVP Awards in 1975 and '76. Only 5'7", he had 268 career homers, 689 stolen bases, 1,133 RBI, 1,650 runs, and 1,865 walks.

STAN MUSIAL
Outfielder; first baseman (1941-1944; 1946-1963)

Originally signed as a pitcher, Musial hurt his arm and transferred to the outfield. Joining the Cardinals in 1941, Musial batted .426 in 12 games, and he went on to lead the NL seven times in batting average. NL MVP in 1943, '46, and '48, he used his "corkscrew" batting stance to hit over .310 16 seasons in a row. At the time of his retirement in 1963, "Stan the Man" held more than 50 major league and NL records. Inducted in 1969, he had a career .331 batting average, 3,630 base hits (fourth all time), 725 doubles (third), 475 home runs, 1,951 RBI, and 1,949 runs scored.

KID NICHOLS
Pitcher (1890-1901; 1904-1906)

Ranked sixth all time in wins with 361, Nichols starred in the 1890s for Boston, leading them to five NL pennants. Winner of 30 games seven times, Nichols started what he finished. In his 501 Boston starts, he was relieved only 25 times. Inducted in 1949, he had a lifetime 361-208 record and a 2.94 ERA.

JIM O'ROURKE
Outfielder (1872-1893; 1904)
In 1876, O'Rourke collected the first base hit in NL history, one of 2,304 he'd gather for his career. A lifetime .310 hitter, O'Rourke's manner of speaking earned him the nickname "Orator Jim." He was inducted in 1945.

MEL OTT
Outfielder (1926-1947)
Despite his small stature (5'9", 170 pounds), this Giant outfielder stands as a colossus among the game's sluggers. Ott's unique leg kick enabled him to generate the power for 511 home runs, the first man in NL history to hit 500. He led the NL in homers six times, in HR percentage 10 times, but in RBI only once. When he retired in 1947, he held the NL career mark for homers, runs scored (1,859), RBI (1,861), and walks (1,708). Inducted in 1951, "Master Melvin" retired with a .304 average.

SATCHEL PAIGE
Pitcher (Negro Leagues years 1926-1947; 1950; AL years 1948-1949; 1951-1953; 1965)
The first African-American elected to the Hall of Fame, Paige was the Negro Leagues' greatest drawing card. He started pitching for the Birmingham Black Barons in 1926 at age 20. His blazing fastball, uncanny control, and effervescent personality made him a legend by age 30. Inducted in 1971, he made his greatest mark on the game by pitching for the Kansas City Monarchs in the 1940s. In 1948, at age 42, he made his major league debut and helped Cleveland to the AL pennant. In 1965, at age 59, he was still able to pitch three scoreless innings for the Athletics.

JIM PALMER
Pitcher (1965-1967; 1969-1984)
Ace of Baltimore's powerful teams of the 1970s, Palmer won 20 games eight times on his way to three Cy Young Awards and 268 career wins. He led the AL in ERA twice and in innings pitched four times. Inducted in 1990, he had a career 2.86 ERA, 2,212 Ks, and 1,311 walks in 3,948 innings pitched.

HERB PENNOCK
Pitcher (1912-1917; 1919-1934)
Pennock finessed his way through 22 big league seasons to earn 240 career wins. He had his greatest success with the Yankees of the 1920s, for whom he went 5-0 in World Series play, sporting a stellar 1.95 ERA. Inducted in 1948, "The Knight of Kennett Square" won in double figures 13 seasons, and he completed 248 of his 421 career starts.

GAYLORD PERRY
Pitcher (1962-1983)
Though he won 314 games, struck out 3,534 batters, and registered a 3.10 ERA during a 22-year career that included tenures with eight different teams, Perry was best known for throwing—or not throwing—a spitball. He won 20 games five times in his career. He won the AL Cy Young Award in 1972 with Cleveland, and the 1978 NL Cy Young Award with San Diego, making him the only pitcher to win the award in both leagues. He was inducted in 1991.

HALL OF FAME

EDDIE PLANK
Pitcher (1901-1917)
A late bloomer, Plank didn't reach Connie Mack's A's until age 26. No matter, the lefthander blossomed to win 327 games. He won at least 20 games in eight seasons, with four in a row from 1902 to 1905. Inducted in 1946, "Gettysburg Eddie" compiled 69 career shutouts, fifth all time, and a 2.34 ERA.

OLD HOSS RADBOURNE
Pitcher (1880-1891)
In 1884, Radbourne won 60 games for NL Providence, still an all-time record, notching a 1.38 ERA and 679 innings pitched. In only 12 seasons he chalked up 311 wins and a 2.67 ERA. Inducted in 1939, Old Hoss's 489 career complete games are seventh on the all-time list.

PEE WEE REESE
Shortstop (1940-1942; 1946-1958)
Reese led the Dodgers to seven pennants between 1941 and 1956. Despite his small size (5'10", 160 pounds), he was the acknowledged leader on the star-laden club. One of the top-fielding shortstops during the 1940s and 1950s, Pee Wee was an All-Star from 1947 to 1954. Inducted in 1984, he scored 1,338 runs in his career, leading the NL in 1947 with 132. When Branch Rickey signed Jackie Robinson, it was Reese, a Southerner, who led his teammates to accept Robinson.

SAM RICE
Outfielder (1915-1934)
Rice, a fleet 150-pounder, smacked 2,987 hits on his way to a .322 career average for Washington. Inducted in 1963, he led the AL in hits twice and had 200 or more base hits six times. He scored 1,515 career runs and stole 351 bases. A master of bat control, in 1929 Rice struck out only nine times in 616 at bats.

BRANCH RICKEY
Executive
One of the game's great innovators, Rickey invented the farm system and built NL dynasties in St Louis and Brooklyn. When he joined the Cardinals in 1919 as president and field manager, the franchise could not compete with richer clubs. "The Mahatma" began to buy minor league clubs, and by 1941, St. Louis had 32 minor league affiliates. He moved to Brooklyn in 1942 to build that franchise. Rickey's most historic act, however, was to integrate the major leagues when he signed Jackie Robinson in 1947. Rickey was enshrined in 1967.

EPPA RIXEY
Pitcher (1912-1917; 1919-1933)
Rixey was a very good pitcher for some not very good teams, winning 266 games while losing 251. A workhorse and a master of control, Rixey won in double figures in 14 seasons and won 20 games four times. He was inducted in 1963. In 1925, his best season, he went 25-13 for Cincinnati.

ROBIN ROBERTS
Pitcher (1948-1966)
Despite a penchant for throwing the gopher ball, Roberts won 20 games for six consecutive seasons from 1950 to 1955. He topped the NL in wins four straight years, and in innings pitched and complete games five times each. While not remembered as a strikeout artist, Robin did lead the NL two years in row in Ks. In 1952, he went 28-7 for

the sixth-place Phillies. Inducted in 1976, Roberts was 286-245 with a 3.41 ERA in his 19 years.

BROOKS ROBINSON
Third baseman (1955-1977)
One of the greatest fielding third basemen ever, Robinson won the Gold Glove 16 times in 23 seasons. The AL MVP in 1964, Brooks turned in a .317 average, 28 homers, and a league-leading 118 RBI. He sparkled in postseason play, posting a .348 average in 18 ALCS games. In the 1970 World Series, he led the Orioles over the Reds, hitting .429 and turning in one spectacular fielding play after another. Inducted in 1983, he had 268 career homers, 1,357 RBI, and 1,232 runs.

FRANK ROBINSON
Outfielder (1956-1976)
Robinson was the first and only player to be selected MVP in both leagues. He was named NL Rookie of the Year in 1956 and the loop's MVP in 1961, when he paced the NL with a .611 slugging average and led the Reds to a pennant. Traded to Baltimore after the '65 season, Frank responded in '66 by hitting .316, 49 home runs, and knocking in 122 RBI to win the Triple Crown. Inducted in 1982, he hit 30 homers in 11 seasons, and his 586 career homers rank fourth all time. He also had 1,812 career RBI and 1,829 runs scored. Named manager of the Indians in 1975, Robinson was the first African-American to manage a major league team.

JACKIE ROBINSON
Second baseman (1947-1956)
The first African-American to play major league baseball since 1884, Robinson succeeded under almost unbearable pressure to secure the black player a permanent place in the game. He endured numerous racial slights, even from his own teammates, without yielding his dignity, while leading the Dodgers to six pennants. A tremendous athlete, Robinson was a four-sport star at UCLA and served in the Army during World War II, before reaching the Dodgers. As a 28-year-old rookie for Brooklyn in 1947, Robinson's aggressive base-running and hitting earned him Rookie of the Year honors. Two years later, in 1949, he led the NL with a .342 average and was named NL MVP. In ten years of major league service, he accumulated a .311 batting average. He was enshrined in 1962.

WILBERT ROBINSON
Manager (1902; 1914-1931)
A catching star for Baltimore in the 1890s, Robinson coached under the Giants' John McGraw before becoming Brooklyn's manager in 1914. "Uncle Robbie" won pennants in 1916 and 1920 but never won a World Series. Inducted in 1945, he had a career 1,399-1,398 record.

EDD ROUSH
Outfielder (1913-1929; 1931)
One of the great defensive outfielders, Roush swung his 48-ounce bat with enough authority to attain two NL batting titles and a .323 lifetime average. In his 10 years in Cincinnati, he never hit lower than .321. Inducted in 1962, he had 1,099 career runs and 981 RBI. Roush habitually held out of spring train-

RED RUFFING
Pitcher (1924-1942; 1945-1947)
In six seasons with the Red Sox, Ruffing couldn't win, going 39-96 from 1924 to 1930 and leading the AL in losses twice. After he was traded to the Yankees, he couldn't lose, with a career 273-225 record and a 7-2 mark in 10 World Series games. Inducted in 1967, he won 20 games four seasons in a row from 1936 to 1939.

AMOS RUSIE
Pitcher (1889-1895; 1897-1898; 1901)
Rusie's fastball forced the rule makers to move the pitching distance from 45 feet to 60 feet 6 inches. From 1890 to 1895, the Giants pitcher led the NL in Ks five times, yet he walked nearly a man for every strikeout. "The Hoosier Thunderbolt" had eight 20-win seasons and 246 career victories in only nine full seasons, before he was traded to Cincinnati for Christy Mathewson. Rusie was inducted in 1977.

BABE RUTH
Outfielder; pitcher (1914-1935)
George Herman Ruth is arguably the greatest player of all time. A man of gargantuan appetites and ability, the Babe's mystique has transcended the sport of baseball and has become ingrained in American mythology. Starting his career as a pitcher with Boston, he was one of the best in the AL. In 1916, the Babe led the AL with a 1.75 ERA while going 23-12. He had 24 wins in '17 with a loop-high 35 complete games. Converted to the outfield part-time in 1918, he led the AL in homers with 11. After he was sold to the Yankees in 1920, he became a full-time flycatcher, and all but invented the home run, slugging 714 for his career, including a then-record 60 in 1927. Inducted in 1936, he led the AL in homers 12 seasons, RBI six seasons, slugging percentage 13 times, and bases on balls 11 times. He had a career .342 batting average, .690 slugging average (first all time), 506 doubles, 2,211 RBI (second all time), 2,174 runs (second all time), and 2,056 walks (first all time).

RAY SCHALK
Catcher (1912-1929)
Although Schalk's career average was .253, few complained when he was elected to the Hall. A superb catcher, Ray's game was defense. In 1920, he caught four 20-game winners for the White Sox, and four no-hitters, more than any other catcher. Inducted in 1955, he holds the AL record for assists by a catcher (1,811). Untainted by the 1919 Black Sox scandal, "Cracker" went on to play another decade.

RED SCHOENDIENST
Second baseman (1945-1963)
Schoendienst teamed with shortstop Marty Marion to form one of baseball's best-ever double-play combinations. Red could also hit, reaching a career-high .342 in 1953. Despite contracting tuberculosis in 1958, he returned to play parts of five more seasons. Inducted in 1989, he had 2,449 career hits and 1,223 runs scored.

HALL OF FAME

JOE SEWELL
Shortstop (1920-1933)
Sewell replaced Ray Chapman in the Cleveland lineup following Chapman's tragic death in 1920. One of the game's best fielding shortstops, Sewell struck out only 114 times in 7,132 at bats. Inducted in 1977, he had 1,141 career runs and 1,051 RBI.

AL SIMMONS
Outfielder (1924-1941; 1943-1944)
An unlikely looking hitter due to his "foot in the bucket" batting stance, Simmons was a leading slugger of his era. From 1929 to 1931, he helped the Athletics to three consecutive pennants, winning batting titles in both 1930 and 1931 with averages of .381 and .390. Inducted in 1953, "Bucketfoot Al" batted over .300 in the first 11 seasons of his career, racking up 2,927 hits and a career .334 batting average.

GEORGE SISLER
First baseman (1915-1922; 1924-1930)
Like Babe Ruth, Sisler's hitting was too good to be on a pitcher's schedule. He was switched to first full-time in 1916 for the Browns and became one of the best, defensively. At bat he was simply unbelievable, hitting .407, .371, and .420 from 1920 to 1922. In 1920, "Gorgeous George" collected 257 base hits, still the all-time record. A sinus infection affected his vision sidelined him in 1923. He returned to play seven more seasons. He was inducted in 1939.

ENOS SLAUGHTER
Outfielder (1938-1942; 1946-1959)
Slaughter would do anything—and often did—in order to win, using hustle to make up for any shortcomings in talent. His mad dash from first to home on a double won the 1946 World Series for the Cardinals. He led the NL in base hits in 1942 before going to war; he led the league in RBI when he came back. Inducted in 1985, "Country" played on four world champions.

DUKE SNIDER
Outfielder (1947-1964)
Known as the "Duke of Flatbush" to his Brooklyn fans, Snider was one of a trio of Hall of Fame center fielders in New York during the 1950s. The others were named Willie Mays and Mickey Mantle. Inducted in 1980, from 1953 to 1957 Snider hit 40 homers. He had 407 career homers, 1,333 RBI, and 1,259 runs scored.

WARREN SPAHN
Pitcher (1942; 1946-1965)
Baseball's winningest lefthander, Spahn didn't even stick in the majors until he was age 25. With the Braves, he won 20 games or more in 13 seasons, tying the major league record. Inducted in 1973, he led the league in wins eight times, complete games nine times, and strikeouts four times. He won the Cy Young Award in 1957, its second year of existence. After 21 years, Spahn retired with 363 wins (fifth all time), 245 losses, a 3.09 ERA, 382 complete games, and 63 shutouts (sixth all time) in 5,243⅔ innings pitched.

AL SPALDING
Pitcher (1871-1878); executive
A star pitcher in the 1870s, Spalding started a sporting goods company and took over NL Chicago. As a pitcher, he had a .787 career win-

HALL OF FAME

ning percentage. Inducted in 1939 as an executive he helped write the new NL's constitution.

TRIS SPEAKER
Outfielder (1907-1928)
The best center fielder of his time, Speaker played close enough to the infield to take pick-off throws at second. "The Grey Eagle" hit over .300 in 18 seasons and topped .375 six times on his way to a career .344 mark (seventh all time). Traded from Boston to Cleveland in 1916, he won his only batting title, at .386. Inducted in 1937, Tris hit a record 792 career doubles, and had 3,515 base hits (fifth all time).

WILLIE STARGELL
Outfielder; first baseman (1962-1982)
One of the strongest players ever, Stargell made tape-measure homers common. He had 13 consecutive years of 20 or more home runs, pacing the NL in 1971 and 1973. He was named season, NLCS, and World Series MVP in 1979, when he led the world champion Bucs. Inducted in 1988, he had 475 career homers and 1,540 RBI.

CASEY STENGEL
Manager (1934-1936; 1938-1943; 1949-1960; 1962-1965)
A good outfielder, Stengel's two homers in the 1923 World Series helped the Giants beat the Yankees. As manager of Brooklyn and Boston, he earned a reputation as an entertaining, if not very effective, skipper. His creative use of the language, dubbed "Stengelese," made him a fan favorite. Named Yankee manager in 1949, "The Old Professor" won 10 pennants in 12 years, plus seven world championships. Inducted in 1966, he had a career 1,905-1,842 record.

BILL TERRY
First baseman (1923-1936)
A career .341 hitter, Terry was the last National Leaguer to hit over .400, batting .401 in 1930 with an amazing 254 hits. Inducted in 1954, "Memphis Bill" had more than 100 RBI from 1927 to 1932. A fine defensive first baseman. He took over as Giant manager in 1932 and led the team to three pennants.

SAM THOMPSON
Outfielder (1885-1898; 1906)
Thompson was a home run hitter in an era when the talent was not much appreciated. He had his greatest success with the Phillies in the 1890s, where in 1894, he hit .404 and fellow outfielders, Billy Hamilton (.399), Ed Delahanty (.400), and Tuck Turner (.416) all had big years. "Big Sam" led the NL in base hits three times, and in homers and RBI twice each. Inducted in 1974, he had 128 career homers, with a .331 average and 1,299 RBI.

JOE TINKER
Shortstop (1902-1916)
Oddly, Tinker, Johnny Evers, and Frank Chance were all elected to the Hall in the same year. Shortstop Tinker was a fielding whiz who keyed the success of that double-play combo. Although not a great hitter, he stole 336 career bases to augment his .263 average. His batting averages from 1902 to 1912 (the years he was with the Cubs) were better than most starting NL shortstops of the time. He was inducted in 1946.

PIE TRAYNOR
Third baseman (1920-1935; 1937)
Traynor earned his way into the Hall of Fame as the best fielding third baseman of his era. A career .320 hitter for Pittsburgh, he hit .300 or better 10 times and had more than 100 RBI seven times. He was selected in 1969 as a member of the all-time team for baseball's centennial. Inducted in 1948, Pie had 1,273 career RBI and 1,183 runs.

DAZZY VANCE
Pitcher (1915; 1918; 1922-1935)
As a 31-year-old rookie with Brooklyn in 1922, Vance won 18 games. Two years later his mark of 28-6 earned him league MVP honors. Armed with an incredible fastball, he led the major leagues in Ks each of his first seven seasons and paced the NL in ERA three times. Inducted in 1955, Dazzy had a career 197-140 record, with a 3.24 ERA and 2,045 Ks.

ARKY VAUGHAN
Shortstop (1932-1943; 1947-1948)
One of the game's best hitting shortstops, only twice in 14 seasons did Vaughan fail to hit .300. In 1935, his .385 average for Pittsburgh led the NL. Arky notched a career .406 on-base percentage, .318 batting average, 1,173 runs, and 926 RBI. Inducted in 1985, he scored more than 100 runs in five seasons, and he led the NL in putouts and assists three times.

BILL VEECK
Executive
One of baseball's most colorful showmen, Veeck integrated the AL when he signed Larry Doby while the Indians' owner. He owned three AL teams—Cleveland, St. Louis, and Chicago. His 1948 Tribe club was the first to top two million in attendance. While owner of the Browns, he sent midget Eddie Gaedel up to bat, and as the chief of the White Sox, introduced baseball's first exploding scoreboard. He was inducted in 1991.

RUBE WADDELL
Pitcher (1897; 1899-1910)
Waddell threw hard and lived even harder. In the AL's first six seasons, Rube was the circuit's best lefthander, under the watchful eye of Connie Mack, winning 20 games four straight years and leading the league in Ks six consecutive years. An eccentric, Waddell couldn't confine himself to baseball, as alligator wrestling, fire-fighting, acting, marbles, and the demon alcohol all competed for his attention. Inducted in 1946, he had a career 191-145 record with 2,316 Ks.

HONUS WAGNER
Shortstop (1897-1917)
One of the game's first five inductees to the Hall of Fame, Wagner hit over .300 17 consecutive seasons. Bowlegged and awkward looking, Wagner possessed tremendous speed and range afield. For his 21-year career, the shortstop had 722 stolen bases and a .327 batting average, highest of any shortstop. Honus led the NL in batting eight times, slugging six times, RBI four times, runs scored twice, and doubles eight times. Inducted in 1936, "The Flying Dutchman" accumulated 3,418 career hits, 643 doubles, 252 triples, 1,732 RBI, 1,735 runs scored, and 963 walks. Some consider Wagner the greatest player of all time.

HALL OF FAME

BOBBY WALLACE
Shortstop (1894-1918)
The first AL shortstop elected to the Hall, during the first decade of the league Wallace was the best at his position. He made his mark with the glove, leading the league in putouts three times and assists four times. He averaged 6.1 chances per game lifetime. Inducted in 1953, he twice notched more than 100 RBI in a season.

ED WALSH
Pitcher (1904-1917)
Perhaps no other pitcher threw the spitball as successfully as Walsh. While his arm gave out after only seven full seasons as a starter, he recorded nearly 170 of his career 195 wins during that span. In 1908, he pitched 464 innings for the White Sox on his way to 40 victories. He led the AL in games pitched five times, innings pitched four times, games started three times, and in strikeouts twice. Inducted in 1946, "Big Ed" had a career 195-126 record with a 1.82 ERA, the lowest of all time.

LLOYD WANER
Outfielder (1927-1942; 1944-1945)
"Little Poison," to older brother Paul's "Big Poison," Lloyd Waner was to the single what Babe Ruth was to the home run. In 1927, Waner's rookie year, the little leadoff man hit 198 one-baggers. He used his speed to cover the vast Forbes Field outfield, leading the NL in putouts four times. Inducted in 1967, Waner had a .316 career batting average, 2,459 hits, and 1,201 runs scored.

PAUL WANER
Outfielder (1926-1945)
"Big Poison" didn't settle for singles as did his little brother; 905 of Paul Waner's 3,152 career hits were for extra bases. He led the NL in hitting three times, peaking at .380 in 1927, when he led Pittsburgh to the pennant and was named league MVP. Inducted in 1952, Waner retired with a .333 batting average, 603 doubles, 1,626 runs scored, and 1,309 RBI. When Lloyd was inducted, the Waners became the second brother combination to be so honored, after the Wrights.

MONTE WARD
Pitcher; shortstop (1878-1894)
Perhaps no figure in baseball had distinguished himself in so many areas as did Ward. As a pitcher for Providence, he led the NL in ERA in 1878 and in wins in 1879. Switched to shortstop in 1885, he became the best in the league for New York. Unhappy with the reserve clause, in 1890 he helped form the Player's League. Becoming a manager, he led the Giants to a championship in 1894. Retiring at age 34 to practice law, Ward returned to the game as part-owner of the Braves in 1911. He was inducted in 1964.

GEORGE WEISS
Executive
As farm director and general manager of the Yankees from 1932 through 1960, Weiss deserves much of the credit for creating the Yankee dynasty. He built the farm system to 21 teams, then became general manager and dealt from strength, constantly picking up precisely the player the Yankees needed in exchange for several prospects plucked from the system

he created. He joined the Mets as the club's first president in 1961. He was inducted in 1971.

MICKEY WELCH
Pitcher (1880-1892)
The third man to win 300 games, Welch starred in the 1880s for Troy (New York) and New York of the NL. In 1885 he won 17 consecutive decisions on his way to 44 wins for the year. Inducted in 1973, "Smiling Mickey" won at least 20 games nine times, with four seasons of more than 30. He had a career 311-209 record with a 2.71 ERA.

ZACK WHEAT
Outfielder (1909-1927)
The Dodgers' first star, Wheat played left field in Ebbets Field for 18 seasons. A line-drive hitter, he topped the .300 mark in 14 seasons, including an NL-best .335 in 1918. He was a complete ballplayer who did everything well. Inducted in 1959, he had a career .317 average, 2,884 hits, 1,261 RBI, 1,289 runs scored, and 205 stolen bases.

HOYT WILHELM
Pitcher (1952-1972)
Wilhelm was the first pitcher elected to the Hall (in 1985) solely on his merits as a reliever. A knuckleballer, he toiled for nine teams, pitching in a record 1,070 games and winning 124 in relief. He started only 52 games in his 21-year career, compiling 227 saves and a 2.52 ERA. Oddly, in his first big league at bat, Wilhelm homered; he never hit another.

BILLY WILLIAMS
Outfielder (1959-1976)
Williams's much admired swing produced 426 career homers and a .290 batting average. The NL Rookie of the Year in 1961, he had at least 20 home runs and 84 RBI in 13 consecutive seasons. His two best seasons were in 1970 and 1972. In 1970, Billy hit .322 with 42 homers, a league-best 137 runs scored, and 129 RBI. He led the NL with a .333 batting average and a .606 slugging average, with 37 homers and 122 RBI in 1972. Playing most of his career for the Cubs, between 1963 and 1970 Williams played in a NL-record 1,117 consecutive games. He was inducted in 1987.

TED WILLIAMS
Outfielder (1939-1942; 1946-1960)
Williams's one desire was to walk down the street and have people say, "There goes the greatest hitter that ever lived." Arguably, he was. Despite missing nearly five years to the military, the Red Sox left fielder won two MVP Awards, six batting and four home run titles, and two Triple Crowns. "The Splendid Splinter" batted over .316 in each of his 19 seasons except one, including a .406 mark in 1941 that makes him the last man to reach that plateau. Inducted in 1966, he had 30 or more homers in eight seasons, 20 or more in 16 seasons. "Teddy Ballgame" retired with the sixth highest career batting average (.344), the second highest slugging average (.634), the second most bases on balls (2,019), and the tenth most in both home runs (521) and RBI (1,839).

HACK WILSON
Outfielder (1923-1934)
For five seasons, from 1926 to 1930, the muscular, midgetlike Wilson was one of the game's greatest sluggers. In 1930, the Cub outfielder hit an NL-record 56 homers and

knocked in a major league record 190 runs. Inducted in 1979, he led the NL in homers four times and in RBI twice. Liquor, nonetheless, was Wilson's downfall, and by the end of 1934, he was out of baseball.

GEORGE WRIGHT
Shortstop (1871-1882)
The star shortstop for the original Cincinnati Red Stockings team that went undefeated for the entire 1869 season, Wright played through 1882. He then started a successful sporting goods firm and helped start the Union Association in 1884. Later in life he served on baseball's Centennial Commission, and was instrumental in the creation of the National Baseball Hall of Fame, to which he was inducted in 1937.

HARRY WRIGHT
Manager (1871-1893)
Harry Wright, the older brother of George, was player-manager of the Cincinnati Red Stockings (the first overtly all-professional team), which Harry led to some 130 consecutive victories, fathering professional baseball in the process. He helped start the National Association in 1871, and later managed a number of NL teams, going 225-60 in the National Association and 1,000-825 in the National League. He was inducted in 1953.

EARLY WYNN
Pitcher (1939; 1941-1944; 1946-1963)
After a so-so career with the Senators, Wynn was traded to Cleveland in 1949 and became a big winner. He won 20 games for the Indians four times and had eight consecutive winning seasons. Traded to the White Sox after the '57 season, "Gus" led Chicago to the pennant in 1959 by winning 22 games, plus the Cy Young Award. Inducted in 1972, he had a 300-244 career record and a 3.54 ERA.

CARL YASTRZEMSKI
Outfielder (1961-1983)
Spending his entire 23-year career with the Red Sox, Yastrzemski is the only AL player to collect over 3,000 hits and 400 home runs. "Yaz" will always be remembered for one remarkable season, 1967, when he won the Triple Crown, and one remarkable month of that season, September, when he single-handedly won the pennant for Boston. Taking over left field for Ted Williams, Yaz soon proved that he belonged in the same category, winning batting titles in 1963, '67, and '68. Inducted in 1989, he had 3,419 career hits, a .285 average, 646 doubles, 452 home runs, 1,844 RBI, 1,816 runs scored, and 1,845 bases on balls.

TOM YAWKEY
Executive
Yawkey is one of the few inducted to the Hall (in 1980) who neither played, coached, umpired, nor served as a general manager. In 1933, at age 30, he received his inheritance and bought the Red Sox. Boston at that time was a doormat and Fenway Park was falling apart. Over the next 44 seasons he spent lavishly on the club and the stadium. He failed in his one, singular quest: While they became winners, the Red Sox never won the World Series for Tom Yawkey.

CY YOUNG
Pitcher (1890-1911)

Young won 511 games, which is 95 victories more than runner-up Walter Johnson. In a career that bridged three decades and several eras of play, Cy was consistently superb. Blessed with speed, control, stamina, and just about every quality a successful pitcher needs, Young won 20 or more games 15 times, including nine seasons in a row from 1891 to 1899. He led his league in victories four times, and in ERA, winning percentage, and strikeouts twice each. Inducted in 1937, Cy is also first on the complete-game list with 750 and innings pitched list with 7,356. When they decided to give an award to the season's top pitcher, they named it after Young.

ROSS YOUNGS
Outfielder (1917-1926)

Youngs was a star on four straight pennant winners for John McGraw's Giants in the early 1920s, becoming McGraw's favorite and one of the game's best hitters. On the verge of greatness, in 1925 Youngs's skills deserted him and his average fell nearly 100 points. Diagnosed with Bright's disease, a terminal kidney disorder, Youngs gamely played one more season and died in 1927. Inducted in 1972, he had a .322 career batting average with 1,491 hits and 812 runs scored.

Prior to his death in 1988, Hall of Famer Edd Roush was both the last surviving former Federal League player and the last surviving participant in the infamous 1919 World Series.

Awards and Highlights

Baseball's top achievements and tributes are listed in this section. The all-time career leaders in several batting and pitching categories are included, as well as the leaders among active players. The all-time single-season leaders are next. The Most Valuable Players, the Cy Young Award winners, and the Rookies of the Year follow. Fielding excellence is acknowledged with the Gold Glove Award winners. Finally, the winners and losers of the World Series and the National League and American League Championship Series are listed.

ALL-TIME LEADERS

BATTING AVERAGE
1. Ty Cobb......................367
2. Rogers Hornsby..........358
3. Joe Jackson................356
4. Ed Delahanty..............346
5. **Wade Boggs..............345**
6. Ted Williams...............344
7. Tris Speaker...............344
8. Billy Hamilton..............344
9. Wee Willie Keeler........343
10. Dan Brouthers............342
11. Babe Ruth..................342
12. Harry Heilmann..........342
13. Pete Browning............341
14. Bill Terry.....................341
15. George Sisler.............340
16. Lou Gehrig..................340
17. Jesse Burkett.............339
18. Nap Lajoie..................338
19. Riggs Stephenson......336
20. Al Simmons................334

HITS
1. Pete Rose.................4,256
2. Ty Cobb....................4,191
3. Hank Aaron..............3,771
4. Stan Musial...............3,630
5. Tris Speaker.............3,515
6. Carl Yastrzemski......3,419
7. Honus Wagner..........3,418
8. Eddie Collins.............3,311
9. Willie Mays................3,283
10. Nap Lajoie...............3,244
11. Paul Waner..............3,152
12. Rod Carew...............3,053
13. Lou Brock.................3,023
14. Al Kaline...................3,007
15. Cap Anson................3,000
    Roberto Clemente....3,000
17. Sam Rice..................2,987
18. Sam Crawford..........2,964
19. Wee Willie Keeler....2,947
20. Frank Robinson.......2,943

DOUBLES
1. Tris Speaker................792
2. Pete Rose....................746
3. Stan Musial..................725
4. Ty Cobb.......................724
5. Nap Lajoie...................658
6. Carl Yastrzemski.........646
7. Honus Wagner............643
8. Hank Aaron.................624
9. Paul Waner..................603
10. **George Brett.............599**
11. Charlie Gehringer........574
12. Harry Heilmann...........542
13. Rogers Hornsby..........541
14. Joe Medwick...............540
15. Al Simmons.................539
16. Lou Gehrig...................535
17. Al Oliver......................529
18. Cap Anson...................528
    Frank Robinson...........528
20. **Dave Parker................526**

TRIPLES
1. Sam Crawford..............312
2. Ty Cobb.......................297
3. Honus Wagner.............252
4. Jake Beckley................243
5. Roger Connor..............233
6. Tris Speaker.................223
7. Fred Clarke..................220
8. Dan Brouthers..............205
9. Joe Kelley...................194
10. Paul Waner.................190
11. Bid McPhee................188
12. Eddie Collins..............187
13. Sam Rice....................184
14. Ed Delahanty.............183
    Jesse Burkett.............183
16. Edd Roush.................182
17. Ed Konetchy..............181
18. Buck Ewing................178
19. Rabbit Maranville.......177

473

AWARDS AND HIGHLIGHTS

Harry Stovey..............177
Stan Musial................177

HOME RUNS
1. Hank Aaron 755
2. Babe Ruth 714
3. Willie Mays 660
4. Frank Robinson 586
5. Harmon Killebrew 573
6. Reggie Jackson 563
7. Mike Schmidt..............548
8. Mickey Mantle 536
9. Jimmie Foxx 534
10. Ted Williams 521
    Willie McCovey..........521
12. Eddie Mathews 512
    Ernie Banks 512
14. Mel Ott 511
15. Lou Gehrig 493
16. Willie Stargell 475
    Stan Musial...............475
18. Carl Yastrzemski 452
19. Dave Kingman 442
20. Billy Williams 426

HOME RUN PERCENTAGE
1. Babe Ruth 8.5
2. Ralph Kiner 7.1
3. Harmon Killebrew 7.0
4. Ted Williams 6.8
5. Dave Kingman 6.6
6. Mickey Mantle 6.6
7. Jimmie Foxx 6.6
8. Mike Schmidt...............6.6
9. Hank Greenberg 6.4
10. Willie McCovey 6.4
11. Darryl Strawberry 6.4
12. Lou Gehrig 6.2
13. Hank Aaron 6.1
14. Willie Mays 6.1
15. Hank Sauer 6.0
16. Eddie Mathews 6.0
17. Willie Stargell 6.0
18. Frank Howard 5.9
19. Frank Robinson 5.9
20. Roy Campanella 5.8

RUNS BATTED IN
1. Hank Aaron 2,297
2. Babe Ruth 2,211
3. Lou Gehrig 1,990
4. Ty Cobb 1,961
5. Stan Musial...............1,951
6. Jimmie Foxx 1,921
7. Willie Mays 1,903
8. Mel Ott 1,861
9. Carl Yastrzemski 1,844
10. Ted Williams 1,839
11. Al Simmons 1,827
12. Frank Robinson 1,812
13. Honus Wagner 1,732
14. Cap Anson 1,715
15. Reggie Jackson 1,702
16. Tony Perez 1,652
17. Ernie Banks 1,636
18. Goose Goslin 1,609
19. Dave Winfield............1,602
20. Nap Lajoie 1,599

SLUGGING AVERAGE
1. Babe Ruth 690
2. Ted Williams 634
3. Lou Gehrig 632
4. Jimmie Foxx 609
5. Hank Greenberg 605
6. Joe DiMaggio 579
7. Rogers Hornsby 577
8. Johnny Mize 562
9. Stan Musial..................559
10. Willie Mays 557
11. Mickey Mantle 557
12. Hank Aaron 555
13. Ralph Kiner 548
14. Hack Wilson 545
15. Chuck Klein 543
16. Duke Snider 540
17. Frank Robinson 537
18. Al Simmons 535
19. Dick Allen 534
20. Earl Averill 533

STOLEN BASES
1. Rickey Henderson 994
2. Lou Brock 938
3. Ty Cobb 892
4. Eddie Collins 743
5. Max Carey 738
6. Honus Wagner 703
7. Joe Morgan 689
8. Tim Raines 685
9. Bert Campaneris 649
10. Willie Wilson 632
11. Vince Coleman 586
    Maury Wills 586
13. Davey Lopes 557
14. Cesar Cedeno 550
15. Luis Aparicio 506
16. Ozzie Smith 499
17. Clyde Milan 495
18. Omar Moreno 487
19. Bobby Bonds 461
20. Jimmy Sheckard.........460

RUNS SCORED
1. Ty Cobb 2,245
2. Babe Ruth 2,174
3. Hank Aaron 2,174
4. Pete Rose................2,165
5. Willie Mays 2,062
6. Stan Musial..............1,949
7. Lou Gehrig 1,888
8. Tris Speaker 1,881
9. Mel Ott 1,859
10. Frank Robinson 1,829
11. Eddie Collins 1,818
12. Carl Yastrzemski 1,816
13. Ted Williams 1,798
14. Charlie Gehringer 1,774
15. Jimmie Foxx 1,751
16. Honus Wagner 1,735
17. Wee Willie Keeler 1,727
18. Cap Anson 1,719
19. Jesse Burkett...........1,718
20. Billy Hamilton...........1,692

TOTAL BASES
1. Hank Aaron 6,856
2. Stan Musial..............6,134
3. Willie Mays 6,066
4. Ty Cobb 5,863
5. Babe Ruth 5,793
6. Pete Rose................5,752
7. Carl Yastrzemski 5,539
8. Frank Robinson 5,373
9. Tris Speaker 5,104
10. Lou Gehrig 5,059
11. Mel Ott 5,041
12. Jimmie Foxx 4,956
13. Ted Williams 4,884
14. Honus Wagner 4,868
15. Al Kaline 4,852
16. Reggie Jackson 4,834
17. Rogers Hornsby 4,712
18. Ernie Banks 4,706
19. Al Simmons 4,685
20. Billy Williams 4,599

BASES ON BALLS
1. Babe Ruth 2,056
2. Ted Williams 2,019
3. Joe Morgan 1,865
4. Carl Yastrzemski 1,845
5. Mickey Mantle 1,734
6. Mel Ott 1,708
7. Eddie Yost 1,614
8. Darrell Evans 1,605
9. Stan Musial.............1,599
10. Pete Rose...............1,566
11. Harmon Killebrew 1,559

474

AWARDS AND HIGHLIGHTS

12. Lou Gehrig 1,508
13. Mike Schmidt 1,507
14. Eddie Collins 1,503
15. Willie Mays 1,463
16. Jimmie Foxx 1,452
17. Eddie Mathews 1,444
18. Frank Robinson 1,420
19. Hank Aaron 1,402
20. **Dwight Evans** **1,391**

WINS
1. Cy Young 511
2. Walter Johnson 416
3. Christy Mathewson .. 373
   Grover Alexander 373
5. Warren Spahn 363
6. Pud Galvin 361
   Kid Nichols 361
8. Tim Keefe 342
9. Steve Carlton 329
10. Eddie Plank 327
11. John Clarkson 326
12. Don Sutton 324
13. Phil Niekro 318
14. **Nolan Ryan** **314**
    Gaylord Perry 314
16. Tom Seaver 311
17. Old Hoss Radbourn .. 311
18. Mickey Welch 308
19. Lefty Grove 300
20. Early Wynn 300

WINNING PERCENTAGE
1. Bob Caruthers 692
2. Dave Foutz 690
3. Whitey Ford 690
4. Lefty Grove 680
5. Vic Raschi 667
6. Christy Mathewson .. 665
7. Larry Corcoran 663
8. Sam Leever 658
9. Sal Maglie 657
10. Sandy Koufax 655
11. Johnny Allen 654
12. Ron Guidry 651
13. Lefty Gomez 649
14. Three Finger Brown .. 649
15. John Clarkson 648
16. Dizzy Dean 644
17. Grover Alexander ... 642
18. Deacon Phillippe ... 639
19. Jim Palmer 638
20. Kid Nichols 634

EARNED RUN AVERAGE
1. Ed Walsh 1.82

2. Addie Joss 1.88
3. Three Finger Brown .. 2.06
4. Monte Ward 2.10
5. Christy Mathewson .. 2.13
6. Rube Waddell 2.16
7. Walter Johnson 2.17
8. Orval Overall 2.24
9. Tommy Bond 2.25
10. Will White 2.28
11. Ed Reulbach 2.28
12. Jim Scott 2.32
13. Eddie Plank 2.34
14. Larry Corcoran 2.36
15. Eddie Cicotte 2.37
16. George McQuillan .. 2.38
17. Ed Killian 2.38
18. Doc White 2.38
19. Nap Rucker 2.42
20. Jeff Tesreau 2.43

STRIKEOUTS
1. **Nolan Ryan** **5,511**
2. Steve Carlton 4,136
3. Tom Seaver 3,640
4. **Bert Blyleven** **3,631**
5. Don Sutton 3,574
6. Gaylord Perry 3,534
7. Walter Johnson ... 3,508
8. Phil Niekro 3,342
9. Ferguson Jenkins .. 3,192
10. Bob Gibson 3,117
11. Jim Bunning 2,855
12. Mickey Lolich 2,832
13. Cy Young 2,796
14. Warren Spahn ... 2,583
15. Bob Feller 2,581
16. **Frank Tanana** **2,566**
17. Jerry Koosman .. 2,556
18. Tim Keefe 2,527
19. Christy Mathewson .. 2,502
20. Don Drysdale 2,486

SAVES
1. Rollie Fingers 341
2. **Jeff Reardon** **327**
3. **Lee Smith** **312**
4. **Goose Gossage** **308**
5. Bruce Sutter 300
6. **Dave Righetti** **248**
7. Dan Quisenberry .. 244
8. Sparky Lyle 238
9. Hoyt Wilhelm 227
10. Gene Garber 218
11. **Dave Smith** **216**
12. **John Franco** **211**
13. Roy Face 193

14. **Dennis Eckersley** **188**
    Mike Marshall 188
16. **Tom Henke** **186**
17. **Steve Bedrosian** **184**
    Kent Tekulve 184
18. Tug McGraw 180
19. Ron Perranoski 179
20. **Bobby Thigpen** **178**

COMPLETE GAMES
1. Cy Young 750
2. Pud Galvin 639
3. Tim Keefe 557
4. Kid Nichols 532
5. Walter Johnson 531
6. Mickey Welch 525
7. Old Hoss Radbourn .. 489
8. John Clarkson 485
9. Tony Mullane 469
10. Jim McCormick ... 466
11. Gus Weyhing 448
12. Grover Alexander .. 438
13. Christy Mathewson .. 435
14. Jack Powell 422
15. Eddie Plank 412
16. Will White 394
17. Amos Rusie 392
18. Vic Willis 388
19. Warren Spahn ... 382
20. Jim Whitney 377

SHUTOUTS
1. Walter Johnson 110
2. Grover Alexander .. 90
3. Christy Mathewson .. 80
4. Cy Young 76
5. Eddie Plank 69
6. Warren Spahn 63
7. **Nolan Ryan** **61**
   Tom Seaver 61
9. **Bert Blyleven** **60**
10. Don Sutton 58
11. Ed Walsh 57
    Three Finger Brown .. 57
    Pud Galvin 57
14. Bob Gibson 56
15. Steve Carlton 55
16. Jim Palmer 53
    Gaylord Perry 53
18. Juan Marichal 52
19. Rube Waddell 50
    Vic Willis 50

GAMES PITCHED
1. Hoyt Wilhelm 1,070
2. Kent Tekulve 1,050

AWARDS AND HIGHLIGHTS

3. Lindy McDaniel 987
4. Rollie Fingers 944
5. Gene Garber 931
6. Cy Young 906
7. Sparky Lyle 899
8. Jim Kaat 898
9. **Goose Gossage 897**
10. Don McMahon 874
11. Phil Niekro 864
12. Roy Face 848
13. Tug McGraw 824
14. Walter Johnson 801
15. Gaylord Perry 777
16. **Charlie Hough 776**
17. Don Sutton 774
18. **Nolan Ryan 767**
19. Darold Knowles 765
20. Tommy John 760

INNINGS PITCHED
1. Cy Young 7,356
2. Pud Galvin 5,941
3. Walter Johnson 5,923
4. Phil Niekro 5,403
5. Gaylord Perry 5,351
6. Don Sutton 5,280
7. Warren Spahn 5,244
8. Steve Carlton 5,217

9. Grover Alexander 5,189
10. **Nolan Ryan 5,164**
11. Kid Nichols 5,084
12. Tim Keefe 5,061
13. **Bert Blyleven 4,837**
14. Mickey Welch 4,802
15. Tom Seaver 4,783
16. Christy Mathewson .. 4,782
17. Tommy John 4,708
18. Robin Roberts 4,689
19. Early Wynn 4,564
20. Tony Mullane 4,540

WALKS ALLOWED
1. **Nolan Ryan 2,686**
2. Steve Carlton 1,833
3. Phil Niekro 1,809
4. Early Wynn 1,775
5. Bob Feller 1,764
6. Bobo Newsom 1,732
7. Amos Rusie 1,704
8. Gus Weyhing 1,566
9. Red Ruffing 1,541
10. **Charlie Hough 1,476**
11. Bump Hadley 1,442
12. Warren Spahn 1,434
13. Earl Whitehill 1,431
14. Tony Mullane 1,409

15. Sad Sam Jones 1,396
16. Tom Seaver 1,390
17. Gaylord Perry 1,379
18. Mike Torrez 1,371
19. Walter Johnson 1,355
20. Don Sutton 1,343

RELIEF WINS
1. Hoyt Wilhelm 124
2. Lindy McDaniel 119
3. **Goose Gossage 108**
4. Rollie Fingers 107
5. Sparky Lyle 99
6. Roy Face 96
7. Gene Garber 94
   Kent Tekulve 94
9. Mike Marshall 92
10. Don McMahon 90
11. Tug McGraw 89
12. Clay Carroll 88
13. Bob Stanley 85
14. Bill Campbell 80
    Gary Lavelle 80
16. Stu Miller 79
    Ron Perranoski 79
    Tom Burgmeier 79
19. Johnny Murphy 73
20. John Hiller 72

ACTIVE LEADERS

HITS
1. Robin Yount 2,878
2. George Brett 2,836
3. Dave Parker 2,712
4. Dave Winfield 2,697
5. Eddie Murray 2,502
6. Dwight Evans 2,446
7. Andre Dawson 2,354
8. Carlton Fisk 2,303
9. Keith Hernandez 2,181
10. Willie Randolph 2,138

HOME RUNS
1. Dave Winfield 406
2. Eddie Murray 398
3. Dale Murphy 396
4. Dwight Evans 385
5. Andre Dawson 377
6. Carlton Fisk 372
7. Dave Parker 339
8. Jack Clark 335
9. Gary Carter 319
10. Lance Parrish 304

RUNS BATTED IN
1. Dave Winfield 1,602
2. Dave Parker 1,493
3. Eddie Murray 1,469
4. George Brett 1,459
5. Dwight Evans 1,384
6. Andre Dawson 1,335
7. Carlton Fisk 1,305
8. Robin Yount 1,278
9. Dale Murphy 1,252
10. Gary Carter 1,196

BATTING AVERAGE
(Minimum 2,000 at bats.)
1. Wade Boggs 345
2. Tony Gwynn 328
3. Kirby Puckett 320
4. Don Mattingly 314
5. Mike Greenwell 311
6. George Brett 308
7. Rafael Palmeiro 302
8. Pedro Guerrero 302
9. Julio Franco 302
10. Luis Polonia 302

WINS
1. Nolan Ryan 314
2. Bert Blyleven 279
3. Frank Tanana 220
4. Jack Morris 216
5. Rick Reuschel 214
6. Charlie Hough 195
7. Bob Welch 188
8. Dennis Martinez 177
9. John Candelaria 175
10. Dennis Eckersley 174

GAMES PITCHED
1. Goose Gossage 897
2. Charlie Hough 776
3. Nolan Ryan 767
4. Jeff Reardon 751
5. Lee Smith 717
6. Dennis Eckersley 671
7. Bert Blyleven 667
8. Dennis Lamp 618
9. Steve Bedrosian 608
10. Dave Smith 598
    Jesse Orosco 598

AWARDS AND HIGHLIGHTS

STRIKEOUTS
1. Nolan Ryan 5,511
2. Bert Blyleven 3,631
3. Frank Tanana 2,566
4. Jack Morris 2,144
5. Charlie Hough 2,096
6. Dennis Eckersley 2,025
7. Rick Reuschel 2,015
8. Bob Welch 1,815
9. Fernando Valenzuela 1,764
10. Roger Clemens 1,665

SAVES
1. Jeff Reardon 327
2. Lee Smith 312
3. Goose Gossage 308
4. Dave Righetti 248
5. Dave Smith 216
6. John Franco 211
7. Dennis Eckersley 188
8. Tom Henke 186
9. Steve Bedrosian 184
10. Bobby Thigpen 178

SINGLE SEASON LEADERS (Since 1900)

BATTING AVERAGE

		BA	YEAR
1.	Rogers Hornsby STL(NL)	.424	1924
2.	Nap Lajoie PHI(AL)	.422	1901
3.	George Sisler STL(AL)	.420	1922
4.	Ty Cobb DET	.420	1911
5.	Ty Cobb DET	.410	1912
6.	Joe Jackson CLE	.408	1911
7.	George Sisler STL(AL)	.407	1920
8.	Ted Williams BOS(AL)	.406	1941
9.	Rogers Hornsby STL(NL)	.403	1925
10.	Harry Heilmann DET	.403	1923
11.	Rogers Hornsby STL(NL)	.401	1922
12.	Bill Terry NY(NL)	.401	1930
13.	Ty Cobb DET	.401	1922
14.	Lefty O'Doul PHI(NL)	.398	1929
15.	Harry Heilmann DET	.398	1927
16.	Rogers Hornsby STL(NL)	.397	1921
17.	Joe Jackson CLE	.395	1912
18.	Harry Heilmann DET	.394	1921
19.	Babe Ruth NY(AL)	.393	1923
20.	Harry Heilmann DET	.393	1925

HITS

		H	YEAR
1.	George Sisler STL(AL)	257	1920
2.	Bill Terry NY(NL)	254	1930
	Lefty O'Doul PHI(NL)	254	1929
4.	Al Simmons PHI(AL)	253	1925
5.	Rogers Hornsby STL(NL)	250	1922
	Chuck Klein PHI(NL)	250	1930
7.	Ty Cobb DET	248	1911
8.	George Sisler STL(AL)	246	1922
9.	Babe Herman BKN	241	1930
	Heinie Manush STL(AL)	241	1928
11.	Wade Boggs BOS	240	1985
12.	Rod Carew MIN	239	1977
13.	Don Mattingly NY(AL)	238	1986
14.	Harry Heilmann DET	237	1921
	Paul Waner PIT	237	1927
	Joe Medwick STL(NL)	237	1937
17.	Jack Tobin STL(AL)	236	1921
18.	Rogers Hornsby STL(NL)	235	1921
19.	Lloyd Waner PIT	234	1929
	Kirby Puckett MIN	234	1988

DOUBLES

		2B	YEAR
1.	Earl Webb BOS(AL)	67	1931
2.	George Burns CLE	64	1926
	Joe Medwick STL(NL)	64	1936
4.	Hank Greenberg DET	63	1934
5.	Paul Waner PIT	62	1932
6.	Charlie Gehringer DET	60	1936
7.	Tris Speaker CLE	59	1923
	Chuck Klein PHI(NL)	59	1930
9.	Billy Herman CHI(NL)	57	1936
	Billy Herman CHI(NL)	57	1935
11.	Joe Medwick STL(NL)	56	1937
	George Kell DET	56	1950
13.	Gee Walker DET	55	1936
14.	Hal McRae KC	54	1977
15.	Don Mattingly NY(AL)	53	1986
	Tris Speaker BOS(AL)	53	1912
	Al Simmons PHI(AL)	53	1926
	Paul Waner PIT	53	1936
	Stan Musial STL(NL)	53	1953

TRIPLES

		3B	YEAR
1.	Owen Wilson PIT	36	1912
2.	Joe Jackson CLE	26	1912
	Sam Crawford DET	26	1914
	Kiki Cuyler PIT	26	1925
5.	Tommy Long STL(NL)	25	1915
	Larry Doyle NY(NL)	25	1911
	Sam Crawford DET	25	1903
8.	Ty Cobb DET	24	1911

HOME RUNS

		HR	YEAR
1.	Roger Maris NY(AL)	61	1961
2.	Babe Ruth NY(AL)	60	1927
3.	Babe Ruth NY(AL)	59	1921
4.	Jimmie Foxx PHI(AL)	58	1932
	Hank Greenberg DET	58	1938
6.	Hack Wilson CHI(NL)	56	1930
7.	Babe Ruth NY(AL)	54	1920
	Babe Ruth NY(AL)	54	1928
	Ralph Kiner PIT	54	1949
	Mickey Mantle NY(AL)	54	1961

AWARDS AND HIGHLIGHTS

11. Mickey Mantle NY(AL)	52	1956
Willie Mays SF	52	1965
George Foster CIN	52	1977
14. Ralph Kiner PIT	51	1947
Johnny Mize NY(NL)	51	1947
Willie Mays NY(NL)	51	1955
Cecil Fielder DET	51	1990
18. Jimmie Foxx BOS(AL)	50	1938

HOME RUN PERCENTAGE

	HR%	YEAR
1. Babe Ruth NY(AL)	11.8	1920
2. Babe Ruth NY(AL)	11.1	1927
3. Babe Ruth NY(AL)	10.9	1921
4. Mickey Mantle NY(AL)	10.5	1961
5. Hank Greenberg DET	10.4	1938
6. Roger Maris NY(AL)	10.3	1961
7. Babe Ruth NY(AL)	10.1	1928
8. Jimmie Foxx PHI(AL)	9.9	1932
9. Ralph Kiner PIT	9.8	1949
10. Mickey Mantle NY(AL)	9.8	1956
11. Hack Wilson CHI(NL)	9.6	1930
12. Hank Aaron ATL	9.5	1971
Babe Ruth NY(AL)	9.5	1926
14. Jim Gentile BAL	9.5	1961
15. Babe Ruth NY(AL)	9.5	1930
16. Willie Stargell PIT	9.4	1971
17. Rudy York DET	9.3	1937
18. Willie Mays SF	9.3	1965
19. Babe Ruth NY(AL)	9.2	1929
20. Willie McCovey SF	9.2	1969

RUNS BATTED IN

	RBI	YEAR
1. Hack Wilson CHI(NL)	190	1930
2. Lou Gehrig NY(AL)	184	1931
3. Hank Greenberg DET	183	1937
4. Jimmie Foxx BOS(AL)	175	1938
Lou Gehrig NY(AL)	175	1927
6. Lou Gehrig NY(AL)	174	1930
7. Babe Ruth NY(AL)	171	1921
8. Hank Greenberg DET	170	1935
Chuck Klein PHI(NL)	170	1930
10. Jimmie Foxx PHI(AL)	169	1932
11. Joe DiMaggio NY(AL)	167	1937
12. Al Simmons PHI(AL)	165	1930
Lou Gehrig NY(AL)	165	1934
14. Babe Ruth NY(AL)	164	1927
15. Babe Ruth NY(AL)	163	1931
Jimmie Foxx PHI(AL)	163	1933
17. Hal Trosky CLE	162	1936

SLUGGING AVERAGE

	SA	YEAR
1. Babe Ruth NY(AL)	.847	1920
2. Babe Ruth NY(AL)	.846	1921
3. Babe Ruth NY(AL)	.772	1927
4. Lou Gehrig NY(AL)	.765	1927
5. Babe Ruth NY(AL)	.764	1923
6. Rogers Hornsby STL(NL)	.756	1925
7. Jimmie Foxx PHI(AL)	.749	1932
8. Babe Ruth NY(AL)	.739	1924
9. Babe Ruth NY(AL)	.737	1926
10. Ted Williams BOS(AL)	.735	1941
11. Babe Ruth NY(AL)	.732	1930
12. Ted Williams BOS	.731	1957
13. Hack Wilson CHI(NL)	.723	1930
14. Rogers Hornsby STL(NL)	.722	1922
15. Lou Gehrig NY(AL)	.721	1930
16. Babe Ruth NY(AL)	.709	1928
17. Al Simmons PHI(AL)	.708	1930
18. Lou Gehrig NY(AL)	.706	1934
19. Mickey Mantle NY(AL)	.705	1956
20. Jimmie Foxx BOS(AL)	.704	1938

TOTAL BASES

	TB	YEAR
1. Babe Ruth NY(AL)	457	1921
2. Rogers Hornsby STL(NL)	450	1922
3. Lou Gehrig NY(AL)	447	1927
4. Chuck Klein PHI(NL)	445	1930
5. Jimmie Foxx PHI(AL)	438	1932
6. Stan Musial STL(NL)	429	1948
7. Hack Wilson CHI(NL)	423	1930
8. Chuck Klein PHI(NL)	420	1932
9. Lou Gehrig NY(AL)	419	1930
10. Joe DiMaggio NY(AL)	418	1937
11. Babe Ruth NY(AL)	417	1927
12. Babe Herman BKN	416	1930
13. Lou Gehrig NY(AL)	410	1931
14. Lou Gehrig NY(AL)	409	1934
Rogers Hornsby CHI(NL)	409	1929
16. Joe Medwick STL(NL)	406	1937
Jim Rice BOS	406	1978
18. Chuck Klein PHI(NL)	405	1929
Hal Trosky CLE	405	1936
20. Jimmie Foxx PHI(AL)	403	1933
Lou Gehrig NY(AL)	403	1936

BASES ON BALLS

	BB	YEAR
1. Babe Ruth NY(AL)	170	1923
2. Ted Williams BOS(AL)	162	1947
Ted Williams BOS(AL)	162	1949
4. Ted Williams BOS(AL)	156	1946
5. Eddie Yost WAS	151	1956
6. Eddie Joost PHI(AL)	149	1949
7. Babe Ruth NY(AL)	148	1920
Jimmy Wynn HOU	148	1969
Eddie Stanky BKN	148	1945
10. Jimmy Sheckard CHI(AL)	147	1911
11. Mickey Mantle NY(AL)	146	1957

AWARDS AND HIGHLIGHTS

12. Ted Williams BOS(AL)	145	1941
Ted Williams BOS(AL)	145	1942
Harmon Killebrew MIN	145	1969
15. Babe Ruth NY(AL)	144	1926
Eddie Stanky NY(NL)	144	1950
Babe Ruth NY(AL)	144	1921
18. Ted Williams BOS(AL)	143	1951
19. Babe Ruth NY(AL)	142	1924
20. Eddie Yost WAS	141	1950

RUNS SCORED

	RS	YEAR
1. Babe Ruth NY(AL)	177	1921
2. Lou Gehrig NY(AL)	167	1936
3. Babe Ruth NY(AL)	163	1928
Lou Gehrig NY(AL)	163	1931
5. Babe Ruth NY(AL)	158	1920
Babe Ruth NY(AL)	158	1927
Chuck Klein PHI(NL)	158	1930
8. Rogers Hornsby CHI(NL)	156	1929
9. Kiki Cuyler CHI(NL)	155	1930
10. Lefty O'Doul PHI(NL)	152	1929
Woody English CHI(NL)	152	1930
Al Simmons PHI(AL)	152	1930
Chuck Klein PHI(NL)	152	1932
14. Babe Ruth NY(AL)	151	1923
Jimmie Foxx PHI(AL)	151	1932
Joe DiMaggio NY(AL)	151	1937
17. Babe Ruth NY(AL)	150	1930
Ted Williams BOS(AL)	150	1949

STOLEN BASES

	SB	YEAR
1. Rickey Henderson OAK	130	1982
2. Lou Brock STL	118	1974
3. Vince Coleman STL	110	1985
4. Vince Coleman STL	109	1987
5. Rickey Henderson OAK	108	1983
6. Vince Coleman STL	107	1986
7. Maury Wills LA	104	1962
8. Rickey Henderson OAK	100	1980
9. Ron LeFlore MON	97	1980
10. Ty Cobb DET	96	1915
Omar Moreno PIT	96	1980
12. Maury Wills LA	94	1965
13. Rickey Henderson NY(AL)	93	1988
14. Tim Raines MON	90	1983
15. Clyde Milan WAS	88	1912
16. Rickey Henderson NY(AL)	87	1986
17. Willie Wilson KC	83	1979
Ty Cobb DET	83	1911
19. Eddie Collins PHI(AL)	81	1910
Bob Bescher CIN	81	1911
Vince Coleman STL	81	1988

WINS

	W	YEAR
1. Jack Chesbro NY(NL)	41	1904
2. Ed Walsh CHI(AL)	40	1908
3. Christy Mathewson NY(NL)	37	1908
4. Walter Johnson WAS	36	1913
5. Joe McGinnity NY(NL)	35	1904
6. Smoky Joe Wood BOS(AL)	34	1912
7. Cy Young BOS(AL)	33	1901
Grover Alexander PHI(NL)	33	1916
Christy Mathewson NY(NL)	33	1904
10. Cy Young BOS(AL)	32	1902
Walter Johnson WAS	32	1912
12. Joe McGinnity NY(NL)	31	1903
Christy Mathewson NY(NL)	31	1905
Jack Coombs PHI(AL)	31	1910
Grover Alexander PHI(NL)	31	1915
Jim Bagby CLE	31	1920
Lefty Grove PHI(AL)	31	1931
Denny McLain DET	31	1968

WINNING PERCENTAGE

	W%	YEAR
1. Roy Face PIT	.947	1959
2. Johnny Allen CLE	.938	1937
3. Ron Guidry NY(AL)	.893	1978
4. Freddie Fitzsimmons BKN	.889	1940
5. Lefty Grove PHI(AL)	.886	1931
6. Bob Stanley BOS	.882	1978
7. Preacher Roe BKN	.880	1951
8. Tom Seaver CIN	.875	1981
9. Smoky Joe Wood BOS(AL)	.872	1912
10. David Cone NY(NL)	.870	1988
11. Orel Hershiser LA	.864	1985
12. Wild Bill Donovan DET	.862	1907
Whitey Ford NY(AL)	.862	1961
14. Roger Clemens BOS	.857	1986
Dwight Gooden NY(NL)	.857	1985

EARNED RUN AVERAGE

	ERA	YEAR
1. Dutch Leonard BOS(AL)	1.01	1914
2. Three Finger Brown CHI(NL)	1.04	1906
3. Walter Johnson WAS	1.09	1913
4. Bob Gibson STL	1.12	1968
5. Christy Mathewson NY(NL)	1.14	1909
6. Jack Pfiester CHI(NL)	1.15	1907
7. Addie Joss CLE	1.16	1908
8. Carl Lundgren CHI(NL)	1.17	1907
9. Grover Alexander PHI(NL)	1.22	1915
10. Cy Young BOS(AL)	1.26	1908
11. Ed Walsh CHI(AL)	1.27	1910
12. Walter Johnson WAS	1.27	1918
13. Christy Mathewson NY(NL)	1.27	1905
14. Jack Coombs PHI(AL)	1.30	1910
15. Three Finger Brown CHI(NL)	1.31	1909

AWARDS AND HIGHLIGHTS

STRIKEOUTS

	SO	YEAR
1. Nolan Ryan CAL	383	1973
2. Sandy Koufax LA	382	1965
3. Nolan Ryan CAL	367	1974
4. Rube Waddell PHI(AL)	349	1904
5. Bob Feller CLE	348	1946
6. Nolan Ryan CAL	341	1977
7. Nolan Ryan CAL	329	1972
8. Nolan Ryan CAL	327	1976
9. Sam McDowell CLE	325	1965
10. Sandy Koufax LA	317	1966
11. J.R. Richard HOU	313	1979
Walter Johnson WAS	313	1910
13. Steve Carlton PHI	310	1972
14. Mickey Lolich DET	308	1971
15. Mike Scott HOU	306	1986
Sandy Koufax LA(NL)	306	1963

SHUTOUTS

	ShO	YEAR
1. Grover Alexander PHI(NL)	16	1916
2. Jack Coombs PHI(AL)	13	1910
Bob Gibson STL	13	1968
4. Grover Alexander PHI(NL)	12	1915
Christy Mathewson NY(NL)	12	1908
6. Dean Chance LA(AL)	11	1964
Walter Johnson WAS	11	1913
Sandy Koufax LA(NL)	11	1963
Ed Walsh CHI(AL)	11	1908

COMPLETE GAMES

	CG	YEAR
1. Jack Chesbro NY(NL)	48	1904
2. Vic Willis BOS(NL)	45	1902
3. Joe McGinnity NY(NL)	44	1903
4. Ed Walsh CHI(AL)	42	1908
George Mullin DET	42	1904
6. Noodles Hahn CIN	41	1901
Cy Young BOS(AL)	41	1902
Irv Young BOS(NL)	41	1905
9. Cy Young BOS(AL)	40	1904

GAMES PITCHED

	G	YEAR
1. Mike Marshall LA	106	1974
2. Kent Tekulve PIT	94	1979
3. Mike Marshall MON	92	1973
4. Kent Tekulve PIT	91	1978
5. Wayne Granger CIN	90	1969
Mike Marshall MIN	90	1979
Kent Tekulve PHI	90	1987
8. Mark Eichhorn TOR	89	1987
9. Wilbur Wood CHI(AL)	88	1968
10. Rob Murphy CIN	87	1987
11. Kent Tekulve PIT	85	1982
Mitch Williams TEX	85	1987
Frank Williams CIN	85	1987

INNINGS PITCHED

	IP	YEAR
1. Ed Walsh CHI(AL)	464	1908
2. Jack Chesbro NY(NL)	455	1904
3. Joe McGinnity NY(NL)	434	1903
4. Ed Walsh CHI(AL)	422	1907
5. Vic Willis BOS(NL)	410	1902
6. Joe McGinnity NY(NL)	408	1904
7. Ed Walsh CHI(AL)	393	1912
8. Christy Mathewson NY(NL)	391	1908
9. Jack Powell NY	390	1904
10. Togie Pittinger BOS(NL)	389	1902
Grover Alexander PHI(NL)	389	1916

SAVES

	SV	YEAR
1. Bobby Thigpen CHI(AL)	57	1990
2. Dennis Eckersley OAK	48	1990
3. Lee Smith STL	47	1991
4. Dave Righetti NY(AL)	46	1986
Bryan Harvey CAL	46	1991
6. Dan Quisenberry KC	45	1983
Bruce Sutter STL	45	1984
Dennis Eckersley OAK	45	1988
9. Dan Quisenberry KC	44	1984
Mark Davis SD	44	1989
11. Doug Jones CLE	43	1990
Dennis Eckersley OAK	43	1991
13. Jeff Reardon MIN	42	1988
Rick Aguilera MIN	42	1991
15. Jeff Reardon MON	41	1985
16. Steve Bedrosian PHI	40	1987
Jeff Reardon BOS	40	1991

WINS PLUS SAVES

	W+S	YEAR
1. Bobby Thigpen CHI(AL)	61	1990
2. Dave Righetti NY(AL)	54	1986
3. Lee Smith STL	53	1991
4. Dennis Eckersley OAK	52	1990
5. Dan Quisenberry KC	50	1984
Bruce Sutter STL	50	1984
Dan Quisenberry KC	50	1983
8. Dennis Eckersley OAK	49	1988
9. John Hiller DET	48	1973
Mark Davis SD	48	1989
Doug Jones CLE	48	1990
Bryan Harvey CAL	48	1991
Dennis Eckersley OAK	48	1991

AWARDS AND HIGHLIGHTS

MOST VALUABLE PLAYERS

NATIONAL LEAGUE

CHALMERS
1911 Wildfire Schulte CHI (OF)
1912 Larry Doyle NY (2B)
1913 Jake Daubert BKN (1B)
1914 Johnny Evers BOS (2B)
1915-21 No Selection

LEAGUE
1922-23 No Selection
1924 Dazzy Vance BKN (P)
1925 Rogers Hornsby STL (2B)
1926 Bob O'Farrell STL (C)
1927 Paul Waner PIT (OF)
1928 Jim Bottomley STL (1B)
1929 Rogers Hornsby CHI (2B)
1930 No Selection

BASEBALL WRITERS ASSOCIATION OF AMERICA
1931 Frankie Frisch STL (2B)
1932 Chuck Klein PHI (OF)
1933 Carl Hubbell NY (P)
1934 Dizzy Dean STL (P)
1935 Gabby Hartnett CHI (C)
1936 Carl Hubbell NY (P)
1937 Joe Medwick STL (OF)
1938 Ernie Lombardi CIN (C)
1939 Bucky Walters CIN (P)
1940 Frank McCormick CIN (1B)
1941 Dolph Camilli BKN (1B)
1942 Mort Cooper STL (P)
1943 Stan Musial STL (OF)
1944 Marty Marion STL (SS)
1945 Phil Cavarretta CHI (1B)
1946 Stan Musial STL (1B)
1947 Bob Elliott BOS (3B)
1948 Stan Musial STL (OF)
1949 Jackie Robinson BKN (2B)
1950 Jim Konstanty PHI (P)
1951 Roy Campanella BKN (C)
1952 Hank Sauer CHI (OF)
1953 Roy Campanella BKN (C)
1954 Willie Mays NY (OF)
1955 Roy Campanella BKN (C)
1956 Don Newcombe BKN (P)
1957 Hank Aaron MIL (OF)
1958 Ernie Banks CHI (SS)
1959 Ernie Banks CHI (SS)
1960 Dick Groat PIT (SS)
1961 Frank Robinson CIN (OF)
1962 Maury Wills LA (SS)
1963 Sandy Koufax LA (P)
1964 Ken Boyer STL (3B)
1965 Willie Mays SF (OF)
1966 Roberto Clemente PIT (OF)
1967 Orlando Cepeda STL (1B)
1968 Bob Gibson STL (P)
1969 Willie McCovey SF (1B)
1970 Johnny Bench CIN (C)
1971 Joe Torre STL (3B)
1972 Johnny Bench CIN (C)
1973 Pete Rose CIN (OF)
1974 Steve Garvey LA (1B)
1975 Joe Morgan CIN (2B)
1976 Joe Morgan CIN (2B)
1977 George Foster CIN (OF)
1978 Dave Parker PIT (OF)
1979 Keith Hernandez STL (1B)
Willie Stargell PIT (1B)
1980 Mike Schmidt PHI (3B)
1981 Mike Schmidt PHI (3B)
1982 Dale Murphy ATL (OF)
1983 Dale Murphy ATL (OF)
1984 Ryne Sandberg CHI (2B)
1985 Willie McGee STL (OF)
1986 Mike Schmidt PHI (3B)
1987 Andre Dawson CHI (OF)
1988 Kirk Gibson LA (OF)
1989 Kevin Mitchell SF (OF)
1990 Barry Bonds PIT (OF)
1991 Terry Pendleton ATL (3B)

AMERICAN LEAGUE

CHALMERS
1911 Ty Cobb DET (OF)
1912 Tris Speaker BOS (OF)
1913 Walter Johnson WAS (P)
1914 Eddie Collins PHI (2B)
1915-21 No Selection

LEAGUE
1922 George Sisler STL (1B)
1923 Babe Ruth NY (OF)
1924 Walter Johnson WAS (P)
1925 Roger Peckinpaugh WAS (SS)
1926 George Burns CLE (1B)
1927 Lou Gehrig NY (1B)
1928 Mickey Cochrane PHI (C)
1929-30 No Selection

BASEBALL WRITERS ASSOCIATION OF AMERICA
1931 Lefty Grove PHI (P)
1932 Jimmie Foxx PHI (1B)
1933 Jimmie Foxx PHI (1B)
1934 Mickey Cochrane DET (C)
1935 Hank Greenberg DET (1B)
1936 Lou Gehrig NY (1B)
1937 Charlie Gehringer DET (2B)
1938 Jimmie Foxx BOS (1B)
1939 Joe DiMaggio NY (OF)
1940 Hank Greenberg DET (1B)
1941 Joe DiMaggio NY (OF)
1942 Joe Gordon NY (2B)
1943 Spud Chandler NY (P)
1944 Hal Newhouser DET (P)
1945 Hal Newhouser DET (P)
1946 Ted Williams BOS (OF)
1947 Joe DiMaggio NY (OF)
1948 Lou Boudreau CLE (SS)
1949 Ted Williams BOS (OF)
1950 Phil Rizzuto NY (SS)
1951 Yogi Berra NY (C)
1952 Bobby Shantz PHI (P)
1953 Al Rosen CLE (3B)
1954 Yogi Berra NY (C)
1955 Yogi Berra NY (C)
1956 Mickey Mantle NY (OF)
1957 Mickey Mantle NY (OF)
1958 Jackie Jensen BOS (OF)
1959 Nellie Fox CHI (2B)
1960 Roger Maris NY (OF)
1961 Roger Maris NY (OF)
1962 Mickey Mantle NY (OF)
1963 Elston Howard NY (C)
1964 Brooks Robinson BAL (3B)
1965 Zoilo Versalles MIN (SS)
1966 Frank Robinson BAL (OF)
1967 Carl Yastrzemski BOS (OF)
1968 Denny McLain DET (P)
1969 Harmon Killebrew MIN (3B)
1970 Boog Powell BAL (1B)
1971 Vida Blue OAK (P)
1972 Richie Allen CHI (1B)

481

AWARDS AND HIGHLIGHTS

1973 Reggie Jackson OAK (OF)
1974 Jeff Burroughs TEX (OF)
1975 Fred Lynn BOS (OF)
1976 Thurman Munson NY (C)
1977 Rod Carew MIN (1B)
1978 Jim Rice BOS (OF)
1979 Don Baylor CAL (DH)
1980 George Brett KC (3B)
1981 Rollie Fingers MIL (P)
1982 Robin Yount MIL (SS)
1983 Cal Ripken BAL (SS)
1984 Willie Hernandez DET (P)
1985 Don Mattingly NY (1B)
1986 Roger Clemens BOS (P)
1987 George Bell TOR (OF)
1988 Jose Canseco OAK (OF)
1989 Robin Yount MIL (OF)
1990 Rickey Henderson OAK (OF)
1991 Cal Ripken BAL (SS)

CY YOUNG AWARD WINNERS (one selection 1956-66)

NATIONAL LEAGUE
1956 Don Newcombe BKN (RH)
1957 Warren Spahn MIL (LH)
1960 Vern Law PIT (RH)
1962 Don Drysdale LA (RH)
1963 Sandy Koufax LA (LH)
1965 Sandy Koufax LA (LH)
1966 Sandy Koufax LA (LH)
1967 Mike McCormick SF (LH)
1968 Bob Gibson STL (RH)
1969 Tom Seaver NY (RH)
1970 Bob Gibson STL (RH)
1971 Ferguson Jenkins CHI (RH)
1972 Steve Carlton PHI (LH)
1973 Tom Seaver NY (RH)
1974 Mike Marshall LA (RH)
1975 Tom Seaver NY (RH)
1976 Randy Jones SD (LH)
1977 Steve Carlton PHI (LH)
1978 Gaylord Perry SD (RH)
1979 Bruce Sutter CHI (RH)
1980 Steve Carlton PHI (LH)
1981 Fernando Valenzuela LA (LH)
1982 Steve Carlton PHI (LH)
1983 John Denny PHI (RH)
1984 Rick Sutcliffe CHI (RH)
1985 Dwight Gooden NY (RH)
1986 Mike Scott HOU (RH)
1987 Steve Bedrosian PHI (RH)
1988 Orel Hershiser LA (RH)
1989 Mark Davis SD (LH)
1990 Doug Drabek PIT (RH)
1991 Tom Glavine ATL (LH)

AMERICAN LEAGUE
1958 Bob Turley NY (RH)
1959 Early Wynn CHI (RH)
1961 Whitey Ford NY (LH)
1964 Dean Chance LA (RH)
1967 Jim Lonborg BOS (RH)
1968 Denny McLain DET (RH)
1969 Mike Cuellar BAL (LH)
    Denny McLain DET (RH)
1970 Jim Perry MIN (RH)
1971 Vida Blue OAK (LH)
1972 Gaylord Perry CLE (RH)
1973 Jim Palmer BAL (RH)
1974 Jim (Catfish) Hunter OAK (RH)
1975 Jim Palmer BAL (RH)
1976 Jim Palmer BAL (RH)
1977 Sparky Lyle NY (LH)
1978 Ron Guidry NY (LH)
1979 Mike Flanagan BAL (LH)
1980 Steve Stone BAL (RH)
1981 Rollie Fingers MIL (RH)
1982 Pete Vuckovich MIL (RH)
1983 LaMarr Hoyt CHI (RH)
1984 Willie Hernandez DET (LH)
1985 Bret Saberhagen KC (RH)
1986 Roger Clemens BOS (RH)
1987 Roger Clemens BOS (RH)
1988 Frank Viola MIN (LH)
1989 Bret Saberhagen KC (RH)
1990 Bob Welch OAK (RH)
1991 Roger Clemens BOS (RH)

ROOKIE OF THE YEAR (one selection 1947-48)

NATIONAL LEAGUE
1947 Jackie Robinson BKN (1B)
1948 Alvin Dark BOS (SS)
1949 Don Newcombe BKN (P)
1950 Sam Jethroe BOS (OF)
1951 Willie Mays NY (OF)
1952 Joe Black BKN (P)
1953 Junior Gilliam BKN (2B)
1954 Wally Moon STL (OF)
1955 Bill Virdon STL (OF)
1956 Frank Robinson CIN (OF)
1957 Jack Sanford PHI (P)
1958 Orlando Cepeda SF (1B)
1959 Willie McCovey SF (1B)
1960 Frank Howard LA (OF)
1961 Billy Williams CHI (OF)
1962 Ken Hubbs CHI (2B)
1963 Pete Rose CIN (2B)
1964 Richie Allen PHI (3B)
1965 Jim Lefebvre LA (2B)
1966 Tommy Helms CIN (2B)
1967 Tom Seaver NY (P)
1968 Johnny Bench CIN (C)
1969 Ted Sizemore LA (2B)
1970 Carl Morton MON (P)
1971 Earl Williams ATL (C)
1972 Jon Matlack NY (P)
1973 Gary Matthews SF (OF)
1974 Bake McBride STL (OF)
1975 Jon Montefusco SF (P)
1976 Pat Zachry CIN (P)
    Butch Metzger SD (P)
1977 Andre Dawson MON (OF)
1978 Bob Horner ATL (3B)
1979 Rick Sutcliffe LA (P)
1980 Steve Howe LA (P)
1981 Fernando Valenzuela LA (P)
1982 Steve Sax LA (2B)
1983 Darryl Strawberry NY (OF)
1984 Dwight Gooden NY (P)
1985 Vince Coleman STL (OF)
1986 Todd Worrell STL (P)
1987 Benito Santiago SD (C)
1988 Chris Sabo CIN (3B)
1989 Jerome Walton CHI (OF)
1990 Dave Justice ATL (OF)
1991 Jeff Bagwell HOU (1B)

482

AWARDS AND HIGHLIGHTS

AMERICAN LEAGUE
1949 Roy Sievers STL (OF)
1950 Walt Dropo BOS (1B)
1951 Gil McDougald NY (3B)
1952 Harry Byrd PHI (P)
1953 Harvey Kuenn DET (SS)
1954 Bob Grim NY (P)
1955 Herb Score CLE (P)
1956 Luis Aparicio CHI (SS)
1957 Tony Kubek NY (SS)
1958 Albie Pearson WAS (OF)
1959 Bob Allison WAS (OF)
1960 Ron Hansen BAL (SS)
1961 Don Schwall BOS (P)
1962 Tom Tresh NY (SS)
1963 Gary Peters CHI (P)

1964 Tony Oliva MIN (OF)
1965 Curt Blefary BAL (OF)
1966 Tommie Agee CHI (OF)
1967 Rod Carew MIN (2B)
1968 Stan Bahnsen NY (P)
1969 Lou Piniella KC (OF)
1970 Thurman Munson NY (C)
1971 Chris Chambliss CLE (1B)
1972 Carlton Fisk BOS (C)
1973 Al Bumbry BAL (OF)
1974 Mike Hargrove TEX (1B)
1975 Fred Lynn BOS (OF)
1976 Mark Fidrych DET (P)
1977 Eddie Murray BAL (DH)
1978 Lou Whitaker DET (2B)

1979 Alfredo Griffin TOR (SS)
   John Castino MIN (3B)
1980 Joe Charboneau CLE (OF)
1981 Dave Righetti NY (P)
1982 Cal Ripken BAL (SS)
1983 Ron Kittle CHI (OF)
1984 Alvin Davis SEA (1B)
1985 Ozzie Guillen CHI (SS)
1986 Jose Canseco OAK (OF)
1987 Mark McGwire OAK (1B)
1988 Walt Weiss OAK (SS)
1989 Gregg Olson BAL (P)
1990 Sandy Alomar CLE (C)
1991 Chuck Knoblauch MIN (2B)

GOLD GLOVE AWARD

COMBINED SELECTION-1957
P Bobby Shantz NY(AL)
C Sherm Lollar CHI(AL)
1B Gil Hodges BKN
2B Nellie Fox CHI(AL)
3B Frank Malzone BOS
SS Roy McMillan CIN
LF Minnie Minoso CHI(AL)
CF Willie Mays NY(NL)
RF Al Kaline DET

PITCHERS

NATIONAL LEAGUE
1958 Harvey Haddix CIN
1959-60 Harvey Haddix PIT
1961 Bobby Shantz PIT
1962-63 Bobby Shantz STL
1964 Bobby Shantz PHI
1965-73 Bob Gibson STL
1974-75 Andy Messersmith LA
1976-77 Jim Kaat PHI
1978-80 Phil Niekro ATL
1981 Steve Carlton PHI
1982-83 Phil Niekro ATL
1984 Joaquin Andujar STL
1985 Rick Reuschel PIT
1986 Fernando Valenzuela LA
1987 Rick Reuschel SF
1988 Orel Hershiser LA
1989 Ron Darling NY
1990-91 Greg Maddux CHI

AMERICAN LEAGUE
1958-60 Bobby Shantz NY
1961 Frank Lary DET
1962-72 Jim Kaat MIN

1973 Jim Kaat MIN,CHI
1974-75 Jim Kaat CHI
1976-79 Jim Palmer BAL
1980-81 Mike Norris OAK
1982-86 Ron Guidry NY
1987-88 Mark Langston SEA
1989 Bret Saberhagen KC
1990 Mike Boddicker BOS
1991 Mark Langston CAL

CATCHERS

NATIONAL LEAGUE
1958-60 Del Crandall MIL
1961 Johnny Roseboro LA
1962 Del Crandall MIL
1963-64 Johnny Edwards CIN
1965 Joe Torre MIL
1966 Johnny Roseboro LA
1967 Randy Hundley CHI
1968-77 Johnny Bench CIN
1978-79 Bob Boone PHI
1980-82 Gary Carter MON
1983-85 Tony Pena PIT
1986 Jody Davis CHI
1987 Mike LaValliere PIT
1988-90 Benito Santiago SD
1991 Tom Pagnozzi STL

AMERICAN LEAGUE
1958-59 Sherm Lollar CHI
1960 Earl Battey WAS
1961-62 Earl Battey MIN
1963-64 Elston Howard NY
1965-69 Bill Freehan DET
1970-71 Ray Fosse CLE
1972 Carlton Fisk BOS

1973-75 Thurman Munson NY
1976-81 Jim Sundberg TEX
1982 Bob Boone CAL
1983-85 Lance Parrish DET
1986-88 Bob Boone CAL
1989 Bob Boone KC
1990 Sandy Alomar CLE
1991 Tony Pena BOS

FIRST BASEMEN

NATIONAL LEAGUE
1958-59 Gil Hodges LA
1960-65 Bill White STL
1966 Bill White PHI
1967-72 Wes Parker LA
1973 Mike Jorgenson MON
1974-77 Steve Garvey LA
1978-82 Keith Hernandez STL
1983 Keith Hernandez STL, NY
1984-88 Keith Hernandez NY
1989-90 Andres Galarraga MON
1991 Will Clark SF

AMERICAN LEAGUE
1958-61 Vic Power CLE
1962-63 Vic Power MIN
1964 Vic Power LA
1965-66 Joe Pepitone NY
1967-68 George Scott BOS
1969 Joe Pepitone NY
1970 Jim Spencer CAL
1971 George Scott BOS
1972-76 George Scott MIL
1977 Jim Spencer CHI
1978 Chris Chambliss NY

AWARDS AND HIGHLIGHTS

1979-80 Cecil Cooper MIL
1981 Mike Squires CHI
1982-84 Eddie Murray BAL
1985-89 Don Mattingly NY
1990 Mark McGwire OAK
1991 Don Mattingly NY

SECOND BASEMEN

NATIONAL LEAGUE
1958 Bill Mazeroski PIT
1959 Charlie Neal LA
1960-61 Bill Mazeroski PIT
1962 Ken Hubbs CHI
1963-67 Bill Mazeroski PIT
1968 Glenn Beckert CHI
1969 Felix Millan ATL
1970-71 Tommy Helms CIN
1972 Felix Millan ATL
1973-77 Joe Morgan CIN
1978 Davey Lopes LA
1979 Manny Trillo PHI
1980 Doug Flynn NY
1981-82 Manny Trillo PHI
1983-91 Ryne Sandberg CHI

AMERICAN LEAGUE
1958 Frank Bolling DET
1959-60 Nellie Fox CHI
1961-65 Bobby Richardson NY
1966-68 Bobby Knoop CAL
1969-71 Dave Johnson BAL
1972 Doug Griffin BOS
1973-76 Bobby Grich BAL
1977-82 Frank White KC
1983-85 Lou Whitaker DET
1986-87 Frank White KC

1988-90 Harold Reynolds SEA
1991 Roberto Alomar TOR

THIRD BASEMEN

NATIONAL LEAGUE
1958-61 Ken Boyer STL
1962 Jim Davenport SF
1963 Ken Boyer STL
1964-68 Ron Santo CHI
1969 Clete Boyer ATL
1970-74 Doug Rader HOU
1975 Ken Reitz STL
1976-84 Mike Schmidt PHI
1985 Tim Wallach MON
1986 Mike Schmidt PHI
1987 Terry Pendleton STL
1988 Tim Wallach MON
1989 Terry Pendleton STL
1990 Tim Wallach MON
1991 Matt Williams SF

AMERICAN LEAGUE
1958-59 Frank Malzone BOS
1960-75 Brooks Robinson BAL
1976 Aurelio Rodriguez DET
1977-78 Graig Nettles NY
1979-84 Buddy Bell TEX
1985 George Brett KC
1986-89 Gary Gaetti MIN
1990 Kelly Gruber TOR
1991 Robin Ventura CHI

SHORTSTOPS

NATIONAL LEAGUE
1958-59 Roy McMillan CIN
1960 Ernie Banks CHI

1961-62 Maury Wills LA
1963 Bobby Wine PHI
1964 Ruben Amaro PHI
1965 Leo Cardenas CIN
1966-67 Gene Alley PIT
1968 Dal Maxvill STL
1969-70 Don Kessinger CHI
1971 Bud Harrelson NY
1972 Larry Bowa PHI
1973 Roger Metzger HOU
1974-77 Dave Concepcion CIN
1978 Larry Bowa PHI
1979 Dave Concepcion CIN
1980-81 Ozzie Smith SD
1982-91 Ozzie Smith STL

AMERICAN LEAGUE
1958-62 Luis Aparicio CHI
1963 Zoilo Versalles MIN
1964 Luis Aparicio BAL
1965 Zoilo Versalles MIN
1966 Luis Aparicio BAL
1967 Jim Fregosi CAL
1968 Luis Aparicio CHI
1969 Mark Belanger BAL
1970 Luis Aparicio CHI
1971 Mark Belanger BAL
1972 Eddie Brinkman DET
1973-78 Mark Belanger BAL
1979 Rick Burleson BOS
1980-81 Alan Trammell DET
1982 Robin Yount MIL
1983-84 Alan Trammell DET
1985 Alfredo Griffin OAK
1986-89 Tony Fernandez TOR
1990 Ozzie Guillen CHI
1991 Cal Ripken BAL

NATIONAL LEAGUE OUTFIELDERS

1958
Frank Robinson CIN (LF)
Willie Mays SF (CF)
Hank Aaron MIL (RF)

1959
Jackie Brant SF (LF)
Willie Mays SF (CF)
Hank Aaron MIL (RF)

1960
Wally Moon LA (LF)

Willie Mays SF (CF)
Hank Aaron MIL (RF)

1961
Willie Mays SF
Roberto Clemente PIT
Vada Pinson CIN

1962
Willie Mays SF
Roberto Clemente PIT
Bill Virdon PIT

1963
Willie Mays SF
Roberto Clemente PIT
Curt Flood STL

1964
Willie Mays SF
Roberto Clemente PIT
Curt Flood STL

1965
Willie Mays SF
Roberto Clemente PIT
Curt Flood STL

1966
Willie Mays SF
Curt Flood STL
Roberto Clemente PIT

1967
Roberto Clemente PIT

Curt Flood STL
Willie Mays SF

1968
Willie Mays SF
Roberto Clemente PIT
Curt Flood STL

1969
Roberto Clemente PIT
Curt Flood STL
Pete Rose CIN

1970
Roberto Clemente PIT
Tommy Agee NY
Pete Rose CIN

AWARDS AND HIGHLIGHTS

1971
Roberto Clemente PIT
Bobby Bonds SF
Willie Davis LA

1972
Roberto Clemente PIT
Cesar Cedeno HOU
Willie Davis LA

1973
Bobby Bonds SF
Cesar Cedeno HOU
Willie Davis LA

1974
Cesar Cedeno HOU
Cesar Geronimo CIN
Bobby Bonds SF

1975
Cesar Cedeno HOU
Cesar Geronimo CIN
Garry Maddox PHI

1976
Cesar Cedeno HOU
Cesar Geronimo CIN
Garry Maddox PHI

1977
Cesar Geronimo CIN
Garry Maddox PHI
Dave Parker PIT

1978
Garry Maddox PHI
Dave Parker PIT
Ellis Valentine MON

1979
Garry Maddox PHI
Dave Parker PIT
Dave Winfield SD

1980
Andre Dawson MON
Garry Maddox PHI
Dave Winfield SD

1981
Andre Dawson MON
Garry Maddox PHI
Dusty Baker LA

1982
Andre Dawson MON
Dale Murphy ATL
Garry Maddox PHI

1983
Andre Dawson MON
Dale Murphy ATL
Willie McGee STL

1984
Dale Murphy ATL
Bob Dernier CHI
Andre Dawson MON

1985
Willie McGee STL
Andre Dawson MON
Dale Murphy ATL

1986
Dale Murphy ATL
Willie McGee STL
Tony Gwynn SD

1987
Eric Davis CIN
Tony Gwynn SD
Andre Dawson CHI

1988
Andre Dawson CHI
Eric Davis CIN
Andy Van Slyke PIT

1989
Eric Davis CIN
Tony Gwynn SD
Andy Van Slyke PIT

1990
Barry Bonds PIT
Tony Gwynn SD
Andy Van Slyke PIT

1991
Barry Bonds PIT
Tony Gwynn SD
Andy Van Slyke PIT

AMERICAN LEAGUE OUTFIELDERS

1958
Norm Siebern NY (LF)
Jimmy Piersall BOS (CF)
Al Kaline DET (RF)

1959
Minnie Minoso CLE (LF)
Al Kaline DET (CF)
Jackie Jenson BOS (RF)

1960
Minnie Minoso CHI (LF)
Jim Landis CHI (CF)
Roger Maris NY (RF)

1961
Al Kaline DET
Jimmy Piersall CLE
Jim Landis CHI

1962
Jim Landis CHI
Mickey Mantle NY
Al Kaline DET

1963
Al Kaline DET
Carl Yastrzemski BOS
Jim Landis CHI

1964
Al Kaline DET
Jim Landis CHI
Vic Davalillo CLE

1965
Al Kaline DET
Tom Tresh NY
Carl Yastrzemski BOS

1966
Al Kaline DET
Tommy Agee CHI
Tony Oliva MIN

1967
Carl Yastrzemski BOS
Paul Blair BAL
Al Kaline DET

1968
Mickey Stanley DET
Carl Yastrzemski BOS
Reggie Smith BOS

1969
Paul Blair BAL
Mickey Stanley DET
Carl Yastrzemski BOS

1970
Mickey Stanley DET
Paul Blair BAL
Ken Berry CHI

1971
Paul Blair BAL
Amos Otis KC
Carl Yastrzemski BOS

1972
Paul Blair BAL
Bobby Murcer NY
Ken Berry CAL

1973
Paul Blair BAL
Amos Otis KC
Mickey Stanley DET

1974
Paul Blair BAL
Amos Otis KC
Joe Rudi OAK

1975
Paul Blair BAL
Joe Rudi OAK
Fred Lynn BOS

1976
Joe Rudi OAK
Dwight Evans BOS
Rick Manning CLE

1977
Juan Beniquez TEX
Carl Yastrzemski BOS
Al Cowens KC

1978
Fred Lynn BOS
Dwight Evans BOS
Rick Miller CAL

1979
Dwight Evans BOS
Sixto Lezcano MIL
Fred Lynn BOS

1980
Fred Lynn BOS
Dwayne Murphy OAK
Willie Wilson KC

1981
Dwayne Murphy OAK
Dwight Evans BOS
Rickey Henderson OAK

1982
Dwight Evans BOS
Dave Winfield NY
Dwayne Murphy OAK

1983
Dwight Evans BOS
Dave Winfield NY
Dwayne Murphy OAK

AWARDS AND HIGHLIGHTS

1984
Dwight Evans BOS
Dave Winfield NY
Dwayne Murphy OAK

1986
Jesse Barfield TOR
Kirby Puckett MIN
Gary Pettis CAL

1988
Devon White CAL
Gary Pettis CAL
Kirby Puckett MIN

1990
Ken Griffey Jr. SEA
Ellis Burks BOS
Gary Pettis TEX

1985
Gary Pettis CAL
Dave Winfield NY
Dwight Evans BOS
Dwayne Murphy OAK

1987
Jesse Barfield TOR
Kirby Puckett MIN
Dave Winfield NY

1989
Devon White CAL
Gary Pettis DET
Kirby Puckett MIN

1991
Ken Griffey Jr. SEA
Devon White TOR
Kirby Puckett MIN

THE WORLD SERIES 1903-90

YEAR	WINNER	SERIES	LOSER
1903	BOS Pilgrims	5-3	PIT Pirates (NL)
1904	NO SERIES		
1905	NY Giants (NL)	4-1	PHI Athletics (AL)
1906	CHI White Sox (AL)	4-2	CHI Cubs (NL)
1907	CHI Cubs (NL)	4-0	DET Tigers (AL)
1908	CHI Cubs (NL)	4-1	DET Tigers (AL)
1909	PIT Pirates (NL)	4-3	DET Tigers (AL)
1910	PHI Athletics (AL)	4-1	CHI Cubs (NL)
1911	PHI Athletics (AL)	4-2	NY Giants (NL)
1912	BOS Red Sox (AL)	4-3	NY Giants (NL)
1913	PHI Athletics (AL)	4-1	NY Giants (NL)
1914	BOS Braves (NL)	4-0	PHI Athletics (AL)
1915	BOS Red Sox (AL)	4-1	PHI Phillies (NL)
1916	BOS Red Sox (AL)	4-1	BKN Robins (NL)
1917	CHI White Sox (AL)	4-2	NY Giants (NL)
1918	BOS Red Sox (AL)	4-2	CHI Cubs (NL)
1919	CIN Reds (NL)	5-3	CHI White Sox (AL)
1920	CLE Indians (AL)	5-2	BKN Robins (NL)
1921	NY Giants (NL)	5-3	NY Yankees (AL)
1922	NY Giants (NL)	4-0	NY Yankees (AL)
1923	NY Yankees (AL)	4-2	NY Giants (NL)
1924	WAS Senators (AL)	4-3	NY Giants (NL)
1925	PIT Pirates (NL)	4-3	WAS Senators (AL)
1926	STL Cardinals (NL)	4-3	NY Yankees (AL)
1927	NY Yankees (AL)	4-0	PIT Pirates (NL)
1928	NY Yankees (AL)	4-0	STL Cardinals (NL)
1929	PHI Athletics (AL)	4-1	CHI Cubs (NL)
1930	PHI Athletics (AL)	4-2	STL Cardinals (NL)
1931	STL Cardinals (NL)	4-3	PHI Athletics (AL)
1932	NY Yankees (AL)	4-0	CHI Cubs (NL)
1933	NY Giants (NL)	4-1	WAS Senators (AL)
1934	STL Cardinals (NL)	4-3	DET Tigers (AL)
1935	DET Tigers (AL)	4-2	CHI Cubs (NL)
1936	NY Yankees (AL)	4-2	NY Giants (NL)
1937	NY Yankees (AL)	4-1	NY Giants (NL)
1938	NY Yankees (AL)	4-0	CHI Cubs (NL)
1939	NY Yankees (AL)	4-0	CIN Reds (NL)
1940	CIN Reds (NL)	4-3	DET Tigers (AL)
1941	NY Yankees (AL)	4-1	BKN Dodgers (NL)
1942	STL Cardinals (NL)	4-1	NY Yankees (AL)
1943	NY Yankees (AL)	4-1	STL Cardinals (NL)
1944	STL Cardinals (NL)	4-2	STL Browns (AL)
1945	DET Tigers (AL)	4-3	CHI Cubs (NL)
1946	STL Cardinals (NL)	4-3	BOS Red Sox (AL)
1947	NY Yankees (AL)	4-3	BKN Dodgers (NL)
1948	CLE Indians (AL)	4-2	BOS Braves (NL)
1949	NY Yankees (AL)	4-1	BKN Dodgers (NL)
1950	NY Yankees (AL)	4-0	PHI Phillies (NL)
1951	NY Yankees (AL)	4-2	NY Giants (NL)
1952	NY Yankees (AL)	4-3	BKN Dodgers (NL)
1953	NY Yankees (AL)	4-2	BKN Dodgers (NL)
1954	NY Giants (NL)	4-0	CLE Indians (AL)
1955	BKN Dodgers (NL)	4-3	NY Yankees (AL)
1956	NY Yankees (AL)	4-3	BKN Dodgers (NL)
1957	MIL Braves (NL)	4-3	NY Yankees (AL)
1958	NY Yankees (AL)	4-3	MIL Braves (NL)
1959	LA Dodgers (NL)	4-2	CHI White Sox (AL)
1960	PIT Pirates (NL)	4-3	NY Yankees (AL)
1961	NY Yankees (AL)	4-1	CIN Reds (NL)
1962	NY Yankees (AL)	4-3	SF Giants (NL)
1963	LA Dodgers (NL)	4-0	NY Yankees (AL)
1964	STL Cardinals (NL)	4-3	NY Yankees (AL)
1965	LA Dodgers (NL)	4-3	MIN Twins (AL)
1966	BAL Orioles (AL)	4-0	LA Dodgers (NL)
1967	STL Cardinals (NL)	4-3	BOS Red Sox (AL)
1968	DET Tigers (AL)	4-3	STL Cardinals (NL)
1969	NY Mets (NL)	4-1	BAL Orioles (AL)
1970	BAL Orioles (AL)	4-1	CIN Reds (NL)
1971	PIT Pirates (NL)	4-3	BAL Orioles (AL)
1972	OAK Athletics (AL)	4-3	CIN Reds (NL)
1973	OAK Athletics (AL)	4-3	NY Mets (NL)
1974	OAK Athletics (AL)	4-1	LA Dodgers (NL)
1975	CIN Reds (NL)	4-3	BOS Red Sox (AL)
1976	CIN Reds (NL)	4-0	NY Yankees (AL)
1977	NY Yankees (AL)	4-2	LA Dodgers (NL)
1978	NY Yankees (AL)	4-2	LA Dodgers (NL)
1979	PIT Pirates (NL)	4-3	BAL Orioles (AL)
1980	PHI Phillies (NL)	4-2	KC Royals (AL)
1981	LA Dodgers (NL)	4-2	NY Yankees (AL)
1982	STL Cardinals (NL)	4-3	MIL Brewers (AL)
1983	BAL Orioles (AL)	4-1	PHI Phillies (NL)
1984	DET Tigers (AL)	4-1	SD Padres (NL)
1985	KC Royals (AL)	4-3	STL Cardinals (NL)
1986	NY Mets (NL)	4-3	BOS Red Sox (AL)
1987	MIN Twins (AL)	4-3	STL Cardinals (NL)
1988	LA Dodgers (NL)	4-1	OAK Athletics (AL)
1989	OAK Athletics (AL)	4-0	SF Giants (NL)
1990	CIN Reds (NL)	4-0	OAK Athletics (AL)
1991	MIN Twins (AL)	4-3	ATL Braves (NL)

AWARDS AND HIGHLIGHTS

LEAGUE CHAMPIONSHIP SERIES 1969-1990

NLCS

YEAR	WINNER	SERIES	LOSER
1969	NY Mets (E)	3-0	ATL Braves (W)
1970	CIN Reds (W)	3-0	PIT Pirates (E)
1971	PIT Pirates (E)	3-1	SF Giants (W)
1972	CIN Reds (W)	3-2	PIT Pirates (E)
1973	NY Mets (E)	3-2	CIN Reds (W)
1974	LA Dodgers (W)	3-1	PIT Pirates (E)
1975	CIN Reds (W)	3-0	PIT Pirates (E)
1976	CIN Reds (W)	3-0	PHI Phillies (E)
1977	LA Dodgers (W)	3-1	PHI Phillies (E)
1978	LA Dodgers (W)	3-1	PHI Phillies (E)
1979	PIT Pirates (W)	3-0	CIN Reds (W)
1980	PHI Phillies (E)	3-2	HOU Astros (W)
1981	NL EAST PLAYOFF		
	MON Expos	3-2	PHI Phillies
	NL WEST PLAYOFF		
	LA Dodgers	3-2	HOU Astros
	LCS		
	LA Dodgers (W)	3-2	MON Expos (E)
1982	STL Cardinals (E)	3-0	ATL Braves (W)
1983	PHI Phillies (E)	3-1	LA Dodgers (W)
1984	SD Padres (W)	3-2	CHI Cubs (E)
1985	STL Cardinals (E)	4-2	LA Dodgers (W)
1986	NY Mets (E)	4-2	HOU Astros (W)
1987	STL Cardinals (E)	4-3	SF Giants (W)
1988	LA Dodgers (W)	4-3	NY Mets (E)
1989	SF Giants (W)	4-1	CHI Cubs (E)
1990	CIN Reds (W)	4-2	PIT Pirates (E)
1991	ATL Braves (W)	4-3	PIT Pirates (E)

ALCS

YEAR	WINNER	SERIES	LOSER
1969	BAL Orioles (E)	3-0	MIN Twins (W)
1970	BAL Orioles (E)	3-0	MIN Twins (W)
1971	BAL Orioles (E)	3-0	OAK Athletics (W)
1972	OAK Athletics (W)	3-2	DET Tigers (E)
1973	OAK Athletics (W)	3-2	BAL Orioles (E)
1974	OAK Athletics (W)	3-1	BAL Orioles (E)
1975	BOS Red Sox (E)	3-0	OAK Athletics (W)
1976	NY Yankees (E)	3-2	KC Royals (W)
1977	NY Yankees (E)	3-2	KC Royals (W)
1978	NY Yankees (E)	3-1	KC Royals (W)
1979	BAL Orioles (E)	3-1	CAL Angels (W)
1980	KC Royals (W)	3-0	NY Yankees (E)
1981	AL EAST PLAYOFF		
	NY Yankees	3-2	MIL Brewers
	AL WEST PLAYOFF		
	OAK Athletics	3-0	KC Royals
	LCS		
	NY Yankees (E)	3-0	OAK Athletics (W)
1982	MIL Brewers (E)	3-2	CAL Angels (W)
1983	BAL Orioles (E)	3-1	CHI White Sox (W)
1984	DET Tigers (E)	3-0	KC Royals (W)
1985	KC Royals (W)	4-3	TOR Blue Jays (E)
1986	BOS Red Sox (E)	4-3	CAL Angels (W)
1987	MIN Twins (W)	4-1	DET Tigers (E)
1988	OAK Athletics (W)	4-0	BOS Red Sox (E)
1989	OAK Athletics (W)	4-1	TOR Blue Jays (E)
1990	OAK Athletics (W)	4-0	BOS Red Sox (E)
1991	MIN Twins (W)	4-2	TOR Blue Jays (E)

Yearly Team and Individual Leaders

In this section, you will find how each National League and American League organization did in each season since 1900. Included also are each league's individual leaders in batting and pitching for each year.

Above the team names is a standard won-loss line. The abbreviations are: **W** = wins; **L** = losses; **PCT** = winning percentage; **GB** = games the team finished behind the league winner or the division winner; **R** = runs scored by the team; **OR** = runs scored by the team's opponents; **BA** = team batting average; **FA** = team fielding average; **ERA** = team earned run average. The league's total runs, opponents runs, batting average, fielding average, and earned run average are shown totaled below the columns.

The year's individual leaders in each league follow, beginning with hitters' categories—batting average, hits, doubles, triples, home runs, runs batted in, slugging average, stolen bases, and runs scored. Pitchers' categories follow—wins, winning percentage, earned run average, strikeouts, saves, complete games, shutouts, games pitched, and innings pitched. Most of these categories will have the top three leaders in the league. When two or more players tied for a position, it is indicated. If there are two who were far and away the leaders in any one category, and many who either tied or were among the ordinary, only two players are listed. The minimum requirements to be considered as a league leader have changed many times over the years. As a rule, this publication lists those players who at the time were the acknowledged leaders in their categories. For example, if Ty Cobb was recognized by his contemporaries as the batting champion in 1914, he is listed as the batting average leader in 1914, even though he may not have had enough plate appearances to qualify recently. The leaders listed under a particular year would have been eligible under the rules of that year. Others who may have been eligible under current rules—or another generally accepted minimum, such as 3.1 plate appearances per scheduled game—do not appear.

NATIONAL LEAGUE STANDINGS

1900 NL

	W	L	PCT	GB	R	OR	BA	FA	ERA
BROOKLYN	82	54	.603	—	816	722	.293	.948	3.89
PITTSBURGH	79	60	.568	4.5	733	612	.272	.945	3.06
PHILADELPHIA	75	63	.543	8	810	791	.290	.945	4.12
BOSTON	66	72	.478	17	778	739	.283	.953	3.72
CHICAGO	65	75	.464	19	635	751	.260	.933	3.23
ST. LOUIS	65	75	.464	19	743	747	.291	.943	3.75
CINCINNATI	62	77	.446	21.5	702	745	.266	.945	3.83
NEW YORK	60	78	.435	23	713	823	.279	.928	3.96
					5930	5930	.279	.942	3.69

BATTING AVERAGE
Honus Wagner PIT..... .381
Elmer Flick PHI .... .378
W. Keeler BKN .... .368

HITS
W. Keeler BKN............ 208
Elmer Flick PHI 207
Jesse Burkett STL 203

DOUBLES
Honus Wagner PIT 45
Elmer Flick PHI 33
two tied at 32

TRIPLES
Honus Wagner PIT 22
Hickman NY.................. 17
Joe Kelley BKN............ 17

HOME RUNS
Herman Long BOS 12
Elmer Flick PHI 11
Mike Donlin STL 10

RUNS BATTED IN
Elmer Flick PHI 110
Ed Delahanty PHI 109
Honus Wagner PIT 100

SLUGGING AVERAGE
Honus Wagner PIT .... .573
Elmer Flick PHI .... .545
Nap Lajoie PHI............ .517

STOLEN BASES
Patsy Donovan STL...... 45
Van Haltren NY............. 45
Jimmy Barrett CIN 44

RUNS SCORED
Roy Thomas PHI 134
Jimmy Slagle PHI 115
two tied at 114

WINS
Joe McGinnity BKN........ 29
four tied at...................... 20

WINNING PERCENTAGE
Jesse Tannehill PIT .... .769
Joe McGinnity BKN.... .763
Chick Fraser PHI .... .615

EARNED RUN AVERAGE
Rube Waddell PIT...... 2.37
Ned Garvin CHI 2.41
Jack Taylor CHI 2.55

STRIKEOUTS
Rube Waddell PIT....... 130
Noodles Hahn CIN...... 127
Cy Young STL 119

SAVES
Frank Kitson BKN 4
Bill Bernhard PHI 2
five tied at 1

COMPLETE GAMES
Pink Hawley NY 34
Bill Dinneen BOS 33
four tied at..................... 32

SHUTOUTS
four tied at........................ 4

GAMES PITCHED
Bill Carrick NY............... 45
Joe McGinnity BKN....... 45
Ed Scott CIN................. 43

INNINGS PITCHED
Joe McGinnity BKN..... 347
Bill Carrick NY............. 342
Pink Hawley NY 329

AMERICAN LEAGUE STANDINGS

1901 AL

	W	L	PCT	GB	R	OR	BA	FA	ERA
CHICAGO	83	53	.610	—	819	631	.276	.941	2.98
BOSTON	79	57	.581	4	759	608	.279	.943	3.04
DETROIT	74	61	.548	8.5	741	694	.279	.930	3.30
PHILADELPHIA	74	62	.544	9	805	761	.288	.942	4.00
BALTIMORE	68	65	.511	13.5	760	750	.294	.926	3.73
WASHINGTON	61	73	.455	21	678	767	.269	.943	4.09
CLEVELAND	55	82	.401	28.5	663	827	.271	.942	4.12
MILWAUKEE	48	89	.350	35.5	641	828	.261	.934	4.06
					5866	5866	.277	.938	3.66

BATTING AVERAGE
Nap Lajoie PHI............ .422
Buck Freeman BOS... .345
Mike Donlin BAL .... .341

HITS
Nap Lajoie PHI............ 229
John Anderson MIL..... 190
Jimmy Collins BOS 187

DOUBLES
Nap Lajoie PHI.............. 48
John Anderson MIL...... 46
Jimmy Collins BOS....... 42

TRIPLES
Jimmy Williams BAL 21
Bill Keister BAL.............. 21
Sam Mertes CHI 17

HOME RUNS
Nap Lajoie PHI.............. 13
Buck Freeman BOS...... 12
Mike Grady WAS 9

RUNS BATTED IN
Nap Lajoie PHI............. 125
Buck Freeman BOS.... 114
John Anderson MIL........ 99

SLUGGING AVERAGE
Nap Lajoie PHI............ .635
Buck Freeman BOS... .527
Socks Seybold PHI..... .499

STOLEN BASES
Frank Isbell CHI 52
Sam Mertes CHI 46
two tied at 38

RUNS SCORED
Nap Lajoie PHI............. 145
Fielder Jones CHI 120
Jimmy Williams BAL ... 113

WINS
Cy Young BOS 33
Joe McGinnity BAL 26
Clark Griffith CHI............ 24

WINNING PERCENTAGE
Clark Griffith CHI......... .774
Cy Young BOS .... .767
Nixie Callahan CHI ..... .652

EARNED RUN AVERAGE
Cy Young BOS 1.62
Nixie Callahan CHI 2.42
Joe Yeager DET 2.61

STRIKEOUTS
Cy Young BOS 158
Roy Patterson CHI...... 127
Dowling CLE, MIL 124

SAVES
Bill Hoffer CLE 3
Joe McGinnity BAL 3
Ned Garvin MIL 2

COMPLETE GAMES
Joe McGinnity BAL 39
Cy Young BOS 38
two tied at 35

SHUTOUTS
Clark Griffith CHI............. 5
Cy Young BOS 5
tw tied at 4

GAMES PITCHED
Joe McGinnity BAL 48
Dowling CLE, MIL 43
Cy Young BOS 43

INNINGS PITCHED
Joe McGinnity BAL 382
Cy Young BOS 371
Roscoe Miller DET...... 332

NATIONAL LEAGUE STANDINGS

1901 NL

	W	L	PCT	GB	R	OR	BA	FA	ERA
PITTSBURGH	90	49	.647	—	776	534	.286	.950	2.58
PHILADELPHIA	83	57	.593	7.5	668	543	.267	.954	2.87
BROOKLYN	79	57	.581	9.5	744	600	.288	.950	3.14
ST. LOUIS	76	64	.543	14.5	792	689	.285	.949	3.68
BOSTON	69	69	.500	20.5	531	556	.250	.952	2.90
CHICAGO	53	86	.381	37	578	699	.258	.943	3.33
NEW YORK	52	85	.380	37	544	755	.255	.941	3.87
CINCINNATI	52	87	.374	38	561	818	.251	.940	4.17
					5194	5194	.268	.947	3.32

BATTING AVERAGE
Jesse Burkett STL ...... .382
Ed Delahanty PHI ...... .357
W. Keeler BKN............ .355

HITS
Jesse Burkett STL 228
W. Keeler BKN............. 209
J. Sheckard BKN 197

DOUBLES
Jake Beckley CIN 39
Honus Wagner PIT 39
Ed Delahanty PHI 39

TRIPLES
Jimmy Sheckard BKN... 19
three tied at.................... 17

HOME RUNS
Sam Crawford CIN........ 16
Jimmy Sheckard BKN... 11
Jesse Burkett STL 10

RUNS BATTED IN
Honus Wagner PIT 126
Ed Delahanty PHI 108
two tied at 104

SLUGGING AVERAGE
J. Sheckard BKN 536
Ed Delahanty PHI .... .533
Sam Crawford Cin ...... .528

STOLEN BASES
Honus Wagner PIT 49
Topsy Hartsel CHI 41
Sammy Strang NY 40

RUNS SCORED
Jesse Burkett STL 139
W. Keeler BKN............. 123
G. Beaumont PIT......... 120

WINS
B. Donovan BKN............ 25
Jack Harper STL............ 23
two tied at 22

WINNING PERCENTAGE
Jack Chesbro PIT .... .677
Jack Harper STL.......... .657
D. Phillippe PIT .... .647

EARNED RUN AVERAGE
Jesse Tannehill PIT ... 2.18
D. Phillippe PIT.......... 2.22
Al Orth PHI................. 2.27

STRIKEOUTS
Noodles Hahn CIN...... 239
B. Donovan BKN......... 226
T. Hughes CHI 225

SAVES
Jack Powell STL 3
three tied at..................... 2

COMPLETE GAMES
Noodles Hahn CIN........ 41
Dummy Taylor NY 37
two tied at 36

SHUTOUTS
Vic Willis BOS................. 6
Jack Chesbro PIT 6
Al Orth PHI...................... 6

GAMES PITCHED
B. Donovan BKN............ 45
Jack Powell STL 45
Dummy Taylor NY 45

INNINGS PITCHED
Noodles Hahn CIN...... 375
Dummy Taylor NY 353
B. Donovan BKN......... 351

AMERICAN LEAGUE STANDINGS

1902 AL

	W	L	PCT	GB	R	OR	BA	FA	ERA
PHILADELPHIA	83	53	.610	—	775	636	.287	.953	3.29
ST. LOUIS	78	58	.574	5	619	607	.265	.953	3.34
BOSTON	77	60	.562	6.5	664	600	.278	.955	3.02
CHICAGO	74	60	.552	8	675	602	.268	.955	3.41
CLEVELAND	69	67	.507	14	686	667	.289	.950	3.28
WASHINGTON	61	75	.449	22	707	790	.283	.945	4.36
DETROIT	52	83	.385	30.5	566	657	.251	.943	3.56
BALTIMORE	50	88	.362	34	715	848	.277	.938	4.33
					5407	5407	.275	.949	3.57

BATTING AVERAGE
Ed Delahanty WAS .... .376
N. Lajoie PHI, CLE ..... .366
Hickman BOS, CLE ... .363

HITS
Hickman BOS, CLE ... 195
Lave Cross PHI........... 191
Bill Bradley CLE.......... 187

DOUBLES
Ed Delahanty WAS....... 43
Harry Davis PHI............ 43
two tied at 39

TRIPLES
Jimmy Williams BAL 21
Buck Freeman BOS...... 19
two tied at 14

HOME RUNS
Socks Seybold PHI....... 16
three tied at.................. 11

RUNS BATTED IN
Buck Freeman BOS.... 121
Hickman BOS, CLE 110
Lave Cross PHI........... 108

SLUGGING AVERAGE
Ed Delahanty WAS .... .590
N. Lajoie PHI, CLE ..... .551
Hickman BOS, CLE ... .541

STOLEN BASES
Topsy Hartsel PHI........ 47
Sam Mertes CHI 46
Dave Fultz PHI.............. 44

RUNS SCORED
Topsy Hartsel PHI...... 109
Dave Fultz PHI............ 109
Sammy Strang CHI..... 108

WINS
Cy Young BOS 32
Rube Waddell PHI 24
two tied at 22

WINNING PERCENTAGE
B. Bernhard PHI, CLE.. .783
Rube Waddell PHI ..... .774
Cy Young BOS .... .744

EARNED RUN AVERAGE
Ed Siever DET 1.91
Rube Waddell PHI 2.05
two tied at 2.15

STRIKEOUTS
Rube Waddell PHI 210
Cy Young BOS 160
Jack Powell STL 137

SAVES
Jack Powell STL 3

COMPLETE GAMES
Cy Young BOS 41
Bill Dinneen BOS.......... 39
two tied at 36

SHUTOUTS
Addie Joss CLE 5
three tied at..................... 4

GAMES PITCHED
Cy Young BOS 45
Jack Powell STL............ 42
Bill Dinneen BOS.......... 42

INNINGS PITCHED
Cy Young BOS 385
Bill Dinneen BOS........ 371
Jack Powell STL 328

NATIONAL LEAGUE STANDINGS

1902 NL

	W	L	PCT	GB	R	OR	BA	FA	ERA
PITTSBURGH	103	36	.741	—	775	440	.287	.958	2.30
BROOKLYN	75	63	.543	27.5	564	519	.257	.952	2.69
BOSTON	73	64	.533	29	572	516	.250	.959	2.61
CINCINNATI	70	70	.500	33.5	633	566	.282	.945	2.67
CHICAGO	68	69	.496	34	530	501	.251	.946	2.21
ST. LOUIS	56	78	.418	44.5	517	695	.258	.944	3.47
PHILADELPHIA	56	81	.409	46	484	649	.247	.946	3.50
NEW YORK	48	88	.353	53.5	401	590	.238	.943	2.82
					4476	4476	.259	.949	2.78

BATTING AVERAGE
G. Beaumont PIT .... .357
W. Keeler BKN .... .338
Sam Crawford CIN ..... .333

HITS
G. Beaumont PIT 194
W. Keeler BKN 188
Sam Crawford CIN 185

DOUBLES
Honus Wagner PIT 33
Fred Clarke PIT 27
Duff Cooley BOS 26

TRIPLES
Sam Crawford CIN 23
Tommy Leach PIT 22
Honus Wagner PIT 16

HOME RUNS
Tommy Leach PIT 6
Jake Beckley CIN 5
two tied at 4

RUNS BATTED IN
Honus Wagner PIT 91
Tommy Leach PIT 85
Sam Crawford CIN 78

SLUGGING AVERAGE
Honus Wagner PIT .... .467
Sam Crawford CIN ..... .461
Fred Clarke PIT .... .453

STOLEN BASES
Honus Wagner PIT 42
Jimmy Slagle CHI 40
Patsy Donovan STL 34

RUNS SCORED
Honus Wagner PIT 105
Fred Clarke PIT 104
G. Beaumont PIT 100

WINS
Jack Chesbro PIT 28
Togie Pittinger BOS 27
Vic Willis BOS 27

WINNING PERCENTAGE
Jack Chesbro PIT .... .824
Ed Doheny PIT .... .800
Jesse Tannehill PIT ... .769

EARNED RUN AVERAGE
Jack Taylor CHI 1.33
Noodles Hahn CIN 1.76
Jesse Tannehill PIT ... 1.95

STRIKEOUTS
Vic Willis BOS 225
Doc White PHI 185
Togie Pittinger BOS 174

SAVES
Vic Willis BOS 3
Sam Leever PIT 2
nine tied at 1

COMPLETE GAMES
Vic Willis BOS 45
Togie Pittinger BOS 36
two tied at 34

SHUTOUTS
Christy Mathewson NY ... 8
Jack Chesbro PIT 8
Jack Taylor CHI 8

GAMES PITCHED
Vic Willis BOS 51
Togie Pittinger BOS 46
Stan Yerkes STL 39

INNINGS PITCHED
Vic Willis BOS 410
Togie Pittinger BOS ... 389
Jack Taylor CHI 325

AMERICAN LEAGUE STANDINGS

1903 AL

	W	L	PCT	GB	R	OR	BA	FA	ERA
BOSTON	91	47	.659	—	708	504	.272	.959	2.57
PHILADELPHIA	75	60	.556	14.5	597	519	.264	.960	2.97
CLEVELAND	77	63	.550	15	639	579	.270	.946	2.66
NEW YORK	72	62	.537	17	579	573	.250	.953	3.08
DETROIT	65	71	.478	25	567	539	.268	.950	2.75
ST. LOUIS	65	74	.468	26.5	500	525	.242	.953	2.77
CHICAGO	60	77	.438	30.5	516	613	.247	.949	3.02
WASHINGTON	43	94	.314	47.5	437	691	.231	.954	3.82
					4543	4543	.256	.953	2.95

BATTING AVERAGE
Nap Lajoie CLE.......... .355
Sam Crawford DET..... .335
P. Dougherty BOS ..... .331

HITS
P. Dougherty BOS 195
Sam Crawford DET..... 184
Nap Lajoie CLE............ 173

DOUBLES
Socks Seybold PHI....... 45
Nap Lajoie CLE............. 40
Buck Freeman BOS...... 39

TRIPLES
Sam Crawford DET........ 25
Bill Bradley CLE............. 22
Buck Freeman BOS...... 20

HOME RUNS
Buck Freeman BOS...... 13
Hickman CLE................. 12
Hobe Ferris BOS 9

RUNS BATTED IN
Buck Freeman BOS.... 104
Hickman CLE................. 97
Nap Lajoie CLE.............. 93

SLUGGING AVERAGE
Nap Lajoie CLE.......... .533
Hickman CLE.............. .502
Buck Freeman BOS... .496

STOLEN BASES
Harry Bay CLE............... 45
Ollie Pickering PHI........ 40
two tied at 35

RUNS SCORED
P. Dougherty BOS 108
Bill Bradley CLE........... 103
two tied at 95

WINS
Cy Young BOS 28
Eddie Plank PHI............. 23
four tied at..................... 21

WINNING PERCENTAGE
Cy Young BOS .... .757
Tom Hughes BOS....... .741
Earl Moore CLE .... .679

EARNED RUN AVERAGE
Earl Moore CLE 1.77
Cy Young BOS 2.08
Bill Bernhard CLE 2.12

STRIKEOUTS
Rube Waddell PHI 302
Bill Donovan DET 187
two tied at 176

SAVES
five tied at. 2

COMPLETE GAMES
Bill Donovan DET 34
Cy Young BOS 34
Rube Waddell PHI 34

SHUTOUTS
Cy Young BOS 7
Bill Dinneen BOS............ 6
George Mullin DET 6

GAMES PITCHED
Eddie Plank PHI............. 43
George Mullin DET 41
two tied at 40

INNINGS PITCHED
Cy Young BOS 342
Eddie Plank PHI........... 336
Jack Chesbro NY........ 325

NATIONAL LEAGUE STANDINGS

1903 NL

	W	L	PCT	GB	R	OR	BA	FA	ERA
PITTSBURGH	91	49	.650	—	793	613	.287	.951	2.91
NEW YORK	84	55	.604	6.5	729	567	.272	.951	2.95
CHICAGO	82	56	.594	8	695	599	.275	.942	2.77
CINCINNATI	74	65	.532	16.5	765	656	.288	.946	3.07
BROOKLYN	70	66	.515	19	667	682	.265	.951	3.44
BOSTON	58	80	.420	32	578	699	.245	.937	3.34
PHILADELPHIA	49	86	.363	39.5	617	738	.268	.947	3.97
ST. LOUIS	43	94	.314	46.5	505	795	.251	.940	3.76
					5349	5349	.269	.946	3.27

BATTING AVERAGE
Honus Wagner PIT .... .355
Fred Clarke PIT .... .351
Mike Donlin CIN .... .351

HITS
G. Beaumont PIT 209
Cy Seymour CIN......... 191
George Browne NY..... 185

DOUBLES
Sam Mertes NY 32
Harry Steinfelt CIN........ 32
Fred Clarke PIT 32

TRIPLES
Honus Wagner PIT 19
Mike Donlin CIN............ 18
Tommy Leach PIT 17

HOME RUNS
Jimmy Sheckard BKN..... 9
six tied at......................... 7

RUNS BATTED IN
Sam Mertes NY 104
Honus Wagner PIT 101
Jack Doyle BKN............ 91

SLUGGING AVERAGE
Fred Clarke PIT .... .532
Honus Wagner PIT .... .518
Mike Donlin CIN.......... .516

STOLEN BASES
Jimmy Sheckard BKN... 67
Frank Chance CHI 67
two tied at 46

RUNS SCORED
G. Beaumont PIT 137
Mike Donlin CIN.......... 110
George Browne NY..... 105

WINS
Joe McGinnity NY 31
C. Mathewson NY.......... 30
Sam Leever PIT............. 25

WINNING PERCENTAGE
Sam Leever PIT.......... .781
D. Phillippe PIT .... .774
Jake Weimer CHI........ .700

EARNED RUN AVERAGE
Sam Leever PIT......... 2.06
C. Mathewson NY....... 2.26
Jake Weimer CHI........ 2.30

STRIKEOUTS
C. Mathewson NY....... 267
Joe McGinnity NY....... 171
Ned Garvin BKN 154

SAVES
Carl Lundgren CHI......... 3
Roscoe Miller NY 3
six tied at......................... 2

COMPLETE GAMES
Joe McGinnity NY......... 44
C. Mathewson NY......... 37
Togie Pittinger BOS...... 35

SHUTOUTS
Sam Leever PIT.............. 7
Henry Schmidt BKN 5
Noodles Hahn CIN.......... 5

GAMES PITCHED
Joe McGinnity NY......... 55
C. Mathewson NY......... 45
Togie Pittinger BOS...... 44

INNINGS PITCHED
Joe McGinnity NY....... 434
C. Mathewson NY....... 366
Togie Pittinger BOS.... 352

AMERICAN LEAGUE STANDINGS

1904 AL

	W	L	PCT	GB	R	OR	BA	FA	ERA
BOSTON	95	59	.617	—	608	466	.247	.962	2.12
NEW YORK	92	59	.609	1.5	598	526	.259	.958	2.57
CHICAGO	89	65	.578	6	600	482	.242	.964	2.30
CLEVELAND	86	65	.570	7.5	647	482	.262	.959	2.22
PHILADELPHIA	81	70	.536	12.5	557	503	.249	.959	2.35
ST. LOUIS	65	87	.428	29	481	604	.239	.960	2.83
DETROIT	62	90	.408	32	505	627	.231	.959	2.77
WASHINGTON	38	113	.252	55.5	437	743	.227	.951	3.62
					4433	4433	.245	.959	2.60

BATTING AVERAGE
Nap Lajoie CLE .381
W. Keeler NY .343
Harry Davis PHI .309

HITS
Nap Lajoie CLE 211
W. Keeler NY 186
Bill Bradley CLE 182

DOUBLES
Nap Lajoie CLE 50
Jimmy Collins BOS 33
four tied at 31

TRIPLES
Joe Cassidy WAS 19
Buck Freeman BOS 19
Chick Stahl BOS 19

HOME RUNS
Harry Davis PHI 10
Buck Freeman BOS 7
Danny Murphy PHI 7

RUNS BATTED IN
Nap Lajoie CLE 102
Buck Freeman BOS 84
Bill Bradley CLE 83

SLUGGING AVERAGE
Nap Lajoie CLE .554
Harry Davis PHI .490
Danny Murphy PHI .440

STOLEN BASES
Elmer Flick CLE 42
Harry Bay CLE 38
Emmet Heidrick STL 35

RUNS SCORED
P. Dougherty BOS, NY 113
Elmer Flick CLE 97
Bill Bradley CLE 94

WINS
Jack Chesbro NY 41
Eddie Plank PHI 26
Cy Young BOS 26

WINNING PERCENTAGE
Jack Chesbro NY .774
J. Tannehill BOS .656
Frank Smith CHI .640

EARNED RUN AVERAGE
Addie Joss CLE 1.59
Rube Waddell PHI 1.62
Otto Hess CLE 1.67

STRIKEOUTS
Rube Waddell PHI 349
Jack Chesbro NY 239
Cy Young BOS 203

SAVES
Casey Patten WAS 3
eight tied at 1

COMPLETE GAMES
Jack Chesbro NY 48
George Mullin DET 42
Cy Young BOS 40

SHUTOUTS
Cy Young BOS 10
Rube Waddell PHI 8
two tied at 7

GAMES PITCHED
Jack Chesbro NY 55
Jack Powell NY 47
Rube Waddell PHI 46

INNINGS PITCHED
Jack Chesbro NY 455
Jack Powell NY 390
Rube Waddell PHI 383

NATIONAL LEAGUE STANDINGS

1904 NL

	W	L	PCT	GB	R	OR	BA	FA	ERA
NEW YORK	106	47	.693	—	744	476	.262	.956	2.17
CHICAGO	93	60	.608	13	599	517	.248	.954	2.30
CINCINNATI	88	65	.575	18	695	547	.255	.954	2.35
PITTSBURGH	87	66	.569	19	675	592	.258	.955	2.89
ST. LOUIS	75	79	.487	31.5	602	595	.253	.952	2.64
BROOKLYN	56	97	.366	50	497	614	.232	.945	2.70
BOSTON	55	98	.359	51	491	749	.237	.946	3.43
PHILADELPHIA	52	100	.342	53.5	571	784	.248	.937	3.39
					4874	4874	.249	.950	2.73

BATTING AVERAGE
Honus Wagner PIT .... .349
M. Donlin CIN, NY ..... .329
Jake Beckley STL ...... .325

HITS
G. Beaumont PIT 185
Jake Beckley STL 179
Honus Wagner PIT 171

DOUBLES
Honus Wagner PIT 44
Sam Mertes NY 28
Joe Delahanty BOS 27

TRIPLES
Harry Lumley BKN 18
Honus Wagner PIT 14
two tied at 13

HOME RUNS
Harry Lumley BKN 9
Dave Brain STL 7
four tied at 6

RUNS BATTED IN
Bill Dahlen NY 80
Sam Mertes NY 78
Harry Lumley BKN 78

SLUGGING AVERAGE
Honus Wagner PIT .... .520
Mike Grady STL .... .474
M. Donlin CIN, NY ..... .457

STOLEN BASES
Honus Wagner PIT 53
Bill Dahlen NY 47
Sam Mertes NY 47

RUNS SCORED
George Browne NY 99
Honus Wagner PIT 97
Ginger Beaumont PIT ... 97

WINS
Joe McGinnity NY 35
C. Mathewson NY 33
Jack Harper CIN 23

WINNING PERCENTAGE
Joe McGinnity NY ...... .814
C. Mathewson NY ...... .733
Jack Harper CIN .... .719

EARNED RUN AVERAGE
Joe McGinnity NY 1.61
Ned Garvin BKN 1.68
T. Brown CHI 1.86

STRIKEOUTS
C. Mathewson NY 212
Vic Willis BOS.............. 196
Jake Weimer CHI 177

SAVES
Joe McGinnity NY 5
Red Ames NY 3
Hooks Wiltse NY 3

COMPLETE GAMES
Jack Taylor STL............. 39
Vic Willis BOS 39
two tied at 38

SHUTOUTS
Joe McGinnity NY 9
Jack Harper CIN 6
two tied at 5

GAMES PITCHED
Joe McGinnity NY 51
C. Mathewson NY 48
Oscar Jones BKN 46

INNINGS PITCHED
Joe McGinnity NY 408
Oscar Jones BKN
C. Mathewson NY 368

AMERICAN LEAGUE STANDINGS

1905 AL

	W	L	PCT	GB	R	OR	BA	FA	ERA
PHILADELPHIA	92	56	.622	—	623	492	.255	.958	2.19
CHICAGO	92	60	.605	2	612	451	.237	.968	1.99
DETROIT	79	74	.516	15.5	512	602	.243	.957	2.83
BOSTON	78	74	.513	16	579	564	.234	.953	2.84
CLEVELAND	76	78	.494	19	567	587	.255	.963	2.85
NEW YORK	71	78	.477	21.5	586	622	.248	.952	2.93
WASHINGTON	64	87	.424	29.5	559	623	.223	.951	2.87
ST. LOUIS	54	99	.353	40.5	511	608	.232	.955	2.74
					4549	4549	.241	.957	2.65

BATTING AVERAGE
Elmer Flick CLE .... .306
W. Keeler NY .... .302
Harry Bay CLE .... .298

HITS
George Stone STL 187
Sam Crawford DET 171
Harry Davis PHI 171

DOUBLES
Harry Davis PHI 47
Sam Crawford DET 40
two tied at 37

TRIPLES
Elmer Flick CLE 19
Hobe Ferris BOS 16
Terry Turner CLE 14

HOME RUNS
Harry Davis PHI 8
George Stone STL 7
four tied at 6

RUNS BATTED IN
Harry Davis PHI 83
Lave Cross PHI 77
Jiggs Donahue CHI 76

SLUGGING AVERAGE
Elmer Flick CLE .... .466
Frank Isbell CHI .... .440
Sam Crawford DET .... .433

STOLEN BASES
Danny Hoffman PHI 46
Dave Fultz NY 44
Jake Stahl WAS 41

RUNS SCORED
Harry Davis PHI 92
Fielder Jones CHI 91
Harry Bay CLE 90

WINS
Rube Waddell PHI 26
Eddie Plank PHI 25
Ed Killian DET 23

WINNING PERCENTAGE
Andy Coakley PHI ...... .741
J. Tannehill BOS .... .710
Rube Waddell PHI ..... .703

EARNED RUN AVERAGE
Rube Waddell PHI 1.48
Doc White CHI 1.76
Cy Young BOS 1.82

STRIKEOUTS
Rube Waddell PHI 287
Eddie Plank PHI 210
Cy Young BOS 208

SAVES
Rube Waddell PHI 4
Clark Griffith NY 3
Chief Bender PHI 3

COMPLETE GAMES
Eddie Plank PHI 36
Harry Howell STL 35
George Mullin DET 35

SHUTOUTS
Ed Killian DET 8
Rube Waddell PHI 7
two tied at 6

GAMES PITCHED
Rube Waddell PHI 46
George Mullin DET 44
two tied at 42

INNINGS PITCHED
George Mullin DET 348
Eddie Plank PHI 347
Frank Owen CHI 334

NATIONAL LEAGUE STANDINGS

1905 NL

	W	L	PCT	GB	R	OR	BA	FA	ERA
NEW YORK	105	48	.686	—	778	505	.273	.960	2.39
PITTSBURGH	96	57	.627	9	692	570	.266	.961	2.86
CHICAGO	92	61	.601	13	667	442	.245	.962	2.04
PHILADELPHIA	83	69	.546	21.5	708	602	.260	.957	2.81
CINCINNATI	79	74	.516	26	735	698	.269	.953	3.01
ST. LOUIS	58	96	.377	47.5	535	734	.248	.957	3.59
BOSTON	51	103	.331	54.5	468	731	.234	.951	3.52
BROOKLYN	48	104	.316	56.5	506	807	.246	.936	3.76
					5089	5089	.255	.954	2.99

BATTING AVERAGE
Cy Seymour CIN......... .377
Honus Wagner PIT .... .363
Mike Donlin NY .... .356

HITS
Cy Seymour CIN.......... 219
Mike Donlin NY 216
Honus Wagner PIT 199

DOUBLES
Cy Seymour CIN............ 40
John Titus PHI................ 36
Honus Wagner PIT 32

TRIPLES
Cy Seymour CIN............ 21
Sam Mertes NY 17
Sherry Magee PHI 17

HOME RUNS
Fred Odwell CIN 9
Cy Seymour CIN.............. 8
three tied at...................... 7

RUNS BATTED IN
Cy Seymour CIN.......... 121
Sam Mertes NY 108
Honus Wagner PIT 101

SLUGGING AVERAGE
Cy Seymour CIN......... .559
Honus Wagner PIT .... .505
Mike Donlin NY .... .495

STOLEN BASES
Billy Maloney CHI 59
Art Devlin NY 59
Honus Wagner PIT 57

RUNS SCORED
Mike Donlin NY 124
Roy Thomas PHI 118
Miller Huggins CIN...... 117

WINS
C. Mathewson NY.......... 31
Togie Pittinger PHI......... 23
two tied at 22

WINNING PERCENTAGE
C. Mathewson NY....... .795
Sam Leever PIT .... .760
Red Ames NY .... .733

EARNED RUN AVERAGE
C. Mathewson NY 1.27
Ed Reulbach CHI 1.42
Bob Wicker CHI 2.02

STRIKEOUTS
C. Mathewson NY........ 206
Red Ames NY 198
Orval Overall CIN......... 173

SAVES
Claude Elliott NY.............. 6
Joe McGinnity NY 3
Hooks Wiltse NY.............. 3

COMPLETE GAMES
Irv Young BOS............... 41
Vic Willis BOS................ 36
Chick Fraser BOS.......... 35

SHUTOUTS
C. Mathewson NY............ 8
Irv Young BOS................. 7
two tied at 5

GAMES PITCHED
Togie Pittinger PHI......... 46
Joe McGinnity NY 46
two tied at 43

INNINGS PITCHED
Irv Young BOS............. 378
Vic Willis BOS.............. 342
C. Mathewson NY....... 339

AMERICAN LEAGUE STANDINGS

1906 AL

	W	L	PCT	GB	R	OR	BA	FA	ERA
CHICAGO	93	58	.616	—	570	460	.230	.963	2.13
NEW YORK	90	61	.596	3	644	543	.266	.957	2.78
CLEVELAND	89	64	.582	5	663	482	.279	.967	2.09
PHILADELPHIA	78	67	.538	12	561	542	.247	.956	2.60
ST. LOUIS	76	73	.510	16	558	498	.247	.954	2.23
DETROIT	71	78	.477	21	518	599	.242	.959	3.06
WASHINGTON	55	95	.367	37.5	518	664	.238	.955	3.25
BOSTON	49	105	.318	45.5	462	706	.239	.949	3.41
					4494	4494	.249	.958	2.69

BATTING AVERAGE
George Stone STL ..... .358
Nap Lajoie CLE .... .355
Hal Chase NY .... .323

HITS
Nap Lajoie CLE 214
George Stone STL 208
Elmer Flick CLE 194

DOUBLES
Nap Lajoie CLE 49
Harry Davis PHI 42
Elmer Flick CLE 34

TRIPLES
Elmer Flick CLE 22
George Stone STL 20
Sam Crawford DET 16

HOME RUNS
Harry Davis PHI 12
Hickman WAS 9
George Stone STL 6

RUNS BATTED IN
Harry Davis PHI 96
Nap Lajoie CLE 91
George Davis CHI 80

SLUGGING AVERAGE
George Stone STL ...... .501
Nap Lajoie CLE .... .460
Harry Davis PHI .... .459

STOLEN BASES
Elmer Flick CLE 39
John Anderson WAS 39
two tied at 37

RUNS SCORED
Elmer Flick CLE 98
Topsy Hartsel PHI 96
Wee Willie Keeler NY ... 96

WINS
Al Orth NY 27
Jack Chesbro NY 24
two tied at 22

WINNING PERCENTAGE
Eddie Plank PHI .... .760
Doc White CHI .... .750
Addie Joss CLE .... .700

EARNED RUN AVERAGE
Doc White CHI 1.52
Barney Pelty STL 1.59
Addie Joss CLE 1.72

STRIKEOUTS
Rube Waddell PHI 196
Cy Falkenberg WAS ... 178
Ed Walsh CHI 171

SAVES
Otto Hess CLE 3
Chief Bender PHI 3
seven tied at 2

COMPLETE GAMES
Al Orth NY 36
George Mullin DET 35
Otto Hess CLE 33

SHUTOUTS
Ed Walsh CHI 10
Addie Joss CLE 9
Rube Waddell PHI 8

GAMES PITCHED
Jack Chesbro NY 49
Al Orth NY 45
Otto Hess CLE 44

INNINGS PITCHED
Al Orth NY 339
Otto Hess CLE 334
George Mullin DET 330

NATIONAL LEAGUE STANDINGS

1906 NL

	W	L	PCT	GB	R	OR	BA	FA	ERA
CHICAGO	116	36	.763	—	705	381	.262	.969	1.76
NEW YORK	96	56	.632	20	625	510	.255	.963	2.49
PITTSBURGH	93	60	.608	23.5	623	470	.261	.964	2.21
PHILADELPHIA	71	82	.464	45.5	528	564	.241	.956	2.58
BROOKLYN	66	86	.434	50	496	625	.236	.955	3.13
CINCINNATI	64	87	.424	51.5	533	582	.238	.959	2.69
ST. LOUIS	52	98	.347	63	470	607	.235	.957	3.04
BOSTON	49	102	.325	66.5	408	649	.226	.947	3.17
					4388	4388	.244	.959	2.63

BATTING AVERAGE
Honus Wagner PIT .... .339
Harry Steinfeldt CHI... .327
Harry Lumley BKN ...... .324

HITS
Harry Steinfeldt CHI.... 176
Honus Wagner PIT 175
Seymour CIN, NY 165

DOUBLES
Honus Wagner PIT 38
Sherry Magee PHI 36
Kitty Bransfield PHI....... 28

TRIPLES
Wildfire Schulte CHI...... 13
Fred Clarke PIT 13
two tied at 12

HOME RUNS
Tim Jordan BKN 12
Harry Lumley BKN 9
Cy Seymour CIN, NY...... 8

RUNS BATTED IN
Jim Nealon PIT 83
Harry Steinfeldt CHI....... 83
Cy Seymour CIN, NY.... 80

SLUGGING AVERAGE
Harry Lumley BKN ...... .477
Honus Wagner PIT .... .459
Sammy Strang NY ..... .435

STOLEN BASES
Frank Chance CHI........ 57
Sherry Magee PHI 55
Art Devlin NY 54

RUNS SCORED
Frank Chance CHI...... 103
Honus Wagner PIT 103
Jimmy Sheckard CHI.... 90

WINS
Joe McGinnity NY 27
T. Brown CHI 26
three tied at.................. 22

WINNING PERCENTAGE
Ed Reulbach CHI........ .826
T. Brown CHI .... .813
Sam Leever PIT.......... .759

EARNED RUN AVERAGE
T. Brown CHI 1.04
Jack Pfiester CHI 1.56
Ed Reulbach CHI........ 1.65

STRIKEOUTS
F. Beebe CHI, STL 171
Big Jeff Pfeffer BOS.... 158
Red Ames NY 156

SAVES
George Ferguson NY...... 6
Hooks Wiltse NY 5
Elmer Stricklett BKN 5

COMPLETE GAMES
Irv Young BOS.............. 37
Big Jeff Pfeffer BOS...... 33
four tied at..................... 32

SHUTOUTS
T. Brown CHI 10
Lefty Leifield PIT 8
Jake Weimer CIN............ 7

GAMES PITCHED
Joe McGinnity NY 45
Irv Young BOS.............. 43
two tied at 42

INNINGS PITCHED
Irv Young BOS............ 358
Joe McGinnity NY 340
Vic Willis PIT................ 322

AMERICAN LEAGUE STANDINGS

1907 AL

	W	L	PCT	GB	R	OR	BA	FA	ERA
DETROIT	92	58	.613	—	694	532	.266	.959	2.33
PHILADELPHIA	88	57	.607	1.5	582	511	.255	.958	2.35
CHICAGO	87	64	.576	5.5	588	474	.237	.966	2.22
CLEVELAND	85	67	.559	8	530	525	.241	.960	2.26
NEW YORK	70	78	.473	21	605	665	.249	.947	3.03
ST. LOUIS	69	83	.454	24	542	555	.253	.959	2.61
BOSTON	59	90	.396	32.5	464	558	.234	.959	2.45
WASHINGTON	49	102	.325	43.5	506	691	.243	.952	3.11
					4511	4511	.247	.958	2.54

BATTING AVERAGE
Ty Cobb DET .... .350
Sam Crawford DET ..... .323
George Stone STL ...... .320

HITS
Ty Cobb DET 212
George Stone STL 191
Sam Crawford DET 188

DOUBLES
Harry Davis PHI 36
Sam Crawford DET 34
two tied at 30

TRIPLES
Elmer Flick CLE 18
Sam Crawford DET 17
Ty Cobb DET 15

HOME RUNS
Harry Davis PHI 8
Socks Seybold PHI 5
Ty Cobb DET 5

RUNS BATTED IN
Ty Cobb DET 116
Socks Seybold PHI 92
Harry Davis PHI 87

SLUGGING AVERAGE
Ty Cobb DET .... .473
Sam Crawford DET ..... .460
Elmer Flick CLE .... .412

STOLEN BASES
Ty Cobb DET 49
Wid Conroy NY 41
Elmer Flick CLE 41

RUNS SCORED
Sam Crawford DET 102
Davy Jones DET 101
Ty Cobb DET 97

WINS
Addie Joss CLE 27
Doc White CHI 27
two tied at 25

WINNING PERCENTAGE
Bill Dovovan DET .... .862
Jimmy Dygert PHI ...... .724
Addie Joss CLE .... .711

EARNED RUN AVERAGE
Ed Walsh CHI 1.60
Ed Killian DET 1.78
Addie Joss CLE 1.83

STRIKEOUTS
Rube Waddell PHI 232
Ed Walsh CHI 206
Eddie Plank PHI 183

SAVES
Ed Walsh CHI 4
Tom Hughes WAS 4
Bill Dinneen BOS, STL ... 4

COMPLETE GAMES
Ed Walsh CHI 37
George Mullin DET 35
Addie Joss CLE 34

SHUTOUTS
Eddie Plank PHI 8
Doc White CHI 7
Rube Waddell PHI 7

GAMES PITCHED
Ed Walsh CHI 56
Doc White CHI 47
George Mullin DET 46

INNINGS PITCHED
Ed Walsh CHI 422
George Mullin DET 357
Eddie Plank PHI 344

NATIONAL LEAGUE STANDINGS

1907 NL

	W	L	PCT	GB	R	OR	BA	FA	ERA
CHICAGO	107	45	.704	—	572	390	.250	.967	1.73
PITTSBURGH	91	63	.591	17	634	510	.254	.959	2.30
PHILADELPHIA	83	64	.565	21.5	512	476	.236	.957	2.43
NEW YORK	82	71	.536	25.5	574	510	.251	.963	2.45
BROOKLYN	65	83	.439	40	446	522	.232	.959	2.38
CINCINNATI	66	87	.431	41.5	526	519	.247	.963	2.41
BOSTON	58	90	.392	47	502	652	.243	.961	3.33
ST. LOUIS	52	101	.340	55.5	419	606	.232	.947	2.70
					4185	4185	.243	.959	2.46

BATTING AVERAGE
Honus Wagner PIT .... .350
Sherry Magee PHI ..... .328
G. Beaumont BOS ..... .322

HITS
G. Beaumont BOS 187
Honus Wagner PIT 180
Tommy Leach PIT 166

DOUBLES
Honus Wagner PIT 38
Sherry Magee PHI 28
two tied at 25

TRIPLES
W. Alperman BKN......... 16
John Ganzel CIN 16
two tied at 14

HOME RUNS
Dave Brain BOS 10
Harry Lumley BKN 9
Red Murray STL 7

RUNS BATTED IN
Sherry Magee PHI 85
Honus Wagner PIT 82
Ed Abbaticchio PIT 82

SLUGGING AVERAGE
Honus Wagner PIT ..... .513
Sherry Magee PHI ..... .455
Harry Lumley BKN ..... .425

STOLEN BASES
Honus Wagner PIT 61
Johnny Evers CHI 46
Sherry Magee PHI 46

RUNS SCORED
Spike Shannon NY 104
Tommy Leach PIT 102
Honus Wagner PIT 98

WINS
C. Mathewson NY 24
Orval Overall CHI 23
two tied at 22

WINNING PERCENTAGE
Ed Reulbach CHI .... .810
T. Brown CHI .... .769
Orval Overall CHI .... .742

EARNED RUN AVERAGE
Jack Pfiester CHI 1.15
Carl Lundgren CHI..... 1.17
T. Brown CHI 1.39

STRIKEOUTS
C. Mathewson NY 178
Buck Ewing CIN 147
Red Ames NY 146

SAVES
Joe McGinnity NY 4
T. Brown CHI 3
Orval Overall CHI............. 3

COMPLETE GAMES
Stoney McGlynn STL.... 33
Buck Ewing CIN............. 32
C. Mathewson NY.......... 31

SHUTOUTS
Christy Mathewson NY ... 8
Orval Overall CHI............. 8
Carl Lundgren CHI.......... 7

GAMES PITCHED
Joe McGinnity NY 47
Stoney McGlynn STL.... 45
two tied at 41

INNINGS PITCHED
S. McGlynn STL............ 352
Buck Ewing CIN 333
C. Mathewson NY 316

AMERICAN LEAGUE STANDINGS

1908 AL

	W	L	PCT	GB	R	OR	BA	FA	ERA
DETROIT	90	63	.588	—	647	547	.264	.953	2.40
CLEVELAND	90	64	.584	.5	568	457	.239	.962	2.02
CHICAGO	88	64	.579	1.5	537	470	.224	.966	2.22
ST. LOUIS	83	69	.546	6.5	544	483	.245	.964	2.15
BOSTON	75	79	.487	15.5	564	513	.246	.955	2.27
PHILADELPHIA	68	85	.444	22	486	562	.223	.957	2.57
WASHINGTON	67	85	.441	22.5	479	539	.235	.958	2.34
NEW YORK	51	103	.331	39.5	459	713	.236	.947	3.16
					4284	4284	.239	.958	2.39

BATTING AVERAGE
Ty Cobb DET .... .324
Sam Crawford DET .... .311
Doc Gessler BOS ...... .308

HITS
Ty Cobb DET 188
Sam Crawford DET 184
two tied at 168

DOUBLES
Ty Cobb DET 36
Sam Crawford DET 33
C. Rossman DET 33

TRIPLES
Ty Cobb DET 20
Sam Crawford DET 16
Jake Stahl BOS, NY 16

HOME RUNS
Sam Crawford DET 7
Bill Hinchman CLE 6
three tied at 5

RUNS BATTED IN
Ty Cobb DET 108
Sam Crawford DET 80
two tied at 74

SLUGGING AVERAGE
Ty Cobb DET .... .475
Sam Crawford DET .... .457
Doc Gessler BOS ...... .423

STOLEN BASES
Patsy Dougherty CHI 47
Charlie Hemphill NY 42
G. Schaefer DET 40

RUNS SCORED
Matty McIntyre DET 105
Sam Crawford DET 102
G. Schaefer DET 96

WINS
Ed Walsh CHI 40
Addie Joss CLE 24
Ed Summers DET 24

WINNING PERCENTAGE
Ed Walsh CHI .... .727
Bill Donovan DET ...... .720
Addie Joss CLE .... .686

EARNED RUN AVERAGE
Addie Joss CLE 1.16
Cy Young BOS 1.26
Ed Walsh CHI 1.42

STRIKEOUTS
Ed Walsh CHI 269
Rube Waddell STL 232
Tom Hughes WAS 165

SAVES
Ed Walsh CHI 6
Tom Hughes WAS 4
two tied at 3

COMPLETE GAMES
Ed Walsh CHI 42
Cy Young BOS 30
Addie Joss CLE 29

SHUTOUTS
Ed Walsh CHI 11
Addie Joss CLE 9
two tied at 6

GAMES PITCHED
Ed Walsh CHI 66
Rube Vickers PHI 53
Jack Chesbro NY 45

INNINGS PITCHED
Ed Walsh CHI 464
Addie Joss CLE 325
Harry Howell STL 324

NATIONAL LEAGUE STANDINGS

1908 NL

	W	L	PCT	GB	R	OR	BA	FA	ERA
CHICAGO	99	55	.643	—	624	461	.249	.969	2.14
NEW YORK	98	56	.636	1	652	456	.267	.962	2.14
PITTSBURGH	98	56	.636	1	585	469	.247	.964	2.12
PHILADELPHIA	83	71	.539	16	504	445	.244	.963	2.10
CINCINNATI	73	81	.474	26	489	544	.227	.959	2.37
BOSTON	63	91	.409	36	537	622	.239	.962	2.79
BROOKLYN	53	101	.344	46	377	516	.213	.961	2.47
ST. LOUIS	49	105	.318	50	371	626	.223	.946	2.64
					4139	4139	.239	.961	2.35

BATTING AVERAGE
Honus Wagner PIT .... .354
Mike Donlin NY .... .334
Larry Doyle NY .... .308

HITS
Honus Wagner PIT 201
Mike Donlin NY 198
two tied at 167

DOUBLES
Honus Wagner PIT 39
Sherry Magee PHI 30
Frank Chance CHI 27

TRIPLES
Honus Wagner PIT 19
Hans Lobert CIN 18
two tied at 16

HOME RUNS
Tim Jordan BKN 12
Honus Wagner PIT 10
Red Murray STL 7

RUNS BATTED IN
Honus Wagner PIT 109
Mike Donlin NY 106
Cy Seymour NY 92

SLUGGING AVERAGE
Honus Wagner PIT .... .542
Mike Donlin NY .... .452
Sherry Magee PHI ..... .417

STOLEN BASES
Honus Wagner PIT 53
Red Murray STL 48
Hans Lobert CIN 47

RUNS SCORED
Fred Tenney NY 101
Honus Wagner PIT 100
Tommy Leach PIT 93

WINS
C. Mathewson NY 37
T. Brown CHI 29
Ed Reulbach CHI 24

WINNING PERCENTAGE
Ed Reulbach CHI .... .774
C. Mathewson NY ...... .771
T. Brown CHI .... .763

EARNED RUN AVERAGE
C. Mathewson NY 1.43
T. Brown CHI 1.47
G. McQuillan PHI 1.53

STRIKEOUTS
C. Mathewson NY 259
Nap Rucker BKN 199
Orval Overall CHI........ 167

SAVES
T. Brown CHI 5
Christy Mathewson NY ... 5
Joe McGinnity NY 4

COMPLETE GAMES
C. Mathewson NY 34
Kaiser Wilhelm BKN 33
G. McQuillan PHI 32

SHUTOUTS
C. Mathewson NY.......... 12
T. Brown CHI 9
two tied at 7

GAMES PITCHED
C. Mathewson NY.......... 56
G. McQuillan PHI 48
Bugs Raymond STL....... 48

INNINGS PITCHED
C. Mathewson NY....... 391
G. McQuillan PHI 360
Nap Rucker BKN 333

AMERICAN LEAGUE STANDINGS

1909 AL

	W	L	PCT	GB	R	OR	BA	FA	ERA
DETROIT	98	54	.645	—	666	493	.267	.959	2.26
PHILADELPHIA	95	58	.621	3.5	605	408	.257	.961	1.92
BOSTON	88	63	.583	9.5	597	550	.263	.955	2.60
CHICAGO	78	74	.513	20	492	463	.221	.964	2.04
NEW YORK	74	77	.490	23.5	590	587	.248	.948	2.68
CLEVELAND	71	82	.464	27.5	493	532	.241	.957	2.39
ST. LOUIS	61	89	.407	36	441	575	.232	.958	2.88
WASHINGTON	42	110	.276	56	380	656	.223	.957	3.04
					4264	4264	.244	.957	2.47

BATTING AVERAGE
Ty Cobb DET .... .377
Eddie Collins PHI .... .346
Nap Lajoie CLE .... .324

HITS
Ty Cobb DET 216
Eddie Collins PHI 198
Sam Crawford DET 185

DOUBLES
Sam Crawford DET 35
Nap Lajoie CLE 33
Ty Cobb DET 33

TRIPLES
Frank Baker PHI 19
Danny Murphy PHI 14
Sam Crawford DET 14

HOME RUNS
Ty Cobb DET 9
Tris Speaker BOS 7
two tied at 6

RUNS BATTED IN
Ty Cobb DET 107
Sam Crawford DET 97
Frank Baker PHI 85

SLUGGING AVERAGE
Ty Cobb DET .... .517
Sam Crawford DET .... .452
Eddie Collins PHI .... .449

STOLEN BASES
Ty Cobb DET 76
Eddie Collins PHI 67
Donie Bush DET 53

RUNS SCORED
Ty Cobb DET 116
Donie Bush DET 114
Eddie Collins PHI 104

WINS
George Mullin DET 29
Frank Smith CHI 25
Ed Willett DET 21

WINNING PERCENTAGE
George Mullin DET ..... .784
Harry Krause PHI .... .692
Chief Bender PHI .... .692

EARNED RUN AVERAGE
Harry Krause PHI 1.39
Ed Walsh CHI 1.41
Chief Bender PHI 1.66

STRIKEOUTS
Frank Smith CHI 177
W. Johnson WAS 164
Heinie Berger CLE 162

SAVES
Frank Arellanes BOS .. 8
Jack Warhop NY 4
two tied at 3

COMPLETE GAMES
Frank Smith CHI 37
Cy Young CLE 30
George Mullin DET 29

SHUTOUTS
Ed Walsh CHI 8
Harry Krause PHI 7
Frank Smith CHI 7

GAMES PITCHED
Frank Smith CHI 51
Frank Arellanes BOS .. 45
Bob Groom WAS 44

INNINGS PITCHED
Frank Smith CHI 365
George Mullin DET 304
W. Johnson WAS 297

NATIONAL LEAGUE STANDINGS

1909 NL

	W	L	PCT	GB	R	OR	BA	FA	ERA
PITTSBURGH	110	42	.724	—	699	447	.260	.964	2.07
CHICAGO	104	49	.680	6.5	635	390	.245	.961	1.75
NEW YORK	92	61	.601	18.5	623	546	.255	.954	2.27
CINCINNATI	77	76	.503	33.5	606	599	.250	.952	2.52
PHILADELPHIA	74	79	.484	36.5	516	518	.244	.961	2.44
BROOKLYN	55	98	.359	55.5	444	627	.229	.954	3.10
ST. LOUIS	54	98	.355	56	583	731	.243	.950	3.41
BOSTON	45	108	.294	65.5	435	683	.223	.947	3.20
					4541	4541	.244	.955	2.59

BATTING AVERAGE
Honus Wagner PIT ..... .339
Mike Mitchell CIN .... .310
Dick Hoblitzell CIN ...... .308

HITS
Larry Doyle NY 172
Eddie Grant PHI.......... 170
Honus Wagner PIT 168

DOUBLES
Honus Wagner PIT 39
Sherry Magee PHI 33
Dots Miller PIT 31

TRIPLES
Mike Mitchell CIN 17
Sherry Magee PHI 14
Ed Konetchy STL.......... 14

HOME RUNS
Red Murray NY 7
three tied at..................... 6

RUNS BATTED IN
Honus Wagner PIT 100
Red Murray NY 91
Dots Miller PIT 87

SLUGGING AVERAGE
Honus Wagner PIT ..... .489
Mike Mitchell CIN .... .430
Larry Doyle NY .... .419

STOLEN BASES
Bob Bescher CIN........... 54
Red Murray NY 48
Dick Egan CIN 39

RUNS SCORED
Tommy Leach PIT 126
Fred Clarke PIT 97
two tied at 92

WINS
T. Brown CHI 27
Howie Camnitz PIT....... 25
C. Mathewson NY......... 25

WINNING PERCENTAGE
C. Mathewson NY..... .806
Howie Camnitz PIT ... .806
T. Brown CHI .... .750

EARNED RUN AVERAGE
C. Mathewson NY...... 1.14
T. Brown CHI 1.31
Orval Overall CHI........ 1.42

STRIKEOUTS
Orval Overall CHI........ 205
Nap Rucker BKN 201
Earl Moore PHI 173

SAVES
T. Brown CHI 7
Doc Crandall NY 4
four tied at........................ 3

COMPLETE GAMES
T. Brown CHI 32
George Bell BKN 29
Nap Rucker BKN 28

SHUTOUTS
Orval Overall CHI............. 9
C. Mathewson NY........... 8
T. Brown CHI 8

GAMES PITCHED
T. Brown CHI 50
Al Mattern BOS............. 47
two tied at 44

INNINGS PITCHED
T. Brown CHI 343
Al Mattern BOS........... 316
Nap Rucker BKN 309

AMERICAN LEAGUE STANDINGS

1910 AL

	W	L	PCT	GB	R	OR	BA	FA	ERA
PHILADELPHIA	102	48	.680	—	673	441	.266	.965	1.79
NEW YORK	88	63	.583	14.5	626	557	.248	.956	2.59
DETROIT	86	68	.558	18	679	582	.261	.956	3.00
BOSTON	81	72	.529	22.5	638	564	.259	.954	2.46
CLEVELAND	71	81	.467	32	548	657	.244	.964	2.89
CHICAGO	68	85	.444	35.5	457	479	.211	.954	2.01
WASHINGTON	66	85	.437	36.5	501	550	.236	.959	2.46
ST. LOUIS	47	107	.305	57	451	743	.220	.944	3.09
					4573	4573	.243	.956	2.53

BATTING AVERAGE
Ty Cobb DET .... .385
Nap Lajoie CLE .... .384
Tris Speaker BOS .... .340

HITS
Nap Lajoie CLE 227
Ty Cobb DET 196
Eddie Collins PHI 188

DOUBLES
Nap Lajoie CLE 51
Ty Cobb DET 36
Duffy Lewis BOS 29

TRIPLES
Sam Crawford DET 19
Danny Murphy PHI 18
Bris Lord CLE, PHI 18

HOME RUNS
Jake Stahl BOS 10
Ty Cobb DET 8
Duffy Lewis BOS 8

RUNS BATTED IN
Sam Crawford DET 120
Ty Cobb DET 91
Eddie Collins PHI 81

SLUGGING AVERAGE
Ty Cobb DET .... .554
Nap Lajoie CLE .... .514
Tris Speaker BOS .... .468

STOLEN BASES
Eddie Collins PHI 81
Ty Cobb DET 65
two tied at 49

RUNS SCORED
Ty Cobb DET 106
Nap Lajoie CLE 92
Tris Speaker BOS 92

WINS
Jack Coombs PHI 31
Russ Ford NY 26
Walter Johnson WAS.... 25

WINNING PERCENTAGE
Chief Bender PHI .... .821
Russ Ford NY .... .813
Jack Coombs PHI .... .775

EARNED RUN AVERAGE
Ed Walsh CHI 1.27
Jack Coombs PHI 1.30
W. Johnson WAS 1.35

STRIKEOUTS
W. Johnson WAS 313
Ed Walsh CHI 258
Jack Coombs PHI 224

SAVES
Ed Walsh CHI 5
Charley Hall BOS 5
Frank Browning DET 3

COMPLETE GAMES
Walter Johnson WAS 38
Jack Coombs PHI 35
Ed Walsh CHI 33

SHUTOUTS
Jack Coombs PHI 13
Russ Ford NY 8
Walter Johnson WAS...... 8

GAMES PITCHED
Walter Johnson WAS.... 45
Ed Walsh CHI 45
Jack Coombs PHI 45

INNINGS PITCHED
W. Johnson WAS 373
Ed Walsh CHI 370
Jack Coombs PHI 353

NATIONAL LEAGUE STANDINGS

1910 NL

	W	L	PCT	GB	R	OR	BA	FA	ERA
CHICAGO	104	50	.675	—	712	499	.268	.963	2.51
NEW YORK	91	63	.591	13	715	567	.275	.955	2.68
PITTSBURGH	86	67	.562	17.5	655	576	.266	.961	2.83
PHILADELPHIA	78	75	.510	25.5	674	639	.255	.960	3.05
CINCINNATI	75	79	.487	29	620	684	.259	.955	3.08
BROOKLYN	64	90	.416	40	497	623	.229	.964	3.07
ST. LOUIS	63	90	.412	40.5	639	718	.248	.959	3.78
BOSTON	53	100	.346	50.5	495	701	.246	.954	3.22
					5007	5007	.256	.959	3.02

BATTING AVERAGE
Sherry Magee PHI ..... .331
Vin Campbell PIT .... .326
Solly Hofman CHI ...... .325

HITS
Bobby Byrne PIT 178
Honus Wagner PIT 178
two tied at 172

DOUBLES
Bobby Byrne PIT 43
Sherry Magee PHI 39
Zack Wheat BKN 36

TRIPLES
Mike Mitchell CIN 18
Sherry Magee PHI 17
two tied at 16

HOME RUNS
Fred Beck BOS 10
Wildfire Schulte CHI 10
two tied at 8

RUNS BATTED IN
Sherry Magee PHI 123
Mike Mitchell CIN 88
Red Murray NY 87

SLUGGING AVERAGE
Sherry Magee PHI ..... .507
Solly Hofman CHI ...... .461
Wildfire Schulte CHI... .460

STOLEN BASES
Bob Bescher CIN 70
Red Murray NY 57
Dode Paskert CIN 51

RUNS SCORED
Sherry Magee PHI 110
Miller Huggins STL 101
Bobby Byrne PIT 101

WINS
C. Mathewson NY 27
T. Brown CHI 25
two tied at 20

WINNING PERCENTAGE
King Cole CHI .... .833
Doc Crandall NY .... .810
C. Mathewson NY ...... .750

EARNED RUN AVERAGE
G. McQuillan PHI 1.60
King Cole CHI 1.80
T. Brown CHI 1.86

STRIKEOUTS
Earl Moore PHI 185
C. Mathewson NY 184
S. Frock PIT, BOS 171

SAVES
T. Brown CHI 7
Harry Gaspar CIN 5
two tied at 4

COMPLETE GAMES
T. Brown CHI 27
C. Mathewson NY 27
Nap Rucker BKN 27

SHUTOUTS
T. Brown CHI 7
three tied at..................... 6

GAMES PITCHED
Al Mattern BOS 51
Harry Gaspar CIN 48
two tied at 46

INNINGS PITCHED
Nap Rucker BKN 320
C. Mathewson NY 318
George Bell BKN 310

AMERICAN LEAGUE STANDINGS

1911 AL

	W	L	PCT	GB	R	OR	BA	FA	ERA
PHILADELPHIA	101	50	.669	—	861	601	.296	.965	3.01
DETROIT	89	65	.578	13.5	831	776	.292	.951	3.73
CLEVELAND	80	73	.523	22	691	712	.282	.954	3.37
CHICAGO	77	74	.510	24	719	624	.269	.961	3.01
BOSTON	78	75	.510	24	680	643	.274	.949	2.73
NEW YORK	76	76	.500	25.5	684	724	.272	.949	3.54
WASHINGTON	64	90	.416	38.5	625	766	.258	.953	3.52
ST. LOUIS	45	107	.296	56.5	567	812	.239	.945	3.83
					5658	5658	.273	.953	3.34

BATTING AVERAGE
Ty Cobb DET .... .420
Joe Jackson CLE .... .408
Sam Crawford DET .... .378

HITS
Ty Cobb DET 248
Joe Jackson CLE 233
Sam Crawford DET 217

DOUBLES
Ty Cobb DET 47
Joe Jackson CLE 45
Frank Baker PHI 40

TRIPLES
Ty Cobb DET 24
Birdie Cree NY 22
Joe Jackson CLE 19

HOME RUNS
Frank Baker PHI 11
Ty Cobb DET 8
Tris Speaker BOS 8

RUNS BATTED IN
Ty Cobb DET 144
Frank Baker PHI 115
Sam Crawford DET 115

SLUGGING AVERAGE
Ty Cobb DET .... .621
Joe Jackson CLE .... .590
Sam Crawford DET .... .526

STOLEN BASES
Ty Cobb DET 83
Clyde Milan WAS 58
Birdie Cree NY 48

RUNS SCORED
Ty Cobb DET 147
Joe Jackson CLE 126
Donie Bush DET 126

WINS
Jack Coombs PHI 28
Ed Walsh CHI 27
Walter Johnson WAS.... 25

WINNING PERCENTAGE
Chief Bender PHI .... .773
Vean Gregg CLE .... .767
Eddie Plank PHI .... .742

EARNED RUN AVERAGE
Vean Gregg CLE 1.81
W. Johnson WAS 1.89
Joe Wood BOS 2.02

STRIKEOUTS
Ed Walsh CHI 255
Joe Wood BOS 231
W. Johnson WAS 207

SAVES
Eddie Plank PHI 5
Charley Hall BOS 4
Ed Walsh CHI 4

COMPLETE GAMES
Walter Johnson WAS 36
Ed Walsh CHI 33
two tied at 26

SHUTOUTS
Eddie Plank PHI 6
Walter Johnson WAS 6
two tied at 5

GAMES PITCHED
Ed Walsh CHI 56
Jack Coombs PHI 47
Joe Wood BOS 44

INNINGS PITCHED
Ed Walsh CHI 369
Jack Coombs PHI 337
W. Johnson WAS 323

NATIONAL LEAGUE STANDINGS

1911 NL

	W	L	PCT	GB	R	OR	BA	FA	ERA
NEW YORK	99	54	.647	—	756	542	.279	.959	2.69
CHICAGO	92	62	.597	7.5	757	607	.260	.960	2.90
PITTSBURGH	85	69	.552	14.5	744	557	.262	.963	2.84
PHILADELPHIA	79	73	.520	19.5	658	669	.259	.963	3.30
ST. LOUIS	75	74	.503	22	671	745	.252	.960	3.68
CINCINNATI	70	83	.458	29	682	706	.261	.955	3.26
BROOKLYN	64	86	.427	33.5	539	659	.237	.962	3.39
BOSTON	44	107	.291	54	699	1021	.267	.947	5.08
					5506	5506	.260	.958	3.39

BATTING AVERAGE
Honus Wagner PIT ..... .334
Dots Miller BOS .... .333
Chief Meyers NY .... .332

HITS
Dots Miller BOS 192
Dick Hoblitzell CIN 180
Jake Daubert BKN 176

DOUBLES
Ed Konetchy STL........... 38
Dots Miller BOS 36
Owen Wilson PIT 34

TRIPLES
Larry Doyle NY 25
Mike Mitchell CIN 22
Wildfire Schulte CHI...... 21

HOME RUNS
Wildfire Schulte CHI...... 21
Fred Luderus PHI 16
Sherry Magee PHI 15

RUNS BATTED IN
Wildfire Schulte CHI.... 121
Owen Wilson PIT 107
Fred Luderus PHI 99

SLUGGING AVERAGE
Wildfire Schulte CHI... .534
Larry Doyle NY .... .527
Honus Wagner PIT ..... .507

STOLEN BASES
Bob Bescher CIN 81
Josh Devore NY............ 61
Fred Snodgrass NY 51

RUNS SCORED
J. Sheckard CHI........... 121
Miller Huggins STL 106
Bob Bescher CIN 106

WINS
Grover Alexander PHI... 28
C. Mathewson NY 26
Rube Marquard NY....... 24

WINNING PERCENTAGE
Rube Marquard NY.... .781
Doc Crandall NY .... .750
King Cole CHI .... .720

EARNED RUN AVERAGE
C. Mathewson NY...... 1.99
Lew Richie CHI........... 2.31
Babe Adams PIT........ 2.33

STRIKEOUTS
Rube Marquard NY..... 237
G. Alexander PHI........ 227
Nap Rucker BKN 190

SAVES
T. Brown CHI 13
Doc Crandall NY 5
four tied at...................... 4

COMPLETE GAMES
Grover Alexander PHI... 31
C. Mathewson NY......... 29
Bob Harmon STL........... 28

SHUTOUTS
Grover Alexander PHI... 7
Babe Adams PIT............. 7
two tied at 5

GAMES PITCHED
T. Brown CHI 53
Bob Harmon STL........... 51
two tied at 48

INNINGS PITCHED
G. Alexander PHI........ 367
Bob Harmon STL........ 348
Lefty Leifield PIT......... 318

AMERICAN LEAGUE STANDINGS

1912 AL

	W	L	PCT	GB	R	OR	BA	FA	ERA
BOSTON	105	47	.691	—	799	544	.277	.957	2.76
WASHINGTON	91	61	.599	14	698	581	.256	.954	2.69
PHILADELPHIA	90	62	.592	15	779	658	.282	.959	3.32
CHICAGO	78	76	.506	28	638	646	.255	.956	3.06
CLEVELAND	75	78	.490	30.5	676	680	.273	.954	3.30
DETROIT	69	84	.451	36.5	720	777	.267	.950	3.78
ST. LOUIS	53	101	.344	53	552	764	.249	.947	3.71
NEW YORK	50	102	.329	55	630	842	.259	.940	4.13
					5492	5492	.265	.952	3.34

BATTING AVERAGE
Ty Cobb DET .... .410
Joe Jackson CLE .... .395
Tris Speaker BOS ...... .383

HITS
Ty Cobb DET 227
Joe Jackson CLE 226
Tris Speaker BOS 222

DOUBLES
Tris Speaker BOS 53
Joe Jackson CLE 44
Frank Baker PHI 40

TRIPLES
Joe Jackson CLE 26
Ty Cobb DET 23
two tied at 21

HOME RUNS
Frank Baker PHI 10
Tris Speaker BOS 10
Ty Cobb DET 7

RUNS BATTED IN
Frank Baker PHI 133
Duffy Lewis BOS 109
Sam Crawford DET 109

SLUGGING AVERAGE
Ty Cobb DET .... .586
Joe Jackson CLE .... .579
Tris Speaker BOS ...... .567

STOLEN BASES
Claude Milan WAS 88
Eddie Collins PHI 63
Ty Cobb DET 61

RUNS SCORED
Eddie Collins PHI 137
Tris Speaker BOS 136
Joe Jackson CLE 121

WINS
Joe Wood BOS 34
Walter Johnson WAS 32
Ed Walsh CHI 27

WINNING PERCENTAGE
Joe Wood BOS .... .872
Eddie Plank PHI .... .813
W. Johnson WAS .... .727

EARNED RUN AVERAGE
W. Johnson WAS 1.39
Joe Wood BOS 1.91
Ed Walsh CHI 2.15

STRIKEOUTS
W. Johnson WAS 303
Joe Wood BOS 258
Ed Walsh CHI 254

SAVES
Ed Walsh CHI 10
three tied at 3

COMPLETE GAMES
Joe Wood BOS 35
Walter Johnson WAS ... 34
two tied at 32

SHUTOUTS
Joe Wood BOS 10
Walter Johnson WAS 7
Ed Walsh CHI 6

GAMES PITCHED
Ed Walsh CHI 62
Walter Johnson WAS ... 50
two tied at 43

INNINGS PITCHED
Ed Walsh CHI 393
W. Johnson WAS 368
Joe Wood BOS 344

NATIONAL LEAGUE STANDINGS

1912 NL

	W	L	PCT	GB	R	OR	BA	FA	ERA
NEW YORK	103	48	.682	—	823	571	.286	.956	2.58
PITTSBURGH	93	58	.616	10	751	565	.284	.972	2.85
CHICAGO	91	59	.607	11.5	756	668	.277	.960	3.42
CINCINNATI	75	78	.490	29	656	722	.256	.960	3.42
PHILADELPHIA	73	79	.480	30.5	670	688	.267	.963	3.25
ST. LOUIS	63	90	.412	41	659	830	.268	.957	3.85
BROOKLYN	58	95	.379	46	651	754	.268	.959	3.64
BOSTON	52	101	.340	52	693	861	.273	.954	4.17
					5659	5659	.272	.960	3.40

BATTING AVERAGE
H. Zimmerman CHI .... .372
Chief Meyers NY .... .358
Bill Sweeney BOS ...... .344

HITS
H. Zimmerman CHI 207
Bill Sweeney BOS 204
Vin Campbell BOS 185

DOUBLES
H. Zimmerman CHI 41
Dode Paskert PHI 37
Honus Wagner PIT 35

TRIPLES
Owen Wilson PIT 36
Honus Wagner PIT 20
Red Murray NY 20

HOME RUNS
H. Zimmerman CHI 14
Wildfire Schulte CHI 13
three tied at 11

RUNS BATTED IN
H. Zimmerman CHI 103
Honus Wagner PIT 102
Bill Sweeney BOS 100

SLUGGING AVERAGE
H. Zimmerman CHI .... .571
Owen Wilson PIT .... .513
Honus Wagner PIT .... .496

STOLEN BASES
Bob Bescher CIN 67
Max Carey PIT 45
Fred Snodgrass NY 43

RUNS SCORED
Bob Bescher CIN 120
Max Carey PIT 114
two tied at 102

WINS
Larry Cheney CHI 26
Rube Marquard NY 26
Claude Hendrix PIT 24

WINNING PERCENTAGE
Claude Hendrix PIT ... .727
Larry Cheney CHI ...... .722
Jeff Tesreau NY .... .708

EARNED RUN AVERAGE
Jeff Tesreau NY 1.96
C. Mathewson NY 2.12
Nap Rucker BKN 2.21

STRIKEOUTS
G. Alexander PHI 195
Claude Hendrix PIT 176
Rube Marquard NY 175

SAVES
Slim Sallee STL 6
Nap Rucker BKN 4
Christy Mathewson NY ... 4

COMPLETE GAMES
Larry Cheney CHI 28
C. Mathewson NY 27
Grover Alexander PHI... 26

SHUTOUTS
Nap Rucker BKN 6
Marty O'Toole PIT 6
George Suggs CIN 5

GAMES PITCHED
Rube Benton CIN 50
Slim Sallee STL 48
Grover Alexander PHI... 46

INNINGS PITCHED
G. Alexander PHI 310
C. Mathewson NY 310
two tied at 303

AMERICAN LEAGUE STANDINGS

1913 AL

	W	L	PCT	GB	R	OR	BA	FA	ERA
PHILADELPHIA	96	57	.627	—	794	592	.280	.966	3.19
WASHINGTON	90	64	.584	6.5	596	561	.252	.960	2.72
CLEVELAND	86	66	.566	9.5	633	536	.268	.962	2.52
BOSTON	79	71	.527	15.5	631	610	.269	.961	2.93
CHICAGO	78	74	.513	17.5	488	498	.236	.960	2.33
DETROIT	66	87	.431	30	624	716	.265	.954	3.41
NEW YORK	57	94	.377	38	529	668	.237	.954	3.27
ST. LOUIS	57	96	.373	39	528	642	.237	.954	3.06
					4823	4823	.256	.959	2.93

BATTING AVERAGE
Ty Cobb DET .... .390
Joe Jackson CLE .... .373
Tris Speaker BOS .... .365

HITS
Joe Jackson CLE 197
Sam Crawford DET 193
Frank Baker PHI 190

DOUBLES
Joe Jackson CLE 39
Tris Speaker BOS 35
Frank Baker PHI 34

TRIPLES
Sam Crawford DET 23
Tris Speaker BOS 22
Joe Jackson CLE 17

HOME RUNS
Frank Baker PHI 12
Sam Crawford DET 9
Ping Bodie CHI 8

RUNS BATTED IN
Frank Baker PHI 126
Duffy Lewis BOS 90
Stuffy McInnis PHI 90

SLUGGING AVERAGE
Joe Jackson CLE .... .551
Ty Cobb DET .... .535
Tris Speaker BOS .... .535

STOLEN BASES
Clyde Milan WAS 75
Danny Moeller WAS 62
Eddie Collins PHI 55

RUNS SCORED
Eddie Collins PHI 125
Frank Baker PHI 116
Joe Jackson CLE 109

WINS
Walter Johnson WAS 36
Cy Falkenberg CLE 23
Reb Russell CHI 22

WINNING PERCENTAGE
W. Johnson WAS .... .837
Ray Collins BOS .... .714
Joe Boehling WAS ...... .708

EARNED RUN AVERAGE
W. Johnson WAS 1.09
Eddie Cicotte CHI 1.58
Willie Mitchell CLE 1.74

STRIKEOUTS
W. Johnson WAS 243
Vean Gregg CLE 166
Cy Falkenberg CLE 166

SAVES
Chief Bender PHI 12
Tom Hughes WAS 6
Hugh Bedient BOS 5

COMPLETE GAMES
W. Johnson WAS 29
Reb Russell CHI 26
Jim Scott CHI 25

SHUTOUTS
Walter Johnson WAS 11
Reb Russell CHI 8
Eddie Plank PHI 7

GAMES PITCHED
Reb Russell CHI 51
Jim Scott CHI 48
Chief Bender PHI 48

INNINGS PITCHED
W. Johnson WAS 346
Reb Russell CHI 316
Jim Scott CHI 312

NATIONAL LEAGUE STANDINGS

1913 NL

	W	L	PCT	GB	R	OR	BA	FA	ERA
NEW YORK	101	51	.664	—	684	515	.273	.961	2.43
PHILADELPHIA	88	63	.583	12.5	693	636	.265	.968	3.15
CHICAGO	88	65	.575	13.5	720	625	.257	.959	3.13
PITTSBURGH	78	71	.523	21.5	673	585	.263	.964	2.90
BOSTON	69	82	.457	31.5	641	690	.256	.957	3.19
BROOKLYN	65	84	.436	34.5	595	613	.270	.961	3.13
CINCINNATI	64	89	.418	37.5	607	717	.261	.961	3.46
ST. LOUIS	51	99	.340	49	523	755	.247	.965	4.24
					5136	5136	.262	.962	3.20

BATTING AVERAGE
Jake Daubert BKN ..... .350
Gavvy Cravath PHI .... .341
two tied at .... .317

HITS
Gavvy Cravath PHI 179
Jake Daubert BKN 178
George Burns NY 173

DOUBLES
Red Smith BKN............ 40
George Burns NY 37
Sherry Magee PHI 36

TRIPLES
Vic Saier CHI 21
Dots Miller PIT 20
Ed Konetchy STL........... 17

HOME RUNS
Gavvy Cravath PHI....... 19
Fred Luderus PHI 18
Vic Saier CHI 14

RUNS BATTED IN
Gavvy Cravath PHI...... 128
H. Zimmerman CHI...... 95
Vic Saier CHI 92

SLUGGING AVERAGE
Gavvy Cravath PHI.... .568
B. Becker CIN, PHI .... .502
H. Zimmerman CHI.... .490

STOLEN BASES
Max Carey PIT.............. 61
Hy Myers BOS 57
Hans Lobert PHI 41

RUNS SCORED
Max Carey PIT.............. 99
Tommy Leach CHI........ 99
Hans Lobert PHI 98

WINS
Tom Seaton PHI 27
C. Mathewson NY......... 25
Rube Marquard NY....... 23

WINNING PERCENTAGE
Bert Humphries CHI... .800
G. Alexander PHI........ .733
Rube Marquard NY.... .697

EARNED RUN AVERAGE
C. Mathewson NY...... 2.06
Babe Adams PIT........ 2.15
Jeff Tesreau NY......... 2.17

STRIKEOUTS
Tom Seaton PHI 168
Jeff Tesreau NY.......... 167
G. Alexander PHI........ 159

SAVES
Larry Cheney CHI 11
T. Brown CIN 6
Doc Crandall NY 6

COMPLETE GAMES
Lefty Tyler BOS 28
C. Mathewson NY......... 25
Larry Cheney CHI 25

SHUTOUTS
Grover Alexander PHI..... 9
Tom Seaton PHI 6

GAMES PITCHED
Larry Cheney CHI 54
Tom Seaton PHI 52
Slim Sallee STL 49

INNINGS PITCHED
Tom Seaton PHI 322
Babe Adams PIT......... 314
two tied at 306

AMERICAN LEAGUE STANDINGS

1914 AL

	W	L	PCT	GB	R	OR	BA	FA	ERA
PHILADELPHIA	99	53	.651	—	749	529	.272	.966	2.78
BOSTON	91	62	.595	8.5	588	511	.250	.963	2.35
WASHINGTON	81	73	.526	19	572	519	.244	.961	2.54
DETROIT	80	73	.523	19.5	615	618	.258	.958	2.86
ST. LOUIS	71	82	.464	28.5	523	614	.243	.952	2.85
CHICAGO	70	84	.455	30	487	560	.239	.955	2.48
NEW YORK	70	84	.455	30	538	550	.229	.963	2.81
CLEVELAND	51	102	.333	48.5	538	709	.245	.953	3.21
					4610	4610	.248	.959	2.73

BATTING AVERAGE
Ty Cobb DET .... .368
Eddie Collins PHI .... .344
two tied at .... .338

HITS
Tris Speaker BOS 193
Sam Crawford DET 183
Frank Baker PHI 182

DOUBLES
Tris Speaker BOS 46
Duffy Lewis BOS 37
two tied at 34

TRIPLES
Sam Crawford DET 26
Larry Gardner BOS 19
Tris Speaker BOS 18

HOME RUNS
Frank Baker PHI 9
Sam Crawford DET 8
two tied at 6

RUNS BATTED IN
Sam Crawford DET 104
Frank Baker PHI 97
Stuffy McInnis PHI 95

SLUGGING AVERAGE
Ty Cobb DET .... .513
Tris Speaker BOS ...... .503
Sam Crawford DET .... .483

STOLEN BASES
Fritz Maisel NY 74
Eddie Collins PHI 58
Tris Speaker BOS 42

RUNS SCORED
Eddie Collins PHI 122
Eddie Murphy PHI 101
Tris Speaker BOS 100

WINS
Walter Johnson WAS 28
Harry Coveleski DET 22
Ray Collins BOS 20

WINNING PERCENTAGE
Chief Bender PHI .... .850
Dutch Leonard BOS ... .783
Eddie Plank PHI .... .682

EARNED RUN AVERAGE
Dutch Leonard BOS ... 1.01
Rube Foster BOS 1.65
W. Johnson WAS 1.72

STRIKEOUTS
W. Johnson WAS 225
Willie Mitchell CLE 179
Dutch Leonard BOS 174

SAVES
six tied at 4

COMPLETE GAMES
W. Johnson WAS 33
Harry Coveleski DET 23
two tied at 22

SHUTOUTS
Walter Johnson WAS 9
Chief Bender PHI 7
Dutch Leonard BOS 7

GAMES PITCHED
Walter Johnson WAS 51
Doc Ayers WAS 49
two tied at 48

INNINGS PITCHED
W. Johnson WAS 372
H. Coveleski DET 303
two tied at 302

NATIONAL LEAGUE STANDINGS

1914 NL

	W	L	PCT	GB	R	OR	BA	FA	ERA
BOSTON	94	59	.614	—	657	548	.251	.963	2.74
NEW YORK	84	70	.545	10.5	672	576	.265	.961	2.94
ST. LOUIS	81	72	.529	13	558	540	.248	.964	2.38
CHICAGO	78	76	.506	16.5	605	638	.243	.951	2.71
BROOKLYN	75	79	.487	19.5	622	618	.269	.961	2.82
PHILADELPHIA	74	80	.481	20.5	651	687	.263	.950	3.06
PITTSBURGH	69	85	.448	25.5	503	540	.233	.966	2.70
CINCINNATI	60	94	.390	34.5	530	651	.236	.952	2.94
					4798	4798	.251	.958	2.78

BATTING AVERAGE
Jake Daubert BKN ..... .329
Beals Becker PHI .... .325
two tied at .... .319

HITS
Sherry Magee PHI 171
George Burns NY 170
Zack Wheat BKN 170

DOUBLES
Sherry Magee PHI 39
H. Zimmerman CHI 36
George Burns NY 35

TRIPLES
Max Carey PIT 17
three tied at 12

HOME RUNS
Gavvy Cravath PHI 19
Vic Saier CHI 18
Sherry Magee PHI 15

RUNS BATTED IN
Sherry Magee PHI 103
Gavvy Cravath PHI 100
Zack Wheat BKN 89

SLUGGING AVERAGE
Sherry Magee PHI ..... .509
Gavvy Cravath PHI .... .499
Joe Connolly BOS ..... .494

STOLEN BASES
George Burns NY 62
Buck Herzog CIN 46
Cozy Dolan STL 42

RUNS SCORED
George Burns NY 100
Sherry Magee PHI 96
Jake Daubert BKN 89

WINS
Dick Rudolph BOS 27
Grover Alexander PHI... 27
two tied at 26

WINNING PERCENTAGE
Bill James BOS .... .788
Bill Doak STL .... .769
Dick Rudolph BOS ..... .730

EARNED RUN AVERAGE
Bill Doak STL 1.72
Bill James BOS 1.90
Jeff Pfeffer BKN 1.97

STRIKEOUTS
G. Alexander PHI 214
Jeff Tesreau NY 189
Hippo Vaughn CHI 165

SAVES
Red Ames CIN 6
Slim Sallee STL 6
Larry Cheney CHI 5

COMPLETE GAMES
Grover Alexander PHI... 32
Dick Rudolph BOS 31
Bill James BOS 30

SHUTOUTS
Jeff Tesreau NY 8
Bill Doak STL 7
two tied at 6

GAMES PITCHED
Larry Cheney CHI 50
Erskine Mayer PHI 48
Red Ames CIN 47

INNINGS PITCHED
G. Alexander PHI 355
Dick Rudolph BOS 336
Bill James BOS 332

AMERICAN LEAGUE STANDINGS

1915 AL

	W	L	PCT	GB	R	OR	BA	FA	ERA
BOSTON	101	50	.669	—	668	499	.260	.964	2.39
DETROIT	100	54	.649	2.5	778	597	.268	.961	2.86
CHICAGO	93	61	.604	9.5	717	509	.258	.965	2.43
WASHINGTON	85	68	.556	17	569	491	.244	.964	2.31
NEW YORK	69	83	.454	32.5	584	588	.233	.966	3.09
ST. LOUIS	63	91	.409	39.5	521	679	.246	.949	3.07
CLEVELAND	57	95	.375	44.5	539	670	.241	.957	3.13
PHILADELPHIA	43	109	.283	58.5	545	888	.237	.947	4.33
					4921	4921	.248	.959	2.94

BATTING AVERAGE
Ty Cobb DET .... .369
Eddie Collins CHI .... .332
two tied at .... .322

HITS
Ty Cobb DET 208
Sam Crawford DET 183
Bobby Veach DET 178

DOUBLES
Bobby Veach DET 40
three tied at 31

TRIPLES
Sam Crawford DET 19
Jack Fournier CHI 18
two tied at 17

HOME RUNS
Braggo Roth CHI, CLE ... 7
Rube Oldring PHI 6

RUNS BATTED IN
Bobby Veach DET 112
Sam Crawford DET 112
Ty Cobb DET 99

SLUGGING AVERAGE
Jack Fournier CHI .... .491
Ty Cobb DET .... .487
M. Kavanagh DET ...... .452

STOLEN BASES
Ty Cobb DET 96
Fritz Maisel NY 51
Eddie Collins CHI 46

RUNS SCORED
Ty Cobb DET 144
Eddie Collins CHI 118
Ossie Vitt DET 116

WINS
Walter Johnson WAS 28
three tied at 24

WINNING PERCENTAGE
Joe Wood BOS 750
Rube Foster BOS .... .704
two tied at .... .692

EARNED RUN AVERAGE
Joe Wood BOS 1.49
W. Johnson WAS 1.55
Ernie Shore BOS 1.64

STRIKEOUTS
W. Johnson WAS 203
Red Faber CHI 182
John Wyckoff PHI 157

SAVES
Carl Mays BOS 5
four tied at 4

COMPLETE GAMES
W. Johnson WAS 35
Ray Caldwell NY 31
Hooks Dauss DET 27

SHUTOUTS
Walter Johnson WAS 7
Jim Scott CHI 7
Guy Morton CLE 6

GAMES PITCHED
Harry Coveleski DET 50
Red Faber CHI 50
two tied at 48

INNINGS PITCHED
W. Johnson WAS 337
H. Coveleski DET 313
Hooks Dauss DET 310

NATIONAL LEAGUE STANDINGS

1915 NL

	W	L	PCT	GB	R	OR	BA	FA	ERA
PHILADELPHIA	90	62	.592	—	589	463	.247	.966	2.17
BOSTON	83	69	.546	7	582	545	.240	.966	2.57
BROOKLYN	80	72	.526	10	536	560	.248	.963	2.66
CHICAGO	73	80	.477	17.5	570	620	.244	.958	3.11
PITTSBURGH	73	81	.474	18	557	520	.246	.966	2.60
ST. LOUIS	72	81	.471	18.5	590	601	.254	.964	2.89
CINCINNATI	71	83	.461	20	516	585	.253	.966	2.84
NEW YORK	69	83	.454	21	582	628	.251	.960	3.11
					4522	4522	.248	.964	2.75

BATTING AVERAGE
Larry Doyle NY .... .320
Fred Luderus PHI .... .315
two tied at .... .307

HITS
Larry Doyle NY 189
Tommy Griffith CIN 179
Bill Hinchman PIT 177

DOUBLES
Larry Doyle NY 40
Fred Luderus PHI 36
Vic Saier CHI 35

TRIPLES
Tommy Long STL 25
Honus Wagner PIT 17
Tommy Griffith CIN 16

HOME RUNS
Gavvy Cravath PHI 24
Cy Williams CHI 13
Wildfire Schulte CHI...... 12

RUNS BATTED IN
Gavvy Cravath PHI 115
Sherry Magee BOS 87
Tommy Griffith CIN 85

SLUGGING AVERAGE
Gavvy Cravath PHI .... .510
Fred Luderus PHI ...... .457
Tommy Long STL ...... .446

STOLEN BASES
Max Carey PIT 36
Buck Herzog CIN 35
two tied at 29

RUNS SCORED
Gavvy Cravath PHI 89
Larry Doyle NY 86
Dave Bancroft PHI 85

WINS
G. Alexander PHI 31
Dick Rudolph BOS 22
two tied at 21

WINNING PERCENTAGE
G. Alexander PHI .... .756
Al Mamaux PIT .... .724
Fred Toney CIN .... .714

EARNED RUN AVERAGE
G. Alexander PHI 1.22
Fred Toney CIN 1.58
Al Mamaux PIT 2.04

STRIKEOUTS
G. Alexander PHI 241
Jeff Tesreau NY........... 176
Tom Hughes BOS....... 171

SAVES
Rube Benton CIN, NY..... 5
Tom Hughes BOS.......... 5
Wilbur Cooper PIT 4

COMPLETE GAMES
Grover Alexander PHI... 36
Dick Rudolph BOS........ 30
Jeff Pfeffer BKN............. 26

SHUTOUTS
Grover Alexander PHI... 12
Al Mamaux PIT 8
Jeff Tesreau NY.............. 8

GAMES PITCHED
Tom Hughes BOS.......... 50
Grover Alexander PHI... 49
Gene Dale CIN 49

INNINGS PITCHED
Grover Alexander PHI. 376
Dick Rudolph BOS...... 341
Jeff Tesreau NY........... 306

AMERICAN LEAGUE STANDINGS

1916 AL

	W	L	PCT	GB	R	OR	BA	FA	ERA
BOSTON	91	63	.591	—	550	480	.248	.972	2.48
CHICAGO	89	65	.578	2	601	497	.251	.968	2.36
DETROIT	87	67	.565	4	670	595	.264	.968	2.97
NEW YORK	80	74	.519	11	577	561	.246	.967	2.77
ST. LOUIS	79	75	.513	12	588	545	.245	.963	2.58
CLEVELAND	77	77	.500	14	630	602	.250	.965	2.89
WASHINGTON	76	77	.497	14.5	536	543	.242	.964	2.66
PHILADELPHIA	36	117	.235	54.5	447	776	.242	.951	3.84
					4599	4599	.248	.965	2.81

BATTING AVERAGE
Tris Speaker CLE ...... .386
Ty Cobb DET .... .371
Joe Jackson CHI .... .341

HITS
Tris Speaker CLE 211
Joe Jackson CHI 202
Ty Cobb DET 201

DOUBLES
Jack Graney CLE 41
Tris Speaker CLE 41
Joe Jackson CHI 40

TRIPLES
Joe Jackson CHI 21
Eddie Collins CHI 17
two tied at 15

HOME RUNS
Wally Pipp NY 12
Frank Baker NY 10
two tied at 7

RUNS BATTED IN
Del Pratt STL 103
Wally Pipp NY 93
Bobby Veach DET 91

SLUGGING AVERAGE
Tris Speaker CLE ...... .502
Joe Jackson CHI .... .495
Ty Cobb DET .... .493

STOLEN BASES
Ty Cobb DET 68
A. Marsans STL 46
Burt Shotton STL 41

RUNS SCORED
Ty Cobb DET 113
Jack Graney CLE 106
Tris Speaker CLE 102

WINS
Walter Johnson WAS.... 25
Bob Shawkey NY 24
Babe Ruth BOS 23

WINNING PERCENTAGE
Eddie Cicotte CHI ...... .682
Babe Ruth BOS .... .657
H. Coveleski DET ...... .656

EARNED RUN AVERAGE
Babe Ruth BOS 1.75
Eddie Cicotte CHI 1.78
W. Johnson WAS 1.89

STRIKEOUTS
W. Johnson WAS 228
Elmer Myers PHI 182
Babe Ruth BOS 170

SAVES
Bob Shawkey NY 8
Allan Russell NY 6
three tied at 5

COMPLETE GAMES
W. Johnson WAS 36
Elmer Myers PHI 31
Joe Bush PHI 25

SHUTOUTS
Babe Ruth BOS 9
Joe Bush PHI 8
Dutch Leonard BOS 6

GAMES PITCHED
Dave Davenport STL 59
Reb Russell CHI 56
Bob Shawkey NY 53

INNINGS PITCHED
W. Johnson WAS 371
H. Coveleski DET 324
Babe Ruth BOS 324

NATIONAL LEAGUE STANDINGS

1916 NL

	W	L	PCT	GB	R	OR	BA	FA	ERA
BROOKLYN	94	60	.610	—	585	471	.261	.965	2.12
PHILADELPHIA	91	62	.595	2.5	581	489	.250	.963	2.36
BOSTON	89	63	.586	4	542	453	.233	.967	2.19
NEW YORK	86	66	.566	7	597	504	.253	.966	2.60
CHICAGO	67	86	.438	26.5	520	541	.239	.957	2.65
PITTSBURGH	65	89	.422	29	484	586	.240	.959	2.76
CINCINNATI	60	93	.392	33.5	505	617	.254	.965	3.10
ST. LOUIS	60	93	.392	33.5	476	629	.243	.957	3.14
					4290	4290	.247	.963	2.61

BATTING AVERAGE
Hal Chase CIN............ .339
Jake Daubert BKN ...... .316
Bill Hinchman PIT .... .315

HITS
Hal Chase CIN............ 184
Dave Robertson NY.... 180
Zack Wheat BKN 177

DOUBLES
Bert Niehoff PHI............ 42
Zack Wheat BKN 32
Dode Paskert PHI 30

TRIPLES
Bill Hinchman PIT 16
three tied at................... 15

HOME RUNS
Dave Robertson NY...... 12
Cy Williams CHI............ 12
Gavvy Cravath PHI....... 11

RUNS BATTED IN
H. Zimmerman CHI, NY 83
Hal Chase CIN.............. 82
Bill Hinchman PIT 76

SLUGGING AVERAGE
Zack Wheat BKN .... .461
Hal Chase CIN........... .459
Cy Williams CHI......... .459

STOLEN BASES
Max Carey PIT.............. 63
Benny Kauff NY 40
Bob Bescher STL.......... 39

RUNS SCORED
George Burns NY 105
Max Carey PIT.............. 90
Dave Robertson NY...... 88

WINS
Grover Alexander PHI... 33
Jeff Pfeffer BKN............ 25
Eppa Rixey PHI 22

WINNING PERCENTAGE
Tom Hughes BOS...... .842
G. Alexander PHI....... .733
Jeff Pfeffer BKN .... .694

EARNED RUN AVERAGE
G. Alexander PHI....... 1.55
R. Marquard BKN 1.58
Eppa Rixey PHI 1.85

STRIKEOUTS
G. Alexander PHI........ 167
Larry Cheney BKN...... 166
Al Mamaux PIT 163

SAVES
Red Ames STL 7
three tied at...................... 5

COMPLETE GAMES
G. Alexander PHI.......... 38
Jeff Pfeffer BKN 30
Dick Rudolph BOS........ 27

SHUTOUTS
Grover Alexander PHI... 16
Lefty Tyler BOS 6
Jeff Pfeffer BKN 6

GAMES PITCHED
Lee Meadows STL......... 51
G. Alexander PHI.......... 48
two tied at 45

INNINGS PITCHED
G. Alexander PHI........ 389
Jeff Pfeffer BKN 329
Dick Rudolph BOS...... 312

AMERICAN LEAGUE STANDINGS

1917 AL

	W	L	PCT	GB	R	OR	BA	FA	ERA
CHICAGO	100	54	.649	—	656	464	.253	.967	2.16
BOSTON	90	62	.592	9	555	454	.246	.972	2.20
CLEVELAND	88	66	.571	12	584	543	.245	.964	2.52
DETROIT	78	75	.510	21.5	639	577	.259	.964	2.56
WASHINGTON	74	79	.484	25.5	543	566	.241	.961	2.77
NEW YORK	71	82	.464	28.5	524	558	.239	.965	2.66
ST. LOUIS	57	97	.370	43	510	687	.245	.957	3.20
PHILADELPHIA	55	98	.359	44.5	529	691	.254	.961	3.27
					4540	4540	.248	.964	2.66

BATTING AVERAGE
Ty Cobb DET .... .383
George Sisler STL ...... .353
Tris Speaker CLE .... .352

HITS
Ty Cobb DET 225
George Sisler STL 190
Tris Speaker CLE 184

DOUBLES
Ty Cobb DET 44
Tris Speaker CLE 42
Bobby Veach DET 31

TRIPLES
Ty Cobb DET 23
Joe Jackson CHI........... 17
Joe Judge WAS............ 15

HOME RUNS
Wally Pipp NY................. 9
Bobby Veach DET 8
two tied at 7

RUNS BATTED IN
Bobby Veach DET 103
Ty Cobb DET 102
Happy Felsch CHI....... 102

SLUGGING AVERAGE
Ty Cobb DET .... .571
Tris Speaker CLE ...... .486
Bobby Veach DET ..... .457

STOLEN BASES
Ty Cobb DET 55
Eddie Collins CHI.......... 53
Ray Chapman CLE....... 52

RUNS SCORED
Donie Bush DET......... 112
Ty Cobb DET 107
Ray Chapman CLE....... 98

WINS
Eddie Cicotte CHI 28
Babe Ruth BOS 24
two tied at 23

WINNING PERCENTAGE
Reb Russell CHI .... .750
Dave Danforth CHI .... .714
Carl Mays BOS .... .710

EARNED RUN AVERAGE
Eddie Cicotte CHI 1.53
Carl Mays BOS 1.74
Stan Coveleski CLE... 1.81

STRIKEOUTS
W. Johnson WAS........ 188
Eddie Cicotte CHI 150
Dutch Leonard BOS.... 144

SAVES
Dave Danforth CHI 9
Jim Bagby CLE 7
Bernie Boland DET 6

COMPLETE GAMES
Babe Ruth BOS 35
Walter Johnson WAS.... 30
Eddie Cicotte CHI 29

SHUTOUTS
Stan Coveleski CLE........ 9
Walter Johnson WAS...... 8
Jim Bagby CLE 8

GAMES PITCHED
Dave Danforth CHI 50
Jim Bagby CLE 49
Eddie Cicotte CHI 49

INNINGS PITCHED
Eddie Cicotte CHI 347
W. Johnson WAS........ 328
Babe Ruth BOS 326

NATIONAL LEAGUE STANDINGS

1917 NL

	W	L	PCT	GB	R	OR	BA	FA	ERA
NEW YORK	98	56	.636	—	635	457	.261	.968	2.27
PHILADELPHIA	87	65	.572	10	578	500	.248	.967	2.46
ST. LOUIS	82	70	.539	15	531	567	.250	.967	3.03
CINCINNATI	78	76	.506	20	601	611	.264	.962	2.66
CHICAGO	74	80	.481	24	552	567	.239	.959	2.62
BOSTON	72	81	.471	25.5	536	552	.246	.966	2.77
BROOKLYN	70	81	.464	26.5	511	559	.247	.962	2.78
PITTSBURGH	51	103	.331	47	464	595	.238	.961	3.01
					4408	4408	.249	.964	2.70

BATTING AVERAGE
Edd Roush CIN .... .341
R. Hornsby STL .... .327
Zack Wheat BKN .... .312

HITS
Heinie Groh CIN 182
George Burns NY 180
Edd Roush CIN 178

DOUBLES
Heinie Groh CIN 39
F. Merkle BKN, CHI 31
Red Smith BOS 31

TRIPLES
Rogers Hornsby STL 17
Gavvy Cravath PHI 16
Hal Chase CIN 15

HOME RUNS
Dave Robertson NY 12
Gavvy Cravath PHI 12
Rogers Hornsby STL 8

RUNS BATTED IN
H. Zimmerman NY 102
Hal Chase CIN 86
Gavvy Cravath PHI 83

SLUGGING AVERAGE
R. Hornsby STL .... .484
Gavvy Cravath PHI .... .473
Edd Roush CIN .... .454

STOLEN BASES
Max Carey PIT 46
George Burns NY 40
Benny Kauff NY 30

RUNS SCORED
George Burns NY 103
Heinie Groh CIN 91
Benny Kauff NY 89

WINS
Grover Alexander PHI... 30
Fred Toney CIN 24
Hippo Vaughn CHI 23

WINNING PERCENTAGE
Ferdie Schupp NY ..... .750
Slim Sallee NY .... .720
Pol Perritt NY .... .708

EARNED RUN AVERAGE
G. Alexander PHI 1.86
Pol Perritt NY 1.88
Ferdie Schupp NY 1.95

STRIKEOUTS
G. Alexander PHI 201
Hippo Vaughn CHI 195
Phil Douglas CHI 151

SAVES
Slim Sallee NY 4
five tied at 3

COMPLETE GAMES
Grover Alexander PHI... 35
Fred Toney CIN 31
two tied at 27

SHUTOUTS
Grover Alexander PHI..... 8
Wilbur Cooper PIT 7
Fred Toney CIN 7

GAMES PITCHED
Phil Douglas CHI 51
Jesse Barnes BOS 50
Pete Schneider CIN 46

INNINGS PITCHED
G. Alexander PHI 388
Pete Schneider CIN 342
Fred Toney CIN 340

AMERICAN LEAGUE STANDINGS

1918 AL

	W	L	PCT	GB	R	OR	BA	FA	ERA
BOSTON	75	51	.595	—	474	380	.249	.971	2.31
CLEVELAND	73	54	.575	2.5	504	447	.260	.962	2.63
WASHINGTON	72	56	.563	4	461	412	.256	.960	2.14
NEW YORK	60	63	.488	13.5	493	475	.257	.970	3.03
ST. LOUIS	58	64	.475	15	426	448	.259	.963	2.75
CHICAGO	57	67	.460	17	457	446	.256	.967	2.69
DETROIT	55	71	.437	20	476	557	.249	.960	3.40
PHILADELPHIA	52	76	.406	24	412	538	.243	.959	3.22
					3703	3703	.254	.964	2.77

BATTING AVERAGE
Ty Cobb DET .... .382
George Burns PHI ..... .352
George Sisler STL ..... .341

HITS
George Burns PHI 178
Ty Cobb DET 161
two tied at 154

DOUBLES
Tris Speaker CLE ... 33
Harry Hooper BOS 26
Babe Ruth BOS 26

TRIPLES
Ty Cobb DET 14
Harry Hooper BOS 13
Bobby Veach DET 13

HOME RUNS
Tilly Walker PHI 11
Babe Ruth BOS 11
two tied at 6

RUNS BATTED IN
Bobby Veach DET 78
George Burns PHI 70
Frank Baker NY 68

SLUGGING AVERAGE
Babe Ruth BOS .... .555
Ty Cobb DET .... .515
George Burns PHI ..... .467

STOLEN BASES
George Sisler STL 45
Braggo Roth CLE 35
Ty Cobb DET 34

RUNS SCORED
Ray Chapman CLE 84
Ty Cobb DET 83
Harry Hooper BOS 81

WINS
Walter Johnson WAS 23
Stan Coveleski CLE 22
two tied at 21

WINNING PERCENTAGE
Sam Jones BOS .... .762
W. Johnson WAS .... .639
Stan Coveleski CLE ... .629

EARNED RUN AVERAGE
W. Johnson WAS 1.27
Stan Coveleski CLE ... 1.82
Allen Sothoron STL 1.94

STRIKEOUTS
W. Johnson WAS 162
Jim Shaw WAS 129
Joe Bush BOS 125

SAVES
George Mogridge NY 7
Jim Bagby CLE 6
two tied at 4

COMPLETE GAMES
Carl Mays BOS 30
Scott Perry PHI 30
Walter Johnson WAS 29

SHUTOUTS
Carl Mays BOS 8
Walter Johnson WAS 8
Joe Bush BOS 7

GAMES PITCHED
Jim Bagby CLE 45
George Mogridge NY 45
Scott Perry PHI 44

INNINGS PITCHED
Scott Perry PHI 332
W. Johnson WAS 325
Stan Coveleski CLE 311

NATIONAL LEAGUE STANDINGS

1918 NL

	W	L	PCT	GB	R	OR	BA	FA	ERA
CHICAGO	84	45	.651	—	538	393	.265	.966	2.18
NEW YORK	71	53	.573	10.5	480	415	.260	.970	2.64
CINCINNATI	68	60	.531	15.5	530	496	.278	.964	3.00
PITTSBURGH	65	60	.520	17	466	412	.248	.966	2.48
BROOKLYN	57	69	.452	25.5	360	463	.250	.963	2.81
PHILADELPHIA	55	68	.447	26	430	507	.244	.961	3.15
BOSTON	53	71	.427	28.5	424	469	.244	.965	2.90
ST. LOUIS	51	78	.395	33	454	527	.244	.962	2.96
					3682	3682	.254	.965	2.76

BATTING AVERAGE
Zack Wheat BKN .... .335
Edd Roush CIN .... .333
Heinie Groh CIN .... .320

HITS
C. Hollocher CHI 161
Heinie Groh CIN 158
Edd Roush CIN 145

DOUBLES
Heinie Groh CIN 28
Les Mann CHI 27
Gavvy Cravath PHI 27

TRIPLES
Jake Daubert BKN 15
three tied at 13

HOME RUNS
Gavvy Cravath PHI 8
Walt Cruise STL 6
Cy Williams PHI 6

RUNS BATTED IN
Sherry Magee CIN 76
George Cutshaw PIT 68
Fred Luderus PHI 67

SLUGGING AVERAGE
Edd Roush CIN .... .455
Jake Daubert BKN ..... .429
R. Hornsby STL .... .416

STOLEN BASES
Max Carey PIT 58
George Burns NY 40
Charlie Hollocher CHI ... 26

RUNS SCORED
Heinie Groh CIN 88
George Burns NY 80
Max Flack CHI 74

WINS
Hippo Vaughn CHI 22
four tied at 19

WINNING PERCENTAGE
Claude Hendrix CHI ... .731
E. Mayer PHI, PIT ...... .696
Hippo Vaughn CHI ..... .688

EARNED RUN AVERAGE
Hippo Vaughn CHI 1.74
Lefty Tyler CHI 2.00
Wilbur Cooper PIT 2.11

STRIKEOUTS
Hippo Vaughn CHI 148
Wilbur Cooper PIT 117
B. Grimes BKN 113

SAVES
four tied at 3

COMPLETE GAMES
Art Nehf BOS 28
Hippo Vaughn CHI 27
Wilbur Cooper PIT 26

SHUTOUTS
Hippo Vaughn CHI 8
Lefty Tyler CHI 8
Burleigh Grimes BKN 7

GAMES PITCHED
Burleigh Grimes BKN 40
Wilbur Cooper PIT 38
Hod Eller CIN 37

INNINGS PITCHED
Hippo Vaughn CHI 290
Art Nehf BOS 284
Wilbur Cooper PIT 273

AMERICAN LEAGUE STANDINGS

1919 AL

	W	L	PCT	GB	R	OR	BA	FA	ERA
CHICAGO	88	52	.629	—	667	534	.287	.969	3.04
CLEVELAND	84	55	.604	3.5	636	537	.278	.965	2.92
NEW YORK	80	59	.576	7.5	578	506	.267	.968	2.78
DETROIT	80	60	.571	8	618	578	.283	.964	3.30
ST. LOUIS	67	72	.482	20.5	533	567	.264	.963	3.13
BOSTON	66	71	.482	20.5	564	552	.261	.975	3.30
WASHINGTON	56	84	.400	32	533	570	.260	.960	3.01
PHILADELPHIA	36	104	.257	52	457	742	.244	.956	4.26
					4586	4586	.268	.965	3.21

BATTING AVERAGE
Ty Cobb DET .... .384
Bobby Veach DET ..... .355
George Sisler STL ..... .352

HITS
Bobby Veach DET 191
Ty Cobb DET 191
Joe Jackson CHI 181

DOUBLES
Bobby Veach DET 45
Tris Speaker CLE 38
Ty Cobb DET 36

TRIPLES
Bobby Veach DET 17
George Sisler STL 15
Harry Heilmann DET..... 15

HOME RUNS
Babe Ruth BOS 29
three tied at................... 10

RUNS BATTED IN
Babe Ruth BOS 114
Bobby Veach DET 101
Joe Jackson CHI............ 96

SLUGGING AVERAGE
Babe Ruth BOS .... .657
George Sisler STL ..... .530
Bobby Veach DET ..... .519

STOLEN BASES
Eddie Collins CHI........... 33
George Sisler STL 28
Ty Cobb DET 28

RUNS SCORED
Babe Ruth BOS 103
George Sisler STL 96
Ty Cobb DET 92

WINS
Eddie Cicotte CHI 29
Stan Coveleski CLE...... 24
Lefty Williams CHI 23

WINNING PERCENTAGE
Eddie Cicotte CHI ...... .806
Hooks Dauss DET ..... .700
Lefty Williams CHI ..... .676

EARNED RUN AVERAGE
W. Johnson WAS........ 1.49
Eddie Cicotte CHI 1.82
Carl Weilman STL....... 2.07

STRIKEOUTS
W. Johnson WAS........ 147
Jim Shaw WAS............ 128
Lefty Williams CHI 125

SAVES
Allan Russell NY, BOS ... 5
three tied at...................... 4

COMPLETE GAMES
Eddie Cicotte CHI 30
Walter Johnson WAS.... 27
Lefty Williams CHI 27

SHUTOUTS
Walter Johnson WAS...... 7
three tied at...................... 5

GAMES PITCHED
Jim Shaw WAS............. 45
A. Russell NY, BOS...... 44
two tied at 43

INNINGS PITCHED
Eddie Cicotte CHI 307
Jim Shaw WAS............ 307
Lefty Williams CHI 297

NATIONAL LEAGUE STANDINGS

1919 NL

	W	L	PCT	GB	R	OR	BA	FA	ERA
CINCINNATI	96	44	.686	—	577	401	.263	.974	2.23
NEW YORK	87	53	.621	9	605	470	.269	.964	2.70
CHICAGO	75	65	.536	21	454	407	.256	.969	2.21
PITTSBURGH	71	68	.511	24.5	472	466	.249	.970	2.88
BROOKLYN	69	71	.493	27	525	513	.263	.972	2.73
BOSTON	57	82	.410	38.5	465	563	.253	.966	3.17
ST. LOUIS	54	83	.394	40.5	463	552	.256	.963	3.23
PHILADELPHIA	47	90	.343	47.5	510	699	.251	.963	4.17
					4071	4071	.258	.968	2.91

BATTING AVERAGE
Edd Roush CIN .... .321
R. Hornsby STL .... .318
Ross Youngs NY .... .311

HITS
Ivy Olsen BKN 164
R. Hornsby STL 163
two tied at 162

DOUBLES
Ross Youngs NY 31
George Burns NY 30
Fred Luderus PHI 30

TRIPLES
Billy Southworth PIT 14
Hy Myers BKN 14
Edd Roush CIN 13

HOME RUNS
Gavvy Cravath PHI 12
Benny Kauff NY 10
Cy Williams PHI 9

RUNS BATTED IN
Hy Myers BKN 73
Edd Roush CIN 71
Rogers Hornsby STL 71

SLUGGING AVERAGE
Hy Myers BKN .... .436
Larry Doyle NY .... .433
two tied at .... .431

STOLEN BASES
George Burns NY 40
George Cutshaw PIT 36
Carson Bigbee PIT 31

RUNS SCORED
George Burns NY 86
Jake Daubert CIN 79
Heinie Groh CIN 79

WINS
Jesse Barnes NY 25
Slim Sallee CIN............. 21
Hippo Vaughn CHI........ 21

WINNING PERCENTAGE
Dutch Ruether CIN .... .760
Slim Sallee CIN........... .750
Jesse Barnes NY .... .735

EARNED RUN AVERAGE
G. Alexander CHI........ 1.72
Hippo Vaughn CHI..... 1.79
Dutch Ruether CIN 1.82

STRIKEOUTS
Hippo Vaughn CHI...... 141
Hod Eller CIN............... 137
G. Alexander CHI........ 121

SAVES
Oscar Tuero STL 4
five tied at 3

COMPLETE GAMES
Wilbur Cooper PIT 27
Jeff Pfeffer BKN 26
Hippo Vaughn CHI 25

SHUTOUTS
Grover Alexander CHI 9
Babe Adams PIT............. 7
Hod Eller CIN.................. 7

GAMES PITCHED
Oscar Tuero STL 45
Meadows PHI, STL....... 40
two tied at 38

INNINGS PITCHED
Hippo Vaughn CHI...... 307
Jesse Barnes NY 296
Wilbur Cooper PIT 287

AMERICAN LEAGUE STANDINGS

1920 AL

	W	L	PCT	GB	R	OR	BA	FA	ERA
CLEVELAND	98	56	.636	—	857	642	.303	.971	3.41
CHICAGO	96	58	.623	2	794	665	.295	.968	3.59
NEW YORK	95	59	.617	3	838	629	.280	.970	3.31
ST. LOUIS	76	77	.497	21.5	797	766	.308	.963	4.03
BOSTON	72	81	.471	25.5	650	698	.269	.972	3.82
WASHINGTON	68	84	.447	29	723	802	.290	.963	4.17
DETROIT	61	93	.396	37	652	833	.270	.965	4.04
PHILADELPHIA	48	106	.312	50	558	834	.252	.959	3.93
					5869	5869	.283	.966	3.79

BATTING AVERAGE
George Sisler STL ..... .407
Tris Speaker CLE ...... .388
Joe Jackson CHI ...... .382

HITS
George Sisler STL 257
Eddie Collins CHI 222
Joe Jackson CHI 218

DOUBLES
Tris Speaker CLE 50
George Sisler STL 49
Joe Jackson CHI 42

TRIPLES
Joe Jackson CHI 20
George Sisler STL 18
Harry Hooper BOS 17

HOME RUNS
Babe Ruth NY 54
George Sisler STL 19
Tilly Walker PHI 17

RUNS BATTED IN
Babe Ruth NY 137
B. Jacobson STL 122
George Sisler STL 122

SLUGGING AVERAGE
Babe Ruth NY .... .847
George Sisler STL ..... .632
Joe Jackson CHI .... .589

STOLEN BASES
Sam Rice WAS 63
George Sisler STL 42
Braggo Roth WAS 24

RUNS SCORED
Babe Ruth NY 158
George Sisler STL 137
Tris Speaker CLE 137

WINS
Jim Bagby CLE 31
Carl Mays NY 26
Stan Coveleski CLE 24

WINNING PERCENTAGE
Jim Bagby CLE .... .721
Carl Mays NY .... .703
Dickie Kerr CHI .... .700

EARNED RUN AVERAGE
Bob Shawkey NY 2.45
Stan Coveleski CLE ... 2.49
Urban Shocker STL ... 2.71

STRIKEOUTS
Stan Coveleski CLE 133
Lefty Williams CHI 128
Bob Shawkey NY 126

SAVES
Dickie Kerr CHI 5
Urban Shocker STL 5
Bill Burwell STL 4

COMPLETE GAMES
Jim Bagby CLE 30
Red Faber CHI 28
Eddie Cicotte CHI 28

SHUTOUTS
Carl Mays NY 6
Urban Shocker STL 5
Bob Shawkey NY 5

GAMES PITCHED
Jim Bagby CLE 48
Doc Ayers DET 46
two tied at 45

INNINGS PITCHED
Jim Bagby CLE 340
Red Faber CHI 319
Stan Coveleski CLE 315

NATIONAL LEAGUE STANDINGS

1920 NL

	W	L	PCT	GB	R	OR	BA	FA	ERA
BROOKLYN	93	61	.604	—	660	528	.277	.966	2.62
NEW YORK	86	68	.558	7	682	543	.269	.969	2.80
CINCINNATI	82	71	.536	10.5	639	569	.277	.968	2.84
PITTSBURGH	79	75	.513	14	530	552	.257	.971	2.89
CHICAGO	75	79	.487	18	619	635	.264	.965	3.27
ST. LOUIS	75	79	.487	18	675	682	.289	.961	3.43
BOSTON	62	90	.408	30	523	670	.260	.964	3.54
PHILADELPHIA	62	91	.405	30.5	565	714	.263	.964	3.63
					4893	4893	.270	.966	3.13

BATTING AVERAGE
R. Hornsby STL .... .370
Ross Youngs NY .... .351
Edd Roush CIN .... .339

HITS
R. Hornsby STL 218
Milt Stock STL 204
Ross Youngs NY 204

DOUBLES
Rogers Hornsby STL 44
three tied at 36

TRIPLES
Hy Myers BKN 22
Rogers Hornsby STL 20
Edd Roush CIN 16

HOME RUNS
Cy Williams PHI 15
Irish Meusel PHI 14
George Kelly NY 11

RUNS BATTED IN
George Kelly NY 94
Rogers Hornsby STL 94
Edd Roush CIN 90

SLUGGING AVERAGE
R. Hornsby STL .... .559
Cy Williams PHI .... .497
Ross Youngs NY. .... .477

STOLEN BASES
Max Carey PIT 52
Edd Roush CIN 36
Frankie Frisch NY 34

RUNS SCORED
George Burns NY 115
Bancroft PHI, NY 102
Jake Daubert CIN 97

WINS
G. Alexander CHI 27
Wilbur Cooper PIT 24
Burleigh Grimes BKN.... 23

WINNING PERCENTAGE
B. Grimes BKN .... .676
G. Alexander CHI .... .659
Fred Toney NY .... .656

EARNED RUN AVERAGE
G. Alexander CHI 1.91
Babe Adams PIT 2.16
B. Grimes BKN 2.22

STRIKEOUTS
G. Alexander CHI 173
Hippo Vaughn CHI 131
B. Grimes BKN 131

SAVES
Bill Sherdel STL 6
Grover Alexander CHI 5
Hugh McQuillan BOS 5

COMPLETE GAMES
G. Alexander CHI 33
Wilbur Cooper PIT 28
two tied at 25

SHUTOUTS
Babe Adams PIT 8
G. Alexander CHI 7

GAMES PITCHED
Jesse Haines STL 47
G. Alexander CHI 46
Phil Douglas NY 46

INNINGS PITCHED
G. Alexander CHI 363
Wilbur Cooper PIT 327
B. Grimes BKN 304

AMERICAN LEAGUE STANDINGS

1921 AL

	W	L	PCT	GB	R	OR	BA	FA	ERA
NEW YORK	98	55	.641	—	948	708	.300	.965	3.79
CLEVELAND	94	60	.610	4.5	925	712	.308	.967	3.90
ST. LOUIS	81	73	.526	17.5	835	845	.304	.964	4.62
WASHINGTON	80	73	.523	18	704	738	.277	.963	3.97
BOSTON	75	79	.487	23.5	668	696	.277	.975	3.98
DETROIT	71	82	.464	27	883	852	.316	.963	4.40
CHICAGO	62	92	.403	36.5	683	858	.283	.969	4.94
PHILADELPHIA	53	100	.346	45	657	894	.274	.958	4.60
					6303	6303	.292	.965	4.28

BATTING AVERAGE
Harry Heilmann DET .. .394
Ty Cobb DET .... .389
Babe Ruth NY .... .378

HITS
Harry Heilmann DET ... 237
Jack Tobin STL 236
George Sisler STL 216

DOUBLES
Tris Speaker CLE 52
Babe Ruth NY 44
two tied at 43

TRIPLES
Howard Shanks WAS ... 19
Jack Tobin STL 18
George Sisler STL 18

HOME RUNS
Babe Ruth NY 59
Ken Williams STL 24
Bob Meusel NY 24

RUNS BATTED IN
Babe Ruth NY 171
Harry Heilmann DET ... 139
Bob Meusel NY 135

SLUGGING AVERAGE
Babe Ruth NY .... .846
Harry Heilmann DET .. .606
Ty Cobb DET .... .596

STOLEN BASES
George Sisler STL 35
Bucky Harris WAS 29
Sam Rice WAS 25

RUNS SCORED
Babe Ruth NY 177
Jack Tobin STL 132
R. Peckinpaugh NY 128

WINS
Carl Mays NY 27
Urban Shocker STL 27
Red Faber CHI 25

WINNING PERCENTAGE
Carl Mays NY .... .750
Urban Shocker STL ... .692
Joe Bush BOS .... .640

EARNED RUN AVERAGE
Red Faber CHI 2.48
G. Mogridge WAS 3.00
Carl Mays NY 3.05

STRIKEOUTS
W. Johnson WAS 143
Urban Shocker STL 132
Bob Shawkey NY 126

SAVES
Jim Middleton DET 7
Carl Mays NY 7
four tied at 4

COMPLETE GAMES
Red Faber CHI 32
Urban Shocker STL 31
Carl Mays NY 30

SHUTOUTS
Sad Sam Jones BOS 5
three tied at 4

GAMES PITCHED
Carl Mays NY 49
Urban Shocker STL 47
Bill Bayne STL 47

INNINGS PITCHED
Carl Mays NY 337
Red Faber CHI 331
Urban Shocker STL 327

NATIONAL LEAGUE STANDINGS

1921 NL

	W	L	PCT	GB	R	OR	BA	FA	ERA
NEW YORK	94	59	.614	—	840	637	.298	.971	3.55
PITTSBURGH	90	63	.588	4	692	595	.285	.973	3.17
ST. LOUIS	87	66	.569	7	809	681	.308	.965	3.62
BOSTON	79	74	.516	15	721	697	.290	.969	3.90
BROOKLYN	77	75	.507	16.5	667	681	.280	.964	3.70
CINCINNATI	70	83	.458	24	618	649	.278	.969	3.46
CHICAGO	64	89	.418	30	668	773	.292	.974	4.39
PHILADELPHIA	51	103	.331	43.5	617	919	.284	.955	4.48
					5632	5632	.289	.967	3.78

BATTING AVERAGE
R. Hornsby STL .... .397
Edd Roush CIN .... .352
Austin McHenry STL.. .350

HITS
R. Hornsby STL 235
Frankie Frisch NY 211
Carson Bigbee PIT 204

DOUBLES
Rogers Hornsby STL 44
George Kelly NY 42
Jimmy Johnston BKN ... 41

TRIPLES
Rogers Hornsby STL 18
Ray Powell BOS 18
two tied at 17

HOME RUNS
George Kelly NY 23
Rogers Hornsby STL 21
Cy Williams PHI 18

RUNS BATTED IN
R. Hornsby STL 126
George Kelly NY 122
two tied at 102

SLUGGING AVERAGE
R. Hornsby STL .... .639
Austin McHenry STL... .531
George Kelly NY .... .528

STOLEN BASES
Frankie Frisch NY 49
Max Carey PIT 37
Jimmy Johnston BKN ... 28

RUNS SCORED
R. Hornsby STL 131
Frankie Frisch NY 121
Dave Bancroft NY 121

WINS
Burleigh Grimes BKN.... 22
Wilbur Cooper PIT 22
two tied at 20

WINNING PERCENTAGE
Bill Doak STL .... .714
Art Nehf NY .... .667
B. Grimes BKN .... .629

EARNED RUN AVERAGE
Bill Doak STL 2.59
Babe Adams PIT 2.64
Whitey Glazner PIT.... 2.77

STRIKEOUTS
B. Grimes BKN 136
Wilbur Cooper PIT 134
Dolf Luque CIN 102

SAVES
Lou North STL 7
Jesse Barnes NY 6
Hugh McQuillan BOS....... 5

COMPLETE GAMES
Burleigh Grimes BKN.... 30
Wilbur Cooper PIT 29
Dolf Luque CIN 25

SHUTOUTS
seven tied at 3

GAMES PITCHED
Jim Scott BOS 47
Joe Oeschger BOS........ 46
Hugh McQuillan BOS.... 45

INNINGS PITCHED
Wilbur Cooper PIT 327
Dolf Luque CIN 304
B. Grimes BKN 302

AMERICAN LEAGUE STANDINGS

1922 AL

	W	L	PCT	GB	R	OR	BA	FA	ERA
NEW YORK	94	60	.610	—	758	618	.287	.975	3.39
ST. LOUIS	93	61	.604	1	867	643	.313	.968	3.38
DETROIT	79	75	.513	15	828	791	.305	.970	4.27
CLEVELAND	78	76	.506	16	768	817	.292	.968	4.60
CHICAGO	77	77	.500	17	691	691	.278	.975	3.93
WASHINGTON	69	85	.448	25	650	706	.268	.969	3.81
PHILADELPHIA	65	89	.422	29	705	830	.269	.966	4.59
BOSTON	61	93	.396	33	598	769	.260	.965	4.30
					5865	5865	.284	.969	4.03

BATTING AVERAGE
George Sisler STL ..... .420
Ty Cobb DET .... .401
Tris Speaker CLE .... .378

HITS
George Sisler STL 246
Ty Cobb DET 211
Jack Tobin STL 207

DOUBLES
Tris Speaker CLE 48
Del Pratt BOS 44
two tied at 42

TRIPLES
George Sisler STL 18
Ty Cobb DET 16
B. Jacobson STL 16

HOME RUNS
Ken Williams STL 39
Tilly Walker PHI 37
Babe Ruth NY 35

RUNS BATTED IN
Ken Williams STL 155
Bobby Veach DET 126
Marty McManus STL... 109

SLUGGING AVERAGE
Babe Ruth NY .... .672
Ken Williams STL .... .627
Tris Speaker CLE .... .606

STOLEN BASES
George Sisler STL 51
Ken Williams STL 37
Bucky Harris WAS 25

RUNS SCORED
George Sisler STL 134
Lu Blue DET 131
Ken Williams STL 128

WINS
Eddie Rommel PHI 27
Joe Bush NY 26
Urban Shocker STL 24

WINNING PERCENTAGE
Joe Bush NY .... .788
Eddie Rommel PHI .... .675
Bob Shawkey NY .... .625

EARNED RUN AVERAGE
Red Faber CHI 2.80
H. Pillette DET 2.85
Bob Shawkey NY 2.91

STRIKEOUTS
Urban Shocker STL 149
Red Faber CHI 148
Bob Shawkey NY 130

SAVES
Sad Sam Jones NY 8
Hub Pruett STL 7
Rasty Wright STL 5

COMPLETE GAMES
Red Faber CHI 31
Urban Shocker STL 29
two tied at 23

SHUTOUTS
George Uhle CLE 5
three tied at 4

GAMES PITCHED
Eddie Rommel PHI 51
George Uhle CLE 50
Urban Shocker STL 48

INNINGS PITCHED
Red Faber CHI 353
Urban Shocker STL 348
Bob Shawkey NY 300

NATIONAL LEAGUE STANDINGS

1922 NL

	W	L	PCT	GB	R	OR	BA	FA	ERA
NEW YORK	93	61	.604	—	852	658	.305	.970	3.45
CINCINNATI	86	68	.558	7	766	677	.296	.968	3.53
PITTSBURGH	85	69	.552	8	865	736	.308	.970	3.98
ST. LOUIS	85	69	.552	8	863	819	.301	.961	4.44
CHICAGO	80	74	.519	13	771	808	.293	.968	4.34
BROOKLYN	76	78	.494	17	743	754	.290	.967	4.05
PHILADELPHIA	57	96	.373	35.5	738	920	.282	.965	4.64
BOSTON	53	100	.346	39.5	596	822	.263	.965	4.37
					6194	6194	.292	.967	4.10

BATTING AVERAGE
R. Hornsby STL .... .401
Ray Grimes CHI .... .354
Hack Miller CHI .... .352

HITS
R. Hornsby STL 250
Carson Bigbee PIT 215
Dave Bancroft NY 209

DOUBLES
Rogers Hornsby STL 46
Ray Grimes CHI 45
Pat Duncan CIN 44

TRIPLES
Jake Daubert CIN 22
Irish Meusel NY 17
two tied at 15

HOME RUNS
Rogers Hornsby STL 42
Cy Williams PHI 26
two tied at 17

RUNS BATTED IN
Rogers Hornsby STL .. 152
Irish Meusel NY 132
Zack Wheat BKN 112

SLUGGING AVERAGE
R. Hornsby STL .... .722
Ray Grimes CHI .... .572
Cliff Lee PHI .... .540

STOLEN BASES
Max Carey PIT 51
Frankie Frisch NY 31
George Burns CIN 30

RUNS SCORED
R. Hornsby STL 141
Max Carey PIT 140
two tied at 117

WINS
Eppa Rixey CIN 25
Wilbur Cooper PIT 23
Dutch Ruether BKN 21

WINNING PERCENTAGE
Pete Donohue CIN ..... .667
Eppa Rixey CIN .... .658
Johnny Couch CIN ..... .640

EARNED RUN AVERAGE
Rosy Ryan NY 3.01
Pete Donohue CIN 3.12
Wilbur Cooper PIT 3.18

STRIKEOUTS
Dazzy Vance BKN 134
Wilbur Cooper PIT 129
Jimmy Ring PHI 116

SAVES
Claude Jonnard NY 5
Lou North STL 4
four tied at 3

COMPLETE GAMES
Wilbur Cooper PIT 27
Dutch Ruether BKN 26
Eppa Rixey CIN 26

SHUTOUTS
Dazzy Vance BKN 5
Johnny Morrison PIT 5
two tied at 4

GAMES PITCHED
Lou North STL 53
Bill Sherdel STL 47
two tied at 46

INNINGS PITCHED
Eppa Rixey CIN 313
Wilbur Cooper PIT 295
Johnny Morrison PIT... 286

AMERICAN LEAGUE STANDINGS

1923 AL

	W	L	PCT	GB	R	OR	BA	FA	ERA
NEW YORK	98	54	.645	—	823	622	.291	.977	3.66
DETROIT	83	71	.539	16	831	741	.300	.968	4.09
CLEVELAND	82	71	.536	16.5	888	746	.301	.964	3.91
WASHINGTON	75	78	.490	23.5	720	747	.274	.966	3.99
ST. LOUIS	74	78	.487	24	688	720	.281	.971	3.93
PHILADELPHIA	69	83	.454	29	661	761	.271	.965	4.08
CHICAGO	69	85	.448	30	692	741	.279	.971	4.03
BOSTON	61	91	.401	37	584	809	.261	.963	4.20
					5887	5887	.282	.968	3.99

BATTING AVERAGE
Harry Heilmann DET.. .403
Babe Ruth NY .... .393
Tris Speaker CLE .... .380

HITS
C. Jamieson CLE 222
Tris Speaker CLE 218
Harry Heilmann DET... 211

DOUBLES
Tris Speaker CLE 59
George Burns BOS....... 47
Babe Ruth NY 45

TRIPLES
Goose Goslin WAS....... 18
Sam Rice WAS 18
two tied at 15

HOME RUNS
Babe Ruth NY 41
Ken Williams STL 29
Harry Heilmann DET..... 18

RUNS BATTED IN
Babe Ruth NY 130
Tris Speaker CLE 130
Harry Heilmann DET... 115

SLUGGING AVERAGE
Babe Ruth NY .... .764
Harry Heilmann DET.. .632
Ken Williams STL ...... .623

STOLEN BASES
Eddie Collins CHI.......... 47
Johnny Mostil CHI......... 41
Bucky Harris WAS 23

RUNS SCORED
Babe Ruth NY 151
Tris Speaker CLE 133
C. Jamieson CLE........ 130

WINS
George Uhle CLE 26
Sad Sam Jones NY 21
Hooks Dauss DET 21

WINNING PERCENTAGE
Herb Pennock NY .... .760
Sad Sam Jones NY ... .724
Waite Hoyt NY .... .654

EARNED RUN AVERAGE
Stan Coveleski CLE.... 2.76
Waite Hoyt NY 3.02
Elam Vangilder STL... 3.06

STRIKEOUTS
W. Johnson WAS........ 130
Joe Bush NY 125
Bob Shawkey NY........ 125

SAVES
Allan Russell WAS.......... 9
Jack Quinn BOS 7
Slim Harriss PHI 6

COMPLETE GAMES
George Uhle CLE 29
Howard Ehmke BOS..... 28
Urban Shocker STL 24

SHUTOUTS
Stan Coveleski CLE........ 5
three tied at..................... 4

GAMES PITCHED
Eddie Rommel PHI 56
George Uhle CLE 54
Allan Russell WAS........ 52

INNINGS PITCHED
George Uhle CLE 358
Howard Ehmke BOS... 317
Hooks Dauss DET 316

NATIONAL LEAGUE STANDINGS

1923 NL

	W	L	PCT	GB	R	OR	BA	FA	ERA
NEW YORK	95	58	.621	—	854	679	.295	.972	3.90
CINCINNATI	91	63	.591	4.5	708	629	.285	.969	3.21
PITTSBURGH	87	67	.565	8.5	786	696	.295	.971	3.87
CHICAGO	83	71	.539	12.5	756	704	.288	.967	3.82
ST. LOUIS	79	74	.516	16	746	732	.286	.963	3.87
BROOKLYN	76	78	.494	19.5	753	741	.285	.955	3.73
BOSTON	54	100	.351	41.5	636	798	.273	.964	4.22
PHILADELPHIA	50	104	.325	45.5	748	1008	.278	.966	5.30
					5987	5987	.286	.966	3.99

BATTING AVERAGE
R. Hornsby STL .... .384
Jim Bottomley STL ..... .371
two tied at .... .351

HITS
Frankie Frisch NY 223
Jigger Statz CHI 209
Pie Traynor PIT 208

DOUBLES
Edd Roush CIN 41
G. Grantham CHI 36
C. Tierney PIT, PHI 36

TRIPLES
Pie Traynor PIT 19
Max Carey PIT 19
Edd Roush CIN 18

HOME RUNS
Cy Williams PHI 41
Jack Fournier BKN 22
Hack Miller CHI 20

RUNS BATTED IN
Irish Meusel NY 125
Cy Williams PHI 114
Frankie Frisch NY 111

SLUGGING AVERAGE
R. Hornsby STL .... .627
Jack Fournier BKN ..... .588
Cy Williams PHI .... .576

STOLEN BASES
Max Carey PIT 51
G. Grantham CHI 43
two tied at 32

RUNS SCORED
Ross Youngs NY 121
Max Carey PIT 120
Frankie Frisch NY 116

WINS
Dolf Luque CIN 27
Johnny Morrison PIT 25
G. Alexander CHI 22

WINNING PERCENTAGE
Dolf Luque CIN .... .771
Rosy Ryan NY .... .762
Jack Scott NY .... .696

EARNED RUN AVERAGE
Dolf Luque CIN 1.93
Eppa Rixley CIN 2.80
Vic Keen CHI 3.00

STRIKEOUTS
Dazzy Vance BKN 197
Dolf Luque CIN 151
B. Grimes BKN 119

SAVES
Claude Jonnard NY 5
Rosy Ryan NY 4
five tied at 3

COMPLETE GAMES
Burleigh Grimes BKN 33
Dolf Luque CIN 28
Johnny Morrison PIT 27

SHUTOUTS
Dolf Luque CIN 6
J. Barnes NY, BOS 5
Hugh McQuillan NY 5

GAMES PITCHED
Rosy Ryan NY 45
Claude Jonnard NY 45
Joe Oeschger BOS 44

INNINGS PITCHED
B. Grimes BKN 327
Dolf Luque CIN 322
Jimmy Ring PHI 313

AMERICAN LEAGUE STANDINGS

1924 AL

	W	L	PCT	GB	R	OR	BA	FA	ERA
WASHINGTON	92	62	.597	—	755	613	.294	.972	3.35
NEW YORK	89	63	.586	2	798	667	.289	.974	3.86
DETROIT	86	68	.558	6	849	796	.298	.971	4.19
ST. LOUIS	74	78	.487	17	764	797	.294	.969	4.55
PHILADELPHIA	71	81	.467	20	685	778	.281	.971	4.39
CLEVELAND	67	86	.438	24.5	755	814	.296	.967	4.40
BOSTON	67	87	.435	25	725	801	.277	.967	4.36
CHICAGO	66	87	.431	25.5	793	858	.288	.963	4.75
					6124	6124	.290	.969	4.23

BATTING AVERAGE
Babe Ruth NY .... .378
C. Jamieson CLE .... .359
Bibb Falk CHI .... .352

HITS
Sam Rice WAS 216
C. Jamieson CLE 213
Ty Cobb DET 211

DOUBLES
Harry Heilmann DET 45
Joe Sewell CLE 45
two tied at 41

TRIPLES
Wally Pipp NY 19
Goose Goslin WAS 17
Harry Heilmann DET 16

HOME RUNS
Babe Ruth NY 46
Joe Hauser PHI 27
B. Jacobson STL 19

RUNS BATTED IN
Goose Goslin WAS 129
Babe Ruth NY 121
Bob Meusel NY 120

SLUGGING AVERAGE
Babe Ruth NY .... .739
H. Heilmann DET .... .533
Ken Williams STL ...... .533

STOLEN BASES
Eddie Collins CHI 42
Bob Meusel NY 26
Sam Rice WAS 24

RUNS SCORED
Babe Ruth NY 143
Ty Cobb DET 115
Eddie Collins CHI 108

WINS
Walter Johnson WAS 23
Herb Pennock NY 21
two tied at 20

WINNING PERCENTAGE
W. Johnson WAS .... .767
Herb Pennock NY ...... .700
Earl Whitehill DET ...... .654

EARNED RUN AVERAGE
W. Johnson WAS 2.72
Tom Zachary WAS 2.75
Herb Pennock NY 2.83

STRIKEOUTS
W. Johnson WAS 158
Howard Ehmke BOS ... 119
Bob Shawkey NY 114

SAVES
Firpo Marberry WAS 15
Allan Russell WAS 8
Jack Quinn BOS 7

COMPLETE GAMES
Sloppy Thurston CHI 28
Howard Ehmke BOS 26
Herb Pennock NY 25

SHUTOUTS
Walter Johnson WAS 6
Dixie Davis STL 5
two tied at 4

GAMES PITCHED
Firpo Marberry WAS 50
Ken Holloway DET 49
two tied at 46

INNINGS PITCHED
Howard Ehmke BOS ... 315
S. Thurston CHI 291
Herb Pennock NY 286

NATIONAL LEAGUE STANDINGS

1924 NL

	W	L	PCT	GB	R	OR	BA	FA	ERA
NEW YORK	93	60	.608	—	857	641	.300	.971	3.62
BROOKLYN	92	62	.597	1.5	717	675	.287	.968	3.64
PITTSBURGH	90	63	.588	3	724	588	.287	.971	3.27
CINCINNATI	83	70	.542	10	649	579	.290	.966	3.12
CHICAGO	81	72	.529	12	698	699	.276	.966	3.83
ST. LOUIS	65	89	.422	28.5	740	750	.290	.969	4.15
PHILADELPHIA	55	96	.364	37	676	849	.275	.972	4.87
BOSTON	53	100	.346	40	520	800	.256	.973	4.46
					5581	5581	.283	.970	3.87

BATTING AVERAGE
R. Hornsby STL .... .424
Zack Wheat BKN .... .375
Ross Youngs NY .... .356

HITS
Rogers Hornsby STL .. 227
Zack Wheat BKN 212
Frankie Frisch NY 198

DOUBLES
R. Hornsby STL 43
Zack Wheat BKN 41
George Kelly NY 37

TRIPLES
Edd Roush CIN 21
Rabbit Maranville PIT ... 20
Glenn Wright PIT 18

HOME RUNS
Jack Fournier BKN........ 27
Rogers Hornsby STL 25
Cy Williams PHI 24

RUNS BATTED IN
George Kelly NY 136
Jack Fournier BKN...... 116
two tied at 111

SLUGGING AVERAGE
R. Hornsby STL .... .696
Cy Williams PHI .... .552
Zack Wheat BKN .... .549

STOLEN BASES
Max Carey PIT.............. 49
Kiki Cuyler PIT 32
Cliff Heathcote CHI 26

RUNS SCORED
Frankie Frisch NY 121
R. Hornsby STL 121
Max Carey PIT............ 113

WINS
Dazzy Vance BKN 28
Burleigh Grimes BKN.... 22
two tied at 20

WINNING PERCENTAGE
Emil Yde PIT.............. .842
Dazzy Vance BKN ..... .824
Jack Bentley NY .... .762

EARNED RUN AVERAGE
Dazzy Vance BKN 2.16
Hugh McQuillan NY ... 2.69
Eppa Rixey CIN 2.76

STRIKEOUTS
Dazzy Vance BKN 262
B. Grimes BKN 135
Dolf Luque CIN 86

SAVES
Jackie May Cin 6
Rosy Ryan NY 5
Claude Jonnard NY 5

COMPLETE GAMES
Dazzy Vance BKN 30
Burleigh Grimes BKN.... 30
Wilbur Cooper PIT 25

SHUTOUTS
five tied at 4

GAMES PITCHED
Ray Kremer PIT............. 41
Johnny Morrison PIT..... 41
Vic Keen CHI 40

INNINGS PITCHED
Burleigh Grimes BKN.. 311
Dazzy Vance BKN 309
Wilbur Cooper PIT 269

AMERICAN LEAGUE STANDINGS

1925 AL

	W	L	PCT	GB	R	OR	BA	FA	ERA
WASHINGTON	96	55	.636	—	829	669	.303	.972	3.67
PHILADELPHIA	88	64	.579	8.5	830	714	.307	.966	3.89
ST. LOUIS	82	71	.536	15	897	909	.298	.964	4.85
DETROIT	81	73	.526	16.5	903	829	.302	.972	4.61
CHICAGO	79	75	.513	18.5	811	771	.284	.968	4.34
CLEVELAND	70	84	.455	27.5	782	810	.297	.967	4.49
NEW YORK	69	85	.448	28.5	706	774	.275	.974	4.33
BOSTON	47	105	.309	49.5	639	921	.266	.957	4.97
					6397	6397	.292	.968	4.39

BATTING AVERAGE
H. Heilmann DET .... .393
Tris Speaker CLE ...... .389
Al Simmons PHI .... .384

HITS
Al Simmons PHI 253
Sam Rice WAS 227
Harry Heilmann DET ... 225

DOUBLES
Marty McManus STL 44
Earl Sheely CHI 43
Al Simmons PHI 43

TRIPLES
Goose Goslin WAS 20
Johnny Mostil CHI 16
George Sisler STL 15

HOME RUNS
Bob Meusel NY 33
Ken Williams STL 25
Babe Ruth NY 25

RUNS BATTED IN
Bob Meusel NY 138
Harry Heilmann DET ... 133
Al Simmons PHI 129

SLUGGING AVERAGE
Ken Williams STL .... .613
Ty Cobb DET .... .598
Al Simmons PHI .... .596

STOLEN BASES
Johnny Mostil CHI 43
Sam Rice WAS 26
Goose Goslin WAS 26

RUNS SCORED
Johnny Mostil CHI 135
Al Simmons PHI 122
Earle Combs NY 117

WINS
Eddie Rommel PHI 21
Ted Lyons CHI 21
two tied at 20

WINNING PERCENTAGE
Stan Coveleski WAS .. .800
W. Johnson WAS .... .741
D. Ruether WAS .... .720

EARNED RUN AVERAGE
S. Coveleski WAS 2.84
Herb Pennock NY 2.96
W. Johnson WAS 3.07

STRIKEOUTS
Lefty Grove PHI 116
W. Johnson WAS 108
two tied at 95

SAVES
Firpo Marberry WAS 15
Jess Doyle DET 8
Sarge Connally CHI 8

COMPLETE GAMES
Sherry Smith CLE 22
Howard Ehmke BOS 22
Herb Pennock NY 21

SHUTOUTS
Ted Lyons CHI 5
Joe Giard STL 4
Sam Gray PHI 4

GAMES PITCHED
Firpo Marberry WAS 55
Rube Walberg PHI 53
two tied at 52

INNINGS PITCHED
Herb Pennock NY 277
Ted Lyons CHI 263
Eddie Rommel PHI 261

NATIONAL LEAGUE STANDINGS

1925 NL

	W	L	PCT	GB	R	OR	BA	FA	ERA
PITTSBURGH	95	58	.621	—	912	715	.307	.964	3.87
NEW YORK	86	66	.566	8.5	736	702	.283	.968	3.94
CINCINNATI	80	73	.523	15	690	643	.285	.968	3.38
ST. LOUIS	77	76	.503	18	828	764	.299	.966	4.36
BOSTON	70	83	.458	25	708	802	.292	.964	4.39
BROOKLYN	68	85	.444	27	786	866	.296	.966	4.77
PHILADELPHIA	68	85	.444	27	812	930	.295	.966	5.02
CHICAGO	68	86	.442	27.5	723	773	.275	.969	4.41
					6195	6195	.292	.966	4.27

BATTING AVERAGE
R. Hornsby STL .... .403
Jim Bottomley STL ..... .367
Zack Wheat BKN .... .359

HITS
Jim Bottomley STL 227
Zack Wheat BKN 221
Kiki Cuyler PIT 220

DOUBLES
Jim Bottomley STL 44
Kiki Cuyler PIT 43
Zack Wheat BKN 42

TRIPLES
Kiki Cuyler PIT 26
three tied at 16

HOME RUNS
Rogers Hornsby STL 39
Gabby Hartnett CHI 24
Jack Fournier BKN 22

RUNS BATTED IN
R. Hornsby STL 143
Jack Fournier BKN 130
Jim Bottomley STL 128

SLUGGING AVERAGE
R. Hornsby STL .... .756
Kiki Cuyler PIT .... .593
Jim Bottomley STL ..... .578

STOLEN BASES
Max Carey PIT 46
Kiki Cuyler PIT 41
Sparky Adams CHI 26

RUNS SCORED
Kiki Cuyler PIT 144
R. Hornsby STL 133
Zack Wheat BKN 125

WINS
Dazzy Vance BKN 22
Eppa Rixey CIN 21
Pete Donohue CIN 21

WINNING PERCENTAGE
Bill Sherdel STL .... .714
Dazzy Vance BKN ...... .710
Vic Aldridge PIT .... .682

EARNED RUN AVERAGE
Dolf Luque CIN 2.63
Eppa Rixey CIN 2.88
Art Reinhart STL 3.05

STRIKEOUTS
Dazzy Vance BKN 221
Dolf Luque CIN 140
two tied at 93

SAVES
Johnny Morrison PIT 4
Guy Bush CHI 4
four tied at 3

COMPLETE GAMES
Pete Donohue CIN 27
Dazzy Vance BKN 26
two tied at 22

SHUTOUTS
Dolf Luque CIN 4
Dazzy Vance BKN 4
Hal Carlson PHI 4

GAMES PITCHED
Johnny Morrison PIT 44
Pete Donohue CIN 42
Guy Bush CHI 42

INNINGS PITCHED
Pete Donohue CIN 301
Dolf Luque CIN 291
Eppa Rixey CIN 287

AMERICAN LEAGUE STANDINGS

1926 AL

	W	L	PCT	GB	R	OR	BA	FA	ERA
NEW YORK	91	63	.591	—	847	713	.289	.966	3.86
CLEVELAND	88	66	.571	3	738	612	.289	.972	3.40
PHILADELPHIA	83	67	.553	6	677	570	.269	.972	3.00
WASHINGTON	81	69	.540	8	802	761	.292	.969	4.34
CHICAGO	81	72	.529	9.5	730	665	.289	.973	3.74
DETROIT	79	75	.513	12	793	830	.291	.969	4.41
ST. LOUIS	62	92	.403	29	682	845	.276	.963	4.66
BOSTON	46	107	.301	44.5	562	835	.256	.970	4.72
					5831	5831	.281	.969	4.02

BATTING AVERAGE
Heinie Manush DET... .378
Babe Ruth NY .... .372
two tied at .... .367

HITS
Sam Rice WAS 216
George Burns CLE 216
Goose Goslin WAS..... 201

DOUBLES
George Burns CLE 64
Al Simmons PHI............ 53
Tris Speaker CLE 52

TRIPLES
Lou Gehrig NY 20
C. Gehringer DET......... 17
two tied at 15

HOME RUNS
Babe Ruth NY 47
Al Simmons PHI............ 19
Tony Lazzeri NY 18

RUNS BATTED IN
Babe Ruth NY 145
George Burns CLE 114
Tony Lazzeri NY 114

SLUGGING AVERAGE
Babe Ruth NY .... .737
Al Simmons PHI......... .566
Heinie Manush DET... .564

STOLEN BASES
Johnny Mostil CHI......... 35
Sam Rice WAS 25
Bill Hunnefield CHI........ 24

RUNS SCORED
Babe Ruth NY 139
Lou Gehrig NY 135
Johnny Mostil CHI....... 120

WINS
George Uhle CLE 27
Herb Pennock NY 23
Urban Shocker NY........ 19

WINNING PERCENTAGE
George Uhle CLE ...... .711
Herb Pennock NY ...... .676
Red Faber CHI............ 652

EARNED RUN AVERAGE
Lefty Grove PHI 2.51
George Uhle CLE 2.83
Ted Lyons CHI............ 3.01

STRIKEOUTS
Lefty Grove PHI 194
George Uhle CLE 159
Tommy Thomas CHI... 127

SAVES
Firpo Marberry WAS..... 22
Hooks Dauss DET 9
two tied at 6

COMPLETE GAMES
George Uhle CLE 32
Ted Lyons CHI.............. 24
Walter Johnson WAS.... 22

SHUTOUTS
Ed Wells DET 4

GAMES PITCHED
Firpo Marberry WAS..... 64
Joe Pate PHI................. 47
Lefty Grove PHI 45

INNINGS PITCHED
George Uhle CLE 318
Ted Lyons CHI............ 284
Herb Pennock NY 266

NATIONAL LEAGUE STANDINGS

1926 NL

	W	L	PCT	GB	R	OR	BA	FA	ERA
ST. LOUIS	89	65	.578	—	817	678	.286	.969	3.67
CINCINNATI	87	67	.565	2	747	651	.290	.972	3.42
PITTSBURGH	84	69	.549	4.5	769	689	.285	.965	3.67
CHICAGO	82	72	.532	7	682	602	.278	.974	3.26
NEW YORK	74	77	.490	13.5	663	668	.278	.970	3.77
BROOKLYN	71	82	.464	17.5	623	705	.263	.963	3.82
BOSTON	66	86	.434	22	624	719	.277	.967	4.03
PHILADELPHIA	58	93	.384	29.5	687	900	.281	.964	5.19
					5612	5612	.280	.968	3.84

BATTING AVERAGE
B. Hargrave CIN .... .353
Christenson CIN .... .350
Earl Smith PIT .... .346

HITS
Eddie Brown BOS 201
Kiki Cuyler PIT 197
Sparky Adams CHI 193

DOUBLES
Jim Bottomley STL 40
Edd Roush CIN 37
Hack Wilson CHI 36

TRIPLES
Paul Waner PIT 22
Curt Walker CIN 20
Pie Traynor PIT 17

HOME RUNS
Hack Wilson CHI 21
Jim Bottomley STL 19
Cy Williams PHI 18

RUNS BATTED IN
Jim Bottomley STL 120
Hack Wilson CHI 109
Les Bell STL 100

SLUGGING AVERAGE
Cy Williams PHI .... .568
Hack Wilson CHI .... .539
Paul Waner PIT .... .528

STOLEN BASES
Kiki Cuyler PIT 35
Sparky Adams CHI 27
two tied at 23

RUNS SCORED
Kiki Cuyler PIT 113
Paul Waner PIT 101
two tied at 99

WINS
four tied at 20

WINNING PERCENTAGE
Ray Kremer PIT .... .769
Flint Rhem STL .... .741
Lee Meadows PIT ...... .690

EARNED RUN AVERAGE
Ray Kremer PIT 2.61
Charlie Root CHI 2.82
Jesse Petty BKN 2.84

STRIKEOUTS
Dazzy Vance BKN 140
Charlie Root CHI 127
two tied at 103

SAVES
Chick Davies NY 6
Ray Kremer PIT 5
Jack Scott NY 5

COMPLETE GAMES
Carl Mays CIN 24
Jesse Petty BKN 23
Charlie Root CHI 21

SHUTOUTS
Pete Donohue CIN 5
Sheriff Blake CHI 4
Bob Smith BOS 4

GAMES PITCHED
Jack Scott NY 50
C. Willoughby PHI 47
Pete Donohue CIN 47

INNINGS PITCHED
Pete Donohue CIN 286
Carl Mays CIN 281
Jesse Petty BKN 276

AMERICAN LEAGUE STANDINGS

1927 AL

	W	L	PCT	GB	R	OR	BA	FA	ERA
NEW YORK	110	44	.714	—	975	599	.307	.969	3.20
PHILADELPHIA	91	63	.591	19	841	726	.303	.970	3.95
WASHINGTON	85	69	.552	25	782	730	.287	.969	3.95
DETROIT	82	71	.536	27.5	845	805	.289	.968	4.12
CHICAGO	70	83	.458	39.5	662	708	.278	.971	3.91
CLEVELAND	66	87	.431	43.5	668	766	.283	.968	4.27
ST. LOUIS	59	94	.386	50.5	724	904	.276	.960	4.95
BOSTON	51	103	.331	59	597	856	.259	.964	4.68
					6094	6094	.285	.967	4.12

BATTING AVERAGE
Harry Heilmann DET .398
Al Simmons PHI .392
Lou Gehrig NY .373

HITS
Earle Combs NY 231
Lou Gehrig NY 218
two tied at 201

DOUBLES
Lou Gehrig NY 52
George Burns CLE 51
Harry Heilmann DET 50

TRIPLES
Earle Combs NY 23
Heinie Manush DET 18
Lou Gehrig NY 18

HOME RUNS
Babe Ruth NY 60
Lou Gehrig NY 47
Tony Lazzeri NY 18

RUNS BATTED IN
Lou Gehrig NY 175
Babe Ruth NY 164
two tied at 120

SLUGGING AVERAGE
Babe Ruth NY .772
Lou Gehrig NY .765
Al Simmons PHI .645

STOLEN BASES
George Sisler STL 27
Bob Meusel NY 24
three tied at 22

RUNS SCORED
Babe Ruth NY 158
Lou Gehrig NY 149
Earle Combs NY 137

WINS
Waite Hoyt NY 22
Ted Lyons CHI 22
Lefty Grove PHI 20

WINNING PERCENTAGE
Waite Hoyt NY .759
Urban Shocker NY .750
Wilcy Moore NY .731

EARNED RUN AVERAGE
Waite Hoyt NY 2.63
Urban Shocker NY 2.84
Ted Lyons CHI 2.84

STRIKEOUTS
Lefty Grove PHI 174
Rube Walberg PHI 136
Tommy Thomas CHI 107

SAVES
G. Braxton WAS 13
Wilcy Moore NY 13
two tied at 9

COMPLETE GAMES
Ted Lyons CHI 30
Tommy Thomas CHI 24
Waite Hoyt NY 23

SHUTOUTS
Hod Lisenbee WAS 4

GAMES PITCHED
G. Braxton WAS 58
Firpo Marberry WAS 56
Lefty Grove PHI 51

INNINGS PITCHED
Tommy Thomas CHI 308
Ted Lyons CHI 308
Willis Hudlin CLE 265

NATIONAL LEAGUE STANDINGS

1927 NL

	W	L	PCT	GB	R	OR	BA	FA	ERA
PITTSBURGH	94	60	.610	—	817	659	.305	.969	3.66
ST. LOUIS	92	61	.601	1.5	754	665	.278	.966	3.57
NEW YORK	92	62	.597	2	817	720	.297	.969	3.97
CHICAGO	85	68	.556	8.5	750	661	.284	.971	3.65
CINCINNATI	75	78	.490	*18.5	643	653	.278	.973	3.54
BROOKLYN	65	88	.425	28.5	541	619	.253	.963	3.36
BOSTON	60	94	.390	34	651	771	.279	.963	4.22
PHILADELPHIA	51	103	.331	43	678	903	.280	.972	5.35
					5651	5651	.282	.969	3.91

BATTING AVERAGE
Paul Waner PIT .... .380
Rogers Hornsby NY ... .361
Lloyd Waner PIT .... .355

HITS
Paul Waner PIT 237
Lloyd Waner PIT 223
Frankie Frisch STL 208

DOUBLES
R. Stephenson CHI 46
Paul Waner PIT 40
two tied at 36

TRIPLES
Paul Waner PIT 17
Jim Bottomley STL 15
F. Thompson PHI 14

HOME RUNS
Hack Wilson CHI 30
Cy Williams PHI 30
Rogers Hornsby NY 26

RUNS BATTED IN
Paul Waner PIT 131
Hack Wilson CHI 129
Rogers Hornsby NY 125

SLUGGING AVERAGE
Chick Hafey STL .... .590
Rogers Hornsby NY ... .586
Hack Wilson CHI .... .579

STOLEN BASES
Frankie Frisch STL 48
Max Carey BKN 32
Harvey Hendrick BKN ... 29

RUNS SCORED
Lloyd Waner PIT 133
Rogers Hornsby NY 133
Hack Wilson CHI 119

WINS
Charlie Root CHI 26
Jesse Haines STL 24
Carmen Hill PIT 22

WINNING PERCENTAGE
Benton BOS, NY .... .708
Jesse Haines STL ...... .706
two tied at .... .704

EARNED RUN AVERAGE
Ray Kremer PIT 2.47
G. Alexander STL 2.52
Dazzy Vance BKN 2.70

STRIKEOUTS
Dazzy Vance BKN 184
Charlie Root CHI 145
Jackie May CIN 121

SAVES
Bill Sherdel STL 6
George Mogridge BOS ... 5
Art Nehf CIN, CHI 5

COMPLETE GAMES
Dazzy Vance BKN 25
Jesse Haines STL 25
Lee Meadows PIT 25

SHUTOUTS
Jesse Haines STL 6
Red Lucas CIN 4
Charlie Root CHI 4

GAMES PITCHED
Charlie Root CHI 48
Jack Scott NY 48
Rube Ehrhardt BKN 46

INNINGS PITCHED
Charlie Root CHI 309
Jesse Haines STL 301
Lee Meadows PIT 299

AMERICAN LEAGUE STANDINGS

1928 AL

	W	L	PCT	GB	R	OR	BA	FA	ERA
NEW YORK	101	53	.656	—	894	685	.296	.968	3.74
PHILADELPHIA	98	55	.641	2.5	829	615	.295	.970	3.36
ST. LOUIS	82	72	.532	19	772	742	.274	.969	4.17
WASHINGTON	75	79	.487	26	718	705	.284	.972	3.88
CHICAGO	72	82	.468	29	656	725	.270	.970	3.98
DETROIT	68	86	.442	33	744	804	.279	.965	4.32
CLEVELAND	62	92	.403	39	674	830	.285	.965	4.47
BOSTON	57	96	.373	43.5	589	770	.264	.971	4.39
					5876	5876	.281	.969	4.04

BATTING AVERAGE
Goose Goslin WAS.... .379
Heinie Manush STL ... .378
Lou Gehrig NY .... .374

HITS
Heinie Manush STL 241
Lou Gehrig NY 210
Sam Rice WAS 202

DOUBLES
Lou Gehrig NY 47
Heinie Manush STL 47
Bob Meusel NY 45

TRIPLES
Earle Combs NY 21
Heinie Manush STL 20
C. Gehringer DET 16

HOME RUNS
Babe Ruth NY 54
Lou Gehrig NY 27
Goose Goslin WAS 17

RUNS BATTED IN
Lou Gehrig NY 142
Babe Ruth NY 142
Bob Meusel NY 113

SLUGGING AVERAGE
Babe Ruth NY .... .709
Lou Gehrig NY .... .648
Goose Goslin WAS .... .614

STOLEN BASES
Buddy Myer BOS 30
Johnny Mostil CHI 23
Harry Rice DET 20

RUNS SCORED
Babe Ruth NY 163
Lou Gehrig NY 139
Earle Combs NY 118

WINS
Lefty Grove PHI 24
George Pipgras NY 24
Waite Hoyt NY 23

WINNING PERCENTAGE
G. Crowder STL.......... .808
Waite Hoyt NY .... .767
Lefty Grove PHI .... .750

EARNED RUN AVERAGE
G. Braxton WAS 2.51
Herb Pennock NY 2.56
Lefty Grove PHI 2.58

STRIKEOUTS
Lefty Grove PHI 183
George Pipgras NY..... 139
Tommy Thomas CHI... 129

SAVES
Waite Hoyt NY 8
Willis Hudlin CLE 7
two tied at 6

COMPLETE GAMES
Red Ruffing BOS 25
Lefty Grove PHI 24
Tommy Thomas CHI..... 24

SHUTOUTS
Herb Pennock NY 5
three tied at 4

GAMES PITCHED
Firpo Marberry WAS 48
Ed Morris BOS.............. 47
George Pipgras NY 46

INNINGS PITCHED
George Pipgras NY 301
Red Ruffing BOS 289
Tommy Thomas CHI... 283

NATIONAL LEAGUE STANDINGS

1928 NL

	W	L	PCT	GB	R	OR	BA	FA	ERA
ST. LOUIS	95	59	.617	—	807	636	.281	.974	3.38
NEW YORK	93	61	.604	2	807	653	.293	.972	3.67
CHICAGO	91	63	.591	4	714	615	.278	.975	3.40
PITTSBURGH	85	67	.559	9	837	704	.309	.967	3.95
CINCINNATI	78	74	.513	16	648	686	.280	.974	3.94
BROOKLYN	77	76	.503	17.5	665	640	.266	.965	3.25
BOSTON	50	103	.327	44.5	631	878	.275	.969	4.83
PHILADELPHIA	43	109	.283	51	660	957	.267	.971	5.52
					5769	5769	.281	.971	3.98

BATTING AVERAGE
R. Hornsby BOS .... .387
Paul Waner PIT .... .370
Freddie Lindstrom NY .358

HITS
F. Lindstrom NY 231
Paul Waner PIT 223
Lloyd Waner PIT 221

DOUBLES
Paul Waner PIT 50
Chick Hafey STL........... 46
two tied at 42

TRIPLES
Jim Bottomley STL... 20
Paul Waner PIT 19
Lloyd Waner PIT 14

HOME RUNS
Hack Wilson CHI............ 31
Jim Bottomley STL........ 31
Chick Hafey STL........... 27

RUNS BATTED IN
Jim Bottomley STL...... 136
Pie Traynor PIT........... 124
Hack Wilson CHI......... 120

SLUGGING AVERAGE
R. Hornsby BOS .... .632
Jim Bottomley STL..... .628
Chick Hafey STL........ .604

STOLEN BASES
Kiki Cuyler CHI 37
Frankie Frisch STL 29
two tied at 19

RUNS SCORED
Paul Waner PIT 142
Jim Bottomley STL...... 123
Lloyd Waner PIT 121

WINS
Larry Benton NY 25
Burleigh Grimes PIT 25
Dazzy Vance BKN 22

WINNING PERCENTAGE
Larry Benton NY .... .735
Jesse Haines STL....... .714
Guy Bush CHI............. .714

EARNED RUN AVERAGE
Dazzy Vance BKN 2.09
Sheriff Blake CHI 2.47
Art Nehf CHI 2.65

STRIKEOUTS
Dazzy Vance BKN 200
Pat Malone CHI 155
Charlie Root CHI......... 122

SAVES
Bill Sherdel STL............. 5
Hal Haid STL 5
two tied at 4

COMPLETE GAMES
Burleigh Grimes PIT 28
Larry Benton NY 28
Dazzy Vance BKN 24

SHUTOUTS
five tied at 4

GAMES PITCHED
Burleigh Grimes PIT 48
Ray Kolp CIN................. 44
Eppa Rixey CIN 43

INNINGS PITCHED
Burleigh Grimes PIT ... 331
Larry Benton NY 310
Eppa Rixey CIN 291

AMERICAN LEAGUE STANDINGS

1929 AL

	W	L	PCT	GB	R	OR	BA	FA	ERA
PHILADELPHIA	104	46	.693	—	901	615	.296	.975	3.44
NEW YORK	88	66	.571	18	899	775	.295	.971	4.17
CLEVELAND	81	71	.533	24	717	736	.294	.968	4.05
ST. LOUIS	79	73	.520	26	733	713	.276	.975	4.08
WASHINGTON	71	81	.467	34	730	776	.276	.968	4.34
DETROIT	70	84	.455	36	926	928	.299	.961	4.96
CHICAGO	59	93	.388	46	627	792	.268	.970	4.41
BOSTON	58	96	.377	48	605	803	.267	.965	4.43
					6138	6138	.284	.969	4.24

BATTING AVERAGE
Lew Fonseca CLE ..... .369
Al Simmons PHI.......... .365
Heinie Manush STL ... .355

HITS
Dale Alexander DET ... 215
C. Gehringer DET 215
Al Simmons PHI.......... 212

DOUBLES
Roy Johnson DET......... 45
C. Gehringer DET 45
Heinie Manush STL 45

TRIPLES
C. Gehringer DET 19
Russ Scarritt BOS......... 17
Bing Miller PHI 16

HOME RUNS
Babe Ruth NY 46
Lou Gehrig NY 35
Al Simmons PHI............ 34

RUNS BATTED IN
Al Simmons PHI.......... 157
Babe Ruth NY 154
Dale Alexander DET ... 137

SLUGGING AVERAGE
Babe Ruth NY............. .697
Al Simmons PHI.......... .642
Jimmie Foxx PHI......... .625

STOLEN BASES
C. Gehringer DET 28
Bill Cissell CHI 26
Bing Miller PHI 24

RUNS SCORED
C. Gehringer DET 131
Roy Johnson DET....... 128
Lou Gehrig NY 127

WINS
G. Earnshaw PHI 24
Wes Ferrell CLE 21
Lefty Grove PHI 20

WINNING PERCENTAGE
Lefty Grove PHI .... .769
G. Earnshaw PHI .... .750
Wes Ferrell CLE .... .677

EARNED RUN AVERAGE
Lefty Grove PHI 2.81
F. Marberry WAS 3.06
T. Thomas CHI 3.19

STRIKEOUTS
Lefty Grove PHI 170
G. Earnshaw PHI 149
Geroge Pipgras NY..... 125

SAVES
Firpo Marberry WAS 11
Wilcy Moore NY 8
Bill Shores PHI................ 7

COMPLETE GAMES
Tommy Thomas CHI..... 24
George Uhle DET 23
Sam Gray STL............... 23

SHUTOUTS
four tied at........................ 4

GAMES PITCHED
Firpo Marberry WAS..... 49
G. Earnshaw PHI.......... 44
two tied at 43

INNINGS PITCHED
Sam Gray STL............. 305
Willis Hudlin CLE 280
Lefty Grove PHI 275

NATIONAL LEAGUE STANDINGS

1929 NL

	W	L	PCT	GB	R	OR	BA	FA	ERA
CHICAGO	98	54	.645	—	982	758	.303	.975	4.16
PITTSBURGH	88	65	.575	10.5	904	780	.303	.970	4.36
NEW YORK	84	67	.556	13.5	897	709	.296	.975	3.97
ST. LOUIS	78	74	.513	20	831	806	.293	.971	4.66
PHILADELPHIA	71	82	.464	27.5	897	1032	.309	.969	6.13
BROOKLYN	70	83	.458	28.5	755	888	.291	.968	4.92
CINCINNATI	66	88	.429	33	686	760	.281	.974	4.41
BOSTON	56	98	.364	43	657	876	.280	.967	5.12
					6609	6609	.294	.971	4.71

BATTING AVERAGE
Lefty O'Doul PHI .... .398
Babe Herman BKN .... .381
R. Hornsby CHI .... .380

HITS
Lefty O'Doul PHI 254
Lloyd Waner PIT 234
Rogers Hornsby CHI... 229

DOUBLES
J. Frederick BKN........... 52
Rogers Hornsby CHI..... 47
Chick Hafey STL........... 47

TRIPLES
Lloyd Waner PIT 20
Curt Walker CIN........... 15
Paul Waner PIT 15

HOME RUNS
Chuck Klein PHI............ 43
Mel Ott NY 42
two tied at 39

RUNS BATTED IN
Hack Wilson CHI......... 159
Mel Ott NY 151
Rogers Hornsby CHI... 149

SLUGGING AVERAGE
R. Hornsby CHI........... .679
Chuck Klein PHI......... .657
Mel Ott NY .... .635

STOLEN BASES
Kiki Cuyler CHI 43
Evar Swanson CIN 33
Frankie Frisch STL 24

RUNS SCORED
Rogers Hornsby CHI... 156
Lefty O'Doul PHI 152
Mel Ott NY 138

WINS
Pat Malone CHI 22
Red Lucas CIN 19
Charlie Root CHI........... 19

WINNING PERCENTAGE
Charlie Root CHI......... .760
Guy Bush CHI............. .720
B. Grimes PIT .... .708

EARNED RUN AVERAGE
Bill Walker NY 3.09
B. Grimes PIT 3.13
Charlie Root CHI........ 3.47

STRIKEOUTS
Pat Malone CHI 166
Watty Clark BKN......... 140
Dazzy Vance BKN 126

SAVES
Johnny Morrison BKN..... 8
Guy Bush CHI................. 8
Lou Koupal BKN, PHI 6

COMPLETE GAMES
Red Lucas CIN 28

SHUTOUTS
Pat Malone CHI 5
F. Fitzimmons NY 4
Charlie Root CHI............. 4

GAMES PITCHED
Guy Bush CHI................ 50
C. Willoughby PHI......... 49
two tied at 43

INNINGS PITCHED
Watty Clark BKN.......... 279
Charlie Root CHI......... 272
Guy Bush CHI............. 271

AMERICAN LEAGUE STANDINGS

1930 AL

	W	L	PCT	GB	R	OR	BA	FA	ERA
PHILADELPHIA	102	52	.662	—	951	751	.294	.975	4.28
WASHINGTON	94	60	.610	8	892	689	.302	.974	3.96
NEW YORK	86	68	.558	16	1062	898	.309	.965	4.88
CLEVELAND	81	73	.526	21	890	915	.304	.962	4.88
DETROIT	75	79	.487	27	783	833	.284	.967	4.70
ST. LOUIS	64	90	.416	38	751	886	.268	.970	5.07
CHICAGO	62	92	.403	40	729	884	.276	.962	4.71
BOSTON	52	102	.338	50	612	814	.264	.968	4.70
					6670	6670	.288	.968	4.65

BATTING AVERAGE
Al Simmons PHI......... .381
Lou Gehrig NY .... .379
two tied at .... .359

HITS
Johnny Hodapp CLE... 225
Lou Gehrig NY 220
Al Simmons PHI.......... 211

DOUBLES
Johnny Hodapp CLE... 51
Manush STL, WAS 49
two tied at 47

TRIPLES
Earle Combs NY 22
Carl Reynolds CHI 18
Lou Gehrig NY 17

HOME RUNS
Babe Ruth NY 49
Lou Gehrig NY 41
two tied at 37

RUNS BATTED IN
Lou Gehrig NY 174
Al Simmons PHI........... 165
Jimmie Foxx PHI.......... 156

SLUGGING AVERAGE
Babe Ruth NY .... .732
Lou Gehrig NY .... .721
Al Simmons PHI.......... .708

STOLEN BASES
Marty McManus DET 23
C. Gehringer DET......... 19
three tied at.................. 17

RUNS SCORED
Al Simmons PHI........... 152
Babe Ruth NY 150
C. Gehringer DET......... 144

WINS
Lefty Grove PHI 28
Wes Ferrell CLE 25
two tied at 22

WINNING PERCENTAGE
Lefty Grove PHI .... .848
F. Marberry WAS .... .750
Sam Jones WAS......... .682

EARNED RUN AVERAGE
Lefty Grove PHI 2.54
Wes Ferrell CLE 3.31
Lefty Stewart STL 3.45

STRIKEOUTS
Lefty Grove PHI 209
G. Earnshaw PHI 193
Bump Hadley WAS 162

SAVES
Lefty Grove PHI 9
G. Braxton CHI, WAS 6
Jack Quinn PHI................ 6

COMPLETE GAMES
Ted Lyons CHI............... 29
Crowder STL, WAS 25
Wes Ferrell CLE 25

SHUTOUTS
George Pipgras NY......... 3
George Earnshaw PHI.... 3

GAMES PITCHED
Lefty Grove PHI 50
G. Earnshaw PHI 49
two tied at 44

INNINGS PITCHED
Ted Lyons CHI............. 298
Wes Ferrell CLE 297
G. Earnshaw PHI 296

NATIONAL LEAGUE STANDINGS

1930 NL

	W	L	PCT	GB	R	OR	BA	FA	ERA
ST. LOUIS	92	62	.597	—	1004	784	.314	.970	4.40
CHICAGO	90	64	.584	2	998	870	.309	.973	4.80
NEW YORK	87	67	.565	5	959	814	.319	.974	4.59
BROOKLYN	86	68	.558	6	871	738	.304	.972	4.03
PITTSBURGH	80	74	.519	12	891	928	.303	.965	5.24
BOSTON	70	84	.455	22	693	835	.281	.971	4.91
CINCINNATI	59	95	.383	33	665	857	.281	.973	5.08
PHILADELPHIA	52	102	.338	40	944	1199	.315	.962	6.71
					7025	7025	.303	.970	4.97

BATTING AVERAGE
Bill Terry NY .... .401
Babe Herman BKN .... .393
Chuck Klein PHI .... .386

HITS
Bill Terry NY 254
Chuck Klein PHI 250
Babe Herman BKN 241

DOUBLES
Chuck Klein PHI 59
Kiki Cuyler CHI 50
Babe Herman BKN 48

TRIPLES
Adam Comorosky PIT ... 23
Paul Waner PIT 18
two tied at 17

HOME RUNS
Hack Wilson CHI 56
Chuck Klein PHI 40
Wally Berger BOS 38

RUNS BATTED IN
Hack Wilson CHI 190
Chuck Klein PHI 170
Kiki Cuyler CHI 134

SLUGGING AVERAGE
Hack Wilson CHI .... .723
Chuck Klein PHI .... .687
Babe Herman BKN .... .678

STOLEN BASES
Kiki Cuyler CHI 37
Babe Herman BKN 18
Paul Waner PIT 18

RUNS SCORED
Chuck Klein PHI 158
Kiki Cuyler CHI 155
Woody English CHI 152

WINS
Ray Kremer PIT 20
Pat Malone CHI 20
Fitzsimmons NY 19

WINNING PERCENTAGE
Fitzsimmons NY .... .731
Pat Malone CHI .... .690
Erv Brame PIT .... .680

EARNED RUN AVERAGE
Dazzy Vance BKN 2.61
Carl Hubbell NY 3.76
Bill Walker NY 3.93

STRIKEOUTS
Bill Hallahan STL 177
Dazzy Vance BKN 173
Pat Malone CHI 142

SAVES
Hi Bell STL 8
Joe Heving NY 6
Watty Clark BKN 6

COMPLETE GAMES
Erv Brame PIT 22
Pat Malone CHI 22
Larry French PIT 21

SHUTOUTS
Charlie Root CHI 4
Dazzy Vance BKN 4
two tied at 3

GAMES PITCHED
Hal Elliot PHI 48
Phil Collins PHI 47
Guy Bush CHI 46

INNINGS PITCHED
Ray Kremer PIT 276
Larry French PIT 275
Pat Malone CHI 272

AMERICAN LEAGUE STANDINGS

1931 AL

	W	L	PCT	GB	R	OR	BA	FA	ERA
PHILADELPHIA	107	45	.704	—	858	626	.287	.976	3.47
NEW YORK	94	59	.614	13.5	1067	760	.297	.972	4.20
WASHINGTON	92	62	.597	16	843	691	.285	.976	3.76
CLEVELAND	78	76	.506	30	885	833	.296	.963	4.63
ST. LOUIS	63	91	.409	45	772	870	.271	.963	4.76
BOSTON	62	90	.408	45	625	800	.262	.970	4.60
DETROIT	61	93	.396	47	651	836	.268	.964	4.56
CHICAGO	56	97	.366	51.5	704	939	.260	.961	5.05
					6355	6355	.278	.968	4.38

BATTING AVERAGE
Al Simmons PHI .... .390
Babe Ruth NY .... .373
Ed Morgan CLE .... .351

HITS
Lou Gehrig NY 211
Earl Averill CLE 209
Al Simmons PHI 200

DOUBLES
Earl Webb BOS 67
Dale Alexander DET 47
Red Kress STL 46

TRIPLES
Roy Johnson DET 19
Lou Gehrig NY 15
Lu Blue CHI 15

HOME RUNS
Lou Gehrig NY 46
Babe Ruth NY 46
Earl Averill CLE 32

RUNS BATTED IN
Lou Gehrig NY 184
Babe Ruth NY 163
Earl Averill CLE 143

SLUGGING AVERAGE
Babe Ruth NY .... .700
Lou Gehrig NY .... .662
Al Simmons PHI .... .641

STOLEN BASES
Ben Chapman NY 61
Roy Johnson DET 33
Jack Burns STL 19

RUNS SCORED
Lou Gehrig NY 163
Babe Ruth NY 149
Earl Averill CLE 140

WINS
Lefty Grove PHI 31
Wes Ferrell CLE 22
two tied at 21

WINNING PERCENTAGE
Lefty Grove PHI .... .886
F. Marberry WAS .... .800
Roy Mahaffey PHI ...... .789

EARNED RUN AVERAGE
Lefty Grove PHI 2.06
Lefty Gomez NY 2.63
Lloyd Brown WAS 3.20

STRIKEOUTS
Lefty Grove PHI 175
G. Earnshaw PHI 152
Lefty Gomez NY 150

SAVES
Wilcy Moore BOS 10
Bump Hadley WAS 8
two tied at 7

COMPLETE GAMES
Lefty Grove PHI 27
Wes Ferrell CLE 27
G. Earnshaw PHI 23

SHUTOUTS
Lefty Grove PHI 4
G. Earnshaw PHI 3

GAMES PITCHED
Bump Hadley WAS 55
Wilcy Moore BOS 53
Pat Caraway CHI 51

INNINGS PITCHED
Rube Walberg PHI 291
Lefty Grove PHI 289
G. Earnshaw PHI 282

NATIONAL LEAGUE STANDINGS

1931 NL

	W	L	PCT	GB	R	OR	BA	FA	ERA
ST. LOUIS	101	53	.656	—	815	614	.286	.974	3.45
NEW YORK	87	65	.572	13	768	599	.289	.974	3.30
CHICAGO	84	70	.545	17	828	710	.289	.973	3.97
BROOKLYN	79	73	.520	21	681	673	.276	.969	3.84
PITTSBURGH	75	79	.487	26	636	691	.266	.968	3.66
PHILADELPHIA	66	88	.429	35	684	828	.279	.966	4.58
BOSTON	64	90	.416	37	533	680	.258	.973	3.90
CINCINNATI	58	96	.377	43	592	742	.269	.973	4.22
					5537	5537	.277	.971	3.86

BATTING AVERAGE
Chick Hafey STL .... .349
Bill Terry NY .... .349
Jim Bottomley STL ..... .348

HITS
Lloyd Waner PIT 214
Bill Terry NY 213
two tied at 202

DOUBLES
Sparky Adams STL 46
Wally Berger BOS 44
two tied at 43

TRIPLES
Bill Terry NY 20
Babe Herman BKN 16
Pie Traynor PIT 15

HOME RUNS
Chuck Klein PHI 31
Mel Ott NY 29
Wally Berger BOS 19

RUNS BATTED IN
Chuck Klein PHI 121
Mel Ott NY 115
Bill Terry NY 112

SLUGGING AVERAGE
Chuck Klein PHI .... .584
R. Hornsby CHI .... .574
Chick Hafey STL .... .569

STOLEN BASES
Frankie Frisch STL 28
Babe Herman BKN 17
two tied at 16

RUNS SCORED
Chuck Klein PHI 121
Bill Terry NY 121
Woody English CHI 117

WINS
Bill Hallahan STL 19
Heinie Meine PIT 19
Jumbo Elliott PHI 19

WINNING PERCENTAGE
Paul Derringer STL ..... .692
Bill Hallahan STL .... .679
Guy Bush CHI .... .667

EARNED RUN AVERAGE
Bill Walker NY 2.26
Carl Hubbell NY 2.66
Ed Brandt BOS 2.92

STRIKEOUTS
Bill Hallahan STL 159
Carl Hubbell NY 156
Dazzy Vance BKN 150

SAVES
Jack Quinn BKN 15
Jim Lindsey STL 7
Jumbo Elliott PHI 5

COMPLETE GAMES
Red Lucas CIN 24
Ed Brandt BOS 23
Heinie Meine PIT 22

SHUTOUTS
Bill Walker NY 6
three tied at 4

GAMES PITCHED
Jumbo Elliot PHI 52
Syl Johnson CIN 42
Phil Collins PHI 42

INNINGS PITCHED
Heinie Meine PIT 284
Larry French PIT 276
Syl Johnson CIN 262

AMERICAN LEAGUE STANDINGS

1932 AL

	W	L	PCT	GB	R	OR	BA	FA	ERA
NEW YORK	107	47	.695	—	1002	724	.286	.969	3.98
PHILADELPHIA	94	60	.610	13	981	752	.290	.979	4.45
WASHINGTON	93	61	.604	14	840	716	.284	.979	4.16
CLEVELAND	87	65	.572	19	845	747	.285	.969	4.12
DETROIT	76	75	.503	29.5	799	787	.273	.969	4.30
ST. LOUIS	63	91	.409	44	736	898	.276	.969	5.01
CHICAGO	49	102	.325	56.5	667	897	.267	.958	4.82
BOSTON	43	111	.279	64	566	915	.251	.963	5.02
					6436	6436	.277	.969	4.48

BATTING AVERAGE
Alexander DET, BOS. .367
Jimmie Foxx PHI........ .364
Lou Gehrig NY .... .349

HITS
Al Simmons PHI.......... 216
Heinie Manush WAS... 214
Jimmie Foxx PHI......... 213

DOUBLES
Eric McNair PHI 47
C. Gehringer DET 44
Joe Cronin WAS 43

TRIPLES
Joe Cronin WAS 18
Tony Lazzeri NY 16
Buddy Myer WAS 16

HOME RUNS
Jimmie Foxx PHI............ 58
Babe Ruth NY............... 41
Al Simmons PHI............ 35

RUNS BATTED IN
Jimmie Foxx PHI.......... 169
Lou Gehrig NY 151
Al Simmons PHI........... 151

SLUGGING AVERAGE
Jimmie Foxx PHI........ .749
Babe Ruth NY............. .661
Lou Gehrig NY .... .621

STOLEN BASES
Ben Chapman NY......... 38
Gee Walker DET 30
Johnson BOS, DET 20

RUNS SCORED
Jimmie Foxx PHI.......... 151
Al Simmons PHI........... 144
Earle Combs NY 143

WINS
G. Crowder WAS 26
Lefty Grove PHI 25
Lefty Gomez NY 24

WINNING PERCENTAGE
Johnny Allen NY .... .810
Lefty Gomez NY .... .774
Red Ruffing NY........... .720

EARNED RUN AVERAGE
Lefty Grove PHI 2.84
Red Ruffing NY........... 3.09
Ted Lyons CHI............ 3.28

STRIKEOUTS
Red Ruffing NY........... 190
Lefty Grove PHI 188
Lefty Gomez NY 176

SAVES
Firpo Marberry WAS 13
Wilcy Moore BOS, NY 8
two tied at 7

COMPLETE GAMES
Lefty Grove PHI 27
Wes Ferrell CLE 26
Red Ruffing NY.............. 22

SHUTOUTS
Tommy Bridges DET 4
Lefty Grove PHI 4

GAMES PITCHED
Firpo Marberry WAS..... 54
Sam Gray STL............... 52
G. Crowder WAS 50

INNINGS PITCHED
G. Crowder WAS 327
Lefty Grove PHI 292
Wes Ferrell CLE 288

NATIONAL LEAGUE STANDINGS

1932 NL

	W	L	PCT	GB	R	OR	BA	FA	ERA
CHICAGO	90	64	.584	—	720	633	.278	.973	3.44
PITTSBURGH	86	68	.558	4	701	711	.285	.969	3.75
BROOKLYN	81	73	.526	9	752	747	.283	.971	4.28
PHILADELPHIA	78	76	.506	12	844	796	.292	.968	4.47
BOSTON	77	77	.500	13	649	655	.265	.976	3.53
NEW YORK	72	82	.468	18	755	706	.276	.969	3.83
ST. LOUIS	72	82	.468	18	684	717	.269	.971	3.97
CINCINNATI	60	94	.390	30	575	715	.263	.971	3.79
					5680	5680	.276	.971	3.88

BATTING AVERAGE
Lefty O'Doul BKN .... .368
Bill Terry NY .... .350
Chuck Klein PHI .... .348

HITS
Chuck Klein PHI 226
Bill Terry NY 225
Lefty O'Doul BKN 219

DOUBLES
Paul Waner PIT 62
Chuck Klein PHI 50
R. Stephenson CHI 49

TRIPLES
Babe Herman CIN 19
Gus Suhr PIT 16
Chuck Klein PHI 15

HOME RUNS
Chuck Klein PHI 38
Mel Ott NY 38
Bill Terry NY 28

RUNS BATTED IN
Don Hurst PHI 143
Chuck Klein PHI 137
Pinky Whitney PHI 124

SLUGGING AVERAGE
Chuck Klein PHI .... .646
Mel Ott NY .... .601
Bill Terry NY .... .580

STOLEN BASES
Chuck Klein PHI 20
Tony Piet PIT 19
two tied at 18

RUNS SCORED
Chuck Klein PHI 152
Bill Terry NY 124
Lefty O'Doul BKN 120

WINS
Lon Warneke CHI 22
Watty Clark BKN 20
Guy Bush CHI 19

WINNING PERCENTAGE
Lon Warneke CHI ...... .786
Guy Bush CHI .... .633
two tied at .... .625

EARNED RUN AVERAGE
Lon Warneke CHI 2.37
Carl Hubbell NY 2.50
Huck Betts BOS 2.80

STRIKEOUTS
Dizzy Dean STL 191
Carl Hubbell NY 137
Pat Malone CHI 120

SAVES
Jack Quinn BKN 8
Ray Benge PHI 6
two tied at 5

COMPLETE GAMES
Red Lucas CIN 28
Lon Warneke CHI 25
Carl Hubbell NY 22

SHUTOUTS
Dizzy Dean STL 4
Steve Swetonic PIT 4
Lon Warneke CHI 4

GAMES PITCHED
Larry French PIT 47
Dizzy Dean STL 46
Tex Carleton STL 44

INNINGS PITCHED
Dizzy Dean STL 286
Carl Hubbell NY 284
Lon Warneke CHI 277

AMERICAN LEAGUE STANDINGS

1933 AL

	W	L	PCT	GB	R	OR	BA	FA	ERA
WASHINGTON	99	53	.651	—	850	665	.287	.979	3.82
NEW YORK	91	59	.607	7	927	768	.283	.972	4.36
PHILADELPHIA	79	72	.523	19.5	875	853	.285	.966	4.81
CLEVELAND	75	76	.497	23.5	654	669	.261	.974	3.71
DETROIT	75	79	.487	25	722	733	.269	.971	3.96
CHICAGO	67	83	.447	31	683	814	.272	.970	4.45
BOSTON	63	86	.423	34.5	700	758	.271	.966	4.35
ST. LOUIS	55	96	.364	43.5	669	820	.253	.976	4.82
					6080	6080	.273	.972	4.28

BATTING AVERAGE
Jimmie Foxx PHI........ .356
H. Manush WAS .... .336
Lou Gehrig NY .... .334

HITS
Heinie Manush WAS... 221
C. Gehringer DET....... 204
Jimmie Foxx PHI......... 204

DOUBLES
Joe Cronin WAS 45
Bob Johnson PHI.......... 44
Jack Burns STL 43

TRIPLES
Heinie Manush WAS..... 17
Earl Averill CLE............. 16
Earle Combs NY 16

HOME RUNS
Jimmie Foxx PHI............ 48
Babe Ruth NY................ 34
Lou Gehrig NY............... 32

RUNS BATTED IN
Jimmie Foxx PHI......... 163
Lou Gehrig NY 139
Al Simmons CHI 119

SLUGGING AVERAGE
Jimmie Foxx PHI........ .703
Lou Gehrig NY .... .605
Babe Ruth NY............. .582

STOLEN BASES
Ben Chapman NY......... 27
Gee Walker DET........... 26
Evar Swanson CHI 19

RUNS SCORED
Lou Gehrig NY 138
Jimmie Foxx PHI......... 125
Heinie Manush WAS... 115

WINS
Lefty Grove PHI 24
G. Crowder WAS 24
Earl Whitehill WAS........ 22

WINNING PERCENTAGE
Lefty Grove PHI .... .750
Earl Whitehill WAS..... .733
Lefty Stewart WAS..... .714

EARNED RUN AVERAGE
Monte Pearson CLE .. 2.33
Mel Harder CLE 2.95
T. Bridges DET 3.09

STRIKEOUTS
Lefty Gomez NY 163
Bump Hadley STL........ 149
Red Ruffing NY............ 122

SAVES
Jack Russell WAS 13
Chief Hogsett DET.......... 9
Wilcy Moore NY 8

COMPLETE GAMES
Lefty Grove PHI 21
Bump Hadley STL......... 19
Earl Whitehill WAS........ 19

SHUTOUTS
Oral Hildebrand CLE...... 6
Lefty Gomez NY 4
G. Blaeholder STL 3

GAMES PITCHED
G. Crowder WAS 52
Jack Russell WAS 50
Johnny Welch BOS....... 47

INNINGS PITCHED
Bump Hadley STL....... 317
G. Crowder WAS 299
Lefty Grove PHI 275

NATIONAL LEAGUE STANDINGS

1933 NL

	W	L	PCT	GB	R	OR	BA	FA	ERA
NEW YORK	91	61	.599	—	636	515	.263	.973	2.71
PITTSBURGH	87	67	.565	5	667	619	.285	.972	3.27
CHICAGO	86	68	.558	6	646	536	.271	.973	2.93
BOSTON	83	71	.539	9	552	531	.252	.978	2.96
ST. LOUIS	82	71	.536	9.5	687	609	.276	.973	3.37
BROOKLYN	65	88	.425	26.5	617	695	.263	.971	3.73
PHILADELPHIA	60	92	.395	31	607	760	.274	.970	4.34
CINCINNATI	58	94	.382	33	496	643	.246	.971	3.42
					4908	4908	.266	.973	3.34

BATTING AVERAGE
Chuck Klein PHI......... .368
Spud Davis PHI .... .349
Tony Piet PIT .... .323

HITS
Chuck Klein PHI........... 223
Chick Fullis PHI 200
Paul Waner PIT 191

DOUBLES
Chuck Klein PHI............ 44
Joe Medwick STL 40
F. Lindstrom PIT 39

TRIPLES
Arky Vaughan PIT......... 19
Paul Waner PIT 16
two tied at 12

HOME RUNS
Chuck Klein PHI............ 28
Wally Berger BOS......... 27
Mel Ott NY 23

RUNS BATTED IN
Chuck Klein PHI........... 120
Wally Berger BOS....... 106
Mel Ott NY 103

SLUGGING AVERAGE
Chuck Klein PHI.......... .602
Wally Berger BOS...... .566
Babe Herman CHI ..... .502

STOLEN BASES
Pepper Martin STL........ 26
Chick Fullis PHI 18
Frankie Frisch STL 18

RUNS SCORED
Pepper Martin STL...... 122
Chuck Klein PHI.......... 101
Paul Waner PIT 101

WINS
Carl Hubbell NY 23
three tied at.................. 20

WINNING PERCENTAGE
Ben Cantwell BOS ..... .667
Carl Hubbell NY .... .657
Heine Meine PIT .... .652

EARNED RUN AVERAGE
Carl Hubbell NY 1.66
Lon Warneke CHI 2.00
H. Schumacher NY.... 2.16

STRIKEOUTS
Dizzy Dean STL.......... 199
Carl Hubbell NY 156
Tex Carlton STL.......... 147

SAVES
Phil Collins PHI 6
three tied at..................... 5

COMPLETE GAMES
Dizzy Dean STL............. 26
Lon Warneke CHI 26
Ed Brandt BOS 23

SHUTOUTS
Carl Hubbell NY 10
Hal Schumacher NY 7
Larry French PIT............. 5

GAMES PITCHED
Dizzy Dean STL............. 48
Larry French PIT........... 47
two tied at 45

INNINGS PITCHED
Carl Hubbell NY 309
Dizzy Dean STL........... 293
Larry French PIT......... 291

AMERICAN LEAGUE STANDINGS

1934 AL

	W	L	PCT	GB	R	OR	BA	FA	ERA
DETROIT	101	53	.656	—	958	708	.300	.974	4.06
NEW YORK	94	60	.610	7	842	669	.278	.973	3.76
CLEVELAND	85	69	.552	16	814	763	.287	.972	4.28
BOSTON	76	76	.500	24	820	775	.274	.969	4.32
PHILADELPHIA	68	82	.453	31	764	838	.280	.967	5.01
ST. LOUIS	67	85	.441	33	674	800	.268	.969	4.49
WASHINGTON	66	86	.434	34	729	806	.278	.974	4.68
CHICAGO	53	99	.349	47	704	946	.263	.966	5.41
					6305	6305	.279	.970	4.50

BATTING AVERAGE
Lou Gehrig NY .... .363
C. Gehringer DET .... .356
H. Manush WAS .... .349

HITS
C. Gehringer DET 214
Lou Gehrig NY 210
Hal Trosky CLE............ 206

DOUBLES
Hank Greenberg DET ... 63
C. Gehringer DET 50
Earl Averill CLE.............. 48

TRIPLES
Ben Chapman NY......... 13
Heinie Manush WAS..... 11

HOME RUNS
Lou Gehrig NY 49
Jimmie Foxx PHI............ 44
Hal Trosky CLE.............. 35

RUNS BATTED IN
Lou Gehrig NY 165
Hal Trosky CLE............ 142
H. Greenberg DET 139

SLUGGING AVERAGE
Lou Gehrig NY .... .706
Jimmie Foxx PHI......... .653
H. Greenberg DET..... .600

STOLEN BASES
Bill Werber BOS............ 40
Jo-Jo White DET........... 28
Ben Chapman NY......... 26

RUNS SCORED
C. Gehringer DET 134
Bill Werber BOS........... 129
two tied at.. 128

WINS
Lefty Gomez NY 26
S. Rowe DET 24
Tommy Bridges DET 22

WINNING PERCENTAGE
Lefty Gomez NY .... .839
S.y Rowe DET .... .750
Firpo Marberry DET ... .750

EARNED RUN AVERAGE
Lefty Gomez NY 2.33
Mel Harder CLE......... 2.61
Johnny Murphy NY 3.12

STRIKEOUTS
Lefty Gomez NY 158
T. Bridges DET 151
two tied at 149

SAVES
Jack Russell WAS 7
Lloyd Brown CLE............ 6
Bobo Newsom STL......... 5

COMPLETE GAMES
Lefty Gomez NY 25
Tommy Bridges DET 23
Ted Lyons CHI............... 21

SHUTOUTS
Mel Harder CLE.............. 6
Lefty Gomez NY 6
Red Ruffing NY............... 5

GAMES PITCHED
Jack Russell WAS 54
Bobo Newsom STL....... 47
two tied at 45

INNINGS PITCHED
Lefty Gomez NY 282
T. Bridges DET 275
S. Rowe DET............... 266

NATIONAL LEAGUE STANDINGS

1934 NL

	W	L	PCT	GB	R	OR	BA	FA	ERA
ST. LOUIS	95	58	.621	—	799	656	.288	.972	3.69
NEW YORK	93	60	.608	2	760	583	.275	.972	3.19
CHICAGO	86	65	.570	8	705	639	.279	.977	3.76
BOSTON	78	73	.517	16	683	714	.272	.972	4.11
PITTSBURGH	74	76	.493	19.5	735	713	.287	.975	4.20
BROOKLYN	71	81	.467	23.5	748	795	.281	.970	4.48
PHILADELPHIA	56	93	.376	37	675	794	.284	.966	4.76
CINCINNATI	52	99	.344	42	590	801	.266	.970	4.37
					5695	5695	.279	.972	4.06

BATTING AVERAGE
Paul Waner PIT .... .362
Bill Terry NY .... .354
Kiki Cuyler CHI .... .338

HITS
Paul Waner PIT 217
Bill Terry NY 213
Ripper Collins STL 200

DOUBLES
Kiki Cuyler CHI 42
Ethan Allen PHI 42
Arky Vaughan PIT 41

TRIPLES
Joe Medwick STL 18
Paul Waner PIT 16
Gus Suhr PIT 13

HOME RUNS
Mel Ott NY 35
Ripper Collins STL 35
Wally Berger BOS 34

RUNS BATTED IN
Mel Ott NY 135
Ripper Collins STL 128
Wally Berger BOS 121

SLUGGING AVERAGE
Ripper Collins STL ...... .615
Mel Ott NY .... .591
Wally Berger BOS .... .546

STOLEN BASES
Pepper Martin STL 23
Kiki Cuyler CHI 15
Dick Bartell PHI 13

RUNS SCORED
Paul Waner PIT 122
Mel Ott NY 119
Ripper Collins STL 116

WINS
Dizzy Dean STL 30
Hal Schumacher NY 23
Lon Warneke CHI 22

WINNING PERCENTAGE
Dizzy Dean STL .... .811
Waite Hoyt PIT .... .714
H. Schumacher NY ..... .697

EARNED RUN AVERAGE
Carl Hubbell NY 2.30
Dizzy Dean STL 2.66
Curt Davis PHI 2.95

STRIKEOUTS
Dizzy Dean STL 195
Van Mungo BKN 184
Paul Dean STL 150

SAVES
Carl Hubbell NY 8
Dizzy Dean STL 7
Dolf Luque NY 7

COMPLETE GAMES
Dizzy Dean STL 24
Carl Hubbell NY 23
Lon Warneke CHI 23

SHUTOUTS
Dizzy Dean STL 7
Carl Hubbell NY 5
Paul Dean STL 5

GAMES PITCHED
Curt Davis PHI 51
Dizzy Dean STL 50
Snipe Hansen PHI 50

INNINGS PITCHED
Van Mungo BKN 315
Carl Hubbell NY 313
Dizzy Dean STL 312

AMERICAN LEAGUE STANDINGS

1935 AL

	W	L	PCT	GB	R	OR	BA	FA	ERA
DETROIT	93	58	.616	—	919	665	.290	.978	3.82
NEW YORK	89	60	.597	3	818	632	.280	.974	3.60
CLEVELAND	82	71	.536	12	776	739	.284	.972	4.15
BOSTON	78	75	.510	16	718	732	.276	.969	4.05
CHICAGO	74	78	.487	19.5	738	750	.275	.976	4.38
WASHINGTON	67	86	.438	27	823	903	.285	.972	5.25
ST. LOUIS	65	87	.428	28.5	718	930	.270	.970	5.26
PHILADELPHIA	58	91	.389	34	710	869	.279	.968	5.12
					6220	6220	.280	.972	4.45

BATTING AVERAGE
Buddy Myer WAS ...... .349
Joe Vosmik CLE .... .348
Jimmie Foxx PHI .... .346

HITS
Joe Vosmik CLE 216
Buddy Myer WAS 215
Doc Cramer PHI 214

DOUBLES
Joe Vosmik CLE 47
Hank Greenberg DET ... 46
Solters BOS, STL 45

TRIPLES
Joe Vosmik CLE 20
John Stone WAS 18
Hank Greenberg DET ... 16

HOME RUNS
Hank Greenberg DET ... 36
Jimmie Foxx PHI 36
Lou Gehrig NY 30

RUNS BATTED IN
H. Greenberg DET 170
Lou Gehrig NY 119
Jimmie Foxx PHI 115

SLUGGING AVERAGE
Jimmie Foxx PHI .... .636
H. Greenberg DET ..... .628
Lou Gehrig NY .... .583

STOLEN BASES
Bill Werber BOS 29
Lyn Lary WAS, STL 28
Mel Almada BOS 20

RUNS SCORED
Lou Gehrig NY 125
C. Gehringer DET 123
H. Greenberg DET 121

WINS
Wes Ferrell BOS 25
Mel Harder CLE 22
T. Bridges DET 21

WINNING PERCENTAGE
Eldon Auker DET .... .720
Johnny Broaca NY ..... .682
T. Bridges DET .... .677

EARNED RUN AVERAGE
Lefty Grove BOS 2.70
Ted Lyons CHI 3.02
Red Ruffing NY 3.12

STRIKEOUTS
T. Bridges DET 163
S. Rowe DET 140
Lefty Gomez NY 138

SAVES
Jack Knott STL 7
five tied at 5

COMPLETE GAMES
Wes Ferrell BOS 31
Lefty Grove BOS 23
Tommy Bridges DET 23

SHUTOUTS
Schoolboy Rowe DET..... 6
Tommy Bridges DET 4
Mel Harder CLE 4

GAMES PITCHED
R. Van Atta NY, STL 58
Jim Walkup STL 55
Ivy Andrews STL 50

INNINGS PITCHED
Wes Ferrell BOS 322
Mel Harder CLE 287
Earl Whitehill WAS 279

NATIONAL LEAGUE STANDINGS

1935 NL

	W	L	PCT	GB	R	OR	BA	FA	ERA
CHICAGO	100	54	.649	—	847	597	.288	.970	3.26
ST. LOUIS	96	58	.623	4	829	625	.284	.972	3.54
NEW YORK	91	62	.595	8.5	770	675	.286	.972	3.78
PITTSBURGH	86	67	.562	13.5	743	647	.285	.968	3.42
BROOKLYN	70	83	.458	29.5	711	767	.277	.969	4.22
CINCINNATI	68	85	.444	31.5	646	772	.265	.966	4.30
PHILADELPHIA	64	89	.418	35.5	685	871	.269	.963	4.76
BOSTON	38	115	.248	61.5	575	852	.263	.967	4.93
					5806	5806	.277	.968	4.02

BATTING AVERAGE
Arky Vaughan PIT ...... .385
Joe Medwick STL .... .353
Gabby Hartnett CHI ... .344

HITS
Billy Herman CHI 227
Joe Medwick STL 224
two tied at 203

DOUBLES
Billy Herman CHI 57
Ethan Allen PHI 46
Joe Medwick STL 46

TRIPLES
Ival Goodman CIN 18
Lloyd Waner PIT 14
Joe Medwick STL 13

HOME RUNS
Wally Berger BOS 34
Mel Ott NY 31
Dolf Camilli PHI 25

RUNS BATTED IN
Wally Berger BOS 130
Joe Medwick STL 126
Ripper Collins STL 122

SLUGGING AVERAGE
Arky Vaughan PIT ...... .607
Joe Medwick STL ...... .576
Mel Ott NY .... .555

STOLEN BASES
Augie Galan CHI 22
Pepper Martin STL 20
Bordagaray BKN 18

RUNS SCORED
Augie Galan CHI 133
Joe Medwick STL 132
Pepper Martin STL 121

WINS
Dizzy Dean STL 28
Carl Hubbell NY 23
Paul Derringer CIN 22

WINNING PERCENTAGE
Bill Lee CHI .... .769
Slick Castleman NY ... .714
Dizzy Dean STL .... .700

EARNED RUN AVERAGE
Cy Blanton PIT 2.58
Bill Swift PIT 2.70
H. Schumacher NY 2.89

STRIKEOUTS
Dizzy Dean STL 182
Carl Hubbell NY 150
two tied at 143

SAVES
Dutch Leonard BKN 8
Waite Hoyt PIT 6
Syl Johnson PHI 6

COMPLETE GAMES
Dizzy Dean STL 29
Carl Hubbell NY 24
Cy Blanton PIT 23

SHUTOUTS
five tied at 4

GAMES PITCHED
Orville Jorgens PHI 53
Dizzy Dean STL 50
Jim Biven PHI 47

INNINGS PITCHED
Dizzy Dean STL 324
Carl Hubbell NY 303
Paul Derringer CIN 277

AMERICAN LEAGUE STANDINGS

1936 AL

	W	L	PCT	GB	R	OR	BA	FA	ERA
NEW YORK	102	51	.667	—	1065	731	.300	.973	4.17
DETROIT	83	71	.539	19.5	921	871	.300	.975	5.00
CHICAGO	81	70	.536	20	920	873	.292	.973	5.06
WASHINGTON	82	71	.536	20	889	799	.295	.970	4.58
CLEVELAND	80	74	.519	22.5	921	862	.304	.971	4.83
BOSTON	74	80	.481	28.5	775	764	.276	.972	4.39
ST. LOUIS	57	95	.375	44.5	804	1064	.279	.969	6.24
PHILADELPHIA	53	100	.346	49	714	1045	.269	.965	6.08
					7009	7009	.289	.971	5.04

BATTING AVERAGE
Luke Appling CHI .... .388
Earl Averill CLE .... .378
Bill Dickey NY .... .362

HITS
Earl Averill CLE 232
C. Gehringer DET 227
Hal Trosky CLE 216

DOUBLES
C. Gehringer DET 60
Gee Walker DET 55
two tied at 50

TRIPLES
Earl Averill CLE 15
Red Rolfe NY 15
Joe DiMaggio NY 15

HOME RUNS
Lou Gehrig NY 49
Hal Trosky CLE 42
Jimmie Foxx BOS 41

RUNS BATTED IN
Hal Trosky CLE 162
Lou Gehrig NY 152
Jimmie Foxx BOS 143

SLUGGING AVERAGE
Lou Gehrig NY .... .696
Hal Trosky CLE .... .644
Jimmie Foxx BOS .... .631

STOLEN BASES
Lyn Lary STL 37
J. Powell WAS, NY 26
Bill Werber BOS 23

RUNS SCORED
Lou Gehrig NY 167
Harlond Clift STL 145
C. Gehringer DET 144

WINS
Tommy Bridges DET 23
Vern Kennedy CHI 21
three tied at 20

WINNING PERCENTAGE
Monte Pearson NY .... .731
Vern Kennedy CHI ..... .700
T. Bridges DET .... .676

EARNED RUN AVERAGE
Lefty Grove BOS 2.81
Johnny Allen CLE 3.44
Pete Appleton WAS ... 3.53

STRIKEOUTS
T. Bridges DET 175
Johnny Allen CLE 165
Bobo Newsom WAS ... 156

SAVES
Pat Malone NY 9
Jack Knott STL 6
two tied at 5

COMPLETE GAMES
Wes Ferrell BOS 28
Tommy Bridges DET ... 26
Red Ruffing NY 25

SHUTOUTS
Lefty Grove BOS 6
Tommy Bridges DET 5
two tied at 4

GAMES PITCHED
Russ Van Atta STL 52
Jack Knott STL 47
two tied at 43

INNINGS PITCHED
Wes Ferrell BOS 301
T. Bridges DET 295
Bobo Newsom WAS ... 286

NATIONAL LEAGUE STANDINGS

1936 NL

	W	L	PCT	GB	R	OR	BA	FA	ERA
NEW YORK	92	62	.597	—	742	621	.281	.974	3.46
CHICAGO	87	67	.565	5	755	603	.286	.976	3.53
ST. LOUIS	87	67	.565	5	795	794	.281	.974	4.48
PITTSBURGH	84	70	.545	8	804	718	.286	.967	3.89
CINCINNATI	74	80	.481	18	722	760	.274	.969	4.22
BOSTON	71	83	.461	21	631	715	.265	.971	3.94
BROOKLYN	67	87	.435	25	662	752	.272	.966	3.98
PHILADELPHIA	54	100	.351	38	726	874	.281	.959	4.64
					5837	5837	.278	.969	4.02

BATTING AVERAGE
Paul Waner PIT .... .373
Babe Phelps BKN ...... .367
Joe Medwick STL ...... .351

HITS
Joe Medwick STL 223
Paul Waner PIT 218
Frank Demaree CHI.... 212

DOUBLES
Joe Medwick STL 64
Billy Herman CHI 57
Paul Waner PIT 53

TRIPLES
Ival Goodman CIN 14
Dolf Camilli PHI............. 13
Joe Medwick STL 13

HOME RUNS
Mel Ott NY 33
Dolf Camilli PHI............. 28
two tied at 25

RUNS BATTED IN
Joe Medwick STL 138
Mel Ott NY 135
Gus Suhr PIT 118

SLUGGING AVERAGE
Mel Ott NY .... .588
three tied at................ .577

STOLEN BASES
Pepper Martin STL........ 23
three tied at................... 17

RUNS SCORED
Arky Vaughan PIT....... 122
Pepper Martin STL...... 121
Mel Ott NY 120

WINS
Carl Hubbell NY 26
Dizzy Dean STL............. 24
Paul Derringer CIN 19

WINNING PERCENTAGE
Carl Hubbell NY .... .813
Red Lucas PIT .... .789
Larry French CHI .... .667

EARNED RUN AVERAGE
Carl Hubbell NY 2.31
D. MacFayden BOS... 2.87
Dizzy Dean STL.......... 3.17

STRIKEOUTS
Van Mungo BKN 238
Dizzy Dean STL........... 195
Cy Blanton PIT............. 127

SAVES
Dizzy Dean STL............. 11
Don Brennan CIN 9
Bob Smith BOS............... 8

COMPLETE GAMES
Dizzy Dean STL............. 28
Carl Hubbell NY 25
Van Mungo BKN............ 22

SHUTOUTS
seven tied at 4

GAMES PITCHED
Dizzy Dean STL............. 51
Paul Derringer CIN 51
Claude Passeau PHI 49

INNINGS PITCHED
Dizzy Dean STL........... 315
Van Mungo BKN 312
Carl Hubbell NY 304

AMERICAN LEAGUE STANDINGS

1937 AL

	W	L	PCT	GB	R	OR	BA	FA	ERA
NEW YORK	102	52	.662	—	979	671	.283	.972	3.65
DETROIT	89	65	.578	13	935	841	.292	.976	4.87
CHICAGO	86	68	.558	16	780	730	.280	.971	4.17
CLEVELAND	83	71	.539	19	817	768	.280	.974	4.39
BOSTON	80	72	.526	21	821	775	.281	.970	4.48
WASHINGTON	73	80	.477	28.5	757	841	.279	.972	4.58
PHILADELPHIA	54	97	.358	46.5	699	854	.267	.967	4.85
ST. LOUIS	46	108	.299	56	715	1023	.285	.972	6.00
					6503	6503	.281	.972	4.62

BATTING AVERAGE
C. Gehringer DET ...... .371
Lou Gehrig NY .... .351
Joe DiMaggio NY .... .346

HITS
Beau Bell STL 218
Joe DiMaggio NY 215
Gee Walker DET 213

DOUBLES
Beau Bell STL 51
Hank Greenberg DET ... 49
Wally Moses PHI 48

TRIPLES
Dixie Walker CHI 16
Mike Kreevich CHI 16
two tied at 15

HOME RUNS
Joe DiMaggio NY 46
Hank Greenberg DET ... 40
Lou Gehrig NY 37

RUNS BATTED IN
H. Greenberg DET 183
Joe DiMaggio NY 167
Lou Gehrig NY 159

SLUGGING AVERAGE
Joe DiMaggio NY .... .673
H. Greenberg DET ..... .668
Rudy York DET .... .651

STOLEN BASES
Chapman WAS, BOS ... 35
Bill Werber PHI 35
Gee Walker DET 23

RUNS SCORED
Joe DiMaggio NY 151
Red Rolfe NY 143
Lou Gehrig NY 138

WINS
Lefty Gomez NY 21
Red Ruffing NY 20
Roxie Lawson DET 18

WINNING PERCENTAGE
Johnny Allen CLE ...... .938
Monty Stratton CHI .... .750
Red Ruffing NY .... .741

EARNED RUN AVERAGE
Lefty Gomez NY 2.33
Monty Stratton CHI 2.40
Johnny Allen CLE 2.55

STRIKEOUTS
Lefty Gomez NY 194
Newsom WAS, BOS ... 166
Lefty Grove BOS 153

SAVES
Clint Brown CHI 18
Johnny Murphy NY 10
Jack Wilson BOS 7

COMPLETE GAMES
W. Ferrell BOS, WAS ... 26
Lefty Gomez NY 25
Red Ruffing NY 22

SHUTOUTS
Lefty Gomez NY 6
Monty Stratton CHI 5
two tied at 4

GAMES PITCHED
Clint Brown CHI 53
Jack Wilson BOS 51
two tied at 41

INNINGS PITCHED
Ferrell BOS, WAS 281
Lefty Gomez NY 278
Newsom WAS, BOS ... 275

NATIONAL LEAGUE STANDINGS

1937 NL

	W	L	PCT	GB	R	OR	BA	FA	ERA
NEW YORK	95	57	.625	—	732	602	.278	.974	3.43
CHICAGO	93	61	.604	3	811	682	.287	.975	3.97
PITTSBURGH	86	68	.558	10	704	646	.285	.970	3.56
ST. LOUIS	81	73	.526	15	789	733	.282	.973	3.95
BOSTON	79	73	.520	16	579	556	.247	.975	3.22
BROOKLYN	62	91	.405	33.5	616	772	.265	.964	4.13
PHILADELPHIA	61	92	.399	34.5	724	869	.273	.970	5.06
CINCINNATI	56	98	.364	40	612	707	.254	.966	3.94
					5567	5567	.272	.971	3.91

BATTING AVERAGE
Joe Medwick STL .... .374
Johnny Mize STL .... .364
two tied at .... .354

HITS
Joe Medwick STL 237
Paul Waner PIT 219
Johnny Mize STL 204

DOUBLES
Joe Medwick STL 56
Johnny Mize STL 40
Dick Bartell NY............. 38

TRIPLES
Arky Vaughan PIT......... 17
Gus Suhr PIT 14
two tied at 12

HOME RUNS
Joe Medwick STL 31
Mel Ott NY 31
Dolf Camilli PHI............. 27

RUNS BATTED IN
Joe Medwick STL 154
Frank Demaree CHI.... 115
Johnny Mize STL 113

SLUGGING AVERAGE
Joe Medwick STL .... .641
Johnny Mize STL........ .595
Dolf Camilli PHI........... .587

STOLEN BASES
Augie Galan CHI............ 23
Stan Hack CHI............... 16
four tied at 13

RUNS SCORED
Joe Medwick STL 111
Stan Hack CHI 106
Billy Herman CHI 106

WINS
Carl Hubbell NY............ 22
three tied at.................. 20

WINNING PERCENTAGE
Carl Hubbell NY .... .733
Cliff Melton NY .... .690
two tied at .... .667

EARNED RUN AVERAGE
Jim Turner BOS 2.38
Cliff Melton NY 2.61
Dizzy Dean STL......... 2.69

STRIKEOUTS
Carl Hubbell NY 159
Lee Grissom CIN 149
Cy Blanton PIT............ 143

SAVES
Mace Brown PIT 7
Cliff Melton NY................ 7
Lee Grissom CIN 6

COMPLETE GAMES
Jim Turner BOS............ 24
Lou Fette BOS.............. 23
Bob Weiland STL.......... 21

SHUTOUTS
Jim Turner BOS.............. 5
Lou Fette BOS................ 5
Lee Grissom CIN 5

GAMES PITCHED
Hugh Mulcahy PHI........ 56
Orville Jorgens PHI....... 52
two tied at 50

INNINGS PITCHED
C. Passeau PHI 292
Bill Lee CHI................. 272
Bob Weiland STL........ 264

1938 AL

	W	L	PCT	GB	R	OR	BA	FA	ERA
NEW YORK	99	53	.651	—	966	710	.274	.973	3.91
BOSTON	88	61	.591	9.5	902	751	.299	.968	4.46
CLEVELAND	86	66	.566	13	847	782	.281	.974	4.60
DETROIT	84	70	.545	16	862	795	.272	.976	4.79
WASHINGTON	75	76	.497	23.5	814	873	.293	.970	4.94
CHICAGO	65	83	.439	32	709	752	.277	.967	4.36
ST. LOUIS	55	97	.362	44	755	962	.281	.975	5.80
PHILADELPHIA	53	99	.349	46	726	956	.270	.965	5.48
					6581	6581	.281	.971	4.79

BATTING AVERAGE
Jimmie Foxx BOS ...... .349
Jeff Heath CLE .... .343
Ben Chapman BOS ... .340

HITS
Joe Vosmik BOS 201
Doc Cramer BOS 198
two tied at 197

DOUBLES
Joe Cronin BOS 51
George McQuinn STL ... 42
two tied at 40

TRIPLES
Jeff Heath CLE 18
Earl Averill CLE 15
Joe DiMaggio NY 13

HOME RUNS
Hank Greenberg DET ... 58
Jimmie Foxx BOS 50
Harlond Clift STL 34

RUNS BATTED IN
Jimmie Foxx BOS 175
H. Greenberg DET 146
Joe DiMaggio NY 140

SLUGGING AVERAGE
Jimmie Foxx BOS .... .704
H. Greenberg DET ..... .683
Jeff Heath CLE .... .602

STOLEN BASES
Frank Crosetti NY 27
Lyn Lary CLE 23
Bill Werber PHI 19

RUNS SCORED
H. Greenberg DET 144
Jimmie Foxx BOS 139
C. Gehringer DET 133

WINS
Red Ruffing NY 21
Bobo Newsom STL 20
Lefty Gomez NY 18

WINNING PERCENTAGE
Red Ruffing NY .... .750
Monty Pearson NY ..... .696
Mel Harder CLE .... .630

EARNED RUN AVERAGE
Lefty Grove BOS 3.08
Red Ruffing NY 3.31
Lefty Gomez NY 3.35

STRIKEOUTS
Bob Feller CLE 240
Bobo Newsom STL 226
Lefty Mills STL 134

SAVES
Johnny Murphy NY 11
Archie McKain BOS 6
John Humphries CLE 6

COMPLETE GAMES
Bobo Newsom STL 31
Red Ruffing NY 22
three tied at 20

SHUTOUTS
Red Ruffing NY 4
Lefty Gomez NY 4
two tied at 3

GAMES PITCHED
John Humphries CLE 45
Bobo Newsom STL 44
two tied at 43

INNINGS PITCHED
Bobo Newsom STL 330
George Caster PHI 280
Bob Feller CLE 278

NATIONAL LEAGUE STANDINGS

1938 NL

	W	L	PCT	GB	R	OR	BA	FA	ERA
CHICAGO	89	63	.586	—	713	598	.269	.978	3.37
PITTSBURGH	86	64	.573	2	707	630	.279	.974	3.46
NEW YORK	83	67	.553	5	705	637	.271	.973	3.62
CINCINNATI	82	68	.547	6	723	634	.277	.971	3.62
BOSTON	77	75	.507	12	561	618	.250	.972	3.40
ST. LOUIS	71	80	.470	17.5	725	721	.279	.967	3.84
BROOKLYN	69	80	.463	18.5	704	710	.257	.973	4.07
PHILADELPHIA	45	105	.300	43	550	840	.254	.966	4.93
					5388	5388	.267	.972	3.78

BATTING AVERAGE
Ernie Lombardi CIN ... .342
Johnny Mize STL .... .337
F. McCormick CIN ..... .327

HITS
F. McCormick CIN 209
Stan Hack CHI 195
Lloyd Waner PIT 194

DOUBLES
Joe Medwick STL 47
F. McCormick CIN 40
two tied at 36

TRIPLES
Johnny Mize STL.......... 16
Don Gutteridge STL...... 15
Gus Suhr PIT 14

HOME RUNS
Mel Ott NY 36
Ival Goodman CIN 30
Johnny Mize STL........... 27

RUNS BATTED IN
Joe Medwick STL 122
Mel Ott NY 116
Johnny Rizzo PIT......... 111

SLUGGING AVERAGE
Johnny Mize STL .... .614
Mel Ott NY .... .583
Joe Medwick STL .... .536

STOLEN BASES
Stan Hack CHI.............. 16
Ernie Koy BKN 15
C. Lavagetto BKN 15

RUNS SCORED
Mel Ott NY 116
Stan Hack CHI............ 109
Dolf Camilli BKN 106

WINS
Bill Lee CHI.................. 22
Paul Derringer CIN 21
Clay Bryant CHI 19

WINNING PERCENTAGE
Bill Lee CHI................ .710
Clay Bryant CHI .... .633
Mace Brown PIT .... .625

EARNED RUN AVERAGE
Bill Lee CHI 2.66
Paul Derringer CIN 2.93
MacFayden BOS 2.95

STRIKEOUTS
Clay Bryant CHI 135
Paul Derringer CIN 132
Vander Meer CIN........ 125

SAVES
Dick Coffman NY 12
Charlie Root CHI............. 8
two tied at 6

COMPLETE GAMES
Paul Derringer CIN 26
Jim Turner BOS............ 22
B. Walters PHI, CIN 20

SHUTOUTS
Bill Lee CHI..................... 9
D. MacFayden BOS........ 5
two tied at 4

GAMES PITCHED
Dick Coffman NY 51
Mace Brown PIT 51
Bill McGee STL.............. 47

INNINGS PITCHED
Paul Derringer CIN 307
Bill Lee CHI................. 291
Clay Bryant CHI 270

AMERICAN LEAGUE STANDINGS

1939 AL

	W	L	PCT	GB	R	OR	BA	FA	ERA
NEW YORK	106	45	.702	—	967	556	.287	.978	3.31
BOSTON	89	62	.589	17	890	795	.291	.970	4.56
CLEVELAND	87	67	.565	20.5	797	700	.280	.970	4.08
CHICAGO	85	69	.552	22.5	755	737	.275	.972	4.31
DETROIT	81	73	.526	26.5	849	762	.279	.967	4.29
WASHINGTON	65	87	.428	41.5	702	797	.278	.966	4.60
PHILADELPHIA	55	97	.362	51.5	711	1022	.271	.964	5.79
ST. LOUIS	43	111	.279	64.5	733	1035	.268	.968	6.01
					6404	6404	.279	.969	4.62

BATTING AVERAGE
Joe DiMaggio NY .... .381
Jimmie Foxx BOS ...... .360
Bob Johnson PHI .... .338

HITS
Red Rolfe NY 213
G. McQuinn STL 195
Ken Keltner CLE 191

DOUBLES
Red Rolfe NY 46
Ted Williams BOS 44
Hank Greenberg DET ... 42

TRIPLES
Buddy Lewis WAS 16
B. McCosky DET 14
two tied at 13

HOME RUNS
Jimmie Foxx BOS 35
Hank Greenberg DET ... 33
Ted Williams BOS 31

RUNS BATTED IN
Ted Williams BOS 145
Joe DiMaggio NY 126
Bob Johnson PHI 114

SLUGGING AVERAGE
Jimmie Foxx BOS ...... .694
Joe DiMaggio NY .... .671
H. Greenberg DET ..... .622

STOLEN BASES
George Case WAS 51
Mike Kreevich CHI 23
Pete Fox DET 23

RUNS SCORED
Red Rolfe NY 139
Ted Williams BOS 131
Jimmie Foxx BOS 130

WINS
Bob Feller CLE 24
Red Ruffing NY 21
two tied at 20

WINNING PERCENTAGE
Lefty Grove BOS .... .789
Red Ruffing NY .... .750
Bob Feller CLE .... .727

EARNED RUN AVERAGE
Lefty Grove BOS 2.54
Ted Lyons CHI 2.76
Bob Feller CLE 2.85

STRIKEOUTS
Bob Feller CLE 246
Newsom STL, DET 192
Ted Bridges DET 129

SAVES
Johnny Murphy NY 19
Clint Brown CHI 18
two tied at 7

COMPLETE GAMES
Newsom STL, DET 24
Bob Feller CLE 24
Red Ruffing NY 22

SHUTOUTS
Red Ruffing NY 5
Bob Feller CLE 4

GAMES PITCHED
Clint Brown CHI 61
Chubby Dean PHI 54
E. Dickman BOS 48

INNINGS PITCHED
Bob Feller CLE 297
Newsom STL, DET 292
Dutch Leonard WAS ... 269

NATIONAL LEAGUE STANDINGS

1939 NL

	W	L	PCT	GB	R	OR	BA	FA	ERA
CINCINNATI	97	57	.630	—	767	595	.278	.974	3.27
ST. LOUIS	92	61	.601	4.5	779	633	.294	.971	3.59
BROOKLYN	84	69	.549	12.5	708	645	.265	.972	3.64
CHICAGO	84	70	.545	13	724	678	.266	.970	3.80
NEW YORK	77	74	.510	18.5	703	685	.272	.975	4.07
PITTSBURGH	68	85	.444	28.5	666	721	.276	.972	4.15
BOSTON	63	88	.417	32.5	572	659	.264	.971	3.71
PHILADELPHIA	45	106	.298	50.5	553	856	.261	.970	5.17
					5472	5472	.272	.972	3.92

BATTING AVERAGE
Johnny Mize STL .... .349
F. McCormick CIN ..... .332
Joe Medwick STL .... .332

HITS
F. McCormick CIN 209
Joe Medwick STL 201
Johnny Mize STL 197

DOUBLES
Enos Slaughter STL 52
Joe Medwick STL 48
Johnny Mize STL 44

TRIPLES
Billy Herman CHI 18
Ival Goodman CIN 16
Johnny Mize STL 14

HOME RUNS
Johnny Mize STL 28
Mel Ott NY 27
Dolf Camilli BKN 26

RUNS BATTED IN
Frank McCormick CIN 128
Joe Medwick STL 117
Johnny Mize STL 108

SLUGGING AVERAGE
Johnny Mize STL .... .626
Mel Ott NY .... .581
Hank Leiber CHI .... .556

STOLEN BASES
Lee Handley PIT 17
Stan Hack CHI 17
Bill Werber CIN 15

RUNS SCORED
Bill Werber CIN 115
Stan Hack CHI 112
Billy Herman CHI 111

WINS
Bucky Walters CIN 27
Paul Derringer CIN 25
Curt Davis STL 22

WINNING PERCENTAGE
Paul Derringer CIN .... .781
Bucky Walkers CIN .... .711
Larry French CHI .... .652

EARNED RUN AVERAGE
Bucky Walters CIN 2.29
Carl Hubbell NY 2.75
two tied at 2.93

STRIKEOUTS
Passeau PHI, CHI 137
Bucky Walters CIN 137
Mort Cooper STL 130

SAVES
Bob Bowman STL 9
Clyde Shoun STL 9
three tied at 7

COMPLETE GAMES
Bucky Walters CIN 31
Paul Derringer CIN 28
Bill Lee CHI 20

SHUTOUTS
Lou Fette BOS 6
Bill Posedal BOS 5
Paul Derringer CIN 5

GAMES PITCHED
Clyde Shoun STL 53
Rip Sewell PIT 52
Bob Bowman STL 51

INNINGS PITCHED
Bucky Walters CIN 319
Paul Derringer CIN 301
Bill Lee CHI 282

AMERICAN LEAGUE STANDINGS

1940 AL

	W	L	PCT	GB	R	OR	BA	FA	ERA
DETROIT	90	64	.584	—	888	717	.286	.968	4.01
CLEVELAND	89	65	.578	1	710	637	.265	.975	3.63
NEW YORK	88	66	.571	2	817	671	.259	.975	3.89
BOSTON	82	72	.532	8	872	825	.286	.972	4.89
CHICAGO	82	72	.532	8	735	672	.278	.969	3.74
ST. LOUIS	67	87	.435	23	757	882	.263	.974	5.12
WASHINGTON	64	90	.416	26	665	811	.271	.968	4.59
PHILADELPHIA	54	100	.351	36	703	932	.262	.960	5.22
					6147	6147	.271	.970	4.38

BATTING AVERAGE
Joe DiMaggio NY .... .352
Luke Appling CHI .... .348
Ted Williams BOS ...... .344

HITS
Rip Radcliff STL 200
Doc Cramer BOS 200
B. McCoskey DET 200

DOUBLES
Hank Greenberg DET ... 50
Lou Boudreau CLE 46
Rudy York DET 46

TRIPLES
B. McCoskey DET 19
Lou Finney BOS 15
Charlie Keller NY 15

HOME RUNS
Hank Greenberg DET ... 41
Jimmie Foxx BOS 36
Rudy York DET 33

RUNS BATTED IN
H. Greenberg DET 150
Rudy York DET 134
Joe DiMaggio NY 133

SLUGGING AVERAGE
H. Greenberg DET ..... .670
Joe DiMaggio NY .... .626
Ted Williams BOS ...... .594

STOLEN BASES
George Case WAS 35
Gee Walker WAS 21
Joe Gordon NY 18

RUNS SCORED
Ted Williams BOS 134
H. Greenberg DET 129
B. McCosky DET 123

WINS
Bob Feller CLE 27
Bobo Newsom DET 21
Al Milnar CLE 18

WINNING PERCENTAGE
S. Rowe DET .... .842
Bobo Newsom DET ... .808
Bob Feller CLE .... .711

EARNED RUN AVERAGE
Ernie Bonham NY 1.90
Bob Feller CLE 2.61
Bobo Newsom DET ... 2.83

STRIKEOUTS
Bob Feller CLE 261
Bobo Newsom DET 164
Johnny Rigney CHI 141

SAVES
Al Benton DET 17
Clint Brown CHI 10
Johnny Murphy NY 9

COMPLETE GAMES
Bob Feller CLE 31
Thorton Lee CHI 24
Dutch Leonard WAS 23

SHUTOUTS
Bob Feller CLE 4
Ted Lyons CHI 4
Al Milnar CLE 4

GAMES PITCHED
Bob Feller CLE 43
Al Benton DET 42
two tied at 41

INNINGS PITCHED
Bob Feller CLE 320
Dutch Leonard WAS ... 289
Johnny Rigney CHI 281

NATIONAL LEAGUE STANDINGS

1940 NL

	W	L	PCT	GB	R	OR	BA	FA	ERA
CINCINNATI	100	53	.654	—	707	528	.266	.981	3.05
BROOKLYN	88	65	.575	12	697	621	.260	.970	3.50
ST. LOUIS	84	69	.549	16	747	699	.275	.971	3.83
PITTSBURGH	78	76	.506	22.5	809	783	.276	.966	4.36
CHICAGO	75	79	.487	25.5	681	636	.267	.968	3.54
NEW YORK	72	80	.474	27.5	663	659	.267	.977	3.79
BOSTON	65	87	.428	34.5	623	745	.256	.970	4.36
PHILADELPHIA	50	103	.327	50	494	750	.238	.970	4.40
					5421	5421	.264	.972	3.85

BATTING AVERAGE
Debs Garms PIT .... .355
Ernie Lombardi CIN ... .319
J. Cooney BOS .... .318

HITS
F. McCormick CIN 191
Stan Hack CHI 191
Johnny Mize STL 182

DOUBLES
F. McCormick CIN 44
Arky Vaughan PIT 40
Jim Gleeson CHI 39

TRIPLES
Arky Vaughan PIT 15
Chet Ross BOS 14
two tied at 13

HOME RUNS
Johnny Mize STL 43
Bill Nicholson CHI 25
Rizzo PIT, CIN, PHI 24

RUNS BATTED IN
Johnny Mize STL 137
F. McCormick CIN 127
M. Van Robays PIT 116

SLUGGING AVERAGE
Johnny Mize STL .... .636
Bill Nicholson CHI ...... .534
Dolf Camilli BKN .... .529

STOLEN BASES
Lonny Frey CIN 22
Stan Hack CHI 21
Terry Moore STL 18

RUNS SCORED
Arky Vaughan PIT 113
Johnny Mize STL 111
Bill Werber CIN 105

WINS
Bucky Walters CIN 22
Paul Derringer CIN 20
Claude Passeau CHI 20

WINNING PERCENTAGE
Fitzsimmons BKN ...... .889
Rip Sewell PIT .... .762
Bucky Walters CIN ..... .688

EARNED RUN AVERAGE
Bucky Walters CIN 2.48
C. Passeau CHI 2.50
Rip Sewell PIT 2.80

STRIKEOUTS
Kirby Higbe PHI 137
Whit Wyatt BKN 124
C. Passeau CHI 124

SAVES
Jumbo Brown NY 7
Joe Beggs CIN 7
Mace Brown PIT 7

COMPLETE GAMES
Bucky Walters CIN 29
Paul Derringer CIN 26
Hugh Mulcahy PHI 21

SHUTOUTS
Manny Salvo BOS 5
Bill Lohrman NY 5
Whit Wyatt BKN 5

GAMES PITCHED
Clyde Shoun STL 54
Mace Brown PIT 48
Claude Passeau CHI 46

INNINGS PITCHED
Bucky Walters CIN 305
Paul Derringer CIN 297
Kirby Higbe PHI 283

AMERICAN LEAGUE STANDINGS

1941 AL

	W	L	PCT	GB	R	OR	BA	FA	ERA
NEW YORK	101	53	.656	—	830	631	.269	.973	3.53
BOSTON	84	70	.545	17	865	750	.283	.972	4.19
CHICAGO	77	77	.500	24	638	649	.255	.971	3.52
CLEVELAND	75	79	.487	26	677	668	.256	.976	3.90
DETROIT	75	79	.487	26	686	743	.263	.969	4.18
ST. LOUIS	70	84	.455	31	765	823	.266	.975	4.72
WASHINGTON	70	84	.455	31	728	798	.272	.969	4.35
PHILADELPHIA	64	90	.416	37	713	840	.268	.967	4.83
					5902	5902	.266	.972	4.15

BATTING AVERAGE
Ted Williams BOS ...... .406
Cecil Travis WAS ...... .359
Joe DiMaggio NY ...... .357

HITS
Cecil Travis WAS 218
Jeff Heath CLE 199
Joe DiMaggio NY 193

DOUBLES
Lou Boudreau CLE 45
Joe DiMaggio NY 43
Walt Judnich STL 40

TRIPLES
Jeff Heath CLE 20
Cecil Travis WAS 19
Ken Keltner CLE 13

HOME RUNS
Ted Williams BOS 37
Charlie Keller NY 33
Tommy Henrich NY 31

RUNS BATTED IN
Joe DiMaggio NY 125
Jeff Heath CLE 123
Charlie Keller NY 122

SLUGGING AVERAGE
Ted Williams BOS ...... .735
Joe DiMaggio NY .... .643
Jeff Heath CLE .... .586

STOLEN BASES
George Case WAS 33
Joe Kuhel CHI 20
Jeff Heath CLE 18

RUNS SCORED
Ted Williams BOS 135
Joe DiMaggio NY 122
Dom DiMaggio NY 117

WINS
Bob Feller CLE 25
Thorton Lee CHI 22
Dick Newsome BOS 19

WINNING PERCENTAGE
Lefty Gomez NY .... .750
Al Benton DET .... .714
Red Ruffing NY .... .714

EARNED RUN AVERAGE
Thorton Lee CHI 2.37
C. Wagner BOS 3.07
Marius Russo NY 3.09

STRIKEOUTS
Bob Feller CLE 260
Bobo Newsom DET 175
Thorton Lee CHI 130

SAVES
Johnny Murphy NY 15
Tom Ferrick PHI 7
Al Benton DET 7

COMPLETE GAMES
Thorton Lee CHI 30
Bob Feller CLE 28
Eddie Smith CHI 21

SHUTOUTS
Bob Feller CLE 6
three tied at 4

GAMES PITCHED
Bob Feller CLE 44
Bobo Newsom DET 43
Clint Brown CLE 41

INNINGS PITCHED
Bob Feller CLE 343
Thorton Lee CHI 300
Eddie Smith CHI 263

NATIONAL LEAGUE STANDINGS

1941 NL

	W	L	PCT	GB	R	OR	BA	FA	ERA
BROOKLYN	100	54	.649	—	800	581	.272	.974	3.14
ST. LOUIS	97	56	.634	2.5	734	589	.272	.973	3.19
CINCINNATI	88	66	.571	12	616	564	.247	.975	3.17
PITTSBURGH	81	73	.526	19	690	643	.268	.968	3.48
NEW YORK	74	79	.484	25.5	667	706	.260	.974	3.94
CHICAGO	70	84	.455	30	666	670	.253	.970	3.72
BOSTON	62	92	.403	38	592	720	.251	.969	3.95
PHILADELPHIA	43	111	.279	57	501	793	.244	.969	4.50
					5266	5266	.258	.972	3.63

BATTING AVERAGE
Pete Reiser BKN........ .343
J. Cooney BOS.......... .319
Joe Medwick BKN...... .318

HITS
Stan Hack CHI............ 186
Pete Reiser BKN......... 184
Danny Litwhiler PHI.... 180

DOUBLES
Pete Reiser BKN........... 39
Johnny Mize STL.......... 39
Johnny Rucker NY........ 38

TRIPLES
Pete Reiser BKN........... 17
Elbie Fletcher PIT......... 13
Johnny Hopp STL......... 11

HOME RUNS
Dolf Camilli BKN........... 34
Mel Ott NY................... 27
Bill Nicholson CHI......... 26

RUNS BATTED IN
Dolf Camilli BKN......... 120
Bobby Young NY........ 104
two tied at.................. 100

SLUGGING AVERAGE
Pete Reiser BKN........ .558
Dolf Camilli BKN .... .556
Johnny Mize STL........ .535

STOLEN BASES
Danny Murtaugh PHI.... 18
Stan Benjamin PHI....... 17
two tied at..................... 16

RUNS SCORED
Pete Reiser BKN......... 117
Stan Hack CHI............ 111
Joe Medwick BKN....... 100

WINS
Kirby Higbe BKN........... 22
Whit Wyatt BKN............ 22
two tied at..................... 19

WINNING PERCENTAGE
Elmer Riddle CIN........ .826
Kirby Higbe BKN........ .710
Ernie White STL......... .708

EARNED RUN AVERAGE
Elmer Riddle CIN........ 2.24
Whit Wyatt BKN 2.34
Ernie White STL......... 2.40

STRIKEOUTS
J. Vander Meer CIN.... 202
Whit Wyatt BKN.......... 176
Bucky Walters CIN...... 129

SAVES
Jumbo Brown NY............ 8
Hugh Casey BKN............ 7
Bill Crouch PHI, STL....... 7

COMPLETE GAMES
Bucky Walters CIN........ 27
Whit Wyatt BKN............ 23
two tied at..................... 20

SHUTOUTS
Whit Wyatt BKN.............. 7
J. Vander Meer CIN........ 6
two tied at....................... 5

GAMES PITCHED
Kirby Higbe BKN........... 48
Ike Pearson PHI............ 46
Hugh Casey BKN.......... 45

INNINGS PITCHED
Bucky Walters CIN...... 302
Kirby Higbe BKN......... 298
Whit Wyatt BKN.......... 288

AMERICAN LEAGUE STANDINGS

1942 AL

	W	L	PCT	GB	R	OR	BA	FA	ERA
NEW YORK	103	51	.669	—	801	507	.269	.976	2.91
BOSTON	93	59	.612	9	761	594	.276	.974	3.44
ST. LOUIS	82	69	.543	19.5	730	637	.259	.972	3.59
CLEVELAND	75	79	.487	28	590	659	.253	.974	3.59
DETROIT	73	81	.474	30	589	587	.246	.969	3.13
CHICAGO	66	82	.446	34	538	609	.246	.970	3.58
WASHINGTON	62	89	.411	39.5	653	817	.258	.962	4.58
PHILADELPHIA	55	99	.357	48	549	801	.249	.969	4.48
					5211	5211	.257	.971	3.66

BATTING AVERAGE
Ted Williams BOS....... .356
Johnny Pesky BOS..... .331
Stan Spence WAS...... .323

HITS
Johnny Pesky BOS..... 205
Stan Spence WAS...... 203
two tied at 186

DOUBLES
Don Kolloway CHI......... 40
Harlond Clift STL 39
Jeff Heath CLE 37

TRIPLES
Stan Spence WAS......... 15
Jeff Heath CLE 13
Joe DiMaggio NY........... 13

HOME RUNS
Ted Williams BOS.......... 36
Chet Laabs STL............. 27
Charlie Keller NY 26

RUNS BATTED IN
Ted Williams BOS......... 137
Joe DiMaggio NY......... 114
Charlie Keller NY 108

SLUGGING AVERAGE
Ted Williams BOS....... .648
Charlie Keller NY .... .513
Walt Judnich STL........ .499

STOLEN BASES
George Case WAS 44
Mickey Vernon WAS..... 25
two tied at 22

RUNS SCORED
Ted Williams BOS........ 141
Joe DiMaggio NY......... 123
Dom DiMaggio BOS ... 110

WINS
Tex Hughson BOS......... 22
Ernie Bonham NY......... 21
two tied at 17

WINNING PERCENTAGE
Ernie Bonham NY ...... .808
Hank Borowy NY .... .789
Tex Hughson BOS..... .786

EARNED RUN AVERAGE
Ted Lyons CHI........... 2.10
Ernie Bonham NY...... 2.27
Spud Chandler NY..... 2.38

STRIKEOUTS
Bobo Newsom WAS ... 113
Tex Hughson BOS...... 113
two tied at 110

SAVES
Johnny Murphy NY 11
Mace Brown BOS 6
Joe Haynes CHI.............. 6

COMPLETE GAMES
Ernie Bonham NY......... 22
Tex Hughson BOS......... 22
Ted Lyons CHI............... 20

SHUTOUTS
Ernie Bonham NY 6

GAMES PITCHED
Joe Haynes CHI............. 40
George Castor STL....... 39
two tied at 38

INNINGS PITCHED
Tex Hughson BOS...... 281
Jim Bagby CLE 271
Eldon Auker STL......... 249

NATIONAL LEAGUE STANDINGS

1942 NL

	W	L	PCT	GB	R	OR	BA	FA	ERA
ST. LOUIS	106	48	.688	—	755	482	.268	.972	2.55
BROOKLYN	104	50	.675	2	742	510	.265	.977	2.84
NEW YORK	85	67	.559	20	675	600	.254	.977	3.31
CINCINNATI	76	76	.500	29	527	545	.231	.971	2.82
PITTSBURGH	66	81	.449	36.5	585	631	.245	.969	3.58
CHICAGO	68	86	.442	38	591	665	.254	.973	3.60
BOSTON	59	89	.399	44	515	645	.240	.976	3.76
PHILADELPHIA	42	109	.278	62.5	394	706	.232	.968	4.12
					4784	4784	.249	.973	3.31

BATTING AVERAGE
Ernie Lombardi BOS .330
Enos Slaughter STL .318
Stan Musial STL .315

HITS
Enos Slaughter STL 188
Bill Nicholson CHI 173
two tied at 166

DOUBLES
Marty Marion STL 38
Joe Medwick BKN 37
Stan Hack CHI 36

TRIPLES
Enos Slaughter STL 17
Bill Nicholson CHI 11
Stan Musial STL 10

HOME RUNS
Mel Ott NY 30
Johnny Mize NY 26
Dolf Camilli BKN 26

RUNS BATTED IN
Johnny Mize NY 110
Dolf Camilli BKN 109
Enos Slaughter STL 98

SLUGGING AVERAGE
Johnny Mize NY .521
Mel Ott NY .497
Enos Slaughter STL .494

STOLEN BASES
Pete Reiser BKN 20
N. Fernandez BOS 15
Pee Wee Reese BKN 15

RUNS SCORED
Mel Ott NY 118
Enos Slaughter STL 100
Johnny Mize NY 97

WINS
Mort Cooper STL 22
Johnny Beazley STL 21
two tied at 19

WINNING PERCENTAGE
Larry French BKN .789
J. Beazley STL .778
Mort Cooper STL .759

EARNED RUN AVERAGE
Mort Cooper STL 1.78
J. Beazley STL 2.13
Curt Davis BKN 2.36

STRIKEOUTS
J. Vander Meer CIN 186
Mort Cooper STL 152
Kirby Higbe BKN 115

SAVES
Hugh Casey BKN 13
Ace Adams NY 11
Joe Beggs CIN 8

COMPLETE GAMES
Jim Tobin BOS 28
Claude Passeau CHI 24
Mort Cooper STL 22

SHUTOUTS
Mort Cooper STL 10
three tied at 5

GAMES PITCHED
Ace Adams NY 61
Hugh Casey BKN 50
two tied at 43

INNINGS PITCHED
Jim Tobin BOS 228
Mort Cooper STL 279
C. Passeau CHI 278

AMERICAN LEAGUE STANDINGS

1943 AL

	W	L	PCT	GB	R	OR	BA	FA	ERA
NEW YORK	98	56	.636	—	669	542	.256	.974	2.93
WASHINGTON	84	69	.549	13.5	666	595	.254	.971	3.18
CLEVELAND	82	71	.536	15.5	600	577	.255	.975	3.15
CHICAGO	82	72	.532	16	573	594	.247	.973	3.20
DETROIT	78	76	.506	20	632	560	.261	.971	3.00
ST. LOUIS	72	80	.474	25	596	604	.245	.975	3.41
BOSTON	68	84	.447	29	563	607	.244	.976	3.45
PHILADELPHIA	49	105	.318	49	497	717	.232	.973	4.05
					4796	4796	.249	.973	3.30

BATTING AVERAGE
Luke Appling CHI .... .328
Dick Wakefield DET ... .316
Ron Hodgin CHI .... .314

HITS
Dick Wakefield DET 200
Luke Appling CHI 192
Doc Cramer DET 182

DOUBLES
Dick Wakefield DET 38
George Case WAS 36
two tied at 35

TRIPLES
Johnny Lindell NY 12
Wally Moses CHI 12
two tied at 11

HOME RUNS
Rudy York DET 34
Charlie Keller NY 31
Vern Stephens STL 22

RUNS BATTED IN
Rudy York DET 118
Nick Etten NY 107
Billy Johnson NY 94

SLUGGING AVERAGE
Rudy York DET .... .527
Charlie Keller NY .... .525
Vern Stephens STL ... .482

STOLEN BASES
George Case WAS 61
Wally Moses CHI 56
Thurman Tucker CHI 29

RUNS SCORED
George Case WAS 102
Charlie Keller NY 97
Dick Wakefield DET 91

WINS
Spud Chandler NY 20
Dizzy Trout DET 20
Early Wynn WAS 18

WINNING PERCENTAGE
Spud Chandler NY ...... .833
Al Smith CLE .... .708
Ernie Bonham NY ...... .652

EARNED RUN AVERAGE
Spud Chandler NY 1.64
Ernie Bonham NY 2.27
T. Bridges DET 2.39

STRIKEOUTS
Allie Reynolds CLE 151
Hal Newhouser DET ... 144
Spud Chandler NY 134

SAVES
G. Maltzberger CHI 14
Mace Brown BOS 9
Joe Heving CLE 9

COMPLETE GAMES
Spud Chandler NY 20
Tex Hughson BOS 20
three tied at 18

SHUTOUTS
Spud Chandler NY 5
Dizzy Trout DET 5
two tied at 4

GAMES PITCHED
Mace Brown BOS 49
Dizzy Trout DET 44
Roger Wolff PHI 41

INNINGS PITCHED
Jim Bagby CLE 273
Tex Hughson BOS 266
Early Wynn WAS 257

NATIONAL LEAGUE STANDINGS

1943 NL

	W	L	PCT	GB	R	OR	BA	FA	ERA
ST. LOUIS	105	49	.682	—	679	475	.279	.976	2.57
CINCINNATI	87	67	.565	18	608	543	.256	.980	3.13
BROOKLYN	81	72	.529	23.5	716	674	.272	.972	3.88
PITTSBURGH	80	74	.519	25	669	605	.262	.973	3.06
CHICAGO	74	79	.484	30.5	632	600	.261	.973	3.24
BOSTON	68	85	.444	36.5	465	612	.233	.972	3.25
PHILADELPHIA	64	90	.416	41	571	676	.249	.969	3.79
NEW YORK	55	98	.359	49.5	558	713	.247	.973	4.08
					4898	4898	.258	.974	3.37

BATTING AVERAGE
Stan Musial STL .... .357
Billy Herman BKN ...... .330
Walker Cooper STL ... .318

HITS
Stan Musial STL 220
Mickey Witek NY 195
Billy Herman BKN 193

DOUBLES
Stan Musial STL 48
Vince DiMaggio PIT 41
Billy Herman BKN 41

TRIPLES
Stan Musial STL 20
Lou Klein STL 14
two tied at 12

HOME RUNS
Bill Nicholson CHI 29
Mel Ott NY 18
Ron Northey PHI........... 16

RUNS BATTED IN
Bill Nicholson CHI 128
Bob Elliott PIT 101
Billy Herman BKN 100

SLUGGING AVERAGE
Stan Musial STL .... .562
Bill Nicholson CHI ...... .531
Walker Cooper STL ... .463

STOLEN BASES
Arky Vaughan BKN 20
Peanuts Lowrey CHI..... 13
three tied at.................. 12

RUNS SCORED
Arky Vaughan BKN 112
Stan Musial STL 108
Bill Nicholson CHI 95

WINS
Elmer Riddle CIN 21
Mort Cooper STL 21
Rip Sewell PIT 21

WINNING PERCENTAGE
Mort Cooper STL .... .724
Rip Sewell PIT .... .700
Max Lanier STL .... .682

EARNED RUN AVERAGE
Howie Pollet STL 1.75
Max Lanier STL 1.90
Mort Cooper STL 2.30

STRIKEOUTS
J. Vander Meer CIN 174
Mort Cooper STL 141
Al Javery BOS 134

SAVES
Les Webber BKN 10
Ace Adams NY 9
Clyde Shoun CIN 7

COMPLETE GAMES
Rip Sewell PIT 25
Jim Tobin BOS.............. 24
Mort Cooper STL 24

SHUTOUTS
Hi Bithorn CHI................. 7
Mort Cooper STL 6
two tied at 5

GAMES PITCHED
Ace Adams NY 70
Les Webber BKN 54
Ed Head BKN 47

INNINGS PITCHED
Al Javery BOS 303
J. Vander Meer CIN 289
Nate Andrews BOS..... 284

AMERICAN LEAGUE STANDINGS

1944 AL

	W	L	PCT	GB	R	OR	BA	FA	ERA
ST. LOUIS	89	65	.578	—	684	587	.252	.972	3.17
DETROIT	88	66	.571	1	658	581	.263	.970	3.09
NEW YORK	83	71	.539	6	674	617	.264	.974	3.39
BOSTON	77	77	.500	12	739	676	.270	.972	3.82
CLEVELAND	72	82	.468	17	643	677	.266	.974	3.65
PHILADELPHIA	72	82	.468	17	525	594	.257	.971	3.26
CHICAGO	71	83	.461	18	543	662	.247	.970	3.58
WASHINGTON	64	90	.416	25	592	664	.261	.964	3.49
					5058	5058	.260	.971	3.43

BATTING AVERAGE
Lou Boudreau CLE .... .327
Bobby Doerr BOS ...... .325
Bob Johnson BOS ..... .324

HITS
S. Stirnweiss NY 205
Lou Boudreau CLE 191
Stan Spence WAS 187

DOUBLES
Lou Boudreau CLE 45
Ken Keltner CLE 41
Bob Johnson BOS 40

TRIPLES
Johnny Lindell NY 16
Snuffy Stirnweiss NY 16
Don Gutteridge STL 11

HOME RUNS
Nick Etten NY 22
Vern Stephens STL 20
three tied at 18

RUNS BATTED IN
Vern Stephens STL 109
Bob Johnson BOS 106
Johnny Lindell NY 103

SLUGGING AVERAGE
Bobby Doerr BOS ...... .528
Bob Johnson BOS ..... .528
Johnny Lindell NY ...... .500

STOLEN BASES
Snuffy Stirnweiss NY 55
George Case WAS 49
Glenn Myatt WAS 26

RUNS SCORED
S. Stirnweiss NY 125
Bob Johnson BOS 106
Roy Cullenbine CLE 98

WINS
Hal Newhouser DET 29
Dizzy Trout DET 27
Nels Potter STL 19

WINNING PERCENTAGE
Tex Hughson BOS ..... .783
H. Newhouser DET ..... .763
Nels Potter STL .... .731

EARNED RUN AVERAGE
Dizzy Trout DET 2.12
H. Newhouser DET 2.22
Tex Hughson BOS..... 2.26

STRIKEOUTS
Hal Newhouser DET ... 187
Dizzy Trout DET 144
Bobo Newsom PHI 142

SAVES
Joe Berry PHI 12
G. Maltzberger CHI....... 12
George Caster STL....... 12

COMPLETE GAMES
Dizzy Trout DET 33
Hal Newhouser DET 25
four tied at..................... 19

SHUTOUTS
Dizzy Trout DET 7
Hal Newhouser DET 6
two tied at 4

GAMES PITCHED
Joe Heving CLE............. 63
Joe Berry PHI 53
Dizzy Trout DET 49

INNINGS PITCHED
Dizzy Trout DET 352
Hal Newhouser DET ... 312
Bobo Newsom PHI 265

NATIONAL LEAGUE STANDINGS

1944 NL

	W	L	PCT	GB	R	OR	BA	FA	ERA
ST. LOUIS	105	49	.682	—	772	490	.275	.982	2.67
PITTSBURGH	90	63	.588	14.5	744	662	.265	.970	3.44
CINCINNATI	89	65	.578	16	573	537	.254	.978	2.97
CHICAGO	75	79	.487	30	702	669	.261	.970	3.59
NEW YORK	67	87	.435	38	682	773	.263	.971	4.29
BOSTON	65	89	.422	40	593	674	.246	.971	3.67
BROOKLYN	63	91	.409	42	690	832	.269	.966	4.68
PHILADELPHIA	61	92	.399	43.5	539	658	.251	.972	3.64
					5295	5295	.261	.972	3.61

BATTING AVERAGE
Dixie Walker BKN ...... .357
Stan Musial STL .... .347
Joe Medwick NY .... .337

HITS
Phil Cavarretta CHI 197
Stan Musial STL 197
T. Holmes BOS 195

DOUBLES
Stan Musial STL 51
Augie Galan BKN 43
T. Holmes BOS 42

TRIPLES
Johnny Barrett PIT 19
Bob Elliott PIT 16
Phil Cavarretta CHI 15

HOME RUNS
Bill Nicholson CHI 33
Mel Ott NY 26
Ron Northey PHI 22

RUNS BATTED IN
Bill Nicholson CHI 122
Bob Elliott PIT 108
Ron Northey PHI 104

SLUGGING AVERAGE
Stan Musial STL .... .549
Bill Nicholson CHI ...... .545
Mel Ott NY .... .544

STOLEN BASES
Johnny Barrett PIT 28
Tony Lupien PHI 18
Roy Hughes CHI 16

RUNS SCORED
Bill Nicholson CHI 116
Stan Musial STL 112
Jim Russell PIT 109

WINS
Bucky Walters CIN 23
Mort Cooper STL 22
two tied at 21

WINNING PERCENTAGE
Ted Wilks STL .... .810
H. Brecheen STL .... .762
Mort Cooper STL .... .759

EARNED RUN AVERAGE
Ed Heusser CIN 2.38
Bucky Walters CIN 2.40
Mort Cooper STL 2.46

STRIKEOUTS
Bill Voiselle NY 161
Max Lanier STL 141
Al Javery BOS 137

SAVES
Ace Adams NY 13
Xavier Rescigno PIT 5
Freddie Schmidt STL 5

COMPLETE GAMES
Jim Tobin BOS 28
Bucky Walters CIN 27
Bill Voiselle NY 25

SHUTOUTS
Mort Cooper STL 7
Bucky Walters CIN 6
two tied at 5

GAMES PITCHED
Ace Adams NY 65
Les Webber BKN 48
Xavier Rescigno PIT 48

INNINGS PITCHED
Bill Voiselle NY 313
Jim Tobin BOS 299
Rip Sewell PIT 286

AMERICAN LEAGUE STANDINGS

1945 AL

	W	L	PCT	GB	R	OR	BA	FA	ERA
DETROIT	88	65	.575	—	633	565	.256	.975	2.99
WASHINGTON	87	67	.565	1.5	622	562	.258	.970	2.92
ST. LOUIS	81	70	.536	6	597	548	.249	.976	3.14
NEW YORK	81	71	.533	6.5	676	606	.259	.971	3.45
CLEVELAND	73	72	.503	11	557	548	.255	.977	3.31
CHICAGO	71	78	.477	15	596	633	.262	.970	3.69
BOSTON	71	83	.461	17.5	599	674	.260	.973	3.80
PHILADELPHIA	52	98	.347	34.5	494	638	.245	.973	3.62
					4774	4774	.255	.973	3.36

BATTING AVERAGE
S. Stirnweiss NY .... .309
T. Cuccinello CHI .... .308
J. Dickshot CHI .... .302

HITS
S. Stirnweiss NY 195
Wally Moses CHI 168
Vern Stephens STL 165

DOUBLES
Wally Moses CHI 35
Snufy Stirnweiss NY 32
George Binks WAS....... 32

TRIPLES
Snuffy Stirnweiss NY 22
Wally Moses CHI 15
Joe Kuhel WAS............. 13

HOME RUNS
Vern Stephens STL 24
three tied at................... 18

RUNS BATTED IN
Nick Etten NY 111
Cullenbine CLE, DET... 93
Vern Stephens STL 89

SLUGGING AVERAGE
S. Stirnweiss NY .... .476
Vern Stephens STL ... .473
Cullenbine CLE, DET. .444

STOLEN BASES
Snuffy. Stirnweiss NY ... 33
George Case WAS 30
Glenn Myatt WAS 30

RUNS SCORED
S. Stirnweiss NY 107
Vern Stephens STL 90
Cullenbine CLE, DET.... 83

WINS
Hal Newhouser DET 25
Boo Ferriss BOS........... 21
Roger Wolff WAS.......... 20

WINNING PERCENTAGE
H. Newhouser DET.... .735
D. Leonard WAS......... .708
Steve Gromek CLE..... .679

EARNED RUN AVERAGE
H. Newhouser DET.... 1.81
Al Benton DET 2.02
Roger Wolff WAS....... 2.12

STRIKEOUTS
Hal Newhouser DET ... 212
Nels Potter STL 129
Bobo Newsom PHI 127

SAVES
Jim Turner NY............... 10
Joe Berry PHI 5

COMPLETE GAMES
Hal Newhouser DET..... 29
Boo Ferriss BOS........... 26
three tied at................... 21

SHUTOUTS
Hal Newhouser DET 8
Boo Ferriss BOS............. 5
Al Benton DET 5

GAMES PITCHED
Joe Berry PHI 52
Allie Reynolds CLE....... 44
Marino Pieretti WAS 44

INNINGS PITCHED
Hal Newhouser DET ... 313
Boo Ferriss BOS......... 265
Bobo Newsom PHI 257

NATIONAL LEAGUE STANDINGS

1945 NL

	W	L	PCT	GB	R	OR	BA	FA	ERA
CHICAGO	98	56	.636	—	735	532	.277	.980	2.98
ST. LOUIS	95	59	.617	3	756	583	.273	.977	3.24
BROOKLYN	87	67	.565	11	795	724	.271	.962	3.70
PITTSBURGH	82	72	.532	16	753	686	.267	.971	3.76
NEW YORK	78	74	.513	19	668	700	.269	.973	4.06
BOSTON	67	85	.441	30	721	728	.267	.969	4.04
CINCINNATI	61	93	.396	37	536	694	.249	.976	4.00
PHILADELPHIA	46	108	.299	52	548	865	.246	.962	4.64
					5512	5512	.265	.971	3.80

BATTING AVERAGE
Phil Cavarretta CHI .... .355
T. Holmes BOS .... .352
Goody Rosen BKN ..... .325

HITS
T. Holmes BOS 224
Goody Rosen BKN 197
Stan Hack CHI 193

DOUBLES
Tommy Holmes BOS 47
Dixie Walker BKN 42
two tied at 36

TRIPLES
Luis Olmo BKN 13
Andy Pafko CHI 12
two tied at 11

HOME RUNS
Tommy Holmes BOS 28
Chuck Workman BOS... 25
B. Adams PHI, STL 22

RUNS BATTED IN
Dixie Walker BKN 124
T. Holmes BOS 117
two tied at 110

SLUGGING AVERAGE
T. Holmes BOS .... .577
W. Kurowski STL .... .511
Phil Cavarretta CHI .... .500

STOLEN BASES
R. Schoendienst STL.... 26
Johnny Barrett PIT 25
Dain Clay CIN 19

RUNS SCORED
Eddie Stanky BKN 128
Goody Rosen BKN 126
T. Holmes BOS 125

WINS
R. Barrett BOS, STL 23
Hank Wyse CHI 22
Ken Burkhart STL 19

WINNING PERCENTAGE
Ken Burkhart STL .... .704
Hank Wyse CHI .... .688
Barrett BOS, STL .... .657

EARNED RUN AVERAGE
Hank Borowy CHI.... 2.13
C. Passeau CHI 2.46
H. Brecheen STL 2.52

STRIKEOUTS
Preacher Roe PIT 148
Hal Gregg BKN 139
Bill Voiselle NY 115

SAVES
Ace Adams NY 15
Andy Karl PHI 15
Xavier Rescigno PIT 9

COMPLETE GAMES
R. Barrett BOS, STL 24
Hank Wyse CHI 23
Claude Passeau CHI 19

SHUTOUTS
Claude Passeau CHI 5
three tied at...................... 4

GAMES PITCHED
Andy Karl PHI 67
Ace Adams NY 65
J. Hutchings BOS 57

INNINGS PITCHED
R. Barrett BOS, STL ... 285
Hank Wyse CHI 278
Hal Gregg BKN 254

AMERICAN LEAGUE STANDINGS

1946 AL

	W	L	PCT	GB	R	OR	BA	FA	ERA
BOSTON	104	50	.675	—	792	594	.271	.977	3.38
DETROIT	92	62	.597	12	704	567	.258	.974	3.22
NEW YORK	87	67	.565	17	684	547	.248	.975	3.13
WASHINGTON	76	78	.494	28	608	706	.260	.966	3.74
CHICAGO	74	80	.481	30	562	595	.257	.972	3.10
CLEVELAND	68	86	.442	36	537	637	.245	.975	3.62
ST. LOUIS	66	88	.429	38	621	711	.251	.974	3.95
PHILADELPHIA	49	105	.318	55	529	680	.253	.971	3.90
					5037	5037	.256	.973	3.50

BATTING AVERAGE
M. Vernon WAS .... .353
Ted Williams BOS .... .342
Johnny Pesky BOS ..... .335

HITS
Johnny Pesky BOS 208
Mickey Vernon WAS ... 207
Luke Appling CHI 180

DOUBLES
Mickey Vernon WAS 51
Stan Spence WAS 50
Johnny Pesky BOS 43

TRIPLES
Hank Edwards CLE 16
Buddy Lewis WAS 13
two tied at 10

HOME RUNS
Hank Greenberg DET ... 44
Ted Williams BOS 38
Charlie Keller NY 30

RUNS BATTED IN
H. Greenberg DET 127
Ted Williams BOS 123
Rudy York BOS 119

SLUGGING AVERAGE
Ted Williams BOS .... .667
H. Greenberg DET ..... .604
Charlie Keller NY .... .533

STOLEN BASES
George Case CLE 28
Snuffy Stirnweiss NY 18
Eddie Lake DET 15

RUNS SCORED
Ted Williams BOS 142
Johnny Pesky BOS 115
Eddie Lake DET 105

WINS
Hal Newhouser DET 26
Bob Feller CLE 26
Boo Ferriss BOS 25

WINNING PERCENTAGE
Boo Ferriss BOS .... .806
H. Newhouser DET .... .743
Spud Chandler NY .... .714

EARNED RUN AVERAGE
H. Newhouser DET ... 1.94
Spud Chandler NY 2.10
Bob Feller CLE 2.18

STRIKEOUTS
Bob Feller CLE 348
Hal Newhouser DET ... 275
Tex Hughson BOS 172

SAVES
Bob Klinger BOS 9
Earl Caldwell CHI 8
Johnny Murphy NY 7

COMPLETE GAMES
Bob Feller CLE 36
Hal Newhouser DET 29
Boo Ferris BOS 26

SHUTOUTS
Bob Feller CLE 10
three tied at 6

GAMES PITCHED
Bob Feller CLE 48
Boo Ferriss BOS 40
Bob Savage PHI 40

INNINGS PITCHED
Bob Feller CLE 371
Hal Newhouser DET ... 292
Tex Hughson BOS 278

NATIONAL LEAGUE STANDINGS

1946 NL

	W	L	PCT	GB	R	OR	BA	FA	ERA
ST. LOUIS*	98	58	.628	—	712	545	.265	.980	3.01
BROOKLYN	96	60	.615	2	701	570	.260	.972	3.05
CHICAGO	82	71	.536	14.5	626	581	.254	.976	3.24
BOSTON	81	72	.529	15.5	630	592	.264	.972	3.37
PHILADELPHIA	69	85	.448	28	560	705	.258	.975	3.99
CINCINNATI	67	87	.435	30	523	570	.239	.975	3.07
PITTSBURGH	63	91	.409	34	552	668	.250	.970	3.72
NEW YORK	61	93	.396	36	612	685	.255	.973	3.92
					4916	4916	.256	.974	3.42

*Defeated Brooklyn in a playoff 2 games to 0.

BATTING AVERAGE
Stan Musial STL .... .365
Johnny Hopp BOS ..... .333
Dixie Walker BKN ...... .319

HITS
Stan Musial STL 228
Dixie Walker BKN 184
Enos Slaughter STL.... 183

DOUBLES
Stan Musial STL 50
Tommy Holmes BOS 35
Whitey Kurowski STL.... 32

TRIPLES
Stan Musial STL 20
Phil Cavarretta CHI....... 10
Pee Wee Reese BKN ... 10

HOME RUNS
Ralph Kiner PIT 23
Johnny Mize NY............ 22
Enos Slaughter STL...... 18

RUNS BATTED IN
Enos Slaughter STL.... 130
Dixie Walker BKN 116
Stan Musial STL 103

SLUGGING AVERAGE
Stan Musial STL .... .587
Del Ennis PHI .... .485
Enos Slaughter STL. . .465

STOLEN BASES
Pete Reiser BKN............ 34
Bert Haas CIN................ 22
Johnny Hopp BOS 21

RUNS SCORED
Stan Musial STL 124
Enos Slaughter STL.... 100
Eddie Stanky BKN 98

WINS
Howie Pollet STL 21
Johnny Sain BOS 20
Kirby Higbe BKN............ 17

WINNING PERCENTAGE
Murry Dickson STL .... .714
Kirby Higbe BKN......... .680
Howie Pollet STL .... .677

EARNED RUN AVERAGE
Howie Pollet STL 2.10
Johnny Sain BOS 2.21
Joe Beggs CIN............ 2.32

STRIKEOUTS
Johnny Schmitz CHI ... 135
Kirby Higbe BKN......... 134
Johnny Sain BOS 129

SAVES
Ken Raffensberger PHI... 6
four tied at........................ 5

COMPLETE GAMES
Johnny Sain BOS 24
Howie Pollet STL 22
Dave Koslo NY 17

SHUTOUTS
Ewell Blackwell CIN........ 6
Harry Brecheen STL 5
J. Vander Meer CIN 5

GAMES PITCHED
Ken Trinkle NY................ 48
Murry Dickson STL 47
Hank Behrman BKN 47

INNINGS PITCHED
Howie Pollet STL 266
Dave Koslo NY 265
Johnny Sain BOS 265

AMERICAN LEAGUE STANDINGS

1947 AL

	W	L	PCT	GB	R	OR	BA	FA	ERA
NEW YORK	97	57	.630	—	794	568	.271	.981	3.39
DETROIT	85	69	.552	12	714	642	.258	.975	3.57
BOSTON	83	71	.539	14	720	669	.265	.977	3.81
CLEVELAND	80	74	.519	17	687	588	.259	.983	3.44
PHILADELPHIA	78	76	.506	19	633	614	.252	.976	3.51
CHICAGO	70	84	.455	27	553	661	.256	.975	3.64
WASHINGTON	64	90	.416	33	496	675	.241	.976	3.97
ST. LOUIS	59	95	.383	38	564	744	.241	.977	4.33
					5161	5161	.256	.977	3.71

BATTING AVERAGE
Ted Williams BOS ...... .343
B. McCosky PHI .... .328
two tied at .... .324

HITS
Johnny Pesky BOS 207
George Kell DET 188
Ted Williams BOS 181

DOUBLES
Lou Boudreau CLE 45
Ted Williams BOS 40
Tommy Henrich NY 35

TRIPLES
Tommy Henrich NY 13
Mickey Vernon WAS 12
Dave Philley CHI 11

HOME RUNS
Ted Williams BOS 32
Joe Gordon CLE 29
Jeff Heath STL 27

RUNS BATTED IN
Ted Williams BOS 114
Tommy Henrich NY 98
Joe DiMaggio NY 97

SLUGGING AVERAGE
Ted Williams BOS ...... .634
Joe DiMaggio NY .... .522
Joe Gordon CLE .... .496

STOLEN BASES
Bob Dillinger STL 34
Dave Philley CHI 21
two tied at 12

RUNS SCORED
Ted Williams BOS 125
Tommy Henrich NY 109
Johnny Pesky BOS 106

WINS
Bob Feller CLE 20
Allie Reynolds NY 19
Phil Marchildon PHI 19

WINNING PERCENTAGE
Allie Reynolds NY ...... .704
Joe Dobson BOS .... .692
Phil Marchildon PHI ... .679

EARNED RUN AVERAGE
Spud Chandler NY 2.46
Bob Feller CLE 2.68
two tied at 2.81

STRIKEOUTS
Bob Feller CLE 196
Hal Newhouser DET ... 176
W. Masterson WAS 135

SAVES
Joe Page NY 17
Eddie Klieman CLE 17
Russ Christopher PHI ... 12

COMPLETE GAMES
Hal Newhouser DET 24
Early Wynn WAS 22
Eddie Lopat CHI 22

SHUTOUTS
Bob Feller CLE 5
three tied at 4

GAMES PITCHED
Eddie Klieman CLE 58
Joe Page NY 56
Earl Johnson BOS 45

INNINGS PITCHED
Bob Feller CLE 299
Hal Newhouser DET ... 285
Phil Marchildon PHI 277

NATIONAL LEAGUE STANDINGS

1947 NL

	W	L	PCT	GB	R	OR	BA	FA	ERA
BROOKLYN	94	60	.610	—	774	668	.272	.978	3.82
ST. LOUIS	89	65	.578	5	780	634	.270	.979	3.53
BOSTON	86	68	.558	8	701	622	.275	.974	3.62
NEW YORK	81	73	.526	13	830	761	.271	.974	4.44
CINCINNATI	73	81	.474	21	681	755	.259	.977	4.41
CHICAGO	69	85	.448	25	567	722	.259	.975	4.10
PHILADELPHIA	62	92	.403	32	589	687	.258	.974	3.96
PITTSBURGH	62	92	.403	32	744	817	.261	.975	4.68
					5666	5666	.265	.976	4.07

BATTING AVERAGE
H. Walker STL, PHI ... .363
Bob Elliott BOS .... .317
Phil Cavarretta CHI .... .314

HITS
T. Holmes BOS 191
H. Walker STL, PHI ... 186
two tied at 183

DOUBLES
Eddie Miller CIN 38
Bob Elliott BOS 35
two tied at 33

TRIPLES
H. Walker STL, PHI 16
Stan Musial STL 13
Enos Slaughter STL 13

HOME RUNS
Ralph Kiner PIT 51
Johnny Mize NY 51
Willard Marshall NY 36

RUNS BATTED IN
Johnny Mize NY 138
Ralph Kiner PIT 127
Walker Cooper NY 122

SLUGGING AVERAGE
Ralph Kiner PIT .... .639
Johnny Mize NY .... .614
Walker Cooper NY ..... .586

STOLEN BASES
Jackie Robinson BKN ... 29
Pete Reiser BKN 14
two tied at 13

RUNS SCORED
Johnny Mize NY 137
J. Robinson BKN 125
Ralph Kiner PIT 118

WINS
Ewell Blackwell CIN 22
four tied at 21

WINNING PERCENTAGE
Larry Jansen NY .... .808
G. Munger STL .... .762
Ewell Blackwell CIN ... .733

EARNED RUN AVERAGE
Warren Spahn BOS ... 2.33
Ewell Blackwell CIN ... 2.47
Ralph Branca BKN 2.67

STRIKEOUTS
Ewell Blackwell CIN 193
Ralph Branca BKN 148
Johnny Sain BOS 132

SAVES
Hugh Casey BKN 18
Harry Gumbert CIN 10
Ken Trinkle NY 10

COMPLETE GAMES
Ewell Blackwell CIN 23
Johnny Sain BOS 22
Warren Spahn BOS 22

SHUTOUTS
Warren Spahn BOS 7
George Munger STL 6
Ewell Blackwell CIN 6

GAMES PITCHED
Ken Trinkle NY 62
Kirby Higbe BKN, PIT ... 50
H. Behrman PIT, BKN... 50

INNINGS PITCHED
Warren Spahn BOS 290
Ralph Branca BKN 280
Ewell Blackwell CIN 273

AMERICAN LEAGUE STANDINGS

1948 AL

	W	L	PCT	GB	R	OR	BA	FA	ERA
CLEVELAND*	97	58	.626	—	840	568	.282	.982	3.22
BOSTON	96	59	.619	1	907	720	.274	.981	4.20
NEW YORK	94	60	.610	2.5	857	633	.278	.979	3.75
PHILADELPHIA	84	70	.545	12.5	729	735	.260	.981	4.43
DETROIT	78	76	.506	18.5	700	726	.267	.974	4.15
ST. LOUIS	59	94	.386	37	671	849	.271	.972	5.01
WASHINGTON	56	97	.366	40	578	796	.244	.974	4.65
CHICAGO	51	101	.336	44.5	559	814	.251	.974	4.89
					5841	5841	.266	.977	4.28

* Defeated Boston in a 1 game playoff

BATTING AVERAGE
Ted Williams BOS ...... .369
Lou Boudreau CLE .... .355
Dale Mitchell CLE ...... .336

HITS
Bob Dillinger STL 207
Dale Mitchell CLE 204
Lou Boudreau CLE 199

DOUBLES
Ted Williams BOS 44
Tommy Henrich NY 42
Hank Majeski PHI 41

TRIPLES
Tommy Henrich NY 14
B. Stewart NY, WAS 13
two tied at 11

HOME RUNS
Joe DiMaggio NY 39
Joe Gordon CLE 32
Ken Keltner CLE 31

RUNS BATTED IN
Joe DiMaggio NY 155
Vern Stephens BOS ... 137
Ted Williams BOS 127

SLUGGING AVERAGE
Ted Williams BOS ...... .615
Joe DiMaggio NY .... .598
Tommy Henrich NY ... .554

STOLEN BASES
Bob Dillinger STL 28
Gill Coan WAS 23
Mickey Vernon WAS 15

RUNS SCORED
Tommy Henrich NY 138
Dom DiMaggio BOS ... 127
two tied at 124

WINS
Hal Newhouser DET 21
Gene Bearden CLE 20
Bob Lemon CLE 20

WINNING PERCENTAGE
Jack Kramer BOS ...... .783
Gene Bearden CLE ... .741
Vic Raschi NY .... .704

EARNED RUN AVERAGE
Gene Bearden CLE ... 2.43
Bob Lemon CLE 2.82
H. Newhouser DET 3.01

STRIKEOUTS
Bob Feller CLE 164
Bob Lemon CLE 147
Hal Newhouser DET ... 143

SAVES
R. Christopher CLE 17
Joe Page NY 16
two tied at 10

COMPLETE GAMES
Bob Lemon CLE 20
Hal Newhouser DET 19
two tied at 18

SHUTOUTS
Bob Lemon CLE 10
Gene Bearden CLE 6
Vic Raschi NY 6

GAMES PITCHED
Joe Page NY 55
Al Widmar STL 49
Frank Biscan STL 47

INNINGS PITCHED
Bob Lemon CLE 294
Bob Feller CLE 280
Hal Newhouser DET ... 272

NATIONAL LEAGUE STANDINGS

1948 NL

	W	L	PCT	GB	R	OR	BA	FA	ERA
BOSTON	91	62	.595	—	739	584	.275	.976	3.38
ST. LOUIS	85	69	.552	6.5	742	646	.263	.980	3.91
BROOKLYN	84	70	.545	7.5	744	667	.261	.973	3.75
PITTSBURGH	83	71	.539	8.5	706	699	.263	.977	4.15
NEW YORK	78	76	.506	13.5	780	704	.256	.974	3.93
PHILADELPHIA	66	88	.429	25.5	591	729	.259	.964	4.08
CINCINNATI	64	89	.418	27	588	752	.247	.973	4.47
CHICAGO	64	90	.416	27.5	597	706	.262	.972	4.00
					5487	5487	.261	.974	3.95

BATTING AVERAGE
Stan Musial STL .... .376
Richie Ashburn PHI ... .333
T. Holmes BOS .... .325

HITS
Stan Musial STL 230
T. Holmes BOS 190
Stan Rojek PIT 186

DOUBLES
Stan Musial STL 46
Del Ennis PHI 40
Alvin Dark BOS 39

TRIPLES
Stan Musial STL 18
Johnny Hopp PIT 12
Enos Slaughter STL 11

HOME RUNS
Johnny Mize NY 40
Ralph Kiner PIT 40
Stan Musial STL 39

RUNS BATTED IN
Stan Musial STL 131
Johnny Mize NY 125
Ralph Kiner PIT 123

SLUGGING AVERAGE
Stan Musial STL .... .702
Johnny Mize NY .... .564
Sid Gordon NY .... .537

STOLEN BASES
Richie Ashburn PHI 32
Pee Wee Reese BKN .. 25
Stan Rojek PIT 24

RUNS SCORED
Stan Musial STL 135
Whitey Lockman NY ... 117
Johnny Mize NY 110

WINS
Johnny Sain BOS 24
Harry Brecheen STL 20
two tied at 18

WINNING PERCENTAGE
H. Brecheen STL .... .741
Sheldon Jones NY ..... .667
Johnny Sain BOS .... .615

EARNED RUN AVERAGE
H. Brecheen STL 2.24
Dutch Leonard PHI 2.51
Johnny Sain BOS 2.60

STRIKEOUTS
Harry Brecheen STL ... 149
Rex Barney BKN 138
Johnny Sain BOS 137

SAVES
Harry Gumbert CIN 17
Ted Wilks STL 13
Kirby Higbe PIT 10

COMPLETE GAMES
Johnny Sain BOS 28
Harry Brecheen STL 21
Johnny Schmitz CHI 18

SHUTOUTS
Harry Brecheen STL 7
three tied at 4

GAMES PITCHED
Harry Gumbert CIN 61
Ted Wilks STL 57
Kirby Higbe PIT 56

INNINGS PITCHED
Johnny Sain BOS 315
Larry Jansen NY 277
Warren Spahn BOS 257

AMERICAN LEAGUE STANDINGS

1949 AL

	W	L	PCT	GB	R	OR	BA	FA	ERA
NEW YORK	97	57	.630	—	829	637	.269	.977	3.69
BOSTON	96	58	.623	1	896	667	.282	.980	3.97
CLEVELAND	89	65	.578	8	675	574	.260	.983	3.36
DETROIT	87	67	.565	10	751	655	.267	.978	3.77
PHILADELPHIA	81	73	.526	16	726	725	.260	.976	4.23
CHICAGO	63	91	.409	34	648	737	.257	.977	4.30
ST. LOUIS	53	101	.344	44	667	913	.254	.971	5.21
WASHINGTON	50	104	.325	47	584	868	.254	.973	5.10
					5776	5776	.263	.977	4.20

BATTING AVERAGE
George Kell DET .... .343
Ted Williams BOS ...... .343
Bob Dillinger STL .... .324

HITS
Dale Mitchell CLE 203
Ted Williams BOS 194
Dom DiMaggio BOS ... 186

DOUBLES
Ted Williams BOS 39
George Kell DET 38
Dom DiMaggio BOS 34

TRIPLES
Dale Mitchell CLE 23
Bob Dillinger STL 13
Elmer Valo PHI 12

HOME RUNS
Ted Williams BOS 43
Vern Stephens BOS 39
four tied at 24

RUNS BATTED IN
Vern Stephens BOS ... 159
Ted Williams BOS 159
Vic Wertz DET 133

SLUGGING AVERAGE
Ted Williams BOS ...... .650
V. Stephens BOS .... .539
Tommy Henrich NY ... .526

STOLEN BASES
Bob Dillinger STL 20
Phil Rizzuto NY 18
Elmer Valo PHI 14

RUNS SCORED
Ted Williams BOS 150
Eddie Joost PHI 128
Dom DiMaggio BOS ... 126

WINS
Mel Parnell BOS 25
Ellis Kinder BOS 23
Bob Lemon CLE 22

WINNING PERCENTAGE
Ellis Kinder BOS .... .793
Mel Parnell BOS .... .781
Allie Reynolds NY ...... .739

EARNED RUN AVERAGE
Mel Parnell BOS 2.77
Virgil Trucks DET 2.81
Bob Lemon CLE 2.99

STRIKEOUTS
Virgil Trucks DET 153
Hal Newhouser DET ... 144
two tied at 138

SAVES
Joe Page NY 27
Al Benton CLE 10
Tom Ferrick STL 6

COMPLETE GAMES
Mel Parnell BOS 27
Bob Lemon CLE 22
Hal Newhouser DET 22

SHUTOUTS
Ellis Kinder BOS 6
Virgil Trucks DET 6
Mike Garcia CLE 5

GAMES PITCHED
Joe Page NY 60
Dick Welteroth WAS 52
Tom Ferrick STL 50

INNINGS PITCHED
Mel Parnell BOS 295
Hal Newhouser DET ... 292
Bob Lemon CLE 280

NATIONAL LEAGUE STANDINGS

1949 NL

	W	L	PCT	GB	R	OR	BA	FA	ERA
BROOKLYN	97	57	.630	—	879	651	.274	.980	3.80
ST. LOUIS	96	58	.623	1	766	616	.277	.976	3.45
PHILADELPHIA	81	73	.526	16	662	668	.254	.974	3.89
BOSTON	75	79	.487	22	706	719	.258	.976	3.99
NEW YORK	73	81	.474	24	736	693	.261	.973	3.82
PITTSBURGH	71	83	.461	26	681	760	.259	.978	4.57
CINCINNATI	62	92	.403	35	627	770	.260	.977	4.33
CHICAGO	61	93	.396	36	593	773	.256	.970	4.50
					5650	5650	.262	.975	4.04

BATTING AVERAGE
J. Robinson BKN .... .342
Stan Musial STL .... .338
Enos Slaughter STL.... .336

HITS
Stan Musial STL 207
J. Robinson BKN 203
Bobby Thomson NY.... 198

DOUBLES
Stan Musial STL 41
Del Ennis PHI 39
two tied at 38

TRIPLES
Stan Musial STL 13
Enos Slaughter STL...... 13
Jackie Robinson BKN ... 12

HOME RUNS
Ralph Kiner PIT 54
Stan Musial STL 36
Hank Sauer CIN, CHI ... 31

RUNS BATTED IN
Ralph Kiner PIT 127
J. Robinson BKN 124
Stan Musial STL 123

SLUGGING AVERAGE
Ralph Kiner PIT .... .658
Stan Musial STL .... .624
J. Robinson BKN .... .528

STOLEN BASES
Jackie Robinson BKN ... 37
P. Reese BKN............... 26
four tied at..................... 12

RUNS SCORED
P. Reese BKN............. 132
Stan Musial STL 128
J. Robinson BKN 122

WINS
Warren Spahn BOS 21
Howie Pollet STL 20
K. Raffensberger CIN ... 18

WINNING PERCENTAGE
Preacher Roe BKN .... .714
Howie Pollet STL .... .690
two tied at .... .680

EARNED RUN AVERAGE
Dave Koslo NY 2.50
Howie Pollet STL 2.77
Preacher Roe BKN 2.79

STRIKEOUTS
Warren Spahn BOS.... 151
D. Newcombe BKN..... 149
Larry Jansen NY 113

SAVES
Ted Wilks STL 9
Jim Konstanty PHI 7
Nels Potter BOS 7

COMPLETE GAMES
Warren Spahn BOS 25
K. Raffensberger CIN ... 20
Don Newcombe BKN.... 19

SHUTOUTS
four tied at....................... 5

GAMES PITCHED
Ted Wilks STL 59
Jim Konstanty PHI 53
Erv Palica BKN 49

INNINGS PITCHED
Warren Spahn BOS.... 302
Raffensberger CIN...... 284
Larry Jansen NY 260

AMERICAN LEAGUE STANDINGS

1950 AL

	W	L	PCT	GB	R	OR	BA	FA	ERA
NEW YORK	98	56	.636	—	914	691	.282	.980	4.15
DETROIT	95	59	.617	3	837	713	.282	.981	4.12
BOSTON	94	60	.610	4	1027	804	.302	.981	4.88
CLEVELAND	92	62	.597	6	806	654	.269	.978	3.74
WASHINGTON	67	87	.435	31	690	813	.260	.972	4.66
CHICAGO	60	94	.390	38	625	749	.260	.977	4.41
ST. LOUIS	58	96	.377	40	684	916	.246	.967	5.20
PHILADELPHIA	52	102	.338	46	670	913	.261	.974	5.49
					6253	6253	.271	.976	4.58

BATTING AVERAGE
Billy Goodman BOS... .354
George Kell DET........ .340
D. DiMaggio BOS ...... .328

HITS
George Kell DET.......... 218
Phil Rizzuto NY............ 200
Dom DiMaggio BOS ... 193

DOUBLES
George Kell DET............ 56
Vic Wertz DET 37
Phil Rizzuto NY 36

TRIPLES
Dom DiMaggio BOS 11
Bobby Doerr BOS 11
Hoot Evers DET............. 11

HOME RUNS
Al Rosen CLE 37
Walt Dropo BOS 34
Joe DiMaggio NY 32

RUNS BATTED IN
Vern Stephens BOS ... 144
Walt Dropo BOS 144
Yogi Berra NY 124

SLUGGING AVERAGE
Joe DiMaggio NY........ .585
Walt Dropo BOS .... .583
Hoot Evers DET 551

STOLEN BASES
Dom DiMaggio BOS 15
Elmer Valo PHI 12
Phil Rizzuto NY.............. 12

RUNS SCORED
Dom DiMaggio BOS ... 131
Vern Stephens BOS ... 125
Phil Rizzuto NY........... 125

WINS
Bob Lemon CLE 23
Vic Raschi NY................ 21
Art Houtteman DET 19

WINNING PERCENTAGE
Vic Raschi NY..............724
Eddie Lopat NY...........692
Early Wynn CLE .... .692

EARNED RUN AVERAGE
Early Wynn CLE 3.20
Ned Garver STL......... 3.39
Bob Feller CLE 3.43

STRIKEOUTS
Bob Lemon CLE 170
Allie Reynolds NY 160
Vic Raschi NY.............. 155

SAVES
Mickey Harris WAS....... 15
Joe Page NY 13
Tom Ferrick STL, NY ... 11

COMPLETE GAMES
Ned Garver STL............. 22
Bob Lemon CLE 22
two tied at 21

SHUTOUTS
Art Houtteman DET 4
three tied at..................... 3

GAMES PITCHED
Mickey Harris WAS....... 53
Ellis Kinder BOS 48
two tied at 46

INNINGS PITCHED
Bob Lemon CLE 288
Art Houtteman DET 275
Ned Garver STL........... 260

588

NATIONAL LEAGUE STANDINGS

1950 NL

	W	L	PCT	GB	R	OR	BA	FA	ERA
PHILADELPHIA	91	63	.591	—	722	624	.265	.975	3.50
BROOKLYN	89	65	.578	2	847	724	.272	.979	4.28
NEW YORK	86	68	.558	5	735	643	.258	.977	3.71
BOSTON	83	71	.539	8	785	736	.263	.970	4.14
ST. LOUIS	78	75	.510	12.5	693	670	.259	.978	3.97
CINCINNATI	66	87	.431	24.5	654	734	.260	.976	4.32
CHICAGO	64	89	.418	26.5	643	772	.248	.968	4.28
PITTSBURGH	57	96	.373	33.5	681	857	.264	.977	4.96
					5760	5760	.261	.975	4.14

BATTING AVERAGE
Stan Musial STL .... .346
J. Robinson BKN .... .328
Duke Snider BKN....... .321

HITS
Duke Snider BKN........ 199
Stan Musial STL 192
Carl Furillo BKN 189

DOUBLES
R. Schoendienst STL.... 43
Stan Musial STL 41
Jackie Robinson BKN ... 39

TRIPLES
Richie Ashburn PHI 14
Gus Bell PIT.................. 11
Duke Snider BKN.......... 10

HOME RUNS
Ralph Kiner PIT 47
Andy Pafko CHI 36
two tied at 32

RUNS BATTED IN
Del Ennis PHI 126
Ralph Kiner PIT 118
Gil Hodges BKN.......... 113

SLUGGING AVERAGE
Stan Musial STL .... .596
Andy Pafko CHI .... .591
Ralph Kiner PIT .... .590

STOLEN BASES
Sam Jethroe BOS......... 35
Pee Wee Reese BKN ... 17
Duke Snider BKN.......... 16

RUNS SCORED
Earl Torgeson BOS..... 120
Eddie Stanky NY......... 115
Ralph Kiner PIT 112

WINS
Warren Spahn BOS...... 21
Robin Roberts PHI........ 20
Johnny Sain BOS 20

WINNING PERCENTAGE
Sal Maglie NY .... .818
Jim Konstanty PHI ..... .696
Curt Simmons PHI...... .680

EARNED RUN AVERAGE
Jim Hearn STL, NY 2.49
Sal Maglie NY 2.71
Ewell Blackwell CIN ... 2.97

STRIKEOUTS
Warren Spahn BOS.... 191
Ewell Blackwell CIN.... 188
Larry Jansen NY 161

SAVES
Jim Konstanty PHI 22
Bill Werle PIT 8
two tied at 7

COMPLETE GAMES
Vern Bickford BOS........ 27
Warren Spahn BOS...... 25
Johnny Sain BOS 25

SHUTOUTS
four tied at....................... 5

GAMES PITCHED
Jim Konstanty PHI 74
Murry Dickson PIT 51
Bill Werle PIT 48

INNINGS PITCHED
Vern Bickford BOS...... 312
Robin Roberts PHI...... 304
Warren Spahn BOS.... 293

AMERICAN LEAGUE STANDINGS

1951 AL

	W	L	PCT	GB	R	OR	BA	FA	ERA
NEW YORK	98	56	.636	—	798	621	.269	.975	3.56
CLEVELAND	93	61	.604	5	696	594	.256	.978	3.38
BOSTON	87	67	.565	11	804	725	.266	.977	4.14
CHICAGO	81	73	.526	17	714	644	.270	.975	3.50
DETROIT	73	81	.474	25	685	741	.265	.973	4.29
PHILADELPHIA	70	84	.455	28	736	745	.262	.978	4.47
WASHINGTON	62	92	.403	36	672	764	.263	.973	4.49
ST. LOUIS	52	102	.338	46	611	882	.247	.971	5.17
					5716	5716	.262	.975	4.12

BATTING AVERAGE
Ferris Fain PHI .... .344
Minoso CLE, CHI .... .326
George Kell DET .... .319

HITS
George Kell DET 191
Dom DiMaggio BOS ... 189
Nellie Fox CHI 189

DOUBLES
Sam Mele WAS 36
George Kell DET 36
Eddie Yost WAS 36

TRIPLES
Minoso CLE, CHI 14
Nellie Fox CHI 12
R. Coleman STL, CHI ... 12

HOME RUNS
Gus Zernial CHI, PHI 33
Ted Williams BOS 30
Eddie Robinson CHI 29

RUNS BATTED IN
G. Zernial CHI, PHI 129
Ted Williams BOS 126
Eddie Robinson CHI ... 117

SLUGGING AVERAGE
Ted Williams BOS ...... .556
Larry Doby CLE .... .512
two tied at .... .511

STOLEN BASES
Minoso CLE, CHI 31
Jim Busby CHI 26
Phil Rizzuto NY 18

RUNS SCORED
Dom DiMaggio BOS ... 113
Minoso CLE, CHI 112
two tied at 109

WINS
Bob Feller CLE 22
Eddie Lopat NY 21
Vic Raschi NY 21

WINNING PERCENTAGE
Bob Feller CLE .... .733
Eddie Lopat NY .... .700
Allie Reynolds NY .... .680

EARNED RUN AVERAGE
Rogovin DET, CHI 2.78
Eddie Lopat NY 2.91
Early Wynn CLE 3.02

STRIKEOUTS
Vic Raschi NY 164
Early Wynn CLE 133
Bob Lemon CLE 132

SAVES
Ellis Kinder BOS 14
Carl Scheib PHI 10
Lou Brissie PHI, CLE 9

COMPLETE GAMES
Ned Garver STL 24
Early Wynn CLE 21
Eddie Lopat NY 20

SHUTOUTS
Allie Reynolds NY 7
Eddie Lopat NY 5
two tied at 4

GAMES PITCHED
Ellis Kinder BOS 63
Lou Brissie PHI, CLE 56
Mike Garcia CLE 47

INNINGS PITCHED
Early Wynn CLE 274
Bob Lemon CLE 263
Vic Raschi NY 258

NATIONAL LEAGUE STANDINGS

1951 NL

	W	L	PCT	GB	R	OR	BA	FA	ERA
NEW YORK*	98	59	.624	—	781	641	.260	.972	3.48
BROOKLYN	97	60	.618	1	855	672	.275	.979	3.88
ST. LOUIS	81	73	.526	15.5	683	671	.264	.980	3.95
BOSTON	76	78	.494	20.5	723	662	.262	.976	3.75
PHILADELPHIA	73	81	.474	23.5	648	644	.260	.977	3.81
CINCINNATI	68	86	.442	28.5	559	667	.248	.977	3.70
PITTSBURGH	64	90	.416	32.5	689	845	.258	.972	4.78
CHICAGO	62	92	.403	34.5	614	750	.250	.971	4.34
					5552	5552	.260	.975	3.96

*Defeated Brooklyn in a playoff 2 games to 1.

BATTING AVERAGE
Stan Musial STL .... .355
Richie Ashburn PHI ... .344
J. Robinson BKN .... .338

HITS
Richie Ashburn PHI 221
Stan Musial STL 205
Carl Furillo BKN 197

DOUBLES
Alvin Dark NY 41
Ted Kluszewski CIN...... 35
two tied at 33

TRIPLES
Stan Musial STL 12
Gus Bell PIT.................. 12
Monte Irvin NY 11

HOME RUNS
Ralph Kiner PIT 42
Gil Hodges BKN............ 40
Roy Campanella BKN... 33

RUNS BATTED IN
Monte Irvin NY 121
Sid Gordon BOS 109
Ralph Kiner PIT 109

SLUGGING AVERAGE
Ralph Kiner PIT .... .627
Stan Musial STL .... .614
R. Campanella BKN ... .590

STOLEN BASES
Sam Jethroe BOS......... 35
Richie Ashburn PHI 29
Jackie Robinson BKN... 25

RUNS SCORED
Stan Musial STL 124
Ralph Kiner PIT 124
Gil Hodges BKN.......... 118

WINS
Sal Maglie NY 23
Larry Jansen NY 23
two tied at 22

WINNING PERCENTAGE
Preacher Roe BKN .... .880
Sal Maglie NY .... .793
D. Newcombe BKN.... .690

EARNED RUN AVERAGE
Chet Nichols BOS...... 2.88
Sal Maglie NY 2.93
Warren Spahn BOS ... 2.98

STRIKEOUTS
Warren Spahn BOS.... 164
D. Newcombe BKN..... 164
Sal Maglie NY 146

SAVES
Ted Wilks STL, PIT....... 13
Frank Smith CIN 11
Jim Konstanty PHI 9

COMPLETE GAMES
Warren Spahn BOS...... 26
Robin Roberts PHI........ 22
Sal Maglie NY 22

SHUTOUTS
Robin Roberts PHI.......... 6
K. Raffensberger CIN 5
two tied at 4

GAMES PITCHED
Ted Wilkes STL, PIT..... 65
Bill Werle PIT................ 59
Jim Konstanty PHI 58

INNINGS PITCHED
Robin Roberts PHI...... 315
Warren Spahn BOS.... 311
Sal Maglie NY 298

AMERICAN LEAGUE STANDINGS

1952 AL

	W	L	PCT	GB	R	OR	BA	FA	ERA
NEW YORK	95	59	.617	—	727	557	.267	.979	3.14
CLEVELAND	93	61	.604	2	763	606	.262	.975	3.32
CHICAGO	81	73	.526	14	610	568	.252	.980	3.25
PHILADELPHIA	79	75	.513	16	664	723	.253	.977	4.15
WASHINGTON	78	76	.506	17	598	608	.239	.978	3.37
BOSTON	76	78	.494	19	668	658	.255	.976	3.80
ST. LOUIS	64	90	.416	31	604	733	.250	.974	4.12
DETROIT	50	104	.325	45	557	738	.243	.975	4.25
					5191	5191	.253	.977	3.67

BATTING AVERAGE
Ferris Fain PHI............ .327
Dale Mitchell CLE .... .323
two tied at .... .311

HITS
Nellie Fox CHI............. 192
Bobby Avila CLE......... 179
two tied at 176

DOUBLES
Ferris Fain PHI.............. 43
Mickey Mantle NY......... 37
two tied at 33

TRIPLES
Bobby Avila CLE............ 11
three tied at.................. 10

HOME RUNS
Larry Doby CLE 32
Luke Easter CLE........... 31
Yogi Berra NY............... 30

RUNS BATTED IN
Al Rosen CLE 105
Eddie Robinson CHI ... 104
Larry Doby CLE 104

SLUGGING AVERAGE
Larry Doby CLE .... .541
Mickey Mantle NY....... .530
Al Rosen CLE .... .524

STOLEN BASES
Minnie Minoso CHI 22
Jim Rivera STL, CHI 21
J. Jensen NY, WAS 18

RUNS SCORED
Larry Doby CLE 104
Bobby Avila CLE......... 102
Al Rosen CLE 101

WINS
Bobby Shantz PHI 24
Early Wynn CLE 23
two tied at 22

WINNING PERCENTAGE
Bobby Shantz PHI ..... .774
Vic Raschi NY............ .727
Allie Reynolds NY....... .714

EARNED RUN AVERAGE
Allie Reynolds NY...... 2.06
Mike Garcia CLE........ 2.37
Bobby Shantz PHI 2.48

STRIKEOUTS
Allie Reynolds NY 160
Early Wynn CLE 153
Bobby Shantz PHI 152

SAVES
Harry Dorish CHI 11
Satchel Paige STL........ 10
Johnny Sain NY 7

COMPLETE GAMES
Bob Lemon CLE 28
Bobby Shantz PHI 27
Allie Reynolds NY 24

SHUTOUTS
Allie Reynolds NY 6
Mike Garcia CLE.............. 6
two tied at 5

GAMES PITCHED
Bill Kennedy CHI............ 47
Mike Garcia CLE............ 46
Satchel Paige STL......... 46

INNINGS PITCHED
Bob Lemon CLE 310
Mike Garcia CLE......... 292
Early Wynn CLE 286

NATIONAL LEAGUE STANDINGS

1952 NL

	W	L	PCT	GB	R	OR	BA	FA	ERA
BROOKLYN	96	57	.627	—	775	603	.262	.982	3.53
NEW YORK	92	62	.597	4.5	722	639	.256	.974	3.59
ST. LOUIS	88	66	.571	8.5	677	630	.267	.977	3.66
PHILADELPHIA	87	67	.565	9.5	657	552	.260	.975	3.07
CHICAGO	77	77	.500	19.5	628	631	.264	.976	3.58
CINCINNATI	69	85	.448	27.5	615	659	.249	.982	4.01
BOSTON	64	89	.418	32	569	651	.233	.975	3.78
PITTSBURGH	42	112	.273	54.5	515	793	.231	.970	4.65
					5158	5158	.253	.976	3.73

BATTING AVERAGE
Stan Musial STL .... .336
F. Baumholtz CHI .... .325
Ted Kluszewski CIN... .320

HITS
Stan Musial STL 194
Schoendienst STL 188
Bobby Adams CIN 180

DOUBLES
Stan Musial STL 42
Schoendienst STL 40
Roy McMillan CIN 32

TRIPLES
Bobby Thomson NY.... 14
Enos Slaughter STL..... 12
Ted Kluszewski CIN...... 11

HOME RUNS
Hank Sauer CHI............. 37
Ralph Kiner PIT 37
Gil Hodges BKN............. 32

RUNS BATTED IN
Hank Sauer CHI............. 121
Bobby Thomson NY.... 108
Del Ennis PHI 107

SLUGGING AVERAGE
Stan Musial STL .... .538
Hank Sauer CHI.......... .531
Ted Kluszewski CIN... .509

STOLEN BASES
Pee Wee Reese BKN ... 30
Sam Jethroe BOS......... 28
Jackie Robinson BKN... 24

RUNS SCORED
Stan Musial STL 105
Solly Hemus STL 105
J. Robinson BKN 104

WINS
Robin Roberts PHI........ 28
Sal Maglie NY 18
three tied at................... 17

WINNING PERCENTAGE
Hoyt Wilhelm NY......... .833
Robin Roberts PHI..... .800
Joe Black BKN .... .789

EARNED RUN AVERAGE
Hoyt Wilhelm NY......... 2.43
Warren Hacker CHI ... 2.58
Robin Roberts PHI..... 2.59

STRIKEOUTS
Warren Spahn BOS.... 183
Bob Rush CHI.............. 157
Robin Roberts PHI...... 148

SAVES
Al Brazle STL................. 16
Joe Black BKN............... 15
two tied at 11

COMPLETE GAMES
Robin Roberts PHI........ 30
Murry Dickson PIT 21
Warren Spahn BOS...... 19

SHUTOUTS
Curt Simmons PHI 6
K. Raffensberger CIN 6
two tied at 5

GAMES PITCHED
Hoyt Wilhelm NY........... 71
Joe Black BKN............... 56
Eddie Yuhas STL........... 54

INNINGS PITCHED
Robin Roberts PHI...... 330
Warren Spahn BOS.... 290
Murry Dickson PIT 278

AMERICAN LEAGUE STANDINGS

1953 AL

	W	L	PCT	GB	R	OR	BA	FA	ERA
NEW YORK	99	52	.656	—	801	547	.273	.979	3.20
CLEVELAND	92	62	.597	8.5	770	627	.270	.979	3.64
CHICAGO	89	65	.578	11.5	716	592	.258	.980	3.41
BOSTON	84	69	.549	16	656	632	.264	.975	3.59
WASHINGTON	76	76	.500	23.5	687	614	.263	.979	3.66
DETROIT	60	94	.390	40.5	695	923	.266	.978	5.25
PHILADELPHIA	59	95	.383	41.5	632	799	.256	.977	4.67
ST. LOUIS	54	100	.351	46.5	555	778	.249	.974	4.48
					5512	5512	.262	.978	4.00

BATTING AVERAGE
M. Vernon WAS .... .337
Al Rosen CLE .... .336
two tied at .... .313

HITS
Harvey Kuenn DET 209
Mickey Vernon WAS... 205
Al Rosen CLE 201

DOUBLES
Mickey Vernon WAS..... 43
George Kell BOS 41
Sammy White BOS....... 34

TRIPLES
Jim Rivera CHI............... 16
Mickey Vernon WAS..... 11
two tied at 9

HOME RUNS
Al Rosen CLE 43
Gus Zernial PHI 42
Larry Doby CLE 29

RUNS BATTED IN
Al Rosen CLE 145
Mickey Vernon WAS... 115
Boone CLE, DET 114

SLUGGING AVERAGE
Al Rosen CLE .... .613
Gus Zernial PHI .... .559
Yogi Berra NY .... .523

STOLEN BASES
Minnie Minoso CHI 25
Jim Rivera CHI............... 22
Jackie Jensen WAS...... 18

RUNS SCORED
Al Rosen CLE 115
Eddie Yost WAS 107
Mickey Mantle NY....... 105

WINS
Bob Porterfield WAS..... 22
Bob Lemon CLE 21
Mel Parnell BOS 21

WINNING PERCENTAGE
Eddie Lopat NY........... .800
Whitey Ford NY .... .750
Mel Parnell BOS .... .724

EARNED RUN AVERAGE
Eddie Lopat NY.......... 2.42
Billy Pierce CHI 2.72
Trucks STL, CHI 2.93

STRIKEOUTS
Billy Pierce CHI........... 186
V. Trucks STL, CHI..... 149
Early Wynn CLE 138

SAVES
Ellis Kinder BOS 27
Harry Dorish CHI 18
Allie Reynolds NY 13

COMPLETE GAMES
Bob Porterfield WAS..... 24
Bob Lemon CLE 23
Mike Garcia CLE........... 21

SHUTOUTS
Bob Porterfield WAS....... 9
Billy Pierce CHI............... 7
two tied at 5

GAMES PITCHED
Ellis Kinder BOS 69
Marlan Stuart STL......... 60
Morrie Martin PHI.......... 58

INNINGS PITCHED
Bob Lemon CLE 287
Mike Garcia CLE......... 272
Billy Pierce CHI........... 271

NATIONAL LEAGUE STANDINGS

1953 NL

	W	L	PCT	GB	R	OR	BA	FA	ERA
BROOKLYN	105	49	.682	—	955	689	.285	.980	4.10
MILWAUKEE	92	62	.597	13	738	589	.266	.976	3.30
PHILADELPHIA	83	71	.539	22	716	666	.265	.975	3.80
ST. LOUIS	83	71	.539	22	768	713	.273	.977	4.23
NEW YORK	70	84	.455	35	768	747	.271	.975	4.25
CINCINNATI	68	86	.442	37	714	788	.261	.978	4.64
CHICAGO	65	89	.422	40	633	835	.260	.967	4.79
PITTSBURGH	50	104	.325	55	622	887	.247	.973	5.22
					5914	5914	.266	.975	4.29

BATTING AVERAGE
Carl Furillo BKN .... .344
Schoendienst STL ...... .342
Stan Musial STL .... .337

HITS
Richie Ashburn PHI 205
Stan Musial STL 200
Duke Snider BKN........ 198

DOUBLES
Stan Musial STL 53
Alvin Dark NY 41
two tied at 38

TRIPLES
Jim Gilliam BKN............. 17
Bill Bruton MIL 14
two tied at 11

HOME RUNS
Eddie Mathews MIL 47
Duke Snider BKN.......... 42
Roy Campanella BKN... 41

RUNS BATTED IN
R. Campanella BKN.... 142
Eddie Mathews MIL ... 135
Duke Snider BKN........ 126

SLUGGING AVERAGE
Duke Snider BKN........ .627
Eddie Mathews MIL ... .627
R. Campanella BKN... .611

STOLEN BASES
Bill Bruton MIL 26
Pee Wee Reese BKN ... 22
Jim Gilliam BKN............. 21

RUNS SCORED
Duke Snider BKN........ 132
Stan Musial STL 127
Alvin Dark NY 126

WINS
Warren Spahn MIL......... 23
Robin Roberts PHI......... 23
two tied at 20

WINNING PERCENTAGE
Carl Erskine BKN........ .769
Warren Spahn MIL...... .767
two tied at .... .750

EARNED RUN AVERAGE
Warren Spahn MIL..... 2.10
Robin Roberts PHI..... 2.75
Bob Buhl MIL 2.97

STRIKEOUTS
Robin Roberts PHI...... 198
Carl Erskine BKN........ 187
Mizell STL 173

SAVES
Al Brazle STL................ 18
Hoyt Wilhelm NY............ 15
Jim Hughes BKN 9

COMPLETE GAMES
Robin Roberts PHI........ 33
Warren Spahn MIL....... 24
two tied at 19

SHUTOUTS
Harvey Haddix STL.......... 6
Robin Roberts PHI.......... 5
Warren Spahn MIL.......... 5

GAMES PITCHED
Hoyt Wilhelm NY 68
Al Brazle STL................. 60
Johnny Hetki PIT 54

INNINGS PITCHED
Robin Roberts PHI...... 347
Warren Spahn MIL...... 266
Harvey Haddix STL..... 253

AMERICAN LEAGUE STANDINGS

1954 AL

	W	L	PCT	GB	R	OR	BA	FA	ERA
CLEVELAND	111	43	.721	—	746	504	.262	.979	2.78
NEW YORK	103	51	.669	8	805	563	.268	.979	3.26
CHICAGO	94	60	.610	17	711	521	.267	.982	3.05
BOSTON	69	85	.448	42	700	728	.266	.972	4.01
DETROIT	68	86	.442	43	584	664	.258	.978	3.81
WASHINGTON	66	88	.429	45	632	680	.246	.977	3.84
BALTIMORE	54	100	.351	57	483	668	.251	.975	3.88
PHILADELPHIA	51	103	.331	60	542	875	.236	.972	5.18
					5203	5203	.257	.977	3.72

BATTING AVERAGE
Bobby Avila CLE .... .341
Minnie Minoso CHI .... .320
two tied at .... .319

HITS
Nellie Fox CHI 201
Harvey Kuenn DET 201
Bobby Avila CLE 189

DOUBLES
Mickey Vernon WAS 33
Minnie Minoso CHI 29
Al Smith CLE 29

TRIPLES
Minnie Minoso CHI 18
Pete Runnels WAS 15
Mickey Vernon WAS 14

HOME RUNS
Larry Doby CLE 32
Ted Williams BOS 29
Mickey Mantle NY 27

RUNS BATTED IN
Larry Doby CLE 126
Yogi Berra NY 125
Jackie Jensen BOS 117

SLUGGING AVERAGE
Ted Williams BOS ...... .635
Minnie Minoso CHI .... .535
Mickey Mantle NY ...... .525

STOLEN BASES
Jackie Jensen BOS 22
Jim Rivera CHI 18
Minnie Minoso CHI 18

RUNS SCORED
Mickey Mantle NY 129
Minnie Minoso CHI 119
Bobby Avila CLE 112

WINS
Bob Lemon CLE 23
Early Wynn CLE 23
Bob Grim NY 20

WINNING PERCENTAGE
S. Consuegra CHI ...... .842
Bob Grim NY .... .769
Bob Lemon CLE .... .767

EARNED RUN AVERAGE
Mike Garcia CLE 2.64
S. Consuegra CHI 2.69
Bob Lemon CLE 2.72

STRIKEOUTS
Bob Turley BAL 185
Early Wynn CLE 155
Virgil Trucks CHI 152

SAVES
Johnny Sain NY 22
Ellis Kinder BOS 15
Ray Narleski CLE 13

COMPLETE GAMES
Bob Porterfield WAS 21
Bob Lemon CLE 21
Early Wynn CLE 20

SHUTOUTS
Virgil Trucks CHI 5
Mike Garcia CLE 5

GAMES PITCHED
S. Dixon WAS, PHI 54
three tied at 48

INNINGS PITCHED
Early Wynn CLE 271
Virgil Trucks CHI 265
Mike Garcia CLE 259

NATIONAL LEAGUE STANDINGS

1954 NL

	W	L	PCT	GB	R	OR	BA	FA	ERA
NEW YORK	97	57	.630	—	732	550	.264	.975	3.09
BROOKLYN	92	62	.597	5	778	740	.270	.978	4.31
MILWAUKEE	89	65	.578	8	670	556	.265	.981	3.19
PHILADELPHIA	75	79	.487	22	659	614	.267	.975	3.59
CINCINNATI	74	80	.481	23	729	763	.262	.977	4.50
ST. LOUIS	72	82	.468	25	799	790	.281	.976	4.50
CHICAGO	64	90	.416	33	700	766	.263	.974	4.51
PITTSBURGH	53	101	.344	44	557	845	.248	.971	4.92
					5624	5624	.265	.976	4.07

BATTING AVERAGE
Willie Mays NY .... .345
Don Mueller NY .... .342
Duke Snider BKN .... .341

HITS
Don Mueller NY 212
Duke Snider BKN 199
two tied at 195

DOUBLES
Stan Musial STL 41
three tied at 39

TRIPLES
Willie Mays NY 13
Granny Hamner PHI 11
Duke Snider BKN 10

HOME RUNS
Ted Kluszewski CIN 49
Gil Hodges BKN 42
two tied at 41

RUNS BATTED IN
Ted Kluszewski CIN 141
Gil Hodges BKN 130
Duke Snider BKN 130

SLUGGING AVERAGE
Willie Mays NY .... .667
Duke Snider BKN .... .647
Ted Kluszewski CIN .. .642

STOLEN BASES
Bill Bruton MIL 34
Johnny Temple CIN 21
Dee Fondy CHI 20

RUNS SCORED
Duke Snider BKN 120
Stan Musial STL 120
Willie Mays NY 119

WINS
Robin Roberts PHI 23
Johnny Antonelli NY 21
Warren Spahn MIL 21

WINNING PERCENTAGE
Johnny Antonelli NY ... .750
B. Lawrence STL .... .714
Ruben Gomez NY ...... .654

EARNED RUN AVERAGE
J. Antonelli NY 2.30
Lew Burdette MIL 2.76
Curt Simmons PHI 2.81

STRIKEOUTS
Robin Roberts PHI 185
Harvey Haddix STL 184
Carl Erskine BKN 166

SAVES
Jim Hughes BKN 24
Frank Smith CIN 20
Marv Grissom NY 19

COMPLETE GAMES
Robin Roberts PHI 29
Warren Spahn MIL 23
Curt Simmons PHI 21

SHUTOUTS
Johnny Antonelli NY 6
three tied at 4

GAMES PITCHED
Jim Hughes BKN 60
Al Brazle STL 58
Johnny Hetki PIT 58

INNINGS PITCHED
Robin Roberts PHI 337
Warren Spahn MIL 283
two tied at 260

AMERICAN LEAGUE STANDINGS

1955 AL

	W	L	PCT	GB	R	OR	BA	FA	ERA
NEW YORK	96	58	.623	—	762	569	.260	.978	3.23
CLEVELAND	93	61	.604	3	698	601	.257	.981	3.39
CHICAGO	91	63	.591	5	725	557	.268	.981	3.37
BOSTON	84	70	.545	12	755	652	.264	.977	3.72
DETROIT	79	75	.513	17	775	658	.266	.976	3.79
KANSAS CITY	63	91	.409	33	638	911	.261	.976	5.35
BALTIMORE	57	97	.370	39	540	754	.240	.972	4.21
WASHINGTON	53	101	.344	43	598	789	.248	.974	4.62
					5491	5491	.258	.977	3.96

BATTING AVERAGE
Al Kaline DET .... .340
Vic Power KC............. .319
George Kell CHI......... .312

HITS
Al Kaline DET 200
Nellie Fox CHI............ 198
two tied at 190

DOUBLES
Harvey Kuenn DET...... 38
Vic Power KC.............. 34
Billy Goodman BOS..... 31

TRIPLES
Andy Carey NY............ 11
Mickey Mantle NY........ 11
Vic Power KC.............. 10

HOME RUNS
Mickey Mantle NY........ 37
Gus Zernial KC 30
Ted Williams BOS........ 28

RUNS BATTED IN
Ray Boone DET.......... 116
Jackie Jensen BOS 116
Yogi Berra NY............. 108

SLUGGING AVERAGE
Mickey Mantle NY....... .611
Al Kaline DET .... .546
Gus Zernial KC .... .508

STOLEN BASES
Jim Rivera CHI............. 25
Minnie Minoso CHI 19
Jackie Jensen BOS 16

RUNS SCORED
Al Smith CLE 123
Al Kaline DET 121
Mickey Mantle NY....... 121

WINS
Whitey Ford NY 18
Bob Lemon CLE 18
Frank Sullivan BOS 18

WINNING PERCENTAGE
Tommy Byrne NY .... .762
Whitey Ford NY .... .720
Billy Hoeft DET .... .696

EARNED RUN AVERAGE
Billy Pierce CHI 1.97
Whitey Ford NY 2.63
Early Wynn CLE 2.82

STRIKEOUTS
Herb Score CLE.......... 245
Bob Turley NY 210
Billy Pierce CHI........... 157

SAVES
Ray Narleski CLE 19
Tom Gorman KC........... 18
Ellis Kinder BOS 18

COMPLETE GAMES
Whitey Ford NY 18
Billy Hoeft DET 17

SHUTOUTS
Billy Hoeft DET 7
three tied at...................... 6

GAMES PITCHED
Ray Narleski CLE 60
Don Mossi CLE............. 57
Tom Gorman KC........... 57

INNINGS PITCHED
Frank Sullivan BOS 260
Whitey Ford NY 254
Bob Turley NY 247

NATIONAL LEAGUE STANDINGS

1955 NL

	W	L	PCT	GB	R	OR	BA	FA	ERA
BROOKLYN	98	55	.641	—	857	650	.271	.978	3.68
MILWAUKEE	85	69	.552	13.5	743	668	.261	.975	3.85
NEW YORK	80	74	.519	18.5	702	673	.260	.976	3.77
PHILADELPHIA	77	77	.500	21.5	675	666	.255	.981	3.93
CINCINNATI	75	79	.487	23.5	761	684	.270	.977	3.95
CHICAGO	72	81	.471	26	626	713	.247	.975	4.17
ST. LOUIS	68	86	.442	30.5	654	757	.261	.975	4.56
PITTSBURGH	60	94	.390	38.5	560	767	.244	.972	4.39
					5578	5578	.259	.976	4.04

BATTING AVERAGE
Richie Ashburn PHI ... .338
Willie Mays NY .... .319
Stan Musial STL .... .319

HITS
Ted Kluszewski CIN.... 192
Hank Aaron MIL......... 189
Gus Bell CIN............... 188

DOUBLES
Hank Aaron MIL............ 37
Johnny Logan MIL 37
Duke Snider BKN.......... 34

TRIPLES
Willie Mays NY.............. 13
Dale Long PIT............... 13
Bill Bruton MIL 12

HOME RUNS
Willie Mays NY.............. 51
Ted Kluszewski CIN...... 47
Ernie Banks CHI 44

RUNS BATTED IN
Duke Snider BKN........ 136
Willie Mays NY............ 127
Del Ennis PHI 120

SLUGGING AVERAGE
Willie Mays NY............ .659
Duke Snider BKN....... .628
Eddie Mathews MIL ... .601

STOLEN BASES
Bill Bruton MIL 25
Willie Mays NY............... 24
Ken Boyer STL 22

RUNS SCORED
Duke Snider BKN........ 126
Willie Mays NY............ 123
two tied at 116

WINS
Robin Roberts PHI........ 23
Don Newcombe BKN.... 20
two tied at 17

WINNING PERCENTAGE
D. Newcombe BKN..... .800
Robin Roberts PHI...... .622
Joe Nuxhall CIN.......... .586

EARNED RUN AVERAGE
Bob Friend PIT........... 2.83
D. Newcombe BKN..... 3.20
Bob Buhl MIL 3.21

STRIKEOUTS
Sheldon Jones CHI..... 198
Robin Roberts PHI...... 160
Harvey Haddix STL..... 150

SAVES
Jack Meyer PHI 16
Ed Roebuck BKN.......... 12
two tied at 11

COMPLETE GAMES
Robin Roberts PHI........ 26
Don Newcombe BKN.... 17
Warren Spahn MIL........ 16

SHUTOUTS
Joe Nuxhall CIN.............. 5
Murry Dickson PHI.......... 4
Sheldon Jones CHI......... 4

GAMES PITCHED
Clem Labine BKN 60
Hoyt Wilhelm NY............ 59
Paul LaPalme STL......... 56

INNINGS PITCHED
Robin Roberts PHI...... 305
Joe Nuxhall CIN.......... 257
Warren Spahn MIL...... 246

AMERICAN LEAGUE STANDINGS

1956 AL

	W	L	PCT	GB	R	OR	BA	FA	ERA
NEW YORK	97	57	.630	—	857	631	.270	.977	3.63
CLEVELAND	88	66	.571	9	712	581	.244	.978	3.32
CHICAGO	85	69	.552	12	776	634	.267	.979	3.73
BOSTON	84	70	.545	13	780	751	.275	.972	4.17
DETROIT	82	72	.532	15	789	699	.279	.976	4.06
BALTIMORE	69	85	.448	28	571	705	.244	.977	4.20
WASHINGTON	59	95	.383	38	652	924	.250	.972	5.33
KANSAS CITY	52	102	.338	45	619	831	.252	.973	4.86
					5756	5756	.260	.975	4.16

BATTING AVERAGE
Mickey Mantle NY ...... .353
Ted Williams BOS ...... .345
Harvey Kuenn DET .... .332

HITS
Harvey Kuenn DET 196
Al Kaline DET 194
Nellie Fox CHI 192

DOUBLES
Jimmy Piersall BOS 40
Al Kaline DET 32
Harvey Kuenn DET 32

TRIPLES
four tied at 11

HOME RUNS
Mickey Mantle NY 52
Vic Wertz CLE 32
Yogi Berra NY 30

RUNS BATTED IN
Mickey Mantle NY 130
Al Kaline DET 128
Vic Wertz CLE 106

SLUGGING AVERAGE
Mickey Mantle NY ...... .705
Ted Williams BOS ...... .605
two tied at .... .534

STOLEN BASES
Luis Aparicio CHI 21
Jim Rivera CHI 20
Bobby Avila CLE 17

RUNS SCORED
Mickey Mantle NY 132
Nellie Fox CHI 109
Minnie Minoso CHI 106

WINS
Frank Lary DET 21
five tied at 20

WINNING PERCENTAGE
Whitey Ford NY .... .760
three tied at .... .690

EARNED RUN AVERAGE
Whitey Ford NY 2.47
Herb Score CLE 2.53
Early Wynn CLE 2.72

STRIKEOUTS
Herb Score CLE 263
Billy Pierce CHI 192
Paul Foytack DET 184

SAVES
George Zuverink BAL ... 16
Tom Morgan NY 11
Don Mossi CLE 11

COMPLETE GAMES
Billy Pierce CHI 21
Bob Lemon CLE 21
Frank Lary DET 20

SHUTOUTS
Herb Score CLE 5
three tied at 4

GAMES PITCHED
George Zuverink BAL ... 62
Jack Crimian KC 54
Tom Gorman KC 52

INNINGS PITCHED
Frank Lary DET 294
Early Wynn CLE 278
Billy Pierce CHI 276

NATIONAL LEAGUE STANDINGS

1956 NL

	W	L	PCT	GB	R	OR	BA	FA	ERA
BROOKLYN	93	61	.604	—	720	601	.258	.981	3.57
MILWAUKEE	92	62	.597	1	709	569	.259	.979	3.11
CINCINNATI	91	63	.591	2	775	658	.266	.981	3.85
ST. LOUIS	76	78	.494	17	678	698	.268	.978	3.97
PHILADELPHIA	71	83	.461	22	668	738	.252	.975	4.20
NEW YORK	67	87	.435	26	540	650	.244	.976	3.78
PITTSBURGH	66	88	.429	27	588	653	.257	.973	3.74
CHICAGO	60	94	.390	33	597	708	.244	.976	3.96
					5275	5275	.256	.977	3.77

BATTING AVERAGE
Hank Aaron MIL .... .328
Bill Virdon STL, PIT ... .319
R. Clemente PIT .... .311

HITS
Hank Aaron MIL 200
Richie Ashburn PHI 190
Bill Virdon STL, PIT 185

DOUBLES
Hank Aaron MIL 34
three tied at 33

TRIPLES
Bill Bruton MIL 15
Hank Aaron MIL 14
two tied at 11

HOME RUNS
Duke Snider BKN 43
Frank Robinson CIN 38
Joe Adcock MIL 38

RUNS BATTED IN
Stan Musial STL 109
Joe Adcock MIL 103
Ted Kluszewski CIN.... 102

SLUGGING AVERAGE
Duke Snider BKN .... .598
Joe Adcock MIL .... .597
two tied at .... .558

STOLEN BASES
Willie Mays NY 40
Jim Gilliam BKN 21
Bill White NY 15

RUNS SCORED
Frank Robinson CIN ... 122
Duke Snider BKN 112
Hank Aaron MIL 106

WINS
Don Newcombe BKN 27
Warren Spahn MIL 20
Johnny Antonelli NY 20

WINNING PERCENTAGE
D. Newcombe BKN .... .794
Bob Buhl MIL .... .692
two tied at .... .655

EARNED RUN AVERAGE
Lew Burdette MIL......... 2.70
Warren Spahn MIL........ 2.78
J. Antonelli NY 2.86

STRIKEOUTS
Sheldon Jones CHI 176
Haddix STL, PHI 170
Bob Friend PIT............. 166

SAVES
Clem Labine BKN 19
Hersh Freeman CIN...... 18
Turk Lown CHI 13

COMPLETE GAMES
Robin Roberts PHI........ 22
Warren Spahn MIL....... 20
Bob Friend PIT.............. 19

SHUTOUTS
Johnny Antonelli NY 6
Lew Burdette MIL........... 6
Don Newcombe BKN 5

GAMES PITCHED
Roy Face PIT 68
Hersh Freeman CIN...... 64
Hoyt Wilhelm NY............ 64

INNINGS PITCHED
Bob Friend PIT............ 314
Robin Roberts PHI...... 297
Warren Spahn MIL...... 281

AMERICAN LEAGUE STANDINGS

1957 AL

	W	L	PCT	GB	R	OR	BA	FA	ERA
NEW YORK	98	56	.636	—	723	534	.268	.980	3.00
CHICAGO	90	64	.584	8	707	566	.260	.982	3.35
BOSTON	82	72	.532	16	721	668	.262	.976	3.88
DETROIT	78	76	.506	20	614	614	.257	.980	3.56
BALTIMORE	76	76	.500	21	597	588	.252	.981	3.46
CLEVELAND	76	77	.497	21.5	682	722	.252	.974	4.05
KANSAS CITY	59	94	.386	38.5	563	710	.244	.979	4.19
WASHINGTON	55	99	.357	43	603	808	.244	.979	4.85
					5210	5210	.255	.979	3.79

BATTING AVERAGE
Ted Williams BOS ...... .388
Mickey Mantle NY ...... .365
G. Woodling CLE .... .321

HITS
Nellie Fox CHI 196
Frank Malzone BOS ... 185
Minnie Minoso CHI 176

DOUBLES
Billy Gardner BAL 36
Minnie Minoso CHI 36
Frank Malzone BOS 31

TRIPLES
Harry Simpson KC, NY ... 9
Gil McDougald NY 9
Hank Bauer NY 9

HOME RUNS
Roy Sievers WAS 42
Ted Williams BOS 38
Mickey Mantle NY 34

RUNS BATTED IN
Roy Sievers WAS 114
Vic Wertz CLE 105
three tied at 103

SLUGGING AVERAGE
Ted Williams BOS ...... .731
Mickey Mantle NY ...... .665
Roy Sievers WAS ...... .579

STOLEN BASES
Luis Aparicio CHI 28
Minnie Minoso CHI 18
Jim Rivera CHI 18

RUNS SCORED
Mickey Mantle NY 121
Nellie Fox CHI 110
Jimmy Piersall BOS 103

WINS
Jim Bunning DET 20
Billy Pierce CHI 20
three tied at 16

WINNING PERCENTAGE
Dick Donovan CHI ...... .727
Tom Sturdivant NY .... .727
Jim Bunning DET .... .714

EARNED RUN AVERAGE
Bobby Shantz NY 2.45
Tom Sturdivant NY 2.54
Jim Bunning DET 2.69

STRIKEOUTS
Early Wynn CLE 184
Jim Bunning DET 182
C. Johnson BAL 177

SAVES
Bob Grim NY 19
Ray Narleski CLE 16
Ike Delock BOS 11

COMPLETE GAMES
Dick Donovan CHI 16
Billy Pierce CHI 16
Tom Brewer BOS 15

SHUTOUTS
Jim Wilson CHI 5
Billy Pierce CHI 4
Bob Turley NY 4

GAMES PITCHED
George Zuverink BAL ... 56
Tex Clevenger WAS 52
Dick Hyde WAS 52

INNINGS PITCHED
Jim Bunning DET 267
Early Wynn CLE 263
Billy Pierce CHI 257

NATIONAL LEAGUE STANDINGS

1957 NL

	W	L	PCT	GB	R	OR	BA	FA	ERA
MILWAUKEE	95	59	.617	—	772	613	.269	.981	3.47
ST. LOUIS	87	67	.565	8	737	666	.274	.979	3.78
BROOKLYN	84	70	.545	11	690	591	.253	.979	3.35
CINCINNATI	80	74	.519	15	747	781	.269	.982	4.62
PHILADELPHIA	77	77	.500	18	623	656	.250	.976	3.80
NEW YORK	69	85	.448	26	643	701	.252	.974	4.01
CHICAGO	62	92	.403	33	628	722	.244	.975	4.13
PITTSBURGH	62	92	.403	33	586	696	.268	.972	3.88
					5426	5426	.260	.977	3.88

BATTING AVERAGE
Stan Musial STL .... .351
Willie Mays NY .... .333
two tied at .... .322

HITS
Schoendienst NY, MIL 200
Hank Aaron MIL 198
Frank Robinson CIN ... 197

DOUBLES
Don Hoak CIN 39
Stan Musial STL 38
Ed Bouchee PHI 35

TRIPLES
Willie Mays NY 20
Bill Virdon PIT 11
two tied at 9

HOME RUNS
Hank Aaron MIL 44
Ernie Banks CHI 43
Duke Snider BKN 40

RUNS BATTED IN
Hank Aaron MIL 132
Del Ennis STL 105
two tied at 102

SLUGGING AVERAGE
Willie Mays NY .... .626
Stan Musial STL .... .612
Hank Aaron MIL .... .600

STOLEN BASES
Willie Mays NY 38
Jim Gilliam BKN 26
Don Blasingame STL 21

RUNS SCORED
Hank Aaron MIL 118
Ernie Banks CHI 113
Willie Mays NY 112

WINS
Warren Spahn MIL 21
Jack Sanford PHI 19
Bob Buhl MIL 18

WINNING PERCENTAGE
Bob Buhl MIL .... .720
Jack Sanford PHI .... .704
Warren Spahn MIL ..... .656

EARNED RUN AVERAGE
J. Podres BKN 2.66
Don Drysdale BKN 2.69
Warren Spahn MIL 2.69

STRIKEOUTS
Jack Sanford PHI 188
Dick Drott CHI 170
Moe Drabowsky CHI ... 170

SAVES
Clem Labine BKN 17
Marv Grissom NY 14
Turk Lown CHI 12

COMPLETE GAMES
Warren Spahn MIL 18
Bob Friend PIT 17
Ruben Gomez NY 16

SHUTOUTS
Johnny Podres BKN 6
three tied at 4

GAMES PITCHED
Turk Lown CHI 67
Roy Face PIT 59
Clem Labine BKN 58

INNINGS PITCHED
Bob Friend PIT 277
Warren Spahn MIL 271
Lew Burdette MIL 257

AMERICAN LEAGUE STANDINGS

1958 AL

	W	L	PCT	GB	R	OR	BA	FA	ERA
NEW YORK	92	62	.597	—	759	577	.268	.978	3.22
CHICAGO	82	72	.532	10	634	615	.257	.981	3.61
BOSTON	79	75	.513	13	697	691	.256	.976	3.92
CLEVELAND	77	76	.503	14.5	694	635	.258	.974	3.73
DETROIT	77	77	.500	15	659	606	.266	.982	3.59
BALTIMORE	74	79	.484	17.5	521	575	.241	.980	3.40
KANSAS CITY	73	81	.474	19	642	713	.247	.979	4.15
WASHINGTON	61	93	.396	31	553	747	.240	.980	4.53
					5159	5159	.254	.979	3.77

BATTING AVERAGE
Ted Williams BOS...... .328
Pete Runnels BOS...... .322
Harvey Kuenn DET..... .319

HITS
Nellie Fox CHI............. 187
Frank Malzone BOS ... 185
Vic Power KC, CLE..... 184

DOUBLES
Harvey Kuenn DET........ 39
Vic Power KC, CLE........ 37
Al Kaline DET 34

TRIPLES
Vic Power KC, CLE....... 10
three tied at..................... 9

HOME RUNS
Mickey Mantle NY......... 42
Rocky Colavito CLE...... 41
Roy Sievers WAS 39

RUNS BATTED IN
Jackie Jensen BOS 122
Rocky Colavito CLE.... 113
Roy Sievers WAS 108

SLUGGING AVERAGE
Rocky Colavito CLE... .620
Bob Cerv KC.............. .592
Mickey Mantle NY...... .592

STOLEN BASES
Luis Aparicio CHI.......... 29
Jim Rivera CHI.............. 21
Jim Landis CHI 19

RUNS SCORED
Mickey Mantle NY....... 127
Pete Runnels BOS...... 103
Vic Power KC, CLE....... 98

WINS
Bob Turley NY 21
Billy Pierce CHI............. 17
two tied at 16

WINNING PERCENTAGE
Bob Turley NY .... .750
Cal McLish CLE .... .667
Bill Pierce CHI............ .607

EARNED RUN AVERAGE
Whitey Ford NY 2.01
Billy Pierce CHI.......... 2.68
J. Harshman BAL....... 2.89

STRIKEOUTS
Early Wynn CHI 179
Jim Bunning DET........ 177
Bob Turley NY 168

SAVES
Ryne Duren NY............. 20
Dick Hyde WAS 18
Leo Kiely BOS 12

COMPLETE GAMES
Bob Turley NY 19
Billy Pierce CHI............. 19
Frank Lary DET 19

SHUTOUTS
Whitey Ford NY 7
Bob Turley NY 6
two tied at 4

GAMES PITCHED
Tex Clevenger WAS 55
D. Tomanek CLE, KC ... 54
Dick Hyde WAS 53

INNINGS PITCHED
Frank Lary DET 260
Pedro Ramos WAS..... 259
Dick Donovan CHI 248

NATIONAL LEAGUE STANDINGS

1958 NL

	W	L	PCT	GB	R	OR	BA	FA	ERA
MILWAUKEE	92	62	.597	—	675	541	.266	.980	3.21
PITTSBURGH	84	70	.545	8	662	607	.264	.978	3.56
SAN FRANCISCO	80	74	.519	12	727	698	.263	.975	3.98
CINCINNATI	76	78	.494	16	695	621	.258	.983	3.73
CHICAGO	72	82	.468	20	709	725	.265	.975	4.22
ST. LOUIS	72	82	.468	20	619	704	.261	.974	4.12
LOS ANGELES	71	83	.461	21	668	761	.251	.975	4.47
PHILADELPHIA	69	85	.448	23	664	762	.266	.978	4.32
					5419	5419	.262	.977	3.95

BATTING AVERAGE
Richie Ashburn PHI .... .350
Willie Mays SF .... .347
Stan Musial STL .... .337

HITS
Richie Ashburn PHI 215
Willie Mays SF 208
Hank Aaron MIL........... 196

DOUBLES
Orlando Cepeda SF...... 38
Dick Groat PIT 36
Stan Musial STL 35

TRIPLES
Richie Ashburn PHI 13
three tied at................... 11

HOME RUNS
Ernie Banks CHI 47
Frank Thomas PIT 35
two tied at 31

RUNS BATTED IN
Ernie Banks CHI 129
Frank Thomas PIT 109
Harry Anderson PHI...... 97

SLUGGING AVERAGE
Ernie Banks CHI .... .614
Willie Mays SF .... .583
Hank Aaron MIL.......... .546

STOLEN BASES
Willie Mays SF 31
Richie Ashburn PHI 30
Tony Taylor CHI............. 21

RUNS SCORED
Willie Mays SF 121
Ernie Banks CHI 119
Hank Aaron MIL........... 109

WINS
Bob Friend PIT............... 22
Warren Spahn MIL........ 22
Lew Burdette MIL.......... 20

WINNING PERCENTAGE
Warren Spahn MIL..... .667
Lew Burdette MIL....... .667
Bob Friend PIT............ .611

EARNED RUN AVERAGE
Stu Miller SF 2.47
Sam Jones STL 2.88
Lew Burdette MIL....... 2.91

STRIKEOUTS
Sam Jones STL 225
Warren Spahn MIL...... 150
two tied at 143

SAVES
Roy Face PIT 20
Clem Labine LA 14
Dick Farrell PHI............. 11

COMPLETE GAMES
Warren Spahn MIL........ 23
Robin Roberts PHI........ 21
Lew Burdette MIL.......... 19

SHUTOUTS
Carl Willey MIL................ 4
three tied at..................... 3

GAMES PITCHED
Don Elston CHI 69
Klippstein CIN, LA......... 57
Roy Face PIT................. 57

INNINGS PITCHED
Warren Spahn MIL...... 290
Lew Burdette MIL........ 275
Bob Friend PIT............ 274

605

AMERICAN LEAGUE STANDINGS

1959 AL

	W	L	PCT	GB	R	OR	BA	FA	ERA
CHICAGO	94	60	.610	—	669	588	.250	.979	3.29
CLEVELAND	89	65	.578	5	745	646	.263	.978	3.75
NEW YORK	79	75	.513	15	687	647	.260	.978	3.60
DETROIT	76	78	.494	18	713	732	.258	.978	4.20
BOSTON	75	79	.487	19	726	696	.256	.978	4.17
BALTIMORE	74	80	.481	20	551	621	.238	.976	3.56
KANSAS CITY	66	88	.429	28	681	760	.263	.973	4.35
WASHINGTON	63	91	.409	31	619	701	.237	.973	4.01
					5391	5391	.253	.977	3.86

BATTING AVERAGE
Harvey Kuenn DET .... .353
Al Kaline DET .... .327
Pete Runnels BOS ..... .314

HITS
Harvey Kuenn DET 198
Nellie Fox CHI 191
Pete Runnels BOS 176

DOUBLES
Harvey Kuenn DET 42
Frank Malzone BOS 34
Nellie Fox CHI 34

TRIPLES
Bob Allison WAS 9
Gil McDougald NY 8
two tied at 7

HOME RUNS
Rocky Colavito CLE 42
H. Killebrew WAS 42
Jim Lemon WAS 33

RUNS BATTED IN
Jackie Jensen BOS 112
Rocky Colavito CLE 111
H. Killebrew WAS 105

SLUGGING AVERAGE
Al Kaline DET .... .530
H. Killebrew WAS ...... .516
Mickey Mantle NY ...... .514

STOLEN BASES
Luis Aparicio CHI 56
Mickey Mantle NY 21
two tied at 20

RUNS SCORED
Eddie Yost DET 115
Mickey Mantle NY 104
Vic Power CLE 102

WINS
Early Wynn CHI 22
Cal McLish CLE 19
Bob Shaw CHI 18

WINNING PERCENTAGE
Bob Shaw CHI .... .750
Cal McLish CLE .... .704
Early Wynn CHI .... .688

EARNED RUN AVERAGE
Hoyt Wilhelm BAL 2.19
C. Pascual WAS 2.64
Bob Shaw CHI 2.69

STRIKEOUTS
Jim Bunning DET 201
C. Pascual WAS 185
Early Wynn CHI 179

SAVES
Turk Lown CHI 15
three tied at 14

COMPLETE GAMES
Camilo Pascual WAS 17
Don Mossi DET 15
Milt Pappas BAL 15

SHUTOUTS
Camilo Pascual WAS 6
Early Wynn CHI 5
Milt Pappas BAL 4

GAMES PITCHED
George Staley CHI 67
Turk Lown CHI 60
Tex Clevenger WAS 50

INNINGS PITCHED
Early Wynn CHI 256
Jim Bunning DET 250
Paul Foytack DET 240

NATIONAL LEAGUE STANDINGS

1959 NL

	W	L	PCT	GB	R	OR	BA	FA	ERA
LOS ANGELES*	88	68	.564	—	705	670	.257	.981	3.79
MILWAUKEE	86	70	.551	2	724	623	.265	.979	3.51
SAN FRANCISCO	83	71	.539	4	705	613	.261	.974	3.47
PITTSBURGH	78	76	.506	9	651	680	.263	.975	3.90
CHICAGO	74	80	.481	*13	673	688	.249	.977	4.01
CINCINNATI	74	80	.481	13	764	738	.274	.978	4.31
ST. LOUIS	71	83	.461	16	641	725	.269	.975	4.34
PHILADELPHIA	64	90	.416	23	599	725	.242	.973	4.27
					5462	5462	.260	.977	3.95

* Defeated Milwaukee in a playoff 2 games to 0.

BATTING AVERAGE
Hank Aaron MIL .... .355
J. Cunningham STL.... .345
Orlando Cepeda SF... .317

HITS
Hank Aaron MIL 223
Vada Pinson CIN 205
Orlando Cepeda SF.... 192

DOUBLES
Vada Pinson CIN 47
Hank Aaron MIL 46
Willie Mays SF 43

TRIPLES
Charlie Neal LA............. 11
Wally Moon LA.............. 11
two tied at 9

HOME RUNS
Eddie Mathews MIL 46
Ernie Banks CHI 45
Hank Aaron MIL............ 39

RUNS BATTED IN
Ernie Banks CHI 143
Frank Robinson CIN ... 125
Hank Aaron MIL........... 123

SLUGGING AVERAGE
Hank Aaron MIL .... .636
Ernie Banks CHI .... .596
Eddie Mathews MIL ... .593

STOLEN BASES
Willie Mays SF 27
three tied at 23

RUNS SCORED
Vada Pinson CIN 131
Willie Mays SF 125
Eddie Mathews MIL 118

WINS
Lew Burdette MIL.......... 21
Sam Jones SF 21
Warren Spahn MIL........ 21

WINNING PERCENTAGE
Roy Face PIT............. .947
Vern Law PIT .... .667
Johnny Antonelli SF... .655

EARNED RUN AVERAGE
Sam Jones SF 2.83
Stu Miller SF 2.84
Bill Buhl MIL............... 2.86

STRIKEOUTS
Don Drysdale LA.......... 242
Sam Jones SF 209
Sandy Koufax LA 173

SAVES
Lindy McDaniel STL...... 15
Don McMahon MIL 15
Don Elston CHI 13

COMPLETE GAMES
Warren Spahn MIL........ 21
Vern Law PIT................. 20
Lew Burdette MIL.......... 20

SHUTOUTS
seven tied at 4

GAMES PITCHED
Bill Henry CHI 65
Don Elston CHI 65
Lindy McDaniel STL...... 62

INNINGS PITCHED
Warren Spahn MIL...... 292
Lew Burdette MIL......... 290
Johnny Antonelli SF.... 282

AMERICAN LEAGUE STANDINGS

1960 AL

	W	L	PCT	GB	R	OR	BA	FA	ERA
NEW YORK	97	57	.630	—	746	627	.260	.979	3.52
BALTIMORE	89	65	.578	8	682	606	.253	.982	3.52
CHICAGO	87	67	.565	10	741	617	.270	.982	3.60
CLEVELAND	76	78	.494	21	667	693	.267	.978	3.95
WASHINGTON	73	81	.474	24	672	696	.244	.973	3.77
DETROIT	71	83	.461	26	633	644	.239	.977	3.64
BOSTON	65	89	.422	32	658	775	.261	.976	4.62
KANSAS CITY	58	96	.377	39	615	756	.249	.979	4.38
					5414	5414	.255	.978	3.87

BATTING AVERAGE
Pete Runnels BOS ..... .320
Al Smith CHI .... .315
Minnie Minoso CHI .... .311

HITS
Minnie Minoso CHI 184
Nellie Fox CHI 175
B. Robinson BAL 175

DOUBLES
Tito Francona CLE 36
Bill Skowron NY 34
two tied at 32

TRIPLES
Nellie Fox CHI 10
Brooks Robinson BAL 9

HOME RUNS
Mickey Mantle NY 40
Roger Maris NY 39
Jim Lemon WAS 38

RUNS BATTED IN
Roger Maris NY 112
Minnie Minoso CHI 105
Vic Wertz BOS 103

SLUGGING AVERAGE
Roger Maris NY .... .581
Mickey Mantle NY ...... .558
two tied at .... .534

STOLEN BASES
Luis Aparicio CHI 51
Jim Landis CHI 23
Lenny Green WAS 21

RUNS SCORED
Mickey Mantle NY 119
Roger Maris NY 98
two tied at 89

WINS
Jim Perry CLE 18
Chuck Estrada BAL 18
Buddy Daley KC 16

WINNING PERCENTAGE
Jim Perry CLE .... .643
Art Ditmar NY .... .625
Chuck Estrada BAL ... .621

EARNED RUN AVERAGE
F. Baumann CHI 2.67
Jim Bunning DET 2.79
two tied at 3.06

STRIKEOUTS
Jim Bunning DET 201
Pedro Ramos WAS 160
Early Wynn CHI 158

SAVES
Mike Fornieles BOS 14
J. Klippstein CLE 14
Ray Moore CHI, WAS ... 13

COMPLETE GAMES
Frank Lary DET 15
Pedro Ramos WAS 14
Ray Herbert KC 14

SHUTOUTS
Jim Perry CLE 4
Whitey Ford NY 4
Early Wynn CHI 4

GAMES PITCHED
Mike Fornieles BOS 70
Gerry Staley CHI 64
Tex Clevenger WAS 53

INNINGS PITCHED
Frank Lary DET 274
Pedro Ramos WAS 274
Jim Perry CLE 261

NATIONAL LEAGUE STANDINGS

1960 NL

	W	L	PCT	GB	R	OR	BA	FA	ERA
PITTSBURGH	95	59	.617	—	734	593	.276	.979	3.49
MILWAUKEE	88	66	.571	7	724	658	.265	.976	3.76
ST. LOUIS	86	68	.558	9	639	616	.254	.976	3.64
LOS ANGELES	82	72	.532	13	662	593	.255	.979	3.40
SAN FRANCISCO	79	75	.513	16	671	631	.255	.972	3.44
CINCINNATI	67	87	.435	28	640	692	.250	.979	4.00
CHICAGO	60	94	.390	35	634	776	.243	.977	4.35
PHILADELPHIA	59	95	.383	36	546	691	.239	.974	4.01
					5250	5250	.255	.977	3.76

BATTING AVERAGE
Dick Groat PIT .... .325
Willie Mays SF .... .319
R. Clemente PIT .... .314

HITS
Willie Mays SF 190
Vada Pinson CIN 187
Dick Groat PIT 186

DOUBLES
Vada Pinson CIN 37
Orlando Cepeda SF 36
two tied at 33

TRIPLES
Bill Bruton MIL 13
Willie Mays SF 12
Vada Pinson CIN 12

HOME RUNS
Ernie Banks CHI 41
Hank Aaron MIL 40
Eddie Mathews MIL 39

RUNS BATTED IN
Hank Aaron MIL 126
Eddie Mathews MIL 124
Ernie Banks CHI 117

SLUGGING AVERAGE
F. Robinson CIN .... .595
Hank Aaron MIL .... .566
Ken Boyer STL .... .562

STOLEN BASES
Maury Wills LA 50
Vada Pinson CIN 32
Tony Taylor CHI, PHI.... 26

RUNS SCORED
Bill Bruton MIL 112
Eddie Mathews MIL 108
two tied at 107

WINS
Ernie Broglio STL.......... 21
Warren Spahn MIL........ 21
Vern Law PIT 20

WINNING PERCENTAGE
Ernie Broglio STL........ .700
Vern Law PIT .... .690
Warren Spahn MIL...... .677

EARNED RUN AVERAGE
Mike McCormick SF ... 2.70
Ernie Broglio STL 2.74
Don Drysdale LA 2.84

STRIKEOUTS
Don Drysdale LA......... 246
Sandy Koufax LA 197
Sam Jones SF 190

SAVES
Lindy McDaniel STL...... 26
Roy Face PIT 24
Bill Henry CIN 17

COMPLETE GAMES
Warren Spahn MIL......... 18
Vern Law PIT 18
Lew Burdette MIL.......... 18

SHUTOUTS
Jack Sanford SF 6
Don Drysdale LA............. 5

GAMES PITCHED
Roy Face PIT 68
Lindy McDaniel STL...... 65
Don Elston CHI 60

INNINGS PITCHED
Larry Jackson STL....... 282
Lew Burdette MIL........ 276
Bob Friend PIT............. 276

AMERICAN LEAGUE STANDINGS

1961 AL

	W	L	PCT	GB	R	OR	BA	FA	ERA
NEW YORK	109	53	.673	—	827	612	.263	.980	3.46
DETROIT	101	61	.623	8	841	671	.266	.976	3.55
BALTIMORE	95	67	.586	14	691	588	.254	.980	3.22
CHICAGO	86	76	.531	23	765	726	.265	.980	4.06
CLEVELAND	78	83	.484	30.5	737	752	.266	.977	4.15
BOSTON	76	86	.469	33	729	792	.254	.977	4.29
MINNESOTA	70	90	.438	38	707	778	.250	.971	4.28
LOS ANGELES	70	91	.435	38.5	744	784	.245	.969	4.31
KANSAS CITY	61	100	.379	47.5	683	863	.247	.972	4.74
WASHINGTON	61	100	.379	47.5	618	776	.244	.975	4.23
					7342	7342	.256	.976	4.02

BATTING AVERAGE
Norm Cash DET .... .361
Al Kaline DET .... .324
Jimmy Piersall CLE.... .322

HITS
Norm Cash DET 193
B. Robinson BAL 192
Al Kaline DET 190

DOUBLES
Al Kaline DET 41
Tony Kubek NY............. 38
Brooks Robinson BAL... 38

TRIPLES
Jake Wood DET............. 14
Marty Keough WAS 9
Jerry Lumpe KC.............. 9

HOME RUNS
Roger Maris NY 61
Mickey Mantle NY......... 54
two tied at 46

RUNS BATTED IN
Roger Maris NY 142
Jim Gentile BAL........... 141
Rocky Colavito DET.... 140

SLUGGING AVERAGE
Mickey Mantle NY....... .687
Norm Cash DET .... .662
Jim Gentile BAL.......... .646

STOLEN BASES
Luis Aparicio CHI 53
Dick Howser KC............ 37
Jake Wood DET............. 30

RUNS SCORED
Roger Maris NY 132
Mickey Mantle NY....... 132
Rocky Colavito DET.... 129

WINS
Whitey Ford NY 25
Frank Lary DET 23
Steve Barber BAL......... 18

WINNING PERCENTAGE
Whitey Ford NY .... .862
Ralph Terry NY .... .842
Luis Arroyo NY........... .750

EARNED RUN AVERAGE
Dick Donovan WAS ... 2.40
Bill Stafford NY 2.68
Don Mossi DET.......... 2.96

STRIKEOUTS
Camilo Pascual MIN ... 221
Whitey Ford NY 209
Jim Bunning DET........ 194

SAVES
Luis Arroyo NY.............. 29
Hoyt Wilhelm BAL......... 18
Mike Fornieles BOS...... 15

COMPLETE GAMES
Frank Lary DET 22
Camilo Pascual MIN 15
Steve Barber BAL......... 14

SHUTOUTS
Camilo Pascual MIN 8
Steve Barber BAL........... 8
two tied at 4

GAMES PITCHED
Luis Arroyo NY.............. 65
Tom Morgan LA............ 59
Turk Lown CHI.............. 59

INNINGS PITCHED
Whitey Ford NY 283
Frank Lary DET 275
Jim Bunning DET........ 268

NATIONAL LEAGUE STANDINGS

1961 NL

	W	L	PCT	GB	R	OR	BA	FA	ERA
CINCINNATI	93	61	.604	—	710	653	.270	.977	3.78
LOS ANGELES	89	65	.578	4	735	697	.262	.975	4.04
SAN FRANCISCO	85	69	.552	8	773	655	.264	.977	3.77
MILWAUKEE	83	71	.539	10	712	656	.258	.982	3.89
ST. LOUIS	80	74	.519	13	703	668	.271	.972	3.74
PITTSBURGH	75	79	.487	18	694	675	.273	.975	3.92
CHICAGO	64	90	.416	29	689	800	.255	.970	4.48
PHILADELPHIA	47	107	.305	46	584	796	.243	.976	4.61
					5600	5600	.262	.976	4.03

BATTING AVERAGE
R. Clemente PIT .... .351
Vada Pinson CIN .... .343
Ken Boyer STL .... .329

HITS
Vada Pinson CIN 208
R. Clemente PIT 201
Hank Aaron MIL.......... 197

DOUBLES
Hank Aaron MIL............ 39
Vada Pinson CIN 34
two tied at 32

TRIPLES
George Altman CHI 12
three tied at................... 11

HOME RUNS
Orlando Cepeda SF...... 46
Willie Mays SF.............. 40
Frank Robinson CIN 37

RUNS BATTED IN
Orlando Cepeda SF... 142
Frank Robinson CIN ... 124
Willie Mays SF............ 123

SLUGGING AVERAGE
F. Robinson CIN .... .611
Orlando Cepeda SF.... .609
Hank Aaron MIL.......... .594

STOLEN BASES
Maury Wills LA.............. 35
Vada Pinson CIN 23
Frank Robinson CIN 22

RUNS SCORED
Willie Mays SF............ 129
Frank Robinson CIN ... 117
Hank Aaron MIL.......... 115

WINS
Joey Jay CIN 21
Warren Spahn MIL....... 21
Jim O'Toole CIN 19

WINNING PERCENTAGE
Johnny Podres LA ..... .783
Jim O'Toole CIN .... .679
Joey Jay CIN .... .677

EARNED RUN AVERAGE
Warren Spahn MIL..... 3.02
Jim O'Toole CIN 3.10
Curt Simmons STL 3.13

STRIKEOUTS
Sandy Koufax LA........ 269
Stan Williams LA......... 205
Don Drysdale LA......... 182

SAVES
Stu Miller SF 17
Roy Face PIT................ 17
two tied at 16

COMPLETE GAMES
Warren Spahn MIL........ 21
Sandy Koufax LA 15
two tied at 14

SHUTOUTS
Joey Jay CIN 4
Warren Spahn MIL........... 4

GAMES PITCHED
Jack Baldschun PHI...... 65
Stu Miller SF 63
Roy Face PIT................ 62

INNINGS PITCHED
Lew Burdette MIL........ 272
Warren Spahn MIL...... 263
Don Cardwell CHI....... 259

AMERICAN LEAGUE STANDINGS

1962 AL

	W	L	PCT	GB	R	OR	BA	FA	ERA
NEW YORK	96	66	.593	—	817	680	.267	.979	3.70
MINNESOTA	91	71	.562	5	798	713	.260	.979	3.89
LOS ANGELES	86	76	.531	10	718	706	.250	.972	3.70
DETROIT	85	76	.528	10.5	758	692	.248	.974	3.81
CHICAGO	85	77	.525	11	707	658	.257	.982	3.73
CLEVELAND	80	82	.494	16	682	745	.245	.977	4.14
BALTIMORE	77	85	.475	19	652	680	.248	.980	3.69
BOSTON	76	84	.475	19	707	756	.258	.979	4.22
KANSAS CITY	72	90	.444	24	745	837	.263	.979	4.79
WASHINGTON	60	101	.373	35.5	599	716	.250	.978	4.04
					7183	7183	.255	.978	3.97

BATTING AVERAGE
Pete Runnels BOS..... .326
Floyd Robinson CHI... .312
Chuck Hinton WAS.... .310

HITS
B. Richardson NY 209
Jerry Lumpe KC........... 193
B. Robinson BAL 192

DOUBLES
Frank Robinson CHI 45
C. Yastrzemski BOS..... 43
Ed Bressoud BOS......... 40

TRIPLES
Gino Cimoli KC 15
three at.......................... 10

HOME RUNS
H. Killebrew MIN 48
Norm Cash DET 39
two tied at 37

RUNS BATTED IN
H. Killebrew MIN 126
Norm Siebern KC........ 117
Rocky Colavito............. 112

SLUGGING AVERAGE
H. Killebrew MIN .... .545
Rocky Colavito DET... .514
Norm Cash DET .... .513

STOLEN BASES
Luis Aparicio CHI 31
Chuck Hinton WAS....... 28
Jake Wood DET............ 24

RUNS SCORED
Albie Pearson LA........ 115
Norm Siebern KC........ 114
Bob Allison MIN 102

WINS
Ralph Terry NY 23
three tied at.................. 20

WINNING PERCENTAGE
Ray Herbert CHI .... .690
Whitey Ford NY .... .680
two tied at .... .667

EARNED RUN AVERAGE
Hank Aguirre DET...... 2.21
Robin Roberts BAL ... 2.78
Whitey Ford NY 2.90

STRIKEOUTS
Camilo Pascual MIN ... 206
Jim Bunning DET........ 184
Ralph Terry NY 176

SAVES
Dick Radatz BOS.......... 24
Marshall Bridges NY..... 18
Terry Fox DET 16

COMPLETE GAMES
Camilo Pascual MIN 18
Jim Kaat MIN 16
Dick Donovan CLE 16

SHUTOUTS
Camilo Pascual MIN 5
Dick Donovan CLE 5
Jim Kaat MIN 5

GAMES PITCHED
Dick Radatz BOS.......... 62
John Wyatt KC............... 59
two tied at 57

INNINGS PITCHED
Ralph Terry NY 299
Jim Kaat MIN 269
two tied at 258

NATIONAL LEAGUE STANDINGS

1962 NL

	W	L	PCT	GB	R	OR	BA	FA	ERA
SAN FRANCISCO*103	62	.624	—	878	690	.278	.977	3.79
LOS ANGELES	102	63	.618	1	842	697	.268	.970	3.62
CINCINNATI	98	64	.605	3.5	802	685	.270	.977	3.75
PITTSBURGH	93	68	.578	8	706	626	.268	.976	3.37
MILWAUKEE	86	76	.531	15.5	730	665	.252	.980	3.68
ST. LOUIS	84	78	.519	17.5	774	664	.271	.979	3.55
PHILADELPHIA	81	80	.503	20	705	759	.260	.977	4.28
HOUSTON	64	96	.400	36.5	592	717	.246	.973	3.83
CHICAGO	59	103	.364	42.5	632	827	.253	.977	4.54
NEW YORK	40	120	.250	60.5	617	948	.240	.967	5.04
*Defeated Los Angeles in a playoff 2 games to 1					7278	7278	.261	.975	3.94

BATTING AVERAGE
Tommy Davis LA .... .346
F. Robinson CIN .... .342
Stan Musial STL .... .330

HITS
Tommy Davis LA 230
Frank Robinson CIN ... 208
Maury Wills LA............ 208

DOUBLES
Frank Robinson CIN 51
Willie Mays SF 36
Dick Groat PIT 34

TRIPLES
four tied at..................... 10

HOME RUNS
Willie Mays SF 49
Hank Aaron MIL............ 45
Frank Robinson CIN 39

RUNS BATTED IN
Tommy Davis LA 153
Willie Mays SF 141
Frank Robinson CIN ... 136

SLUGGING AVERAGE
F. Robinson CIN .... .624
Hank Aaron MIL.......... .618
Willie Mays SF .... .615

STOLEN BASES
Maury Wills LA............ 104
Willie Davis LA.............. 32
two tied at 26

RUNS SCORED
Frank Robinson CIN ... 134
Maury Wills LA............ 130
Willie Mays SF 130

WINS
Don Drysdale LA........... 25
Jack Sanford SF 24
Bob Purkey CIN 23

WINNING PERCENTAGE
Bob Purkey CIN .... .821
Jack Sanford SF .... .774
Don Drysdale LA........ .735

EARNED RUN AVERAGE
Sandy Koufax LA....... 2.54
Bob Shaw MIL 2.80
Bob Purkey CIN 2.81

STRIKEOUTS
Don Drysdale LA.......... 232
Sandy Koufax LA........ 216
Bob Gibson STL 208

SAVES
Roy Face PIT................ 28
Ron Perranoski LA........ 20
Stu Miller SF 19

COMPLETE GAMES
Warren Spahn MIL........ 22
Art Mahaffey PHI 20
Billy O'Dell SF............... 20

SHUTOUTS
Bob Gibson STL 5
Bob Friend PIT................ 5
two tied at 4

GAMES PITCHED
Ron Perranoski LA........ 70
Jack Baldshun PHI 67
Ed Roebuck LA............. 64

INNINGS PITCHED
Don Drysdale LA......... 314
Bob Purkey CIN 288
Billy O'Dell SF............. 281

AMERICAN LEAGUE STANDINGS

1963 AL

	W	L	PCT	GB	R	OR	BA	FA	ERA
NEW YORK	104	57	.646	—	714	547	.252	.982	3.07
CHICAGO	94	68	.580	10.5	683	544	.250	.979	2.97
MINNESOTA	91	70	.565	13	767	602	.255	.976	3.28
BALTIMORE	86	76	.531	18.5	644	621	.249	.984	3.45
CLEVELAND	79	83	.488	25.5	635	702	.239	.977	3.79
DETROIT	79	83	.488	25.5	700	703	.252	.981	3.90
BOSTON	76	85	.472	28	666	704	.252	.978	3.97
KANSAS CITY	73	89	.451	31.5	615	704	.247	.980	3.92
LOS ANGELES	70	91	.435	34	597	660	.250	.974	3.52
WASHINGTON	56	106	.346	48.5	578	812	.227	.971	4.42
					6599	6599	.247	.978	3.63

BATTING AVERAGE
Yastrzemski BOS .... .321
Al Kaline DET .... .312
Rich Rollins MIN .... .307

HITS
C. Yastrzemski BOS ... 183
Pete Ward CHI 177
Albie Pearson LA 176

DOUBLES
C. Yastrzemski BOS 40
Pete Ward CHI 34
two tied at 32

TRIPLES
Zoilo Versalles MIN 13
Jim Fregosi LA 12
Chuck Hinton WAS 12

HOME RUNS
H. Killebrew MIN 45
Dick Stuart BOS 42
Bob Allison MIN 35

RUNS BATTED IN
Dick Stuart BOS 118
Al Kaline DET 101
H. Killebrew MIN 96

SLUGGING AVERAGE
H. Killebrew MIN .... .555
Bob Allison MIN .... .533
Elston Howard NY ..... .528

STOLEN BASES
Luis Aparicio BAL 40
Chuck Hinton WAS 25
two tied at 18

RUNS SCORED
Bob Allison MIN 99
Albie Pearson LA 92
two tied at 91

WINS
Whitey Ford NY 24
Jim Bouton NY 21
Camilo Pascual MIN 21

WINNING PERCENTAGE
Whitey Ford NY .... .774
Jim Bouton NY .... .750
Dick Radatz BOS .... .714

EARNED RUN AVERAGE
Gary Peters CHI 2.33
Juan Pizarro CHI 2.39
C. Pascual MIN 2.46

STRIKEOUTS
Camilo Pascual MIN ... 202
Jim Bunning DET 196
Dick Stigman MIN 193

SAVES
Stu Miller BAL 27
Dick Radatz BOS 25
three tied at 21

COMPLETE GAMES
Ralph Terry NY 18
Camilo Pascual MIN 18
Dick Stigman MIN 15

SHUTOUTS
Ray Herbert CHI 7
Jim Bouton NY 6

GAMES PITCHED
Stu Miller BAL 71
Dick Radatz BOS 66
Bill Dailey MIN 66

INNINGS PITCHED
Whitey Ford NY 269
Ralph Terry NY 268
Monbouquette BOS 267

NATIONAL LEAGUE STANDINGS

1963 NL

	W	L	PCT	GB	R	OR	BA	FA	ERA
LOS ANGELES	99	63	.611	—	640	550	.251	.975	2.85
ST. LOUIS	93	69	.574	6	747	628	.271	.976	3.32
SAN FRANCISCO	88	74	.543	11	725	641	.258	.975	3.35
PHILADELPHIA	87	75	.537	12	642	578	.252	.978	3.09
CINCINNATI	86	76	.531	13	648	594	.246	.978	3.29
MILWAUKEE	84	78	.519	15	677	603	.244	.980	3.26
CHICAGO	82	80	.506	17	570	578	.238	.976	3.08
PITTSBURGH	74	88	.457	25	567	595	.250	.972	3.10
HOUSTON	66	96	.407	33	464	640	.220	.974	3.44
NEW YORK	51	111	.315	48	501	774	.219	.967	4.12
					6181	6181	.245	.975	3.29

BATTING AVERAGE
Tommy Davis LA .... .326
R. Clemente PIT .... .320
two tied at .... .319

HITS
Vada Pinson CIN 204
Hank Aaron MIL 201
Dick Groat STL 201

DOUBLES
Dick Groat STL 43
Vada Pinson CIN 37
two tied at 36

TRIPLES
Vada Pinson CIN 14
Tony Gonzalez PHI 12
two tied at 11

HOME RUNS
Willie McCovey SF 44
Hank Aaron MIL 44
Willie Mays SF 38

RUNS BATTED IN
Hank Aaron MIL 130
Ken Boyer STL 111
Bill White STL 109

SLUGGING AVERAGE
Hank Aaron MIL .... .586
Willie Mays SF .... .582
Willie McCovey SF ..... .566

STOLEN BASES
Maury Wills LA 40
Hank Aaron MIL 31
Vada Pinson CIN 27

RUNS SCORED
Hank Aaron MIL 121
Willie Mays SF 115
Curt Flood STL 112

WINS
Sandy Koufax LA 25
Juan Marichal SF 25
two tied at 23

WINNING PERCENTAGE
Ron Perranoski LA ..... .842
Sandy Koufax LA .... .833
two tied at .... .767

EARNED RUN AVERAGE
Sandy Koufax LA 1.88
Dick Ellsworth CHI 2.11
Bob Friend PIT 2.34

STRIKEOUTS
Sandy Koufax LA 306
Jim Maloney CIN 265
Don Drysdale LA 251

SAVES
Lindy McDaniel CHI 22
Ron Perranoski LA 21
two tied at 16

COMPLETE GAMES
Warren Spahn MIL 22
Sandy Koufax LA 20
Dick Ellsworth CHI 19

SHUTOUTS
Sandy Koufax LA 11
Warren Spahn MIL 7
two tied at 6

GAMES PITCHED
Ron Perranoski LA 69
Jack Baldschun PHI 65
Larry Bearnarth NY 58

INNINGS PITCHED
Juan Marichal SF 321
Don Drysdale LA 315
Sandy Koufax LA 311

AMERICAN LEAGUE STANDINGS

1964 AL

	W	L	PCT	GB	R	OR	BA	FA	ERA
NEW YORK	99	63	.611	—	730	577	.253	.983	3.15
CHICAGO	98	64	.605	1	642	501	.247	.981	2.72
BALTIMORE	97	65	.599	2	679	567	.248	.985	3.16
DETROIT	85	77	.525	14	699	678	.253	.982	3.84
LOS ANGELES	82	80	.506	17	544	551	.242	.978	2.91
CLEVELAND	79	83	.488	20	689	693	.247	.981	3.75
MINNESOTA	79	83	.488	20	737	678	.252	.977	3.57
BOSTON	72	90	.444	27	688	793	.258	.977	4.50
WASHINGTON	62	100	.383	37	578	733	.231	.979	3.98
KANSAS CITY	57	105	.352	42	621	836	.239	.974	4.71
					6607	6607	.247	.980	3.63

BATTING AVERAGE
Tony Oliva MIN .... .323
B. Robinson BAL .... .317
Elston Howard NY ..... .313

HITS
Tony Oliva MIN 217
B. Robinson BAL 194
B. Richardson NY 181

DOUBLES
Tony Oliva MIN 43
Ed Bressoud BOS......... 41
Brooks Robinson BAL... 35

TRIPLES
Rich Rollins MIN 10
Zoilo Versalles MIN....... 10
two tied at 9

HOME RUNS
H. Killebrew MIN 49
Boog Powell BAL........... 39
Mickey Mantle NY 35

RUNS BATTED IN
B. Robinson BAL 118
Dick Stuart BOS.......... 114
two tied at 111

SLUGGING AVERAGE
Boog Powell BAL .... .606
Mickey Mantle NY .... .591
Tony Oliva MIN .... .557

STOLEN BASES
Luis Aparicio BAL 57
Al Weis CHI 22
Vic Davalillo CLE 21

RUNS SCORED
Tony Oliva MIN 109
Dick Howser CLE........ 101
H. Killebrew MIN 95

WINS
Gary Peters CHI 20
Dean Chance LA 20
three tied at................... 19

WINNING PERCENTAGE
Wally Bunker BAL........ .792
Whitey Ford NY .... .739
Gary Peters CHI .... .714

EARNED RUN AVERAGE
Dean Chance LA 1.65
Joe Horlen CHI 1.88
Whitey Ford NY 2.13

STRIKEOUTS
Al Downing NY............ 217
Camilo Pascual MIN ... 213
Dean Chance LA 207

SAVES
Dick Radatz BOS.......... 29
Hoyt Wilhelm CHI 27
Stu Miller BAL............... 23

COMPLETE GAMES
Dean Chance LA 15
Camilo Pascual MIN 14
three tied at................... 13

SHUTOUTS
Dean Chance LA 11
Whitey Ford NY 8
Milt Pappas BAL 7

GAMES PITCHED
John Wyatt KC.............. 81
Dick Radatz BOS.......... 79
Hoyt Wilhelm CHI 73

INNINGS PITCHED
Dean Chance LA 278
Gary Peters CHI 274
Jim Bouton NY............. 271

NATIONAL LEAGUE STANDINGS

1964 NL

	W	L	PCT	GB	R	OR	BA	FA	ERA
ST. LOUIS	93	69	.574	—	715	652	.272	.973	3.43
CINCINNATI	92	70	.568	1	660	566	.249	.979	3.07
PHILADELPHIA	92	70	.568	1	693	632	.258	.975	3.36
SAN FRANCISCO	90	72	.556	3	656	587	.246	.975	3.19
MILWAUKEE	88	74	.543	5	803	744	.272	.977	4.12
LOS ANGELES	80	82	.494	13	614	572	.250	.973	2.95
PITTSBURGH	80	82	.494	13	663	636	.264	.972	3.52
CHICAGO	76	86	.469	17	649	724	.251	.975	4.08
HOUSTON	66	96	:407	27	495	628	.229	.976	3.41
NEW YORK	53	109	.327	40	569	776	.246	.974	4.25
					6517	6517	.254	.975	3.54

BATTING AVERAGE
R. Clemente PIT .... .339
Hank Aaron MIL .... .328
Joe Torre MIL .... .321

HITS
Curt Flood STL 211
R. Clemente PIT 211
two tied at 201

DOUBLES
Lee Maye MIL 44
R. Clemente PIT 40
Billy Williams CHI 39

TRIPLES
Dick Allen PHI 13
Ron Santo CHI 13
two tied at 11

HOME RUNS
Willie Mays SF 47
Billy Williams CHI 33
three tied at 31

RUNS BATTED IN
Ken Boyer STL 119
Ron Santo CHI 114
Willie Mays SF 111

SLUGGING AVERAGE
Willie Mays SF .... .607
Ron Santo CHI .... .564
Dick Allen PHI .... .557

STOLEN BASES
Maury Wills LA 53
Lou Brock CHI, STL 43
Willie Davis LA 42

RUNS SCORED
Dick Allen PHI 125
Willie Mays SF 121
Lou Brock CHI, STL 111

WINS
Larry Jackson CHI 24
Juan Marichal SF 21
Ray Sadecki STL 20

WINNING PERCENTAGE
Sandy Koufax LA .... .792
Juan Marichal SF .... .724
Jim O'Toole CIN .... .708

EARNED RUN AVERAGE
Sandy Koufax LA 1.74
Don Drysdale LA 2.18
Chris Short PHI 2.20

STRIKEOUTS
Bob Veale PIT 250
Bob Gibson STL 245
Don Drysdale LA 237

SAVES
Hal Woodeshick HOU ... 23
Al McBean PIT 22
Jack Baldschun PHI 21

COMPLETE GAMES
Juan Marichal SF 22
Don Drysdale LA 21
Larry Jackson CHI 19

SHUTOUTS
Sandy Koufax LA 7
three tied at 5

GAMES PITCHED
Bob Miller LA 74
Ron Perranoski LA 72
Jack Baldschun PHI 71

INNINGS PITCHED
Don Drysdale LA 321
Larry Jackson CHI 298
Bob Gibson STL 287

AMERICAN LEAGUE STANDINGS

1965 AL

	W	L	PCT	GB	R	OR	BA	FA	ERA
MINNESOTA	102	60	.630	—	774	600	.254	.973	3.14
CHICAGO	95	67	.586	7	647	555	.246	.980	2.99
BALTIMORE	94	68	.580	8	641	578	.238	.980	2.98
DETROIT	89	73	.549	13	680	602	.238	.981	3.35
CLEVELAND	87	75	.537	15	663	613	.250	.981	3.30
NEW YORK	77	85	.475	25	611	604	.235	.978	3.28
CALIFORNIA	75	87	.463	27	527	569	.239	.981	3.17
WASHINGTON	70	92	.432	32	591	721	.228	.976	3.93
BOSTON	62	100	.383	40	669	791	.251	.974	4.24
KANSAS CITY	59	103	.364	43	585	755	.240	.977	4.24
					6388	6388	.242	.978	3.46

BATTING AVERAGE
Tony Oliva MIN .... .321
Yastrzemski BOS .... .312
Vic Davalillo CLE .... .301

HITS
Tony Oliva MIN 185
Zoilo Versalles MIN 182
Rocky Colavito CLE 170

DOUBLES
C. Yastrzemski BOS 45
Zoilo Versalles MIN 45
Tony Oliva MIN 40

TRIPLES
Bert Campaneris KC 12
Zoilo Versalles MIN 12
Luis Aparicio BAL 10

HOME RUNS
Tony Conigliaro BOS 32
Norm Cash DET 30
Willie Horton DET 29

RUNS BATTED IN
Rocky Colavito CLE 108
Willie Horton DET 104
Tony Oliva MIN 98

SLUGGING AVERAGE
Yastrzemski BOS .... .536
T. Conigliaro BOS ...... .512
Norm Cash DET .... .512

STOLEN BASES
Bert Campaneris KC 51
Jose Cardenal CAL 37
Zoilo Versalles MIN 27

RUNS SCORED
Zoilo Versalles MIN 126
Tony Oliva MIN 107
Tom Tresh NY 94

WINS
Mudcat Grant MIN 21
Mel Stottlemyre NY 20
Jim Kaat MIN 18

WINNING PERCENTAGE
Mudcat Grant MIN ..... .750
Denny McLain DET .... .727
Mel Stottlemyre NY .... .690

EARNED RUN AVERAGE
Sam McDowell CLE ... 2.18
Eddie Fisher CHI 2.40
Sonny Siebert CLE 2.43

STRIKEOUTS
Sam McDowell CLE 325
Mickey Lolich DET 226
Denny McLain DET 192

SAVES
Ron Kline WAS 29
Eddie Fisher CHI 24
Stu Miller BAL 24

COMPLETE GAMES
Mel Stottlemyre NY 18
Mudcat Grant MIN 14
Sam McDowell CLE 14

SHUTOUTS
Mudcat Grant MIN 6
three tied at..................... 4

GAMES PITCHED
Eddie Fisher CHI 82
Ron Kline WAS 74
Bob Lee CAL 69

INNINGS PITCHED
Mel Stottlemyre NY 291
Sam McDowell CLE 273
Mudcat Grant MIN 270

NATIONAL LEAGUE STANDINGS

1965 NL

	W	L	PCT	GB	R	OR	BA	FA	ERA
LOS ANGELES	97	65	.599	—	608	521	.245	.979	2.81
SAN FRANCISCO	95	67	.586	2	682	593	.252	.976	3.20
PITTSBURGH	90	72	.556	7	675	580	.265	.977	3.01
CINCINNATI	89	73	.549	8	825	704	.273	.981	3.88
MILWAUKEE	86	76	.531	11	708	633	.256	.978	3.52
PHILADELPHIA	85	76	.528	11.5	654	667	.250	.975	3.53
ST. LOUIS	80	81	.497	16.5	707	674	.254	.979	3.77
CHICAGO	72	90	.444	25	635	723	.238	.974	3.78
HOUSTON	65	97	.401	32	596	711	.237	.974	3.84
NEW YORK	50	112	.309	47	495	752	.221	.974	4.06
					6558	6558	.249	.977	3.54

BATTING AVERAGE
R. Clemente PIT .... .329
Hank Aaron MIL .... .318
Willie Mays SF .... .317

HITS
Pete Rose CIN 209
Vada Pinson CIN 204
Billy Williams CHI 203

DOUBLES
Hank Aaron MIL 40
Billy Williams CHI 39
two tied at 35

TRIPLES
Johnny Callison PHI 16
three tied at 14

HOME RUNS
Willie Mays SF 52
Willie McCovey SF 39
Billy Williams CHI 34

RUNS BATTED IN
Deron Johnson CIN 130
Frank Robinson CIN ... 113
Willie Mays SF 112

SLUGGING AVERAGE
Willie Mays SF .... .645
Hank Aaron MIL .... .560
Billy Williams CHI .... .552

STOLEN BASES
Maury Wills LA 94
Lou Brock STL 63
Jimmy Wynn HOU 43

RUNS SCORED
Tommy Harper CIN 126
Willie Mays SF 118
Pete Rose CIN 117

WINS
Sandy Koufax LA 26
Tony Cloninger MIL 24
Don Drysdale LA 23

WINNING PERCENTAGE
Sandy Koufax LA .... .765
Jim Maloney CIN .... .690
Sammy Ellis CIN .... .688

EARNED RUN AVERAGE
Sandy Koufax LA 2.04
Juan Marichal SF 2.13
Vern Law PIT 2.15

STRIKEOUTS
Sandy Koufax LA 382
Bob Veale PIT 276
Bob Gibson STL 270

SAVES
Ted Abernathy CHI 31
Billy McCool CIN 21
Frank Linzy SF 21

COMPLETE GAMES
Sandy Koufax LA 27
Juan Marichal SF 24
two tied at 20

SHUTOUTS
Juan Marichal SF 10
Sandy Koufax LA 8
two tied at 7

GAMES PITCHED
Ted Abernathy CHI 84
Woodeshick HOU, STL.. 78
Lindy McDaniel CHI 71

INNINGS PITCHED
Sandy Koufax LA 336
Don Drysdale LA 308
Bob Gibson STL 299

AMERICAN LEAGUE STANDINGS

1966 AL

	W	L	PCT	GB	R	OR	BA	FA	ERA
BALTIMORE	97	63	.606	—	755	601	.258	.981	3.32
MINNESOTA	89	73	.549	9	663	581	.249	.977	3.13
DETROIT	88	74	.543	10	719	698	.251	.980	3.85
CHICAGO	83	79	.512	15	574	517	.231	.976	2.68
CLEVELAND	81	81	.500	17	574	586	.237	.977	3.23
CALIFORNIA	80	82	.494	18	604	643	.232	.979	3.56
KANSAS CITY	74	86	.463	23	564	648	.236	.977	3.55
WASHINGTON	71	88	.447	25.5	557	659	.234	.977	3.70
BOSTON	72	90	.444	26	655	731	.240	.975	3.92
NEW YORK	70	89	.440	26.5	611	612	.235	.977	3.42
					6276	6276	.240	.978	3.44

BATTING AVERAGE
F. Robinson BAL .... .316
Tony Oliva MIN .... .307
Al Kaline DET .... .288

HITS
Tony Oliva MIN 191
Frank Robinson BAL... 182
Luis Aparicio BAL 182

DOUBLES
C. Yastrzemski BOS 39
Brooks Robinson BAL... 35
Frank Robinson BAL..... 34

TRIPLES
Bobby Knoop CAL 11
Bert Campaneris KC 10
Ed Brinkman WAS 9

HOME RUNS
Frank Robinson BAL..... 49
H. Killebrew MIN 39
Boog Powell BAL 34

RUNS BATTED IN
Frank Robinson BAL... 122
H. Killbrew MIN 110
Boog Powell BAL 109

SLUGGING AVERAGE
F. Robinson BAL .... .637
H. Killebrew MIN .... .538
Al Kaline DET .... .534

STOLEN BASES
Bert Campaneris KC..... 52
Don Buford CHI 51
Tommy Agee CHI 44

RUNS SCORED
Frank Robinson BAL... 122
Tony Oliva MIN 99
two tied at 98

WINS
Jim Kaat MIN 25
Denny McLain DET....... 20
E. Wilson BOS, DET..... 18

WINNING PERCENTAGE
Sonny Siebert CLE .... .667
Jim Kaat MIN .... .658
Wilson BOS, DET ...... .621

EARNED RUN AVERAGE
Gary Peters CHI 1.98
Joe Horlen CHI 2.43
Steve Hargan CLE..... 2.48

STRIKEOUTS
Sam McDowell CLE.... 225
Jim Kaat MIN 205
E. Wilson BOS, DET ... 200

SAVES
Jack Aker KC 32
Ron Kline WAS 23
Larry Sherry DET 20

COMPLETE GAMES
Jim Kaat MIN 19
Denny McLain DET....... 14
E. Wilson BOS, DET..... 13

SHUTOUTS
Luis Tiant CLE 5
Sam McDowell CLE........ 5
Tommy John CHI............ 5

GAMES PITCHED
E. Fisher CHI, BAL 67
Casey Cox WAS 66
Jack Aker KC 66

INNINGS PITCHED
Jim Kaat MIN 305
Denny McLain DET..... 264
E. Wilson BOS, DET... 264

NATIONAL LEAGUE STANDINGS

1966 NL

	W	L	PCT	GB	R	OR	BA	FA	ERA
LOS ANGELES	95	67	.586	—	606	490	.256	.979	2.62
SAN FRANCISCO	93	68	.578	1.5	675	626	.248	.974	3.24
PITTSBURGH	92	70	.568	3	759	641	.279	.978	3.52
PHILADELPHIA	87	75	.537	8	696	640	.258	.982	3.57
ATLANTA	85	77	.525	10	782	683	.263	.976	3.68
ST. LOUIS	83	79	.512	12	571	577	.251	.977	3.11
CINCINNATI	76	84	.475	18	692	702	.260	.980	4.08
HOUSTON	72	90	.444	23	612	695	.255	.972	3.76
NEW YORK	66	95	.410	28.5	587	761	.239	.975	4.17
CHICAGO	59	103	.364	36	644	809	.254	.974	4.33
					6624	6624	.256	.977	3.61

BATTING AVERAGE
Matty Alou PIT .... .342
Felipe Alou ATL .... .327
Rico Carty ATL .... .326

HITS
Felipe Alou ATL 218
Pete Rose CIN............. 205
R. Clemente PIT 202

DOUBLES
Johnny Callison PHI 40
Pete Rose CIN............. 38
Vada Pinson CIN 35

TRIPLES
Tim McCarver STL........ 13
Lou Brock STL 12
R. Clemente PIT 11

HOME RUNS
Hank Aaron ATL 44
Dick Allen PHI................ 40
Willie Mays SF 37

RUNS BATTED IN
Hank Aaron ATL 127
R. Clemente PIT 119
Dick Allen PHI.............. 110

SLUGGING AVERAGE
Dick Allen PHI............. .632
Willie McCovey SF...... .586
Willie Stargell PIT .... .581

STOLEN BASES
Lou Brock STL 74
Sonny Jackson HOU 49
Maury Wills LA............... 38

RUNS SCORED
Felipe Alou ATL 122
Hank Aaron ATL 117
Dick Allen PHI.............. 112

WINS
Sandy Koufax LA........... 27
Juan Marichal SF........... 25
two tied at 21

WINNING PERCENTAGE
Juan Marichal SF........... .806
Sandy Koufax LA......... .750
Gaylord Perry SF .... .724

EARNED RUN AVERAGE
Sandy Koufax LA....... 1.73
Mike Cuellar HOU 2.22
Juan Marichal SF....... 2.23

STRIKEOUTS
Sandy Koufax LA........ .317
Jim Bunning PHI 252
Bob Veale PIT............. 229

SAVES
Phil Regan LA................ 21
Billy McCool CIN........... 18
Roy Face PIT................ 18

COMPLETE GAMES
Sandy Koufax LA........... 27
Juan Marichal SF........... 25
Bob Gibson STL 20

SHUTOUTS
five tied at 5

GAMES PITCHED
Clay Carroll ATL 73
Pete Mikkelsen PIT....... 71
Darold Knowles PHI...... 69

INNINGS PITCHED
Sandy Koufax LA......... 323
Jim Bunning PHI 314
Juan Marichal SF........ 307

AMERICAN LEAGUE STANDINGS

1967 AL

	W	L	PCT	GB	R	OR	BA	FA	ERA
BOSTON	92	70	.568	—	722	614	.255	.977	3.36
DETROIT	91	71	.562	1	683	587	.243	.979	3.32
MINNESOTA	91	71	.562	1	671	590	.240	.978	3.14
CHICAGO	89	73	.549	3	531	491	.225	.979	2.45
CALIFORNIA	84	77	.522	7.5	567	587	.238	.982	3.19
BALTIMORE	76	85	.472	15.5	654	592	.240	.980	3.32
WASHINGTON	76	85	.472	15.5	550	637	.223	.978	3.38
CLEVELAND	75	87	.463	17	559	613	.235	.981	3.25
NEW YORK	72	90	.444	20	522	621	.225	.976	3.24
KANSAS CITY	62	99	.385	29.5	533	660	.233	.978	3.68
					5992	5992	.236	.979	3.23

BATTING AVERAGE
Yastrzemski BOS ...... .326
F. Robinson BAL .... .311
Al Kaline DET .... .308

HITS
C. Yastrzemski BOS ... 189
Cesar Tovar MIN 173
two tied at 171

DOUBLES
Tony Oliva MIN 34
Cesar Tovar MIN 32
C. Yastrzemski BOS 31

TRIPLES
Paul Blair BAL 12
Don Buford CHI 9

HOME RUNS
H. Killebrew MIN 44
C. Yastrzemski BOS 44
Frank Howard WAS 36

RUNS BATTED IN
C. Yastrzemski BOS ... 121
H. Killebrew MIN 113
Frank Robinson BAL..... 94

SLUGGING AVERAGE
Yastrzemski BOS .... .622
F. Robinson BAL .... .576
H. Killebrew MIL .... .558

STOLEN BASES
Bert Campaneris KC 55
Don Buford CHI 34
Tommy Agee CHI 28

RUNS SCORED
C. Yastrzemski BOS ... 112
H. Killebrew MIN 105
Cesar Tovar MIN 98

WINS
Jim Lonborg BOS 22
Earl Wilson DET 22
Dean Chance MIN 20

WINNING PERCENTAGE
Joe Horlen CHI .... .731
Jim Lonborg BOS ...... .710
Earl Wilson DET .... .667

EARNED RUN AVERAGE
Joe Horlen CHI 2.06
Gary Peters CHI 2.28
Sonny Siebert CLE 2.38

STRIKEOUTS
Jim Lonborg BOS 246
Sam McDowell CLE.... 236
Dean Chance MIN 220

SAVES
Minnie Rojas CAL 27
John Wyatt BOS 20
Bob Locker CHI 20

COMPLETE GAMES
Dean Chance MIN 18
Jim Lonborg BOS 15
Steve Hargan CLE 15

SHUTOUTS
four tied at 6

GAMES PITCHED
Bob Locker CHI 77
Minnie Rojas CAL 72
Bill Kelso CAL 69

INNINGS PITCHED
Dean Chance MIN 284
Jim Lonborg BOS 273
Earl Wilson DET 264

NATIONAL LEAGUE STANDINGS

1967 NL

	W	L	PCT	GB	R	OR	BA	FA	ERA
ST. LOUIS	101	60	.627	—	695	557	.263	.978	3.05
SAN FRANCISCO	91	71	.562	10.5	652	551	.245	.979	2.92
CHICAGO	87	74	.540	14	702	624	.251	.981	3.48
CINCINNATI	87	75	.537	14.5	604	563	.248	.980	3.05
PHILADELPHIA	82	80	.506	19.5	612	581	.242	.978	3.10
PITTSBURGH	81	81	.500	20.5	679	693	.277	.978	3.74
ATLANTA	77	85	.475	24.5	631	640	.240	.978	3.47
LOS ANGELES	73	89	.451	28.5	519	595	.236	.975	3.21
HOUSTON	69	93	.426	32.5	626	742	.249	.974	4.03
NEW YORK	61	101	.377	40.5	498	672	.238	.975	3.73
					6218	6218	.249	.978	3.38

BATTING AVERAGE
R. Clemente PIT .... .357
Tony Gonzalez PHI.... .339
Matty Alou PIT .... .338

HITS
R. Clemente PIT 209
Lou Brock STL 206
Vada Pinson CIN 187

DOUBLES
Rusty Staub HOU 44
Orlando Cepeda STL.... 37
Hank Aaron ATL 37

TRIPLES
Vada Pinson CIN 13
Lou Brock STL 12
Billy Williams CHI.......... 12

HOME RUNS
Hank Aaron ATL 39
Jimmy Wynn HOU 37
two tied at 31

RUNS BATTED IN
O. Cepeda STL............ 111
R. Clemente PIT 110
Hank Aaron ATL 109

SLUGGING AVERAGE
Hank Aaron ATL .... .573
Dick Allen PHI............. .566
R. Clemente PIT .... .554

STOLEN BASES
Lou Brock STL.............. 52
Maury Wills PIT............. 29
Joe Morgan HOU.......... 29

RUNS SCORED
Lou Brock STL 113
Hank Aaron ATL 113
Ron Santo CHI............ 107

WINS
Mike McCormick SF...... 22
F. Jenkins CHI 20
two tied at 17

WINNING PERCENTAGE
Dick Hughes STL........ .727
Mike McCormick SF... .688
Bob Veale PIT............. .667

EARNED RUN AVERAGE
Phil Niekro ATL.......... 1.87
Jim Bunning PHI........ 2.29
Chris Short PHI.......... 2.39

STRIKEOUTS
Jim Bunning PHI 253
F. Jenkins CHI 236
Gaylord Perry SF 230

SAVES
Ted Abernathy CIN 28
Frank Linzy SF............... 17
Roy Face PIT................. 17

COMPLETE GAMES
F. Jenkins CHI 20
three tied at................... 18

SHUTOUTS
Jim Bunning PHI 6
three tied at..................... 5

GAMES PITCHED
Ron Perranoski LA........ 70
Ted Abernathy CIN 70
Ron Willis STL 65

INNINGS PITCHED
Jim Bunning PHI 302
Gaylord Perry SF 293
F. Jenkins CHI 289

AMERICAN LEAGUE STANDINGS

1968 AL

	W	L	PCT	GB	R	OR	BA	FA	ERA
DETROIT	103	59	.636	—	671	492	.235	.983	2.71
BALTIMORE	91	71	.562	12	579	497	.225	.981	2.66
CLEVELAND	86	75	.534	16.5	516	504	.234	.979	2.66
BOSTON	86	76	.531	17	614	611	.236	.979	3.33
NEW YORK	83	79	.512	20	536	531	.214	.979	2.79
OAKLAND	82	80	.506	21	569	544	.240	.976	2.94
MINNESOTA	79	83	.488	24	562	546	.237	.973	2.89
CALIFORNIA	67	95	.414	36	498	615	.227	.977	3.43
CHICAGO	67	95	.414	36	463	527	.228	.977	2.75
WASHINGTON	65	96	.404	37.5	524	665	.224	.976	3.64
					5532	5532	.230	.978	2.98

BATTING AVERAGE
Yastrzemski BOS .... .301
Danny Cater OAK ...... .290
Tony Oliva MIN .... .289

HITS
B. Campaneris OAK ... 177
Cesar Tovar MIN 167
two tied at 164

DOUBLES
Reggie Smith BOS 37
Brooks Robinson BAL ... 36
C. Yastrzemski BOS 32

TRIPLES
Jim Fregosi CAL 13
Tom McCraw CHI 12
two tied at 10

HOME RUNS
Frank Howard WAS 44
Willie Horton DET 36
Ken Harrelson BOS 35

RUNS BATTED IN
Ken Harrelson BOS 109
Frank Howard WAS 106
Jim Northrup DET 90

SLUGGING AVERAGE
Frank Howard WAS ... .552
Willie Horton DET ...... .543
Ken Harrelson BOS ... .518

STOLEN BASES
B. Campaneris OAK 62
Jose Cardenal CLE 40
Cesar Tovar MIN 35

RUNS SCORED
Dick McAuliffe DET 95
C. Yastrzemski BOS 90
two tied at 89

WINS
Denny McLain DET 31
Dave McNally BAL 22
two tied at 21

WINNING PERCENTAGE
Denny McLain DET .... .838
Ray Culp BOS .... .727
Luis Tiant CLE .... .700

EARNED RUN AVERAGE
Luis Tiant CLE 1.60
Sam McDowell CLE ... 1.81
Dave McNally BAL 1.95

STRIKEOUTS
Sam McDowell CLE 283
Denny McLain DET 280
Luis Tiant CLE 264

SAVES
Al Worthington MIN 18
Wilbur Wood CHI 16
Dennis Higgins WAS 13

COMPLETE GAMES
Denny McLain DET 28
Luis Tiant CLE 19
Mel Stottlemyre NY 19

SHUTOUTS
Luis Tiant CLE 9
three tied at 6

GAMES PITCHED
Wilbur Wood CHI 88
Hoyt Wilhelm CHI 72
Bob Locker CHI 70

INNINGS PITCHED
Denny McLain DET 336
Dean Chance MIN 292
Mel Stottlemyre NY 279

NATIONAL LEAGUE STANDINGS

1968 NL

	W	L	PCT	GB	R	OR	BA	FA	ERA
ST. LOUIS	97	65	.599	—	583	472	.249	.978	2.49
SAN FRANCISCO	88	74	.543	9	599	529	.239	.975	2.71
CHICAGO	84	78	.519	13	612	611	.242	.981	3.41
CINCINNATI	83	79	.512	14	690	673	.273	.978	3.56
ATLANTA	81	81	.500	16	514	549	.252	.980	2.92
PITTSBURGH	80	82	.494	17	583	532	.252	.979	2.74
LOS ANGELES	76	86	.469	21	470	509	.230	.977	2.69
PHILADELPHIA	76	86	.469	21	543	615	.233	.980	3.36
NEW YORK	73	89	.451	24	473	499	.228	.979	2.72
HOUSTON	72	90	.444	25	510	588	.231	.975	3.26
					5577	5577	.243	.978	2.99

BATTING AVERAGE
Pete Rose CIN .... .335
Matty Alou PIT .... .332
Felipe Alou ATL .... .317

HITS
Pete Rose CIN 210
Felipe Alou ATL 210
Glenn Beckert CHI 189

DOUBLES
Lou Brock STL 46
Pete Rose CIN 42
Johnny Bench CIN 40

TRIPLES
Lou Brock STL 14
R. Clemente PIT 12
Willie Davis LA 10

HOME RUNS
Willie McCovey SF 36
Dick Allen PHI 33
Ernie Banks CHI 32

RUNS BATTED IN
Willie McCovey SF 105
Billy Williams CHI 98
Ron Santo CHI 98

SLUGGING AVERAGE
Willie McCovey SF ..... .545
Dick Allen PHI .... .520
Billy Williams CHI .... .500

STOLEN BASES
Lou Brock STL 62
Maury Wills PIT 52
Wilie Davis LA 36

RUNS SCORED
Glenn Beckert CHI 98
Pete Rose CIN 94
Tony Perez CIN 93

WINS
Juan Marichal SF 26
Bob Gibson STL 22
F. Jenkins CHI 20

WINNING PERCENTAGE
Steve Blass PIT .... .750
Juan Marichal SF .... .743
Bob Gibson STL .... .710

EARNED RUN AVERAGE
Bob Gibson STL 1.12
Bobby Bolin SF 1.99
Bob Veale PIT 2.05

STRIKEOUTS
Bob Gibson STL 268
F. Jenkins CHI 260
Bill Singer LA 227

SAVES
Phil Regan LA, CHI 25
Joe Hoerner STL 17
Clay Carroll ATL, CIN ... 17

COMPLETE GAMES
Juan Marichal SF 30
Bob Gibson STL 28
F. Jenkins CHI 20

SHUTOUTS
Bob Gibson STL 13
Don Drysdale LA 8
two tied at 7

GAMES PITCHED
Ted Abernathy CIN 78
Phil Regan LA, CHI 73
Clay Carroll ATL, CIN ... 68

INNINGS PITCHED
Juan Marichal SF 326
F. Jenkins CHI 308
Bob Gibson STL 305

AMERICAN LEAGUE STANDINGS

1969 AL

	W	L	PCT	GB	R	OR	BA	FA	ERA
BALTIMORE	109	53	.673	—	779	517	.265	.984	2.83
DETROIT	90	72	.556	19	701	601	.242	.979	3.32
BOSTON	87	75	.537	22	743	736	.251	.975	3.93
WASHINGTON	86	76	.531	23	694	644	.251	.978	3.49
NEW YORK	80	81	.497	28.5	562	587	.235	.979	3.23
CLEVELAND	62	99	.385	46.5	573	717	.237	.976	3.94

WEST	W	L	PCT	GB	R	OR	BA	FA	ERA
MINNESOTA	97	65	.599	—	790	618	.268	.977	3.25
OAKLAND	88	74	.543	9	740	678	.249	.978	3.71
CALIFORNIA	71	91	.438	26	528	652	.230	.978	3.55
KANSAS CITY	69	93	.426	28	586	688	.240	.975	3.72
CHICAGO	68	94	.420	29	625	723	.247	.981	4.21
SEATTLE	64	98	.395	33	639	799	.234	.974	4.35
					7960	7960	.246	.978	3.63

BATTING AVERAGE
Rod Carew MIN .... .332
Reggie Smith BOS .... .309
Tony Oliva MIN .... .309

HITS
Tony Oliva MIN 197
Horace Clarke NY 183
Paul Blair BAL 178

DOUBLES
Tony Oliva MIN 39
Reggie Jackson OAK 36
Davey Johnson BAL 34

TRIPLES
Del Unser WAS 8
Horace Clarke NY 7
Reggie Smith BOS 7

HOME RUNS
Harmon Killebrew MIN 49
Frank Howard WAS 48
Reggie Jackson OAK 47

RUNS BATTED IN
Harmon Killebrew MIN 140
Boog Powell BAL 121
Reggie Jackson OAK 118

SLUGGING AVERAGE
Reggie Jackson OAK ...... .608
Rico Petrocelli BOS .... .589
Harmon Killebrew MIN .... .584

STOLEN BASES
Tommy Harper SEA 73
Bert Campaneris OAK 62
Cesar Tovar MIN 45

RUNS SCORED
Reggie Jackson OAK 123
Frank Howard WAS 111
Frank Robinson BAL 111

WINS
Denny McLain DET 24
Mike Cuellar BAL 23
four tied at 20

WINNING PERCENTAGE
Jim Palmer BAL .... .800
Jim Perry MIN .... .769
Dave McNally BAL .... .741

EARNED RUN AVERAGE
Dick Bosman WAS 2.19
Jim Palmer BAL 2.34
Mike Cuellar BAL 2.38

STRIKEOUTS
Sam McDowell CLE 279
Micky Lolich DET 271
Andy Messersmith CAL.... 211

SAVES
Ron Perranoski MIN 31
Ken Tatum CAL 22
Sparky Lyle BOS 17

COMPLETE GAMES
Mel Stottlemyre NY 24
Denny McLain DET 23
two tied at 18

SHUTOUTS
Denny McLain DET 9
Jim Palmer BAL 6
Mike Cuellar BAL 5

GAMES PITCHED
Wilbur Wood CHI 76
Ron Perranoski MIN 75
Sparky Lyle BOS 71

INNINGS PITCHED
Denny McLain DET 325
Mel Stottlemyre NY 303
Mike Cuellar BAL 291

NATIONAL LEAGUE STANDINGS

1969 NL

EAST	W	L	PCT	GB	R	OR	BA	FA	ERA
NEW YORK	100	62	.617	—	632	541	.242	.980	2.99
CHICAGO	92	70	.568	8	720	611	.253	.979	3.34
PITTSBURGH	88	74	.543	12	725	652	.277	.975	3.61
ST. LOUIS	87	75	.537	13	595	540	.253	.978	2.94
PHILADELPHIA	63	99	.389	37	645	745	.241	.978	4.17
MONTREAL	52	110	.321	48	582	791	.240	.971	4.33

WEST	W	L	PCT	GB	R	OR	BA	FA	ERA
ATLANTA	93	69	.574	—	691	631	.258	.981	3.53
SAN FRANCISCO	90	72	.556	3	713	636	.242	.974	3.25
CINCINNATI	89	73	.549	4	798	768	.277	.973	4.13
LOS ANGELES	85	77	.525	8	645	561	.254	.980	3.09
HOUSTON	81	81	.500	12	676	668	.240	.975	3.60
SAN DIEGO	52	110	.321	41	468	746	.225	.975	4.24
					7890	7890	.250	.977	3.60

BATTING AVERAGE
Pete Rose CIN .... .348
Roberto Clemente PIT .... .345
Cleon Jones NY .... .340

HITS
Matty Alou PIT 231
Pete Rose CIN 218
Lou Brock STL 195

DOUBLES
Matty Alou PIT 41
Don Kessinger CHI 38
two tied at 33

TRIPLES
Roberto Clemente PIT 12
Pete Rose CIN 11
two tied at 10

HOME RUNS
Willie McCovey SF 45
Hank Aaron ATL 44
Lee May CIN 38

RUNS BATTED IN
Willie McCovey SF 126
Ron Santo CHI 123
Tony Perez CIN 122

SLUGGING AVERAGE
Willie McCovey SF .... .656
Hank Aaron ATL .... .607
Dick Allen PHI .... .573

STOLEN BASES
Lou Brock STL 53
Joe Morgan HOU 49
Bobby Bonds SF 45

RUNS SCORED
Pete Rose CIN 120
Bobby Bonds SF 120
Jimmy Wynn HOU 113

WINS
Tom Seaver NY 25
Phil Niekro ATL 23
two tied at 21

WINNING PERCENTAGE
Tom Seaver NY .... .781
Juan Marichal SF .... .656
two tied at .... .654

EARNED RUN AVERAGE
Juan Marchial SF 2.10
Steve Carlton STL 2.17
Bob Gibson STL 2.18

STRIKEOUTS
Ferguson Jenkins CHI 273
Bob Gibson STL 269
Bill Singer LA 247

SAVES
Fred Gladding HOU 29
Wayne Granger CIN 27
Cecil Upshaw ATL 27

COMPLETE GAMES
Bob Gibson STL 28
Juan Marichal SF 27
Gaylord Perry SF 26

SHUTOUTS
Juan Marichal SF 8
Ferguson Jenkins CHI 7
Claude Osteen LA 7

GAMES PITCHED
Wayne Granger CIN 90
Dan McGinn MON 74
two tied at 71

INNINGS PITCHED
Gaylord Perry SF 325
Claude Osteen LA 321
Bill Singer LA 316

AMERICAN LEAGUE STANDINGS

1970 AL

EAST	W	L	PCT	GB	R	OR	BA	FA	ERA
BALTIMORE	108	54	.667	—	792	574	.257	.981	3.15
NEW YORK	93	69	.574	15	680	612	.251	.980	3.25
BOSTON	87	75	.537	21	786	722	.262	.974	3.90
DETROIT	79	83	.488	29	666	731	.238	.978	4.09
CLEVELAND	76	86	.469	32	649	675	.249	.979	3.91
WASHINGTON	70	92	.432	38	626	689	.238	.982	3.80

WEST	W	L	PCT	GB	R	OR	BA	FA	ERA
MINNESOTA	98	64	.605	—	744	605	.262	.980	3.23
OAKLAND	89	73	.549	9	678	593	.249	.977	3.30
CALIFORNIA	86	76	.531	12	631	630	.251	.980	3.48
KANSAS CITY	65	97	.401	33	611	705	.244	.976	3.78
MILWAUKEE	65	97	.401	33	613	751	.242	.978	4.20
CHICAGO	56	106	.346	42	633	822	.253	.975	4.54
					8109	8109	.250	.978	3.72

BATTING AVERAGE
Alex Johnson CAL .... .329
Carl Yastrzemski BOS .... .329
Tony Oliva MIN .... .325

HITS
Tony Oliva MIN 204
Alex Johnson CAL 202
Cesar Tovar MIN 195

DOUBLES
Cesar Tovar MIN 36
Tony Oliva MIN 36
Amos Otis KC 36

TRIPLES
Cesar Tovar MIN 13
Mickey Stanley DET 11
Amos Otis KC 9

HOME RUNS
Frank Howard WAS 44
Harmon Killebrew MIN 41
Carl Yastrzemski BOS 40

RUNS BATTED IN
Frank Howard WAS 126
Tony Conigliaro BOS 116
Boog Powell BAL 114

SLUGGING AVERAGE
Carl Yastrzemski BOS .... .592
Boog Powell BAL .... .549
Harmon Killebrew MIN .... .546

STOLEN BASES
Bert Campaneris OAK 42
Tommy Harper MIL 38
Sandy Alomar CAL 35

RUNS SCORED
Carl Yastrzemski BOS 125
Cesar Tovar MIN 120
two tied at 109

WINS
Dave McNally BAL 24
Jim Perry MIN 24
Mike Cuellar BAL 24

WINNING PERCENTAGE
Mike Cuellar BAL .... .750
Dave McNally BAL .... .727
two tied at .... .667

EARNED RUN AVERAGE
Diego Segui OAK 2.56
Jim Palmer BAL 2.71
Clyde Wright CAL 2.83

STRIKEOUTS
Sam McDowell CLE 304
Mickey Lolich DET 230
Bob Johnson KC 206

SAVES
Ron Perranoski MIN 34
Lindy McDaniel NY 29
two tied at 27

COMPLETE GAMES
Mike Cuellar BAL 21
Sam McDowell CLE 19
Jim Palmer BAL 17

SHUTOUTS
Jim Palmer BAL 5
Chuck Dobson OAK 5
two tied at 4

GAMES PITCHED
Wilbur Wood CHI 77
Mudcat Grant OAK 72
Darold Knowles WAS 71

INNINGS PITCHED
Sam McDowell CLE 305
Jim Palmer BAL 305
Mike Cuellar BAL 298

NATIONAL LEAGUE STANDINGS

1970 NL

EAST	W	L	PCT	GB	R	OR	BA	FA	ERA
PITTSBURGH	89	73	.549	—	729	664	.270	.979	3.70
CHICAGO	84	78	.519	5	806	679	.259	.978	3.76
NEW YORK	83	79	.512	6	695	630	.249	.979	3.46
ST. LOUIS	76	86	.469	13	744	747	.263	.977	4.05
PHILADELPHIA	73	88	.453	15.5	594	730	.238	.981	4.17
MONTREAL	73	89	.451	16	687	807	.237	.977	4.50

WEST	W	L	PCT	GB	R	OR	BA	FA	ERA
CINCINNATI	102	60	.630	—	775	681	.270	.976	3.71
LOS ANGELES	87	74	.540	14.5	749	684	.270	.978	3.82
SAN FRANCISCO	86	76	.531	16	831	826	.262	.973	4.50
HOUSTON	79	83	.488	23	744	763	.259	.978	4.23
ATLANTA	76	86	.469	26	736	772	.270	.977	4.35
SAN DIEGO	63	99	.389	39	681	788	.246	.975	4.38
					8771	8771	.258	.977	4.05

BATTING AVERAGE
Rico Carty ATL .366
Joe Torre STL .325
Manny Sanguillen PIT .325

HITS
Billy Williams CHI 205
Pete Rose CIN 205
Joe Torre STL 203

DOUBLES
Wes Parker LA 47
Willie McCovey SF 39
Pete Rose CIN 37

TRIPLES
Willie Davis LA 16
Don Kessinger CHI 14
two tied at 10

HOME RUNS
Johnny Bench CIN 45
Billy Williams CHI 42
Tony Perez CIN 40

RUNS BATTED IN
Johnny Bench CIN 148
Billy Williams CHI 129
Tony Perez CIN 129

SLUGGING AVERAGE
Willie McCovey SF .612
Tony Perez CIN .589
Johnny Bench CIN .587

STOLEN BASES
Bobby Tolan CIN 57
Lou Brock STL 51
Bobby Bonds SF 48

RUNS SCORED
Billy Williams CHI 137
Bobby Bonds SF 134
Pete Rose CIN 120

WINS
Gaylord Perry SF 23
Bob Gibson STL 23
Ferguson Jenkins CHI 22

WINNING PERCENTAGE
Bob Gibson STL .767
Gary Nolan CIN .720
Luke Walker PIT .714

EARNED RUN AVERAGE
Tom Seaver NY 2.81
Wayne Simpson CIN 3.02
Luke Walker PIT 3.04

STRIKEOUTS
Tom Seaver NY 283
Bob Gibson STL 274
Ferguson Jenkins CHI 274

SAVES
Wayne Granger CIN 35
Dave Giusti PIT 26
Jim Brewer LA 24

COMPLETE GAMES
Ferguson Jenkins CHI 24
Gaylord Perry SF 23
Bob Gibson STL 23

SHUTOUTS
Gaylord Perry SF 5
three tied at 4

GAMES PITCHED
Ron Herbel SD, NY 76
Dick Selma PHI 73
two tied at 67

INNINGS PITCHED
Gaylord Perry SF 329
Ferguson Jenkins CHI 313
Bob Gibson STL 294

AMERICAN LEAGUE STANDINGS

1971 AL

EAST	W	L	PCT	GB	R	OR	BA	FA	ERA
BALTIMORE	101	57	.639	—	742	530	.261	.981	3.00
DETROIT	91	71	.562	12	701	645	.254	.983	3.64
BOSTON	85	77	.525	18	691	667	.252	.981	3.83
NEW YORK	82	80	.506	21	648	641	.254	.981	3.45
WASHINGTON	63	96	.396	38.5	537	660	.230	.977	3.70
CLEVELAND	60	102	.370	43	543	747	.238	.981	4.28

WEST	W	L	PCT	GB	R	OR	BA	FA	ERA
OAKLAND	101	60	.627	—	691	564	.252	.981	3.06
KANSAS CITY	85	76	.528	16	603	566	.250	.978	3.25
CHICAGO	79	83	.488	22.5	617	597	.250	.975	3.13
CALIFORNIA	76	86	.469	25.5	511	576	.231	.980	3.10
MINNESOTA	74	86	.463	26.5	654	670	.260	.980	3.82
MILWAUKEE	69	92	.429	32	534	609	.229	.977	3.38
					7472	7472	.247	.980	3.47

BATTING AVERAGE
Tony Oliva MIN .... .337
Bobby Murcer NY .... .331
Merv Rettenmund BAL .... .318

HITS
Cesar Tovar MIN 204
Sandy Alomar CAL 179
Rod Carew MIN 177

DOUBLES
Reggie Smith BOS 33
Paul Schaal KC 31
two tied at 30

TRIPLES
Freddie Patek KC 11
Rod Carew MIN 10
Paul Blair BAL 8

HOME RUNS
Bill Melton CHI 33
Norm Cash DET 32
Reggie Jackson OAK 32

RUNS BATTED IN
Harmon Killebrew MIN ... 119
Frank Robinson BAL 99
Reggie Smith BOS 96

SLUGGING AVERAGE
Tony Oliva MIN .... .546
Bobby Murcer NY .... .543
Norm Cash DET .... .531

STOLEN BASES
Amos Otis KC 52
Freddie Patek KC 49
Sandy Alomar CAL 39

RUNS SCORED
Don Buford BAL 99
Bobby Murcer NY 94
Cesar Tovar MIN 94

WINS
Mickey Lolich DET 25
Vida Blue OAK 24
Wilbur Wood CHI 22

WINNING PERCENTAGE
Dave McNally BAL .... .808
Vida Blue OAK .... .750
Chuck Dobson OAK .... .750

EARNED RUN AVERAGE
Vida Blue OAK 1.82
Wilbur Wood CHI 1.91
Jim Palmer BAL 2.68

STRIKEOUTS
Mickey Lolich DET 308
Vida Blue OAK 301
Joe Coleman DET 236

SAVES
Ken Sanders MIL 31
Ted Abernathy KC 23
Fred Scherman DET 20

COMPLETE GAMES
Mickey Lolich DET 29
Vida Blue OAK 24
Wilbur Wood CHI 22

SHUTOUTS
Vida Blue OAK 8
Mel Stottlemyre NY 7
Wilbur Wood CHI 7

GAMES PITCHED
Ken Sanders MIL 83
Fred Scherman DET 69
Tom Burgmeier KC 67

INNINGS PITCHED
Mickey Lolich DET 376
Wilbur Wood CHI 334
Vida Blue OAK 312

NATIONAL LEAGUE STANDINGS

1971 NL

EAST	W	L	PCT	GB	R	OR	BA	FA	ERA
PITTSBURGH	97	65	.599	—	788	599	.274	.979	3.31
ST. LOUIS	90	72	.556	7	739	699	.275	.978	3.87
CHICAGO	83	79	.512	14	637	648	.258	.980	3.61
NEW YORK	83	79	.512	14	588	550	.249	.981	3.00
MONTREAL	71	90	.441	25.5	622	729	.246	.976	4.12
PHILADELPHIA	67	95	.414	30	558	688	.233	.981	3.71

WEST	W	L	PCT	GB	R	OR	BA	FA	ERA
SAN FRANCISCO	90	72	.556	—	706	644	.247	.972	3.33
LOS ANGELES	89	73	.549	1	663	587	.266	.979	3.23
ATLANTA	82	80	.506	8	643	699	.257	.977	3.75
CINCINNATI	79	83	.488	11	586	581	.241	.984	3.35
HOUSTON	79	83	.488	11	585	567	.240	.983	3.13
SAN DIEGO	61	100	.379	28.5	486	610	.233	.974	3.23
					7601	7601	.252	.979	3.47

BATTING AVERAGE
Joe Torre STL .... .363
Ralph Garr ATL .... .343
Glenn Beckert CHI .... .342

HITS
Joe Toore STL 230
Ralph Garr ATL 219
Lou Brock STL 200

DOUBLES
Cesar Cedeno HOU 40
Lou Brock STL 37
two tied at 34

TRIPLES
Joe Morgan HOU 11
Roger Metzger HOU 11
Willie Davis LA 10

HOME RUNS
Willie Stargell PIT 48
Hank Aaron ATL 47
Lee May CIN 39

RUNS BATTED IN
Joe Torre STL 137
Willie Stargell PIT 125
Hank Aaron ATL 118

SLUGGING AVERAGE
Hank Aaron ATL .... .669
Willie Stargell PIT .... .628
Joe Torre STL .... .555

STOLEN BASES
Lou Brock STL 64
Joe Morgan HOU 40
Ralph Garr ATL 30

RUNS SCORED
Lou Brock STL 126
Bobby Bonds SF 110
Willie Stargell PIT 104

WINS
Ferguson Jenkins CHI 24
three tied at 20

WINNING PERCENTAGE
Don Gullett CIN .... .727
Steve Carlton STL .... .690
Al Downing LA .... .690

EARNED RUN AVERAGE
Tom Seaver NY 1.76
Dave Roberts SD 2.10
Don Wilson HOU 2.45

STRIKEOUTS
Tom Seaver NY 289
Ferguson Jenkins CHI 263
Bill Stoneman MON 251

SAVES
Dave Giusti PIT 30
Mike Marshall MON 23
Jim Brewer LA 22

COMPLETE GAMES
Ferguson Jenkins CHI 30
Tom Seaver NY 21
two tied at 20

SHUTOUTS
four tied at 5

GAMES PITCHED
Wayne Granger CIN 70
Jerry Johnson SF 67

INNINGS PITCHED
Ferguson Jenkins CHI 325
Bill Stoneman MON 295
Tom Seaver NY 286

AMERICAN LEAGUE STANDINGS

1972 AL

EAST	W	L	PCT	GB	R	OR	BA	FA	ERA
DETROIT	86	70	.551	—	558	514	.237	.984	2.96
BOSTON	85	70	.548	.5	640	620	.248	.978	3.47
BALTIMORE	80	74	.519	5	519	430	.229	.983	2.54
NEW YORK	79	76	.510	6.5	557	527	.249	.978	3.05
CLEVELAND	72	84	.462	14	472	519	.234	.981	2.97
MILWAUKEE	65	91	.417	21	493	595	.235	.977	3.45

WEST	W	L	PCT	GB	R	OR	BA	FA	ERA
OAKLAND	93	62	.600	—	604	457	.240	.979	2.58
CHICAGO	87	67	.565	5.5	566	538	.238	.977	3.12
MINNESOTA	77	77	.500	15.5	537	535	.244	.974	2.86
KANSAS CITY	76	78	.494	16.5	580	545	.255	.980	3.24
CALIFORNIA	75	80	.484	18	454	533	.242	.981	3.06
TEXAS	54	100	.351	38.5	461	628	.217	.972	3.53
					6441	6441	.239	.979	3.07

BATTING AVERAGE
Rod Carew MIN................ .318
Lou Piniella KC................ .312
two tied at......................... .308

HITS
Joe Rudi OAK 181
Lou Piniella KC................ 179
Bobby Murcer NY 171

DOUBLES
Lou Piniella KC.................. 33
Joe Rudi OAK 32
Bobby Murcer NY 30

TRIPLES
Joe Rudi OAK 9
Carlton Fisk BOS 9
Paul Blair BAL 8

HOME RUNS
Dick Allen CHI 37
Bobby Murcer NY 33
two tied at 26

RUNS BATTED IN
Dick Allen CHI 113
John Mayberry KC 100
Bobby Murcer NY 96

SLUGGING AVERAGE
Dick Allen CHI .... .603
Carlton Fisk BOS .... .538
Bobby Murcer NY .... .537

STOLEN BASES
Bert Campaneris OAK........ 52
Dave Nelson TEX............... 51
Freddie Patek KC............... 33

RUNS SCORED
Bobby Murcer NY 102
Joe Rudi OAK 94
Tommy Harper BOS........... 92

WINS
Wilbur Wood CHI 24
Gaylord Perry CLE 24
Mickey Lolich DET 22

WINNING PERCENTAGE
Catfish Hunter OAK.......... .750
Blue Moon Odom OAK.....714
Luis Tiant BOS .... .714

EARNED RUN AVERAGE
Luis Tiant BOS 1.91
Gaylord Perry CLE 1.92
Catfish Hunter OAK......... 2.04

STRIKEOUTS
Nolan Ryan CAL 329
Mickey Lolich DET 250
Gaylord Perry CLE........... 234

SAVES
Sparky Lyle NY 35
Terry Forster CHI 29
Rollie Fingers OAK............. 21

COMPLETE GAMES
Gaylord Perry CLE 29
Mickey Lolich DET 23
two tied at........................... 20

SHUTOUTS
Nolan Ryan CAL 9
Wilbur Wood CHI 8
Mel Stottlemyre NY 7

GAMES PITCHED
Paul Lindblad TEX 66
Rollie Fingers OAK............. 65
Wayne Granger MIN 63

INNINGS PITCHED
Wilbur Wood CHI 377
Gaylord Perry CLE 343
Mickey Lolich DET 327

NATIONAL LEAGUE STANDINGS

1972 NL

EAST	W	L	PCT	GB	R	OR	BA	FA	ERA
PITTSBURGH	96	59	.619	—	691	512	.274	.978	2.81
CHICAGO	85	70	.548	11	685	567	.257	.979	3.22
NEW YORK	83	73	.532	13.5	528	578	.225	.980	3.27
ST. LOUIS	75	81	.481	21.5	568	600	.260	.977	3.42
MONTREAL	70	86	.449	26.5	513	609	.234	.978	3.60
PHILADELPHIA	59	97	.378	37.5	503	635	.236	.981	3.67

WEST	W	L	PCT	GB	R	OR	BA	FA	ERA
CINCINNATI	95	59	.617	—	707	557	.251	.982	3.21
HOUSTON	84	69	.549	10.5	708	636	.258	.980	3.77
LOS ANGELES	85	70	.548	10.5	584	527	.256	.974	2.78
ATLANTA	70	84	.455	25	628	730	.258	.974	4.27
SAN FRANCISCO	69	86	.445	26.5	662	649	.244	.974	3.70
SAN DIEGO	58	95	.379	36.5	488	665	.227	.976	3.78
					7265	7265	.248	.978	3.46

BATTING AVERAGE
Billy Williams CHI .... .333
Ralph Garr ATL .... .325
Cesar Cedeno HOU .... .320

HITS
Pete Rose CIN 198
Lou Brock STL 193
Billy Williams CHI 191

DOUBLES
Cesar Cedeno HOU 39
Willie Montanez PHI 39
Ted Simmons STL 36

TRIPLES
Larry Bowa PHI 13
Pete Rose CIN 11
two tied at 8

HOME RUNS
Johnny Bench CIN 40
Nate Colbert SD 38
Billy Williams CHI 37

RUNS BATTED IN
Johnny Bench CIN 125
Billy Williams CHI 122
Willie Stargell PIT 112

SLUGGING AVERAGE
Billy Williams CHI .... .606
Willie Stargell PIT .... .558
Johnny Bench CIN .... .541

STOLEN BASES
Lou Brock STL 63
Joe Morgan CIN 58
Cesar Cedeno HOU 55

RUNS SCORED
Joe Morgan CIN 122
Bobby Bonds SF 118
Jimmy Wynn HOU 117

WINS
Steve Carlton PHI 27
Tom Seaver NY 21
two tied at 20

WINNING PERCENTAGE
Gary Nolan CIN .... .750
Steve Carlton PHI .... .730
Milt Pappas CHI .... .708

EARNED RUN AVERAGE
Steve Carlton PHI 1.97
Gary Nolan CIN 1.99
Don Sutton LA 2.08

STRIKEOUTS
Steve Carlton PHI 310
Tom Seaver NY 249
Bob Gibson STL 208

SAVES
Clay Carroll CIN 37
Tug McGraw NY 27
Dave Giusti PIT 22

COMPLETE GAMES
Steve Carlton PHI 30
Ferguson Jenkins CHI 23
Bob Gibson STL 23

SHUTOUTS
Don Sutton LA 9
Steve Carlton PHI 8
Fred Norman SD 6

GAMES PITCHED
Mike Marshall MON 65
Clay Carroll CIN 65
Pedro Borbon CIN 62

INNINGS PITCHED
Steve Carlton PHI 346
Ferguson Jenkins CHI 289
Phil Niekro ATL 282

AMERICAN LEAGUE STANDINGS

1973 AL

EAST	W	L	PCT	GB	R	OR	BA	FA	ERA
BALTIMORE	97	65	.599	—	754	561	.266	.981	3.07
BOSTON	89	73	.549	8	738	647	.267	.979	3.65
DETROIT	85	77	.525	12	642	674	.254	.982	3.90
NEW YORK	80	82	.494	17	641	610	.261	.976	3.34
MILWAUKEE	74	88	.457	23	708	731	.253	.977	3.98
CLEVELAND	71	91	.438	26	680	826	.256	.978	4.58

WEST	W	L	PCT	GB	R	OR	BA	FA	ERA
OAKLAND	94	68	.580	—	758	615	.260	.978	3.29
KANSAS CITY	88	74	.543	6	755	752	.261	.974	4.21
MINNESOTA	81	81	.500	13	738	692	.270	.978	3.77
CALIFORNIA	79	83	.488	15	629	657	.253	.975	3.57
CHICAGO	77	85	.475	17	652	705	.256	.977	3.86
TEXAS	57	105	.352	37	619	844	.255	.974	4.64
					8314	8314	.259	.977	3.82

BATTING AVERAGE
Rod Carew MIN .... .350
George Scott MIL .... .306
Tommy Davis BAL .... .306

HITS
Rod Carew MIN 203
Dave May MIL 189
Bobby Murcer NY 187

DOUBLES
Sal Bando OAK 32
Pedro Garcia MIL 32
two tied at 30

TRIPLES
Rod Carew MIN 11
Al Bumbry BAL 11
Jorge Orta CHI 10

HOME RUNS
Reggie Jackson OAK 32
Frank Robinson CAL 30
Jeff Burroughs TEX 30

RUNS BATTED IN
Reggie Jackson OAK 117
George Scott MIL 107
John Mayberry KC 100

SLUGGING AVERAGE
Reggie Jackson OAK ...... .531
Sal Bando OAK .... .498
Frank Robinson CAL .... .489

STOLEN BASES
Tommy Harper BOS 54
Billy North OAK 53
Dave Nelson TEX 43

RUNS SCORED
Reggie Jackson OAK 99
three tied at 98

WINS
Wilbur Wood CHI 24
Joe Coleman DET 23
Jim Palmer BAL 22

WINNING PERCENTAGE
Catfish Hunter OAK .... .808
Jim Palmer BAL .... .710
Vida Blue OAK .... .690

EARNED RUN AVERAGE
Jim Palmer BAL 2.40
Bert Blyleven MIN 2.52
Bill Lee BOS 2.74

STRIKEOUTS
Nolan Ryan CAL 383
Bert Blyleven MIN 258
Bill Singer CAL 241

SAVES
John Hiller DET 38
Sparky Lyle NY 27
Rollie Fingers OAK 22

COMPLETE GAMES
Gaylord Perry CLE 29
Nolan Ryan CAL 26
Bert Blyleven MIN 25

SHUTOUTS
Bert Blyleven MIN 9
Gaylord Perry CLE 7
Jim Palmer BAL 6

GAMES PITCHED
John Hiller DET 65
Rollie Fingers OAK 62
Doug Bird KC 54

INNINGS PITCHED
Wilbur Wood CHI 359
Gaylord Perry CLE 344
Nolan Ryan CAL 326

NATIONAL LEAGUE STANDINGS

1973 NL

EAST	W	L	PCT	GB	R	OR	BA	FA	ERA
NEW YORK	82	79	.509	—	608	588	.246	.980	3.27
ST. LOUIS	81	81	.500	1.5	643	603	.259	.975	3.25
PITTSBURGH	80	82	.494	2.5	704	693	.261	.976	3.74
MONTREAL	79	83	.488	3.5	668	702	.251	.974	3.73
CHICAGO	77	84	.478	.5	614	655	.247	.975	3.66
PHILADELPHIA	71	91	.438	11.5	642	717	.249	.979	4.00

WEST	W	L	PCT	GB	R	OR	BA	FA	ERA
CINCINNATI	99	63	.611	—	741	621	.254	.982	3.43
LOS ANGELES	95	66	.590	3.5	675	565	.263	.981	3.00
SAN FRANCISCO	88	74	.543	11	739	702	.262	.974	3.79
HOUSTON	82	80	.506	17	681	672	.251	.981	3.78
ATLANTA	76	85	.472	22.5	799	774	.266	.974	4.25
SAN DIEGO	60	102	.370	39	548	770	.244	.973	4.16
					8062	8062	.254	.977	3.67

BATTING AVERAGE
Pete Rose CIN .... .338
Cesar Cedeno HOU .... .320
Garry Maddox SF .... .319

HITS
Pete Rose CIN 230
Ralph Garr ATL 200
Lou Brock STL 193

DOUBLES
Willie Stargell PIT 43
Al Oliver PIT 38
two tied at 36

TRIPLES
Roger Metzger HOU 14
Garry Maddox SF 10
Gary Matthews SF 10

HOME RUNS
Willie Stargell PIT 44
Davey Johnson ATL 43
Darrell Evans ATL 41

RUNS BATTED IN
Willie Stargell PIT 119
Lee May HOU 105
two tied at 104

SLUGGING AVERAGE
Willie Stargell PIT .... .646
Darrell Evans ATL .... .556
Davey Johnson ATL .... .546

STOLEN BASES
Lou Brock STL 70
Joe Morgan CIN 67
Cesar Cedeno HOU 56

RUNS SCORED
Bobby Bonds SF 131
Joe Morgan CIN 116
Pete Rose CIN 115

WINS
Ron Bryant SF 24
Tom Seaver NY 19
Jack Billingham CIN 19

WINNING PERCENTAGE
Tommy John LA .... .696
Don Gullett CIN .... .692
Ron Bryant SF .... .667

EARNED RUN AVERAGE
Tom Seaver NY 2.08
Wayne Twitchell PHI 2.50
Mike Marshall MON 2.66

STRIKEOUTS
Tom Seaver NY 251
Steve Carlton PHI 223
John Matlack NY 205

SAVES
Mike Marshall MON 31
Tug McGraw NY 25
two tied at 20

COMPLETE GAMES
Tom Seaver NY 18
Steve Carlton PHI 18
Jack Billingham CIN 16

SHUTOUTS
Jack Billingham CIN 7
Dave Roberts HOU 6
two tied at 5

GAMES PITCHED
Mike Marshall MON 92
Pedro Borbon CIN 80
Elias Sosa SF 71

INNINGS PITCHED
Steve Carlton PHI 293
Jack Billingham CIN 293
Tom Seaver NY 290

AMERICAN LEAGUE STANDINGS

1974 AL

EAST	W	L	PCT	GB	R	OR	BA	FA	ERA
BALTIMORE	91	71	.562	—	659	612	.256	.980	3.27
NEW YORK	89	73	.549	2	671	623	.263	.977	3.32
BOSTON	84	78	.519	7	696	661	.264	.977	3.72
CLEVELAND	77	85	.475	14	662	694	.255	.977	3.80
MILWAUKEE	76	86	.469	15	647	660	.244	.980	3.77
DETROIT	72	90	.444	19	620	768	.247	.975	4.17

WEST	W	L	PCT	GB	R	OR	BA	FA	ERA
OAKLAND	90	72	.556	—	689	551	.247	.977	2.95
TEXAS	84	76	.525	5	690	698	.272	.974	3.82
MINNESOTA	82	80	.506	8	673	669	.272	.976	3.64
CHICAGO	80	80	.500	9	684	721	.268	.977	3.94
KANSAS CITY	77	85	.475	13	667	662	.259	.976	3.51
CALIFORNIA	68	94	.420	22	618	657	.254	.977	3.52
					7976	7976	.258	.977	3.62

BATTING AVERAGE
Rod Carew MIN .... .364
Jorge Orta CHI .... .316
Hal McRae KC .... .310

HITS
Rod Carew MIN 218
Tommy Davis BAL 181
Don Money MIL 178

DOUBLES
Joe Rudi OAK 39
George Scott MIL 36
Hal McRae KC 36

TRIPLES
Mickey Rivers CAL 11
Amos Otis KC 9
two tied at 8

HOME RUNS
Dick Allen CHI 32
Reggie Jackson OAK 29
Gene Tenace OAK 26

RUNS BATTED IN
Jeff Burroughs TEX 118
Sal Bando OAK 103
Joe Rudi OAK 99

SLUGGING AVERAGE
Dick Allen CHI .... .563
Reggie Jackson OAK .... .514
Jeff Burroughs TEX .... .504

STOLEN BASES
Billy North OAK 54
Rod Carew MIN 38
John Lowenstein CLE 36

RUNS SCORED
Carl Yastrzemski BOS 93
Bobby Grich BAL 92
Reggie Jackson OAK 90

WINS
Catfish Hunter OAK 25
Ferguson Jenkins TEX 25
four tied at 22

WINNING PERCENTAGE
Mike Cuellar BAL .... .688
Catfish Hunter OAK .... .676
Ferguson Jenkins TEX .... .676

EARNED RUN AVERAGE
Catfish Hunter OAK 2.49
Gaylord Perry CLE 2.52
Andy Hassler CAL 2.61

STRIKEOUTS
Nolan Ryan CAL 367
Bert Blyleven MIN 249
Ferguson Jenkins TEX 225

SAVES
Terry Forster CHI 24
Tom Murphy MIL 20
Bill Campbell MIN 19

COMPLETE GAMES
Ferguson Jenkins TEX 29
Gaylord Perry CLE 28
Mickey Lolich DET 27

SHUTOUTS
Luis Tiant BOS 7
Catfish Hunter OAK 6
Ferguson Jenkins TEX 6

GAMES PITCHED
Rollie Fingers OAK 76
Tom Murphy MIL 70
Steve Foucault 69

INNINGS PITCHED
Nolan Ryan CAL 333
Ferguson Jenkins TEX 328
Gaylord Perry CLE 322

NATIONAL LEAGUE STANDINGS

1974 NL

EAST	W	L	PCT	GB	R	OR	BA	FA	ERA
PITTSBURGH	88	74	.543	—	751	657	.274	.975	3.49
ST. LOUIS	86	75	.534	1.5	677	643	.265	.977	3.48
PHILADELPHIA	80	82	.494	8	676	701	.261	.976	3.92
MONTREAL	79	82	.491	8.5	662	657	.254	.976	3.60
NEW YORK	71	91	.438	17	572	646	.235	.975	3.42
CHICAGO	66	96	.407	22	669	826	.251	.969	4.28

WEST	W	L	PCT	GB	R	OR	BA	FA	ERA
LOS ANGELES	102	60	.630	—	798	561	.272	.975	2.97
CINCINNATI	98	64	.605	4	776	631	.260	.979	3.42
ATLANTA	88	74	.543	14	661	563	.249	.979	3.05
HOUSTON	81	81	.500	21	653	632	.263	.982	3.48
SAN FRANCISCO	72	90	.444	30	634	723	.252	.972	3.80
SAN DIEGO	60	102	.370	42	541	830	.229	.973	4.61
					8070	8070	.255	.976	3.62

BATTING AVERAGE
Ralph Garr ATL .... .353
Al Oliver PIT .... .321
two tied at .... .314

HITS
Ralph Garr ATL 214
Dave Cash PHI 206
Steve Garvey LA 200

DOUBLES
Pete Rose CIN 45
Al Oliver PIT 38
Johnny Bench CIN 38

TRIPLES
Ralph Garr ATL 17
Al Oliver PIT 12
Dave Cash PHI 11

HOME RUNS
Mike Schmidt PHI 36
Johnny Bench CIN 33
Jimmy Wynn LA 32

RUNS BATTED IN
Johnny Bench CIN 129
Mike Schmidt PHI 116
Steve Garvey LA 111

SLUGGING AVERAGE
Mike Schmidt PHI .... .546
Willie Stargell PIT .... .537
Reggie Smith STL .... .528

STOLEN BASES
Lou Brock STL 118
Davey Lopes LA 59
Joe Morgan CIN 58

RUNS SCORED
Pete Rose CIN 110
Mike Schmidt PHI 108
Johnny Bench CIN 108

WINS
Phil Niekro ATL 20
Andy Messersmith LA 20
two tied at 19

WINNING PERCENTAGE
Andy Messersmith LA ..... .769
Don Sutton LA .... .679
Buzz Capra ATL .... .667

EARNED RUN AVERAGE
Buzz Capra ATL 2.28
Phil Niekro ATL 2.38
John Matlack NY 2.41

STRIKEOUTS
Steve Carlton PHI 240
Andy Messersmith LA 221
Tom Seaver NY 201

SAVES
Mike Marshall LA 21
Randy Moffitt SF 15
Pedro Borbon CIN 14

COMPLETE GAMES
Phil Niekro ATL 18
Steve Carlton PHI 17
Jim Lonborg PHI 16

SHUTOUTS
John Matlack NY 7
Phil Niekro ATL 6
two tied at 5

GAMES PITCHED
Mike Marshall LA 106
Larry Hardy SD 76
Pedro Borbon CIN 73

INNINGS PITCHED
Phil Niekro ATL 302
Andy Messersmith LA 292
Steve Carlton PHI 291

AMERICAN LEAGUE STANDINGS

1975 AL

EAST	W	L	PCT	GB	R	OR	BA	FA	ERA
BOSTON	95	65	.594	—	796	709	.275	.977	3.99
BALTIMORE	90	69	.566	4.5	682	553	.252	.983	3.17
NEW YORK	83	77	.519	12	681	588	.264	.978	3.29
CLEVELAND	79	80	.497	15.5	688	703	.261	.978	3.84
MILWAUKEE	68	94	.420	28	675	793	.250	.971	4.34
DETROIT	57	102	.358	37.5	570	786	.249	.972	4.29

WEST	W	L	PCT	GB	R	OR	BA	FA	ERA
OAKLAND	98	64	.605	—	758	606	.254	.977	3.29
KANSAS CITY	91	71	.562	7	710	649	.261	.976	3.49
TEXAS	79	83	.488	19	714	733	.256	.971	3.90
MINNESOTA	76	83	.478	20.5	724	736	.271	.973	4.05
CHICAGO	75	86	.466	22.5	655	707	.255	.978	3.93
CALIFORNIA	72	89	.447	25.5	628	723	.246	.971	3.89
					8281	8281	.258	.975	3.79

BATTING AVERAGE
Rod Carew MIN .... .359
Fred Lynn BOS .... .331
Thurman Munson NY .... .318

HITS
George Brett KC 195
Rod Carew MIN 192
Thurman Munson NY 190

DOUBLES
Fred Lynn BOS 47
Reggie Jackson OAK 39
two tied at 38

TRIPLES
Mickey Rivers CAL 13
George Brett KC 13
Jorge Orta CHI 10

HOME RUNS
George Scott MIL 36
Reggie Jackson OAK 36
Johnny Mayberry KC 34

RUNS BATTED IN
George Scott MIL 109
John Mayberry KC 106
Fred Lynn BOS 105

SLUGGING AVERAGE
Fred Lynn BOS .... .566
John Mayberry KC .... .547
George Scott MIL .... .515

STOLEN BASES
Mickey Rivers CAL 70
C. Washington OAK 40
Amos Otis KC 39

RUNS SCORED
Fred Lynn BOS 103
John Mayberry KC 95
Bobby Bonds NY 93

WINS
Jim Palmer BAL 23
Catfish Hunter NY 23
Vida Blue OAK 22

WINNING PERCENTAGE
Mike Torrez BAL .... .690
Dennis Leonard KC .... .682
Jim Palmer BAL .... .676

EARNED RUN AVERAGE
Jim Palmer BAL 2.09
Catfish Hunter NY 2.58
Dennis Eckersley CLE 2.60

STRIKEOUTS
Frank Tanana CAL 269
Bert Blyleven MIN 233
G. Perry CLE, TEX 233

SAVES
Goose Gossage CHI 26
Rollie Fingers OAK 24
Tom Murphy MIL 20

COMPLETE GAMES
Catfish Hunter NY 30
Jim Palmer BAL 25
Gaylord Perry CLE, TEX 25

SHUTOUTS
Jim Palmer BAL 10
Catfish Hunter NY 7
two tied at 5

GAMES PITCHED
Rollie Fingers OAK 75
Paul Lindblad OAK 68
Goose Gossage CHI 62

INNINGS PITCHED
Catfish Hunter NY 328
Jim Palmer BAL 323
G. Perry CLE, TEX 306

NATIONAL LEAGUE STANDINGS

1975 NL

EAST	W	L	PCT	GB	R	OR	BA	FA	ERA
PITTSBURGH	92	69	.571	—	712	565	.263	.976	3.02
PHILADELPHIA	86	76	.531	6.5	735	694	.269	.976	3.82
NEW YORK	82	80	.506	10.5	646	625	.256	.976	3.39
ST. LOUIS	82	80	.506	10.5	662	689	.273	.973	3.58
CHICAGO	75	87	.463	17.5	712	827	.259	.972	4.57
MONTREAL	75	87	.463	17.5	601	690	.244	.973	3.73

WEST	W	L	PCT	GB	R	OR	BA	FA	ERA
CINCINNATI	108	54	.667	—	840	586	.271	.984	3.37
LOS ANGELES	88	74	.543	20	648	534	.248	.979	2.92
SAN FRANCISCO	80	81	.497	27.5	659	671	.259	.976	3.74
SAN DIEGO	71	91	.438	37	552	683	.244	.971	3.51
ATLANTA	67	94	.416	40.5	583	739	.244	.972	3.93
HOUSTON	64	97	.398	43.5	664	711	.254	.979	4.05
					8014	8014	.257	.976	3.63

BATTING AVERAGE
Bill Madlock CHI .... .354
Ted Simmons STL .... .332
Manny Sanguillen PIT ..... .328

HITS
Dave Cash PHI 213
Steve Garvey LA 210
Pete Rose CIN 210

DOUBLES
Pete Rose CIN 47
Dave Cash PHI 40
two tied at 39

TRIPLES
Ralph Garr ATL 11
three tied at 10

HOME RUNS
Mike Schmidt PHI 38
Dave Kingman NY 36
Greg Luzinski PHI 34

RUNS BATTED IN
Greg Luzinski PHI 120
Johnny Bench CIN 110
Tony Perez CIN 109

SLUGGING AVERAGE
Dave Parker PIT .... .541
Greg Luzinski PHI .... .540
Mike Schmidt PHI .... .523

STOLEN BASES
Davey Lopes LA 77
Joe Morgan CIN 67
Lou Brock STL 56

RUNS SCORED
Pete Rose CIN 112
Dave Cash PHI 111
Davey Lopes LA 108

WINS
Tom Seaver NY 22
Randy Jones SD 20
Andy Messersmith LA 19

WINNING PERCENTAGE
Tom Seaver NY .... .710
Burt Hooton CHI, LA .... .667
four tied at .... .625

EARNED RUN AVERAGE
Randy Jones SD 2.24
Andy Messersmith LA 2.29
Tom Seaver NY 2.38

STRIKEOUTS
Tom Seaver NY 243
John Montefusco SF 215
Andy Messersmith LA 213

SAVES
Rawley Eastwick CIN 22
Al Hrabosky STL 22
Dave Giusti PIT 17

COMPLETE GAMES
Andy Messersmith LA 19
Randy Jones SD 18
two tied at 15

SHUTOUTS
Andy Messersmith LA 7
Randy Jones SD 6
Jerry Reuss PIT 6

GAMES PITCHED
Gene Garber PHI 71
Will McEnaney CIN 70
two tied at 67

INNINGS PITCHED
Andy Messersmith LA 322
Randy Jones SD 285
Tom Seaver NY 280

AMERICAN LEAGUE STANDINGS

1976 AL

EAST	W	L	PCT	GB	R	OR	BA	FA	ERA
NEW YORK	97	62	.610	—	730	575	.269	.980	3.19
BALTIMORE	88	74	.543	10.5	619	598	.243	.982	3.31
BOSTON	83	79	.512	15.5	716	660	.263	.978	3.52
CLEVELAND	81	78	.509	16	615	615	.263	.980	3.48
DETROIT	74	87	.460	24	609	709	.257	.974	3.87
MILWAUKEE	66	95	.410	32	570	655	.246	.975	3.64

WEST	W	L	PCT	GB	R	OR	BA	FA	ERA
KANSAS CITY	90	72	.556	—	713	611	.269	.978	3.21
OAKLAND	87	74	.540	2.5	686	598	.246	.977	3.26
MINNESOTA	85	77	.525	5	743	704	.274	.973	3.72
CALIFORNIA	76	86	.469	14	550	631	.235	.977	3.36
TEXAS	76	86	.469	14	616	652	.250	.976	3.47
CHICAGO	64	97	.398	25.5	586	745	.255	.979	4.25
					7753	7753	.256	.977	3.52

BATTING AVERAGE
George Brett KC.............. .333
Hal McRae KC .... .332
Rod Carew MIN............... .331

HITS
George Brett KC.......... 215
Rod Carew MIN.............. 200
Chris Chambliss NY 188

DOUBLES
Amos Otis KC..................... 40
three tied at 34

TRIPLES
George Brett KC................ 14
Phil Garner OAK 12
Rod Carew MIN.................. 12

HOME RUNS
Graig Nettles NY 32
Sal Bando OAK 27
Reggie Jackson BAL......... 27

RUNS BATTED IN
Lee May BAL..................... 109
Thurman Munson NY 105
Carl Yastrzemski BOS 102

SLUGGING AVERAGE
Reggie Jackson BAL....... .502
Jim Rice BOS.................. .482
Graig Nettles NY .... .475

STOLEN BASES
Billy North OAK 75
Ron LeFlore DET 58
Bert Campaneris OAK....... 54

RUNS SCORED
Roy White NY.................. 104
Rod Carew MIN................ 97
Mickey Rivers NY.............. 95

WINS
Jim Palmer BAL 22
Luis Tiant BOS.................. 21
Wayne Garland BAL 20

WINNING PERCENTAGE
Bill Campbell MIN............ .773
Wayne Garland BAL .... .741
Doc Ellis NY .... .680

EARNED RUN AVERAGE
Mark Fidrych DET 2.34
Vida Blue OAK 2.36
Frank Tanana CAL.......... 2.44

STRIKEOUTS
Nolan Ryan CAL 327
Frank Tanana CAL........... 261
B. Blyleven MIN, TEX....... 219

SAVES
Sparky Lyle NY 23
Dave LaRoche CLE 21
two tied at........................... 20

COMPLETE GAMES
Mark Fidrych DET 24
Frank Tanana CAL............. 23
Jim Palmer BAL 23

SHUTOUTS
Nolan Ryan CAL 7
three tied at 6

GAMES PITCHED
Bill Campbell MIN............... 78
Rollie Fingers OAK............. 70
Paul Lindblad OAK.............. 65

INNINGS PITCHED
Jim Palmer BAL 315
Catfish Hunter NY 299
Vida Blue OAK 298

NATIONAL LEAGUE STANDINGS

1976 NL

EAST	W	L	PCT	GB	R	OR	BA	FA	ERA
PHILADELPHIA	101	61	.623	—	770	557	.272	.981	3.10
PITTSBURGH	92	70	.568	9	708	630	.267	.975	3.37
NEW YORK	86	76	.531	15	615	538	.246	.979	2.94
CHICAGO	75	87	.463	26	611	728	.251	.978	3.93
ST. LOUIS	72	90	.444	29	629	671	.260	.973	3.61
MONTREAL	55	107	.340	46	531	734	.235	.976	3.99

WEST	W	L	PCT	GB	R	OR	BA	FA	ERA
CINCINNATI	102	60	.630	—	857	633	.280	.984	3.51
LOS ANGELES	92	70	.568	10	608	543	.251	.980	3.02
HOUSTON	80	82	.494	22	625	657	.256	.978	3.55
SAN FRANCISCO	74	88	.457	28	595	686	.246	.971	3.53
SAN DIEGO	73	89	.451	29	570	662	.247	.978	3.65
ATLANTA	70	92	.432	32	620	700	.245	.973	3.87
					7739	7739	.255	.977	3.50

BATTING AVERAGE
Bill Madlock CHI .... .339
Ken Griffey CIN .... .336
Garry Maddox PHI .... .330

HITS
Pete Rose CIN 215
W. Montanez SF, ATL 206
Steve Garvey LA 200

DOUBLES
Pete Rose CIN 42
Jay Johnstone PHI 38
two tied at 37

TRIPLES
Dave Cash PHI 12
Cesar Geronimo CIN 11
two tied at 10

HOME RUNS
Mike Schmidt PHI 38
Dave Kingman NY 37
Rick Monday CHI 32

RUNS BATTED IN
George Foster CIN 121
Joe Morgan CIN 111
Mike Schmidt PHI 107

SLUGGING AVERAGE
Joe Morgan CIN .... .576
George Foster CIN .... .530
Mike Schmidt PHI .... .524

STOLEN BASES
Davey Lopes LA 63
Joe Morgan CIN 60
two tied at 58

RUNS SCORED
Pete Rose CIN 130
Joe Morgan CIN 113
Mike Schmidt PHI 112

WINS
Randy Jones SD 22
Jerry Koosman NY 21
Don Sutton LA 21

WINNING PERCENTAGE
Steve Carlton PHI .... .741
John Candelaria PIT .... .696
two tied at .... .677

EARNED RUN AVERAGE
John Denny STL 2.52
Doug Rau LA 2.57
Tom Seaver NY 2.59

STRIKEOUTS
Tom Seaver NY 235
J. R. Richard HOU 214
Jerry Koosman NY 200

SAVES
Rawley Eastwick CIN 26
Skip Lockwood NY 19
Ken Forsch HOU 19

COMPLETE GAMES
Randy Jones SD 25
Jerry Koosman NY 17
John Matlack NY 16

SHUTOUTS
John Matlack NY 6
John Montefusco SF 6
two tied at 5

GAMES PITCHED
Dale Murray MON 81
Charlie Hough LA 77
Butch Metzger NY 77

INNINGS PITCHED
Randy Jones SD 315
J. R. Richard HOU 291
two tied at 271

AMERICAN LEAGUE STANDINGS

1977 AL

EAST	W	L	PCT	GB	R	OR	BA	FA	ERA
NEW YORK	100	62	.617	—	831	651	.281	.979	3.61
BALTIMORE	97	64	.602	2.5	719	653	.261	.983	3.74
BOSTON	97	64	.602	2.5	859	712	.281	.978	4.16
DETROIT	74	88	.457	26	714	751	.264	.978	4.13
CLEVELAND	71	90	.441	28.5	676	739	.269	.979	4.10
MILWAUKEE	67	95	.414	33	639	765	.258	.978	4.32
TORONTO	54	107	.335	45.5	605	882	.252	.974	4.57

WEST	W	L	PCT	GB	R	OR	BA	FA	ERA
KANSAS CITY	102	60	.630	—	822	651	.277	.978	3.52
TEXAS	94	68	.580	8	767	657	.270	.982	3.56
CHICAGO	90	72	.556	12	844	771	.278	.974	4.25
MINNESOTA	84	77	.522	17.5	867	776	.282	.978	4.38
CALIFORNIA	74	88	.457	28	675	695	.255	.976	3.76
SEATTLE	64	98	.395	38	624	855	.256	.976	4.83
OAKLAND	63	98	.391	38.5	605	749	.240	.970	4.05
					10247	10247	.266	.977	4.07

BATTING AVERAGE
Rod Carew MIN .... .388
Lyman Bostock MIN .... .336
Ken Singleton BAL .... .328

HITS
Rod Carew MIN 239
Ron LeFlore DET 212
Jim Rice Bos 206

DOUBLES
Hal McRae KC 54
Reggie Jackson NY 39
two tied at 38

TRIPLES
Rod Carew MIN 16
Jim Rice BOS 15
Al Cowens KC 14

HOME RUNS
Jim Rice BOS 39
Graig Nettles NY 37
Bobby Bonds CAL 37

RUNS BATTED IN
Larry Hisle MIN 119
Bobby Bonds CAL 115
Jim Rice BOS 114

SLUGGING AVERAGE
Jim Rice BOS .... .593
Rod Carew MIN .... .570
Reggie Jackson NY .... .550

STOLEN BASES
Freddie Patek KC 53
Mike Page OAK 42
two tied at 41

RUNS SCORED
Rod Carew MIN 128
Carlton Fisk BOS 106
George Brett KC 105

WINS
Jim Palmer BAL 20
Dave Goltz MIN 20
Dennis Leonard KC 20

WINNING PERCENTAGE
Paul Splittorff KC .... .727
Ron Guidry NY .... .696
Dave Rozema DET .... .682

EARNED RUN AVERAGE
Frank Tanana CAL 2.54
Bert Blyleven TEX 2.72
Nolan Ryan CAL 2.77

STRIKEOUTS
Nolan Ryan CAL 341
Dennis Leonard KC 244
Frank Tanana CAL 205

SAVES
Bill Campbell BOS 31
Sparky Lyle NY 26
Lerrin LaGrow CHI 25

COMPLETE GAMES
Jim Palmer BAL 22
Nolan Ryan CAL 22
two tied at 21

SHUTOUTS
Frank Tanana CAL 7
three tied at 5

GAMES PITCHED
Sparky Lyle NY 72
Tom Johnson MIN 71
Bill Campbell BOS 69

INNINGS PITCHED
Jim Palmer BAL 319
Dave Goltz MIN 303
Nolan Ryan CAL 299

NATIONAL LEAGUE STANDINGS

1977 NL

EAST	W	L	PCT	GB	R	OR	BA	FA	ERA
PHILADELPHIA	101	61	.623	—	847	668	.279	.981	3.71
PITTSBURGH	96	66	.593	5	734	665	.274	.977	3.61
ST. LOUIS	83	79	.512	18	737	688	.270	.978	3.81
CHICAGO	81	81	.500	20	692	739	.266	.977	4.01
MONTREAL	75	87	.463	26	665	736	.260	.980	4.01
NEW YORK	64	98	.395	37	587	663	.244	.978	3.77

WEST	W	L	PCT	GB	R	OR	BA	FA	ERA
LOS ANGELES	98	64	.605	—	769	582	.266	.981	3.22
CINCINNATI	88	74	.543	10	802	725	.274	.984	4.22
HOUSTON	81	81	.500	17	680	650	.254	.978	3.54
SAN FRANCISCO	75	87	.463	23	673	711	.253	.972	3.75
SAN DIEGO	69	93	.426	29	692	834	.249	.971	4.43
ATLANTA	61	101	.377	37	678	895	.254	.972	4.85
					8556	8556	.262	.977	3.91

BATTING AVERAGE
Dave Parker PIT .... .338
Garry Templeton STL ...... .322
George Foster CIN .... .320

HITS
Dave Parker PIT 215
Pete Rose CIN 204
Garry Templeton STL 200

DOUBLES
Dave Parker PIT 44
Dave Cash MON 42
two tied at 41

TRIPLES
Garry Templeton STL 18
three tied at 11

HOME RUNS
George Foster CIN 52
Jeff Burroughs ATL 41
Greg Luzinski PHI 39

RUNS BATTED IN
George Foster CIN 149
Greg Luzinski PHI 130
Steve Garvey LA 115

SLUGGING AVERAGE
George Foster CIN .... .631
Greg Luzinski PHI .... .594
Reggie Smith LA .... .576

STOLEN BASES
Frank Taveras PIT 70
Cesar Cedeno HOU 61
Gene Richards SD 56

RUNS SCORED
George Foster CIN 124
Ken Griffey CIN 117
Mike Schmidt PHI 114

WINS
Steve Carlton PHI 23
Tom Seaver NY, CIN 21
four tied at 20

WINNING PERCENTAGE
John Candelaria PIT .... .800
Tom Seaver NY, CIN .... .778
Larry Christenson PHI ..... .760

EARNED RUN AVERAGE
John Candelaria PIT 2.34
Tom Seaver NY, CIN 2.58
Burt Hooton LA 2.62

STRIKEOUTS
Phil Niekro ATL 262
J. R. Richard HOU 214
Steve Rogers MON 206

SAVES
Rollie Fingers SD 35
Bruce Sutter CHI 31
Goose Gossage PIT 26

COMPLETE GAMES
Phil Niekro ATL 20
Tom Seaver NY, CIN 19
two tied at 17

SHUTOUTS
Tom Seaver NY, CIN 7
Rick Reuschel CHI 4
Steve Rogers MON 4

GAMES PITCHED
Rollie Fingers SD 78
Dan Spillner SD 76
Dave Tomlin SD 76

INNINGS PITCHED
Phil Niekro ATL 330
Steve Rogers MON 302
Steve Carlton PHI 283

AMERICAN LEAGUE STANDINGS

1978 AL

EAST	W	L	PCT	GB	R	OR	BA	FA	ERA
NEW YORK*	100	63	.613	—	735	582	.267	.982	3.18
BOSTON	99	64	.607	1	796	657	.267	.977	3.54
MILWAUKEE	93	69	.574	6.5	804	650	.276	.977	3.65
BALTIMORE	90	71	.559	9	659	633	.258	.982	3.56
DETROIT	86	76	.531	13.5	714	653	.271	.981	3.64
CLEVELAND	69	90	.434	29	639	694	.261	.980	3.97
TORONTO	59	102	.366	40	590	775	.250	.979	4.55

WEST	W	L	PCT	GB	R	OR	BA	FA	ERA
KANSAS CITY	92	70	.568	—	743	634	.268	.976	3.44
CALIFORNIA	87	75	.537	5	691	666	.259	.978	3.65
TEXAS	87	75	.537	5	692	632	.253	.976	3.42
MINNESOTA	73	89	.451	19	666	678	.267	.977	3.69
CHICAGO	71	90	.441	20.5	634	731	.264	.977	4.22
OAKLAND	69	93	.426	23	532	690	.245	.971	3.62
SEATTLE	56	104	.350	35	614	834	.248	.978	4.72
					9509	9509	.261	.978	3.77

* Defeated Boston in a 1 game playoff.

BATTING AVERAGE
Rod Carew MIN .... .333
Al Oliver TEX .... .324
Jim Rice BOS .... .315

HITS
Jim Rice BOS 213
Ron LeFlore DET 198
Rod Carew MIN 188

DOUBLES
George Brett KC 45
Carlton Fisk BOS 39
Hal McRae KC 39

TRIPLES
Jim Rice BOS 15
Rod Carew MIN 10
Dan Ford MIN 10

HOME RUNS
Jim Rice BOS 46
Larry Hisle MIL 34
Don Baylor CAL 34

RUNS BATTED IN
Jim Rice BOS 139
Rusty Staub DET 121
Larry Hisle MIL 115

SLUGGING AVERAGE
Jim Rice BOS .... .600
Larry Hisle MIL .... .533
Doug DeCinces BAL .... .526

STOLEN BASES
Ron LeFlore DET 68
Julio Cruz SEA 59
Bump Wills TEX 52

RUNS SCORED
Ron LeFlore DET 126
Jim Rice BOS 121
Don Baylor CAL 103

WINS
Ron Guidry NY 25
Mike Caldwell MIL 22
two tied at 21

WINNING PERCENTAGE
Ron Guidry NY .... .893
Bob Stanley BOS .... .882
Larry Gura KC .... .800

EARNED RUN AVERAGE
Ron Guidry NY 1.74
John Matlack TEX 2.27
Mike Caldwell MIL 2.36

STRIKEOUTS
Nolan Ryan CAL 260
Ron Guidry NY 248
Dennis Leonard KC 183

SAVES
Goose Gossage NY 27
Dave LaRoche CAL 25
Don Stanhouse BAL 24

COMPLETE GAMES
Mike Caldwell MIL 23
Dennis Leonard KC 20
Jim Palmer BAL 19

SHUTOUTS
Ron Guidry NY 9
Mike Caldwell MIL 6
Jim Palmer BAL 6

GAMES PITCHED
Bob Lacey OAK 74
Dave Heaverlo OAK 69
Elias Sosa OAK 68

INNINGS PITCHED
Jim Palmer BAL 296
Dennis Leonard KC 295
Mike Caldwell MIL 293

NATIONAL LEAGUE STANDINGS

1978 NL

EAST	W	L	PCT	GB	R	OR	BA	FA	ERA
PHILADELPHIA	90	72	.556	—	708	586	.258	.983	3.33
PITTSBURGH	88	73	.547	1.5	684	637	.257	.973	3.41
CHICAGO	79	83	.488	11	664	724	.264	.978	4.05
MONTREAL	76	86	.469	14	633	611	.254	.979	3.42
ST. LOUIS	69	93	.426	21	600	657	.249	.978	3.58
NEW YORK	66	96	.407	24	607	690	.245	.979	3.87

WEST	W	L	PCT	GB	R	OR	BA	FA	ERA
LOS ANGELES	95	67	.586	—	727	573	.264	.978	3.12
CINCINNATI	92	69	.571	2.5	710	688	.256	.978	3.81
SAN FRANCISCO	89	73	.549	6	613	594	.248	.977	3.30
SAN DIEGO	84	78	.519	11	591	598	.252	.975	3.28
HOUSTON	74	88	.457	21	605	634	.258	.978	3.63
ATLANTA	69	93	.426	26	600	750	.244	.975	4.08
					7742	7742	.254	.978	3.58

BATTING AVERAGE
Dave Parker PIT .... .334
Steve Garvey LA .... .316
Jose Cruz HOU .... .315

HITS
Steve Garvey LA 202
Pete Rose CIN 198
Enos Cabell HOU 195

DOUBLES
Pete Rose CIN 51
Jack Clark SF 46
Ted Simmons STL 40

TRIPLES
Garry Templeton STL 13
Dave Parker PIT 12
Gene Richards SD 12

HOME RUNS
George Foster CIN 40
Greg Luzinski PHI 35
Dave Parker PIT 30

RUNS BATTED IN
George Foster CIN 120
Dave Parker PIT 117
Steve Garvey LA 113

SLUGGING AVERAGE
Dave Parker PIT .... .585
Reggie Smith LA .... .559
George Foster CIN .... .546

STOLEN BASES
Omar Moreno PIT 71
Frank Taveras PIT 46
Davey Lopes LA 45

RUNS SCORED
Ivan DeJesus CHI 104
Pete Rose CIN 103
Dave Parker PIT 102

WINS
Gaylord Perry SD 21
Ross Grimsley MON 20
two tied at 19

WINNING PERCENTAGE
Gaylord Perry SD .... .778
Don Robinson PIT .... .700
Burt Hooton LA .... .655

EARNED RUN AVERAGE
Craig Swan NY 2.43
Steve Rogers MON 2.47
Pete Vuckovich STL 2.55

STRIKEOUTS
J. R. Richard HOU 303
Phil Niekro ATL 248
Tom Seaver CIN 226

SAVES
Rollie Fingers SD 37
Kent Tekulve PIT 31
Doug Bair CIN 28

COMPLETE GAMES
Phil Niekro ATL 22
Ross Grimsley MON 19
two tied at 16

SHUTOUTS
Bob Knepper SF 6
three tied at 4

GAMES PITCHED
Kent Tekulve PIT 91
Mark Littell STL 72
Donnie Moore CHI 71

INNINGS PITCHED
Phil Niekro ATL 334
J. R. Richard HOU 275
Ross Grimsley MON 263

AMERICAN LEAGUE STANDINGS

1979 AL

EAST	W	L	PCT	GB	R	OR	BA	FA	ERA
BALTIMORE	102	57	.642	—	757	582	.261	.980	3.26
MILWAUKEE	95	66	.590	8	807	722	.280	.980	4.03
BOSTON	91	69	.569	11.5	841	711	.283	.977	4.03
NEW YORK	89	71	.556	13.5	734	672	.266	.981	3.83
DETROIT	85	76	.528	18	770	738	.269	.981	4.28
CLEVELAND	81	80	.503	22	760	805	.258	.978	4.57
TORONTO	53	109	.327	50.5	613	862	.251	.975	4.82

WEST	W	L	PCT	GB	R	OR	BA	FA	ERA
CALIFORNIA	88	74	.543	—	866	768	.282	.978	4.34
KANSAS CITY	85	77	.525	3	851	816	.282	.977	4.45
TEXAS	83	79	.512	5	750	698	.278	.979	3.86
MINNESOTA	82	80	.506	6	764	725	.278	.979	4.13
CHICAGO	73	87	.456	14	730	748	.275	.972	4.10
SEATTLE	67	95	.414	21	711	820	.269	.978	4.58
OAKLAND	54	108	.333	34	573	860	.239	.972	4.75
					10527	10527	.270	.978	4.22

BATTING AVERAGE
Fred Lynn BOS .... .333
George Brett KC .... .329
Brian Downing CAL .... .326

HITS
George Brett KC 212
Jim Rice BOS 201
Buddy Bell TEX 200

DOUBLES
Cecil Cooper MIL 44
Chet Lemon CHI 44
two tied at 42

TRIPLES
George Brett KC 20
Paul Molitor MIL 16
two tied at 13

HOME RUNS
Gorman Thomas MIL 45
Fred Lynn BOS 39
Jim Rice BOS 39

RUNS BATTED IN
Don Baylor CAL 139
Jim Rice BOS 130
Gorman Thomas MIL 123

SLUGGING AVERAGE
Fred Lynn BOS .... .637
Jim Rice BOS .... .596
Sixto Lezcano MIL .... .573

STOLEN BASES
Willie Wilson KC 83
Ron LeFlore DET 78
Julio Cruz SEA 49

RUNS SCORED
Don Baylor CAL 120
George Brett KC 119
Jim Rice BOS 117

WINS
Mike Flanagan BOS 23
Tommy John NY 21
Jerry Koosman MIN 20

WINNING PERCENTAGE
Mike Caldwell MIL .... .727
Mike Flanagan BAL .... .719
Jack Morris DET .... .708

EARNED RUN AVERAGE
Ron Guidry NY 2.78
Tommy John NY 2.97
Dennis Eckersley BOS 2.99

STRIKEOUTS
Nolan Ryan CAL 223
Ron Guidry NY 201
Mike Flanagan BAL 190

SAVES
Mike Marshall MIN 32
Jim Kern TEX 29
two tied at 21

COMPLETE GAMES
Dennis Martinez BAL 18
three tied at 17

SHUTOUTS
Dennis Leonard KC 5
Mike Flanagan BAL 5
Nolan Ryan CAL 5

GAMES PITCHED
Mike Marshall MIN 90
Sid Monge CLE 76
Jim Kern TEX 71

INNINGS PITCHED
Dennis Martinez BAL 292
Tommy John NY 276
Mike Flanagan BAL 266

NATIONAL LEAGUE STANDINGS

1979 NL

EAST	W	L	PCT	GB	R	OR	BA	FA	ERA
PITTSBURGH	98	64	.605	—	775	643	.272	.979	3.41
MONTREAL	95	65	.594	2	701	581	.264	.979	3.14
ST. LOUIS	86	76	.531	12	731	693	.278	.980	3.72
PHILADELPHIA	84	78	.519	14	683	718	.266	.983	4.16
CHICAGO	80	82	.494	18	706	707	.269	.975	3.88
NEW YORK	63	99	.389	35	593	706	.250	.978	3.84

WEST	W	L	PCT	GB	R	OR	BA	FA	ERA
CINCINNATI	90	71	.559	—	731	644	.264	.980	3.58
HOUSTON	89	73	.549	1.5	583	582	.256	.978	3.19
LOS ANGELES	79	83	.488	11.5	739	717	.263	.981	3.83
SAN FRANCISCO	71	91	.438	19.5	672	751	.246	.974	4.16
SAN DIEGO	68	93	.422	22	603	681	.242	.978	3.69
ATLANTA	66	94	.413	23.5	669	763	.256	.970	4.18
					8186	8186	.261	.978	3.73

BATTING AVERAGE
Keith Hernandez STL ...... .344
Pete Rose PHI .... .331
Ray Knight CIN .... .318

HITS
Garry Templeton STL 211
Keith Hernandez STL 210
Pete Rose PHI 208

DOUBLES
Keith Hernandez STL 48
Warren Cromartie MON 46
Dave Parker PIT 45

TRIPLES
Garry Templeton STL 19
three tied at 12

HOME RUNS
Dave Kingman CHI 48
Mike Schmidt PHI 45
Dave Winfield SD 34

RUNS BATTED IN
Dave Winfield SD 118
Dave Kingman CHI 115
Mike Schmidt PHI 114

SLUGGING AVERAGE
Dave Kingman CHI .... .613
Mike Schmidt PHI .... .564
Dave Winfield SD .... .558

STOLEN BASES
Omar Moreno PIT 77
Billy North SF 58
two tied at 44

RUNS SCORED
Keith Hernandez STL 116
Omar Moreno PIT 110
two tied at 109

WINS
Phil Niekro ATL 21
Joe Niekro HOU 21
three tied at 18

WINNING PERCENTAGE
Tom Seaver CIN .... .727
Joe Niekro HOU .... .656
Silvio Martinez STL .... .652

EARNED RUN AVERAGE
J. R. Richard HOU 2.71
Tom Hume CIN 2.76
Dan Schatzeder MON 2.83

STRIKEOUTS
J. R. Richard HOU 313
Steve Carlton PHI 213
Phil Niekro ATL 208

SAVES
Bruce Sutter CHI 37
Kent Tekulve PIT 31
Gene Garber ATL 25

COMPLETE GAMES
Phil Niekro ATL 23
J. R. Richard HOU 19
two tied at 13

SHUTOUTS
Tom Seaver CIN 5
Steve Rogers MON 5
Joe Niekro HOU 5

GAMES PITCHED
Kent Tekulve PIT 94
Enrique Romo PIT 84
Grant Jackson PIT 72

INNINGS PITCHED
Phil Niekro ATL 342
J. R. Richard HOU 292
Joe Niekro HOU 264

AMERICAN LEAGUE STANDINGS

1980 AL

EAST	W	L	PCT	GB	R	OR	BA	FA	ERA
NEW YORK	103	59	.636	—	820	662	.267	.978	3.58
BALTIMORE	100	62	.617	3	805	640	.273	.985	3.64
MILWAUKEE	86	76	.531	17	811	682	.275	.977	3.71
BOSTON	83	77	.519	19	757	767	.283	.977	4.38
DETROIT	84	78	.519	19	830	757	.273	.979	4.25
CLEVELAND	79	81	.494	23	738	807	.277	.983	4.68
TORONTO	67	95	.414	36	624	762	.251	.979	4.19

WEST	W	L	PCT	GB	R	OR	BA	FA	ERA
KANSAS CITY	97	65	.599	—	809	694	.286	.978	3.83
OAKLAND	83	79	.512	14	686	642	.259	.979	3.46
MINNESOTA	77	84	.478	19.5	670	724	.265	.977	3.93
TEXAS	76	85	.472	20.5	756	752	.284	.977	4.02
CHICAGO	70	90	.438	26	587	722	.259	.973	3.92
CALIFORNIA	65	95	.406	31	698	797	.265	.978	4.52
SEATTLE	59	103	.364	38	610	793	.248	.977	4.38
					10201	10201	.269	.978	4.03

BATTING AVERAGE
George Brett KC .... .390
Cecil Cooper MIL .... .352
Miguel Dilone CLE .... .341

HITS
Willie Wilson KC 230
Cecil Cooper MIL 219
Mickey Rivers TEX 210

DOUBLES
Robin Yount MIL 49
Al Oliver TEX 43
Jim Morrison CHI 40

TRIPLES
Willie Wilson KC 15
Alfredo Griffin TOR 15
two tied at 11

HOME RUNS
Reggie Jackson NY 41
Ben Oglivie MIL 41
Gorman Thomas MIL 38

RUNS BATTED IN
Cecil Cooper MIL 122
George Brett KC 118
Ben Oglivie MIL 118

SLUGGING AVERAGE
George Brett KC .... .664
Reggie Jackson NY .... .597
Ben Oglivie MIL .... .563

STOLEN BASES
R. Henderson OAK 100
Willie Wilson KC 79
Miguel Dilone CLE 61

RUNS SCORED
Willie Wilson KC 133
Robin Yount MIL 121
Al Bumbry BAL 118

WINS
Steve Stone BAL 25
Tommy John NY 22
Mike Norris OAK 22

WINNING PERCENTAGE
Steve Stone BAL .... .781
Rudy May NY .... .750
Scott McGregor BAL .... .714

EARNED RUN AVERAGE
Rudy May NY 2.47
Mike Norris OAK 2.54
Britt Burns CHI 2.84

STRIKEOUTS
Len Barker CLE 187
Mike Norris OAK 180
Ron Guidry NY 166

SAVES
Dan Quisenberry KC 33
Goose Gossage NY 33
Ed Farmer CHI 30

COMPLETE GAMES
Rick Langford OAK 28
Mike Norris OAK 24
Matt Keough OAK 20

SHUTOUTS
Tommy John NY 6
Geoff Zahn MIN 5
two tied at 4

GAMES PITCHED
Dan Quisenberry KC 75
Doug Corbett MIN 73
two tied at 67

INNINGS PITCHED
Rick Langford OAK 290
Mike Norris OAK 284
Larry Gura KC 283

NATIONAL LEAGUE STANDINGS

1980 NL

EAST	W	L	PCT	GB	R	OR	BA	FA	ERA
PHILADELPHIA	91	71	.562	—	728	639	.270	.979	3.43
MONTREAL	90	72	.556	1	694	629	.257	.977	3.48
PITTSBURGH	83	79	.512	8	666	646	.266	.978	3.58
ST. LOUIS	74	88	.457	17	738	710	.275	.981	3.93
NEW YORK	67	95	.414	24	611	702	.257	.975	3.85
CHICAGO	64	98	.395	27	614	728	.251	.974	3.89

WEST	W	L	PCT	GB	R	OR	BA	FA	ERA
HOUSTON*	93	70	.571	—	637	589	.261	.978	3.10
LOS ANGELES	92	71	.564	1	663	591	.263	.981	3.24
CINCINNATI	89	73	.549	3.5	707	670	.262	.983	3.85
ATLANTA	81	80	.503	11	630	660	.250	.975	3.77
SAN FRANCISCO	75	86	.466	17	573	634	.244	.975	3.46
SAN DIEGO	73	89	.451	19.5	591	654	.255	.980	3.65
					7852	7852	.259	.978	3.60

*Defeated Los Angeles in a 1 game playoff

BATTING AVERAGE
Bill Buckner CHI .... .324
Keith Hernandez STL .... .321
Garry Templeton STL ...... .319

HITS
Steve Garvey LA 200
Gene Richards SD 193
Keith Hernandez STL 191

DOUBLES
Pete Rose PHI 42
Bill Buckner CHI 41
Andre Dawson MON 41

TRIPLES
Rodney Scott MON 13
Omar Moreno PIT 13
two tied at 11

HOME RUNS
Mike Schmidt PHI 48
Bob Horner ATL 35
Dale Murphy ATL 33

RUNS BATTED IN
Mike Schmidt PHI 121
George Hendrick STL 109
Steve Garvey LA 106

SLUGGING AVERAGE
Mike Schmidt PHI .... .624
Jack Clark SF .... .517
Dale Murphy ATL .... .510

STOLEN BASES
Ron LeFlore MON 97
Omar Moreno PIT 96
Dave Collins CIN 79

RUNS SCORED
Keith Hernandez STL 111
Mike Schmidt PHI 104
Dale Murphy ATL 98

WINS
Steve Carlton PHI 24
Joe Niekro HOU 20
Jim Bibby PIT 19

WINNING PERCENTAGE
Jim Bibby PIT .... .760
Jerry Reuss LA .... .750
Steve Carlton PHI .... .727

EARNED RUN AVERAGE
Don Sutton LA 2.21
Steve Carlton PHI 2.34
Jerry Reuss LA 2.52

STRIKEOUTS
Steve Carlton PHI 286
Nolan Ryan HOU 200
Mario Soto CIN 182

SAVES
Bruce Sutter CHI 28
Tom Hume CIN 25
Rollie Fingers SD 23

COMPLETE GAMES
Steve Rogers MON 14
Steve Carlton PHI 13
two tied at 11

SHUTOUTS
Jerry Reuss LA 6
J. R. Richard HOU 4
Steve Rogers MON 4

GAMES PITCHED
Dick Tidrow CHI 84
Tom Hume CIN 78
Kent Tekulve PIT 78

INNINGS PITCHED
Steve Carlton PHI 304
Steve Rogers MON 281
Phil Niekro ATL 275

AMERICAN LEAGUE STANDINGS

1981 AL

EAST	W	L	PCT	GB	R	OR	BA	FA	ERA
MILWAUKEE**	62	47	.569	—	493	459	.257	.982	3.91
BALTIMORE*†	59	46	.562	1	429	437	.251	.983	3.70
NEW YORK	59	48	.551	2	421	343	.252	.982	2.90
DETROIT	60	49	.550	2	427	404	.256	.984	3.53
BOSTON	59	49	.546	2.5	519	481	.275	.979	3.81
CLEVELAND	52	51	.505	7	431	442	.263	.978	3.88
TORONTO	37	69	.349	23.5	329	466	.226	.975	3.82

WEST	W	L	PCT	GB	R	OR	BA	FA	ERA
OAKLAND*†	64	45	.587	—	458	403	.247	.980	3.30
TEXAS	57	48	.543	5	452	389	.270	.984	3.40
CHICAGO	54	52	.509	8.5	476	423	.272	.979	3.47
KANSAS CITY**	50	53	.485	11	397	405	.267	.982	3.56
CALIFORNIA	51	59	.464	13.5	476	453	.256	.977	3.70
SEATTLE	44	65	.404	20	426	521	.251	.979	4.23
MINNESOTA	41	68	.376	23	378	486	.240	.978	3.98
					6112	6112	.256	.980	3.66

BATTING AVERAGE
Carney Lansford BOS ..... .336
Tom Paciorek SEA .... .326
Cecil Cooper MIL .... .320

HITS
R. Henderson OAK 135
Carney Lansford BOS 134
two tied at 133

DOUBLES
Cecil Cooper MIL 35
Al Oliver TEX 29
Tom Paciorek SEA 28

TRIPLES
John Castino MIN 9
three tied at 7

HOME RUNS
four tied at 22

RUNS BATTED IN
Eddie Murray BAL 78
Tony Armas OAK 76
Ben Oglivie MIL 72

SLUGGING AVERAGE
Bobby Grich CAL .... .543
Eddie Murray BAL .... .534
Dwight Evans BOS .... .522

STOLEN BASES
Rickey Henderson OAK 56
Julio Cruz SEA 43
Ron LeFlore CHI 36

RUNS SCORED
Rickey Henderson OAK 89
Dwight Evans BOS 84
Cecil Cooper MIL 70

WINS
four tied at 14

WINNING PERCENTAGE
Pete Vuckovich MIL .... .778
Mike Torrez BOS .... .769
Dennis Martinez BAL ...... .737

EARNED RUN AVERAGE
Steve McCatty OAK 2.32
Sammy Stewart BAL 2.33
Dennis Lamp CHI 2.41

STRIKEOUTS
Len Barker CLE 127
Britt Burns CHI 108
two tied at 107

SAVES
Rollie Fingers MIL 28
Goose Gossage NY 20
Dan Quisenberry KC 18

COMPLETE GAMES
Rick Langford OAK 18
Steve McCatty OAK 16
Jack Morris DET 15

SHUTOUTS
four tied at 4

GAMES PITCHED
Doug Corbett MIN 54
Rollie Fingers MIL 47
Shane Rawley SEA 46

INNINGS PITCHED
Dennis Leonard KC 202
Jack Morris DET 198
Rick Langford OAK 195

NATIONAL LEAGUE STANDINGS

1981 NL

EAST	W	L	PCT	GB	R	OR	BA	FA	ERA
ST. LOUIS	59	43	.578	—	464	417	.265	.981	3.63
MONTREAL**†	60	48	.556	2	443	394	.246	.980	3.30
PHILADELPHIA*	59	48	.551	2.5	491	472	.273	.980	4.05
PITTSBURGH	46	56	.451	13	407	425	.257	.979	3.56
NEW YORK	41	62	.398	18.5	348	432	.248	.968	3.55
CHICAGO	38	65	.369	21.5	370	483	.236	.974	4.01

WEST	W	L	PCT	GB	R	OR	BA	FA	ERA
CINCINNATI	66	42	.611	—	464	440	.267	.981	3.73
LOS ANGELES*†	63	47	.573	4	450	356	.262	.980	3.01
HOUSTON**	61	49	.555	6	394	331	.257	.980	2.66
SAN FRANCISCO	56	55	.505	11.5	427	414	.250	.977	3.28
ATLANTA	50	56	.472	15	395	416	.243	.976	3.45
SAN DIEGO	41	69	.373	26	382	455	.256	.977	3.72
					5035	5035	.255	.978	3.49

*Winner of first half. **Winner of second half. †Winner of playoff.

BATTING AVERAGE
Bill Madlock PIT .341
Pete Rose PHI .325
Dusty Baker LA .320

HITS
Pete Rose PHI 140
Bill Buckner CHI 131
Dave Concepcion CIN 129

DOUBLES
Bill Buckner CHI 35
Ruppert Jones SD 34
Dave Concepcion CIN 28

TRIPLES
Craig Reynolds HOU 12
Gene Richards SD 12
Tommy Herr STL 9

HOME RUNS
Mike Schmidt PHI 31
Andre Dawson MON 24
two tied at 22

RUNS BATTED IN
Mike Schmidt PHI 91
George Foster CIN 90
Bill Buckner 75

SLUGGING AVERAGE
Mike Schmidt PHI .664
Andre Dawson MON .553
George Foster CIN .519

STOLEN BASES
Tim Raines MON 71
Omar Moreno PIT 39
Rodney Scott MON 30

RUNS SCORED
Mike Schmidt PHI 78
Pete Rose PHI 73
Andre Dawson MON 71

WINS
Tom Seaver CIN 14
Steve Carlton PHI 13
F. Valenzuela LA 13

WINNING PERCENTAGE
Tom Seaver CIN .875
Steve Carlton PHI .765
Jerry Reuss LA .714

EARNED RUN AVERAGE
Nolan Ryan HOU 1.69
Bob Knepper HOU 2.18
Burt Hooton LA 2.28

STRIKEOUTS
F. Valenzuela LA 180
Steve Carlton PHI 179
Mario Soto CIN 151

SAVES
Bruce Sutter STL 25
Greg Minton SF 21
Neil Allen NY 18

COMPLETE GAMES
F. Valenzuela LA 11
Mario Soto CIN 10
Steve Carlton PHI 10

SHUTOUTS
Fernando Valenzuela LA 8
Bob Knepper HOU 5
Burt Hooton LA 4

GAMES PITCHED
Gary Lucas SD 57
Greg Minton SF 55
two tied at 51

INNINGS PITCHED
F. Valenzuela LA 192
Steve Carlton PHI 190
Mario Soto CIN 175

AMERICAN LEAGUE STANDINGS

1982 AL

EAST	W	L	PCT	GB	R	OR	BA	FA	ERA
MILWAUKEE	95	67	.586	—	891	717	.279	.980	3.98
BALTIMORE	94	68	.580	1	774	687	.266	.984	3.99
BOSTON	89	73	.549	6	753	713	.274	.981	4.03
DETROIT	83	79	.512	12	729	685	.266	.981	3.80
NEW YORK	79	83	.488	16	709	716	.256	.979	3.99
CLEVELAND	78	84	.481	17	683	748	.262	.980	4.11
TORONTO	78	84	.481	17	651	701	.262	.978	3.95

WEST	W	L	PCT	GB	R	OR	BA	FA	ERA
CALIFORNIA	93	69	.574	—	814	670	.274	.983	3.82
KANSAS CITY	90	72	.556	3	784	717	.285	.979	4.08
CHICAGO	87	75	.537	6	786	710	.273	.976	3.87
SEATTLE	76	86	.469	17	651	712	.254	.978	3.88
OAKLAND	68	94	.420	25	691	819	.236	.974	4.54
TEXAS	64	98	.395	29	590	749	.249	.981	4.28
MINNESOTA	60	102	.370	33	657	819	.257	.982	4.72
					10163	10163	.264	.980	4.07

BATTING AVERAGE
Willie Wilson KC .332
Robin Yount MIL .331
Rod Carew CAL .319

HITS
Robin Yount MIL 210
Cecil Cooper MIL 205
Paul Molitor MIL 201

DOUBLES
Robin Yount MIL 46
Hal McRae KC 46
Frank White KC 45

TRIPLES
Willie Wilson KC 15
Larry Herndon DET 13
Robin Yount MIL 12

HOME RUNS
Reggie Jackson CAL 39
Gorman Thomas MIL 39
Dave Winfield NY 37

RUNS BATTED IN
Hal McRae KC 133
Cecil Cooper MIL 121
Andre Thornton CLE 116

SLUGGING AVERAGE
Robin Yount MIL .578
Dave Winfield NY .560
Eddie Murry BAL .549

STOLEN BASES
R. Henderson OAK 130
Damaso Garcia TOR 54
Julio Cruz SEA 46

RUNS SCORED
Paul Molitor MIL 136
Robin Yount MIL 129
Dwight Evans BOS 122

WINS
LaMarr Hoyt CHI 19
three tied at 18

WINNING PERCENTAGE
Pete Vuckovich MIL .750
Jim Palmer BAL .750
Britt Burns CHI .722

EARNED RUN AVERAGE
Rick Sutcliffe CLE 2.96
Bob Stanley BOS 3.10
Jim Palmer BAL 3.13

STRIKEOUTS
Floyd Bannister SEA 209
Len Barker CLE 187
Dave Righetti NY 163

SAVES
Dan Quisenberry KC 35
Goose Gossage NY 30
Rollie Fingers MIL 29

COMPLETE GAMES
Dave Stieb TOR 19
Jack Morris DET 17
Rick Langford OAK 15

SHUTOUTS
Dave Stieb TOR 5
Geoff Zahn CAL 4
Ken Forsch CAL 4

GAMES PITCHED
Ed Vande Berg SEA 78
Tippy Martinez BAL 76
Dan Quisenberry KC 72

INNINGS PITCHED
Dave Stieb TOR 288
Jim Clancy TOR 267
Jack Morris DET 266

NATIONAL LEAGUE STANDINGS

1982 NL

EAST	W	L	PCT	GB	R	OR	BA	FA	ERA
ST. LOUIS	92	70	.568	—	685	609	.264	.981	3.37
PHILADELPHIA	89	73	.549	3	664	654	.260	.981	3.61
MONTREAL	86	76	.531	6	697	616	.262	.980	3.31
PITTSBURGH	84	78	.519	8	724	696	.273	.977	3.81
CHICAGO	73	89	.451	19	676	709	.260	.979	3.92
NEW YORK	65	97	.401	27	609	723	.247	.972	3.88

WEST	W	L	PCT	GB	R	OR	BA	FA	ERA
ATLANTA	89	73	.549	—	739	702	.256	.979	3.82
LOS ANGELES	88	74	.543	1	691	612	.264	.979	3.26
SAN FRANCISCO	87	75	.537	2	673	687	.253	.973	3.64
SAN DIEGO	81	81	.500	8	675	658	.257	.976	3.52
HOUSTON	77	85	.475	12	569	620	.247	.978	3.41
CINCINNATI	61	101	.377	28	545	661	.251	.980	3.66
					7947	7947	.258	.978	3.60

BATTING AVERAGE
Al Oliver MON .... .331
Bill Madlock PIT .... .319
Leon Durham CHI .... .312

HITS
Al Oliver MON 204
Bill Buckner CHI 201
Andre Dawson MON 183

DOUBLES
Al Oliver MON 43
Terry Kennedy SD.............. 42
Andre Dawson MON 37

TRIPLES
Dickie Thon HOU 10
three tied at 9

HOME RUNS
Dave Kingman NY............... 37
Dale Murphy ATL 36
Mike Schmidt PHI 35

RUNS BATTED IN
Dale Murphy ATL 109
Al Oliver MON 109
Bill Buckner CHI 105

SLUGGING AVERAGE
Mike Schmidt PHI............ .547
Pedro Guerrero LA.......... .536
Leon Durham CHI .... .521

STOLEN BASES
Tim Raines MON................. 78
Lonnie Smith STL............... 68
Omar Moreno PIT 60

RUNS SCORED
Lonnie Smith STL.............. 120
Dale Murphy ATL 113
Mike Schmidt PHI 108

WINS
Steve Carlton PHI 23
Steve Rogers MON 19
F. Valenzuela LA................. 19

WINNING PERCENTAGE
Phil Niekro ATL .... .810
Steve Rogers MON .... .704
Manny Sarmiento PIT ..... .692

EARNED RUN AVERAGE
Steve Rogers MON 2.40
Joe Niekro HOU 2.47
Joaquin Andujar STL....... 2.47

STRIKEOUTS
Steve Carlton PHI 286
Mario Soto CIN.................. 274
Nolan Ryan HOU 245

SAVES
Bruce Sutter STL................ 36
Greg Minton SF 30
Gene Garber ATL................ 30

COMPLETE GAMES
Steve Carlton PHI 19
F. Valenzuela LA................. 18
Joe Niekro HOU 16

SHUTOUTS
Steve Carlton PHI 6
Joaquin Andujar STL............ 5
Joe Niekro HOU 5

GAMES PITCHED
Kent Tekulve PIT................. 85
Greg Minton SF 78
Rod Scurry PIT 76

INNINGS PITCHED
Steve Carlton PHI 296
F. Valenzuela LA............... 285
Steve Rogers MON 277

AMERICAN LEAGUE STANDINGS

1983 AL

EAST	W	L	PCT	GB	R	OR	BA	FA	ERA
BALTIMORE	98	64	.605	—	799	652	.269	.981	3.63
DETROIT	92	70	.568	6	789	679	.274	.980	3.80
NEW YORK	91	71	.562	7	770	703	.273	.978	3.85
TORONTO	89	73	.549	9	795	726	.277	.981	4.12
MILWAUKEE	87	75	.537	11	764	708	.277	.982	4.02
BOSTON	78	84	.481	20	724	775	.270	.979	4.34
CLEVELAND	70	92	.432	28	704	785	.265	.980	4.43

WEST	W	L	PCT	GB	R	OR	BA	FA	ERA
CHICAGO	99	63	.611	—	800	650	.262	.981	3.67
KANSAS CITY	79	83	.488	20	696	767	.271	.974	4.25
TEXAS	77	85	.475	22	639	609	.255	.982	3.31
OAKLAND	74	88	.457	25	708	782	.262	.974	4.35
CALIFORNIA	70	92	.432	29	722	779	.260	.977	4.31
MINNESOTA	70	92	.432	29	709	822	.261	.980	4.67
SEATTLE	60	102	.370	39	558	740	.240	.978	4.12
					10177	10177	.266	.979	4.06

BATTING AVERAGE
Wade Boggs BOS .... .361
Rod Carew CAL .... .339
Lou Whitaker DET .... .320

HITS
Cal Ripken BAL 211
Wade Boggs BOS 210
Lou Whitaker DET 206

DOUBLES
Cal Ripken BAL 47
Wade Boggs BOS 44
two tied at 42

TRIPLES
Robin Yount MIL 10
three tied at 9

HOME RUNS
Jim Rice BOS 39
Tony Armas BOS 36
Ron Kittle CHI 35

RUNS BATTED IN
Cecil Cooper MIL 126
Jim Rice BOS 126
Dave Winfield NY 116

SLUGGING AVERAGE
George Brett KC .... .563
Jim Rice BOS .... .550
Eddie Murray BAL .... .538

STOLEN BASES
R. Henderson OAK 108
Rudy Law CHI 77
Willie Wilson KC 59

RUNS SCORED
Cal Ripken BAL 121
Eddie Murray BAL 115
Cecil Cooper MIL 106

WINS
LaMarr Hoyt CHI 24
Rich Dotson CHI 22
Ron Guidry NY 21

WINNING PERCENTAGE
Moose Haas MIL .... .813
Rich Dotson CHI .... .759
Scott McGregor BAL .... .720

EARNED RUN AVERAGE
Rick Honeycutt TEX 2.42
Mike Boddicker BAL 2.77
Dave Stieb TOR 3.04

STRIKEOUTS
Jack Morris DET 232
Floyd Bannister CHI 193
Dave Stieb TOR 187

SAVES
Dan Quisenberry KC 45
Bob Stanley BOS 33
Ron Davis MIN 30

COMPLETE GAMES
Ron Guidry NY 21
Jack Morris DET 20
Dave Stieb TOR 14

SHUTOUTS
Mike Boddicker BAL 5
Britt Burns CHI 4
Dave Stieb TOR 4

GAMES PITCHED
Dan Quisenberry KC 69
Ed Vande Berg SEA 68
Ron Davis MIN 66

INNINGS PITCHED
Jack Morris DET 294
Dave Stieb TOR 278
Dan Petry DET 266

NATIONAL LEAGUE STANDINGS

1983 NL

EAST	W	L	PCT	GB	R	OR	BA	FA	ERA
PHILADELPHIA	90	72	.556	—	696	635	.249	.976	3.34
PITTSBURGH	84	78	.519	6	659	648	.264	.982	3.55
MONTREAL	82	80	.506	8	677	646	.264	.981	3.58
ST. LOUIS	79	83	.488	11	679	710	.270	.976	3.79
CHICAGO	71	91	.438	19	701	719	.261	.982	4.07
NEW YORK	68	94	.420	22	575	680	.241	.976	3.68

WEST	W	L	PCT	GB	R	OR	BA	FA	ERA
LOS ANGELES	91	71	.562	—	654	609	.250	.974	3.10
ATLANTA	88	74	.543	3	746	640	.272	.978	3.67
HOUSTON	85	77	.525	6	643	646	.257	.977	3.45
SAN DIEGO	81	81	.500	10	653	653	.250	.979	3.62
SAN FRANCISCO	79	83	.488	12	687	697	.247	.973	3.70
CINCINNATI	74	88	.457	17	623	710	.239	.981	3.98
					7993	7993	.255	.978	3.63

BATTING AVERAGE
Bill Madlock PIT .323
Lonnie Smith STL .321
two tied at .318

HITS
Jose Cruz HOU 189
Andre Dawson MON 189
Rafael Ramirez ATL 185

DOUBLES
Al Oliver MON 38
Johnny Ray PIT 38
Bill Buckner CHI 38

TRIPLES
Brett Butler ATL 13
Omar Moreno HOU 11
two tied at 10

HOME RUNS
Mike Schmidt PHI 40
Dale Murphy ATL 36
two tied at 32

RUNS BATTED IN
Dale Murphy ATL 121
Andre Dawson MON 113
Mike Schmidt PHI 109

SLUGGING AVERAGE
Dale Murphy ATL .540
Andre Dawson MON .539
Pedro Guerrero LA .531

STOLEN BASES
Tim Raines MON 90
Alan Wiggins SD 66
Steve Sax LA 56

RUNS SCORED
Tim Raines MON 133
Dale Murphy ATL 131
two tied at 104

WINS
John Denny PHI 19
three tied at 17

WINNING PERCENTAGE
John Denny PHI .760
three tied at .652

EARNED RUN AVERAGE
Atlee Hammaker SF 2.25
John Denny PHI 2.37
Bob Welch LA 2.65

STRIKEOUTS
Steve Carlton PHI 275
Mario Soto CIN 242
Larry McWilliams PIT 199

SAVES
Lee Smith CHI 29
Al Holland PHI 25
Greg Minton SF 22

COMPLETE GAMES
Mario Soto CIN 18
Steve Rogers MON 13
Bill Gullickson MON 10

SHUTOUTS
Steve Rogers MON 5
three tied at 4

GAMES PITCHED
Bill Campbell CHI 82
Kent Tekulve PIT 76
G. Hernandez CHI, PHI 74

INNINGS PITCHED
Steve Carlton PHI 284
Mario Soto CIN 274
Steve Rogers MON 273

AMERICAN LEAGUE STANDINGS

1984 AL

EAST	W	L	PCT	GB	R	OR	BA	FA	ERA
DETROIT	104	58	.642	—	829	643	.271	.979	3.49
TORONTO	89	73	.549	15	750	696	.273	.980	3.86
NEW YORK	87	75	.537	17	758	679	.276	.977	3.78
BOSTON	86	76	.531	18	810	764	.283	.977	4.18
BALTIMORE	85	77	.525	19	681	667	.252	.981	3.72
CLEVELAND	75	87	.463	29	761	766	.265	.977	4.25
MILWAUKEE	67	94	.416	36.5	641	734	.262	.978	4.06

WEST	W	L	PCT	GB	R	OR	BA	FA	ERA
KANSAS CITY	84	78	.519	—	673	686	.268	.979	3.91
CALIFORNIA	81	81	.500	3	696	697	.249	.980	3.96
MINNESOTA	81	81	.500	3	673	675	.265	.980	3.86
OAKLAND	77	85	.475	7	738	796	.259	.975	4.49
CHICAGO	74	88	.457	10	679	736	.247	.981	4.13
SEATTLE	74	88	.457	10	682	774	.258	.979	4.31
TEXAS	69	92	.429	14.5	656	714	.261	.977	3.91
					10027	10027	.264	.979	3.99

BATTING AVERAGE
Don Mattingly NY .... .343
Dave Winfield NY .... .340
Wade Boggs BOS .... .325

HITS
Don Mattingly NY 207
Wade Boggs BOS 203
Cal Ripken BAL 195

DOUBLES
Don Mattingly NY 44
Larry Parrish TEX 42
George Bell TOR 39

TRIPLES
Dave Collins TOR 15
Lloyd Moseby TOR 15
two tied at 10

HOME RUNS
Tony Armas BOS 43
Dave Kingman OAK 35
three tied at 33

RUNS BATTED IN
Tony Armas BOS 123
Jim Rice BOS 122
Dave Kingman OAK 118

SLUGGING AVERAGE
Harold Baines CHI .... .541
Don Mattingly NY .... .537
Dwight Evans BOS .... .532

STOLEN BASES
Rickey Henderson OAK 66
Dave Collins TOR 60
Brett Butler CLE 52

RUNS SCORED
Dwight Evans BOS 121
R. Henderson OAK 113
Wade Boggs BOS 109

WINS
Mike Boddicker BAL 20
Bert Blyleven CLE 19
Jack Morris DET 19

WINNING PERCENTAGE
Doyle Alexander TOR ..... .739
Bert Blyleven CLE .... .731
Dan Petry DET .... .692

EARNED RUN AVERAGE
Mike Boddicker BAL 2.79
Dave Stieb TOR 2.83
Bert Blyleven CLE 2.87

STRIKEOUTS
Mark Langston SEA 204
Dave Stieb TOR 198
Mike Witt CAL 196

SAVES
Dan Quisenberry KC 44
Bill Caudill OAK 36
G. Hernandez DET 32

COMPLETE GAMES
Charlie Hough TEX 17
Mike Boddicker BAL 16
Rich Dotson CHI 14

SHUTOUTS
Geoff Zahn CAL 5
Bob Ojeda BOS 5
two tied at 4

GAMES PITCHED
G. Hernandez DET 80
Dan Quisenberry KC 72
Aurelio Lopez DET 71

INNINGS PITCHED
Dave Stieb TOR 267
Charlie Hough TEX 266
Doyle Alexander TOR 262

NATIONAL LEAGUE STANDINGS

1984 NL

EAST	W	L	PCT	GB	R	OR	BA	FA	ERA
CHICAGO	96	65	.596	—	762	658	.260	.981	3.75
NEW YORK	90	72	.556	6.5	652	676	.257	.979	3.60
ST. LOUIS	84	78	.519	12.5	652	645	.252	.982	3.58
PHILADELPHIA	81	81	.500	15.5	720	690	.266	.975	3.62
MONTREAL	78	83	.484	18	593	585	.251	.978	3.31
PITTSBURGH	75	87	.463	21.5	615	567	.255	.980	3.11

WEST	W	L	PCT	GB	R	OR	BA	FA	ERA
SAN DIEGO	92	70	.568	—	686	634	.259	.978	3.48
ATLANTA	80	82	.494	12	632	655	.247	.978	3.57
HOUSTON	80	82	.494	12	693	630	.264	.979	3.32
LOS ANGELES	79	83	.488	13	580	600	.244	.975	3.17
CINCINNATI	70	92	.432	22	627	747	.244	.977	4.16
SAN FRANCISCO	66	96	.407	26	682	807	.265	.973	4.39
					7894	7894	.255	.978	3.59

BATTING AVERAGE
Tony Gwynn SD .... .351
Lee Lacy PIT .... .321
Chili Davis SF .... .315

HITS
Tony Gwynn SD 213
Ryne Sandberg CHI 200
Tim Raines MON 192

DOUBLES
Johnny Ray PIT 38
Tim Raines MON 38
two tied at 36

TRIPLES
Juan Samuel PHI 19
Ryne Sandberg CHI 19
Jose Cruz HOU 13

HOME RUNS
Dale Murphy ATL 36
Mike Schmidt PHI 36
Gary Carter MON 27

RUNS BATTED IN
Gary Carter MON 106
Mike Schmidt PHI 106
Dale Murphy ATL 100

SLUGGING AVERAGE
Dale Murphy ATL .... .547
Mike Schmidt PHI .... .536
Ryne Sandberg CHI .... .520

STOLEN BASES
Tim Raines MON 75
Juan Samuel PHI 72
Alan Wiggins SD 70

RUNS SCORED
Ryne Sandberg CHI 114
Tim Raines MON 106
Alan Wiggins SD 106

WINS
Joaquin Andujar STL 20
Mario Soto CIN 18
Dwight Gooden NY 17

WINNING PERCENTAGE
Mario Soto CIN .... .720
Alejandro Pena LA .... .667
Dwight Gooden NY .... .654

EARNED RUN AVERAGE
Alejandro Pena LA 2.48
Dwight Gooden NY 2.60
Orel Hershiser LA 2.66

STRIKEOUTS
Dwight Gooden NY 276
F. Valenzuela LA 240
Nolan Ryan HOU 197

SAVES
Bruce Sutter STL 45
Lee Smith CHI 33
Jesse Orosco NY 31

COMPLETE GAMES
Mario Soto CIN 13
F. Valenzuela LA 12
Joaquin Andujar STL 12

SHUTOUTS
Alejandro Pena LA 4
Joaquin Andujar STL 4
Orel Hershiser LA 4

GAMES PITCHED
Ted Power CIN 78
Gary Lavelle SF 77
Greg Minton SF 74

INNINGS PITCHED
Joaquin Andujar STL 261
F. Valenzuela LA 261
Joe Niekro HOU 248

AMERICAN LEAGUE STANDINGS

1985 AL

EAST	W	L	PCT	GB	R	OR	BA	FA	ERA
TORONTO	99	62	.615	—	759	588	.269	.980	3.31
NEW YORK	97	64	.602	2	839	660	.267	.979	3.69
DETROIT	84	77	.522	15	729	688	.253	.977	3.78
BALTIMORE	83	78	.516	16	818	764	.263	.979	4.38
BOSTON	81	81	.500	18.5	800	720	.282	.977	4.06
MILWAUKEE	71	90	.441	28	690	802	.263	.977	4.39
CLEVELAND	60	102	.370	39.5	729	861	.265	.977	4.91
WEST	**W**	**L**	**PCT**	**GB**	**R**	**OR**	**BA**	**FA**	**ERA**
KANSAS CITY	91	71	.562	—	687	639	.252	.980	3.49
CALIFORNIA	90	72	.556	1	732	703	.251	.982	3.91
CHICAGO	85	77	.525	6	736	720	.253	.982	4.07
MINNESOTA	77	85	.475	14	705	782	.264	.980	4.48
OAKLAND	77	85	.475	14	757	787	.264	.977	4.41
SEATTLE	74	88	.457	17	719	818	.255	.980	4.68
TEXAS	62	99	.385	28.5	617	785	.253	.980	4.56
					10317	10317	.261	.979	4.15

BATTING AVERAGE
Wade Boggs BOS .... .368
George Brett KC .... .335
Don Mattingly NY .... .324

HITS
Wade Boggs BOS 240
Don Mattingly NY 211
Bill Buckner BOS 201

DOUBLES
Don Mattingly NY 48
Bill Buckner BOS 46
Wade Boggs BOS 42

TRIPLES
Willie Wilson KC 21
Brett Butler CLE 14
Kirby Puckett MIN 13

HOME RUNS
Darrell Evans DET 40
Carlton Fisk CHI 37
Steve Balboni KC 36

RUNS BATTED IN
Don Mattingly NY 145
Eddie Murray BAL 124
Dave Winfield NY 114

SLUGGING AVERAGE
George Brett KC .... .585
Don Mattingly NY .... .567
Jesse Barfield TOR .... .536

STOLEN BASES
Rickey Henderson NY 80
Gary Pettis CAL 56
Brett Butler CLE 47

RUNS SCORED
Rickey Henderson NY 146
Cal Ripken BAL 116
Eddie Murray BAL 111

WINS
Ron Guidry NY 22
Bret Saberhagen KC 20
two tied at 18

WINNING PERCENTAGE
Ron Guidry NY .... .786
Bret Saberhagen KC .... .769
Jimmy Key TOR .... .700

EARNED RUN AVERAGE
Dave Stieb TOR 2.48
Charlie Leibrandt KC 2.69
Bret Saberhagen KC 2.87

STRIKEOUTS
B. Blyleven CLE, MIN 206
Floyd Bannister CHI 198
Jack Morris DET 191

SAVES
Dan Quisenberry KC 37
Bob James CHI 32
two tied at 31

COMPLETE GAMES
Bert Blyleven CLE, MIN 24
Charlie Hough TEX 14
Mike Moore SEA 14

SHUTOUTS
Bert Blyleven CLE, MIN 5
Jack Morris DET 4
Britt Burns CHI 4

GAMES PITCHED
Dan Quisenberry KC 84
Ed Vande Berg SEA 76
two tied at 74

INNINGS PITCHED
B. Blyleven CLE, MIN 294
Oil Can Boyd BOS 272
Dave Stieb TOR 265

NATIONAL LEAGUE STANDINGS

1985 NL

EAST	W	L	PCT	GB	R	OR	BA	FA	ERA
ST. LOUIS	101	61	.623	—	747	572	.264	.983	3.10
NEW YORK	98	64	.605	3	695	568	.257	.982	3.11
MONTREAL	84	77	.522	16.5	633	636	.247	.981	3.55
CHICAGO	77	84	.478	23.5	686	729	.254	.979	4.16
PHILADELPHIA	75	87	.463	26	667	673	.245	.978	3.68
PITTSBURGH	57	104	.354	43.5	568	708	.247	.979	3.97

WEST	W	L	PCT	GB	R	OR	BA	FA	ERA
LOS ANGELES	95	67	.586	—	682	579	.261	.974	2.96
CINCINNATI	89	72	.553	5.5	677	666	.255	.980	3.71
HOUSTON	83	79	.512	12	706	691	.261	.976	3.66
SAN DIEGO	83	79	.512	12	650	622	.255	.980	3.41
ATLANTA	66	96	.407	29	632	781	.246	.976	4.19
SAN FRANCISCO	62	100	.383	33	556	674	.233	.976	3.61
					7899	7899	.252	.979	3.59

BATTING AVERAGE
Willie McGee STL .... .353
Pedro Guerrero LA .... .320
Tim Raines MON .... .320

HITS
Willie McGee STL 216
Dave Parker CIN 198
Tony Gwynn SD 197

DOUBLES
Dave Parker CIN 42
Glenn Wilson PHI 39
Tommy Herr STL 38

TRIPLES
Willie McGee STL 18
Juan Samuel PHI 13
Tim Raines MON 13

HOME RUNS
Dale Murphy ATL 37
Dave Parker CIN 34
two tied at 33

RUNS BATTED IN
Dave Parker CIN 125
Dale Murphy ATL 111
Tommy Herr STL 110

SLUGGING AVERAGE
Pedro Guerrero LA .... .577
Dave Parker CIN .... .551
Dale Murphy ATL .... .539

STOLEN BASES
Vince Coleman STL 110
Tim Raines MON 70
Willie McGee STL 56

RUNS SCORED
Dale Murphy ATL 118
Tim Raines MON 115
Willie McGee STL 114

WINS
Dwight Gooden NY 24
John Tudor STL 21
Joaquin Andujar STL 21

WINNING PERCENTAGE
Orel Hershiser LA .... .864
Dwight Gooden NY .... .857
Bryn Smith MON .... .783

EARNED RUN AVERAGE
Dwight Gooden NY 1.53
John Tudor STL 1.93
Orel Heshiser LA 2.03

STRIKEOUTS
Dwight Gooden NY 268
Mario Soto CIN 214
Nolan Ryan HOU 209

SAVES
Jeff Reardon MON 41
Lee Smith CHI 33
two tied at 27

COMPLETE GAMES
Dwight Gooden NY 16
F. Valenzuela LA 14
John Tudor STL 14

SHUTOUTS
John Tudor STL 10
Dwight Gooden NY 8
two tied at 5

GAMES PITCHED
Tim Burke MON 78
Mark Davis SF 77
Scott Garrelts SF 74

INNINGS PITCHED
Dwight Gooden NY 277
John Tudor STL 275
F. Valenzuela LA 272

AMERICAN LEAGUE STANDINGS

1986 AL

EAST	W	L	PCT	GB	R	OR	BA	FA	ERA
BOSTON	95	66	.590	—	794	696	.271	.979	3.93
NEW YORK	90	72	.556	5.5	797	738	.271	.979	4.11
DETROIT	87	75	.537	8.5	798	714	.263	.982	4.02
TORONTO	86	76	.531	9.5	809	733	.269	.984	4.08
CLEVELAND	84	78	.519	11.5	831	841	.284	.975	4.57
MILWAUKEE	77	84	.478	18	667	734	.255	.976	4.01
BALTIMORE	73	89	.451	22.5	708	760	.258	.978	4.30

WEST	W	L	PCT	GB	R	OR	BA	FA	ERA
CALIFORNIA	92	70	.568	—	786	684	.255	.983	3.84
TEXAS	87	75	.537	5	711	743	.267	.980	4.11
KANSAS CITY	76	86	.469	16	654	673	.252	.980	3.82
OAKLAND	76	86	.469	16	731	760	.252	.978	4.31
CHICAGO	72	90	.444	20	644	699	.247	.981	3.93
MINNESOTA	71	91	.438	21	741	839	.261	.980	4.77
SEATTLE	67	95	.414	25	718	835	.253	.975	4.65
					10449	10449	.262	.979	4.18

BATTING AVERAGE
Wade Boggs BOS .... .357
Don Mattingly NY .... .352
Kirby Puckett MIN .... .328

HITS
Don Mattingly NY 238
Kirby Pucket MIN 223
Tony Fernandez TOR 213

DOUBLES
Don Mattingly NY 53
Wade Boggs BOS 47
two tied at 39

TRIPLES
Brett Butler CLE 14
Ruben Sierra TEX 10
two tied at 9

HOME RUNS
Jesse Barfield TOR 40
Dave Kingman OAK 35
Gary Gaetti MIN 34

RUNS BATTED IN
Joe Carter CLE 121
Jose Canseco OAK 117
Don Mattingly NY 113

SLUGGING AVERAGE
Don Mattingly NY .... .573
Jesse Barfield TOR .... .559
Kirby Puckett MIN .... .537

STOLEN BASES
Rickey Henderson NY 87
Gary Pettis CAL 50
John Cangelosi CHI 50

RUNS SCORED
Rickey Henderson NY 130
Kirby Puckett MIN 119
Don Mattingly NY 117

WINS
Roger Clemens BOS 24
Jack Morris DET 21
Ted Higuera MIL 20

WINNING PERCENTAGE
Roger Clemens BOS .... .857
Dennis Rasmussen NY ... .750
Jack Morris DET .... .724

EARNED RUN AVERAGE
Roger Clemens BOS 2.48
Ted Higuera MIL 2.79
Mike Witt CAL 2.84

STRIKEOUTS
Mark Langston SEA 245
Roger Clemens BOS 238
Jack Morris DET 223

SAVES
Dave Righetti NY 46
Don Aase BAL 34
Tom Henke TOR 27

COMPLETE GAMES
Tom Candiotti CLE 17
Bert Blyleven MIN 16
two tied at 15

SHUTOUTS
Jack Morris DET 6
Bruce Hurst BOS 4
Ted Higuera MIL 4

GAMES PITCHED
Mitch Williams TEX 80
Dave Righetti NY 74
Greg Harris TEX 73

INNINGS PITCHED
Bert Blyleven MIN 272
Mike Witt CAL 269
Jack Morris DET 267

NATIONAL LEAGUE STANDINGS

1986 NL

EAST	W	L	PCT	GB	R	OR	BA	FA	ERA
NEW YORK	108	54	.667	—	783	578	.263	.978	3.11
PHILADELPHIA	86	75	.534	21.5	739	713	.253	.978	3.85
ST. LOUIS	79	82	.491	28.5	601	611	.236	.981	3.37
MONTREAL	78	83	.484	29.5	637	688	.254	.979	3.78
CHICAGO	70	90	.438	37	680	781	.256	.980	4.49
PITTSBURGH	64	98	.395	44	663	700	.250	.978	3.90

WEST	W	L	PCT	GB	R	OR	BA	FA	ERA
HOUSTON	96	66	.593	—	654	569	.255	.979	3.15
CINCINNATI	86	76	.531	10	732	717	.254	.978	3.91
SAN FRANCISCO	83	79	.512	13	698	618	.253	.977	3.33
SAN DIEGO	74	88	.457	22	656	723	.261	.978	3.99
LOS ANGELES	73	89	.451	23	638	679	.251	.971	3.76
ATLANTA	72	89	.447	23.5	615	719	.250	.978	3.97
					8096	8096	.253	.978	3.72

BATTING AVERAGE
Tim Raines MON .... .334
Steve Sax LA .... .332
Tony Gwynn SD .... .329

HITS
Tony Gwynn SD 211
Steve Sax LA 210
Tim Raines MON 194

DOUBLES
Von Hayes PHI 46
Steve Sax LA 43
Sid Bream PIT 37

TRIPLES
Mitch Webster MON 13
Juan Samuel PHI 12
Tim Raines MON 10

HOME RUNS
Mike Schmidt PHI 37
Glenn Davis HOU 31
Dave Parker CIN 31

RUNS BATTED IN
Mike Schmidt PHI 119
Dave Parker CIN 116
Gary Carter NY 105

SLUGGING AVERAGE
Mike Schmidt PHI .... .547
Darryl Strawberry NY ...... .507
Kevin McReynolds SD .... .504

STOLEN BASES
Vince Coleman STL 107
Eric Davis CIN 80
Tim Raines MON 70

RUNS SCORED
Tony Gwynn SD 107
Von Hayes PHI 107
two tied at 97

WINS
F. Valenzuela LA 21
Mike Krukow SF 20
two tied at 18

WINNING PERCENTAGE
Bob Ojeda NY .... .783
Dwight Gooden NY .... .739
Sid Fernandez NY .... .727

EARNED RUN AVERAGE
Mike Scott HOU 2.22
Bob Ojeda NY 2.57
Ron Darling NY 2.81

STRIKEOUTS
Mike Scott HOU 306
F. Valenzuela LA 242
Floyd Youmans MON 202

SAVES
Todd Worrell STL 36
Jeff Reardon MON 35
Dave Smith HOU 33

COMPLETE GAMES
F. Valenzuela LA 20
Rick Rhoden PIT 12
Dwight Gooden NY 12

SHUTOUTS
Mike Scott HOU 5
Bob Knepper HOU 5
two tied at 3

GAMES PITCHED
Craig Lefferts SD 83
Roger McDowell NY 75
two tied at 74

INNINGS PITCHED
Mike Scott HOU 275
F. Valenzuela LA 269
Bob Knepper HOU 258

AMERICAN LEAGUE STANDINGS

1987 AL

EAST	W	L	PCT	GB	R	OR	BA	FA	ERA
DETROIT	98	64	.605	—	896	735	.272	.980	4.02
TORONTO	96	66	.593	2	845	655	.269	.982	3.74
MILWAUKEE	91	71	.562	7	862	817	.276	.976	4.62
NEW YORK	89	73	.549	9	788	758	.262	.983	4.36
BOSTON	78	84	.481	20	842	825	.278	.982	4.77
BALTIMORE	67	95	.414	31	729	880	.258	.982	5.01
CLEVELAND	61	101	.377	37	742	957	.263	.975	5.28

WEST	W	L	PCT	GB	R	OR	BA	FA	ERA
MINNESOTA	85	77	.525	—	786	806	.261	.984	4.63
KANSAS CITY	83	79	.512	2	715	691	.262	.979	3.86
OAKLAND	81	81	.500	4	806	789	.260	.977	4.32
SEATTLE	78	84	.481	7	760	801	.272	.980	4.48
CHICAGO	77	85	.475	8	748	746	.258	.981	4.29
CALIFORNIA	75	87	.463	10	770	803	.252	.981	4.38
TEXAS	75	87	.463	10	823	849	.266	.976	4.63
					11112	11112	.265	.980	4.46

BATTING AVERAGE
Wade Boggs BOS .... .363
Paul Molitor MIL .... .353
Alan Trammell DET .... .343

HITS
Kevin Seitzer KC 207
Kirby Puckett MIN 207
Alan Trammell DET 205

DOUBLES
Paul Molitor MIL 41
Wade Boggs BOS 40
two tied at 38

TRIPLES
Willie Wilson KC 15
Luis Polonia OAK 10
Phil Bradley SEA 10

HOME RUNS
Mark McGwire OAK 49
George Bell TOR 47
four tied at 34

RUNS BATTED IN
George Bell TOR 134
Dwight Evans BOS 123
Mark McGwire OAK 118

SLUGGING AVERAGE
Mark McGwire OAK .... .618
George Bell TOR .... .605
Wade Boggs BOS .... .588

STOLEN BASES
Harold Reynolds SEA 60
Willie Wilson KC 59
Gary Redus CHI 52

RUNS SCORED
Paul Molitor MIL 114
George Bell TOR 111
two tied at 110

WINS
Roger Clemens BOS 20
Dave Stewart OAK 20
Mark Langston SEA 19

WINNING PERCENTAGE
Roger Clemens BOS .... .690
Tommy John NY .... .684
Jimmy Key TOR .... .680

EARNED RUN AVERAGE
Jimmy Key TOR 2.76
Frank Viola MIN 2.90
Roger Clemens BOS 2.97

STRIKEOUTS
Mark Langston SEA 262
Roger Clemens BOS 256
Ted Higuera MIL 240

SAVES
Tom Henke TOR 34
Jeff Reardon MIN 31
Dave Righetti NY 31

COMPLETE GAMES
Roger Clemens BOS 18
Bruce Hurst BOS 15
Bret Saberhagen KC 15

SHUTOUTS
Roger Clemens BOS 7
Bret Saberhagen KC 4

GAMES PITCHED
Mark Eichhorn TOR 89
Mitch Williams TEX 85
Dale Mohorcic TEX 74

INNINGS PITCHED
Charlie Hough TEX 285
Roger Clemens BOS 282
Mark Langston SEA 272

NATIONAL LEAGUE STANDINGS

1987 NL

EAST	W	L	PCT	GB	R	OR	BA	FA	ERA
ST. LOUIS	95	67	.586	—	798	693	.263	.982	3.91
NEW YORK	92	70	.568	3	823	698	.268	.978	3.84
MONTREAL	91	71	.562	4	741	720	.265	.976	3.92
PHILADELPHIA	80	82	.494	15	702	749	.254	.980	4.18
PITTSBURGH	80	82	.494	15	723	744	.264	.980	4.20
CHICAGO	76	85	.472	18.5	720	801	.264	.979	4.55

WEST	W	L	PCT	GB	R	OR	BA	FA	ERA
SAN FRANCISCO	90	72	.556	—	783	669	.260	.980	3.68
CINCINNATI	84	78	.519	6	783	752	.266	.979	4.25
HOUSTON	76	86	.469	14	648	678	.253	.981	3.84
LOS ANGELES	73	89	.451	17	635	675	.252	.975	3.72
ATLANTA	69	92	.429	20.5	747	829	.258	.982	4.63
SAN DIEGO	65	97	.401	25	668	763	.260	.976	4.27
					8771	8771	.261	.979	4.08

BATTING AVERAGE
Tony Gwynn SD .... .370
Pedro Guerrero LA .... .338
Tim Raines MON .... .330

HITS
Tony Gwynn SD 218
Pedro Guerrero LA 184
Ozzie Smith STL 182

DOUBLES
Tim Wallach MON 42
Ozzie Smith STL 40
Andres Galarraga MON 40

TRIPLES
Juan Samuel PHI 15
Tony Gwynn SD 13
two tied at 11

HOME RUNS
Andre Dawson CHI 49
Dale Murphy ATL 44
Darryl Strawberry NY 39

RUNS BATTED IN
Andre Dawson CHI 137
Tim Wallach MON 123
Mike Schmidt PHI 113

SLUGGING AVERAGE
Jack Clark STL .... .597
Eric Davis CIN .... .593
Darryl Strawberry NY ..... .583

STOLEN BASES
Vince Coleman STL 109
Tony Gwynn SD 56
Billy Hatcher HOU 53

RUNS SCORED
Tim Raines MON 123
Vince Coleman STL 121
Eric Davis CIN 120

WINS
Rick Sutcliffe CHI 18
Shane Rawley PHI 17
two tied at 16

WINNING PERCENTAGE
Mike Dunne PIT .... .684
Dwight Gooden NY .... .682
Rick Sutcliffe CHI .... .643

EARNED RUN AVERAGE
Nolan Ryan HOU 2.76
Mike Dunne PIT 3.03
Orel Hershiser LA 3.06

STRIKEOUTS
Nolan Ryan HOU 270
Mike Scott HOU 233
Bob Welch LA 196

SAVES
Steve Bedrosian PHI 40
Lee Smith CHI 36
Todd Worrell STL 33

COMPLETE GAMES
Rick Reuschel PIT, SF 12
F. Valenzuela LA 12
Orel Hershiser LA 10

SHUTOUTS
Rick Reuschel PIT, SF 4
Bob Welch LA 4

GAMES PITCHED
Kent Tekulve PHI 90
Rob Murphy CIN 87
Frank Williams CIN 85

INNINGS PITCHED
Orel Hershiser LA 265
Bob Welch LA 252
F. Valenzuela LA 251

AMERICAN LEAGUE STANDINGS

1988 AL

EAST	W	L	PCT	GB	R	OR	BA	FA	ERA
BOSTON	89	73	.549	—	813	689	.283	.984	3.97
DETROIT	88	74	.543	1	703	658	.250	.982	3.71
MILWAUKEE	87	75	.537	2	682	616	.257	.981	3.45
TORONTO	87	75	.537	2	763	680	.268	.982	3.80
NEW YORK	85	76	.528	3.5	772	748	.263	.978	4.26
CLEVELAND	78	84	.481	11	666	731	.261	.980	4.16
BALTIMORE	54	107	.335	34.5	550	789	.238	.980	4.54

WEST	W	L	PCT	GB	R	OR	BA	FA	ERA
OAKLAND	104	58	.642	—	800	620	.263	.983	3.44
MINNESOTA	91	71	.562	13	759	672	.274	.986	3.93
KANSAS CITY	84	77	.522	19.5	704	648	.259	.980	3.66
CALIFORNIA	75	87	.463	29	714	771	.261	.979	4.31
CHICAGO	71	90	.441	32.5	631	757	.244	.976	4.12
TEXAS	70	91	.435	33.5	637	735	.252	.979	4.05
SEATTLE	68	93	.422	35.5	664	744	.257	.980	4.15
					9858	9858	.259	.981	3.97

BATTING AVERAGE
Wade Boggs BOS .... .366
Kirby Puckett MIN .... .356
Mike Greenwell BOS .... .325

HITS
Kirby Puckett MIN 234
Wade Boggs BOS 214
Mike Greenwell BOS 192

DOUBLES
Wade Boggs BOS 45
three tied at 42

TRIPLES
Willie Wilson KC 11
Harold Reynolds SEA 11
Robin Yount MIL 11

HOME RUNS
Jose Canseco OAK 42
Fred McGriff TOR 34
Mark McGuire OAK 32

RUNS BATTED IN
Jose Canseco OAK 124
Kirby Puckett MIN 121
Mike Greenwell BOS 119

SLUGGING AVERAGE
Jose Canseco OAK .... .569
Fred McGriff TOR .... .552
Gary Gaetti MIN .... .551

STOLEN BASES
Rickey Henderson NY 93
Gary Pettis DET 44
Paul Molitor MIL 41

RUNS SCORED
Wade Boggs BOS 128
Jose Canseco OAK 120
Rickey Henderson NY 118

WINS
Frank Viola MIN 24
Dave Stewart OAK 21
Mark Gubicza KC 20

WINNING PERCENTAGE
Frank Viola MIN .... .774
Bruce Hurst BOS .... .750
Mark Gubicza KC .... .714

EARNED RUN AVERAGE
Allan Anderson MIN 2.45
Ted Higuera MIL 2.45
Frank Viola MIN 2.64

STRIKEOUTS
Roger Clemens BOS 291
Mark Langston SEA 235
Frank Viola MIN 193

SAVES
Dennis Eckersley OAK 45
Jeff Reardon MIN 42
Doug Jones CLE 37

COMPLETE GAMES
Roger Clemens BOS 14
Dave Stewart OAK 14
Bobby Witt TEX 13

SHUTOUTS
Roger Clemens BOS 8
three tied at 4

GAMES PITCHED
Chuck Crim MIL 70
Bobby Thigpen CHI 68
Mitch Williams TEX 67

INNINGS PITCHED
Dave Stewart OAK 276
Mark Gubicza KC 270
Roger Clemens BOS 264

NATIONAL LEAGUE STANDINGS

1988 NL

EAST	W	L	PCT	GB	R	OR	BA	FA	ERA
NEW YORK	100	60	.625	—	703	532	.256	.981	2.91
PITTSBURGH	85	75	.531	15	651	616	.247	.980	3.47
MONTREAL	81	81	.500	20	628	592	.251	.978	3.08
CHICAGO	77	85	.475	24	660	694	.261	.980	3.84
ST. LOUIS	76	86	.469	25	578	633	.249	.981	3.47
PHILADELPHIA	65	96	.404	35.5	597	734	.239	.976	4.14

WEST	W	L	PCT	GB	R	OR	BA	FA	ERA
LOS ANGELES	94	67	.584	—	628	544	.248	.977	2.97
CINCINNATI	87	74	.540	7	641	596	.246	.980	3.35
SAN DIEGO	83	78	.516	11	594	583	.247	.981	3.28
SAN FRANCISCO	83	79	.512	11.5	670	626	.248	.980	3.39
HOUSTON	82	80	.506	12.5	617	631	.244	.978	3.40
ATLANTA	54	106	.338	39.5	555	741	.242	.976	4.09
					7522	7522	.248	.979	3.45

BATTING AVERAGE
Tony Gwynn SD .... .313
Rafael Palmeiro CHI .... .307
Andre Dawson CHI .... .303

HITS
A. Galarraga MON 184
Andre Dawson CHI 179
Rafael Palmeiro CHI 178

DOUBLES
Andres Galarraga MON 42
Rafael Palmeiro CHI 41
Chris Sabo CIN 40

TRIPLES
Andy Van Slyke PIT 15
Vince Coleman STL 10
two tied at 9

HOME RUNS
Darryl Strawberry NY 39
Glenn Davis HOU 30
two tied at 29

RUNS BATTED IN
Will Clark SF 109
Darryl Strawberry NY 101
two tied at 100

SLUGGING AVERAGE
Darryl Strawberry NY ...... .545
A. Galarraga MON .... .540
Will Clark SF .... .508

STOLEN BASES
Vince Coleman STL 81
Gerald Young HOU 65
Ozzie Smith STL 57

RUNS SCORED
Brett Butler SF 109
Kirk Gibson LA 106
Will Clark SF 102

WINS
Orel Hershiser LA 23
Danny Jackson CIN 23
David Cone NY 20

WINNING PERCENTAGE
David Cone NY .... .870
Tom Browning CIN .... .783
two tied at .... .742

EARNED RUN AVERAGE
Joe Magrane STL 2.18
David Cone NY 2.22
Orel Hershiser LA 2.26

STRIKEOUTS
Nolan Ryan HOU 228
David Cone NY 213
Jose DeLeon STL 208

SAVES
John Franco CIN 39
Jim Gott PIT 34
Todd Worrell STL 32

COMPLETE GAMES
Orel Hershiser LA 15
Danny Jackson CIN 15
Eric Show SD 13

SHUTOUTS
Orel Hershiser LA 8
Tim Leary LA 6
Danny Jackson CIN 6

GAMES PITCHED
Rob Murphy CIN 76
Jeff Robinson PIT 75
Juan Agosto HOU 75

INNINGS PITCHED
Orel Hershiser LA 267
Danny Jackson CIN 261
Tom Browning CIN 251

AMERICAN LEAGUE STANDINGS

1989 AL

EAST	W	L	PCT	GB	R	OR	BA	FA	ERA
TORONTO	89	73	.549	—	731	651	.260	.980	3.58
BALTIMORE	87	75	.537	2	708	686	.252	.986	4.00
BOSTON	83	79	.512	6	774	735	.277	.980	4.01
MILWAUKEE	81	81	.500	8	707	679	.259	.975	3.80
NEW YORK	74	87	.460	14.5	698	792	.269	.980	4.50
CLEVELAND	73	89	.451	16	604	654	.245	.981	3.65
DETROIT	59	103	.364	30	617	816	.242	.979	4.53

WEST	W	L	PCT	GB	R	OR	BA	FA	ERA
OAKLAND	99	63	.611	—	712	576	.261	.979	3.09
KANSAS CITY	92	70	.568	7	690	635	.261	.982	3.55
CALIFORNIA	91	71	.562	8	669	578	.256	.985	3.28
TEXAS	83	79	.512	16	695	714	.263	.978	3.91
MINNESOTA	80	82	.494	19	740	738	.276	.982	4.28
SEATTLE	73	89	.451	26	694	728	.257	.977	4.00
CHICAGO	69	92	.429	29.5	693	750	.271	.975	4.23
					9732	9732	.261	.980	3.88

BATTING AVERAGE
Kirby Puckett MIN .... .339
Carney Lansford OAK ..... .336
Wade Boggs BOS .... .330

HITS
Kirby Puckett MIN 215
Wade Boggs BOS 205
Steve Sax NY 205

DOUBLES
Wade Boggs BOS 51
Kirby Puckett MIN 45
Jody Reed BOS 42

TRIPLES
Ruben Sierra TEX 14
Devon White CAL 13
Phil Bradley BAL 10

HOME RUNS
Fred McGriff TOR 36
Joe Carter CLE 35
Mark McGwire OAK 33

RUNS BATTED IN
Ruben Sierra TEX 119
Don Mattingly NY 113
Nick Esasky BOS 108

SLUGGING AVERAGE
Ruben Sierra TEX .... .543
Fred McGriff TOR .... .525
Robin Yount MIL .... .511

STOLEN BASES
R. Henderson NY, OAK 77
Cecil Espy TEX 45
Devon White CAL 44

RUNS SCORED
R. Henderson NY, OAK ... 113
Wade Boggs BOS 113
two tied at 101

WINS
Bret Saberhagen KC 23
Dave Stewart OAK 21
two tied at 19

WINNING PERCENTAGE
Bret Saberhagen KC .... .793
Bert Blyleven CAL .... .773
Storm Davis OAK .... .731

EARNED RUN AVERAGE
Bret Saberhagen KC 2.16
Chuck Finley CAL 2.57
Mike Moore OAK 2.61

STRIKEOUTS
Nolan Ryan TEX 301
Roger Clemens BOS 230
Bret Saberhagen KC 193

SAVES
Jeff Russell TEX 38
Bobby Thigpen CHI 34
three tied at 33

COMPLETE GAMES
Bret Saberhagen KC 12
Jack Morris DET 10
Chuck Finley CAL 9

SHUTOUTS
Bert Blyleven CAL 5
Kirk McCaskill CAL 4
Bret Saberhagen KC 4

GAMES PITCHED
Chuck Crim MIL 76
Rob Murphy BOS 74
Kenny Rogers TEX 73

INNINGS PITCHED
Bret Saberhagen KC 262
Dave Stewart OAK 258
Mark Gubicza KC 255

NATIONAL LEAGUE STANDINGS

1989 NL

EAST	W	L	PCT	GB	R	OR	BA	FA	ERA
CHICAGO	93	69	.574	—	702	623	.261	.980	3.43
NEW YORK	87	75	.537	6	683	595	.246	.976	3.29
ST. LOUIS	86	76	.531	7	632	608	.258	.982	3.36
MONTREAL	81	81	.500	12	632	630	.247	.979	3.48
PITTSBURGH	74	88	.457	19	637	680	.241	.975	3.64
PHILADELPHIA	67	95	.414	26	629	735	.243	.979	4.04

WEST	W	L	PCT	GB	R	OR	BA	FA	ERA
SAN FRANCISCO	92	70	.568	—	699	600	.250	.982	3.30
SAN DIEGO	89	73	.549	3	642	626	.251	.976	3.38
HOUSTON	86	76	.531	6	647	669	.239	.977	3.65
LOS ANGELES	77	83	.481	14	554	536	.240	.981	2.95
CINCINNATI	75	87	.463	17	632	691	.247	.980	3.73
ATLANTA	63	97	.394	28	584	680	.234	.976	3.70
					7673	7673	.246	.978	3.50

BATTING AVERAGE
Tony Gwynn SD .... .336
Will Clark SF .... .333
Lonnie Smith ATL .... .315

HITS
Tony Gwynn SD 203
Will Clark SF 196
Roberto Alomar SD 184

DOUBLES
Pedro Guerrero STL 42
Tim Wallach MON 42
Howard Johnson NY 41

TRIPLES
Robby Thompson SF 11
Bobby Bonilla PIT 10
two tied at 9

HOME RUNS
Kevin Mitchell SF 47
Howard Johnson NY 36
two tied at 34

RUNS BATTED IN
Kevin Mitchell SF 125
Pedro Guerrero STL 117
Will Clark SF 111

SLUGGING AVERAGE
Kevin Mitchell SF .... .635
Howard Johnson NY ...... .559
Will Clark SF .... .546

STOLEN BASES
Vince Coleman STL 65
Juan Samuel PHI, NY 42
Roberto Alomar SD 42

RUNS SCORED
Howard Johnson NY 104
Will Clark SF 104
Ryne Sandberg CHI 104

WINS
Mike Scott HOU 20
Greg Maddux CHI 19
two tied at 18

WINNING PERCENTAGE
Scott Garrelts SF .... .737
Sid Fernandez NY .... .737
Mike Bielecki CHI .... .720

EARNED RUN AVERAGE
Scott Garrelts SF 2.28
Orel Hershiser LA 2.31
Mark Langston MON 2.39

STRIKEOUTS
Jose DeLeon STL 201
Tim Belcher LA 200
Sid Fernandez NY 198

SAVES
Mark Davis SD 44
Mitch Williams CHI 36
John Franco CIN 32

COMPLETE GAMES
Tim Belcher LA 10
Bruce Hurst SD 10
three tied at 9

SHUTOUTS
Tim Belcher LA 8
Doug Drabek PIT 5
two tied at 4

GAMES PITCHED
Mitch Williams CHI 76
Rob Dibble CIN 74
Jeff Parrett PHI 72

INNINGS PITCHED
Orel Hershiser LA 257
Tom Browning CIN 250
two tied at 245

AMERICAN LEAGUE STANDINGS

1990 AL

EAST	W	L	PCT	GB	R	OR	BA	FA	ERA
BOSTON	88	74	.543	—	699	664	.272	.980	3.72
TORONTO	86	76	.531	2	767	661	.265	.986	3.84
DETROIT	79	83	.488	9	750	754	.259	.979	4.39
CLEVELAND	77	85	.475	11	732	737	.267	.981	4.26
BALTIMORE	76	85	.472	11.5	669	698	.245	.985	4.04
MILWAUKEE	74	88	.457	14	732	760	.256	.976	4.08
NEW YORK	67	95	.414	21	603	749	.241	.980	4.21

WEST	W	L	PCT	GB	R	OR	BA	FA	ERA
OAKLAND	103	59	.636	—	733	570	.254	.986	3.18
CHICAGO	94	68	.580	9	682	633	.258	.980	3.61
TEXAS	83	79	.512	20	676	696	.259	.979	3.83
CALIFORNIA	80	82	.494	23	690	706	.260	.978	3.79
SEATTLE	77	85	.475	26	640	680	.259	.979	3.69
KANSAS CITY	75	86	.466	27.5	707	709	.267	.980	3.93
MINNESOTA	74	88	.457	29	666	729	.265	.983	4.12
					9746	9746	.259	.981	3.91

BATTING AVERAGE
George Brett KC .... .329
R. Henderson OAK .... .325
Rafael Palmeiro TEX .... .319

HITS
Rafael Palmeiro TEX 191
Wade Boggs BOS 187
Roberto Kelly NY 183

DOUBLES
George Brett KC 45
Jody Reed BOS 45
two tied at 44

TRIPLES
Tony Fernandez TOR 17
Sammy Sosa CHI 10
three tied at 9

HOME RUNS
Cecil Fielder DET 51
Mark McGwire OAK 39
Jose Canseco OAK 37

RUNS BATTED IN
Cecil Fielder DET 132
Kelly Gruber TOR 118
Mark McGwire OAK 108

SLUGGING AVERAGE
Cecil Fielder DET .... .592
R. Henderson OAK .... .577
Jose Canseco OAK .... .543

STOLEN BASES
R. Henderson OAK 65
Steve Sax NY 43
Roberto Kelly NY 42

RUNS SCORED
Rickey Henderson OAK ... 119
Cecil Fielder DET 104
Harold Reynolds SEA 100

WINS
Bob Welch OAK 27
Dave Stewart OAK 22
Roger Clemens BOS 21

WINNING PERCENTAGE
Bob Welch OAK .... .818
Roger Clemens BOS .... .778
two tied at .... .750

EARNED RUN AVERAGE
Roger Clemens BOS 1.93
Chuck Finley CAL 2.40
Dave Stewart OAK 2.56

STRIKEOUTS
Nolan Ryan TEX 232
Bobby Witt TEX 221
Erik Hanson SEA 211

SAVES
Bobby Thigpen CHI 57
Dennis Eckersley OAK 48
Doug Jones CLE 43

COMPLETE GAMES
Jack Morris DET 11
Dave Stewart OAK 11
five tied at 7

SHUTOUTS
Roger Clemens BOS 4
Dave Stewart OAK 4
three tied at 3

GAMES PITCHED
Bobby Thigpen CHI 77
Jeff Montgomery KC 73
Duane Ward TOR 73

INNINGS PITCHED
Dave Stewart OAK 267
Jack Morris DET 250
Bob Welch OAK 238

668

NATIONAL LEAGUE STANDINGS

1990 NL

EAST	W	L	PCT	GB	R	OR	BA	FA	ERA
PITTSBURGH	95	67	.586	—	733	619	.259	.979	3.40
NEW YORK	91	71	.562	4	775	613	.256	.978	3.43
MONTREAL	85	77	.525	10	662	598	.250	.982	3.37
CHICAGO	77	85	.475	18	690	774	.263	.980	4.34
PHILADELPHIA	77	85	.475	18	646	729	.255	.981	4.07
ST. LOUIS	70	92	.432	25	599	698	.256	.979	3.87

WEST	W	L	PCT	GB	R	OR	BA	FA	ERA
CINCINNATI	91	71	.562	—	693	597	.265	.983	3.39
LOS ANGELES	86	76	.531	5	728	685	.262	.979	3.72
SAN FRANCISCO	85	77	.525	6	719	710	.262	.983	4.08
HOUSTON	75	87	.463	16	573	656	.242	.978	3.61
SAN DIEGO	75	87	.463	16	673	673	.257	.977	3.68
ATLANTA	65	97	.401	26	682	821	.250	.974	4.58
					8173	8173	.256	.980	3.79

BATTING AVERAGE
Willie McGee STL .... .335
Eddie Murray LA .... .330
Dave Magadan NY .... .328

HITS
Brett Butler SF................. 192
Lenny Dykstra PHI 192
Ryne Sandberg CHI 188

DOUBLES
Gregg Jefferies NY............ 40
Bobby Bonilla PIT.............. 39
Chris Sabo CIN 38

TRIPLES
Mariano Duncan CIN......... 11
Tony Gwynn SD 10
three tied at 9

HOME RUNS
Ryne Sandberg CHI 40
Darryl Strawberry NY 37
Kevin Mitchell SF 35

RUNS BATTED IN
Matt Williams SF.............. 122
Bobby Bonilla PIT............ 120
Joe Carter SD 115

SLUGGING AVERAGE
Barry Bonds PIT.............. .565
Ryne Sandberg CHI .... .559
Kevin Mitchell SF .... .544

STOLEN BASES
Vince Coleman STL 77
Eric Yelding HOU 64
Barry Bonds PIT 52

RUNS SCORED
Ryne Sandberg CHI 116
Bobby Bonilla PIT............ 112
Brett Butler SF................ 108

WINS
Doug Drabek PIT 22
Ramon Martinez LA 20
Frank Viola NY 20

WINNING PERCENTAGE
Doug Drabek PIT .... .786
Ramon Martinez LA .... .769
John Tudor STL .... .750

EARNED RUN AVERAGE
Danny Darwin HOU........ 2.21
Zane Smith MON, PIT..... 2.55
Ed Whitson SD................ 2.60

STRIKEOUTS
David Cone NY 233
Dwight Gooden NY 223
Ramon Martinez LA 223

SAVES
John Franco NY 33
Randy Myers CIN.............. 31
Lee Smith STL 27

COMPLETE GAMES
Ramon Martinez LA 12
Doug Drabek PIT 9
Bruce Hurst SD 9

SHUTOUTS
Mike Morgan LA 4
Bruce Hurst SD 4
six tied at 3

GAMES PITCHED
Juan Agosto HOU 82
Paul Assenmacher CHI...... 74
Greg Harris SD.................. 73

INNINGS PITCHED
Frank Viola NY 250
Greg Maddux CHI 237
Ramon Martinez LA 234

AMERICAN LEAGUE STANDINGS

1991 AL

EAST	W	L	PCT	GB	R	OR	BA	FA	ERA
TORONTO	91	71	.562	—	684	622	.257	.980	3.50
BOSTON	84	78	.519	7	731	712	.269	.981	4.01
DETROIT	84	78	.519	7	817	794	.247	.983	4.51
MILWAUKEE	83	79	.512	8	799	744	.271	.981	4.14
NEW YORK	71	91	.438	20	674	777	.256	.979	4.42
BALTIMORE	67	95	.414	24	686	796	.254	.985	4.59
CLEVELAND	57	105	.352	34	576	759	.254	.976	4.23

WEST	W	L	PCT	GB	R	OR	BA	FA	ERA
MINNESOTA	95	67	.586	—	776	652	.280	.985	3.69
CHICAGO	87	75	.534	8	758	681	.262	.982	3.79
TEXAS	85	77	.525	10	829	814	.270	.979	4.47
OAKLAND	84	78	.519	11	760	776	.248	.982	4.57
SEATTLE	83	79	.512	12	702	674	.255	.983	3.79
KANSAS CITY	82	80	.506	13	727	722	.264	.980	3.92
CALIFORNIA	81	81	.500	14	653	649	.255	.984	3.69
					10172	10172	.260	.981	4.09

BATTING AVERAGE
Julio Franco TEX............. .341
Wade Boggs BOS .... .332
Ken Griffey Jr SEA .... .327

HITS
Paul Molitor MIL 216
Cal Ripken BAL................ 210
two tied at............................ 203

DOUBLES
Rafael Palmeiro TEX........... 49
Cal Ripken BAL.................. 46
Ruben Sierra TEX 44

TRIPLES
Lance Johnson CHI............ 13
Paul Molitor MIL 13
Roberto Alomar TOR 11

HOME RUNS
Cecil Fielder DET 44
Jose Canseco OAK............ 44
Cal Ripken BAL.................. 34

RUNS BATTED IN
Cecil Fielder DET 133
Jose Canseco OAK........... 122
Ruben Sierra TEX 116

SLUGGING AVERAGE
Danny Tartabull KC.......... .593
Cal Ripken BAL................ .566
Jose Canseco OAK........... .556

STOLEN BASES
Rickey Henderson OAK 58
Roberto Alomar TOR 53
Tim Raines CHI 51

RUNS SCORED
Paul Molitor MIL 133
Jose Canseco OAK........... 115
Rafael Palmeiro TEX......... 115

WINS
Scott Erickson MIN............. 20
Bill Gullickson DET............. 20
Mark Langston CAL 19

WINNING PERCENTAGE
Scott Erickson MIN...........714
Mark Langston CAL .... .704
Bill Gullickson DET........... .690

EARNED RUN AVERAGE
Roger Clemens BOS........ 2.62
T. Candiotti CLE,TOR 2.65
Bill Wegman MIL.............. 2.84

STRIKEOUTS
Roger Clemens BOS........ 241
Randy Johnson SEA 228
Nolan Ryan TEX 203

SAVES
Bryan Harvey CAL 46
Dennis Eckersley OAK....... 43
Rick Aguilera MIN 42

COMPLETE GAMES
Jack McDowell CHI 15
Roger Clemens BOS.......... 13
two tied at............................ 10

SHUTOUTS
Roger Clemens BOS............ 4
four tied at 3

GAMES PITCHED
Duane Ward TOR 81
Mike Jackson SEA 72
Gregg Olson BAL 72

INNINGS PITCHED
Roger Clemens BOS........ 271
Jack McDowell CHI.......... 254
Jack Morris MIN 247

NATIONAL LEAGUE STANDINGS

1991 NL

EAST	W	L	PCT	GB	R	OR	BA	FA	ERA
PITTSBURGH	98	64	.605	—	768	632	.263	.981	3.44
ST. LOUIS	84	78	.519	14	651	648	.255	.982	3.69
PHILADELPHIA	78	84	.481	20	629	680	.241	.981	3.86
CHICAGO	77	83	.481	20	695	734	.253	.982	4.03
NEW YORK	77	84	.478	20.5	640	646	.244	.977	3.56
MONTREAL	71	90	.441	26.5	579	655	.246	.979	3.64

WEST	W	L	PCT	GB	R	OR	BA	FA	ERA
ATLANTA	94	68	.580	—	749	644	.258	.978	3.49
LOS ANGELES	93	69	.574	1	665	565	.253	.980	3.06
SAN DIEGO	84	78	.519	10	636	646	.244	.982	3.57
SAN FRANCISCO	75	87	.463	19	649	697	.246	.982	4.03
CINCINNATI	74	88	.457	20	689	691	.258	.979	3.83
HOUSTON	65	97	.401	29	605	717	.244	.974	4.00
					7975	7975	.250	.980	3.68

BATTING AVERAGE
Terry Pendleton ATL .... .319
Hal Morris CIN .... .318
Tony Gwynn SD .... .317

HITS
Terry Pendleton ATL 187
Brett Butler LA 182
Chris Sabo CIN 175

DOUBLES
Bobby Bonilla PIT 44
Felix Jose STL 40
two tied at 36

TRIPLES
Ray Lankford STL 15
Tony Gwynn SD 11
Steve Finley HOU 10

HOME RUNS
Howard Johnson NY 38
Matt Williams SF 34
Ron Gant ATL 32

RUNS BATTED IN
Howard Johnson NY 117
Barry Bonds PIT 116
Will Clark SF 116

SLUGGING AVERAGE
Will Clark SF .... .536
Howard Johnson NY .... .535
Terry Pendleton ATL .... .517

STOLEN BASES
Marquis Grissom MON 76
Otis Nixon ATL 72
Delino DeShields MON 56

RUNS SCORED
Brett Butler LA 112
Howard Johnson NY 108
Ryne Sandberg CHI 104

WINS
John Smiley PIT 20
Tom Glavine ATL 20
Steve Avery ATL 18

WINNING PERCENTAGE
Jose Rijo CIN .... .714
John Smiley PIT .... .714
Steve Avery ATL .... .692

EARNED RUN AVERAGE
Dennis Martinez MON 2.39
Jose Rijo CIN 2.51
Tom Glavine ATL 2.55

STRIKEOUTS
David Cone NY 241
Greg Maddux CHI 198
Tom Glavine ATL 192

SAVES
Lee Smith STL 47
Rob Dibble CIN 31
two tied at 30

COMPLETE GAMES
Tom Glavine ATL 9
Dennis Martinez 9
Terry Mulholland PHI 8

SHUTOUTS
Dennis Martinez MON 5
Ramon Martinez LA 4
three tied at 3

GAMES PITCHED
Barry Jones MON 77
Paul Assenmacher CHI 75
Mike Stanton ATL 74

INNINGS PITCHED
Greg Maddux CHI 263
Tom Glavine ATL 247
Mike Morgan LA 236

1991 AWARDS

NL MOST VALUABLE PLAYER VOTING

PLAYER	1st	2nd	3rd	Tot
Terry Pendleton ATL	12	10	2	274
Barry Bonds PIT	10	10	1	259
Bobby Bonilla PIT	1	3	14	191
Will Clark SF	0	0	3	118
Howard Johnson NY	0	0	1	112
Ron Gant ATL	0	0	1	110
Brett Butler LA	1	1	1	103
Lee Smith STL	0	0	1	89
Darryl Strawberry LA	0	0	0	76
Fred McGriff SD	0	0	0	23
Tom Glavine ATL	0	0	0	16
Dave Justice ATL	0	0	0	11
Jay Bell PIT	0	0	0	11
Andre Dawson CHI	0	0	0	5
John Smiley PIT	0	0	0	5
Tony Gwynn SD	0	0	0	4
John Kruk PHI	0	0	0	2
Ryne Sandberg CHI	0	0	0	2
Barry Larkin CIN	0	0	0	2
Dennis Martinez MON	0	0	0	1
Chris Sabo CIN	0	0	0	1
Ozzie Smith STL	0	0	0	1

AL MOST VALUABLE PLAYER VOTING

PLAYER	1st	2nd	3rd	Tot
Cal Ripken BAL	15	8	4	318
Cecil Fielder DET	9	12	6	286
Frank Thomas CHI	1	4	5	181
Jose Canseco OAK	0	0	3	145
Joe Carter TOR	1	2	2	136
Roberto Alomar TOR	2	2	3	128
Kirby Puckett MIN	0	0	2	78
Ruben Sierra TEX	0	0	0	63
Ken Griffey Jr. SEA	0	0	1	62
Roger Clemens BOS	0	0	1	57
Paul Molitor MIL	0	0	0	51
Danny Tartabull KC	0	0	0	32
Jack Morris MIN	0	0	0	29
Chili Davis MIN	0	0	0	21
Julio Franco TEX	0	0	0	17
Devon White TOR	0	0	0	15
Scott Erickson MIN	0	0	1	12
Rick Aguilera MIN	0	0	0	11
Rafael Palmeiro TEX	0	0	0	6
Robin Ventura CHI	0	0	0	3
Dave Henderson OAK	0	0	0	1

NL ROOKIE OF THE YEAR VOTING

PLAYER	1st	2nd	3rd	Tot
Jeff Bagwell HOU	23	1	0	118
Orlando Merced PIT	1	13	9	53
Ray Lankford STL	0	7	7	28
Brian Hunter ATL	0	1	4	7
Bret Barberie MON	0	1	0	3
Wes Chamberlain PHI	0	0	3	3
Chuck McElroy CHI	0	1	0	3
Mike Stanton ATL	0	0	1	1

AL ROOKIE OF THE YEAR VOTING

PLAYER	1st	2nd	3rd	Tot
Chuck Knoblauch MIN	26	2	0	136
Juan Guzman TOR	1	20	3	68
Milt Cuyler DET	1	2	11	22
Ivan Rodriguez TEX	0	2	4	10
Rich DeLucia SEA	0	2	1	7
Mike Timlin TOR	0	0	2	2
Mark Whiten TOR, CLE	0	0	2	2
Leo Gomez BAL	0	0	1	1
Doug Henry MIL	0	0	1	1
Brent Mayne KC	0	0	1	1
Charles Nagy CLE	0	0	1	1
Phil Plantier BOS	0	0	1	1

NL CY YOUNG AWARD VOTING

PLAYER	1st	2nd	3rd	Tot
Tom Glavine ATL	19	5	0	110
Lee Smith STL	4	12	4	60
John Smiley PIT	0	4	14	26
Jose Rijo CIN	1	2	2	13
Dennis Martinez MON	0	1	1	4
Steve Avery ATL	0	0	1	1
Andy Benes SD	0	0	1	1
Mitch Williams PHI	0	0	1	1

AL CY YOUNG AWARD VOTING

PLAYER	1st	2nd	3rd	Tot
Roger Clemens BOS	21	4	2	119
Scott Erickson MIN	3	12	5	56
Jim Abbott CAL	0	5	11	26
Jack Morris MIN	3	0	2	17
Bryan Harvey CAL	0	3	1	10
Mark Langston CAL	0	2	1	7
Kevin Tapani MIN	1	0	1	6
Bill Gullickson DET	0	0	5	5
Jack McDowell CHI	0	1	0	3
Duane Ward TOR	0	1	0	3